SWANSEA UNIVERSITY
PRIFYSGOL ABERTAWE
LIBRARY/LLYFRGELL

Classmark HV6025 .B6575 2003

Location Miners Library

WITHDRAWN FROM STOCK

Crime and Criminology

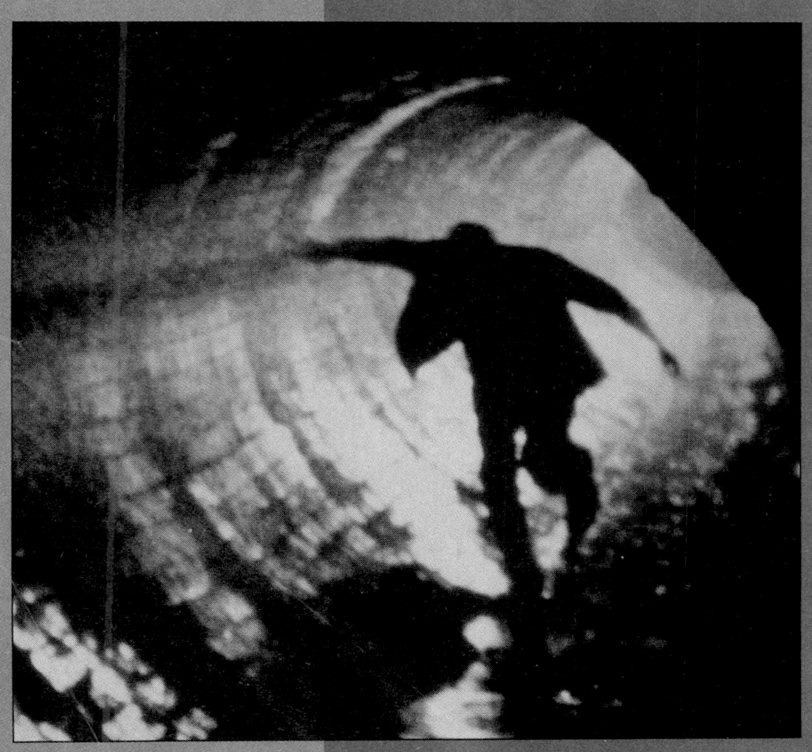

10TH EDITION

Crime and Criminology

SUE TITUS REID, J.D., Ph.D.
Florida State University

Boston Burr Ridge, IL Dubuque, IA Madison, WI New York
San Francisco St. Louis Bangkok Bogotá Caracas Kuala Lumpur
Lisbon London Madrid Mexico City Milan Montreal New Delhi
Santiago Seoul Singapore Sydney Taipei Toronto

McGraw-Hill Higher Education

A Division of The ***McGraw-Hill*** *Companies*

CRIME and CRIMINOLOGY

Published by McGraw-Hill, a business unit of The McGraw-Hill Companies, Inc., 1221 Avenue of the Americas, New York, NY, 10020. Copyright © 2003, 2000, 1997, 1994, 1991, 1988, 1985, 1982, 1979, 1976 by The McGraw-Hill Companies, Inc. All rights reserved. No part of this publication may be reproduced or distributed in any form or by any means, or stored in a database or retrieval system, without the prior written consent of The McGraw-Hill Companies, Inc., including, but not limited to, in any network or other electronic storage or transmission, or broadcast for distance learning.
Some ancillaries, including electronic and print components, may not be available to customers outside the United States.

This book is printed on acid-free paper.

1 2 3 4 5 6 7 8 9 0 WCK/WCK 0 9 8 7 6 5 4 3 2

ISBN 0-07-248595-7

Editorial director: *Phillip A. Butcher*
Senior sponsoring editor: *Carolyn Henderson Meier*
Senior marketing manager: *Daniel M. Loch*
Media producer: *Shannon Rider*
Project manager: *Christina Thornton-Villagomez*
Production supervisor: *Carol A. Bielski*
Senior designer: *Matthew Baldwin*
Photo research coordinator: *Judy Kausal*
Photo researcher: *Romy Charlesworth*
Lead supplement producer: *Marc Mattson*
Cover/interior design: *Lucy Lesiak*
Cover image: *GettyImages/John Schlesinger*
Typeface: *10/12 Palatino*
Compositor: *Carlisle Communications, Ltd.*
Printer: *Quebecor World Versailles Inc.*

Library of Congress Cataloging-in-Publication Data

Reid, Sue Titus.
Crime and criminology / Sue Titus Reed.—10th ed.
p. cm.
Includes index.
ISBN 0-07-248595-7 (alk. paper)
1. Criminology. 2. Crime—United States. 3. Criminal justice, Administration of—United States. I. Title.
HV6025 .R515 2003
364—dc21

2002025452

SWANSEA UNIVERSITY LIBRARY

www.mhhe.com

To Robin Reid, with my appreciation for 30 years of support for this text and for your friendship.

ABOUT THE AUTHOR

Sue Titus Reid, a professor and director of the Undergraduate Program in the Reubin O'D. Askew School of Public Administration and Policy at Florida State University, Tallahassee, has taught law students, graduate students, and undergraduate students in many states. She has served on the board of the Midwest Sociological Society and the executive staff of the American Sociological Association. She has served as chairperson, associate dean, and dean. In 1985 she held the prestigious George Beto Chair in criminal justice at the Criminal Justice Center, Sam Houston State University, Huntsville, Texas.

Dr. Reid was influenced in her choice of career by her family background and early experiences in a small East Texas community. She graduated with honors from Texas Woman's University in 1960 and received graduate degrees in sociology (M.A. in 1962 and Ph.D. in 1965) from the University of Missouri–Columbia. In 1972 she graduated with distinction from the University of Iowa College of Law. She was admitted to the Iowa bar that year and later to the District of Columbia Court of Appeals. She has been admitted to practice before the U.S. Supreme Court as well.

Dr. Reid is unique among authors in the criminal justice field because of her distinguished qualifications in both law and the social sciences. She launched her publishing career in 1976 with *Crime and Criminology,* which has been widely adopted throughout the United States and in foreign countries. Dr. Reid's other titles include *Criminal Justice,* sixth edition; *The Correctional System: An Introduction;* and *Criminal Law,* fifth edition. She has contributed a chapter to the *Encyclopedia of Crime and Justice,* as well as to other books, in addition to publishing scholarly articles in law, sociology, and public administration.

Dr. Reid has traveled extensively to widen her knowledge of criminal justice systems in the United States and in other countries. In 1982 she was a member of the People-to-People Crime Prevention delegation to the People's Republic of China. Her several trips to Europe included a three-month study and lecture tour of 10 countries in 1985.

Dr. Reid's contributions to her profession have been widely recognized nationally and abroad. In 1982 the American Society of Criminology elected her a fellow "for outstanding contributions to the field of Criminology." Other national honors include the following: Who's Who among Women; Who's Who in Criminal Law; 2,000 Notable Women (Hall of Fame for Outstanding Contributions to Criminal Law, 1990); Personalities of America; and Most Admired Woman of the Decade, 1992. Her international honors include International Woman of the Year, 1991–92; International Who's Who of Intellectuals; and International Order of Merit, 1993. In 1998 she was elected to the International Professional and Business Women's Hall of Fame. In 1999 she was included in the Marquis Who's Who in America and appointed to the School of Justice Studies Advisory Board of Roger Williams University; she was also a featured speaker at the Oberlin Conference on Crime and Punishment at Oberlin College. In 1998 she received a university teaching award at Florida State University.

CONTENTS IN BRIEF

LIST OF MEDIA FOCUS BOXES

CONTENTS

PREFACE

As a discipline, criminology is concerned with the causes of crime—the traditional emphasis of sociologists—as well as with criminal justice and correctional systems. The exploration of these areas in this text features the integration of law with pertinent theories and empirical studies from the social sciences. This integrated approach is the result of my years of teaching criminology to undergraduates, my background as a law professor and legal consultant, and my experience as a social scientist.

In teaching undergraduates, I have been impressed with their eagerness to learn how law relates to the traditional topics covered in criminology and criminal justice courses, even to the point that they enjoy reading and briefing court cases. For this reason I have included within the text some excerpts from appellate opinions to illustrate concepts and to demonstrate the role of courts in criminal justice systems.

The responses to the nine previous editions of this text confirm that students and faculty find the integration of law and social science to be an interesting and effective approach to the study of criminal behavior. No less important to users of earlier editions has been the text's assessment of society's response to criminal behavior. Therefore, I have retained the text's integrated approach but have made some significant revisions and numerous updates, the most important of which are detailed in the section below titled "The 10th Edition."

As a social scientist, I want to ensure that the text discusses the results of sociological research on criminal justice systems and does so in a context of sociological theory. Summaries and critiques of classic works in criminology, analyses of recent social science research, and attention to major social science theorists who have contributed significantly to the study of crime are included.

Features

As in the previous editions, I have included many learning aids to help students comprehend the text's wealth of material. The book has also been completely redesigned not only for visual appeal but also to better draw students into the text material. New photographs, figures, maps, graphs, and charts bring text material to life even further. Each chapter of the 10th edition begins with a brief overview, outline, and list of key terms that together serve as the student's road map to the chapter. To help students master criminology's vast array of vocabulary, key terms are identified in boldface within the text and are defined in the margins throughout; they are also collected in a comprehensive glossary at the end of the text for easy reference later. Finally, each chapter closes with a built-in study guide consisting of a chapter summary, plentiful review questions, brief essay assignments, Internet activities, and Internet resources for use when writing papers.

The numerous boxed inserts support the book's integration of social science research and law. Additional inserts, labeled "Exhibits," provide insights and background information on current events, legal decisions, and other topics of interest. The legal excerpts within the text show how legal decisions affect criminal justice systems. All legal citations have been checked to determine whether any changes have been made on appeal; all statutes are updated to the latest possible time during the production process.

New to this edition are boxed inserts featuring how the media have treated a particular subject (see page viii for a complete list). These additions illustrate how the media treatment of a crime can distort our views. For example, Media

Focus 2.1 (see Chapter 2, p. 27), "Media Headlines concerning Crime Data," demonstrates how media headlines and discussions can be misleading, depending on the sources used for the report as well as the time periods it covers. But the media can also enhance our understanding of an event or issue. For example, Media Focus 12.1 (see Chapter 12, p. 396) summarizes a recent *New York Times* article that emphasizes the need to make policing more attractive to potential recruits, thus perhaps creating more public awareness of this critical need. Likewise, Media Focus 14.1 (see Chapter 14, p. 485), "The Crisis in Recruiting Correctional Officers," also based on a *New York Times* article, explores the need to find ways to attract individuals to the profession of correctional officer.

Finally, Appendix A contains selected constitutional amendments to provide quick and easy reference to the reader who wishes to read the full amendment mentioned in the text. Appendix B discusses how to read a case citation. The indexes are divided by cases, names, and general subject topics.

The 10th Edition

Significant content changes have been made in this edition as well. Although the text retains its 15-chapter format for ease of use in semester/quarter-length courses, changes have been made to some chapter titles and to the outlines within some chapters. These changes are enumerated within each part and chapter.

Part I, "Introduction to the Study of Crime and Criminology," introduces the study of criminology and criminal law. Chapter 1, "Crime, Criminal Law, and Criminology," explains and analyzes the concept of crime. Its discussion of the concept of law covers the nature and purpose as well as the limits of law, looking in particular at law as a method of social control. At the suggestion of reviewers, the chapter was simplified, with the discussion of torts eliminated, but the chapter contains considerable new material. It features two 2001 U.S. Supreme Court cases to illustrate the following topics: the legalization of marijuana for medicinal purposes, and the extent to which the criminal law should cover behavior such as failure to wear a seat belt and shoulder restraint while driving an automobile. The issue of using the criminal law to cover voluntary sexual behavior by adults is illustrated by a discussion of the recent changes in Vermont's laws concerning same-gender relationships.

Chapter 2, "The Measurement of Crime and Its Impact," focuses on the compilation of crime data through official and unofficial methods, using the most recent data available. In addition to overall data, this chapter includes information on social class and crime as well as a more extensive discussion of age and crime, including the topics of juveniles as criminals and as victims and the growing problem of crimes among the elderly. The section on the Cartographic School was deleted at the suggestion of reviewers and the previous edition's Chapter 3 discussion of research was moved to Chapter 2 and revised.

Part II, "Explanations of Criminal Behavior," contains four chapters on causation. Chapter 3, "Early Explanations of Criminal Behavior and Their Modern Counterparts," begins with an exploration of the historical explanations of criminal behavior that have strongly influenced modern developments. The classical and positive schools of thought are explained, contrasted, and related to current philosophies of punishment and sentencing. I have updated the discussions of rehabilitation, retribution and revenge, and deterrence. In particular, the California movement toward treatment rather than punishment of first- and second-time nonviolent drug offenders is noted. The new edition features an enhanced discussion of the early philosophers, such as Beccaria and Bentham, along with the addition of the contributions of Montesquieu and Rousseau in the Classical School and Lombroso, Garofalo, and Ferri in the Positive School. Additional critiques of these contributors are also included. This and the following theory chapters all contain exhibits that summarize the major theorists and their contributions discussed in the respective chapters.

Chapter 4, "Biological and Psychological Theories of Criminal Behavior," recognizes the increasing attention that is being given to variables such as chemical imbalance, substance abuse, psychological problems, and intelligence that may be related to criminal behavior, especially violence. A complete discussion of criminology cannot ignore these issues even though they remain controversial. This version of the chapter features several new boxed inserts, with topics such as "Policy Implications of Drug Addiction," "Can the Media Introduce the Public to Science?" and "The Human Genome Project."

Part II concludes with two chapters on sociological explanations of criminal behavior. Chapter 5, "Sociological Theories of Criminal Behavior I: The Social-Structural Approach," focuses on the relationship between social structure and criminal behavior. Due to the increased focus on juvenile crimes, this edition contains more on this topic. Traditional theories are utilized to explain such crimes; for example, Media Focus 5.1 is entitled "The Media and School Shootings: A Look at Feminist Theory."

Chapter 6, "Sociological Theories of Criminal Behavior II: The Social-Process Approach," deals with the processes by which criminal behavior may be acquired. Some changes have been made in the organization and outline. The discussion of Sutherland's theory of differential association is enlarged, and Exhibit 6.1 contains the listing of the theory's nine propositions. Akers's social learning theory is expanded, and several of the theories in the chapter have enlarged discussions on recent research. A new section in this edition is a discussion of the policy implications of all theories discussed in this and previous chapters to assist students in their applications of theory to real-world issues.

Part III, "Types of Crime," includes Chapter 7, "Violent Crimes," which introduces the study of criminology typologies. This chapter has several new additions. The section on terrorism was moved to this chapter and expanded to include the sentencing in the American embassy bombing case, the execution of Timothy McVeigh, the appeals of Michael Fortier and Terry Nichols, the June 2001 suicide bombings in Israel, the attack on America on 11 September 2001, and the latest data (December 2001) showing an increase in murders in some large cities despite the overall leveling off of crime in the United States.

The discussion on pornography was moved to Chapter 7 and enlarged to include the latest U.S. Supreme Court case concerning children and pornography, along with a reference to the case on virtual pornography that the Court has agreed to decide. The discussion of hate crimes was moved from Chapter 2 to this chapter and updated; the discussion of marital rape was moved from the section on domestic violence to the section on forcible rape. More information is included on the four major violent crimes. The inclusion of state statutes illustrates the various ways of defining the serious violent crimes. The chapter also includes more information on gun control, the fear of crime, and stalking.

Chapter 8, "Property Crimes," includes expanded and updated information on the four index property crimes—burglary, larceny-theft, motor vehicle theft, and arson—as well as some property crimes considered to be lesser offenses. Particular attention is given to crimes such as credit card theft as well as the problems of repeat offenders. The discussion of the crime of carjacking is updated. New to this chapter is an enhanced analysis of computer crimes (previously in Chapter 9) and the topics of cyberstalking and identity theft. The control of pornography on the Internet was moved from the previous edition's Chapter 6 and updated in this chapter.

Chapter 9, "Business and Government-Related Crimes," features several new or revised exhibits. Exhibit 9.2 includes a focus on Marc Rich and his controversial pardon by President Bill Clinton and the subsequent investigation of that action. Exhibit 9.3, "Workplace Violations and Criminal Law," details the case of an employer who was sentenced to 17 years in prison for providing an unsafe working environment, which led to the brain damage of a 20-year-old employee. Exhibit 9.4 includes discussion of 2001 cases on health care fraud. The chapter updates information on Bill Gates and Microsoft, Terry Nichols, Susan McDougal, Valujet and SabreTech, and Michael Milken, as well as the New York City Police Department case regarding the beating and sodomization of Abner Louima. That same department is featured in the case of Amadou Diallo, who was killed by four white police officers, all of whom were acquitted.

Chapter 10, has been renamed "Drug Abuse, Drug Trafficking, and Organized Crime" to reflect the move of the discussion on terrorism to Chapter 7 and the increased emphasis on drug abuse and drug trafficking. Data on drug abuse are discussed, along with the effects of the problem, such as fetal abuse, the economic cost, criminal activity, prison and jail overcrowding, and the influence of drugs on criminal justice personnel. The war-on-drugs discussion has been updated, and the discussion of the efforts to decriminalize marijuana, especially for medical purposes, is enhanced by a notation of the increased violence attributed to marijuana sales in New York City. New York's unsuccessful efforts to reduce drug penalties by revising the Rockefeller laws is noted, along with a more detailed discussion of California's new provisions for treatment rather than incarceration of first- and second-time nonviolent drug offenders.

The final focus of Chapter 10 is organized crime, featuring the history of the subject as well as a discussion of some of the modern players. The infiltration of organized crime into legitimate businesses—such as health care, food, construction, and cartage—is updated, as are attempts to control organized crime.

Part IV, "Criminal Justice Systems," includes three chapters. The outline of Chapter 11, "U.S. Criminal Justice Systems," has been revised. The chapter now begins with the concepts of U.S. criminal justice, followed by a discussion of the special characteristics of criminal justice systems and then the stages within the systems. Media Focus 11.1 discusses the changes that correctional officials are making due to the influx of teens in adult prisons. All legal discussions are updated, featuring many new cases, including *Illinois* v. *McArthur* (2001), *Dickerson* v. *United States* (2000), *Indianapolis* v. *Edmone* (2000), *Burdine* v. *Johnson* (1999), *Kyllo* v. *United States* (2001), and *Roe* v. *Flores-Ortega* (2000).

With its overview of the constitutional rights of defendants in the adversary system, this chapter, as in the previous edition, sets the stage for subsequent chapters in Part IV. It focuses on four major constitutional rights of defendants: the right to be free from unreasonable search and seizure, the right not to testify against onself, the right to counsel, and the right to a trial by jury. This edition features expanded discussions of due process and equal protection, more material on victims' rights, and a notation of the $50 million settlement that New York City is paying for the illegal strip searches of 50,000 or more people.

Chapter 12, "Police," has some outline changes, with the deletion of subheads, but it retains the major topics of the previous edition. The discussion on female and minority hiring is enhanced, and extensive information is included in the discussion of the FBI. Most exhibits are new to this edition, including one focusing on the security problems within the FBI, illustrated by the case of convicted spy Robert P. Hanssen, the Community Policing Act (COPS) of 1994, and one on the ways in which the media portray police in a negative light. Information is also included on the role police played after the terrorist acts against America on 11 September 2001. This edition features a discussion on the zero tolerance policy, illustrated by the New York City administration, more information on police subculture and racial profiling, and a recent case (*United States* v. *Monero-Camargo*) holding that police cannot use ethnicity as a factor in deciding whether to stop an individual suspected of a crime. The discussion of the Los Angeles Police Department's Rampart scandal is updated, as is the discussion of the New York City Diallo case.

Chapter 13, "Court Systems," provides an overview of the criminal justice processes that occur in the courts, from pretrial to posttrial. Significant changes in court systems, especially in sentencing, are an important part of this chapter, with particular attention given in this edition to three-strikes legislation and the call for a moratorium on capital punishment. A new feature exhibit illustrates both the violence of young teens and the problems of plea bargaining, as it focuses on two Florida offenders, one of whom rejected a plea bargain of three years and was sentenced to life in prison. The U.S. Supreme Court's two most recent terms are summarized in Media Focus 13.1.

Part V, "Social Reactions to Crime: Corrections," contains two chapters. Chapter 14, "The Confinement of Offenders," includes a brief historical account of the emergence of prisons and jails for punishment; discusses U.S. contributions to this movement; and distinguishes jails, prisons, and community corrections. Jail and prison overcrowding is one focus of this chapter; the review includes an analysis of the attempted solutions to this serious problem. The inmate's social world within prison is discussed, as are prison violence and control. The chapter's overview of inmates' legal rights is updated, with discussion of a federal judge in Alabama who imposed fines for contempt of court for officials who do not remove inmates from county jails to state prisons as per his orders. New data on female inmates and their children are included, along with updates on the sexual abuse of female inmates by correctional officers. The topic of juvenile inmates being held in adult jails and prisons is highlighted, while new material on riots in adult prisons is summarized. The alleged beating that resulted in the death of a Florida death row inmate is featured, (including the results of the trial of the guards accused in that death. Health issues within prisons are noted, along with the effects of maxi-maxi prisons on prison conditions and inmate conduct. The impact of the Americans with Disabilities Act (ADA) is examined, and additional information is provided on privatization of prisons.

Chapter 15, "Corrections in the Community" contains a discussion of the types of community correctional facilities and programs along with updated information on probation and parole. Megan's laws continue to attract court attention, and those changes are updated. The discussion of shock incarceration and boot camps takes on a new focus, as some jurisdictions have eliminated their programs. Special attention is given to the recent death of a young offender in boot camp. Chapter 15 closes the text with a new discussion on the future of corrections. This analysis includes such topics as an evaluation of community corrections, the privatization issue, and juvenile justice.

Supplements Package

As a full-service publisher of quality educational products, McGraw-Hill does much more than just sell textbooks. The company creates and publishes an extensive array of print, video, and digital supplements for students and instructors. This edition of *Crime and Criminology* is accompanied by the following valuable supplements:

- *Instructor's Manual/Testbank:* chapter outlines, key terms, overviews, lecture notes, discussion questions, a complete testbank, and more.

- *Computerized Testbank:* easy-to-use computerized testing program for both Macintosh and Windows computers.
- *Videotapes:* a wide variety of videotapes from the *Films for the Humanities and Social Sciences* series is available to adopters of the text.

All of the above supplements are provided free of charge to instructors. Orders of new (versus used) textbooks help us defray the cost of developing such supplements, which is substantial. Please contact your local McGraw-Hill representative for more information about any of the above supplements.

Acknowledgments

The writing and production of a text requires the assistance and cooperation of many people. This one in particular was difficult because every phase of it occurred while the author was moving, building a home, moving again, and getting settled. The patience and understanding of my editor, Carolyn Henderson Meier, and my project manager, Christina Thornton-Villagomez is greatly appreciated. Christina has produced many of my texts and perhaps knows me too well, but she is uncanny in her ability to locate me, even when I am on the highway and almost out of cell-phone territory! The tedious process of selecting photographs to illustrate the book, deciding where they should be placed, and writing captions was easier than ever before because of the extraordinarily organized efforts of my photo researcher, Romy Charlesworth. As with several of the previous editions, the copy editing was done by Janet Renard. The end-of-chapter sections on brief essay assignments, Internet activities, and net resources were contributed by Leigh Herbst, from the University of Nebraska–Omaha.

The many editions of *Crime and Criminology* have benefited tremendously from the suggestions of reviewers. For this edition, I am grateful for the efforts of the following:

Robert Mutchnick—Indiana University of Pennsylvania
Debra Kelley—Longwood College
Anthony W. Zumpetta—Chester University
Antonia Keane—Loyola College
Joan Luxenburg—University of Central Oklahoma
Greg Scott—DePaul University
Robert Turner—Virgina Polytechnic Institute and State University
Michael Brown—Ball State University
Terry V. Alston Sr.—Chesapeake College
David Pilgrim—Ferris State University
Kathryn England Aytes—American Behavioral Studies Institute
Ellen G. Cohn—Florida International University
Pamela Tontodonato—Kent State University

As always, I am grateful to the undergraduates who take my course in The American Legal Systems at Florida State University. All sections of this seminar involve students who are planning to attend law school or graduate school in criminology or a related field. They are inspiring and rewarding as they show their enthusiasm for many of the topics discussed in this text. Many of them keep in touch after the course, and I delight in hearing about their studies, jobs, and personal lives.

Along with my family, I would like to thank three colleagues who have supported this text for a combination of over 90 years! Professors H.H.A. Cooper, David Fabianic, and Marlyn Mather have always been there, encouraging me in my teaching and writing experiences, and to each of them I owe a big debt for their professional assistance and personal friendship.

My move to New Hampshire has brought new friends, some of whom eased the problems of moving to a new home. Bob and Ann McGraw, Ed Cremo, and Judy Coleman transported and unpacked boxes and took care of many of the mechanical problems a move involves, while Pat and Paul Belluche took over the tedious job of hanging pictures to make the house look like a home. Judy, along with Amber Marsh, provided loving and efficient cat care while I traveled weekly to Florida. Thanks to all of them for helping me move and get settled while working on this book.

The pains of moving the contents of one's office (most of which was in storage for over six months)—along with selecting and adjusting to a new computer and other office equipment and trying to find files in a new environment—can be overwhelming. My computer issues were greatly eased by the work of Robin Reid, who not only set up my new equipment and transferred all the files from the old but served as a frequent phone or e-mail contact when I encountered a problem. Without his efforts this edition would not have been completed on time, and perhaps without his encouragement in 1972 the contract for the first edition of this text might not have been signed and the text written. Thanks, Robin, for your continued support. To you this book is dedicated.

Sue Titus Reid, J. D., Ph.D.
Professor and Director of the Undergraduate Program
Reubin O'D. Askew School of Public Administration and Policy,
Florida State University

A Visual Walkthrough

This text is unique in its integration of law with theory and social science research in criminology. The text presents all of the material one would expect to find in any criminology text, from the definition and measurement of crime to sociological theories regarding the causes of crime, detailed discussion of types of crimes, and material on the criminal justice system. But what this text does better and more completely than any other criminology text available is consistently discuss the law as it relates to all of these topics.

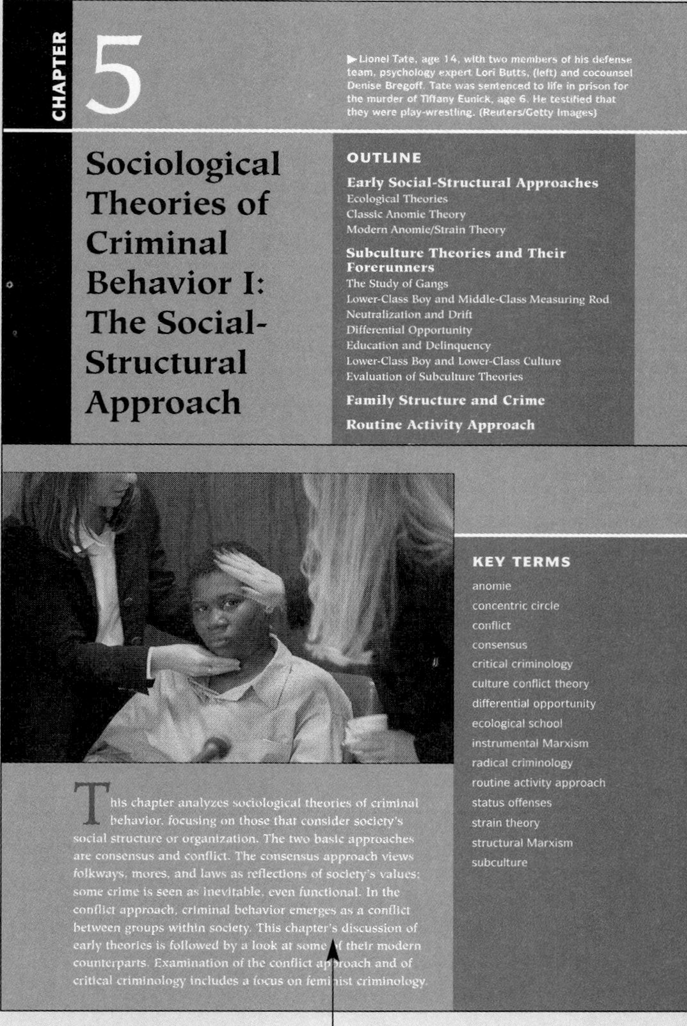

CHAPTER 5

▶ Lionel Tate, age 14, with two members of his defense team, psychology expert Lori Butts, (left) and cocounsel Denise Bregoff. Tate was sentenced to life in prison for the murder of Tiffany Eunick, age 6. He testified that they were play-wrestling. (Reuters/Getty Images)

Sociological Theories of Criminal Behavior I: The Social-Structural Approach

OUTLINE

Early Social-Structural Approaches
Ecological Theories
Classic Anomie Theory
Modern Anomie/Strain Theory

Subculture Theories and Their Forerunners
The Study of Gangs
Lower-Class Boy and Middle-Class Measuring Rod
Neutralization and Drift
Differential Opportunity
Education and Delinquency
Lower-Class Boy and Lower-Class Culture
Evaluation of Subculture Theories

Family Structure and Crime

Routine Activity Approach

KEY TERMS

anomie
concentric circle
conflict
consensus
critical criminology
culture conflict theory
differential opportunity
ecological school
instrumental Marxism
radical criminology
routine activity approach
status offenses
strain theory
structural Marxism
subculture

This chapter analyzes sociological theories of criminal behavior, focusing on those that consider society's social structure or organization. The two basic approaches are consensus and conflict. The consensus approach views folkways, mores, and laws as reflections of society's values; some crime is seen as inevitable, even functional. In the conflict approach, criminal behavior emerges as a conflict between groups within society. This chapter's discussion of early theories is followed by a look at some of their modern counterparts. Examination of the conflict approach and of critical criminology includes a focus on feminist criminology.

Absolutely critical to any course in criminology is early, clear, comprehensive coverage of the major theoretical approaches to explaining criminal behavior—which you will find in Part II of this text.

Media Focus 6.1

Should the Media Be Legally Liable for Violence?

The text discusses the impact the media are alleged to have on violence in real life. Exhibit 6.2 enumerates specific cases in which the media are cited as the reason for the criminal acts. Media company representatives deny any responsibility for criminal acts that follow their programs. With regard to his show, mentioned in one of the examples in Exhibit 6.2, Jerry Springer said some of the episodes are silly but that he should not be responsible for what some folks find entertaining.[1]

The parents of the three shooting victims of the December 1997 school shooting at Heath High School in Paducah, Kentucky, filed a lawsuit against 25 media companies. The parents argued that violent video games "trained" Michael Carneal, the shooter, to point and shoot a gun and thus become a more effective killer. Therefore, the parents argued, the media should be legally liable. The trial court dismissed the lawsuit, ruling that the defendants had no legal duty to the parents under Kentucky laws. The parents have appealed.[2]

In a second recent lawsuit, a federal appellate court ruled that an Indianapolis, Indiana, city ordinance limiting minors' access to violent video games probably would not pass the constitutional tests regarding the First Amendment's right to free speech.[3]

1. "Brothers Molest Sister, Blame Talk Show Episode," *Tallahassee Democrat* (7 January 1999), p. 6C.
2. James v. Meow Media Inc., 90 F.Supp. 2d 798 (W.D.Ky. 2000), discussed in "Broadcasting Violence: Debate Intensifies on Whether Media Should Be Liable for School Shootings," *ABA Journal* 87 (May 2001), p. 29.
3. American Amusement Machine Association v. Kendrick, 244 F.3d 572 (7th Cir. 2001), discussed in "Broadcasting Violence," ibid.

CONTROL THEORY

In addition to trying to determine the process by which people become criminals, sociologists and psychologists have developed explanations of how behavior can be controlled. According to control theorists, deviance results when social controls are weakened or broken down; when controls are strong, deviance does not occur. The problem is to try to explain what can be done in a positive way to elicit appropriate behavior. The question is not how to prevent criminal behavior but how to train people to engage in law-abiding behavior.

Control theory An explanation of criminal behavior that focuses on the control mechanisms, techniques, and strategies for regulating human behavior, leading to conformity or obedience to society's rules, and that argues that deviance results when social controls are weakened or break down so that individuals are not motivated to conform to them.

Like many other explanations of criminal behavior, **control theory** is not a theory in the sense of rigorous scientific procedures of developing and testing hypotheses; rather, it is an approach or an explanation. Several theorists have articulated variations of control theory. In reading the discussion that follows, keep in mind that all of the variations have some common assumptions, articulated by one sociologist as follows:

1. That the human animal requires nurturing.
2. That differences in nurturing account for variations in attachment to others and commitment to an ordered way of living.
3. That attachment and commitment may be described as "internal controls," commonly called "conscience" and recognized in *guilt*, and "external controls," usually tested by the production of *shame*.
4. That evidence from experimental studies, longitudinal research, comparative studies, and cross-cultural investigation tells us *how* attachment and commitment are developed. Conversely, such evidence describes the situations that loosen the moral bond with others and that are, therefore, productive of crime.[46]

Reiss's and Nye's Control Theory

One of the first to apply control theory to delinquent or criminal behavior was Albert J. Reiss Jr., who maintained that such behavior results from the failures of personal and social controls. *Personal controls* are internalized, while *social*

This critical coverage is neatly encapsulated throughout Part II of the text, making it easier for students to grasp the differences between important theories and study for exams.

Thorough updates throughout the text ensure that the text remains relevant to today's students; in Chapter 7, for instance, students will find a detailed discussion of terrorism, including the events of 11 September 2001 and their aftermath; in Chapter 8, coverage of cyberstalking, identity theft, and the rise in computer crime in general; and in Chapter 9, discussion of the Amadou Diallo and Abner Louima cases in New York, the Marc Rich pardon, and an important 2001 health care fraud case.

EXHIBIT 7.3

Recent Terrorist Acts

WORLD TRADE CENTER, NEW YORK CITY; PENTAGON, WASHINGTON, D.C., 11 SEPTEMBER 2001

Chapter 1 introduced us to the greatest terrorist acts that have ever occurred on American soil. More than 3,000 people died when carefully coordinated hijacked airplanes were flown into the twin towers of the World Trade Center in New York City—two of the tallest buildings in the world, representing the financial strength of the United States—and the Pentagon in Washington, D.C., one of the sources of U.S. government and military strength. A fourth hijacked plane, apparently headed for another Washington, D.C., building (perhaps the U.S. Congress or the White House), crashed in Pennsylvania after passengers presumably fought with the hijackers. The death toll would have been much higher, but thousands were able to evacuate the World Trade Center towers before they collapsed. The area, subsequently referred to as Ground Zero, became a hallowed burial ground as Americans, supported by allies around the world, mourned their dead and tried to reconstruct their lives.

President George W. Bush responded by freezing the bank accounts of persons thought to have financed the attacks, which he and others alleged were masterminded by Osama bin Laden, a Saudi Arabian millionaire hiding in Afghanistan, the leader of al Qaeda, the network blamed for the terrorist attacks. The president ordered air strikes and subsequently sent troops to Afghanistan in an attempt to destroy Afghanistan's ruling Taliban organization and capture or kill bin Laden. Although significant progress was made in the war, by the time of this publication it appeared that bin Laden remained at large.

vate automobiles and homes as well as businesses, and large numbers of people wore flag pins or other patriotic symbols.

President Bush appointed Pennsylvania governor Tom Ridge to head the newly created White House Office of Homeland Security and charged him and his agency to coordinate the efforts of dozens of agencies, ranging from the Federal Bureau of Investigation to the Federal Aviation Administration. Another key figure in the U.S. war against terrorism was U.S. attorney general John Ashcroft, charged with the investigation and possible trials of living persons connected to the terrorist acts.

As this manuscript went into production, many questions remained not only about the terrorist acts but also about the possibility of additional acts. Public debate centered on how to secure peace and safety in U.S. airports and other places in which large numbers of people gather. The terrorist acts of 11 September targeted the United States, but the nation's allies were aware that other countries could be next.

Shortly after the events of 11 September 2001, another form of what appeared to be a terrorist attack occurred when deadly anthrax spores were found in mail sent to various targets, including news media offices, the U.S. Congress, and the U.S. Supreme Court. Several people died after they came into contact with the anthrax-tainted letters, but no suspect has yet been connected with these events.

TEL AVIV SUICIDE BOMBER, JUNE 2001

In a deadly terrorist attack outside a nightclub in Tel Aviv, Israel, in early June 2001, at least 17 people were killed and several others injured. Most of the victims were teenagers and young adults who were wait- ... tclub. The city's mayor ... e whole country is the ... other suicide bombings ... e previous week. The ... eral expressed his hor- ... that the crime under- ... the cycle of violence."[1]

... MBASSIES,

... he American embassies ... zania, resulted in the ... cluding 12 Americans)

(continued)

Computer hacker Kevin Mitnick arrives at a news conference early on 21 January 2000 after being released from the Federal Correction Institute in Lompoc, California. After five years behind bars, Mitnick, one of the nation's most notorious computer hackers, was released under the ... ent that for the next three years he keeps his ... computers, modems, cell phones, and anything ... could give him Internet access. Mitnick, 36, ... caused millions of dollars of damage by hacking ... orate and university computers. He was once the ... st wanted hacker. (AP)

Types of Computer Crimes

Computer crimes may involve the same kinds of crimes discussed elsewhere in this chapter as well as those discussed in previous chapters except that a computer is used in the perpetration of the crime. According to a white-collar crime expert, "Computer crime may also take the form of threats of force directed against the computer itself. These crimes are usually 'sabotage' or 'ransom' cases. Computer crime cases have one commonality: the computer is either the tool or the target of the felon."[50]

A special jargon has been developed to describe computer crimes:

1. *Data diddling*, the most common, the easiest, and the safest technique, involves changing the data that will be put into the computer or that are in the computer.
2. *The Trojan horse* method involves instructing the computer to perform unauthorized functions along with its intended functions.
3. *The salami technique* involves taking small amounts of assets from a larger source without significantly reducing the whole. In a bank account situation, for example, one might instruct the computer to reduce specified accounts by 1 percent and place those assets in another account.
4. *Superzapping* involves taking control of a computer's contents. Because computers at times malfunction, there is a need for what is sometimes called a "break glass in case of emergency" computer program. This program will "bypass all controls to modify or disclose any of the contents of the computer." In the hands of the wrong person, it can be an extremely powerful tool for crime.
5. *Data leakage* involves removing information from the computer system or computer facility.[51]

Controlling Computer Crimes

Legislation regulating computer crimes is relatively recent and reflects the varying definitions of this type of theft. Passage of a federal statute did not occur until the enactment of the Comprehensive Crime Control Act of 1984. Before that act, computer crimes were prosecuted under other statutes, such as those covering mail fraud and wire fraud, which excluded some types of computer crimes. In addition, the penalties were considered inadequate for computer crimes. The 1984 act has been amended several times, most recently as part of the Violent Crime Control and Law Enforcement Act of 1994.[52]

In 1995 Connecticut became one of the first states to enact legislation making harassment by computer a crime. Other jurisdictions have followed suit, but it is possible that the enactment of statutes designed to prevent computer crimes will not be as effective as some would like to think. First, many establishments might not want the public to know that their employees committed crimes with the company's computers. Second, in addition to a lack of reporting or willingness to prosecute and the difficulties of apprehension and prosecution, law

Justin A. Volpe, former New York City police officer, with his attorney before entering a guilty plea for the charge of beating and sodomizing Haitian immigrant Abner Louima. Volpe entered the plea after the trial began and damaging testimony was introduced. Volpe was sentenced to 30 years in prison. (© AFP/Corbis)

A. Volpe pleaded guilty to sodomizing Abner Louima, a Haitian immigrant, and threatening to kill Louima if he reported the incident. Volpe was sentenced to 30 years in prison. In 2001 Louima accepted an $8.7 million settlement of his claims against the city for this brutality.[71]

In 2000 a jury acquitted four white New York City police officers who fired 41 times, killing an unarmed West African immigrant, Amadou Diallo. An anonymous juror reported that the prosecution did not prove its case beyond a reasonable doubt. In 2001 Diallo's mother criticized the police department for permitting the four officers to return to their jobs.[72]

CONTROLLING BUSINESS AND GOVERNMENT-RELATED CRIMES

The sampling of business and government-related crimes in this chapter pertains to those that may be committed by individuals in a business or government setting or by executives acting on behalf of the corporation. One issue in analyzing government or business-related crimes is whether the civil or criminal law should be invoked. Another is whether corporate managers should be held criminally liable for the actions of their employees or whether the civil law is sufficient for these cases.

Chapter 1 distinguishes between criminal and civil law and notes that in some cases corporations (or noncorporate employers) may be held criminally

Chapter-Opening abstracts, outlines, and key-terms list serve as the student's road map to the chapter.

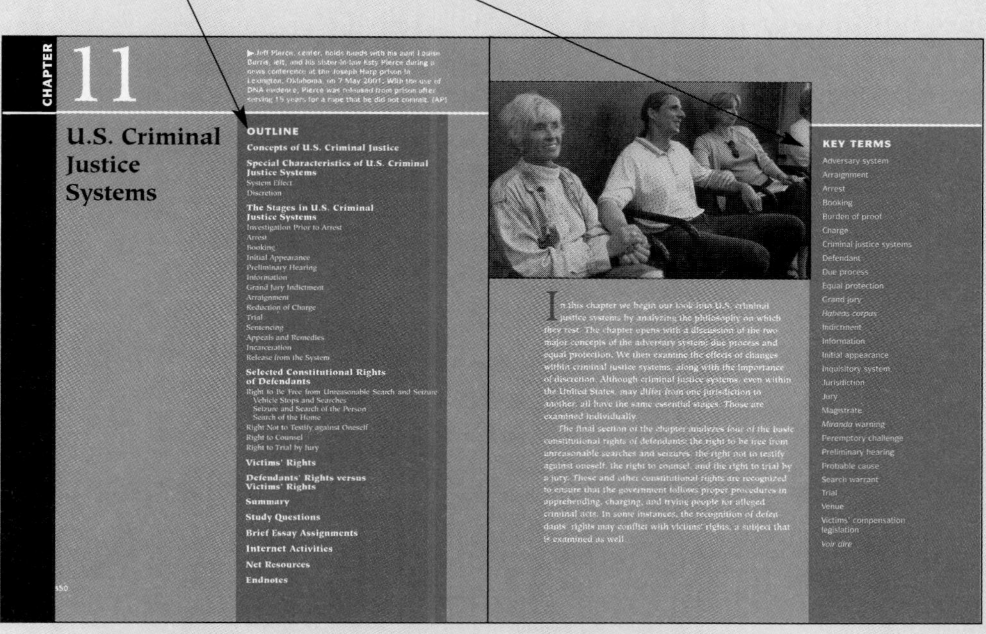
CHAPTER 11

▶ Jeff Pierce, center, holds hands with his aunt Louise Burris, left, and his sister-in-law Esty Pierce during a news conference at the Joseph Harp prison in Lexington, Oklahoma, on 7 May 2001. With the use of DNA evidence, Pierce was released from prison after serving 15 years for a rape that he did not commit. (AP)

U.S. Criminal Justice Systems

OUTLINE

Concepts of U.S. Criminal Justice

Special Characteristics of U.S. Criminal Justice Systems
System Effect
Discretion

The Stages in U.S. Criminal Justice Systems
Investigation Prior to Arrest
Arrest
Booking
Initial Appearance
Preliminary Hearing
Information
Grand Jury Indictment
Arraignment
Reduction of Charge
Trial
Sentencing
Appeals and Remedies
Incarceration
Release from the System

Selected Constitutional Rights of Defendants
Right to Be Free from Unreasonable Search and Seizure
Vehicle Stops and Searches
Seizure and Search of the Person
Search of the Home
Right Not to Testify against Oneself
Right to Counsel
Right to Trial by Jury

Victims' Rights

Defendants' Rights versus Victims' Rights

Summary

Study Questions

Brief Essay Assignments

Internet Activities

Net Resources

Endnotes

350

In this chapter we begin our look into U.S. criminal justice systems by analyzing the philosophy on which they rest. The chapter opens with a discussion of the two major concepts of the adversary system: due process and equal protection. We then examine the effects of changes within criminal justice systems, along with the importance of discretion. Although criminal justice systems, even within the United States, may differ from one jurisdiction to another, all have the same essential stages. Those are examined individually.

The final section of the chapter analyzes four of the basic constitutional rights of defendants: the right to be free from unreasonable searches and seizures, the right not to testify against oneself, the right to counsel, and the right to trial by a jury. These and other constitutional rights are recognized to ensure that the government follows proper procedures in apprehending, charging, and trying people for alleged criminal acts. In some instances, the recognition of defendants' rights may conflict with victims' rights, a subject that is examined as well.

KEY TERMS
Adversary system
Arraignment
Arrest
Booking
Burden of proof
Charge
Criminal justice systems
Defendant
Due process
Equal protection
Grand jury
Habeas corpus
Indictment
Information
Initial appearance
Inquisitory system
Jurisdiction
Jury
Magistrate
Miranda warning
Peremptory challenge
Preliminary hearing
Probable cause
Search warrant
Trial
Venue
Victims' compensation legislation
Voir dire

Each chapter then closes with a built-in study guide consisting of a chapter summary, plentiful review questions, essay assignments, Internet activities, and Internet resources for use when writing papers.

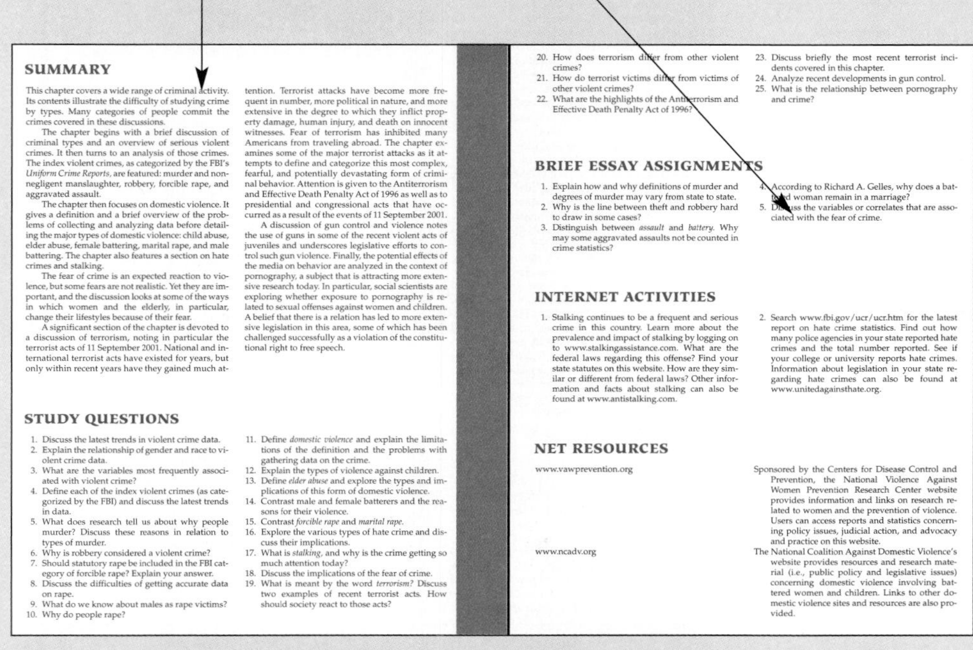
SUMMARY

This chapter covers a wide range of criminal activity. Its contents illustrate the difficulty of studying crime by types. Many categories of people commit the crimes covered in these discussions.

The chapter begins with a brief discussion of criminal types and an overview of serious violent crimes. It then turns to an analysis of those crimes. The index violent crimes, as categorized by the FBI's *Uniform Crime Reports*, are featured: murder and nonnegligent manslaughter, robbery, forcible rape, and aggravated assault.

The chapter then focuses on domestic violence. It gives a definition and a brief overview of the problems of collecting and analyzing data before detailing the major types of domestic violence: child abuse, elder abuse, female battering, marital rape, and male battering. The chapter also features a section on hate crimes and stalking.

The fear of crime is an expected reaction to violence, but some fears are not realistic. Yet they are important, and the discussion looks at some of the ways in which women and the elderly, in particular, change their lifestyles because of their fear.

A significant section of the chapter is devoted to a discussion of terrorism, noting in particular the terrorist acts of 11 September 2001. National and international terrorist acts have existed for years, but only within recent years have they gained much attention. Terrorist attacks have become more frequent in number, more political in nature, and more extensive in the degree to which they inflict property damage, human injury, and death on innocent witnesses. Fear of terrorism has inhibited many Americans from traveling abroad. The chapter examines some of the major terrorist attacks as it attempts to define and categorize this most complex, fearful, and potentially devastating form of criminal behavior. Attention is given to the Antiterrorism and Effective Death Penalty Act of 1996 as well as to presidential and congressional acts that have occurred as a result of the events of 11 September 2001.

A discussion of gun control and violence notes the use of guns in some of the recent violent acts of juveniles and underscores legislative efforts to control such gun violence. Finally, the potential effects of the media on behavior are analyzed in the context of pornography, a subject that is attracting more extensive research today. In particular, social scientists are exploring whether exposure to pornography is related to sexual offenses against women and children. A belief that there is a relation has led to more extensive legislation in this area, some of which has been challenged successfully as a violation of the constitutional right to free speech.

STUDY QUESTIONS

1. Discuss the latest trends in violent crime data.
2. Explain the relationship of gender and race to violent crime data.
3. What are the variables most frequently associated with violent crime?
4. Define each of the index violent crimes (as categorized by the FBI) and discuss the latest trends in data.
5. What does research tell us about why people murder? Discuss these reasons in relation to types of murder.
6. Why is robbery considered a violent crime?
7. Should statutory rape be included in the FBI category of forcible rape? Explain your answer.
8. Discuss the difficulties of getting accurate data on rape.
9. What do we know about males as rape victims?
10. Why do people rape?
11. Define *domestic violence* and explain the limitations of the definition and the problems with gathering data on the crime.
12. Explain the types of violence against children.
13. Define *elder abuse* and explore the types and implications of this form of domestic violence.
14. Contrast male and female batterers and the reasons for their violence.
15. Contrast *forcible rape* and *marital rape*.
16. Explore the various types of hate crime and discuss their implications.
17. What is *stalking*, and why is the crime getting so much attention today?
18. Discuss the implications of the fear of crime.
19. What is meant by the word *terrorism?* Discuss two examples of recent terrorist acts. How should society react to those acts?
20. How does terrorism differ from other violent crimes?
21. How do terrorist victims differ from victims of other violent crimes?
22. What are the highlights of the Antiterrorism and Effective Death Penalty Act of 1996?
23. Discuss briefly the most recent terrorist incidents covered in this chapter.
24. Analyze recent developments in gun control.
25. What is the relationship between pornography and crime?

BRIEF ESSAY ASSIGNMENTS

1. Explain how and why definitions of murder and degrees of murder may vary from state to state.
2. Why is the line between theft and robbery hard to draw in some cases?
3. Distinguish between *assault* and *battery*. Why may some aggravated assaults not be counted in crime statistics?
4. According to Richard A. Gelles, why does a battered woman remain in a marriage?
5. Discuss the variables or correlates that are associated with the fear of crime.

INTERNET ACTIVITIES

1. Stalking continues to be a frequent and serious crime in this country. Learn more about the prevalence and impact of stalking by logging on to www.stalkingassistance.com. What are the federal laws regarding this offense? Find your state statutes on this website. How are they similar or different from federal laws? Other information and facts about stalking can also be found at www.antistalking.com.
2. Search www.fbi.gov/ucr/ucr.htm for the latest report on hate crime statistics. Find out how many police agencies in your state reported hate crimes and the total number reported. See if your college or university reports hate crimes. Information about legislation in your state regarding hate crimes can also be found at www.unitedagainsthate.org.

NET RESOURCES

www.vawprevention.org — Sponsored by the Centers for Disease Control and Prevention, the National Violence Against Women Prevention Research Center website provides information and links on research related to women and the prevention of violence. Users can access reports and statistics concerning policy issues, judicial action, and advocacy and practice on this website.

www.ncadv.org — The National Coalition Against Domestic Violence's website provides resources and research material (i.e., public policy and legislative issues) concerning domestic violence involving battered women and children. Links to other domestic violence sites and resources are also provided.

Unique Media Focus boxes in every chapter further heighten the book's accessibility and relevancy and illustrate how the media treatment of a crime can at times distort our views and at other times enhance our understanding of an event or issue, perhaps creating greater public awareness of critical needs.

Media Focus 8.1

Identity Theft: Statements by the Media

During the past few years the media have frequently focused on the growing crime of identity theft, which, they claim, is reaching epidemic proportions. These informative accounts have alerted people to a crime that can cause severe economic damage as well as loss of personal time as victims cope with the results. Reports have appeared in media from the national television news to small-town newspapers.

Typical of the media reports was a 12 March 2002 news clip on CBS, which referred to identity theft as one of our fastest-growing crimes. According to this report, identity theft claims 750,000 new victims each year in the United States. Some victims spend weeks or even months trying to unravel the problems caused by identity theft. The report noted the need to maintain careful control over financial and other documents that contain numbers and other information that constitute an identity that can be stolen.[1]

On 5 February 2002 a small-town paper in New Hampshire reported that identity theft is becoming "an increasing problem" in that state. Identity theft was the number one consumer complaint made in New Hampshire in 2001. The article noted that the state had enacted an identity theft law in 2000, following the national law passed in 1998. Finally, the report emphasized that New Hampshire might become a leader in the national fight against identity theft. The Franklin Pierce Law Center in Concord, New Hampshire, will offer a degree program in e-commerce and cyberlaw. The program will feature identity theft.[2]

Finally, an article reprinted in a Tallahassee, Florida, paper noted that, although most people eventually recoup the money they lose through identity theft, "they also suffer damage to their credit records and invasion of privacy."[3]

1. *CBS National News*, 12 March 2002.
2. "Identity Theft an Increasing Problem in New Hampshire," *Conway Daily Sun* (5 February 2002), p. 3. (24 January 2002), p. 1E.
3. "Identity Theft Tops List of Frauds," *Tallahassee Democrat* 2.

enforcement officials may not have the technical expertise to solve computer crimes, and most cases that go to trial are highly technical, costly, and extremely time-consuming.

Media Focus 1.1

Crime in the Media

Television, movies, newspapers, and news magazines carry a recurrent theme of crime, especially violence. A recent *New York Times* article entitled "On TV, Crime Will Pay" enumerated the current popular crime-focused television shows and concluded,

> New York may have many fancy addresses, but where prime-time television is concerned, the most impressive is One Police Plaza. So many New York badges glisten in the lights of the cameras these days, it might behoove the police brass to think about recruiting from the drama schools.[1]

The media also provide an important function in time of crisis, such as the events of 11 September 2001, when hijacked planes flew into the twin towers of the World Trade Center, demolishing those buildings and some surrounding ones, while another plane was flown into the Pentagon in Washington, D.C. A fourth hijacked plane crashed in Pennsylvania, apparently after passengers fought with the hijackers. Presumably the hijackers on that aircraft were headed for Washington, D.C., as well. The death toll is not final, but it is estimated that close to 3,000 people, including several hundred police and firefighters, died in these terrorist attacks. This most severe of all terrorist attacks on American soil has changed a nation and its people, many of whom now fear flying commercial airlines or occupying tall buildings. Following the 11 September events, letters contaminated with anthrax were sent to Senator Tom Daschle, NBC News anchor Tom Brokaw and others, leading to several deaths. According to a *New York Times* article, "Anthrax is what the Nobel laureate Joshua Lederberg calls a 'professional pathogen,' a hardy germ that could wreak havoc if inhaled. The trick was turning it into an aerosol that lingers."[2] led the United States into war in Afghanistan, where the suspected terrorist was thought to be in hiding while directing his followers. As of this writing bin Laden has not been captured, but many of his allies have. Throughout the aftermath of 11 September, the media have played a key role in communicating the unfolding events to the American people. Although at times their presentations may have been excessive or misleading, the media probably have accounted for the intense display of loyalty and patriotism of the American people. The American flag is exhibited at homes, on cars, in businesses, and on mail boxes, and its image imprinted on clothing and numerous other objects. Patriotic songs are sung often, and signs outside businesses and churches proclaim GOD BLESS AMERICA, WE WILL NOT BE DEFEATED, or other statements that indicate a determination to eradicate terrorism.

The media also play a role in relaying trials to the public. Criminal trials are televised in some courts (although others refuse to permit this practice), illustrated by the so-called trial of the century, the trial of O. J. Simpson for the murders of his former wife Nicole Brown and her friend Ronald Goldman. Each step in the lengthy trial was followed by legal commentary, which was reported in detail by the media, while even the lawyers on the losing side made fortunes from publications, media appearances, and new jobs. Simpson was acquitted of those murders, and his civil trial, in which he was found liable for them, was followed with far less publicity.

Such intense media coverage of crimes raises the issue of whether the media actually contribute to future criminal acts by providing a forum for those who seek attention, even if in a socially unapproved manner.

1. "On TV, Crime Will Pay," *New York Times* (11 May 2001),

To help students master criminology's vast array of vocabulary, key terms are identified in boldface within the text and are defined in the margins throughout; they are also collected in a comprehensive glossary at the end of the text for easy reference later.

FIGURE 7.8
Hate Crimes: Percent Distribution, 2000[1]

Source: Federal Bureau of Investigation, *Crime in the United States: Uniform Crime Reports 2000* (Washington, DC: U.S. Government Printing Office, 2001), p. 62.

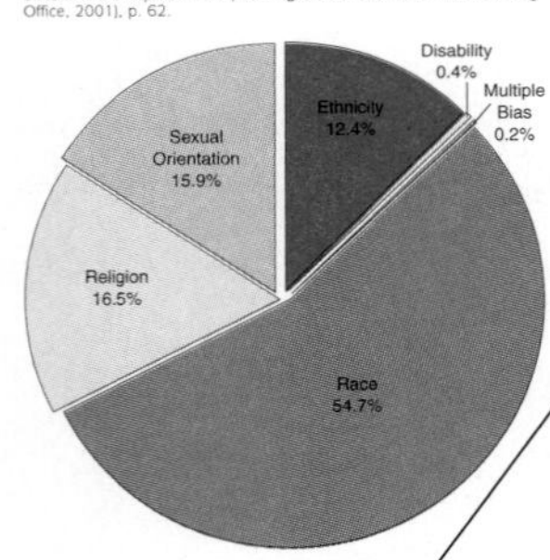

[1] Due to rounding, the percentages do not add to 100.0.

tims, and 7,642 known offenders. Most of the crimes (4,368) were motivated by racial bias, with religious bias accounting for 1,483; sexual-orientation bias for 1,330; ethnicity–national origin bias for 927, disability bias for 36; and multiple biases for 8. The percentages for each of these categories are noted on Figure 7.8. Crimes against persons accounted for 65.3 percent of 2000 hate crimes, with 34 percent against property and 0.6 percent against society. Of those property hate crimes, 85.3 percent consisted of damage, destruction, or vandalism. The most frequently reported single offense was intimidation, which accounted for 34.6 percent of the total bias crimes.[62]

Several hate crimes have been publicized widely in recent years, although not all of these were actually prosecuted under hate crime statutes. In 1998 university student Matthew Shephard became a symbol of hate crimes after Russell A. Henderson and Aaron J. McKinney tortured and killed him, allegedly because he was gay. Both defendants were sentenced to life in prison. In Texas that same year, James Byrd Jr., an African American, was tortured and dragged by a truck by three white men, all of whom were convicted of the crime. Two of the defendants received capital sentences, while the third will spend at least four decades in prison for his lesser role in the crime. Although Texas had no hate crime statute, its laws permit enhanced sentencing if during the sentencing hearing "the court determines that the defendant intentionally selected the victim primarily because of the defendant's bias or prejudice against a group." The statute does not enumerate specific groups.[63]

Stalking Defined in the National Violence Against Women Survey as "a course of conduct directed at a specific person that involves repeated visual or physical proximity, nonconsensual communication, or verbal, written or implied threats, or a combination thereof, that would cause a reasonable person fear." The term *repeated* means two or more times.

Stalking

Some acts do not rise to the level of actual physical contact but are still frightening to potential victims. **Stalking** is an example. Stalking statutes are relatively new, with the federal one established in the fall of 1996, when President Bill Clinton signed into law the Interstate Stalking Punishment and Prevention Act. This act is aimed at stalking on federal property or across state lines.[64]

State stalking statutes are also relatively new, and they differ in their coverage. In general, stalking statutes are designed to punish individuals who watch, follow, and harass others repeatedly over a period of time. Some of the statutes, however, have been invalidated by courts taking the position that the laws are vague or too broad. For example, the Kansas antistalking statute was

GLOSSARY

acquired immune deficiency syndrome (AIDS) A deadly disease discovered in 1979 and spreading throughout the world. The virus that causes AIDS (the human immunodeficiency virus, or HIV) is spread through the exchange of bodily fluids, which occurs most frequently during sexual contact but may occur in other ways such as blood transfusions and the use of contaminated needles. There is no known cure for the disease.

administrative law Rules and regulations made by agencies to which power has been delegated by the state legislature or the U.S. Congress. Administrative agencies investigate and decide cases concerning potential violations of these rules.

adversary system One of two primary systems for settling disputes in court. The accused is presumed to be innocent. A defense attorney and a prosecuting attorney attempt to convince a judge or a jury of their respective versions of a criminal case. *See also* **inquisitory system.**

aggravated assault Technically, an assault is a threat to commit a battery, but often the term is used to refer to a **battery.** In that case, aggravated assault involves an assault or a battery intended to cause serious injury or death and often includes the use of a deadly weapon.

anomie A state of normlessness in society that may be caused by decreased homogeneity and that provides a setting conducive to crimes and other antisocial acts.

antitrust laws State and federal statutes designed to protect trade and commerce from unlawful restraints, such as price fixing, price discrimination, and monopolies.

appeal A step in a judicial proceeding, petitioning a higher court to review a lower court's decision.

appellant The losing party in a lower court who appeals to a higher court for review of the decision.

appellee The winning party in a lower court who argues on appeal that the lower court's decision should not be reversed.

arraignment In criminal practice, the stage in criminal justice systems when the defendant appears before the court, hears the charges, is given instructions on his or her legal rights, and enters a plea.

arrest The act of depriving persons of their liberty; taking suspects into custody for the purpose of charging them formally with a crime.

arson The willful and malicious burning of the property of another with or without the intent to defraud. Burning of one's own property with the intent to defraud is included in some jurisdictions.

assault *See* **aggravated assault.**

attempt crimes Crimes in which the offender engages in some effort to commit a crime but does not carry through with it. Planning is not sufficient; some step must be taken toward committing the criminal act, and a criminal intent must be shown.

bail The release of a defendant from custody pending a legal proceeding, such as a trial. *See also* **bail bond.**

bail bond A legal document stating the terms under which a defendant is granted release from jail prior to a legal proceeding, such as a trial. The bail bond may or may not be secured with money or property pledged by the defendant or others. Technically, if the defendant does not appear at the time and place designated in the document, the court may require the forfeiture of any money or property used to secure the bail bond.

battered person syndrome A syndrome arising from a cycle of abuse by a special person, often a parent or a spouse, that leads the battered person to perceive that violence against the offender is the only way to end the abuse. In some cases the battered person murders the batterer, and in some jurisdictions evidence of the battered person syndrome constitutes a defense to the murder.

battery See **assault.**

behavior theory Theory based on the belief that all behavior is learned and can be unlearned. It is the basis for behavior modification, one approach used for changing behavior in both institutionalized and noninstitutionalized settings.

biocriminology The introduction of biological variables into the study of criminology.

blackmail The unlawful demand for money or property by threatening bodily harm or exposure of information that is disgraceful or criminal. *See also* **extortion.**

booking The process of recording an arrest officially by entering the suspect's name, offense charged, place, time, arresting officer, and reason for arrest; usually done at a police station by the arresting officer.

boot camps Correctional facilities designed to detain offenders, primarily juveniles or young adults, for short periods, such as six months; they usually include a regimented daily routine of physical exercise, work, and discipline, resembling military training. Most of the programs include rehabilitative measures such as drug treatment and educational courses.

bootlegging The illegal production, use, or sale of alcoholic beverages; the term was used particularly during Prohibition.

bribery Offering money, goods, services, information, or anything else of value for the purpose of denied when Grimshaw accepted a reduction of the punitive award from $125 million to $2.5 million. Ford appealed on a number of legal issues; Grimshaw appealed on other issues. The appellate court upheld the lower court and the judgment stood.

The Pinto represented Ford's attempt in the early 1970s to produce a compact car that would sell for $2,000. The design and production were on a rush schedule. The reasons for considering the design of this car defective are complicated, but at issue was the location of the fuel tank. For design reasons, it was placed behind rather than over the rear axle, as was the custom in other compacts at that time. Because this made the car less crush-resistant, death by fire was more probable in a Pinto than in other compact cars. Evidence revealed that the design defects were known to Ford's corporate executives and that they were warned of the dangers. The cost of adding additional crush space was $15.30 per car, but high-level officials decided to go ahead with the project for cost-saving reasons. The court concluded as follows:[41]

Grimshaw v. Ford Motor Company

Through the results of the crash tests Ford knew that the Pinto's fuel tank and rear structure would expose consumers to serious injury or death in a 20 to 30 mile-per-hour collision. There was evidence that Ford could have corrected the hazardous design defects at minimal cost but decided to defer correction of the shortcomings by engaging in a cost-benefit analysis balancing human lives and limbs against corporate profits. Ford's institutional mentality was shown to be one of callous indifference to public safety. There was substantial evidence that Ford's conduct constituted "conscious disregard" of the probability of injury to members of the consuming public.

The *Grimshaw* case illustrates how gross negligence can be used in a civil suit to award punitive damages to a plaintiff. The fact that Ford was acquitted in the criminal trial does not mean that in a similar case another corporation will not be convicted. Corporations engaging in conduct that is grossly negligent or reckless may find themselves convicted of crimes.

In fact, in December 1999 SabreTech, a corporation dealing with aircraft maintenance, was convicted of charges stemming from the 11 May 1996 fatal crash of a ValuJet Airlines plane. All 110 persons on board the flight from Miami to Atlanta were killed when the plane went down in fire in the Florida Everglades. SabreTech was ordered to pay $11 million in damages to the families of the victims. The company was convicted of improper handling of the hazardous materials that caused the fire in the aircraft.[42]

Defective design and defective manufacture may occur in any product, and the law may ... deceased). ... criminal pe... other consu... imposed on... in deciding...

In a de... Food, Drug... tance of pr... Court, rats... the Court, t... that he or s...

In keeping with the text's commitment to integrating law, theory, social science research, and the criminal justice system in a single text, excerpts detailing legal decisions are included throughout the text to show how such decisions affect the study of criminology. Also included are two unique appendixes to aid in this same effort: Appendix A, with selected constitutional amendments to provide quick and easy reference to the reader who wishes to read the entire amendment mentioned in the text, and Appendix B, on how to read a case citation.

APPENDIX A

Selected Amendments of the U.S. Constitution

Amendment I (1791)

Congress shall make no law respecting an establishment of religion, or prohibiting the free exercise thereof; or abridging the freedom of speech, or of the press, or the right of the people peaceably to assemble, and to petition the Government for a redress of grievances.

Amendment IV (1791)

The right of the people to be secure in their persons, houses, papers, and effects, against unreasonable searches and seizures, shall not be violated, and no Warrants shall issue, but upon probable cause, supported by Oath or affirmation, and particularly describing the place to be searched, and the persons or things to be seized.

Amendment V (1791)

No person shall be held to answer for a capital, ... unless on a presentment or indictment of a Grand ... the land or naval forces, or in the Militia, when i... or public danger; nor shall any person be subject ... put in jeopardy of life or limb; nor shall be comp... a witness against himself, nor be deprived of lif... due process of law; nor shall private property be ... just compensation.

Amendment VI (1791)

In all criminal prosecutions, the accused shall e... public trial, by an impartial jury of the State and ... have been committed; which district shall have b... law, and to be informed of the nature and caus... fronted with the witnesses against him; to have ... ing witnesses in his favor, and to have the assista...

Amendment VIII (1791)

Excessive bail shall not be required, nor excessiv... unusual punishments inflicted.

Amendment X (1791)

The powers not delegated to the United States b... ited by it to the States, are reserved to the States ...

APPENDIX B

Guide to Legal Citations of Reported Decisions

Pugh v. Locke, 406 F.Supp. 318 (M.D.Ala. 1976), aff'd., remanded sub nom., Newman v. Alabama, 559 F.2d 283 (5th Cir. 1977), *reh'g. denied*, 564 F.2d 97 (5th Cir. 1977), *and rev'd. in part sub nom.*, 438 U.S. 781 (1978), *later proceeding sub nom.*, 466 F.Supp. 628 (M.D.Ala. 1979), *later proceeding*, Newman v. Alabama, 688 F.2d 1312 (11th Cir. 1982), *cert. denied*, 460 U.S. 1083 (1983), *later proceeding sub nom.*, 740 F.2d 1513 (11th Cir. 1984), *dismissed*, 1988 U.S.Dist LEXIS 18634 (M.D.Ala., Dec. 28, 1988).

This case has a number of citations, which is not common among all cases but is common among those involving unconstitutional conditions in prisons and jails. The case is used here because it illustrates so many elements of case citations. There are other citations to *later proceedings* that have been eliminated from the lengthy citation.

Original Citation

[Pugh v. Locke][1] [406][2] [F.Supp.][3] [318][4] [M.D.Ala.][5] [1976].[6]

1. Name of case.
2. Volume number of reporter in which case is published.
3. Name of reporter; see Abbreviations for Commonly Used Reporters, later in this appendix.
4. Page in the reporter where the decision begins.
5. Court deciding the case.
6. Year decided.

Additional Case History

[*aff'd., remanded sub nom.*][7] [Newman v. Alabama][8] [559][9] [F.2d][10] [283][11] [(5th Cir. 1977)][12] [*and rev'd. in part sub nom.*][13] [438][14] [U.S.][15] [781][16] [1978][17] [*later proceeding sub nom.*] or [*later proceeding*][18] [*cert. denied*][19] [*dismissed*][20]

7. Affirmed and remanded (sent back for further proceedings) under a different name. The appellate court told the lower court that it agreed with part of its decision but that some aspect of the decision needed to be reconsidered.
8. The name under which the case was affirmed and remanded.
9. Volume number of the reporter in which case is published.
10. Abbreviated name of reporter (Federal Reporter, second series).
11. Page number on which the opinion begins.
12. The court deciding the case and the date decision was given.
13. Additional history—appeal to U.S. Supreme Court, which reversed the

PART

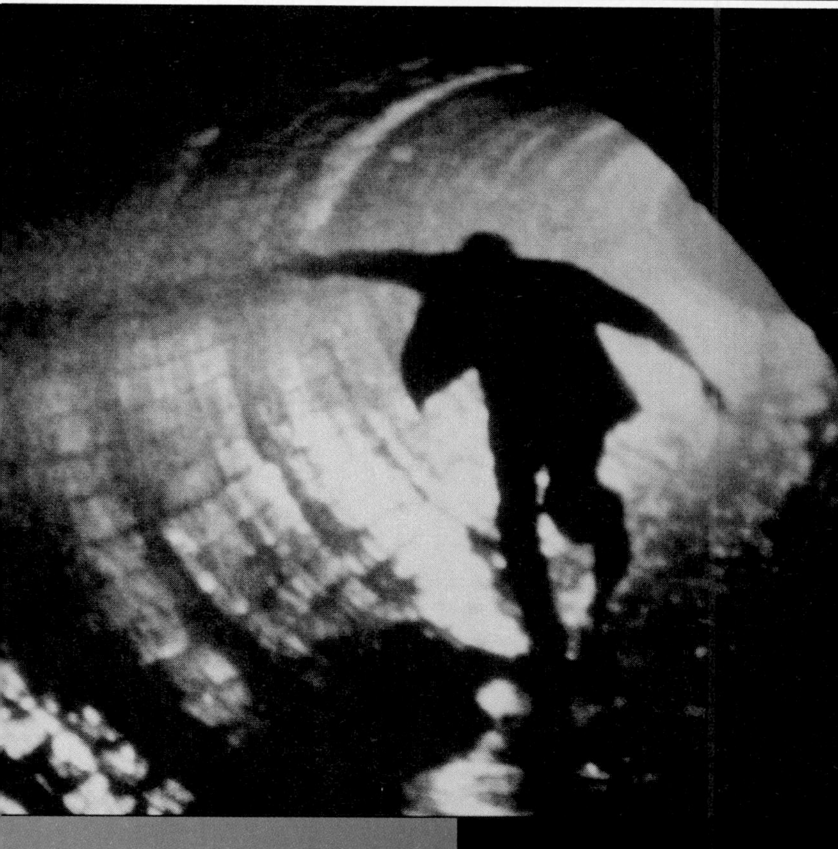

Introduction to the Study of Crime and Criminology

The study of crime and criminology is a complex but fascinating venture. It should begin with an understanding of the basic concepts of crime, criminal law, and criminology, and that is the focus of the first chapter of Part I. The chapter explores the meaning of these concepts in the context of which behaviors should be covered by the criminal law and whether the discipline of criminology should focus on a broader range of behaviors.

Chapter 2 concludes the introductory material with a focus on how crime is measured. It looks at the characteristics of offenders and of victims, giving close attention to the variables of gender, race, and age.

1

▶ Hijacked United Airlines flight 175 flies toward the World Trade Center's twin towers shortly before slamming into the south tower. The north tower is burning following an earlier attack by another hijacked airliner. The stunning aerial assaults on the high commercial complex, where more than 40,000 people worked, were part of a coordinated attack, which included attacks on the Pentagon in Washington, and a fourth plane, apparently heading for another Washington, D.C. target, that crashed in a Pennsylvania field. The events of 11 September 2001, which resulted in the deaths of about 3,000 people, constitued the most severe attack on U.S. soil in the nation's history. (Sean Adair/Reuters/Getty Images)

Crime, Criminal Law, and Criminology

OUTLINE

This first chapter provides an introduction to the study of crime and the criminal. The concept of crime is explored, followed by an analysis of the concept of law and a distinction between civil and criminal law. The purpose of criminal law as an agent of social control is discussed in relationship to efforts to control sexual behavior. In its final section the chapter discusses criminology and the study of crime.

KEY TERMS

acquired immune deficiency syndrome (AIDS)

administrative law

case law

causation

civil law

crime

criminal law

criminology

felony

felony-murder doctrine

intent

mala in se

mala prohibita

mens rea

misdemeanor

stare decisis

statutory law

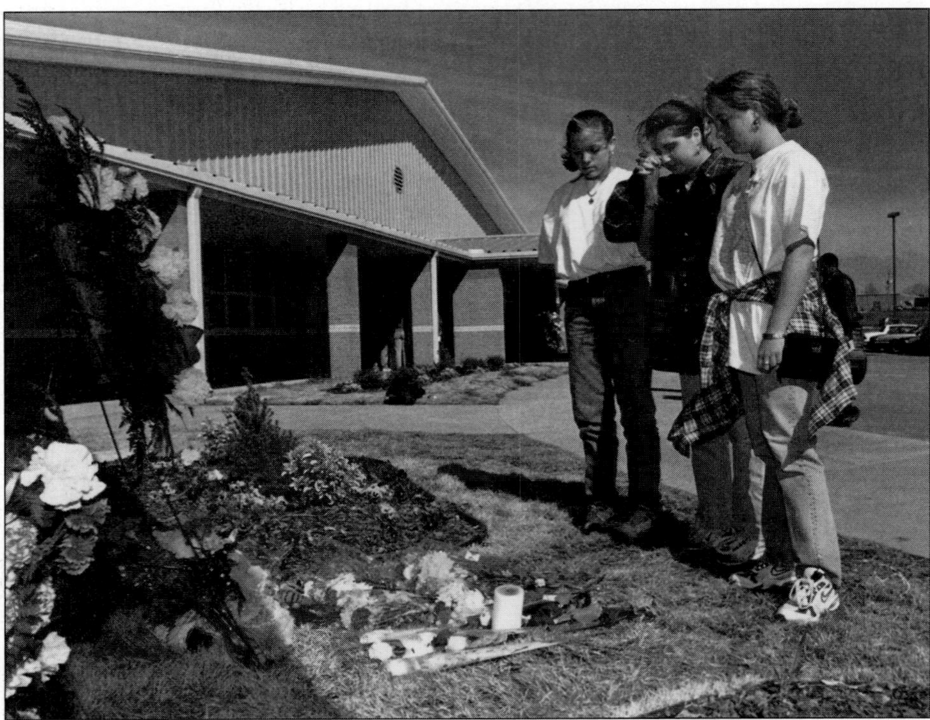

Local college students stand by a makeshift memorial at the scene of the shooting at the Westside Middle School in Jonesboro, Arkansas, on 25 March 1998. One teacher and four students were killed, and 10 other people were injured. (Jeff Mitchell/Reuters/Getty Images)

In recent years shocking crimes such as the 11 September 2001 terrorist attacks on the World Trade Center's twin towers in New York City and the Pentagon in Washington, D.C.; the dissemination of the deadly agent anthrax in 2001; the 1995 bombing of the federal building in Oklahoma City; the sending of mail bombs by the Unabomber; and the shootings by teenagers in schools in several U.S. cities have led many to ask why people engage in violent acts. Chapter 2 notes that U.S. crime rates have been dropping, but the senseless and unexplainable violence of certain crimes, especially the terrorist acts of 1995 and 2001 and the violent crimes committed by young persons, are frightening and baffling. It is the purpose of this text to explore the possible explanations for these and other crimes as well as to consider changes that might be made in U.S. criminal justice systems.

Attempts to explain and control criminal behavior involve many disciplines. Although other disciplines are mentioned, this text focuses on the social sciences and their interaction with criminal law, the legal mechanism by which society reacts to crime and through which it attempts to prevent criminal behavior. But the social sciences do not tell the full story of the country's interest in crime. In fact, probably few read the scientific reports of the scholars who study criminal behavior. Rather, public attention is captured by the media, as Media Focus 1.1 notes.

THE CONCEPT OF CRIME

The concept of **crime** formulates the basis for a study of criminal behavior. The word is difficult to explain, for not all agree on how it should be defined. This text uses the

On 19 April 2000, the fifth anniversary of the bombing of the federal building in Oklahoma City, the above memorial was dedicated to the memory of the 168 persons who died in the attack. An empty chair contains the name of each victim. Timothy McVeigh was convicted and executed for this terrorist act. At his federal trial, Terry L. Nichols was found guilty of conspiracy and of manslaughter but not of murder. A third suspect, Michael Fortier, entered a plea negotiation with federal prosecutors in which he agreed to testify against McVeigh and Nichols. (Bob Daemmerich/Stock Boston)

Crime An international act or omission that violates criminal statutory or case law and for which the state provides punishment.

legal approach because that is the basis for permitting the state to take action against persons accused of crimes, but before dissecting a definition of the word *crime* it is important to understand that other approaches are important as well.

Social scientists argue that if we are interested in knowing why people engage in behavior that is detrimental to society, we should go beyond the legal definition and include behavior that is defined as criminal but for which no arrests have been made. Accused persons who are not prosecuted because of legal technicalities should be included. The focus is on the behavior: Why do people do what they do? This approach claims that the legal technicalities are not relevant to a study of criminal behavior. In addition, some would claim that *deviant behavior,* which is behavior that is different from that of the generally held social norms but not normally covered by the criminal law, should also be studied.

These positions are important in the analysis of why people do what they do. But in U.S. legal systems, only those persons who have actually been convicted of crimes are considered criminal, and thus it is important to focus on that approach. The term *crime* should be limited to its strict legal definition, and the term *criminal* used only to refer to those who have been convicted in criminal courts. The terms *crime* and *criminal* have severe implications and repercussions. They should be used only after proper procedures have been followed to establish which acts are criminal, as in the case of defining *crime,* or in the case of *criminal,* after a guilty plea or the determination of guilt by a judge or jury. This is not to suggest that nonlegal definitions are not relevant. From the point of view of the causes of human behavior, it is important for social scientists to study the behavior of persons who have committed criminal acts but who have not been processed through criminal justice systems to the point of conviction.

Media Focus 1.1

Crime in the Media

Television, movies, newspapers, and news magazines carry a recurrent theme of crime, especially violence. A recent *New York Times* article entitled "On TV, Crime Will Pay" enumerated the current popular crime-focused television shows and concluded,

> New York may have many fancy addresses, but where prime-time television is concerned, the most impressive is One Police Plaza. So many New York badges glisten in the lights of the cameras these days, it might behoove the police brass to think about recruiting from the drama schools.[1]

The media also provide an important function in time of crisis, such as the events of 11 September 2001, when hijacked planes flew into the twin towers of the World Trade Center, demolishing those buildings and some surrounding ones, while another plane was flown into the Pentagon in Washington, D.C. A fourth hijacked plane crashed in Pennsylvania, apparently after passengers fought with the hijackers. Presumably the hijackers on that aircraft were headed for Washington, D.C., as well. The death toll is not final, but it is estimated that close to 3,000 people, including several hundred police and firefighters, died in these terrorist attacks. This most severe of all terrorist attacks on American soil has changed a nation and its people, many of whom now fear flying commercial airlines or occupying tall buildings. Following the 11 September events, letters contaminated with anthrax were sent to Senator Tom Daschle, NBC News anchor Tom Brokaw and others, leading to several deaths. According to a *New York Times* article, "Anthrax is what the Nobel laureate Joshua Lederberg calls a 'professional pathogen,' a hardy germ that could wreak havoc if inhaled. The trick was turning it into an aerosol that lingers."[2]

The events of 11 September, allegedly masterminded by Osama bin Laden, a Muslim extremist, led the United States into war in Afghanistan, where the suspected terrorist was thought to be in hiding while directing his followers. As of this writing bin Laden has not been captured, but many of his allies have. Throughout the aftermath of 11 September, the media have played a key role in communicating the unfolding events to the American people. Although at times their presentations may have been excessive or misleading, the media probably have accounted for the intense display of loyalty and patriotism of the American people. The American flag is exhibited at homes, on cars, in businesses, and on mail boxes, and its image imprinted on clothing and numerous other objects. Patriotic songs are sung often, and signs outside businesses and churches proclaim GOD BLESS AMERICA, WE WILL NOT BE DEFEATED, or other statements that indicate a determination to eradicate terrorism.

The media also play a role in relaying trials to the public. Criminal trials are televised in some courts (although others refuse to permit this practice), illustrated by the so-called trial of the century, the trial of O. J. Simpson for the murders of his former wife Nicole Brown and her friend Ronald Goldman. Each step in the lengthy trial was followed by legal commentary, which was reported in detail by the media, while even the lawyers on the losing side made fortunes from publications, media appearances, and new jobs. Simpson was acquitted of those murders, and his civil trial, in which he was found liable for them, was followed with far less publicity.

Such intense media coverage of crimes raises the issue of whether the media actually contribute to future criminal acts by providing a forum for those who seek attention, even if in a socially unapproved manner.

1. "On TV, Crime Will Pay," *New York Times* (11 May 2001), p. 1B.
2. "Anthrax Letter Awaits Discovery, C.D.C. Chief Hints," *New York Times* (27 October 2001), p. 1.

The concept of crime must be examined more closely. In U.S. criminal justice systems, the definition of a crime must be precise, unambiguous, and usable. It must clarify who is and who is not a criminal.

Crime is an act defined by law. Unless the elements specified by criminal law are present and proved beyond a reasonable doubt, a person should not be convicted of a crime. The following legal definition serves as our reference point:

> Crime is an intentional act or omission in violation of criminal law (statutory and case law), committed without defense or justification and sanctioned by the state as a felony or misdemeanor.[1]

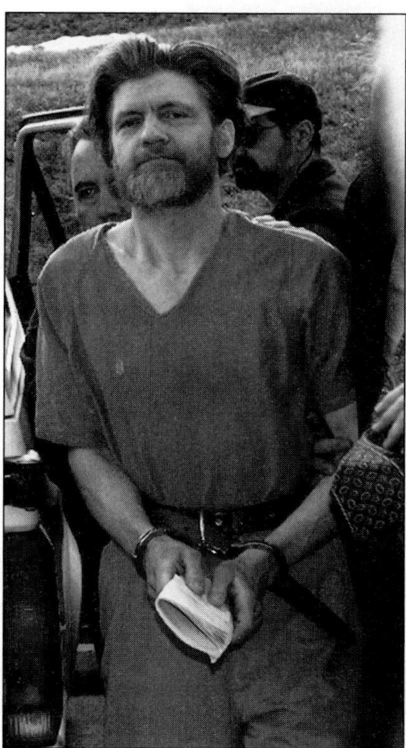

Theodore J. Kaczynski was living in a mountain cabin in Montana when he was arrested in April 1996. The former math professor was accused of crimes committed by the so-called Unabomber, who sent mail bombs over a 17-year period, killing 3 persons and wounding 23 others, some seriously. At the beginning of his trial for a murder in California, Kaczynski entered a guilty plea in exchange for a life rather than a death sentence. (AP Photo/Elaine Thompson)

An Act or Omission

The first part of the definition of crime embodies philosophies central to U.S. legal systems. A person may not be punished for his or her thoughts; crimes must involve actions. Under U.S. legal systems an individual cannot be punished for thinking about committing a crime if no elements are put into action toward the commission of that crime. To consider murdering a spouse but to do nothing toward the commission of that act is not a crime; hiring someone to murder a spouse is a crime.

There is one important exception to the act requirement: In some cases a failure to act may be criminal, but that is true only when there is a legal duty to act. Moral duty does not suffice. According to an 1897 court decision, "With purely moral obligations the law does not deal."[2] For example, a Michigan judge dismissed murder charges against a female defendant who did not give assistance to a woman locked in a car trunk and crying for help. The victim died of dehydration. The female defendant was a passenger in the car, but there was no evidence that she was involved in (or even knew about) the crimes for which the driver was charged. The judge dismissed the charges against her because he could not find a law that required her to aid the victim "even if she knew or suspected someone was locked in the trunk."[3]

In general we do not have affirmative duties to prevent people from being injured or killed. We may watch while people are brutalized by others or while a child is drowning. Unless there is a legal duty to aid, the law may not be invoked even though it would have been easy for us to prevent the injury or death in these situations. We may be moral monsters, but we have not violated the civil or criminal law. A legal duty may exist, however, if we are the parent, spouse, or other close relative, or if we have assumed a duty through a contractual relationship such as operating a licensed day care center. Legal duties may be imposed in other special relationships as well.

In order to be criminal, acts or omissions must be voluntary, and the actor must have control over his or her actions. If a person has a heart attack while driving a car and kills another human being, he or she should not be charged with a crime if the heart attack was an involuntary act over which the person had no control. The case might be different, however, if the individual had had a series of heart attacks and therefore knew it might be dangerous to drive an automobile.

The Intent Requirement and Its Exceptions

Intent In the legal sense, the design, determination, or purpose with which a person uses a particular means to effect a certain result; it shows the presence of will in the act that consummates a crime.

Mens rea Criminal intent; the guilty or wrongful purpose of the defendant at the time he or she committed a criminal act.

An act or the omission of an act is not sufficient to constitute a crime. The law requires **intent,** or ***mens rea***—the mental element—to establish criminal culpability. In many cases intent is the critical factor in determining whether an act was or was not a crime. In addition, it may determine the degree of crime committed (for example, whether a killing is first- or second-degree murder). Despite the importance of *mens rea,* historically the term has not been defined clearly or developed thoroughly.

The Texas Penal Code provides an example of a frequently used approach to defining criminal intent. Texas divides culpability into four mental states: intentional, knowing, reckless, and criminal negligence. Each of these mental states is defined in Exhibit 1.1. The interpretation of these four tiers of culpability has been the subject of considerable dispute. It is clear, however, that a person may be held criminally liable for the unintended consequences of an intended act. In addition, a person may be held criminally liable for injury or death to a victim other than the intended victim or for a more serious degree of harm than that intended. Consider the following examples.

EXHIBIT 1.1

General Requirements of Culpability

TEXAS PENAL CODE, CHAPTER 6 (2001)

Section 6.02. Requirement of Culpability.

(a) Except as provided in Subsection (b), a person does not commit an offense unless he intentionally, knowingly, recklessly, or with criminal negligence engages in conduct as the definition of the offense requires.

(b) If the definition of an offense does not prescribe a culpable mental state, a culpable mental state is nevertheless required unless the definition plainly dispenses with any mental element. . . .

Section 6.03. Definitions of Culpable Mental States.

(a) A person acts intentionally, or with intent, with respect to the nature of his conduct or to a result of his conduct when it is his conscious objective or desire to engage in the conduct or cause the result.

(b) A person acts knowingly, or with knowledge, with respect to the nature of his conduct or to circumstances surrounding his conduct when he is aware of the nature of his conduct or that the circumstances exist. A person acts knowingly, or with knowledge, with respect to a result of his conduct when he is aware that his conduct is reasonably certain to cause the result.

(c) A person acts recklessly, or is reckless, with respect to circumstances surrounding his conduct or the result of his conduct when he is aware of but consciously disregards a substantial and unjustifiable risk that the circumstances exist or the result will occur. The risk must be of such a nature and degree that its disregard constitutes a gross deviation from the standard of care that an ordinary person would exercise under all the circumstances as viewed from the actor's standpoint.

(d) A person acts with criminal negligence, or is criminally negligent with respect to circumstances surrounding his conduct or the result of his conduct when he ought to be aware of a substantial and unjustifiable risk that the circumstances exist or the result will occur. The risk must be of such a nature and degree that the failure to perceive it constitutes a gross deviation from the standard of care that an ordinary person would exercise under all the circumstances as viewed from the actor's standpoint.

In the first case, Jones shot at Anders with the intent of killing him; but, being a bad shot, he missed Anders and killed Williams instead. Jones can be charged with the death of the victim. In the second case, an unhappy husband wanted to scare his wife to convince her that they should move to another neighborhood. The husband hired a man to fire several shots into the air while his wife was walking the dog, but the accomplice was a bad shot and killed the woman. Even though there was no specific intent to kill the woman, both men could be charged with murder. They plotted, and one carried out, an act that a reasonable person should have known could result in serious injury or death. It is possible that in this case the charge would be reduced to reckless or negligent homicide, but the point is that the actors could be charged with murder.

There are exceptions to the requirement of a criminal intent. In some situations employers may be liable for acts of their employees, even if the employers do not know their employees are committing the acts. For example, the president of a drug company was found guilty of violating a provision of the Pure Food and Drug Act, which requires proper labeling of drugs. He did not know that the drugs had been mislabeled by employees who were responsible for repackaging and labeling the drugs received from the manufacturer, but the U.S. Supreme Court upheld the conviction.[4]

Felony-murder doctrine Doctrine used to hold a defendant liable for murder if a human life is taken during another felony, such as armed robbery, kidnapping, or arson, even if the defendant did not commit the murder.

Statutory law Law created or defined in a written enactment by the legislative body, as opposed to case law.

Case law The aggregate of reported judicial decisions, which are legally binding court interpretations of written statutes and previous court decisions or rules made by courts in the absence of written statutes *or* other sources of law.

Administrative law Rules and regulations made by agencies to which power has been delegated by the state legislature or the U.S. Congress. Administrative agencies investigate and decide cases concerning potential violations of these rules.

Causation Causation assumes a relationship between two phenomena in which the occurrence of the former brings about changes in the latter. In the legal sense, causation is the element of a crime that requires the existence of a causal relationship between the offender's conduct and the particular harmful consequences.

Acquired immune deficiency syndrome (AIDS) A deadly disease discovered in 1979 and spreading throughout the world. The virus that causes AIDS (the human immunodeficiency virus, or HIV) is spread through the exchange of bodily fluids, most frequently during sexual contact but it may occur in other ways such as blood transfusions and the use of contaminated needles. There is no known cure for the disease.

Another exception to the intent requirement is the **felony-murder doctrine,** under which a person may be held criminally liable for murder when death results from the commission of another felony. To illustrate, a person who commits arson by setting fire to a house in which several children die as a result may be charged with both murder and arson. In many jurisdictions the felony-murder doctrine is limited to deaths that follow the commission of inherently dangerous felonies such as forcible rape, robbery, arson, and burglary.

Violation of the Elements of Criminal Law

To be convicted of a crime, a person must violate the criminal law. Criminal law comes from three sources: the federal and state constitutions, statutes, and court decisions. Statutes enacted by state legislatures and the U.S. Congress constitute **statutory law,** in contrast to **case law,** the term applied to law that develops from judicial decisions.

Another source of criminal law is **administrative law.** State legislatures and the U.S. Congress may delegate to administrative agencies—the Federal Trade Commission, the Internal Revenue Service, public universities, human rights commissions, and others—the power to make rules, interpret those rules, and process violations. The rule-making procedures must follow specified guidelines. These rules and the decisions concerning them constitute administrative law, which is civil law, although a violation of administrative law may result in a criminal penalty if it becomes necessary to ask a criminal court to enforce the administrative decision. Even in that case, however, society normally does not look upon the individual in the same negative light as it does upon those who are convicted in criminal courts.

In order for a defendant to be convicted, all elements of a crime must be proved beyond a reasonable doubt. Establishing proof of any element may be difficult, but one of the most difficult is **causation.** In recent years the causation element has been a hindrance to prosecuting many of the charges brought against individuals who have engaged in sexual and other acts after having been diagnosed with **acquired immune deficiency syndrome (AIDS),** a deadly disease first discovered in 1979 and spreading rapidly throughout the world today. Even in these cases, however, both the criminal law and the civil law have been used successfully. For example, a New York court has held that under some circumstances an individual may bring a civil suit for the negligent infliction of emotional distress in situations in which the alleged victim could have reasonable fear of contracting AIDS.[5] As Exhibit 1.2 notes, AIDS has become the focus of some lawsuits.

Without Justification or Defense

Individuals are not always held responsible for acts that cause harm or injury to others; the law recognizes some extenuating circumstances. An act or omission of an act is not a crime if the individual has a legally recognized justification or defense for the act. For example, a person faced with the possibility of being killed might use the defense of justifiable homicide. A police officer in pursuit of an armed robbery suspect who fires at the officer may be justified in killing that suspect. People may be excused from criminal liability for inflicting serious bodily harm on others if they are in danger of being injured by these persons, but they may use only the force necessary for their own protection.

An individual charged with a crime may offer evidence to defeat the criminal charge. A variety of defenses are recognized; the extent and complexity of legal defenses are beyond the scope of this discussion. Chapter 4 mentions the insanity defense, one of the more publicized—although infrequently used and seldom successful—defenses.

EXHIBIT 1.2

The Spread of AIDS Leads to Numerous Lawsuits

Institutions and social relationships are affected by the spread of the deadly virus that causes acquired immune deficiency syndrome (AIDS), a condition that results in the inability of the body to fight infections. The prevalence of AIDS has created medical, social, and legal problems.

AIDS was first diagnosed among previously healthy gay and bisexual males in New York City and in San Francisco in 1981, although as early as 1979, signs of the condition were found in blood that had been donated to blood banks. AIDS is caused by the human immunodeficiency virus (HIV), which attacks certain white blood cells and renders them unable to combat infections. After entering a host cell the virus may remain dormant for a long period; thus, AIDS symptoms may not show up immediately after the virus is contracted. But once the virus is stimulated into action (and scientists do not know what causes that to happen), it reproduces rapidly.

Thus far, there is no known cure for AIDS. HIV is transmitted through the exchange of bodily fluids (such as during sexual contact), through inoculation with blood or blood products, and from a pregnant woman to her fetus. Sexual contact is the most frequent method of transmission, accounting for a majority of AIDS cases. The virus may be transmitted through heterosexual as well as same-gender sexual contacts.

Since its discovery AIDS has spread rapidly. It has threatened to reach epidemic proportions in many countries and has been transmitted frequently among heterosexual as well as gay couples. AIDS has resulted in civil and criminal actions. AIDS patients have sued insurance carriers for canceling health insurance policies. Some who contracted AIDS through artificial insemination, blood transfusions, or organ transplants have sued health care providers. Discrimination in employment cases has been attributed to AIDS. Criminal cases alleging that an AIDS patient tried to infect another person have been brought, most without much success. Some have succeeded, however, as the following case illustrates.

Curtis Weeks, a Texas drifter with advanced AIDS who was incarcerated for robbing a Kmart, spat on a correctional officer twice and hit the officer in the lips, nostrils, eyes, and cheeks. Weeks yelled that he had AIDS when he spat on the officer. Weeks was charged and convicted of attempted murder and sentenced to life in prison. The American Civil Liberties Union described the case as "the most outrageous AIDS-related case ever." The conviction was upheld by an appellate court, which ruled that the jury could find that the prosecution had offered sufficient evidence to support all elements of the crime of attempted murder beyond a reasonable doubt.[1]

Most cases of this type are dismissed for lack of proof of criminal intent. In the *Weeks* case, prosecutors argued that the fact that Weeks yelled that he had AIDS demonstrated his intent to transmit the deadly disease. Weeks claimed his intent was to stop the officers. In Weeks's case defense attorneys questioned the credibility of the experts and argued that AIDS cannot be spread through spittle. The jury believed the experts, however, and brought back a quick guilty verdict.

1. Weeks v. State, 834 S.W.2d 559 (Tex.App. 1992).

Felony A serious type of offense, such as murder, armed robbery, or rape, punishable by a year or longer in prison or a more serious penalty, such as capital punishment.

Misdemeanor An offense less serious than a felony and generally having a penalty of short-term incarceration in a local facility, a fine, or probation.

Felony or Misdemeanor

Historically, the primary distinction between a **felony** and a **misdemeanor** was that a person could be required to forfeit all property upon conviction of a felony but not upon conviction of a misdemeanor. In addition, during some time periods most if not all felonies were capital offenses. Today the two crime categories are distinguished primarily in terms of the sentences that may be imposed. Usually, a felony is a crime for which a person may be sentenced to death or a long prison term, while a misdemeanor is a less serious offense for which a short jail term (less than a year), a fine, a period of probation, or some other alternative to incarceration may be imposed.

The Judge or Jury as Final Decision Makers

A crime is defined as an act or an omission of an act that violates criminal statutory or case law and for which the state has provided a penalty. But not all acts that meet these criteria result in convictions. In cases that are tried before a jury, jurors may refuse to return a guilty verdict even when the facts point to the defendant's guilt. In cases tried without a jury, the judge may do the same. In other cases, the defendant may be convicted of a crime by the jury, but the judge may grant the defendant's motion for acquittal because he or she does not think the evidence is sufficient to show guilt beyond a reasonable doubt. Alternatively, the judge may allow the conviction to stand but reduce the sentence.

THE CONCEPT OF LAW

A study of crime, the criminal, and criminal law should rest on an understanding of the nature and purpose of law. Law is important because it touches virtually every area of human interaction. Law is used to protect ownership, to define the parameters of private and public property, to regulate business, to raise revenue, and to provide compensation when agreements are broken. Laws define the nature of institutions such as the family. Laws regulate marriage and divorce or dissolution, adoption, the handling of dependent and neglected children, and the inheritance of property.

Laws are designed to protect legal and political systems. Laws organize power relationships. They establish who is superordinate and who is subordinate. Laws maintain the status quo while permitting flexibility when times change. Laws, particularly criminal laws, are designed to preserve order as well as to protect private and public interests. Society determines that some interests are so important that a formal system of control is necessary to preserve them; therefore, laws must be passed to give the state enforcement power. Law is a formal system of social control that may be exercised when other forms of control are not effective.

The Source and Nature of Law

Earlier discussions of criminal law note that laws derive from constitutions, statutes, administrative law, or court decisions. Philosophers and other scholars have argued over the source of law, some contending that laws derived from rulers, referred to as *positive law,* are not the only laws. *Natural law,* also referred to as higher law, comes from a source higher than the rulers and is understood to be binding on people even in the absence of, or in conflict with, laws of the sovereigns.

The concept of natural law is seen in the first known written legal document, the Code of Hammurabi, dated approximately 1900 BC. This embodiment of existing rules and customs of Babylonia was named in honor of King Hammurabi. The code incorporated the religious habits of the people and emphasized the importance of religious beliefs. It reflected the economic problems of Babylonian society, giving specific regulations about how commodities were to be priced and marketed. The "eye for an eye, tooth for a tooth" philosophy was ingrained in the code. If a physician performed a careless operation, his hand was removed; if he was responsible for the death of a woman by causing a miscarriage, the life of one of his daughters was taken. The code "presented the idea that justice was man's inherent right, derived from supernatural forces rather than by royally bestowed favor."[6]

The late civil rights leader Martin Luther King Jr. appealed to higher law, or natural law, in his "Letter from the Birmingham Jail," in which he wrote that there are two types of laws, just and unjust. According to King, people have a moral responsibility to disobey unjust laws as well as to obey just laws. A just law is in accordance with God's moral law; an unjust law is in conflict with that law. An unjust law, King wrote, is not "rooted in eternal law and natural law. Any law that uplifts human personality is just. Any law that degrades human personality is unjust."[7]

King's position was the basis of the civil rights movement that began in the 1960s, and many people still use it to protest laws they perceive as unfair. This concept is important because it is one of the reasons some people who violate statutory law and case law do not believe that they are committing wrongful acts. Another rationalization for violating law is the belief that laws are enforced in an arbitrary and discriminatory manner. These positions raise issues about the use of law as a method of social control.

Law as Social Control

Law is one method of social control. Prior to the emergence of law, social control was achieved in less formal ways. Customs and taboos regulated civilization. Most people took care of their own needs and lived at a subsistence level. They grew or captured their own food and made their own clothing and housing; they had no need for exchanging goods and services. Submission to custom controlled most of their behavior, and laws were not necessary. Those who deviated from the norms of the group were spotted easily; the community could react with nonlegal sanctions. These informal sanctions, which can be more effective than laws, could include a disapproving glance, an embarrassed silence, a smile, a nod, a frown, a social invitation, or social ostracism. The threat of being banished from society (or a smaller group) can be a serious deterrent to deviant behavior. These informal methods of social control are most successful when the group is closely knit; thus, it is relatively easy to know the norms and the general will of the group and to identify transgressors.[8]

The Evolution of Formal Social Control

Why did it become necessary for human societies to move beyond the informal methods of social control and develop law? Sociologist Émile Durkheim believed that as societies grew more complex, they developed a division of labor; as that occurred, they moved from mechanical (the less complex type of society in which members are highly integrated through their cultural and functional similarities) to organic solidarity (the more complex type of society in which members are integrated because they are functionally interdependent). Along with these developments, repressive sanctions were replaced by restitutive sanctions, leading to a more formal system of social control.[9]

Sociologists have suggested that the development of a formal system of social control was necessary for society to progress. Max Weber studied modern capitalism and reasoned that a precondition of its growth was the development of formal legal rationality. As societies became more complex and economically advanced, there was an increasing rationality.[10]

A Comparison of Law and Other Social Controls

Although there are similarities between law and other methods of social control, there are significant differences, too. At least in theory, law is more specific than less formal methods of social control. In criminal law, the law defines the nature of the offense and the punishment (or range of types of punishments) to be imposed for conviction of that offense. Laws cannot define every possible situation that would constitute a violation, but in the United States, they may be declared unconstitutional if they are vague. Laws must be clear enough to give adequate notice to potential transgressors that they are in danger of violating them. Exhibit 1.3 provides an example of a city ordinance that was declared void for vagueness.

EXHIBIT 1.3

Statutes Will Be Declared Void If They Are Vague: The Case of *State* v. *Metzger*

[The case involves Douglas E. Metzger, who was convicted of violating a city code that provided in part, "It shall be unlawful for any person within the City of Lincoln . . . to commit any indecent, immodest or filthy act in the presence of any person, or in such a situation that persons passing might ordinarily see the same."]

According to the evidence, Metzger lived in a garden-level apartment located in Lincoln, Nebraska. A large window in the apartment faces a parking lot which is situated on the north side of the apartment building. At about 7:45 AM on April 30, 1981, another resident of the apartment, while parking his automobile in a space directly in front of Metzger's apartment window, observed Metzger standing naked with his arms at his sides in his apartment window for a period of five seconds.

The resident testified that he saw Metzger's body from his thighs on up. The resident called the police department and two officers arrived at the apartment at about 8 AM. The officers testified that they observed Metzger standing in front of the window eating a bowl of cereal. They testified that Metzger was standing within a foot of the window and his nude body, from the mid-thigh on up, was visible.

. . . The more basic issue presented to us by this appeal is whether the ordinance, as drafted, is so vague as to be unconstitutional. We believe that it is. There is no argument that a violation of the municipal ordinance in question is a criminal act. Since the ordinance in question is criminal in nature, it is a fundamental requirement of due process of law that such criminal ordinance be reasonably clear and definite.

Moreover, a crime must be defined with sufficient definiteness and there must be ascertainable standards of guilt to inform those subject thereto as to what conduct will render them liable to punishment thereunder. The dividing line between what is lawful and unlawful cannot be left to conjecture. A citizen cannot be held to answer charges based upon penal statutes whose mandates are so uncertain that they will reasonably admit of different constructions. A criminal statute cannot rest upon an uncertain foundation. The crime and the elements constituting it must be so clearly expressed that the ordinary person can intelligently choose in advance what course it is lawful for him to pursue. Penal statutes prohibiting the doing of certain things and providing a punishment for their violation should not admit of such a double meaning that the citizen may act upon one conception of its requirements and the courts upon another. A statute which forbids the doing of an act in terms so vague that men of common intelligence must necessarily guess as to its meaning and differ as to its application violates the first essential elements of due process of law. It is not permissible to enact a law which in effect spreads an all-inclusive net for the feet of everybody upon the chance that, while the innocent will surely be entangled in its meshes, some wrongdoers may also be caught.

The ordinance in question makes it unlawful for anyone to commit any "indecent, immodest or filthy act." We know of no way in which the standards required of a criminal act can be met in those broad, general terms. There may be those few who believe persons of opposite sex holding hands in public are immodest, and certainly more who might believe that kissing in public is immodest. Such acts cannot constitute a crime. Certainly one could find many who would conclude that today's swimming attire found on many beaches or beside many pools is immodest. Yet, the fact that it is immodest does not thereby make it illegal, absent some requirement related to the health, safety, or welfare of the community. The dividing line between what is lawful and what is unlawful in terms of "indecent," "immodest," or "filthy" is simply too broad to satisfy the constitutional requirements of due process. Both lawful and unlawful acts can be embraced within such broad definitions. That cannot be permitted. One is not able to determine in advance what is lawful and what is unlawful . . .

BOSLAUGH, Justice, dissenting.

The ordinance in question prohibits indecent acts, immodest acts, *or* filthy acts in the presence of any person . . . The exhibition of his genitals under the circumstances of this case was, clearly, an indecent act.

Source: State v. Metzger, 319 N.W.2d 459, 460–463 (Neb. 1982), citations omitted.

A second distinction between law and other forms of social control is that law arises from a more rational procedure. It is a formal enactment by a legislative body or a court that occurs presumably after discussion and reflection. The law is to be applied to all who transgress its provisions, unless there are justifications or defenses for the otherwise illegal acts. Law specifies sanctions, and only those sanctions may be applied. Law differs from other types of social control in that its sanctions are applied exclusively by organized political agencies. Physical force may be involved in enforcing the sanctions, although this is limited to reasonable action applied by an official party.

Stare decisis Literally, "let the decision stand." The doctrine that courts will abide by or adhere to the rulings of previous court decisions when deciding cases with sibstantially the same facts.

Law is characterized by regularity, which does not mean absolute certainty. It adheres to the principle of ***stare decisis,*** which means to abide by or adhere to settled cases. It is based on the assumption that security and certainty are important in the law. Decided cases establish precedent for the future, but courts may overrule prior decisions in light of new facts, reasoning, or changing social conditions.

Unlike other social controls, law does not reward conforming behavior; it is concerned primarily with negative sanctions. Another difference between other social controls and law is that in most cases the legal system provides the right of appeal but other social controls do not.

Criminal Law and Civil Law Compared

Criminal law The statutes and norms the violation of which may subject the accused person to government prosecution. In general, criminal laws encompass those wrongs considered to be so serious as to threaten the welfare of society.

Civil law That part of the law concerned with the rules and enforcement of private or civil rights as distinguished from criminal law. In a civil suit, an individual who has been harmed seeks personal compensation in court rather than criminal punishment through prosecution.

Another feature of the concept of law is that it may be divided into categories. This text focuses on **criminal law,** rather than **civil law** because criminal law provides the framework for the state's jurisdiction over crime. There is considerable overlap between criminal and civil law, but there are important distinctions as well. When a criminal wrong has been committed, the state (or federal government) initiates action against the person accused of the crime. The state becomes involved because a crime is considered a serious threat to the welfare of the entire society as well as to the alleged victim.

In contrast, a noncriminal or civil wrong is considered to be a wrong against a particular individual. In such cases the person wronged may initiate legal action against the accused. Noncriminal law refers primarily to laws (such as divorce, property, or contract law) that regulate the legal rights between individuals or organizations and others.

Civil wrongs and crimes may be distinguished in other ways as well. They may be tried in different courts, although that is not always the case. Different procedural rules apply, with criminal cases involving more extensive legal safeguards because of the potentially more serious results for those found guilty of crimes. Whereas in a civil case the party at fault may be required to pay financial damages to the injured party, in a criminal case the state may impose penalties that restrict the liberty of the individual. In some cases the state may take the life of the convicted person.

THE PURPOSE OF CRIMINAL LAW

We should not expect to regulate all behavior by the criminal law. Criminal law should provide some standards, goals, and guidelines—a statement of what conduct is so important that it must be sanctioned. It should provide some moral guidance as well, but controversy arises over the extent to which the law should be used to regulate morality.

The serious impact of the criminal law should lead us to question what kinds of behavior ought to be covered by its reach. For example, some people question the use of the criminal law to enforce wearing helmets while riding bicycles or motorcycles or wearing seat belts and shoulder straps in automobiles. In the case of seat belts and shoulder straps, some jurisdictions permit arrest only if a moving violation occurs, but in 2001 the U.S. Supreme Court upheld the right of police to make a full custodial arrest even when a motorist is committing only a minor infraction, such as violating the seat belt requirement.

In *Atwater* v. *City of Lago Vista,* the Court ruled in favor of the police who arrested Gail Atwater, who was not wearing her seat belt in violation of a Texas statute that provided a maximum fine of $50 for the offense, a misdemeanor. In writing for the Court, Justice David Souter stated that although Atwater had suffered "gratuitious humiliations" and "pointless indignity" when she was arrested (with her children in the car), taken in handcuffs to the police station, and held in jail until she posted $310 for bail, the police had the legal authority to make the arrest.[11]

This case and many others raise the question of how extensive the law should be. Requiring motorists to wear seat belts may be a worthwhile cause, especially now that data published in 2001 show a strong correlation between lack of seat belt use and deaths from automobile accidents among teens (compared to very few deaths of children; all states require that children be in proper restraints while cars are in motion),[12] but should we use the criminal law to achieve this purpose? Would civil sanctions suffice? How should the law respond to activities such as same-gender sexual acts, prostitution, the use of alcohol or other drugs, and attempted suicide? In short, we are faced with the critical question of whether the criminal law should be used to regulate activities that may be considered religious or moral issues but not *legal* issues.

The Control of Crime

Clearly, the criminal law should be used to regulate criminal activity. The problem is to define which acts should be considered criminal. We have looked at the legal definition of crime and explored its elements, but that definition does not solve the problem of which behaviors *should* be included. It may be helpful to distinguish between acts that are criminal within themselves and those that are criminal because they are defined as such.

Mala in se Acts morally wrong in themselves, such as rape, murder, or robbery.

Mala prohibita Acts that are wrong because they are prohibited by legislation although they may not be recognized by most people as morally wrong.

Mala in se crimes are those that are evil in themselves, such as rape, murder, robbery, arson, and aggravated assault. There is general agreement that these acts are criminal. In contrast, ***mala prohibita*** crimes, such as public drunkenness, are considered evil because they are forbidden. Historically, there was little difference between *mala in se* and *mala prohibita* crimes, because most primitive societies did not distinguish morality, sin, and law.

The Control of Morality

Some argue that, in addition to regulating criminal behavior, another purpose of the criminal law is to regulate moral behavior. Others disagree and conclude that our law overreaches or overcriminalizes. The illegal use of alcohol and other drugs (discussed in Chapter 10) and private sexual behavior between consenting adults (regardless of the genders involved) are examples of actions that may not affect other people directly and thus, it is argued, should not be classified as crimes. When they are criminalized, they may be referred to as *victimless crimes.*

Edwin Schur defined *victimless crimes* as "the willing exchange, among adults, of strongly demanded but legally proscribed goods or services." Schur points out that there is a lack of public consensus on laws that govern gambling, prostitution, the use of narcotics, and other such behavior. Schur distinguished these laws from other laws characterized by a lack of consensus, such as income tax laws, by articulating the difference in the exchange of the elements of transaction: "Crimes without victims may be limited to those situations in which one person obtains from another, in a fairly direct exchange, a commodity or personal service which is socially disapproved and legally proscribed." These behaviors are distinguished further by the lack of apparent harm to others and by the difficulty in enforcing the laws against them because of low visibility and the absence of a complainant.[13]

Norval Morris and Gordon Hawkins, who have written extensively on this subject, emphasized that, with the possible exception of John Calvin's 16th-century Geneva, the United States has the most moralistic criminal laws in history. Morris and Hawkins refer to sex offense laws as possibly designed "to provide an enormous legislative chastity belt encompassing the whole population and proscribing everything but solitary and joyless masturbation and 'normal coitus' inside wedlock."[14]

In addition to laws prohibiting prostitution or other forms of commercial sex, some states have retained statutes prohibiting private consensual sexual behavior between unmarried persons. The following Idaho statute is an example:

> Any unmarried person who shall have sexual intercourse with an unmarried person of the opposite sex shall be deemed guilty of fornication, and, upon conviction thereof, shall be punished by a fine of not more than $300 or by imprisonment for not more than six months or both such fine and imprisonment; provided that the sentence imposed or any part thereof may be suspended with or without probation in the discretion of the court.[15]

Although many states have repealed their fornication statutes, most have retained the prohibition against adultery, defined as sexual relations between a married person and someone other than his or her spouse. Some jurisdictions still criminalize oral and anal sex, with the proponents of these prohibitions arguing that the acts are unnatural. Some statutes refer to these acts as "crimes against nature." An example is the Idaho statute, which refers to them as "the infamous crime against nature, committed with mankind or with any animal." Idaho courts have interpreted these acts to include "all unnatural carnal copulations, whether with man or beast, committed per os [mouth] or per anum [anus]."[16]

A traditional reason given for criminalizing oral and anal sex is to prevent the spread of disease. The recent focus on AIDS has called attention to same-gender sexual behavior as a health problem because the incidence of the disease is higher among gay males than among any other group. The public argues that it must be protected from the possibility of contracting the deadly disease and that this can be done only by controlling same-gender sexual behavior. But as Exhibit 1.2 notes, the disease is transmitted in other ways also.

Some of the sex statutes are written to apply only to gay men; some are gender neutral and thus could apply to lesbians. Other statutes apply to heterosexual behavior between persons not married to each other, while some even extend to sexual behavior between married persons. Most of these statutes are not enforced except in cases involving gay men or an adult involved with a minor of either gender. This development has led to allegations of discrimination in the enforcement of the statutes, along with allegations of a violation of privacy rights. Some states have changed their statutes to permit any sexual behavior between consenting adults in private; others have revised statutes to permit certain behaviors only between consenting married persons acting in private. These statutes and the court decisions interpreting them are crucial to this discussion, as they raise the issue of whether prohibiting private, consensual sexual behavior among adults is legal. The trend in this area is demonstrated by two cases involving Georgia statutes.

In 1986 the U.S. Supreme Court decided a case upholding the Georgia sodomy statute. *Bowers* v. *Hardwick,* decided by a 5-to-4 vote, has created considerable controversy over the role of the government in the regulation of sexual behavior.[17] The case involved two men engaging in oral sex in their bedroom, where they were seen by a police officer who went to the house with a warrant for the arrest of Hardwick (who had not paid a fine owed for conviction of drinking on a public street in Atlanta). The case raises the issue of state regulation of sexual behavior between consenting adults of the same gender in the privacy of a home. The Court emphasized that "otherwise illegal conduct is not always immunized whenever it occurs in the home" and that prohibitions against sodomy have been upheld historically and do not constitute an invasion of privacy.[18]

In 1996 the Georgia Supreme Court upheld the misdemeanor conviction of a man who solicited an undercover male police officer for sex. The court also upheld the sentence of 12-months' probation against a challenge that the Georgia statute violated the defendant's privacy rights under the state's constitution. The following brief excerpt from *Christensen* v. *State* gives the court's reasoning. The U.S. Supreme Court refused to review the case.[19]

Christensen v. State

In the exercise of its police power the state has a right to enact laws to promote the public health, safety, morals, and welfare of its citizens. There is also a concomitant interest in curtailing criminal activities wherever they may be committed. As was acknowledged in *Bowers* v. *Hardwick,* the law "is constantly based on notions of morality, and if all laws representing essentially moral choices are to be invalidated under the Due Process Clause, the courts will be very busy indeed." We hold that the proscription against sodomy is a legitimate and valid exercise of state police power in furtherance of the moral welfare of the public. Our constitution does not deny the legislative branch the right to prohibit such conduct . . .

The right to determine what is harmful to health and morals or what is criminal to the public welfare belongs to the people through their elected representatives. We decline to usurp what is the power of the legislature.

In 1998, however, the Georgia Supreme Court held that the state's sodomy statute (the one that was featured in *Bowers* v. *Hardwick,* involving actual sex, not just solicitation) violated the state's constitution. The excerpt below from that case, *Powell* v. *State,* gives the facts and the court's reasoning. Note that the facts involve a man and a woman and thus, strictly speaking, the case does not apply to sex between two members of the same gender, as in *Hardwick.* It is probable that, given its stated reasons in *Powell,* the Georgia Supreme Court would apply the same reasoning to oral or anal sex between two consenting adults of the same gender, but that may not be the case.[20]

Powell v. State

Anthony San Juan Powell was charged in an indictment with rape and aggravated sodomy in connection with sexual conduct involving his and his wife's 17-year-old niece in Powell's apartment. The niece testified that appellant had sexual intercourse with her and [performed oral sex on her] . . . without her consent and against her will. Powell testified and admitted he performed the acts with the consent of the complainant. In light of Powell's testimony, the trial court included in its jury charge instructions on the law of sodomy. The jury acquitted Powell of the rape and aggravated sodomy charges and found him guilt of sodomy, thereby establishing that the State did not prove beyond a reasonable doubt that the act was committed "with force and against the will" of the niece . . .

[The Georgia statute in question defines sodomy as] the performance of or submission to "any sexual act involving the sex organs of one person and the mouth or anus of another." Appellant's admission at trial that he placed his mouth upon the genitalia of his wife's niece, and the niece's testimony similarly describing appellant's conduct constitute sufficient evidence to authorize a rational trier of fact to conclude beyond a reasonable doubt that appellant committed sodomy . . .

Today we are faced with whether the constitutional right of privacy screens from governmental interference a non-commercial sexual act that occurs without force in a private home between persons legally capable of consenting to the act . . .

In undertaking the judiciary's constitutional duty, it is not the prerogative of members of the judiciary to base decisions on their personal notions of morality. Indeed, if we were called upon to pass upon the propriety of the conduct herein involved, we would not condone it. Rather, the judiciary is charged with the task of examining a legislative enactment when it is alleged to impinge upon the freedoms and guarantees contained in the Georgia Bill of Rights and the U.S. Constitution, and scrutinizing the law, the interests it promotes, and the means by which it seeks to achieve those interests, to ensure that the law meets constitutional standards. While many believe that acts of sodomy, even those involving consenting adults, are morally reprehensible, this repugnance alone does not create a compelling justification for state regulation of the activity . . .

We conclude that [the statute], insofar as it criminalizes the performance of private, non-commercial acts of sexual intimacy between persons legally able to consent, "manifestly infringes upon a constitutional provision" which guarantees to the citizens of Georgia the sexual intimacy with one legally capable of consenting thereto in the privacy of his home. Accordingly, appellant's conviction for such behavior must be reversed.

In 1992 the Kentucky Supreme Court ruled that the state's sodomy law was unconstitutional in that it denied the right of privacy to gay males. According to that court, "We need not sympathize, agree with or even understand the sexual preference of homosexuals in order to recognize their right to equal treatment before the bar of criminal justice."[21] Other states have followed this position, while in some states the laws prohibiting private sexual behavior between consenting, unmarried adults remain unchallenged—and they may remain unchallenged, as most are not enforced.

Several issues are involved in these and similar cases, but for purposes of our discussion here, the primary issue is whether the state should regulate consensual, private sexual behavior through the criminal law. If the answer to that is yes, it would be necessary to analyze whether the criminal law should distinguish between the private, consensual behavior of heterosexual persons as compared to gay males and lesbians or between married and unmarried heterosexuals. If the answer is no, the statutes should be revoked or declared invalid by the courts.

The issues are not that simple, however, as we analyze the overall changes occurring in America with regard to same-gender sexual behavior. On the one hand, some religious denominations have spoken out against it, and organized groups are protesting the movement toward equal rights. On the other hand, some jurisdictions have expanded the rights of gay men and lesbians beyond equal employment opportunities to such matters as the right to share medical benefits with a same-gender partner, the right to adopt children, and the right to be appointed legal guardian of a partner. And the state supreme court in Vermont has extended full rights to same-gender couples who requested them, although the term *marriage* is not used.

Whether or not the criminal law should be used to regulate same-gender sexual behavior will continue to be a matter of great controversy.

An Analysis of the Purpose of Criminal Law

The preceding discussion of the use of the criminal law to regulate morality raises the question of whether law is the best method of social control in certain

In 1993 New York began allowing same-gender as well as opposite-gender couples to register as domestic partners. This acknowledgment of the relationship gives the couple many of the same rights as those of married persons. Diana Flood Goldstick, left, and Patricia Flood Goldstick were among those who participated in a ceremony celebrating their status as domestic partners. (Sara Kulwich/New York Times)

areas of behavior. Whether the law serves its purpose of deterrence is a controversial issue (see Chapter 3). Whether the law serves as an adequate symbol of morality can be questioned when the law is enforced infrequently. Whether the law is used to discriminate against particular groups—such as poor people, minorities, foreigners, or persons with a same-gender sexual orientation—is an important issue, too.

Other examples could be raised. Should the law be used to protect people against themselves, requiring, for example, motorcyclists or bicyclists to wear helmets? As noted earlier, some states require drivers and passengers to use seat belts and shoulder straps in automobiles. Failure to do so may result in a fine. Should the criminal law be employed to regulate this behavior? If this concept were carried further, it could be argued that the state should regulate the diet of its citizens and prohibit cigarette smoking and excessive drinking.

There are limits to how far the law should go in protecting people against themselves and others, but there is little consensus on exactly how to set those limits. Attempts to legislate morality have not been successful when the laws lacked substantial support by the American people, as illustrated by the widespread violation of Prohibition in the 1920s and of drug laws today.

The state does have an interest in preserving the morals of its people, and there is concern about the weakening of moral fiber in the United States. Clearly, the law must be concerned with some moral principles and cannot permit people to abuse one another; it should provide moral guidance. But can that happen if people disrespect the law because it is applied unfairly or because it is difficult or impossible to enforce? Some laws—those regulating sexual behavior, for example—cannot be enforced without violating one or more of our basic freedoms, such as the right to privacy. Therefore, in many cases no attempt is made to enforce them, and this creates disrespect for the law. If these criminal laws do not deter the behavior at which they are aimed, do they serve any positive function in society?

To some extent laws regulating moral behavior are functional. Edwin Schur suggested that attaching the label of *deviant* or *criminal* to some persons who violate these laws may serve a positive function for the conformists in that the process may increase their group cohesion.[22] But selective enforcement of the laws also serves to preserve the power of the majority—the weaker, unimportant members of society are kept in their places. In that sense, unequal administration of the law is functional because it keeps the status arrangements of society from being disrupted.

For example, when drunks appear in public, police may react differently depending on the offenders' social status. Lower-class offenders may have a greater probability of being arrested. Upper- or middle-class offenders, in contrast, may just be driven home by police or permitted to call someone else to drive them.

Laws regulating morality may serve the function of making the majority feel that something is being done to preserve the morals of society. That is, these laws may create the impression that certain questionable behavior is disapproved officially. It is argued that repealing these laws would condone the behavior and would not be a wise move for politicians. However, some of the statutes that regulate victimless crimes or morality may have negative repercussions. Violation of privacy to obtain evidence of criminal conduct may drive demanded services underground. Laws may give the impression that something is being done when actually this is not the case. For example, laws that criminalize the act of spreading AIDS may look good on the books but may have little effect on sexual behavior because of the difficulties in getting convictions in these cases.

CRIMINOLOGY AND THE STUDY OF CRIME

Criminology The scientific study of crime, criminals, criminal behavior, and efforts to regulate crime.

The study of crime, criminals, and criminal law is of ancient origin, although the development of **criminology** as a discipline took place in the 1900s, with the first textbooks in the field published in the 1920s. But earlier attempts should be recognized. Chapter 3 of this text discusses some pertinent historical developments in criminal law. Other developments are also important. In June 1909 the American Institute of Criminal Law and Criminology was organized at the National Conference of Criminal Law and Criminology held at Northwestern University in Chicago. A resolution was passed that allowed the president to appoint a committee of five persons to select criminological treatises that should be translated into English. An early writer on criminology noted: "For the community at large, it is important to recognize that criminal science is a larger thing than criminal law. The legal profession in particular has a duty to familiarize itself with the principles of that science, as the sole means for intelligent and systematic improvement of the criminal law."[23] Despite this step, the legal profession has until recently remained aloof from the developments in the field of criminology, and even now the recognition is not significant.

Today, however, most colleges and universities teach criminology courses; many offer graduate degrees in criminology or criminal justice. A Ph.D. program in juvenile justice was recently started at PrairieView A&M in Texas. Professional journals in the field include one that focuses on education—the *Journal of Criminal Justice Education,* published by the Academy of Criminal Justice Sciences (ACJS). In addition to the ACJS, the field boasts another national and highly recognized professional association, the American Society of Criminology. Regional professional organizations exist throughout the country.

Most early teachers of criminology and related subjects were educated in sociology, psychology, political science, or some other related discipline or were practitioners in various fields of criminal justice. Today many professors in the field have a Ph.D. in criminal justice or criminology, although the emphasis on interdisciplinary studies remains strong among many scholars. Perhaps, however, we will never dispute the statement of the noted theorist Thorsten Sellin, who stated in 1938 that the "criminologist does not exist who is an expert in all the disciplines which converge in the study of crime."[24] It could be argued that a criminologist needs training in sociology, law, medicine, psychiatry, psychology, history, anthropology, chemistry, biology, architecture, systems engineering, political science, social work, public administration, business, communications, and economics.

Great progress has been made, however, since the introduction of criminology textbooks in the 1920s. Today the discipline of criminology is characterized by an interdisciplinary approach, sophisticated research methods, and an intense emphasis on empirical research. Many departments emphasize the interrelationship of theory and practice, and student demand for courses has increased significantly.

Modern criminologists have moved away from the discipline's historical primary focus on explaining the behavior of criminals. The causes of crime are explored through discussions of biological, psychological, economic, and sociological theories, as the subsequent theory chapters of this text illustrate. But the modern study of crime involves more than an attempt to understand why people violate the law. The discipline of criminology includes the sociology of law, which analyzes why some acts and not others are defined as crimes, and a study of the social responses to crime, which examines why some people are processed through the system while others who commit the same acts are not. These areas of focus are not always separable (there is considerable overlap), nor is there agreement on which areas should receive research priorities. This text includes information on all three areas—law, criminology, and sociology—in addition to materials from other disciplines where pertinent.

SUMMARY

This chapter explores the meaning of crime and the nature and purpose of criminal law. Because criminal law defines criminal behavior, thus formulating the basis for the kinds of behavior on which this study of criminology focuses, the discussion is important in setting the stage for this text. Many of the questions raised throughout the text are related to the central issues of this chapter—the purpose of criminal law and the kinds of behavior that should be included within its reach. The answers to these questions determine who is and who is not a criminal and therefore who does and who does not constitute a basis for the study of criminology.

The inclusion or exclusion of morality within the reach of the criminal law affects all elements of criminal justice systems, including defendants' rights, victims' rights, and society's right to be protected from criminal behavior. Central to the entire discussion is the underlying theme of law as social control. A basic question is whether imposing sanctions discourages people from engaging in the proscribed behavior. Sociological contributions to our understanding of whether or not laws deter are crucial in the analysis of this issue.

What, then, should be the purpose of law? It has been argued that the main purpose of criminal law is to protect persons and property from abuse. Norval Morris and Gordon Hawkins have stated: "When the criminal law invades the spheres of private morality . . . it exceeds its proper limits at the cost of neglecting its primary tasks. This unwarranted extension is expensive, ineffective, and criminogenic."[25]

What should be included within the province of criminal law? Certainly criminal law should be used to protect individuals from being forced to engage in certain behaviors. For example, no person, adult or juvenile, should be forced to engage in a sexual act. Criminal law should penalize those who participate in sexual acts with persons under the age of consent; that is, immature persons should be protected from sexual exploitation. Also, consensual sex between adults should be restricted to places where it is reasonable to expect privacy so that others are not forced to view it.

The law, however, cannot control the behavior of all people in a complex society. The law should provide some standards, goals, and guidelines—a statement that defines which conduct is so important that it must be sanctioned formally. The law should provide some moral guidance, but it should not be used to regulate behavior that could be regulated more effectively and more appropriately by other agencies or by individuals.

Nor should the law interfere with privacy rights. As one expert noted, "Any attempt to criminalize all wrongful conduct would involve intolerable intrusions into citizens' lives and choices. Much wrongdoing in people's private and working lives should not be legally punishable because it involves areas of behavior which a free society should keep clear of the drastic intervention of the criminal law."[26]

Finally, law is social. Sociological perspectives and inquiries are necessary if we are to appreciate the social nature of law.[27]

These and numerous other questions can be answered only when society has a thorough understanding of the causes and consequences of crime and the subsequent criminal law designed to deal with crime. This text is an effort to provide you with that understanding.

STUDY QUESTIONS

1. What is meant by the concept of *crime?*
2. Distinguish between criminal law and civil law.
3. Give a legal definition of *crime,* and explain the meaning of the terms within that definition.
4. Discuss the meaning and importance of *mens rea* and the exceptions to the concept.
5. Distinguish statutory law, case law, constitutional law, and administrative law.
6. What impact has AIDS had on the concept of crime?
7. What is meant by a *defense* to crime?
8. Distinguish between *felony* and *misdemeanor.*
9. Why should a jury be permitted to determine guilt or innocence?
10. How is law used to control people?
11. What are the sources of criminal law?
12. Why does law adhere to the principle of *stare decisis?*
13. Distinguish *mala in se* and *mala prohibita* crimes, and explain the importance of this distinction in criminal law.
14. What should be the role of criminal law with regard to regulating private, consensual sexual behavior among adults?

BRIEF ESSAY ASSIGNMENTS

1. Discuss why an act or an omission of an act is not sufficient to constitute a crime. What is required?
2. Why aren't all individuals who cause harm or injury to others not held responsible?
3. Describe the concept of natural law, and provide an example.
4. Explain the differences between law and other forms of social control.
5. Discuss the debate concerning whether the law should be used to control morality.

INTERNET ACTIVITIES

1. Much debate surrounds the criminalization of "victimless" crimes such as drug use, gambling, and prostitution. For information concerning the issue of prostitution, check out the website for the organization Coalition on Trafficking Against Women at www.catwinternational.org. This website includes facts, statistics, and issues on prostitution from several countries plus an article on sex trafficking in the United States.
2. Search for information about cases that involve the prosecution of defendants with HIV/AIDS. Under what conditions were these cases prosecuted? (That is, what type of crime was involved?) What has been the outcome of these cases? Do you think the rulings were fair? Sites such as www.crimelibrary.com and www.crimelynx.com, which provide stories and news about crimes, are a good place to start.

NET RESOURCES

www.refdesk.com — The Reference Desk website provides information and facts from a variety of sources, including reference resources, news, government, and statistical sites and information categorized by subject. In addition to a search engine, this site also offers guidelines on writing and grammar, and on how to cite references from articles and information obtained from the Internet.

www.findlaw.com — Find Law includes various links to legal and business law sources; international, federal, and state resources; daily legal news; and U.S. Supreme Court cases.

www.megalaw.com — MegaLaw provides search engines for legal sources; other law site search engines; news links; and links to websites on federal and state laws, and local court rules.

www.fedworld.gov — A program of the U.S. Department of Commerce, Fedworld offers links on all government research and development publications and links to government Web pages and government-sponsored science and technology websites.

www.law.cornell.edu — The Cornell Law School-Legal Information Institute website includes recent law events in the news, links to law topics listed alphabetically, topical libraries, directories to law journals and bulletins, and a search engine to find information about specific subjects concerning law.

ENDNOTES

1. Paul W. Tappan, *Crime, Justice and Correction* (New York: McGraw-Hill, 1960), p. 10.
2. Buch v. Amory Manufacturing Co., 69 N.H. 257 (1897), *overruled in part by* Ouellette v. Blanchard, 364 A.2d 631 (N.H. 1976).
3. "Cries Ignored, Charges Dropped," *Tampa Tribune* (20 July 1991), p. 3.
4. United States v. Dotterweich, 320 U.S. 277 (1943).
5. Ordway v. County of Suffolk, 583 N.Y.S.2d 1014 (N.Y.Sup. 1992).
6. Henry J. Abraham, *The Judicial Process* (New York: Oxford University Press, 1968), p. 5.
7. Martin Luther King Jr., *Why We Can't Wait* (New York: Harper & Row, 1963), pp. 84–85.
8. See, for example, Richard D. Schwartz, "Social Factors in the Development of Legal Control: A Case Study of Two Israeli Settlements," *Yale Law Journal* 63 (February 1954): 471–91.
9. Émile Durkheim, *The Division of Labor in Society,* trans. George Simpson (New York: Free Press, 1947).
10. Max Weber, *Law in Economy and Society,* Max Rheinstein, ed. (Cambridge, MA: Harvard University Press, 1954).
11. Atwater v. City of Lago Vista, 2001 U.S. LEXIS 3366 (2001).
12. "Low Seat Belt Use Linked to Teenage Death Rates," *New York Times* (21 May 2001), p. 12, referring to a report released that day by the National Safety Council.
13. Edwin M. Schur, *Crimes without Victims: Deviant Behavior and Public Policy* (Englewood Cliffs, NJ: Prentice Hall, 1965), pp. 169, 170–71.
14. Norval Morris and Gordon P. Hawkins, *The Honest Politician's Guide to Crime Control* (Chicago: University of Chicago Press, 1969), p. 15.
15. Idaho Criminal Code, Section 18-6603 (2000).
16. Idaho Criminal Code, Section 18-6605 (2000), State v. Altwatter, 157, p. 256, 257 (Idaho 1916).
17. Bowers v. Hardwick, 478 U.S. 186 (1986).
18. Bowers v. Hardwick, 478 U.S. 186 (1986).
19. Christensen v. State, 468 S.E.2d 188 (Ga. 1996), *cert. denied sub nom.,* 522 U.S. 1128 (1998), citations omitted. The statute at issue is OCGA, Section 16-6-15(a) (2001).
20. Powell v. State, 510 S.E.2d 18 (Ga. 1998), cases and citations omitted. The statute is codified at OCGA, Section 16-6-2 (2001).
21. Commonwealth v. Wasson, 842 S.W.2d 487 (Ky. 1992).
22. Schur, *Crimes Without Victims,* p. 4. See also Durkheim, *The Division of Labor in Society,* pp. 96–110.
23. Willem A. Bonger, *Criminality and Economic Conditions,* trans. Henry P. Horton (Boston: Little, Brown, 1916), p. xi.
24. Thorsten Sellin, "A Sociological Approach," in Marvin E. Wolfgang et al., eds., *The Sociology of Crime and Delinquency,* 2nd ed. (New York: Wiley, 1970), p. 6.
25. Morris and Hawkins, *The Honest Politician's Guide,* p. 2.
26. Andrew von Hirsch, "Desert and Previous Convictions in Sentencing," *Minnesota Law Review* 65 (April 1981): 607.
27. Edwin M. Schur, *Law and Society: A Sociological View* (New York: Random House, 1968).

CHAPTER 2

▶ Today police are more informed and sensitive to the needs of victims than in the past. In this picture two officers trained in the process are interviewing a young woman who has alleged that she was beaten by her domestic partner. (Mark Burnett/Stock Boston)

The Measurement of Crime and Its Impact

OUTLINE

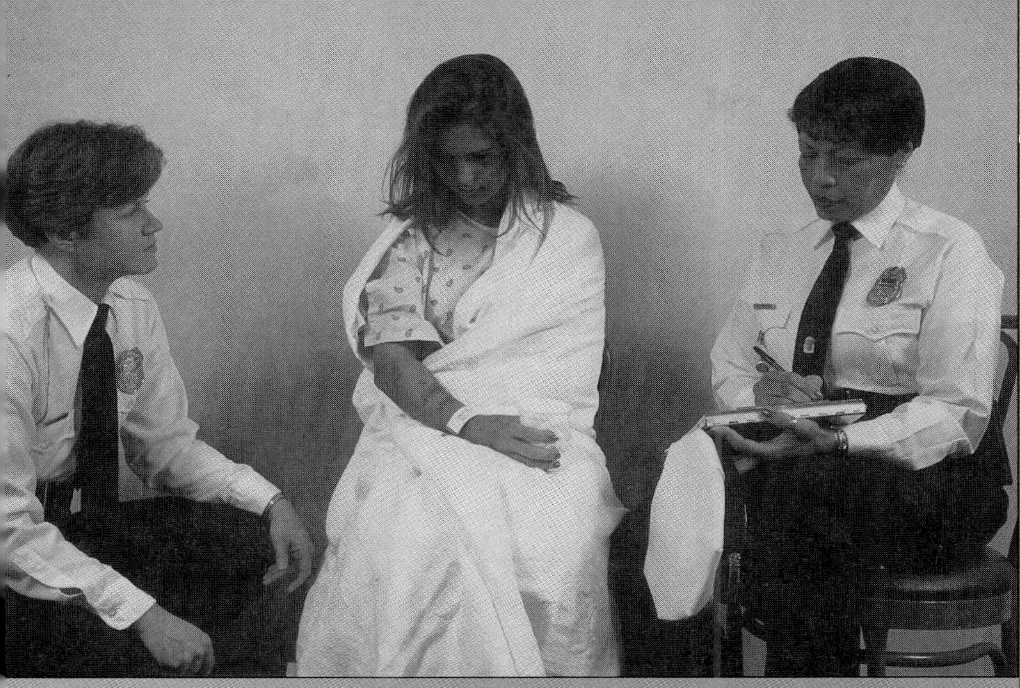

The focus of this chapter is crime data. We examine the official and unofficial ways in which data on crimes, criminals, and crime victims are collected. Variables affecting the accuracy of crime data collection include police discretion, reporting methods, victims' cooperation or refusal to cooperate, and administrative and bureaucratic changes. Following this background on the problems of collecting data, we look at the most recent data on crime and crime victims with regard to the variables of age, race, and gender. After an analysis of crime data collection, the chapter concludes with a look at research in criminology.

KEY TERMS

Bureau of Justice Statistics (BJS)

Crime Classification System (CCS)

crime rate

crimes known to the police

discretion

dualistic fallacy

ex post facto method

index offense

Megan's laws

National Crime Victimization Survey (NCVS)

National Criminal History Improvement Program (NCHIP)

National Incident-Based Reporting System (NIBRS)

National Youth Survey (NYS)

property crime

self-report data (SRD)

three strikes and you're out

Uniform Crime Reports (UCR)

violent crimes

Crime is a topic of national and international concern. During elections in the United States and other countries, discussions of crime dominate the news media. Concern with crime led the U.S. Congress to enact a new federal crime bill in 1994. The bombing of the federal building in Oklahoma City in April 1995 led to a call for stricter controls on terrorism, as the city and a nation mourned the deaths and injuries caused by the massive destruction. In Washington, D.C., following the bombing, Pennsylvania Avenue was closed to traffic in front of the White House and three other contiguous streets were blocked off as an extra precautionary measure. A May 1995 *USA Today* article reported, "U.S. institutions that once were the symbol of openness, like the Capitol, are now surrounded by tank-stopping barriers and metal detectors."[1]

The situation became much worse, however, on 11 September 2001, when, as noted in Chapter 1, terrorists hijacked and crashed four U.S. domestic airplanes, resulting in the destruction of the twin towers of the World Trade Center (and damage to adjacent buildings) in New York City, damage to the Pentagon in Washington, D.C., and the deaths of approximately 3,000 people. These terrorist attacks are discussed in more detail in Chapter 7.

Some crimes lead to legislation attempting to prevent such crimes in the future. For example, shortly before the first anniversary of the Oklahoma City bombing, a new counterterrorism bill was signed by President Bill Clinton.[2] The resulting Antiterrorism and Effective Death Penalty Act is discussed in Chapter 7 of this text.

Two other high-profile crimes led to extensive state legislation. First, the 1993 sexual assault and murder of 12-year-old Polly Klaas by a repeat offender in California led to the enactment in that state, and subsequently in most other jurisdictions, of legislation referred to as **three strikes and you're out.** The statutes differ but essentially provide for mandatory, severe penalties for persons convicted of a third felony. Second, the 1994 sexual assault and murder of Megan Kanka by her New Jersey neighbor, who had two prior sexual assault convictions, led to **Megan's laws,** adopted first in New Jersey and then throughout the country. These laws require released sex offenders to register when they move to into a community; (for some require community notification more details, see Chapter 15, p. 519).

Three strikes and you're out Legislation enacted in most states and in the federal government in recent years and designed to impose long sentences on persons who commit three or more serious crimes or felonies.

Megan's laws Refers to laws requiring the registration of sex offenders when they move to a community. Some jurisdictions require the offenders to notify neighbors; others require only that law enforcement authorities be notified. These laws are named after Megan Kanka, who was raped and murdered by a neighbor who was a released sex offender living with two other such offenders.

The 1999 shootings at Columbine High School in Littleton, Colorado, led to new proposals on gun control, while the continuing problem of young children and teenagers engaging in violent acts in schools has led to the use of metal detectors in many institutions. Special programs designed to train teachers and school administrators to recognize potential problem behavior have become commonplace.

The greatest changes, however, have been made as a result of the 11 September 2001 terrorist attacks. Security at U.S. airports has been altered dramatically, with armed guards and police dogs patrolling while passengers wait in lines, sometimes for hours, to be searched more thoroughly than ever before.

Actual violence and the perception of increasing violence have led many Americans to fear being on the streets in the daytime as well as at night. Others are terrified even in their own homes. The fear of violent crime has led to a boom in the sales of locks, bars, and sophisticated home alarm systems. And the events of 11 September 2001 have led many people to reduce or eliminate flying as a means of travel; some refuse to enter tall buildings, and many are staying closer to home, even for the major holidays.

This chapter looks carefully at official and unofficial crime data. The importance of this discussion cannot be overemphasized. The reader should realize that, in many respects, all other discussions of crime hinge on these data. How we count crime and criminals influences the causation theories we advance and affects resource allocations in criminal justice systems.

SOURCES OF CRIME DATA

Measurement of crime today is more sophisticated and more extensive than in earlier times, but serious disagreement remains over how crime should be measured. Even official crime data vary according to their sources; unofficial sources differ from official sources. As we look at crime data we must keep in mind that data collection methods differ; that they are not always comparable; and that conclusions about how much crime exists, what kinds of crimes are committed, who commits them, and who is victimized differ according to the measurement methods used. (See Media Focus 2.1.)

Most media reports and most analyses of crime data are based on official data. The major sources of official data are the *Uniform Crime Reports (UCR)* and the National Crime Victimization Survey (NCVS). Official compilers are government

Media Focus 1.1

Media Headlines concerning Crime Data

Information on crime makes headlines, and periodic reports on crime data are no exceptions. A few headlines from the year 2000 illustrate the impact the written news media might have on perceptions.

In May 2000 the *New York Times* carried this headline: "Serious Crimes Fall for 8th Consecutive Year." The article, based on the preliminary *UCR* data for 1999, stated that the decline in serious crimes had been continuous since 1992, although it did note that murders increased in some cities, such as New York City.[1]

Three months later, in August 2000, the same paper published an article with the headline "New York's Murder Rate, After Upturn, Starts to Slide Down." This article noted that, although by the end of 1999 the number of murders in New York City had surpassed those of the previous year by 6 percent and by the end of March 2000 the number was up 13 percent over the same period in 1999, the number of murders in the city was down 1 percent for the first seven months of the year 2000 compared to the same period in 1999. Police and politicians claimed credit for this decrease, but they had difficulty explaining why some of the efforts they said were responsible for the overall decrease did not lead to a decline in murders in the Bronx.[2]

Even so, it would be reasonable for New Yorkers to have concluded in August 2000 that, once again, murder was becoming less of a threat in their city. However, by the end of the year another *New York Times* article, entitled "Data Hint Crime Plunge May Be Leveling Off," pointed out that although the nationwide murder rate during the first six months of 2000 fell by 1.8 percent, murders increased in New York City, Los Angeles, Dallas, and New Orleans "for the first time since the early 1990's."[3]

Such news articles can be very confusing to the public, that is, if anyone is reading them carefully. The end-of-year article stated that the number of murders in New York City increased in 2000 for the first time in years; yet the two that appeared earlier in the year claimed that murders in New York City had increased in 1999. So what is the public to believe?

Adding to the potential for confusion are the politicians who rush to claim victory when crime rates are reported as falling. President Bill Clinton credited the overall decline in serious crimes in the United States to his program that put more police on the streets. The New York City police commissioner and the city's mayor proclaimed the city's efforts at reducing drug-related crimes to be responsible for the decrease in murders.[4]

An important point, however, is that short-term changes in crime data do not present a reason to proclaim victory over crime. Further, some of the data for these short-term reports were "fragmentary and contradictory."[5]

1. "Serious Crimes Fall for 8th Consecutive Year," *New York Times* (8 May 2000), p. 21.
2. "New York's Murder Rate, After Upturn, Starts to Slide Down," *New York Times* (8 August 2000), p. 8.
3. "Data Hint Crime Plunge May Be Leveling Off," *New York Times* (19 December 2000), p. 18.
4. "Serious Crimes Fall for 8th Consecutive Year"; "New York's Murder Rate, After Upturn, Starts to Slide Down."
5. "Data Hint Crime Plunge May Be Leveling Off."

agencies that collect crime data for a variety of different purposes. The most common source is agency reports. At the state level, data about criminal justice systems are updated routinely, but the systems differ in scope, definition, and quality. As a result, state-by-state comparison of crime data is difficult.

The situation is not much better at the federal level. Many agencies have independent data systems; the usefulness of the data is reduced because of different definitions, reporting periods, and classification schemes. The sources of federal crime data include many agencies, such as the Federal Bureau of Investigation; the National Criminal Justice Information and Statistics Service; the Drug Enforcement Administration; the National Institute on Drug Abuse; the Federal Aviation Administration; the Secret Service; the Administrative Office of the United States Courts; the Federal Prison System; the Bureau of Alcohol, Tobacco and Firearms; the Customs Service; the Census Bureau; the National Council on Crime and Delinquency; the Institute for Law and Social Research; the National Institute for Juvenile Justice and Delinquency Prevention; the National Center for Juvenile Justice; and the National Center for Health Statistics.

Partly as a response to this fragmentation, in 1981 Congress authorized the creation of the **Bureau of Justice Statistics (BJS).** Its main goal is to furnish an objective, independent, and competent source of police-relevant data to the government and to criminal justice and academic communities. Goals of the BJS are the unification of data, development of a program to follow an offender from the time of entering the criminal justice process until release from the correctional system, and provision of services to states and local communities to aid in comprehensive data gathering. The bureau is not to be involved in policy decisions.

Although BJS data are useful, the most frequently cited and most comprehensive source of crime data is the ***Uniform Crime Reports (UCR)*** under the jurisdiction of the Federal Bureau of Investigation (FBI).

Bureau of Justice Statistics (BJS) An agency authorized by Congress to furnish an objective, independent, and competent source of crime data to the government. Agency researchers analyze data and issue reports on the amount and characteristics of crime as measured by surveys of the general population who are asked questions about crime victimization.

Uniform Crime Reports (UCR) The official government source of national crime data; collected, compiled, and published by the Federal Bureau of Investigation.

Violent crimes Serious crimes against the person (as contrasted to serious crimes against property). The four serious violent crimes as defined as index offenses by the FBI in its *Uniform Crime Reports* are murder and nonnegligent manslaughter, forcible rape, robbery, and aggravated assault.

Property crimes Those serious crimes not directed toward the person, such as burglary, larceny-theft, motor vehicle theft, or arson.

Crimes known to the police The record of serious offenses for which the police find evidence that the alleged crimes occurred.

Index offense A serious crime as reported by the FBI's *Uniform Crime Reports*. Index offenses include murder and nonnegligent manslaughter, forcible rape, robbery, aggravated assault, burglary, larceny-theft, motor vehicle theft, and arson.

The *Uniform Crime Reports (UCR)*

In the 1920s the International Association of Chiefs of Police (IACP) appointed a committee to develop a system for securing crime data on a national scale. By 1929 the committee had developed a plan that became the basis for the *UCR*. A 1930 law requires the U.S. attorney general to report annually on the amount of crime in the United States. Also in 1930 the FBI began issuing its publication on national crime data, the *Uniform Crime Reports.* At first the *UCR* was issued monthly, then quarterly, then semiannually; finally, in 1958 the present format of one annual publication was begun. The *UCR* is also available on the Internet.

Standardized definitions were drafted for all included offenses in order to provide uniformity in reporting data. Local agencies compile data and submit them through state *UCR* agencies. Although the FBI has the responsibility for administering the *UCR* program, it has no authority to compel reporting by state and local jurisdictions. Even though it is voluntary, the national *UCR* program covers 98 percent of the U.S. population.

Originally seven crimes (because of their seriousness and frequency) were selected to constitute the *UCR* crime index; arson, the eighth, was added in 1978. The eight index crimes are known as Part I offenses. They are the serious **violent crimes**—murder and nonnegligent manslaughter, forcible rape, robbery, and aggravated assault—and the serious **property crimes**—burglary, larceny-theft, motor vehicle theft, and arson. Each month law enforcement agencies report the number of **crimes known to the police,** the number of Part I offenses verified by police investigation. The number of actual crimes in the index category is reported whether or not there is any further action in the case; that is, a crime known to the police is counted even if no suspect is arrested and no prosecution occurs.

If a criminal act involves several different crimes, only the most serious is reported as an **index offense.** For example, if a victim is raped, robbed, and mur-

Crime rate In the *Uniform Crime Reports,* the number of offenses recorded per 100,000 population.

dered, only the murder is counted in the *UCR.* In addition to reporting crimes known to the police, the *UCR* reports a **crime rate,** which is calculated by dividing the number of reported crimes by the number of people in the country. The result is expressed as a rate of crime per 100,000 people. In addition, the *UCR* reports trends in offenses and crime rates.

The number of Part I offenses that are cleared by arrest is also reported. Offenses are cleared in two ways: (1) by arrest when a suspect is arrested, charged, and turned over to the judicial system for prosecution; or (2) by circumstances beyond the control of the police. For example, normally the death of a suspect or a victim's refusal to press charges ends police involvement. Crimes are considered cleared whether or not the person arrested is convicted.

Several persons may be arrested and one crime cleared, or one person may be arrested and many crimes cleared. The *clearance rate* is the number of crimes solved expressed as a percentage of the total number of crimes reported to the police. The clearance rate is critical in policy decisions because it is one measure used to evaluate police departments. The higher the number of crimes solved by arrest, the better the police force looks in the eyes of the public. As Figure 2.1 shows, the clearance rate is higher for violent than for property crimes.

The *UCR* records and publishes arrest data for Part II offenses, the less serious crimes, as well as for Part I, or index, offenses. The *UCR* lists the number of arrests made during one year for each offense per 100,000 population. The *UCR* does not report the number of persons arrested each year because some individuals are arrested more than once during the year. The actual number of arrested persons is likely to be smaller than the number of arrests.

Official reports have been criticized for excluding some crimes. The *UCR* does not include federal offenses. It does not include computer crime, organized crime, and white-collar crime (all discussed in subsequent chapters). Some of these offenses, although they are violations of criminal law, are handled by

FIGURE 2.1
Crimes Cleared by Arrest, 2000

Source: Federal Bureau of Investigation, *Crime in the United States, Uniform Crime Reports 2000* (Washington, DC: U.S. Government Printing Office, 2001), p. 206.

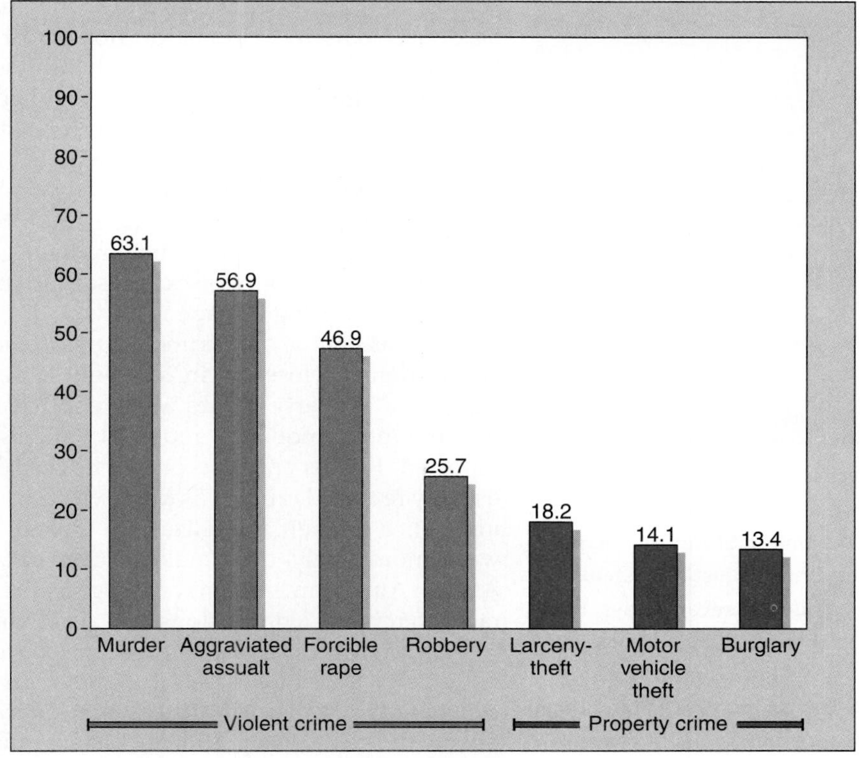

administrative agencies rather than by criminal courts. Since these crimes, which are more often committed by people in the middle and upper classes, are not included in the crime index, by looking only at official data we can conclude erroneously that there is a high correlation between crime and socioeconomic status, with the greatest proportion of crimes being committed by persons in the lowest socioeconomic classes.

Although considerable empirical research on crime and social class has been conducted, the results vary, and most of the studies are not comparable due to a lack of agreement on how to measure social class. However, one study, based on a sample of 555 adults, "demonstrated that regardless of how class or crime [was] measured, social class exerted little direct influence on adult criminality in the general population . . . [although there was some evidence that] social class was related to criminal involvement for nonwhites."[3]

Discretion In criminal justice systems, the authority to make decisions and choose among options according to one's own judgment rather than to specific legal rules and facts. Discretionary decision making may result in positive actions tailored to individual circumstances or in the inconsistent handling of offenders.

In addition to the exclusion of some serious crimes, the *UCR* has several other limitations. First, the use of "crimes known to the police" as a measure of crime may result in a serious underestimation of actual crime. Police do not know about all criminal incidents, as many crimes are not reported. Moreover, police departments do not use uniform procedures for coding a complaint. For example, a sexual offense may be coded as rape, indecent assault, sexual battery, assault with intent to harm, or another sex offense.

Another variable that may limit crime data accuracy is police **discretion** in deciding whether a complaint is a crime. Several variables may influence police decision making. Police may decide not to file a complaint in cases involving close relationships, although that is changing as departments have altered their arrest policies in domestic violence cases. Police may decide not to file when the complainant does not want charges pressed. They may decide not to file if the alleged offenders show proper deference to police. Socioeconomic status, race, gender, or other factors might be influential as well.

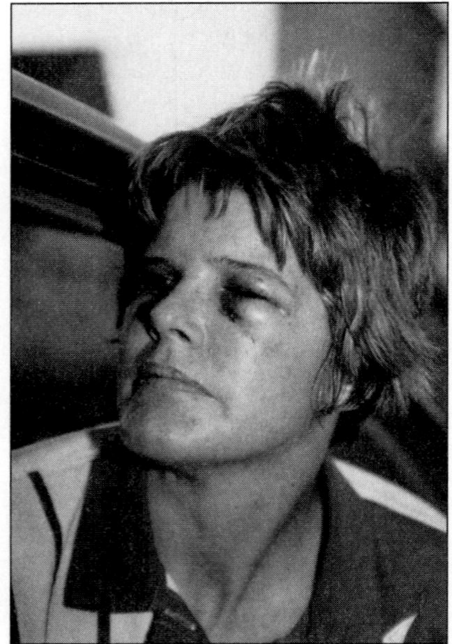

Domestic violence has received increasing attention in recent years both in the United States and in other countries. Criminal justice systems have responded in several ways, with the result that reporting of domestic violence cases has risen. It is also possible that an increase in the crime accounts for some of the increase in data. (Michael Newman/Photo Edit)

A third additional variable affecting the measurement of crime is victims' cooperation. Reporting of crimes may be affected by the climate surrounding crime victims and the belief that something will (or will not) be done. Some individuals do not report crimes because they do not think the police will do anything. In the case of rape, the beliefs that nothing will be done and that the victim will be suspected of having encouraged the crime often lead to underreporting. Therefore, an increase in reported rapes might not reflect an actual increase in rape but rather an increase in victims' willingness to report the crimes. Many cities have developed rape counseling centers that provide assistance for rape victims. In addition, some jurisdictions have given police special training in the handling of rape cases; these and other changes may result in increased reporting by rape victims.

Rape is not the only crime victims do not report to the police. Victim-survey data disclose that in 2000 only 48 percent of violent crimes and 36 percent of property crimes were reported to police. Aggravated assault was the most frequently reported violent crime, with 57 percent being reported. Robbery was second, with 56 percent reported. The least frequently reported crime was rape, with only 28 percent of persons informing police of their victimization. Overall, female victims (54 percent) were more likely than male victims (42.0 percent) to report crimes. African American women were slightly more likely than women of other races to report victimizations (see also Exhibit 2.3, p. 37).[4]

Even when victims or witnesses decide to report a crime, there is always some delay, the length of which depends on factors such as the time it may take to notice or discover the crime, the decision to report, the search for a phone, the call to the police, and actual police arrival on the scene. These delays may be decisive in determining whether police arrest a suspect.

Victims' decisions to report a crime may be determined by their experiences with police, judges, and attorneys. Criminal justice systems can make a more positive response to victims by keeping victims better informed, improving social services for victims, requiring restitution more frequently, and treating offenders more harshly. Improvements in victims' attitudes would increase crime reporting and enhance police ability to clear crimes by arrest.

A third variable that might influence official crime data is a change in the administration or organization of police departments. A reduction in the size or location of police forces might affect data; methods of reporting may be changed, resulting in an apparent increase or decrease in the data.

A fourth variable that may influence crime data collection is the method of counting crime. Crime data may be affected by decisions such as whether a series of criminal acts by one perpetrator is counted as one crime or as several. If a person appears before a group of people, pulls a gun, and asks each of the group for money, has the individual committed one act of armed robbery or several? If a perpetrator twice engages in sexual intercourse with force and without the consent of the victim, have two rapes been committed or only one? England and Wales follow the one-victim, one-crime rule, although the English rule with regard to property crime is not clear. The one-operation, one-crime rule is followed in the United States and Canada. Official reports record crimes as single events, but victim surveys may record each victim separately.[5] The two sources are not comparable in this regard.

The method of counting crimes has implications for sentencing, too, as illustrated by the case of *People* v. *Harrison,* decided in 1989 by the California Supreme Court. The case involved a defendant who was convicted of burglary and of three counts of violating a statute prohibiting sexual intercourse by instrumentation. The defendant argued that it was improper to convict him of three counts because his acts occurred during a brief period. The court disagreed. In the following excerpt, which begins with the author's summary of the facts, the court gives its reasons.[6]

People v. Harrison

[The defendant broke into the home of the legally blind victim who lived alone. He attacked her sexually by reaching inside her underwear and inserting his finger into her vagina. The victim struggled and screamed, pulled away, and eventually dislodged his finger, which had been inserted for approximately four seconds. Defendant managed to insert his finger a second time for approximately five seconds and after another struggle and another dislodging, managed to do so a third time for approximately five seconds. The victim estimated that the entire attack lasted from seven to ten minutes. The statute prohibited "any penetration, however slight."]

It follows logically that a *new and separate* violation of [the statute] is "completed" each time a *new and separate* "penetration, however slight" occurs. Here, defendant does not dispute that his finger actually penetrated the victim's vagina against her will three *separate* times; that *each* penetration was accomplished with the statutorily prescribed intent; that the requisite degree of force or fear preceded, and was used to accomplish *each* penetration; or that a finger is a foreign object within the meaning of the statute . . .

Obviously, *one* purpose of the "slight penetration" language used throughout this family of sex-offense statutes is to make clear that prolonged or deep insertion, or emission or orgasm, is unnecessary to "complete" the crime . . . [T]he "essential guilt" of sex offenses lies in the "outrage to the person and feelings of the victim . . ." The "slight penetration" language confirms that this peculiar "outrage" is deemed to occur each time the victim endures a new, unconsented sexual insertion. The Legislature, by devising a distinctly harsh sentencing scheme, has emphasized the seriousness with which society views each separate unconsented sexual act, even when all are committed on a single occasion.

One final point regarding categories is that the *UCR*'s method of counting crimes does not take into account the differing degrees of seriousness of crimes that have the same legal label. Even serious crimes such as rape or robbery differ in circumstances and severity. Some investigators measure crime by using an index that takes into account the components of the criminal act and the aggravating factors accompanying it. For example, greater weight is given to a rape aggravated by use of a dangerous weapon than to one in which no weapon is used.

National Incident-Based Reporting System (NIBRS) A method of collecting crime data that views crimes as involving numerous elements. Twenty-two crimes are categorized in this system.

Because of the deficiencies in the *UCR*'s traditional methods of collecting crime data, a new collection method was approved by the FBI and is being implemented. The new system, the **National Incident-Based Reporting System (*NIBRS*)**, categorizes crime and collects data according to numerous elements, such as the relationship between the offender and the victim, the use of alcohol and/or drugs by one or both, the type of weapon used, and the type of victims. Twenty-two crimes are categorized. Exhibit 2.1 contains a comparison of the *UCR* and the NIBRS approaches. According to the 2001 *UCR* the implementation of the NIBRS is moving at a "pace commensurate with the resources, abilities, and limitations of the contributing law enforcement agencies." Twenty-one states have programs certified for NIBRS participation, with an additional 15 state programs and some federal agencies having submitted data under the program.[7]

In a November 2001 press release the U.S. Department of Justice announced awards of approximately $13 million to 24 states under the NIBRS program. The release stated that the system will permit "law enforcement executives, analysts and the public to better understand trends in different types of crime, including domestic violence, the victimization of children and alcohol-involved crime, and to evaluate the harm to victims, including injuries as well as monetary and other losses."[8]

A recent analysis of the differences in crime rates between the two approaches revealed only small differences. On the average, the *UCR* rates were about 2 percent higher than those recorded by the NIBRS method.[9]

The National Crime Victimization Survey (NCVS)

Victimization surveys were developed in response to criticisms of the FBI's *Uniform Crime Reports*, which do not record all crimes, since many crimes are not reported to the police. To determine actual crime trends and to ascertain the true level of crime in society, it is important to know the dark figure of crime, that is, the amount of crime that is not reported to police. One purpose of victimization surveys is to determine why citizens do not report crime. Victims are the most important link in the system. If they do not report the crime to the police, in most cases it will not be recorded as a crime. The more serious the crime, the more likely it is that the victim will bring it to the attention of authorities. Similarly, if a weapon is used, or if the victim sustains serious physical or financial injury, the crime is more likely to be reported. In fact, the seriousness of the crime is the most important factor in the decision to report.

National Crime Victimization Survey (NCVS) Victimization data collected and published annually by the Bureau of Justice Statistics (BJS).

The major source of victimization data is the **National Crime Victimization Survey (NCVS),** which comes from the Bureau of Justice Statistics. The NCVS measures six crimes: rape, robbery, assault, household burglary, personal and household larceny, and motor vehicle theft. As Exhibit 2.2 shows, two crimes included in the index offenses of the *UCR* are omitted: murder and arson. Murder cannot be measured by this survey since the victim is dead. Arson is excluded because of the difficulty of determining whether the property owner was the perpetrator of the crime. The NCVS includes research on large samples in 20 of the nation's largest cities, along with 8 impact cities. Business and personal victimizations are included in the survey. In the early 1990s the NCVS

EXHIBIT 2.1

Contrasts between the *Uniform Crime Reports (UCR)* and the National Incident-Based Reporting System (NIBRS)

DIFFERENCES BETWEEN SUMMARY UCR AND NIBRS

Summary UCR

- Consists of monthly aggregate crime counts for eight Index crimes.
- Records one offense per incident as determined by *hierarchy rule.*
- *Hierarchy rule* suppresses counts of lesser offenses in multiple-offense incidents.
- Does not distinguish between attempted and completed crimes.
- Applies *hotel rule* to burglary.
- Records rape of females only.
- Collects weapon information for murder, robbery, and aggravated assault.
- Provides counts on arrests for the 8 Index crimes and 21 other offenses.

NIBRS

- Consists of individual incident records for the 8 Index crimes and 38 other offenses with details on—
  - Offense
  - Victim
  - Offender
  - Property
- Records each offense occurring in incident.
- Distinguishes between attempted and completed crimes.
- Expands burglary *hotel rule* to include rental storage facilities.
- Records rape of males and females.
- Restructures definition of assault.
- Collects weapon information for all violent offenses.
- Provides details on arrests for the 8 Index crimes and 49 other offenses.

SOURCE OF DATA DISCREPANCIES BETWEEN SUMMARY UCR AND (NIBRS)

Human error

Misclassifications of—

- Aggravated assault.
- Motor vehicle theft.
- Larceny.

Hierarchy

- Suppression of multiple offenses by *hierarchy rule.*

Operational

- Modified offense definitions.
- Converting State penal code to FBI crime definitions.
- Over-reporting because of State practices.
- Recording every possible offense with which offender may be charged.

Computer

- Inadequate programming.

When comparing data from the same year for the jurisdictions in this study, NIBRS rates differ only slightly from Summary UCR—

- Murder rates are the same.
- Rape, robbery, and aggravated assault rates in NIBRS are about 1% higher, on average, than in Summary UCR.
- NIBRS burglary rates are lower by an average 0.5%.
- NIBRS larceny rates are higher by an average 3.4%.
- NIBRS motor vehicle theft rates are higher by an average 4.5%.

Source: Bureau of Justice Statistics, *Effects of NIBRS on Crime Statistics* (Washington, DC: U.S. Department of Justice, July 2000), p. 1.

underwent extensive changes in its design, resulting in the introduction of a new instrument in 1992.

The NCVS should be considered a valuable addition to, not a substitute for, the *UCR.* The NCVS includes data on crimes that victims did not report to the police as well as the reasons for not reporting the crimes. The NCVS has been criticized because it depends on the willingness and ability of alleged victims to report data accurately. BJS data have been praised as "a storehouse of information on who is being victimized under what conditions." The bureau's design principles have been adopted by numerous foreign countries as well as by the United Nations.[10]

EXHIBIT 2.2
Comparison of the *Uniform Crime Reports* and the National Crime Victimization Survey

	Uniform Crime Reports	National Crime Victimization Survey
Offenses measured	Homicide Rape Robbery (personal and commercial) Assault (aggravated) Burglary (commercial and household) Larceny (commercial and household) Motor vehicle theft Arson	 Rape Robbery (personal) Assault (aggravated and simple) Household burglary Larceny (personal and household) Motor vehicle theft
Scope	Crimes reported to the police in most jurisdictions; considerable flexibility in developing small-area data	Crimes both reported and not reported to police; all data are available for a few large geographic areas
Collection method	Police department reports to FBI or to centralized State agencies that then report to FBI	Survey interviews; periodically measures the total number of crimes committed by asking a national sample of 49,000 households encompassing 101,000 persons age 12 and over about their experiences as victims of crime during a specified period
Kinds of information	In addition to offense counts, provides information on crime clearances, persons arrested, persons charged, law enforcement officers killed and assaulted, and characteristics of homicide victims	Provides details about victims (such as age, race, sex, education, income, and whether the victim and offender were related to each other) and about crimes (such as time and place of occurrence, whether or not reported to police, use of weapons, occurrence of injury, and economic consequences)
Sponsor	Department of Justice Federal Bureau of Investigation	Department of Justice Bureau of Justice Statistics

Source: Bureau of Justice Statistics, *Report to the Nation on Crime and Justice: The Data,* 2d ed. (Washington, DC: U.S. Department of Justice, 1988), p. 11.

Several scholars have compared crime data provided by the *UCR* with data from the NCVS surveys, but they disagree on the results. The authors of one study concluded that "over the years, the two major national crime series have tracked each other quite closely, at least for the serious crime types of burglary and robbery," while another concluded that those authors exaggerated the extent to which the results of the two measures converge. The authors of the first study responded that the second focused too much on "minor technical issues."[11] In comments on these two approaches, other scholars argue that "such controversy is inevitable. In part this is due to limitations of the data, and in part it reflects problems in defining comparability."[12]

Although in previous years crime data from the *UCR* and the NCVS have been relatively close, the data for 2000 defy that fact. Just a few weeks after the FBI announced that its preliminary data for the year 2000 showed that crime leveled off, the Bureau of Justice Statistics (BJS) published its 2000 victimization data, which showed a 15 percent drop in crime. This apparently wide discrepancy between the two sources caused some experts to question whether one or both sources are significantly inaccurate. Most insist that more than a year is needed for comparison purposes, while others suggest that the differences are not as great as they might at first appear. Recall that the BJS data include simple as well as aggravated assaults but that they do not include murder. This may account for most of the wide difference. Or it may be that the real explanation of the difference between the two reports is, as one criminologist stated, "They are telling us that crime is very difficult to measure."[13]

Observers hope that some of the methodological problems in comparing data from the NCVS and the *UCR* can be solved. Additional research may result in using one source to test or predict the other or to measure criminal activity in areas not measured effectively by either approach. In the meantime, when analyzing data from each source it is important to understand that scholars disagree on the comparability of the two measures.

One limitation common to both the NCVS and the *UCR* is that neither can estimate the extent to which a few offenders are responsible for large numbers of crimes. These reports tell us how many crimes occurred (not how many can be traced to the same offenders) and how many arrests were made (not how many times a particular person was arrested).

Self-Report Data (SRD)

Official crime data report the number of crimes that come to the attention of law enforcement officials. Victimization surveys report the number of crimes that occur regardless of whether they are reported to the police. Another way to measure crime is to survey people about their own criminal activity.

A 1994 publication takes the position that most of us engage in some form of criminal activity and that criminality is only a matter of degree "rather than an attribute that we either possess or lack."[14] Earlier **self-report data (SRD)** disclosed that much criminal activity is not reported to officials. In 1947 two investigators reported the results of their sample of upper-income persons, 99 percent of whom answered that they had committed one or more acts for which they could have been arrested.[15]

Self-report data (SRD) The method of collecting data by asking people to give information about their prior involvement in crime; based on selected samples of the total population or a subset such as juveniles or incarcerated criminals. Data may be obtained in several ways, such as by anonymous questionnaires or interviews.

Similar results were reported in an earlier study of college students and institutionalized delinquents. College students reported types of delinquency similar to those of youths who had been judged to be delinquent. That is, although probably with less frequency of commission, college students admitted to having engaged in delinquent and criminal acts as serious as those for which delinquents had been adjudicated. Some of these students were honors students and leaders of school organizations.[16] These studies were somewhat unsystematic. The systematic use of the self-report method of measuring delinquency was introduced by James F. Short and F. Ivan Nye in 1957 and since that time has been improved upon and used extensively.[17]

Self-report data are secured through interviews or anonymous questionnaires. Although originally the SRD approach was used primarily with juveniles, the method is employed today to measure adult criminality as well. Several studies by the Rand Corporation, which conducts extensive research in many areas of criminal justice, have relied on the SRD approach to obtain data on the past criminal behavior of incarcerated persons. These studies reveal interesting facts about career criminals, those few who commit most of the crimes. They also disclose that individuals serving time after conviction of a crime were not arrested for most of the crimes they reported having committed.[18] Another use of the SRD method has been to measure the extent of rule breaking by incarcerated offenders by comparing inmates' self-reports to reports of correctional officers concerning their observations of rule breaking.[19]

The SRD method provides data on criminal acts that do not come to the attention of official authorities. In addition, it provides information on unapprehended law violators. The approach has been criticized because of the possibility that respondents may overreport or underreport their criminal activities purposely; others may forget. This problem may be reduced by comparing SRD responses with official data when available.

Crime data secured by the SRD method have been criticized for excluding serious crimes and for including too few African Americans in the samples surveyed. These criticisms raise serious questions since research shows that African American respondents tend to report illegal acts that are less frequent but more serious, whereas white respondents tend to report greater involvement in less serious crimes that occur more frequently.[20]

The National Youth Survey (NYS)

National Youth Survey (NYS) A program for gathering crime data by interviewing adolescents over a five-year period. The program has been structured to overcome many of the criticisms of other self-report studies.

Self-report studies may yield more useful data in the future. The **National Youth Survey (NYS),** has been structured to overcome many of the criticisms of older self-report studies. The NYS, based on interviews conducted with adolescents over a five-year period, includes all *UCR* offenses except homicide and records crimes that are likely to be relevant to a delinquent lifestyle or culture, such as gang fights, sexual activity, and misdemeanors. The NYS may be more useful for comparison because it measures criminal activity from Christmas to Christmas. This period is close to the *UCR* calendar period and coincides with the more recent victimization surveys. The NYS allows researchers to pinpoint many types and levels of delinquent behavior and shows promise for gathering more accurate data.

The Crime Classification System (CCS)

Crime Classification System (CCS) Collection of crime data based on the severity of crimes and the effect of the crimes on victims.

A final approach that is utilized as an alternative to the *UCR* and the NCVS is the **Crime Classification System (CCS).** The focus of the CCS is the harm suffered by the victim and the context in which the criminal activity occurs. Unlike the *UCR,* the CCS has the capacity to measure the degree of severity, giving more refined measures of the harm suffered by victims and the type of circumstances in which that harm occurred. This system might provide a more useful database for criminal justice agencies and a better understanding of victimization risk.

The National Criminal History Improvement Program (NCHIP)

National Criminal History Improvement Program (NCHIP) A federal program that provides grants to assist states in improving their crime record systems.

In November 2001 the BJS and the FBI announced that they were awarding $40 million to state agencies for the purpose of improving the completeness, quality, and accessibility of the nation's crime record systems. The **National Criminal History Improvement Program (NCHIP)** provides grants to assist states "in automating and upgrading records that link to record systems administered by the FBI, including the National Sex Offender Registry and the National Instant Criminal Background Check Systems (NICS), which supports instant background checks on persons attempting to purchase firearms." Such awards, which have been made to all states, have totaled over $354 million since 1995.[21]

CRIME IN THE UNITED STATES: AN OVERVIEW

The preceding discussion of sources should be kept in mind as we look at crime data throughout the rest of this text. When analyzing data, we must consider the source and the time period covered. For example, the media may report what appear to be conflicting crime data, but the conflict comes from reporting two sources that cover two different time periods. Some examples of this problem are provided in the following discussion, which contains a brief look at the most recent official crime data as reported by the Bureau of Justice Statistics and the *Uniform Crime Reports.* Data on all serious crimes and on some less serious ones are analyzed more carefully in later chapters as we discuss the nature and elements of those crimes.

National Crime Victimization Survey (NCVS) Data

The NCVS data for 2000 recorded a dramatic drop in victimization over 1999, as graphed in Exhibit 2.3. Violent crime rates were down 15 percent, with property rates declining 10 percent. The exhibit also shows other highlights of the 2000 data. The decline in violent crimes was the largest ever recorded by the NCVS and was experienced by most groups of victims as categorized by the program.

EXHIBIT 2.3

Highlights of the National Crime Victimization Survey, 2000

Violent crime rates fell 15% between 1999 and 2000, resulting in the greatest annual percentage decline and the lowest rates of violent crime recorded since the inception of the NCVS in 1973.

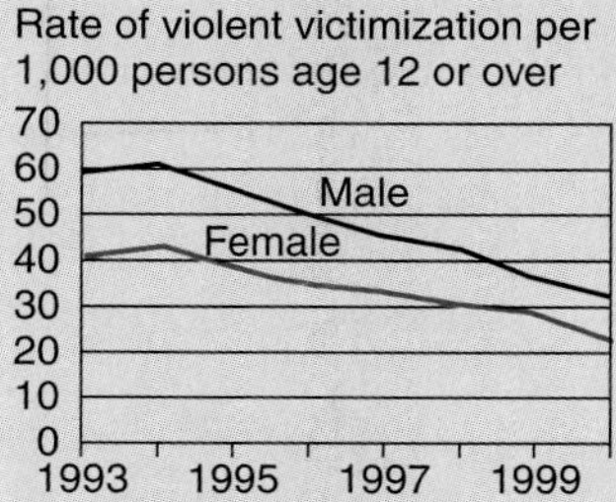

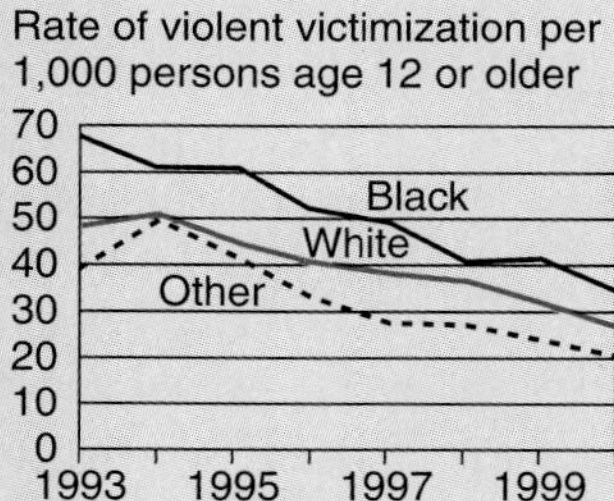

- According to the National Crime Victimization Survey, the violent crime rate fell 15% and the property crime rate fell 10%, 1999–2000.
- Violent victimization and property crime rates in 2000 are the lowest recorded since the NCVS' inception in 1973.[1]
- The overall violent crime rate decline resulted from a decrease in simple assault and rape/sexual assault coupled with a slight fall in aggravated assault during 2000.
- Overall property crime rates fell between 1999 and 2000 due to a decrease in theft and a slight decline in motor vehicle theft.
- From 1999 to 2000 violent crime rates fell for almost every demographic group considered: males, females, whites, blacks, non-Hispanics, and 12-to-24-year-olds. Violent crime against Hispanics also fell somewhat during the period.
- 48% of violent victimizations and 36% of property crimes were reported to the police in 2000.
- From 1999 to 2000 the number of crimes of violence, completed or threatened, dropped about 1 million from 7.4 million to 6.3 million.
- The majority of violent crime victims (67%) do not face an armed offender. Rape/sexual assault victims (6%) were the least likely, while robbery victims (55%) were the most likely, to face an armed offender.

1. Based on adjustments to pre-1992 estimates to account for the 1992 redesign of the NCVS.

Source: Bureau of Justice Statistics, *Criminal Victimization 2000* (Washington, DC: U.S. Department of Justice, August 2001), p. 1.

Even the age group that normally experiences the highest violent crime victimization rates, those between 12 and 24, experienced a significant decline. Males, teenagers, and African Americans, however, continued to be the most frequent violent crime victims. Fifty-three percent of the violent crime victims were attacked by an intimate, friend, relative, or acquaintance. Property crimes most often victimized African Americans. Motor vehicle thefts were, as usual, the most frequently reported crimes (80 percent); larceny-theft was the most infrequently reported property crime (30 percent).[22]

Uniform Crime Report Data

In the foreword to the *Uniform Crime Reports* for 1982, William H. Webster, then director of the FBI, announced with cautious optimism that the rate of serious or index offenses was down 3 percent from 1981. The cautiousness of his optimism stemmed from the fact that in the 1970s crime rates dropped twice, only to turn upward again shortly thereafter. The estimated 12.9 million crime index offenses of 1982, although up 47 percent from 1973 and 15 percent from 1978, represented the first significant decline since 1977. The figures were down in both violent and property crimes.[23]

Both the number of offenses and the rate per 100,000 inhabitants continued their downward trends in 1983 and 1984 but started back up in 1985. Although the 1985 figures were below those of 1981, there was cause for concern after three consecutive years of declines in serious offenses. All property and violent crimes comprising index offenses increased in number in 1985. In reaction to these data, Webster emphasized that data must be analyzed over time, that data do not represent all the human suffering that results from crime, and that they do not reflect the tremendous economic losses from crime. Declines in offenses and crime rates are welcome; they may be due to any number of factors and, Webster noted, "their accuracy is often questionable and certainly controversial." With regard to the increases in 1985, Webster commented, "There are few social statements more tragic than these."[24]

The upward trend continued through 1991. The crime index total in 1991 was 3 percent higher than that of 1990, representing a 15 percent increase over 1982 and a 10 percent increase over 1987.[25] In 1992 the number of crimes known to the police and the crime rate began a decline that continued through 1999, the latest official yearly data. Figure 2.2 graphs the percentage change in the number of offenses known and the crime rate from 1996 through 2000.

The *UCR* recorded a 2 percent decrease in the volume of serious crimes, or index offenses from 1998 to 1999, representing the seventh consecutive year in which offenses declined "and the lowest annual serious crime count since 1985." Serious violent crimes were down 3.2 percent; serious property crimes dropped by 2 percent.[26]

U.S. crime leveled off in 2000, with the estimated 11.6 million offenses representing only a .2 percent decline over 1999, but these figures were the lowest since 1978. The crime rate of 4,124 offenses per 100,000 inhabitants was the lowest since 1972. Of the total crime index offenses, 12.3 percent were violent crimes and 87.7 percent were property crimes. A total of 2.2 million arrests for index crimes were reported; 20.5 percent were cleared.[27]

Experts do not agree on the reasons for the decline in crime rates nationally. Although some public officials proclaim that the declines are the result of stronger and larger police forces, others are not so sure. In a 1998 symposium of articles on the dramatic drop in crime to that point, scholars did not agree on the explanations. Various causes were suggested, and most of them focused on a reversal of the factors that were viewed as driving up crime rates in the 1980s. One professor suggested that the drop in murder rates among adults, espe-

FIGURE 2.2
Crime Index: Percent Change from 1996 to 2000
Source: Federal Bureau of Investigation, *Crime in the United States, Uniform Crime Reports 2000* (Washington, DC: U.S. Government Printing Office, 2001), p. 8.

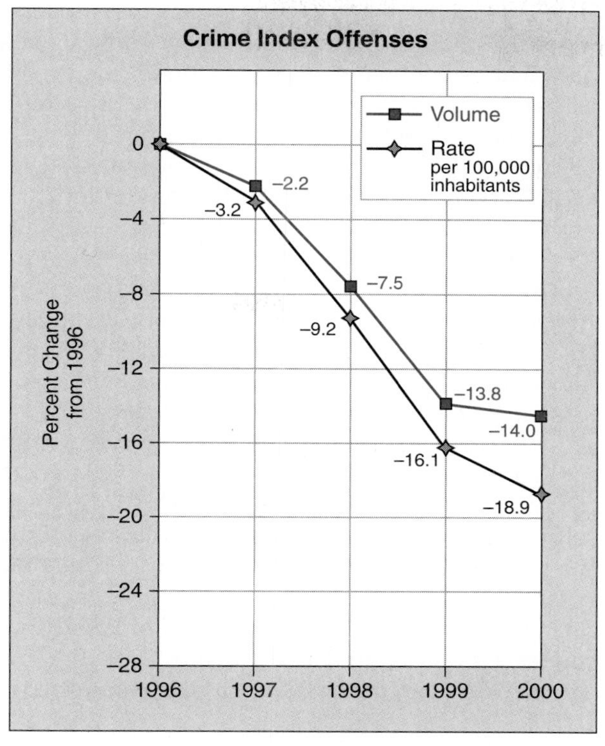

cially spouses, might be related to the changing social structure: fewer barroom brawls in the neighborhood taverns and more adults in prison. Among young people the decline in overall crime might be related to changes in the drug culture, reflecting a decline in the crack cocaine epidemic of the 1980s, with more young people finding legitimate jobs and abandoning the rough drug culture. Greater stability and an improved economy as well as the increase in the number of young people who are in schools, were also cited as reasons for declines in crimes. In summary, however, the scholars concluded that they were no closer to explaining the decrease in crime than they were when it began in the early 1990s.[28]

By the end of 2000, however, experts were faced with explaining the *increase* in violent crime in some cities, in particular New York City, Los Angeles, Dallas, and New Orleans. During the first six months of 2000, the number of murders in these cities rose, although the numbers fell by 1.8 percent nationally. The New York City murder rate, however, appeared to be leveling off toward the end of 2000, and it was declining in December 2001, mayor Rudolph W. Giuliani proclaiming New York City as one of the safest cities in the United States.[29] In late June 2002, however, the FBI released preliminary data indicating that crime rates were increasing.

Criminologist James Alan Fox said, "To some extent, we are victims of our own success . . . With eight straight years of declining crime rates, we are at a level that is difficult to continue and certainly hard to improve upon."[30]

CHARACTERISTICS OF OFFENDERS

A thorough study of crime includes not only an analysis of the number and type of crimes but also information on the characteristics of those who commit crimes. Data on offenders are discussed by the variables of age, race, and gender.

Age

Of the 14 million arrests (excluding traffic violations) reported by the *UCR* in 2000, 46 percent were of persons under the age of 25; 32.1 percent were of persons under 21; 17.1 percent were of persons under 18; and 5.5 percent were of persons under 15. When only the eight index offenses are considered, persons under 25 accounted for 55.1 percent of all arrests; 43.1 percent of arrestees were under 21; 27.5 percent were under 18. Persons under 25 accounted for 44.4 percent of all arrests for violent crimes and 59.2 percent of all property crime arrests.[31]

Despite the high percentage of crimes committed by the young, the 2000 arrest rate of juveniles for murder was the lowest it had been since 1966. Arrest rates for other serious crimes among juveniles also dropped, with robbery falling 53 percent between 1994 and 1999, to its lowest level since 1980. Rape arrest rates were also at their lowest level since 1980, while the aggravated assault rates fell to their lowest level since 1989.[32]

A word of caution is in order, however, with regard to these data. A report issued by the U.S. surgeon general's office in early 2001 warns that we should not conclude that youth violence is over or even decreasing significantly. The official data are based on arrest records, and, according to this report, those represent only a portion of youth violence: "For every youth arrested in any given year in the late 1990s, at least ten were engaged in some form of violent behavior that could have seriously injured or killed another person." The report continues, emphasizing that, according to confidential surveys, 13 to 15 percent of high school seniors "report having committed an act of serious violence in

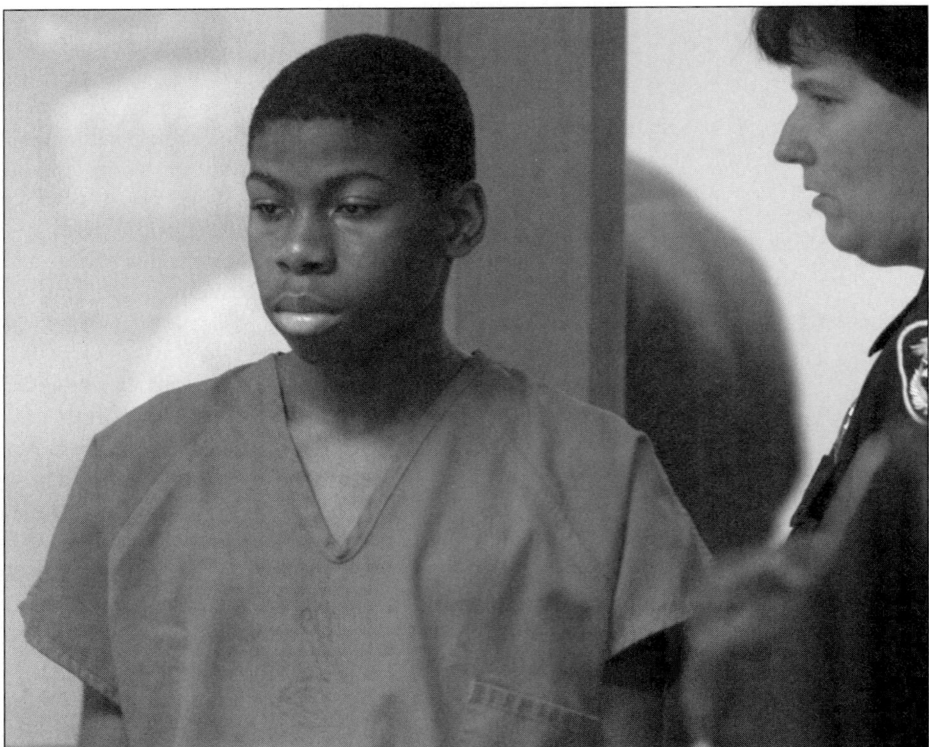

Nathaniel Brazill was 13 when he was accused of the shooting death of his favorite teacher. Brazill was tried as an adult when he was 14. He was convicted by a Florida court of second-degree murder and sentenced to 28 years in prison. (Richard Graulich/Reuters/Getty Images)

recent years." In conclusion, "The best available evidence from multiple sources indicates that youth violence is an ongoing national problem, albeit one that is largely hidden from public view."[33]

Additional crimes by juveniles are processed in juvenile courts and are not reflected in the *UCR* data. A report issued in October 2000 stated that between 1988 and 1997 the number of such cases rose by 48 percent, but the numbers leveled off. Approximately the same number, 1.8 million, were processed in 1997 as in 1996. Between 1996 and 1997 the number of juvenile homicide cases processed in juvenile courts fell by 17 percent.[34]

These data show clearly that the young are arrested more often than the elderly. There are some reports, however, that crime is becoming more of a problem with the elderly, especially in areas in which they are heavily concentrated. In Florida, for example, the percentage of elderly people who are committing crimes is growing faster than adults of younger ages who are doing so. Between 1980 and 1998 the rate of forcible sex offenses by Floridians age 60 or over increased by 171 percent, while robberies increased 168 percent and aggravated assaults by 13 percent. The director of the Miami, Florida, institute responsible for training police to handle the elderly stated, "Much to their surprise, officers now sometimes find themselves handcuffing someone over age sixty-five . . . [W]e try to caution them that just because someone is old doesn't mean they are innocent."[35]

Nationally, however, the elderly account for little crime. *UCR* data for 2000 reported that persons 65 and older accounted for only 0.6 percent of the total arrests for that year. The crime for which the elderly were most frequently arrested was driving under the influence. Among index crimes, the elderly were most frequently arrested for larceny-theft, followed by aggravated assault.[36]

Crime rates generally decrease with age. Various explanations have been given for this phenomenon. Scholars who have studied career criminals have reported that normal biological and sociopsychological maturation processes decrease criminal activity, and that age enables people to calculate the probability of success in crime more accurately. Most criminals do not have financial gains over a long period of years, nor do they avoid arrest, conviction, and incarceration with great success. Whatever the reasons, it appears that "the allure of crime diminishes substantially as offenders get older."[37]

Perhaps this is true, but some scholars are warning that there may be problems in predicting future crime rates based primarily on age demographics. Thus, if we look at the fact that most crimes are committed by young people, and we consider the predicted increase in the population in that age group, we could conclude that there will be more crime and that we should prepare by building more prisons, courts, and so on. For example, scholars as well as the popular media made dire predictions, such as this 1996 statement from *Scientific American*, which quotes criminologist James Alan Fox:

> The baby boom generation has produced 39 million people who are now under the age of 10. During the next decade, this "baby boomerang," . . . will enter their most crime-prone years. Unless steps are taken immediately, "the next crime wave will get so bad that it will make 1995 look like the good old days."[38]

Some scholars argue, however, that changes in the demographics of age have a "limited impact on aggregate crime rates." Steven D. Levitt examined the population decline between the ages of 15 and 24 (those who commit most of the crimes) between 1980 and 1995.[39] Although general crime rates did go down during most of those years, Levitt notes that homicides among the young increased. Levitt's analysis led him to the conclusion that only about a 1 percent crime decrease was accounted for by the changes in age demographics. "In predicting a future demographically driven crime wave, analysts have dramatically overstated the magnitude of the anticipated changes," says Levitt. He concludes with a policy note:

At a minimum, the results of this analysis suggest that caution should be exercised when making large investments in criminal justice resources in anticipation of rising crime rates. For instance, arguments for continued expansion of prison capacity to house the future wave of criminals would seem misplaced given the results of this analysis.[40]

Race

The National Commission on the Causes and Prevention of Violence reported in 1969 that African American crime rates were four times higher than white crime rates for the four major violent crimes of homicide, rape, robbery, and aggravated assault. In 1967 African American arrest rates for murder were about 17 times higher than those for whites, and for forcible rape the arrest rates were 12 times higher. Among juveniles, the murder rate for African Americans was 17 times higher than for whites. The commission reported that African American rates for violent crimes had increased more rapidly than the rates for whites during the previous decade.[41]

The most recent official data on arrests by race show that although 69.7 percent of all arrests were of whites, compared with 27.9 percent for African Americans, the percentages were much closer in the serious crimes, the greater differences occurring in arrests for less serious offenses. For example, 76.3 percent of arrests for runaways, 88.2 percent of arrests for driving under the influence, and 85.6 percent of arrests for violating liquor laws were white. Arrests for sex offenses (except forcible rape and prostitution) more often involved whites than African Americans—74.4 percent compared with 23.2 percent. For index crimes, 64.5 percent of all arrestees were white, compared with 32.9 percent African American. African Americans constituted 53.9 percent of the robbery arrests, 48.8 percent of arrests for murder and nonnegligent manslaughter, and 34.1 percent of arrests for forcible rape (compared to 63.7 percent for whites). African Americans were responsible for 41.6 percent of arrests for motor vehicle theft, while whites were arrested for 55.4 percent of those crimes. Whites accounted for 63.5 percent of arrests for aggravated assault, compared to 34 percent for African Americans.[42]

While analyzing these data, we must realize that even in cases in which the arrest rates are higher for whites than for African Americans, the rates may still be disproportionate, as African Americans constitute only approximately 11 percent of the total population. Second, we must consider not only arrest data but also the fact that official and unofficial crime data show differences between African Americans and whites at all levels of criminal justice systems.[43]

Gender

Historically, crime rates for men have been higher than those for women, with the exception of such crimes as prostitution. Men accounted for 77.8 percent of all arrests in 2000, compared to 22.2 percent for women. The index crime for which women were most frequently arrested in 2000 was larceny-theft, for which they constituted 35.9 percent of all arrests. Women accounted for 10.6 percent of arrests for murder and nonnegligent manslaughter, 1.1 percent for forcible rape, 10.1 percent for robbery, 20.1 percent for aggravated assault, 13.3 percent for burglary, 15.8 percent for motor vehicle theft, and 15.1 percent for arson. Among less serious crimes women had their highest arrests for prostitution and commercialized vice (62.1 percent of the total arrests), embezzlement

Although most criminal offenders are male, the rate of women involved in crimes has been increasing faster than that of men, and some of the crimes are violent. In this picture Andrea Yates, 37, is led into a Houston, Texas, court on 8 August 2001, to face charges of drowning her five children. Yates, who had been taking medicine for depression, used the insanity defense in her trial that began in early 2002. She was convicted and sentenced to life in prison. (Buster Dean/Getty Images)

(50 percent), fraud (44.9 percent), and forgery and counterfeiting (39 percent). The arrests of women for runaways, which involves juveniles, was also high, at 58.8 percent of the total arrests.[44]

When trend data on the arrests of men and women in the United States are examined, some interesting findings emerge. Between 1991 and 2000 the total arrests of women increased by 17.6 percent, compared to an increase of 3.8 percent for men. During that period arrests of women for index violent crimes were up 32.7 percent, compared to a decrease of 17.1 percent for men; arrests for serious property crimes were up 16.7 percent for women, compared to a 38.1 percent for men.[45]

If the index violent and property crimes are examined individually in terms of increases in arrests by gender between 1991 and 2000, some significant results are also evident. Arrests of women for index offenses increased in only one category, aggravated assault, up 46.2 percent compared to a decrease of 15.7 percent for men. Arrests for murder and nonnegligent manslaughter decreased by 34.2 percent for women, compared to 67.3 percent for men. For all index violent crimes arrests for women increased by 32.7 percent, while those for men decreased by 22.7 percent. For property index crimes, there were 16.7 percent fewer arrests of women in the period, compared to a decrease of 37.1 percent for men.[46]

Between 1991 and 2000 the increases in arrests of women compared to men were high in a few categories of non-index serious offenses as well. For example, the increase in arrests of women for offenses against the family and children was 93.6 percent, compared to a 24.3 percent increase for men. For the crime of other assaults, the increase for women was 68.6 percent, compared to an increase of 23.7 percent for men. Arrests for drug abuse violations were up 50.2 percent among women, compared to 47.5 percent for men, while forgery and counterfeiting arrests increased 19.5 percent for women, compared to only 2.7 percent for men.[47]

CRIME VICTIMS

Earlier we noted that surveys of victims have produced significant insights into the nature and extent of crime. In addition, studies have given us information on the characteristics of victims, who for years were ignored by scholars, researchers, and institutions. In recent years, however, professional societies have been formed, workshops on victims have been held, journals have been established, and a national organization has been actively pursuing victims' rights. Other changes have been made in court systems, with a greater emphasis being placed on victims' needs and rights.

An analysis of victimization data shows that there are differences in the victimization rates of specific groups. The most common victims of violent crimes are younger people, men, African Americans, Hispanics, the poor, and residents of central cities. This discussion gives individual attention to the factors of age, race, and gender, but in addition to those critical variables, it is important to consider a few others.

Although the *UCR* does not contain official data on the socioeconomic status of arrestees, we know by analyzing prison populations that most persons who are processed through all of the stages of criminal justice systems are from lower income groups. The official victimization data from the Bureau of Justice Statistics (BJS) also show that persons from lower income households are more frequently victims of violent crimes than are those from higher income households. For example, in 2000 the highest rates of violent crimes were committed against those whose household incomes were $7,500 or less. But the relationship between household income and property victimizations depends on the type of crime. Households at the upper income level as well as those at the lower level suffer about the same amounts of victimization in overall property crimes, but households in which the income is $75,000 or higher are more likely to be victimized by theft although less likely to be victimized by burglary than are lower income households.[48]

Another variable that is related to victimization is marital status. In 2000 the most likely category of violent crime victims (when marital status is considered) were persons who had never married. They were six times as likely as widowed persons and four times as likely as married persons to be victimized by violent crimes. Location is also an important variable, with those living in urban areas more likely to be victimized by violent crimes than those who live in suburban areas, and their chances are higher than those living in rural areas. Some differences were obvious in property crimes, with urban residents more vulnerable to most property crimes, followed by suburban residents; but rural residents were more likely than suburban ones to be burglary victims. Finally, rental households were more often victimized by property crimes than those in which the individuals owned their homes.[49]

Age

Age is an important variable in the study of victims. For crimes of violence, the elderly are least frequently the victims, and persons between the ages of 12 and 24 are most frequently victimized. The same is true with property crimes, although the elderly are affected at about the same rate as younger persons in the crime of larceny-theft, which includes picking pockets as well as snatching purses.[50]

The incidence of crimes against the elderly may not be as important, however, as the elderly's perception of the probability of such crimes. This fear may be unrealistic, but its impact is dramatic. Many older people change their lifestyles, relocating if possible, in an effort to avoid becoming victims of crime. Others become prisoners in their own dwellings, afraid to venture out even during the daylight hours. For many elderly people it is not the *probability* of becoming a victim that is crucial; it is the *possibility,* as well as the potential impact of an attack, that is of concern. A purse snatching can have a far more serious effect on an elderly person than it might have on a younger victim. The elderly are more likely to be injured seriously if there is any altercation between the assailant and the victim, and the direct contact may be much more frightening. The loss of money may be more harmful, too, because many elderly people live on fixed incomes.

Just as the elderly may be peculiarly susceptible to some kinds of crime because they are so defenseless, the very young may be easy prey, too. Children as victims of sexual abuse, physical abuse, and other forms of family violence are discussed in Chapter 7. In addition, many young people are victimized by the growing incidence of violence in schools, with some of the most shocking and tragic examples having occurred in the past few years.

Finally with regard to the age of victims, it is important to note that for male juveniles, in particular for those who are African American, "the risk of being murdered begins to rise sharply as they reach age fourteen."[51]

Race

African Americans are more likely than other nonwhites or whites to be crime victims, especially violent crime victims. In 2000, for every 1,000 African Americans in the United States, 35.5 were violent crime victims, compared to 27.1 whites and 20.7 persons of other races. The differences are greater for robbery, in which African Americans experienced 7.2 victimizations per 1,000 individuals in 2000, compared to 2.7 for whites and 2.8 for other races. Rape and other sexual assaults per 1,000 occurred at the rate of 1.1 among whites, 1.2 among African Americans, and 1.1 among persons of other races. Property crimes were also highest among African Americans, while Hispanics were victimized more frequently than non-Hispanics.[52]

Various explanations have been given for the high rates of violent crimes against African Americans. A large percentage of African Americans live in highly populated and poor areas, which generally have higher crime rates. Victimization rates are higher among the unemployed and the poor than among the employed and the higher-income populations; African Americans, compared to whites, represent a higher proportion of these groups. African American children are more likely to attend inner-city schools, which are often characterized by a lower quality of education. Further, it may be argued that police are more likely to arrest African Americans than whites and that the other aspects of criminal justice systems have a more negative impact on African Americans than on others.

In a recent analysis of crime victimization, race, and social class in Cleveland, Ohio, researchers concluded, "The cost of being black, of being segregated

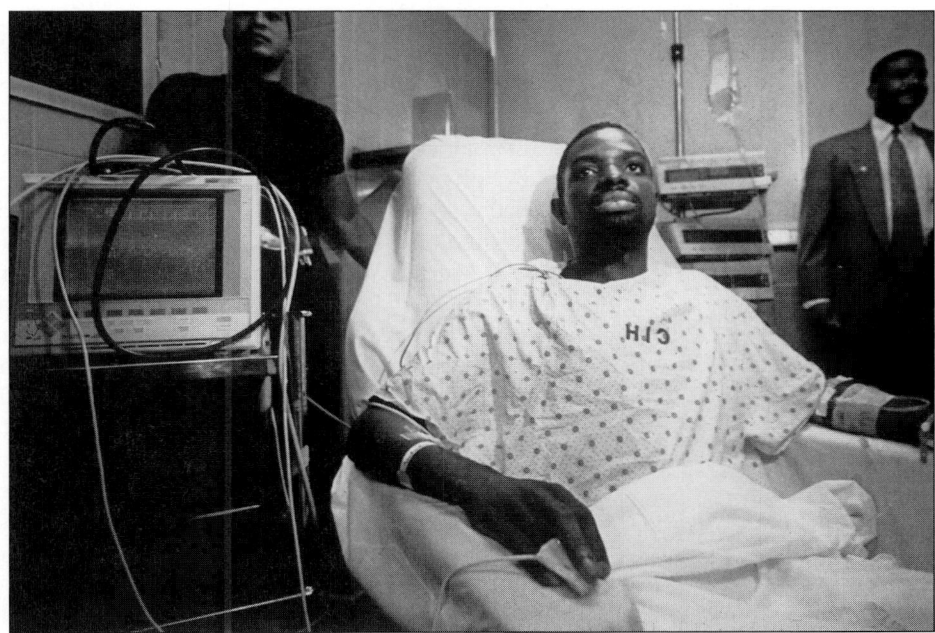

Abner Louima, Haitian immigrant who alleged that he was sodomized and beaten by New York City police officers in 1997, talks to the press from his hospital bed. After the trial of five officers began, Justin A. Volpe entered a guilty plea; the jury found officer Charles Schwarz guilty of aiding in the attack; three other officers were acquitted. In 2001 Louima settled with New York City for $8.7 million, while the spouse and other supporters of Charles Schwarz continued to work for his release, claiming that he was innocent. (Stephen Ferry/Getty Images)

into the least advantaged parts of the metropolis, is high." The authors found that both poor whites and poor blacks shared this disadvantage equally. With respect to violent crime, they noted, "There are class differences, but there are equal or even stronger effects of race itself . . . The . . . results suggest that the racial differences extend to the 'truly disadvantaged' in suburbia, and even the most affluent black residents do not fully escape its reach."[53]

Gender

Men are the most frequent victims in almost every violent crime category. (The only exception is rape/sexual assault; for that crime in 2000, women were victims at a significantly higher rate than men.) Men were twice as often victimized by aggravated assault or robbery as women.[54]

Even though men are much more likely than women to be violent crime victims, many studies disclose that the fear of violent crime is greater among women, mainly because of the crime of forcible rape.[55] Female violent crime victims may be at a greater disadvantage because of the reaction (or lack thereof) of criminal justice systems to the types of violent crimes that victimize women more often than men. In addition to forcible rape by strangers, women are more frequently the victims of family violence. In addition to being more likely to become a violent crime victim at the hands of a spouse, ex-spouse, or boyfriend, women are more likely than men to be victimized by relatives. Men, on the other hand, are more likely to be victimized by friends, acquaintances, and strangers.[56] The issue of what type of relationship exists between victim and offender is given further attention in the next section.

Relationship of Victim and Offender

One final issue regarding victims is important—the relationship between the victim and the offender. Most violence in the form of assault or murder is preceded by social interaction. Physical violence is more likely if both the offender and the victim define the situation as one calling for violence. In this sense, the victim may contribute to his or her own injury or death. If only one is prone toward physical violence, the altercation probably will not become physical. Often the social interactions have been preceded by numerous other interactions, some of these recent. In a classic study of homicide victims, noted criminologist Marvin Wolfgang found that 25 percent of homicide victims precipitated the event that led to their deaths. In these cases the victim was the first to strike a blow, show force with a deadly weapon, or use that weapon.[57]

Victimization data published in 2001 showed that 53 percent of all violent crime victims in 2000 knew their assailants. The percentages were highest among rape/sexual assault victims, 62 percent of whom knew the person who victimized them. Least likely to have known their assailants were robbery victims (28 percent). In 10 percent of all violent crimes, 17 percent of rape or sexual assault crimes, and 5 percent of aggravated assaults, respondents reported that they were victimized by an intimate partner. Women were more likely than men to report victimization by an intimate.[58]

ANALYSIS OF CRIME DATA COLLECTION

Crime data collection is critical to an understanding of crime and criminal justice systems. This chapter notes that data from official and unofficial sources do not always agree, and considers the pros and cons of using the different methods of measuring crime. In the final analysis, the debate has been over which method is most accurate—that is, which minimizes the dark figures of unreported crime most successfully.

One sociologist concluded that in trying to understand crime data, the important concern is not the accuracy with which data describe the extent of criminal behavior or illuminate the dark figures of unreported crime. Instead, the main concern is the way in which the data reflect the complex relationship between society and criminal behavior, providing a barometer of society's attitudes toward deviant behavior.[59] Others emphasize that official crime data are the product of decisions to classify some behavior as criminal and that therefore crime rates "can be viewed as indices of organizational processes rather than as indices of the incidence of certain forms of behavior."[60] The official data represent decisions by those in authority, and the decision to detain is based on a whole network of social action.[61]

These and other positions have led some social scientists to argue that new approaches should be taken toward official crime data. Instead of being criticized for not including all crimes, the data should be recognized for what they are—data concerning the social control of crime. They should be considered an end in themselves rather than a means to an end. Crime rates are phenomena that are part of the social system, and therefore they cannot be evaluated as inaccurate or unreliable. As an aspect of social organization and from a sociological point of view, crime rates cannot be wrong.[62] Thus, official crime rates may be viewed as rates of socially recognized deviant behavior. Any social system has rates of deviance that are not socially or officially recognized, but deviance should be regarded in terms of the reaction of legal and social control systems.

It is relevant sociologically to determine from the official data what behaviors are defined as deviant and how society organizes, classifies, and treats those forms of behavior. Official data indicate that deviants are distinguished from nondeviants. It is relevant sociologically to analyze the difference between a convicted person and one whose crime stops at the crimes-known-to-the-police stage. That both persons may have committed the same deviant act is important sociologically, as is the fact that officially they have been treated differently. Thus, official crime data may be viewed as the structural response to crime rather than as indicators of the actual incidence of deviancy.[63] In addition, they provide important information about crime victims, changing policies of the courts (increases or decreases in the number of offenders placed on probation or fined), or trends in the length of sentencing; that is, they can be viewed as an *index of official action.*

Sociologist Stanton Wheeler suggested that the concept of crime data should be reformulated and considered as the interrelationship of three elements: (1) the person who commits the crime, (2) the victim or other citizens who may report the crime, and (3) the official agents of the state who are charged with controlling crime. Wheeler recommends this reformulation because there is increasing recognition that deviance depends on a social definition. Therefore, any analysis of crime data should recognize not only those who commit crimes but also those who define the behavior as criminal. Wheeler compares crime data to data on admission to and release from mental hospitals, arguing that neither can be understood by referring only to the characteristics of the subjects. Patients referred to child guidance clinics by doctors are admitted more quickly than are those referred by members of their families; people with a higher socioeconomic status can get their family members into mental hospitals more quickly than people from lower classes can. In these cases the reaction of others is important in determining who is labeled deviant.

Wheeler discussed three practical consequences of this reformulation. First, police forces can be analyzed; perhaps the crime rates are high because the police are efficient. The police organizations of high-rate and low-rate areas can be compared; for example, the crime rates might reflect the relationship of the

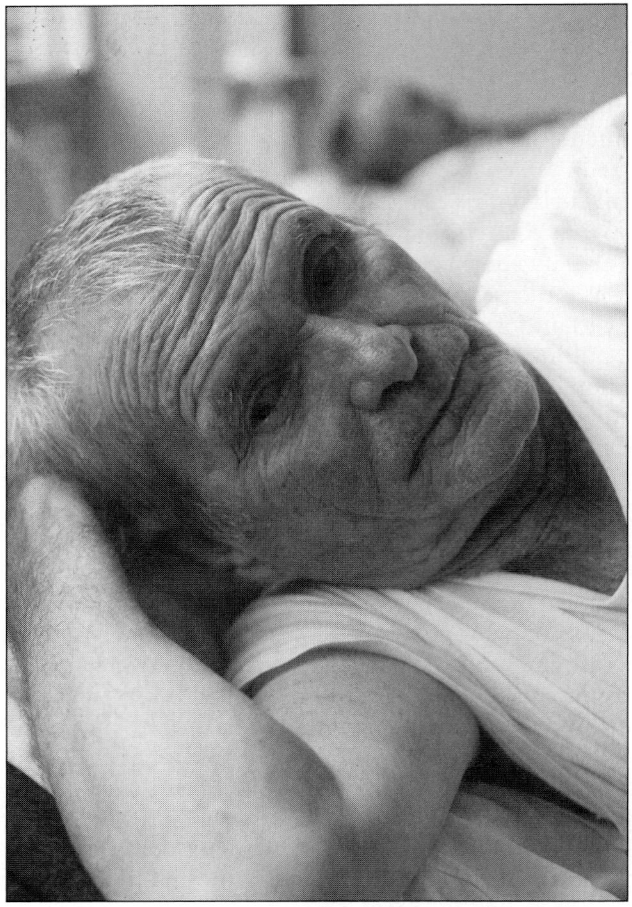

The aging of the population is creating problems within correctional facilities, whose administrators must make provisions for the special medical and other needs of the elderly. This gentleman is an inmate at a correctional facility in Alabama. (Ramey/Stock Boston)

number of police cars to the number of people in an area. Differences among individual police could be analyzed also.

A second consequence would be an improved understanding of citizens and social control. Citizens who observe crimes being committed or who are victims affect the crime rate by their decision on whether to report the crimes. Third, Wheeler's approach would lead to the development of consumer-oriented crime data. Crime data classify criminals by age, gender, and race. But more relevant to consumers is the *probability* that a crime will be committed against them. It is important to know that the crime rate went up because of an increase of people in the age bracket that commits most crimes, but it is more important to citizens to know the increase or decrease of their chances of being victimized. Empirical data could be used to describe the victims, not just the criminals.

Wheeler concluded that the result of this approach would be an improved understanding of criminals and criminal acts. Currently, comparisons of crime rates of one community with another have little meaning because of all the variables that make such comparisons of data unreliable. But within a community, crime could be understood better if the relevant variables were examined. Wheeler suggested that his new orientation toward crime data begin by collecting data on (1) the complaining witnesses, (2) the social characteristics of the community, (3) the reporting or arresting officer, and (4) the nature of the police system as a whole.[64]

Wheeler made these suggestions in 1967, and we have made some progress in our collection of crime data. Clearly, more needs to be done. But it is also important to take a brief look at how research is conducted in criminology.

RESEARCH IN CRIMINOLOGY

Research in criminology is conducted to understand criminal behavior. If we can understand criminal behavior, we will have a better chance of predicting it and thus will be able to take policy steps to control, eliminate, or prevent it. All of these purposes—control, elimination, and prevention—are, however, controversial.

Basing Policy Decisions on Research

Although it might seem obvious to the casual observer that the purpose of research in criminology is to control human behavior, traditionally there has been disagreement within the social sciences over the role of the social scientist in a society's decision-making process. In a provocative book entitled *Can Science Save Us?*, sociologist George Lundberg stated the problem succinctly: "If we want results in improved human relations we must direct our research to the solution of these problems."[65] Early sociologists were interested in social reform; later sociologists argued that they should not be involved in making decisions based on their research results because scientists should be value-free. They should conduct their research rigorously but leave policy making to others.

Some scholars maintain that criminal justice systems are political and that they are used to discriminate against people who are not in positions of power, for example, minorities. More recently, because of the widespread belief that nothing works in criminal justice, there has been a tendency to disregard research findings and to use common sense in setting policy. Sociologist Daniel Glaser contended in the late 1970s that public officials and many criminologists had abandoned crime causation theories. But, said Glaser, "Explanatory theory cannot disappear, for it is inherent in human thinking, even in that of persons who disavow it." Glaser emphasized that anytime we explain, we theorize, "and we theorize scientifically whenever we offer explanations that observation could prove erroneous." It is important to recognize these processes, for unless "it is made explicit, it cannot have cumulative growth and improvement." Most important, claimed Glaser, "The foundations of any science are the basic statements of its theory—its principles."[66]

The Search for Explanations

The need for adequate research on criminal behavior has long been emphasized by social scientists and in the 1980s gained the attention of the President's Task Force on Violent Crime. In its preliminary report in 1981, the task force stated, "It is imperative that we discover what works—what does not."[67] If we are to discover the answer to that question—what works?—we must conduct scientific research. The discussion in this chapter is limited to analyzing the pitfalls and problems that we need to consider as we review the results of empirical research throughout this text.

Many different types of errors may occur in scientific research in the physical and social sciences. Some may be avoidable, and others may be due to the nature of the material being studied. Social scientists study human beings who are capable of thinking, reflecting, forgetting, misrepresenting, and refusing to tell the truth. Given this practical reality, no criminal behavior research is without problems for the social scientist.

Selection of a Research Method

Several methods are used to gather data. We have already looked at official data collected and published by the FBI, by the BJS, and by social scientists using self-report data (SRD). Data may be secured by asking agencies to report data from their files, by asking individuals to complete questionnaires about their own behavior or the behavior of others, or by interviewing people about their involvement in crime or their perceptions of others' behavior.

There are advantages and disadvantages to selecting a particular method of securing data. Before selecting a method, the researcher should consider the nature of the study to be conducted. For example, although an in-depth study or a case study of a few inmates convicted of murder may give detailed information on the history of those criminals, this information would not be sufficient to permit generalization about all murderers. Case studies are very helpful, however, in identifying variables that might be studied in larger populations. Depending on our purposes, it might be more valuable to survey a large number of murderers even though we would not find out as much about each murderer as we would if we conducted intensive individual case studies.

Research might take place over a period of time in which multiple sets of data are gathered. For example, if we wanted to know whether persons released from prison commit further crimes, we might decide to gather information six months or a year after their release. We could continue the research further into the future as well. If we did not want the time variable to be considered, we might select samples of subjects (for example, male inmates and female inmates) at the same time and collect data for comparative purposes. The method of gathering data depends on the nature of the study and the cost of the project. Following a sample over a period of years is expensive, and research funds for studies of this type are limited. Selecting a large sample for an in-depth study is costly, particularly if the subjects are located in different cities and numerous researchers are needed to conduct the study.

***Ex post facto* method** Referring to a law that provides punishment for an act that was not defined as a crime when the act was committed, or to a law that increases the penalty for a crime committed prior to the enactment of the statute.

In some cases the activities the researcher wishes to study have already taken place and cannot be repeated. In these cases, an ***ex post facto* method** is appropriate. (The Latin phrase *ex post facto* means "after the fact.") A sample of people already convicted of murder might be selected and studied to find out whether any past events or characteristics of these persons could explain why they murdered. In contrast, when researchers want to study ongoing activities, they might go into the field to study behavior as it occurs. But they must be careful not to get so involved in the behavior under study that they lose their objectivity.[68]

Errors in Interpreting Data

Social scientists must take care in analyzing empirical data, for the meaning of most facts is not obvious. Facts must be interpreted. Researchers must be careful not to go beyond the data—that is, not to use it to explain something that was not measured or to generalize the findings beyond the scope of the study. For example, if all members of a given sample are men, we cannot conclude that the research findings apply also to women, because gender might be an important variable in explaining the delinquent or criminal behavior under study.

Dualistic fallacy In criminoligical studies, the assumption that a population has two mutually exclusive subclasses, such as criminals and noncriminals.

One of the most common errors in interpreting crime data is the **dualistic fallacy,** the assumption that there is necessarily a distinct difference between two groups: criminals and noncriminals. The assumption is that each group is homogeneous, and that studies can compare the two groups on a given trait and conclude that the findings represent the differences between them—that is, criminals violate the law and noncriminals do not. As noted earlier, research shows that this assumption is not correct. The dualistic fallacy is so serious that all empirical studies of criminal behavior involving the error must be assumed to have limited scientific validity in distinguishing between those who commit crimes and those who do not.

Science assumes that a phenomenon can be measured empirically with valid and reliable tools and distinguished from something that is similar but not of the same classification. Even if the phenomenon cannot be measured with the senses, science presumes that it has consistent indicators of its existence, which can be measured.

When these assumptions are applied to the study of crime, the critical issue is what phenomenon is assumed to exist. Is there something called crime that is unique behavior? Can it be distinguished from all other behavior? The answer to both questions must be no. There is nothing intrinsically unique or distinguishable about crime. A crime is defined not in terms of the properties or attributes of an act but in terms of the social situation in which it occurs. For example, sexual intercourse may be a lawful relationship between a husband and wife; it is a physical act that can be described. In different circumstances, however, sexual intercourse may be incest, adultery, rape, statutory rape, or fornication—all of which are crimes in some jurisdictions. Furthermore, even though certain acts are defined as crimes, many violators are not prosecuted, in which case they should not be considered criminals as the term is defined legally.

Crime is a definitional term. It exists because certain acts are defined as such. But those acts cannot be distinguished clearly from similar acts, or even from identical acts, except by social reaction, because intrinsically crime is just like noncrime. A given behavior may be a crime when committed by some people in some situations and not a crime when committed by others in different situations. In trying to understand criminal behavior, we must understand not only why people commit acts that are defined as crimes—the approach taken by many sociological theorists—but also the *process* by which some but not all people who engage in the acts are labeled criminal.

We could conclude from the discussion in this section that social science research is inherently suspect and that it never will be free of methodological problems to the extent that it can be used to explain crime. But many of the problems can be resolved with adequate planning. As one methodologist observed, "Many of the fruits of science . . . can be used to advantage while still in the process of development. Science is at best a growth, not a sudden revelation." Research in the social sciences can be used "imperfectly and in part while it is developing."[69]

We have come a long way from the writings and thinking of the people whose ideas dominated the 20th century, but those ideas were important in establishing the foundation for our current knowledge, and attention should be given to their contributions. That is the purpose of Chapter 3.

SUMMARY

This chapter examines the official and unofficial sources of data on criminal activity. Its focus is on the collection and interpretation of crime data. The two major official sources of crime and victimization data, the *Uniform Crime Reports (UCR)* and the National Crime Victimization Survey (NCVS), are examined.

The official source of crime data, the *UCR*, is examined in terms of its coverage and its limitations. The source reports the most serious crimes, those referred to as index (or Part I) offenses, by two major categories: violent crimes and property crimes. The total number of crimes known to the police are reported. In addition, the *UCR* reports crime rates and clearance rates for index (serious) offenses. Recent crime rates have shown a decrease in serious crimes, with a leveling off in the year 2000, but officials warn that this trend may be temporary. For less serious offenses, the *UCR* reports only arrest data.

After describing what the *UCR* does, the chapter turns to an analysis of the limitations of this source. Data may be influenced by police discretion in determining whether a crime has been committed, deciding whether to report the crime, or even by policy changes within police departments. Victims may refuse to cooperate with police or refuse to report crimes. Administrative and bureaucratic changes within police departments, such as a change in the size of the police force, may affect crime data. Changes in personnel may be influential.

The ways in which crimes are counted also influence crime data. Another factor is the method of categorizing an event. Thus, rape might be categorized either as rape or as a lesser offense, such as simple assault, and the decision will influence the number of crimes in each of those categories.

Another limitation of the *UCR* is that it excludes some crimes, such as computer crimes, organized crime, and white-collar crimes that may be frequent in occurrence but that do not fall within any of the categories contained within the *UCR*.

Recognition of these and other limitations of the *UCR* led the FBI to develop and implement the National Incident-Based Reporting System (NIBRS), which includes such elements of crimes as the relationship between the offender and the victim, and the type of weapon used. Another reaction to the limitations of the *UCR* has been to utilize data from victimization surveys such as the Bureau of Justice Statistics' National Crime Victimization Survey (NCVS). These reports are based on the responses of alleged crime victims. Comparisons of data from the NCVS and the *UCR* must be made carefully and in light of the differences in the databases of the two sources.

Another source of crime and victimization data is self-report data (SRD), which are secured through anonymous questionnaires or interviews. This method is limited by factors such as nonresponsiveness or inaccurate reporting of the sample. Some of the methodological problems of the SRD may be overcome by the National Youth Survey (NYS), which involves interviews with young people over a five-year period. A final method is the Crime Classification System (CCS), which focuses on the harm suffered by victims and the context in which the crime occurs.

From a discussion of methods of collecting data, the chapter turns to a focus on the actual data. Crime and victimization data are discussed in terms of trends as well as the demographic characteristics of criminals and their victims. The age, race, and gender of offenders and of victims are discussed. This analysis indicates the necessity of carefully examining the crime and victimization data as well as the variables associated with those data. At relevant points throughout the text, attention will be given to age, gender, and race as variables that influence decision making in criminal justice systems. This chapter establishes the background on which those discussions are based. In the final section regarding victims, the chapter discusses the relationship between offenders and victims.

The next focus of the chapter is the position taken some years ago by a prominent sociologist, Stanton Wheeler, who proposed an expanded view of crime data collection. Wheeler's suggestion that crime is a social phenomenon is shared by others, some of whose views are represented throughout the text. It is important to view crime in the context in which it occurs, but it is also important to keep in mind the restrictions the law places on the use of the terms *crime* and *criminal*, as discussed in Chapter 1.

The chapter's final section contains a brief overview of the importance of research and a glance at the methods of social science research and its problems. This background is necessary for understanding the modern empirical studies on which subsequent chapters are based.

It is easy to become discouraged by the problems of data collection. We should not conclude that, because no one source is accurate, the situation is hopeless. The secret nature of crime, the shame and fear with which some victims react, and many other factors may contribute to the inaccuracy of crime data, but our sources are better today than they were in the past, and they continue to improve.

STUDY QUESTIONS

1. Distinguish the *UCR* and the NCVS as sources of crime data and discuss the primary limitations of each.
2. Explain the NIBRS.
3. Is the crime rate going up or down? Discuss.
4. Do self-report data shed any light on crime?
5. What contributions do the National Youth Survey and the Crime Classification System make to crime data collection?
6. Discuss the implications of age, race, and gender on crime and on victimization.
7. How important is the relationship between offender and crime victim?
8. Evaluate crime data in view of Stanton Wheeler's position.
9. What is the importance of the research methods used by those who study criminal behavior?
10. What is an *ex post facto* study?
11. Explain what is meant by the dualistic fallacy.

BRIEF ESSAY ASSIGNMENTS

1. Discuss the criticisms of self-report data (SRD).
2. Assess the possible explanations for the national decrease in crime rates.
3. Explain the relationship between victimization and the variables of socioeconomic status, marital status, and resident location.
4. Describe how the elderly perceive victimization compared to their true victimization rates. What is the impact of this perception?
5. Why can crime not be considered unique behavior that is distinguishable from all other behavior?

INTERNET ACTIVITIES

1. Check out your school's website for crime statistics. If your school has a police or security department, it may be listed in a directory of campus law enforcement agencies at http:// dpsw.usc.edu/ UnivPDWeb.html. The website for Security on Campus (www.campussafety. org) also has campus crime statistics. What has been the most frequently reported crime? How many serious violent and property crimes have been reported?
2. To learn more about information on race and victimization, go to the Bureau of Justice Statistics website at www.ojp.usdoj.gov/bjs/press.htm and find the article "Violent Victimization and Race, 1993–1998."

NET RESOURCES

www.fbi.gov

The Federal Bureau of Investigation website contains statistics from the *Uniform Crime Reports (UCR)*, FBI press releases, a library and reference section, "most wanted" information, and links to interagency programs. Users can also enter keywords to search the site for various articles and information.

www.ojp.usdoj.gov/bjs

The Bureau of Justice Statistics website provides data and statistics on several aspects of the criminal justice system including victims, law enforcement, courts and sentencing. This site also has statistics from the Sourcebook of Criminal Justice, National Crime Victimization Survey (NCVS), the National Crime History Improvement Program (NCHIP), and the National Incident-Based Reporting System (NIBRS).

http://fjsrc.urban.org/

The Federal Justice Statistics Resource Center website contains statistics on defendants and suspects processed through the federal criminal justice system, and a database compiled from information from several federal agencies such as the U.S. Marshals Service, the U.S. Sentencing Commission and Federal Bureau of Prisons, and the U.S. Court of Appeals.

www.fedstats.gov/

FedStats includes statistics from over 100 federal agencies. Statistical abstracts, press releases, links to other government sites, and access to online databases are provided. Users can also look for data by state name, geographic region, and federal agency.

www.icpsr.umich.edu/NACJD

The National Archive of Criminal Justice Data (NACJD) website provides archived data collected through the Inter-University Consortium for Political and Social Research (ICPSR) at the University of Michigan. Data collections include topics in all areas of the criminal justice system comprised from federal, state, local agencies and private research organizations.

www.apbonline.com/

APB includes a news center, special reports on criminal events, safety and justice news, criminal justice system information, crime statistics, and a link to criminal justice professionals.

www.ncpc.org/ncpc1.htm — The National Crime Prevention Council is a nonprofit educational organization that provides information and links to crime statistics and information. This site also provides a link to the Crime Prevention Coalition of America, a site that allows users to access information on criminal-justice-related legislation and issues, and media resources catalogued by zip codes.

www.interpol.int/ — The Interpol website contains press releases, fact sheets, and crime information covering the international community. This site also includes criminal-justice-related topics such as fingerprinting, DNA profiling, computer crime, and offenses against children.

ENDNOTES

1. "Pa. Ave. Closing Is Expected to Spur Traffic Chaos," *USA Today* (22 May 1995), p. 5. The 1994 bill is the Violent Crime Control and Law Enforcement Act of 1994, Public Law 103–322 (13 September 1994).
2. Antiterrorism and Effective Death Penalty Act of 1996, 104th Cong., 2d Session, No. 104–518 (1996).
3. R. Gregory Dunaway et al., "The Myth of Social Class and Crime Revisited: An Examination of Class and Adult Criminality," *Criminology* 38 (May 2000); 589–632; quotation is from p. 589.
4. Bureau of Justice Statistics, *Criminal Victimization 2000* (Washington, DC: U.S. Department of Justice, August 2001), p. 10.
5. Gwynn Nettler, *Explaining Crime,* 3d ed. (New York: McGraw-Hill, 1984), p. 41.
6. People v. Harrison, 768 P.2d 1078, 1082 (Cal. 1989), citations omitted; emphasis in the original.
7. *Crime in the United States, Uniform Crime Reports 2000* (Washington, DC: U.S. Government Printing office, 2001), p. 3.
8. U.S. Department of Justice Office of Justice Programs News Release, www.ojp.usdoj.gov/bjs/pub/press/nibrspr.htm (10 November 2001).
9. Bureau of Justice Statistics, *Effects of NIBRS on Crime Statistics* (Washington, DC: U.S. Department of Justice, July 2000), p. 3.
10. National Institute of Justice and Bureau of Justice Statistics, *Supplementing the National Crime Survey: Research Solicitation* (Washington, DC: U.S. Department of Justice, 1987).
11. Alfred Blumstein et al., "Trend and Deviation in Crime Rates: A Comparison of UCR and NCS Data for Burglary and Robbery," *Criminology* 29 (May 1991): 237–63; quotation is from pp. 259–60; Scott Menard, "Residual Gains, Reliability, and the UCR-NCS Relationship: A Comment on Blumstein, Cohen, and Rosenfeld," *Criminology* 30 (February 1992): 105–13; and Blumstein et al., "The UCR-NCS Relationship Revisited: A Reply to Menard," *Criminology* 30 (February 1992): 115–24.
12. David McDowall and Colin Loftin, "Comparing the UCR and NCVS over Time," *Criminology* 30 (February 1992): 125–32; quotation is from p. 125.
13. "Victim Poll on Violent Crime Finds 15 Percent Drop Last Year," *New York Times* (14 June 2001), p. 14.
14. Thomas Gabor, *Everybody Does It! Crime by the Public* (Toronto, Canada: University of Toronto Press, 1994), p. xiii.
15. James S. Wallerstein and C. J. Wyle, "Our Law-Abiding Lawbreakers," *Probation* 25 (April 1947): 107–12.
16. See Austin Porterfield, "Delinquency and Its Outcome in Courts and College," *American Journal of Sociology* 49 (November 1943): 199–208; Maynard L. Erikson and Lamar T. Empey, "Court Records, Undetected Delinquency, and Decision Making," *Journal of Criminal Law, Criminology, and Police Science* 54 (December 1963): 456–69; and Jay R. Williams and Martin Gold, "From Delinquent Behavior to Official Delinquency," *Social Problems* 20 (Fall 1962): 209–13.
17. James F. Short and F. Ivan Nye, "Extent of Unrecorded Juvenile Delinquency: Tentative Conclusions," *Journal of Criminal Law, Criminology, and Police Science* 49 (November/December 1957): 296–302. For an analysis, see Michael J. Hindelang, Travis Hirschi, and Joseph G. Weis, *Measuring Delinquency* (Beverly Hills, CA: Sage Publications, 1981).
18. See "Career Criminals and Criminal Careers," *Criminal Justice Research at Rand* (Santa Monica, CA: Rand Corporation, 1985), pp. 3–7.
19. John D. Hewitt et al., "Self-Reported and Observed Rule-Breaking in Prison: A Look at Disciplinary Response," *Justice Quarterly* 1, no. 3 (1983): 437–47.
20. Michael J. Hindelang et al., "Correlates of Delinquency: The Illusion of Discrepancy between Self-Report and Official Measures," *American Sociological Review* 44 (December 1979): 995–1014.
21. U.S. Department of Justice Office of Justice Programs news release (10 Novenber 2001), www.ojp.usdoj.gov/bjs/pub/press/nch01pr.htm.
22. Bureau of Justice Statistics, *Criminal Victimization 2000* (Washington, DC: U.S. Department of Justice, August 2001), pp. 1–11.
23. Federal Bureau of Investigation, *Crime in the United States, Uniform Crime Reports 1982* (Washington, DC: U.S. Government Printing Office, 1983), p. iii.
24. Federal Bureau of Investigation, *Crime in the United States, Uniform Crime Reports 1985* (Washington, DC: U.S. Government Printing Office, 1986), p. iii.
25. Federal Bureau of Investigation, *Crime in the United States, Uniform Crime Reports 1991* (Washington, DC: U.S. Government Printing Office, 1992), p. 6.
26. Federal Bureau of Investigation, *Crime in the United States 1999* (Washington, DC: U.S. Government Printing Office, 2000), pp. 7, 37.
27. Federal Bureau of Investigation, *Crime in the United States 2000* (Washington, DC: U.S. Government Printing Office, 2001), pp. 5, 6.
28. "Reasons for Dramatic Drop in Crime Puzzles the Experts," *New York Times* (29 March 1998), p. 14.
29. "New York's Murder Rate, After Upturn, Starts to Slide Down," *New York Times* (8 August 2000), p. 8; "Murders Finally Fall in New York City," *New York Times* (18 December 2001), p. 19.
30. "Data Hint Crime Plunge May Be Leveling Off," *New York Times* (19 December 2000), p. 18.
31. *Uniform Crime Reports 2000,* p. 232.
32. Howard N. Snyder, Office of Justice Programs, *Juvenile Arrests 1999* (Washington, DC: U.S. Department of Justice, 2000), p. 1.
33. *Youth Violence: A Report of the Surgeon General,* available at the surgeon general's website (www.surgeongeneral.gov) and cited in "Surgeon General Warns of 'Hidden' Violence by Youths," *Criminal Justice Newsletter* 31 (9 February 2001): 4.
34. Office of Justice Programs, *Offenders in Juvenile Court, 1997* (Washington, DC: U.S. Department of Justice, October 2000), p. 1.
35. "State Senior Citizens Increasingly Violent," *Tallahassee Democrat* (26 June 2000), p. 2B.
36. *Uniform Crime Reports 2000,* p. 227.
37. Neal Shover and Carol Y. Thompson, "Age, Differential Expectations, and Crime Desistance," *Criminology* 30 (February 1992): 88.
38. "Profile: James Alan Fox—Catching a Coming Crime Wave," *Scientific American* (June 1996): 40–41, quoted in Steven D. Levitt, "The Limited Role of Changing Age Structure in Explaining Aggregate Crime Rates,"

Criminology 37 (August 1999): 581–98; quotation is from p. 582.

39. Levitt, "The Limited Role of Changing Age Structure."
40. Ibid., pp. 582, 594.
41. U.S. National Commission on the Causes and Prevention of Violence, *Violent Crime: Homicide, Assault, Rape, Robbery,* introduction by Daniel Patrick Moynihan (New York: Braziller, 1969).
42. *Uniform Crime Reports 2000,* p. 234.
43. For a general discussion of the impact of U.S. criminal justice systems on African Americans, see Michael Tonry, *Malign Neglect, Race, Crime, and Punishment in America* (New York: Oxford University Press, 1995).
44. *Uniform Crime Reports 2000,* p. 233.
45. Ibid, p. 221.
46. Ibid.
47. Ibid.
48. *Criminal Victimization 2000,* pp. 7, 9.
49. Ibid., pp. 7, 11.
50. Ibid., p. 6; Bureau of Justice Statistics, *Crimes Against Persons Age 65 or Older, 1992–97* (Washington, DC: U.S. Department of Justice, January 2000), p. 5.
51. "Juvenile Arrests for Murder Reach Lowest Level Since 1966," *Criminal Justice Newsletter* 31 (9 February 2001), p. 5, referring to data from the Bureau of Justice Statistics.
52. *Criminal Victimization 2000,* pp. 6, 9.
53. John R. Logan and Brian J. Stults, "Racial Differences in Exposure to Crime: The City and Suburbs of Cleveland in 1990," *Criminology* 37 (May 1999): 251–76; quotation is from p. 271.
54. *Criminal Victimization 2000,* p. 6.
55. Other studies question this conclusion and maintain that the apparent differences are the result of measurement problems in the research. See, for example, Randy L. LaGrange and Kenneth F. Ferraro, "Assessing Age and Gender Differences in Perceived Risk and Fear of Crime," *Criminology* 27 (November 1989): 697–715.
56. Bureau of Justice Statistics, *Female Victims of Violent Crime* (Washington, DC: U.S. Department of Justice, December 1996), p. 2.
57. See Marvin Wolfgang, *Patterns in Criminal Homicide* (Philadelphia: University of Pennsylvania Press, 1958).
58. *Criminal Victimization 2000,* p. 8.
59. Keith Bottomley, *Decisions in the Penal Process* (South Hackensack, NJ: Fred B. Rothman, 1973), p. 21.
60. John I. Kitsuse and Aaron V. Cicourel, "A Note on the Uses of Official Statistics," *Social Problems* 11 (Fall 1963): 137.
61. Aaron V. Cicourel, *The Social Organization of Juvenile Justice* (New York: John Wiley, 1968), p. 37.
62. See Kitsuse and Cicourel, "A Note on the Uses of Official Statistics," pp. 131–39.
63. Ibid., p. 137.
64. Stanton Wheeler, "Criminal Statistics: A Reformulation of the Problem," *Journal of Criminal Law, Criminology and Police Science* 58 (September 1967): 317–24.
65. George A. Lundberg, *Can Science Save Us?* (New York: Longman, 1961), p. 134.
66. Daniel Glaser, "A Review of Crime-Causation Theory and Its Application," in *Crime and Justice: An Annual Review of Research,* vol. 1, ed. Norval Morris and Michael Tonry (Chicago: University of Chicago Press, 1979), pp. 204–5.
67. Attorney General William French Smith, "Federal, State, and Local Law Enforcement Must Cooperate to Fight Crime in America," *Justice Assistance News* (August 1981), p. 2.
68. See Hans Toch, "Cast the First Stone: Ethics as a Weapon," *Criminology* 19 (August 1981): 185–94; and Marvin E. Wolfgang, "Confidentiality in Criminological Research and Other Ethical Issues," *Journal of Criminal Law and Criminology* 71 (Spring 1981): 345–61.
69. Lundberg, *Can Science Save Us?,* pp. 143–44.

PART 

Explanations of Criminal Behavior

Part II covers the major concepts and theories utilized in attempts to explain criminal behavior. Chapter 3 opens the discussion with an analysis of the earlier explanations of criminal behavior. The chapter compares those explanations to their modern counterparts by looking at punishment philosophies.

Chapter 4 covers biological and psychological theories. Both areas are gaining recognition among some scholars in criminology, although both remain controversial. Sociological theories, which comprise the major focus of criminological explanations of behavior, are divided into two chapters. Chapter 5 analyzes theories that focus on society's structure and its impact, while Chapter 6 is composed of social-processes approaches.

CHAPTER

3

▶ Crime rates declined for several years and in 2001 leveled off, but violent crimes such as the 1999 shootings at Columbine High School in Littleton, Colorado— which claimed the lives of 15, including the student perpetrators—leave us wondering why, as this photo from Columbine illustrates. (Renato Rotolo/Getty Images)

Early Explanations of Criminal Behavior and Their Modern Counterparts

OUTLINE

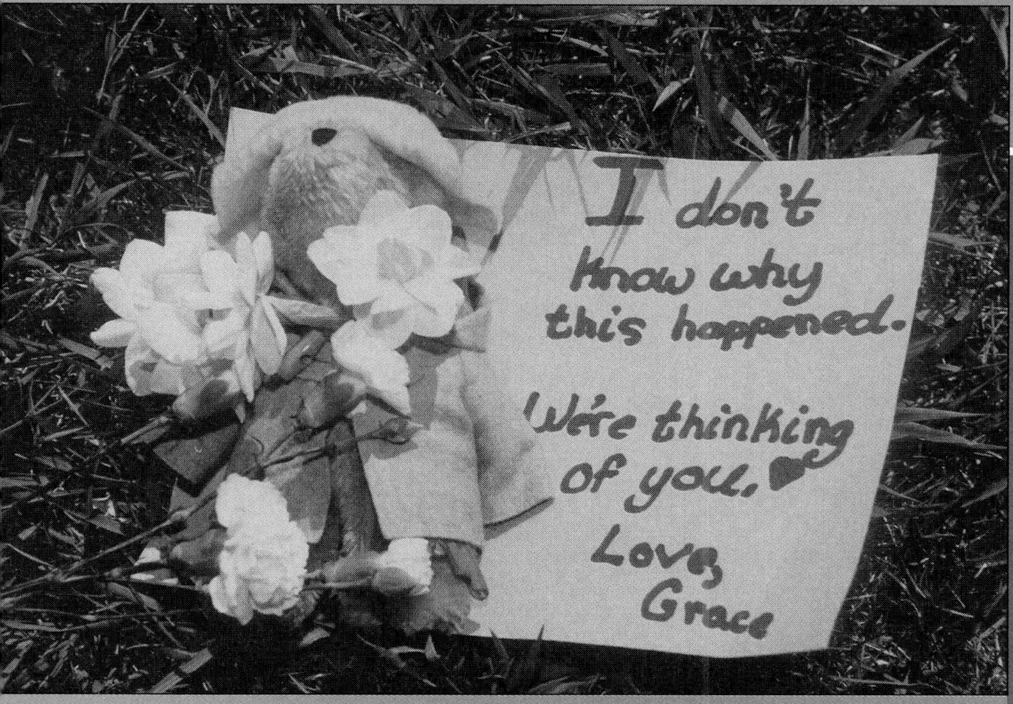

This chapter begins with an analysis of the contributions of the classical, neoclassical, and positive schools to the development of the study of crime. It examines the impact of these schools on modern punishment philosophies. The classical position of "Let the punishment fit the crime," with its emphasis on the beliefs that we are rational in our thoughts and that we make rational choices to seek pleasure and avoid pain, argues that sufficient punishment is a deterrent to criminal behavior. If the punishment is a little worse than the pleasure of committing the crime, individuals will not commit the crimes. The chapter analyzes empirical research on this issue and contrasts the current emphasis on deterrence and retribution or, in the more palatable terms of today, just deserts, with the former emphasis on the need to reform or rehabilitate the criminal.

KEY TERMS

castration
classical theorists
constitutional approach
cruel and unusual punishment
determinate sentence
determinism
deterrence
free will
general deterrence
hedonism
incapacitation
indeterminate sentence
individual (or specific) deterrence
just deserts
justice model
neoclassical school
positive school
punishment
rehabilitation
retribution
revenge
social contract
theory
utilitarianism

Chapter 2 discussed the measurement of crime and considered some of the variables, such as age, gender, and race, that are related to crime data. It also covered methods of studying crime. Collecting data on crime is the first step toward the goals of punishing, controlling, and preventing criminal behavior. In order to achieve one or more of these goals, we must develop ways to evaluate the data. Why are crime rates higher among men than among women? What are the reasons, the explanations? If we can understand why people engage in criminal behavior, we may be able to predict and to control that behavior.

Simple facts are not sufficient; for example, it is not very helpful to know only that there are more arrests of men than of women. We need to know what the patterns and the variables are that might explain the differences in arrest rates. To come up with such explanations, social scientists, like physical scientists, engage in research, developing and testing their theories. A **theory** is part of an explanation, an attempt to relate two or more variables in ways that can be tested. If properly constructed and tested, a theory can be either supported, shown to be incorrect, or at least questioned. Thus, a theory is more than an assumption. It involves efforts to test the reality of thoughts or explanations about how variables (such as gender) are related to phenomena (such as criminal behavior). Research that involves empirical testing of theories can be, and usually is, very complex and therefore beyond the scope of this text. We do, however, look briefly at the research *process*, with the view of understanding its overall purpose.

Theory Part of an explanation, an attempt to relate two or more variables in ways that can be tested. If property constructed and tested, a theory can be shown to be incorrect or at least questioned. Thus, a theory is more than an assumption. It involves efforts to test the reality of thoughts or explanations about how variables (such as gender) are related to phenomenon (such as criminal behavior).

Research findings may influence the decisions that are made regarding the processing of offenders. For example, if we believe that stiff penalties are more effective than light ones in deterring criminal activity, we will probably institute harsher penalties. Unfortunately, too often we make such decisions on the basis of intuition or "common sense," without any reference to existing social science findings or any attempt to conduct research if no findings are available. This chapter sets the stage for subsequent chapters on social science research and theories that have been developed to explain criminal behavior.

THE CLASSICAL BEGINNINGS

The development of criminology as a formal discipline is recent, but the ideas of people who might be called early criminologists can be traced historically. Most of these people were lawyers, doctors, philosophers, or sociologists whose primary interest was in reforming the criminal law, not in creating a science of criminal behavior. Nevertheless, their contributions to criminology are immense, and some familiarity with these earlier approaches is essential to an adequate understanding of current criminological theories.

Ideas and philosophies do not exist within a vacuum; they must be understood in light of the social context in which they appear. To understand the classical writers and their contributions to criminology, we must know something about the social conditions that existed at that time.

The **classical theorists** were rebelling against an arbitrary system of law in which judges held an absolute and almost tyrannical power over those who were brought before them. The law was applied unequally, and corruption was widespread. Confessions were obtained by means of torture, and the death penalty was used for many offenses.

Classical theorists Writers and philosophers who argued that punishment should fit the crime. The popularization of this school of thought led to the abolition of the death penalty and torture in some countries and generally to more humane treatment of criminals.

Cesare Beccaria

The leader of the classical school was Cesare Beccaria, born in Milan, Italy, on 15 March 1738. Before his death in 1794, Beccaria published only one major

This statue of Cesare Beccaria (1738–1794) in Milan, Italy, where he was born, pays tribute to the leader of the classical school of criminology. Beccaria is best known for his philosophy that the punishment should fit the crime rather than be individualized for the criminal. He is a controversial figure among modern criminologists. (Courtesy R. E. Kania)

book, a slim volume titled *On Crimes and Punishments.* It was not entirely original, for many of Beccaria's ideas were syntheses of those already expressed by others, but it was well received because many people in Europe were ready to hear about and to implement the kinds of changes Beccaria proposed.[1]

Beccaria's work is extremely important today. As one scholar stated, "It is not an exaggeration to regard Beccaria's work as being of primary importance in paving the way for penal reform for approximately the last two centuries."[2] His short essay contains the basis for almost all modern penal reforms, but its greatest contribution was "the foundation it laid for subsequent changes in criminal legislation."[3]

At the time in which Beccaria wrote, many philosophers and intellectuals were speaking about the **social contract.** This concept held that an individual was bound to society only by his or her consent and that therefore society was responsible to the individual as well as vice versa. Beccaria believed in the concept of the social contract and felt that each individual surrendered only enough liberty to the state to make the society viable. Laws should therefore merely be the necessary conditions of the social contract, and punishments should exist only to defend the total sacrificed liberties against the usurpation of those liberties by other individuals. He also believed that the basic principle that should guide legislation and, indeed, form its backbone is that of the greatest happiness to be shared by the greatest number of people.[4]

Another philosophy that strongly influenced Beccaria was that of **free will.** He maintained that behavior is purposive and is based on **hedonism,** the pleasure–pain principle: Human beings choose those actions that give pleasure and avoid those that bring pain. Therefore, punishment should be assigned to each crime in a degree that results in more pain than pleasure for those who commit the forbidden acts. The *punishment should fit the crime.* This hedonistic view of conduct implies that laws must be written clearly and not be open to judicial interpretation. Only the legislature can specify punishment. The law must apply equally to all citizens; no defenses for criminal acts are permitted. The issue in court is whether a person committed the act; if so, the particular penalty prescribed by law for that act must be imposed. Judges are mere instruments of the law, allowed only to determine innocence or guilt and thereafter to prescribe punishment. Under this system the law is rigid, structured, and theoretically impartial.[5]

Social contract The philosophy that for greater protection, people voluntarily surrender their rights to protect themselves to the government, which must govern by the consent of the people.

Free will A philosophy advocating punishment severe enough for people to choose to avoid criminal acts. It includes the belief that a certain criminal act warrants a specific punishment without any variation.

The impact of Beccaria's arguments on modern American criminal law can be seen in this statement by a jurist: "Our substantive criminal law is based upon a theory of punishing the vicious will. It postulates a free moral agent, confronted with a choice between doing right and doing wrong, and choosing freely to do wrong."[6] In other words, the person who chooses to do wrong *deserves* to be punished. Beccaria's position may be seen as a forerunner to the modern justice model of punishment discussed later in this chapter.

Beccaria has been praised for helping to make the law impartial. Contemporary American philosophy holds that all people should be equal under the law and that all cases must be weighed on an impartial scale of justice. Although that ideal has never been implemented fully, Beccaria should be recognized for his contributions to the concept of justice.

Beccaria's contributions were honored at the United Nations' Seventh Congress on the Prevention of Crime and Treatment of Offenders in 1985. At a conference in Milan, Italy, commemorating the 250th anniversary of Beccaria's birth, one speaker called him a prophet.[7]

Hedonism The belief that people choose pleasure and avoid pain. In law, its proponents advocate clearly written laws and certainty of punishment without any departure from the prescribed penalty.

Some modern scholars are critical of Beccaria, maintaining that his attacks on the criminal justice systems of his day were misplaced. Perhaps the most critical is Graeme Newman, who refers to Beccaria as a "pampered intellectual who had no firsthand knowledge of the criminal justice system."[8] In a later publication, Newman and his collaborator review the praise social scientists and others had bestowed on Beccaria and conclude that it was misplaced. They take the position that "the majority of reforms that occurred during and soon after Beccaria's treatise can as easily be ascribed to prevailing social and political conditions as to Beccaria or his tract."[9]

The major weaknesses of Beccaria's ideas were the rigidity of his concepts and his lack of provision for justifiable criminal acts. These problems were acknowledged by the neoclassical school, discussed below after a brief look at another classical theorist, Jeremy Bentham.

Jeremy Bentham

Jeremy Bentham, born in 1748 and thus a contemporary of Beccaria, was a British philosopher trained in law. He died in 1832. Bentham's legal thinking was described by one critic as original, enormous, and many-sided, with universal influence and far-reaching practical results. The critic concluded that he was tempted to proclaim Bentham the "greatest legal philosopher and reformer the world has ever seen."[10]

Among Bentham's contributions was his belief that the greatest good must go to the greatest number. In addition, he assumed that people are rational creatures who will consciously choose pleasure and avoid pain. Therefore, a punishment should be assigned to each crime so that the pain would outweigh any pleasure. Like Beccaria, Bentham believed that the punishment should fit the crime. Bentham referred to his philosophy of social control as **utilitarianism:** "An act is not to be judged by an irrational system of absolutes but by a supposedly verifiable principle . . . [which is] 'the greatest happiness for the greatest number' or simply 'the greatest happiness.' " Despite his belief in utilitarianism and the free will of individuals, however, Bentham hinted at the theory of learned behavior in contrast to a deterministic explanation of criminal behavior. One noted scholar summed up his opinion of Bentham by stating, "He deserves considerable credit . . . for his adherence to a theory of social (i.e., pleasure pursuit) causation of crime rather than a concept of biological, climatic or other non-social causation."[11]

Utilitarianism The philosophy that makes the happiness of the individual or society the main goal and the criterion for determining what is morally good and right. In politics, this means that the greatest happiness of the greatest number is the sole end and criterion of all public action.

Other Influential Scholars

All of the writers of the 18th century who emphasized the importance of human rights were important in establishing a framework in which the ideas of criminal reform would flourish. Voltaire contributed indirectly and directly to the success of Beccaria's reform measures. Voltaire's indirect contribution was his work in laying the foundation for the Enlightenment. According to one scholar, "By fighting religious intolerance and fanaticism, he contributed, more than any other, to the building of a more reasonable and humane society in which there was no longer any place for a criminal law based on superstitution and cruelty."[12] Without Voltaire's work, criminal reform would have been greatly delayed. Beccaria's essay on crime and punishment probably would not have appeared. Voltaire contributed directly to the success of penal reform by publicizing Beccaria's work.[13]

Montesquieu also had considerable influence, primarily by "stimulating the crusading zeal of . . . Beccaria."[14] Philosopher Jean-Jacques Rousseau's writings on the social contract also influenced the classical school in its philosophy of crime and punishment.

The philosophy of the classical school was reflected in the changes in French penal codes, with the French Code of 1795 completing the process of replacing the arbitrary power of judges with fixed, determinate penalties. These penalties were harsh, however, and in many cases juries would not convict defendants, thus avoiding all penalties. This situation led to the development of the neoclassical school.

THE NEOCLASSICAL SCHOOL

Neoclassical school Those who argued that situations or circumstances that made it impossible to exercise free will are reasons to exempt the accused from conviction.

The **neoclassical school** of criminology, which flourished during the 19th century, had the same basis as the classical school—a belief in free will. But the neoclassical criminologists, most of whom were British, viewed the penalties that resulted from the classical doctrine as too severe and all-encompassing for the humanitarian spirit of the time. The neoclassical school emphasized the need for individualized reaction to offenders. Under their influence criminal codes permitted more judicial discretion, although only under objective circumstances. Still, no consideration was given by the criminal code to the intent of the offender.

Perhaps the most shocking aspect of the early 19th century's harsh penal codes was that they did not provide for the separate treatment of children. One of the changes of the neoclassical period was that children under seven years of age were exempt from the law because they were presumed to be unable to understand the difference between right and wrong. Mental disease became a reason to exempt a suspect from conviction, too. It was seen as a sufficient cause of impaired responsibility, and thus defense by reason of insanity crept into the law. Any situation or circumstance that made it impossible to exercise free will was seen as reason to exempt a person from legal responsibility for what otherwise might be a criminal act.

Although the neoclassical school was not a scientific school of criminology, it did begin to explore the causation issue. The neoclassical theorists made exceptions to the law and implied multiple causation. The doctrine of free will could no longer stand alone as an explanation for criminal behavior. Even today, much modern law is based on the neoclassical philosophy of free will tempered by exceptions.

Although the classical and neoclassical schools were based on philosophy and armchair thinking rather than empirical research, they have influenced the thinking and policies of Europeans as well as Americans. According to Andrew von Hirsch,

> There has been growing support for a "neoclassical" sentencing rationale that would emphasize penalties proportionate to the gravity of the criminal conduct. This movement has had its great impact in Finland, where "neoclassicism" has come to be official policy.[15]

Before a science of criminology could emerge, however, it was necessary to gather and analyze empirical data on crime and criminals. The use of data to explain criminal behavior is characteristic of the positive school of thought.

THE POSITIVE SCHOOL

Positive school Early writers and philosophers who advocated that the study of crime should emphasize the individual,

The **positive school** of criminology was composed of several Italians whose approaches differed to some extent but all of whom agreed that, in the study of crime, the emphasis should be on the scientific treatment of the criminal, not on the penalties to be imposed after conviction.

scientific treatment of the criminal, not the postconviction punishment. Adherents believed that the punishment should fit the criminal, not the crime.

Determinism A doctrine holding that one's options, decisions, and actions are decided by inherited or environmental factors.

Constitutional approach An approach to explaining criminal behavior that assumes that behavior is influenced by the structure or physical characteristics of a person's body.

The classical school, defining crime in legal terms, emphasized the concept of free will and the position that punishment gauged to fit the crime would be a deterrent. The positivists rejected the harsh legalism of the classical school and substituted the doctrine of **determinism** for that of free will. They focused on the **constitutional approach** to crime, claiming that the structure or physical characteristics of an individual determine that person's behavior. Noting that these characteristics are not uniform, the positivists emphasized a philosophy of individualized, scientific treatment of criminals, based on the findings of the physical and social sciences. According to Stephen Schafer, "Their emergence [in the late 18th century] symbolized clearly that the era of faith was over and the scientific age had begun."[16]

Cesare Lombroso

Cesare Lombroso (1835–1909), the leader of the positive school, has been called "the father of modern criminology."[17] Lombroso rejected the classical doctrine of free will, but he was influenced by the contemporary writings on positivism of early sociologists. He was most famous for his biological theory of crime, which is discussed in Chapter 4, but although Lombroso obviously emphasized the biological causes of crime, he did not, as some critics have argued, neglect the sociological causes.

Lombroso was concerned about these critics, who came to what he considered a false conclusion concerning his work. In the preface to one of his books, Lombroso referred to those who accused his school "of having confined itself to the study of the born criminal, thus teaching that the criminal is riveted irrevocably to his destiny, and that humanity has no escape from his atavistic ferocity." If this were true, he said, his school could not be criticized merely for discovering this truth. But, he added, the truth is that while the old system of cruel punishment had nothing to propose for the prevention of crime, "my school has devised a new strategic method of proceeding against crime, based upon a study of its aetiology and nature."[18]

Lombroso described himself as a slave to facts, and he should be recognized for his emphasis on careful measurement in securing data. Despite his conscientiousness, Lombroso may be criticized for his failure to interpret the data in light of his theory. It was his belief that the data, even if they appeared unrelated at the moment, would evolve subsequently into a theory of universal applicability. His method was to draw conclusions primarily from analogy and anecdote.

The reactions to Lombroso range from severe criticism to high praise. In an early edition of their text on criminology, Edwin H. Sutherland and Donald R. Cressey asserted that Lombroso and his school "delayed for fifty years the work which was in progress at the time of its origin and in addition made no lasting contribution of its own." In an edition published 19 years later, the criticism was milder, stating only that the Lombrosian school "fell into disrepute."[19]

Cesare Lombroso (1836–1909), Italian leader of the positive school of criminology, was criticized for his methodology and his attention to the biological characteristics of offenders, but his emphasis on the need to study offenders scientifically earned him the title "father of modern criminology." (Corbis/Bettmann)

Criminologist Marvin E. Wolfgang argued that the concern of critics that Lombroso "diverted attention from social to individual phenomena reveals their basic misunderstanding of his work and its effect." Wolfgang concluded, "Lombroso served to redirect emphasis from the crime to the criminal, not from social to individual factors."[20]

Although Wolfgang acknowledged the serious methodological problems in Lombroso's research, as evaluated by modern techniques and knowledge, he believed strongly that Lombroso "also manifested imaginative insight, good intuitive judgment, intellectual honesty, awareness of some of his limitations, attempts to use control groups and a desire to have his theories tested impartially. Many researchers of today fare little better than this."[21]

Raffaele Garofalo

Baron Raffaele Garofalo (1852–1934) was born in Naples, Italy. He studied law, was interested in criminal law reform, and served as a professor of criminal law and procedure during part of his career. Garofalo's major work was *Criminology,* published in 1885. The second edition was published in 1891 and translated into English in 1914. Garofalo was clearly a member of the positivist, or Italian, school of thought. He rejected most of the philosophies of the classical school. He saw the need for empirical research to establish theories of criminal behavior. Although Garofalo embraced some of Lombroso's ideas, he was critical of others.

Garofalo and Lombroso differed in the emphasis they each placed on the physical abnormality of the criminal. Garofalo agreed that criminals are abnormal, that they are lacking in the degree of "sentiments and certain repugnances" held by others in society. But Garofalo thought that the question of whether or not this abnormality is caused by physiological factors must remain unanswered. He did note some physical differences between criminals and noncriminals, but he was cautious in his analysis of this phenomenon since he did not think the scientific evidence existed to substantiate the theories. He spoke of psychic anomalies and moral degeneracy, admitting that environmental factors *might* play a role in some crimes. But Garofalo also believed that there was in the instincts of the true criminal one element that was congenital, inherited, or somehow acquired in early infancy, which becomes inseparable from the criminal's psychic organism. He did not believe in the *casual* offender, "if by the use of this term we grant the possibility of a morally well-organized man committing a crime by the force of external circumstances."[22] Finally, Garofalo disagreed with the classification of criminals used by Lombroso and by Ferri (discussed in the next section), basing his own classification on the degree of moral inferiority of criminal types.

Enrico Ferri

Enrico Ferri (1856–1929), the son of a poor shopkeeper had already published some of his main ideas and become a positivist before he spent a year studying with Lombroso. Ferri, a professor of criminal law, wrote his book *Criminal Sociology* before he reached the age of 25. He rejected the doctrine of free will, believing instead that it is not the criminal who wills to act, but the situation that influences the criminal's action. Ferri believed that crime was primarily produced by the type of society from which the criminal came. He postulated the *law of criminal saturation,* which states that "in a given social environment with definite individual and physical conditions, a fixed number of [crimes], no more and no less, can be committed."[23] Thus, crime can only be corrected by making changes in society.

Contributions of the Positive School

The positive school made extensive contributions to the development of a scientific approach to the study of criminal behavior and to the reform of criminal law. The positivists emphasized the importance of empirical research. They believed that punishment should fit the criminal, not the crime (reversing the recommendation of the classical school). The positivists developed the doctrine of determinism, some arguing that the cause of crime was physical, others that it was psychological, social, or economic, thus introducing the concept of environment into the study of crime.

The research of the positivists can be criticized for serious errors in methodology. Their samples were not scientifically selected, and their subjects usually came from institutionalized populations. They made little use of follow-up studies; the concepts they measured were not clearly defined. They did not use sophisticated statistical analyses, as those had not been developed at the time. But despite these and other criticisms, the positive school had an important impact on the emergence and development of criminology, as emphasized by a noted sociological theorist:

> Few today can fail to appreciate that Lombroso, together with Ferri and Garofalo, the "holy three of criminology," revolutionalized the way of looking at the criminal and excited the world towards the scientific study of crime. The works of these three Italians may well last as long as criminology itself.[24]

THE CLASSICAL AND POSITIVE SCHOOLS COMPARED

The positive and the classical schools had an important impact on the emergence and development of criminology. The basic differences between these schools of thought are listed in the following table. The premises on which our policies of punishment, treatment, and sentencing have been based for the past quarter of a century may be traced to these schools of thought.

Classical School	Positive School
1. Legal definition of crime	1. Rejection of legal definition
2. Let the punishment fit the crime	2. Let the punishment fit the criminal
3. Doctrine of free will	3. Doctrine of determinism
4. Death penalty for some offenses	4. Abolition of the death penalty
5. Anecdotal method—no empirical research	5. Empirical research, inductive method
6. Definite sentence	6. Indeterminate sentence

Exhibit 3.1 contains a summary of the contributions of the various individuals of the two schools.

PUNISHMENT PHILOSOPHIES

Punishment Any of a series of impositions (such as a fine, probation, work service, or incarceration) imposed by the authority of law on a person who has been determined to be a criminal offender.

The nineteenth-century explanations of criminal behavior and those that preceded them by thousands of years were attempts to explain behavior in a way that would justify **punishment.** Punishments within the criminal law may involve fines to the state, restitution to the victim or others, community service or work, probation with or without supervision, imprisonment, corporal punishment, participation in programs such as drug treatment, or other provisions. Some of these punishments, such as corporal punishment, are not recognized by U.S. courts today although they were in the past.

Historically corporal punishment played a significant role in the reaction of individual victims and of society to criminals. The Eighth Amendment of the U.S. Constitution (see Appendix A) prohibits the imposition of **cruel and unusual punishment,** which has been interpreted to include any punishment that amounts to barbarity or torture, or punishments that are not proportionate to the offense committed, such as capital punishment for the rape of an adult woman.

EXHIBIT 3.1

Major Contributors to Early Criminology

THE CLASSICAL SCHOOL

1. **Cesare Beccaria**—Wrote *On Crimes and Punishments;* believed that the punishment should fit the crime.
2. **Jeremy Bentham**—Developed the doctrine of free will, arguing that behavior is purposive and is based on hedonism, or the pleasure–pain principle.
3. **Voltaire**—Laid the foundation for the Enlightenment; publicized Beccaria's contributions.
4. **Montesquieu**—Stimulated the reform crusade of Beccaria.
5. **Jean-Jacques Rousseau**—Influenced the classical school through his writings on the social contract.

THE POSITIVE SCHOOL

1. **Cesare Lombroso**—Rejected the classical doctrine of free will and advocated determinism, both biological and environmental; emphasized empirical research.
2. **Raffaele Garofalo**—Placed less emphasis than Lombroso on the biological and more on the psychic or environmental causes of crime.
3. **Enrico Ferri**—Rejected free will, believing that it is not the criminal who wills to act, but the situation that determines the criminal's actions.

Cruel and unusual punishment Punishment prohibited by the Eighth Amendment of the U.S. Constitution. The interpretation rests with the courts. Some examples are excessive lengths or conditions in sentences and the death penalty for rape but not murder of an adult woman.

In criminal law, punishment refers to penalties that are inflicted by the power of the state, that is, the authority of law after a court has found the defendant guilty of a crime. In the past the authority of private individuals to impose punishment on offenders was recognized; today in most countries that power is granted only to the state. The question is not whether the state should punish offenders but under what circumstances, to what extent, and in what manner. Some of these issues are discussed in a subsequent chapter, but for our purposes here, it is important to analyze the philosophies that are used to justify punishment.

The classical, neoclassical, and positive schools of thought did not originate either the major punishment philosophies of incapacitation, retribution, deterrence, and rehabilitation or the variations of these philosophies, although they set the stage for the emphasis placed on some of them. It is important to examine punishment philosophies historically and in terms of modern developments, for our social policies are determined in large measure by the punishment philosophies in which we believe. Exhibit 3.2 defines each of the philosophies briefly.

U.S. courts have recognized some or all of these philosophies. Consider the following excerpt from a 1930 decision.[25]

Commonwealth v. Ritter

Generally speaking, there have been advanced four theories as the basis upon which society should act in imposing penalties upon those who violate its laws. These are: (1) To bring about the reformation of the evil-doer; (2) to effect retribution or revenge upon him; (3) to restrain him physically, so as to make it impossible for him to commit further crimes; and (4) to deter others from similarly violating the law.

EXHIBIT 3.2
Punishment Philosophies

Throughout history four philosophies or purposes have been used to justify punishment:

1. *Incapacitation*—doing whatever is necessary to keep the offender from repeating the offense. Today incapacitation generally takes the form of incarceration, but in earlier times it might have involved cutting off the hand of the thief, castrating the sex offender, or disfiguring the prostitute.
2. *Retribution*—taking action to get even with the offender. Retribution is similar to *revenge*, the term used most frequently in earlier times. For an eye-for-an-eye, tooth-for-a-tooth approach meant to harm the offender in the same way he or she harmed the victim. Today retribution is a popular justification for punishment, although some refer to the philosophy by the term *just deserts*, which means to give the offender what he or she deserves in light of the offense committed. The modern approach is thought to be more humane than traditional revenge, although some argue that nothing has changed but the name.
3. *Deterrence*—devising punishment to keep offenders from committing the offenses again *(individual deterrence)*, while setting an example that will keep others from engaging in criminal activities *(general deterrence)*. Scholars debate whether punishment deters, how much punishment is needed for deterrence, and so on.
4. *Rehabilitation*—attempting to change the offender through proper treatment. Early criminologists talked about repenting and emphasized religious training as a prerequisite. Criminals were kept in solitary confinement so that they would not be corrupted by others and would have time to contemplate their actions. The more recent approach involves the establishment of treatment programs within prisons, along with diversion programs to keep juveniles and others who might be salvageable from going to prison. Rehabilitation was the dominant theory of punishment in the United States until recently, when many jurisdictions rejected it and implemented a policy of retribution, or just deserts, usually coupled with an emphasis on deterrence.

Incapacitation A punishment theory and a sentencing goal, generally implemented by incarcerating an offender to prevent him or her from committing any other crimes. In earlier times incapacitation involved such measures as removing the hands of thieves or castrating rapists.

Castration Removal of the testes in the male or the ovaries in the female; in earlier times used as a punishment for male rape offenders. In recent times some courts have ordered chemical castration of sex offenders. This process involves using female hormones to alter

More recent cases illustrate that today U.S. courts recognize one or all of these major punishment philosophies. As an example, a 1992 decision by the Idaho Supreme Court recognized that sentencing may be imposed "to accomplish the primary objective of protecting society and to achieve any or all of the related goals of deterrence, rehabilitation or retribution applicable to a given case."[26] Subsequent discussions demonstrate that one or more of these philosophies has been rejected by modern courts in recent years.

Incapacitation

The excerpt from *Commonwealth* v. *Ritter* states that one purpose of punishment is to restrain the offender physically. In modern times the term *selective incapacitation* is used frequently, referring to the restraint of select rather than all offenders. Thus, serious offenders may be incarcerated whereas minor offenders are handled in less restrictive ways. In previous times (and in some countries today), deterring an offender from committing additional crimes took the form of physical **incapacitation.** For example, thieves' hands were amputated and rapists were castrated. Incapacitation of this type still occurs in some countries.

Some recent attempts to incapacitate offenders have focused on sex offenders. Efforts to incapacitate sex offenders through **castration** are controversial. In earlier times, surgical castration was acceptable in the United States; in recent the male's chemical balance to reduce his sex drive and potency.

years, voluntary chemical castration has been permitted in some jurisdictions. This procedure involves treatment with a drug that reduces but does not eliminate the male sex drive. The normal sex drive is restored when the drug is discontinued. Mandatory chemical or surgical castration has not been permitted, although voluntary surgical castration is under consideration, as illustrated by the discussion in Exhibit 3.3.

Montana has enacted a statute that provides that, in addition to other punishments, a sex offender may be required to undergo a medically safe drug treatment "that reduces sexual fantasies, sex drive, or both."[27]

Retribution and Revenge

Retribution A punishment theory that contends that an offender should be punished for the crimes committed because he or she deserves it.

Revenge A punishment doctrine under which a person who violates the law should be punished in the same way the victim suffered.

Historically, victims (or their families) were permitted to take measures to avenge crime. This practice is referred to as revenge, retaliation, or retribution. **Retribution,** which focuses on the conduct of the wrongdoer, is the concept in vogue today and is discussed below. **Revenge,** or retaliation, reflects the practices of earlier days when victims were permitted to inflict on their attackers the same or similar kind of offenses as those victims had suffered.

Some modern jurisdictions permit victims to take revenge or retaliate against criminals, but long ago it was recognized that private revenge or retaliation can get out of control. Consequently, in most jurisdictions the state has taken over the responsibility of avenging criminal offenses. In a few cases, however, some people would argue that courts may not go far enough, as, for example, in the case of Judge Robert E. Cahill Sr., who sentenced a man to an 18-month prison term for killing his wife several hours after he found her in bed with another man. According to the judge, "I seriously wonder how many married men . . . would have the strength to walk away . . . without inflicting some corporal punishment . . . I shudder to think what I would do."[28]

The judge's sentence and comments brought an uproar of reaction, including a revision of the method by which Maryland judges are investigated. Cahill was the first judge charged under the new procedures. At the hearing on Judge Cahill's case, representatives of women's groups criticized the judge as sexist; law professors and judges, including one woman, said his comments were not indicative of sexism or disrespect for the law. Judge Cahill testified that his remarks were imperfect but that he did not intend to offend. The Judicial Disabilities Commission ruled that although the judge's decision and comments may have been unwise, they did not show prejudice against women. Judge Cahill convinced the commission members that he would have rendered the same sentence in the case of a woman killing her husband under similar circumstances. The commission concluded that none of the evidence proved that the judge is unfit to remain on the bench. In October 1995 the husband, whose case was the focus of this hearing, was released after serving one year of the sentence imposed after he entered a guilty plea to voluntary manslaughter.[29]

Revenge is a harsh word, and public reaction to the defendant's killing in the above case suggests that private revenge may not be acceptable today. But throughout history revenge has been one of the most important justifications for punishment. The philosophy of revenge, or retaliation, is referred to as the eye-for-an-eye, tooth-for-a-tooth doctrine. This Old Testament doctrine has been quoted by modern courts. For example, in a 1963 case involving a 15-year-old boy who was sentenced to life upon his conviction for slaying a young woman, the court noted that a life sentence must seem like a long time to the young defendant. "But," the court continued, "we must remember that as judge, jury and executioner he imposed a sentence to eternity [upon his victim]." The court added this reference to the Bible: "The Old Testament doctrine of an 'eye for an eye and a tooth for a tooth,' [may seem harsh to the criminal, who prefers the] modern trend toward rehabilitation." But the court noted that the victim may

EXHIBIT 3.3

Incapacitation as Punishment: How Far Can We Go?

In 1991 Steven Allen Butler, a Houston, Texas, sex offender, raped a 13-year-old repeatedly while on probation for molesting a 7-year-old. Butler's attorney proposed a plea bargain to the judge, who had spoken publicly about castrating rapists. The defendant would undergo castration if he could be freed at once and placed on probation. The judge agreed to castration and a 10-year probationary term. Critics responded that castration (in which the testicles are removed) reduces but does not eliminate the ability to have an erection. Furthermore, many sex crimes are about power, not sex, and castration would not eliminate the hostility a sex offender has toward women or girls. Among other problems in this case was that officials could not find a physician who would castrate the offender. There was significant opposition by civil liberties groups as well as allegations of racism.[1]

The issue of castration but not of race arose in Texas again in 1996. Larry Don McQuay, a 32-year-old offender who had almost completed his term for child molesting, stated that he had molested at least 240 children and that he would do so again unless he was castrated. McQuay was sentenced to eight years for having oral sex with a six-year-old boy. He served six years. With his good-time credits he was ready for mandatory release to supervised parole, which meant that he would live under supervision in a halfway house. The state had no legal authority to keep McQuay in prison. Although he was indicted for aggravated sexual assault, through a plea bargain he pleaded guilty to indecency. Under the statute in effect when McQuay was sentenced, early release was permitted for indecency although not for aggravated sexual assault. (Subsequently, the statute was changed to include indecency as an offense for which early release is not permitted.)

McQuay asked the state to castrate him. The attorney general said the state could do so under certain conditions, but the parole board insisted that they cannot make castration a condition of release on parole. Under Texas law a paroled inmate must be sent to his home county. In 1996 victims' families were complaining that McQuay would be sent back to the area in which he committed his crimes and that he had threatened to kill the victims and their families if they reported his offenses.[2]

In May 1998 McQuay was still incarcerated and continuing to demand to be castrated. Texas officials were processing paperwork for having the procedure done by a medical center, while the state senator who heads the Criminal Justice Commitee proclaimed that McQuay was "not going anywhere. I assure you he will serve his full 20 years."[3]

McQuay was not castrated, but he was out on parole only a short time before he was indicted for a another sex crime committed before he entered prison; he was convicted and reincarcerated, where he remains.

An unusual case occurred in Arkansas, where in November 1998 a convicted pedophile was facing surgical castration. James Ray Stanley entered guilty pleas to soliciting a teenage boy for sex and to raping an 11-year-old boy. He could have received life in prison on the rape charge and six years for the solicitation. Stanley pleaded guilty and was sentenced to 30 years in prison, with 10 years suspended if he agreed to be castrated, along with other requirements ordered by the court.

The American Civil Liberties Union (ACLU) intervened in the case but was unsuccessful in its argument that castration constitutes cruel and unusual punishment. The state said it would not carry out the castration for lack of authority, at which point Stanley asked the court to permit him to withdraw his guilty plea. His case was set for retrial, but Stanley and his attorney arranged with a private doctor for the defendant to be castrated. After the surgery, Stanley again entered a plea of guilty and was sentenced to 20 years in prison.[4]

1. "Court Abandons Castration Plan in a Rape Case," *New York Times* (17 March 1992), p. 6.
2. "Molester Seeks Castration; Texas Agrees," *New York Times* (5 April 1996), p. 9; "Castration Is Allowable, Attorney General Says," *Houston Chronicle* (5 April 1996), p. 1.
3. "Pedophile Pushes Texas for Castration: Surgical Procedure Would Be First in U.S.," *Washington Times* (17 May 1998), p. 6.
4. "Pedophile Agrees to Go under Knife: Apparently a State First," *Arkansas Democrat-Gazette* (11 November 1998), p. 1; "Fort Smith Castrated Sex Criminal Sentenced: After State Won't Do Job, He Gets Private Operation, Pleads Guilty, Gets 30 Years," *Arkansas Democrat-Gazette* (20 May 2000), p. 1B.

have a different point of view, as should those who have not yet lost their eyes or teeth or lives.[30]

The classical thinkers did not accept the extreme eye-for-an-eye punishment philosophy. They rejected punishments that were too harsh, believing that the criminal law should not be used as vengeance against offenders. As noted earlier, they believed the punishment should fit the crime. Beccaria insisted that the state had no right to impose a punishment greater than is necessary. One scholar explained Beccaria's view as follows: "Any law or punishment in excess of this limit is an abuse of power, not justice, and no unjust punishment may be tolerated, however useful it seems."[31]

Although the concept of retribution was severely criticized in much of the scholarly social science literature and in judicial opinions in the first two-thirds of the 20th century, it was recognized in 1972 by the U.S. Supreme Court as an appropriate reason for capital punishment.[32] In a 1976 opinion, the Court discussed retribution as a justification for capital punishment. It stated that, although retribution is no longer the dominant philosophy,

> neither is it a forbidden objective nor one inconsistent with our respect for the dignity of men . . . Indeed, the decision that capital punishment may be the appropriate sanction in extreme cases is an expression of the community's belief that certain crimes are themselves so grievous an affront to humanity that the only adequate response may be the penalty of death.[33]

The Court suggested that the instinct for retribution is a part of human nature and that if the courts do not handle these situations, private individuals might take the law into their own hands. Regarding retribution, the Court concluded,

> In part, capital punishment is an expression of society's moral outrage at particularly offensive conduct. This function may be unappealing to many, but it is essential in an ordered society that asks its citizens to rely on legal processes rather than self-help to vindicate their wrongs.[34]

It has been argued that in recent years Supreme Court justices have given more support to the doctrine of retribution as a justification for capital punishment because they realize that the evidence on deterrence is not strong and that the public has become disillusioned with rehabilitation. Retribution is the only doctrine supporting punishment in general, and the death penalty in particular, in which there need be no question of effectiveness. Effectiveness is not an issue. The argument supporting retribution is that people are punished in a specific way because that is the punishment they deserve. Retribution is *not* utilitarian. Because its goal is " 'doing justice' rather than preventing crimes, it makes no instrumental claims," and that is its principal merit.[35]

Another current justification for retribution is that it serves the important social function of legitimizing punishment. The argument is that society desires to see crime punished because "the criminal has pursued his interests, or gratified his desires, by means noncriminals have restrained themselves from using for the sake of the law and in fear of its punishments." Therefore, the offender's act must be punished to justify the self-restraint of noncriminals. Finally, society punishes because it feels it wants to or it ought to; the sole purpose of retribution is to express moral outrage.[36]

Justice model A philosophy holding that justice is achieved when offenders receive punishments based on what is deserved by their offenses as written in the law; the crime determines the punishment. In sentencing, this model presumes that prison should be used only as a last resort. Determinate or flat-time sentences are set for each offense. Parole is abolished, and early release can be achieved only through good-time credits.

The Justice Model of Punishment

That retribution provides the rationale for the modern **justice model** of punishment and sentencing is illustrated by the writings of Andrew von Hirsch,

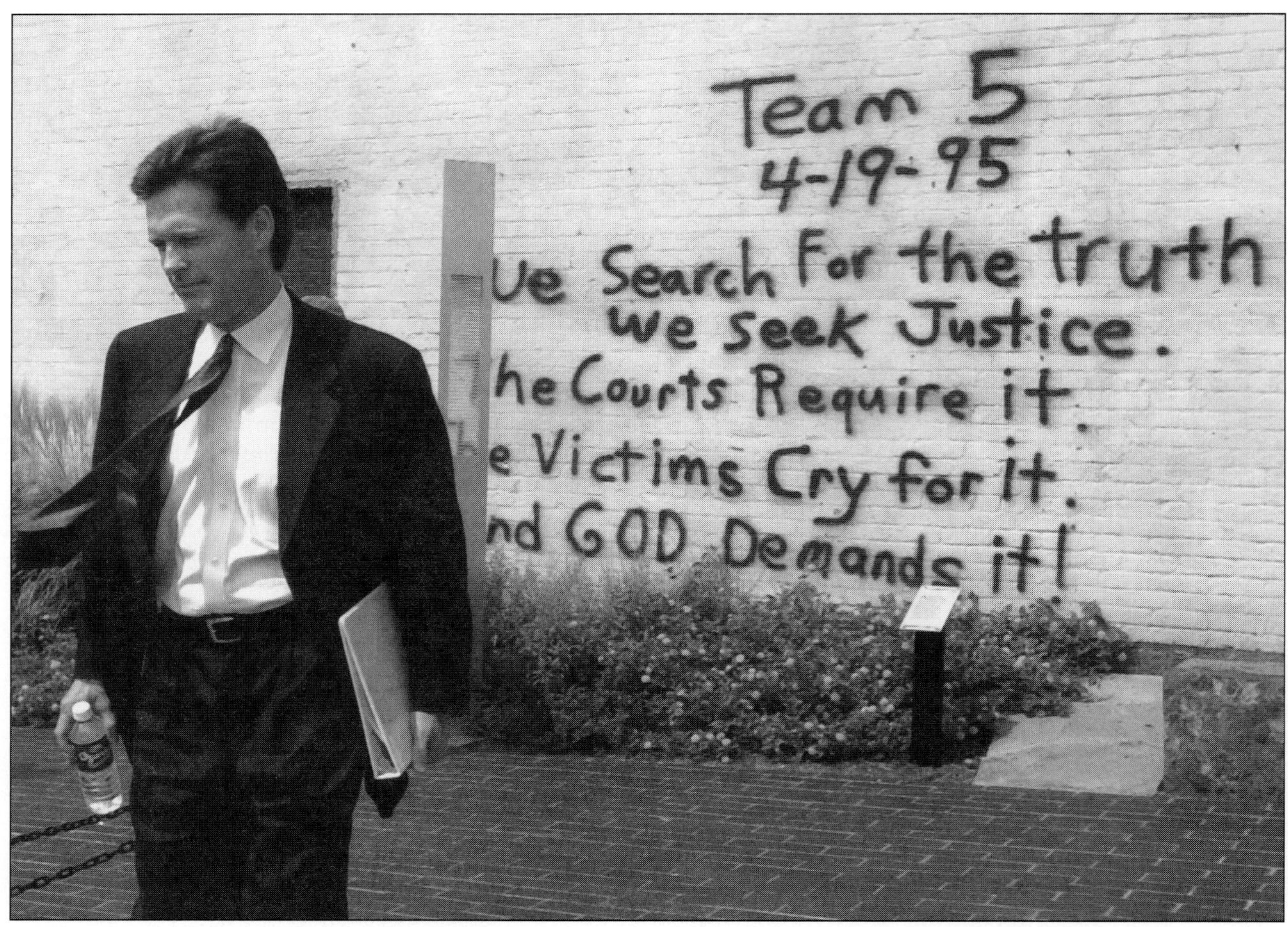

In September 2001 Oklahoma County District Attorney Wes Lane announced that the state would try Terry Nichols for murder for his role in the 19 April 1995 bombing of the federal building in Oklahoma City. Timothy McVeigh was convicted of federal murder charges and executed for his terrorist acts. Nichols was tried on federal charges and convicted of conspiracy to commit murder but not of murder. Behind Lane is a quotation that rescue workers painted on the side of an Oklahoma City building—their version of what justice required in this case. (AP Photo/J. Pat Carter)

Just deserts The philosophy that an individual who commits a crime deserves to suffer for it; also called *retribution*.

representing the position of the Committee for the Study of Incarceration in his book *Doing Justice: The Choice of Punishments.* Articulating their basic mistrust of the state's power, the committee members rejected rehabilitation and the indeterminate sentence and turned to deterrence and **just deserts** as reasons for punishment. The committee advocated shorter sentences and a sparing use of incarceration.[37]

The justice model was supported by David Fogel in his book *We Are the Living Proof: The Justice Model for Corrections.* Fogel formulated 12 propositions on which he believed the justice model could be based. He argued that punishment is necessary to implement the criminal law, a law based on the belief that people act as a result of their own free will and must be held responsible for their actions. Inmates should be considered and treated as "responsible, volitional and aspiring human beings." All the processes of the agencies of criminal justice systems should be carried out "in a milieu of justice." This requirement precludes a correctional system that "becomes mired in the dismal swamp of preaching, exhorting, and treatment." According to Fogel, discretion cannot be eliminated, but under the justice model it can be controlled, narrowed, and subjected to review.[38]

In the justice model, the emphasis is shifted away from the processor (the public, the administration, and others) to criminal justice system consumers.

According to Fogel, justice for the offender must not stop with sentencing but must continue throughout the correctional process: "*Properly understood, the justice perspective is not so much concerned with administration of justice as it is with the justice of administration.*"[39]

Under Fogel's justice model, an incarcerated person should retain all the rights "accorded free citizens consistent with mass living and the execution of a sentence restricting the freedom of movement." Inmates should be allowed to choose whether or not to participate in rehabilitation programs. The purpose of the prison is to confine for a specified period of time, not to rehabilitate the criminal. Offenders receive only the sentences they deserve, and those sentences are implemented according to fair principles.

The influence of the classical school may be seen in this return to a theory of just deserts or retribution. The theory is related to Bentham's and Beccaria's argument that the punishment should fit the crime. The just and humane approach is to punish the criminal for what he or she has done, not to follow the treatment-rehabilitation approach.

The justice model, with its emphasis on retribution and just deserts, sounds fair and simple. Offenders get the punishment they deserve—no more, no less. The problem is in determining what is fair and just punishment for a particular offense. The justice model does not answer the important question "How much punishment is deserved?" That question must be answered by legislators, judges, or administrators, and the argument is made that those in power will use punishment to discriminate against certain groups, such as minorities. When that happens, we do not have a just and fair system, and the justice model is a farce.

Even if sentencing is not used to discriminate against minorities, there are problems with deciding how much punishment to impose. Consider the case discussed in Exhibit 3.4. Do you agree with the original punishment decision or the subsequent one?

Indeterminate sentence The length of the sentence is determined not by the legislature or the court but by professionals at the institution or by parole boards, which decide when an offender is ready to return to society. The sentence imposed by the judge may range from one day to life.

Determinate sentence A sentence whose length is determined by the legislature, precluding adjustment by the judge, the correctional institution, or the parole board.

Rehabilitation The rationale for reformation of offenders, based on the premise that human behavior is the result of antecedent causes that may be discovered by objective analysis and that permit the scientific control of human behavior. The focus is on treatment, not punishment, of the offender.

Reform or Rehabilitation

Retribution and deterrence were the philosophies of the classical and neoclassical schools, with their emphasis on "Let the punishment fit the crime." The positive school emphasized the importance of the "punishment fitting the criminal"; the individual criminal, not the crime, was the focal point. Positivists believed that, to prevent crime, changes must be made in the social environment. They favored the **indeterminate sentence** (in contrast to the **determinate sentence**), tailored to meet the needs of individual criminals. They set the stage for further development of the philosophy of **rehabilitation,** a philosophy that dominated U.S. criminal justice systems until recently.

Rehabilitation: A Modern Ideal?

In 1982 a *Time* magazine article phrased a key question in the title and then answered it in the subtitle: " 'What Are Prisons For?' No Longer Rehabilitation, but to Punish—and to Lock the Worst Away." The article referred briefly to the original purpose of U.S. prisons: to punish but also to transform offenders "from idlers and hooligans into good, industrious citizens." The article concluded that "no other country was so seduced for so long by that ambitious charter. The language, ever malleable, conformed to the ideal: when a monkish salvation was expected of inmates, prisons became penitentiaries, then reformatories, correctional centers and rehabilitation facilities." The simple fact is that prisons did not work as intended.[40]

The **rehabilitation** philosophy became the modern philosophy of incarceration. It was described by one authority as the rehabilitative ideal, based on the premise that human behavior is the result of antecedent causes that may be

EXHIBIT 3.4
Punishment and Just Deserts

According to the just deserts philosophy, punishment should be commensurate with the crime or crimes for which it is imposed. The philosophy became quite popular during the 1994 elections, when the cry "three strikes and you're out" referred to sentencing rather than baseball. Numerous jurisdictions enacted three-strikes legislation, but this get-tough approach to crime was criticized by many judges, with 80 percent of federal judges resisting the mandatory minimum sentences typical of the three-strikes approach, discussed in more detail in Chapter 13 (see Exhibit 13.3).

The first case under the California three-strikes legislation illustrates the problem. Jerry Dewayne Williams was sentenced to a 25-years-to-life prison term upon conviction of stealing a slice of pepperoni pizza in 1994. Williams was the first to be sentenced under the new California statute, which provides for enhanced penalties for those who are convicted of three or more felonies. Williams was convicted of felony petty theft in the pizza incident, but he had prior convictions for robbery, attempted robbery, drug possession, and unauthorized use of a vehicle. Under California law, Williams would have been required to serve 20 years before he was eligible for parole.[1]

The California statute did not permit the sentencing judge to have any discretion in repeat-offender cases. It was assumed that the sentence was appropriate for the offender's cumulative crimes if not the last crime for which he was convicted. Thus, the judge should not be permitted to consider any mitigating factors in sentencing. Do you agree?

In a 1996 decision the California Supreme Court held that the state's three-strikes statute did not eliminate all discretion by the trial judge, who, according to the court, retains the power to disregard a prior conviction in assessing punishment in a particular case. According to the court, if a trial judge believes that "in the interest of justice" a prior conviction should be disregarded, he or she has the power to do just that.[2]

Williams was resentenced to a six-year term, and in April 2002 the U.S. Supreme Court agreed to hear two California cases in which offenders were sentenced to from 25 years to life for a minor property offense following earlier convictions for felonies.[3]

1. "Theft of Pizza Slice Nets a Twenty-Five Year Term," *New York Times* (5 March 1995), p. 11.
2. People v. Superior Court, 917 P.2d 628 (Cal. 1996), *modified*, 1996 Cal. LEXIS 4699 (Cal., 21 August 1996).
3. See Lockyer v. Andrade, No. 01–1127, and Ewing v. California, No. 1–6978, which will be heard during the Court's 2002–2003 term.

known by objective analysis and that permit scientific control. The assumption was that the offender should be *treated*, not punished.[41]

Many social scientists endorsed the rehabilitative ideal and began developing treatment programs for institutionalized inmates. The ideal was incorporated into statutes, proclaimed by courts, and supported by the 1967 President's Commission on Crime and the Administration of Justice.

The Indeterminate Sentence

The backbone of the rehabilitation philosophy was the indeterminate sentence. No longer would a judge sentence an offender to a definite term, as it could not be predicted in advance how much time would be needed for treatment and rehabilitation. Consequently, in most jurisdictions the legislature established minimum and maximum terms for each offense. In its purest form, the indeterminate sentence means that a person is sentenced to prison for one day to life. Treatment personnel evaluate the person, recommend and implement treatment, and decide when that individual has been rehabilitated and can be released safely. The punishment fits the criminal, not the crime. In short, the basic philosophy is that we should incarcerate people until they are cured or rehabilitated.[42]

The Decline of the Rehabilitative Ideal

The rehabilitative ideal is based on the belief that we can predict when offenders have been rehabilitated and are ready for release from prison or a treatment program. Prediction is not so accurate in the social sciences, however, although individuals trained in the behavioral sciences may be more qualified to make a decision about release after working with an offender than the judge is at the time of sentencing.

In the 1970s many people began to question the rehabilitation philosophy. It was alleged that treatment did not work, a position popularized by a 1974 article titled "What Works? Questions and Answers about Prison Reform."[43] Acceptance of the rehabilitative ideal declined in the judicial system, too. In 1977 David L. Bazelon, then chief judge of the U.S. Court of Appeals in Washington, D.C., and a strong supporter of using social science research findings in court decisions, concluded, "The guiding faith of corrections—rehabilitation—has been declared a false god." Judge Bazelon argued that the problem with rehabilitation as a justification for punishment was that it

> should never have been sold on the promise that it would reduce crime. Recidivism rates cannot be the only measure of what is valuable in corrections. Simple decency must count too. It is amoral, if not immoral, to make cost-benefit equations a lodestar in corrections.[44]

Perhaps an even stronger criticism of the rehabilitation philosophy as a basis for punishment was the allegation of administrative abuse of the power to release. For example, under the indeterminate system in California, though offenders served longer terms than they would have served under determinate sentences, there was no evidence that these longer terms were necessary for rehabilitation. Another criticism of the indeterminate sentence was that it caused feelings of hostility. Offenders never knew when they would be released. According to one report, inmates referred to the indeterminate sentence as the "never-knowing system," which created psychological problems for them.[45]

Another serious problem was the lack of guidelines, rules, or standards for release. This lack, along with the general unwillingness of appellate courts to review trial judges' sentencing decisions, led to serious attacks on the indeterminate sentence.[46] It was alleged that indeterminate sentencing was unjust and that the rehabilitative ideal removes the concept of just deserts. In effect, critics said, the criminal gets more than he or she deserves. The foundation for this position was raised in the early 1950s by the British theologian C. S. Lewis, who advocated a return to the philosophy of retribution and just deserts. In analyzing the treatment/rehabilitation approach, Lewis said:

> Merciful though it appears, [this approach] really means that each one of us, from the moment he breaks the law, is deprived of the rights of a human being . . . when we cease to consider what the criminal deserves and consider only what will cure him or deter others, we have tacitly removed him from the sphere of justice altogether; instead of a person, a subject of rights, we now have a mere object, a patient, a case.[47]

The belief that the criminal should be processed in accordance with the act committed, not with his or her chances of rehabilitation, was supported in the 1970s by recognized scholars such as Norval Morris and Andrew von Hirsch.[48] Increasing dissatisfaction with the rehabilitative ideal and concern about the extent of crime, especially violent crime, led many to favor a get-tough sentencing policy. The argument was this: treatment does not work, so let us try incarceration for longer periods of time. According to the 1982 *Time* article cited earlier, "Lock 'em up and throw away the key! Crudely put, that increasingly is the rallying cry in an America fed up with violent crime."[49]

By the late 1970s and early 1980s, many states had revised their sentencing statutes. Maine led the way toward the adoption of determinate sentencing, a position followed by several other states and federal government. Changes were made in the use of parole, with some jurisdictions (including federal) abolishing this practice. In the legislation adopting federal sentencing guidelines, Congress expressed its position that rehabilitation is no longer the goal of sentencing. According to the statute,

> The [Sentencing] Commission shall insure that the guidelines reflect the inappropriateness of imposing a sentence to a term of imprisonment for the purpose of *rehabilitating* the defendant or providing the defendant with needed educational or vocational training, medical care, or other correctional treatment.[50]

In 1989, in reference to this federal sentencing reform, the U.S. Supreme Court stated that the act as adopted revises former sentencing processes in several ways, including its rejection of "imprisonment as means of promoting *rehabilitation,* and it states that punishment should serve retributive, educational, deterrent, and incapacitative goals."[51]

A Return to Rehabilitation?

Recently, some scholars have encouraged a return to rehabilitation as a viable reason for punishment. Prison overcrowding and rising crime rates have made it necessary for us to reevaluate our get-tough sentencing policies. In 1982 two scholars, Francis T. Cullen and Karen E. Gilbert, published their approach to the issue in a book entitled *Reaffirming Rehabilitation.* According to Cullen and Gilbert, we should be careful in attributing all of the problems of criminal justice systems to the rehabilitative ideal. Cullen spoke before the National Center on Institutions and Alternatives' 1990 conference, Reaffirming Rehabilitation II: Beyond the "Nothing Works" Myth. He said that the American people "have not given up on rehabilitation"; they want the correctional system to do more than "punish and cage."[52]

In a later article based on a nationwide study, Cullen and his colleagues reported that prison wardens are committed to rehabilitation as well as to custody and security.[53] A correctional counseling text author espoused the position that rehabilitation is necessary for effective criminal justice programs.[54] Furthermore, a survey of citizens revealed that although the get-tough policy toward offenders is supported, "strong support was also expressed for rehabilitative programs, particularly among the young, poor, and minority populations."[55]

Early in the Clinton administration the word *rehabilitation* was heard in connection with drug offenders. In the fall of 1993 the administration issued a 31-page report that emphasized education and rehabilitation rather than punishment of drug offenders, but no specifics were given. The Violent Crime Control and Law Enforcement Act of 1994 increased penalties for numerous drug offenses.[56]

A different approach is taken in a 1993 article in which the authors (one from the Federal Bureau of Prisons) argued that we do not know "what works" in the way of rehabilitation. Furthermore, the primary job of prison administrators is to "administer justice, not treatment." Rejecting the proposition that treatment makes punishment more humane, the authors concluded: "Individualized treatment muddles the punishment message, making it less principled and not necessarily more inhumane." These authors reject rehabilitation as an *official goal* of incarceration but recommend that programs permitting offenders to engage in work, education, and other activities should be one mission of prisons.[57]

Some court decisions within the last decade or so have recognized the importance of rehabilitation as a reason for punishment. Idaho's Supreme Court recognizes four goals of criminal punishment: protection of society, deterrence of the individual and the public generally, possibility of rehabilitation, and punishment or retribution for wrongdoing.[58] Some statutes retained rehabilitation as a reason for punishment. For example, Montana provided that its correctional policy was

> to protect society by preventing crime through punishment and rehabilitation of the convicted . . . Furthermore, it is the state's policy that persons convicted of a crime shall be dealt with in accordance with their individual characteristics, circumstances, needs, and potentialities.

In 1997, however, Montana amended that statute, removing the language about rehabilitation and adding a statement that the purpose of punishment is to "protect the public by incarcerating violent offenders and serious repeat offenders." The statute does provide that another purpose is to "encourage and provide opportunities for the offender's self-improvement."[59]

A dramatic move toward rehabilitation occurred in the fall of 2000, when 61 percent of voting Californians passed Proposition 36. The change provides for treatment for specified nonviolent drug offenders. The state's prison system, the largest in the Western hemisphere, with a total population of over 162,000, is crowded primarily by drug offenders. They represent almost one of three of California's inmates. The new approach views drug use as a health issue, not a matter of concern for the criminal law.[60]

On the whole, rehabilitation is no longer considered the dominant reason for punishment. It has been replaced with a deterrence approach.

Deterrence

In addition to emphasizing a philosophy of punishment based on what the criminal deserves, the classical thinkers believed that a major purpose of punishment is **deterrence. Individual (or specific) deterrence** refers to the effect of punishment in preventing a particular individual from committing additional crimes. **General deterrence** is based on the assumption that punishing individuals who are convicted of crimes provides an example to potential violators, who, being rational persons and wishing to avoid pain, will not violate the law. Again, we see the influence of the classical thinkers' emphasis on free will and rational choice.

Individual (or specific) deterrence A punishment philosophy based on the belief that the threat of punishment may prevent an individual from committing any crimes. The use of incarceration is an example.

Deterrence A justification for punishment based on the prevention or discouragement of crime through fear or danger, as by punishing offenders to serve as examples to potential criminals, or by incarcerating offenders to prevent them from committing further criminal acts.

General deterrence The philosophy of punishment resting on the belief that punishment in an individual case inhibits others from committing the same offense.

Deterrence theory is based on the assumption that appropriate punishments deter criminal activity because rational humans will not choose behavior that brings more pain than pleasure. Thus, punishment deters.

Empirical Evidence regarding Deterrence

Many reactions to the question of whether punishment deters crime are based on conjecture, faith, or emotion, with little or no empirical data. That advocates simply "know" that punishment does or does not deter is the case, particularly in the death penalty debate, the focus of many deterrence studies.

Sociologist Jack P. Gibbs addressed the issue of deterrence in an insightful and provocative book in which he reviewed the empirical findings on punishment and deterrence. Noting that much of the earlier sociological research on deterrence was concerned solely with the relationship of crime rates and the statutory existence of the death penalty, Gibbs pointed out that, more recently, sociologists have turned to an "examination of the relation between actual legal punishments (imprisonment in particular) and crime rates." According to Gibbs, the findings of the earlier studies cannot be generalized to other types of punishment. They are limited also in their application to our understanding of the deterrent effect of capital punishment, since most ignore the variable of certainty of actual execution. Gibbs argued that studies of the deterrent effect of punishment must allow for the differences between general and individual deterrence and take into account properties of punishment such as the perceived certainty that one would suffer a punishment. If a potential criminal thinks the law will not be enforced, he or she might not be deterred from criminal activity simply because the law provides a severe penalty for violation.[61] It might be reasonable to conclude that with most death row inmates filing numerous appeals over many years, potential violators will assume that capital punishment is unlikely to occur.

Some social scientists have agreed that we cannot test deterrence until we can refine our research models and specify the variables determining whether or not punishment deters.[62] For example, there is some evidence that punishment may have a quick but not a long-term deterrent effect.[63] Some studies of the deterrent effect of jailing drunk drivers support this position.[64] An earlier study found some evidence that mandatory jail sentences for offenders convicted of driving while under the influence (DUI) are not a significant deterrent for future convictions.[65] A more recent analysis of increased penalties for DUI offenders found that "the increasing severity of penalties throughout the decade is not associated with any corresponding significant decrease in recidivism rates for the offender population as a whole, or for particular subgroups."[66]

There is evidence that arrests are no greater deterrent to spouse abuse than is advising or issuing a citation.[67] One scholar has concluded that there is "reason to doubt that prevention of domestic violence has moved much beyond where it was fifty years ago."[68] Other studies have examined gun control and deterrence. In suggesting that the knowledge that potential victims may be armed might deter offenders, one researcher stated that "much social order in America may precariously depend on the fact that millions of people are armed and dangerous to each other."[69] Others say the evidence does not support the conclusion that "publicity about gun ownership measurably deters criminal behavior."[70]

Deterrence of juvenile crime is the major reason that states have passed statutes providing for automatic transfer of juveniles accused of violent crimes to the adult criminal court. A study of Idaho's practice, however, found no evidence that these measures deter violent crimes by juveniles.[71] Furthermore, it is questionable that severe punishment, for example capital punishment, is a significant deterrence for murder. In a study and review of the literature, one scholar concluded that his findings "support the large number of studies at state and national levels that have found no deterrent effect of capital punishment."[72] Another researcher has concluded that stalking statutes are not very effective in protecting stalking victims.[73]

Deterrence of Types of Crime and Types of People

Although in this book we cannot fully discuss the wide array of empirical research on deterrence, the small sampling given above demonstrates that the findings are contradictory. One of the reasons for this is the controversy over how to define and measure deterrence. In addition, the research should be more focused. We will consider two ways in which that might be accomplished.

First, deterrence research should be narrowed to types of crime and types of people. Perhaps punishment (or the threat of punishment) is effective in deterring people from shoplifting but not from killing their spouses. Perhaps certain types of people are deterred by laws, but other types are not. Or perhaps punishment perceptions may have a deterrent effect on some but not all persons. For example, many offenders who commit murder and other violent crimes do so while under the influence of alcohol or other drugs or while involved in an emotional experience, usually connected with the family or close friends. Probably most of these offenders are not thinking rationally at the moment they commit the crime. In that case, such behavior will not be deterred by criminal statutes. This rationale may also apply to those who violate criminal laws prohibiting driving while intoxicated.

Second, researchers should consider the following question: What types of people need stiff penalties and what types are more likely to be deterred by publicity or lesser penalties? For an executive who must drive to conduct business and to entertain clients, the revocation of a driver's license and publication of the arrest and type of punishment might be sufficient deterrence; that is, the executive may not be likely to repeat the offense. This sanction might be sufficient to deter other professionals from driving while intoxicated, too. But even if those sanctions are sufficient deterrents, the effect may be short-lived and may be lost if people *perceive* that they will not be caught or that, if they are caught, the probability of punishment is slim.

Prior experiences of potential offenders might affect deterrence as well. Two investigators who followed a cohort of men over a period of years found evidence to support a specific deterrence theory but noted that the deterrent effect of arrest operates differently for novice and experienced offenders. Among novice offenders, arrest is somewhat more likely to terminate their criminal careers. Among more experienced offenders, arrest significantly reduces future rates of offending.[74]

Perceived Deterrence

Some researchers say that what we are considering is *perceived deterrence*—what people think will happen will determine whether they are deterred. The perception of the certainty and severity of punishment may be the key variable in explaining deterrence. It is said that the *actual* certainty of punishment influences people's perceptions of certainty. If they believe that punishment is certain, they will be afraid to violate the law. The relationship between the certainty of punishment and the perceived certainty of punishment is difficult to test empirically, although there have been some suggestions of ways in which it might be done. One study reported the results of a test of the hypothesis that a person's perception of the severity of legal punishments will be increased when that person has an experience with the sanction. The authors concluded that their findings

> suggest that more severe legal sanctions are more successful than less severe sanctions in achieving the first goal of deterrence, namely, raising perceptions of severity of formal legal sanctions and transmitting the message that legal sanctions are costly.[75]

Perceived deterrence may involve more variables than perceived legal punishment. Two investigators studied the deterrent effect of three variables: moral commitment (internalization of legal norms), fear of social disapproval, and fear of legal punishment. They found that all three forms of social control were important as inhibitors of illegal behavior. They noted that, according to some deterrence theorists, many people who internalize norms behave in legal ways not because they fear punishment but because they believe this is the proper way to behave. For these people, internalization of norms is a more effective form of social control than is fear of legal apprehension and punishment. The researchers concluded, however, that the perceived threat of punishment is somewhat effective at all levels of moral commitment.[76]

The relationship between people's perceptions of what will happen if they violate a law and whether they decide to take that course may be far more complex

Media Focus 3.1

Will Television Deter Crime?

When the execution of a well-known criminal is scheduled, it is not uncommon to hear requests for television coverage. Thus far, U.S. courts have refused to permit such coverage, although the U.S. attorney general did make arrangements for closed-circuit television of the scheduled May 2001 execution of Timothy McVeigh, convicted in the 1995 bombing of the federal building in Oklahoma City.

The scheduled execution was postponed until June 2001 after it was discovered that the Federal Bureau of Investigation (FBI) failed to release thousands of documents to McVeigh's attorneys to consider in the preparation of their client's defense. McVeigh's attorneys prepared a motion for a further delay, but the trial judge refused to grant it. The first appellate court agreed, and McVeigh decided not to appeal to the U.S. Supreme Court. He was executed on 11 June 2001. Only a small number of persons were permitted to view the actual execution, which occurred at the federal prison in Terre Haute, Indiana.

The attorney general permitted victims' family members to view the execution by satellite at a designated facility in Oklahoma City as a means of allowing them to bring closure to the horrendous crime. It is not uncommon to permit victims' families to view executions, but in the McVeigh case there were too many people for the Terre Haute facility.

Do you believe that if judges (or the U.S. Supreme Court justices) permit the filming of executions to be shown on television the events would serve as a deterrent to persons who might be considering committing the crime of murder? Would the type of murder under consideration be significant? For example, would televised executions be more likely to deter murders that occur within the home or those that are the result of terrorist activities? Would age be a factor—the viewing might deter older but not younger people? Would television of executions have any harmful effects on society?

than the classical theorists envisioned when they argued that all behavior is rational and that people will choose to avoid behavior that might result in pain. In a 1986 study researchers questioned the validity of the classical approach. They found that persons in high-risk groups for receiving criminal sanctions (for example, drug addicts) were not deterred significantly from criminal acts because of their perception of the risk of being caught and sanctioned formally. They were, however, influenced by their perceptions of their opportunities to commit crime and by their respect for criminal activities. The researchers emphasized the need to refine research on the deterrent effect of criminal law.[77]

In a study published in 2001, one researcher found that "objective information about the certainty of punishment was used moderately, but it was used only for some offenses," concluding that if individuals use objective information concerning the certainty of punishment only moderately, their decisions regarding whether to commit crimes will not be significantly affected.[78]

Finally, consider the impact that televised executions might have on potential criminal activity. Media Focus 3.1 contains some questions you might ponder in your analysis.

PUNISHMENT: AN ANALYSIS

Where does the preceding discussion leave us? The classical thinkers argued that the punishment should fit the crime; some modern thinkers have taken that statement to mean that criminals should get the punishment they deserve. Others have interpreted classical thinking in terms of its utilitarian principle of deterrence—that people behave rationally and seek pleasure and avoid pain.

Therefore, for the criminal law to deter, it must be swift and sure. It must provide penalties that are perceived to be just a little worse than the pleasure that would be gained from engaging in the criminal behavior. Others argue that people do not always behave rationally and may choose criminal behavior even when they know the chances of getting caught are high and that the penalty is severe.

Other problems arise from the justice model based on the classical position. If we assume that criminals should get what they deserve but that punishment should be severe enough to deter others from committing crimes, what do we do when these two are in conflict? Let us assume that the degree of punishment deserved by a particular criminal is not sufficient to deter others. Under the justice model, a criminal must not be punished more than he or she deserves; that would be as unfair as too little punishment. Thus, if this criminal gets what is deserved, the result may be punishment that has little or no deterrent effect on others.

What might happen if the only punishment that is a sufficient deterrent is one considered to be unfair or unjust? How do the principles of just deserts, utilitarianism, and deterrence apply to the punishment of corporate offenders? Should the corporation be punished by fine or by a withdrawal of its charter, or should its individual executives be punished? If so, how? Would it ever be just to punish the corporate executive for the criminal behavior of his or her employees? Would it be just to punish the employees if they were acting as directed? Which would be the greater deterrent?

Although many questions about individual and general deterrence remain, one result is obvious: Many U.S. jails and prisons are overcrowded. This overcrowding is caused primarily by the recently increased and extended penalties imposed on drug offenders as well as by mandatory minimum sentences for these and other crimes. Meanwhile, drug problems have increased, and law enforcement officials seem powerless to do anything about them.

This is not to suggest that we should retreat from our attempts to control drug-related offenses, but it does mean that government officials should consider the total effect of any action before implementing the proposed reform. The federal sentencing guidelines, enacted in an effort to reduce both sentence disparity and crime rates, are an example. Many federal judges and others questioned the wisdom of this legislation before and after its passage, and recently it has come under judicial fire. The legislation has achieved some of its goals: More federal offenders are going to prison, and they are staying there longer. But in 1992 a chorus of federal judges called the sentencing guidelines a "hobgoblin of U.S. courts." Some judges "liken them [federal sentencing guidelines] to Prohibition: a utopian experiment gone haywire."[79] Discussions elsewhere in this text note some of the criticisms of the guidelines: They may discriminate against minorities (for example, in the greater sentences for possession of crack cocaine as compared to powder cocaine); they raise constitutional issues; they exacerbate prison overcrowding; and they may not have a significant deterrent effect.

States have reported negative results of determinate sentencing. In New York, which had one of the toughest drug laws ever enacted in the United States, a study of this subject led a researcher to conclude that determinate sentencing, which she called punishment "for the sake of punishment," had not lived up to the expectations of its proponents.[80]

The controversy over reasons for punishment can be expected to continue; it can be expected, too, that some people will argue that the criminal law is the most appropriate mechanism for social control. As social problems such as crime and AIDS become more life threatening, we might expect the controversies to take on greater importance.

SUMMARY

This chapter begins with the relationship between the modern views of punishment and sentencing and the view of the thinkers of the classical, neoclassical, and positivist periods. It discusses the debate over how much punishment we should have in order to deter criminal behavior.

Because the classical, neoclassical, and positivist thinkers had an impact on the development of punishment philosophy, their views are examined and critiqued in this chapter. That discussion is followed by a more intensive analysis of the major punishment philosophies: incapacitation, retribution and revenge, the justice model, and rehabilitation. The previous emphasis on rehabilitation as the primary reason for punishment is examined in light of historical developments that led to its partial demise. The indeterminate sentence was replaced by determinate sentencing in many jurisdictions as legislators and others became convinced that tougher and more definite sentencing was needed to deter crime.

The rehabilitation philosophy did not die, however, and the chapter notes its reemergence as a viable punishment philosophy in recent years. It is obvious, though, that deterrence theory is very important in explaining recent sentence reform. Deterrence theory is examined in terms of individual and general deterrence, with an analysis of some of the recent empirical studies. The chapter emphasizes that deterrence is difficult to determine and that the issues must be broken down into relevant variables, such as deterrence of specific types of crime or persons, and the relationship between deterrence and perception of the reality and severity of punishment.

The final section of the chapter assesses the impact of a return to determinate sentences, noting the problems of jail and prison overcrowding as well as negative judicial reaction to mandatory sentences.

A reassessment of punishment philosophies is in order. Was it a mistake to abandon the rehabilitative ideal during the return to retribution, deterrence, and just deserts as the dominant reasons for punishment? Some who approved the demise of the rehabilitative ideal as the primary purpose of punishment have emphasized the importance of maintaining the *opportunity* for treatment. For example, David Fogel's justice model does not preclude treatment; it merely precludes *coercive* treatment. As Fogel said in 1975, "What I suggest we do is give up this nonsense [coerced treatment] and return to a very open system . . . where we don't try to screw people's heads on right." In reporting those comments from his speech, the *Seattle Times* ran the headline "Ex–Prison Director Mocks Rehabilitation."[81] But that headline is not correct. It was only the *coerced* treatment, the attempt to *force* rehabilitation, that was being rejected.

The previous year, Norval Morris, a noted authority on criminal justice and a professor and former dean of the University of Chicago College of Law, had posed a similar argument for salvaging something of the rehabilitative ideal: "Rehabilitative programs in prisons have been characterized more by false rhetoric than by solid achievement. They have been corrupted to punitive purposes. But it does not follow that they should be discarded." According to Morris, we should not send people to prison *for* treatment; we should keep treatment programs but distinguish between the purposes of incarceration and the opportunities that might be provided for the incarcerated person: "Rehabilitation can be given only to a volunteer."[82]

STUDY QUESTIONS

1. Contrast the approaches of the classical, neoclassical, and the positive schools of thought. Who were the leaders of each?
2. Define, compare, and give examples of the major punishment philosophies.
3. Comment on the recent change in California concerning treatment rather than punishment of drug offenders.
4. How has the emphasis on punishment philosophies changed over time?
5. Define *indeterminate sentence* and explain its relationship to punishment philosophies.
6. How effective do you think deterrence is in preventing criminal behavior? Does the type of behavior matter? Does the severity or the certainty of punishment matter?
7. Which punishment philosophy do you think should form the basis of sentencing? Why?
8. What impact have longer sentences for drug offenses had on criminal justice systems?

BRIEF ESSAY ASSIGNMENTS

1. Define *social contract*. What was Beccaria's position on the social contract?
2. Explain the methodological weaknesses of the positivists.
3. According to Fogel's justice model, what rights should incarcerated persons have?
4. What are the criticisms of indeterminate sentencing?
5. Explain why it might be more valuable to examine perceived deterrence rather than deterrence by itself.

INTERNET ACTIVITIES

1. Check out the website www.faculty.newc.edu/toconnor/default.htm, which includes links to various sources on criminal justice topics. Click on the "criminology" link, which provides information on the history of criminology, history of theories, terms, and policy implications for many of the theories that will be addressed in this book.
2. Does your state have a law or proposed legislation concerning sex offenders? Search for the law in your state and learn about some issues concerning the treatment of sex offenders (e.g., sex offender registries, chemical and physical castration) by using a legal and news resource site such as www.law.about.com.

NET RESOURCES

www.crimetheory.com
Designed and maintained by an individual, crimetheory provides information on criminology and criminologists as well as a glossary of criminology terms. Resources such as bibliographies and links to other criminological sites are included.

www.utm.edu/research/iep
The Internet Encyclopedia of Philosophy allows users to access copyrighted articles on various philosophy topics that are categorized alphabetically. Links to a time line on Western philosophy and keywords are also provided.

www.sentencingproject.org/nasa/
The National Association of Sentencing Advocates website provides access to publications and reports from a professional organization of sentencing advocates. This site includes links to policy reports, fact sheets from the Sentencing Project, and links to other agencies related to sentencing advocacy.

www.famm.org/home.htm
Families Against Mandatory Minimums is a national organization working to improve sentencing guidelines and to reform state and federal mandatory sentencing laws. The site provides news updates and information on the history and issues related to mandatory sentencing.

www.sentence.org
The Determinate Sentence Clearinghouse website provides public information about sentencing laws, including issues related to prisons, the war on drugs and a specific focus on three strikes laws. Research findings on three strikes laws and links to all aspects of the criminal justice system are available on this website.

www.prevent-abuse-now.com/ The Prevent Abuse Now website, maintained by an individual, includes an index of topics on sexual offenders that includes news and information on sex offender registries (Megan's law), juvenile offenders, and law and the courts.

ENDNOTES

1. Eliott Monochese, "Cesare Beccaria," in *Pioneers in Criminology*, ed. Herman Mannheim (Montclair, NJ: Patterson Smith, 1973), p. 48. Beccaria's book (originally published in 1764 as *Dei deletti e delle pene*) is *On Crime and Punishments*, trans. Henry Paolucci (Indianapolis: Bobbs-Merrill, 1963).
2. Monochese, "Cesare Beccaria," p. 49.
3. Stephen Schafer, *Theories in Criminology* (New York: Random House, 1969), p. 106.
4. Beccaria, *On Crime and Punishments*, pp. 11–13.
5. For an article questioning Beccaria's contributions to the free will philosophy of crime, see Piers Beirne, "Inventing Criminology: The 'Science of Man' in Cesare Beccaria's *Dei deletti e delle pene* (1764)," *Criminology* 29 (November 1991): 777–820.
6. Roscoe Pound, quoted in Frank Tannenbaum, *Crime and the Community* (New York: Ginn, 1938), p. 4.
7. Gerhard Mueller, "Cesare Beccaria and the Social Significance of His Concept of Criminal Policy," paper presented at the International Congress on Cesare Beccaria and Modern Criminal Policy (Milan, Italy, 1988), referred to in Graeme Newman and Pietro Marongiu, "Penological Reform and the Myth of Beccaria," *Criminology* 28 (May 1990): 325.
8. Graeme Newman, *Just and Painful: A Case for the Corporal Punishment of Criminals* (New York: Free Press, 1983), p. 71.
9. Newman and Marongiu, "Penological Reform," p. 326.
10. Coleman Phillipson, *Three Criminal Law Reformers: Beccaria, Bentham, and Romilly* (New York: Dutton, 1923), p. 234.
11. Gilbert Geis, "Jeremy Bentham," in *Pioneers in Criminology*, ed. Herman Mannheim (Montclair, NJ: Patterson Smith, 1973), pp. 54, 57.
12. M. T. Maestro, *Voltaire and Beccaria as Reformers of the Criminal Law* (New York: Columbia University Press, 1942), p. 152.
13. Ibid., pp. 152–57.
14. Harry Elmer Barnes and Negley K. Teeters, *New Horizons in Criminology* (Englewood Cliffs, NJ: Prentice Hall, 1959), p. 322.
15. Andrew von Hirsch, "Neoclassicism, Proportionality, and the Rationale for Punishment: Thoughts on the Scandinavia Debate," *Crime & Delinquency* 29 (January 1983): 52.
16. Schafer, *Theories in Criminology*, p. 123.
17. Marvin E. Wolfgang, "Cesare Lombroso," in *Pioneers in Criminology*, ed. Herman Mannheim (Montclair, NJ: Patterson Smith, 1973), pp. 232–91. See also Cesare Lombroso, *Crime, Its Causes and Remedies*, trans. H. P. Horton (Boston: Little, Brown, 1911), p. 33.
18. Lombroso, *Crime, Its Causes and Remedies*, p. 33.
19. Edwin H. Sutherland and Donald Cressey, *Criminology*, 5th ed. (Philadelphia: Lippincott, 1978), pp. 55, 59.
20. Wolfgang, "Cesare Lombroso," p. 288.
21. Ibid., p. 271.
22. Raffaele Garofalo, *Criminology*, trans. Robert W. Millar (Boston: Little, Brown, 1914), pp. 95, 96.
23. Enrico Ferri, *Criminal Sociology*, trans. Joseph Killey and John Lisle (Boston: Little, Brown, 1917), p. 209.
24. Shafer, *Theories in Criminology*, p. 123.
25. Commonwealth v. Ritter, Court of Oyer and Terminer, Philadelphia, 13 D. & C. 285 (1930).
26. State v. Elliot, 828 P.2d 349, 350 (Ida.App. 1992).
27. Mont. Code Anno., Title 45, Section 45-5-512(1) (2001).
28. "Md. Judge Taking Heat in Cuckolded Killer Case," *Washington Post* (30 October 1994), p. 1.
29. See "Final Verdict on Judge Cahill; Judicial Commission Ruling: He Made Poor Decision, but It's Time to Move On," *Baltimore Sun* (8 May 1996), p. 18.
30. State v. Rinehart, 125 N.W.2d 242 (Iowa 1963).
31. Francis Edward Devine, "Cesare Beccaria and the Theoretical Foundation of Modern Penal Jurisprudence," *New England Journal of Prison Law* 7 (Winter 1981): 13.
32. Furman v. Georgia, 408 U.S. 238 (1972).
33. Gregg v. Georgia, 428 U.S. 153, 184–85 (1976).
34. Gregg v. Georgia, 428 U.S. 153, 183 (1976).
35. Jack P. Gibbs, "The Death Penalty, Retribution and Penal Policy," *Journal of Criminal Law and Criminology* 69 (Fall 1978): 294.
36. Ernest van den Haag, "Punishment as a Device for Controlling the Crime Rate," *Rutgers Law Review* 33 (Spring 1981): 719–30.
37. Andrew von Hirsch, *Doing Justice: The Choice of Punishments* (New York: Hill & Wang, 1976).
38. David Fogel, *We Are the Living Proof: The Justice Model for Corrections*, 2d ed. (Cincinnati, OH: Anderson, 1979), pp. 183–84.
39. Ibid., p. 192; emphasis in the original.
40. " 'What Are Prisons For?' No Longer Rehabilitation, but to Punish—and to Lock the Worst Away," *Time* (13 September 1982), p. 38.
41. Francis A. Allen, "Criminal Justice, Legal Values and the Rehabilitative Ideal," *Journal of Criminal Law, Criminology, and Police Science* 50 (September/October 1959): 226–32.
42. For a more detailed discussion of the indeterminate sentence, see Sue Titus Reid, "A Rebuttal to the Attack on the Indeterminate Sentence," *Washington Law Review* 51 (July 1976): 565–606.
43. Robert Martinson, "What Works? Questions and Answers about Prison Reform," *The Public Interest* 35 (Spring 1974): 22–54. The complete work is published in Douglas Lipton, Robert Martinson, and Judith Wilks, *The Effectiveness of Correctional Treatment: A Survey of Treatment Education Studies* (New York: Holt, Rinehart & Winston, 1975).
44. David L. Bazelon, "Street Crime and Correctional Potholes," *Federal Probation* 42 (March 1977): 3.
45. David A. Ward, "Evaluation Research for Corrections," in *Prisoners in America*, ed. Lloyd E. Ohlin (Englewood Cliffs, NJ: Prentice Hall, 1973), pp. 196, 198.
46. See, for example, the report of the American Friends Service Committee, *Struggle for Justice* (New York: Hill & Wang, 1971); and Jessica Mitford, *Kind and Unusual Punishment* (New York: Knopf, 1973).
47. C. S. Lewis, "The Humanitarian Theory of Punishment," *Res Judicatae* 6 (June 1953): 224–25.
48. Norval Morris, *The Future of Imprisonment* (Chicago: University of Chicago Press, 1974); Andrew von Hirsch, *Doing Justice: The Choice of Punishments* (New York: Hill & Wang, 1976).
49. " 'What Are Prisons For?,' " p. 38.
50. U.S. Code, Title 28, Section 994(k) (2001), emphasis added.
51. Mistretta v. United States, 488 U.S. 361 (1989).
52. "Believers in Prison Rehabilitation Told at Confab to 'Hang on to Hope,' " *Miami Herald* (24 June 1990), p. 5. See also Francis T. Cullen et al., "Is Rehabilitation Dead? The Myth of the Punitive Public," *Journal of Criminal Justice* 16, no. 4 (1988): 303–17.
53. Francis T. Cullen et al., "The Correctional Orientation of Prison Wardens: Is the Rehabilitative Ideal Supported?" *Criminology* 31 (February 1993): 69–92.
54. David Lester et al., *Correctional Counseling*, 2d ed. (Cincinnati, OH: Anderson, 1992).
55. Richard C. McCorkle, "Research Note: Punish and Rehabilitate? Public Attitude toward Six Common Crimes," *Crime & Delinquency* 39 (April 1993): 240–52; quotation is from p. 240.
56. See Violent Crime Control and Law Enforcement Act of 1994, Public Law 103–322 (13 September 1994), Title IX.
57. Charles H. Logan and Gerald G. Gaes, "Meta-Analysis and the Rehabilitation of Punishment," *Justice Quarterly* 10 (June 1993): 245–63.
58. State v. Romero, 775 P.2d 1233 (Ida. 1989).
59. Montana Code Annotated, Title 46, Section 46-18-101(2) (2001).
60. "California Gets Set to Shift on Sentencing Drug Users," *New York Times* (10 November 2000), p. 18.
61. Jack P. Gibbs, *Crime, Punishment and Deterrence* (New York: Elsevier, 1975), pp. ix, 11.
62. See Robert F. Meier, "Correlates of Deterrence: Problems of Theory and Method," *Journal of Criminal Justice* 7 (Spring 1979): 18–19.
63. See Robert F. Meier et al., "Sanctions, Peers, and Deviance: Preliminary Models of a

Social Control Process," *Sociological Quarterly* 25 (Winter 1984): 67–82; and Robert F. Meier, "Perspectives on the Concept of Social Control," *Annual Review of Sociology* 8 (1982): 35–55.

64. See, for example, National Institute of Justice, *Jailing Drunk Drivers: Impact on the Criminal Justice System* (Washington, DC: U.S. Government Printing Office, May 1985).
65. See Gerald R. Wheeler and Rodney V. Hissong, "Effects of Criminal Sanctions on Drunk Drivers: Beyond Incarceration," *Crime & Delinquency* 34 (January 1988): 29–42; and Harold G. Gransmick et al., "Reduction in Drunk Driving as a Response to Increased Threats of Shame, Embarrassment, and Legal Sanctions," *Criminology* 31 (February 1993): 41–68.
66. Rodney F. Kingsnorth et al., "Specific Deterrence and the DUI Offender: The Impact of a Decade of Reform," *Justice Quarterly* 10 (June 1993): 265–88; quotation is from p. 283.
67. J. David Hirschel et al., "The Failure of Arrest to Deter Spouse Abuse," *Journal of Research in Crime and Delinquency* 29 (February 1992): 7–33.
68. Joan McCord, "Deterrence of Domestic Violence: A Critical View of Research," *Journal of Research in Crime and Delinquency* 29 (May 1992): 229–39; quotation is from p. 237.
69. Gary Kleck, "Crime Control through the Private Use of Armed Force," *Social Problems* 35 (1988): 1–21. See also Gary Kleck, *Point Blank: Guns and Violence in America* (New York: Aldine de Gruyter, 1991).
70. David McDowall et al., "General Deterrence through Civilian Gun Ownership: An Evaluation of the Quasi-Experimental Evidence," *Criminology* 29 (November 1991): 554.
71. Eric L. Jensen and Linda K. Metsger, "A Test of the Deterrent Effect of Legislative Waiver on Violent Juvenile Crime," *Crime & Delinquency* 40 (January 1994): 96–104.
72. Derral Cheatwood, "Capital Punishment and the Deterrence of Violent Crime in Comparable Counties," *Criminal Justice Review* 18 (Autumn 1993): 165–81; quotation is from p. 165.
73. Ellen F. Sohn, "Antistalking Statutes: Do They Actually Protect Victims?" *Criminal Law Bulletin* (May/June 1994): 203–42.
74. Douglas A. Smith and Patrick R. Gartin, "Specifying Specific Deterrence: The Influence of Arrest on Future Criminal Activity," *American Sociological Review* 54 (February 1989): 94–106; quotation is from p. 102.
75. Eleni Apospori and Geoffrey Alpert, "Research Note: The Role of Differential Experience with the Criminal Justice System in Changes in Perceptions of Severity of Legal Sanctions over Time," *Crime & Delinquency* 39 (April 1993): 184–94; quotation is from p. 192.
76. Harold G. Grasmick and Donald E. Green, "Deterrence and the Morally Committed," *Sociological Quarterly* 22 (Winter 1981): 2, 13; and "Legal Punishment, Social Disapproval and Internalization as Inhibitors of Illegal Behavior," *Journal of Criminal Law and Criminology* 71 (Fall 1980): 325–35.
77. Irving Piliavin et al., "Crime, Deterrence, and Rational Choice," *American Sociological Review* 51 (February 1986): 101–19.
78. Matthew C. Scheider, "Deterrence and the Base Rate Fallacy: An Examination of Perceived Certainty," *Justice Quarterly* 18 (March 2001): 63–86; quotation is from p. 84.
79. "Chorus of Judicial Critics Assail Sentencing Guides," *New York Times* (17 April 1992), p. 1.
80. Pamala L. Griset, *Determinate Sentencing: The Promise and the Reality of Retributive Justice* (Albany: State University of New York Press, 1992).
81. "Ex–Prison Director Mocks Rehabilitation," *Seattle Times* (18 June 1975), p. 10.
82. Morris, *The Future of Imprisonment,* pp. 13, 15, 27.

CHAPTER

4

▶ Explaining delinquent and criminal behavior was a primary focus after the shootings in Littleton, Colorado, in April 1999. This photo from the Columbine High School yearbook features the Trenchcoat Mafia, a group to which the two student killers belonged. (Renato Rotolo/Getty Images)

Biological and Psychological Theories of Criminal Behavior

OUTLINE

Trenchcoat Mafia,
e are Josh, Joe, Chris, Horst, Chuck, Brian, Pauline, Nicole,
Kristen, Krista, plus Tad, Alex, Cory. Who says we're
rent? Insanity's healthy!
ember rocking parties at
isten's, foos-ball at Joe's,
and fencing at
hristopher's! Stay alive,
ay different, stay crazy!
Oh, and stay away from
CREAM SODA!!
Love Always,
The Chicks

This chapter brings together a wide variety of approaches to understanding criminal behavior, many of which were popular in the past, lost favor, and have been revived but with more sophisticated research. The current developments in biological and psychological theories are discussed against the background of the earlier contributions of the positive school and those who studied the relationship between body type and crime. We also consider the importance of genetic background as well as the possible relationship of the nervous system, endocrinology, and body chemistry to criminal behavior. We conclude with an analysis of the practical and legal implications of recent developments.

KEY TERMS

- behavior theory
- biocriminology
- cognitive development theory
- constitutional approach
- control group
- demonology
- guilty but mentally ill
- insanity defense
- learning theory
- phrenology
- psychiatry
- psychoanalysis
- sociobiology
- XYY chromosome abnormality

Fashions and fads in human thought affect many fields, and criminology is no exception. We have seen that in the 18th century the major emphasis regarding criminals was on a punishment philosophy that lost favor in the following century. During the 19th century the concept of the influence of biology on criminal behavior was strong, stemming from the theory of evolution of Charles Darwin, whose 1859 publication, *On the Origin of Species by Means of Natural Selection,* is ranked by some as one of the most important books ever written and criticized bitterly by others.

In criminology, biological and psychological explanations of behavior have been out of style for some time, but recently there has been a resurgence of interest in these explanations. This chapter presents some of the recent findings from studies of how the body and mind may affect behavior. Taken together, studies on the relationship between biology and crime leave no doubt that social and biological variables and their interactions are important to our understanding of the origins of antisocial behavior.

BIOLOGICAL FACTORS AND CRIME

Phrenology Theory of behavior based on the belief that the exterior of the skull corresponds to the interior and to the brain's conformation; thus phrenologists claim that a propensity toward certain types of behavior may be discovered by examining the bumps on the head.

Although the major biological theories of criminal behavior were developed in the 19th century, their origins can be found much earlier. One criminologist has traced back to Aristotle the belief that personality is determined by the shape of the skull. Belief in a relationship between criminal behavior and body type has been traced back to the 1500s, and the study of facial features and their relationship to crime, to the 1700s. In the latter part of the 1700s **phrenology** emerged as a discipline. Its development is associated mainly with the work of Franz Joseph Gall (1758–1828), who investigated the bumps and other irregularities of the skulls of those confined in penal and mental institutions. In addition, Gall studied the heads and head casts of persons who were not institutionalized and compared those findings to data on criminals. Phrenology is based on several propositions: that the exterior of the skull corresponds to the interior and to the brain's conformation; that the brain can be divided into functions or faculties that are related to the shape of the skull; and that, by measuring the shape of the skull, we can measure behavior.

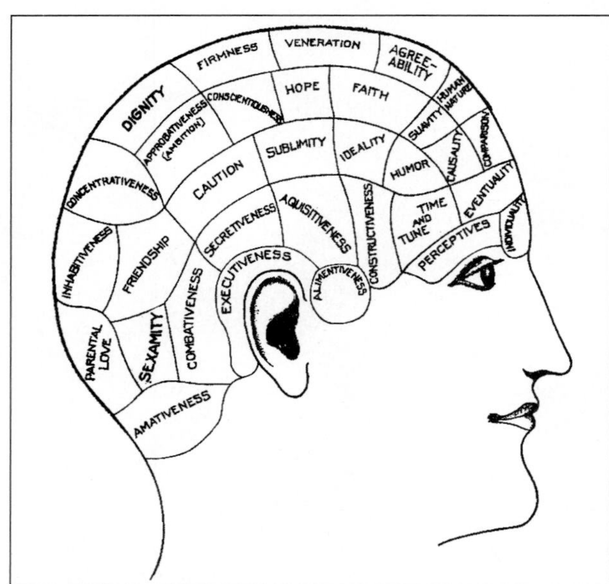

The association of brain functions with configurations of the brain was a concept espoused by early thinkers such as Franz Joseph Gall (1748–1828). Gall and others believed that the functions corresponded to bumps or irregularities on the head. (Bob McCoy)

Lombroso and the Positivists

If the study of phrenology is considered applicable, we are placing the beginning of scientific criminology about 70 years before the contributions of Cesare Lombroso and other positivists (see Chapter 3). With historical perspective, this may become a more commonly accepted conclusion, but today most scholars begin that study with Lombroso and his colleagues.

According to one criminologist, Lombroso (1835–1909) is "rarely discussed in a neutral tone; he is either adulated or condemned. 'In the history of criminology probably no name has been eulogized or attacked so much as [his].' "[1] Lombroso developed several categories of criminals, but he was best known for his concept of the biological, or born, criminal. He called such a person an *atavism,* a throwback or a reversion to prehuman creatures, and believed that he saw in criminals some of the characteristics of savages.[2]

Theories of evolution introduced during Lombroso's time argued that as humans evolved, their physical constitution changed, becoming more complex as it developed to a higher stage. Lombroso used these theories of evolution to support his belief that criminals were not merely physically different from noncriminals but physically inferior to them; criminals had not evolved as far as noncriminals. Lombroso also claimed that he had found biological characteristics that distinguished criminals according to the *kind* of crime they committed. Lombroso compared criminals to wild animals; both must be restrained to keep them from endangering others. But reforming the guilty is almost always an exception, claimed Lombroso. Most inmates are not rehabilitated in prison; many are worse for the experience. The state incarcerates offenders, and after they have served their sentences, they are released, which increases the danger to society because "the criminal always becomes more depraved in the promiscuity of the prison, and goes out more irritated and better armed against society."[3]

Lombroso was not in favor of short prison terms, which he felt only exposed inmates to other offenders and left no time for rehabilitation. He advocated alternatives such as "confinement at home, judicial admonition, fines, forced labor without imprisonment, local exile, corporal punishment, [and] conditional sentence." He advocated the probation system, which he claimed had been very successful in the United States. He supported the death penalty only as a last resort. He believed in restitution for crime victims, and he placed great emphasis on crime prevention.[4]

Besides the biological criminal, Lombroso recognized two other types, the criminaloid and the insane criminal. The *criminaloid* he defined as a person who is motivated by passion or some other emotional characteristic that, coupled with various factors, leads to criminal behavior. The *insane criminal* is one who is epileptic or psychotic and who, along with the idiot and the imbecile, is unfit for society. Like born criminals, Lambroso said, insane criminals cannot control their behavior, but they do not suffer the same stigma as born criminals.

Despite his development of the concepts of the insane criminal and the criminaloid, Lombroso's concept of the born criminal remained central to his analysis and was viewed by others as his main focus. According to a modern sociologist, "This basic concept of innate criminality became the dominant perspective on crime and triggered an onslaught of biological theorizing about crime."[5]

Other members of the positive school, such as Raffaelle Garofalo and Enrico Ferri (discussed in Chapter 3), shared Lombroso's explanations of criminal behavior but also emphasized the possible role of environmental or psychic factors. The belief that criminal behavior is inherited was tempered with the suggestion that inherited traits were not sufficient to *cause* criminal behavior.

Lombroso and the other positivists generated heated responses, ranging from high praise to scathing criticism. One scholar proclaimed that "his ideas proved so challenging that they gave an unprecedented impetus to the study of the offender. Any scholar . . . whose ideas after half a century possess vitality, merits an honorable place in the history of thought."[6]

Considerable criticism has been hurled at the positivists, especially at Lombroso, because of an *overemphasis* on biological causes of criminal behavior to the neglect of environmental factors.[7] One writer responded with these words:

> The fears of these critics that Lombroso diverted attention from social to individual phenomena reveal their basic misunderstanding of his work and its effect . . . Lombroso served to redirect emphasis from the crime to the criminal, not from social to individual factors.[8]

One criminological analysis of the work of Lombroso and other earlier contributors to our understanding of criminology from a positivist perspective focuses on the impact they had on the development of criminal anthropology in the United States. "Because criminal anthropologists' doctrine of the criminal as a physically anomalous human type has long been discredited, we tend to ignore their work." The result is that we do not recognize the impact these earlier criminal anthropologists had on some of the problems in criminology today, such as defining the methods that should be used for research, establishing the boundaries of the discipline, and deciding whether crime control or the production of knowledge should be the primary goal of anthropology. It is alleged that although a study of early criminal anthropology cannot solve these current issues, it can give us an understanding of how our problems evolved.[9]

Lombroso and the other positivists of his time are also important because they laid the foundation for a scientific and biological analysis of criminal behavior. In addition, some of the writers foresaw the need for changing the social structure and environment to ensure the effectiveness of crime prevention.

Physique and Crime

Constitutional approach An approach to explaining criminal behavior that assumes that behavior is influenced by the structure or physical characteristics of a person's body.

The **constitutional** (or physical) **approach** to the study of human behavior rests on the assumption that function is determined by structure. Applied to crime, constitutional approaches maintain that behavior is determined by the body's build, which may be the body type, the endocrine system, or some other physical or mental characteristic. The belief that criminal behavior is related to body type can be traced back to a 1926 translation by Ernst Kretschmer,[10] but the first real development of this approach began in the 1940s with the work of William H. Sheldon, who measured physique and compared body type with temperament. Sheldon defined three body types: ectomorph, endomorph, and mesomorph. The *ectomorph* is the tall, skinny body; the *endomorph,* the short, fat body; and the *mesomorph,* the athletic body. Sheldon identified three types of temperament that he claimed were associated with the three body types. His purpose was to lay a foundation for a systematic study of human behavior and human personality.[11]

Sheldon has been criticized for his samples, the implication being that he selected only persons who would support his theory,[12] and for failure to define the three body types precisely enough so that they could be distinguished.[13] He is also alleged to have overemphasized constitutional factors to the exclusion of environmental causes of crime. Sheldon reacted to the latter criticism by saying that he was not excluding environmental factors but only emphasizing constitutional factors because their importance had been neglected previously.

Two other researchers who focused on body type were Sheldon Glueck and Eleanor Glueck. They conducted many studies on the relationship of body type and criminal behavior, although they concentrated most of their research on juvenile delinquents. The Gluecks were two of the most prolific and most controversial writers in the field of constitutional criminology. They claimed that their research was of high quality, skillfully utilizing the precision control of samples of 500 delinquents and 500 nondelinquents, matched on age, general intelligence, ethnic/racial origins, and residence in underprivileged neighborhoods. Physicians, psychiatrists, anthropologists, and others were involved in gathering the data from the samples. They found delinquency to be associated with the mesomorphic body type.[14]

Some critics point out that the Gluecks' findings were not surprising, as many delinquent activities require a strong body build. After examining the researchers' data, others have concluded that the information was complicated and not significant because there was no specific combination of character, physique, and temperament that would permit a prediction about whether or not a young person would become delinquent.[15] Critics have also argued that since the delinquent sample was taken from "persistently delinquent" boys, the data could not be generalized to the total population of delinquents. Another criticism is that the Gluecks' concepts and measuring techniques were vague.[16]

Criticisms of the body-type studies of Sheldon and of the Gluecks led many to discredit the entire approach of explaining crime in terms of physique. Juan B. Cortés and others thought the approach had merit. In 1972 Cortés and Florence M. Gotti published the results of 10 years of research in which they reported finding a high correlation between mesomorphy and delinquency. Cortés warned, however, that his research did not show that body type *causes* delinquency, only that the two often occur together.[17]

Cortés's work has been criticized because it was based on small samples that were not selected randomly, did not precisely define measurement terms, and neglected the importance of the environment. His work is important, however, in establishing the *foundation* for a return to some concern with the genetic factor in criminal behavior. Cortés emphasized that *constitution* (which he said was a term used almost synonymously with *physique* and *body build*) was not fixed and unalterable but was a result of genetics and environment: "It is not, therefore, and should not be, heredity or environment, nor heredity versus environment nor heredity under or over environment, but only and always heredity *and* environment."[18] Therefore, it is necessary to look at heredity and examine what, if any, role genetic factors play in human behavior.

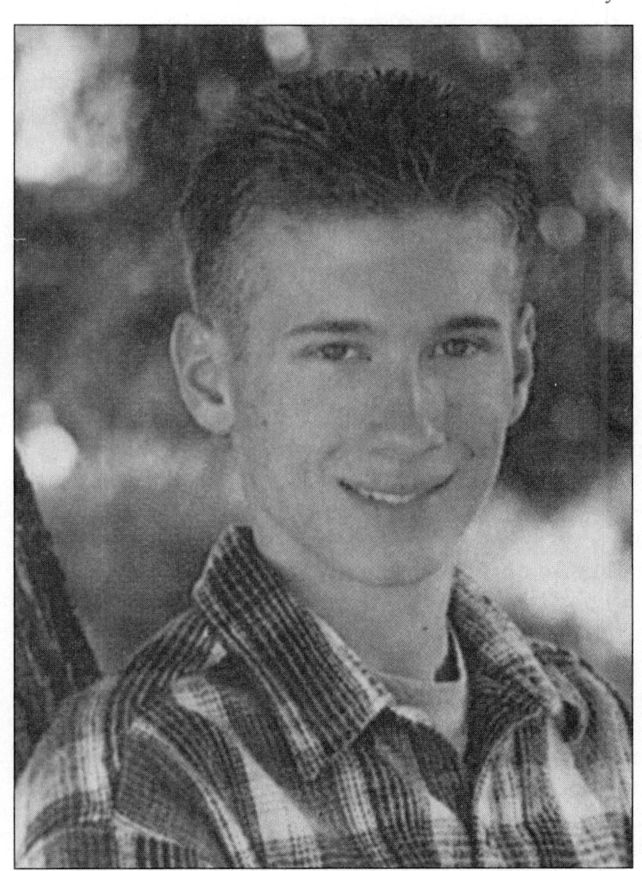

Eric Harris, one of two students who opened fire at Columbine High School in Littleton, Colorado, on 20 April 1999, killing 14 students (including themselves) and one teacher. This photograph appears in the school yearbook. (Getty Images)

Genetic Factors

Perhaps it was not too difficult for some of the early students of criminal behavior to conclude that the differences between criminals and noncriminals *caused* the criminal behavior and that these differences are inherited. The criminal was seen as one who was predisposed or predetermined by biological factors to commit crimes. The next step was to look at the family background to see whether the family had a history of criminal behavior. If so, it was assumed that criminality must be inherited.

Family Studies

Most of the early studies of family histories, conducted in an effort to show the relationship between heredity and crime as well as other forms of deviant behavior, have been discredited as lacking enough methodological sophistication to permit significant conclusions.[19]

Sheldon and Eleanor Glueck included family histories in their comparisons of delinquents and nondelinquents. They found that more delinquent than nondelinquent boys came from families characterized by a history of delinquency and crime, with the criminality of the father as the best predictor.[20]

In his pursuit of evidence to disprove Lombroso's theory of the born criminal, Charles Goring used statistical techniques to measure the degree of correlation, or resemblance, of members within a family line. He compared brothers as well as fathers and sons, attempting to show that the correlations for general criminality, as measured by imprisonment, were as high as for two other categories he measured: (1) ordinary physical traits and features and (2) inherited defects, insanity, and mental disease. He attempted to show that the correlations were the result of heredity, not environment. He used several arguments to support his position, such as the discovery that boys who were taken out of the home early in life became criminals as frequently as did those who remained longer in the home with their fathers. Also, he found the correlations as high for sex crimes (in which presumably the fathers would try to conceal their activities) as for stealing (in which the fathers might set an example for their sons).[21]

Goring's findings may be criticized on several grounds. He did not measure environmental influences adequately; indeed, it is questionable whether all environmental variables can be isolated. He did not consider criminality among sisters. He offered no proof of his assumption that mental ability is inherited. He assumed that removing a boy from his criminal father's home and placing him in some other environment at an early age was putting him into a noncriminal environment.

Although the earlier studies of families have been criticized severely, they influenced some policy decisions. The belief that criminality was inherited led to the passage of laws that permitted compulsory sterilization of persons thought to be capable of passing on to their children genes that would result in criminal behavior. These statutes were upheld by earlier courts.[22]

The basic problem with these family studies was that they could not control for environment. Exhibit 4.1 illustrates the problem. In the studies, the parents who produced the children, thereby determining their genetic background, socialized them as well; thus, genetics and environment were inseparable. This problem led to two other methods of studying genetic factors and criminality: the study of twins and adoptees, discussed below. It led also to the development of environmental and learning theories of behavior to explain generations of deviance and violence within families.[23]

Studies of Twins

If behavior is inherited, we would expect to find the same behavior among people with identical genes. Thus, identical twins should behave alike. Fraternal twins (nonidentical) of the same gender have about 50 percent identical genes; they should engage in similar behaviors.

Early studies of twins led researchers to conclude that heredity plays a major role in explaining behavior, but most of these studies were based on small samples. Until recently, the most recognized studies of twins were those conducted by Karl O. Christiansen, who avoided many of the sampling problems of the earlier studies. Christiansen studied the incidence of criminal behavior among 3,586 twins in one region of Denmark between 1881 and 1910. He reported that if one twin engaged in criminal behavior, the probability that his or her identical twin also would do so was 35 percent, compared with only 12 percent if the twins were not identical.[24]

Sarnoff A. Mednick and his associates updated the Christiansen study and concluded "that genetic factors account for some of the variables associated with anti-social behavior."[25] The twin studies of Mednick and others have been criticized on methodological grounds. Two scholars concluded that, despite the methodological errors, there is evidence of a correlation between genetic factors and criminality,

> but the large number of methodological flaws and limitations in the research should make one cautious in drawing any causal inferences at this point in time. Our review leads us to the inevitable conclusion that current genetic research on crime has been

EXHIBIT 4.1
Families and Crime

A *New York Times* article related the events surrounding the life of 15-year-old Garland Hampton, incarcerated in a county jail while awaiting trial for the murder of a fellow gang member. At age 10 Hampton was apprehended for stealing a bicycle, at age 12 he was accused of shooting and wounding a gang rival, and at age 14 he was apprehended for carrying a gun and being in possession of cocaine.

Hampton's home life might have suggested to earlier theorists (and perhaps to some of the lay public today) that he had *inherited* a criminal lifestyle. According to the *Times*,

> When other children were hearing fairy tales, Garland Hampton heard bedtime stories about the day Uncle Robert killed two Milwaukee police officers, or the time Grandma, with both barrels, blew away the father of two of her children back in '62. By the time he was nine, he had seen his mother kill her boyfriend.[1]

Hampton said he did not want people to feel sorry for him, but he described his life as "running through hell with a gasoline suit on." He claims that nothing good has happened to him during his young life. Hampton has been abused and neglected, experienced violence in his home, and been subjected to inconsistent treatment by his family—all variables that are predictive of violence among youth. Garland Hampton grew up in an environment in which he saw parents, grandparents, neighbors, and acquaintances beating and killing. He had no time for childhood. In his own words, "I feel like I been grown my whole life."

In previous times, criminologists and others concluded that violence among such youths was caused by their families. Today criminologists recognize that although a child might experience one or more factors conducive to becoming violent, not all children who experience those factors become violent. Today it is the *interaction* of biological, social, and cultural factors that is used to explain the violence of families over time.

1. "When the Family Heirloom Is Homicide," *New York Times* (12 December 1994), p. 1. The facts about Garland Hampton are summarized from this article.

> poorly designed, ambiguously reported, and exceedingly inadequate in addressing the relevant issues . . . These studies have muddied the already turbid waters of genetic research on crime.[26]

Mednick and one of his graduate students responded to this article by alleging that the criticisms were too general and amounted to little more than name-calling. They referred to the article as one that denigrates "the work of the many serious and honest researchers in this field."[27]

Among other critics of the Danish twin studies are Michael Gottfredson and Travis Hirschi, whose extensive criticism has "raised doubts as to how much [each study] validates the theory of inherited criminal potential."[28]

Finally, a more recent study of the criminal and psychiatric histories of twins found no evidence of an independent genetic basis for behavior. Rather, the study found that the number and types of criminal convictions were related to psychiatric diagnosis. For example, diagnosed male schizophrenics were significantly more likely to be convicted than males diagnosed with affective psychosis. Furthermore, the schizophrenics were more likely than the affective group to be younger at first conviction and to commit more violent offenses.[29]

Adoption Studies

Concern with the problem of separating the influence of environment and of heredity, even in the study of twins, has led some researchers to select samples of adoptees for study. Most adoptees are placed at birth, and many do not know their biological parents. Many do not even know they are adopted, at least not during their formative years.

American parents pose with their newly adopted Korean children. Although many children are adopted at birth, an increasing number of foreign-born children are being adopted as infants or even toddlers by American couples. Social scientists study these and other adoptions in their efforts to determine the influence of genetics and environment in human behavior. (Laura Dwight/Corbis)

Mednick and his associates conducted adoption studies utilizing a sample of about 72,000 from Denmark's adoption register. According to the investigators, these and other studies of adoptees suggest that we should not ignore the genetic factor in explaining criminal behavior.[30] Mednick's studies have come under fire, and even he and his associates have raised some pertinent questions about the research. In Denmark efforts are made to place adoptable children in homogeneous environments, and the evidence shows that this approach is successful. Most babies born to lower-class parents are adopted by lower-class parents. It is also important to understand that Denmark is a rather homogeneous society. These and other factors suggesting that environment may play a part in criminal behavior have been studied by Mednick and his associates, but these researchers remain firm in their belief that there is also some association between genetic factors and criminal behavior. Critics are not so sure!

Chromosomal Abnormality

The possible relationship between chromosomal abnormality and criminal behavior has been the subject of research in recent years. The most common area of investigation has been the **XYY chromosome abnormality.** The X chromosome is female; the Y, male. Men are XY, and women XX. The XYY is a man with an extra Y chromosome. The abnormality was discovered in 1961, but it did not receive much attention until papers were published in the mid-1960s by Scottish researchers who studied 197 inmates and found that a significant number of them were XYY.[31]

XYY chromosome abnormality Presence of an extra Y chromosome in a male. It has been argued that this abnormality is related to criminal behavior, but the evidence of a relationship is not supported strongly. Most courts refuse to admit evidence of this abnormality as a defense to a criminal act.

Later studies have not consistently found that XYY men are more likely to be criminals than are men without the chromosomal abnormality, but the studies were based on very small and nonrandom samples that prevent generalization. They did show that XYY men are more introverted and have more asocial attitudes than the rest of the population, and that they have a tendency to be both gay and aggressive.[32]

Control group In an experiment with two or more groups, the control group is used as a standard and is not introduced to the experimental variable. The control group is similar to the experimental group in all other relevant factors. Investigators measure the differences between the control and experimental groups before and after the variable is used with the experimental group.

What was needed was a larger study using a **control group** of noncriminals. In 1977 several investigators reported the results of a study conducted in Denmark on all of the 31,436 men who were born in Copenhagen during a four-year period and who were over a certain height. Their blood was checked for chromosome composition; only 12 XYY men were found. The investigators discovered that the XYY men had engaged in "significantly more criminal behavior than did the XY men of their age, height, intelligence, and social class," but they had not engaged in violent behavior. The small number of XYY men in the sample, however, limits the conclusions that can be drawn.[33] One author noted, "Even major contemporary proponents of biological explanations dismiss the XYY theory as scientifically invalid."[34]

Genetics and Behavior: A Modern View

The early criminologists did not have modern research tools; most of their studies were based on small samples, and their analyses of data were simplistic. In the past hundred years, with the development of modern tools of analysis and the increased sophistication of the study of genetics, the conclusions of the early studies have been questioned and, in many cases, rejected. In recent decades, little attention has been paid to genetic explanations of criminal behavior; many criminologists have thought it unnecessary to tell their students about these earlier approaches.

Numerous studies have explored the relationship between heredity and behavior. These studies are controversial, but it is significant that they are gaining more attention and that scholars are trying to improve our understanding of the relationship between biology and behavior. Some of these studies suggest that sexual orientation is related to heredity, that alcoholism is linked to heredity, that the ability to learn grammar might be controlled by genes, and that body fat may be controlled by heredity. But despite the renewed interest in the relationship between genetics and behavior, the findings draw the skepticism of many, and the studies must be interpreted carefully.

Two criminologists who reviewed the major studies of the relationship between biology and crime concluded:

> [C]urrent genetic research on crime has been poorly designed, ambiguously reported, and exceedingly inadequate in addressing the relevant issues.[35]

Perhaps this will change with the development of scientific knowledge about human genomes, discussed in Exhibit 4.2. In her presidential address to the American Society of Criminology at its 1998 annual meeting, sociologist Margaret A. Zahn spoke directly to the potentially rich source of data contained in an application of genomic sciences to the understanding of human behavior: "It is important, if not imperative, that we become aware of the biological and biochemical bases for behavior and incorporate them, *where relevant*, into our theories about violent crime and its consequences."[36]

Anthony Walsh, who was challenged by Zahn's appeal, suggested that "it is time for mainstream criminology to at least pull back its blinders and peek at what behavior genetics has to offer." Walsh attempted to show how behavior genetics could enhance our understanding of criminal behavior through the theory of anomie/strain, which is discussed in Chapter 5 (see p. 126). Walsh emphasized that behavior genetics is not a *biological* perspective of human behavior but rather a *biosocial perspective* "that takes seriously the proposition that all human traits, abilities, and behaviors are the result of the interplay of genetics and environments, and it is the only perspective with the research tools to untangle their effects." Walsh concludes:

> The question is no longer if genes affect human behavior, but how and under what circumstances they do. When we are able to dispassionately explore the individual

EXHIBIT 4.2

The Human Genome Project

Humans are more closely related to dogs than to mice, reported some of the professional research teams attending a genome conference in Cold Spring Harbor, New York, in May 2001. The *genome,* first deciphered in 2000, maps or "spells" all of our genes. It is being studied by two major groups: the publicly funded Human Genome Project, composed of the U.S. Department of Energy, the National Institutes of Health, universities and colleges in the United States and other nations, and the Wellcome Trust in England. It is directed by Francis Collins, a molecular geneticist. The second group, Gelera Genomics, which is privately funded, is based in Rockville, Maryland.

The success of these research projects is remarkable. "Results from the Human Gene Project are coming in at such a furious pace, in such astounding detail, that gene scientists can't scramble fast enough to keep up."[1]

These discoveries may enable geneticists to identify the causes of diseases, such as cancer, arthritis, and diabetes, as well as to ascertain what causes hair and eye color. The implications for analyzing human behavior, including criminal behavior, are exciting.

1. "Fast-Moving Research Is Changing View of Life; Discoveries with Human Genome Open New Vistas," *Milwaukee Journal Sentinel* (23 May 2001), p. 7.

correlates of criminal behavior, we will be in a much better position to develop theories that are vertically integrated with propositions from the more fundamental sciences. The history of science tells us that cross-disciplinary fertilization by a more mature science has, without exception, proven to be of immense value to the immature science. Criminology will be no exception."[37]

Another area of biology that some believe is associated with criminal behavior is that of the nervous system.

Neurological Factors[38]

All the nervous systems enclosed within the body portions of the skull and spine are part of the *central nervous system (CNS).* Complex sensory information is processed in the CNS, which controls voluntary muscle movement as well. One basic test of the CNS's functioning is the electroencephalogram (EEG), which creates graphic images of the brain's activities. The EEG has been the most common tool for research on the relationship between the CNS and criminal behavior, with some findings that "incarcerated individuals tend to have higher proportions of abnormal EEGs than do individuals in the general population."[39] The relationship between epilepsy and criminal behavior has been tested, too, but the results have failed as yet to resolve the issue of whether or not epilepsy is related significantly to crime.[40]

A second way to examine the CNS's functioning is through neuropsychological tests, which combine psychological observation with neurological evidence from the nervous system. These tests include X rays; computerized axial tomography (CAT), which takes X rays of the brain; magnetic resonance imaging (MRI), which permits viewing detailed images of the brain or other parts of the body; and spinal taps, which determine whether the brain has been damaged. The results may be used to analyze the relationship between brain damage and criminal behavior. "Results of neuropsychological tests administered to criminals suggest that violent, impulsive individuals suffer from damage to specific brain areas," which may occur before birth or at delivery. Studies show, too, that criminals suffer injury with resulting unconsciousness earlier in life than noncriminals do.[41]

Another method of studying the neurological system and its relationship to behavior is positron emission tomography (PET), described by Mayo Clinic Rochester's researchers as "the most sophisticated nuclear imaging tool to date."[42] PET scanning monitors the brain's radioactive substances, showing which areas of the brain are working hardest when the individual is engaged in a particular thought process. PET is also used to measure other organs and is diagnostic in discovering diseases, such as cancer, before they are detected by other measures.

PET has been used to determine differences between the thought processes and emotions of men and women as well as to differentiate between murderers and nonviolent criminals. More recently, PET has been used to reveal underlying causes of psychiatric illness and mental diseases of aging, which affect 1 in 10 people and consume about one-half of the national health budget. Depression and other emotional problems also may be investigated through the use of PET scans. Researchers from various disciplines are working together to understand and explain "evolution's greatest achievement"—the human brain.[43]

Some researchers have concluded that "aggressive or violent behavior has to be explained in part by biology" and in part by the fact that the brain adapts physically to the environmental threats of poverty, abuse, neglect, and sensory deprivation. The adaptations may "make some genetically vulnerable children more prone to violence."[44] Adrian Raine, a psychologist at the University of Southern California in Los Angeles, studied 4,000 Danish babies and concluded that an "overwhelming number of the babies who suffered birth complications were also rejected by their mothers and went on to become criminals." According to Raine, there is evidence that the brains of murderers function differently from those of nonmurderers, and this provides "objective evidence of the connection between brain function and criminal behavior."[45]

The use of scientific findings, such as those of Raine, may be enhanced by media exposure. Consider, for example, the article highlighted in Media Focus 4.1. Do you think that such information helps the public understand such atrocities as the 1999 shootings at Columbine High School?

Researchers at the University of Iowa, the National Institute of Mental Health, and the University of Arizona have engaged in independent studies utilizing PET to map the brain's differences. They report that damage to only the part of the brain that controls social and personal decisions can leave a person with an inability to make those decisions. Depression, fear arousal, and self-induced anxiety may be measured by brain scans such as PET. Emotional responses of men and women may differ in degree; some researchers believe they differ in kind as well. Whatever the case, researchers say they can pinpoint "where emotions reside in the brain, and how they work in concert with the physical body."[46]

According to an article in the *Journal of the American Medical Association:*

> CAT and PET scans and MRI are powerful tools that should provide us with a tremendous amount of information about how the brain develops in association with behavioral development. These instruments may help us solve some of biology's greatest remaining mysteries, such as how the brain establishes connections, how experiences alter development, how the tremendous changes that occur in the brain during the first year or two of a child's life are related to the profound changes that occur in his or her behavior.[47]

Neuroendocrinology

Neuroendocrinologists have attributed criminal behavior to an imbalance of the body's chemicals. The endocrine, or glandular, system and its relationship to criminal behavior were the focus of a 1928 book entitled *The New Criminology.* At

Media Focus 4.1

Can the Media Introduce the Public to Science?

The maxim "Publish or perish," which is often imposed on research university faculties, leads to numerous scientific publications in professional journals. If read at all, most of these articles are read only by colleagues (or administrators evaluating the authors) and are generally unavailable to the average person. They are also quite difficult to read for the individual who is not professionally educated in that particular science.

The media are criticized for saturating the public with too much information on crimes of national and international interest. It is even suggested (as noted in Media Focus 5.1, p. 150) that media attention to some crimes may cause others to copy those crimes, thus increasing the crime rates. But what about media attempts to familiarize the public with scientific findings in language that ordinary people can understand?

Consider, for example, a *USA Today* headline on 29 April 1999, nine days after the 20 April 1999 shootings at Columbine High School in Littleton, Colorado. Two students, Eric Harris and Dylan Klebold, opened fire in their school, killing a teacher and 12 students, and wounding several others, before taking their own lives.

The *USA Today* article is entitled "Chemistry of a Killer: Is It in the Brain?" The article discusses the scientific works of scholars who have studied the relationship between the brain and behavior, especially criminal behavior. In particular, it mentions the works of Dr. Adrian Raine of the University of Southern California, who is referred to in this text. The article quotes Dr. Raine as stating, "There is clearly a biological predisposition to violence." Raine, who compared the brains of 41 murderers to those of 41 nonviolent persons who were matched for gender and age, concluded that "murderers have poorer functioning of the . . . part of the brain . . . that controls regulating behaviors—the part that says, 'wait a minute.' " In another study, in which the brains of murderers from healthy, stable backgrounds were compared to those of murderers from abusive, dysfunctional backgrounds, Raine found that those from the better home environments had the poorest brain functioning.[1]

The *USA Today* article also presented the views of scientists who do not agree that there are genetic links to violence. For example, it referred to psychologist John Cole of Duke University, who says there was no evidence of dysfunction in the brains of the two involved in the Columbine shootings.

1. "Chemistry of a Killer: Is It in the Brain?" *USA Today* (29 April 1999), p. 2.

that time, it was alleged that "the glandular theory of crime accounts for all the discrepancies, errors, oversights and inadequacies of the earlier explanations," a conclusion that was cited and criticized by a well-known anthropologist in 1941.[48]

Research on animals and humans has disclosed a relationship between male hormones and behavior, with lower levels of certain hormones in men who are more dominant, aggressive, and hostile than the average man.[49] Research suggesting a relationship between female hormones and the reduction of the male sex drive and potency has led to chemical castration as a method of treating sex offenders. Researchers claim that these findings should be considered tentative, as other research does not show a significant relationship between hormones and male behavior.[50]

Among women, premenstrual tension, which affects about 25 percent of the female population, appears to be associated with the imbalance of the two female hormones, estrogen and progesterone. Also, there appears to be a relationship between the presence of premenstrual and menstrual tension and the number of suicides, suicide attempts, admissions to a medical facility for psychiatric illness or acute medical and surgical reasons, and criminal acts. Researchers are quick to point out, however, that a cause-and-effect relationship between endocrine factors and behavior cannot be assumed, because endocrine factors do not work independently of other factors. For example, one researcher found that women who complained that they were irritable during premenstrual and menstrual periods were more likely to be irritable at other times than were women who did not complain.[51]

In 1995 researchers at the Johns Hopkins University in Baltimore announced their findings that male mice bred to lack a gene that is essential to the production of nitric oxide were more aggressive than other mice. Nitric oxide is a "molecule that allows nerve cells to communicate." According to the researchers mice that lack this chemical are "relentlessly aggressive against their fellow males, often to the point of killing them." They pursue female mice "monomaniacally, mounting them repeatedly even when the females are not in heat and screech vocally in apparent protest." The researchers warned their readers that drawing conclusions about humans from these studies was not reasonable, but they suggested that nitric oxide serves as a brake on aggressive behavior and that the lack of the chemical leads to "wild, impulsive activity."[52]

Scientists have reported that the size of a certain region at the base of the brain may be associated with transsexuality. The roots of sexuality are thought to be within this area, which has been found to be about 50 percent larger in men than in women, and almost 60 percent larger in men than in male-to-female transsexuals (men who undergo surgery to change their bodies from male to female). It may explain why male-to-female transsexuals describe themselves as "women trapped in men's bodies." Because transsexuality is rare, it took the researchers 11 years to collect six brains from deceased transsexuals in order to study them. Obviously the study is limited in its implications, but it may suggest a biological basis for sexual orientation, similar to the biological differences found between the brains of heterosexual and gay males. Some researchers have found the brains of the latter more similar to those of women than to those of other men.[53]

Neurochemistry

Scientists have been looking at a possible relationship between criminal behavior and diet. In October 1983 the National Conference on Nutrition and Behavior focused on an issue of growing recognition—the effects on human behavior of nutrition (or its lack) and of chemicals, food additives, or preservatives. A later publication supported by the Robert J. Kutak Foundation and the National Institute of Corrections summarizes briefly the current complex information on the relationship between behavior and diet and its implications for understanding criminal behavior. Diana Fishbein and Susan Pease begin their publication with a brief review of the study of **biocriminology,** which is the introduction of biological variables into modern criminology.[54]

Biocriminology The introduction of biological variables into the study of criminology.

After a literature review Fishbein and Pease conclude that the evidence is not yet sufficient to support a causal relationship between diet and criminal behavior. "Nevertheless," they add, "we do feel that current findings justify further attention to the possibility of a diet/behavior link that is relevant to the criminal justice system."[55]

The relationship between diet and behavior may also be illustrated by examples from other cultures. For example, millions of Chinese children have been diagnosed with having a serious lack of iodine in their diet. The Chinese Public Health Ministry estimates that approximately 10 million Chinese children are mentally retarded as a result of this deficiency. The Chinese government has plans to eradicate the problem in the near future, but the implications are serious for now. The chair of the Department of International Health at Emory University in Atlanta, Georgia, concluded:

> The whole intellectual fabric of a large portion of the population is being dulled . . . With the lack of iodine, the brain just does not wire correctly in early development.[56]

Autonomic Nervous System Studies

Another area of biological study involves the autonomic nervous system (ANS), which "mediates physiological activity associated with emotions . . . Examples of peripheral manifestations of ANS activity include changes in heart rate, blood pressure, respiration, muscle tension, pupillary size, and electrical activity of the skin," the last being the most frequently used measure of the psychophysiological characteristics of antisocial persons.[57]

Psychologists have studied aggressive, highly impulsive, antisocial criminals who appear to have little or no concern for society's values. This lack of concern contributes to their difficulties in establishing meaningful relationships and in behaving in an acceptable manner.

We might consider a simple example. In order to learn not to steal, a child must be taught—socialized—that it is wrong to take the property of others without their permission. Usually this socialization occurs within the family, which acts as a censuring agent. The appropriate fear response is developed. Children learn to fear punishment if they steal, and that fear enables them to inhibit their stealing impulses. Antisocial children do not learn adequate initial fear responses; thus, they may not anticipate negative reactions if they steal. The fear inhibitor does not work to repress their stealing impulses.

How does this factor relate to ANS? The ANS is the primary control of the fear response. If children have quick ANS responses, they learn to react to stimuli with fear, and generally that fear inhibits their desire to steal. Children who have slow ANS responses learn slowly to inhibit stealing, if at all. A number of studies suggest that those who exhibit criminal behavior tend to have slower-than-average ANS responses.[58]

Attention Deficit Disorder (ADD)

The most commonly diagnosed psychiatric condition among U.S. children today is attention deficit disorder (ADD) or, to use the more recent name, attention deficit hyperactivity disorder (ADHD). The disorder has also been referred to as minimal brain dysfunction, hyperactivity, and hyperkinesis. It affects approximately 3 percent of U.S. children and is manifested by inattentiveness, difficulty in stifling inconvenient impulses, daydreaming, not finishing projects, repeatedly making careless mistakes, switching haphazardly from one activity to another, problems with obeying instructions, and other behaviors that inhibit school, work, and social relationships. Some of the symptoms are common in many people, but in ADD or ADHD children the characteristics reach such a critical level that the children are diagnosed as having the psychiatric disorder.[59]

It is difficult to diagnosis ADD because the symptoms are not consistent. The disorder, which is more common among boys than among girls (although in adults the prevalence of the disorder may be equally common among women and men), may result in a child's disruptive behavior in the classroom and difficulty on the playground. Or the child might be unruly in the classroom one day and show no symptoms of ADD on another day. There is a lack of agreement concerning when to determine that a child's behavior constitutes a psychiatric disorder. Scholars have described children with ADD as follows:

> Many of these children are also impulsive. They seem irritable and impatient, unable to tolerate delay or frustration. They act before thinking and do not wait their turn. In conversation they interrupt, talk too much, too loud, and too fast, and blurt out whatever comes to mind. They seem to be constantly pestering parents, teachers, and other children. They cannot keep their hands to themselves, and often appear to be reckless, clumsy, and accident-prone.[60]

It is the association of ADD with other disorders in children that is a cause for concern in those studying delinquent and criminal behavior. ADD children are more likely to suffer from "atypical depression, anxiety disorders, impaired speech or hearing, mild retardation, and traumatic stress reactions." Many of them (one-third to one-half) develop major depression or anxiety disorders. Many are "easily angered and provoked to agression, or seemingly callous, manipulative, and egocentric. They intimidate other children, start fights, and throw tantrums." In addition to these types of conduct disorder, many ADD children also suffer from learning disabilities.[61]

ADD has at one time or another been blamed on allergies, vitamin deficiencies, radiation, lead, sugar, and fluorescent lights. All of these alleged causes are rejected today. Although there is no agreement on the precise cause of ADD, "[m]ost experts agree that ADD is a brain disorder with a biological basis. A genetic influence is suggested by studies comparing identical with fraternal twins and by the high rates of ADD . . . found in the families of children with the disorder."[62]

Experts do not agree on the extent to which children diagnosed with ADD should be medicated, if at all. Nor do they agree on the drugs to prescribe. It does appear, however, that ADD children can be diagnosed and treated, although treatment is expensive. The diagnosis process may involve numerous medical tests as well as examinations of intelligence and academic achievement; interviews with parents, siblings, teachers, and others who work with the children; and discussions with the subjects themselves.[63]

PSYCHOLOGICAL THEORIES OF CRIMINAL BEHAVIOR

Biologists and chemists are not the only professionals to link behavior to physical characteristics. Psychologists have done so, too. Early psychologists attempted to explain criminal behavior by means of the trait we call *intelligence,* which they assumed to be inherited. Family studies were their sources of data. As the researchers traced criminality through generations of the same families, they concluded that inherited mental retardation was the *cause* of crime. Earlier in the chapter we noted some of the problems with these early studies, which were preceded by other, also problematic attempts to explain criminal behavior in terms of the mind or spirit.[64]

Demonology Belief that persons are possessed by evil spirits that cause crime and other evil behavior and that this behavior can be eliminated only when the spirits are eliminated.

One of the most popular explanations of criminal behavior was **demonology.** Individuals were thought to be possessed by spirits, which caused good or evil behavior. In medieval times people believed that the deviant behavior could not be changed unless the bad spirits were banished. One method of treating criminal behavior was to use a crude stone to cut a hole in the skull of a person thought to be possessed by devils. The process, called *trephining,* supposedly permitted the evil spirits to escape. (There is evidence that some people survived the surgery.) But the usual treatment for evil spirits was *exorcism,* which included having the "possessed" person drink horrible concoctions, pray, and make strange noises. Later it was assumed that the only way to drive out the devils was to insult them or to make the body an unpleasant place for them to inhabit; sufferers underwent flogging and other forms of corporal punishment. During the latter part of the 15th century, the belief arose that some possessed people were actively and deliberately working with the devil of their own free will. Society reacted to this alleged witchcraft by imposing the death penalty.

In the 18th century, scholars began developing knowledge about human anatomy, physiology, neurology, general medicine, and chemistry. The discovery of an organic basis for many physical illnesses led to similar applications for some mental illnesses. These findings replaced the demonological theory of causation and dominated the fields of psychology and psychiatry until 1915. By the beginning of the 20th century, a new viewpoint in psychiatry had been created with the argument that psychological problems could *cause* mental illness.

SWANSEA UNIVERSITY LIBRARY

Psychiatric Approach

Psychiatry A field of medicine that specializes in the understanding, diagnosis, treatment, and prevention of mental problems.

Psychoanalysis A special branch of psychiatry based on the theories of Sigmund Freud and employing a particular personality theory and method of treatment; the approach concentrates on individual case study.

The field of medicine that specializes in the understanding, diagnosis, treatment, and prevention of mental problems is **psychiatry. Psychoanalysis** is a branch of psychiatry based on the theories of Sigmund Freud; it employs particular personality theory and a specific treatment method, usually the individual case study. Psychiatry views each individual as a unique personality who can be understood only by a thorough case study.

The use of the case study in psychiatry characterized the work of William Healy, who is credited with shifting the positivists' emphasis from anatomical characteristics to psychological and social elements. Healy and his colleagues believed that the only way to find the roots or causes of delinquent behavior was to delve deeply into the individual's background, especially his or her emotional development. They measured personality disorders and environmental pathologies as well, maintaining that delinquency is purposive behavior that results when children are frustrated in their attempts to fulfill some of their basic needs. Healy and his associates found that delinquents had a higher frequency of personality defects and disorders than nondelinquents.[65]

Despite their popularization of the case study method, Healy and his colleagues may be criticized for basing their studies on vaguely defined terms, giving little information on how they measured the concepts and characteristics, and using samples too small to permit generalization to the total population of delinquents.

Sigmund Freud (1856–1939), who is credited with having made the greatest contribution to the development of psychoanalytic theory, did not advance a theory of criminality per se. However, his theories attempted to explain all behavior and, in so doing, have implications for criminology. The psychoanalytic theories of Freud and his colleagues introduced the concept of the *unconscious,* along with techniques for probing that element of the personality, and emphasized that all human behavior is motivated and purposive.

The works of Sigmund Freud (1856–1939), an Austrian neurologist and the founder of psychoanalysis, have been influential in the development of psychological theories of human behavior for over half a century. (Getty Images)

According to Freud, humans have mental conflicts because of desires and energies that are repressed into the unconscious. These urges, ideas, desires, and instincts are basic, but they are repressed because of society's morality. People try frequently to express these natural drives in some way, often indirect, to avoid the reactions of others. Dreams are one example of indirect expression.

Freud saw original human nature as assertive and aggressive. Aggression is not learned but is rooted deeply in early childhood experiences. We all have criminal tendencies, but during the socialization process most of us learn to control those tendencies by developing strong and effective inner controls. The improperly socialized child does not develop an ability to control impulses and instead either acts them out or projects them inward. In the case of the latter, the child may become neurotic; in the case of the former, delinquent.[66]

The main exhibit hall of the 1992 meeting of the American Psychiatric Association (APA) suggested the waning influence of Freud: "No sign of Freud was evident," reported a news article on the meeting. Rather, the hall featured drug therapy displays, and many of the professional papers carried titles suggesting that drug prescriptions are in vogue for treating psychological and psychiatric problems. There was some evidence of an attempt to integrate social and biological sciences, but the APA president and others suggested that the profession had gone overboard for the biomedical model of mental disease. Clearly the use of drug therapy dominated.[67]

The dominance of drug therapy over psychoanalysis continues to draw media attention. For example, the prescription drug Prozac is used widely to treat depression. A typical news article notes this trend:

> [P]sychiatry is moving increasingly toward biological explanations. Researchers have linked physical and chemical disturbances in the synthesizing of new compounds that affect these disturbances. Prozac, for example, offsets imbalances of serotonin, a brain chemical that has been linked to depression.[68]

The psychiatric approach may be criticized for several reasons. The terms are vague, no operational definitions for most concepts are given, and most of the data are open to the analyst's subjective interpretation. Moreover, the research has been based on small samples that are selected primarily from psychiatric patients, many of whom are institutionalized. The use of control groups has not been adequate. The individual is the focus of the psychiatric approach, and this focus does not permit generalizations of *patterns* of behavior. The emphasis on early childhood experiences has been questioned by social scientists, who de-emphasize the deterministic nature of these experiences, arguing that their impact can be decreased or even eliminated through proper training.[69]

Personality Theory

Emotional conflict and personality deviation characterize many criminals, especially habitual offenders, leading some theorists to conclude that such deviations cause criminal behavior. But the critical questions are whether these factors distinguish criminals from law-abiding persons and, if so, whether the traits *cause* the illegal behavior. A number of early researchers found such differences,[70] but others found evidence that questioned the relationship between personality traits and criminal behavior.[71]

The earlier studies emphasized the frequency of an association between mental disorders and crime. The belief that mental disorders cause criminal behavior led to confinement of the mentally ill in jails and prisons rather than in public hospitals. A report from the National Institute of Justice points out that, although mental disorders are found more often among criminals than among noncriminals, the explanation is not that mental disorders *cause* crime but that mental disorders and crime are both associated with some of the same demographic factors, such as age, gender, and race.[72]

Later research reports that the evidence is mixed, with some studies supporting the position that there is a causal relationship between personality and behavior and others concluding that there is no evidence to support that position. After reviewing the literature, sociologist Ronald L. Akers stated:

> The research using personality inventories and other methods of measuring personality characteristics [has] not been able to produce findings to support personality variables as major causes of criminal and delinquent behavior.[73]

Intelligence and Crime

Closely associated with the mental disorder approach is the linking of crime and intelligence. It is argued that low intelligence causes crime. This approach has long historical roots. As noted, early studies of family histories that found many people of lower intelligence in a family line of criminals concluded that the criminal behavior was caused by low intelligence. These studies were discredited when researchers found few differences between the intelligence of criminals and that of World War I army draftees. In the 1960s, however, attention turned to intelligence and crime once again.

The idea that crime and intelligence are related got a boost with the 1985 publication of *Crime & Human Nature,* whose authors, Harvard professors James Q. Wilson (political scientist) and Richard J. Herrnstein (psychologist), stated that there is a "clear and consistent link between criminality and low intelligence" and criticized criminology textbook authors for ignoring the research in this area.[74] However, critics have argued that the authors showed only that low intelligence and crime *appear* together frequently in the same groups; they did not demonstrate that low intelligence is the *cause* of crime.

Shortly after Herrnstein's death in 1994, his book *The Bell Curve: Intelligence and Class Structure in American Life,* coauthored with Charles Murray, was published. Herrnstein and Murray argued that success in life is dictated and influenced by intelligence, which is linked also to criminal behavior, dependence on welfare, and economic success. They further argued that the link is inherited and thus cannot be changed by environment.[75]

Critics take the position that environment is a *factor* in determining intelligence and in how intelligence affects behavior. For example, several studies show a correlation between low intelligence and delinquency; the higher the intelligence, the less likelihood there is of delinquent behavior. Furthermore, there is some evidence that this correlation remains even when researchers control for other variables associated with delinquency, such as social class, family interaction, and race. Critics argue that it is unreasonable to assume that intelligence is *determined* solely by biology and that therefore it cannot be altered.

Finally, in a study released in November 2001, Dr. Paul M. Thompson and his colleagues mapped brain structure using magnetic resonance imaging (MRI) and concluded that the size of certain regions of the human brain is controlled by genetics and that the larger these areas, the more intelligent the individual. These researchers utilized a sample of twins in Finland, discovering that the parts of the brain controlled by genetic differ only slightly in identical twins but differ considerably among fraternal twins and significantly among unrelated persons. According to Dr. Thompson, these findings are "the first maps of the degree to which the genes control brain structure." Although the sample consisted of only 40 subjects, Dr. Thompson believes the results give "enough statistical power to identify the key brain systems." A neurologist and expert on brain changes among patients with Alzheimer's disease, Dr. Bruce L. Miller, concluded that Dr. Thompson's work is "an exciting study that starts to show there are some brain areas in which there are very significant genetic influences on structure."[76]

Cognitive Development Theory

Cognitive development theory Psychological theory of behavior based on the belief that people organize their thoughts into rules and laws and that the way in which those thoughts are organized results in either criminal or noncriminal behavior. This organization of thoughts is called *moral reasoning,* and when applied to law, *legal reasoning*.

Another type of psychological theory that has been used to explain criminal behavior is **cognitive development theory.** This approach is based on the belief that the way in which people organize their thoughts about rules and laws results in either criminal or noncriminal behavior. Psychologists refer to this organization of thoughts as *moral reasoning.* When that reasoning is applied to law, it is termed *legal reasoning,* although that term has a different meaning to persons trained in law. The approach stems from the early works of Swiss psychologist Jean Piaget (1896–1980), who believed that there are two stages in the development of moral reasoning: (1) the belief that rules are sacred and immutable, and (2) the belief that rules are the products of humans. According to Piaget, we leave the first stage at about the age of 13, and the second stage leads to more moral behavior than the first.[77]

In 1958 psychologist Lawrence Kohlberg (1927–1987) made some changes in the cognitive development approach. He called the first stage *preconventional* and the second *conventional*. He added a third and higher stage, *postconventional reasoning*. According to Kohlberg, between the ages of 10 and 13, most people move from preconventional to conventional reasoning or thinking; those who do not make this transition may be considered arrested in their development of moral reasoning, and they may become delinquent.[78] He and others refined this position, with a development of stages of moral judgment that are applicable to all kinds of behavior. The progression to higher stages should preclude criminal behavior, but most criminals do not progress beyond the earlier stages.[79]

Other modern scholars have developed the thesis that both criminal behavior and noncriminal behavior are related to cognitive development and that people choose the behavior in which they wish to engage, just like the classical writers proclaimed in the 18th century. For example, psychologists at the U.S penitentiary at Leavenworth, Kansas, emphasize that although environmental factors such as family background, peer relationships, and poverty may limit a person's choices, they do not *determine* them. They conclude, "The root causes of crime . . . are thought and choice." Criminal behavior exists because of the way people think and the choices they make. Thus, either criminals must be confined forever or they must be taught how to change their ways of thinking.[80]

Behavior Theory

Behavior theory Theory based on the belief that all behavior is learned and can be unlearned. It is the basis for behavior modification, one approach used for changing behavior in both institutional and noninstitutional settings.

Originating in the late 1800s, **behavior theory** gained attention in this century through the work of B. F. Skinner (1904–1990). Behavior theory is the basis for behavior modification, one approach used in institutionalized and noninstitutionalized settings for changing behavior. The primary thesis is that all behavior is learned and can be unlearned. The approach is concerned with observable behavior, in contrast to the traditional psychoanalytic emphasis on deep, underlying personality problems that must be uncovered and treated.

Behavior theory is based on the belief that what is important is not the unconscious but rather behavior that can be observed and manipulated. It is assumed that neurotic symptoms and some deviant behaviors are acquired through an unfortunate quirk of learning and that they are rewarding to the patient. The undesirable behavior can be eliminated, modified, or replaced by taking away the reward value or by rewarding a more appropriate behavior that is incompatible with the deviant one. It is argued that behavior is controlled by its consequences. In dealing directly with behaviors that are undesirable, behavioral therapy attempts to change a person's long-established patterns of response to him- or herself and to others.

Learning Theory

Learning theory Theory based on the assumption that although human aggression may be influenced by physiological characteristics, the activation of those characteristics depends on learning and is subject to the person's control. Social learning determines whether aggressive behavior occurs and, if so, the nature of that behavior.

Another contrasting theory, **learning theory,** acknowledges that individuals have physiological mechanisms that permit them to behave aggressively, but whether or not they will do so is learned, as is the nature of their aggressive behavior. This theory may be contrasted with behavior theory in that the latter emphasizes performance and reinforcement, whereas learning theory emphasizes that learning may be accomplished by using other people as models. It is not necessary to engage in all the behavior that we learn; we engage in the behavior only if we have incentives and motivations to do so. Motivations may come from biological factors or from mental factors, the latter giving us the ability to imagine the behavior's consequences.

Learning theorists view consequences as the factors that influence behavior. There are three types of consequences: (1) *external reinforcement*, such as goods, money, social status, and punishment (effective in restraining behavior); (2) *vicarious reinforcement,* such as noting the status of others whom one observes being reinforced for their behavior; and (3) *self-regulatory mechanisms,* such as people responding to their own actions in ways that bring self-rewards or self-punishment. Learning theorists focus on the importance of the family, the subculture, and the media.

Learning theories have been combined with biological approaches to explain criminal behavior. English scholar and psychologist Hans J. Eysenck stressed the interrelationship between psychology and biology in explaining how humans learn to behave. He related his approach directly to criminal behavior.[81]

Eysenck's approach was based on the principle of *conditioning.* We learn appropriate and inappropriate behavior through a process of training that involves rewards for appropriate behavior, punishment for inappropriate behavior, and the establishment of models of appropriate behavior. Through these processes, we learn moral preferences as well as behavior. The process is slow and subtle. Often we do not realize how we obtained our moral preferences, but in the process of learning, most of us develop a conscience. This conscience provides us with feelings of responsibility and duty, shame and guilt, of the need to do the right thing. If we do the wrong thing, we feel guilty—assuming, of course, that our conscience incorporates the moral preferences that define that activity as wrong.[82]

The process of training uses three tools: classical conditioning, operant conditioning, and modeling. Most of us have heard about classical conditioning in terms of Pavlov's dogs, who began to salivate when a bell rang because they knew from conditioning that the bell meant they would be fed. *Classical conditioning* is a learned response to a stimulus.

Operant conditioning is based on a reaction after we have acted. It is argued that this is the most powerful form of training. We are rewarded, or reinforced, when we behave appropriately, and we are punished when we misbehave. We learn by *models,* too; social learning occurs through the observation of others and from the media. In many languages, the verb *to teach* is synonymous with the verb *to show.*[83]

Eysenck's approach, based almost entirely on classical conditioning, took the position that "criminality can be understood in terms of conditioning principles." Criminals do not condition adequately to stimuli that society deems should be incorporated in a conscience.[84]

Eysenck believed that conditioning depends on the sensitivity of the inherited autonomic nervous system as well as the quality of conditioning that is received during the socialization process. In the third edition of his book, he emphasized that his original plan in 1964 was to outline a theory of antisocial behavior, relate that theory to personality, "and indicate some of the biological factors underlying both personality and criminality." Biological and psychological approaches were not given much credit at the time, but in 1977 Eysenck argued that we had much more evidence of the relationship between genetic factors and criminality, more evidence that personality traits are strongly determined by genetic factors, and much more empirical work "on the biological causes of personality differences, and by implication, of psychopathic and criminal conduct." Eysenck took the position that some of the sociological theories that previously had overshadowed biological and psychological theories were now less acceptable in explaining criminal behavior. He cited the variables of poverty, poor housing, and social inequality. Eysenck has been criticized for his overemphasis on classical conditioning to the exclusion of operant conditioning and modeling.[85]

The various theories and approaches discussed thus far are summarized in Exhibit 4.3.

EXHIBIT 4.3

Summary of Major Biological and Psychological Theories

BIOLOGICAL THEORIES

- **Lombroso and the positivists**—Cesare Lombroso developed the theory of born criminals, who have specified physical characteristics that distinguish them from noncriminals. Lombroso also recognized the criminaloid and the insane criminal.
- **Physique and crime—Constitutional approaches** rest on the assumption that function is determined by structure. The primary early proponent was **William H. Sheldon,** who categorized body types as the ectomorph (tall, skinny); the endomorph (short, fat); and the mesomorph (athletic build), with a temperament type identified for each. Researchers **Sheldon and Eleanor Glueck** focused on juvenile offenders and found most were mesomorphic types. Their findings were later supported by **Juan Cortés.**
- **Genetic factors**—Early proponents associated criminality with inherited family traits. **Charles Goring's** research in this area was severely criticized. Studies of twins by **Karl O. Christiansen** and **Sarnoff A. Mednick** and his associates found associations between heredity and crime. Subsequent studies of adoptions were conducted. Existence of a **chromosomal abnormality** was also thought to be evidence of inherited behavior.
- **Genetics and behavior today**—Some scholars have argued for increased attention to genetics and behavior, with an emphasis today on genomic research.
- **Neurological factors**—Some scientists view crime as related to the body's nervous system, stating that aggressive or violent behavior is at least in part explained by the brain.
- **Neuroendocrinology**—Some researchers relate behavior at least in part to an imbalance of the body's chemicals. Aggressive men may have lower levels of certain hormones, while among women problems such as premenstrual tension appear to be related to the imbalance of two female hormones.
- **Neurochemistry**—Some scientists have looked at the possibility that nutrition, chemicals, food additives, or preservatives may affect behavior.
- **Autonomic nervous system**—Changes in this system, such as in blood pressure, may affect behavior.
- **Attention deficit disorder (ADD)**—The most commonly diagnosed psychiatric condition among U.S. children today, ADD causes inattentiveness, daydreaming, and many other characteristics that may be associated with behavioral patterns, such as anxiety disorders, traumatic stress reactions, or atypical depression.

PSYCHOLOGICAL THEORIES

- **Psychiatric approach**—Psychiatry is a field of medicine that specializes in the understanding, diagnosis, treatment, and prevention of mental problems. One of its branches, **psychoanalysis,** based on **Sigmund Freud's** concept of the unconscious, looks at the unique personalty of each person by conducting case studies. These were typical of the work of **William Healy,** who believed that the roots of delinquency were embedded deeply in a person's background. Freud believed that early childhood experiences affected adults' behavior and that original human nature was assertive and aggressive.
- **Personality theory**—Some theorists look to emotional conflict and personality deviations to explain behavior, with the early studies focusing primarily on mental disorders and crime.
- **Intelligence and crime**—Crime has been associated with low intelligence. Early studies in this area focused on family histories. More recently, **James Q. Wilson** and **Richard J. Herrnstein** have stated that there is a clear and consistent link between low intelligence and crime.
- **Cognitive development theory**—According to this theory, the way in which people organize their thoughts about rules and laws results in either criminal or noncriminal behavior; the organization process is called *moral reasoning*. **Lawrence Kohlberg** listed three stages of moral reasoning: preconventional, conventional, and postconventional.

(continued)

EXHIBIT 4.3

Summary of Major Biological and Psychological Theories, *(continued)*

- **Behavior theory**—This theory, which forms the basis for behavior modification, states that all behavior is learned and can be unlearned. Its primary proponent was **B. F. Skinner.**
- **Learning theory**—Learning theorists accept that persons have physiological mechanisms that permit them to behave aggressively, but whether or not they do so is learned behavior. Consequences influence the learning, and they are of three categories: *external reinforcement,* such as goods, money, social status; *vicarious reinforcement,* such as noting the status of others whose behavior is reinforced; and *self-regulatory mechanisms,* such as responding to one's own actions in ways that bring self-rewards or self-punishment. **Hans J. Eysenck** based his learning theory approach on the principle of *conditioning* and discussed three types: classical (for example, Pavlov's dogs' response to stimuli); operant (learned response to a stimuli); and modeling (reaction based on what we see in others' behaviors).

IMPLICATIONS OF BIOLOGICAL AND PSYCHOLOGICAL THEORIES

The thesis of our discussion thus far is that the social, physical, and psychological sciences should be integrated in our attempt to understand criminal behavior.

Increased attention to biological and psychological explanations of human behavior and their implications for studying crime was fueled in 1985 by Wilson and Herrnstein's *Crime & Human Nature,* mentioned earlier. This comprehensive book, replete with pages of summaries of criminological literature, received national attention through television talk shows, popular magazines, and newspapers. The authors, who refocused attention on genetic and biological components of criminal behavior, were well received by some but criticized by others. One sociologist warned that colleagues "who suffer from high blood pressure should be cautious in reading it."[86]

In contrast, biologist Sarnoff Mednick and his associates (writing just a few years before Wilson and Herrnstein) concluded:

> A half century of research and common sense leaves no doubt that social and cultural factors play a considerable role in the etiology of crime. The biological factors . . . must be seen as another set of variables involved in the etiology of crime. Both social and biological variables *and their interactions* are important for our complete understanding of the origins of antisocial behavior.[87]

The key word in this statement is *interactions.* Today many scholars argue that the issue is not nature *or* nurture but nature *and* nurture. It is not a question of whether human behavior is the result of biology *or* environment, but what effect each has on the other.

Sociobiology The application of principles of biology to the study of social behavior.

The combination of the physical and social sciences to explain behavior is seen in the work of sociobiologists. Edward O. Wilson, who introduced the concept of **sociobiology,** defines the term as "the systematic study of the biological basis of all social behavior."[88] Some scientists denounce the concept as just another deterministic approach,[89] but others view the work of Wilson and his colleagues as a framework for the future unification of the social and natural sciences.[90]

Other scholars are writing about the interaction of biology (and other physical sciences) and the social sciences in an effort to explain criminal behavior. Diana H. Fishbein has explored the relationship between psychobiology and female aggression and concluded that "pre- or postnatal biological experiences, combined with a socially disadvantageous environment, predispose certain women to antisocial behavior."[91]

Thomas J. Bernard has analyzed aggressive behavior among the "truly disadvantaged" members of our society. He points out that research on violent behavior, especially homicides, shows that many of the violent acts occur after relatively insignificant or trivial incidents, such as an insult. Why is it that among some people these incidents escalate into violent behavior? Bernard looks at three social-structural variables—urban environment, low social position, and racial and ethnic discrimination—which he believes explain why some people react violently to the incidents while others do not. He stresses that although the arousal of aggressive feelings occurs through the autonomic nervous system, there is evidence that individual cognition determines the level and type of that arousal. Some people are able to cope; others are not. Bernard maintains that the difference is in the variation of the social factors (low social position, racial and ethnic discrimination, and urban environment), not the biological factors. Thus, social variables operate with biological reactions to influence behavior.[92]

The policy implications of the biological and psychological approaches to explaining human behavior are extremely important. Exhibit 4.4 discusses what drug addiction suggests for criminal justice systems' policies.

U.S. legal systems are based on the premise that people are responsible legally only for those criminal acts over which they have control; they are not responsible if they cannot control their behavior. Thus, if someone forces you to shoot at another person, you may have a duress defense. In Chapter 1 we noted that the law permits defenses to criminal behavior. A defense may mitigate the criminal act or eliminate criminal responsibility entirely.

Insanity defense A defense that enables the defendant to be found not guilty because he or she does not have the mental ability required for legal responsibility for criminal behavior.

Guilty but mentally ill An alternative to the insanity defense: permits finding that defendants were mentally ill but not insane at the time they committed the crimes charged. They are guilty, and they may be punished, but generally the jurisdictions that have this concept require that these defendants must receive psychiatric treatment while they are confined.

A full discussion of legal defenses is beyond the scope of this text, but it is important to understand that criminal defenses may (and often do) rest on the decisions we make concerning the relationship that biology and psychology have to the law. This may be illustrated by one of the best-known but least frequently used defenses, the **insanity defense.** A defendant who is judged by the jury to be insane may be totally excused from criminal liability; that is, he or she is found to be not guilty by reason of insanity. Various insanity tests are used, but there is little agreement on these tests or, for that matter, whether the insanity defense should be permitted. Some jurisdictions have abolished the defense.

The all-or-nothing aspect of "not guilty by reason of insanity" has led some jurisdictions to provide for a defense of **guilty but mentally ill,** under which the defendant may be found guilty of the offense charged and mentally ill but not insane at the time it was committed. He or she may be incarcerated but also provided with psychiatric treatment.[93]

These and other defenses have been criticized as removing responsibility from criminal defendants who should be liable for their behavior.[94] The debate over defenses will continue to be important in light of new evidence concerning the relationship between behavior and biology or psychology. The same issues arise with sociology, too; the next two chapters are devoted to sociological theories of criminal behavior.

EXHIBIT 4.4

Policy Implications of Drug Addiction

In a 1998 article entitled "Addiction Is a Brain Disease—and It Matters," Alan I. Leshner, the director of the National Institute on Drug Abuse (NIDA), discussed the nature of drug addiction and its policy implications for criminal justice systems. Leshner emphasized that "virtually all drugs of abuse have common effects . . . on a single pathway deep within the brain." Brain function is modified in many ways by acute drug use, and these changes persist even after the individual discontinues using the drug. In short, the addicted brain "is significantly different from the unaddicted brain." Leshner maintains that drug addiction is a brain disease. It would seem reasonable, then, in dealing with addiction, to attempt to stop or reverse the changes that have occurred in the brain.

Furthermore, addiction is rarely an acute illness; rather, it is chronic and should therefore be approached as a health issue, akin to chronic pain, diabetes, or hypertension. Unlike acute illnesses, addiction cannot be cured by antibiotics or other medicines. This has definite implications for policy development within criminal justice systems, as Leshner notes in this passage:

> For example, if we know criminals are also drug addicted, it is no longer reasonable to simply incarcerate them. If they have a brain disease, imprisoning them without treatment will be futile. If they are left untreated, their crime and drug use recidivism rates are frighteningly high. However, if addicted criminals are treated while in prison, both types of recidivism can be reduced dramatically. It is therefore counterproductive not to treat addicts while they are in prison.[1]

Leshner emphasizes that even if the original behavior is voluntary, the fact that the brain of an addict is different from that of a nonaddict means that we must react differently to that individual, recognizing the illness as just that—an illness. He says that we should react to drug addicts as we react to those who have Alzheimer's disease, which is also a brain disease.

Such a position has definite implications for criminal justice systems, and some jurisdictions are recognizing this. Recall Chapter 3's notation (see p. 77) that in 2000 California voters approved providing treatment rather than incarceration for drug users in most cases.

1. Alan I. Leshner, "Addiction Is a Brain Disease—and It Matters," *National Institute of Justice Journal* (Washington, DC: October 1998), 2–6, footnotes omitted; quotation is from p. 5.

SUMMARY

In this chapter we have continued our inquiry into the explanations of criminal behavior by concentrating on the contributions of biologists and psychologists. Once again, we see the impact of the positive school, how its constitutional approach to criminal behavior influenced the body type theories of Sheldon and the Gluecks. These researchers, along with Cortés, saw the importance of environmental factors.

Following a discussion of genetic factors, including family studies, studies of twins and adoptees, chromosomal abnormalities, and a modern view of genetics, the chapter considers the importance of the central nervous system, neuroendocrinology and neurochemistry, and the autonomic nervous system. The chapter features a discussion of attention deficit disorder (ADD), which bridges the discussions of biology and psychology. ADD is the most commonly diagnosed psychiatric problem among U.S. children, but it is believed to have a biological basis.

Psychiatry and psychology are discussed, beginning with a brief glance at demonology. The psychiatric and personality theory approaches are discussed, too. Intelligence and crime, cognitive development theory, behavior theory, learning theory, and the relationship between psychological conditioning and biology are discussed. The implications of current research in biology and psychology, as well as the impact of these findings on criminology, enhance our understanding of criminal behavior. But they also raise significant policy questions, some of which are explored in Exhibit 4.4. Other issues raised are legal ones; these center primarily on defenses to criminal behavior.

It may be that biological implications of criminal behavior will have a greater impact in the courtroom than in the social science journals. To date, however, social science theories of criminal behavior continue to dominate the literature; the next two chapters are devoted to their explanation and analysis.

STUDY QUESTIONS

1. Explain the contributions of the classical school to our understanding of criminal behavior. Compare the classical contributions to those of Sheldon and the Gluecks.
2. Compare and contrast the historical studies of families and crime to the more modern approach.
3. How important are XYY studies?
4. How would you react to the statement that heredity *causes* crime?
5. What is a *genome* and what are the implications of genome research for studying crime?
6. Discuss the importance of neurological factors in explaining crime.
7. Contrast neuroendocrinology and neurochemistry in explaining crime.
8. Has the study of the autonomic nervous system shown any promise in explaining criminal behavior?
9. What is attention deficit disorder? How do you think it might relate to delinquent or criminal behavior?
10. What is the role of psychiatry in explaining criminal behavior?
11. Does low intelligence cause crime? Explain.
12. Explain cognitive development theory.
13. What is behavior theory?
14. What effect should biology and psychology have on criminal defenses?
15. What effect should biology and psychology have on policy decisions in criminal justice?

BRIEF ESSAY ASSIGNMENTS

1. What was Lombroso's approach to explaining criminality? What types of criminal punishment did he advocate?
2. Discuss the relationship between physique and crime and Sheldon's contribution to this concept.
3. What were the problems of early family studies? What impact did they have on policy decisions?
4. Assess the criticisms of the psychiatric approach to explain criminality
5. Distinguish between the insanity defense and the guilty-but-mentally-ill defense. What are the criticisms of these legal defenses?

INTERNET ACTIVITIES

1. Find out more about the study and applicability of genetics research in the criminal justice system by logging onto the Humane Genome Project's website at www.ornl.gov/hgmis/. Under the link "Genetics in the Courtroom," read the article entitled "The Impact of Behavioral Genetics on the Law and the Courts." What future implications do you think the study of genetics on behavior will have on the law and the criminal justice system? What other types of systems/institutions might this type of research affect?
2. Go to www.crimelibrary.com/criminology/insanity/ 4.htm and learn more about the history and use of the insanity defense. When did the practice of the insanity defense begin? What are the M'Naghten rules? Do all states permit the use of the insanity defense?

NET RESOURCES

www.crime-times.org

The Crime Times website contains articles that address the relationship between aberrant behavior and variables associated with biological and psychological disorders. Articles featured in the *Crime Times* newsletter related to this subject and other criminal justice topics can be accessed by issue, subject, title and author(s).

www.psychologicalscience.net	Psychological Science on the Net provides links to psychological organizations, student resources, and access to the American Psychological Association archives and psychology topics. Users can also enter keywords to search various topics included in the site.
www.psycline.org/journals/psycline.html	Managed by an individual psychologist, psychline offers both a journal and article locator that can be used to access a collection of psychology and social science journals on the Web. There are links to some international journals and articles as well.
www.apa.org	The website for the American Psychological Association includes information about the organization, links to issues and news items related to psychology, press releases, access to articles, and a site search engine.
www.psych.org	The website for the American Psychiatric Association provides organizational information, news in psychiatry, press releases, and a link to publications and article abstracts. Users can also subscribe to psychiatric journals.

ENDNOTES

1. Stephen Schafer, *Theories in Criminology* (New York: Random House, 1969), p. 24, quoting Marvin E. Wolfgang, "Cesare Lombroso," in *Pioneers in Criminology,* 2d ed., ed. Hermann Mannheim (Montclair, NJ: Patterson Smith, 1973), pp. 232–91.
2. Cesare Lombroso, *Crime, Its Causes and Remedies,* trans. H. P. Horton (Boston: Little, Brown, 1911), p. 365.
3. Ibid., pp. 381–83.
4. Ibid., pp. 388, 391, 426; Wolfgang, "Cesare Lombroso," p. 280.
5. Ronald L. Akers, *Criminological Theories: Introduction and Evaluation,* 3d ed. (Los Angeles: Roxbury, 2000), p. 43.
6. Thorsten Sellin, "The Lombrosian Myth in Criminology," *American Journal of Sociology* 42 (May 1937): 898–99. For a scathing criticism of Lombroso, see Alfred Lindesmith and Yale Levin, in this same issue, pp. 653–71.
7. See Edwin H. Sutherland and Donald R. Cressey, *Principles of Criminology,* 5th ed. (Philadelphia: Lippincott, 1955), p. 55; 9th ed. (1974), p. 54; and the discussion in Chapter 3 of this text.
8. Wolfgang, "Cesare Lombroso," p. 288.
9. Nicole Hahn Rafter, "Criminal Anthropology in the United States," *Criminology* 30 (November 1992): 525–45; quotation is from p. 525.
10. Ernst Kretschmer, *Physique and Character,* trans. W. J. H. Sprott (New York: Harcourt, Brace, 1926).
11. William H. Sheldon, *The Varieties of Human Physique: An Introduction to Constitutional Psychology* (New York: Harper & Row, 1940); *The Varieties of Temperament* (New York: Harper & Row, 1942); *Varieties of Delinquent Youth: An Introduction to Constitutional Psychiatry* (New York: Harper & Row, 1949); and *Atlas of Men* (New York: Harper & Row, 1954).
12. Juan B. Cortés with Florence M. Gatti, *Delinquency and Crime: A Biopsychosocial Approach* (New York: Seminar Press, 1972), p. 8.
13. Albert K. Cohen, Alfred Lindesmith, and Karl Schuessler, *The Sutherland Papers* (Bloomington: Indiana University Press, 1956), p. 289.
14. See Sheldon Glueck and Eleanor Glueck, *Physique and Delinquency* (New York: Harper & Row, 1956); *Five Hundred Criminal Careers* (New York: Knopf, 1930); *Later Criminal Careers* (New York: Commonwealth Fund, 1937); *Criminal Careers in Retrospect* (New York: Commonwealth Fund, 1943); and *Unraveling Juvenile Delinquency* (New York: Commonwealth Fund, 1950).
15. Hermann Mannheim, *Comparative Criminology* (Boston: Houghton Mifflin, 1965), p. 241.
16. Cortés, *Delinquency and Crime,* p. 19.
17. Ibid., p. 19.
18. Ibid., p. 58.
19. See Richard L. Dugdale, *The Jukes: A Study in Crime, Pauperism, Disease, and Heredity,* 4th ed. (New York: Putnam's, 1942); and Henry H. Goddard, *Feeblemindedness, Its Causes and Consequences* (New York: Macmillan, 1914).
20. Sheldon Glueck and Eleanor Glueck, *Of Delinquency and Crime* (Springfield, IL: Charles C. Thomas, 1974).
21. Charles Goring, *The English Convict* (London: H. M. Stationery Office, 1919).
22. See Buck v. Bell, 274 U.S. 200 (1927).
23. See, for example, Ronald L. Simons et al., "A Test of Various Perspectives on the Intergenerational Transmission of Domestic Violence," *Criminology* 33 (February 1995): 141–71.
24. For a detailed review of these early studies, see Karl O. Christiansen, "A Review of Studies of Criminality among Twins" and "A Preliminary Study of Criminality among Twins," in *Biosocial Bases of Criminal Behavior,* eds. Sarnoff A. Mednick and Karl O. Christiansen (New York: Gardner Press, 1977), pp. 89–108.
25. Sarnoff A. Mednick and Jan Volavka, "Biology and Crime," in *Crime and Justice: An Annual Review of Research,* vol. 2, eds. Norval Morris and Michael Tonry (Chicago: University of Chicago Press, 1980), p. 97.
26. Glenn D. Walters and Thomas W. White, "Heredity and Crime: Bad Genes or Bad Research?," *Criminology* 27 (August 1989): 478.
27. Patricia A. Brennan and Sarnoff A. Mednick, "A Reply to Walters and White: 'Heredity and Crime,' " *Criminology* 28 (November 1990): 660–61. For a response see Glenn D. Walters, "Heredity, Crime, and the Killing-the-Bearer-of-Bad-News Syndrome: A Reply to Brennan and Mednick," *Criminology* 28 (November 1990): 663–67.
28. Akers, *Criminological Theories,* p. 53, referring to Michael Gottfredson and Travis Hirschi, *A General Theory of Crime* (Palo Alto, CA: Stanford University Press, 1990), pp. 46–63.
29. Bira Coid, "A Twin Study of Psychosis and Criminality," *British Journal of Psychiatry* 162 (January 1993): 87–92.
30. See Sarnoff A. Mednick et al., "Genetic Factors in Criminal Behavior: A Review," in *Development of Antisocial and Prosocial Behavior: Research, Theories, and Issues,* eds. Dan Olweus et al. (New York: Academic Press, 1986), pp. 33–50.
31. P. A. Jacobs et al., "Aggressive Behavior, Mental Subnormality, and the XYY Male," *Nature* 208 (December 1965): 1351.

32. See, for example, T R. Sarbin and J. E. Miller, "Demonism Revisited: The XYY Chromosomal Anomaly," *Issues in Criminology* 5 (1970): 195–207.
33. Mednick and Volavka, "Biology and Crime," p. 93.
34. Akers, *Criminological Theories,* p. 48.
35. Walters and White, "Heredity and Crime," p. 478.
36. Margaret A. Zahn, "Thoughts on the Future of Criminology—the American Society of Criminology 1998 Presidential Address," *Criminology* 37 (February 1999): 1–16; quotation is from p. 3.
37. Anthony Walsh, "Behavior Genetics and Anomie/Strain Theory," *Criminology* 38 (November 2000): 1075–1108; quotations are from pp. 1077, 1097, 1098–99.
38. Unless otherwise noted, the information in this and the following sections on neuroendocrinology and neurochemistry and the autonomic nervous system are taken from Vicki Pollock et al., "Crime Causation: Biological Theories," in *Encyclopedia of Crime and Justice,* vol. 1, ed. Sanford H. Kadish (New York: Macmillan, 1983), pp. 311–15.
39. Ibid., p. 311, referring to the study of Sarnoff A. Mednick et al., "EEG as a Predictor of Antisocial Behavior," *Criminology* 19 (August 1981): 219–29.
40. Mednick and Volavka, "Biology and Crime," pp. 130–32, 143.
41. Pollock et al., "Crime Causation," p. 312.
42. "PET Imaging Brings New Advances in Patient Care and Research," *Mayo Magazine* (Fall/Winter 1999), p. 46.
43. "Science: The Last GRE: At Frontier," *The Independent* (21 May 1995), p. 52.
44. "Why Some Kids Turn Violent: Abuse and Neglect Can Reset Brain's Chemistry," *Chicago Tribune* (14 December 1993), p. 1.
45. "Diminished Capacity Examined: Experts Give Support to View That the Criminal Mind Is Different," *St. Louis Post-Dispatch* (26 July 1994), p. 1.
46. "New Studies Show That Chemical Reactions in the Brain Are at the Core of Emotional Responses," *Newsday* (7 March 1995), p. 23B.
47. "Neuroscientist/Psychiatrist Takes Helm at Flagship Primate Research Center," *Journal of the American Medical Association* 272 (28 September 1994): 907.
48. Quoted in Ashley Montagu, "The Biologist Looks at Crime," *Annals of the American Academy of Social and Political Science* 217 (September 1941): 55–56.
49. Saleem A. Shah and Loren H. Roth, "Biological and Psychophysiological Factors in Criminality," in *Handbook of Criminology,* ed. Daniel Glaser (Chicago: Rand McNally, 1974), pp. 101, 123.
50. See Dan Olweus, "Aggression and Hormones: Behavioral Relationship with Testosterone and Adrenaline," in *Development of Antisocial and Prosocial Behavior,* ed. Dan Olweus et al. (New York: Academic Press, 1986), pp. 51–74.
51. Shah and Roth, "Biological and Psychophysiological Factors in Criminality," pp. 124–25.
52. "Gene Defect Tied to Violence in Male Mice," *New York Times* (23 November 1995), p. 14.
53. "Size of Region of Brain May Hold Crucial Clue to Transsexuality, a Study Finds," *New York Times* (2 November 1995), p. 12. The research was conducted in the Netherlands.
54. Diana Fishbein and Susan Pease, *The Effects of Diet on Behavior: Implications for Criminology and Corrections* (Boulder, CO: National Institute of Corrections, June 1988), pp. 2–3.
55. Ibid., p. 32.
56. "Lacking Iodine in their Diets, Millions in China Are Retarded," *New York Times* (4 June 1996), p. 1.
57. Mednick and Volavka, "Biology and Crime," p. 106.
58. Pollock et al., "Crime Causation," p. 315.
59. "Attention Deficit Disorder, Part I," *Harvard Mental Health Letter* 11, no. 10 (April 1995), p. 1.
60. Ibid.
61. Ibid.
62. Ibid.
63. Ibid.
64. For an overview of the study of psychology and crime, see S. Giora Shoham and Mark C. Seis, *A Primer in the Psychology of Crime* (New York: Harrow and Heston, 1993).
65. See William Healy, *The Individual Delinquent* (Boston: Little, Brown, 1915); Franz Alexander and William Healy, *Roots of Crime* (New York: Knopf, 1935); and William Healy and Augusta Bronner, *New Light on Delinquency and Its Treatment* (New Haven, CT: Yale University Press, 1931).
66. See Sigmund Freud, *New Introductory Lectures on Psychoanalysis,* ed. and trans. James Strachey (New York: Norton, 1933).
67. "Drugs vs. Couch: Psychiatric Convention Hears Both Sides," *Miami Herald* (10 May 1992), p. 2J.
68. "Is Prozac Changing Traditional Notions of Psychiatry?" *Rocky Mountain News* (7 September 1994), p. 12D.
69. Herbert C. Quay, "Crime Causation: Psychological Theories," in *Encyclopedia of Crime and Justice,* vol. 1, ed. Sanford H. Kadish (New York: Macmillan, 1983), p. 332.
70. See, for example, Cyril Burt, *The Young Delinquent* (New York: D. Appleton, 1925); Sheldon Glueck and Eleanor Glueck, *One Thousand Juvenile Delinquents: Their Treatment by Court and Clinic* (Cambridge, MA: Harvard University Press, 1934); and Healy and Bronner, *New Light on Delinquency and Its Treatment.*
71. See, for example, Karl F. Schuessler and Donald R. Cressey, "Personality Characteristics of Criminals," *American Journal of Sociology* 55 (March 1950): 476–86. One of the earlier researchers, Cyril Burt, was accused of altering the data he reported. See *Psychology Today* 10 (February 1977): 33.
72. John Monahan and Henry J. Steadman, *Crime and Mental Disorder,* National Institute of Justice (Washington, D.C.: U.S. Department of Justice, September 1984).
73. Akers, *Criminological Theories,* 3d ed., p. 63.
74. James Q. Wilson and Richard J. Herrnstein, *Crime & Human Nature* (New York: Simon & Schuster, 1985), pp. 148–72.
75. Richard J. Herrnstein and Charles Murray, *The Bell Curve: Intelligence and Class Structure in American Life* (New York: Free Press, 1994).
76. "Study Finds Genetic Link Between Intelligence and Size of Some Regions of the Brain," *New York Times* (5 November 2001), p. 12.
77. See Jean Piaget, *The Moral Judgment of the Child* (New York: Harcourt Brace Jovanovich, 1932).
78. Lawrence Kohlberg, *The Development of Modes of Moral Thinking and Choice in Years Ten to Sixteen,* Ph.D. dissertation (Cambridge, MA: Harvard University, 1958).
79. Lawrence Kohlberg et al., *The Just Community Approach to Corrections: A Manual* (Niantic: Connecticut Department of Corrections, 1973).
80. Glenn D. Walters and Thomas W. White, "The Thinking Criminal: A Cognitive Model of Lifestyle Criminality," Sam Houston State University Criminal Justice Center, *Criminal Justice Research Bulletin* 4, no. 4 (1989): 8.
81. Hans J. Eysenck, *Crime and Personality* (London: Routledge & Kegan Paul, 1977).
82. Gwynn Nettler, *Explaining Crime,* 3d ed. (New York: McGraw-Hill, 1984), p. 207.
83. Eysenck, *Crime and Personality,* p. 13.
84. Nettler, *Explaining Crime,* p. 297.
85. Ibid.
86. Wilson and Herrnstein, *Crime & Human Nature;* Jack P. Gibbs, "Review Essay," *Criminology* 23 (May 1985): 381.
87. Mednick and Volavka, "Biology and Crime," pp. 143–44; emphasis in the original.
88. Edward O. Wilson, *Sociobiology: The New Synthesis* (Cambridge, MA: Harvard University Press, 1975), p. 4. See also Wilson, *On Human Nature* (Cambridge, MA: Harvard University Press, 1978).
89. See, for example, Sociobiology Study Group of Science for the People, "Sociobiology—Another Biological Determinism," in *The Sociobiology Debate: Readings on the Ethical and Scientific Issues Concerning Sociobiology,* ed. Arthur L. Caplan (New York: Harper & Row, 1978), pp. 280–90.
90. Boyce Rensberger, "The Nature-Nurture Debate I: On Becoming Human," *Science* 83 (April 1983): 41.
91. Diana H. Fishbein, "The Psychobiology of Female Aggression," *Criminal Justice and Behavior* 19 (June 1992): 99.
92. Thomas J. Bernard, "Angry Aggression among the 'Truly Disadvantaged,' " *Criminology* 28 (February 1990): 73–96.
93. See the Michigan provision, as explained in People v. Ramsey, 375 N.W.2d 297 (Mich. 1985). The statute is codified at MSA 28.1059(2) (2001).
94. See, for example, Alan Dershowitz, *The Abuse Excuse and Other Cop-Outs, Sob Stories, and Evasions of Responsibility* (Boston: Little, Brown, 1994).

5

▶Lionel Tate, age 14, with two members of his defense team, psychology expert Lori Butts, (left) and cocounsel Denise Bregoff. Tate was sentenced to life in prison for the murder of Tiffany Eunick, age 6. He testified that they were play-wrestling. (Reuters/Getty Images)

Sociological Theories of Criminal Behavior I: The Social-Structural Approach

OUTLINE

KEY TERMS

anomie
concentric circle
conflict
consensus
critical criminology
culture conflict theory
differential opportunity
ecological school
instrumental Marxism
radical criminology
routine activity approach
status offenses
strain theory
structural Marxism
subculture

This chapter analyzes sociological theories of criminal behavior, focusing on those that consider society's social structure or organization. The two basic approaches are consensus and conflict. The consensus approach views folkways, mores, and laws as reflections of society's values; some crime is seen as inevitable, even functional. In the conflict approach, criminal behavior emerges as a conflict between groups within society. This chapter's discussion of early theories is followed by a look at some of their modern counterparts. Examination of the conflict approach and of critical criminology includes a focus on feminist criminology.

"Just tell me *the* cause of crime, and I won't have to read all these theories." I hear this statement frequently when I am discussing crime causation with students who find theory not only difficult to begin with but complicated further by the lack of agreement among scholars in the field. Some professors who serve as reviewers of this text suggest that many of the theories should be eliminated because the material is too confusing for students. However, it would be a disservice to students to tell them that one theory explains all criminal behavior. Consider the examples of crimes in Exhibit 5.1 and try to develop your own sociological (or other) explanations for why those acts were committed.

Social science theory can be very complicated, and this gives rise to much disagreement. Nevertheless, theory is important, and sociologists and criminologists have made great strides in their analyses of criminal behavior and other aspects of criminal justice systems. This chapter and Chapter 6 present the major approaches, along with evaluations, research, and current events that illustrate different crimes and criminals. This approach is intended to enable the reader to see how a particular theory might be useful in explaining criminal behavior.[1]

Contemporary sociologists study the causes of crime from two perspectives: structure and process. The first views crime in relation to the social organization or structure of society and asks how crime is related to the social system. What are the characteristics of the situation or social *structure* in which crime takes place? Do crime rates vary as these situations or structures change? The second approach looks at the *process* by which criminals are produced, but it is not an individualistic approach. Sociologists look for *patterns* of variables and relationships that might explain how and why people engage in criminal acts.

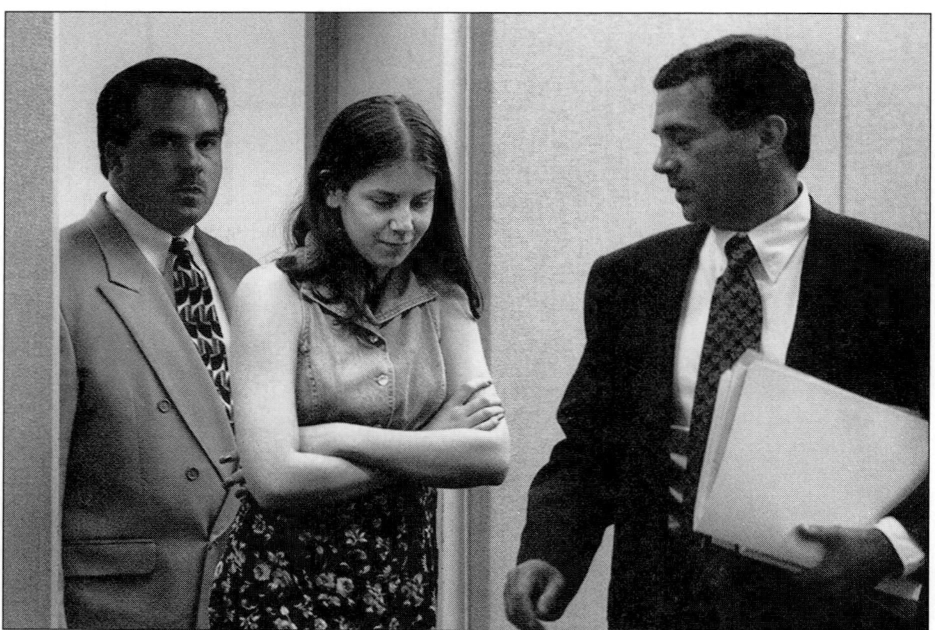

In 1997 Melissa Drexler, seen here with her lawyer Steven Secare (right), pleaded guilty to manslaughter in the 1996 death of her baby boy, whom she delivered in the restroom during her school prom. Drexler was sentenced to a 15-year prison term, but she was released after 5 years. (AP Photo/Pool, Thomas P. Costello)

EXHIBIT 5.1

Crimes of the Young: Do the Theories Explain Them?

In recent years the media have focused on violent crimes committed by young people, many of whom are very young. In addition to the shootings at Columbine High School in Colorado, mentioned in Chapter 1, consider the facts of the following cases and determine whether any of the theories discussed in Chapter 5 might be used to explain the behavior.

1. In 2001 in Florida, two juveniles were found guilty of murder. Lionel Tate, age 14, said he was imitating wrestling when at the age of 12 he killed his 6-year-old playmate. Tate, who refused a plea bargain that included 3 years in prison followed by 10 years on probation, was convicted of first-degree murder and given the mandatory penalty under Florida law: life in prison with no chance of parole. In June 2001 Florida's governor refused to waive the state's two-year requirement for petitioning for early clemency. Governor Jeb Bush said that although he was troubled by the sentence and concerned that Florida offers no alternative for one so young who is convicted in criminal court of first-degree murder, he is also aware of the gravity of the crime committed.

   Nathaniel Brazill, also 14, was 13 when he shot and killed his favorite teacher. Brazill was convicted of second-degree rather than first-degree murder and thus, unlike Tate, avoided the mandatory penalty of life without parole. Brazill could have been sentenced to 25 years to life; he was sentenced to 28 years in prison.
2. In February 2000 a 6-year-old boy shot and killed a 6-year-old girl in front of their teacher at Buell Elementary School in Mount Morris Township, Michigan. The boy's name was not released and he was not charged because of his age.
3. In November 1998 Joshua Phillips, age 14, was accused of killing 8-year-old Maddie Clifton, whose body was found "securely entombed" under Joshua's water bed. The victim, a neighbor, had been stabbed and hit in the head. Joshua's attorney confirmed that his client had admitted responsibility for Maddie's death. Joshua's friends and teachers were shocked, and no one had an explanation for the killing. He was described by those who knew him as: "a very intelligent young man" who had minor problems, "one you never had to call down," and "always so polite, so well-mannered."[1]

   Phillips was convicted of second-degree murder and sentenced to life in prison without parole.
4. Kip Kinkel, age 15, was accused of opening fire at his high school in Springfield, Oregon, in May 1998. Two students were killed and several others were wounded seriously; still others suffered minor injuries from gunfire or from being trampled by students trying to escape the bullets. Earlier that week the suspect had been arrested and suspended after reportedly trying to buy a gun at

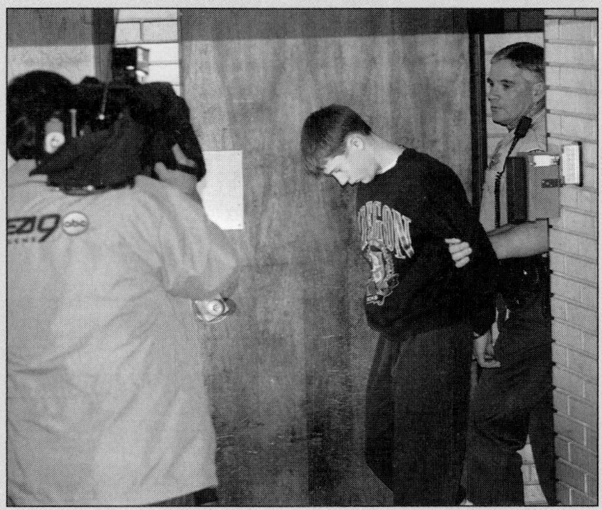

Kipland (Kip) P. Kinkel, age 15, was accused of killing 2 students and wounding 20 others at his Springfield, Oregon, high school in May 1998. When asked why he did it, he allegedly said, "I had no other choice." Kinkel, who is from a middle-class home, was also accused of killing his parents. He was tried as an adult, convicted, and sentenced to 112 years. He is incarcerated in a youth facility and his attorney is appealing the sentence. (Craig Strong/Getty Images)

(continued)

EXHIBIT 5.1

Crimes of the Young: Do the Theories Explain Them? *(continued)*

school. He made threats, but no one took him seriously. He had a history of bad behavior, but no one thought he would be violent. Kinkel was also accused in the deaths of his parents, who were killed shortly before the school rampage. Kinkel, who was tried as an adult, was sentenced to 112 years and is working on his high school diploma at the youth facility in which he is incarcerated. In May 2001 an attorney for Kinkel filed an appeal for his client, arguing that the sentencing judge placed more emphasis on protecting society than on reformation of the offender.

5. In June 1998 Luke Woodham, age 17, was convicted of charges stemming from his acts in the fall of 1997. After stabbing his mother to death, Woodham went to his high school in Pearl, Mississippi, and shot nine students, killing two, including his ex-girlfriend. Seven other students were wounded. Woodham is serving life in prison.

According to prosecutors, Woodham slaughtered numerous cats in the weeks prior to the shootings for which he was convicted, and he is said to have laughed when he killed his own dog. Animal abuse has been tied by some authorities to violence against humans. For example, there is evidence that Russell Eugene Weston Jr., charged with killing two police officers at the U.S. Capitol in the summer of 1998, shot and killed a dozen cats the day before the Capitol shootings. The Federal Bureau of Investigation considers the slaughter of animals as one of its "predictors of violence," especially domestic violence.[2]

6. Several young people were convicted in 1998 of killing their babies. Amy S. Grossberg, age 19, was sentenced to two and a half years in prison, and her boyfriend, Brian C. Peterson Jr., also 19, to two years for killing the baby boy to whom Amy had given birth in a motel room. Both Grossberg and Peterson have been released from custody.

Melissa Drexler entered a guilty plea to aggravated manslaughter to avoid the possibility of a life sentence if she were convicted of murder in the killing of the baby to whom she gave birth in a restroom at her senior prom. She was sentenced to a 15-year prison term, but under the terms of a plea agreement, she may be released in less than 3 years.

Drexler's attorney, Steven Secare, stated that young people who kill their newborns should not be treated like other murderers. They engage in these criminal acts because of "fear, immaturity, confusion, loneliness, depression, and denial," rather than because of a premeditated act. Secare has called for a separate crime to cover these acts: neonaticide. According to him, his client suffered from a disassociative disorder; she was in denial and did not believe the baby was hers, even when she delivered it.[3]

Source: Summarized from media accounts.

1. "Slaying of a Girl, 8, Tests Ties in Florida," *New York Times* (13 November 1998), p. 16; "Always So Nice," *Baltimore Sun* (13 November 1998), p. 20.
2. "Animal Killing Foretells Violence to Humans," *Rocky Mountain News* (15 August 1998), p. 2D.
3. "Fifteen Years for Baby Killing at Prom," *The Record* (Bergen County, NJ) (30 October 1998), p. 1.

Although sociological theories may be classified abstractly as structural or process, most do not fall exclusively into either category. Likewise, it is not possible to isolate sociological from nonsociological theories. For analysis, however, some categorizations may be made. This chapter focuses on social-structural approaches, and Chapter 6 discusses social process approaches.

One further distinction is important. Some sociologists attempt to develop a *general* theory that will explain most, if not all, deviant or criminal behavior, whereas others focus on *specific* approaches, such as the study of persons who

Joshua Phillips, age 14, admitted responsibility for killing 8-year-old Maddie Clifton, whose body was found securely entombed under Joshua's water bed in November of 1998, in Jacksonville, Florida. Joshua was charged with first-degree murder and tried as an adult. He was convicted of second-degree murder and sentenced to life without parole. (AP Photo/Florida Times Union, John White)

commit robbery as contrasted to those who commit murder. Some try to identify variables that may be linked in criminal behavior. For example, the variables of cigarette smoking, problem drinking, illicit sexual behavior, illegal use of drugs, aggressive behavior, and stealing have been found to occur together with enough frequency that some scholars refer to these variables as constituting problem behavior or a problem behavior syndrome. *Problem behavior* includes behavior that is defined as problematic, undesirable, or a source of concern for which societal response is required. Scholars have found that problem behavior is related to environmental and personality variables.[2] Some research suggests that problem behavior differs by gender.[3] These studies focus on delinquent behavior, as do many of the sociological theories. Others focus on adult criminal behavior.

Specifically, with juveniles, a recent study conducted by 22 researchers working over a two-year period under the sponsorship of the Office of Juvenile Justice and Delinquency Prevention of the U.S. Department of Justice, located a number of predictors that appear to be related to deliquent behavior. The list is shown in Exhibit 5.2. Note that the first group of predictors consists of individual factors, and those would be included under the theories discussed in Chapter 4.

The first two factors listed in Exhibit 5.2 are medical and physical factors; other individual factors include psychological ones, such as internalizing disorders (nervousness or withdrawal, worrying, and anxiety). Most of Exhibit 5.2 refers to facts that might be considered part of the social structure in which delinquency occurs; a few apply to the theories discussed in Chapter 6.

EARLY SOCIAL-STRUCTURAL APPROACHES

Early scholars studied crime through a variety of approaches, some of which influenced modern sociological theory.

EXHIBIT 5.2

Predictors of Youth Violence

Individual Factors

- Pregnancy and delivery complications.
- Low resting heart rate [which might predispose one to aggressive and violent behavior].
- Internalizing disorders [nervousness or withdrawal, worrying, and anxiety].
- Hyperactivity, concentration problems, restlessness, and risk taking.
- Aggressiveness.
- Early initiation of violent behavior.
- Involvement in other forms of antisocial behavior.
- Beliefs and attitudes favorable to deviant or antisocial behavior.

Family Factors

- Parental criminality.
- Child maltreatment.
- Poor family management practices.
- Low levels of parental involvement.
- Poor family bonding and family conflict.
- Parental attitudes favorable to substance use and violence.
- Parent–child separation.

School Factors

- Academic failure.
- Low bonding to school.
- Truancy and dropping out of school.
- Frequent school transitions.

Peer-Related Factors

- Delinquent siblings.
- Delinquent peers.
- Gang membership.

Community and Neighborhood Factors

- Poverty.
- Community disorganization.
- Availability of drugs and firearms.
- Neighborhood adults involved in crime.
- Exposure to violence and racial prejudices.

Source: J. David Hawkins et al., Office of Juvenile and Delinquency Prevention *Predictors of Youth Violence* (Washington, DC: U.S. Department of Justice, April 2000), p. 2.

Ecological Theories

Ecological school In criminology, an approach that studies the quantitative relationship between geographic phenomena and crime.

Ecology is the study of the distribution of phenomena and their relationship to their environment. The **ecological school** attempts to explain crime as a function of social change that occurs along with environmental change.

The early ecological school in the United States was centered during the 1920s and 1930s at the University of Chicago, where it was dominated by the works of Ernest W. Burgess, Robert Ezra Park, and others who attempted to explain the relationship between ecology and crime in Chicago. They saw the city as a living, growing, organic whole, and the various areas of the city as organs that served different functions.[4]

Studies of Chicago's areas of high crime rates and other forms of deviance suggested to researchers that even the deviant's world was characterized by differentiated social roles, which were ordered and stratified with rules that were enforced. Subjects in the study had rewards and satisfactions, not all of which were deviant.[5] Some researchers noted evidence of this approach in their studies of hobos and homeless men, who were found to have a stratified society, defined social roles, regulations, and traditions.[6]

Concentric circle An ecological theory that divides cities into zones based on environmental and other characteristics and attempts to find a relationship between them and the crime and delinquency rates.

The city's characteristics, social change, and distribution of people and their behavior have been studied by means of the **concentric circle,** an approach developed to study Chicago but thought to be applicable to other cities. The concentric circle theory divides the city into five zones. At the center of the city is Zone 1, the *central business district.* This zone is characterized by light manufacturing, retail trade, and commercialized recreation. Zone 2, surrounding the central business district, is the *zone of transition* from residential to business. This zone is populated primarily by low-income people, although typically it has an area of high-cost luxury housing as well. Zone 3 is the *zone of working-class homes,* which is less deteriorated than the zone of transition and populated largely by "workers whose economic status enables them to have many of the comforts and even some of the luxuries the city has to offer." Zone 4, the *area of middle-class dwellers,* is populated largely by professional people, clerical forces, owners of small businesses, and the managerial class. On the outer edge of the city is Zone 5, *the commuters' zone.* This zone includes satellite towns and suburbs. Many of the occupants vacate the area during the day and commute to the city for their employment.[7]

To explain crime, delinquency, and other vices, Burgess and Park stated that the key zone is Zone 2, the zone of transition. Because of the movement of businesses into this zone, it becomes an undesirable place to live, even though previously it claimed some of the most desirable housing in the city. Houses deteriorate. Zoning laws change. People who can afford to move out do so, and there is no prospect of improving the housing in the area without public subsidy. The population in the city is segregated by economic and occupational forces. Low-income persons, mostly unskilled workers, live in Zone 2, and frequently this leads to racial and ethnic segregation. The zone is characterized by warehouses, pawnshops, cheap theaters, restaurants, and a breakdown in the usual institutional methods of social control. The investigators hypothesized that crime, vice, and other forms of deviance would flourish in these socially disorganized environments.

Clifford R. Shaw and Henry D. McKay, early ecological researchers, conducted several projects to determine the relationship between school truancy, young adult offenders, infant mortality, tuberculosis, mental disorders, and other factors—and rates of delinquency and adult crime. They "noted that there is not a single instance in which they do not vary together . . . On the basis of the facts presented, it is clear that delinquency is not an isolated phenomenon."[8]

Numerous criticisms have been directed at the early ecological studies, but these must be analyzed in light of the investigators' actual claims. Shaw and McKay did not conclude that the Zone 2 area *causes* crime, as some have suggested. In fact, they warned that cause-and-effect relationships should not be assumed just because high correlations between variables exist. Although Zone 2 may attract or collect criminals, another explanation of the higher rates may be differential law enforcement. Police may be more likely to make arrests in Zone 2 than in other zones.

The Chicago studies found that areas with high rates and those with low rates of crime and delinquency were distinguished on the basis of physical status, economic status, and population composition, as well as social values. Data from other cities supported these findings. Furthermore, despite changes in the population, rates of crime and delinquency remained highest in the zone of transition. Shaw and McKay concluded that crime-producing factors were inherent in the social and economic fabric of the community and constituted a normal reaction to living in a disorganized area.

Several sociologists have written critical analyses of Shaw and McKay's work. They have questioned the methodology of the studies, the representativeness of the data, and the logic of the research. They have noted that the ecological approach does not explain varying rates of crime when ethnic groups are compared.[9] Many modern scholars approach ecology by a careful analysis of the geography of crime. For example, researchers have shown a relationship between crime (and the development of gangs, discussed later in this chapter) and the "transformation of the U.S. economy from manufacturing-based to service-based," resulting in a lower demand for unskilled workers. Further, it is argued that the decrease in demand for unskilled workers is related to the increase in the number of people on social welfare and the number of female-headed families. These findings underscore "the continued criminogenic importance of urban change."[10]

Other scholars have conducted research that shows support of the early ecologists at least to some extent. The ecological approach of the Chicago sociologists has been confirmed by a study of the Washington, D.C., zone of transition. The investigators computed the commuting distance of criminals and found that most of them victimize people who live in transitional areas—areas with a high proportion of construction, demolition, and temporary lodgings. The correlation is highest for robbery and burglary but is significant for rape as well. Business areas are hit heavily by criminal activity, too. The areas of high crime rates are characterized by multiple-family dwellings, as contrasted with single-family homes.[11]

Research also shows that most offenders live in or near the area where they commit their crimes. This does not mean that offenders never travel to commit their crimes; some commuting does take place. But when it does, it appears to be related to the characteristics of the offenders, where they live, the crimes they intend to commit, the attractiveness of the area, and the location of potential targets. Commuting to commit a crime is an investment—it takes time and expense and may increase the risk. By traveling outside their own environments to commit the crime, the offenders may be suggesting that they see the crime as worth the increased risk.[12] If that is the case, opportunity theory and economic theory may be combined. That is, the economic motivation to commit a crime may be related to the existing opportunities or the need to expand the opportunities for successful criminal behavior.

The impact of environment on crime was developed further by the contributions of Oscar Newman. Newman introduced the concept of *defensible space.* He believed that crime can be reduced by modifying the environment's physical features to the point that crime is more difficult to commit because the area gives the impression that the residents are in control.[13] For example, on the one hand, houses in certain neighborhoods may be considered too risky in the summer because more people are outdoors and neighbors have a better view of the potential target. On the other hand, the fact that people go on vacation in the summer can make these houses more attractive targets during this time. Lighting is important, too—a well-lighted area is less likely to become a target because of the increased possibility of detection.[14]

Newman's approach has been criticized as difficult to test empirically because many of his concepts are not articulated and defined clearly. Yet numerous social scientists, many in Great Britain, have conducted research on his concepts, with strong support for his position coming from studies of burglary that show that the "border blocks in city housing areas are much more vulnerable to burglary offenses than the interior blocks."[15]

Another criticism is that changing the environment does not reduce crime; it just displaces it—the potential criminals go elsewhere. This may be desirable for a potential victim, but it does not reduce the community's crime rate. It raises serious problems for research, for it is difficult, if not impossible, to measure the displacement process.

It is important to emphasize that the early ecological theorists and their modern counterparts do not advocate that social disorganization *causes* crime. Indeed, many people who live in Zone 2 do not engage in criminal or delinquent activities. Scholars point out that social disorganization within an area interferes with normal social control processes and thus enables crime and delinquency to persist and, in some cases, flourish.[16]

Classic Anomie Theory

Émile Durkheim (1858–1917), a noted French sociologist, made significant contributions to the study of human behavior. According to Durkheim, crime has functional (or positive) consequences, such as fostering flexibility. It is impossible for all people to be alike and to hold the same moral consciousness. Some individuals differ from the collective type; inevitably some of these divergences include criminal behavior—not because the act is intrinsically criminal but because the collectivity defines it as criminal. Durkheim saw crime as the product of norms. The concept of wrong is necessary to give meaning to right and is inherent in that concept. Even a community of saints will create sinners. For a society to be flexible enough to permit positive deviation, it must permit negative deviation as well. If no deviation is permitted, societies become stagnant. Crime helps prepare society for such changes; it is one of the prices we pay for freedom.[17] Furthermore, crime is normal. No society can be exempt from crime: "There is . . . no phenomenon that presents more indisputably all the symptoms of normality, since it appears closely connected with the conditions of all collective life."[18]

Émile Durkheim (1858–1917), a French sociologist, introduced and developed the concept of anomie in his writings about crime and suicide. His work has influenced modern sociologists, who have expanded and tested his concepts. (Corbis/Bettmann)

In 1893 Durkheim introduced his version of the concept of **anomie,** which derives from a Greek word meaning "without norms." Durkheim was not the first to use the term, nor did he develop the concept as extensively as the American sociologist Robert K. Merton. But Durkheim was responsible for making the concept an integral part of sociology and criminology. He believed that one of society's most important elements is its social cohesion, or *social solidarity,* which represents a *collective conscience.* The absence of a sense of community is viewed by some as a major problem in modern society. In explaining this phenomenon, Durkheim defined two types of solidarity, mechanical and organic.

Anomie A state of normlessness in society that may be caused by decreased homogeneity and that provides a setting conducive to crimes and other antisocial acts.

According to Durkheim, primitive societies are characterized by *mechanical solidarity,* which is dominated by the collective conscience. The type of law manifests this dominance—the reason for law is to discourage individuals from acting in a way that threatens the collective conscience. As societies become larger and more complex, the emphasis in law shifts from the collective conscience to the individual wronged, and law becomes *restitutive.* This shift from mechanical to *organic solidarity* is characterized by an increased need for a division of labor, a division that may be forced and therefore abnormal, leading to the creation of unnatural differences in class and status. People are less homogeneous, and the traditional forms of social control, appropriate to a simple homogeneous society, are not effective in controlling behavior. Greater loneliness, more social isolation, and a loss of identity result, with a consequent state of anomie, or normlessness, replacing the former state of solidarity and providing an atmosphere in which crimes and other antisocial acts may develop and flourish.[19]

Durkheim had a strong impact on scholarly theorists, including most of those discussed in this chapter. His theory of the relationship between anomie and suicide and other social problems remains important today.

Durkheim's belief that crime is normal and his theory of anomie form the basis of Robert K. Merton's contributions toward an understanding of criminal behavior.[20] Merton's thesis is that social structures exert pressure on some persons to behave in nonconforming rather than conforming ways. If evidence is found for this thesis, it will follow that nonconforming behavior is as normal as conforming behavior.

Merton begins by suggesting that all social and cultural structures are characterized by two elements that are not always separable but that may be categorized separately for analysis. First are the *goals,* which are the aspirations of all individuals in the society. Goals are those things that individuals believe are worth striving for. Second are the *means* by which those goals may be obtained. The means are socially approved methods and thus involve the norms, which are defined culturally. A society's norms define (1) the goals and (2) the methods by which those goals may be obtained. According to Merton, when there is a focus on the goals to the virtual exclusion of the norms, and when the socially approved means for obtaining the goals are not equally available to all, many people turn to unapproved and unacceptable means to achieve them. The result is a situation of normlessness, or anomie. Merton suggests that in contemporary American culture the primary emphasis is on goals, not means, and the main goal is a monetary one.[21]

After examining American cultural patterns, Merton designed a typology to describe the methods, or modes, of adaptation that are available to those who react to society's goals and means. He identifies five modes: conformity, innovation, ritualism, retreatism, and rebellion. These are *modes of adaptation,* not personality types. The first mode, *conformity,* refers to the acceptance of a society's goals and its approved means for achieving those goals. Conformity is the adaptation used most frequently. *Innovation* represents acceptance of the goals but rejection of the means for obtaining them. For example, if a college degree is the goal, the student who adopts that goal but chooses to reject the acceptable means for attaining it may cheat.

The third mode of adaptation is *ritualism,* which refers to rejection of the goals but acceptance of the means. Often people lose sight of the reasons for doing things, such as going to church, but continue the socially approved methods, thus making a ritual out of the method. *Retreatism,* the least common of the five adaptations, refers to the rejection of both the goals and the means. This adaptation occurs after a person has accepted both the goals and means but has failed repeatedly to achieve the goals by legitimate means. At the same time, because of prior socialization, this individual is not able to adopt illegitimate means. The retreatist mode of adaptation represents a nonproductive liability to conventional society, and it is characteristic of psychotics, autistic persons, outcasts, tramps, chronic drunkards, drug addicts, vagrants, and vagabonds. The final type of adaptation, *rebellion,* consists of rejecting the goals and means of the present society and attempting to establish a new social order. Merton says this adaptation is different from the others, as it represents an attempt to change the social structure rather than to make an individual adaptation within that structure. Merton's five types of adaptations are listed in Exhibit 5.3, along with an indication of whether each type accepts or rejects society's goals and the means of achieving those goals.

Merton raised some criticisms of his own theory. It does not take into account social-psychological variables that might explain the adoption of one adaptation over the other. It does not examine rebellious behavior thoroughly, and it does not consider the social-structural elements that might predispose an individual toward one adaptation over another.[22]

Others have argued that Merton's theory of anomie does not explain the nonutilitarian element of much juvenile delinquency, which its perpetrators appear to engage in just for fun and not to meet society's specific goals. It has been argued also that the theory neither explains the destructive nature of some delinquent and criminal acts nor accounts for crime in societies where some goals are not seen as available to everyone. Finally, some critics argue that the theory has not been sufficiently tested empirically.[23]

Some scholars advocate abandoning Merton's approach;[24] others maintain that it remains a viable theory to explain delinquent and criminal behavior.[25] Alternatively, revisions of the theory have been suggested.[26] Steven F. Messner

EXHIBIT 5.3

Summary of Merton's Anomie Theory

Robert K. Merton's approach to explaining the effect of anomie, or strain on adaptations, is to present five types of adaptations, which are based on acceptance or rejection of the society's goals and its institutionlized means for achieving those goals.

Type of Adaptation	Goals	Means
1. Conformity	Accept	Accept
2. Innovation	Accept	Reject
3. Ritualism	Reject	Accept
4. Retreatism	Reject	Reject
5. Rebellion	Accept Reject	Accept Reject

and Richard Rosenfeld recommend extending Merton's ideas about the relationship between crime rates and such variables as culture, social structure, and anomie. They base their *institutional anomie theory* approach around an analysis of profit-motivated crimes, including both white-collar and common law crimes. They go beyond Merton's emphasis on the legitimate opportunity structure and maintain that eliminating social-structural obstacles to achieving goals will not reduce crime rates significantly. Their point is that the desire to succeed economically is so strong in America that all of the country's social institutions have lost their ability to control behavior. They promote the goals of economic success and so do not provide alternative definitions of success. For example, education "is regarded largely as a means to occupational attainment, which in turn is valued primarily insofar as it promises economic rewards."[27] No matter how much wealth one has, there is pressure to accumulate more, while social institutions have little power to control the means of achieving goals.

This approach is predicted to generate considerable theoretical analysis and empirical research, although scholars have found some difficulties in empirical testing of the propositions of Messner and Rosenfeld. Specifically, it is difficult to operationalize and measure the variables of culture, social structure, and institutional controls and compare them with crime rates.[28] Despite these problems, two authors have researched the relationship between social altruism and crime, concluding that "communities that effectively teach their members to respect and engage in behaviors that promote the welfare of others enjoy relatively lower rates of crime."[29]

In a 1997 publication, representing the largest study to date of the relationships among delinquency, crime, values, and a sense of community, a psychiatrist found lower rates of violence in areas characterized by social cohesion.[30]

Finally, the study conducted by research scientists and sponsored by the Office of Juvenile Justice and Delinquency Prevention (see again Exhibit 5.2) found that community and neighborhood factors such as social disorganization, poverty, low neighborhood attachment, and the availability of drugs and guns may contribute to violence.

Modern Anomie/Strain Theory

Strain theory Refers to the theories of social disorganization, anomie, and subculture that focus on negative social structures and relationships.

More recent developments in anomie may be analyzed by looking at **strain theory,** which refers to the theories of social disorganization, anomie, and subculture that focus on negative social structures and relationships. As stated by sociologist Robert Agnew, "Strain theory has typically focused on relationships in which others prevent the individual from achieving positively valued goals." Agnew maintains that strain theory should be expanded beyond the traditional emphasis on an individual's failure to achieve goals and include "all types of negative relations between the individual and others." Agnew believes that there is more to strain than a person's failure to achieve desired goals. He argues for a more comprehensive approach to the analysis of how strain is related to delinquent and criminal behavior but recognizes that his theory is not developed fully.[31]

Agnew has developed three types of strain that may produce deviance. First is the individual's failure to achieve his or her goals, which he divides into three subtypes. He includes immediate as well as future goals, and he goes beyond Merton's anomie theory to include the inability to achieve goals because of one's own inadequacies. In addition, he notes that the gap between one's expectations and achievements may result not only in disappointment but also in resentment or even anger. The third subtype includes the person's impression that there is a difference between the actual outcome and what the outcome should be—that is, a fair and just outcome. This might be illustrated by the student who expects an A on a test because he or she studied so hard: An A would be a just result!

Agnew's second type of strain occurs when an individual loses a source of stability, such as a loved one, through death or the dissolution of the personal relationship, such as the end of a romantic involvement. The person suffers strain through the loss of a stimuli that had a positive valuation.

The third of Agnew's strain types occurs when the individual is confronted with negative stimuli, such as difficulties in school, crime victimization, or even abuse by his or her own family members. The young person cannot get away from school or family without acting in a deviant way, and that appears to be the solution to the troubled youth. Agnew's typology of strain theory is summarized in Exhibit 5.4.

One test of strain theory verified Agnew's position generally but failed to support some of his findings. The researcher concluded: "In expanding the

EXHIBIT 5.4
Robert Agnew's Major Types of Strains

1. Strain as the failure to achieve positively valued goals.
   a. Strain as the disjunction between anticipations and expectations/actual achievements.
   b. Strain as the disjunction between expectations and actual achievements.
   c. Strain as the disjunction between just/fair outcomes and actual outcomes.
2. Strain as the removal of positively valued stimuli from the individual.
3. Strain as the presentation of negative stimuli.

Source: Summarized from Robert Agnew, "A General Strain Theory of Crime and Delinquency," in *Criminological Theory: Past to Present,* eds. Francis T. Cullen and Robert Agnew (Los Angeles, CA: Roxbury, 1999), pp. 152–56.

scope of strain theory, Agnew has only begun an important line of both theoretical and empirical work that we wish to see undertaken."[32]

A 1997 publication by Agnew and Lisa M. Broidy utilizes strain theory to explain why crime rates are higher among men than among women as well as why women commit crime. The authors suggest that men and women suffer different types of strain, which explains the differences in their behavior.[33] An empirical test of this approach found some support for its ability to explain male versus female criminality.[34]

In a 2001 publication Broidy noted that most tests of strain theory concentrated on the relationship between strain and crime. She extended her research on a sample of college students to include the role of negative emotions, such as anger, and legitimate coping strategies (cognitive, behavioral, emotional). She found some support for strain theory: "Central general strain theory variables—strain, negative emotions, and legitimate coping—all appear to be important in explaining the likelihood of criminal/illegitimate outcomes." However, Broidy concluded that the "nature of the relationship among these variables appears to be more complex than the theory suggests."[35]

Finally, researchers delving into general strain theory suggest that although it may not be possible to remove all strain from the lives of adolescents, "It is not unreasonable to equip [adolescents] with techniques enabling them to manage their reactions to that strain more positively."[36]

The influence of classic anomie and modern strain theory may be seen in some of the subculture theories discussed below.

SUBCULTURE THEORIES AND THEIR FORERUNNERS

Subculture An identifiable segment of society or group having specific patterns of behavior, folkways, and mores that set that group apart from the others within a culture or society.

The theory of anomie as developed by Durkheim and Merton established a framework for the development of **subculture** theories of delinquent and criminal behavior. These theories focus on an identifiable segment or group characterized by specific patterns of behavior, folkways, and mores that set it apart from the rest of society. The subculture theorists do not agree on why certain norms exist within subcultures, but all their studies may be characterized by their attempt to understand delinquent behavior as sanctioned by the subculture and influenced by its status requirements.

The Study of Gangs

Modern subculture theories and studies of gangs were preceded by Frederic M. Thrasher's classic study (published in 1927). Thrasher saw juvenile gangs developing in Chicago as a result of social disorganization in the zone of transition. He studied 1,313 Chicago gangs and noted that they emerged as a result of innocent play groups that came into conflict over space in the crowded and physically deteriorated areas of the inner city. Thrasher did not deny that gangs existed outside the slums, but he thought most were located in that area of the city.[37]

In his classic study, *Street Corner Society* (published in 1943), William F. Whyte disputed Thrasher's social disorganization theory. Whyte showed that slums are characterized by social organization but that inhabitants may face a conflict between the status system of their culture within the slums and the system of mainstream society. Thus, to move up within their milieu means to excel in the rackets or in the politics of the slum. But this success is frowned on by the rest of society.[38]

For many years little attention was paid to these early studies or, for that matter, any studies of gangs. Recent gang-related crimes, especially those associated with substance abuse and illegal drug sales, have resulted in a refocusing of attention on gangs.

Since gangs are linked to the spread of violence throughout the United States today, many school administrators have taken measures to decrease gang activities. Extra security officers and metal detectors are utilized in an effort to eliminate the problem of lethal weapons. In some schools students are forbidden to wear certain colors and insignia or to engage in activities, such as handshakes, commonly associated with local gangs. These restrictions are being challenged in the courts.

As part of the Violent Crime Control and Law Enforcement Act of 1994, Congress included increased penalties for certain gang-related crimes and provided for the attorney general to "develop a national strategy to coordinate gang-related investigations by Federal law enforcement agencies."[39]

Attempts have been made to document the extent of gang membership, although this is difficult because definitions of gangs and gang activities differ from jurisdiction to jurisdiction. There are some criteria, however, and in one government study students were asked to identify gangs based on one of the following criteria:

Name
Recognized leader
Territory or turf
Tagging or marking turf with graffiti
Violence
Time spent with other gang members
Clothing or other identifying items
Tatoos[40]

Students reporting the presence of gangs in their schools differed by age, as illustrated by Exhibit 5.5. The older the student, the more likely he or she was to report the presence of gangs in school. Responses also differed by race and ethnicity, with African American and Hispanic students more likely than whites to report gangs in their schools.[41]

Research suggests that gang activity has changed significantly since the early studies of Thrasher and others. Unlike those in the past, many of today's gangs are associated with violence and illegal drugs. Some studies show that today's gangs are more organized and more formal than past gangs, manifesting clear leadership structures and significant control over members.[42] But other scholars describe gangs as "loosely confederated groups generally lacking persistent forms of cohesion or organization."[43] An alternative view is that the modern gang represents "a semiorganized response of young people to decreased opportunities in the postindustrial era."[44]

One final issue related to gangs is that of gender. The early 1990s saw an increase in female gang memberships. It is suggested that young women enter gangs because gangs provide "a social structure and sense of identity that members may not find elsewhere." The member is given a new name (a nickname) and welcomed into the group of members who "are willing to die for her."[45]

It appears that girls and women in gangs are becoming more violent, which may be a reflection of a generally more violent society. After a two-year study of women and gangs, the Chicago Crime Commission concluded that girls in gangs "are stepping to the forefront, selling their own drugs, making their own decisions and avenging their own wrongs. Females are willing to participate in

EXHIBIT 5.5

Percentage of Students Reporting Gang Presence in School, by Age

Age	*Gang Presence* Yes	No
12	26%	74%
13	34	66
14	40	60
15	43	57
16	40	60
17	41	59
18	40	60
19	43	57
Total	37%	63%

Source: James C. Howell and James P. Lynch, Office of Juvenile Justice and Deliquency Prevention, Office of Justice Programs, *Youth Gangs in Schools* (Washington, DC: U.S. Department of Justice, August 2000), p. 3.

the full range of violent criminal activity at the same rate and the same level—and sometimes more—as their male counterparts."[46]

A review of two recent studies of gangs concluded that researchers need to spend more time studying the phenomenon, noting that the publications portray a "sobering perspective on gang life that normally is not portrayed in the popular media."[47]

Finally, in studying the involvement of girls and women within gangs, it is important to analyze the social structure of the gangs of boys and young men to ascertain their attitudes toward female members. For example, there is evidence that, in gangs to which both boys and girls belong, the boys view girls with much greater acceptance than is the case in gangs to which only men belong. In the latter, the boys tend to view girls and young women as unacceptable for gang membership.[48]

The nature of female gang membership continues to be debated, with scholars unable to agree on whether young women are becoming more violent and less willing to assume traditional female roles within gangs.[49]

The study of gangs is important to an understanding of the specific subculture theories developed by sociologists and criminologists. These subculture theories may also be viewed in terms of both classic anomie and modern anomie/strain theories.

Lower-Class Boy and Middle-Class Measuring Rod

The 1955 publication of Albert K. Cohen's *Delinquent Boys* set the stage for a new look at subculture theories as an explanation for delinquency. Cohen focused on young males who live in economically disadvantaged neighborhoods but who are judged by the standards of the more affluent population. This discussion utilizes Cohen's language, as he referred to the "lower-class boy and the middle-class measuring rod." According to Cohen, the lower-class boy accepts the goals of the middle class but is unable to meet those goals by socially approved means. He must function within institutions that are run by middle-class people who judge him according to their standards and who expect everyone to strive for accomplishments and to succeed.

According to Cohen, the lower-class boy does not have the prior socialization that the middle-class boy has had and thus is unprepared for aspiring to and achieving middle-class goals. He has been socialized to live for today and to place more value on physical aggression than does the middle-class boy. He is less likely to have played with educational toys as a child and has lower aspirations. He finds himself deprived of status, as compared with middle-class norms, and his problem is complicated further because he accepts middle-class standards. He learns this acceptance from his parents, who want him to achieve at a higher level than they did; from the mass media; from the realization that some people do move up in the social hierarchy; and from the cultural emphasis on competition. The lower-class boy learns that the way to status and success is to adopt middle-class values, but he is not able to do so. The results are low self-esteem and major adjustment problems. In answer to these problems, lower-class boys develop a subculture that inverts middle-class values.[50]

Cohen says the subculture is *nonutilitarian* (boys steal items "for the hell of it," not necessarily out of need); *malicious* (boys delight in the discomfort they cause others); *negativistic* (the boys' norms are opposite those of society); and *versatile* (boys steal a variety of items). Also, it is characterized by *short-run hedonism* (emphasis on momentary pleasures) and *group automony* (resistance to outside pressures to conform).

Most of the reviews of Cohen's book have been positive; moreover, his theory has been given considerable recognition in sociological literature. Nevertheless, some criticisms have been raised. Cohen's statement that the lower-class boy measures himself by middle-class norms has been questioned. Cohen himself noted that some lower-class boys may not be concerned about middle-class values. But he argued that most children seek the approval of adults with whom they have significant contacts. Critics have responded that Cohen was not convincing, and that if there are class differences in socialization, it is reasonable to expect that they will affect the working-class boy's perspective of how he is perceived by middle-class people. In addition, Cohen's description of the delinquent subculture as nonutilitarian, malicious, and negativistic has been criticized. Some of the activities Cohen described are not characteristic of the lower-class gang today but are characteristic of some middle-class delinquent groups, which are excluded from Cohen's theories. In contrast, many of today's lower-class gang activities are much more serious than those Cohen identified.[51]

Neutralization and Drift

In one sense, the *techniques of neutralization* approach developed by Gresham Sykes and David Matza and Matza's theory of *delinquency and drift* are social-process theories. They are considered here (rather than in Chapter 6) because of their relationship to the subculture theories, which involve an analysis of the social structure.

In stating their theory, Sykes and Matza attack Cohen's assertion that delinquents develop values that differ from those of middle-class adult society as a reaction to their initial failure to accept those values and meet middle-class goals. First, they argue that if delinquents had established a subculture with norms that differ from those of the larger society, they would not exhibit shame or guilt when violating the social order. Such feelings are evident, however. Second, many juvenile delinquents admire law-abiding citizens. They resent the attribution of criminal or immoral behavior to those who are important to them, for example, their mothers. They appear to be recognizing the "moral validity of the dominant normative system in many instances." Third, juvenile delinquents distinguish between appropriate victims and persons or groups considered inappropriate targets for their activities. Finally, delinquents do internalize and accept some of society's norms.

Sykes and Matza contend that delinquents may become committed to the dominant norms but may rationalize their deviance from those norms. They describe the delinquents' attitudes not as a rejection of society's values, as Cohen suggests, but as an "apologetic failure . . . We call these justifications of deviant behavior techniques of neutralization." Sykes and Matza argue that delinquents are "at least partially committed to the dominant social order," but they may rationalize their deviance from these norms. They are not rejecting society's values, as Cohen states, but apologizing for their failure to attain society's goals.[52]

Problems of testing neutralization theory have led some social scientists to conclude that it has not been substantiated or tested empirically.[53] In one analysis, the importance of neutralization theory in "bridging the gulf that exists between social-structural analysis and social-psychological analysis" was emphasized.[54] Support for neutralization theory was found by another researcher, who analyzed the self-report responses of almost 10,000 persons in the workplace. The researcher concluded that those who have dismissed the theory are premature in their judgment.[55]

Similar to neutralization theory is David Matza's theory of delinquency and drift. Matza's studies of delinquency adopted an approach that he called *soft determinism.* It is a middle-of-the-road position between the extremes of the classicists, who believed that crime was the product of free will, and the positivists, who argued that crime was the result of forces beyond the criminal's control. Matza argued that although modern-day criminologists' theories incorporate different elements of determinism compared with those of the positivists of Cesare Lombroso's day, they have gone to an extreme. Although Matza did not adopt the doctrine of free will, he did argue that some movement should be made back in that direction, hence his "soft" determinism. He suggested that the delinquent *drifts* between conventional and criminal behavior, "responding in turn to the demands of each, flirting now with one, now with the other, but postponing commitment, evading decision."[56]

Differential Opportunity

Differential opportunity A theory that attempts to combine the concepts of anomie and differential association by analyzing both the legitimate and the illegitimate opportunity structures available to individuals. Criminal behavior is possible because the environment has models of crime as well as opportunities to interact with those models.

When Richard Cloward and Lloyd Ohlin introduced their theory of **differential opportunity,** they said that their work was influenced by two schools of thought: Durkheim's and Merton's concepts of anomie, which focus on the pressures associated with deviance, and Edwin H. Sutherland's differential association theory, discussed in Chapter 6.[57]

Cloward and Ohlin maintain that sociological and psychological factors limit a person's access to both illegitimate *and* legitimate roles but that this is not recognized by other approaches. For example, the anomie approach views individuals from the perspective of the legitimate opportunity structure. The focus is on differential access to *legitimate* means of achieving goals, but the approach assumes either that illegitimate routes to success are freely available to all or that there is little significance in any differential to their availability. Thus, anomie theory recognizes that not all persons have equal access to the approved ways of becoming a doctor, but it does not recognize that many persons do not have easy access to unapproved methods of achieving success, such as cheating, stealing, and so on. In contrast, Sutherland's differential association theory recognizes differential access to *illegitimate* opportunities but does not recognize differential access to legitimate opportunities.

Cloward and Ohlin's theory of differential opportunity structures unites the theories of anomie and differential association and considers the individual in terms of the legitimate *and* the illegitimate systems. Differential opportunity theory contains three types of subcultures: criminal, conflict, and retreatist. *Criminal subcultures* exist primarily in what Cloward and Ohlin describe as lower-class neighborhoods, in which successful criminals are more available and willing to assist young people in committing crimes. Conventional role models are less available. The *conflict subculture* features violence as a way of gaining status. Social controls are weak, and the area is populated with failures from conventional and criminal groups. Transiency and instability create disorganization in this area, and young people turn to violence due to lack of an organized way to address their frustrations. Those who fail in the conflict and criminal subcultures tend to resort to the *retreatist subculture,* which is characterized by drug use.

Differential opportunity theory fostered extensive early research and provided the basis for numerous programs aimed at crime prevention.[58] More recently, criminologist Francis T. Cullen has argued that the theory is more than a variation of Merton's strain theory. Differential opportunity theory is rooted in the Chicago school of ecology, and because of that, some have relegated it to historical status only. Cullen suggests that the theory be reexamined for its potential contributions to an analysis of crime causation.[59]

One of the problems with the differential opportunity theory is the lack of precise, measurable definitions of the relevant concepts. In addition, Cloward and Ohlin do not specify the degree of organization that is required for a gang to fall within their theoretical framework. The empirical validity of the theory has been questioned also. Despite these criticisms, the theory identifies an important element in the development of deviant behavior: the differences in the deviant's perceptions of the availability of illegitimate as compared to legitimate opportunities and the belief in a greater chance of success through illegitimate sources.[60]

Education and Delinquency

In a study of delinquency and school dropouts, Delbert S. Elliott and Harwin L. Voss attempted to modify and expand the differential opportunity theory of Cloward and Ohlin. Unlike Cloward and Ohlin, Elliott and Voss studied both genders and all social classes.

The guiding principle for this extension of differential opportunity theory was that "both delinquent behavior and dropping out are alternative responses to failure, alienation, and selective exposure to these forms of behavior" and that of the three contexts in which the investigators studied delinquency and dropout—the home, the school, and the community—the school would be the most important. For male and female dropouts, the strongest predictors are academic failure, school normlessness and social isolation, exposure to dropout in the home, and commitment to peers. School "dropout is related to class while delinquency is not," and "a strong commitment to one's peers was conducive to delinquency, regardless of the extent of delinquency in that group." The investigators concluded that "peer culture itself is conducive to delinquency."[61]

The results of this study shown in the following list are relevant because they challenge the conclusions of some other subculture studies of delinquency:

1. There appeared to be no relationship between delinquent behavior and social class or ethnic origins.
2. The degree to which students participated in extracurricular activities was not predictive of delinquency.
3. Delinquency among females compared to that of males was more frequently a response to alienation and rejection.
4. For males and females the school context was more important socially than home or community.
5. Associations with delinquent friends, along with alienation and normlessness, were both causes and results of delinquency in both males and females.[62]

Refer back to Exhibit 5.2, which lists factors predictive of future violence. In elaborating on the school factors, the publication notes that academic failure, truancy, poor-quality schools, and dropping out of school have long been recognized as predictive of youth violence. The predictive value of poor academic achievement and subsequent violence has long been recognized, and is higher for girls than for boys.

One other facet of education that should be considered and that constitutes a social-structural approach to explaining delinquency is that of the size of the school. About a month after the Littleton, Colorado, shootings at Columbine High School, experts gathered in Washington, D.C., to discuss the causes of youth violence. One of the suggestions made there was that large high schools (those with more than 500 students) may be a factor because of the greater possibility that some students will be on the outer fringes of the social structure and the resulting difficulty faculty and staff have in identifying and helping these students.

One media article focused on an Arizona high school of 1,800 students, describing in detail its social structure, which provides a place for the athletes and other select groups but may lead to significant alienation of others. The "winners" among high school students constitute a smaller group than we might imagine, "and high school life is very different for those who experience it as the losers. They become part of the invisible middle and suffer in silence, aleinated and without any real connection to any adult."[63]

The large high schools in which many of the recent violent acts have occurred are not located in the inner city and are not populated by lower-class students. They represent the mainstream of society, and most of the young people involved are from middle- or upper-class families; their parents are professionals, but they themselves are alienated from most of their peers as well as from adults. For example, Michael Carneal, who at age 15 entered a plea of guilty but mentally ill for the shooting deaths of three fellow students in West Paducah, Kentucky, on 1 December 1997, was from a family of "average churchgoing Americans." His father was a lawyer and his sister was valedictorian of her class, yet Carneal was an "alienated, sensitive, and nerdy juvenile who had been bullied from his childhood," according to one of the defense experts. Carneal turned to violent movies and video games, and may have been sent "over the edge," said the expert, by the suggestion in a school newspaper's gossip column that he was gay.[64]

Lower-Class Boy and Lower-Class Culture

Walter B. Miller focused his class theory of delinquent subcultures on what he termed lower-class delinquents responding to lower-class subcultures. First, Miller viewed the lower class as characterized by a *female-based household;* the family is organized around a woman. Men may be present but not in the stable form of marriage that is characteristic of the middle and upper classes. When present, the man in the lower class does not participate as fully in the rearing of children and in the economic support of the family as do men of other social classes. Second, Miller stated that the *one-sex peer unit* is the most significant unit for men and women in the lower class, in contrast to the two-parent unit that is the focus of other social classes.[65]

The lower class is characterized by six *focal concerns,* which Miller defined as "areas or issues which command widespread and persistent attention and a high degree of emotional involvement." He labeled them *trouble, toughness, smartness, excitement, fate,* and *autonomy,* resulting in a *cultural system* that distinguishes the lower class from the middle and upper classes. Miller argued that this cultural system was growing more distinctive and that the size of the group that shared the tradition was growing larger, too.

In contrast with Cohen's theory that the lower-class boy is engaging in reaction formation against middle-class values that he cannot attain, Miller suggested that lower-class values come from the inherent characteristics of the lower class itself. When lower-class males act according to the focal concerns that dominate the socialization within their social class, they conflict with middle-class values.

The author of an ecological study in Portland, Oregon, concluded that Miller's theory, although relevant as a tool for understanding the African American lower class, is not applicable to all lower-class areas.[66] A study in Seattle, Washington, reported that social class was not a significant factor in predicting delinquency.[67]

Evaluation of Subculture Theories

Subculture theorists seek to explain the high rates of delinquency in the lower class. These researchers and their critics, who have assumed a significant place in criminology, cannot be ignored. However, their approaches have limitations. Tests of these theories, many of which are based on samples from institutionalized populations, have been questioned by studies based on noninstitutionalized populations, such as questionnaires administered anonymously to the general population. Some studies suggest that most people commit acts for which they could be adjudicated delinquent or criminal (although the extent and severity of the delinquent and criminal activity vary) and that social class is not significantly related to criminal behavior among the general population.[68]

Other studies note that class is an important variable in explaining delinquent and criminal behavior but that the middle or upper class may be as significant as the lower class. Thus, access to power may be as important as lack of access to power.[69] In short, several variables might be involved in the analysis of social class and crime or delinquency, and the results may differ according to whether one uses official data or self-report studies as measures of crime and delinquency.[70]

Status offenses A class of crime that does not consist of proscribed action or inaction, but of the personal condition or characteristic of the accused, for example, being a vagrant. In juvenile law, may refer to a variety of acts that would not be considered criminal if committed by an adult. Examples are being insubordinate, truant, or running away.

Another issue is how social class is measured. The usual measure is income (or, in the case of juveniles, parental income). Scholars who reviewed the literature on delinquency and class report that the results varied according to how delinquency was measured. Furthermore, in their study of adolescents in a small midwestern town, these investigators "did not find class differences in reported delinquency" on either of two scales used for the research, but they did find that "having money enhances rather than diminishes delinquency." Delinquency may be a pleasurable pursuit, not a desperate move to acquire status. The more money adolescents have, the more likely they are to engage in **status offenses,** or alcohol/drug and property violations, although the amount of money to which they have access does not seem to affect their involvement in violent crimes.[71]

In short, the relationship between social class and delinquent or criminal behavior is complex; one researcher has noted that, "depending mainly on the measure of social class used, the relationship between class and violence is nonexistent, moderate, or relatively strong."[72]

FAMILY STRUCTURE AND CRIME

Just as social class per se may not be a cause of delinquency or crime, any other variables thought to be related must be considered along with other factors. For example, a traditional approach is that delinquency and broken homes are related variables. In Chapter 4 brief attention was given to the early studies associating crime and family structure. More recent research suggests that the relationship between these variables is complex. There is evidence that school and justice officials "discriminate on the basis of family structure alone." They are more likely to intervene in families of adolescents when the adolescent in question is a girl with a mother but no father. Another family structure that is predictive of delinquency is that of an adolescent boy with a stepfather in the home. Although there is evidence that some family structures are not closely related to delinquency,[73] other research has found some relationship between adult criminality and (*a*) family structure;[74] (*b*) family size (with delinquent and criminal behavior more frequent among those from large families);[75] and (*c*) the absence of one parent, although that relationship is not a strong one, and exists mainly in cases of status offenses.[76]

Some studies have disclosed subsequent delinquency by both male and female child abuse victims, with more extensive delinquency reported among the victims of more severe abuse.[77] Furthermore, substance abuse by parents prior to conception as well as by the mother during pregnancy may cause injury to a fetus. Some of these children later exhibit disruptive behavior.[78] The relationship between substance abuse and injuries to the fetus is discussed in Chapter 10 (see p. 312).

Basing their study on a reconstruction of the research data of Sheldon and Eleanor Glueck (discussed in Chapter 4), Robert J. Sampson and John H. Laub found that although childhood family experiences are important, adult family experiences are also important. Specifically, Sampson and Laub found that "job stability and marital attachment in adulthood are significantly related to changes in adult crime—the stronger the adult ties to work and family, the less crime and deviance."[79]

In 1993 Sampson and Laub published a book about their expansion of the Gluecks' research. One critic referred to this book as a "tour de force in criminology. It brings to fruition Sheldon and Eleanor Glueck's pioneering research on juvenile delinquency, which, until now, has never completely received its rightful acclaim." The reviewer called Sampson and Laub "consummate theorists and statisticians" and noted that their work enhances our understanding of social control theory (discussed in Chapter 6):

> In a nutshell, when people have a reason and an opportunity to become interested in their school work, families, and jobs, they are more likely to view crime as a costly and untenable option—a basic message that should be heeded by policymakers interested in alleviating America's intractable crime problem.[80]

Finally, refer back to Exhibit 5.2, which enumerates the factors found to be associated with youth violence. One group of those is family factors. Research has shown the following:

1. Juveniles with criminal fathers are much more likely to commit juvenile or criminal acts.

2. Those who are sexually abused (or abused physically in other ways) as children are more likely than others to engage in delinquent and criminal acts.
3. Lack of good family management is associated with subsequent delinquency and substance abuse. Poor family management includes the following: lack of clear parental expectations; poor supervision and monitoring by parents; severe and inconsistent discipline.
4. Low levels of parental involvement in children's activities may precipitate aggressive and violent behavior.
5. Exposure to high levels of parental discord may increase the probability of deliquent behavior.
6. Positive parental attitudes toward substance abuse may increase the chances the children will become violent.
7. Separation of children from their parents before those children are ten may predict future violence.[81]

ROUTINE ACTIVITY APPROACH

Routine activity approach An approach explaining crime by means of three elements: (1) likely offenders (people who are motivated to commit crimes), (2) suitable targets (presence of things that are valuable and that can be transported fairly easily), and (3) absence of capable guardians (people who can prevent the criminal activity).

Another recent social-structural approach to explaining crime is the **routine activity approach.** Lawrence Cohen and Marcus Felson take the position that crime may be explained as the convergence of three elements: (1) likely offenders (people who are motivated to commit crimes), (2) suitable targets (the presence of things that are valued and that can be transported fairly easily), and (3) absence of capable guardians (people to prevent the criminal activity). Human ecology is used to explain how legal activities increase the probability of illegal activities. For example, the movement of women into the workforce reduces the number of women at home during the day and increases the absence of capable guardians. Two-income families have greater spending power, and this may increase the number of desirable goods or suitable targets for crime. If these two elements converge in time and space with likely offenders, the crime rate increases. The absence of any of these elements may inhibit or prevent crime. Furthermore, "the convergence in time and space of suitable targets and the absence of capable guardians can lead to large increases in crime rates without any increase or change in the structural conditions that motivate individuals to engage in crime."[82]

In a private letter to this author, Felson explained his approach more fully as follows:

> The idea of the routine activity approach is to *bypass* traditional sociological theories, including those dealing with motivation and those of Cloward and Ohlin. Indeed, I selected the term "routine activity" to *distinguish* this approach from differential opportunity, which means something entirely different from what I mean. I also deliberately avoided the word "theory," calling it instead an "approach," hoping that this might exempt it from the usual muddle.[83]

The routine activity approach has been found useful in explaining urban homicides;[84] the importance of facilities (such as taverns and barrooms) in explaining crime rates;[85] victimization of youth;[86] victimization of single-parent families;[87] differences between violence among men and women;[88] the subculture of violence;[89] victimization in property crimes;[90] reactions to natural disasters, such as Florida's Hurricane Andrew;[91] and, most recently, street robberies.[92]

The emphasis in this approach is on a *crime of places* rather than a *crime of persons.* It has some of the same problems as a crime-of-persons approach: It cannot explain all crime, and changes in high-crime places will not eliminate all crime just as changes in high-risk persons will not do so.[93]

THE CONFLICT PERSPECTIVE

Consensus An explanation of the evolution of law that considers law to be the formalized views and values of the people, arising from the aggregate of social values and developing through social interaction. Criminal law is viewed as a reflection of societal values broader than the values of special-interest groups and individuals.

Conflict In contrast with the **consensus** approach, the conflict approach views values, norms, and laws as creating dissension and conflict. Conflict thinkers do not agree on the nature or the source of the conflict; nor do they agree on what to call this perspective. The *pluralistic* approach sees conflict emerging from multiple sources, and the *critical* approach assumes that the conflict reflects the political power of the society's elite groups. Also called *Marxist, new conflict approach, new criminology, materialist criminology, critical criminology, radical criminology,* and *socialist criminology.*

Earlier in this chapter we noted Durkheim's position that crime is functional and normal. A society that permits any kind of deviation can expect negative deviation, thus crime. We have seen that some scholars believe that laws emerge because societies understand the need to institute a more formal system of social control. The laws emerge out of **consensus.** In addition, we have looked at numerous studies, both historical and recent, in which social scientists have studied criminals and compared them with noncriminals, the assumption being that these are two distinct groups.

These and other aspects of the traditional approaches to the study of crime are rejected by those who believe that laws emerge out of **conflict,** not consensus. Laws are enacted by the group in power as a means of controlling those who are not in power. Furthermore, criminals do not necessarily differ from noncriminals. The difference may be in the way society *reacts* to their behavior. Thus, a person who embezzles millions of dollars from his or her company may be handled quietly by the company's management, whereas a hungry homeless person who takes food from the farmer's market may be processed through the criminal justice system. Members of minority groups may be treated more harshly than those who come from the majority; women and men may be treated differentially, too. Power and conflict may explain these differences.

The consensus approach views the emerging norms and laws of society as representative of the common feeling about what is right and proper; that is, they represent a consensus of views—a mechanism for maintaining social order. The conflict perspective views norms, values, and laws as creating dissension. Conflict thinkers do not agree on the nature of this process; in fact, they do not agree on what to call it. Nor have the thinkers in this field agreed with one another over time; for some, the process has been an evolving one, and their current positions differ from their earlier ones.

Background of the Modern Conflict Approach

Many of today's scholars trace criminology conflict theory back to the social and economic upheavals of the 1960s, including racial conflicts and the civil rights movement, protests against the Vietnam War, the recognition of inmates' constitutional rights, and the beginning of the modern feminist movement. The conflict approach can be traced much further back in history, however, and some scholars have done so. The study is a fascinating and informative one. In criminology, particular attention is given to the works of Karl Marx and Friedrich Engels and the impact that their writings have had on theoretical and political perspectives.

Marx has had a significant impact on the thinking and policies of the modern world. His works, along with those of Engels, were not focused directly on crime, but they have implications for its study.[94] Their ideas, from the mid-19th century, should not be associated only with the development of communism, and their influence may be even more important today than ever before.

In the conflict perspective of Marx and Engels, crime may be viewed in terms of the social structure characterized by social class conflict, which they saw as an inevitable by-product of capitalism. They argued that private ownership of property results in the poverty of some members of society, as those who own the means of production exploit those who do not. The latter turn to crime as a result of poverty. Marx and Engels believed that the capitalistic system is the sole determinant of crime as well as the causative element in all social, political, religious, ethical, psychological, and material life—and that the only way to eliminate social problems is to change the system through social revolution. Marx and Engels believed that eliminating social class would eliminate conflict;

The philosophies and writings of Karl Marx (1818–1883) form the basis for modern conflict perspectives. Marx, along with Friedrich Engels, presented a deterministic view that had implications for understanding criminal behavior from a social-structural vantage. (Library of Congress)

crime could be abolished. Obviously this position differs from that of Durkheim's functional approach, which maintains that crime is a normal and inevitable part of society.

The deterministic approach of Marx and Engels may be contrasted to the *facilitating* approach of Frank Tannenbaum. Tannenbaum argued that criminals are as much a part of the community as scholars, inventors, scientists, and businesspersons, and that the community must provide a facilitating environment for their behavior to exist. According to Tannenbaum, the community facilitates the development of criminal methods as well as its ideals and goals.[95]

A similar view was taken by Willem A. Bonger, a Dutch criminologist who examined the lives of primitive peoples and noted that they were characterized by altruism. They were very social and helped one another. According to Bonger, this altruistic way of life, based on mutual help, could be explained only by the social environment, which was determined by the mode of production. Among these people, production was for personal consumption and not for trade. Furthermore, neither property nor wealth existed. When there was abundance all were fed, and when food was scarce all were hungry. Finally, primitive people were subordinate to nature. As a result of these three characteristics, they were not egotistic. Society was characterized by social solidarity, which was the result of the economic system.[96]

In contrast, in a capitalist system people concentrate only on themselves, and this leads to selfishness. Capitalism breeds social irresponsibility and contributes to crime. It does not determine criminal behavior but makes people more capable of becoming criminals. The economic system provides a *climate of motivation* for criminal behavior. Although influenced by Marx and his economic determinism, Bonger recognized the influence of facilitating factors in the environment.[97]

Culture and Group Conflict

Culture conflict theory An analysis of crime resting on a clash of conduct norms, both of which are accepted partially and lead to contradictory standards and opposing loyalties. *Primary conflict* refers to the clash of conduct norms between two different cultures; *secondary conflict* refers to the clash of conduct norms between groups within a single culture.

Conflict may exist between cultures, between subcultures within cultures, and between interest groups. **Culture conflict theory** is concerned with the first of these possibilities and is illustrated by the work of sociologist Thorsten Sellin. Sellin argued that criminal acts must be analyzed as conflicts among norms. For every person there is a right (normal) and wrong (abnormal) way of acting in specific situations, and these conduct norms are defined by the groups to which the individual belongs. In the process of social differentiation, these norms clash with other norms; culture conflict is the inevitable result of conflict between conduct norms.

Sellin distinguished between *primary conflict,* which occurs when the norms of two cultures clash, and *secondary conflict,* which occurs within the evolution of a single culture. The first is exemplified by a father from Sicily, who, while living in New Jersey, killed the man who seduced his 16-year-old daughter. The father was surprised to be arrested for committing a crime. In his country, such an act by a father was viewed as a defense of the family's honor. In contrast, secondary conflicts "grow out of the process of social differentiation which characterizes the evolution of our own culture."[98] They develop when, during the normal growth of cultures from homogeneous to heterogeneous, social differentiation occurs. This in turn produces different social groupings, each with its own values and its lack of understanding of the values of other groups. The result is an increase in social conflict.

Criminologists disagree with Sellin's thesis that criminals and delinquents are responding to different norms. They argue that they are responding to the same norms but that there is a scarcity of rewards associated with them. Perhaps the way to resolve these differences is to recognize that cultural conflicts may account for some types of crime, especially among subculture groups, such as gangs, and among the foreign born, but that they do not explain all types of crime.

Conflict may also exist between interest groups within the same society, an approach developed by sociologist George B. Vold. Vold did not suggest that the conflicts between groups are caused by any abnormality. Rather, they are made by "natural human beings struggling in understandably normal and natural situations for the maintenance of the way of life to which they stand committed."[99] Examples are racial conflicts that involve violence between interest groups and the violent behavior accompanying conflict between the interest groups of management and labor. The focus is on conflicts between interest groups, not between subcultures or cultures.

Power and Conflict

Conflicts between groups involve another dimension emphasized by conflict theorists—power and authority. The concept of power has been explored by historians, sociologists, economists, and philosophers, one of whom in particular—Max Weber—became critical to the development of our understanding of social stratification and power. Weber was influenced by Marx but expanded Marxist views of class beyond economics and included the dimensions of power and prestige. By *power* Weber meant the ability to secure compliance from an unwilling person.[100]

Another advocate of the power concept is Austin T. Turk, who in his early works viewed society as organized into weak and powerful groups, the powerful dictating the norms that are proper for all and establishing the sanctions that are imposed if those norms are violated. Turk's position has some similarity with the labeling theory (discussed in Chapter 6), thereby taking a social-process approach, for he suggests that the persons most likely to be designated criminal because of their law violations are members of the least powerful groups in society.[101] Turk's position is a social-structural one in that he sees the *structure* of social institutions as relevant to the labeling process.

Turk emphasizes that criminologists must study the differences between the status and roles of legal *authorities* and *subjects.* He argues that these two roles are differentiated in all societies and that authority–subject relationships are accepted because it is felt that they are necessary for the preservation of a social order that permits individuals to coexist. Turk is a modern conflict theorist who views political organization as the result of, and characterized by, conflicts. Those in power have some control over the goods and services that might be available to others. That control is exercised through the use of power.[102]

Turk's conflict theory has been criticized for dismissing research suggesting that there is considerable consensus regarding crime, a criticism leveled at most conflict theorists. Turk's approach, however—viewing crime as a status that is conferred on those who do not follow the laws of society—points out the conflict between those in power and those not in power.[103] One attempt to test Turk's position empirically led the authors to conclude that there is support for his theory but that it should be tested further.[104]

CRITICAL CRIMINOLOGY

Critical criminology *See* **radical criminology.**

The influence of Marx and Engels and the early conflict theorists is seen in a broader scope of criminological thought that has emerged in the past two decades. The approach is called **critical criminology** or **radical criminology.**

Radical criminology Approach to the study of crime and criminals that explores and verifies the connection between economic reality and social phenomena; most radical theorists express a desire to change situations for the betterment of suppressed classes. *See also* **conflict.**

The literal meaning of *radical* is "origin" or "to get to the root of". *Critical* is used in the context of skillful judgment or judging with severity. *Radical criminology* refers to the process of exploring and verifying "connections between social phenomena and economic reality." It refers to a policy of "changing things for the better," although "there is no firm consensus or precise definition of radical criminology, either with respect to its key concepts or its primary theoretical emphasis."[105]

In 1973, Ian Taylor and his colleagues published *The New Criminology,* the first noted work to challenge traditional criminology and invite a new critical look at American criminal justice systems. This volume was followed two years later by *Critical Criminology,* by the same authors.[106] These classic works were followed by numerous other Marxist critiques of all aspects of criminal justice systems.

The emergence of critical criminology came on the heels of the social turbulence that rocked the United States in the 1960s. Social conflict between different groups affected most Americans, causing many to admit that discrimination and economic inequality were so widespread that new approaches were required to address the nation's problems.

Despite the recency of critical criminology as an approach to the study of crime and its lack of unity, there are at least two basic elements common to all critical theorists: (1) a reliance on economic explanations of behavior, and (2) a belief that the problem of crime cannot be solved within the existing confines of capitalism. Critical theorists are united also in their conviction that serious crimes (included in the FBI's *Uniform Crime Reports* as the eight index crimes) are not the most serious criminal threat to an organized society. They assert that corporate, political, and environmental crimes pose a greater danger.

Critical criminologists direct attention to how structural conditions and social inequality in class affect criminal behavior and official responses to crime. The emphasis is on social and economic conditions rather than on the characteristics of individual criminals. Critical theorists draw upon a Marxist orientation to analyze social relations and processes.

The critical theorists' redefinition of crime emphasizes violations of human rights on grounds of racism and sexism, unsafe and exploitive working conditions, substandard housing, political and military crimes, inadequate medical care, environmental pollution, and the lack of opportunity for every person to excel to his or her greatest potential because of policies dictated by the powerful. Marxism, they claim, promotes an equitable distribution of wealth and decision-making power.[107]

According to critical theory, capitalism is an economic system that creates a class structure that benefits some members of society at the cost of others. Class membership determines how individuals relate to one another both economically and politically since economic ownership is related to political power. According to critical criminologists, the class bias contained in laws is reflected in social control. For example, individuals belonging to the lower class are more likely to be arrested, convicted, and given harsh sentences than persons from the upper class. Self-report studies (unofficial data) show that crime is more evenly distributed among all classes than official figures reveal.

Critical criminologists contend that the social control of criminals is biased because criminal law focuses on behaviors in which the powerless are most likely to engage, such as public drunkenness. The class bias in law is evident also in the fact that many cases of harmful social behaviors of the upper classes are processed through civil and administrative law and not through criminal justice systems.

Critical criminologists focus on existing social and economic conditions in society and examine how these conditions affect individuals and classes as well as criminal activity. This is in direct contrast to conventional criminology, which concentrates on the actions of individuals. Critical criminologists also focus on criminal justice systems, analyzing the emergence and development of law as well as law enforcement. For purposes of analysis, the work of many critical criminologists may be categorized as *instrumental Marxism* or *structural Marxism.*

Instrumental Marxism

Instrumental Marxism A school of thought in Marxist criminology, which takes the position that the state is the instrument used by those in power to control those they dominate. Instrumental Marxists view the law, the state, and the ruling class as one, which enables the ruling class to take advantage of other classes by determining the nature and enforcement of law.

One school of thought in Marxist criminology is that in a capitalist society the state is the instrument used by those in power to control everyone else, a position called **instrumental Marxism.** Those who espouse this approach believe that "the state, law and the ruling class are one: the economic, social, and political interests of the ruling class find expression in law, which is constructed and used by the ruling class to the advantage of that class and that class alone."[108] One of the most prolific writers in this area has been Richard Quinney, who stated in 1974 that the "role of the state in capitalist society is to defend the interests of the ruling class."[109]

In his early writings, Quinney viewed both the theory and practice of criminology as "a form of cultural production," or cultural politics, whose purposes should be to move us from the acceptance of a capitalist to a socialist society. He attempted to develop a social theory that supports socialist rather than capitalist development and that "provides the knowledge and politics for the working class, rather than knowledge for the survival of the capitalist class." According to Quinney, the necessary basis for the development of this theory is Marxist theory and practice.[110]

In earlier developments of his perspective, Quinney examined and rejected the traditional criminological approaches and developed his own approach, which he called *critical philosophy.* According to Quinney, this approach permits us to question everything and to develop a new form of social life. Specifically, Quinney argued that traditional criminology has not questioned the legal order critically. He claimed that the state is a political organization that serves to maintain the interests of the ruling class over and against those of the ruled.[111]

Quinney proposed a socialist society in which the "goal is a world that is free from the oppressions produced by capitalism." In a socialist society, all will be equal, and all will share equally in the society's material benefits. A new human nature will arise, one that is liberated from acquisitive individualism and "no longer suffers the alienation otherwise inherent in the relations of capitalism." There will be no need for the state once classes, bureaucracy, and centralized authority are abolished. Law as it is known now will exist only in history.[112]

According to Quinney, the traditional notion of causality in criminology should be abandoned, and the attempt to discover "what is" should be replaced by an approach that would try to understand "what is in terms of what *could* be." His purpose in developing what he called a theory of the *social reality of crime* was to "provide the ideas for correct thought and action. Only with a critical theory are we able to adequately understand crime in American society."[113]

Like many critical criminologists, Quinney's position changed over time. His most radical work was written during the late 1960s and early 1970s, but during the middle 1970s he became more closely identified with the Marxist position, arguing that the real conflict is between the ruling class and those who are victimized by that class. He maintained his belief, however, that the solution is the establishment of a socialist system.[114]

In more recent years, Quinney has been comparing the spiritualism of Christianity with the moral position of Marxist philosophy.[115] In 1991 he and his coauthor reaffirmed Quinney's Marxist position but added a new dimension—a "*criminology of peacemaking*—a nonviolent criminology of compassion and service . . . There can be no solution to the problem of crime without peace and social justice. They are the beginning of a world free of crime."[116] Quinney and others expanded the field of inquiry beyond crime to include other areas in which they saw the state as an instrument of oppression: sexism, racism, imperialism, unsafe working conditions, inadequate medical care, substandard education and employment opportunities, and so on.

Two other early conflict writers of significance are Herman Schwendinger and Julia Schwendinger. In 1970 the Schwendingers published an article in which they argued that criminologists should extend their analyses beyond those acts traditionally defined as crime and include violations of human rights.[117]

In subsequent writings the Schwendingers reported the results of their analyses. Their study of rape is one example. They maintain that women who are raped feel guilty because of the oppression and discrimination that they suffer in a capitalist society.[118] The Schwendingers have conducted research in other areas of criminology, too—for example, on social class and delinquency, in which they question the conclusion that membership in the lower class explains most delinquency.[119]

William J. Chambliss describes the Schwendingers' work, along with the similar position of David Greenberg, as

> ground breaking in that they recognize the necessity to begin with the widespread nature of delinquency among youths and explain patterns and types of delinquent subcultures. They do not propose to answer the unscientific question of why some people commit delinquency; they focus instead on the question of what the varieties of adolescent subcultures are and why they have the shape and distribution they do.[120]

Structural Marxism

Chambliss and others have criticized the instrumental Marxist approach as static, too deterministic, too focused on economics, and inaccurate in its assumption that all law is used to the advantage of the ruling class and the disadvantage of those ruled. For example, laws regulating trade and commerce (e.g., antitrust laws designed to protect business from unlawful restraints that would reduce competition), employment discrimination, working conditions, wages, consumer laws, and many other areas aid the capitalist system, but they do not necessarily work to the interests of the ruling class.[121]

Structural Marxism Marxist position that although law may be explained by capitalism, it does not always reflect the interests of the ruling class. Structural Marxists look for the underlying forces that shape law, and those forces may create a conflict between capitalism in general and any particular capitalist.

Although there is some divergence, in general the adherents of **Structural Marxism** believe that although law may be explained by capitalism, it does not always work in the interests of the ruling class. They look for the underlying forces that shape law, and those forces may create a conflict between capitalism in general and any particular capitalist. Thus, to keep the system in effect, some laws that operate against the interests of some capitalists (such as those mentioned above) may be enacted to keep capitalism running.[122]

In their earlier work William J. Chambliss and Robert Seidman analyzed the impact of bureaucracy on various elements of the legal system: law enforcement, appellate courts, police, prosecutors, sentencing practices, and so on, and concluded that it led to injustice.[123] In a later work Chambliss focused on the political aspects of crime as well as on the relationship between economics and bureaucracy and how that relationship affects criminal justice systems.[124]

Integrated Structural-Marxist Theory

Mark Colvin and John Pauly have developed the concept of *integrated structural-Marxist theory,* which analyzes several control structures: work, family, school, peer groups, and social class. They analyze socialization within the family in terms of marketplace control, as follows: Parents' class position is determined by the marketplace (those who own and control production exert control over workers). Negative work experiences resulting from the control structure of work (for example, disagreements with those in power) alienate parents, who then develop more coercive controls within the family. These controls alienate juveniles, who have a greater probability of being placed in coercive control situations at school. These youth are more likely to be in inferior schools and to perform poorly. They have a greater tendency to associate with other alienated juveniles and to develop peer group control structures, which in interaction with class-related, community, and neighborhood distributions of opportunities, lead to delinquency. In short, major changes in delinquency cannot be made without changes in the root causes of that delinquency.[125]

One test of the Colvin-Pauly approach drew mixed results. The authors concluded that their "reconceptualized construct of social class, their incorporation of family and school compliance structures in their causal model is a promising contribution to the development of integrated theories of delinquency." The researchers found, however, "very minor effects of the class variables" in their study.[126]

In his analysis of the approach, Chambliss claims that Colvin and Pauly "make the classic error that we have seen over and over in the literature on delinquency and crime: they assume that delinquency is primarily a lower-class phenomenon when all the evidence indicates it is not."[127]

Power-Control Theory

Social control theories of delinquent and criminal behavior are discussed in Chapter 6. Another type of control theory, however, builds on the Marxist tradition and is relevant to this chapter's discussion of social-structural theories. The primary thesis of *power-control theory* is that authority within the workplace affects power within the family structure. These power relationships between parents affect the way they socialize and control their sons and daughters. Those practices "influence gender differences in both perceived risks of sanctions and risk preferences," which are "translated into gender differences in delinquency."[128] Or, in the words of power-control theory's major proponent, John Hagan, and his colleagues, "The core assumption of our theory is that the presence of power and the absence of control create conditions of freedom that permit common forms of delinquency."[129] The authors tested their theory on a Toronto, Canada, population. After responding to their critics, they proclaimed that the theory has merit.[130]

Hagan's power-control theory is an example of Marxist theory that introduces us to another variable ignored by many—gender. According to Hagan, power-control theory "asserts that the class structure of the family plays a significant role in explaining the social distribution of delinquent behavior through the social reproduction of gender relations."[131] Parental power affects delinquency in terms of the way in which children are socialized into accepted gender roles. Parental power is determined by factors within the family as well as by the workforce outside the family.

In the development of power-control theory, Hagan and others note that gender is important in explaining delinquency because most reported delinquent acts are committed by boys. Class is not as important as many theorists have claimed, but class and gender are seldom analyzed in the same study, a serious omission. Hagan and his associates also consider the power relationships of husbands *and* wives, emphasizing that the family's power structure is determined by the wife's outside employment as well as by that of the husband. In families characterized as *patriarchal,* meaning that the husband/father assumes the traditional breadwinner role and the wife/mother the traditional domestic role, fathers have more power and resources at work and at home, while mothers have less power, less ownership, and fewer resources at work and at home. This has been the dominant family type in contemporary Western industrial societies. Women are expected to keep greater control over their daughters, socializing them in traditional female gender roles. The daughter will have less freedom to take risks and engage in nontraditional gender behavior. When daughters are groomed for domestic life, their delinquency is not as likely.

The opposite of the patriarchal is the *matriarchal* family, in which the female has the dominant work job and more power and resources at work and at home. In more balanced, or *egalitarian,* family structures, husbands and wives have jobs with similar power and authority, which is reflected in more equal authority and power within the family. The roles mothers and fathers play within the family are different. In the egalitarian family, for example, daughters "gain a kind of freedom that is reflected in a reduced control by fathers and mothers and an increased openness to risk taking that, among adolescents, includes some common forms of delinquent behavior."[132] Power-control theory states that as families become more balanced, there are changes in the ways in which parents socialize their children. For example, it might be expected that females would be more likely to take risks and become involved in traditionally male-oriented activities, such as delinquency.

Although Hagan began his power-control theory development in an attempt to explain why males are generally more involved than females in delinquent behavior, in a later study he and his colleagues extended the theory to include the variable of how parental influence and support for dominant attitudes influence male as well as female delinquency. They found that differences in family structure, especially within patriarchal families, result in variations in the way families interact. This is particularly true with regard to the interaction between mothers and their sons. Hagan and his colleagues found support for their belief that in less patriarchal families "the most pronounced effects of changes in family life may be in altering the control of sons by mothers." Specifically, mothers may lessen the impact of traditional patriarchal roles of power, "thereby discouraging a preference [among their sons] for risks and delinquency."[133]

The work of Hagan and his colleagues has generated considerable reaction, although some have questioned its validity. One critic, quoting from Hagan himself, suggests that his approach "deals not so much with a testable theory of crime as it does with the means by which 'meaningful questions about crime and delinquency can be asked, and begin to be answered.' "[134]

Other critics claim that power-control theory omits some variables used traditionally to explain delinquency (such as rational choice and routine activities, discussed earlier in this text) and does not include normative or moral variables. Nor does it include social bond variables characteristic of other theories.

In a recent challenge to power-control theory, Brenda Sims Blackwell reviews the position of Hagan and others, along with empirical tests of the theory. She notes that the assumption that the type of household or family structure influences gender perceptions of risks and of being caught is not complete. The power-control position that females, compared with males, perceive a greater risk in being caught and punished if they engage in delinquent or criminal behavior and that the perception is greater for those females reared in patriarchal family structures, is supported but limited. It fails to account for the influence of informal social controls on females—specifically the fear of shame or embarrassment. Blackwell argues that research supports the fact that these variables "are at least equally, if not more, important for females."[135] In her own research Blackwell claims that the evidence supports the conclusion that "[a]mong those individuals reared in more patriarchal households, the perceived threat of shame accounts for a significant proportion of the gender-crime relationship."[136]

Evaluation of Critical Criminology

The most serious criticism of critical criminology is that it is a "viewpoint, a perspective, or an orientation."[137] The concepts that are crucial to the theory, such as social class, are not defined clearly in terms that facilitate empirical testing. Consequently, little testing has been, or can be, done. Others disagree. For example, critical criminologist Michael J. Lynch maintains that a Marxist approach to the explanation of crime can be assessed quantitatively.[138]

Critical criminology has produced a large body of literature, not all of which is Marxist. But it is the Marxist, or radical, approach that has drawn the greatest criticism. In a review and critique of a series of original papers written by conflict criminologists, some of whom were Marxists, Ronald L. Akers, a sociologist and criminologist, commented on Marxist criminology. Akers, who acknowledged that he was acquainted personally and professionally with all the authors whose papers he reviewed, stated that he found little empirical support for Marxist theory in criminology and that he disagreed with Marxism, thus rejecting Quinney's argument for the need for a socialist society. Akers accused Quinney of making static conclusions rather than deriving them from empirically tested propositions. Despite his criticism of critical criminology, Akers concluded, "[H]owever much I disagree with Marxist criminology, I believe we should continue to hear about it and respond to it."[139]

Others have pointed out that critical criminology "holds out the promise of having a profound impact on our thinking about crime and society." Conflict or critical criminology forces a reexamination of notions of equality before the law and a consideration of whether it really exists, or whether "there is ample evidence that our ideals of equality before the law are being compromised by the facts of income and race in an industrial, highly bureaucratized social order. If a 'critical criminology' can help us solve that issue, while still confronting the need to control crime, it will contribute a great deal."[140]

Finally, it is argued that "[f]ar from crisis and impending doom, the radical position appears to be on the verge of revitalization and redirection."[141]

SOCIAL-STRUCTURAL THEORIES AND FEMALE CRIMINALITY

Social-structural theories, especially opportunity theory, have been utilized to explain female criminality. Some criminologists reject this approach as an explanation of why women engage in criminal behavior. In fact, scholars do not agree on the nature or extent of female criminality.

Until recently, little attention was given to female offenders. Various reasons have been given for this neglect. Female offenders constitute a much smaller percentage of offenders than their proportion in the population. Most of their crimes do not present a serious threat to society, except perhaps to its moral fiber, as in the case of prostitution. Female inmates have not been seen as a serious social problem and have not engaged in prison violence to the same extent as male inmates. Because female inmates have been easier to manage than male inmates, most correctional facilities for women are less secure. Some widely

Although historically gang members were usually male, young women are forming their own gangs, and there is evidence that they are becoming increasingly violent. (Deborah Copaken/Getty Images)

held beliefs in this area have been challenged, however, as scholars have begun to take a closer look at women in criminal justice systems.

But crimes among women, as measured by official crime data, have been increasing, and for some crimes, as noted in Chapter 2 (see exhibit), the increases for women have exceeded those for men. Furthermore, although violent crimes among women remain rare, there have been several cases in recent years in which women engaged in violence against their children (as in the case of Susan Smith of South Carolina, who strapped her little boys into the backseat of a car and drove into a lake, jumping out to save herself, or Andrea Yates of Houston, Texas, who in 2001 drowned all of her five children); against their newborns (as noted in Exhibit 5.1); or against others (as illustrated by the pickax murders for which Texas executed Karla Faye Tucker).

Execution of women is not common in the United States, and considerable attention was generated by Tucker's 1998 execution. Tucker was convicted of the brutal murders of two people; she claimed to have been rehabilitated in prison, and numerous people throughout the world called for Texas to spare her life. That call was refused. The cases of Smith, Yates, and Tucker received far more media attention than the "normal" crimes committed by women. Although these high-profile cases are unusual, the fact is that women are being convicted of more violent crimes today than in the past, and their participation in property crimes is increasing, too, even though men still surpass women in the official data of most crimes.

Attempts to explain female criminality today focus on three areas: opportunity and women's liberation; conflict; and feminist theories.

Opportunity Theory and Women's Liberation

One explanation of the increase in crimes among women is that as women have become more liberated and have participated more extensively (and more equally) in the workforce, they have had greater opportunities to commit crimes and have done so. Illustrative of those who give this explanation are Freda Adler and Rita James Simon.

In *Sisters in Crime,* published in 1975 Adler set the stage for the debate on the extent and nature of female criminality from the perspective of women's liberation. According to Adler, the data revealed that crime among women was increasing and that more women were engaging in acts traditionally considered to be male rather than female crimes. Women were becoming murderers, muggers, bank robbers, and members of organized crime (although they had not attained much success in the latter venture).[142]

Some supported Adler's position that female crime was increasing and becoming more violent, although not all agreed on why this was occurring.[143] Others criticized her approach, suggesting that any differences in data might be the result of methodological problems in collecting or analyzing the data.[144] Adler's *Sisters in Crime* became a controversial work and, nearly three decades since its publication, continues to generate debate.

The second approach to the opportunity theory involving women's liberation is that of Rita James Simon. In one of her early works, Simon argued that female crime rates increased only in certain property crimes—such as larceny-theft, fraud, and embezzlement—and that the increase in those crimes could be explained by opportunity theory. More women were in the labor force, and they were working in a larger variety of jobs, leading to greater opportunities for committing crimes. Simon suggested that the propensities of men and women to commit crimes do not differ significantly; the difference is in opportunities. Simon's position is that women are more involved in economic crimes because they have more opportunities to commit these crimes, and they are less involved in violent crimes because the frustrations that lead to the latter are decreased as women become liberated.[145]

The women's liberation approach has not received significant empirical support,[146] and Darrell J. Steffensmeier and others have argued that the increase in female criminality actually began before the women's liberation movement. Steffensmeier agrees that there has been an increase in some kinds of crime among women, but he takes the position that women are involved *primarily* in traditional female crimes such as shoplifting.[147] Steffensmeier notes also the lack of success of women in organized crime.[148] He concludes that, among male delinquents and criminals, women are regarded primarily as sex objects, wives, and mothers. Female delinquency continues to reflect traditional female gender roles; the women's movement has had little effect on this phenomenon.[149]

The findings of more recent research by Steffensmeier and Cathy Streifel "do not support the traditional liberation thesis" of female criminality. "Instead they show that trends in the female share of offending are largely a function of trends in formal policing, and less so of trends in the economic marginalization of females."[150]

Other scholars have supported Steffensmeier's argument that women are engaging in traditional female gender roles even when they commit crimes generally considered to be masculine.[151] Meda Chesney-Lind and Randall G. Shelden claim the same is the case with juveniles, with the relationship between male and female delinquency remaining about the same.[152]

Conflict Theory

Conflict theory has also been utilized to explain the nature and extent of female criminality. Under this approach the analysis of gender and crime emphasizes the subordinate position of women. Historically, women have been treated as property, first of their fathers and then of their husbands. Women were expected to take care of their families, bear and rear children, and engage in sexual relations with their husbands. Under the law in many jurisdictions, women did not have the authority to decline these roles. When they began working outside the home, they held inferior economic positions. There have been some changes in the law and social expectations; many would argue that those changes have not been sufficient.

Critical criminologists look at female offenders in terms of the economic structure and other conflicts within the social structure. Some radical criminologists suggest that female criminality is a function of the capitalist system that denies women equal access to the economic advantages men enjoy. If women spend most of their time at home, they do not have many opportunities to commit crimes. When they do engage in crime, they do so primarily in conjunction with their traditional roles as wives, homemakers, and mothers; they are prostitutes; they shoplift; or they engage in fraud. When they engage in violence, usually it is directed toward their children, husbands, or lovers. Critical criminologists' analysis of gender and crime goes beyond an attempt to explain the cause of crime and delinquency to an explanation of all elements of criminal justice systems in terms of gender roles and power.

In his critical approach to explaining the relationship between gender and crime, James Messerschmidt emphasizes the need to consider hierarchical structures as well as economics. Most societies are patriarchal, with specific divisions of labor for men and women within the family. Primarily, women's roles have been related to their biological reproductive function. That women are subordinate to men economically and biologically, he asserts, explains why women engage in less criminal activity than men and why any criminal activity they do engage in is less serious. "Gender and class shape one's possibilities . . . Criminality is related, then, to the interaction of patriarchy and capitalism and the structural possibilities this interaction creates."[153]

According to Messerschmidt, the lack of power explains female criminality as well as the violent crimes of lower-class men. Corporate crimes and sexual crimes committed by men against women (and children) may be explained by male power. These power relationships may explain particular types of crime, too, such as prostitution by women, and rape and domestic violence by men.

Messerschmidt also examines the roles of class, race, and gender in explaining criminal behavior. His effort has been described by one critic as follows: "superb on every dimension of scholarship . . . The passions of his profeminist ideology are apparent at every turn. Arguably the most progressive of contemporary criminological theorists . . . A Classic in the making."[154]

Gender inequality has been used to explain domestic violence leading to battering of women by men. In many cases domestic violence is accompanied by heavy drinking, and it is argued that violence and alcoholism "both represent the politics of domination" that exists between men and women in a domestic relationship.[155]

On the one hand, some scholars believe that the addition of the analysis of gender inequality to critical criminology has advanced and enriched the field. "New questions are being asked, new perspectives are being introduced, and new solutions are being advanced."[156] On the other hand, some criminologists have been criticized for falling "into their own brand of reductionism by assuming that the experiences of women (as a social category and distinct from the category of men) are universal and distinct from those of men." It is suggested that race and social class as well as gender are important in explaining the differences between male and female criminality.[157]

Feminist Theory

Meda Chesney-Lind and others have taken the position that the contributions of Adler and Simon do not constitute a sufficient explanation of female criminality, which requires the rethinking of criminological theory. Chesney-Lind and Kathleen Daly describe the latter as "a product of white, economically privileged men's experiences."[158] They do not consider the contributions of Adler and Simon to constitute feminist theory, and Chesney-Lind refers to those works as "flawed theory building" that has been, for the most part, discredited by other researchers.[159]

Although feminist scholars are not clear on what constitutes feminist theory in criminology, they do agree that the contributions may be made by male as well as female scholars and that the focus on female crime alone is not sufficient to qualify. The trend today is toward looking at the dominance of men over women (the patriarchal society) and the impact that has on crimes by and against women. This focus on the power of one gender over the other is similar to the conflict focus on the power of one group over another, as illustrated by the above discussion of Messerschmidt's work. The use of the term *feminist* rather than *conflict* or *critical*, however, may connote a more special place or focus on the subject of women and crime. Given the years of neglect of any attempt to explain female crime from a theoretical perspective, this labeling may be significant.

Feminist scholars go beyond an attempt to explain female criminality; they look at female victimization and at the treatment of women by criminal justice systems, too. They have been particularly important in sensitizing us to the manner in which female victims of rape and other sexual assaults have been treated by police, prosecutors, and judges.[160]

Feminist scholars have also contributed to our understanding of the possible explanations of gender differences in violent delinquency. For example, Karen Heimer and Stacy De Coster examined gender and violence among juveniles, utilizing differential association theory as well as feminist theory and gender studies. They found that more subtle, indirect mechanisms control female violence, with more direct, overt ways affecting the violence of young males:

> In short, the conclusion of our research is that violent delinquency is "gendered" in significant ways [through the socialization process] . . . Specifically, boys are more violent than girls largely because they are taught more definitions favoring such behavior; girls are less violent than boys because they are controlled through subtle mechanisms, which included learning that violence is incompatible with the meaning of gender for them and being restrained by emotional bonds to family.[161]

Heimer and De Coster state that just as traditional patterns of socialization of young males contribute to male violence, they also contribute to inhibiting young women from such positive goals as "climbing the corporate ladder." Given this situation, they argue, "socializing either gender similarly to the other could have negative consequences. The best scenario may prove to be a middle ground, where both genders learn distaste for violence and learn to pursue their positive potentials."[162] Much remains to be done, however, as Media Focus 5.1 suggests.

Finally, feminist explanations may have sensitized us to many issues regarding gender and crime, but there have been insufficient empirical studies to support their positions. "Indirect tests by feminist theorists have found no or weak support for the hypothesis of major differences in the etiology of male and female crime."[163] Ronald L. Akers concludes, "Feminist theory is still in formation, and the paucity of direct tests of its hypotheses has not yet provided a clear evaluation of its empirical validity."[164]

Media Focus 5.1

The Media and School Shootings: A Look at Feminist Theory

The shootings at Columbine High School in Colorado as well as those at other schools have gained international media attention. Although some of the attention has focused on the social class of the schools targeted (most draw students from middle- or upper-class neighborhoods), little attention has been given to an analysis of the gender issues involved.

Two female scholars have studied media reactions to Columbine and other schools that were the scenes of multiple shootings by students.[1] In these studies all of the offenders were male; 59 percent of the victims were female. Mona J. E. Danner and Dianne Cyr Carmody utilized the feminist approach in their analysis of the media treatment of these crimes. They define their approach as one that places women at the center of the inquiry, or, in Danner's words, "a women-centered description and explanation of human experience and the social world."[2] The authors emphasize the importance of asking what the gender issues are in situations such as student shootings in schools.

In their analysis, the authors note that when those persons closest to the shootings—the classmates and teachers—were asked why they thought the violence occurred, they frequently responded with statements such as "he was retaliating against a girlfriend" or "he was responding to being bullied." The grandfather of a suspect in one shooting was quoted as saying that the suspects selected their victims because of their gender: "It was not a random shooting." Yet some of the early media reports, featuring interviews with social scientists, referred to the culture of violence in our society, the easy availability of guns, the breakdown of the family, violence in movies, and so on. "None of these experts commented on the gendered nature of the . . . shootings, suggested that violence is a means of asserting one's masculinity, or implicated violence against women and girls in any way."[3]

The authors conclude: "The relative absence of expert and media attention to the social construction of gender encourages incomplete explanations of school violence, and therefore fosters ineffective policy recommendations."[4]

If policy recommendations are made without looking at the gender issues that may be involved in school shootings, we may have more gun control, less violence in movies, and other changes, but we may still miss the real issue: Sexual harassment is a big problem and may lead to violence. And sexual attacks are increasing in some schools. A June 2001 article based on a study in New York City reported that in the nation's largest school system sexual attacks on students by students or staff rose sharply during the previous two years and that the rate is about four times the national average.[5]

1. Mona J. E. Danner and Dianne Cyr Carmody, "Missing Gender in Cases of Infamous School Violence: Investigating Research and Media Explanations," *Justice Quarterly* 18 (March 2001): 87–114.
2. Ibid., p. 89.
3. Ibid., pp. 107, 108.
4. Ibid., p. 110.
5. "Data Show Sexual Attacks in City Schools Are Up Sharply," *New York Times* (3 June 2001), p. 31.

SUMMARY

Chapters 3 and 4 explore explanations of criminal behavior that focus on the individual criminal and his or her characteristics. This chapter examines explanations that focus on crime as a function of the social structure. Writings on these theories and approaches are extensive and involve numerous contributors. To ease the difficulty students may have in outlining the presentation, Exhibit 5.6 is provided.

During the past several decades, the social-structural approach has been the most popular one of liberals, many of whom concentrated on such characteristics as unemployment and other forms of economic deprivation. They viewed the entire society as being to blame for crime. Even violent crime was seen as the result of the social structure—the oppressed kill and steal to get even with a society that has wronged them.

Although some writers see crime as a reflection of the family and other social institutions, and some offer psychological and psychiatric causes, the consensus of the liberal writings is that whatever or whomever is blamed, severe punishment based on a concept of personal evil and wickedness is not appropriate. The principal problem in dealing with crime is to curb poverty, sexism, and racism.

EXHIBIT 5.6

Dominant Social-Structural Theories or Concepts of Crime

EARLY APPROACHES

Ecological

Attempts to explain crime as a function of social change that occurs along with environmental change; work centered around the University of Chicago in the 1920s and 1930s, dominated by the works of **Ernest W. Burgess** and **Robert Ezra Park** and their concentric circle theory. The impact of environment on crime was developed further by **Oscar Newman's** concept of *defensible space,* stating that crime can be reduced by modifying the environment's physical features so that it appears that residents are in control.

Classic Anomie

Characterized by **Émile Durkheim's** belief that crime is functional and exists in all societies; based on the concept of *anomie,* which means without norms. The concept was developed further by **Robert K. Merton,** who believed that social structures exert pressure on some persons to behave in nonconforming rather than conforming ways. Merton analyzed this proposition by looking at the goals, along with the means of achieving them, in terms of five modes of adaptations, which are listed in Exhibit 5.3.

Modern Anomie/Strain

Focuses "on relationships in which others prevent the individual from achieving positively valued goals," according to **Robert Agnew,** the major proponent. Agnew expands the concept of anomie beyond the failure of one to achieve desired goals. His categories of strain are enumerated in Exhibit 5.4.

SUBCULTURE THEORIES

Gangs

Early developments by **Frederic M. Thrasher,** who studied juvenile gangs in Chicago and viewed them as the result of social disorganization, which emerged as innocent play groups that encountered conflict over space in the crowded and physically deteriorated areas of the inner city. Thrasher's approach was disputed by **William F. Whyte,** who believed that slums were characterized by social organization, not disorganization, but that young people living there may face a conflict between the status system of their culture within the slums and the system of mainstream society. Recent research suggests that today's gangs differ significantly from these earlier ones, are often associated with violence and drugs, and that girls and young women are also affiliated with gangs.

Lower-Class Boy and Middle-Class Measuring Rod

Albert K. Cohen's theory focuses on young males who live in economically disadvantaged neighborhoods but who are judged by middle-class standards, which they accept but are unable to meet because of their lack of proper socialization. The result is the development of a subculture that is nonutilitarian, malicious, negativistic, versatile, and characterized by short-run hedonism and group autonomy.

Neutralization and Drift

Gresham Sykes and **David Matza** disagreed with Cohen's position and argued instead that delinquents have developed values that differ from those of the middle class; in effect they neutralize middle-class values.

Differential Opportunity

Richard Cloward and **Lloyd Ohlin** argue that sociological and psychological factors limit a person's access to both illegitimate and legitimate roles and, in their analysis of delinquency, focus on the differential access to *legitimate* means of achieving goals. They developed three types of subcultures: criminal, conflict, and retreatist. An attempt to modify and verify this approach was made by **Delbert S. Elliott** and **Harwin L. Voss,** who viewed delinquency and school dropouts in terms of academic failure, school normlessness and social isolation, exposure to dropout in the home, and commitment to peers.

Lower-Class Boy and Lower-Class Culture

Walter B. Miller's position that lower-class boys who become delinquent are responding to a lower-class culture, which is characterized by a female-based household and the one-sex peer unit. He views the social structure of this class in terms of six focal concerns: trouble, toughness, smartness, excitement, fate, and autonomy, which combine to distinguish lower-class from middle-class culture.

(continued)

EXHIBIT 5.6

Dominant Social-Structural Theories or Concepts of Crime *(continued)*

FAMILY STRUCTURE AND CRIME

Examines delinquency in terms of the family structure. Earlier works by **Sheldon** and **Eleanor Glueck** are discussed in Chapter 4. **Robert J. Sampson** and **John H. Laub** based their work on that of the Gluecks but extended the analysis beyond that of the childhood family to that of the adult family.

ROUTINE ACTIVITY APPROACH

As stated by **Lawrence Cohen** and **Marcus Felson,** views crime as resulting from the convergence of three elements: likely offenders, suitable targets, and the absence of capable guardians. The emphasis is on a crime of places rather than a crime of persons.

THE CONFLICT PERSPECTIVE

Conflict Theory—Deterministic

Karl Marx and **Friedrich Engels** viewed crime in terms of the social structure characterized by social class conflict, which to them was an inevitable by-product of capitalism. Capitalism produces a system in which some people live in poverty; as a result, they turn to crime.

Conflict Theory—Facilitating

View of **Frank Tannebaum** that the community must provide a facilitating environment before individuals may turn to criminal behavior. **Willem A. Bonger** studied primitive societies, which he viewed as characterized by altruism, meaning that individuals helped one another in various ways and were not egotistic. The society is characterized by social solidarity, which results from the economic system, in contrast to the *climate of motivation,* conducive to criminal behavior, that is created by capitalism in which people concentrate only on their own individual needs.

Culture and Group Conflict

Characterized by the culture conflict theory of **Thorsten Sellin,** who analyzed criminal acts as conflicts among norms. He articulated two types of conflict: primary, which occurs when two cultures clash, and secondary, which occurs within a single culture. **George B. Vold** viewed conflict as existing between interest groups within the same society. An example would be racial conflicts.

Power and Conflict

An approach emphasizing that power is an important concept within the conflict perspective. To **Max Weber,** power meant the ability to secure compliance from an unwilling person. **Austin T. Turk** looks at the differences between the status and roles of legal *authorities* and their *subjects.* He views political organization as the result of, and characterized by, conflicts, with those in power having some control over the goods and services that might be available to others.

CRITICAL CRIMINOLOGY

Directs attention to how structural conditions and social inequality in class affect criminal behavior and official responses to crime. The emphasis is on social and economic conditions rather than on the characteristics of individual criminals. Those who advocate critical criminology draw upon a Marxist orientation of society to analyze social relations and processes. The approach may be divided into two areas: instrumental Marxism and structural Marxism. Two other approaches that come under Critical Criminology are integrated structural-Marxist theory and power-control theory.

Instrumental Marxism

Means that in a capitalist society the state is the instrument used by persons in power to control everyone else. Major proponent is **Richard Quinney,** who in his early work developed the concept of *critial philosophy,* an approach that permits us to question everything critically and to develop a new form of social life. Quinney spoke in favor of a socialist society free from the oppressions produced by capitalism. The emphasis should be on a social reality of crime, looking for what ought to be, not what is. He argued that the real conflict is between the ruling class and its victims. In his later writings he added the dimension of peacemaking, seeking a nonviolent criminology of compassion and service.

Herman Schwendinger and **Julia Schwendinger** argued that criminologists should go beyond analyzing only crime and include the violation of human rights as well.

Structural Marxism

William J. Chambliss and **Robert Seidman** view the instrumental Marxist position as too static, too deterministic, too focused on economics, and inaccurate in its assumption that all law is used to the advantage of the ruling class and the disadvantage of those ruled.

Integrated Structural-Marxist Theory

Works by **Mark Colvin** and **John Pauly** focus on several social control structures, such as work, family, school, peer groups, and social class. Some of these can alienate parents, who then develop more controls within the famly, which can alienate juveniles, who then have a greater probability of joining forces with other alienated youth, leading to delinquency.

Power-Control Theory

John Hagan and others state that the core position of this theory is that "the presence of power and the absence of control create conditions of freedom that permit common forms of delinquency." The position introduces the concept of gender to the Marxist approach, advocating that delinquency is affected by the way parents socialize their children into gender roles. Hagan distinguishes families characterized as *paternalistic* (traditional parental roles) from those that are more *egalitarian* (more equal roles between parents). In the former type, girls are likely to be socialized for traditional female roles in domestic life, and delinquency is not as likely.

THEORIES THAT ADDRESS FEMALE CRIMINALITY

Opportunity Theory and Women's Liberation

Views the increase in female criminality as the result of greater opportunities for women in the workforce. **Freda Adler's** *Sisters in Crime* states that the nature of female crime (toward that previously characterized primarily as male crimes) increased when women began participating more extensively in the workforce. **Rita James Simon** took the position that female crime rates increased only in certain property crimes, and that increase is explained by opportunity theory—they have more chances to engage in crimes such as larceny-theft, fraud, and embezzlement. **Darrell J. Steffensmeier** argues that the increase in female criminality began before the women's liberation movement and that women have been engaged primarily in traditional female crimes, or when engaging in traditional male crimes (such as murder), they assume traditional female gender roles.

Conflict Theory

Emphasizes the subordinate position of women within society's economic structure in explaining the nature and extent of female crime and the criminal justice systems' reactions to those crimes. **James Messerschmidt** looks at hierarchical structures of society as well as economic systems. Women are viewed in most societies as subordinate to men in both areas and thus they engage in less crime and the crimes they do engage in are less serious. Their possibilities in the criminal world are shaped by gender and class as well as by economics.

Feminist Theory

Looks at the dominance of men over women and the impact it has on crimes by and against women. Since criminology has been dominated by male researchers, who have concentrated on male crime, the issue of gender roles in explaining crime and the reaction to crime have been ignored. Feminists aim to eliminate this bias in criminological research. **Meda Chesney-Lind** and **Kathleen Daly** are two of the major proponents of feminist theory; they emphasize that the traditional structure of patriarchy, with men dominating women, is as important as social class in understanding crime. Male dominance is seen in criminal justice systems as well as in criminological research, as men discriminate against women in order to reinforce traditional female gender roles.

The chapter begins with a brief overview of the social-structural approach before focusing on the ecological school of thought. The Chicago-based studies of Park and Burgess, and Shaw and McKay, are examined and critiqued, and their relevance to crime in other countries is noted.

The contributions of Durkheim center on the view that crime is normal and functional. His concept of anomie is discussed in the context of social solidarity and its relationship to deviant and criminal behavior. Anomie is an important concept in criminological theory. It was developed further by Merton, who focused on American culture, which he analyzed by typologies or modes of adaptation to societal goals and the acceptable means of attaining those goals. Attention is also given to more recent scholarly tests of anomie.

The influence of anomie on the emergence of subculture theories to explain crime and especially delinquency is introduced with a look at the ecological theories of early gangs. Particular attention is given to the work of Thrasher in the Chicago area, but current data and research on gangs are highlighted as well. The subculture approaches illustrate various ways of analyzing crime in terms of society's social and economic class structure. These approaches range from viewing the lower socioeconomic class as a subculture with norms differing from those of the rest of society, to the assumption that crime and delinquency may be explained primarily in terms of differential access to legitimate or illegitimate ways of achieving goals. One aspect of opportunity theory is education, and the chapter notes the research on differentials between male and female school dropouts and delinquency. The problem of measuring class is noted in a critique of subculture approaches.

Gender is a relevant variable in any attempt to explain criminal or delinquent behavior. This chapter builds on previous discussions of gender in analyses of the relationship between family structure and delinquency.

Scholars continue to refine social structural analyses of criminal behavior, and the chapter summarizes some of the more recent approaches, such as routine activity. This approach considers the availability of likely offenders, suitable targets, and the absence of "guardians"—people to prevent criminal activity from occurring. It is useful in explaining urban crime.

In recent years considerable attention has been given to the study of crime by conflict theorists. The chapter discusses the early conflict approach, the differences among conflict theorists, and the more recent works in this area. The emergence of the conflict approach is viewed in the context of other societal changes, such as the civil rights movement. This section begins with a look at the theories of Marx and Engels as well as those of Sellin before examining in more detail the contributions of modern conflict theorists. The concept of power in relation to social class is explored. The discussion focuses on the works of critical criminologists, which may be categorized as instrumental Marxism, structural Marxism, or an integration of the approaches.

Closely related to the Marxist approach is John Hagan's power-control theory, which is examined with particular reference to Hagan's analysis of gender and crime. That discussion is followed by a more expansive look at social-structural theories, especially critical criminology, and female criminality.

The social-structural emphasis has lost popularity in this country. The swing is toward the criminal, who is presumed to think rationally and who, it is assumed, can be deterred from criminal activity if the correct disincentives are imposed. The contributions of social-structural theories must not be overlooked, however. In identifying social and political institutions as possible causes of crime, we have made significant changes, some that may be questioned and some that appear to be functional for individuals and for society. We have learned that it is important to consider crime from many perspectives.

Although this chapter's primary emphasis is on social structure, the approaches provide a basis from which process theories may be considered. For example, an environmental explanation of criminal behavior might include not only the ecology of the area in which the criminal behavior occurs but also the impact that the environment has on a person's decision to engage in criminal behavior. The process of becoming a criminal might be intertwined with the structure in which the behavior takes place. Thus, these social-structural explanations are important not only for their own merit in explaining criminal behavior but also for the framework they establish for process theories.

In developing an understanding of how to reduce crime, we need to assess sociological theories that are concerned with the *process* of becoming a criminal. The contributions of sociologists in this area are significant. To those developments the next chapter is devoted.

STUDY QUESTIONS

1. Explain the basis of the ecological school of crime, and discuss some of the early research supporting its position.
2. Contrast Durkheim's concept of anomie with the development by Merton.
3. Describe briefly the reaction to Merton's theory of anomie.
4. What is *strain theory?* Briefly discuss the contributions of Robert Agnew.
5. Evaluate the contributions of Thrasher and Whyte to the study of gangs. Discuss modern gangs, especially with reference to gender.
6. List and distinguish the major subculture theories of delinquency.
7. What is the relationship between education and delinquency? Social class and delinquency? High school size and delinquency?
8. Evaluate the studies of family structure and crime.
9. What is meant by *defensible space,* and how does this concept relate to crime?
10. What is meant by *routine activity?* Is it a reasonable explanation for crime?
11. Explain conflict theory and discuss its history briefly.
12. Evaluate Sellin's contributions to our understanding of conflict.
13. What is Austin Turk's position regarding conflict and criminality?
14. State briefly the history and importance of critical criminology.
15. Distinguish and evaluate instrumental and structural Marxism.
16. What is power-control theory, and how important is it in explaining crime?
17. Evaluate the contributions of critical criminology.
18. Explain the application of opportunity theory and women's liberation to the explanation of gender and crime.
19. Analyze the contributions of conflict criminology to our understanding of crime and gender.
20. What contributions may be made by a feminist approach to the explanation of crime and gender?
21. Evaluate the social-structural approach to understanding criminal behavior.

BRIEF ESSAY ASSIGNMENTS

1. Describe Newman's concept of defensible space and the criticisms of this concept.
2. Discuss Albert Cohen's theory of the lower-class boy and the middle-class measuring rod.
3. What are the criticisms of subculture theories?
4. Contrast the consensus approach with the conflict perspective.
5. Explain the elements and emphasis of critical criminology.

INTERNET ACTIVITIES

1. Go to the Office of Juvenile Justice and Delinquency Prevention's March 2001 Juvenile Justice Bulletin at www.ncjrs.org/html/ojjdp/jjbul2001_3_3/contents.html and find out more about the current research and history on female involvement in gangs.
2. The National Association of School Resource Officers (NASRO) maintains a website at www.nasro.org. Go to this site and find the 2001 SRO survey results. What are the major findings of the survey? In light of the issues discussed in this chapter, do you think the SRO program is an effective way to combat school crime and violence? Do SROs have a positive impact on students? Can their presence curb deviant and/or delinquent behavior? Explain your answers.

NET RESOURCES

www.ojjdp.ncjrs.org — The Office of Juvenile Justice and Delinquency Prevention (OJJDP) website provides facts and figures on issues related to juvenile justice, delinquency prevention, and victimization. This site also includes publications and links to other resources that provide juvenile and criminal justice information, and links to programs sponsored by the OJJDP.

www.feminist.org — The Feminist Majority Foundation Online presents a collection of resources, articles, news items and links to related to feminist issues. Links to a research center and the National Center for Women and Policing are also provided.

www.cddc.vt.edu/feminism/ — The Feminist Theory Website has information and resource materials on various aspects of feminist theory. The site is divided into sections that include feminist theory and national/ethnic feminisms. Users can also find information about individual feminists throughout the international community.

www.critcrim.org — Maintained by the American Society of Criminology, this website offers links and articles in critical criminology. Other features include links to theories such as peacemaking, left realism, feminism, and postmodern criminology and links to issues relating to criminology/deviance, government and other resources.

www.sshub.com — The Social Science Hub offers information and links to websites in several areas of social science including psychology, research methods, health, online journals, data archives, and evaluation.

www.ed.gov/offices/OESE/SDFS — Sponsored by the U.S. Department of Education, this website on the Safe & Drug Free Schools Program provides information, publications, and reports in areas such as school crime and safety, youth risk behavior, and legislation related to safe schools.

ENDNOTES

1. For a concise but excellent overview and analysis of criminology theories, see Ronald L. Akers, *Criminological Theories: Introduction, Evaluation, and Application,* 3d ed. (Los Angeles, CA: Roxbury, 2000).
2. Richard Jessor and Shirley Jessor, *Problem Behavior and Psychosocial Development—A Longitudinal Study of Youth* (New York: Academic Press, 1977).
3. Helene Raskin White, "Early Problem Behavior and Later Drug Problems," *Journal of Research in Crime and Delinquency* 29 (November 1992): 412–29.
4. See Robert E. Park, "Human Ecology," *American Journal of Sociology* 42 (1936): 1–15.
5. David Matza, *Becoming Deviant* (Englewood Cliffs, NJ: Prentice Hall, 1969), p. 31.
6. Nels Anderson, *The Hobo* (Chicago: University of Chicago Press, 1923). See also Harvey Zorbaugh, *The Gold Coast and the Slum* (Chicago: University of Chicago Press, 1929); and Paul Cressey, *The Taxi-Dance Hall* (Chicago: University of Chicago Press, 1932).
7. See Francis T. Cullen, *Rethinking Crime and Deviance Theory* (Totowa, NJ: Rowman & Allanheld, 1984), pp. 102–22.
8. Clifford R. Shaw and Henry D. McKay, *Juvenile Delinquency and Urban Areas,* rev. ed. (Chicago: University of Chicago Press, 1972), p. 106; first published in 1942.
9. See, for example, Solomon Kobrin, "The Formal Logical Properties of the Shaw-McKay Delinquency Theory," Chapter 5 in *Ecology, Crime, and Delinquency,* ed. Harwin L. Voss and David M. Petersen (New York: Appleton-Century-Crofts, 1971), pp. 101–31. For information on earlier attempts to test the theory of ecology in Baltimore, see Bernard Lander, *Toward an Understanding of Juvenile Delinquency* (New York: Columbia University Press, 1954).
10. Pamela Irving Jackson, "Crime, Youth Gangs, and Urban Transition: The Social Dislocations of Postindustrial Economic Development," *Justice Quarterly* 8 (September 1991): 381.
11. William M. Rhodes and Catherine Conley, "Crime and Mobility: An Empirical Study," in *Environmental Criminology,* ed. Paul L. Brantingham and Patricia L. Brantingham (Beverly Hills, CA: Sage, 1981), pp. 182–83.

12. Ibid., p. 172.
13. Oscar Newman, *Defensible Space* (London: Architectural Press, 1972).
14. Barbara B. Brown and Irwin Altman, "Territoriality and Residential Crime: A Conceptual Framework," in *Environmental Criminology*, ed. Brantingham and Brantingham, p. 66.
15. John Baldwin, "Ecological and Area Studies in Great Britain and the United States," in *Crime and Justice: An Annual Review of Research*, vol. 1, ed. Norval Morris and Michael Tonry (Chicago: University of Chicago Press, 1979), p. 57.
16. See, for example, Robert J. Bursik Jr., "Social Disorganization and Theories of Crime and Delinquency: Problems and Prospects," *Criminology* 26 (November 1988): 519–51; and Robert J. Sampson, "The Community," in *Crime*, ed. by James Q. Wilson and Joan Petersillia (San Francisco: ICS Press, 1995), pp. 193–216.
17. Émile Durkheim, *The Rules of Sociological Method* (New York: Free Press, 1964), p. 71; first published in 1938.
18. Ibid., p. 66.
19. Émile Durkheim, *The Division of Labour in Society*, paper ed. (New York: Free Press, 1964), pp. 374–88.
20. Robert K. Merton, *Social Theory and Social Structure*, enlarged ed. (New York: Free Press, 1968).
21. Ibid., pp. 189, 190, 192–93.
22. Ibid., p. 241. For a more recent statement by Merton, see Robert K. Merton, "On the Evolving Synthesis of Differential Association and Anomie Theory: Perspective from the Sociology of Science," *Criminology* 35 (August 1997): 517–25.
23. Edward Sagarin, *Deviants and Deviance: An Introduction to the Study of Disvalued People and Behavior* (New York: Holt, Rinehart & Winston, 1975), pp. 108–9.
24. See Ruth Kornhauser, *Social Sources of Delinquency* (Chicago: University of Chicago Press), 1978.
25. Margaret Farnworth and Michael J. Leiber, "Strain Theory Revisited: Economic Goals, Educational Means, and Delinquency," *American Sociological Review* 54 (April 1989): 263–74.
26. See, for example, Scott Menard, "A Developmental Test of Mertonian Anomie Theory," *Journal of Research in Crime and Delinquency* 32 (May 1995): 136–74.
27. Steven F. Messner and Richard Rosenfeld, *Crime and the American Dream* (Belmont, CA: Wadsworth, 1994), p. 78.
28. See, for example, the work of Mitchell B. Chamlin and John K. Cochran, "Assessing Messner and Rosenfeld's Institutional Anomie Theory: A Partial Test," *Criminology* 33 (August 1995): 411–29.
29. Mitchell B. Chamlin and John K. Cochran, "Social Altruism and Crime," *Criminology* 35 (May 1997): 203–28; quotation is from pp. 220–21.
30. "Study Links Violence Rate to Cohesion of Community," *New York Times* (19 September 1997), p. 11, referring to the study of Harvard psychiatrist Dr. Felton Earls.
31. Robert Agnew, "Foundation for a General Strain Theory of Crime and Delinquency," *Criminology* 30 (February 1992): 47–87; quotations are from pp. 74, 75. For the most comprehensive statement of Agnew's version of strain theory, see his article "The Contribution of Social-Psychological Strain Theory to the Explanation of Crime and Delinquency," Chapter 3 in *The Legacy of Anomie Theory*, vol. 6 of *Advances in Criminological Theory*, ed. Freda Adler and William S. Laufer (New Brunswick, NJ: Transaction, 1994), pp. 113–38.
32. Raymond Paternoster and Paul Mazerolle, "General Strain Theory and Delinquency: A Replication and Extension," *Journal of Research in Crime and Delinquency* 31 (August 1994): 235–74; quotation is from p. 254. See also Robert Agnew, "Testing the Leading Crime Theories: An Alternative Strategy Focusing on Motivational Processes," *Journal of Research in Crime and Delinquency* 32 (November 1995): 363–98.
33. See Lisa M. Broidy and Robert Agnew, "Gender and Crime: A General Strain Theory Perspective," *Journal of Research in Crime and Delinquency* 34 (August 1997): 275–306.
34. Paul Mazerolle, "Gender, General Strain, and Delinquency: An Empirical Examination," *Justice Quarterly* 15 (March 1998): 65–92.
35. Lisa M. Broidy, "A Test of General Strain Theory," *Criminology* 39 (February 2001): 9–37; quotation is from p. 30.
36. Miriam D. Sealock and Nicole Leeper Piquero, "Generalizing General Strain Theory: An Examination of an Offending Population," *Justice Quarterly* 17 (September 2000): 449–85; quotation is from p. 475.
37. Frederic M. Thrasher, *The Gang*, abbrev. ed. (Chicago: University of Chicago Press, 1927, 1963).
38. William F. Whyte, *Street Corner Society* (Chicago: University of Chicago Press, 1943).
39. Violent Crime Control and Law Enforcement Act of 1994, Public Law 103-322 (13 September 1994), Title XV, Section 150006(a).
40. James C. Howell and James P. Lynch, Office of Juvenile Justice and Delinquency Prevention, *Youth Gangs in Schools* (Washington, DC: U.S. Department of Justice, August 2000), p. 2.
41. Ibid., pp. 2–3.
42. See Jerome Skolnick, "The Social Structure of Street Drug Dealing," *American Journal of Police* 9 (1990): 1–41.
43. Scott H. Decker and Barrik Van Winkle, " 'Slinging Dope': The Role of Gangs and Gang Members in Drug Sales," *Justice Quarterly* 11 (December 1994): 583–604; quotation is from p. 584.
44. John M. Hagedorn, "Neighborhoods, Markets, and Gang Drug Organization," *Journal of Research in Crime and Delinquency* 31 (August 1994): 264–94; quotation is from p. 291.
45. "Life in Girls' Gang: Colors and Bloody Noses," *New York Times* (29 January 1990), p. 1. See also G. David Curry, "Female Gang Involvement," *Research in Crime and Delinquency* 35 (February 1998): 100–18; and Deborah Burris-Kitchen, *Female Gang Participation: The Role of African-American Women in the Informal Drug Economy and Gang Activities* (Lewiston, NY: Mellen Press, 1997).
46. Quoted in Terry Carter, "Equality with a Vengeance: Violent Crimes and Gang Activity by Girls Skyrocket," *American Bar Association Journal* 85 (November 1999), p. 22.
47. James C. Howell, book review essay, *Justice Quarterly* 17 (September 2000), p. 635, reviewing these books: Jody Miller, *One of the Guys:* (New York: Oxford University Press 2001); and Mark Fleisher, *Dead End Kids: Gang Girls and the Boys They Know* (Madison: University of Wisconsin Press, 1998).
48. Jody Miller and Rod K. Brunson, "Gender Dynamics in Youth Gangs: A Comparison of Males' and Females' Accounts," *Justice Quarterly* 17 (September 2000): 419–48.
49. See James C. Howell, *Youth Gangs: An Overview* (Washington, DC: Office of Justice Programs, U.S. Department of Justice, August 1998), p. 3. See also Finn-Aage Esbensen and Elizabeth Piper Deschenes, "A Multisite Examination of Youth Gang Membership: Does Gender Matter?" *Criminology* 4 (November 1998): 799–828.
50. Albert K. Cohen, *Delinquent Boys: The Culture of the Gang* (New York: Free Press, 1955).
51. John I. Kitsuse and David C. Dietrick, "Delinquent Boys: A Critique," in *Society, Delinquency, and Delinquent Behavior*, ed. Harwin L. Voss (Boston: Little, Brown, 1979), pp. 238–45.
52. Gresham Sykes and David Matza, "Techniques of Neutralization: A Theory of Delinquency," in *The Sociology of Crime and Delinquency*, 2d ed., ed. Marvin E. Wolfgang et al. (New York: John Wiley, 1970), pp. 292–99.
53. See William W. Minor, "The Neutralization of Criminal Offense," *Criminology* 18 (May 1980): 103–20. In a later work, Minor reported finding some support for neutralization theory. See Minor, "Techniques of Neutralization: A Reconceptualization and Empirical Examination," *Journal of Research in Crime and Delinquency* 18 (July 1981): 295–318.
54. John E. Hamlin, "The Misplaced Role of Rational Choice in Neutralization Theory," *Criminology* 26 (August 1988): 425–38.
55. Richard C. Hollinger, "Neutralizing in the Workplace: An Empirical Analysis of Property Theft and Production Deviance," *Deviant Behavior* 12, no. 2 (1991): 169–202.
56. David Matza, *Delinquency and Drift* (New York: John Wiley, 1964), p. 28.
57. Richard A. Cloward and Lloyd E. Ohlin, *Delinquency and Opportunity: A Theory of Delinquent Gangs* (New York: Free Press, 1960). The following comments are from pp. 144–60.
58. See James F. Short Jr. et al., "Perceived Opportunities, Gang Membership, and Delinquency," *American Sociological Review* 30 (February 1956): 56–67.
59. Francis T. Cullen, "Were Cloward and Ohlin Strain Theorists? Delinquency and Opportunity Revisited," *Journal of Research in Crime and Delinquency* 25 (August 1988): 236.
60. Clarence Schrag, "Delinquency and Opportunity: Analysis of a Theory," in *Society, Delinquency, and Delinquent Behavior*, ed. Harwin L. Voss (Boston: Little, Brown, 1979), pp. 259–61.
61. Delbert S. Elliott and Harwin L. Voss, *Delinquency and Dropout* (Lexington, MA: D. C. Heath, 1974), pp. 5, 204–5.
62. Ibid., pp. 206–7.
63. "Arizona High School Provides Glimpse Inside Cliques' Divisive Webs," *New York Times* (2 May 1999), p. 26.
64. "Violent Teens Remain a Puzzle," *Tallahassee Democrat* (18 May 1999), p. 3.
65. Walter B. Miller, "Lower Class Culture as a Generating Milieu of Gang Delinquency," *Journal of Social Issues* 14 (1958): 5–19.
66. Kenneth Polk, "Urban Social Areas and Delinquency," *Social Problems* 14 (Winter

1967): 320–25; reprinted in *Ecology, Crime, and Delinquency,* ed. Harwin L. Voss and David M. Petersen (New York: Appleton-Century-Crofts, 1971), pp. 273–81.

67. Richard E. Johnson, "Social Class and Delinquent Behavior: A New Test," *Criminology* 18 (May 1980): 91.
68. See, for example, James F. Short Jr., "Differential Association and Delinquency," *Social Problems* 4 (January 1957): 233–39; and F. Ivan Nye, *Family Relationships and Delinquent Behavior* (New York: John Wiley, 1958).
69. For a discussion of class and power as they relate to delinquency, see John Hagan et al., "The Class Structure of Gender and Delinquency: Toward a Power-Control Theory of Common Delinquent Behavior," *American Journal of Sociology* 90 (1985): 1151–78.
70. See John Hagan, "The Poverty of a Classless Criminology—The American Society of Criminology 1991 Presidential Address," *Criminology* 30 (February 1992): 1–19.
71. Francis T. Cullen et al., "Having Money and Delinquent Involvement: The Neglect of Power in Delinquency Theory," *Criminal Justice and Behavior* 12 (June 1985): 171–92.
72. David Brownfield, "Social Class and Violent Behavior," *Criminology* 24 (August 1986): 435.
73. Richard E. Johnson, "Family Structure and Delinquency: General Patterns and Gender Differences," *Criminology* 24 (February 1986): 65–84.
74. See, for example, Joan McCord, "Some Child-Rearing Antecedents of Criminal Behavior in Adult Men," *Journal of Personality and Social Psychology* 37 (1979): 1477–86.
75. See Nye, *Family Relationships and Delinquent Behavior.*
76. See Lawrence Rosen, "Family and Delinquency: Structure or Function?" *Criminology* 23 (1985): 553–73, and Patricia Van Voorhis et al., "The Impact of Family Structure and Quality on Delinquency: A Comparative Assessment of Structural and Functional Factors," *Criminology* 26 (May 1988): 235–61.
77. Carolyn Smith and Terence P. Thornberry, "The Relationships between Childhood Maltreatment and Adolescent Involvement in Delinquency," *Criminology* 33 (November 1995): 451–77.
78. See Timothy Brezina, "Adolescent Maltreatment and Delinquency: The Question of Intervening Processes," *Journal of Research in Crime and Delinquency* 35 (February 1998): 71–99.
79. Robert J. Sampson and John H. Laub, "Crime and Deviance Over the Life Course: The Salience of Adult Social Bonds," *American Sociological Review* 55 (October 1990): 625.
80. Arthur J. Lurigio, "Going Backward to Move Forward in Criminological Theory and Research," *Criminal Justice and Behavior* 22 (June 1995): 200, reviewing Robert J. Sampson and John H. Laub, *Crime in the Making: Pathways and Turning Points through Life* (Cambridge, MA: Harvard University Press, 1993).
81. J. David Hawkins et al., Office of Juvenile Justice and Delinquency Prevention, *Predictors of Youth Violence* (Washington, DC: U.S. Department of Justice, April 2000), pp. 3–5.
82. Lawrence E. Cohen and Marcus Felson, "Social Change and Crime Rate Trends: A Routine Activity Approach," *American Sociological Review* 44 (August 1979): 604. See also Marcus Felson, *Crime and Everyday Life: Insights and Implications for Society* (Thousand Oaks, CA: Pine Forge Press, 1994).
83. Private letter from Marcus Felson to the author, 25 January 1988.
84. Steven F. Messner and Kenneth Tardiff, "The Social Ecology of Urban Homicide: An Application of the 'Routine Activities' Approach," *Criminology* 23 (May 1985): 241–67.
85. Dennis W. Roncek and Pamela A. Maier, "Bars, Blocks and Crimes Revisited: Linking the Theory of Routine Activities to the Empiricism of 'Hot Spots,' " *Criminology* 29 (November 1991): 725–53.
86. James Lasley, "Drinking Routines, Lifestyles, and Predatory Victimizations: A Causal Analysis," *Justice Quarterly* 6 (December 1989): 529–42.
87. Michael Maxfield, "Household Composition, Routine Activities, and Victimization: A Comparative Analysis," *Journal of Quantitative Criminology* (1987): 301–20.
88. See Robert M. O'Brien, "Exploring the Intersexual Nature of Violent Crimes," *Criminology* 26 (February 1988): 151–70.
89. See Leslie W. Kennedy and Stephen W. Baron, "Routine Activities and a Subculture of Violence: A Study of Violence on the Street," *Journal of Research in Crime and Delinquency* 30 (February 1993): 88–111.
90. See James L. Massey et al., "Property Crime and the Routine Activities of Individuals," *Journal of Research in Crime and Delinquency* 26 (November 1989): 378–400; and Elizabeth Ehrhardt Mustaine and Richard Tewksbury, "Predicting Risks of Larceny Theft Victimization: A Routine Activity Analysis Using Refined Lifestyle Measures," *Criminology* 36 (November 1998): 829–57.
91. Paul F. Cromwell et al., "Routine Activities and Social Control in the Aftermath of a Natural Catastrophe," *European Journal on Criminal Policy and Research* 3 (1995): 56–69.
92. William R. Smith et al., "Furthering the Integration of Routine Activity and Social Disorganization Theories: Small Units of Analysis and the Study of Street Robbery as a Diffusion Process," *Criminology* 38 (May 2000): 489–524.
93. Lawrence W. Sherman et al., "Hot Spots of Predatory Crime: Routine Activities and the Criminology of Place," *Criminology* 27 (February 1989): 27–55.
94. See Karl Marx and Friedrich Engels, *The German Ideology* (New York: International, 1947); and Marx and Engels, *The Communist Manifesto* (New York: International, 1930).
95. Frank Tannenbaum, *Crime and the Community* (Boston: Ginn, 1938).
96. Willem A. Bonger, *Criminality and Economic Conditions,* trans. Henry P. Horton (Boston: Little, Brown, 1916). This work was reissued with an introduction by criminologist Austin T. Turk (Bloomington: Indiana University Press, 1969).
97. C. Ronald Huff, "Conflict Theory in Criminology," in *Radical Criminology: The Coming Crises,* ed. James A. Inciardi (Beverly Hills, CA: Sage, 1980), p. 69.
98. Thorsten Sellin, *Culture, Conflict, and Crime,* Bulletin no. 41 (New York: Social Science Research Council, 1938), p. 105.
99. George B. Vold, *Theoretical Criminology* (New York: Oxford University Press, 1958), p. 208. See also Vold with T. J. Bernard, *Theoretical Criminology,* 3d ed. (New York: Oxford University Press, 1986).
100. Huff, "Conflict Theory in Criminology," p. 73. See also Max Weber, *The Protestant Ethic and the Spirit of Capitalism,* trans. Talcott Parsons (New York: Charles Scribner's Sons, 1958); *From Max Weber: Essays in Sociology,* trans. and eds. Hans Gerth and C. Wright Mills (New York: Oxford University, 1946); and *The Theory of Social and Economic Organization,* trans. A. M. Henderson and Talcott Parsons (New York: Oxford University Press, 1947).
101. Austin T. Turk, "Law as a Weapon in Social Conflict," *Social Problems* 23 (February 1976): 288.
102. See Austin T. Turk, *Political Criminality: The Defiance and Defense of Authority* (Beverly Hills, CA: Sage, 1982).
103. William V. Pelfrey, *The Evolution of Criminology* (Cincinnati, OH: Anderson, 1980), pp. 64, 68.
104. See Richard G. Greenleaf and Lonn Lanza-Kaduce, "Sophistication, Organization, and Authority-Subject Conflict: Rediscovering and Unraveling Turk's Theory of Norm Resistance," *Criminology* 33 (November 1995): 565–85.
105. Michael J. Lynch and W. Byron Groves, *A Primer in Radical Criminology,* 2d ed. (New York: Harrow & Heston, 1989), pp. viii, ix, 4.
106. Ian Taylor et al., *The New Criminology: For a Social Theory of Deviance* (New York: Harper & Row, 1973); and Ian Taylor et al., eds., *Critical Criminology* (London: Routledge & Kegan Paul, 1975).
107. See Karl Marx, *Critique of Political Economy* (New York: International Library, 1904; originally published 1859).
108. Lynch and Groves, *A Primer in Radical Criminology,* p. 23.
109. Richard Quinney, *Criminal Justice in America* (Boston: Little, Brown, 1974), p. 95.
110. Richard Quinney, "The Production of Criminology," *Criminology* 16 (February 1979): 445, 455.
111. Richard Quinney, *Critique of Legal Order: Crime Control in a Capitalist Society* (Boston: Little, Brown, 1974).
112. Ibid., p. 165.
113. Richard Quinney, *Criminology: Analysis and Critique of Crime in the United States* (Boston: Little, Brown, 1974), pp. 37–41.
114. Richard Quinney, *Class, State and Crime: On the Theory and Practice of Criminal Justice* (New York: McKay, 1977), pp. 61–62, 165.
115. See Richard Quinney, *Social Existence: Metaphysics, Marxism, and the Social Sciences* (Beverly Hills, CA: Sage, 1982); and *Providence: The Development of Social and Moral Order* (New York: Longman, 1980).
116. Richard Quinney and John Wildeman, *The Problem of Crime: A Peace and Social Justice Perspective,* 3d ed. (Mountain View, CA: Mayfield, 1991), p. viii.
117. Herman Schwendinger and Julia Schwendinger, "Defenders of Order or Guardians of Human Rights?" *Issues in Criminology* 5 (1970): 113–46.
118. Herman Schwendinger and Julia Schwendinger, "Rape Victims and the False Sense of Guilt," *Crime and Social Justice* 6 (1976): 4–17.
119. See Herman Schwendinger and Julia Schwendinger, "The Paradigmatic Crisis in Delinquency Theory," *Crime and Social Justice* 18 (Winter 1982): 70–78; and *Adolescent*

Subcultures and Delinquency (New York: Praeger, 1985).

120. William J. Chambliss, *Exploring Criminology* (New York: Macmillan, 1988), p. 294. For more information on Greenberg's position, see David Greenberg, "Delinquency and the Age Structure of Society," *Contemporary Crises* 1 (1977): 189–223.
121. William J. Chambliss and Robert Seidman, *Law, Order, and Power* (Reading, MA: Addison-Wesley, 1971).
122. Lynch and Groves, *A Primer in Radical Criminology,* p. 26.
123. Chambliss and Seidman, *Law, Order, and Power.*
124. William J. Chambliss, *Whose Law? What Order?* (New York: John Wiley, 1976).
125. Mark Colvin and John Pauly, "A Critique of Criminology: Toward an Integrated Structural-Marxist Theory of Delinquency Production," *American Journal of Sociology* 89 (November 1983): 513–51.
126. Steven F. Messner and Marvin D. Krohn, "Class, Compliance Structures, and Delinquency: Assessing Integrated Structural-Marxist Theory," *American Journal of Sociology* 96 (September 1990): 300, 325.
127. Chambliss, *Exploring Criminology,* p. 296.
128. Brenda Sims Blackwell, "Perceived Sanction Threats, Gender, and Crime: A Test and Elaboration of Power-Control Theory," *Criminology* 38 (May 2000): 439–88; quotation is from p. 440.
129. John Hagan et al., "The Class Structure of Gender and Delinquency: Toward a Power-Control Theory of Common Delinquent Behavior," *American Journal of Sociology* 90 (May 1985): 1151–78; quotation is from p. 1174.
130. John Hagan, "Clarifying and Extending Power-Control Theory," *American Journal of Sociology* 95 (1990): 1024–37.
131. John Hagan, *Structural Criminology* (New Brunswick, NJ: Rutgers University Press, 1989), p. 145.
132. John Hagan et al., "Class in the Household: A Power-Control Theory of Gender and Delinquency," *American Journal of Sociology* 92 (January 1987): 788–816; quotation is from p. 813.
133. Bill McCarthy, John Hagan, and Todd S. Woodward, "In the Company of Women: Structure and Agency in a Revised Power-Control Theory of Gender and Delinquency," *Criminology* 37 (November 1999): 761–814; quotation is from p. 784.
134. Kyle L. Snow, "Contemporary Theories of Crime: Control and Socialization," Review Essay in *Criminal Justice and Behavior* 18 (December 1991): 493, quoting Hagan, *Structural Criminology,* p. 14.
135. Brenda Sims Blackwell, "Perceived Sanction Threats, Gender, and Crime: A Test and Elaboration of Power-Control Theory," *Criminology* 38 (May 2000): 439–88; quotations are from p. 477.
136. Ibid., p. 439.
137. Gresham M. Sykes, "The Rise of Critical Criminology," *Journal of Criminal Law and Criminology* 65 (June 1974): 212–13.
138. Michael J. Lynch, "The Extraction of Surplus Value, Crime and Punishment: A Preliminary Examination," *Contemporary Crisis* 12 (1988): 329–44.
139. Ronald L. Akers, "Theory and Ideology in Marxist Criminology: Comments on Turk, Quinney, Toby, and Klockars," *Criminology* 16 (February 1979): 528, 543.
140. Sykes, "The Rise of Critical Criminology," p. 213.
141. Michael J. Lynch et al., "The Rate of Surplus Value and Crime: A Theoretical and Empirical Examination of Marxian Economic Theory and Criminology," *Crime, Law & Social Change* 21 (1994): 15–48; quotation is from p. 39.
142. Freda Adler, *Sisters in Crime* (Prospect Heights, IL: Waveland Press, 1975; reprinted 1985), pp. 19–20.
143. See Richard Deming, *Women: The New Criminals* (Nashville, TN: Thomas Nelson, 1977).
144. See Darrell J. Steffensmeier, "Flawed Arrest 'Rates' and Overlooked Reliability Problems in UCR Arrest Statistics: A Comment on Wilson's 'The Masculinity of Violent Crime—Some Second Thoughts,' " *Journal of Criminal Justice* 11 (1983): 167–71.
145. Rita James Simon, *Women and Crime* (Lexington, MA: D. C. Heath, 1975).
146. See Coramae Richey Mann, *Female Crime and Delinquency* (Tuscaloosa: University of Alabama Press, 1984).
147. Darrell J. Steffensmeier, "Crime and the Contemporary Woman: An Analysis of Changing Levels of Female Property Crime, 1960–75," *Social Forces* 57 (December 1978): 566–84.
148. Darrell J. Steffensmeier, "Organization Properties and Sex-Segregation in the Underworld: Building a Sociological Theory of Sex Differences in Crime," *Social Forces* 61 (June 1983): 1010–32.
149. Darrell J. Steffensmeier and Renee Hoffman Steffensmeier, "Trends in Female Delinquency: An Examination of Arrest, Juvenile Court, Self-Report, and Field Data," *Criminology* 18 (May 1980): 62–85.
150. Darrell J. Steffensmeier and Cathy Streifel, "Time-Series Analysis of the Female Percentage of Arrests for Property Crimes, 1960–1985: A Test of Alternative Explanations," *Justice Quarterly* 9 (March 1992): 77–103; quotation is from p. 77.
151. See Lee H. Bowker, *Women, Crime, and the Criminal Justice System* (Lexington, MA: D. C. Heath, 1978).
152. Meda Chesney-Lind and Randall G. Shelden, *Girls, Delinquency, and Juvenile Justice* (Pacific Grove, CA: Brooks/Cole, 1992).
153. James W. Messerschmidt, *Capitalism, Patriarchy and Crime: Toward Socialist Feminist Criminology* (Totowa, NJ: Rowman & Littlefield, 1986), p. 41.
154. James W. Messerschmidt, *Masculinity and Crime: Critique and Reconceptualization of Theory* (Boston: Rowman & Littlefield, 1993). The review by Ann Goetting is published in "The Connection between Gender and Crime," *Federal Probation* 58 (December 1994): 75.
155. Marsali Hansen and Michele Harway, eds., *Battering and Family Therapy: A Feminist Perspective* (Newbury Park, CA: Sage, 1993), p. 217.
156. Quinney and Wildeman, *The Problem of Crime,* p. 85.
157. Sally S. Simpson and Lori Elis, "Doing Gender: Sorting Out the Caste and Crime Conundrum," *Criminology* 33 (February 1995): 47–81; quotation is from p. 47.
158. Kathleen Daly and Meda Chesney-Lind, "Feminism and Criminology," *Justice Quarterly* 5 (1988) 497–538; quotation is from p. 506.
159. Meda Chesney-Lind, "Girls' Crime and Woman's Place: Toward a Feminist Model of Female Delinquency," *Crime and Delinquency* 35 (1989): 5–29; quotation is from p. 19.
160. See, for example, Daly and Chesney-Lind, "Feminism and Criminology.
161. Karen Heimer and Stacy De Coster, "The Gendering of Violent Delinquency," *Criminology* (May 1999): 277–319; quotation is from pp. 305 and 306.
162. Ibid., p. 306.
163. Akers, *Criminological Theories,* 3d ed., p. 231, referring to Simpson and Ellis, "Doing Gender."
164. Akers, ibid., p. 234.

CHAPTER

6

▶Michael Corneal, age 14, was led to his arraignment on 15 January 1998. Corneal was charged with a shooting rampage that killed three students and injured five others at Heath High School in Paducah, Kentucky, on 1 December 1997. Corneal pleaded guilty. (John Sommes II/ Reuters/ Getty Images)

Sociological Theories of Criminal Behavior II: The Social-Process Approach

OUTLINE

KEY TERMS

containment theory
control theory
differential association
differential association-reinforcement
labeling theory
learning theory
self-concept

This chapter is concerned with the *process* by which people become criminals. Do they learn this behavior and, if so, how, and under what circumstances? The chapter begins with a discussion of the learning theory called *differential association*. The influence of that theory is assessed in light of the recent reformulations of learning theory by sociologists and criminologists. The discussion of learning theory closes with a look at imitation theory, the mass media, and criminal behavior.

The second section of the chapter examines *control theories,* which are based on the assumption that criminal behavior occurs when society's normal methods of controlling people break down. The third section discusses *labeling theory,* which focuses on the process by which people who engage in certain acts come to be called (or labeled) criminal whereas others who engage in those same kinds of behavior are not labeled. The chapter closes with an analysis of the policy implications of the theories of criminality that have been explored in this chapter and in Chapter 5.

Chapter 5 discusses sociological theories that emphasize the relationship of criminal behavior to the social structure, or the organization of society. Whether the environment is seen as a determining or a facilitating factor in the causation of crime, the emphasis is on the environment's structure rather than on individual characteristics, as in the constitutional theories discussed in Chapters 3 and 4. One problem with the social-structural theories, however, is that they do not explain the process through which individuals turn to crime. This chapter analyzes *social-process* theories, which attempt to explain *how* people become criminals.

It is not possible to separate all sociological theories into the categories of social structure and social process. Some theories may be considered in both categories. For example, the neutralization theory of Gresham Sykes and David Matza explains the *process* by which a person neutralizes any inhibitions that he or she might have against violating laws. Yet the theory is also related to subcultures, an aspect of the social structure. Likewise, labeling theory is discussed in this chapter because it explains the *process* by which a person becomes a criminal—the person is labeled by those in a position to make that determination. Others characterize labeling theory as a social-structural theory that has some similarities to conflict theory.

Social-process theories developed as sociologists began to analyze the fact that not all people exposed to the same social-structural conditions respond in the same way. Some become law-abiding citizens, and others become criminals. Not all criminals respond in criminal ways in all circumstances; likewise, not all noncriminals observe the law at all times. To explain these differences, sociologists suggest that human behavior is learned and that criminal behavior may be acquired in the same way as any other behavior. This approach has been taken by other disciplines as well.

LEARNING THEORY

Various scholars have based their research on **learning theory.** One of the most prominent of these scholars is Albert Bandura, who referred to "reciprocal interaction between cognitive, behavioral and environmental determinants."[1] Although learning theory has been developed by sociologists and psychologists to explain a variety of behaviors, this chapter's discussion of the theory will focus on criminal behavior.

Learning theory Theory based on the assumption that although human aggression may be influenced by physiological characteristics, the activation of those characteristics depends on learning and is subject to the person's control. Social learning determines whether aggressive behavior occurs and, if so, the nature of that behavior.

Differential association A person who engages in criminal behavior can be differentiated by the quality or quantity of his or her learning through associations with those who define criminal activity favorably and the relative isolation from lawful social norms.

Sutherland's Differential Association Theory

As an explanation of criminal behavior, **differential association** is based on the premise that criminal behavior is learned in the same way that any other behavior is learned. The term was introduced in 1939 by Edwin H. Sutherland, who is sometimes referred to as the dean of American criminology and whose work has had a significant impact on sociologists and criminologists in the United States.

When Sutherland was asked to write a criminology text in 1921, his primary interest was in the controversy that was raging between environmental and heredity theories of behavior. Sutherland wanted to analyze criminal behavior by utilizing some of the prevailing sociological concepts. He was also interested in finding concrete causes of crime. As he examined the facts and issues, he decided that no concrete variables could explain crime. For example, the condition associated most frequently with crime is gender; that is, most people apprehended for crimes are men. But Sutherland said that it was obvious that gender was not the *cause* of crime. He turned to abstract explanations and decided that a learning process involving communication and interaction must be the principle that would explain all types of crime.[2]

In the 1939 edition of his book, Sutherland introduced the concept of differential association, although he was reluctant to do so. His concern about the hypothesis was expressed in his reference to it as a "hypothesis which might quickly be murdered or commit suicide."[3] The hypothesis was developed into a theory to explain the process by which an individual engages in criminal behavior.

Sutherland's theory has nine statements.[4] They are discussed here, but for easy reference to the statements alone, see Exhibit 6.1.

First, "Criminal behavior is learned." In this proposition Sutherland emphasized his belief that criminal behavior is not inherited. Nor did he believe that a person who has not been trained in criminal behavior invents that behavior. It must be learned.

Second, "Criminal behavior is learned in interaction with other persons in a process of communication." That process involves gestures as well as verbal interactions. Third, "The principal part of the learning of criminal behavior occurs within intimate personal groups." Sutherland did not believe that the media play an important role in the process. His approach should be understood in the context of pretelevision times.

Fourth, "The learning includes (a) techniques of committing the crime, which are sometimes very complicated, sometimes very simple; (b) the specific direction of motives, drives, rationalizations, and attitudes." Fifth, "The specific direction of motives and drives is learned from definitions of the legal codes as favorable or unfavorable." Sutherland pointed out that in American society the definitions of legal codes are mixed: Some favor violating those codes, while others support compliance. The mixture creates cultural conflict with respect to legal codes.

EXHIBIT 6.1

The Nine Propositions of Sutherland's Differential Association Theory

1. Criminal behavior is learned.
2. Criminal behavior is learned in interaction with other persons in a process of communication.
3. The principal part of the learning of criminal behavior occurs within intimate personal groups.
4. When criminal behavior is learned, the learning includes, (a) techniques of committing the crime, which are sometimes very complicated, sometimes very simple; (b) the specific direction of motives, drives, rationalizations, and attitudes.
5. The specific direction of motives and drives is learned from definitions of the legal codes as favorable or unfavorable.
6. A person becomes delinquent because of an excess of definitions favorable to violation of law over definitions unfavorable to violation of law.
7. Differential associations may vary in frequency, duration, priority, and intensity.
8. The process of learning criminal behavior by association with criminal and anticriminal patterns involves all of the mechanisms that are involved in any other learning.
9. While criminal behavior is an expression of general needs and values, it is not explained by those general needs and values since noncriminal behavior is an expression of the same needs and values.

Source: Quoted from Edwin H. Sutherland, *Principles of Criminology,* 4th ed. (Philadelphia: Lippincott, 1947), pp. 6–7. Reprinted by permission of Lippincott, Williams, and Wilkins.

Sixth, "A person becomes delinquent because of an excess of definitions favorable to violation of law over definitions unfavorable to violation of law." Sutherland stated that people learn positive and negative as well as neutral behavior. For example, brushing teeth is neutral in that it does not contribute to or detract from criminal behavior except that it does occupy time. People become assimilated to the surrounding cultural patterns unless there are conflicting ones. This sixth statement is Sutherland's principle of differential association. Those who engage in criminal behavior do so because they have contacts with that type of behavior and are isolated from anticriminal behavior.

The seventh statement reads, "Differential associations may vary in frequency, duration, priority, and intensity." Sutherland believed that the first two components of this proposition were obvious and needed no further explanation. He believed *priority* to be important because unlawful or lawful behavior learned in childhood could persist throughout life but that this proposition had not been documented adequately and that "priority seems to be important principally through its selective influence." He did not have a precise definition for *intensity*, either, but he stated that "it has to do with such things as the prestige of the source of a criminal or noncriminal pattern and with emotional reactions related to the associations."[5] This seventh statement is a crucial one in Sutherland's theory, and it means that associations with criminal and noncriminal behavior vary in terms of those four elements.

The eighth statement provides, "The process of learning criminal behavior by association with criminal and anticriminal patterns involves all of the mechanisms that are involved in any other learning." As stated above, to Sutherland the same learning theory that explains noncriminal behavior explains criminal behavior. He emphasized that criminal behavior is not "restricted to the process of imitation." It involves learning.

The last statement of Sutherland's theory is, "While criminal behavior is an expression of general needs and values, it is not explained by those general needs and values, since noncriminal behavior is an expression of the same needs and values." This statement is important, for it negates the belief that hungry people steal because they are hungry. That belief fails to explain why some hungry people do not steal. To Sutherland, the attempt to explain criminal behavior in terms of a person's needs or desires was as futile as trying to explain the behavior in terms of respiration: Breathing (like a need or desire) does not distinguish criminal from noncriminal behavior, although it is necessary for both.

At the time he developed these nine propositions, Sutherland stated that it was not necessary to explain why a person has the associations he has. But he used the example of two boys growing up in neighborhoods with high rates of criminal behavior. One boy, who is outgoing, active, and athletic, might associate with the criminals in his neighborhood and learn their behavior. A second boy, who is shy and withdrawn, may not become acquainted with other boys in the neighborhood and thus not engage in the same types of delinquent behavior they do. These contacts (or the lack of them) occur within the total social organization in which the boys live (including their families). Thus, behavior may be determined by many other associations within that society.

Sutherland has had a "massive impact on criminology," according to some critics.[6] In one of his efforts to test a portion of Sutherland's theory, James F. Short Jr. called the theory "the most truly sociological of all theories which have been advanced to explain criminal and delinquent behavior."[7] Short, however, pointed out some of the problems with the theory, which he said was not testable in its general terms; some reformulations were necessary. He attempted to measure the terms *frequency, duration, priority,* and *intensity.* Within the limitations of his study, Short found strong support for Sutherland's theory, although in a later study he concluded that a reformulation might be necessary before the theory's concepts could be measured.[8]

One early attempt to test differential association by measuring actual delinquency as reported by best friends led researchers to conclude: "We are led to question the postulate that differential association is a necessary and sufficient condition explaining delinquency."[9] In 1944 Sutherland considered this and other criticisms in "The Swan Song of Differential Association," a paper that was not published until after his death. He acknowledged that some of the criticisms were valid, and he concluded that criminal associations alone do not explain criminal behavior: "Rather, it is those associations plus tendencies toward alternate ways of satisfying whatever needs happen to be involved in a particular situation."[10]

In "The Swan Song," Sutherland considered returning to multiple causation and abandoning the attempt to explain all criminal behavior by means of one theory. But in the 1947 edition of his text, he did not try to incorporate these ideas, and the theory of differential association has remained as he stated it in that edition.

Donald R. Cressey, who revised the text after Sutherland's death in 1950, acknowledged problems with differential association. The theory, he wrote, "is neither precise nor clear . . . Most significantly, the published statement gives the incorrect impression that there is little concern for accounting for variations in crime and delinquency rates. This is a serious error in communication on Sutherland's part."[11] Cressey believed that the theory needed to be reformulated, but he made no attempt to do so in subsequent editions of the text, stating, "The theory is presently in a period of great popularity . . . It would be inappropriate to modify the statement in such a way that research work now in progress would be undermined."[12]

Cressey analyzed the criticisms and defended the theory against some of the attacks. He stated that one result of the theory's ambiguity and the critics' failure to read the theory carefully was the assumption that people become criminals because of their association with criminals or criminal patterns of behavior and attitudes. But, observed Cressey, the theory is that people become criminals because of an *overabundance* of associations with criminal, as compared with anticriminal, behavior patterns.[13]

Some critics argued that a person can become a criminal without associating with criminals; therefore, differential association does not apply. That was not the point, said Cressey. One may be exposed to criminal attitudes and behavior without being exposed to criminals. For example, parents who teach their children not to steal in general may suggest that it is permissible to steal a loaf of bread if they are starving.

According to Cressey, Sutherland was aware of the criticism that differential association does not explain why some but not all people commit crimes when presented with the opporunity to do so. Sutherland believed that his theory accounts for these differential response patterns. Whether or not a person takes money from an open cash register is related to his or her previous associations. According to Cressey, more damaging criticisms are those that point out the difficulties of operationalizing some of the theory's terms: It is impossible to measure the precise mechanism by which people learn criminal behavior, a limitation of differential association as a *theory* from which testable hypotheses may be derived. Cressey noted that the theory of differential association was developed by Sutherland primarily to interpret crime data. He was not trying to devise a theory that would explain individual criminal behavior but, rather, one that would bring some order to the understanding of crime rates. Cressey argued that differential assocation is a principle, not a "precise statement of the process by which one becomes a criminal."[14]

Differential association has produced extensive research findings; one of the most consistent among these in delinquency literature is the relationship between peer associations and delinquency. The influence of Sutherland is seen in empirical research concerning this relationship.[15]

One study has established that the relationship between peer associations and delinquency involves several aspects of peer relations, all of which are consistent with Sutherland's position as well as with explaining (at least in part) the relationship between age and criminal behavior:

1. differential *exposure* to delinquent peers, meaning the number of delinquent peers reported by respondents at different ages,
2. *time* spent in the company of peers,
3. the *importance of friends* to respondents, and
4. respondents' *commitment or loyalty* to their own particular set of friends.[16]

Researchers have emphasized that although peer attitudes affect delinquency, peer behavior is even more important, suggesting that delinquency does not result primarily from the influence of attitudes acquired from peers: "Rather, it more likely stems from other social learning mechanisms, such as imitation or vicarious reinforcement, or from group pressures to conform." It is suggested that, for purposes of analysis, attitudes and behavior should be separated, in that "what peers do appears to be at least as important as what they think."[17]

Another analysis of Sutherland's differential association claims that it "marked a watershed in criminology. The theory was instrumental in bringing the perspective of sociology to the forefront of criminology." Earlier reactions focused on the theory's development and refinement; more recently, scholars have focused on testing it or rejecting it and replacing the theory with control or integrated theories, discussed later. Some argue that differential association theory is sound but that further developments are needed. For example, it is difficult to measure the content of definitions favorable to law violations. In general, the theory "appears supported, but requires additional research to specify the concrete content of its abstract principles."[18]

Of the suggestions for revising Sutherland's theory, the most often cited and tested is Ronald L. Akers's learning theory, which Akers developed more thoroughly after his work with Robert L. Burgess.

Akers's Social Learning Theory

Differential association-reinforcement A crime-causation theory based on the belief that criminal behavior is learned through associations with criminal behaviors and attitudes combined with a learning theory of operant conditioning. Criminal behavior is learned through associations and is continued or discontinued as a result of the positive or negative reinforcement received.

In an effort to provide a "more adequate specification of the learning process" required in the theory of differential association, Burgess and Akers developed a concept of **differential association-reinforcement.** Their purpose was to integrate Sutherland's theory with the principles of modern behavior theory. They assumed that in doing so, they could render differential association propositions more testable and at the same time make the learning processes easier to understand.[19]

Social learning theory is based on the assumption that the "primary learning mechanism in social behavior is operant (instrumental) conditioning in which behavior is shaped by the stimuli which follow, or are consequences of the behavior." Direct conditioning and imitation of others are important in determining this behavior. Rewards, or positive reinforcement, as well as avoidance of punishment, or negative reinforcement, strengthen it. The behavior may be weakened by *aversive stimuli,* or positive punishment, as well as by *loss of reward,* or negative punishment. The determination of whether the behavior is deviant or conforming depends on *differential reinforcement,* defined as "past and present rewards or punishments for the behavior and the rewards and punishments attached to alternative behavior." Furthermore, from others who are important to them, people learn norms, attitudes, and orientations that define certain behaviors as good or bad. These definitions help to reinforce behavior and serve as cues for behavior. The more positive the definitions people have of a given behavior, the more likely they are to engage in it. These definitions are learned from peer groups and from family but also may come from schools, churches, and other groups.[20]

Social learning occurs first in a process of differential association. The person interacts and identifies with groups that provide models for social reinforcements and behavior. The individual learns definitions of behavior through imitation within these groups; the definitions are reinforced by the group and serve as reinforcers for the person's behavior. Akers and his colleagues tested their learning theory in the context of drug and alcohol use and abuse. They found that the theory explained 55 percent of the variance in drinking behavior and 68 percent of the variance in the use of marijuana.[21]

Akers and his students and colleagues have conducted other tests of the theory. It has been used to test smoking among adolescents, deviant drinking among the elderly, and rape and sexual coercion. According to Akers, "The findings . . . demonstrated that the social learning variables of differential association, differential reinforcement, imitation, and definitions, singly and in combination, are strongly related to the various forms of deviant, delinquent, and criminal behavior studied."[22]

In recent years Akers has expanded his social learning theory into the *social structure and social learning (SSSL) model*, which combines social structure and social process. He advances four dimensions of social structure. First is *differential social organization*, which refers to the demographic variables in a given area—such as age and population density—that affect crime rates. Second is *differential location in the social structure*, which encompasses the characteristics of individuals—such as race and ethnicity, class, gender, marital status, and age—that determine their locations within groups. The third dimension of the social structure consists of *theoretically defined structural variables*, which includes anomie, group conflict, social disorganization, and other concepts that have been used by other theorists to identify social-structural conditions that may be related to high delinquency and crime rates. The fourth, and final, dimension is *differential social location*, which refers to memberships in primary, secondary, and reference groups such as the family or peer groups. Akers then concludes:

> The differential social organization of society and community, as well as the differential location of persons in the social class, race, gender, religion, and other structures in society, provides the general learning contexts for individuals that increase or decrease the likelihood of their committing crime.[23]

Akers continues working on and testing the SSSL model, but earlier his work was evaluated by two criminologists, Francis T. Cullen and Robert Agnew, who concluded that Akers's social learning theory is "perhaps the leading theory of crime."[24]

Learning Theory and the Mass Media

It is possible that delinquent and criminal behavior are learned through association with the media rather than through association with other human beings. Whether the process is one of identification or imitation, the result is the same: What the media portray may influence how the audience behaves. Some of that impact may be seen in the concern over whether television has an effect on behavior, a concern that raises the possibility of psychological and sociological explanations of the process by which a person becomes either deviant or law-abiding. Before looking at research on behavior and the mass media, we will take a brief look at an early theorist, Gabriel Tarde, who may be considered a forerunner of modern imitation theory.

Tarde's Imitation Theory

Gabriel Tarde (1843–1904) was born in southern France. After studying law, he was a magistrate for many years. He showed considerable interest in social problems as a judge, and proved to be a deep thinker and profound philosopher. Reacting against Cesare Lombroso and the positive school, Tarde argued that people are not born criminal; they become criminal. He saw criminal behavior as the result primarily of social factors, a belief that constitutes one of his greatest contributions to criminology.[25]

Tarde rejected the biological and physical theories of criminal behavior, but he did not become a social determinist. He thought people had some choice in their behavior, although he did believe that when the ability to choose is impaired, people should not be held responsible for their criminal acts.[26]

Tarde's social-process theory of criminal behavior is reflected in his belief that all of the "important acts of social life are carried out under the domination of example."[27] Upon this belief he formulated his *theory of imitation,* through which he explained the process of acquiring criminal as well as noncriminal behavior. In developing his theory, Tarde distinguished between fashion and custom, both of which are forms of imitation. *Fashion* is characteristic of the imitation that takes place in crowds or cities where contact is close and frequent. *Custom* refers to the phenomenon that occurs in small towns and rural areas where contact is less frequent and change occurs less often. Since both fashion and custom are forms of imitation, each occurs to some degree within a society; fashion may uproot and create a new custom. Since fashion and custom are related to the degree of social contact, Tarde formulated his first law of imitation: "Men imitate one another in proportion as they are in close contact."[28]

Tarde's second law of imitation is that the *inferior imitates the superior.* Peasants imitate royalty; small-town and rural residents imitate the acts of city residents. Tarde wrote, "Infectious epidemics spread with the air or the wind; epidemics of crime follow the line of the telegraph."[29] The third law of imitation is the *law of insertion:* "When two mutually exclusive fashions come together, one can be substituted for the other. When this happens, there is a decline in the older method and an increase in the newer method."[30] Tarde illustrated this position by noting the increase in the use of a gun rather than a knife for murder.

Tarde's neglect of the physical, psychological, and economic influences in behavior and his oversimplification of causation have led most sociologists to reject his imitation theory, but his "emphasis on the social origins of crime had a lasting impact on criminological thought in both Europe and America."[31]

The Modern Media and Imitation

Television is the prime source of news for most Americans, and this is true particularly of those who commit the most violence, as measured by official data sources. In addition, polls show that most Americans believe television is an accurate source of news,[32] although polls also reveal that an increasing number of Americans are concerned about violence on television. One poll showed that 80 percent believed that watching televised violence is harmful, and 57 percent believed that television gives too much attention to violent crimes.[33]

A Cornell University psychologist has called television a "thief of time; it robs children of critical hours required for learning about the world, about one's place in it."[34] The issue here, however, is whether exposure to television (or other media, such as movies) *causes* crime. There are arguments pro and con,

Violence on television and in movies is a common concern to those who believe that the media glamorize violent behavior, and that violence has an adverse influence on children and young people. This picture shows Leonardo DiCaprio, starring in *The Basketball Diaries*, a movie in which he dreams that he goes on a school massacre that resembles the shooting in the Littleton, Colorado, Columbine High School case. (© 1995 Palm Pictures Inc. by Getty Images)

and actual causation is difficult to prove. A Yale University psychology professor who in 1960 began a study of the causes of aggression visited his sample 10 years later and again in another 10 years; he reported a high correlation between violence and the amount of television watched. The professor stated that he "found that the violent programming [his subjects] had watched was related to the seriousness of the crimes they committed, how aggressive they were to their spouses, and even to how aggressive their own kids were."[35]

Writing in the 1970s, psychological learning theorist Albert Bandura said that research had shown that television, the most influential of the media for adolescents, had four types of effects on their social behavior:

1. The teaching of aggressive styles of conduct.
2. The lessening of restraints on aggression.
3. Desensitization and habituation to violence.
4. The shaping of images of reality on which people base their actions.

Bandura claimed that television can distort people's perceptions of the real world: "Heavy viewers see the society at large as more dangerous regardless of their educational level, sex, age, and amount of newspaper reading."[36]

Some of the attention given to the effects that violence on television might have on the behavior of adults and children is anecdotal (i.e., based on individual stories rather than on empirical research). Crimes such as those discussed in Exhibit 6.2 may, however, help form people's attitudes about the influence of the media. Consider those crimes carefully. How do you react to each case in terms of a causal relationship between the criminal act and television viewing?

Researchers remind us that television viewing does not occur in a vacuum. Although most of the surveys of reactions to a particular show occur right after the show in question, we cannot assume a direct cause-and-effect relationship. The behavior must be examined in the total context in which it occurs, and the facts can be misleading. For example, women watch more television than men, yet crime rates are higher among men. Teens watch less television than adults do, yet most property crimes are committed by young adults. Clearly something other than television is involved. A National Institute of Justice review of research on the issue concluded that there is "no clear evidence of causal links."[37] James Q. Wilson and Richard J. Herrnstein, whose work was discussed in Chapter 4, concluded that most of the research does not show a causal link between television and crime.[38]

The critical question is to determine the *processes* that are involved in reactions to media violence. Psychological and sociological theories of behavior must be considered.[39] Many people who view the programs or movies in question do not engage in antisocial behavior. Why do they react in appropriate ways, whereas others who viewed the same material react in antisocial, even violent, ways? One scholar suggested this explanation:

> The empirical and theoretical evidence suggests that . . . the effects of television's content depend in part on the extent to which contradictory messages are available, understood, and consistent. In the case of sex-role attitudes, messages from television are consistent and either absent or reinforced in real life, whereas in the case of aggressive behavior, most viewers receive contradictory messages from both sources. All viewers may learn aggression from television, but whether they act agressively will depend on a variety of factors.[40]

T. J. Solomon, shown here at his sentencing, entered guilty and guilty but mentally ill pleas to all charges filed against him after he opened fire at his high school in Conyers, Georgia, on 20 May 1999. Six students were injured. Solomon is appealing his 40-year sentence. (AP Photo/Ricky Crumbley, Pool)

The influence of television on crime has been measured in the context of publicity over capital punishment. One scholar, William C. Bailey, found no relationship between television viewing of news about capital punishment and the incidence of homicide. The evidence did not support the assumption that publicizing executions deters homicides, nor did it support the assumption that publicity encourages and increases homicides. Bailey noted that such publicity may be communicating the fact that a person convicted of homicide is not likely to be executed, thus reducing any possible deterrent effect of capital punishment. But it seems clear that "the current level of executions and media practices regarding executions in this country neither discourage nor promote murder."[41]

EXHIBIT 6.2

Crime as Imitation: Are the Media Responsible?

The following crimes were reported in the media during recent years. Each case stated that the media were the cause or a major cause of the crime. What questions would you raise in reaction to these cases?

1. In 1999 T. J. Solomon, age 15, was accused of shooting six classmates at his high school in Conyers, Georgia. Police found a letter written by Solomon in which he stated his allegiance to the "brothers and sisters related to the trench coat mafia." That was a group in which Littleton, Colorado's Columbine High School shooters, Eric Harris and Dylan Klebold, were fringe members. Solomon was reported to have boasted to other students that he could do a better job than the Columbine killers and that his school should have had a shooting long before. It was suggested that Solomon's knowledge of the Columbine shootings came from his exposure to television.[1]
2. Also in 1999 another 15-year-old boy, who was accused of sexually abusing his 8-year-old half-sister for the previous three years, said he got the idea for the crime from watching television. The youth (along with his 13-year-old brother) testified that he had oral, anal, and vaginal sex with the child after their mother left for work in the mornings and before she returned in the afternoons. When asked by police how he learned these behaviors, the boy said, "I watched 'The Jerry Springer Show.' " When asked what that meant, he said he watched a show on incest. The program was characterized by lewd language and physical violence, but only one or two episodes had dealt with incest. Still, one of those shows was entitled, "I'm Pregnant by My Brother."[2]
3. After arresting a 17-year-old accused of murdering his stepmother and half-sister, police claimed the suspect was obsessed with the movie *Natural Born Killers*. Friends said the youth had been unhappy, had threatened to kill his family, and after seeing the movie shaved his head and wore tinted glasses similar to those worn by the offender in the movie.[3]
4. A 17-year-old boy was convicted of murdering a woman, whom he stabbed and strangled. His defense was that he had watched the movie *A Clockwork Orange* several times and as a result "did bad things." The movie portrays a "marauding young Briton with a vacant stare who acts on his violent impulses." The movie character and his gang associates engage in random rapes and murders on London's streets. The movie was nominated for several Academy Awards but was criticized for its portrayal of violence. After he received several death threats, the director withdrew the movie from circulation in Britain.

   At his trial, the defendant testified that he did "bad things" only when he wore a black *Clockwork Orange* T-shirt, which he was wearing when he killed the victim.[4]
5. A four-year-old boy accidentally shot and killed his two-year-old sister. Authorities say the boy learned how to load a gun by watching television and learned to shoot by playing with his friend's air gun.[5]
6. The mother of a five-year-old boy who started a fire that killed his younger sister claimed the boy got the idea from the MTV cartoon *Beavis and Butt-Head,* which promoted burning as fun. Shortly after the boy watched the cartoon, his mother caught him playing with matches. According to the fire chief who investigated the fire, "The children admitted they saw it on TV and thought they could do it, too."[6]
7. In 1998 a 16-year-old who, assisted by his 14-year-old cousin, stabbed his mother to death, stated that they were influenced by the "slice-and-dice" *Scream* movies.[7]

1. "Colorado Killers Inspired Youth in Georgia Shooting, Note Says," *New York Times* (10 August 1999), p. 8.
2. "Youth Says He Got Idea for Sexual Abuse from Springer Show," *New York Times* (8 January 1999), p. 10.
3. "Police Seize Suspect Obsessed by a Movie," *New York Times* (11 November 1994), p. 9.
4. "Teen Found Guilty of Murder, Blames *A Clockwork Orange*," *Miami Herald* (23 June 1990), p. 3B.
5. "Boy, Four, Learned How to Load Gun from TV—He Kills Sister," *Miami Herald* (28 August 1991), p. 3B.
6. "Mother Blames a Deadly Fire on an MTV Cartoon," *New York Times* (10 October 1993), p. 14.
7. "Teenager: 'Scream' Films Inspired Me to Kill Mom," *St. Petersburg Times* (15 January 1998), p. 14.

Social scientist Ray Surette's analysis of the impact of the media on crime covers many aspects of the relationship between the media, especially television, and criminal behavior. His research suggests that we are more aggressive socially because of the mass media, but that social aggression is not always criminal and most crime is not violent. Research implies that the relationship between the media and crime may be indirect and that the relationship is greater in property crimes than in violent crimes, with the possible exception of the impact of pornography, discussed in Chapter 7. Further, there is evidence of short-term imitation of media violence by children, but "researchers who have looked for an incorporation of violent behavior into the viewer's overall behavior pattern or a subsequent willingness among children to use violence as a problem-solving method have reported mixed results."[42]

In 1998, after visiting and working with faculty and students who had witnessed the shootings at Westside Middle School in Jonesboro, Arkansas, carried out by Mitchell Johnson, age 14, and Andrew Golden, age 12, psychology professor Dave Grossman related his beliefs concerning the violence by young people in that incident and others. According to Grossman, the behavior of the accused killers at Jonesboro, like many others, can be explained in part by the phenomenon of media-induced violence. The boys, who killed 4 students and a teacher, and wounded 10 others, were characterized by a lack of self-esteem and a sense of inferiority that, combined with media violence, can provoke violent behavior in young people who are "wanna-bes": "They want to be tough, they want to impress people, they want to make a bold statement and they don't know how. And then the media tells them how." Grossman suggests that the media message is that "killing is the route to greatness. Killing is the route to fame." Grossman also believes that specific types of role models on television may precipitate similar types of violence. He alleges that school shootings by white adolescent boys in 1997 and 1998 may have been influenced by the 1995 movie *The Basketball Diaries.* In that movie, the character played by *Titanic* star Leonardo DiCaprio enters a schoolroom and shoots numerous teachers and children. "In doing so," Grossman said, "he became a role model that other white males desire to emulate." Movie producers and others reject that analysis.[43]

Another issue regarding the role of the media in the imitation process is whether the media should be legally liable for acts of violence. The issue is discussed in Media Focus 6.1 in relation to lawsuits filed by the families of victims of violent acts. The families argue that these acts were the result of the offenders' access to media violence.

Even if the media are not legally liable for violence, whether or not they should continue to market violence is an issue of great concern. Even the American Bar Association (ABA) has become involved in the issue. The ABA's section on litigation sponsored a conference on gun and media violence. The venue for that conference was Beverly Hills, California, "practically the front yard of the entertainment industry."[44]

Finally, in 2000 the *Journal of Personality and Social Psychology* carried a research article concerning the effect of media violence on behavior. The authors measured the impact that violent videos had on the behavior of 210 college students. The students were asked questions to measure their level of irritability and anger; some were then permitted to play violent video games, while others played nonviolent games. Those who played the violent games showed more angry thoughts and behavior. The results are debated, though, with some saying evidence of this kind shows that violence in the media is related to violent behavior. Others argue that, if that were the case, given the number of young people who are exposed to violence there would be "hundreds of bodies lying around."[45]

Media Focus 6.1

Should the Media Be Legally Liable for Violence?

The text discusses the impact the media are alleged to have on violence in real life. Exhibit 6.2 enumerates specific cases in which the media are cited as the reason for the criminal acts. Media company representatives deny any responsibility for criminal acts that follow their programs. With regard to his show, mentioned in one of the examples in Exhibit 6.2, Jerry Springer said some of the episodes are silly but that he should not be responsible for what some folks find entertaining.[1]

The parents of the three shooting victims of the December 1997 school shooting at Heath High School in Paducah, Kentucky, filed a lawsuit against 25 media companies. The parents argued that violent video games "trained" Michael Carneal, the shooter, to point and shoot a gun and thus become a more effective killer. Therefore, the parents argued, the media should be legally liable. The trial court dismissed the lawsuit, ruling that the defendants had no legal duty to the parents under Kentucky laws. The parents have appealed.[2]

In a second recent lawsuit, a federal appellate court ruled that an Indianapolis, Indiana, city ordinance limiting minors' access to violent video games probably would not pass the constitutional tests regarding the First Amendment's right to free speech.[3]

1. "Brothers Molest Sister, Blame Talk Show Episode," *Tallahassee Democrat* (7 January 1999), p. 6C.
2. James v. Meow Media Inc., 90 F.Supp. 2d 798 (W.D.Ky. 2000), discussed in "Broadcasting Violence: Debate Intensifies on Whether Media Should Be Liable for School Shootings," *ABA Journal* 87 (May 2001), p. 29.
3. American Amusement Machine Association v. Kendrick, 244 F.3d 572 (7th Cir. 2001), discussed in "Broadcasting Violence," ibid.

CONTROL THEORY

In addition to trying to determine the process by which people become criminals, sociologists and psychologists have developed explanations of how behavior can be controlled. According to control theorists, deviance results when social controls are weakened or broken down; when controls are strong, deviance does not occur. The problem is to try to explain what can be done in a positive way to elicit appropriate behavior. The question is not how to prevent criminal behavior but how to train people to engage in law-abiding behavior.

Control theory An explanation of criminal behavior that focuses on the control mechanisms, techniques, and strategies for regulating human behavior, leading to conformity or obedience to society's rules, and that argues that deviance results when social controls are weakened or break down so that individuals are not motivated to conform to them.

Like many other explanations of criminal behavior, **control theory** is not a theory in the sense of rigorous scientific procedures of developing and testing hypotheses; rather, it is an approach or an explanation. Several theorists have articulated variations of control theory. In reading the discussion that follows, keep in mind that all of the variations have some common assumptions, articulated by one sociologist as follows:

1. That the human animal requires nurturing.
2. That differences in nurturing account for variations in attachment to others and commitment to an ordered way of living.
3. That attachment and commitment may be described as "internal controls," commonly called "conscience" and recognized in *guilt*, and "external controls," usually tested by the production of *shame*.
4. That evidence from experimental studies, longitudinal research, comparative studies, and cross-cultural investigation tells us *how* attachment and commitment are developed. Conversely, such evidence describes the situations that loosen the moral bond with others and that are, therefore, productive of crime.[46]

Reiss's and Nye's Control Theory

One of the first to apply control theory to delinquent or criminal behavior was Albert J. Reiss Jr., who maintained that such behavior results from the failures of personal and social controls. *Personal controls* are internalized, while *social controls* result from formal controls (such as laws) and informal controls (such as social sanctions).[47]

Shortly after Reiss's work was published, sociologist F. Ivan Nye analyzed delinquency using three control categories:

1. Direct control, by which punishment is imposed or threatened for misconduct and compliance is rewarded by parents;
2. Indirect control, by which a youth refrains from delinquency because his or her delinquent act might cause pain and disappointment for parents or others with whom they have close relationships;
3. Internal control, by which a youth's conscience or sense of guilt prevents him or her from engaging in delinquent acts.[48]

Although Nye recognized that formal institutions, such as law, could influence social control, he believed that the informal institutions, such as the family, were most influential. Thus, the more of an adolescent's needs that are met within the family, the less likely the adolescent would be to look for satisfaction in unacceptable ways outside the family. Nye reported that in his research he found associations between delinquent behavior and such family situations as lack of discipline, broken or disintegrated homes, lack of sufficient parental affection toward the children, and even rejection. These associations were weak, however, and Nye has been criticized for not clearly articulating exactly "how a particular aspect of family relationships included in his study was connected to the concepts in his control theory." Furthermore, for some of the family attributes, such as social class, Nye did not show any connection to delinquency.[49]

Reckless's Containment Theory

Containment theory An explanation of criminal behavior that focuses on two insulating factors: first, the individual's favorable **self-concept** (definition of self) and commitment to long-range legitimate goals and, second, the pressure of the external social structure against criminal activity.

Perhaps the best known of the early control theories is Walter C. Reckless's **containment theory,** which stresses that we live in a society that provides a variety of opportunities for conformity or nonconformity. Not everyone chooses the illegal opportunities; thus social-structural theories that stress the availability of illegal and legal opportunities, the existence of a subculture, the location of goods and services within the city, population density, and other variables cannot explain all criminal behavior. What we need to know is *why* those phenomena affect some people and not others. That is, why are some of us immune to such influences in that our exposure to them is not followed by criminal behavior? Reckless suggested that the answer lies in containment theory, which he defined as follows:

> The assumption is that there is a containing external social structure which holds individuals in line and that there is also an internal buffer which protects people against deviation of the social and legal norms. The two containments act as a defense against deviation from the legal and social norms, as an insulation against pressures and pulls, as a protection against demoralization and seduction. If there are "causes" which lead to deviant behavior, they are negated, neutralized, rendered impotent, or are paired by the two containing buffers.[50]

There are two types of containment: outer containment and inner containment. *Outer containment* (or external control) might be called social pressure, and in simple societies this kind of social control works well. The community's social norms are taught to new members, who internalize them and are restrained by the community's reaction to any violation of these norms. Social ostracism may be the most effective social control in simple societies or communities, but as societies become more complex, outer containment loses its effectiveness. People must develop inner containment mechanisms by which to control their own behavior.

Self-concept The image one has of one's self, including an assessment of strengths and weaknesses; a self-image. *See also* **containment theory.**

Inner containment (or internal control) refers to the ability to direct oneself, which is related to one's **self-concept.** Reckless writes: "One of the components of capability of self is a favorable self-image, self-concept, self-perception. The person who conceives of himself as a responsible person is apt to act responsibly."[51] A high goal level, especially regarding societal goals, and a high aspiration level geared to society's expectations are essential components of the self. Frustration tolerance and identification with society's values and laws are important. The opposite of this is alienation—the release of inner containment.

Reckless emphasized that the components of external and internal containment are buffers, not causes. They operate to help the individual refrain from succumbing to pressures to violate laws. If the buffers are strong, the individual is law-abiding; if they are weak, he or she commits a crime.

One way in which these buffers operate is by neutralizing the norms. Research on self-concept gives us more insight into the neutralization process. A sample of white working-class boys was examined in sixth grade and again in ninth grade. When the boys were in sixth grade, their behavior appeared to be controlled more strongly by the norms they attributed to their peers than by their own internalized norms. By the time they were in ninth grade, internalized norms were a stronger factor. This suggests that inner containment theory does not have the same influence at all stages of adolescent development. The study also found that the boys' self-concept "is especially important as an explanation of such behavior and as an intervening variable that affects the relationship between other attitudes and possible behavioral outcomes."[52]

Despite the claims of Reckless and his associates that containment theory explains most delinquency and crime; that the theory might bring psychologists and sociologists together in the study of crime because it involves both disciplines; and that the theory, unlike many others, can be used in an individual case history,[53] the theory has been criticized severely. It cannot explain why people

A positive self-image is important as young people grow into adulthood. Bonding with other adolescents is one way of enhancing self-esteem. Sharing values, social habits, and experiences, as these teenagers in a southern California shopping mall do, reinforces the sense of belonging. (Spencer Grant/Stock Boston)

who do the same things are labeled differentially; it is limited in its predictive ability; and it includes a questionable measure of self-concept, along with a lack of control groups in some of the early works. The difficulty of measuring the strength or weakness of external and internal containment is a problem. Further, the theory does not explain why some children with bad self-concepts are not delinquent.

Containment theory may be most useful when combined with other approaches. In a comparison of containment theory with differential association theory, one sociologist concluded that they are similar, except that the latter emphasizes the *process* of differential association, whereas the former emphasizes the *product* of socialization—the self-concept. Both of these theories can account for delinquency more fully than either can separately.[54]

It has been argued that containment theory is too broad and its concepts too vague to produce testable hypotheses for rigorous empirical research.[55] Travis Hirschi attempted to eliminate these criticisms by refining the elements of control theory.

Hirschi's Bonding Theory

In his review and critique of control theories of criminal behavior, Ronald L. Akers states: "All of the earlier control theories were superseded by the version proposed by Travis Hirschi (1969), who remains today the major control theorist." Hirschi's theory "has come to occupy a central place in criminological theory. Indeed, it is the most frequently discussed and tested of all theories in criminology."[56]

Hirschi's control theory focuses on social bonding. According to Hirschi, it is conforming behavior, not deviance, that we need to explain. The real question is *why,* with so many opportunities and pressures to commit crimes, most of us are law-abiding citizens most of the time. The basic concept of control theory, asserts Hirschi, is "the bond of the individual to society." That bond has four components: *attachment* to conventional persons, *commitment* to conventional behavior, *involvement* with conventional people, and *belief* in conventional norms. Hirschi believes that delinquency becomes more likely as this social bond is weakened.[57]

By *attachment,* Hirschi means the feelings we have toward others. If we have close ties to them, we are more likely to care what they think of our behavior; likewise, if we do not have close ties, we care less. The controlling of delinquency is tied to the attachments young people have to their parents. But Hirschi emphasized that attachment to peers may also control delinquency, even when those peers are not always law-abiding. It is the *attachment* that is most important; it is the lack of attachment that is conducive to delinquency.

Commitment refers to the investment one has in activities, such as getting an education. A person must measure the extent to which that investment would be lost by deviant behavior before he or she engages in that behavior. Thus, commitment to conventional behavior, such as going to school, might be sufficient to cause someone to avoid jeopardizing that education by engaging in delinquent behavior. According to Hirschi, most people acquire goods and services that they do not want to lose; the risk of losing those is "society's insurance that [people] will abide by the rules."[58]

Most people are engaged in conventional activities, and such *involvement* does not permit them sufficient time to engage in delinquent or nonconventional activities. Hirschi notes: "Many people undoubtedly owe a life of virtue to a lack of opportunity to do otherwise."[59] Finally, by *belief,* Hirschi means that a person accepts the conventional norms and rules of society, believing that its general rules and laws (although not necessarily each specific one) are correct and should be obeyed. But individuals vary in the extent to which they have these beliefs, and "the less a person believes he should obey the rules, the more likely he is to violate them."[60]

Hirschi tested his theory on a sample of California youths, using the self-report method of collecting data (discussed and analyzed in Chapter 2). The 4,000 junior and senior high school students were given questionnaires designed to measure their attitudes toward friends, neighborhood, parents, school, teachers, and human relations. They were asked to respond to the following six questions, indicating whether they had (1) never committed the offense, (2) committed the offense more than one year ago, (3) committed the offense during the past year, or (4) committed the offense during the past year as well as more than a year ago:

1. Have you ever taken little things (worth less than $2) that did not belong to you?
2. Have you ever taken things of some value (between $2 and $50) that did not belong to you?
3. Have you ever taken things of large value (worth over $50) that did not belong to you?
4. Have you ever taken a car for a ride without the owner's permission?
5. Have you ever banged up something that did not belong to you on purpose?
6. Not counting fights you may have had with a brother or sister, have you ever beaten up on anyone or hurt anyone on purpose?[61]

The responses to these questions were used as an index of self-reported delinquency. In addition, questions were asked about work, money, expectations, aspirations, participation in school activities, and use of leisure time. School records, including grades, and police records were used as sources of data for the study.

The high association between low socioeconomic class and crime, found in the earlier studies using official crime data, has been questioned by self-report studies. Hirschi found strong evidence that this traditional association does not exist. Indeed, he noted very little association between social class, as measured by the father's occupation, and admitted or official delinquency, with the exception of a low incidence, by both measures, of delinquency among the sons of professionals. He did find, however, that boys "whose fathers have been unemployed and/or whose families are on welfare are more likely than children from fully employed, self-sufficient families to commit delinquent acts." The study also disclosed that positive attitudes toward teachers and school were related to non-delinquent behavior. Hirschi suggested that the closer the ties to parents, the less likely it was that the youths would engage in delinquent acts. It was not the parent's status that was important but, rather, the child's *attachment* to the parent.[62]

Hirschi concluded that young people who are not very attached to their parents and to school are more likely to be delinquent than are those who have these kinds of attachments. He also found that youths who have positive attitudes toward their own accomplishments are more likely to believe in the validity and appropriateness of conventional laws and the moral rules of society than are youths who are negative about their own accomplishments.

Although Hirschi's California study was based on a sample of urban respondents, a study of a rural sample in New York State, conducted by Michael Hindelang, found support for Hirschi's control theory.[63] However, Hindelang "failed to replicate a positive relationship between attachment to parents and attachment to friends . . . he failed to show that attachment to friends increases the likelihood of delinquent behavior." In fact, a critic notes that Hindelang "found a slightly positive relationship between identification with peers and delinquency which is unexplainable in terms of control theory." This does not mean that the theory is incorrect—only that it is incomplete. We need to go beyond attachment to peers and discover the *type* of peer to whom the individual is attached before the analysis has validity for the prediction of delinquent behavior.[64] Others have found that the type of peer does not matter[65] or that the likelihood of delinquent behavior seems to be decreased by attachment to conventional peers but increased by attachment to delinquent peers.[66]

Hirschi recognized that his control theory "does not escape unscathed." In the first place, his theory "underestimated the importance of delinquent friends; it overestimated the significance of involvement in conventional activities." He decided that probably one should look at the relationship between delinquent activities and the person's self-concept or self-esteem. That relationship might be important in explaining "the potency of the adult-status items, such as smoking, drinking, dating, and driving a car." Although control theory can help us understand these relations, Hirschi noted, it leaves a lot unexplained. However, he concluded this early work on an optimistic note with regard to his theory: "I am confident that when the processes through which these variables affect delinquency are spelled out, they will supplement rather than seriously modify the control theory, but that remains to be seen."[67]

Perhaps a more serious challenge to Hirschi's theory has been raised by those who emphasize that most tests of the theory have used cross-sectional data at a particular time rather than measuring the relationship of variables over time. A sample of young men at the beginning of their sophomore year in high school and again near the end of their junior year suggests that Hirschi's control theory is more limited than he claims. This study showed that the theory does not predict delinquency among middle to older adolescents, although it might be important in predicting delinquency among younger adolescents.[68] Similar findings were reported by other investigators, who concluded that adolescence should not be viewed as a unitary period but should be refined further by the age variable.[69]

Another criticism of Hirschi's control theory, discussed here as a social-process theory, comes from one of Hirschi's former doctoral students, Thomas J. Bernard, who argues that the four elements of the theory are not all social-psychological variables, as Hirschi suggests. According to Bernard, *commitment* is a social-structural variable that differs from the other three variables of Hirschi's theory—*attachment, involvement,* and *belief*—which are social psychological variables. Commitment "confuses the definition and the explanation of conformity" and "is properly conceived as an antecedent variable that measures the role of social structure in the origin of delinquency."[70]

Bernard argues that viewing commitment as a social-structural rather than a social-process variable would eliminate the current perception in Hirschi's theory that "the individual's bonding to society is independent of social structural characteristics, and therefore can be enhanced without broader societal changes."[71]

Despite his suggestions for revision of Hirschi's control theory, Bernard emphasizes that none of his ideas should challenge "the substantial contribution of Hirschi's theory to criminology [which has] generated a host of studies that have advanced criminology as a science, whether or not they support Hirschi's conclusions."[72]

Hirschi's contributions have been noted by others. His 1969 work, *Causes of Delinquency,* in which he stated his theory, has been described as "a benchmark for theory construction and research in the delinquency field."[73] As Bernard noted, Hirschi's theory has generated considerable research, some of which has resulted in additional suggestions for modification or extension.

According to some critics, Hirschi's control theory is more complete than subcultural or differential association theory, but it does not give a complete explanation. The theory does not show how the four elements of attachment, commitment, involvement, and belief might operate simultaneously to discourage delinquent behavior. Furthermore, Hirschi does not empirically test the relationships among the social bond's four elements. Consequently, the theory raises three issues:

1. Are the four elements "empirically distinct components of socialization"?
2. Why are only four elements identified?
3. Although Hirschi talks about educational and occupational aspirations, he does not incorporate into the theory elements such as family socioeconomic level, ability, and the influence of significant others, and research has found that all of them are important.[74]

Investigators who attempted to replicate Hirschi's theory and incorporate these additional elements found general support for the theory's four elements, but they found that the theory needed reformulation and expansion.[75]

Some recent analyses of control theory have found support for this approach. For example, control theory suggests that the greater the degree of school bonding, the less likelihood there is of delinquency. It is argued that this occurs despite the race, gender, and socioeconomic status of the juveniles. This proposition was examined among African American juveniles, with the result that bonding was found to be important and not influenced significantly by race. The authors conclude, however, that it is premature to exclude race as a factor in an analysis of school bonding and delinquency. They state that more research is needed before we conclude that race is or is not a relevant variable. The findings challenge the belief that the school environment of African American juveniles is more dysfunctional than that of whites: "The black youths in our sample are not isolated and alienated from school; rather they are just as committed and attached as whites, if not more so."[76]

Hirschi's control theory has been used to explain juvenile behavior other than delinquency. A study of adolescence and smoking found support for control theory but emphasized the need to include an analysis of parental behavior (as well as parental attitudes) in the study of the juvenile's attachment and commitment.[77]

Ronald L. Akers concludes his analysis of Hirschi's control theory by noting that it has received some support empirically. "However," Akers says, "the magnitude of the relationship between social bonding and deviant behavior has ranged from moderate to low."[78]

Before leaving Hirschi's bonding theory, however, it is important to look at research comparing it with Sutherland's differential association theory. In 1982 Ross Matsueda, in an examination of data used by Hirschi, published his comparison of the two theories and concluded that measures of Sutherland's sixth concept—which states that it is "an excess of definitions favorable to violation of law" that leads to delinquency (see again Exhibit 6.1)—superceded Hirschi's social bonding concepts, thus challenging the studies of Hirschi and others.[79]

In 1999 two other scholars, Barbara J. Costello and Paul R. Vowell, reanalyzed the same data and reached the opposite result, concluding that "the social bond and friends' delinquency retain important direct effects on delinquency, and . . . these effects are greater than those of definitions. Thus, our results are more supportive of control theory than differential association theory."[80]

Gottfredson's and Hirschi's Control Theory

In recent years Hirschi has collaborated with Michael Gottfredson in developing a general theory of crime that focuses on self-control. Gottfredson and Hirschi reject the traditional theories of crime, arguing that in an attempt to answer the question "What causes crime?" each discipline looks to its own central concepts: "Thus sociology looks to social class, culture, and organization; psychology looks to personality; biology looks to inheritance; and economics looks to employment or work."[81]

According to Gottfredson and Hirschi, all of these explanations are incompatible with the nature of *crime,* which they define as "an act of force or fraud undertaken in pursuit of self-interest."[82] Crime is distinguished from *criminality,* which refers to a person's predisposition to commit a crime. Criminality is a part of the personality trait that is central to the thesis of this approach: low self-control.

Persons with low self-control have several characteristics. They seek immediate gratification, with a "here-and-now" attitude, in contrast to persons with high self-control, who are able to defer gratification. Second, persons with low self-control look for easy or simple ways to gratify their desires. Crime provides "money without work, sex without courtship, revenge without court delays." Third, they find in crime their need for acts that are exciting, risky, or thrilling. Criminal acts involve "stealth, danger, speed, agility, deception, or power." In contrast, persons with high self-control "tend to be cautious, cognitive, and verbal." Fourth, persons with low self-control have little stability in their lives, for crimes do not provide stability in the form of a job or a career, friendships, or family ties. Little skill or planning is required to pursue crime; thus, persons with low self-control do not need or value cognitive or academic skills. Fifth, people with low self-control are "self-centered, indifferent, or insensitive to the suffering and needs of others." Thus, they can handle the fact that crime causes pain or discomfort for its victims. This does not mean that those with low self-control are "routinely unkind or antisocial. On the contrary, they may discover the immediate and easy rewards of charm and generosity." Finally, persons with low self-control have little tolerance for frustration and tend to respond to situations physically rather than verbally.[83]

Gottfredson and Hirschi maintain that low self-control is a product primarily of poor parenting; and, although it may improve over time as the result of improved parenting or the influence of other social institutions, in most individuals low self-control persists throughout life. Persons with low self-control are much more likely than persons with high self-control to engage in criminal activities throughout their lives.[84] Low self-control does not cause crime, but it interacts with crime opportunities. When an opportunity to commit a crime exists, a person with high self-control is not likely to commit the act; a person with low self-control may succumb.

Gottfredson and Hirschi claim that their theory is a general one in that it "explains all crime, at all times, and, for that matter, many forms of behavior that are not sanctioned by the state." That is a big claim, but the authors note that "modesty per se is not a virtue of a theory."[85]

Some scholars have attempted to test self-control theory, although most of them have not defined and measured self-control directly. Self-control is assumed from the presence of certain behavior. One attempt to measure self-control in terms of the risk-taking and temper-control variables articulated by Gottfredson and Hirschi found some support for self-control theory. The authors offered suggestions for modifying and expanding self-control theory.[86]

The authors of a study published in 1993, in a partial test of self-control theory, "found support for both Hirschi's earlier version of control theory and Gottfredson and Hirschi's self-control conceptualization."[87] A 1999 research analysis concluded that "the general theory's concept of low self-control provides a partial, but not complete, explanation for marked gender differences in offending among [a sample of Canadian secondary school students]."[88] Another study reported in 2000 found support for self-control theory.[89] Finally, a recent analysis of general control theory has found some evidence that self-control may explain variables, such as drug and alcohol abuse, academic probation, excessive partying, friendship loss, and others associated with courtship violence. These variables may be indicators of low self-esteem and self-control. In addition, the theory may explain the fact that many persons who are involved in courtship violence are from homes in which domestic violence was experienced. In short, "self-control theory appears to be consistent with the empirical correlates of courtship violence."[90]

Control theory, although well recognized, remains controversial among researchers, two of whom noted that the disagreement over how to test the theory "is solid evidence of the value of their theoretical framework for contemporary criminological thought."[91]

Robert Agnew's analysis of leading crime theories led him to conclude that, although "Hirschi's social control theory is the leading control theory, Gottfredson and Hirschi's self-control theory is rapidly gaining in popularity."[92]

Finally, Ronald L. Akers, after reviewing the research on self-control theory, concludes: "There has not yet been enough research conducted to test self-control theory directly in order to come to any firm conclusions about its empirical validity."[93]

Control Theory: A Conclusion

Some scholars who have criticized control theory for failing to include the relationship between differential association and delinquency have developed *integrated control theories* in which they combine learning theory and control theory. Some include the strain theories discussed in Chapter 5.[94] One researcher who took this approach found that of strain, control, and learning theory, the strongest support exists for learning theory.[95] Some have attempted to integrate social-process and social-structural theories.[96] Others have emphasized the importance of adding the dimension of social class to a control theory analysis.[97] The conclusion by many is that "the causes of delinquency are more complex than originally thought."[98]

Control theory has produced extensive and significant research that is helpful in understanding and explaining delinquent and criminal behavior. It has the advantage of an individualized approach in that it recognizes that we do not all respond in the same way to the same environment. For that reason, the theory may be popular with the public, but it does not provide blueprints for the kinds of changes that can be implemented by politicians. In that sense, despite its empirical basis, control theory may be less attractive than social-structural approaches that do give a basis for political change. If unemployment is seen as the cause of crime, plans can be implemented to change employment opportunities. But if commitment to an involvement with family is a significant element, change is more difficult. As one expert concluded, "The truth sometimes tells us more clearly what we can*not* have and what will *not* work."[99]

LABELING THEORY

A final approach to explaining crime is different from the others discussed. Most theories and explanations of criminal behavior look for its *cause.* Why did the individual commit the crime and what can be done to prevent future criminal acts? The answer may be found in the individual physique, body build, chemical imbalance, hormones, or chromosomes; it may be found in the environment; or it may be the result of some type of social process. The emphasis is on finding out *why* the person engaged in the behavior.

Labeling theory An attempt to explain deviance as a social process by which some people who commit deviant acts come to be known as deviants and others do not. Deviance is seen as a consequence of society's decision to apply that term to a person, and deviant behavior is behavior that society labels as deviant.

In contrast, **labeling theory** asks why the person was *designated* deviant. The critical issue is not the behavior itself but why the behavior is labeled deviant. Not all who engage in certain kinds of behavior are labeled deviant, but some are. What is the reason for this distinction? Sociologist Kai T. Erikson has described this approach as follows:

> Some men who drink heavily are called alcoholics and others are not, some men who behave oddly are committed to hospitals and others are not . . . and the difference between those who earn a deviant title in society and those who go their own way in peace is largely determined by the way in which the community filters out and codes the many details of behavior which come to its attention.[100]

If criminal behavior is to be explained according to the response of others rather than the characteristics of the offender, the appropriate subject matter is the *audience*, not the individual; for it is the existence of the behavior, not why it occurred, that is significant. Only the audience's response determines whether that behavior is defined as deviant.

This section considers the history and development of the labeling perspective along with a critique of this approach. In some respects it is a social-structural approach, like conflict theory, but it is primarily a social-process theory because it attempts to explain labeling as a process by which some people who commit deviant acts come to be known as deviants whereas others do not.

The Emergence and Development of Labeling Theory

A 1938 statement by Frank Tannenbaum describes the labeling concept as follows:

> The process of making the criminal is a process of tagging, defining, identifying, segregating, describing, emphasizing, making conscious and self-conscious; it becomes a way of stimulating, suggesting, emphasizing, and evoking the very traits that are complained of.
>
> The person becomes the thing he is described as being.[101]

According to Tannenbaum, it does not make any difference whether the label is assessed for the purpose of punishing or of reforming the individual. In both cases the label indicates disapproval of the conduct.

The labeling concept was developed further by Edwin Lemert, who distinguished *primary* and *secondary deviance* (or deviation) as follows:

> Primary deviation is assumed to arise in a wide variety of social, cultural, and psychological contexts, and at best has only marginal implication for the psychic structure of the individual; it does not lead to symbolic reorganization at the level of self-regarding attitudes and social roles.
>
> Secondary deviation is deviant behavior or social roles based upon it, which becomes a means of defense, attack or adaptation to the overt and covert problems created by the societal reaction to primary deviation.[102]

To labeling theorists, primary deviance is relatively unimportant; it is secondary deviance that is most important, for it is the *interaction* between the person labeled deviant and the labeler that counts. This approach is called *interaction theory.*

Another contributor to the early development of labeling theory was Howard S. Becker, who pointed out that because only some of the many people who break rules are considered deviant, we must distinguish between rule breaking and deviance. Rule breaking describes the behavior, but deviance describes the reaction of others to that behavior; thus, rule breaking is defined as deviant when engaged in by *some* people. It is important to find out who is and who is not labeled deviant. According to labeling theorists, the people who are most often labeled deviant for their rule-breaking behavior are those on the margin of society. Once they are labeled deviant, normally they cannot escape the designation. According to Becker:

> Social groups create deviance by making rules whose infractions constitute deviance, and by applying those rules to particular people and labeling them as outsiders. From this point of view, deviance is not a quality of the act a person commits, but rather a consequence of the application by others of rules and sanctions to an "offender." The deviant is one to whom the label has successfully been applied; deviant behavior is behavior that people so label.[103]

The effect of the deviant label extends also to the self-concept of the labeled person who, according to labeling theory, has experienced a socialization process that is virtually irreversible, not only from the point of view of the labeler but also from that of the person labeled. That person develops a self-concept consistent with the deviant label and acquires the knowledge and skills of the labeled status. Whether or not labeling occurs depends on (1) the time the act is committed, (2) who commits the act and who is the victim, and (3) society's perception of the consequences of the act.[104]

The Effects of Labeling

Labeling theory is based on the assumption that people respond to other people in an informal and unorganized way until these others are placed in categories that lead to stereotyping, which causes corresponding responses. The response may become what sociologists call a *self-fulfilling prophecy.* Labeling is important particularly in the area of delinquent behavior because of the discretion police and other authorities have when a juvenile commits a delinquent act. Most youths commit some delinquent acts; only a few are labeled delinquent.

Once labeled, the labelee has an almost impossible task of shedding that status. The effects of labeling may snowball, too, in that once a person is stigmatized by the label, new restrictions are placed on legitimate opportunities and the labelee's probabilities of further deviance are increased. Such a vicious circle is reinforced by the tendency of the public to believe that one who commits a crime will always be a criminal.

One act may not be enough to result in a negative label, but whether or not a person is labeled brings into play the differentials of power. Certain types of groups may be more likely to be labeled deviant than others: groups that do not have political power, groups that are seen to threaten the persons in power, and groups that have low social status. The last is particularly important. Even when middle- and upper-class persons are suspected of committing conventional crimes, they are less likely to be labeled criminal than are lower-class persons.[105]

The upper classes have greater access to attorneys and are more likely to know their legal rights. They are less likely to negotiate a plea or admit guilt. They have the symbols of the middle and upper classes, and those symbols are not associated with criminal status. For example, they are more likely to have strong family ties, to have a job, to have sufficient income, to speak fluently and knowledgeably, to be poised, to be able to rationalize their behavior, to have a record of continuous employment, and to have the respect of the community and of law enforcement officials. They are more likely to have friends who may intervene at any stage in the legal process. They live in areas that are unlikely to be the target of drug raids. They are more likely to get probation if a condition of probation is that they obtain psychiatric or other professional services.[106]

Crime visibility is a factor in determining whether a person is labeled criminal. People who live in ghettos are more likely to be visible in committing crimes. Because of their greater contact with public services, they are also more likely to be visible after crimes are committed. For example, most statutory rape cases are brought to the attention of the police through referrals from public welfare agencies. Thus, statutory rape is punished mainly among the poor, as the victims become visible by applying for maternity aid from welfare authorities.

Empirical Research

Attempts have been made to test labeling theory empirically. In a classic study, Richard D. Schwartz and Jerome H. Skolnick measured the reaction of 100 employers to a potential employee with a *criminal* record. The employers were divided into four groups, and each group was shown a different folder on the prospective employee. Stated simply, the conclusion was that employers would not offer a job to a person with a criminal record. The second phase of this study included 58 doctors who had been sued for medical malpractice (a civil wrong rather than a criminal act) in Connecticut. There was no evidence that these doctors had lost patients because of the malpractice suits. Most of the doctors reported no change, and five specialists reported an increase in the number of their patients.[107]

Schwartz and Skolnick warn of the problems of comparing these two phases of their study. The doctors had a *protective institutional environment* that did not exist for the prospective employee. The doctors were permitted to continue using the facilities of the hospital and had no difficulty getting malpractice insurance, although often at a higher rate. This protective institutional environment may eliminate the negative labeling process that occurs normally after one loses in a court battle. Possibly another reason for the different reactions in the two phases in the study is that physicians were in short supply and unskilled laborers were not. But most probably the difference in reaction was due to the doctors' occupational status and the protection they got from their profession. An interesting question left unanswered by this study is how a doctor would be labeled if he or she had been acquitted of a charge of assault and battery or some other *criminal* offense.

One example of the effect of labeling gained national attention in the 1970s. Eight sane researchers of varied backgrounds sought admission to the psychiatric wards of 12 hospitals in various parts of the United States. The hospitals were of different types, some with excellent treatment facilities and others with poor ones. The researchers called the hospitals for appointments, and upon their arrival for the initial interviews, they feigned mental illness, stating that they heard voices. When asked about the significant events in their backgrounds, all related the events accurately; none had a history of pathological experiences. After admission to the hospital, all the pseudopatients acted like sane persons. All except one had been labeled schizophrenic, and none of the doctors or staff suspected the researchers' pseudopatient status. Once labeled insane, they were presumed insane by the staff, who interacted with them daily. Their behavior did not identify them as insane; the identity came from a label given to them upon admission. Thus, they differed from sane persons only in the label.[108]

Another study involved the simulation of prison life with student volunteers assigned to the roles of correctional officers and inmates. The experiment had to be terminated because of serious problems. Those in the experiment who were assigned the role of correctional officers began behaving as if they derived pleasure "from insulting, threatening, humiliating and dehumanizing" those who were inmates. The ones who were assigned to be inmates became depressed, despondent, and helpless and acted in self-deprecating ways.[109]

Many of the early empirical studies on the effects of labeling focus on juveniles. These studies have been categorized as measuring (1) the effect of labeling on subsequent delinquent behavior, (2) the effect of the family's and the community's reaction to a youth who has contact with the juvenile justice system, and (3) the effect that the labeling has on the juvenile's self-concept. To summarize, the studies report some evidence that white youths are affected more than minority youths by the juvenile delinquency label. The community's reaction to the labeled youths was negative, but the little evidence available on family reaction suggests that the labeled youths found little change in their parents' perceived attitudes toward them after the label had been attached. Juveniles do not feel that the experience is highly stigmatizing, although there is some evidence that some youths, especially whites, change their self-concepts after a juvenile court experience. But "there is a hint in two of the studies . . . that the labeling effects of court contact may erode over time. In summary, we don't know much about the effects of court labeling on juveniles."[110]

Much of the recent research on labeling theory has also focused on juvenile delinquency. This research calls for refining the approach. For example, gender roles should be considered. Male and female juveniles do not necessarily respond to labels in the same way.[111] Other characteristics of the juvenile may be related to the effect of the label; research suggests that those in the higher socioeconomic classes, whites, and first-time offenders are "more susceptible to the labeling processes" than others are.[112] The differences between negative and positive labeling continue to be important.[113] All these findings have practical applications for policymakers who must decide whether to impose formal negative sanctions on juvenile offenders.

In a test of labeling theory in the context of juvenile court cases, researchers found that the juvenile who appears in juvenile court (in contrast to the one who is dismissed or processed in some other social institution) is more likely to appear in juvenile court again. This might suggest an effect from labeling. But the researchers noted that those who appeared in juvenile court were at a higher risk of recidivism than those who did not appear in court; thus, it is possible that labeling had no effect on future behavior.[114]

One attempt to revitalize labeling theory has been conducted by John Braithwaite, who emphasizes that labeling per se is not the issue. Labeling must be examined in the context of the complete social structure. It might cause some to abandon criminal activity or cause others to continue. What are the characteristics of the broader social context in which the behavior occurs that might explain whether the person becomes law-abiding or law-breaking? Braithwaite answers the question with his concept of *shaming,* defined as social disapproval that has the "intention or effect of invoking remorse in the person being shamed and/or condemnation by others who become aware of the shaming."[115]

In the view of Braithwaite, shaming may go further to stigmatize the person labeled, a process he refers to as *disintegrative shaming.* Disintegrative shaming does not involve any attempt to reintegrate the shamed person back into society; it stands in contrast to *reintegrative shaming,* in which attempts are made at reintegration "through words or gestures of forgiveness or ceremonies to decertify the offender as deviant."[116] These reactions are more likely to reduce the negative effect of shaming, thus reducing the chances that the shamed person will continue in crime.

One final contributor to labeling theory in recent years is Ross L. Matsueda.[117] Matsueda based his approach on the much earlier theory of George Herbert Mead, whose classic *Mind, Self, and Society* was published in 1934.[118] Mead explored the concept of *self,* which he said is composed of many dimensions and developed through symbolic interactions with other individuals, some of whom are more significant than others. In the process of interactions, individuals often take the role of the other person and try to discern how that person is evaluating his or her behavior. Later in their development they learn to generalize the roles of others, such as a group, a community, or a society. The behavior children exhibit may initially be labeled as play or mischief by family members, but a larger group or the society may label that same behavior as bad, evil, deviant, or even delinquent. According to Matsueda,

> Eventually, this spiraling labeling process can leave the youth in the hands of juvenile justice officials—cut off from conventional society, stigmatized by parents and teachers, and left with a delinquent self-image. Thus, a self-fulfilling prophecy is set up: through this process of deviance amplification . . . an otherwise conforming child may eventually respond to the initial labeling of harmless acts by confirming the delinquent label.[119]

Matsueda, along with Dawn Jeglum Bartusch, studied data on juvenile delinquency collected by the National Youth Survey and found support for their approach that "reflected appraisals thus are the link between parental labeling and delinquency."[120]

Evaluation of Labeling Theory

Labeling theory has been described as "one of the most influential in the field of deviance over the past two decades."[121] Others have emphasized that the theory "has produced equivocal results."[122] The criticisms have been extensive.

One of the most serious criticisms of labeling theory is that it is not a theory—it is a perspective. No systematic labeling theory has been developed. The empirical assessment of a theory requires that it produce testable propositions. Not only is that difficult with labeling theory, but some of the theorists "unashamedly claim to eschew precise propositional statements in favor of 'sensitizing observations' which 'jostle the imagination,' to create a crisis of consciousness which will lead to new visions of reality." From this perspective, "empirical tests of labeling theory are both impossible and ridiculous."[123]

A systematic theory cannot be created unless it has precisely defined terms that can be measured. Characteristic of the empirical research on labeling is the assumption "that the imposition of any sanction or any official act of negative classification constitutes labeling" without defining that term systematically. Critics have contended that the theory's major propositions have not been supported empirically, but that is no reason for rejecting it. The methodological problems of the empirical efforts are crippling, and the data are poor. Thus, the research cannot be used to support the theory, but neither can it be used to reject it. For adequate testing, it is imperative that specific hypotheses be derived and tested after precise, operational definitions have been articulated.[124]

One of the common criticisms of labeling theory is that it avoids the question of causation and ignores the actual behavior in question. Labeling theory assumes that what one does is not the key to explaining behavior; the key is who that person is and why he or she was labeled deviant. Akers has argued that the labeling process is not "arbitrary and unrelated to the behavior of those detected and labeled." Errors occur, but in general society does not label persons "in a vacuum." There are reasons for tagging persons deviant; there are reasons for arresting individuals for alleged criminal acts.[125] Not all would agree with Akers, either, as the discussion of conflict theory (see again Chapter 5) and evidence of discrimination against racial and ethnic groups or decisions based solely on gender, might suggest.

Another criticism of labeling theory is that it views the actor, or labelee, as too passive and that it does not acknowledge the reciprocal relationship between the actor and the reactor. Most labeling theorists overemphasize the action of society and de-emphasize the action of the subject being labeled. Social interaction should receive greater attention.

Labeling theory has been criticized for its lack of attention to the personality characteristics of those who engage in deviant behavior. To the labeling theorists, characteristics of the individual, such as personality traits, are not important in explaining behavior. It is the *reaction* to the person that is critical. Yet labeling theory does not explain differential law enforcement. Why do police arrest some and not others for the same offense?

A final category of criticisms focuses on the assumption that labeling produces only negative results. Critics argue that labeling a person deviant might deter that person rather than plunge him or her into further deviance. It is suggested that whether or not the labeling process produces negative or positive results depends on a number of factors that have been overlooked by labeling theorists.[126]

First, it appears that labeling has different effects on the deviant at various stages in his or her career. Labeling might thrust a male juvenile delinquent into a criminal career but deter an adult female shoplifter. Perhaps the key element is peer support, not labeling. Labeling may create a subculture, thereby establishing peer support, especially among juveniles.

A second factor concerns the confidentiality of the labeling. If the label is confidential and given to a nonprofessional deviant, that person may be more likely to abandon his or her deviant behavior than if the individual is already a professional and the label is public. Third, the result is more often positive than negative when the subject has some commitment to and is sensitive toward the person doing the labeling. For example, there is some evidence that former alcoholics and drug addicts are more successful than nonpeers, counselors, or psychiatrists in the rehabilitation of fellow deviants. Fourth, a person is more likely to abandon deviant behavior if the label of deviant, once given, can be removed easily.

Fifth, the reaction of friends and society is important to whether the label results in positive or negative behavior. If friends and others are supportive in assisting the individual to improve, the results are more likely to be positive. Sixth, most labeling theorists have overlooked the possibility that positive labeling can increase positive behavior.

Because of these and other criticisms, some have argued that labeling theory is not very important.[127] Others take the position that even if labeling does not cause delinquent and criminal behavior, it does cause problems that should be analyzed. For example, there is evidence that people who have been labeled mentally ill have negative feelings about both that label and the way others respond to them even after they are released from treatment. The more negative these feelings, the more difficult it may be for such persons to interact with others. They may try to hide the fact that they have been treated, they may avoid interaction with others, or they may project negative attitudes that do not exist in others. Labeling theory should be modified and developed further rather than abolished.[128]

Akers concludes his evaluation of labeling theory by stating that it continues to be utilized, but that

> the preponderance of research finds no or very weak evidence of labeling effects. The more carefully the research keeps other factors constant, the less likely it is to find evidence that labeling has a significant independent effect on criminal or deviant behavior. The soundest conclusion is that official sanctions by themselves have neither a strong deterrent nor a substantial labeling effect.[129]

Akers believes that some of the modifications of labeling theory are promising. He suggests that the approach by Braithwaite, which incorporates negative and positive labeling with the community's social characteristics, has more potential than earlier models for empirical testing and support.[130]

Finally, other researchers who have analyzed labeling theory as it has been applied to the study of juvenile delinquency, "suggest that labeling theory is not as invalid as its critics have claimed, and that what is needed is a restatement and revitalization of a labeling theory of delinquency."[131]

CONCLUSION TO CRIMINAL BEHAVIOR THEORIES

We have looked at the various theories of criminal behavior: the economic, biological, physiological, psychological, psychiatric, and sociological approaches. All have methodological problems: Crime is difficult to define in operational terms; samples are limited; and follow-up studies are expensive and time-consuming. All the research today is plagued with an increasing lack of public interest in what caused the behavior; rather, the hue and cry is "Let the punishment fit the crime." Thus, gaining an understanding of the reasons for the behavior does not command a high priority in research funding.

What have we come to know about crime by analyzing official data? We know that most crimes are committed by men but that some crimes have been increasing among women. We know that most crimes are committed by persons who are mobile and who live in large cities. We know that among juveniles, those who are closely bonded to their families and schools are less likely to commit delinquent acts or crimes than those who are not so closely bonded. We know that, according to FBI data, those who are unemployed and hovering at the bottom of society's class structure are more likely than those who are at the top of the social structure to be apprehended for serious property crimes. But the FBI data must be considered along with data about white-collar crimes (discussed in Chapter 9), which involve greater financial losses to society than the serious property crimes of arson, larceny-theft, burglary, and motor vehicle theft.

We know that according to official data, a disproportionate amount of crime is committed by African Americans, and we know that most crimes are committed by persons who are not married. So, how do we make sense of these crime data? That is what the theories, and the tests of those theories, are about. If you become discouraged because we do not know *the* cause of crime, perhaps you can compare this venture to health problems for which we have not found *the* cause, problems such as cancer and the common cold. We know about the virus that causes AIDS, but we have not found a cure. Physical scientists continue forming and testing their theories in an effort to find answers to these and other problems. Likewise, social scientists continue to work toward understanding the causes of crime.

Some social scientists look for a general theory to explain all crime (or perhaps all behavior); we have seen some of those approaches that look at the social-structure or social-process theories. Some say that we have made tremendous progress in empirical research on crime but little progress on theoretical developments.[132] Others express their views that a general theory to explain all crime cannot be discovered: "Crime is too variable, too influenced by moral and political entrepreneurs to be seen as a unitary phenomenon."[133]

These differences and problems do not mean that we should abandon our efforts to develop theories that explain the causes of crime and to test those theories empirically. It does mean that we must be careful in our interpretations of the existing theories, research, and data on crime.

It is important that we do not conclude that research on criminal behavior is hopeless: "Many of the fruits of science . . . can be used to advantage while still in the process of development. Science is at best a growth, not a sudden revelation . . .

We do not abandon cancer research because the patients of today may not be saved by it." Research in the social and physical sciences can be used "imperfectly and in part while it is developing."[134]

In reemphasizing the importance of theory, a 2001 statement by the editor of the leading professional journal in the field noted why the annual meetings of the American Society of Criminology require that research papers be grounded in theory. Editor Robert J. Bursik Jr. quoted a passage from a 1963 book by noted sociologist Peter Berger entitled *Invitation to Sociology:* "Statistical data by themselves do not make sociology. They become sociology only when they are sociologically interpreted, put within a theoretical frame of reference." Bursik emphasized that although anyone can take a set of data and explain what is there—for example, more men than women commit crime—"a truly criminological contribution to the field not only documents the 'what,' but also offers insightful arguments about the 'why.' " Bursik continued by noting that this is possible only "if the selection of variables upon which to focus and the interpretation of the patterns that are identified are grounded in theoretical considerations."[135]

It is also critical that criminologists, sociologists, and other social scientists communicate their theoretical explanations and empirical findings in language that can be understood (and hopefully accepted!) by those who are in a position to make policy decisions.

POLICY IMPLICATIONS OF CRIMINAL BEHAVIOR THEORIES

Public policy decisions regarding how to deal with crime are made at all levels of government as well as within other institutions, such as families, churches, and schools. These decisions may be made after a careful analysis of the research data; they may be made on the basis of intuition; they may be the result of political decisions; or they may involve all of these approaches. In most cases, we really do not know the reasons policy decisions are made. We may be given reasons, but those are not always accurate. Part of the problem lies with social scientists, who do not always communicate their findings and theoretical developments in a manner that is readily accessible and fully understood by those in policymaking positions. At times, however, the latter simply refuse to listen. Still, it is important to consider the policy implications of what we know (or do not know) about crime.

Throughout this text you will read about administrative rules and regulations, local ordinances, state and federal laws, court decisions, and even some constitutional changes that will impact the way we react to deviant, juvenile, and criminal behavior. We have already noted that even the definitions of the word *crime* are not always uniform. And even when we agree on what is a crime, we do not always count the acts or react to them in the same ways in various jurisdictions. It is suggested that as you progress through the text you consider the theories you have learned in Chapters 3, 4, 5, and 6 and question their relevance to the policy decisions that have been made. Let us consider a few examples.

In his presidential address before the American Society of Criminology in November 2000, Roland Chilton spoke about public policy. He referred to a meeting in which a group of scientists were discussing murders that appeared to be drug related. Chilton suggested that it might be time to reexamine the government's policies regarding drug enforcement. The implication was that we might consider legalizing drugs. The response was that such a suggestion would not be "viable policy." In other words, it would not be politically acceptable. Chilton sees this response as a serious problem.[136]

In Chapter 10 we will look at some aspects of the criminalization of drugs in greater detail, but the purpose is not to advocate that drugs should be legalized. Rather, it is to examine the implications of the direction we have taken in the so-called war on drugs. Chilton refers to this war as "the folly of our time." By *folly,* he means "a costly undertaking that has an absurd or ruinous outcome" or "conduct that lacks good sense, understanding, or foresight." According to Chilton, the U.S. drug policies are "one of the best examples of criminal justice folly in our lifetime. Our drug laws are indeed tragically foolish and excessively costly." And, he notes, they consume enormous resources within our criminal justice systems.

If research shows that the long sentences that we have been assessing for minor drug offenses have had little or no impact on drug sales (i.e., no impact on the big drug dealers); have had no impact on rehabilitation of drug offenders; and have crowded many prisons almost beyond our capacity to process more serious offenders, should we refuse to look for new ways to deal with the issue? Or should we look more closely at the position taken in the fall of 2000 by California voters (see p. 77) and provide treatment rather than punishment for minor drug offenses?

Chilton ended his speech by stating, "Political viability is of little value if it produces foolish and unfair policies and practices."[137]

In connection with Chilton's thoughts, we might consider whether marijuana should be permitted for medicinal reasons, a subject discussed in greater detail in Chapter 10. Clearly, it is not politically viable in many jurisdictions to suggest legalizing marijuana, even for a limited worthwhile purpose, and thus proposals to do so are often defeated.

Or consider decriminalizing laws concerning sexual behavior between consenting adults in private, discussed in Chapter 1. It probably is never politically viable to run for office on the platform that you wish to legalize oral or anal sex. So how do these laws get changed, as has happened in most jurisdictions? They become part of a larger package of laws, perhaps a revision of the entire criminal code of the state or the federal government. They are thus "hidden" among more acceptable changes, which get all the attention, and often the opposition will not notice the proposed changes in sex laws.

Today considerable attention is given to the increasing number of shootings at our schools, which were, until these incidents, thought to be safe havens for our children. This concern has led to tougher gun laws in some states, such as Colorado. But changing gun laws may not be the best solution, or even an effective one.

What should we do about repeat offenders? Later in the book (see Chapter 13) we will consider special laws enacted recently in all states and the federal government. These laws provide for very long sentences—such as 25 years to life without parole—for repeat offenders even when the offenses are not serious (although most do require a serious third offense to invoke the statutes). This situation has increased prison populations and contributed little to public safety.

But does it not make sense that putting people in prison for longer periods of time will deter them from committing crimes as well as provide a warning to others? Yes, it might seem logical, but what did we learn from the classical theorists about letting the punishment fit the crime? Did it work then? Will it work now?

Or consider the biological and psychological theories, such as the belief, no longer in vogue, that crime is caused by mental illness, which is inherited. During the early 1900s, when that position was particularly popular, some states had statutes that provided for sterilizing offenders to avoid creating more criminals. As the justice who wrote the 1927 U.S. Supreme Court case upholding the sterilization of a young woman said, "Three generations of imbeciles are enough."[138] Today we do not take that position, as we no longer believe that criminality is inherited. But, as we have already noted, some are calling for castrating sex offenders (see again pp. 69–70) and supporting other forms of punishment thought to fit the crime.

The importance of considering the policy implications of research and theory in criminology is dramatically illustrated by the most recent edition of Ronald L. Akers's criminology theory book. To the previous title, *Criminological Theories: Introduction and Evaluation,* Akers added *Application.* He discusses the policy implications of all theories, giving detailed information on specific programs that have been instituted as a result of an acceptance of that theory. His examples range from policies of involuntary sterilization to fundamental changes within institutions based on the theory that criminal justice policies have been sexist.

SUMMARY

This chapter examines theories that emphasize the *process* by which a person becomes a criminal. Many theories are mentioned, and Exhibit 6.3 summarizes them to assist the reader in assimilating the material.

The chapter begins with a brief overview of learning theory, which provides the framework for Edwin H. Sutherland's theory of differential association. Sutherland viewed his theory as one that explains all behavior, not just deviance, delinquency, or crime. Individuals learn these behaviors in the same ways in which they learn acceptable behaviors.

Sutherland's work influenced other social scientists, many of whom attempted to test the propositions of differential association. The chapter gives attention to differential association-reinforcement theory, in which Burgess and Akers attempt to integrate Sutherland's theory with that of the psychologist B. F. Skinner, while other scholars have considered Sutherland's theory in an analysis of the mass media's influence on behavior. The earlier contributions of Thrasher, who studied how imitation influences behavior (especially gang activities) have gained more attention with the current emphasis on the media's impact on behavior. Like Sutherland, Tarde used his theory to explain how people learn acceptable as well as deviant, delinquent, or criminal behavior.

The influence of sociology may be seen in the application of social-control theories as a supplement (or replacement) to psychological-control theories (discussed in Chapter 4) in explanations of criminal and delinquent behavior. Control theories explain deviance in terms of a breakdown in social controls. Two major approaches are discussed in this chapter. Reckless utilized a containment approach, exploring the impact of personal inner controls and external social structures on behavior. He viewed these controls as providing insulators or buffers against improper behavior rather than as causes of that behavior.

Hirschi developed control theory in terms of his position that it is conforming behavior that must be explained. He did so in terms of four components of social bonds: *attachment* to conventional persons, *commitment* to conventional behavior, *involvement* with conventional people, and *belief* in conventional norms. In testing his approach by means of self-report studies, Hirschi found a lack of support for the traditionally reported high association between low socioeconomic class and crime. Rather, he found that weak attachments to parents and to school are more predictive of delinquent and criminal behavior than class is, and that positive attitudes toward one's own accomplishments are more characteristic of law-abiding than of law-violating youth.

Gottfredson and Hirschi have developed a general theory to explain self-control theory. They argue that low self-control, which results primarily from poor parenting, is the best predictor of criminal behavior. They attempt to measure the characteristics of persons with low self-control and relate them to criminal behavior.

A final area of social-process theories discussed in this chapter is labeling theory, which focuses on why of all people who engage in deviant, delinquent, or criminal behavior some are processed through criminal justice systems while others are ignored. The emphasis is on the labeling process rather than on the reason for the behavior in question. Labeling theory has been applied to criminal behavior since the 1930s but has received more attention in recent years. The chapter discusses the earlier works of Tannenbaum, Becker, and others before focusing on

EXHIBIT 6.3

Summaries of Social-Process Theories

SUTHERLAND'S DIFFERENTIAL ASSOCIATION

Based on nine propositions (see Exhibit 6.1), this theory advocates that all criminal behavior is learned, not inherited. It is learned through social interaction with others in the same way that noncriminal behavior is learned. The learning occurs primarily in small groups and includes techniques as well as motives and drives. Criminal behavior basically occurs when the individual has more definitions favorable to a deviant life rather than to a law-abiding life.

AKERS'S SOCIAL LEARNING THEORY

Ronald L. Akers (joined in some of his early work by Robert L. Burgess) expanded differential association theory to include the principles of modern behavior theory. Behavior is strengthened by positive reinforcement and weakened by negative reinforcement—thus, Akers's differential reinforcement theory. Individuals learn these reinforcements from peers, families, schools, and other institutions. More recently, Akers expanded his position to include four social structural dimensions: differential social organization (such as age); differential location in the social structure (such as social class); theoretically defined structural variables (such as anomie or group conflict); and differential social location (for example, memberships in primary, secondary, and reference groups, such as the family or peer groups).

TARDE'S IMITATION THEORY

Gabriel Tarde was a forerunner in developing theories about what are today called *copycat crimes.* He rejected the biological and psychological theories but did not believe in social determinism; rather, he said, behavior is the process of imitation. Tarde articulated three laws of imitation: (1) people imitate each other in proportion to their close contact; (2) the inferior imitates the superior; and (3) when two mutually exclusive behaviors occur together, one can be substituted for the other, resulting in the decline of the use of the older and an increase in the use of the newer.

REISS'S AND NYE'S CONTROL THEORIES

Albert J. Reiss Jr. maintained that criminal behavior results from the failures of two types of controls: personal (internalized) and social (formal controls, such as laws and informal controls, such as social sanctions). F. Ivan Nye articulated three social control categories, which he believed could occur in formal institutions but took place primarily within the family: (1) direct control (parents threaten punishment for bad behavior and give rewards for good behavior); (2) indirect control (youth refuses to engage in delinquent behavior because it might hurt family or friends); and (3) internal control (youth's conscience or guilt prevents participation in delinquent acts).

RECKLESS'S CONTAINMENT THEORY

According to Walter C. Reckless, there are two forms of containment that control behavior. First is outer containment, or external control, such as social pressure. Second is inner containment, or internal control, which refers to the ability to direct oneself. This ability is related to one's self-concept or self-image. These two control components are not causes of behavior; rather, they are buffers that operate to help the person refrain from engaging in illegal acts. If the buffers are strong, the person is law-abiding; if they are weak, he or she commits a crime. These buffers neutralize the society's norms.

more recent research, much of which tests the approach utilizing juvenile subjects.

The chapter continues with a brief analysis of theories of criminality. Social-process theories in particular have been instrumental in achieving a better understanding of criminal behavior. As a group, social-process theories may be more acceptable than other current approaches of sociologists and criminologists. The theories attempt to explain differential reaction to the social structure; they are based on the sociological proposition that criminal behavior is acquired through social interaction just as noncriminal behavior is acquired. In addition, the research faces fewer methodological problems than the other approaches. Some theorists, for example, Sutherland, tried to avoid the class bias in criminological studies created by selecting samples of convicted criminals, who are mainly from a lower socioeco-

HIRSCHI'S BONDING THEORY

Travis Hirschi looks at the question of why most people do not commit crimes. He believes the answer lies in social bonding, which includes four components: (1) *attachment* to conventional persons; (2) *commitment* to conventional behavior, (3) *involvement* with conventional people; and (4) *belief* in conventional norms.

GOTTFREDSON'S AND HIRSCHI'S CONTROL THEORY

Low self-control is the key element of the theory Travis Hirschi and Michael Gottfredson developed to explain crime. Persons with low self-control have several characteristics in common. They (1) seek immediate gratification; (2) look for easy or simple ways to gratify their desires; (3) find in crime their need for exciting, risky, or thrilling acts; (4) have little stability in their lives; (5) are self-centered and indifferent or insensitive to the needs of others; and (6) have little tolerance for frustration.

LABELING THEORY

Tannebaum

According to Frank Tannenbaum, persons are tagged, labeled, or named—and whether the purpose of this process is punishment or reformation, disapproval is indicated.

Lemert

Edwin Lemert distinguished between (1) *primary deviation,* which arises in a wide variety of contexts and has only marginal implication for the individual's psychic structure; and (2) *secondary deviation,* which consists of deviant behavior that is a defense to society's reaction to one's primary deviation.

Becker

Howard S. Becker distinguished between rule breaking and deviance, as some people who break rules are not considered deviant. Deviance is a label created by society and attached to some but not all people who engage in the described acts.

Braithwaite's Shaming Theory

John Braithwaite examined labeling theory in the context of the total social structure, which might cause some to embrace criminal behavior and others to avoid it. His key word is *shaming,* which is a process of heaping social disapproval on one until it induces remorse. *Disintegrative shaming* stigmatizes the subject, while *reintegrative shaming* consists of attempts to reintegrate that person into law-abiding society.

MATSUEDA'S SELF CONCEPT APPROACH

Based on the symbolic interaction theory of George Herbert Mead, Ross L. Matsueda's approach focuses on the development of the individual's self-concept. This process occurs through social interaction during which the person plays the role of the other in an effort to determine his or her reactions. Some of those reactions are negative, which may lead the roleplayer to a self-fulfilling prophecy: "They say I am bad, so I will be bad." Thus, the initially harmless acts of a child, as defined by his or her parents, may be labeled bad by others. The spiraling labeling process may cause an otherwise conforming child to live up to the labels.

nomic class, by analyzing the crimes of the upper classes as well. The use of random samples has helped in this effort. The studies of self-concept had follow-up studies, although more research on that procedure is needed.

Despite these factors, the social-process theories face some methodological problems, most of which have been noted. In summary, some of the concepts have not been defined precisely, and some of the samples used in empirical research have not been selected properly to avoid bias. Some of the theoretical approaches do not go beyond theory to empirical research.

The chapter closes with a discussion of some of the policy implications of sociological theories.

This chapter concludes our formal analysis of theories. Chapter 7 begins our study of particular crimes.

STUDY QUESTIONS

1. Briefly explain learning theory.
2. Discuss the impact of Edwin H. Sutherland on criminology, and summarize the reactions to his major theoretical developments.
3. State the elements of differential association.
4. Define and evaluate differential association-reinforcement theory.
5. What was Tarde's contribution to criminology, and what is its relevance today?
6. Define *control theory,* and compare the contributions of Reiss, Reckless, and Hirschi.
7. Evaluate Hirschi's control theory.
8. Define and evaluate self-control theory as developed by Gottfredson and Hirschi.
9. What is meant by *integrated control theories?*
10. Explain the primary difference between labeling theory and other explanations of deviant behavior.
11. Discuss the major contributors in the labeling theory field.
12. Explain briefly how labeling theory may influence reactions to doctors who are sued for malpractice. Contrast this with other empirical studies of labeling.
13. Discuss briefly the use of labeling theory to explain juvenile delinquency. What are the racial implications of the theory?
14. Evaluate the concept of shaming.
15. Briefly evaluate labeling theory.
16. Discuss the policy implications of criminological theories.

BRIEF ESSAY ASSIGNMENTS

1. List and describe Tarde's laws of imitation. Why do most sociologists reject his imitation theory?
2. Discuss the arguments, research, and so on concerning whether there is a relationship between the media and crime.
3. What are the criticisms of Hirschi's control theory?
4. Explain Lemert's two types of deviance. According to the labeling theory, which type is more important to examine? Why?
5. Why would a person of a lower-class standing be more vulnerable to labeling than a person of middle- or upper-class standing?

INTERNET ACTIVITIES

1. Learn more about the debate on the media's effect on violent behavior by first logging on to http://interact.uoregon.edu/MediaLit/FA/articles/violence.html. For a different view, go to the American Civil Liberties Union (ACLU) website at www.aclu.org and search for articles on media and violence. What are the opposing viewpoints on the relationship between media and violence? What is your opinion on the subject?
2. Search newspapers, magazines or journals, and the Internet for information on a recent well-publicized crime. Find out as much information as you can about the defendant(s), victims(s), and offense(s). In your opinion, do any of the theories discussed in this and the previous chapters explain or contribute to explaining the defendant(s)' behavior? If so, which one(s)?

NET RESOURCES

www.criminology.fsu.edu/cjlinks/default.htm

Designed and maintained by an individual, Criminal Justice Links, as its name suggests, has numerous links to criminal justice areas and topics including police agencies and resources, drug and alcohol information, corrections, courts, and forensics.

http://people.ne.mediaone.net/dianedemelo/crime/crimetheory.html

Criminological Theory offers information and descriptions on most of the criminological theories discussed in the first portion of this text. Specific theories are organized under general subheadings that range from early criminological thought through radical and feminist criminology.

http://wcr.sonoma.edu	Western Criminology Review is an online journal where users can access past and current articles related to criminology and criminal justice issues. This website also provides links to other criminal justice information.
www.rand.org	A nonprofit institution, Rand Corporation offers information and resources on various social policy issues including access to online publications. Topics range from health, civil and criminal justice, and social welfare to science and technology, national security, and international policy.
www.publicagenda.org/index.htm	Public Agenda is a nonprofit organization that serves to present opinion research and to educate citizens on public policy and social issues. The website includes a section highlighting issues, a pressroom, national issues forums, public engagement, and research assistance.
www.vera.org	The Vera Institute of Justice's website provides links and resources on several areas of the criminal justice system such as crime and victimization, policing, the judicial process, and sentencing and corrections. In addition, this site includes publications and reports concerning Vera's work with local and international institutions, governments, and communities.

ENDNOTES

1. Albert Bandura, *Social Learning Theory* (Englewood Cliffs, NJ: Prentice Hall, 1977), p. vii.
2. Albert K. Cohen et al., *The Sutherland Papers* (Bloomington: Indiana University Press, 1956), p. 19.
3. Ibid., p. 18.
4. Edwin H. Sutherland and Donald R. Cressey, *Criminology,* 10th ed. (Philadelphia: Lippincott, 1978), pp. 80–82, emphasis omitted; Edwin H. Sutherland, Donald R. Cressey, and David F. Luckenbill, *Criminology,* 11th ed. (Dix Hills, NY: General Hall, 1992).
5. Ibid., 10th ed., p. 81.
6. George B. Vold and Thomas J. Bernard, *Theoretical Criminology,* 3d ed. (New York: Oxford University Press, 1986).
7. James F. Short Jr., "Differential Association and Delinquency," *Social Problems* 4 (January 1957): 233.
8. James F. Short Jr., "Differential Association as a Hypothesis: Problems of Empirical Testing," *Social Problems* 8 (Summer 1960): 14–25.
9. Albert J. Reiss Jr., and Albert L. Rhodes, "An Empirical Test of Differential Association Theory," *Journal of Research in Crime and Delinquency* 1 (February 1964): 5–18; quotation is from p. 12.
10. Cohen et al., *The Sutherland Papers,* p. 37.
11. Donald R. Cressey, "The Theory of Differential Association: An Introduction," *Social Problems* 8 (Summer 1960): 3.
12. Edwin H. Sutherland and Donald R. Cressey, *Criminology,* 9th ed. (Philadelphia: Lippincott, 1974), p. 78. This position was retained in the 10th edition, published in 1978.
13. Sutherland and Cressey, *Criminology,* 10th ed., p. 84.
14. Ibid., p. 90.
15. See, for example, Ross L. Matsueda and Karen Heimer, "Race, Family Structure, and Delinquency: A Test of Differential Association and Social Control Theories," *American Sociological Review* 52 (1987): 826–40.
16. Mark Warr, "Age, Peers, and Delinquency," *Criminology* 31 (February 1993): 17–40, emphasis in the original; quotation is from p. 19.
17. Mark Warr and Mark Stafford, "The Influence of Delinquent Peers: What They Think or What They Do," *Criminology* 29 (November 1991): 851–66; quotations are from pp. 851 and 864.
18. Ross L. Matsueda, "The Current State of Differential Association Theory," *Crime & Delinquency* 34 (July 1988): 277–306; quotations are from p. 277.
19. See, for example, Robert L. Burgess and Ronald L. Akers, "A Differential Association-Reinforcement Theory of Criminal Behavior," *Social Problems* 14 (Fall 1966): 128–47.
20. Ronald L. Akers et al., "Social Learning and Deviant Behavior: A Specific Test of a General Theory," *American Sociological Review* 44 (August 1979): 637–38.
21. Ibid., pp. 638–39, 651.
22. Ronald L. Akers, *Criminological Theories: Introduction, Evaluation, and Application,* 3d ed. (Los Angeles: Roxbury, 2000), p. 89.
23. Ibid., pp. 81, 82; quotation is from p. 82.
24. Francis T. Cullen and Robert Agnew, eds. *Criminology Theory: Past to Present* (Los Angeles: Roxbury, 1999), p. 92.
25. See Gabriel Tarde, "Penal Philosophy," in *The Heritage of Modern Criminology,* ed. Sawyer F. Sylvester Jr. (Cambridge, MA: Schenkman, 1972), p. 84.
26. For further details on Tarde's theories, see Margaret S. Wilson Vine, "Gabriel Tarde," in *Pioneers in Criminology,* 2d ed., ed. Hermann Mannheim (Montclair, NJ: Patterson Smith, 1973), p. 292.
27. Tarde, "Penal Philosophy", p. 90.
28. Vine, "Gabriel Tarde," p. 295.
29. Tarde, "Penal Philosophy", p. 94.
30. Vine, "Gabriel Tarde," p. 295.
31. Stephen Schafer, *Theories in Criminology* (New York: Random House, 1969), p. 239.
32. See Robert T. Bower, *The Changing Television Audience in America* (New York: Columbia University, 1985); and Mediamark Research, *Multimedia Audiences* (New York: Mediamark Research, Inc., 1987).
33. "Poll: Americans Concerned about TV Violence," *Orlando Sentinel* (26 February 1993), p. 3.
34. "Kids' TV More of a Wasteland Than Ever, Critics Say," *Miami Herald* (3 May 1993), p. 7.
35. "Television Gets Closer Look as a Factor in Real Violence," *New York Times* (14 December 1994), p. 1.
36. Albert Bandura, "The Social Learning Perspective: Mechanisms of Aggression," in *Psychology of Crime and Criminal Justice,* ed.

Hans Toch (New York: Holt, Rinehart & Winston, 1979), pp. 204–5.
37. J. Ronald Milavsky, *TV and Violence,* National Institute of Justice (Washington, DC: U.S. Department of Justice, 1988), p. 3.
38. James Q. Wilson and Richard J. Herrnstein, *Crime and Human Nature* (New York: Simon & Schuster, 1985).
39. See David Pearl et al., *Television and Behavior: Ten Years of Scientific Progress and Implications for the Eighties* (Washington, DC: U.S. Government Printing Office, 1982). For the full report see J. Ronald Milavsky et al., *Television and Aggression: A Panel Study* (New York: Academic Press, 1983).
40. Tannis MacBeth Williams, "Summary, Conclusions, and Implications," in *The Impact of Television: A Natural Experiment in Three Communities,* ed. Tannis MacBeth Williams (New York: Academic Press, 1986), p. 411.
41. Walter C. Bailey, "Murder, Capital Punishment, and Television: Execution Publicity and Homicide Rates," *American Sociological Review* 55 (October 1990): 628–33; quotation is from p. 633.
42. Ray Surette, *Media, Crime, and Criminal Justice: Images and Realities* (Pacific Grove, CA: Brooks/Cole, 1992), pp. 108, 118.
43. "Media Violence Plays Part in Shootings: Ex-Army Ranger Argues TV, Films Affect Children," *Washington Times* (10 November 1998), p. 2.
44. "Broadcasting Violence: Debate Intensifies on Whether Media Should Be Liable for School Shootings," *American Bar Association Journal* 87 (May 2001), p. 29.
45. "Study Ties Aggression to Violence in Games," *USA Today* (10 May 2000), p. 3D.
46. Gwynn Nettler, *Explaining Crime,* 3d ed. (New York: McGraw-Hill, 1984), p. 290; emphasis in the original.
47. See Albert J. Reiss Jr., "Delinquency as the Failure of Personal and Social Controls," *American Sociological Review* 16 (1951): 196–207.
48. F. Ivan Nye, *Family Relationships and Delinquent Behavior* (New York: John Wiley, 1958), as quoted in Akers, *Criminological Theories,* p. 101.
49. Akers, *Criminological Theories,* p. 102.
50. Walter C. Reckless, "Containment Theory," in *The Sociology of Crime and Delinquency,* 2d ed., ed. Marvin E. Wolfgang et al. (New York: John Wiley, 1970), p. 402.
51. Ibid.
52. Richard A. Ball, "Development of Basic Norm Violation: Neutralization and Self-Concept within a Male Cohort," *Criminology* 21 (February 1983): 90.
53. Walter C. Reckless, *The Crime Problem,* 5th ed. (Englewood Cliffs, NJ: Prentice Hall, 1973), pp. 55–57; reprint of article from *Federal Probation* 25 (December 1961): 42–46.
54. Harwin L. Voss, "Differential Association and Containment Theory: A Theoretical Convergence," in *Society, Delinquency and Delinquent Behavior,* ed. Harwin L. Voss (Boston: Little, Brown, 1970), pp. 198, 206.
55. See Nettler, *Explaining Crime,* p. 293.
56. Akers, *Criminological Theories,* p. 105, referring also to B. Grant Stitt and David J. Giacopassi, "Trends in the Connectivity of Theory and Research in Criminologist," *The Criminologist* 17, no. 1 (1992): 3–6.
57. Travis Hirschi, *Causes of Delinquency* (Berkeley and Los Angeles: University of California Press, 1969), pp. 16–34.
58. Ibid., p. 21.
59. Ibid.
60. Ibid., p. 26.
61. Ibid., pp. 54, 56. Questionnaire, Copyright 1969 The Regents of the University of California. Reprinted by permission of the publisher
62. Ibid., pp. 72, 108, 132, 134.
63. See Michael J. Hindelang, "Causes of Delinquency: A Partial Replication and Extension," *Social Problems* 20 (Spring 1973): 471–87.
64. Rand D. Conger, "Social Control and Social Learning Models of Delinquent Behavior: A Synthesis," *Criminology* 14 (May 1976): 19, 35.
65. See Delbert S. Elliott and Harwin L. Voss, *Delinquency and Dropout* (Lexington, MA: Lexington Books, 1974).
66. Eric Linden and James C. Hackler, "Affective Ties and Delinquency," *Pacific Sociological Review* 16 (January 1973): 27–46.
67. Hirschi, *Causes of Delinquency,* pp. 230–31.
68. Robert Agnew, "Social Control Theory and Delinquency: A Longitudinal Test," *Criminology* 23 (February 1985): 58, 59.
69. Randy L. LaGrange and Helene Raskin White, "Age Differences in Delinquency: A Test of Theory," *Criminology* 23 (February 1985): 36.
70. Thomas J. Bernard, "Structure and Control: Reconsidering Hirschi's Concept of Commitment," *Justice Quarterly* 4 (September 1987): 409.
71. Ibid., p. 422.
72. Ibid., p. 423.
73. Michael D. Wiatrowski et al., "Social Control Theory and Delinquency," *American Sociological Review* 46 (October 1981): 525.
74. Ibid.
75. Ibid., p. 537.
76. Stephen A. Cernkovich and Peggy C. Giordano, "School Bonding, Race, and Delinquency," *Criminology* 30 (May 1992): 261–91; quotation is from p. 286.
77. Vangie Foshee and Karl E. Bauman, "Parental and Peer Characteristics as Modifiers of the Bond-Behavior Relationship: An Elaboration of Control Theory," *Journal of Health and Social Behavior* (March 1992): 66–76.
78. Akers, *Criminological Theories,* pp. 109–10.
79. Ross L. Matsueda, "Testing Control Theory and Differential Association: A Causal Modeling Approach," *American Sociological Review* 47 (1982): 489–504.
80. Barbara J. Costello and Paul R. Vowell, "Testing Control Theory and Differential Association: A Reanalysis of the Richmond Youth Project Data," *Criminology* 37 (November 1999): 815–42; quotation is from p. 815.
81. Michael R. Gottfredson and Travis Hirschi, *A General Theory of Crime* (Stanford, CA: Stanford University Press, 1990), p. xiv.
82. Ibid., p. 15.
83. Ibid., pp. 89–90.
84. Ibid., pp. 89, 95–97.
85. Ibid., p. 117.
86. Harold G. Grasmick et al., "Testing the Core Empirical Implications of Gottfredson and Hirschi's General Theory of Crime," *Journal of Research in Crime and Delinquency* 30 (February 1993): 5–29.
87. David Brownfield and Ann Marie Sorenson, "Self-Control and Juvenile Delinquency: Theoretical Issues and an Empirical Assessment of Selected Elements of a General Theory of Crime," *Deviant Behavior* 14 (July/September 1993): 243–64; quotation is from p. 260.
88. Teresa C. LaGrange and Robert A. Silverman, "Low Self-Control and Opportunity: Testing the General Theory of Crime as an Explanation for Gender Differences in Delinquency," *Criminology* 37 (February 1999): 41–72; quotation is from p. 64.
89. Alex R. Piquero et al., "Does Self-Control Affect Survey Response? Applying Exploratory, Confirmatory, and Item Response Theory Analysis to Grasmick Et Al.'s Self-Control Scale," *Criminology* 38 (August 2000): 897–930.
90. Christine S. Sellers, "Self-Control and Intimate Violence: An Examination of the Scope and Specification of the General Theory of Crime," *Criminology* 37 (May 1999): 375–404; quotation is from p. 396.
91. Raymond Paternoster and Robert Brame, "On the Association Among Self-Control, Crime, and Analogous Behaviors," *Criminology* 38 (August 2000): 971–82; quotation is from p. 980.
92. Robert Agnew, "Testing the Leading Crime Theories: An Alternative Strategy Focusing on Motivational Processes," *Journal of Research in Crime and Delinquency* 32 (November 1995): 363–98; quotation is from p. 370.
93. Akers, *Criminological Theories,* p. 90.
94. See Delbert Elliott et al., *Explaining Delinquency and Drug Use* (Beverly Hills, CA: Sage, 1985).
95. Scott Menard, "Demographic and Theoretical Variables in the Age-Period-Cohort Analysis of Illegal Behavior," *Journal of Research in Crime and Delinquency* 29 (May 1992): 178–99.
96. See Joseph Weis and J. David Hawkins, *Reports of the National Juvenile Assessment Centers, Preventing Delinquency* (Washington, DC: U.S. Department of Justice, 1981).
97. See Terence P. Thornberry, "Toward an Interactional Theory of Delinquency," *Criminology* 25 (1987): 863–91.
98. Terence P. Thornberry et al., "Testing Interactional Theory: An Examination of Reciprocal Causal Relationships among Family, School, and Delinquency," *Journal of Criminal Law and Criminology* 82 (Spring 1991): 3–35; quotation is from p. 4.
99. Nettler, *Explaining Crime,* p. 314; emphasis in the original.
100. Kai T. Erikson, "Notes on the Sociology of Deviance," *Social Problems* 9 (Spring 1962): 308.
101. Frank Tannenbaum, *Crime and the Community* (New York: Columbia University Press, 1938), pp. 19–20.
102. Edwin M. Lemert, *Human Deviance, Social Problems, and Social Control* (Englewood Cliffs, NJ: Prentice Hall, 1967), p. 17.
103. Howard S. Becker, *Outsiders: Studies in the Sociology of Deviance* (New York: Free Press, 1963), p. 9.
104. For more details on the development of labeling theory, see Walter R. Gove, ed., *The Labeling of Deviance: Evaluating a Perspective,* 2d ed. (Beverly Hills, CA: Sage, 1980).
105. See Edwin M. Schur, *Radical Nonintervention: Rethinking the Delinquency Problem* (Englewood Cliffs, NJ: Prentice Hall, 1973).
106. Stuart L. Hills, *Crime, Power and Morality* (Scranton, PA: Chandler, 1971), pp. 19–21.
107. Richard D. Schwartz and Jerome H. Skolnick, "Two Studies of Legal Stigma," *Social Problems* 10 (Fall 1962): 136–41.

108. D. L. Rosenhan, "On Being Sane in Insane Places," *Science* 179 (January 1973): 250.
109. Craig Haney et al., "Interpersonal Dynamics in a Simulated Prison," *International Journal of Criminology and Penology* 1 (1973): 69–97; reprinted in *Examining Deviance Experimentally*, ed. Darrell J. Steffensmeier and Robert M. Terry (Port Washington, NY: Alfred, 1975), p. 223.
110. Anne Rankin Mahoney, "The Effect of Labeling upon Youths in the Juvenile Justice System: A Review of the Evidence," *Law and Society Review* 8 (Summer 1974): 583–614. Quotation is from page 609. See this article for a listing and discussion of the empirical studies.
111. Melvin C. Ray and William R. Down, "An Empirical Test of Labeling Theory Using Longitudinal Data," *Journal of Research in Crime and Delinquency* 23 (May 1986): 169–94.
112. Malcolm W. Klein, "Labeling Theory and Delinquency Policy," *Criminal Justice and Behavior* 13 (March 1986): 47–79.
113. Gordon Bazemore, "Delinquent Reform and the Labeling Perspective," *Criminal Justice and Behavior* 12 (June 1985): 131–69.
114. Douglas A. Smith and Raymond Paternoster, "Formal Processing and Future Delinquency: Deviance Amplification as Selection Artifact," *Law and Society Review* 24 (1990): 1109–31.
115. John Braithwaite, *Crime, Shame, and Reintegration* (Cambridge, UK: Cambridge University Press, 1989), p. 100.
116. Ibid., pp. 100–1.
117. Ross L. Matsueda, "Reflected Appraisals, Parental Labeling, and Delinquency," in *Criminological Theory: Past to Present*, eds. Cullen and Agnew, pp. 279–85.
118. George Herbert Mead, *Mind, Self, and Society* (Chicago: University of Chicago Press, 1934).
119. Matsueda, "Reflected Appraisals," p. 284.
120. Ibid., p. 279. See also Dawn Jeglum Bartusch and Ross L. Matsueda, "Gender, Reflected Appraisals, and Labeling: A Cross-Group Test of an Interactionist Theory of Delinquency," *Social Forces* 75 (1996): 145–77.
121. Daniel L. Dotter and Julian B. Roebuck, "The Labeling Approach Re-Examined: Interactionism and the Components of Deviance," *Deviant Behavior* 9, no. 1 (1988): 19.
122. Matsueda, "Reflected Appraisals," p. 284.
123. Charles T. Tittle, "Labelling and Crime: An Empirical Evaluation," Chapter 6 in *The Labelling of Deviance*, ed. Walter R. Gove (New York: Halsted Press, 1975), pp. 157–79; quotation is from p. 158; citations omitted.
124. Ibid., p. 176.
125. Akers, *Criminological Theories*, p. 127.
126. Bernard A. Thorsell and Lloyd D. Klemke, "The Labeling Process: Reinforcement and Deterrent?" *Law and Society Review* 6 (February 1972): 393–403.
127. See, for example, Walter Gove, "Postscript to Labeling and Crime," in *The Labeling of Deviance: Evaluating a Perspective*, 2d ed., ed. Walter Gove, pp. 53–109.
128. See Bruce G. Link et al., "A Modified Labeling Theory Approach to Mental Disorders: An Empirical Assessment," *American Sociological Review* 54 (June 1989): 400–23; and Bruce G. Link et al., "The Social Rejection of Former Mental Patients: Understanding Why Labels Matter," *American Journal of Sociology* 6 (May 1987): 1461–1500.
129. Akers, *Criminological Theories*, p. 128.
130. Ibid., p. 137.
131. Raymond Paternoster and Leeann Iovanni, "The Labeling Perspective and Delinquency: An Elaboration of the Theory and An Assessment of the Evidence," *Justice Quarterly* 6 (September 1989): 359.
132. See Thomas J. Bernard, "Twenty Years of Testing Theories: What Have We Learned and Why?" *Journal of Research in Crime and Delinquency* 27 (November 1990): 330–47.
133. Roland Chilton, "Urban Crime Trends and Criminological Theory," *Criminal Justice Research Bulletin* 6, no. 3 (Huntsville, TX: Sam Houston State University Criminal Justice Center, 1991), p. 2.
134. George A. Lundberg, *Can Science Save Us?* (New York: Longman, 1961), pp. 143–44.
135. Robert B. Bursik Jr., Editorial Statement, *Criminology* 39 (February 2001): no page number.
136. Roland Chilton, "Viable Policy: The Impact of Federal Funding and the Need for Independent Research Agendas—the American Society of Criminology 2000 Presidential Address," *Criminology* 39 (February 2001): 1.
137. Ibid., p. 7.
138. Buck v. Bell, 274 U.S. 200 (1927).

PART III

Types of Crime

CHAPTER 7
Violent Crimes

CHAPTER 8
Property Crimes

CHAPTER 9
Business and Government-Related Crimes

CHAPTER 10
Drug Abuse, Drug Trafficking, and Organized Crime

The study of crime and criminal behavior necessitates a close look at types of crime, which is the focus of Part III. Chapter 7 opens the discussion with an overview of the crimes people most fear: violent crimes against the person. The chapter explores the four serious violent crimes (or index crimes) as categorized by the *UCR* (murder and nonnegligent manslaughter, forcible rape, robbery, and aggravated assault). It focuses on non-index serious violent offenses, including domestic violence, hate crimes, stalking, and terrorism. The chapter then discusses the fear of crime, followed by an analysis of gun control and violence. It closes with a consideration of the media, pornography, and crime.

Chapter 8 covers the four index property crimes (burglary, larceny-theft, motor vehicle theft, and arson) as well as less serious crimes against property. Attention is given to professional career criminals and their activities.

Chapter 9 considers crimes of the business world. It covers government-related crimes, such as obstruction of justice, political crimes, and official abuse of power such as civil rights violations. The chapter closes with an overview of methods for controlling these crimes. Chapter 10 focuses on three major areas of criminal activity in the world today: illegal drug use, drug trafficking, and organized crime.

7

▶ Muslim mourners pray at the casket of Abdo Ali Ahmed, 4 October 2001. More than 300 people attended the funeral of the slain Arab American shopkeeper. Family and friends believed he was a victim of a hate crime committed against him because of the terrorist acts of 11 September 2001, allegedly by persons from the Middle East. (AP)

Violent Crimes

OUTLINE

This is the first of four chapters on types of crime. After discussing the study of types of crime and looking at an overview of violent crimes, this chapter considers violent crimes in greater detail, focusing first on the *UCR*'s four serious violent crimes (or index crimes): murder and nonnegligent manslaughter, forcible rape, robbery, and aggravated assault. A few of the less serious violent crimes included in *UCR* data are also selected for discussion. Considerable attention is given to the various types of domestic violence, including child abuse, elder abuse, and spouse abuse. Hate crimes and stalking are overviewed, followed by a more intensive analysis of terrorism. All crimes of violence may involve the use of weapons, and particular attention is given to gun control. Finally, the chapter considers the impact of the media and pornography on violence.

KEY TERMS

assault
aggravated assault
battered person syndrome
battery
child abuse
domestic violence
elder abuse
felony-murder doctrine
forcible rape
hate crimes
homicide
incest
involuntary manslaughter
marital rape
murder
nonnegligent manslaughter
rape
robbery
stalking
statutory rape
Stockholm syndrome
terrorism
voluntary manslaughter

The 1980 murder rate in the United States was the highest annual rate in this century. *Newsweek* labeled 1981 as the "year that mainstream America rediscovered violent crime" and concluded, "Defying any cure, it overwhelms the police, the courts and the prisons—and warps U.S. life."[1] By 1989 violence had escalated to the point that one national news magazine headlined an article as follows: "Dead Zones: Whole Sections of Urban America Are Being Written Off as Anarchic Badlands, Places Where Cops Fear to Go and Acknowledge: 'This Is Beirut, U.S.A.' "[2]

Rates of murder and other violent crimes fell in the 1990s, but that was little comfort to a nation that had experienced the Oklahoma City bombing; the killings by the Unabomber; numerous violent acts committed on school grounds by juveniles with guns, some involving multiple murders; and many other crimes that made it clear that our schools, our homes, and our workplaces are no longer safe from violent acts. Highly publicized acts of domestic violence, such as those by O. J. Simpson (who was acquitted of criminal charges but found liable in a civil suit involving the deaths of his ex-wife and her friend); Susan Smith (who strapped her little boys into the back seat of a car and drove it into a lake, jumping out in time to save herself); Andrea Pia Yates, who drowned all of her five children; and teenage parents who kill their newborns (see Chapter 5, Exhibit 5.1) illustrate that dangers of violence lurk even among people who seem to live ordinary lives.

Rescue workers carry fatally injured New York City Fire Department chaplain, the Reverend Mychal Judge, from the wreckage of the World Trade Center in New York City on September 11, 2001. Judge was crushed by falling debris while giving a man last rites. The twin towers collapsed after being struck by hijacked airplanes. (Shannon Stapleton/Reuters/Getty Images)

None of these crimes, however, compared to the terrorist attacks of 11 September 2001, introduced in Chapter 1 and discussed in greater detail in Exhibit 7.3 of this chapter (see p. 227).

This chapter focuses on the four index violent crimes as defined by the Federal Bureau of Investigation, but it also includes discussions of domestic violence (which often involves one or more of the four index violent crimes), hate crime, stalking, and terrorism. Other features are the fear of crime; gun control; and, finally, the mass media, pornography, and crime.

THE STUDY OF TYPES OF CRIME

Thus far the text has analyzed criminal behavior using biological and other physical-characteristic theories of criminal behavior, as well as psychological, psychiatric, social-structural, and social-process approaches and theories. Some social scientists have also attempted to explain criminal behavior by looking at *types* of crime and criminals. Many early studies took this approach, focusing on the robber, the burglar, the thief, or the rapist.

In analyzing the study of criminal behavior in terms of typologies, sociologist Don Gibbons stated in 1975 that "the research . . . indicates that no fully comprehensive offender typology which subsumes most criminality within it yet exists." New types of criminal behavior continue to develop and must be accommodated by the typology. Gibbons concluded that typing criminals may be inappropriate in many cases.[3]

The emphasis in this chapter is on types of crime, not types of criminals. Some sociological analyses of types of criminals are discussed, but it is important to recognize that a rapist may commit armed robbery as well. Furthermore, it does not necessarily follow that a person has committed the particular crime charged. For many reasons, defendants might not be charged with the crimes they are thought to have committed, or they may be charged with those crimes but be allowed to plead guilty to lesser ones. For example, a defendant charged with forcible rape may be permitted to plead guilty to assault and battery (see p. 212). In official data this offender is classified as one who committed assault and battery, not forcible rape.

These chapters on types of crime use the legal approach to define crime. This is not to suggest that other approaches are not important, but it is the legal elements of the definition that must be proved for a conviction in U.S. criminal justice systems. Thus, within the legal system it is inappropriate to label a person a robber if the charges of robbery, a violent crime, have been dismissed and the defendant has been permitted to plead guilty to theft, a property crime. Likewise, it is inappropriate to call a person a rapist after he or she has been acquitted of forcible rape.

In such cases, sociologists studying why people engage in robbery might include this person in their samples. Some sociological studies are discussed, but it is important to understand that they are not always based on legal or mutually exclusive categories.

VIOLENT CRIMES: AN OVERVIEW

For official crime data, originally the FBI's *Uniform Crime Reports (UCR)* selected seven crimes (because of their seriousness and frequency) as the index, or Part I, offenses: murder (including nonnegligent manslaughter), forcible rape, robbery, aggravated assault, burglary, larceny-theft, and motor vehicle theft. In 1978 Congress added arson. The four *violent crimes*—murder, manslaughter,

EXHIBIT 7.1
UCR Definitions of Index Serious Violent Crimes

- *Murder and nonnegligent manslaughter*—the willful (nonnegligent) killing of one human being by another.
- *Forcible rape*—the carnal knowledge of a female forcibly and against her will. Assault or attempts to commit rape by force or threat of force are also included; however, statutory rape (without force) and other sex offenses are excluded.
- *Robbery*—the taking or attempting to take anything of value from the care, custody, or control of a person or persons by force or threat of force or violence and/or by putting the victim in fear.
- *Aggravated assault*—an unlawful attack by one person upon another for the purpose of inflicting severe or aggravated bodily injury. This type of assault is usually accompanied by the use of a weapon or by means likely to produce death or great bodily harm. Attempts are included since it is not necessary that an injury result when a gun, knife, or other weapon is used which could and probably would result in serious personal injury if the crime were successfully completed.

Source: Federal Bureau of Investigation, *Crime in the United States, Uniform Crime Reports 2000* (Washington, DC: U.S. Government Printing Office, 2001), pp. 14, 25, 29, 34.

FIGURE 7.1
Crime Index Offenses: Percent Distribution, 2000[1]

Source: Federal Bureau of Investigation, *Crime in the United States, Uniform Crime Reports 2000* (Washington, DC: U.S. Government Printing Office, 2001), p. 9.

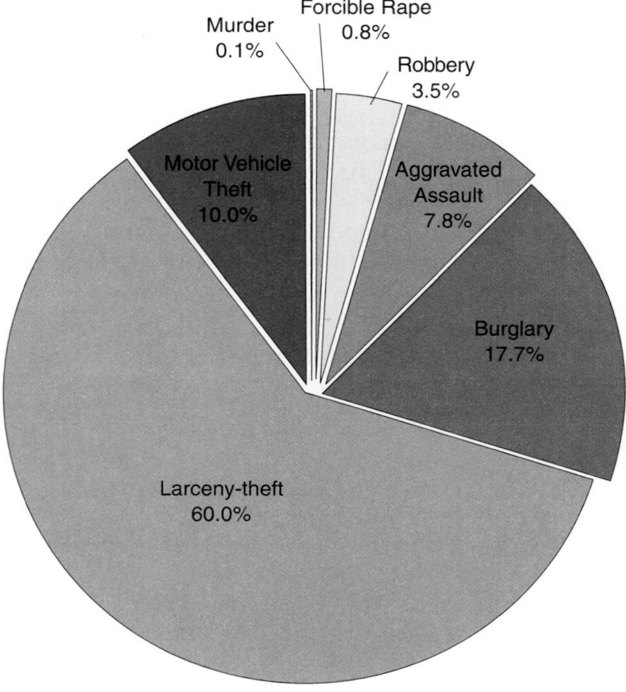

[1] Due to rounding, the percentages do not add to 100.0 percent.

forcible rape, robbery, and aggravated assault—are the focus of this chapter. Exhibit 7.1 provides the *UCR* definition of each. Burglary, larceny-theft, motor vehicle theft, and arson are property crimes; they are discussed in Chapter 8. All of the index offenses are serious crimes, but the category of violent crimes designates those that might result in injury to a person.

Most of the serious crimes in the United States consist of property, not violent crimes, as illustrated by Figure 7.1. As that figure shows, murder constituted only 0.1 percent of all index crimes in the United States in 2000, while the largest percentage, 60 percent, were larceny-theft. Rape accounted for only 0.8 percent of all index crimes, and robbery for only 3.5 percent. Yet it is violent crime that engenders the most fear, attention, and reaction among the public.

Despite the relatively few violent compared to serious property crimes in the United States, of interest to public officials and scholars has been the fluctuation in violence in the United States. According to the FBI's official data on crime, as recorded in the *Uniform Crime Reports* (*UCR*), violent crime rates were high in the 1920s but decreased during the depression and World War II. The rates began climbing again in the 1960s. Between 1976 and 1977 the violent crime rate decreased for the first time since 1961, but in 1978 the rates began climbing again.[4]

In the 1990s violent crime showed some fluctuation, but as Figure 7.2 demonstrates, both the rate and the volume of offenses declined from 1996 to 2000. The official data for 2000 reveal that crime declined for a ninth consecutive year, although the changes

FIGURE 7.2
Trends in U.S. Violent Crime, 1996–2000

Source: Federal Bureau of Investigation, *Crime in the United States, Uniform Crime Reports 2000* (Washington, DC: U.S. Government Printing Office, 2001), p. 13.

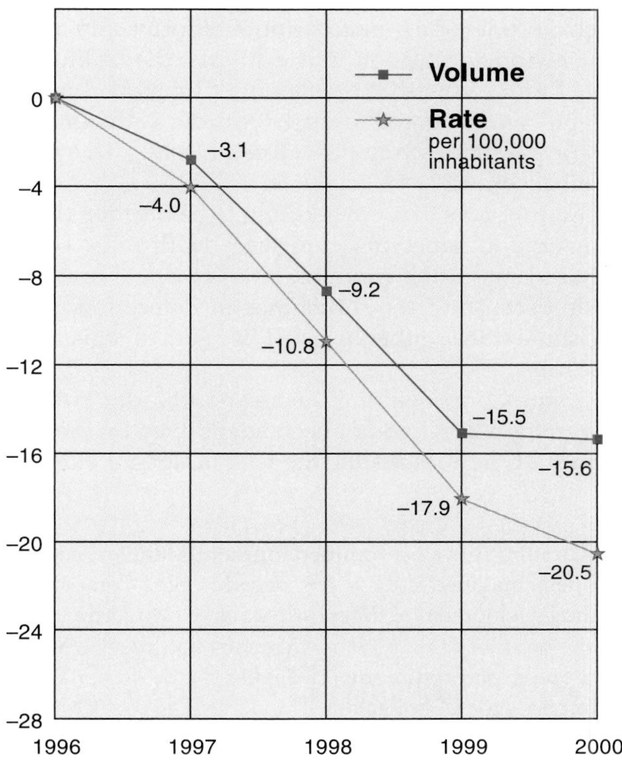

were small. The number of offenses was down only 0.1 percent over the previous year, and the rate per 100,000 decreased by 2.6 percent.[5]

Victimization data for 2000, released in 2001 by the Bureau of Justice Statistics (BJS), reveal an even greater decline in crimes, showing a 15 percent drop in serious crime (recall that the BJS does not measure murder, but unlike the *UCR,* it does cover simple assaults, which are far more numerous than aggravated assaults), with an overall decrease of 15 percent in violent crimes and 10 percent in property crimes. The differences between the two sources puzzle experts, although most agree that more than one year is required for a trend. Further, the larger apparent decrease in crime as measured by the victimization studies, may reflect greater reporting on that survey.[6]

These downward figures are encouraging, but the overall figures can mask changes within segments of the population. Recall the warning from government officials that there appears to be far more juvenile violence than arrest records show; thus, declining crime and arrests may not be as encouraging as we might like. Furthermore, the violence among juveniles, especially in our nation's schools, is cause for grave concern.

And in December 2001 the government released crime data indicating that murders in some cities rose significantly during that year. Despite the fact that in some cities murders decreased after 11 September 2001, compared with the previous year, the overall increases in several large cities led experts to express concern that after years of declining murders, the changes in 2001 might represent a change back in the other direction.[7]

SERIOUS VIOLENT CRIMES: THE INDEX OFFENSES

Murder The unlawful and unjustified killing of a human being (or a fetus in some jurisdictions) with malice aforethought: the intent to kill, the intent to do great bodily harm, an act done in willful disregard of the strong likelihood that death or great injury would result, or a killing committed during the commission of another felony.

Nonnegligent manslaughter *See* **murder.**

Homicide A general term including all killings, some of which are deemed to be justifiable or excusable homicides, while other might constitute manslaughter or murder.

This section discusses individually the four index offenses of the *UCR:* murder, forcible rape, robbery, and aggravated assault, beginning with the most serious but least committed crime of murder.

Murder and Nonnegligent Manslaughter

The *UCR* combines **murder** and **nonnegligent manslaughter,** defined as "the willful (nonnegligent) killing of one human being by another." This definition may appear simple, but not all willful killings are categorized as murder. Generally, the term **homicide** is used to refer to all killings, some of which may be lawful, as implied by this statute from the Washington State criminal code.

> Homicide is the killing of a human being by the act, procurement, or omission of another, death occurring at any time, and is either (1) murder, (2) homicide by abuse, (3) manslaughter, (4) excusable homicide, or (5) justifiable homicide.[8]

Some of those terms need further explanation. The killing of another person might be *justifiable homicide,* as when a police officer kills in the line of duty. A homicide may be *excusable,* such as taking the life of another person who is trying to inflict serious bodily harm or kill you or others. Not all states have the provision of *homicide by abuse,* which involves a death that occurs as the result of abusing a child or even an adult.

Note that the above statute refers to killing "a human being." In most jurisdictions that would preclude including as murder the killing of a fetus, because historically a fetus has not been considered a human being. California and a few other states have altered that historical position. For example, the California statute, which used to state that murder was "the unlawful killing of a human being, with malice aforethought," was changed to read, "Murder is the unlawful killing of a human being, or a fetus, with malice aforethought." There are exclusions for acts such as legal abortions.[9]

The Washington statute also provides that, for a killing to be murder, death may occur "at any time." In some jurisdictions, however, death must occur within the traditional period used under the common law—one year and one day. This limitation was made because of the difficulties in determining the cause of death. In recent years some states, either by court decision or legislative enactment, have changed that rule.

In 1999 the Tennessee Supreme Court held that the year-and-a-day rule no longer existed in that state. Even though it had not been abandoned by the legislature, the court emphasized that the reasons for the rule no longer existed. According to the court,

> Medical science can now sustain the critically wounded for months and even years beyond what might have been imagined only a few decades ago. Comparable progress has been made in the development of diagnostic skills . . . Modern pathologists are able to determine the cause of death with much greater accuracy . . . Moreover, jurors today may rely upon expert testimony . . . Finally, the death penalty is no longer indiscriminately imposed for all homicides.[10]

California has retained the theory of the year-and-a-day rule but expanded the time period. According to the California Penal Code,

> To make the killing either murder or manslaughter, it is requisite that the party die within three years and a day after the stroke received or the cause of death administered . . . In the computation of such time, the whole of the day on which the act was done shall be reckoned the first.[11]

There are other definitions of elements of the crime of murder that might distinguish one state from another and, as a result, affect murder data. For example, murder requires an intent, but states differ in the words they use and the interpretations of those words. Some might refer to an intent to kill, while others might stipulate that an intent to inflict great bodily harm is sufficient. Still others find intent if a victim dies while a felony, such as a robbery or rape, is being committed. This type of murder is referred to as **felony murder.** Its definition might include a list of felonies to which it applies—for example, Maine lists committing or attempting to commit "murder, robbery, burglary, kidnapping, arson, gross sexual assault, or escape" and further requires that the resulting death be reasonably foreseeable.[12]

Felony-murder doctrine Doctrine used to hold a defendant liable if a human life is taken during the commission of another felony, such as armed robbery, kidnapping, or arson, even if the defendant did not commit the murder.

Voluntary manslaughter *See* manslaughter.

In addition to varying definitions of murder, statutes may distinguish degrees of murder, such as first, second, or third, with first-degree murder being the most serious. They may also distinguish murder from manslaughter, which may be divided into types. Generally, **voluntary manslaughter** refers to an intentional killing that takes place while the defendant is in the heat of passion and is provoked by the victim—a situation that mitigates but does not excuse

Involuntary manslaughter *See* manslaughter.

the killing. The circumstances must be examined to determine whether the crime is murder or manslaughter. The provocation must be such that it would cause a reasonable person to kill.

FIGURE 7.3
Murder and Nonnegligent Manslaughter: Percent Change, 1996–2000
Source: Federal Bureau of Investigation, *Crime in the United States, Uniform Crime Reports 2000* (Washington, DC: U.S. Government Printing Office, 2001), p. 16.

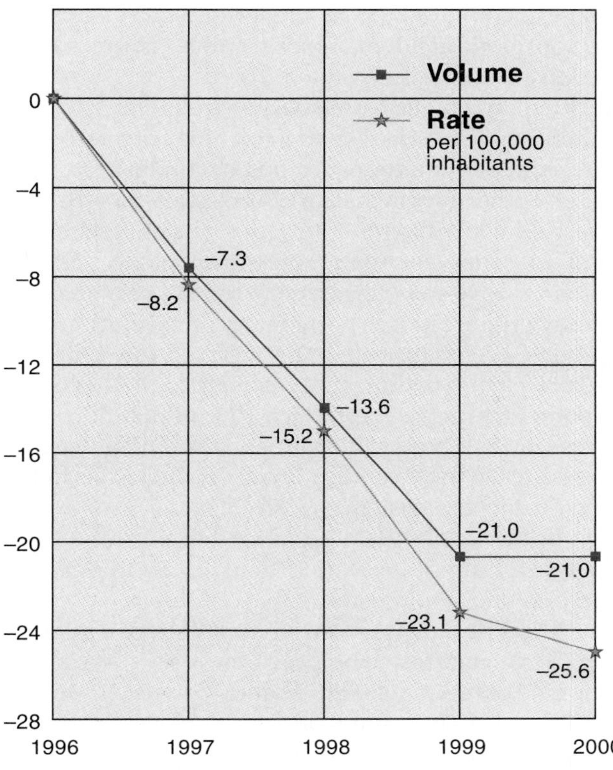

Involuntary manslaughter refers to a killing that was not intended. California defines the term as "the unlawful killing of a human being without malice . . . in the commission of an unlawful act, not amounting to felony; or in the commission of a lawful act which might produce death, in an unlawful manner, or without due caution and circumspection." The provision excludes "acts committed in the driving of a vehicle,"[13] although those acts are included within some statutes and may be referred to as *vehicular homicide, vehicular manslaughter,* or even *DUI* (driving under the influence) *manslaughter.* Involuntary manslaughter may also be categorized as negligent manslaughter (deaths resulting from negligent but not criminal acts).

Although there are other terms relevant to the crime of murder, these definitions give an overview of how complicated the issues may be. Consequently, the simple definition used by the FBI may not mean the same in all jurisdictions, and thus counting murders will differ from area to area.

In 2000 the FBI reported 15,517 murder and nonnegligent manslaughter offenses, down only 0.1 percent from 1999. Figure 7.3 graphs the percentage changes in murder and nonnegligent manslaughter offenses and rates from 1996 through 2000. The rate of these offenses in 2000 was the lowest since 1966. The most populous region, the South, accounted for 44 percent of the crimes. Slightly over 76 percent of the victims were men. Most victims (88.5 percent of males and 90.8 percent of females) were killed by male offenders.[14]

Over 40 percent of murder and nonnegligent manslaughter victims knew their assailants. Figure 7.4 diagrams the nature of the relationships between victims and their assailants.

Rape Unlawful sexual intercourse (limited to female victims in some jurisdictions); called **forcible rape** if committed against the victim's will by the use of threats or force. **Statutory rape** refers to consensual sexual intercourse with a person who is below the legal age of consent. **Marital rape** occurs when the victim of forced intercourse is the spouse of the alleged offender. **Rape by instrumentation,** a relatively new legal concept, refers to any intrusion by the male penis of any part of a person's body that could be interpreted for the purpose of sexual arousal or gratification or as an act of violence, or the forced intrusion of any object into the genital or anal openings of another person's body.

Forcible rape *See* **rape.**

Marital rape *See* **rape.**

Forcible Rape

The FBI's official data on forcible **rape** as an index offense include only the crime of **forcible rape,** defined by the *UCR* as unlawful sexual intercourse involving force by a man with a female victim (see Exhibit 7.1).

Technically the FBI definition would include **marital rape,** which is forcible rape by a husband of his wife, but in fact, prosecutions of such cases are rarely reported and are not very successful when prosecuted. Historically, a husband had unlimited sexual access to his wife; she was expected, and in most cases she herself expected, to comply with his sexual desires. The husband could be charged with rape only if he forced his wife to have sexual intercourse with a third person. This common law provision became a part of most of our rape statutes. Although some jurisdictions retain the common law approach, in recent years many have changed their rules by statute or by judicial holdings to permit forced sexual acts between spouses to be prosecuted as rape.

FIGURE 7.4
Murder by Relationship[1]

Source: Federal Bureau of Investigation, *Crime in the United States, Uniform Crime Reports 2000* (Washington, DC: U.S. Government Printing Office, 2001), p. 21.

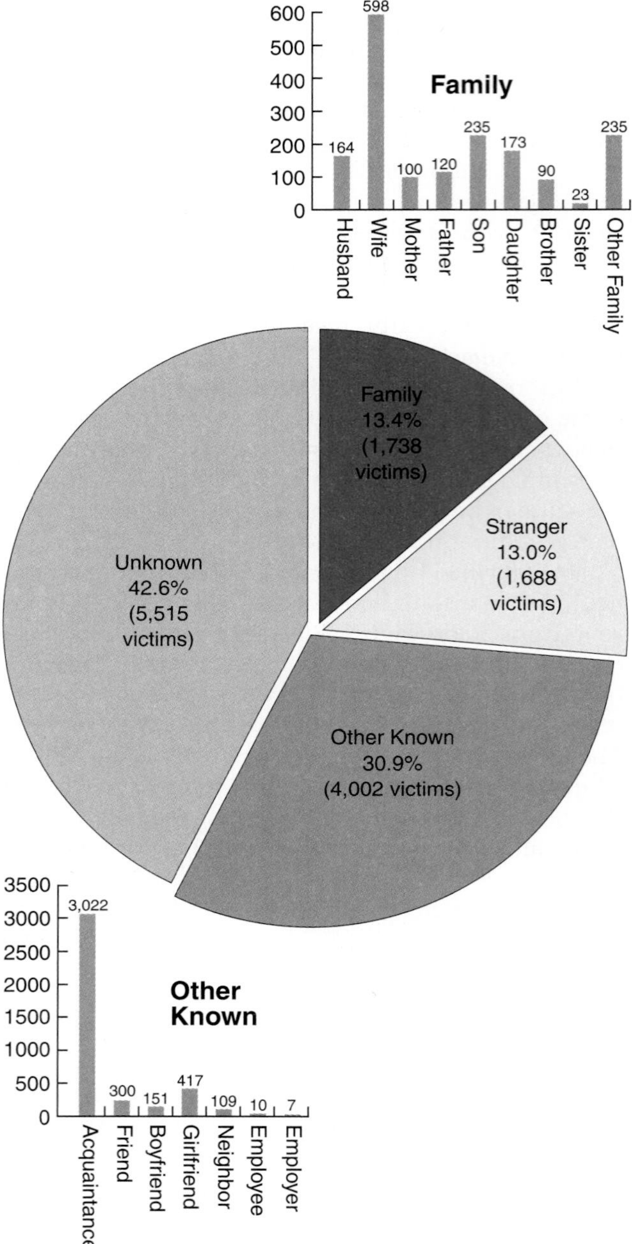

[1] Relationship is that of victim to offender.
Due to rounding, the percentages do not add to 100.0.
Figures are based on 12,943 murder victims for whom Supplementary Homicide Report data were received.

Recent research implies that marital rape is much more prevalent than previously thought and probably exceeds all other kinds of rape. Possibly as many as 1 of every 10 wives is victimized. According to one report, "The offender's goal, in many instances, appears to be to humiliate and retaliate against his wife and the abuse may often include anal intercourse."[15]

State statutes define rape in different ways. Some include only rape of women; others include rape of both genders. Some statutes require actual penetration of the vagina by the penis; others include rape by instrumentation, involving the penetration of the genital or anal openings of another by a foreign object under specified circumstances.

Another factor that may influence rape data is the victim's willingness to report the alleged crime and to cooperate with police and prosecutors in attempting to solve the crime. This can be a problem in any crime, but it is particularly significant in allegations of forcible rape because of the sensitive nature of the victimization as well as the historical "blame-the-victim" approach to investigations and prosecutions. Today most jurisdictions have enacted measures to increase the victim's cooperation in the criminal justice system.

In comparing data on rape, therefore, we must look carefully at the variables involved in defining statutes and implementing those statutes.

The FBI recorded 90,196 forcible rapes in 2000, up 0.9 percent from the previous year. The volume and rate of rapes rose significantly between 1990 and 1992 but began a sharp decline in 1993, continuing until 1999, with the slight upturn in 2000.[16] Figure 7.5 graphs the changes between 1996 and 2000.

Victimization data show higher figures for forcible rape, with reports of rape and other sexual assaults going up under the redesigned National Crime Victimization Survey (NCVS), discussed in Chapter 2. However, there was a significant decrease in the rates of simple assault and rape/sexual assault between 1999 and 2000.[17] Recall that the FBI publishes data on crimes reported to the police, while the NCVS data are secured from a sample of the population who report on questionnaires whether they have been victimized. Both sources should be analyzed carefully because of the refusal by some rape victims to report the crime. After analyzing both sources, one scholar noted that we still do not have the answer to the question of whether the rape rates decreased, increased, or remained stable during recent years.[18]

A number of studies have compared forcible rape data from the *UCR* with data from the NCVS, and some have reported an increase in the willingness of alleged victims to report their experiences. It has been suggested that one rea-

Jennifer W., 26, is consoled by her fiancé, who gave his name only as Ken, during the sentencing of Timothy Mobley in Reno, Nevada, 20 February 2001. Mobley admitted to raping Jennifer and another woman after meeting them on the Internet. Mobley, a fugitive rapist, was sentenced to three consecutive life terms in prison. (AP)

son for the increased willingness to report is the change in attitude toward gender roles and sexual behavior, representing a greater acceptance of sexual behavior by unmarried women. This might increase the willingness of women to report rapes by acquaintances, but others question these assumptions and note evidence that there is no relationship between gender beliefs and rape reporting. Rape data may be influenced by organizational responses to the crime, such as police departments, paying more attention to rape and showing more sensitivity to victims and their allegations.

Recent forcible rape data must be analyzed in light of the results of the first National Violence Against Women Survey estimates. This study indicates that rape is far more prevalent than the official data would suggest; indeed, this survey reports approximately twice as many rapes as the victimization surveys. In addition, the survey gave the following data: over one-half (54 percent) of rape victims were under 18 at the time of their first rape. Over 21 percent of the women reported being first raped before they were 12 years old. The typical female rape victim is raped nearly three times a year; about 111,000 men each year report being raped, most by other men; and over three-fourths of the women who report being raped say the offender was a current or former domestic partner. Most of the female victims reported that they were attacked by someone they knew: a boyfriend, husband or former husband, lover, date. Of those who reported a sexual attack after they were 18 years old, three-fourths said the perpetrator was a date or an intimate partner. In this survey rape included oral, anal, or vaginal intercourse by force or the threat of force.[19]

Most studies of rapists do not separate out the violent rapist, who is thought to account for only a small percentage of rapes. Thus, it is not surprising that these studies suggest that most people convicted of rape are not deviant psychologically. In fact, an earlier study showed that most men who rape adult women are not distinguishable from other men except for their sexual conduct, although those who are convicted of **statutory rape** are rather impulsive individuals.[20]

Statutory rape *See* **rape.**

Further insight into rapists has come from the work of Menachem Amir, who studied a sample of 646 forcible rape cases in Philadelphia. Amir found that most rapes were intraracial, with the rate much higher among African Americans than among whites; the offenders and victims were young, usually under 25, and were unmarried. Most of the offenders were unemployed and from the lower socioeconomic class. About one-half of the victims had a previous relationship, often a primary one, with the offenders. The majority of the victims were found to be submissive (although that could be because of fear), and the majority of the incidents did not involve repeated intercourse, fellatio, cunnilingus, or brutality.

FIGURE 7.5
Rape: Percent Change, 1996–2000

Source: Federal Bureau of Investigation, *Crime in the United States, Uniform Crime Reports 2000* (Washington, DC: U.S. Government Printing Office, 2001), p. 28.

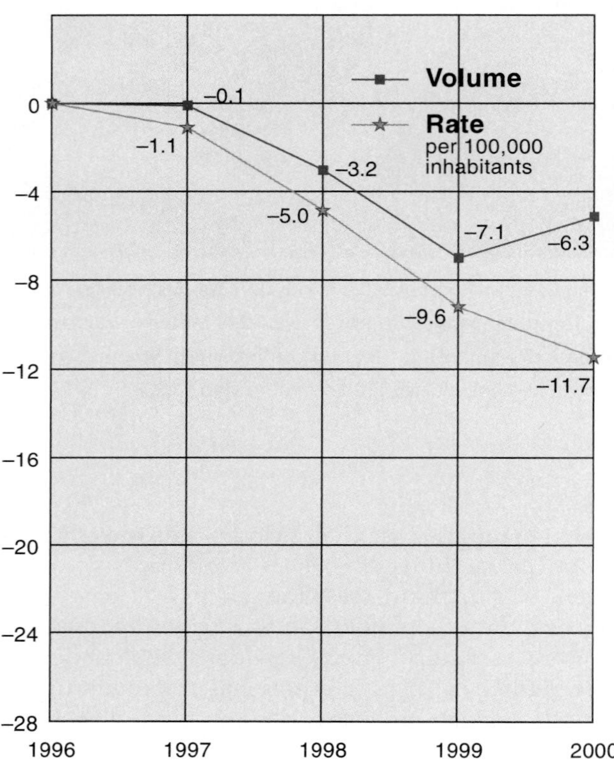

Myths about rapists were discussed by A. Nicholas Groth and H. Jean Birnbaum, who conducted clinical studies of 500 rapists and reported that rape is more often an expression of nonsexual than of sexual needs. One-third of the sample were married men who had active sex lives with their wives, and the majority of the unmarried offenders had active sex lives with consenting women. According to Groth and Birnbaum, rape is not the result of sexual arousal but rather of an emotional problem. Most rapists are persons who lack secure and close emotional relationships with others.[21] Groth and Birnbaum argue that sex is a motivating factor in some rapes, usually those occurring between persons who had a previous acquaintance, but sex is not the primary motivation for rape. In many cases, sex is not even a relevant variable.

A further position is that sociological explanations are more relevant than other approaches in explaining the rapist. According to one analysis, "Rape is a socially patterned phenomenon, not just a manifestation of individual psychopathology or other defects of personality, character or physiology." Rape is explained in terms of four theoretical approaches: gender inequality, pornography, social disorganization, and legitimate violence.[22]

Rape has been related to pornography as a negative influence on men as well as on potential female victims, but scholars do not agree on the relationship between pornography and criminal behavior (discussed later in this chapter). Labeling theory, learning theory, and conflict theory are employed in the explanation of rape. Others suggest that rape is the result of sexual desire as well as a desire for power and control.

Robbery

Robbery Taking personal property from the possession of another against his or her will by the use of force or fear.

Two elements distinguish **robbery,** a form of theft, from larceny-theft, which is discussed in Chapter 8. In robbery, possessions are taken from a person by the use or threat of force (see Exhibit 7.1). Thus, robbery is not just a property crime but also a crime against the person, a crime that might result in personal violence. The use or threat of force must be such that it would make a reasonable person fearful.

The line between theft and robbery is difficult to draw in some cases. For example, if an offender grabs a purse, billfold, or other piece of property from the victim so quickly that he or she cannot offer any resistance, the act may be classified either as larceny-theft or as robbery. If there is a struggle between the victim and the offender, the act is more likely to be classified as a robbery. Some jurisdictions classify robbery according to the degree of force used or threatened; thus, a state might define armed robbery as a more serious crime than robbery without a weapon.

A weapon may be defined in various ways and does not necessarily mean a gun, a knife, or some other obviously dangerous instrument. Some courts have held that a toy pistol may meet the weapon requirement, while others have held that hands can be a weapon.

The *UCR* reported that the volume of robbery offenses declined only 0.4 percent from 1999 to 2000, with the rate showing a decline of 3.5 percent. As Figure 7.6 shows, the volume of offenses was 23.9 percent lower than in 1996, with the rate 28.2 percent lower. The area with the highest volume of robberies was the South (the most populous area of the country), with 37.4 percent of all reported robberies. The average dollar loss per robbery was $1,170, up from the 1999 figure of $1,131. The average bank robbery resulted in a $4,437 loss. Of the 2000 robberies, 40.9 percent involved the use of firearms, while 40.4 percent were perpetrated by strong-arm tactics. Knives or other cutting instruments were used in 8.4 percent of the 2000 robberies. Of the reported robberies, 25.7 percent were cleared by arrest. Of the persons arrested for robbery in 2000, 89.9 percent were men, 53.9 percent were African American, and 44.2 percent were white.[23]

FIGURE 7.6
Robbery: Percent Change, 1996–2000

Source: Federal Bureau of Investigation, *Crime in the United States, Uniform Crime Reports 2000* (Washington, DC: U.S. Government Printing Office, 2001), p. 32.

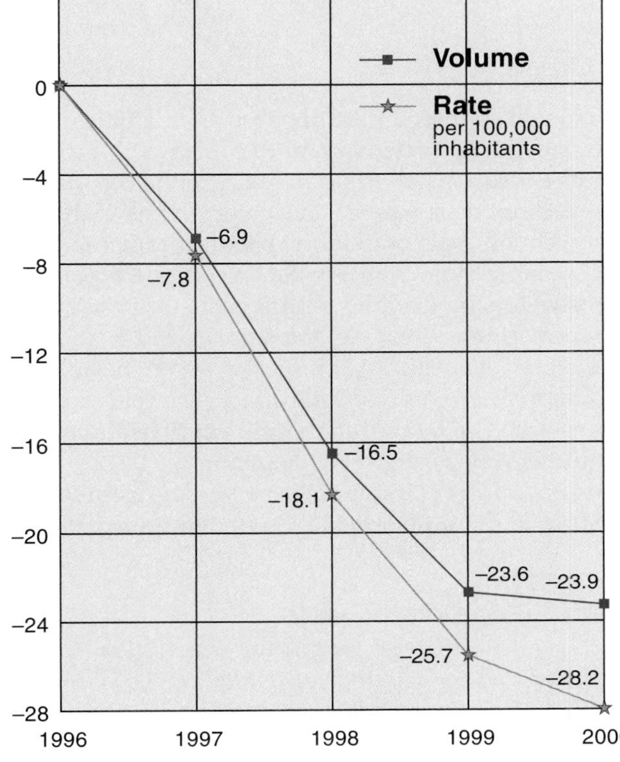

Robbery, which occurs more frequently than rape or homicide, often results in injury to its victims, and robbery victims are much more likely than rape or assault victims to be victimized by two or more offenders at the same time.[24]

Social scientists have studied robbery in an effort to explain this criminal behavior. Stewart D'Alessio and Lisa Stolzenberg looked at the role of the social and physical environment, analyzing convenience store robberies in Florida. They found that although "environmental factors are not important predictors of whether a convenience store is robbed," significant factors in determining the frequency of robbery are "parking lot size, degree of social disorganization surrounding the store, number of hours open, and whether gasoline service is provided." D'Alessio and Stolzenberg note that it is difficult to predict where robberies will occur because robbers are not consistent in their target selections.[25]

An in-depth study of 49 inmates serving time for armed robbery in a medium-security facility in California disclosed that all of them had served more than one prison term. The inmates had committed a total of 10,500 crimes; individuals had committed multiple crimes, ranging from six rapes to 3,620 drug sales. The inmates averaged 20 crimes per person per year. The level of criminal activity diminished with age. Most of the inmates had started their criminal careers with auto theft in their juvenile years, then moved to burglary and, as they got older, to robbery. They shifted to robbery because they could do it alone and therefore did not run the risk of being implicated by a partner. Robbery has the additional advantages of requiring few tools, having unlimited targets, and not usually requiring that the offender hurt anyone. Most of the career robbers did not earn much money from their crimes. Drugs and alcohol were involved in many cases.[26]

Criminologists have also looked at gender differences in robbery offenses. Jody Miller has pointed out that "robbery is perhaps the most gender differentiated serious crime in the United States," with the exception of rape. Miller focused her attention on female as compared to male street robbers. She reported that although the motivations of male and female robbers reveal gender similarities, the methods for committing the crimes show striking differences. "These differences," "she continued, "highlight the clear gender hierarchy that exists on the streets."[27]

In particular, Miller found that women are more likely to rob other women, which is considered by both male and female robbers to be an easier task than robbing men. Men are more likely to rob other men, which Miller suggested is one way of showing their masculinity. When women do rob men they accomplish the task by reverting to behaviors that make men more vulnerable, such as flirting:

> Because they recognize men's perceptions of women, they also recognize that men are more likely to resist being robbed by a female, and thus they commit these robberies in ways that minimize their risk of losing control and maximize their ability to show that they're "for real."

Miller concluded that women, compared to men, do not engage in different techniques in order to meet specific needs while committing robberies. Rather, they are making practical choices in the gender-stratified environment of street crime. This is an environment in which "men are perceived as strong and women are perceived as weak."[28]

Aggravated Assault

Aggravated assault Technically, an assault is a threat to commit a battery, but often the term is used to refer to a **battery.** In that case, aggravated assault involves an assault or a battery intended to cause serious injury or death and often includes the use of a deadly weapon.

Battery *See* assault.

Assault *See* aggravated assault.

An unlawful attack by one person on another for the purpose of inflicting severe or aggravated bodily injury is called **aggravated assault** (see Exhibit 7.1). Usually this type of assault involves a weapon. *Attempts* are included in the official data for this category; that is, it is not necessary that an injury result if the act involves a gun, knife, or other weapon that could inflict serious harm.

An assault should be distinguished from a battery. Technically, **battery** is the unauthorized harmful or offensive touching, while **assault** is the threat to inflict immediate bodily harm. In common use, however, the term *assault* is used to refer to the actual physical attack for the purpose of inflicting severe harm. The FBI category of *aggravated assault* includes only serious attacks; simple assaults are included under lesser offenses. Recall, however, that BJS victimization data on serious crimes include simple as well as aggravated assaults.

As with most crimes, jurisdictions differ in the way they define assault and battery. For example, the District of Columbia Penal Code defines *aggravated assault* as follows:

> (a) A person commits the offense of aggravated assault if:
> (1) By any means, that person knowingly or purposely causes serious bodily injury to another person; or
> (2) Under circumstances manifesting extreme indifference to human life, that person intentionally or knowingly engages in conduct which creates a grave risk of serious bodily injury to another person, and thereby causes serious bodily injury.[29]

FIGURE 7.7
Aggravated Assault: Percent Change, 1996–2000

Source: Federal Bureau of Investigation, *Crime in the United States, Uniform Crime Reports 2000* (Washington, DC: U.S. Government Printing Office, 2001), p. 36.

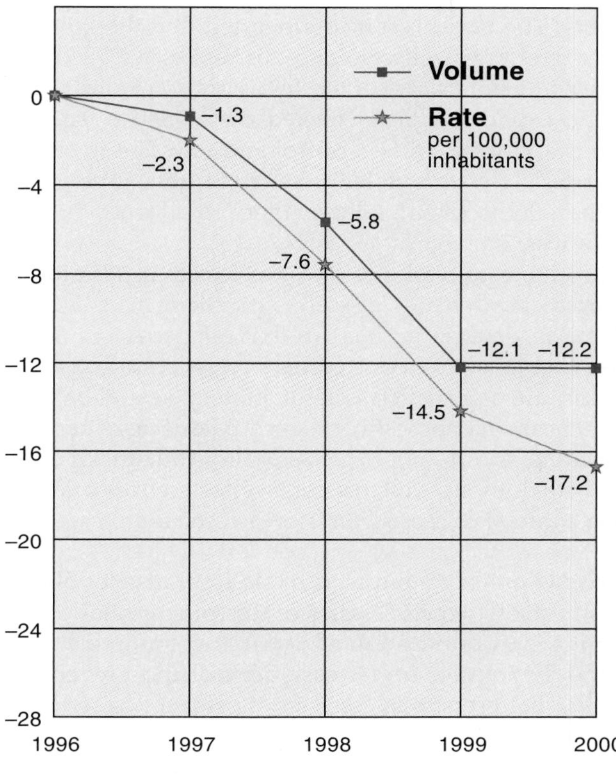

Florida defines *aggravated battery* as follows:

(1) (a) A person commits aggravated battery who, in committing battery:

1. Intentionally or knowingly causes great bodily harm, permanent disability, or permanent disfigurement; or
2. Uses a deadly weapon.

(b) A person commits aggravated battery if the person who was the victim of the battery was pregnant at the time of the offense and the offender knew or should have known that the victim was pregnant.[30]

Aggravated assault is the most common serious violent crime, according to official FBI data, accounting for 63.9 percent of index violent crimes in 2000. Aggravated assaults in 2000 were 0.1 percent lower than in 1999, representing a decline, although slight, in this crime for the seventh consecutive year. As Figure 7.7 shows, between 1996 and 2000 aggravated assaults decreased by 12.2 percent, with the rate of the offenses showing a 17.2 percent decline. Slightly over 63 percent of those arrested for aggravated assault in 2000 were white, and 34 percent were African American.[31]

In considering data on aggravated assault, it is important to understand that some aggravated assaults may not actually be counted as such because they have been defined as specific crimes occurring within the family. Domestic violence is a significant type of violence in today's world. It constitutes the first of the non-index violent crimes covered in this chapter.

LESS SERIOUS VIOLENT CRIMES

Despite the emphasis on index violent crimes, many other crimes of violence are committed against victims. Some of those are discussed in this section.

Domestic Violence

Domestic violence Violence within the family or other close associations, and including violence against spouses, lovers, housemates, children, and parents.

A discussion of violent crime is not complete without an analysis of **domestic violence,** which is an example of behavior that historically was not considered as a serious violent crime. Domestic violence occurs within the setting where people can and should expect warmth, reinforcement, support, trust, and love. It has been considered a personal, domestic problem, not an act of violence. In early Roman and English law, parents had almost exclusive rights to discipline their children. These rights permitted physical punishment and even death. The Bible provides that a stubborn and rebellious child could be taken by the parents into the city and there stoned to death by the elders. The death sentence was permitted for children who cursed or killed their parents. Historically, wives were the property first of their fathers and then of their husbands, who were allowed to punish them virtually without penalty and, as noted in the discussion of rape, engage them in sexual relations by force.

Even after the abuse of family members was no longer sanctioned as proper, little attention was paid to such abuse. It was considered to be a domestic matter and of little or no concern to the rest of society. Thus, although we have known about family violence for a long time, it has been only recently that facts have been pulled together into a general analysis of violence in the home.

In the 1982 reports, the Task Force on Victims emphasized the seriousness of domestic violence. The report stated that domestic violence is more complex than violence against strangers. The task force recommended that the government appoint a new task force to study family violence. In September 1983, the U.S. attorney general announced the formation of the Task Force on Family Violence, but it was not until 1994 that Congress enacted the Violence Against Women Act, which is part of the Violent Crime Control and Law Enforcement Act. The act makes gender-based violence a violation of civil rights, giving victims a civil cause of action that, if successful, entitles them to attorney fees as well as compensatory and punitive damages.[32]

The difficulty of defining domestic violence and the fact that definitions vary from jurisdiction to jurisdiction creates a serious problem in collecting accurate data. Other problems in data gathering are that alleged victims are reluctant to report the crimes; cases that are reported may be processed as some other crime (such as simple assault, aggravated assault, battery, sexual battery, and so on) and thus not be recorded as domestic violence. Many cases are dismissed without formal processing and do not become part of the official data. This may be true particularly with domestic violence cases reported from middle- and upper-income families in contrast to those from low-income families, especially those on welfare.

In recent years some jurisdictions have initiated mandatory arrest policies when there is evidence of domestic violence. Studies of this practice have produced inconsistent results, but a 2001 publication of research sponsored by the U.S. Department of Justice and the Centers for Disease Control and Prevention reports findings that "arresting batterers was consistently related to reduced subsequent aggression." The researchers also stated that they did not find evidence that arresting the batterer resulted in an increased risk of subsequent violence against that alleged victim by the accused.[33]

Child Abuse

Child abuse Physical and emotional abuse of children, including sexual abuse and child pornography.

In recent years considerable media attention has focused on **child abuse,** a broad term used to include neglect as well as physical and sexual abuse. Child abuse may include child stealing or parental kidnapping, in which the parent who does not have legal custody takes the child without permission and refuses to return the youngster to his or her legal guardian or parent. Child abuse may include the involvement of children in pornography. Sexual abuse includes sexual activities that are voluntary in the sense that no force is used, but in which the child is coerced to act by the parent or other person.

Within the family, child abuse may take the form of physical abuse without sexual contact. According to health officials, child abuse is a leading cause of death for small children, claiming at least 2,000 lives each year. Approximately 140,000 other children are injured by physical abuse. The U.S. Advisory Board on Child Abuse and Neglect, established by Congress in 1988 to study child abuse, conducted a national study for two and a half years, releasing its report in April 1995. According to the report, many children die from head trauma as a result of the "shaken baby syndrome," with approximately 25 percent of children abused in that manner dying and most of the rest sustaining brain damage.[34] This type of child abuse gained international attention in the 1990s, when a young English woman, Louise Woodward, was charged in the death of an infant, Matthew Eppen, who was in her care. Woodward was convicted of second-

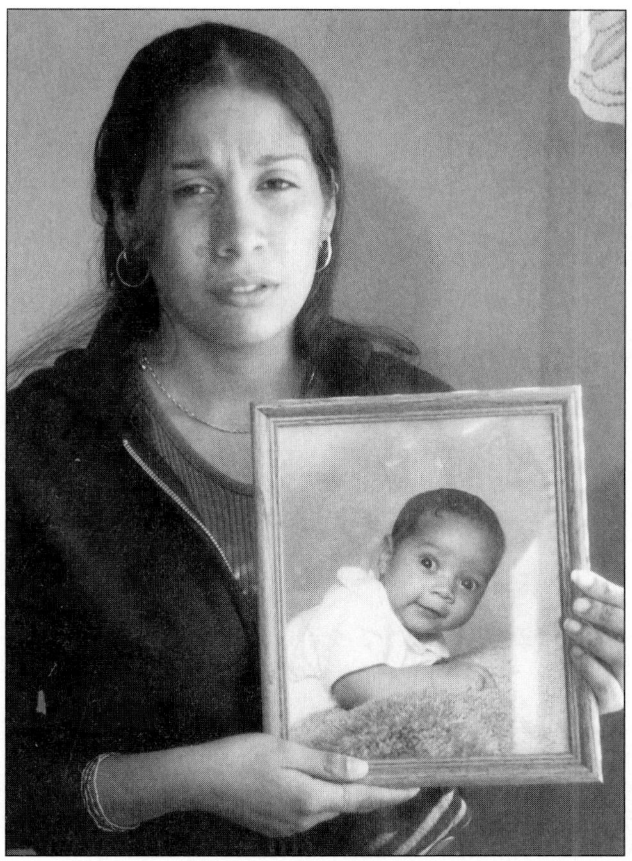

Yadira Guevara, 19, holds a portrait of her five-month-old son, Michael Arzuaga-Guevara, in this 13 November 2001 photo. The little boy died after his mother approved the removal of life support systems that kept the brain-damaged child alive. After a legal battle that reached the state supreme court, Guevara made the painful decision, one that left her husband charged with murder and facing a possible life sentence in prison. Jonathon Arzuaga, 22, was suspected of abusing the child, who was found with a bite mark on his body. (AP)

degree murder, but the judge permitted her to enter a plea to manslaughter (her attorneys had refused to request that the judge give a manslaughter charge to the jury, apparently assuming the jury would not convict their client of murder and thus would acquit her). She was sentenced to time served and permitted to return to England.

Although most research in the area of child abuse focuses on girls (thought to be abused more frequently than boys), a study conducted by Louis Harris and Associates for the Commonwealth Fund and released in 1998 reported that one in eight boys in high school had suffered abuse and that usually the abuse was a recurring pattern. One-third of the male sample said the abuse occurred at home; 45 percent said they were abused by a family member. As compared to female abuse victims, boys were less likely to report the abuse or talk to anyone, with almost one-half of the boys saying they did not talk about the abuse. Boys were twice as likely as girls to consider suicide. While only 3 percent of white and African American boys reported abuse, among Asian American boys, 9 percent reported sexual abuse and 17 percent reported nonsexual physical abuse. Seven percent of Hispanic boys reported sexual abuse; 13 percent reported physical abuse. The nature of abuse was not specified in the study.[35]

Sexual abuse of children, especially within the family, is a major type of child abuse today. The increased attention given nationally to this abuse has created a greater awareness of the crime of **incest,** which refers to sexual relations between family members who are considered by law to be related too closely to marry. Usually children cooperate with the abusing parent or sibling because they are eager to please and do not understand what is going on. Most children also cooperate in the warning not to tell anyone about the sexual behavior. Because many cases of incest are not reported, the data on this crime are not accurate.[36]

Incest Sexual relations between members of the immediate family who are too close in relationships to marry, such as between siblings or a parent and child, grandparent and grandchildren.

Most cases of incest are between father and daughter. Father/son incest may occur, but less is known about this type of sexual abuse than about the other types. Most of the studies of incest are about father/daughter relationships, reporting that in most cases sexual abuse does not begin with sexual intercourse; other forms of activity may take place for years before sexual penetration. Usually the activity begins with exhibitionism, then masturbation, mutual masturbation, other fondling, digital penetration of the vagina and/or anus, and finally sexual intercourse. Many daughters who are involved have poor relationships with their mothers and do not feel that they can turn to them when their fathers initiate sexual activity. Many men who have sexual relations with their daughters are having problems, often sexual, with their wives, and they see their wives as threatening and rejecting.[37]

Most fathers deny the incestuous relationship or, if it is admitted, attribute it to overindulgence in alcohol or drugs. Many incestuous relationships begin when the daughter is very young. When confronted, some fathers rationalize the behavior in terms of "teaching his daughter the facts of life"; others say, "She seduced me." Often the mother is passive and possesses other traits characteristic of battered wives: extreme dependence on her husband, poor self-image, hostility, and jealousy of her spouse. In some cases, the mother becomes an accomplice or at least a witness.

Very little has been written about brother/sister incest, thought to be the least damaging of all types of incest and usually transitory. Mother/son sexual relationships are reported infrequently, but they do exist. In fact, "Masters and Johnson state that the most traumatic form of incest is mother/son contact. The boy's social relationships with peers of both sexes are badly damaged."[38]

Some studies have reported that children who are abused are more likely than other children to engage in delinquent (or criminal) behavior. In September 2001 the National Council on Crime and Delinquency (NCCD) reported the results of its recent study on the subject, concluding that preventing child abuse is one way to prevent delinquency. The report noted that many juveniles who are serving time for delinquent acts were abused in their homes when they were younger.[39]

Elder Abuse

Elder abuse The mistreatment of elderly persons, usually by the parents of the abuser.

In 1994 the Department of Health and Human Services (HHS) commissioned the National Center on Elder Abuse to begin a three-year investigation of the abuse, neglect, and exploitation of the elderly. Accurate data on **elder abuse** are not available, for many of the crimes are not reported. But it is estimated that 1.5 million Americans over the age of 60 suffer some type of physical or mental abuse. According to an HHS official, "Elder abuse, especially in the family, is one of the most sensitive and embarrassing problems an older person faces . . . It's the hidden shame of the American family."[40]

There are other reasons, too, for inaccurate data on elder abuse. It is difficult to prove. The fact that elderly people fall often and bruise easily accounts for the majority of all home accidents. Because some doctors are not trained to detect abuse, many incidents do not come to the attention of those who collect the data.

One type of elder abuse that has gained attention in recent years is the abuse of elderly parents by members of their own families. This form of violence has been referred to as the *King Lear syndrome* (after the aging character in Shakespeare's play who was mistreated by two of his daughters), *granny bashing,* and *parental abuse* as well as elder abuse. Abuse of the elderly includes not only violent attacks but also such acts as withholding food, stealing savings and social security checks, verbal abuse, and threatening to send an elderly person to a nursing home.

It has been relatively recently that social scientists have begun to study family abuse of the elderly; thus, our knowledge of the problem is limited. The roots of the abuse may lie in child abuse. It may be the result of an attempt to do the right thing but an inability to cope with the problems of an aging parent or grandparent, coupled with the inability, because of guilt or expense, to place that parent in a nursing home. Transferring the responsibility for the person is difficult.

Elder abuse occurs outside the family, too. Many elderly people die from neglect in nursing homes and other residences. With its large elderly population, Florida faces difficult problems in this area, and investigations reveal that most of the victims are elderly women, and most of the cases are reported by social services, followed closely by neighbors or friends. Some are referred by medical personnel. In 1992 the *Miami Herald* reviewed hundreds of Florida cases and reported that "dozens of frail and disabled adults have died sick, starved, ridden with bedsores, bruises and broken bones—the silent casualties of abuse, neglect and a welfare system that did little to protect them."[41] In more recent years elder abuse in Florida had led to civil lawsuits, some of them successful, concerning the deaths of elderly persons in special care facilities.

One final problem for the elderly with regard to violent crime is their fear of becoming victims. This fear is realistic to the elderly but unrealistic in terms of actual data. Most violent crime victims are young, between the ages of 18 and 21. Persons age 50 or over comprise 30 percent of the population but constitute only 12 percent of murder victims and 7 percent of violent crime victims.[42]

Female Battering

Despite the seriousness of child abuse and the apparently growing incidence of parental abuse of elderly parents, the woman (wife, lover, estranged wife, former wife, girlfriend) is the one victimized most frequently by domestic violence.

Historically, by law and by social convention, husbands had the authority to control their wives, considered to be their property. Much of our law comes from English common law, which gave men the authority to chastise their wives. The *rule-of-thumb* measure referred to the specification that a husband could discipline his wife by beating her as long as he used a stick no thicker than his thumb. Medieval practices permitted beating, even killing, a wife or a serf if done for the purpose of disciplining. In the United States, wife beating was permitted by statute. This historical recognition of a husband's legal right to discipline his wife with physical brutality has changed, as the following excerpt from a 1913 case illustrates.[43]

Bailey v. People

This assertion of the right of a husband to control the acts and will of his wife by physical force cannot be tolerated . . .

To say that a court of law will recognize in the husband the power to compel his wife to obey his wishes, by force if necessary, is a relic of barbarism that has no place in an enlightened civilization.

Data on abuse of female companions are probably less accurate than those on any other crime, including forcible rape. Earlier publications by sociologists reported that one out of every six couples in the United States engaged in at least one violent act each year and that during the years of their marriages the chances are greater than one in four that a couple will engage in physical violence.[44]

The redesigned BJS victimization studies offer more recent data on domestic violence. The 1995 report stated that over a half-million violent crimes were committed against a spouse or ex-spouse in 1993. Of those crimes, 9 percent were rapes or other sexual assaults, 6 percent were robberies, 14 percent were aggravated assaults, and 71 percent were simple assaults. Women were four times more likely than men to be victimized by relatives. Recall that the victimization studies do not include murder.[45]

In a publication on intimate violence, the Bureau of Justice Statistics reported that in 1996 an estimated 840,000 women were domestic violence victims, down from 1.1 million in 1993. Approximately 150,000 men were domestic violence victims.[46]

What are the characteristics of those who inflict violence against women in domestic situations? Despite the stereotype of the batterer as a pathological male from the lower socioeconomic class, researchers have found that all races and social classes are involved. Statistically, battering may occur more often in the lower than in the upper classes, but that may be due to variations in reporting. There appear to be three major variables characteristic of men who batter their partners: frustration or stress, gender roles or learned behavior, and alcohol.[47] Stress may occur for many reasons. Frustration and stress may result from the man's sense of inadequacy as a male; as a provider; and as a father, a husband, or a lover. Insecurities may result from his extreme dependency on his partner, coupled with his fear of losing her.

Gender roles, learned through the process of socialization, may be related to partner battering. Men learn to be aggressive and dominant and to expect women to be passive and subservient. Any show of superiority by the partner—for example, if she is employed and he is unemployed or if both are employed and she earns more money—may trigger a violent response. Many men and women adjust to changing gender roles without violence. The point is that those who continue to hold traditional gender-role differentiations may be more likely to explode when the situation gets, by their definition, out of hand. This desire to maintain traditional gender-role stereotypes may explain the willingness of some women to tolerate the physical abuse.

The socialization process may trigger a violent reaction in the man. If he comes from a home in which his mother was battered (a characteristic of many batterers), he may have accepted violence as an appropriate way to handle the problems between men and women. If he was battered as a child, he may have decided that it is acceptable for the one who loves you to beat you as a method of control. Another factor in abusive behavior may be alcohol. Because of the frequent association of alcohol with violence, many battered women have assumed that drinking causes the violence, but the relationship is much more complex. In some situations, both spouses are under the influence of alcohol when violence occurs.

One study reports that men who abuse their wives or other partners are not violent in other relationships; that is, violent men tend to specialize. Either they abuse partners and other family members or they abuse nonfamily members, but they do not abuse both groups. Only 10 percent of the sample reported engaging in violence against both family and nonfamily. Further, those who engaged in violence outside the family are more likely to be blue-collar workers than those who engaged in violence against the family.[48]

What are the characteristics of female victims of domestic battering? There are many myths about domestic violence, especially wife battering. Research has examined the prevalent public attitudes toward the victims, who are thought to be weak, sick, guilty (she nagged him until he beat her), lower class, and willing to take physical abuse for a meal ticket.[49]

Research on the battered woman is limited in scope and depth, but the available studies suggest that the battered woman has characteristics similar to those of the battering man. One writer has described the battered woman in these terms:

> The profile of the battered woman looks almost identical to that of her batterer: she is all ages, all ethnicities, from all socioeconomic groups, has a low level of self-esteem, and for the most part has very traditional notions of male and female behavior. She may feel that her husband is supposed to be in charge of the family, even if that means beating her; she must be supportive of him, even if that means allowing herself to be abused repeatedly. Her role as a woman includes marriage, even a bad marriage, and to leave the home would be to admit that she is a failure as a woman.[50]

Perhaps we can understand the battered woman best by analyzing why she remains in the marriage. The pioneer work on this issue was conducted by Richard J. Gelles, who gives three reasons battered women do not leave their husbands. First, women are less likely to leave if the violence is not frequent or severe. Second, wives who were abused by their own parents are more likely to remain with abusive husbands than are those who were not abused as children. Third, the more resources and options a wife has, the more likely she is to leave an abusive spouse.[51]

Psychologist Lenore E. Walker characterizes the battered woman as one who is

> repeatedly subjected to any forceful or psychological behavior by a man in order to coerce her to do something he wants her to do without concern for her rights . . . Furthermore . . . the couple must go through the battering cycle at least twice . . . [And if] she remains in the situation, she is defined as a battered woman.[52]

Battered person syndrome A syndrome arising from a cycle of abuse by a special person, often a parent or a spouse, that leads the battered person to perceive that violence against the offender is the only way to end the abuse. In some cases the battered person murders the batterer, and in some jurisdictions evidence of the battered person syndrome consitutes a defense to the murder.

In 1977 Walker coined the term **battered person syndrome** in a case involving a battered woman who was accused of murdering her husband. The defendant was acquitted, and Walker was on her way to a career as a recognized expert on the battered person syndrome. The syndrome has been accepted in many courts, though rejected in others. Some jurisdictions have enacted statutes declaring the admissability of expert testimony concerning the syndrome. The battered person syndrome is used in cases in which women claim they have been raped as well as beaten by their partners over a long period of time.

Male Battering

Although data show that most domestic violence acts are committed against women by their spouses, ex-spouses, or lovers, there is evidence that some women batter or even kill within domestic relationships. Many women who strike or kill men allege that they do so in self-defense. In an early study Richard Gelles found that women are seven times more likely than men to engage in domestic violence for self-defense, either to avoid physical attacks or physical violence in the form of rape.[53]

It is the fear of further victimization involving serious injury or even death that is behind the legal movement toward permitting women to use the battered person defense as a self-defense argument when they are charged with killing their husbands. Some experts argue that the fear of future violence is a factor that distinguishes female domestic violence victims from male victims. Sociologist Mildred Daley Pagelow, an expert in domestic violence, argues that a man who lives with a habitually violent woman, unlike a woman who lives with such a man, "is not tied economically or through fear. He mostly needs psychological help."[54] Many female victims of *reported* domestic abuse are tied economically to the men who abuse them. Furthermore, data suggest that once a woman is victimized by her spouse or lover, she is likely to be victimized again.[55]

Explanations of Domestic Violence

The literature on theories of family violence and child abuse is extensive, but the approach has moved from an emphasis on the individual offender's pathology to sociological analyses, such as the social organization of the family and the culture in which family violence occurs.

Both social-process and social-structure theories are used to explain child abuse. For example, the lack of social integration is used to explain why the mother is the most frequent child abuser in the family in those situations not involving sexual abuse. Frequently the female offender in child abuse cases is a socially isolated person who came from a background of inadequate nurturing. Abusive mothers are able to sublimate or redirect their negative emotions, yet they face strains and stresses that contribute to feelings of anger. These mothers have a low threshold for children's typical activities such as crying, soiling themselves, and periodically rejecting food. One study found that battering mothers "yearned for a mature response from their babies, for a show of love that would bolster their sagging egos and lack of self-esteem."[56]

Social-structural variables were the focus of a national study of family violence, including child abuse, conducted by sociologist Richard Gelles and published in 1989. Gelles emphasized that the causes of child abuse are complex. Clearly they are not attributed solely to mental illness or psychiatric disorder. A number of variables are involved, including "stress, unemployment and underemployment, number of children, and social isolation." Gelles examined the social characteristics of the abusing parents, the social characteristics of the abused children, and, finally, the situational or contextual properties of the child abuse itself. Gelles concluded that if we are to treat and prevent the abuse of children, we must stop thinking of the abuser as a sick person who can be cured and begin working on social-structural variables, such as unemployment and child-rearing techniques.[57]

In a later publication, Gelles and a colleague reviewed the research on domestic violence conducted in the 1980s. They noted that the amount of child sexual abuse was substantial, perhaps more extensive than in any other area of social science research. Estimates of the extent of child sexual abuse range from victimization of 6 to 62 percent of girls and 3 to 31 percent of boys. The implications of this abuse are serious, too; studies suggest that many children who are abused sexually exhibit serious problems later in life.[58]

Some child abuse victims engage in violence against other children and their parents while they are children; many become child abusers when they themselves have children. Studies of juvenile offenders reveal that many were victims of child abuse or were witnesses to the abuse of other children. The same is true of adult offenders. A study published in 1998 by the National Institute of Justice reported that two-thirds of convicted male felons in New York State said they had suffered child abuse. Some were abused sexually, while others were abused physically. Some reported being neglected but not physically or sexually abused. Physical abuse, the most frequently cited type, was reported by 35 percent of the inmates. Although only 14 percent reported sexual abuse, of those who were serving time for sexual offenses, 26 percent reported that they were sexually abused as children.[59]

Researchers refer to the continuation of violence in families over generations as the *cycle of violence* or the *intergenerational transmission of violence.* It is important to understand, however, that sexual (or nonsexual) abuse of children does not necessarily *cause* them to engage in the same kind of behavior against others. Other factors may be influential as well.

One final area of discussion important to an understanding of intimate violence is feminist criminology (see again Chapter 5). Two of the noted researchers in this area, Kathleen Daly and Meda Chesney-Lind, have applied feminist theory to an explanation of why men brutalize women in domestic relationships. Daly and Chesney-Lind define rape and other forms of intimate violence as the "rape and the linchpin of patriarchal systems, in which women's bodies and minds are subject to men's domination." They call for more regulations on pornography (discussed later in this chapter) as well as changing laws concerning prostitution and intimate violence and rape. Finally, they argue in favor of gender equality in criminal justice systems.[60]

There are situations in which persons may not be physically harmed by domestic partners or others, but they may still be placed in fear. Hate crimes and stalking are examples.

Hate Crimes

Hate crimes Defined in the federal criminal code as crimes "that manifest evidence of prejudice based on race, religion, disability, sexual orientation, or ethnicity, including where appropriate the crimes of murder; nonnegligent manslaughter; forcible rape; aggravated assault; simple assault; intimidation: arson; and destruction, damage or vandalism of property."

The U.S. Congress enacted the Hate Crime Statistics Act in 1990, requiring that data on **hate crimes** be collected. The FBI uses this definition: "A hate crime, also known as a bias crime, is a criminal offense committed against a person, property, or society which is motivated, in whole or in part, by the offender's bias against a race, religion, disability, sexual orientation, or ethnicity/national origin." Disability was added to the statute in 1994.[61] States may include some or all of these targets in their statutes, and some include gender. Some states do not have hate crime statutes. Hate crimes are not separate or distinct from other crimes. They are traditional crimes committed by persons with an improper bias or motivation.

Since the collection of hate crime data is so recent, trend data are not available for meaningful periods. In 2001 the FBI disclosed that 8,152 hate crimes were reported in 2000. These crimes included 9,524 separate offenses, 10,021 victims, and 7,642 known offenders. Most of the crimes (4,368) were motivated by racial bias, with religious bias accounting for 1,483; sexual-orientation bias for 1,330; ethnicity–national origin bias for 927, disability bias for 36; and multiple biases for 8. The percentages for each of these categories are noted on Figure 7.8. Crimes against persons accounted for 65.3 percent of 2000 hate crimes, with 34 percent against property and 0.6 percent against society. Of those property hate crimes, 85.3 percent consisted of damage, destruction, or vandalism. The most frequently reported single offense was intimidation, which accounted for 34.6 percent of the total bias crimes.[62]

FIGURE 7.8
Hate Crimes: Percent Distribution, 2000[1]
Source: Federal Bureau of Investigation, *Crime in the United States: Uniform Crime Reports 2000* (Washington, DC: U.S. Government Printing Office, 2001), p. 62.

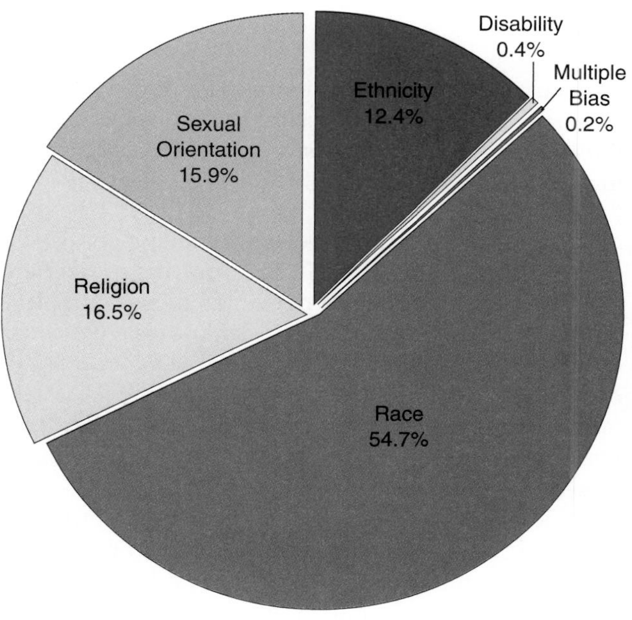

[1] Due to rounding, the percentages do not add to 100.0.

Several hate crimes have been publicized widely in recent years, although not all of these were actually prosecuted under hate crime statutes. In 1998 university student Matthew Shephard became a symbol of hate crimes after Russell A. Henderson and Aaron J. McKinney tortured and killed him, allegedly because he was gay. Both defendants were sentenced to life in prison. In Texas that same year, James Byrd Jr., an African American, was tortured and dragged by a truck by three white men, all of whom were convicted of the crime. Two of the defendants received capital sentences, while the third will spend at least four decades in prison for his lesser role in the crime. Although Texas had no hate crime statute, its laws permit enhanced sentencing if during the sentencing hearing "the court determines that the defendant intentionally selected the victim primarily because of the defendant's bias or prejudice against a group." The statute does not enumerate specific groups.[63]

Stalking Defined in the National Violence Against Women Survey as "a course of conduct directed at a specific person that involves repeated visual or physical proximity, nonconsensual communication, or verbal, written or implied threats, or a combination thereof, that would cause a reasonable person fear." The term *repeated* means two or more times.

Stalking

Some acts do not rise to the level of actual physical contact but are still frightening to potential victims. **Stalking** is an example. Stalking statutes are relatively new, with the federal one established in the fall of 1996, when President Bill Clinton signed into law the Interstate Stalking Punishment and Prevention Act. This act is aimed at stalking on federal property or across state lines.[64]

State stalking statutes are also relatively new, and they differ in their coverage. In general, stalking statutes are designed to punish individuals who watch, follow, and harass others repeatedly over a period of time. Some of the statutes, however, have been invalidated by courts taking the position that the laws are vague or too broad. For example, the Kansas antistalking statute was

Nellie Ruth Shirley, accused of stalking talk-show host David Letterman, is escorted by county sheriffs to the courthouse in Honea Path, South Carolina, in December 1998, where she was sentenced to one year of accelerated probation. Shirley was also ordered to undergo psychiatric evaluation. (AP Photo/Douglas Healey)

invalidated in 1996. That statute defined stalking as follows:

> an intentional and malicious following or course of conduct directed at a specific person when such following or course of conduct seriously alarms, annoys, or harasses the person, and which serves no legitimate purpose.[65]

The Kansas Supreme Court held that the statute was void for vagueness because *alarms* and *annoys* are subjective terms and thus open to many interpretations. The court noted that there were no guidelines to enlighten persons on the meaning of when following a person becomes "alarming, annoying, or harassing." As defined, the crime of stalking "depends upon the sensitivity of the complainant." The court did hold, however, that the word *following* is not vague.[66]

The Kansas statute was changed to read as follows:

> Stalking is an intentional, malicious and repeated following or harassment of another person and making a credible threat with the intent to place such person in reasonable fear for such person's safety.[67]

Courts in Ohio and Delaware have also upheld state stalking statutes. An Ohio court of appeals held that the law prohibiting a person from engaging in a "pattern of conduct" that he or she knows will "cause another to believe that the offender will cause physical harm to the other person or cause mental distress to the other person" is not vague or too broad. A "pattern of conduct" is defined as "two or more incidents closely related in time."[68]

The Delaware Supreme Court held that the state statute that punishes "[a]ny person who willfully, maliciously and repeatedly follows or harasses another person" is not vague. The statute defines *harasses* as "a knowing and willful course of conduct directed at a specific person which seriously alarms, annoys or harasses the person, and which serves no legitimate purpose." It defines *course of conduct* as "a pattern of conduct composed of a series of acts."[69]

North Carolina has a similar statute but states that the person must act "willfully on more than one occasion" and includes not only following but being "in the presence of another person without legal purpose and with the intent to cause death or bodily injury or with the intent to cause emotional distress by placing that person in reasonable fear of death or bodily injury."[70]

A final type of stalking statute is new and does not yet exist in most jurisdictions: electronic stalking. On 1 January 1999 California's computer stalking statute became effective. It constitutes an amendment to the state's stalking statute by adding that the term *credible threat* in the original statute means:

> a verbal or written threat, including that performed through the use of electronic communication device, or a threat implied by a pattern of conduct or a combination of verbal, written, or electronically communicated statements and conduct made with the intent to place the person that is the target of the threat in reasonable fear for his or her safety or the safety of his or her family and made with the apparent ability to carry out the threat so as to cause the person who is the target

> of the threat to reasonably fear for his or her safety or the safety of his or her family. It is not necessary to prove that the defendant had the intent to actually carry out the threat.[71]

The first charge under this new statute came in January 1999, when Gary Steven Dellapenta, a 50-year-old security guard, was accused of sending out an advertisement, via electronic mail, that appeared to be written by the alleged victim and listed her name, address, and phone number, along with information on how to bypass her home security system. The ad further stated that the victim fantasized about being raped. The alleged victim, who had rebuffed Dellapenta and who did not even own a computer, was not injured, but six men showed up at her house over a period of several months. The men stated that they were responding to her advertisment.[72]

Studies of stalking and data on stalking are scarce because of the recentness of the statutes, but the results of the first national study of stalking were published in 1998. The key findings and policy implications of that study, sponsored by the National Institute of Justice and the Centers for Disease Control and Prevention, are presented in Exhibit 7.2.

TERRORISM

Terrorism Violent acts or the use of the threat of violence to create fear, alarm, dread, or coercion, usually against governments.

This section of the chapter focuses on **terrorism,** a crime that frequently involves violence. Most terrorism victims are innocent and unsuspecting persons who become the targets of violent attacks that frequently result in death. This was tragically demonstrated on 19 April 1995, when Timothy McVeigh bombed the federal building in Oklahoma City, killing 168 people, including 19 children in a day care center within the building and injuring hundreds. This was the worst act of terrorism on American soil until the events of 11 September 2001, noted earlier and discussed in more detail in Exhibit 7.3 (see page 227). Also as noted earlier, McVeigh was executed for his terrorist act.

Definitional Issues

Although there is little agreement on a definition of the word *terrorism,* most people have a concept of what it means. A broad legal definition is one found in the American Law Institute's Model Penal Code, which defines *terrorist threats* as follows:

> A person is guilty of a felony if he threatens to commit any crime of violence with purpose to terrorize another or to cause evacuation of a building, place of assembly, or facility of public transportation, or otherwise to cause serious public inconvenience, or in reckless disregard of the risk of causing such terror or inconvenience.[73]

Applied to the political arena, *terrorism* has been defined simply as "motivated violence for political ends."[74] The Task Force on Disorders and Terrorism of the National Advisory Committee on Criminal Justice Standards has defined *terrorism* as "a tactic or technique by means of which a violent act or the threat thereof is used for the prime purpose of creating overwhelming fear for coercive purposes." Terrorism is a political crime but may be a violent personal crime as well. Terrorist acts are planned in advance, and, to be effective, terrorists must manipulate the community to which the message is addressed. The inculcation of fear is paramount and deliberate; it is the real purpose of the activity, and an audience is important. In this respect, the terror involved in an individual robbery, for example, differs from terrorism. In the latter, the immediate victim is

EXHIBIT 7.2

A National Study of Stalking: Key Findings and Policy Implications

- Stalking is more prevalent than previously thought: 8 percent of women and 2 percent of men in the United States have been stalked at some time in their life; an estimated 1,006,970 women and 370,990 men are stalked annually. Given these findings, stalking should be treated as a legitimate criminal justice and public health concern.
- American Indian/Alaska Native women are significantly more likely to report being stalked than women of other racial or ethnic backgrounds. More research is needed to establish the degree of variance and determine how much of the variance may be explained by demographic, social, and environmental factors.
- Although stalking is a gender-neutral crime, most (78 percent) stalking victims are female and most (87 percent) stalking perpetrators are male.
- Adults between 18 and 29 years old are the primary targets of stalking, comprising 52 percent of all victims.
- Most stalking cases involve perpetrators and victims who know each other; 23 percent of all female victims and 36 percent of all male victims are stalked by strangers.
- Women are significantly more likely than men (59 percent and 30 percent, respectively) to be stalked by intimate partners, about half of whom stalk their partners while the relationship is intact. Since most stalking cases involve victims and perpetrators who know each other, future research should focus on intimate and acquaintance stalking, rather than "celebrity" stalking.
- There is a strong link between stalking and other forms of violence in intimate relationships: 81 percent of women who were stalked by a current or former husband or cohabiting partner were also physically assaulted by that partner and 31 percent were also sexually assaulted by that partner. It is imperative, therefore, that America's criminal justice community receive comprehensive training on the special safety needs of victims of intimate partner stalking.
- Less than half of all stalking victims are directly threatened by their stalkers, although the victims, by definition, experience a high level of fear. Thus, "credible threat" requirements should be eliminated from the definition of stalking in all state stalking statutes.
- About half of all stalking victims report their stalking to the police. About a quarter of stalking cases reported to the police result in suspects being arrested. While there is some evidence that antistalking laws have increased reports to the police, more research is needed to determine antistalking laws' full effect on reports to the police.
- About 12 percent of all stalking cases result in criminal prosecution, and about a quarter of female stalking victims and about a tenth of male stalking victims obtain restraining orders against their stalkers. Of all victims with restraining orders, 69 percent of the women and 81 percent of the men said their stalkers violated the order. More research is needed on the effectiveness of formal and informal justice system interventions in stalking cases.
- Thirty percent of female stalking victims and 20 percent of male stalking victims seek psychological counseling as a result of their victimization. Stalking victims are significantly more likely than nonstalking victims to live in fear for their personal safety and to carry something to defend themselves. To better meet the needs of stalking victims, the mental health community should receive comprehensive training on appropriate treatment of stalking victims.
- The average stalking case lasts 1.8 years. Since nearly a fifth of all stalking victims move to new locations to escape their stalkers, it is important that address confidentiality programs be made available to stalking victims.

Source: Patricia Tjaden and Nancy Thoennes, National Institute of Justice/Centers for Disease Control and Prevention, *Stalking in America: Findings from the National Violence against Women Survey* (Washington, DC: U.S. Department of Justice, April 1998), p. 2.

not the important focus; the emphasis is on the larger audience.[75] It is in this respect that terrorism differs significantly from violent personal crimes.

One final definition is relevant. Law professor H. H. A. Cooper, a noted international authority on terrorism, published an article in 2001 in which he referred to his definition of terrorism, which he says has evolved during his 25-year teaching career. According to Cooper, "Terrorism is the intentional generation of massive fear by human beings for the purpose of securing or maintaining control over other human beings." He goes on to say, "Terrorism is not a struggle for the hearts and minds of the victims nor for their immortal souls. Rather, it is, as Humpty Dumpty would have said, about who is to be master, that is all." It is a "naked struggle for power, who shall wield it, and to what ends." Cooper admits that the definition of terrorism is "as needful and as illusory as ever." But, he says, as with pornography, "we know it well enough when we see it."[76]

The Categories of Terrorism

The Task Force on Disorders and Terrorism, directed by Cooper, divided terrorism into six categories:

1. *Civil disorders:* "a form of collective violence interfering with the peace, security, and normal functioning of the community."
2. *Political terrorism:* "violent criminal behavior designed primarily to generate fear in the community, or a substantial segment of it, for political purposes."
3. *Nonpolitical terrorism:* terrorism that is not aimed at political purposes but that exhibits "conscious design to create and maintain a high degree of fear for coercive purposes, but the end is individual or collective gain rather than the achievement of a political objective."
4. *Quasi terrorism:* "Those activities incidental to the commission of crimes of violence that are similar in form and method to true terrorism but which nevertheless lack its essential ingredient." It is not the main purpose of the quasi terrorists "to induce terror in the instant victim," as in the case of true terrorism. Typically, the fleeing felon who takes a hostage is a quasi terrorist, whose methods are similar to those of the true terrorist but whose purposes are quite different.
5. *Limited political terrorism:* "acts of terrorism which are committed for ideological or political motives but which are not part of a concerted campaign to capture control of the State." Limited political terrorism differs from real terrorism in the former's lack of a revolutionary approach.
6. *Official or state terrorism:* Activities carried out by "nations whose rule is based upon fear and oppression that reach terrorist proportions."[77]

Terrorism may consist of acts or threats or both. The Task Force on Disorders and Terrorism discussed several characteristics that distinguish modern terrorism from classical terrorism in its original form. First, as the result of our technological vulnerability, the potential for harm is greater today than in the past. This development, which includes improved intercontinental travel and mass communication, has increased the bargaining power of the modern terrorist. Television has carried the activities of terrorists to the entire world, giving modern terrorists more power than classical terrorists. Finally, modern terrorists believe that through violence they can maintain or increase hope for their causes.

The Objective, Strategy, and Tactics

A primary objective of terrorists is to create violence, or instill the fear of violence, for the sake of effect. In addition, they seek to destroy the confidence people have in government.

Terrorist groups have been categorized as *xenofighters*, who fight for foreigners, or *homofighters*, who fight for their own people. Often xenofighters are seeking removal of a foreign power or a change of political boundaries regarding a foreign power. They have such goals as the following:

1. To attract international attention
2. To harm the relations of the target country with other nations
3. To cause insecurity and to damage the economy and public order in the target country
4. To build feelings of distrust and hostility toward the government among the target country's population
5. To cause actual damage to civilians, security forces, and property in the target country.[78]

Homofighters must win the support of their compatriots in their fight to discredit their own government; thus, they must adopt policies that do not alienate the citizenry. One approach is the Robin Hood demand, in which terrorists use an acceptable cause to justify their unacceptable tactics. The kidnapping of Patricia Hearst in 1974 is an example. The Symbionese Liberation Army demanded that Hearst's family distribute free food to the needy.

Some of the strategies used by homofighters are these:

1. Undermining internal security, public order, and the economy in order to create distrust of the government's ability to maintain control
2. Acquiring popular sympathy and support by positive action
3. Generating popular repulsion from extreme counterterrorist repressive measures
4. Damaging hated foreign interests
5. Harming the international position of the existing regime
6. Causing physical damage and harassing persons and institutions that represent the ruling regime.[79]

The Nature and Extent of Terrorism

Terrorist attacks are not new to this country or to other countries, but it was not until 1981 that the U.S. government perceived the threat of terrorism "to be serious enough to warrant classification as a major component of American foreign policy."[80] Accurate data on terrorism are not available, but it is known that some terrorist attacks have been costly, in terms of both human lives and property.

Terrorism may and usually does result in extensive property damage. More important, it may affect the lives of many persons, as noted in Exhibit 7.3. Many of the victims are innocent bystanders, and attention should be given to victimization and terrorism.

Terrorism Victims

In one sense all of society is victimized by terrorist acts. The action taken against the immediate victim is coercive, designed to impress others. Terrorism is not a victimless crime. The immediate victims may be involved incidentally, as when they are killed by a randomly placed bomb, or they may be selected with considerable discrimination, as, for example, when a prominent politician is assassinated or a businessperson is kidnapped. Terrorism is characterized by gross indifference toward the victims, which includes their dehumanization and their treatment as mere elements in a deadly power play. All of these characteristics are seen clearly in the terrorist acts of 11 September 2001.

The randomness of victimization by terrorism is illustrated by most of the examples discussed in Exhibit 7.3. The ultimate objective of the terrorist, particularly the political terrorist, is the establishment of a bargaining position, so the

EXHIBIT 7.3
Recent Terrorist Acts

WORLD TRADE CENTER, NEW YORK CITY; PENTAGON, WASHINGTON, D.C., 11 SEPTEMBER 2001

Chapter 1 introduced us to the greatest terrorist acts that have ever occurred on American soil. More than 3,000 people died when carefully coordinated hijacked airplanes were flown into the twin towers of the World Trade Center in New York City—two of the tallest buildings in the world, representing the financial strength of the United States—and the Pentagon in Washington, D.C., one of the sources of U.S. government and military strength. A fourth hijacked plane, apparently headed for another Washington, D.C., building (perhaps the U.S. Congress or the White House), crashed in Pennsylvania after passengers presumably fought with the hijackers. The death toll would have been much higher, but thousands were able to evacuate the World Trade Center towers before they collapsed. The area, subsequently referred to as Ground Zero, became a hallowed burial ground as Americans, supported by allies around the world, mourned their dead and tried to reconstruct their lives.

President George W. Bush responded by freezing the bank accounts of persons thought to have financed the attacks, which he and others alleged were masterminded by Osama bin Laden, a Saudi Arabian millionaire hiding in Afghanistan, the leader of al Qaeda, the network blamed for the terrorist attacks. The president ordered air strikes and subsequently sent troops to Afghanistan in an attempt to destroy Afghanistan's ruling Taliban organization and capture or kill bin Laden. Although significant progress was made in the war, by the time of this publication it appeared that bin Laden remained at large.

Immediate reactions to the events of 11 September were swift and significant. All U.S. airports were closed until 13 September, when planes were once again allowed to fly but with intense security, creating waits at airport check-ins and security often of more than two hours, and reduced flight schedules. The government provided over $3 billion to improve airport security; federal funds were made available to assist the airlines financially; Congress appropriated tax-free funds for the families of those who died (provided they agreed not to sue the airlines); and Americans gave over $600 million to the New York Relief Fund. Americans reacted with fear and outrage but also with a renewed loyalty and commitment to their country. The U.S. flag appeared on private automobiles and homes as well as businesses, and large numbers of people wore flag pins or other patriotic symbols.

President Bush appointed Pennsylvania governor Tom Ridge to head the newly created White House Office of Homeland Security and charged him and his agency to coordinate the efforts of dozens of agencies, ranging from the Federal Bureau of Investigation to the Federal Aviation Administration. Another key figure in the U.S. war against terrorism was U.S. attorney general John Ashcroft, charged with the investigation and possible trials of living persons connected to the terrorist acts.

As this manuscript went into production, many questions remained not only about the terrorist acts but also about the possibility of additional acts. Public debate centered on how to secure peace and safety in U.S. airports and other places in which large numbers of people gather. The terrorist acts of 11 September targeted the United States, but the nation's allies were aware that other countries could be next.

Shortly after the events of 11 September 2001, another form of what appeared to be a terrorist attack occurred when deadly anthrax spores were found in mail sent to various targets, including news media offices, the U.S. Congress, and the U.S. Supreme Court. Several people died after they came into contact with the anthrax-tainted letters, but no suspect has yet been connected with these events.

TEL AVIV SUICIDE BOMBER, JUNE 2001

In a deadly terrorist attack outside a nightclub in Tel Aviv, Israel, in early June 2001, at least 17 people were killed and several others injured. Most of the victims were teenagers and young adults who were waiting to enter the crowded nightclub. The city's mayor said, "This just proves that the whole country is the front line." He referred to two other suicide bombings that had occurred within the previous week. The United Nations' secretary general expressed his horror at the bombing and stated that the crime underlined "the urgency of breaking the cycle of violence."[1]

BOMBING OF AMERICAN EMBASSIES, 7 AUGUST 1998

Simultaneous bomb blasts at the American embassies in Africa in Nairobi and Tanzania, resulted in the deaths of over 200 people (including 12 Americans)

(continued)

EXHIBIT 7.3

Recent Terrorist Acts *(continued)*

and the wounding of thousands on 7 August 1998. One journalist stated, "The dead [were] everywhere. Passengers on a bus were incinerated. Motorists who had been driving by . . . lay dead across the smashed windshields of their cars."[2]

In May 2001 four men were convicted of conspiring with Osama bin Laden in these terrorist bombings. Two of the defendants were also convicted of murder and faced the death penalty. But that penalty requires a unanimous jury vote, and in the case of the first to be sentenced, that was not accomplished. Thus, the 24-year-old convicted of 213 counts of murder was sentenced to life in prison.

OKLAHOMA CITY BOMBING, 19 APRIL 1995

The blast that rocked the Alfred P. Murrah Federal Building in Oklahoma City on 19 April 1995 killed 168 people (including 19 children), injured many others, and resulted in millions of dollars in property damage. Shortly after the blast Timothy McVeigh was arrested. He was tried, convicted, and executed for his crime. Terry L. Nichols was convicted of conspiracy to commit murder (but not of murder) and sentenced to life in prison. A third suspect, Michael Fortier, entered a plea negotiation with federal prosecutors and agreed to testify against Nichols and McVeigh. He received 15 years. Both Nichols and Fortier are appealing. The state of Oklahoma has announced that it will try Nichols for the state crimes of murder.

THE REIGN OF THE UNABOMBER, 1978–1995

He terrorized by mail, sending 16 letter bombs—which killed 3 people and injured 29 others—and eluding law enforcement officials for 17 years. In the summer of 1995 he began issuing threats, one of which involved planting a bomb on an airplane in the Los Angeles airport during the Fourth of July holiday period. Authorities increased security, but the Unabomber called off his threat. He communicated that he would stop sending bombs if newspapers would print in full an article he wrote, "Against the Future: The Luddites and Their War on the Industrial Revolution." Editors wrestled with the dilemma; some published part of the essay, and the *Washington Post* published it in full in a special eight-page section in September 1995. The full essay was also distributed to professors throughout the country in hopes that one would recognize the writing as that of a former student. The Unabomber claimed that he was trying to save the world from becoming enslaved to technology. His targets were from what he considered technical fields.

In April 1996 Theodore John Kaczynski, a former University of California–Berkeley math professor, was taken into custody from his one-room mountain shack in Montana. He was held without bail and arraigned on one count of possessing bomb components. It was Theodore's brother David whose information tipped off the FBI. David Kaczynski began to suspect that Theodore might be the Unabomber after reading the Unabomber's published article. He reported this to an attorney, who discussed these

identity of the victims is unimportant in most cases. Kidnapping and taking hostages are terrorist techniques par excellence for this purpose. The victims are treated largely as objects to be traded for what the terrorist wants: money, release of prisoners, publication of manifestos, escape, and so on. These bargains are extralegal and rest on a recognition of the powers of life and death that the terrorist holds over victims. This aspect raises the most serious social, political, and humanitarian issues for those who must make these awesome decisions affecting the lives and safety of the victims.

Stockholm syndrome An incongruous feeling of empathy by hostages toward the hostage takers and a displacement of frustration and aggression on the part of the victims against the authorities.

Terrorist victimization produces special individual and collective traumas. Many hostages and kidnap victims experience incongruous feelings toward their captors, and the events may constitute a serious challenge to their own value systems. The most striking manifestation of this is the **Stockholm syndrome,** named after an incident that occurred in the Swedish capital in 1973. The Stockholm syndrome is an incongruous feeling of empathy toward the hostage takers and a displacement of frustration and aggression on the part of the vic-

fears with authorities. The tip led the FBI to the mountain cabin of the person they suspected to be the nation's most-wanted serial killer.

After lengthy negotiations and a delay in the trial, Theodore Kaczynski and the prosecution agreed on a plea bargain that resulted in a life rather than a death sentence. In the summer of 1998, David Kaczynski was given the $1 million reward that was provided for information leading to the capture of the Unabomber. He stated that the money would be used to assist his brother's victims and their families.

In 1999 Theodore Kaczynski appealed his conviction, alleging that his guilty plea was coerced.

WORLD TRADE CENTER BOMBING, 26 FEBRUARY 1993

Before 11 September 2001 the World Trade Center was the site of another terrorist attack—a bombing on 26 February 1993 that killed 6 people and injured more than 1,000 others. In May 1994 Judge Kevin T. Duffy told one of the four defendants in the World Trade Center bombing trial, "You are the biggest hypocrite in the room . . . What you have done is turn your life into a total lie . . . You violated the laws not only of man but of God," as he sentenced him to 240 years in prison without possibility of parole. The same sentence was imposed on the other three defendants. In August 1998 a federal court ordered that those three be resentenced because they were not represented by counsel at their sentence hearings. The same sentences were imposed on Nidal Ayyad, Mahmud Abouhalima, Ahmad Ajaj, and Mohammad Salameh. The bombing cut a five-story hole in the building and caused, in addition to the deaths and injuries, half a billion dollars in property damage.[3]

In 1998 Ramzi Ahmed Yousef was convicted of masterminding as well as helping to execute the World Trade Center bombing. Judge Duffy added to Yousef's 240-year sentence a recommendation that the defendant spend his time in solitary confinement. Referring to Yousef as an "apostle of evil," the judge recommended that he be incarcerated at the federal prison in Florence, Colorado, where he would have visits only from lawyers, and have little contact with correctional officers because of the high security under which he would be housed. The judge recognized that his recommendations were harsh, but he told the defendant, "It is better that the evil which you espouse be quarantined than to let it loose once again on the world. You have already shown that you are quite capable of attempting to communicate evil even from prison." Yousef commented at his sentencing, "Yes. I am a terrorist, and I am proud of it . . . I support terrorism as long as it is used against the United States and Israel."[4]

1. "Sixteen Killed by Suicide Bomber outside Tel Aviv Nightclub," *New York Times* (2 June 2001).
2. "Staggering Carnage Overwhelms Rescuers," *USA Today* (10 August 1998), p. 6.
3. "Perspectives," *Newsweek* (6 June 1994), p. 15; "Trade Center Bombers Get Prison Terms of 240 Years," *New York Times* (25 May 1994), p. 1; "WTC Bombers Win Resentencing," *Daily News* (New York) (5 August 1998), p. 12.
4. "I Am a Terrorist," *The (Bergen County, NJ) Record* (9 January 1998), p. AO1.

tims toward authorities. In some terrorist acts, such as those of 11 September 2001, death and destruction occur so rapidly that the Stockholm syndrome concept is not applicable.

Another way in which many individuals are victimized by terrorist attacks is in the creation of fear that leads to changes in lifestyle. This result has occurred among many Americans who were not direct victims of the 11 September 2001 events but who fear additional terrorist acts. Perhaps the fear of flying that led many to cancel flights (or refuse to book them) after these events was the greatest manifestation of the fear in reaction to the acts.

The Control of Terrorism

When President Ronald Reagan returned from the 12th annual summit of industrial democracies, held in Tokyo, Japan, in May 1986, he proclaimed the meeting a triumph that had produced a "strong measure of allied unity" on economic, agricultural, and antiterrorism issues. Of primary concern here is the response of the seven summit nations to the increased terrorist acts in the year before the meeting. According to Reagan, "We agreed that the time has come to move beyond words and rhetoric. Terrorists and those who support them—especially governments—have been put on notice. It is going to be tougher from now on."

Reagan's comments followed the U.S. air raids on Libya after the Libyan government was accused of sponsoring terrorist attacks on Americans in foreign countries. The raids had split the nation's allies; some argued against them, whereas Great Britain permitted the use of its bases for launching the attacks. *Time* reported that the United States "had crossed a fateful line in the intensifying battle between civilized society and terrorism, with consequences that no one could truly predict." Some who opposed the raids predicted retaliation; supporters argued that terrorist force could be met only with force. Libya's Colonel Mu'ammar Gadhafi, whose living quarters and command center were the focus of the raids, lost an adopted daughter; two sons were injured. Gadhafi called Prime Minister Margaret Thatcher of Great Britain (who gave the United States permission to use Britain's bases and to fly over the country) and President Reagan "child murderers" and vowed to get revenge.[81]

What is the most effective way to respond to terrorism? If the government meets the demands of the terrorists, does that concession raise the specter of creating inconvenient or unreasonable precedents for the handling of future incidents? Ted Gurr, author of *Why Men Rebel*, says, "The most fundamental human response to the use of force is counterforce. Force threatens and angers men. Threatened, they try to defend themselves; angered, they want to retaliate."[82]

After terrorist attacks on U.S. planes, skyjacked in large numbers in the 1970s, security measures were required in all U.S. airports, and skyjacking decreased. But terrorists are adaptable, as demonstrated by their planting of bombs *outside* the secure areas of airports. It was obvious on 11 September 2001 that, although efforts to secure airports and aircraft had increased, they were not sufficient to prevent such attacks. The hijackers boarded airplanes carrying box cutters, which were apparently used to subdue and murder flight attendants. And even with the increased security that followed those attacks, passengers have boarded planes with knives and guns—and in December 2001 a man boarded a U.S.-bound flight in Paris, France, with explosives in his shoes. Even more stringent security measures were put into effect in the aftermath of these subsequent security breaches.

In the summer of 1995 President Bill Clinton urged Congress to pass his antiterrorism bill. After considerable negotiation the House and Senate passed a bill, and President Clinton signed it shortly before the first anniversary of the Oklahoma City bombing. The Antiterrorism and Effective Death Penalty Act of 1996 restricts the legal opportunities for death row and other inmates to appeal their sentences. It makes it more difficult for foreign terrorist groups to raise money in the United States and provides for easier deportation of alien terrorists. It authorizes an expenditure of $1 billion for fighting terrorism in the United States. The statute contains provisions for terrorism victims such as mandatory restitution and a provision for them to have access to closed-circuit television to view a trial that has been moved more than 350 miles from the venue in which they were victimized by a terrorist act.[83] And after the 11 September 2001 terrorist acts, the White House and the Congress enacted measures to make it more difficult for terrorists to operate—as mentioned earlier, one method was to freeze the financial assets of those thought to have aided the terrorist acts of 11 September. Additional measures concern stringent proposals for processing individuals accused of those crimes.

Legislation will not eliminate terrorism. The root causes of terrorism must be identified and treated if the threat of terrorist attacks is to be reduced significantly. Clearly, those threats have not been eliminated.

FEAR OF CRIME

According to a report of the National Research Council Committee on Law and Justice (the research arm of the National Academy of Sciences), violence has left Americans in fear for their safety and their lives, causing them to resort to locking themselves in at night and to altering their lifestyles significantly.[84] That study was published a decade ago; the fear of crime, especially random terrorist acts, is probably much greater now that Americans have experienced the devastation that was caused by the terrorist acts of 11 September 2001.

Numerous studies have been conducted on the fear of crime, what causes the fear, and how it may be alleviated. Research suggests that fear of crime varies according to where people live. For example, greater fear of crime exists in some cities than in others, or in specific neighborhoods within cities. Fear is affected by where people live within housing projects. Also, the nature of social interaction correlates with the degree of fear. And research confirms what most people think would be obvious: Fear is greater at night than during the day.[85]

Many people believe it is necessary to change their lifestyles because of their fear of crime. The fear of random crime, the belief that "random mayhem has spilled out of bounds and that a sanctuary can become a killing ground almost at whim," may be the greatest fear.[86] This fear of violent crime by strangers who pick their victims randomly led Warren E. Burger, then chief justice of the U.S. Supreme Court, to refer to the "reign of terror in American cities" and caused one privately funded study of crime to conclude, "The fear of crime is slowly paralyzing American society."[87]

This fear of crime has changed our lives in many other ways. We must have exact change for buses and small bills for taxi drivers, who will not change large bills. We must lock our doors, bar our windows, and install burglar alarms, thus paying a high price for security. Many people refuse to go out alone at night. Elderly people have suffered or even died from heat strokes in their apartments because they would not leave their homes during hot weather for fear of being burglarized or attacked. We worry that on Halloween our children might be given candy or other treats that have been laced with poison or have razor blades hidden inside. The fear of terrorist acts has made our lives more regulated, as illustrated by increased security not only at airports throughout the world but also at Times Square on New Year's Eve 2001 as well as at many other large, public events, such as the Winter Olympics in Salt Lake City in February 2002.

Some of these fears are realistic; others are not. Americans are more likely to die from natural causes than from violent crime, but people do not always respond in terms of probabilities. Research suggests that women and the elderly have the greatest fears of violent crime, but (as noted in earlier discussions of victims) they are less likely than young people, or men in general, to become victims. Still, both women and the elderly may perceive themselves as more vulnerable to crime and less able to protect themselves from violent predators than do men and the young. Research shows that, compared with men, women take far more precautions to protect themselves. They are more likely to avoid being on the streets at night and, when on the streets, to use what has been called *street savvy,* meaning the use of "tactics intended to reduce risks when exposed to danger, such as wearing shoes that permit one to run, or choosing a seat on a bus with an eye to who is sitting nearby." They are less likely than men are to go to a public place alone at night.[88]

The nature of crimes against women is important in understanding their fear of violent crime. Although, as mentioned earlier, rape is not a common crime, most of its victims are women; few men are raped. Rape usually takes longer to commit than other crimes, thus increasing the victim's contact with the offender and the probability of additional personal injury. Studies of the effects of rape show that it is one of the most traumatic of all personal crimes. In addition, the victim may be blamed for the rape. Rape may be feared, too, because of the inaccurate belief that in most cases it involves violence that goes beyond that of the rape itself.

The elderly are more vulnerable to crime and thus to fear, for they are less likely to be able to change residences to protect themselves, to be able to afford locks and other protective measures for their homes, and to be able to defend themselves should they be attacked at home or on the streets.

Scholars argue that fear of crime should be analyzed more carefully in terms of the environment and the cues that might create unrealistic fear. One attempt to do so was made by two scholars, who analyzed *fear spots,* defined as "those specific places or areas where individuals feel fear of being victimized but where crime may not be frequent or where the police may not have recorded any criminal incidents either during the day or at night." The results suggested that fear may be greater when people have little chance of escaping, when there are places for potential offenders to hide and wait for their prospective victims, and when there is lack of prospect (the ability to obtain an open view of the area by looking into or walking through the area). For example, lack of sufficient lighting affects a person's ability to look through an area, perhaps even to walk through the area. If these variables are found to be widely applicable to the fear of crime, the relationship raises obvious policy issues; local and state governments may call for more effective lighting, fewer obstructions, more open escape routes, and so on. The researchers concluded, "We believe that understanding the causes of fear will help to better understand the fear-generating process and to develop effective fear reduction strategies."[89]

Another variable that deserves further study is the relationship between race and the fear of crime. A report by the Bureau of Justice Statistics disclosed that African Americans are three times as likely as whites to express fear of crime in their neighborhoods.[90]

Finally, researchers have compared the effects of local to that of national television news in creating fear and found that local news effects are stronger "especially for people who live in high crime places or have recent victim experience."[91]

The fear of crime may have contributed to the current widespread ownership of guns, but this practice has created problems, leading to a controversy over gun control.

GUN CONTROL AND VIOLENT CRIME

The front cover of *Time* magazine on 8 April 1998 featured small pictures of Mitchell Johnson, age 13, and Andrew Golden, age 11, accused of firing on their classmates in Jonesboro, Arkansas, killing 4 young girls and a teacher and wounding 10 other students (see Chapter 6, p. 172). The large picture, however, showed Golden as a toddler, holding a gun; the caption read "Armed & Dangerous." On 26 March 1998 *USA Today* ran a story on recent killings, allegedly by young people, with the caption, "Armed, Alienated and Adolescent." The use of guns in crimes allegedly committed by very young people has amplified the national debate over gun control.[92]

The Department of Health and Human Services projects that, if current trends continue, by the year 2003 more deaths in the United States will be caused by guns than by automobiles.[93] Violent crimes committed by offenders with handguns reached a record high in 1992, accounting for approximately 13 percent of all violent crimes recorded by the Bureau of Justice Statistics (BJS). The most likely victims were young African American males, who were four times as likely as white males in their age group (16 to 19) to be victimized by handgun violence.[94] According to a recent BJS report, firearms are used in approximately 7 out of every 10 murders. In approximately 25 percent of all violent victimizations the offender has a gun (8 percent), knife (7 percent), or other weapon (10 percent). Guns are rarely used by rapists but often used in robberies (26 percent).[95]

In a 1994 announcement of government plans to enforce the federal ban on juvenile gun possession, Attorney General Janet Reno stated, "Unless we act now, a generation of young Americans will grow up in a world where gunfire is as normal as blue jeans and schoolbooks." The 1994 ban, along with numerous other gun control measures, was part of the Violent Crime Control and Law Enforcement Act of 1994.[96]

A scholarly analysis of juveniles and guns found that juveniles in early adolescence who are gang members are more likely to carry guns than are nongang members: "Gangs are more likely to recruit adolescents who own a gun, and gang members are more than twice as likely as nongang members to own a gun for protection . . . At younger ages, gang membership increases the probability of gun violence." Further, the probability of carrying a gun is increased by gang membership in all but the earliest juvenile ages. And juveniles who sell drugs are more likely to carry guns than those who do not; the more drugs they sell, the more likely they are to carry guns.[97]

General legislation at the federal level followed John Hinckley Jr.'s attempted assassination of President Ronald Reagan in 1981. The Brady Handgun Violence Prevention Act, called the Brady bill after Press Secretary James Brady, who was wounded during Hinckley's attack on the president, requires a five-day waiting period for purchasing handguns. When the permanent provisions of the Brady bill became effective, the statute covered all gun purchases, not just handguns.

In 2000 two professors of public policy, one from Duke and one from Georgetown University, published the results of their study of the Brady bill. These authors concluded that the statute has not had a pronounced effect on homicides because it does not go far enough in its background-check requirements. The act requires checks only for guns purchased from federally licensed firearms dealers. It does not cover those purchased at gun shows or other private transactions. The government responded quickly, arguing that the bill is responsible for part of the 52 percent decline (twice the decline of the overall crime rate) in crimes committed with handguns between 1993 and 1998.[98]

In May 2001 President George W. Bush promised to provide increased federal funds for additional prosecutions of gun-related crimes. Bush called for greater enforcement of existing gun laws, such as the Brady bill, rather than enacting additional statutes. In particular the president noted that today young people are more likely to die from a gunshot wound than from all natural causes combined.[99] Exhibit 7.4 provides information concerning the results of background checks for firearm transfers in 1999.

Researchers differ regarding the effect of gun control statutes. Criminologist Lawrence W. Sherman found that "directed police patrols in gun crime 'hot spots' can reduce gun crimes by increasing the seizures of illegally carried guns." When gun seizures by police increased by 65 percent, gun crimes decreased by 49 percent.[100] A University of Maryland study of five urban areas reported an increase in the number of people killed by guns after the passage of laws making it easier for citizens to carry guns.[101] A study conducted by researchers at the center for Gun Policy and Research at Johns Hopkins University and published in the fall of 2001 concluded that gun control laws may be effective in preventing gun-related crimes.[102] Others maintain that gun control may not be effective in reducing crime but that permitting guns for self-defense may inhibit crime.[103]

EXHIBIT 7.4

Background Checks of Applications for Firearm Transfers since Implementation of the Brady Act

	1994[a]–99	1998	1999		
	National Total	National Total	National Total	State and Local Checks	Federal/NICS Checks[b]
Applications and rejections					
Applications received	22,254,000	3,277,000	8,621,000	4,083,000	4,538,000
Applications rejected	536,000	90,000	204,000	123,000	81,000
Rejection rate	2.4%	2.7%	2.4%	3.0%	1.8%

Note: All counts are rounded.

[a] The Brady Act became effective on February 29, 1994, and data collection began on March 1, 1994. Data through November 29, 1998, are primarily for handguns.

[b] Applications are from the FBI's *National Instant Criminal Background Check System (NICS) Operations Report (November 30, 1998–December 31, 1999)*, published March 1, 2000. Rejections are an estimate based on 12 out of the 13 months reported in the *NICS Operations Report.*

- From the inception of the Brady Act on March 1, 1994, to December 31, 1999, about 22 million applications for firearm purchase or pawn transaction were subject to background checks of applicants. About 536,000 were rejected.
- In 1999 alone, 204,000 (2.4%) of approximately 8,621,000 applications for firearm transfer were rejected by the FBI or State and local agencies.
- Over half of the applications for firearm transfers were checked directly by the FBI, while the remainder of applications were checked by State or local agencies.
- The rejection rate was lower in States where background checks were conducted only by the FBI (1.8%) as opposed to States where points of contact were responsible for background investigations (3.0%).
- Two-thirds (68%) of the Nation's population lived in the 26 States that served as POCs for handgun checks.
- Among State and local agencies, about 73% of the rejections were for a felony conviction or indictment, 11% for a disqualifying domestic violence conviction or restraining order, and about 4% for State or local law prohibitions. The FBI's rejections included a slightly higher percentage based on the finding of a domestic violence conviction or restraining order (15%).

Source: Bureau of Justice Statistics, *Background Checks for Firearm Transfers, 1999* (Washington, DC: U.S. Department of Justice, July 2000), p. 1.

THE MEDIA, PORNOGRAPHY, AND VIOLENT CRIME

A final area of concern in violent crime is the impact of the media and pornography on violent crime. Concern with the potential effect of the media on criminal behavior has been raised in particular by those who are fighting to control or eliminate pornography, especially that involving minors. The 1986 publication of the final report of the Commission on Pornography (appointed by Attorney General Edwin Meese) focused nationwide attention on the relationship between pornography and aggressive behavior. The commission concluded that there is a causal relationship between some forms of aggressive behavior and pornography.

Two members of the commission issued a strong dissent from the commission's finding that hard-core pornography may cause violent behavior. According to one of the dissenters, "The idea that eleven individuals studying in their spare time could complete a comprehensive report on so complex a matter in so constricted a time frame is simply unrealistic . . . No self-respecting investigator would accept conclusions based on such a study." Many social scientists agree with this criticism. Others point out that the commission's conclusions contradict those of a 1970 presidential panel "which found no link between violence and sexually explicit material."[104]

In defense of its conclusions, some members of the commission argued that since 1970 the nature of sexually explicit material has changed; today it is more violent and more explicit. This conclusion is questioned by some social scientists, who argue that neither the commission's report nor current scientific evidence supports such a causal relationship.

Psychologists who have studied the effect of pornography on behavior have reported that there is little proof that laboratory studies of sexual aggression give evidence of sexual aggression in real life. It is more likely that antisocial attitudes and behavior toward women in particular occur after exposure to violent material regardless of whether that material is considered obscene. According to one set of researchers, "No scientifically reputable data exist that indicate a pornography–violence connection in serial murders."[105] The issue was raised in the case of Ted Bundy, the convicted killer who was accused of multiple murders in addition to the one for which he was executed in January 1989 in Florida. Shortly before his execution, Bundy confessed to other murders and attributed his problems to stimulation by pornography. Some professionals questioned that conclusion.

Other researchers, however, take the position that there may be a relationship between pornography and violence:

> There is increasing evidence that even nonexplicit, non-X-rated depictions of sexual violence against women may evoke negative social effects such as trivalizing rape and supporting aggression against women, and the potential influence of sexually violent material on predisposed males poses a clear danger.[106]

On the other hand, one study contradicted this statement, finding no relationship between exposure to sexually oriented magazines and rape rates.[107] Still others note that although sexually explicit material may be offensive to some, it has not been shown to be "sufficiently harmful to justify state intrusion."[108]

Along with the complicated and controversial issue of whether pornography causes or is related to violence against women and children are the legal issues. The U.S. Supreme Court has recognized the First Amendment (see Appendix A) right of free speech as embracing the right of adults to view certain forms of pornography. This does not include a right to view pornography involving minors, nor does it include a right to view obscenity. The problem comes in defining the term *obscene.* The Court has held that to be obscene a work must meet all of the following criteria:

1. [T]he average person, applying contemporary community standards, would find that the work, taken as a whole, appeals to the prurient interest.
2. [T]he work depicts or describes, in a patently offensive way, sexual conduct specifically defined by the applicable state [or federal] law, and
3. [T]he work, taken as a whole, lacks serious literary, artistic, political, or scientific value.[109]

Prurient interest is defined legally as "a shameful or morbid interest in nudity, sex, or excretion."[110] The Court has ruled that state statutes must be judged by local, not national, standards.[111]

In addition to problems of defining what is meant by *obscene,* attempts to criminalize what people possess and view have run into other legal issues. In particular, issues have been raised recently with regard to the Internet and the viewing of child pornography.

In 1995 President Clinton signed a bill that provides for longer penalties for persons convicted of engaging children in sex offenses before a camera. The penalties for the respective categories of crimes are doubled if a computer is used to transmit the child pornography. Another effort to protect children from pornographic and other material that might be harmful to them was the enactment of the Communications Decency Act of 1996, signed by President Clinton in early 1996 as part of the Telecommunications Act of 1996. One provision of the act was that it subjected violators to a $250,000 fine and two years in prison if they were convicted of making indecent or patently offensive words or pictures available online where children could find them. In 1997 the U.S. Supreme Court held portions of the Communications Decency Act unconstitutional. Media Focus 7.1 discusses some of the issues.[112]

Finally, in October 2001 the U.S. Supreme Court heard oral arguments in a case involving what has been described as *virtual child pornography*. The case, *Ashcroft* v. *The Free Speech Coalition,* was appealed from a lower federal court decision that held in 1999 that some provisions of the Child Pornography Prevention Act violated the First Amendment of the U.S. Constitution. "The provision at issue in the current case [Ashcroft v. The Free Speech Coalition] prohibits the distribution, receipt, or possession of an image that 'appears to be of a minor engaging in sexually explicit conduct.' In April 2002 the U.S. Supreme Court overturned this portion of the act, which criminalizes what has been referred to as virtual child pornography."[113]

Media Focus 7.1

The Case against Limiting Access to the Internet

In 1997 the U.S. Supreme Court considered two aspects of the Communications Decency Act (CDA) of 1996. These provisions were aimed at preventing minors from accessing pornography on the Internet. After a discussion of the nature of the Internet, the Court stated that the World Wide Web is "both a vast library including millions of readily available and indexed publications and a sprawling mall offering goods and services."

The Court described Internet pornography as extending "from the modestly titillating to the hardest core." The Court noted, however, that generally the sexually explicit materials are preceded by warnings about their content, and that, unlike listening to the radio or watching television, accessing materials on the Internet requires affirmative acts beyond that of turning a dial.

The CDA criminalized the knowing transmission of obscene or indecent messages to any recipient under 18 and prohibited knowingly sending or displaying to a person under 18 any message "that, in context, depicts or describes, in terms patently offensive as measured by community standards, sexual or excretory activities or organs." Affirmative defenses were provided for those acting in good faith to exclude minors from viewing this material.

The Court's analysis is lengthy and involves complicated legal issues, as the justices distinguished this case from those decided previously. In essence, the Court held the provisions unconstitutional because they were too broad. They encompassed material that adults have a First Amendment right to view, and there are no realistic and economically reasonable methods for preventing minors from viewing the material without infringing on the rights of adults. In the words of the Court,

> It is true that we have repeatedly recognized the governmental interest in protecting children from harmful materials. But that interest does not justify an unnecessarily broad suppression of speech addressed to adults. As we have explained, the Government may not "reduc[e] the adult population . . . to . . . only what is fit for children." Regardless of the strength of the government's interest in protecting children, "[t]he level of discourse reaching a mailbox simply cannot be limited to that which would be suitable for a sandbox."[1]

[1] Reno v. American Civil Liberties Union, 521 U.S. 844 (1997).

SUMMARY

This chapter covers a wide range of criminal activity. Its contents illustrate the difficulty of studying crime by types. Many categories of people commit the crimes covered in these discussions.

The chapter begins with a brief discussion of criminal types and an overview of serious violent crimes. It then turns to an analysis of those crimes. The index violent crimes, as categorized by the FBI's *Uniform Crime Reports*, are featured: murder and nonnegligent manslaughter, robbery, forcible rape, and aggravated assault.

The chapter then focuses on domestic violence. It gives a definition and a brief overview of the problems of collecting and analyzing data before detailing the major types of domestic violence: child abuse, elder abuse, female battering, marital rape, and male battering. The chapter also features a section on hate crimes and stalking.

The fear of crime is an expected reaction to violence, but some fears are not realistic. Yet they are important, and the discussion looks at some of the ways in which women and the elderly, in particular, change their lifestyles because of their fear.

A significant section of the chapter is devoted to a discussion of terrorism, noting in particular the terrorist acts of 11 September 2001. National and international terrorist acts have existed for years, but only within recent years have they gained much attention. Terrorist attacks have become more frequent in number, more political in nature, and more extensive in the degree to which they inflict property damage, human injury, and death on innocent witnesses. Fear of terrorism has inhibited many Americans from traveling abroad. The chapter examines some of the major terrorist attacks as it attempts to define and categorize this most complex, fearful, and potentially devastating form of criminal behavior. Attention is given to the Antiterrorism and Effective Death Penalty Act of 1996 as well as to presidential and congressional acts that have occurred as a result of the events of 11 September 2001.

A discussion of gun control and violence notes the use of guns in some of the recent violent acts of juveniles and underscores legislative efforts to control such gun violence. Finally, the potential effects of the media on behavior are analyzed in the context of pornography, a subject that is attracting more extensive research today. In particular, social scientists are exploring whether exposure to pornography is related to sexual offenses against women and children. A belief that there is a relation has led to more extensive legislation in this area, some of which has been challenged successfully as a violation of the constitutional right to free speech.

STUDY QUESTIONS

1. Discuss the latest trends in violent crime data.
2. Explain the relationship of gender and race to violent crime data.
3. What are the variables most frequently associated with violent crime?
4. Define each of the index violent crimes (as categorized by the FBI) and discuss the latest trends in data.
5. What does research tell us about why people murder? Discuss these reasons in relation to types of murder.
6. Why is robbery considered a violent crime?
7. Should statutory rape be included in the FBI category of forcible rape? Explain your answer.
8. Discuss the difficulties of getting accurate data on rape.
9. What do we know about males as rape victims?
10. Why do people rape?
11. Define *domestic violence* and explain the limitations of the definition and the problems with gathering data on the crime.
12. Explain the types of violence against children.
13. Define *elder abuse* and explore the types and implications of this form of domestic violence.
14. Contrast male and female batterers and the reasons for their violence.
15. Contrast *forcible rape* and *marital rape.*
16. Explore the various types of hate crime and discuss their implications.
17. What is *stalking,* and why is the crime getting so much attention today?
18. Discuss the implications of the fear of crime.
19. What is meant by the word *terrorism?* Discuss two examples of recent terrorist acts. How should society react to those acts?

20. How does terrorism differ from other violent crimes?
21. How do terrorist victims differ from victims of other violent crimes?
22. What are the highlights of the Antiterrorism and Effective Death Penalty Act of 1996?
23. Discuss briefly the most recent terrorist incidents covered in this chapter.
24. Analyze recent developments in gun control.
25. What is the relationship between pornography and crime?

BRIEF ESSAY ASSIGNMENTS

1. Explain how and why definitions of murder and degrees of murder may vary from state to state.
2. Why is the line between theft and robbery hard to draw in some cases?
3. Distinguish between *assault* and *battery.* Why may some aggravated assaults not be counted in crime statistics?
4. According to Richard A. Gelles, why does a battered woman remain in a marriage?
5. Discuss the variables or correlates that are associated with the fear of crime.

INTERNET ACTIVITIES

1. Stalking continues to be a frequent and serious crime in this country. Learn more about the prevalence and impact of stalking by logging on to www.stalkingassistance.com. What are the federal laws regarding this offense? Find your state statutes on this website. How are they similar or different from federal laws? Other information and facts about stalking can also be found at www.antistalking.com.
2. Search www.fbi.gov/ucr/ucr.htm for the latest report on hate crime statistics. Find out how many police agencies in your state reported hate crimes and the total number reported. See if your college or university reports hate crimes. Information about legislation in your state regarding hate crimes can also be found at www.unitedagainsthate.org.

NET RESOURCES

www.vawprevention.org

Sponsored by the Centers for Disease Control and Prevention, the National Violence Against Women Prevention Research Center website provides information and links on research related to women and the prevention of violence. Users can access reports and statistics concerning policy issues, judicial action, and advocacy and practice on this website.

www.ncadv.org

The National Coalition Against Domestic Violence's website provides resources and research material (i.e., public policy and legislative issues) concerning domestic violence involving battered women and children. Links to other domestic violence sites and resources are also provided.

www.elderabusecenter.org	Statistics, fact sheets and publications on elder abuse can be found at the National Center on Elder Abuse's website. Also provided is a link to search for research material through the University of Delaware's Clearinghouse on Abuse and Neglect of the Elderly (CANE), this country's largest collection of information on elder abuse.
http://support.jhsph.edu/departments/gunpolicy	At the Johns Hopkins Center for Gun Policy and Research website, users can view the findings of National Gun Policy Surveys, read articles concerning gun policy, obtain fact sheets on gun injury and policy, access links to other resources, and search the site for full-text articles.
www.freespeechcoalition.com	The Free Speech Coalition focuses on First Amendment rights and highlights current news and issues related to these rights across the country. Editorials, opinion statements, and resource links are provided on the website.
www.ncovr.heinz.cmu.edu	The National Consortium on Violence Research provides data, statistics, publications on research related to the investigation and knowledge of causes and factors associated with violence. Contribution to information and resources for the site comes from several academic disciplines, including social, legal, medical, biological and political backgrounds.
www.thecpac.com/index3.html	The website of the Children's Protection and Advocacy Coalition contains information and data on the protection and advocacy of children. Resources and research are provided concerning offenses against children such as missing children, pedophilia, child pornography, and Internet crime targeted toward children.
www.adl.org	The website of the Anti-Defamation League covers all topics related to anti-Semitism, bigotry, civil rights, extremism, and issues related to hate crimes. Topic areas on this site include religious freedom, government affairs, terrorism, and international affairs.

ENDNOTES

1. "The Plague of Violent Crime," *Newsweek* (23 March 1981), p. 46.
2. *U.S. News and World Report* (10 April 1989), pp. 20–21.
3. Don C. Gibbons, "Offender Typologies—Two Decades Later," *British Journal of Criminology* 15 (April 1975): 148, 152, 153.
4. U.S. Department of Justice, National Indicators System Briefing Book, *Violent Crime in the United States* (Washington, DC: U.S. Government Printing Office, 1981), p. 8.
5. Federal Bureau of Investigation, *Crime in the United States: Uniform Crime Reports 2000* (Washington, DC: U.S. Government Printing Office, 2001), p. 13.
6. "Victim Poll on Violent Crime Finds 15% Drop Last Year," *New York Times* (14 June 2001), p. 14.
7. "Killings Increase in Many Big Cities," *New York Times* (21 December 2001), p. 1.
8. Rev. Code Wash., Section 9A.32.010 (2001).
9. Cal. Penal Code, Section 187(a) (2001).
10. State v. Rogers, 992 S.W.2d 393 (Tenn. 1999), *petition for cert. filed* (16 September 1999).
11. Cal. Penal Code, Section 194 (2001).
12. Maine Rev. Stats., Section 202 (2001).
13. Cal. Penal Code, Section 192(b) (1999).
14. *Uniform Crime Reports 2000*, pp. 14–18.
15. David Finkelhor and Kersti Yllo, "Forced Sex in Marriage: A Preliminary Research Report," *Crime & Delinquency* 28 (July 1982): 459.
16. *Uniform Crime Reports 1997*, pp. 26, 27; *Uniform Crime Reports 2000*, p. 25.
17. Bureau of Justice Statistics, *Criminal Victimization 2000* (Washington, DC: U.S. Department of Justice, 2001), p. 3.
18. Gary F. Jensen and Mary Altani Karpos, "Managing Rape: Exploratory Research on the Behavior of Rape Statistics," *Criminology* 31 (August 1993): 363–86.
19. *Report of the Prevalence, Incidence, and Consequences of Violence Against Women: Findings from the National Violence Against Women Survey* (Washington, DC: U.S. Department

of Justice, 2000). The report is available from the National Criminal Justice Reference Service, Box 6000, Rockville, MD 20849–6000 (800–851–3420). On the Internet: www.ojp.usdoj.gov/nij.

20. Paul H. Gebhard et al., *Sex Offenders* (New York: Harper & Row, 1965), pp. 197–205.
21. A. Nicholas Groth and H. Jean Birnbaum, *Men Who Rape: The Psychology of the Offender* (New York: Plenum, 1979), pp. 5–6.
22. Larry Baron and Murray A. Straus, *Four Theories of Rape in American Society: A State Level Analysis* (New Haven, CT: Yale University Press, 1989); quotation is from p. 57.
23. *Uniform Crime Reports 2000,* pp. 29–32.
24. Caroline Wolf Harlow, Bureau of Justice Statistics, *Robbery Victims* (Washington, DC: U.S. Department of Justice, April, 1987), p. 1.
25. Stewart D'Allesio and Lisa Stolzenberg, "A Crime of Convenience: The Environment and Convenience Store Robbery," *Environment and Behavior* 22 (March 1990): 255–71; quotation is from p. 255.
26. Joan Petersilia et al., National Institute of Law Enforcement and Criminal Justice, *Criminal Careers of Habitual Felons* (Washington, DC: U.S. Government Printing Office, 1978), pp. vii and xiii.
27. Jody Miller, "Up It Up: Gender and the Accomplishment of Street Robbery," *Criminology* 36 (February 1998): 37–66; quotation is from p. 60.
28. Ibid., p. 61. See also Jody Miller, "Feminist Theories of Women's Crime: Robbery as a Case Study," in *Of Crime & Criminality,* ed. Sally S. Simpson (Thousand Oaks, CA: Pine Forge Press, 2000), pp. 25–46.
29. D.C. Code, Title 22, Section 22-504.1 (2001).
30. Fla. Stat., Section 784.045 (2001).
31. *Uniform Crime Reports 2000,* pp. 34–37.
32. Violent Crime Control and Law Enforcement Act of 1994, Public Law 103-322 (13 September 1994), Title IV, "Violence Against Women."
33. *The Effects of Arrest on Intimate Partner Violence: New Evidence from the Spouse Assault Replication Program* (Washington, DC: National Criminal Justice Reference Service, 2001); on the Internet: www.ojp.usdoj.gov/nij.
34. Cited in "Abuse a Leading Cause of Death for Small Children, Study Finds," *Miami Herald* (26 April 1995), p. 1.
35. "One in Eight Boys of High-School Age Has Been Abused, Survey Shows," *New York Times* (26 June 1998), p. 11.
36. See Anne L. Horton et al., *The Incest Perpetrator: A Family Member No One Wants to Treat* (Newbury Park, CA: Sage, 1989).
37. See Robert L. Geiser, *Hidden Victims: The Sexual Abuse of Children* (Boston: Beacon Press, 1979).
38. Ibid., p. 68.
39. *Preventing Delinquency through Improved Child Protection Services* (Washington, DC: Juvenile Justice Clearinghouse, 2001).
40. "Abuse of Elderly Is Target of Nationwide Investigation," *Miami Herald* (17 September 1994), p. 12.
41. "Abused Adults: Silent Casualties," *Miami Herald* (22 November 1992), p. 1.
42. Bureau of Justice Statistics Special Report, *Age Patterns of Victims of Serious Violent Crime* (Washington, DC: U.S. Department of Justice, September 1997), p. 1.
43. Bailey v. People, 130 P. 832, 835, 836 (Colo. 1913), footnotes and citations omitted.
44. See Richard J. Gelles, *Family Violence* (Beverly Hills, CA: Sage, 1987), p. 92.
45. Bureau of Justice Statistics, *Criminal Victimization 1993* (Washington, DC: U.S. Department of Justice, May 1995), p. 6.
46. Bureau of Justice Statistics, *Violence by Intimates* (Washington, DC: U.S. Department of Justice, 1998), p. 1.
47. Donna M. Moore, ed., *Battered Women* (Beverly Hills, CA: Sage, 1979), pp. 16–19.
48. Elizabeth Kandel-Englander, "Wife Battering and Violence outside the Family," *Journal of Interpersonal Violence* 7 (December 1992): 462–70.
49. Mildred Daley Pagelow, *Women-Battering: Victims and Their Experiences* (Beverly Hills, CA: Sage, 1981), p. 54.
50. Moore, *Battered Women,* p. 20.
51. Richard J. Gelles, The *Violent Home* (Beverly Hills, CA: Sage, 1974).
52. Quoted in State v. Kelly, 478 A.2d 364, 371 (N.J. 1984). See also Lenore Walker, *The Battered Woman* (New York: Harper & Row, 1979).
53. Gelles, *Family Violence,* p. 137.
54. Quoted in "Striking Back," *Time* (21 December 1987), p. 68.
55. Bureau of Justice Statistics, *Preventing Domestic Violence against Women* (Washington, DC: U.S. Department of Justice, August 1986), pp. 1–2; Bureau of Justice Statistics, *Criminal Victimization 1996.*
56. Study by psychiatrists Brant Steele and Carl Pollock, cited in Ruth Inglis, *Sins of the Fathers: A Study of the Physical and Emotional Abuse of Children* (New York: St. Martin's Press, 1978), p. 69.
57. Gelles, *Family Violence,* pp. 32–37, 42–53.
58. Richard J. Gelles and Jon R. Conte, "Domestic Violence and Sexual Abuse of Children: A Review of Research in the Eighties," *Journal of Marriage and the Family* 52 (November 1990): 1045–58; data are from p. 1050.
59. National Institute of Justice, *Early Childhood Victimization among Incarcerated Adult Male Felons* (Washington, DC: U.S. Department of Justice, 1998), cited in "Two-Thirds of Prisoners Were Abused as Children, Study Finds," *Criminal Justice Newsletter* 29 (15 April 1998), pp. 7–8.
60. Kathleen Daly and Meda Chesney-Lind, "Feminism and Criminology," in *Criminological Theory: Past to Present,* ed. Francis T. Cullen and Robert Agnew (Los Angeles: Roxbury, 1999), pp. 355–74.
61. *Uniform Crime Reports 2000,* p. 59.
62. Ibid., pp. 60–61.
63. Texas Code of Criminal Procedure, Chapter 40, Article 42.041 (2001). See also Texas Penal Code, Title 3, Subchapter D, Section 12.47 (2001).
64. Public Law 104-201 (1997); U.S. Code, Title 18, Section 2261 (2001).
65. Kan. Stat. Ann. 21–3438 (2001).
66. State v. Bryan, 910 P.2d 212 (Kan. 1999).
67. Kan. Stat. Ann., Section 21-3438 (2001).
68. State v. Dario, 665 N.E.2d 759 (Ohio App. 1995). The statute is codified at Ohio Rev. Code, Section 2903.211 (2001).
69. Snoden v. State, 677 A.2d 33 (Del. 1996). The statute is codified at Del. Code, Title 11, Section 1312A(b)(2) (2001).
70. N. C. Gen. Stat., Section 14-277.3 (2001).
71. Cal. Penal Code, Section 646.9(g) (2001).
72. "Computer Stalking Case a First for California," *New York Times* (25 January 1999).
73. American Law Institute, Model Penal Code, Section 211.3.
74. Brian Crozier, *Terroristic Activity, International Terrorism Part 4: Hearings before the Subcommittee to Investigate the Administration of the Internal Security Laws of the Senate Committee on the Judiciary,* 94th Cong., 1st Sess. 180 (1975); quoted in H. H. A. Cooper, "Terrorism: New Dimensions of Violent Criminality," *Cumberland Law Review* 9 (1978): 370.
75. National Advisory Committee on Criminal Justice Standards and Goals, *Disorders and Terrorism* (Washington, DC: U.S. Government Printing Office, 1976), p. 3.
76. H. H. A. Cooper, "Terrorism: The Problem of Definition Revisited," *American Behavioral Scientist* 44 (February 2001): 881–93; quotations are from pp. 883, 890, 891, 892.
77. National Advisory Committee, *Disorders and Terrorism,* pp. 3–7.
78. Ariel Merari, "A Classification of Terrorist Groups," *Terrorism* 1, no. 2 (1978): 332–47.
79. Ibid., p. 339.
80. Robert H. Kupperman, "Terrorism and Public Policy," in *American Violence and Public Policy: An Update on the National Commission on the Causes and Prevention of Violence,* ed. Lynn A. Curtis (New Haven, CT: Yale University, 1985), pp. 184, 188.
81. "Hitting the Source: U.S. Bombers Strike at Libya's Author of Terrorism, Dividing Europe and Threatening a Rash of Retaliations," *Time* (28 April 1986), pp. 16–27.
82. Ted Robert Gurr, *Why Men Rebel* (Princeton, NJ: Princeton University Press, 1970), p. 232; quoted in Robert G. Bell, "The U.S. Response to Terrorism against International Civil Aviation," in *Contemporary Terrorism: Selected Readings,* ed. John D. Elliott and Leslie K. Gibson (Gaithersburg, MD: International Association of Chiefs of Police, 1978), p. 191.
83. Antiterrorism and Effective Death Penalty Act of 1996, 104th Cong., 2d Session, No. 104-518 (1996), codified at U.S. Code, Title 18, Section 2254 (2001).
84. Reported in "Study Finds U.S. Most Violent of All Industrialized Nations," *Tampa Tribune* (13 November 1992), p. 2.
85. For a review of the literature concerning these areas, see Bonnie Fisher and Jack L. Nasar, "Fear Spots in Relation to Microlevel Physical Cues: Exploring the Overlooked," *Journal of Research in Crime and Delinquency* 32 (May 1995): 214–39.
86. "The Plague of Violent Crime," p. 46.
87. "The Curse of Violent Crime: A Pervasive Fear of Robbery and Mayhem Threatens the Way America Lives," *Time* (23 March 1981), p. 16.
88. Stephanie Riger, "On Women," in *Reactions to Crime,* ed. Dan A. Lewis (Beverly Hills, CA: Sage, 1981), pp. 47–52.
89. Fisher and Nasar, "Fear Spots in Relation to Microlevel Physical Cues," pp. 215, 236.
90. Bureau of Justice Statistics, *Crime and Neighborhoods* (Washington, DC: U.S. Department of Justice, 1994).
91. Ted Chiricos et al., "Fear, TV News, and the Reality of Crime," *Criminology* 38 (August 2000): 755–86; quotation is from p. 755.
92. "One in Five Teen-Agers Is Armed, a Survey Finds," *New York Times* (14 August 1998), p. 19.
93. "Guns Gaining on Cars as Bigger Killer in U.S.," *New York Times* (28 January 1994), p. 8.

94. Bureau of Justice Statistics, *Guns and Crime* (Washington, DC: U.S. Department of Justice, April 1994), p. 1.
95. Bureau of Justice Statistics, *Criminal Victimization 2000,* p. 9.
96. Violent Crime Control and Law Enforcement Act of 1994, Public Law 103-322, Title XI, Firearms (13 September 1994).
97. Alan J. Lizotte et al., "Factors Influencing Gun Carrying Among Young Urban Males Over the Adolescent-Young Adult Life Course," *Criminology* 38 (August 2000): 811–34; quotations are from p. 829.
98. "Study Disputes Success of the Brady Law," *New York Times* (2 August 2000), p. 11.
99. "Citing the Drain of Violence, Bush Backs Increased Prosecution of Gun-Related Crimes," *New York Times* (15 May 2001), p. 16.
100. Lawrence W. Sherman et al., *The Kansas City Gun Experiment* (Washington, DC: National Institute of Justice, January 1995), p. 1.
101. "Study Links Rise in Killings with Loosening of Gun Laws," *New York Times* (15 March 1995), p. 16.
102. Reported in "Gun Controls Limit Criminals' Access to Guns, Study Finds," *Criminal Justice Newsletter* 31 (19 September 2001), p. 3.
103. See Gary Kleck, *Point Blank: Guns and Violence in America* (Hawthorne, NY: Aldine de Gruyter, 1991).
104. "Two on U.S. Panel Dissent on Pornography's Impact," *New York Times* (19 May 1986), p. 13.
105. Daniel Linz and Edward Donnerstein, "Research Can Help Us Explain Violence and Pornography," *Chronicle of Higher Education* 39 (30 September 1992), p. 1.
106. Surette, *Media, Crime, and Criminal Justice,* p. 108.
107. Cynthia S. Gentry, "Pornography and Rape: An Empirical Analysis," *Deviant Behavior* 12 (July/September 1991): 277–88.
108. Alexis M. Durham III, "Pornography, Social Harm, and Legal Control: Observations on Bart," *Justice Quarterly* 3 (March 1986): 94–102; quotation is from p. 102. Durham was responding to an article by Pauline B. Bart, "Pornography: Hating Women and Institutionalizing Dominance and Submission for Fun and Profit: Response to Alexis M. Durham III," in the same journal, pp. 102–5.
109. Miller v. California, 413 U.S. 15 (1973), citations omitted.
110. *Black's Law Dictionary,* special deluxe 5th ed. (St. Paul, MN: West, 1979), p. 1104.
111. See, for example, FW/PBS, Inc. v. City of Dallas, 493 U.S. 215 (1990).
112. See Sex Crimes against Children Prevention Act of 1995, Public Law 104-72 (1996). H.R. 1240 (December 1995). The Communications Decency Act of 1996 is part of the 1996 Telecommunications Act of 1996. The case is American Civil Liberties Union v. Reno, 521 U.S. 844 (1997).
113. Ashcroft v. The Free Speech Coalition, No. 00–795 (2002).

8

▶ Tempe police detective John Bier looks through the broken passenger window at the damage to the steering column of a stolen 1988 Oldsmobile on 13 April 2001, in Tempe, Arizona. Tempe is in the Phoenix metropolitan area, which ranks first in the number of car thefts per resident. (AP)

Property Crimes

OUTLINE

KEY TERMS

Arson
Attempt crimes
Burglary
Career criminals
Carjacking
Cohort
Computer crime
Constructive possession
Cybercrime
Cyberphobia
Cyberstalking
Embezzlement
Fence
Forgery
Fraud
Grand larceny
Identity theft
Larceny-theft
Petit larceny
Recidivism
Selective incapacitation
Shoplifting

This chapter discusses property crimes and begins with the four serious property crimes as defined by the FBI's *Uniform Crime Reports:* burglary, larceny-theft, motor vehicle theft, and arson. Because laws defining larceny-theft and burglary can be understood only in light of their historical development, brief attention is given to the history of property crimes. The second section focuses on a few of the less serious property crimes as categorized by the *UCR:* forgery and counterfeiting; buying, receiving, and possessing stolen property; and embezzlement. Next there is a brief look at modern theft crimes, some of which are discussed in more detail in Chapter 9 on business and government-related crimes. The final section explores professional and career criminals, many of whom are engaged in property crimes.

"Law is never a mere abstraction. It is a very practical . . . matter. It represents the sum total of the rules by which the game of life is played . . . but this is quite a different game in different lands and in different times."[1] With those words, a noted law professor began his commentary on the development of property law. The emphasis on different times is significant, for this chapter discusses crimes that are distinct from the personal, violent ones of the previous chapters. Violent crimes and property crimes differ not only according to the degree of personal threat involved but also because, historically, some property crimes discussed in this chapter were not considered criminal. For example, taking something of value from another by fraud, deceit, or embezzlement was considered clever, not criminal.

In business deals between people who knew each other well, it was usually the responsibility of all parties to ensure that they were being treated fairly. Times changed, however, and as business and social conditions became more complex, it became necessary to change the laws governing business life. The problems, statutory or otherwise, of the crimes discussed in this chapter have not yet been solved. We are just beginning to cope with some of them, such as computer crimes.

This chapter also focuses on some crimes that resemble behavior considered acceptable business practice in other contexts. We do not know how to deal with the offenders in these cases. Some are occasional street criminals, others are career property offenders, and still others are "just like us." This may be true also of some offenders involved in family violence, but most people do not condone physical violence.

In the following sections, property crimes are discussed by categories, beginning with the four that are included in the Federal Bureau of Investigation's (FBI's) list of index offenses. The next section enumerates and discusses three crimes included in the FBI's categorization of non-index crimes. Attention there is given to such modern crimes as computer, credit card, and identity thefts. This is followed by a discussion of professional versus amateur thieves, which sets the stage for a look at career criminals in the last section of the chapter.

INDEX PROPERTY CRIMES

The index offenses of the official crime reports of the FBI include four property crimes: burglary, larceny-theft, motor vehicle theft, and arson, all defined according to the FBI categorization in Exhibit 8.1. The percentage of all index crimes accounted for by each property crime discussed in this chapter is noted in Figure 7.1 on page 204.

EXHIBIT 8.1

UCR Definitions of Index Property Crimes

- *Burglary*—the unlawful entry of a structure to commit a felony or theft.
- *Larceny-theft*—the unlawful taking, carrying, leading, or riding away of property from the possession or constructive possession of another.
- *Motor vehicle theft*—the theft or attempted theft of a motor vehicle.
- *Arson*—any willful or malicious burning or attempt to burn, with or without intent to defraud, a dwelling, house, public building, motor vehicle or aircraft, personal property of another, etc.

Source: Federal Bureau of Investigation, *Crime in the United States: Uniform Crime Reports 2000* (Washington, DC: U.S. Department of Justice, 2001), pp. 41, 46, 52, 56.

Burglary

Burglary Breaking and entering any type of enclosed structure without consent and with the intent to commit a felony therein.

Attempt crimes Crimes in which the offender engages in some effort to commit the crime but does not carry through with it. Planning is not sufficient; some step must be taken toward committing the criminal act, and criminal intent must be shown.

The *UCR* defines **burglary** as "the unlawful entry of a structure to commit a felony or theft." The evolution of burglary statutes illustrates the problems the common law courts had in interpreting the elements of the crime; some of these elements have survived in recent legislation.

Under English common law, burglary was defined as breaking and entering the dwelling of another *in the night* with the intent to commit a felony. Burglary was punishable as a separate offense from the felony committed, probably in an attempt to plug legal loopholes regarding **attempt crimes,** which are difficult to prove and carry penalties less severe than for completed crimes. Making burglary a separate offense increased the chances of a conviction even when the state could not prove all the elements of the theft or other crime that took place after the breaking and entering.

Numerous problems arose with the common law definition. What was meant by *breaking and entering?* The cases are fascinating and in some instances absurd. Early cases held that if the owner left the home unsecured, he (women were not permitted to own property) was not entitled to protection. A person who entered the home through an open door or window without permission could not be convicted of burglary. If the door or window was partly opened, opening it further to enter was not breaking and entering. It was not necessary that the home owner lock the doors or windows, only that he close them.

The requirement of *entering* presented problems, too. If a person used an instrument to open the building and if only the instrument entered the building, that action did not constitute entering unless the instrument was used in the commission of the felony for which the premises were entered. However, the entry by any part of the offender could constitute an entry. In addition, the offender could be held to have met the entering element of the crime by sending in a child or another person who could not be held responsible legally. In that situation the adult offender was held to have entered constructively.

The phrase *dwelling of another* raised interesting legal problems. Because a person's home was his castle, breaking and entering that dwelling was a heinous crime punishable by death. The occupant did not have to be present; indeed, he could have been absent for a long time, but it had to be that person's dwelling place. An unfinished house would not count even if the workers slept there. In some circumstances, the word *dwelling* included barns, stables, and other outhouses.

Under common law, to constitute burglary, the offense had to be committed during the night. The difference between night and day was defined as "whether the countenance of a man could be discerned by natural light even though the sun may have set. Artificial light or moonlight, regardless of their intensity, would not suffice." Finally, to be convicted of burglary the offender had to intend to commit a felony while inside the dwelling. Passing through the home to commit a felony elsewhere would not suffice.[2]

Over the years the meaning of *burglary* has been changed to the extent that modern statutes bear little resemblance to the common law definition. They are much broader; most do not require breaking, and they may cover entry at any time into any kind of structure.

An example of a modern statute that differs from the common law is the New York statute, which permits a burglary charge when a person "knowingly enters or remains unlawfully in a building with intent to commit a crime therein." In New York this statement refers to all three degrees of burglary and is the sole definition of third-degree burglary. To constitute first- or second-degree burglary, the act must meet other elements, ranging from being "armed with explosives or a deadly weapon" to displaying "what appears to be a pistol, revolver, rifle, shotgun, machine gun or other firearm." Notice also that the statute refers to an intent to commit a *crime,* not an intent to commit a *felony.* Thus, a burglary charge could be brought against one who entered with the intent to commit a misdemeanor.[3]

Under many modern burglary statutes, a person may be convicted of burglary as well as of the crime for which the burglary was committed. For example, Maine, which provides that one who "enters or surreptitiously remains in a structure, knowing that he is not licensed or privileged to do so, can be charged with burglary," also has the following provision:

> A person may be convicted both of burglary and of the crime which he committed or attempted to commit after entering or remaining in the structure.[4]

Problems of interpreting the elements of burglary remain, but it appears clear that the crime involves invading the right of a person to possess and thus have exclusive control over property. Burglary "remains *an entry which invades a possessory right in a building.* And it still must be committed by a person who has no right to be in the building."[5]

As Figure 7.1 (see p. 204) notes, burglary constituted 17.7 percent of all index crimes in 2000. Figure 8.1 graphs the decline in burglaries in the United States between 1996 and 2000, showing an 18.2 percent decline in the number of offenses and a 22.9 percent decline in the rate of burglaries per 100,000 people. Between 1999 and 2000 burglary offenses fell by 2.4 percent, representing the ninth consecutive year in which burglaries declined. The highest volume of burglaries, 44.2 percent, occurred in the South. The distribution of burglaries in terms of the three FBI categories were as follows: forcible entry, 63.7 percent; unlawful entries without force, 29.5 percent; and forcible entry attempts, 6.8 percent. Two of every three burglaries targeted residences, with 54.55 percent of those burglaries occurring during the day. The total estimated loss in 2000 was nearly $3 billion, with the average dollar loss per burglary at $1,462. Law enforcement officials cleared only 13.4 percent of the burglaries, and the highest percentage of those, 80.8 percent, involved adult offenders. Of those arrested, 86.7 percent were males; 63.8 percent were under age 25; and 69.4 percent were white.[6]

FIGURE 8.1
Percent Change in Burglary, 1996–2000
Source: Federal Bureau of Investigation, *Crime in the United States: Uniform Crime Reports 2000* (Washington, DC: U.S. Department of Justice, 2001), p. 43.

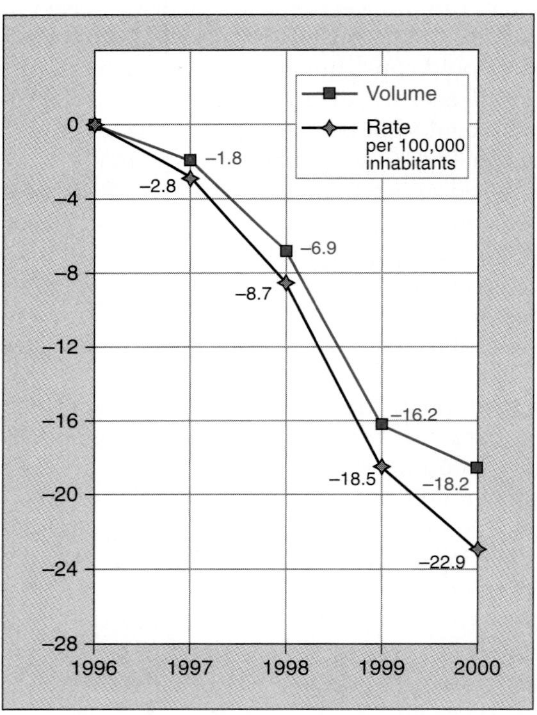

Analysis of Burglary

Burglary and burglars have been studied from several approaches. Some sociologists have studied the people convicted of burglary (often combined with those who commit larceny), trying to discover whether these types of criminals have any distinguishable characteristics. Others have looked at the circumstances surrounding the crime, for example, the *type of establishment* burglarized, the *value of the loss,* the *type of entry,* and the hour of the day or night when the crime occurred. Still others have looked at characteristics of the *area* in which the crime occurred. Some researchers have concentrated on the characteristics of burglary.

The most extensive research on burglary has been in the area of professional or career criminal studies, which may include all serious property crimes. These studies require greater analysis and are discussed later in this chapter. It is not always possible to separate the burglary offenders from the studies of career criminals, but a significant number of persons convicted of burglary are habitual or professional criminals.

Most persons apprehended for burglary are young, unskilled males. In urban areas, they are disproportionately nonwhite. Older and more talented burglars are more likely to steal alone, while young and female burglars are more likely to steal in groups. Most do not travel far from their homes to commit their crimes: "White thieves avoid black neighborhoods and blacks are wary of police patrols in white neighborhoods. Most burglars choose victims by their accessibility." Thus, well-guarded apartments and houses with adequate security are not as likely to be burglarized as those that are less closely guarded.[7]

Neal Shover has written extensively on burglary, beginning with his Ph.D. dissertation in 1971, in which he suggested that we should attempt to "correct" burglars as well as make it more difficult for them to succeed in their crimes. Shover studied 88 incarcerated burglars while gathering data for his dissertation, which, along with his more recent works, is referred to later in this chapter, in the section on career criminals.[8]

Other researchers have studied burglars in the field—active burglars who are not incarcerated. Such fieldwork is difficult and at times dangerous, but researchers who studied 105 active residential burglars concluded that this approach is important and meaningful. Seventy-five percent of the burglars would not have been included in a sample of incarcerated burglars. Of these, 44 percent reported that they had never been arrested for burglary, and 35 percent responded that they had been arrested for burglary one or more times but had not been convicted. An analysis of the data on the 105 burglars supported other studies, discussed later, suggesting that a few offenders commit most of the crimes. Thirty-four percent of the 105 burglars said that they committed fewer than 5 burglaries a year, while 7 percent stated that they committed 50 or more burglaries per year.[9]

Another field study of burglars, which involved a sample of 30 active residential burglars over a two-year period, led researchers to conclude that burglars are less rational and more opportunistic than previous research suggested. Most burglars "are easily deterred or displaced from one target site to another. Situational factors such as the presence of a dog, an alarm system security hardware, and alert neighbors may be the most effective deterrents."[10]

One scholar has looked at burglary from the perspective of multiple variables. In a recent article Matthew B. Robinson summarizes his conclusions concerning crime prevention policy based on his analyses of residential burglary patterns and the environment. The studies were conducted at private apartment complexes near a large state university in a southeastern city. Robinson concluded that burglary prevention can be aided by changes at the individual, group, community, organization, and society levels. Specifically, individuals should alter their lifestyles in such a way as to "promote higher volume of irregular pedestrian and automotive traffic." Those living alone should vary their schedules and activities; those living with others should attempt to maximize the times in which someone is visibly at the residence. At the group level, those looking for roommates should seek persons with different schedules. At the community level, neighbors should become acquainted with each other and look out for other homes. At the organizational level, there are various crime prevention policies that can be adopted by police and other departments. An obvious one is crime prevention alert signs in the area. At the societal level Robinson suggests employer policies that provide more flexible work schedules, thus enabling employees to be home at varying times, and, of course, education campaigns concerning burglary prevention. Robinson concluded: "Citizens who seek to alter their physical and social environments should focus on increasing surveillability, reducing accessibility, changing their lifestyles, and getting involved in community crime prevention activities."[11] This study thus finds some support for the routine activity approach discussed in Chapter 5.

The routine activities approach, along with social disorganization theory, has also been employed in research of economic stress and crime as related to welfare benefits. One study concluded that all property crimes were associated with welfare assistance levels as well as welfare participation rates. The authors argue that reduction in welfare benefits should not be supported as a way to reduce property crimes: "In fact, the results strongly support the view that welfare has operated as a mechanism of crime control . . . [W]elfare can reduce crime . . . [W]elfare allows recipients to obtain desired goods legally, thus reducing criminogenic strain."[12]

Larceny-Theft

Larceny-theft The taking of personal property without the owner's consent and with the intent to deprive the owner of it permanently. Historically, *petit larceny* involved small amounts, with imprisonment as punishment, and *grand larceny* involved larger amounts and the death penalty. Most modern theft statutes abolish the common law distinctions, and U.S. courts have ruled that the death penalty may not be imposed for larceny-theft.

Constructive possession A legal doctrine referring to the condition of having the power to control an item along with the intent to do so.

The crime of **larceny-theft** is defined by the FBI as "the unlawful taking, carrying, leading, or riding away of property from the possession or constructive possession of another." The term **constructive possession** means that an individual has the power and intent to control an item. The crime does not include embezzlement, forgery, passing worthless checks, or confidence games. It does include "crimes such as shoplifting, pocket-picking, purse-snatching, thefts from motor vehicles, thefts of motor vehicle parts and accessories, bicycle thefts, etc., in which no use of force, violence, or fraud occurs."[13] Larceny-theft is a broad category that can be understood only in light of its historical development.

Larceny-theft, the first theft crime in English history, was a common law crime, meaning that it was created by judges in deciding cases, not by Parliament in passing statutes. Larceny was defined as a crime committed when a person misappropriated the property of another by taking that property from the possession and without the consent of the owner. The crime did not include misappropriation of property that one already had; for example, if your boss asked you to take a sheep to a customer and you decided to keep the sheep, that act was not larceny since you already had the sheep in your possession.

One of the reasons for requiring that the property be taken from the possession of another was that the seriousness of the offense lay not in the act of taking possession but in doing so under circumstances that might cause the owner to retaliate, perhaps in a violent way. In addition, taking possession by deceit, fraud, or embezzlement was not considered larceny, because such methods only demonstrated that the thief was smarter than the owner of the property, and that was not a crime. It was the responsibility of the owner of the property to watch business dealings more carefully.

Another feature of early English common law is very important to an understanding of how theft laws evolved. Larceny was a felony, a more serious crime than a misdemeanor. At one period in English history all felonies were punishable by death. Early statutes provided that if the value of what was stolen did not exceed a specified amount, the punishment might be imprisonment rather than death—but the amount was relatively small, equivalent to about the price of a sheep.

Grand larceny A felony involving the theft of property or money over a specified amount or value, in contrast to *petit larceny* (often a misdemeanor), which involves smaller amounts or values. The values for each type of crime differ among the various jurisdictions.

Petit larceny *See* **grand larceny.**

As money depreciated in value over the years and the statutes remained unchanged, the amount required for **grand larceny** (rather than **petit larceny**) was very small. Many judges were reluctant to impose the death penalty in cases of grand larceny, so they began looking for technical ways to avoid finding the defendant guilty. One method was to find something peculiar about the way in which the property had been taken. The results were that many loopholes developed in the law of theft and that statutes were passed to fill the gaps in the law, resulting in a patchwork of laws on theft that "are interesting as a matter of history but embarrassing as a matter of law-enforcement."[14]

Larceny-theft is the serious crime recorded most frequently by the FBI. In 2000, the number of larceny-theft offenses was 6,965,058 (0.2 percent higher than the previous year), constituting 60 percent of the index total (see again Figure 7.1, p. 204) and 68.4 percent of all serious property crimes. Larceny-thefts were at

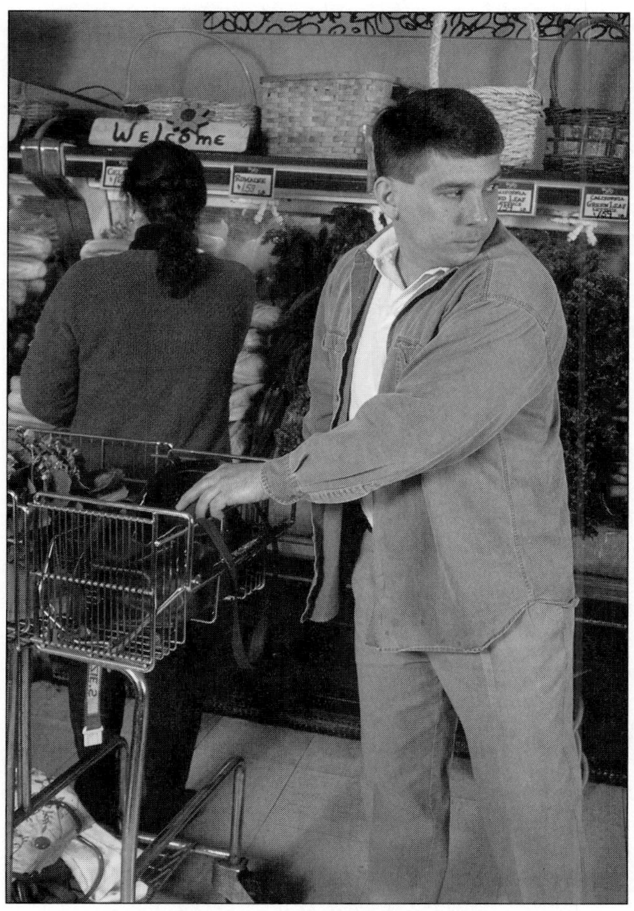

The difficulty in distinguishing robbery from theft is obvious in situations like this, in which an offender takes a wallet from a woman's purse. If the victim is aware and put in fear, the act may be charged as robbery; if she is unaware, the act may be classified as larceny-theft. Both are felonies, but robbery usually carries a more severe penalty. (Mark Burnett/Stock Boston)

their lowest levels in February and peaked in August. The southern states had the highest volume—40 percent of the total.[15]

Only 18.2 percent of larceny-thefts were cleared by arrest in 2000. Of those arrested, 35.9 percent were women, with larceny-theft being the serious offense for which women were most often arrested. Slightly over 66 percent of those arrested for larceny-theft were white; 30.4 percent were African American. Larceny-thefts were distributed by category in 2000 as follows: from motor vehicles (except accessories), 25.2 percent; shoplifting, 13.8 percent; from buildings, 13.1 percent; motor vehicle accessories, 9.7 percent; bicycles, 4.5 percent; from coin-operated machines, 0.7 percent; purse-snatching, 0.5 percent, pocket-picking, 0.5 percent; and all others, 32 percent.[16]

Caution must be used in interpreting these data. In our discussion of robbery we noted that one of the differences between theft and robbery is the use or threat of violence in the latter. We used the example of purse snatching, categorized by the FBI as larceny-theft. But if sufficient force or threat of force is used, the crime should be classified as robbery. This kind of distinction makes it necessary for us to realize that when we compare robbers to thieves, we may not be talking about significantly different types of criminals.

Focus on Shoplifting

Shoplifting is the illegal removal of merchandise from stores by customers or persons posing as customers. Most shoplifters do not take large amounts of merchandise; the average was only $181 in 2000.[17] That is an official figure, however; as noted below, not all suspected shoplifting is reported to police. In fact, one estimate is that retailers lose about $10 billion a year to an approximate 23 million shoplifters.[18]

Shoplifting The illegal removal of merchandise from stores by customers or persons posing as customers.

The total cost of shoplifting is enormous to businesses and goes beyond the amount stolen. Additional costs arise with crime prevention. Most readers are familiar with many of the techniques used to prevent retail theft. Many people have experienced the embarrassment of leaving a store with an item purchased appropriately, only to hear an alarm sounding as the result of the salesclerk's failure to remove the security tag. Some stores have loudspeakers in clothes racks, reminding the potential shoplifter that someone knows he or she is present. Some retail stores use other, less obvious techniques for theft prevention.

Shoplifters come from all income levels and from both minority and majority populations; the types of items they steal vary widely. Most shoplifters are not apprehended, and most of those who are apprehended are not prosecuted. One study, in which respondents were asked to answer questions anonymously about shoplifting, disclosed that 1 in 12 admitted they had shoplifted recently. Most of these respondents were young and white. One in three responded that they had experienced family disruptions recently. They came from all income levels, but they were more likely than nonshoplifters to be experiencing economic and other stresses, to have a negative attitude toward the system, and to place a high value on material possessions. The researcher emphasized that in most cases more than one variable appeared to be related to shoplifting.[19]

FIGURE 8.2
Larceny-Theft Categories: Percent Change, 1996–2000

Source: Federal Bureau of Investigation, *Crime in the United States: Uniform Crime Reports 2000* (Washington, DC: U.S. Department of Justice, 2001), p. 48.

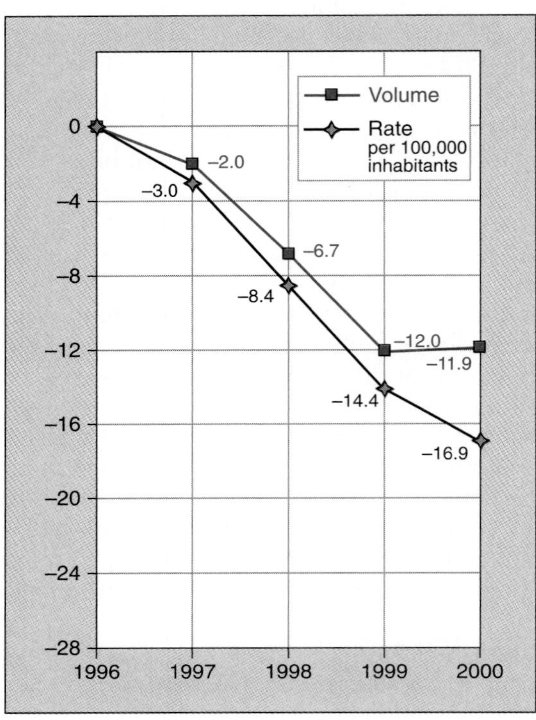

The belief that women shoplift more frequently than men was challenged by a report of the Sensormatic Electronics Corporation of Deerfield Beach, Florida. The company is the country's largest manufacturer of shoplifting-detection systems. The 1995 report was based on shoplifting data from 189 retail stores involving 127,807 shoplifting apprehensions. Fifty-two percent of the cases involved a man taking an average of $20.36 of merchandise, consisting most often of cigarettes, athletic shoes, and clothing (usually designer-type). Sunday was identified as the least frequent day for shoplifting; Saturday was the most popular. In the previous year (1994) the average theft was $60, but there were 37 percent fewer apprehensions.[20]

Findings vary on the quantity and nature of stolen items, although many studies indicate that most of the stolen goods are inexpensive items that the shoplifter could afford to purchase. Both men and women steal cosmetics with some frequency. One study reports that the item stolen most frequently from drugstores is Preparation H. Some stores now use a small magnetic sensor to secure this valuable product.[21]

Many comments about shoplifting are not based on systematic studies, but one recognized study merits attention. In 1964, Mary Owen Cameron's classic study of shoplifting distinguished between the *snitch* (the pilferer) and the *booster* (the commercial or professional shoplifter). Cameron concluded that "most shoplifting, including pilfering, appears to be chronic, habitual or systematic behavior." Cameron found that in addition to the booster and the snitch there might be a group of shoplifters who committed the offense because of an "unexpected urge to steal" or who were overcome "by an unpremeditated desire for a particular object."[22]

Cameron's data showed that the majority of shoplifters were not associated with a criminal subculture. Most were women, and over 90 percent probably were never convicted of another offense. Usually they had not thought about the possibility of being arrested, although they had given consideration to the chance of being caught.

When apprehended, many shoplifters use the excuses and rationalizations characteristic of juveniles caught in a delinquent act. They do not manifest psychotic symptoms, and seldom are they repeat offenders. In many instances they have had childhood experiences with groups in which older children taught them the techniques of successful pilfering. The items taken are generally for the shoplifter's personal use rather than for resale and profit. Most of the female shoplifters are from families with modest budgets. They steal luxury items that cannot come out of the family budget without sacrificing other needs of the family, rather than items they buy frequently. They rationalize that it is better to steal from the department store than from the family budget.

Pilferers, in contrast to other thieves, do not think of themselves as thieves, and when arrested they resist the definition of their behavior as theft. The arrest, however, forces them to realize that the behavior is not just bad but also illegal. At this stage, many pilferers become upset, even hysterical. In contrast, professional shoplifters, upon finding it impossible to talk their way out of an arrest, accept the inevitable. The pilferer fears the family's reaction and does not expect in-group support for the illegal behavior. The act of apprehension is sufficient to deter most of them from further illegal activity of this kind.

Motor Vehicle Theft

The *UCR* tabulates motor vehicle theft separately from other serious thefts. The crime is defined officially as "the theft or attempted theft of a motor vehicle . . . The definition excludes the taking of a motor vehicle for temporary use by those persons having lawful access." An estimated 1.1 million motor vehicle thefts were reported in 2000, up 1.2 percent from the previous year. The estimated total loss from motor vehicle thefts in 2000 was $7.8 billion. Most of the thefts (74.5 percent) involved automobiles. Over 60 percent of the arrestees were under 25 years of age, with 34.3 percent under 18. Males constituted 84.2 percent of those arrested; 55.4 percent were white; 41.6 percent were African American. Only 14.1 percent of the reported thefts were cleared by arrest.[23]

This low level of clearance means that auto theft is a fairly safe crime to commit. A recent study of offenders incarcerated in Illinois for car theft revealed that most of them viewed the crime as a "lucrative, 'low-tech' enterprise . . . in most cases, a screwdriver is the only tool required to break into and steal a targeted vehicle." The offenders said they could break through most safety devices (although they agreed that some of the devices might deter novices, who would just move to other cars). The study also noted that most of the offenders had stolen an average of 30 cars before they were detected.[24]

Some law enforcement efforts to cut car thefts have been successful. In 1991 Newark, New Jersey, police began utilizing a special task force to combat car thefts. By 1998 they had lowered the city's rank from 1st to 16th in car thefts nationally. The officers work in teams, called *wolf packs,* which consist of "a half dozen or more unmarked trucks and cars patrolling in adjacent grids of 10 square blocks, converging to surround their prey"; suspects are identified by the use of high-tech means, such as computer databases. Newark's plan also involves a multicounty effort to reduce the frequency with which a car stolen in one county ends up in another.[25]

Carjacking: Property or Violent Crime?

Carjacking Auto theft by force or threat of force.

The difficulty in differentiating property crimes and violent crimes is illustrated by carjacking. **Carjacking** refers to auto theft by force or threat of force, and, as we noted in Chapter 7, it is the force element that differentiates robbery as a violent crime. The usual procedure is for the carjackers to force people out of their cars and then to steal the cars. Personal injury and death have occurred in some cases, a few of which are described in Exhibit 8.2.

Because of the violent nature of carjacking and the increase in the number of these crimes, in September 1992 the FBI announced that carjacking was a new priority in the bureau's Operation Safe Streets program. This anticrime program was established earlier in approximately 40 cities for the purpose of combating violence associated with drugs and gang activities. According to the FBI director, "We consider carjacking a violent crime that deserves the full attention of the FBI. . . We have the mechanism in place to deal aggressively with this problem."[26]

The Anti Car Theft Act of 1992 became law in October of that year. This statute defines *carjacking* as an act in which a person with a firearm approaches a car and removes the driver forcibly for purposes of stealing the car. The crime carries a sentence of not more than 15 years unless there is bodily injury, in which case the maximum penalty is 25 years. If the driver is killed, the penalty is "any number of years up to life." In addition, the statute increases penalties for other crimes related to car theft. The first trial under this new statute is referred to in Exhibit 8.2. The statute's constitutionality has been challenged, but it was upheld by a federal court in 1995, and the U.S. Supreme Court refused to hear the case on appeal.[27]

EXHIBIT 8.2

Carjacking: A New Fear

She was a 21-year-old college student with a bright future who was in the wrong place at the wrong time. While Kimberly Horton waited for the light to turn green so she could continue on her way to visit her parents in the Los Angeles area, she was forced out of her car, shot in the head, and left dying on the sidewalk. Two hours later her Honda Accord was pulled over by officers. An 18-year-old suspect was arrested but released for lack of evidence that he stole the car or knew anything about the carjacking.

The previous week Pamela Basu, 34, of Maryland, was forced from her BMW by two men who stole the car and drove it two miles. Basu, whose left arm was restrained by the shoulder strap of the car, was dragged to her death. The drivers swerved into a barbed-wire fence, apparently trying to dislodge Basu's body. "Before finally ridding themselves of the fatally injured woman, they stopped to toss her 22-month-old daughter from the car." The daughter, found in her car seat, survived. The two men, aged 27 and 16, were arrested 90 minutes later.[1]

Kissimmee, Florida, home of Disney World and other amusement parks, was the scene of a 1992 carjacking that involved four victims, only two of whom survived. According to three of the four suspects, all of whom are African American, one of the survivors, an African American female, was spared because of her race. During the carjacking, the three male victims were ordered to remove their clothes and lie down in a field, where each was shot in the back of the head. The survivor, who was wounded by a gunshot to the hand he held over his head, feigned death. The female victim was forced to watch the executions.[2]

The suspects were apprehended, and one defendant entered a guilty plea providing that he would testify against the other defendants and that state prosecutors would not seek the death penalty in a pending state case. The trial of the other three accused constituted the first trial under the new federal statute prohibiting carjacking, which became law in October 1992. In April 1993 the three defendants were convicted of abducting three men and murdering two of them. With their husbands at their sides, the mothers of the victims asked the judge to impose the harshest penalties on all the defendants. One said, "They had no sympathy for my son. I have no sympathy for them. . .My son was brutally murdered and I feel no remorse for them. And there has to be a place in hell for the three of them." Calling the crimes "cold-blooded and pitiless," the judge imposed identical terms: life without parole plus 25 years for their convictions in federal court on charges of conspiracy, armed carjacking resulting in death, and using a firearm during a felony.[3]

In the subsequent state trial, two of the defendants were convicted of murder and kidnapping. The defendant who admitted that he pulled the trigger was sentenced to die in Florida's electric chair. Attorneys for one of the others argued that since their client did not pull the trigger he should not be convicted. The prosecutor disagreed and stated,

> The fact that the pack has a leader doesn't change the wolves in the pack into sheep . . .When you run with the pack, you share in the kill. This was a pack, a pack of hungry wolves looking for prey.[4]

This defendant was sentenced to life in prison. The fourth defendant, who testified against his friends in the federal trial, was not tried on state charges.

1. "A New Terror on the Road: Carjacking Puts Fear in the Driver's Seat," *Newsweek* (23 November 1992), p. 31.
2. "Three Men Get Life Plus Twenty-Five Years in Carjacking," *Orlando Sentinel* (27 April 1993), p. 1B.
3. "Two Found Guilty in Carjack Deaths," *St. Petersburg Times* (11 February 1994), p. 5B.
4. "Carjack Killer Sentenced to Electric Chair," *St. Petersburg Times* (26 July 1994), p. 4B.

Analysis of Motor Vehicle Theft

Despite the attention given to the violent aspects of carjacking, most motor vehicle thefts do not involve violence. Some studies report that many arrestees are young people who steal cars for a joy ride. A second reason for car theft is *short-term transportation,* and a third is *long-term transportation.* The latter purpose is given by persons from a lower socioeconomic background who are older than the joy riders. They paint or alter the car in other ways to disguise its appearance. Others steal for *profit,* intending to sell the car (or strip it and sell the parts)

Relatively new statutes involve the crime of carjacking, which, as pictured here, involves taking the car from the driver by force. Personal injury and death have occurred in some cases. (Mark Richards/Photo Edit)

rather than use it for transportation. Many of these offenders operate in groups that resemble highly organized businesses. A final reason for stealing motor vehicles is to use them in the *commission of another crime* such as robbery. This category constitutes a small portion of auto thefts.[28]

Arson

Arson The willful and malicious burning of the structure of another with or without the intent to defraud. Burning of one's own property with the intent to defraud is included in some jurisdictions.

The fourth index property crime is **arson,** defined by the *UCR* as "any willful or malicious burning or attempt to burn, with or without intent to defraud, a dwelling house, public building, motor vehicle or aircraft, personal property of another, etc."[29] The *UCR* definition includes only those fires that are found to be set maliciously or willfully. Fires of unknown or suspicious origin are excluded.

Arson was not categorized by the FBI's *UCR* as an index offense originally. By congressional mandate in October 1978, which became effective in 1979, arson was moved from Part II to Part I, or index offenses. Procedures were developed for reporting the crime, but the *UCR* emphasizes that care must be used in interpreting arson data, particularly trend data, which might be affected significantly by better reporting procedures rather than by increased volume and higher rates of arson.

Arson offenses reported in 2000 totaled 78,280, representing a 0.4 percent increase over 1999. The most frequent structural targets of arson were residences. The average damage amount per arson for all structures was $19,497. Only 16.5 percent of the crimes were cleared by arrest.[30]

Despite its seriousness, arson did not receive much attention historically. The crime was, however, in the news frequently during the 1990s. Numerous church

EXHIBIT 8.3

Church Burnings: Congress Reacts

The frequent burnings of churches in which the congregations are predominantly or entirely African American led Congress to enact the Church Arson Prevention Act of 1996. President Bill Clinton appointed the National Arson Task Force to investigate whether the arsons were racially motivated. In 1997 the task force concluded that the rash of arson against African American churches was not the result of a national conspiracy. The statute provides $10 million in private loans to assist congregations in rebuilding their churches, most of which are located in southern states. It doubles to 20 years the maximum sentence for arson of a house of worship. It permits the federal government to become involved in arson cases in which racial hatred appears to be a factor.[1]

The new statute may not be as effective as hoped, however, for all arson cases are difficult to investigate. Connecting them with racial hatred presents a challenging evidentiary issue.

1. The statute amends U.S. Code, Title 18, Section 247, Damage to Religious Property (2001).

fires, which occurred primarily in southern states and involved very old buildings with predominantly African American congregations, led Congress to enact legislation (see Exhibit 8.3). Also, in March 1990, a blaze in the Happy Land Social Club in New York City killed 87 people. It was the worst fire in that city since 1911 and the worst in the nation since 1986, when 97 people died in a hotel fire in Puerto Rico. The Happy Land Social Club victims died within minutes after the fire began in the club. Julio Gonzalez, convicted of starting the fire, was sentenced to 25 years to life in prison on each of 87 counts of felony murder and murder. By law the sentences must be served concurrently, but Gonzalez will be eligible for parole after serving 25 years. Gonzalez went to the club to talk to his former girlfriend, Lydia Feliciano, who was an employee. The club's bouncer evicted Gonzalez after he quarreled with Feliciano, who had jilted him. Gonzalez returned later and started the fire. Feliciano was among the six survivors of the fire and mass murder.[31]

Arsons have been attributed to children as well as adults. In 1996 the National Fire Protection Association cited examples of young children found guilty of arson or more serious crimes. For example, an 11-year-old who set fire to a newspaper and threw it onto a porch was convicted of manslaughter when the resulting fire took the lives of two elderly people. Association officials emphasized that for the first time, over one-half of all arson arrests are of children and teenagers, with one-third of those apprehended being under the age of 15 and almost 7 percent under the age of 10. *UCR* data for 2000 report that 71.6 percent of all persons arrested for arson were under the age of 25, with 52.8 percent under 18. Males constituted 84.9 percent of the arrestees.[32]

Analysis of Arson

Analysis of arson has focused on the crime, not the criminal, and some sociological theories discussed previously have been utilized. Arson has been attributed to "patterns of systematic speculation in transitional neighborhoods," racial problems, and capitalism, and the scale and complexity of this crime call into question our deviance theories.[33]

An earlier study of convicted arsonists, conducted by two psychiatrists and a sociologist, suggests six types of arsonists. *Revenge arsonsists* are the most prevalent type. Most are family members or friends who have been involved in an argument with the people against whom they seek revenge. Many are intoxicated at the time of the crime; potentially they are more dangerous than other types, and they make little attempt to conceal their acts.

Many *vandalism arsonists* are teenagers who think it is fun to destroy property by fire. Often they work in pairs or groups, in contrast to other types, who work alone most of the time. *Crime-concealment arsonists* are offenders who set fires to conceal other crimes that they have committed, for example, burglary or murder. *Insurance-claim arsonists* set fires so they can make claims against their insurance companies. Often they commit their crimes during the day, in contrast to crime-concealment arsonists, who work at night most of the time.

Excitement arsonists are usually intoxicated and set fire to inhabited buildings at night for the fun they find in the activity. Perhaps *pyromaniacs* best fit the common stereotype of arsonists. They are the pathological fire starters who do not seem to commit the crime for any other practical or financial reason but, rather, because of an irresistible impulse.[34]

A final type, identified more recently, is the person who commits *arson for hire,* or for profit. Most of these arsonists are never caught, and therefore little is known about their characteristics.

NON-INDEX PROPERTY CRIMES: A SAMPLE

The *UCR* enumerates and collects data on less serious offenses, called Part II offenses. Despite the FBI categorization of these crimes as less serious property crimes, it may be argued that, at some levels, they are *more* serious than burglary, larceny-theft, motor vehicle theft, and arson. The total economic loss may be greater, as in embezzlement, and the erosion of society's moral fiber may be more significant. More attention is given to these issues in Chapter 9, which discusses business and government-related crimes. Several of these Part II offenses are property crimes. Three of them—forgery, receiving stolen property, and embezzlement—are the subjects of sociological studies and are discussed in the following sections.

Forgery and Counterfeiting

Forgery Falsely making or altering, with the intent to defraud, a negotiable and legally enforceable instrument, such as a check.

The crime of **forgery** involves falsely making or altering, with the intent to defraud, a legally negotiable instrument such as a bank draft. The most common type of forgery is *check forgery.*

Many people who engage in check forgery are not professionals but amateurs, called *naive check forgers* by Edwin M. Lemert, who applied his closure theory of analysis in studying them. According to Lemert, a person who is isolated socially and facing situations that tend to create further isolation (such as divorce, unemployment, or alcoholism) may encounter problems that can be solved only by money. Check forging is seen as a way to eliminate or at least reduce those problems—a way to get closure. Lemert found that check forgers did not associate with other criminals or engage in other types of crime. Many were nonviolent and likable persons, older and more intelligent than most other criminals.[35]

Although writing checks without sufficient funds in the account is a crime, most people are not prosecuted for this offense.

Stolen Property: Buying, Receiving, Possessing

Fence A person who disposes of stolen goods.

The *UCR* includes the buying, receiving, or possessing of stolen property as a Part II offense. To make money on their acquisitions, thieves must make arrangements to exchange the goods for money or other goods. In many instances a fence is involved. A **fence** is a person who disposes of stolen goods. Often fences are professionals connected with organized crime, discussed in Chapter 10. The fence is an important key to the big business of property crime.

In recent times, researchers have given more attention to the role of the fence in property crimes. For example, sociologist Darrell J. Steffensmeier's *The Fence: In the Shadow of Two Worlds* covers many aspects of fencing, including a discussion of the process of becoming and being a fence.[36] Another sociological analysis of fences was conducted by Neal Shover, whose primary focus was the professional burglar. Shover found that fences can be distinguished by three characteristics: "(1) the *scale* of their operation, (2) the *frequency* of purchase, and (3) their degree of *product specialization.*"[37]

The routine activity approach, discussed in Chapter 5, has been used in the study of offenders who engage in receiving stolen property. According to routine activity theory, demographic variables such as gender, age, ethnicity, and income appear to be related to whether a person is offered stolen property for purchase and whether the individual to whom it is offered is motivated to buy. But these variables do not influence whether or not the person buys the stolen property. It appears that the opportunity to buy stolen property and to a lesser degree the motivation to buy are more important than demographic variables in determining whether the purchase is made. The researchers concluded:

> Routine activities theory predicts that potential buyers and potential sellers of illegal goods must converge in time and space before an illegal transaction can occur. This convergence is facilitated when the lifestyles of buyers and sellers bring them together . . .Younger persons and males were much more likely than older persons or females to be offered stolen goods for sale. These groups are also more likely than other groups to engage in "high risk" activities which might bring them into physical proximity with sellers of stolen goods.[38]

Embezzlement

As mentioned earier, under common law, if the property of another had been entrusted to you and if you had kept the property, even against the wishes of the owner, you would not have committed larceny-theft. Gradually it was decided that misappropriation of the property entrusted by the owner to another person should be a crime. But since larceny-theft was a felony and all felonies carried the death penalty, there was a reluctance to place such acts in that category. The solution was to create a new crime that carried lighter penalties.

Embezzlement Obtaining rightful possession of property with the owner's consent and subsequently wrongfully depriving the owner of that property.

Embezzlement refers to the misappropriation or misapplication of property or money entrusted to the care, custody, or control of the offender. The crime may involve greater economic loss than larceny-theft but result in a less severe sentence. Today many jurisdictions have a general theft statute that covers most if not all types of theft, including larceny-theft and embezzlement.[39]

From both a sociological and a legal point of view, embezzlement and embezzlers present a problem. In analyzing why the crime is committed, should we include embezzlement in the categories of theft in the FBI's *UCR* or with white-collar crime? Sociologically, the crime is more like white-collar crime; legally, however, it probably belongs with other theft crimes. This is true also of modern theft crimes, discussed, along with a sociological analysis of embezzlement, in Chapter 9, on business and government-related crimes.

MODERN THEFT CRIMES

Because of the loopholes that developed in the common law, as well as the belief that other types of "taking" or "stealing" should be included in the crime of theft, modern statutes differ from English common law. The California statute is an example:

> Every person who shall feloniously steal, take, carry, lead, or drive away the personal property of another, or who shall fraudulently appropriate property which has been entrusted to him, or who shall knowingly and designedly by any false or fraudulent representation or pretense, defraud any other person of money, labor or real or personal property . . . is guilty of theft.[40]

A statute as broadly worded as this one includes the new kinds of theft that have come to our attention in recent years. The following paragraphs present a few examples of what has occurred as technology has improved and lifestyles have changed.

Modular telephones that can be plugged into almost any telephone connection are particularly susceptible to theft. These phones permit a hotel guest to dial an outside number without having to go through the hotel operator, a savings in time and cost. They do not have to be wired into the walls, a costly procedure. After several telephone thefts, some hotel owners spent additional money to secure the phones by wiring them to the walls, buying devices that secure the phones in place, or replacing them with ones that are not modular. Handheld and car cellular phones are frequent theft targets, too.

According to some experts, credit card theft has become our fastest-growing crime. Measures to prevent these thefts include eliminating carbon paper in credit receipts or giving the carbons to customers to avoid the possibility that someone, such as an employee, may take the number from the carbon and use it in place of the card. People are warned not to use their credit card numbers for telephone purchases and to keep their cards in sight at all times when using them to make a purchase, to eliminate the possibility that the salesclerk could make out two sales slips with the imprint of the card. A further warning is not to give out the number to people wanting identification for check cashing or other reasons. Use only a driver's license for that purpose.

Fraud Falsely representing a fact, either by conduct or by words or writing, in order to induce a person to rely on the misrepresentation and surrender something of value.

Credit card thefts demonstrate the interrelationship between individual theft and organized crime. Muggers, prostitutes, and burglars connected with organized crime steal credit cards and sell them to credit card rings. Estimated loss per year as a result of credit card theft and **fraud** (which, unlike theft and embezzlement, does not require the actual taking or misappropriation of money or property) is over $3 billion. Most recently, credit cards have been stolen by use of an encoded strip. Offenders are able to put valid account numbers inside the magnetic code of invalid cards. Lee Iacocca, former chair of the Chrysler Corporation, lost $25,000 in cash advances from his Visa account by this method of theft. As authorities note, "This is a very expensive kind of fraud."[41]

Theft of computer chips is another example of technological theft, although in one case the act involved a robbery as well. A gang of robbers, perhaps as many as 10, tied up employees at Centon Electronics in Irvine, California, and stole about $5 million in memory chips. Computer memory chips are easy to steal, easy to carry, and virtually impossible to trace. They are expensive; so the thefts are lucrative. Many of the businesses targeted for these thefts do not have high security. Thefts of computer chips range from simple solo thefts to highly organized and carefully planned crimes that involve insider information (see discussion in Chapter 9, p. 286).[42]

Of ever greater concern, however, are the crimes that are committed by the use of a computer, and the next section focuses on computer crimes.

COMPUTER CRIMES

Computers have revolutionized the way we do business and in many respects the way we think and act. Computers fascinate and challenge many people; others

Cyberphobia An irrational fear of the Internet or of working with computers.

Computer crime Crime that involves the use of a computer.

Cybercrime Type of computer crime that involves the Internet.

Identity theft The stealing of an individual's social security number or other important information about his or her identity and using that information to commit crimes, such as removing funds from the victim's bank account.

Cyberstalking Stalking someone by use of a computer.

may develop an intense fear of computers, called **cyberphobia;** and a few people may even become violent, attacking the computer. Unfortunately, computers are also used to commit crimes, and cracking computer codes has become a rite of passage for some teenagers and college students.

The cost of **computer crime** is unknown, but estimates run into the billions of dollars. Within the category of computer crime is **cybercrime,** or computer crime that involves the Internet. In his June 2001 testimony before a congressional subcommittee on cybercrime, a newly appointed assistant attorney general from the U.S. Department of Justice estimated that cybercrimes such as disseminating an e-mail virus could cause millions, if not billions, of dollars in damages.[43]

Specifically, it has been estimated that the computer virus known as the *Love Bug* infected the computers of 45 million people in 2000 and cost at least $10 billion. The FBI estimates that every hour there are three computer hacking attempts somewhere in the United States; 57,000 viruses and 22,000 hacking jobs were reported in the year 2000.[44]

In addition to viruses and other forms of hacking, *Internet fraud* is a serious crime today, affecting over 700,000 victims yearly. In 2001 the Department of Justice warned Congress of the growing problem, estimating a $745 million loss in 1997. Much of the fraud involves **identity theft,** in which the hacker steals a personal identity (usually by accessing a person's accounts through his or her social security number). Typical victims spend two years "trying to erase $18,000 in false charges from their credit reports," while the "anonymous nature of computer crime often makes catching the crooks almost impossible."[45]

Federal officials estimate that identity theft victimizes half a million people per year in the United States. As one victim said, "What has taken me a lifetime to build—my trust, my integrity and my identity—has been tainted."[46]

Some well-known examples of cybercrime are discussed in Exhibit 8.4. In addition, persons have been convicted of using computers to distribute pornography, but detection and successful prosecution of computer pornography are difficult because of the widespread use of computer bulletin boards (about 45,000 currently) and the lack of legislation dealing explicitly with computer pornography. In addition, the First Amendment rights of citizens may not be infringed by laws regulating the Internet. Privacy laws need revision and must be considered in any attempts to regulate the Internet. Media Focus 8.1 explains a U.S. Supreme Court case that was concerned with this issue.

One final type of computer crime that is becoming a growing menace is **cyberstalking.** Stalking is discussed in Chapter 7 (see p. 221) and should be reviewed here. In cyberstalking, the Internet, e-mail, or some other form of electronic communicating is used for stalking, harassing, or annoying an individual, and in some cases individuals have been physically threatened by their stalkers. In a 1999 report to the vice president, who requested the study, the U.S. Department of Justice recommended that the government improve training of law enforcement personnel, increase resources, and consider whether current stalking statutes (all 50 states and the federal government have them) are sufficient to prosecute cyberstalking.[47]

To emphasize how serious the problem can be, the report summarized the first case prosecuted under California's cyberstalking statute, which became effective on 1 January 1999. Gary Steven Dellapenta, age 50, pleaded guilty to stalking and other charges for soliciting on the Internet the rape of a 28-year-old woman who had rejected him. The defendant impersonated the woman in Internet chat rooms, listed her phone number and her address, along with information on how to bypass her security system, and suggested that she fantasized about being raped. On at least six occasions men knocked on the door of the victim (who does not even own a computer) during the night and said

EXHIBIT 8.4

Computer Hackers and Their Victims

In 1988 national attention was focused on computer crimes when Robert T. Morris Jr., apparently intending no harm, made one programming error that resulted in jamming more than 6,000 computers in what was called at that time the "country's most serious computer 'virus' attack." Morris's father was the chief scientist at the government's National Computer Security Center. Friends reported that young Morris, a Cornell University graduate student, was horrified by his mistake.[1]

In June 1989 Cornell officials suspended Morris, saying they found unauthorized passwords in Morris's computer. In January 1990 Morris was convicted and faced up to five years in prison and a $250,000 fine, but he was placed on three years' probation, fined $10,000, and ordered to perform 400 hours of community service, which included answering the phone for a bar association. He lost his appeal, in which he argued several issues, such as his lack of intent to cause harm.[2]

In 1990 three members of the nationwide computer-hacker group known as Legion of Doom (named after one of the villains in Superman comic books) became the first persons convicted of electronic intruding to be sent to federal prison. The defendants caused an estimated $4.5 million in damage to Bell South computers. Two of the defendants pleaded guilty to possessing illegal access devices, and another to conspiracy. Each faced up to 10 years in prison and a $250,000 fine. One of the defense attorneys argued that his client meant no harm or malice and that the court should be lenient because his client cooperated with authorities. One defendant testified that the act was a learning experience for him. Two of the defendants were sentenced to seven months in prison and ordered to pay $233,800 in restitution. The third, who had a prior computer-hacking conviction, was sentenced to 21 months in prison. All were barred from owning personal computers for three years and ordered to assist private companies and colleges with computer security. The judge called the acts a "major electronic vandalism case."[3]

In July 1998, according to a professional computer expert, Stephen James, who was hired to test computer systems, the Legion of Doom attacked over 350 websites. A news article reported: "In one fell swoop, it hit the Indonesian police, Stanford University, the Pentagon, the Los Angeles Police Department, the US National Aerronautics and Space Administration, the British Labour Party and the Spice Girls."[4]

The Legion of Doom was itself a target of another computer hacker group, the Masters of Deception, a group of young men in New York who had code names such as Acid Phreak and Outlaw. The Masters of Deception used their computers to play pranks on other computer hackers by tapping into their computer systems, pulling up confidential credit reports, and engaging in other menacing behavior. Federal prosecutors thought the actions went beyond harmless pranks. In July 1992, five members of the group pleaded not guilty to numerous federal computer crime charges. They were charged with breaking into some of the most sophisticated computer systems in the country, stealing information, and selling it to private investigators. According to prosecutors, previous hackers were primarily joy riders through computers whereas these defendants committed computer crimes to harass and intimidate.[5]

Kevin Lee Poulsen was indicted in December 1992 after a 17-month manhunt. Poulson was convicted and ordered to serve 51 months in prison, the longest term given to a computer hacker, for using a computer to break into a telephone system and rig a radio contest. As a result of his computer hacking, he won a new Porsche, a vacation to Hawaii, and cash prizes. Poulsen was ordered to pay restitution for those prizes. When he was released from prison he had to begin serving three years of supervision, during which time he could not own or touch a computer without permission from federal authorities.[6]

Poulson was released from prison in 1996. He commented that he wanted to pursue a college degree but could not do so in the field in which he was most qualified, so he chose English because it required less use of a computer. Poulsen was also charged with espionage, a charge on which he was to be tried after his prison term for the computer crime. That charge was dropped as part of a plea negotiation while he was in prison.

In December 1988 Kevin Mitnick was charged with computer crimes consisting of stealing programs and tapping into Digital Equipment's computer network. He was convicted and sentenced to a year in jail. Mitnick's attorneys argued that their

(continued)

EXHIBIT 8.4
Computer Hackers and Their Victims *(continued)*

client was addicted to computers. As part of his treatment program, Mitnick was ordered not to touch a computer or modem, but by 1994 the computer wizard was named to the FBI's "Most Wanted" list, suspected of numerous other computer crimes involving millions of dollars. He was captured in 1995, and by the spring of 1996 he and his attorney had agreed with federal prosecutors on a plea agreement concerning charges against Mitnick for crimes committed in North Carolina.[7]

In March of 1999 Mitnick and the federal authorities reached a plea agreement. Mitnick pleaded guilty to seven computer and fraud charges and was assessed a 54-month prison sentence, the longest to date for a computer hacker. In exchange, the federal prosecutors dropped the remainder of their 25 charges and agreed to the sentence, which is much more lenient than the sentence Mitnick could have received for the crimes to which he pleaded guilty: 35 years in prison and a fine of $1.75 million. The sentencing judge also ordered that for three years after his release from prison, Mitnick could not own or even use a computer, and he could not profit financially from his experiences for at least seven years after his release. Mitnick received credit for the four years he served in jail after his arrest in 1995. He was released in January 2000 and was challenging the probation conditions that he could not use a computer, cellular telephone, television, or any equipment that would permit him access to the Internet and that he could not profit from his crime. Mitnick said he had lined up writing and speaking fees of $20,000. Noted First Amendment attorney and law professor Floyd Abrams was supporting Mitnick, arguing that his First Amendment rights to express his own views were being violated.[8]

In 1998 an Israeli teen, Ehud Tenebaum, who is also known as "The Analyzer," claimed that he mentored two teens who were arrested for hacking Pentagon computers. In February 2001 Tenebaum, age 21, pleaded guilty in Israel to breaking into American and Israeli defense computers. Prosecutors were asking for a sentence of at least six months to negate the possibility that the defendant would qualify for house arrest.[9]

1. John Markoff, "How a Need for Challenge Seduced Computer Expert," *New York Times* (6 November 1988), p. 1.
2. United States v. Morris, 928 F.2d 504 (2d Cir. 1991), *cert. denied*, 502 U.S. 817 (1991).
3. "Elite Trio of Hackers Sentenced for Damaging Phone Computers," *Atlanta Journal and Constitution* (17 November 1990), p. 1C.
4. "This Man Can Hack into Your Computer System," *The (Singapore) Straits Times* (30 July 1998), p. 31.
5. "Urban Hackers Charged in High-Tech Crime," *New York Times* (23 July 1992), p. 1.
6. "Hacker Gets Record Sentence for Invading FBI Files," *Arizona Republic* (17 April 1995), p. 4F; "Filmmakers Follow Trend, Plug into Computer Themes," *Sun-Sentinel* (Fort Lauderdale) (28 May 1995), p. 2D.
7. "Hacker Plea Bargains: He Could Serve Eight Months," *Orlando Sentinel* (2 July 1995), p. 16; "Filmmakers Follow Trend," ibid.; "Leading Computer Hacker Pleads Guilty to Two Counts," *New York Times* (24 April 1996), p. 11.
8. "Judge Accepts Mitnick's Guilty Plea on 7 Counts," *Los Angeles Times* (27 March 1999), p. 1C; "Famed Hacker Fights for His Right to Seek Fortune," *Legal Times* (15 May 2000), p. 15.
9. "Ex-Hackers Hack Away at New Generation of Techno-Punks," *Tallahasse Democrat* (21 September 1998), p. 1.

they were responding to her advertisement on the Internet.[48] Dellapenta was prosecuted under the following section, which constitutes an amendment to the state's stalking statute by adding that the term *credible threat* in the original statute means:

> a verbal or written threat, including that performed through the use of electronic communication device, or a threat implied by a pattern of conduct or a combination of verbal, written, or electronically communicated statements and conduct made with the intent to place the person that is the target of the threat in reasonable fear for his or her safety or the safety of his or her family and made with the apparent ability to carry out the threat so as to cause the person who is the target of the threat to reasonably fear for his or her safety or the safety of his or her family. It is not necessary to prove that the defendant had the intent to actually carry out the threat.[49]

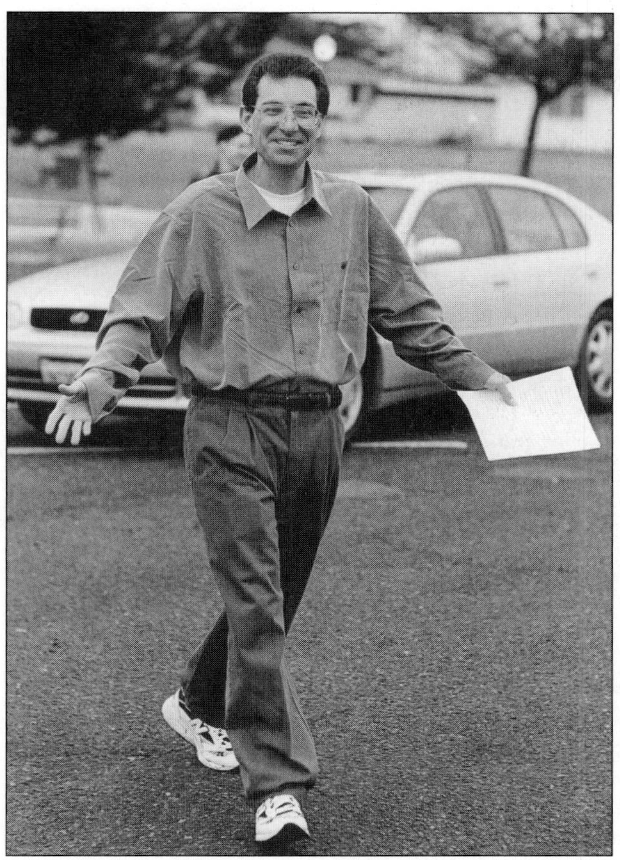

Computer hacker Kevin Mitnick arrives at a news conference early on 21 January 2000 after being released from the Federal Correction Institute in Lompoc, California. After five years behind bars, Mitnick, one of the nation's most notorious computer hackers, was released under the requirement that for the next three years he keeps his hands off computers, modems, cell phones, and anything else that could give him Internet access. Mitnick, 36, allegedly caused millions of dollars of damage by hacking into corporate and university computers. He was once the FBI's most wanted hacker. (AP)

Types of Computer Crimes

Computer crimes may involve the same kinds of crimes discussed elsewhere in this chapter as well as those discussed in previous chapters except that a computer is used in the perpetration of the crime. According to a white-collar crime expert, "Computer crime may also take the form of threats of force directed against the computer itself. These crimes are usually 'sabotage' or 'ransom' cases. Computer crime cases have one commonality: the computer is either the tool or the target of the felon."[50]

A special jargon has been developed to describe computer crimes:

1. *Data diddling,* the most common, the easiest, and the safest technique, involves changing the data that will be put into the computer or that are in the computer.
2. *The Trojan horse* method involves instructing the computer to perform unauthorized functions along with its intended functions.
3. *The salami technique* involves taking small amounts of assets from a larger source without significantly reducing the whole. In a bank account situation, for example, one might instruct the computer to reduce specified accounts by 1 percent and place those assets in another account.
4. *Superzapping* involves taking control of a computer's contents. Because computers at times malfunction, there is a need for what is sometimes called a "break glass in case of emergency" computer program. This program will "bypass all controls to modify or disclose any of the contents of the computer." In the hands of the wrong person, it can be an extremely powerful tool for crime.
5. *Data leakage* involves removing information from the computer system or computer facility.[51]

Controlling Computer Crimes

Legislation regulating computer crimes is relatively recent and reflects the varying definitions of this type of theft. Passage of a federal statute did not occur until the enactment of the Comprehensive Crime Control Act of 1984. Before that act, computer crimes were prosecuted under other statutes, such as those covering mail fraud and wire fraud, which excluded some types of computer crimes. In addition, the penalties were considered inadequate for computer crimes. The 1984 act has been amended several times, most recently as part of the Violent Crime Control and Law Enforcement Act of 1994.[52]

In 1995 Connecticut became one of the first states to enact legislation making harassment by computer a crime. Other jurisdictions have followed suit, but it is possible that the enactment of statutes designed to prevent computer crimes will not be as effective as some would like to think. First, many establishments might not want the public to know that their employees committed crimes with the company's computers. Second, in addition to a lack of reporting or willingness to prosecute and the difficulties of apprehension and prosecution, law

Media Focus 8.1

Identity Theft: Statements by the Media

During the past few years the media have frequently focused on the growing crime of identity theft, which, they claim, is reaching epidemic proportions. These informative accounts have alerted people to a crime that can cause severe economic damage as well as loss of personal time as victims cope with the results. Reports have appeared in media from the national television news to small-town newspapers.

Typical of the media reports was a 12 March 2002 news clip on CBS, which referred to identity theft as one of our fastest-growing crimes. According to this report, identity theft claims 750,000 new victims each year in the United States. Some victims spend weeks or even months trying to unravel the problems caused by identity theft. The report noted the need to maintain careful control over financial and other documents that contain numbers and other information that constitute an identity that can be stolen.[1]

On 5 February 2002 a small-town paper in New Hampshire reported that identity theft is becoming "an increasing problem" in that state. Identity theft was the number one consumer complaint made in New Hampshire in 2001. The article noted that the state had enacted an identity theft law in 2000, following the national law passed in 1998. Finally, the report emphasized that New Hampshire might become a leader in the national fight against identity theft. The Franklin Pierce Law Center in Concord, New Hampshire, will offer a degree program in e-commerce and cyberlaw. The program will feature identity theft.[2]

Finally, an article reprinted in a Tallahassee, Florida, paper noted that, although most people eventually recoup the money they lose through identity theft, "they also suffer damage to their credit records and invasion of privacy."[3]

1. *CBS National News*, 12 March 2002.
2. "Identity Theft an Increasing Problem in New Hampshire," *Conway Daily Sun* (5 February 2002), p. 3. (24 January 2002), p. 1E.
3. "Identity Theft Tops List of Frauds," *Tallahassee Democrat* 2.

enforcement officials may not have the technical expertise to solve computer crimes, and most cases that go to trial are highly technical, costly, and extremely time-consuming.

As quickly as officials learn how to protect computers and detect those who violate them, offenders learn new ways to commit computer crimes. One technique developed by hackers, *spoofing*, is used to trick a computer into thinking that it is being accessed by a friendly computer. According to a government-funded group called the Computer Emergency Response Team, spoofing can lead to high-level computer hijacking. By spoofing, a cyberthief can elude firewalls (electronic gates that keep out all but friendly users); enter computers; and alter, copy, or delete data.[53]

Finally, some businesspersons have decided that the way to handle cybercrime is to employ former computer hackers as consultants or full-time employees. Gregory D. Evans, who was arrested at age 28 and paid millions in fines to the government and to private companies for his computer hacking, is the founder and chief executive officer of the Cyber Group Network Corporation, a research and development firm with Internet software sales and contracted services with private and governmental agencies. The company specializes in computer and software security. Neal O'Farrell, also a former hacker, uses his computer skills to teach others how to avoid hackers. In the summer of 2001 he was presenting seminars entitled Breach of Trust. These presentations were one-day "bootcamps" designed to teach lawyers how to secure their computer records from hackers.[54]

PROFESSIONAL AND CAREER CRIMINALS

Some criminals work alone. Occasional thieves may steal for something they need; employees may embezzle money from their employers. Such people steal consistently over a number of years but never develop the skills, techniques, and attitudes of professional thieves. Other criminals are considered, and consider themselves, trained professionals; they may possess the skills, techniques, and attitudes that are common to many professional people. Usually they steal for profit. They may have long criminal careers, during which they may serve prison terms, one of the hazards of their occupation.

For years professional thieves have captured the interest of the public. They have been featured in the media, and they have provided sociologists with interesting research opportunities. This discussion begins with an analysis of the professional thief before proceeding to the more recent approach that focuses on the career of the persistent offender.

Professional Criminal Behavior: The Early Approach

Numerous writers on professional crime have pointed out that over time there has been little change in conceptual categories of professional crime. The professional criminal, such as the professional thief, manifests highly developed career behavior patterns characterized by nonviolence, a high degree of skill, loyalty toward the loosely organized group rather than toward individuals, association with other professional as opposed to amateur criminals, long careers with few arrests, and an outlook that views noncriminals as people who deserve to be victimized. Professional criminals have a status hierarchy that is related to a combination of skill and an expectation of high profits. They are not from the extremes of poverty. They start crime later in life than other criminals, and the peer group becomes important in terms of reinforcing their deviant self-concepts and attitudes.[55]

The classic study of professional criminals was conducted by Edwin H. Sutherland, who talked extensively with a thief who had been in the profession for more than 20 years. Sutherland asked the thief to write on several topics. He submitted the manuscript to other professional thieves and talked with still others, finding that none disagreed with the account. Sutherland described the theft profession as a group way of life that has all the characteristics of other groups—techniques, codes, status, traditions, consensus, and organization. He pointed out that these characteristics are not pathological. In addition, apprenticeship and tutelage by professional thieves is a prerequisite, and an individual must be recognized by professional thieves in order to become one.[56]

Contemporary Conceptualizations of Professional Thieves

Traditional conceptions of professional criminals are criticized for relying mainly on anecdotes and case studies, and for not utilizing systematic sociological approaches.[57] Few attempts were made to test hypotheses; professional crime was confused with full-time crime, the latter being engaged in by individuals who did not have the skills and other characteristics of professional criminals. More recent studies have attempted to alleviate these problems.

Under the auspices of the 1967 President's Crime Commission, several investigators determined that the professional thief is characterized by decreased specialization. The professional "is in business to cash in on opportunities and thus must not specialize too narrowly, for that increases the possibility of missing opportunities. Such characterizations of professional criminals indicate a radical change from the more traditional conceptualizations." They have to be versatile because of an emphasis on hustling, which means using all available means for victimizing others to make illegal gains for oneself. Further characteristics of contemporary professional criminals, in contrast to prior ones, are an increased reliance on fences and longer careers because of increased agreements with prosecutors, which may reduce the probability of incarceration and the time spent behind bars if incarcerated. In many cases their selection of work depends on available opportunities rather than on their preferred criminal activity.[58]

Neal Shover's studies of burglars suggest that they are not highly specialized, although there is some evidence of short-term specialization. Shover found that, in contrast to the rest of the population, who might be viewed as honest, burglars do not see themselves as thieves: "The *good burglar* sees himself, then, as different from most people only in the methods he uses to steal."[59] Shover found also that most burglars are young African American men. Most of them perform their work in concert with others. The social organization and other characteristics may differ according to the type of burglar. For example, the *high-level* burglar's social organization might resemble that of the military. High-level burglars earn more than low- or middle-level burglars; for them, burglary is a way of life:

> Misfits in a world that values precise schedules, punctuality, and disciplined subordination to authority, high-level thieves value the autonomy to structure life and work as they wish . . . Only the infirmities of age and diminishing connections significantly dampen their criminal activities.[60]

The study of professional crime shows the intricate pattern of social interaction that develops, which in many cases is a subculture. It shows the close relationship to acceptable patterns of business relationships, emphasizing shrewdness and even condoning fraud and swindles. According to one criminologist, "The law violator is no less a product of society than the moral, upright citizen, and both of them have much more in common than they are likely to acknowledge."[61]

Career Criminals: The Modern Approach

The skills, knowledge, attitudes, and values of professional criminals that were emphasized by early researchers may not be as much of a concern to the public as **career criminals** are. Today the emphasis is on the repeat offender, especially when that offender is violent. Most people are not concerned with whether the offender is professional—in fact, an amateur violent criminal may be more feared than a professional nonviolent criminal. Nor is there a great concern for the attitudes and group affiliations of the person who burglarizes a home.

Career criminals Persons who commit a variety of offenses over an extended period of time or offenders who specialize in particular types of crime, for example, burglary.

Semiprofessional property offenders are distinguished from professional criminals in the former's lack of skill and absence of a complex interactional pattern. These criminals see themselves as society's victims. They do not feel guilty about their behavior. In comparison to professional criminals, they are more hostile toward law enforcement officials and toward society, their parents, and occupational roles. Most remain in crime through middle age, at which point some change to noncriminal activities. Some studies suggest that an increasing number of amateurs are involved in bank robberies and car thefts; others suggest that these offenders have rather stable criminal careers. It has also been reported that semiprofessional burglars are predominantly young nonwhite men, and that most burglary victims are from the lower socioeconomic class. A study of African American armed robbers disclosed that most are older than other felons, with predominantly lower-class urban origins, a history of criminal activity as teenagers, and an unstable family background.[62]

Cohort The total universe of people defined by an event or events. For example, all children living in Minneapolis in 2002 and enrolled in the eighth grade constitute a cohort. This cohort might be interviewed or given questionnaires to gather data on delinquent behavior. At specified intervals, for example, every five years in the future, the cohort might be tested again to discover the existence of delinquent behavior.

Wolfgang's Studies of Delinquency Cohorts

Many modern studies of chronic career offenders are based on the approach developed most extensively in the now-classic studies of Marvin E. Wolfgang and his colleagues. These researchers utilized a **cohort** (a universe of persons defined by some characteristic) of 10,000 boys born in Philadelphia in 1945, who were available for study when they became 18 in 1963. According to official police reports, 65 percent of the boys had not been arrested before their 18th birthday. About one-third had prior contact with police. Forty-six percent of the delinquents stopped after the first offense, and of those who committed more than one offense, 35 percent had no more than three offenses. Less than 7 percent had five or more arrests; these chronic offenders committed 57 percent of all crimes attributed to the cohort of 10,000.[63]

Wolfgang repeated this approach in a study of 14,000 boys born in 1958, and he found some similarities with the earlier study. A small percentage, around 7 percent, committed most of the crimes. In this second study, they committed an even higher percentage of the crimes of their cohort, including 75 percent of the reported rapes and robberies. They constituted a chronically violent, although small, group of young men who began their criminal careers early and continued engaging in criminal activities into adult life.[64]

Other studies of delinquent cohorts have disclosed similar patterns of involvement with law enforcement, with a small percentage of the sample showing relatively high rates of repeat offenses.[65] There is evidence that these high-rate juvenile offenders continue their criminal activities into adulthood.[66] Such findings raise interesting research as well as ethical questions, such as "How can we identify the potential career criminals prior to the beginning of their careers and, if that can be done, with what result?" If effective prediction scales can be constructed, the results could be used for crime prevention and other social programs.[67] If most crimes are committed by only a few people, it can be argued that taking those people out of circulation, a process called **selective incapacitation,** would cut the crime rate significantly and "take the criminal justice system out of the business of dealing with social problems and put it to work doing what it alone can do: Identifying and removing from circulation people whose continued freedom would jeopardize the safety of the community."[68]

Selective incapacitation The selection of certain offenders, usually the most serious, for incarceration.

Earlier policy expectations of reduced crime through selective incapacitation seemed obvious to many law enforcement officials; special units to identify and track career criminals were established. Few of these programs were evaluated, however, and "those which were evaluated failed to show strong positive results in either conviction rates or sentence severity." Evaluations of recent police department repeat-offender programs suggest that the programs have had some success, but even success in identification and prosecution raises important issues. First, which suspects should be targeted? Second, will the improved efforts of defense lawyers erase the efforts of police and prosecution?[69] Finally, the programs raise the ethical and legal question of invading the privacy of targeted persons.

In addition to the ethical problems involved in predicting which juveniles (or adults) might become recidivists, there are practical problems. In short, the scales are not highly predictive of **recidivism.** Research on career criminals who engaged in dangerous behavior in California and Massachusetts found some characteristics that assist in the identification of offenders who commit violent crimes frequently. This information may be useful to prosecutors in deciding priority in prosecution.[70]

Recidivism Further violations of the law by released suspects or inmates, or noncriminal violations of conditions by probationers and parolees.

Rand Studies of Career Criminals

Rand Corporation researchers have published numerous documents based on their extensive studies of habitual or career offenders. Their research, which collected data through the self-reports of offenders, focuses on the small percentage of offenders who commit many offenses. In analyzing these studies, we should recall the discussion in Chapter 2 of the pros and cons of collecting data by the self-report data (SRD) method.

The first Rand sample involved 49 California prison inmates. The next study utilized a sample of 624 inmates from five California prisons selected to represent all male inmates in that state in terms of custody level, age, offense, and race. The study focused on the criminal activities of the inmates during the three years prior to their current incarcerations.[71] A third sample was larger: 2,190 jail and prison inmates in California, Michigan, and Texas.

The first Rand study found that most offenders were not specialized in their crimes. At any given time, they engaged in a variety of criminal activities. Few criminals committed crimes at a high rate; most did so at a fairly low rate, and the rate of violent crime among these inmates was very low. These findings were confirmed in the second study. During the three years prior to their current incarcerations, most of the inmates committed several other kinds of crime. Of those who reported having committed a crime other than the type for which they had been incarcerated, 49 percent listed more than four other crimes. As in the earlier study, a few inmates committed most of the reported crimes.

The Rand investigators found that neither age nor a prior prison term was associated strongly with offense rates, but self-concept was significant: "High-rate offenders tended to share a set of beliefs that were consistent with their criminal lifestyle—e.g., that they could beat the odds, that they were better than the average criminal, that crime was exciting, and that regular work was boring."[72]

The larger sample in the third Rand study was selected to check on possible problems in the first two samples and to include lesser offenses normally represented by jail populations. Analysis of data from this study confirmed that most offenders report committing few crimes, while only a few reported committing many crimes. Offenders were placed into categories, the most serious being those who reported robberies, assaults, and drug deals. These were termed *violent predators.* Most reported having committed these crimes at high rates while also engaging in numerous other property crimes. The factors that distinguished the violent predators from other inmates were:

Youth.
Onset of crime (especially violent crime) before age 16.
Frequent commission of both violent and property crime before age 18.
Multiple commitments to state juvenile facilities.
Unmarried and with few family obligations.
Employed irregularly and for short times.
Frequent use of hard drugs as a juvenile.
Use of heroin at costs exceeding $50 per day.
Use of multiple combinations of drugs.[73]

Researchers listed the following conclusions: Offenders identified as career criminals see themselves as criminals; they expect to return to crime after release from prison; they began their criminal careers early in their juvenile years; they are hedonistic, viewing crime as "a safe and enjoyable way to obtain the good life"; and they view themselves as proficient criminals. They represent only 25 percent of the sample, but they committed 58 percent of all reported armed robberies, 65 percent of burglaries, 60 percent of auto thefts, and 46 percent of assaults. The investigators point out that criminal justice systems might benefit by directing their incarceration efforts at these types of offenders rather than at other offenders (the majority) who do not exhibit these characteristics. The study notes that career property offenders can be identified and that some of them commit violent crimes, but "it provides no evidence of an identifiable group of career criminals who commit only violence."[74]

Many studies are limited by the fact that the data represent official reports only, but the Rand research, based on self-report data, is said to be more reliable.

In addition, the Rand studies have "stimulated both secondary analysis of the data and several replications with modifications."[75]

The BJS Report

The Bureau of Justice Statistics (BJS) issued a Special Report on Career Criminals, which utilized data on offenders from across the country. A random sample of 11,397 male and female inmates was interviewed; respondents were questioned extensively about their criminal careers. Since the major purpose of the study was to examine careers, only inmates who were at least 40 years old at the date of last admission to prison were selected for intensive study.[76] Data in the BJS study were analyzed by four types of offenders. The typologies were concerned with three of the major stages of life: adolescence (7 through 17 years), young adulthood (18 through 39 years), middle age (40 years and over). The sample was divided as follows:

Type 1: offenders who engaged in criminal activity in all three stages.
Type 2: offenders who engaged in criminal activity in all but young adulthood.
Type 3: offenders who engaged in criminal activity in all but adolescence.
Type 4: offenders who engaged in criminal activity in middle age only.

Type 1 and Type 2 offenders engaged in some criminal activity during adolescence. Type 2 offenders did not engage in criminal activity during young adulthood. They were law-abiding during that time but returned to criminal activity in middle age. They represent a small percentage of the inmate population, but it is significant that 92 percent of those offenders who reported criminal activity during adolescence continued with criminal activity during young adulthood and into middle age. These are the Type 1 offenders.

Perhaps the most surprising finding of this study is that the Type 4 offenders, those middle-aged offenders who did not engage in criminal activity as adolescents or as young adults, represented almost half of all the inmates who entered prison in middle age. The BJS report explained this finding in terms of the reasons for incarceration. Many persons arrested for property offenses are incarcerated for those offenses only if they have prior criminal records. But those who commit violent personal crimes are likely to be incarcerated even without a prior criminal record. Therefore, in an analysis of the crimes for which offenders are incarcerated currently, it is important to consider their prior records. Thus, the fact that 40 percent of the inmates in the BJS study were serving time for property offenses, not violent crimes, does not necessarily mean that society is incarcerating too many people for nonviolent crimes. Violence has been a part of the past record of many of these property offenders. The BJS report suggested that although the study did not investigate the issue, it is likely that the high rates of incarceration for violent crimes of the offenders over the age of 40 represent domestic violence.

The NIJ Overview of Repeat Offenders

The National Institute of Justice (NIJ), under the authorship of Lawrence Sherman, has published an overview on repeat offenders, defining them as "people who commit serious criminal offenses at a high rate and over a long period." According to Sherman, these criminals do not specialize; they commit a variety of crimes, and they differ in the extent to which they commit crimes. They commit the majority of serious, detected crimes, although they do not constitute a majority of criminals.

Sherman notes that ethical, practical, and technological problems exist when authorities track these repeat offenders. One view shared by many is that offenders are responsible for crimes they have committed but not for crimes they *may* commit at some future date. Yet identifying repeat offenders and arresting them for crimes may reduce crime significantly. Some cities have attempted to do this, establishing repeat-offender programs among the police as well as prosecutors. Sherman concluded:

> Repeat offender programs seem likely to expand and proliferate. With the scarce resources of modern criminal justice confronted by growing demands, policy makers must increasingly establish priorities. The idea of focusing scarce resources on repeat offender programs—even with all the errors of prediction and ethical questions of such programs—provides an attractive basis for choosing which criminal justice course to take.[77]

The Young Criminal Years of the Violent Few

Another study of criminal careers that has gained wide attention is that by Donna Martin Hamparian. In writing an introduction to one of Hamparian's works, the administrator of the Office of Juvenile Justice and Delinquency Prevention, which funded the research, explained that the study extended those of Wolfgang and his associates and of the Rand Corporation, whose research he described "as important as anything else we have learned in recent years." He continued, referring to the Hamparian study: "Probably the most significant contribution of this study is the increased knowledge of the characteristics of those offenders who are likely to continue their criminality into adulthood."[78] Hamparian's work was based on a cohort of 1,222 people born between 1956 and 1960. She describes the juvenile arrests of these young people from 1962 to 1978 and "follows the cohort members through their early adult careers, if any, up to mid-1983." The major conclusions of Hamparian's study are as follows:

1. Most violent juvenile offenders make the transition to adult offenders.
2. There is a continuity between juvenile and adult criminal careers.
3. A relatively few chronic offenders are responsible for a disproportionate number of crimes.
4. The frequency of arrests as adults declines with age.
5. Incarceration has not slowed the rate of arrest—in fact, the subsequent rate of arrest increases after each incarceration.[79]

Recent Research

Criminal careers have been the focus of considerable research in recent years. The researchers do not agree on all of the issues. One approach, led by Michael Gottfredson and Travis Hirschi, takes the position that it is not important to study criminals over a time period and analyze the progression of their activities in order to understand crime. Gottfredson and Hirschi maintain that their self-control, or general, theory of crime (discussed in Chapter 6 of this text) explains all crime, and it is not relevant how many crimes were committed: "[T]he causes of criminal acts are the same regardless of the number of such acts."[80] Furthermore, it is not important to look at stages in the careers of criminals in an effort to distinguish criminal types and when they cease committing crimes or increase their activities. Gottfredson and Hirschi argue that, over time, all criminals lose their propensity to engage in crime. There is no need to study the impact of unemployment or other variables on crime, for the variables are unimportant in explaining the behavior.

The second position, illustrated by the work of Alfred Blumstein and his collaborators, views career criminal behavior in terms of its stages. They argue that factors that influence the beginning of crime may not influence a criminal career or its decline. For example, people might begin stealing or selling illegal drugs because they have no other source of income. But as their income needs are fulfilled, they may not abandon theft; some other reason might be necessary to explain the continuation of the criminal activity at this subsequent stage.

Yet other factors might explain why an individual ceases engaging in criminal activity, a process Blumstein and his colleagues refer to as *desisting*. Further, career criminals differ in characteristics and may be analyzed by groups. Career criminals must be studied over a time period (longitudinal studies) in an effort to understand the factors that might be influential at various stages of their criminal careers. Such a study should distinguish between criminals and noncriminals, analyze a criminal career by frequency of offending, and analyze the termination of a criminal career. These three categories are referred to as *innocents, desisters,* and *persisters. Innocents* have never been involved with law enforcement. *Desisters* are offenders with a relatively low probability of repeating criminal behavior, while *persisters* have a relatively high probability of repeating criminal acts.[81]

Blumstein and his colleagues conclude that their approach, in contrast to the single-factor approach of Gottfredson and Hirschi, "allows for the possibility that different factors could influence these different facets of a criminal career, whereas the single-factor approach presumes that all aspects of a criminal career are influenced by the same factors in the same way."[82]

Both approaches have been analyzed by David Greenberg, who developed a mathematical formula model of criminal careers and concluded that much of the empirical research utilized in the dispute concerning the study of criminal careers "is entirely irrelevant to it . . . Findings that seem to point to one conclusion can take on a different significance when viewed from a different perspective."[83]

Blumstein and his colleagues conclude that Greenberg's position does not detract at all from their work and that he has made an important contribution to the debate on research on criminal careers "by presenting a much more explicit representation of the Gottfredson-Hirschi position than had previously been available." They concede that the study of criminal careers needs more work and that in the future it might become obvious that a simpler approach to the study is warranted. They point out that their main contention with Gottfredson and Hirschi is not their single-factor approach per se but "their unwillingness to consider more complex possibilities."[84]

In a response, Greenberg argues that the debate over criminal careers has been mainly empirical, not theoretical, and the lack of a link to theory means that much work is left to be done. Greenberg states that when research on criminal careers "is conducted with greater attention to procedures that do not bias the research in favor of one model over the other, I predict that both positions will require modification."[85]

When asked to write a comment on the debate concerning the two models for approaching the study of criminal careers, one professor said, "I responded that this would be somewhat like trying to referee a fight between King Kong and Godzilla—with a substantial likelihood of being crushed in the middle, regardless of what I say." He proceeded to suggest some ways to move beyond the current debate,[86] but thus far no consensus has been reached.

In terms of policy, however, it is being assumed that repeat offenders are different from other offenders and that they should be punished more severely. The issues surrounding the enhancement of penalties for repeat offenders are discussed further in Chapter 13.

SUMMARY

This chapter explores the most prevalent property crimes historically and currently. It begins with a look at the index offense property crimes as defined by the FBI's *Uniform Crime Reports:* burglary, larceny-theft, motor vehicle theft, and arson.

Burglary is a common law crime with a fascinating history, which is necessary for a complete understanding of the treatment of this serious property crime today. Burglary has been studied by sociologists, but since many burglars are repeat offenders, frequently the analysis of this crime is included within studies of career criminals.

Originally larceny-theft was a felony and carried the death penalty. The intricacies of the traditional laws concerning this serious crime are explored historically to see how the law has developed. Larceny-theft remains a serious crime, but it no longer carries the death penalty in the United States, and some of the elements required for the crime have changed. Larceny-theft, however, continues to embody a variety of crimes such as shoplifting. Motor vehicle theft is a serious property crime and one that is committed frequently in the United States, but the clearance rate is so low that it has not permitted significant sociological research on those who commit the crime. Carjacking is a serious but less frequent crime and one that may, and often does, result in violence.

Arson was moved by the FBI from its list of less serious crimes to an index offense status in 1979. That means that data are not available for long-term trends. Estimates suggest that arson is increasing; some saying it is one of the fastest-growing index property crimes.

The second section of the chapter covers some Part II property offenses as defined by the *UCR:* forgery and counterfeiting; buying, receiving, and possessing stolen property; and embezzlement. These crimes may be categorized officially as less serious, but the economic and other losses from these crimes cause some people to consider them more serious than index property crimes.

The section on modern theft crimes is brief as many of these crimes are similar to white-collar crimes and organized crime, discussed in Chapters 9 and 10. More attention is given to the growing number of computer crimes, including cyberstalking, Internet fraud, and identity theft. Since many property crimes do involve career criminals and professional thieves, the final section of the chapter is devoted to the major studies of career criminals. That discussion shows the extent of disagreements among scholars in the field.

Property crimes do not always receive as much popular press as violent crimes because they are less dramatic, but the effect on the American public is significant, and the volume of property crimes far exceeds the volume of violent crimes. Many of the property crimes are subtle in their execution, and unlike common street crimes, they are committed by people with white-collar positions. The importance of these and other crimes related to business organizations makes it necessary to devote an entire chapter to them—Chapter 9.

STUDY QUESTIONS

1. Discuss the historical and current general requirements for establishing that the crime of burglary has occurred.
2. Briefly discuss sociological findings about burglary.
3. Define *larceny-theft* and discuss the historical development of the crime.
4. Has larceny-theft increased or decreased in recent years?
5. What do we know about shoplifting?
6. Did motor vehicle thefts increase or decrease in recent years? What are the characteristics of the most frequent victims of this crime?
7. Why was it necessary to have a federal carjacking statute? Do you think it is effective?
8. State three reasons for motor vehicle theft.
9. Explain why we do not have long-term trend data on arson.
10. List and explain six types of arsonists.
11. Explain briefly the following crimes: forgery; buying, receiving, and possessing stolen property; and embezzlement.
12. Define and give examples of criminal fraud.
13. What is *cybercrime?*
14. Define *cyberstalking.*
15. What are the issues regarding attempts to curb cybercrime and, in particular, cyberstalking?
16. Discuss two major studies of career criminals.

BRIEF ESSAY ASSIGNMENTS

1. Discuss Mary Owen Cameron's findings from her classic study on shoplifting. What two types of shoplifters did she define?
2. Explain Edwin M. Lemert's concept of naive check forgers. According to this concept, why do people commit check forgery?
3. Why might the enactment of statutes against computer crime be ineffective?
4. Describe the characteristics of a professional criminal. What makes a professional criminal different from a full-time criminal?
5. In studies involving incarcerated offenders, why is it important to consider an offender's prior record?

INTERNET ACTIVITIES

1. Go to the Bureau of Justice Statistics website (www.ojp.usdoj.gov/bjs) and find the article entitled "Carjackings in the United States, 1992–1996." How does carjacking differ from motor vehicle theft? According to the findings, how often were weapons used in the crime? What percent of carjackings were committed by a lone offender? How many carjackings resulted in death?
2. Check out the U.S. Department of Justice's Computer Crime and Intellectual Property Section (CCIPS) website at www.cybercrime.gov. This site provides a comprehensive collection of publications, reports, and news updates involving various types of crimes involving intellectual property, computers, and the Internet.

NET RESOURCES

www.atf.treas.gov

The Bureau of Alcohol Tobacco and Firearms (ATF) provides statistics, publications and reports on ATF activities and investigations at its website. In addition to alcohol, tobacco and firearms, this site has information on arson and explosives, the church arson task force, school safety, and the National Integrated Ballistics Information Network (NIBIN).

www.privacyrights.org/identity.htm

A nonprofit consumer education organization, the Privacy Rights Clearinghouse uses its website to teach consumers how to protect their personal privacy. Topics include financial and Internet privacy, fact sheets, publications, and reports related to identity theft. Links to other sites concerning identity theft are also provided.

www.fraud.org

Maintained by the National Consumer's League, the National Fraud Information Center provides information on fraud against businesses and the elderly, and Internet and telemarketing fraud. Users can also access statistics, reports, fraud alerts, and additional links on fraud.

www.ckfraud.org

The National Check Fraud Center is a comprehensive site that includes links and data for topics ranging from counterfeit checks and check fraud to forgery and white-collar crimes. A section on recent news media coverage pertaining to these crimes is provided.

www.ustreas.gov/fincen — Maintained by the U.S. Department of the Treasury, the site for the Financial Crimes Enforcement Network is designed as a network to address the problems of both domestic and international money laundering. Law enforcement, regulatory actions, international issues, and publications comprise the topic areas for the site.

www.cert.org — The Computer Emergency Response Team addresses Internet, network, and computer security issues through reports, statistics, and publications from staff at the Software Engineering Institute, a development center operated by the Carnegie Mellon University.

www.ojp.usdoj.gov/ovc — The United States Department of Justice Office for Victims of Crime provides sources and information on victimization from several types of crimes on its website. In addition to a site search engine, this site offers speeches, press releases, updates, and publications all pertaining to criminal victimization.

www.cfenet.com — The Association of Certified Fraud Examiners is a professional organization that provides resources, a media center, and links concerning the detection, investigation, and deterrence of fraud and white-collar crime. Users can obtain up-to-date headlines and order free newsletters from the site.

ENDNOTES

1. Rollin M. Perkins, *Criminal Law,* 3d ed. (Mineola, NY: Foundation Press, 1982), p. 289.
2. For a discussion of the historical development of the law of burglary, see Wayne R. LaFave and Austin W. Scott Jr., *Criminal Law,* 2d ed. (St. Paul, MN: West, 1986), pp. 702–6, from which this summary was taken.
3. New York Penal Code, Sections 140.20–140.30 (2001).
4. Maine Rev. Stats, Title 17-A, Section 401 (2001).
5. People v. Salemme, 3 Cal.Rptr.2d 398 (Cal.App.3d Dist. 1992), *review denied,* 1992 Cal. LEXIS 1617 (Cal. 1992), quoting a previous case; emphasis in the original.
6. Federal Bureau of Investigation, *Crime in the United States: Uniform Crime Reports 2000* (Washington, DC: U.S. Department of Justice, 2001), pp. 42–45.
7. Gwynn Nettler, *Lying, Cheating, Stealing* (Cincinnati, OH: Anderson, 1982), p. 109.
8. Neal Shover, *Burglary as an Occupation,* Ph.D. dissertation (Urbana-Champaign: University of Illinois Department of Sociology, 1971).
9. Richard Wright et al., "A Snowball's Chance in Hell: Doing Fieldwork with Active Residential Burglars," *Journal of Research in Crime and Delinquency* 29 (May 1992): 148–61.
10. Paul F. Cromwell et al., *Breaking and Entering: An Ethnographic Analysis of Burglary* (Newbury Park, CA: Sage, 1991), p. 40.
11. Matthew B. Robinson, "From Research to Policy: Preventing Residential Burglary through a Systems Approach," *American Journal of Criminal Justice* 24 (Spring 2000): 169–79; quotation is from p. 178.
12. Lance Hannon and James DeFronzo, "Welfare and Property Crime," *Justice Quarterly* 15 (June 1998): 273–88; quotation is from p. 284.
13. *Uniform Crime Reports 2000,* p. 46.
14. Perkins, *Criminal Law,* 3d ed., p. 291. For a history of the development of the law of theft, see Jerome Hall, *Theft, Law and Society,* rev. ed. (Indianapolis: Bobbs-Merrill, 1952), Chapters 1–4.
15. *Uniform Crime Reports 2000,* pp. 46–47.
16. Ibid., pp. 50, 51.
17. Ibid., p. 47.
18. "Shoplifting Has Enormous Costs," *San Diego Union-Tribune* (5 May 2001), p. 3E.
19. Jo Ann Ray, "Every Twelfth Shopper: Who Shoplifts and Why?" *Social Casework* 68 (April 1987): 234–39.
20. "Profile of the Average Shoplifter," *Miami Herald* (7 July 1995), p. 1C.
21. "Shoplifting: Retailers Lose $25 Million a Day to Fast-Growing Crime," *Tallahassee Democrat* (8 April 1990), p. 1E; "Sensormatic Corp.'s Electronic Security Tags Reaping Huge Sales," *Los Angeles Times* (13 April 1994), p. 7D.
22. Mary Owen Cameron, "An Interpretation of Shoplifting," in *Criminal Behavior Systems: A Typology,* ed. Marshall B. Clinard and Richard Quinney (New York: Holt, Rinehart & Winston, 1967; Cincinnati, OH: Anderson, 1986), p. 109; reprinted from Mary Owen Cameron, *The Booster and the Snitch: Department Store Shoplifting* (New York: Free Press, 1964).
23. *Uniform Crime Reports 2000,* pp. 53, 55.
24. "Offenders Consider Car Theft a Low-Tech, Lucrative Crime," *Criminal Justice Newsletter* 21 (1 November 1996), p. 5.
25. "Teamwork Reducing Newark Car Thievery," *New York Times* (7 May 1998), p. 31.
26. "FBI Announces Plans for Anti-Carjacking Task Forces," *Criminal Justice Newsletter* 23 (1 September 1992): 5.
27. United States v. Bishop, 66 F.3d 569 (3d Cir. 1995), *cert. denied,* 516 U.S. 1066 (1996). The Anti Car Theft Act of 1992 is codified at U.S. Code, Title 18, Section 2119 (2001).
28. Charles McCaghy et al., "Auto Theft," *Criminology* 15 (November 1977): 367–81.
29. *Uniform Crime Reports 2000,* p. 56.
30. Ibid., pp. 57–58.
31. "Happy Land Arsonist Sentenced to 25 Years to Life for 87 Deaths," *New York Times* (20 September 1991), p. 12B.
32. "Kids Are Getting a Taste for Arson," *Tallahassee Democrat* (20 January 1996), p. 1; "Juveniles Lead in Arson Cases," *Pittsburgh Post-Gazette* (20 January 1996), p. 5; *Uniform Crime Reports 2000,* p. 58.
33. James P. Brady, "Arson, Fiscal Crisis, and Community Action: Dialectics of an Urban Crime and Popular Response," *Crime & Delinquency* 28 (April 1982): 247–70.
34. Nolan D. C. Lewis and Helen Yarnell, *Pathological Firesetting (Pyromania)* (New York:

Nervous and Mental Disease Monographs, 1951), and James A. Inciardi, "The Adult Firesetter: A Typology," *Criminology* 8 (August 1970): 145–55.

35. Edwin M. Lemert, "An Isolation and Closure Theory of Naive Check Forgery," *Journal of Criminal Law, Criminology and Police Science* 44 (September/October 1953): 301–4. See also Norman S. Hayner, "Characteristics of Five Offender Types," *American Sociological Review* 16 (February 1961): 96–102.
36. Darrell J. Steffensmeier, *The Fence: In the Shadow of Two Worlds* (Totowa, NJ: Rowman & Littlefield, 1986). See also Marilyn E. Walsh, *The Fence: A New Look at the World of Property Theft* (Westport, CT: Greenwood Press, 1977).
37. Shover, *Burglary as an Occupation,* p. 152.
38. Paul F. Cromwell and Karen McElrath, "Buying Stolen Property: An Opportunity Perspective," *Journal of Research in Crime and Delinquency* 31 (August 1994): 295–310; quotation is from p. 306.
39. Louis B. Schwartz, "Theft," in *Encyclopedia of Crime and Justice,* vol. 4, ed. Sanford Kadish (New York: Macmillan, 1984), p. 1544.
40. Cal. Penal Code, Section 484 (2001).
41. "Card Thieves May Have Your Number," *Miami Herald* (3 June 1995), p. 1B.
42. "A New Target for Thieves: Silicon Chips," *New York Times* (21 May 1995), p. 11.
43. "Top DOJ Official Outlines Priority List to Combat Cybercrime," 2001 Industry Standard Communications Inc. The Industry Standard.com (25 June 2001).
44. "Guarding Against Cybercrime: Technology Fair Addresses Attacks of Hackers, Viruses," *(Norfolk) Virginian-Pilot* (22 June 2001), p. 1D.
45. "Law Needs to Catch Up with Thieves," *Dayton Daily News* (9 June 2001), p. 1.
46. "Identity Thieves in Information Age: Rise of Online Data Brokers Makes Criminal Impersonation Easier," *Washington Post* (31 May 2001), p. 1.
47. *Cyberstalking: A New Challenge for Law Enforcement and Industry: A Report from the Attorney General to the Vice President,* available on the Internet at www.usdoj/ag/cyberstalkingreport.htm.
48. "Computer Stalking Case a First for California," *New York Times* (25 January 1999).
49. Cal. Penal Code, Section 646.9(g) (2001).
50. August Bequai, *Computer Crime* (Lexington, MA: D. C. Heath, 1978), p. 4.
51. Discussed in National Criminal Justice Information and Statistics Service, *Computer Crime: Criminal Resource Manual* (Washington, DC: U.S. Government Printing Office, 1979), pp. 9–29.
52. U.S. Code, Title 18, Section 1030 (2001).
53. "New Breed of Hacker Breaking and Entering on Internet," *Miami Herald* (24 January 1995), p. 1.
54. "Protecting Firm from Hackers Doesn't Need to Cost a Fortune," *Broward Daily Business Review* (2 May 2001), p. 9.
55. For a more complete discussion of these issues, along with numerous citations of sociological works on professional criminals, see Gregory R. Staats, "Changing Conceptualizations of Professional Criminals: Implications for Criminology Theory," *Criminology* 15 (May 1977): 49–65.
56. Edwin H. Sutherland, *The Professional Thief* (Chicago: University of Chicago Press, 1937).
57. For an example of some of the earlier works, see David Maurer: *The Big Con* (New York: Signet, 1962); and *Wiz Mob: A Correlation of the Technical Argot of Pickpockets with Their Behavior Pattern* (Gainesville, FL: American Dialect Society, 1955).
58. Leroy Gould et al., *Crime as a Profession* (Washington, DC: U.S. Government Printing Office), cited in Staats, "Changing Conceptualizations of Professional Criminals," p. 60.
59. Shover, *Burglary as an Occupation,* p. 194, emphasis in the original.
60. Neal Shover, "Burglary," in *Crime and Justice: A Review of Research,* vol. 14, ed. Michael Tonry (Chicago: University of Chicago Press, 1991), p. 92.
61. Don C. Gibbons, *Society, Crime, and Criminal Careers: An Introduction to Criminology,* 4th ed. (Englewood Cliffs, NJ: Prentice Hall, 1983), p. 279.
62. For a general discussion, see Gibbons, Ibid., pp. 284–88.
63. Marvin E. Wolfgang et al., *Delinquency in a Birth Cohort* (Chicago: University of Chicago Press, 1972). See also Marvin E. Wolfgang et al., *From Boy to Man, from Delinquency to Crime* (Chicago: University of Chicago Press, 1987).
64. See Marvin E. Wolfgang, "Delinquency in a Birth Cohort II: Some Preliminary Results." Paper prepared for the Attorney General's Task Force on Violent Crime, Chicago, Illinois, 17 June 1982, cited in Patrick A. Langan and Lawrence A. Greenfeld, Bureau of Justice Statistics, *Career Patterns in Crime* (Washington, DC: U.S. Department of Justice, June 1983), p. 2.
65. See, for example, Lyle W. Shannon, *Assessing the Relationship of Adult Criminal Careers to Juvenile Careers* (Iowa City: Iowa Urban Community Research Center, University of Iowa, 1981).
66. See Jan Chaiken et al., *Varieties of Criminal Behavior: Summary and Policy Implications* (Santa Monica, CA: Rand Corporation, 1982).
67. See Alfred Blumstein et al., "Delinquency Careers: Innocents, Desisters, and Persisters," in *Crime and Justice: An Annual Review of Research,* vol. 6, ed. Michael Tonry and Norval Morris (Chicago: University of Chicago, 1985), pp. 187–219.
68. Michael Gottfredson and Travis Hirschi, "Career Criminals and Selective Incapacitation," in *Controversial Issues in Crime and Justice,* ed. Joseph E. Scott and Travis Hirschi (Newbury Park, CA: Sage, 1988), p. 291.
69. Allan F. Abrahamse et al., "An Experimental Evaluation of the Phoenix Repeat Offender Program," *Justice Quarterly* 8 (June 1991): 141–68; quotation is from p. 143.
70. Marcia Chaiken and Jan Chaiken, *Redefining the Career Criminal: Priority Prosecution of High-Rate, Dangerous Offenders* (Washington, DC: U.S. Department of Justice, National Institute of Justice, 1990).
71. See Mark A. Peterson et al., *Who Commits Crimes: A Survey of Prison Inmates* (Cambridge, MA: Oelgeschlager, Gunn & Hain, 1981).
72. Peter W. Greenwood with Allan Abraham, *Selective Incapacitation,* prepared for the National Institute of Justice (Santa Monica, CA: Rand Corporation, 1982), p. 19.
73. Jan Chaiken et al., *Varieties of Criminal Behavior,* pp. v, vi, vii.
74. Mark A. Peterson et al., *Doing Crime: A Survey of California Prison Inmates* (Santa Monica, CA: Rand Corporation, 1980), pp. vii-xii.
75. Julie Horney and Ineke Haen Marshall, "An Experimental Comparison of Two Self-Report Methods for Measuring Lambda," *Journal of Research in Crime and Delinquency* 29 (February 1992): 102–21; quotation is from p. 117.
76. Langan and Greenfeld, *Career Patterns in Crime.*
77. Lawrence Sherman, *Repeat Offenders,* National Institute of Justice (Washington, DC: U.S. Department of Justice, 1989), p. 3.
78. Alfred S. Regnery, quoted in the Introduction to Donna Martin Hamparian et al., *Young Criminal Years of the Violent Few* (Washington, DC: U.S. Department of Justice, June 1985).
79. Hamparian, ibid., p. 22.
80. Michael Gottfredson and Travis Hirschi, *A General Theory of Crime* (Stanford, CA: Stanford University Press, 1990), p. 241.
81. Alfred Blumstein et al., "Delinquency Careers: Innocents, Desisters, and Persisters," in *Crime and Justice: An Annual Review of Research,* vol. 6, ed. Tonry and Morris, pp. 187–219.
82. Arnold Barnett et al., "Not All Criminal Career Models Are Equally Valid," *Criminology* 30 (February 1992): 133–40; quotation is from p. 133.
83. David F. Greenberg, "Modeling Criminal Careers," *Criminology* 29 (February 1991): 17–46; quotation is from pp. 17–18.
84. Barnett et al., "Not All Criminal Career Models Are Equally Valid," p. 138.
85. David F. Greenberg, "Comparing Criminal Career Models," *Criminology* 30 (February 1992): 141–47; quotation is from p. 144.
86. Kenneth Land, "Models of Criminal Careers: Some Suggestions for Moving Beyond the Current Debate," *Criminology* 30 (February 1992): 149.

CHAPTER 9

▶View of the logo outside Enron Headquarters in Houston, Texas. The company collapsed and, along with its auditors at the Arthur Andersen auditing firm, members of the Enron board are being investigated for allegations of insider trading and other offenses. Enron employees lost their jobs as well as their retirement accounts consisting of stock in the company. (© Greg Smith/Corbis SABA)

Business and Government-Related Crimes

OUTLINE

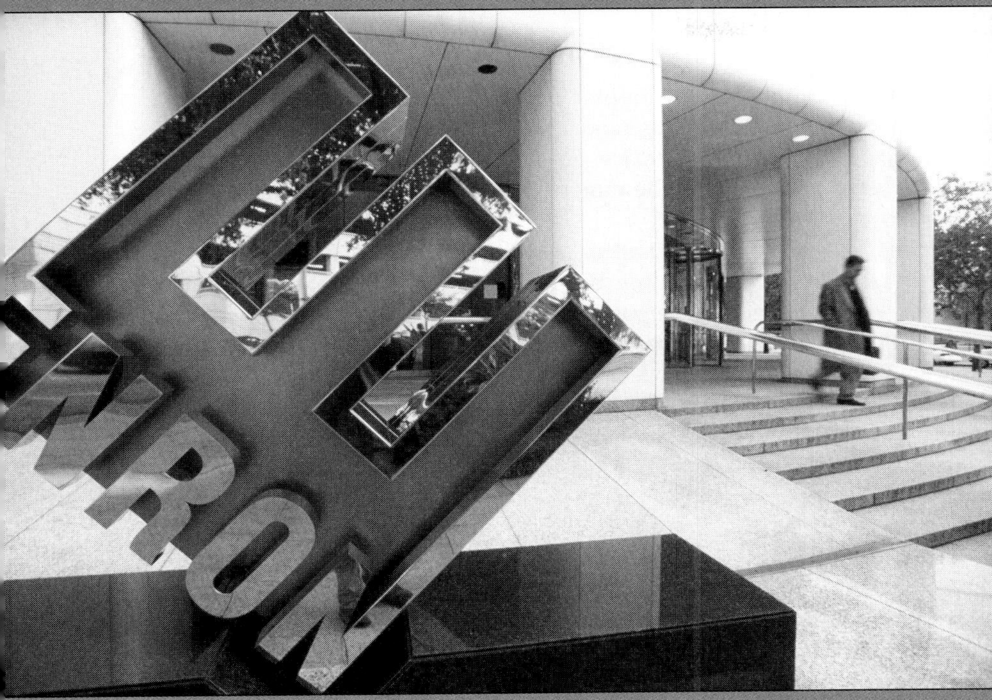

KEY TERMS

Antitrust laws
Blackmail
Bribery
Conspiracy
Contempt
Conversion
Corporate crime
Enterprise liability
Extortion
False advertising
False pretense
Graft
Insider information
Insider trading
Irangate
Obstruction of justice
Official misconduct in office
Pardon
Strict liability
Under color of law
Vicarious liability
Watergate
White-collar crime

This chapter covers crimes committed within business and in government, although many of them may be committed in other contexts as well. Most of the chapter focuses on crimes of the business world. The history of larceny-theft, discussed in Chapter 8, provides a background for this chapter. Many of the business activities that are defined as crimes are not viewed by everyone as crimes but rather as shrewd business transactions, just as they were perceived historically. There is little agreement on the definitions of business (or white-collar) crimes or on how to control these illegal activities. The chapter begins with a discussion of the problem of defining business-related crimes and proceeds to an analysis of the concepts, extent, history, types, research, and issues involved.

In a similar vein, the discussion of government-related crimes covers some acts that previously were considered acceptable or at least overlooked in our society. Today those acts are crimes, and government officials are coming under closer scrutiny in their personal as well as their public lives.

The analysis of types of crime, which began in Chapter 7 with violent crimes and continued in Chapter 8 with ordinary property crimes, proceeds in this chapter to look at business (or white-collar) as well as government-related crimes. These crimes involve property and may involve violence, but they can be distinguished from the violent and property crimes discussed in the previous two chapters.

The crimes discussed in this chapter have less obvious victims than those covered in Chapters 7 and 8. The victims may be individual consumers or the general public. Even when the victim is a particular person, the relationship between the offender and the victim is not always obvious. Business-related crimes differ from ordinary serious property crimes and personal violent crimes in the violation of public trust that is involved in many cases. Likewise, the government-related crimes described in the latter part of this chapter may not have obvious victims, and certainly the violation of public trust is a factor there, too.

However, there are similarities between the crimes discussed in this chapter and those discussed in Chapter 8. In many cases the same kinds of actions are involved. In the past, as we saw in Chapter 8, some of these practices were accepted, even admired; others were considered unethical but not illegal. Today, enhanced technology, combined with the complexity and heterogeneity of business transactions and the inability of individual consumers to protect themselves, has brought about increased regulation of business transactions. Likewise, many actions (private as well as public) of government officials that were acceptable in the past are illegal today. Or if they were illegal in the past, they were virtually ignored. Some of the new regulations of business and the government involve the criminal law; others involve civil or administrative law.

BUSINESS-RELATED CRIMES: AN OVERVIEW

Before looking at specific business-related crimes, it is important to look at problems of defining these crimes. That discussion will be followed by a brief look at the nature and impact of the crimes, a sociological analysis, and the basis of legal liability for business-related crimes.

Definitional Problems

The most difficult problem in analyzing business-related crimes is to define the concept. Social scientists disagree about the best way to categorize crimes associated with occupations and businesses. The most familiar term, *white-collar crime,* is not defined uniformly, as Exhibit 9.1 demonstrates. The term was coined by Edwin H. Sutherland in his 1939 presidential address to the American Sociological Society and developed in a later published work.[1]

White-collar crime The term used to describe violations of the law by persons with higher status; usually the term refers to corporate or individual crimes in connection with businesses or occupations regarded as a legitimate part of society.

By **white-collar crime,** Sutherland meant "a crime committed by a person of respectability and high social status in the course of his occupation." Embezzlement by a banker, illegal sales of alcohol and other drugs, and price fixing by physicians are examples. This definition excludes crimes such as murder, adultery, and intoxication, "since these are not customarily a part of [a person's] occupational procedures. Also, it excludes the confidence games of wealthy members of the underworld, since they are not persons of respectability and high social status."[2]

Sutherland became interested in white-collar crime because most studies of crime were based on samples of institutionalized criminals, who were predominantly poor. Sutherland observed that upper-class people commit crimes but that most of their crimes, particularly those connected with their occupations,

EXHIBIT 9.1

The Nature and Extent of White-Collar Crime

White-collar crime refers to a group of nonviolent crimes that generally involve deception or abuse of power.

There is much debate about how to define "white-collar" crime.

Reiss and Biderman define it as violations of law "that involve the use of a violator's position of significant power, influence or trust . . . for the purpose of illegal gain, or to commit an illegal act for personal or organizational gain." Another researcher, Sutherland, defines white-collar crime as "a crime committed by a person of respectability and high social status in the course of his occupation." Edelhertz defines it as "an illegal act or series of illegal acts committed by nonphysical means and by concealment or guile to obtain money or property, to avoid the payment or loss of money or property, or to obtain business or personal advantage."

Although specific definitions vary, the term is generally construed to include business-related crimes, abuse of political office, some (but not all) aspects of organized crime, and the newly emerging areas of high-technology crime. White-collar crimes often involve deception of a gullible victim and generally occur where an individual's job, power, or personal influence provide the access and opportunity to abuse lawful procedures for unlawful gain.

Specific white-collar crimes include embezzlement, bribery, fraud (including procurement fraud, stock fraud, fraud in government programs, and investment and other "schemes"), theft of services, theft of trade secrets, tax evasion, and obstruction of justice.

Unlike violent crimes, white-collar crimes do not necessarily cause injury to identifiable persons.

White-collar crime instead can cause loss to society in general as in cases of tax evasion, for example. For this reason, white-collar crimes, unlike violent crimes, may not always be detected and are more difficult to investigate.

Little data are available on the extent of white-collar crime.

Measuring white-collar crime presents special problems:

- No uniform definitions exist that define either the overall scope of white-collar crime or individual criminal acts.
- Wide variations in commercial record-keeping procedures make it difficult to collect and classify data on the loss.
- Uncertainty over the legal status of financial and technical transactions complicates the classification of data.
- Computer technology can conceal losses resulting from computer crimes.
- Crimes may not be reported to protect consumer confidence.

Source: Bureau of Justice Statistics, *Report to the Nation on Crime and Justice,* 2d ed. (Washington, DC: U.S. Department of Justice, 1988), p. 9, footnotes and citations omitted.

were not handled by criminal courts. Rather, they were covered by administrative law and processed through administrative agencies. The offenders were not considered criminals and were not included in studies and theories of criminal behavior. Sutherland was not trying to redefine white-collar crime, nor was he saying that we should consider white-collar offenders as criminals and process them in the criminal courts rather than through administrative agencies. He was saying that if we want to know why crimes are committed, it is just as important to study white-collar crimes as it is to study the crimes of those who are processed through the criminal courts and incarcerated in penal institutions.

Sutherland's limitation of white-collar crimes to occupational crimes of the upper class is rejected by most authorities today. In defense of Sutherland's approach, August Bequai emphasized that Sutherland was reacting to the social and economic situation of the 1930s, in which "only the wealthier classes had access to the requisite machinery necessary for the enactment of many of the crimes included in his concept of white-collar crime."[3] With improvements in technology and mass communications, more people have acquired the opportunity to engage in white-collar crime. Bequai argued that instead of defining white-collar criminals by social class, we should define them by the methods they use to commit the crimes. He pointed out that even though white-collar criminals may use force occasionally, they are distinguished primarily from the common felon by "guile, deceit, and concealment."[4]

The definition of *white-collar crime* developed by the Congressional Committee on the Judiciary's Subcommittee on Crime, was as follows: "an illegal act or series of illegal acts committed by nonphysical means and by concealment or guile, to obtain money or property, to avoid the payment or loss of money or property, or to obtain personal or business advantage." This definition was adopted by Congress in the Justice System Improvement Act of 1979, although the statute was later repealed.[5]

Since the crimes that might be included in a definition of white-collar crime are extensive, categorization is difficult. Herbert Edelhertz concludes that the best categorization is to classify the various crimes "by the general environment and motivation of the perpetrator," and for that purpose he suggests the following:

1. Crimes by persons operating on an individual, ad hoc basis, for personal gain in a nonbusiness context . . .
2. Crimes in the course of their occupations by those operating inside businesses, Government, or other establishments, or in a professional capacity, in violation of their duty of loyalty and fidelity to employer or client . . .
3. Crimes incidental to and in furtherance of business operations, but not the central purpose of such business operations . . .
4. White-collar crimes as a business, or as the central activity of the business . . .[6]

Numerous specific crimes may be included within the category of white-collar or business crimes, and in some circumstances it is difficult to draw the line between these crimes and legitimate activities. Most people would agree that the crimes discussed in the first part of this chapter should be included as white-collar crimes, but in some cases the acts might be considered sharp business practice rather than crimes.

Corporate crime An intentional act (or omission of an act when there is a legal duty to act) that violates criminal statutory or case law and that is committed by individuals in a corporate organization for its benefit.

It is important to an understanding of business-related crime that *corporate crime* be distinguished from white-collar crime and other business crimes. **Corporate crime** is a form of white-collar crime, but, unlike the latter, it may involve individuals or small groups of individuals acting within their professional or occupational capacity. Corporate crime is organizational crime that occurs "in the context of extremely complex inter-relationships. . . Here it is the organization, not the occupation, that is of prime importance."[7] A more precise distinction between the two is this:

> If a policymaking corporate executive is acting in the name of the corporation and the individual's decision to violate the law is for the benefit of the corporation, as in price-fixing violations, the violation would constitute corporate crime.
>
> If, on the other hand, the corporate official acts against the corporation, as in the case of embezzlement, and is financing benefits in a personal way from his official connections with the corporation, his acts would constitute white-collar or occupational crime.[8]

Early studies of white-collar crime focused on *individuals* who committed their crimes in secret. The lack of attention to corporate crime may have been due, first, to the complexity of the crimes and of the corporate structure. A thorough understanding of corporate crime requires expertise in areas that have not been a part of the traditional training of social scientists. Second, the regulation of corporate crime is frequently carried out in administrative agencies rather than in courts. Many sociologists and criminologists have not been as familiar with the functions of these agencies as they are with the judicial court process.

Investigation and prosecution of white-collar crime cases have been problems, too. Third, research funds have been more readily available for the study of conventional crime than for corporate crime. Fourth, the public has not been as concerned with white-collar crime as it has been with conventional crime.

Why change the emphasis today from individual white-collar or business crimes to corporate crime? First, the number and size of corporations increased significantly in the 20th century. Today most business activities, along with many social and political activities, are influenced or controlled by corporations. The number of federal and state regulations has increased dramatically, too.

Second, although the media gave little publicity to the prosecution of corporate crimes during the time of Sutherland's studies, that is not the case today. The media give considerable attention to modern business-related crimes, particularly when public officials are involved. Third, the efforts of consumer advocate Ralph Nader and others have had a significant impact on public concern with corporate crime and on the increasing legislative efforts to curb such crime. Fourth, increasing concern with the environment, coupled with the realization that many corporations contribute to its pollution, led to the creation of the federal Environmental Protection Agency (EPA) and to legislation in this area.

A fifth reason for today's focus on corporate crime is the realization that, in concentrating crime control on the poor (which in the 1960s included an emphasis on the eradication of poverty), the crime problem was not being solved. Furthermore, crimes committed by middle- and upper-class persons and by corporations were being ignored. Similarly, the civil rights and prison reform movements of the 1960s and 1970s, along with the short sentences imposed on business and government offenders, focused attention on differential treatment in criminal justice systems. Finally, both Marxist and neo-Marxist writings in criminology have focused on this differential treatment.[9]

Extent and Impact

Estimates of the cost of business-related crimes vary considerably, but clearly the cost—which may be more than $100 billion annually—by far exceeds that of street crime. Furthermore, there is evidence that few of the offenders are prosecuted and that those who are convicted generally receive lighter sentences than other felons do.

Although most of the violent and property crimes discussed in Chapters 7 and 8 are prosecuted and tried in state courts because they involve violations of state statutes, many of the prosecutions of crimes discussed in this and the following chapter occur in federal courts. These cases are prosecuted by U.S. attorneys, who are appointed by the president and confirmed by the Senate. U.S. attorneys report to the U.S. attorney general through the deputy attorney general. They are aided by staff and assistant attorneys, and the numbers of these personnel have almost doubled in the last decade.

U.S. attorneys and their assistant attorneys and staffs handle civil as well as criminal cases. Although the caseload is higher for civil cases than for criminal cases, approximately 62 percent of personnel time is spent on criminal matters. The criminal caseload is more diverse than ever before, including "emotionally charged violent crime and international and domestic terrorism, . . . financial institution fraud, computer fraud and environmental crime, sensitive public corruption and organized crime, organized crime drug enforcement, and cases involving multiple defendants and international organizations." In recent years U.S. attorneys have focused on the following priority areas for criminal prosecutions: violent crime, narcotics, immigration, organized crime, white-collar crime, government regulatory offenses, child support recovery crimes, and civil rights violations.[10]

Another important aspect of white-collar or business-related as well as government-related crimes is the cost to society in terms of the loss of trust and security. This cost was noted often during the scandals caused by President Bill Clinton, who was impeached by the U.S. House of Representatives and tried by the U.S. Senate on charges of perjury and obstruction of justice stemming from his improper behavior with intern Monica Lewinsky and his testimony in the Paula Jones case. (Jones accused Clinton of unwanted sexual advances; that case was settled out of court with no admission of guilt.) The Senate acquitted Clinton of the charges in the Lewinsky case. (This case is discussed further later in this chapter.)

Perhaps the actions and words of the outgoing chair of the Securities and Exchange Commission in 1987, explaining why he donated $20 million to the Harvard Business School for an ethics program, best emphasize the impact on the moral fiber of the country that can result when persons of status and power engage in illegal acts:

> I've been very disturbed most recently with the large numbers of graduates of leading business and law schools who have become convicted felons. Some of those we're bringing cases against are . . . the cream of the crop, and that's what is so shocking and causes concern.[11]

A Sociological Analysis

Despite the difficulties of defining and categorizing business-related crimes, sociologists have identified some characteristics that distinguish offenders in these cases from other offenders. Most often sociologists use the term *white-collar offenders,* noting that they differ primarily in their higher socioeconomic status and their occupational respectability and prestige. Most white-collar offenders do not perceive themselves as criminals but rather as honest people taking advantage of a good business situation. Often, even when they recognize the law-breaking aspect of their behavior, they rationalize it by claiming that the laws either are wrong or do not apply to them. Donald R. Cressey illustrated this self-concept in his study of trust violators, who were able to redefine their positions and convince themselves that their behavior was noncriminal. They were not stealing; they were borrowing. They acted as they did because of unusual circumstances, a financial problem that they could not share with others, and a belief that the only way to solve that problem was through embezzling.[12]

Is white-collar crime learned? Sutherland argued that his theory of differential association (discussed in Chapter 6) was an appropriate theory for explaining the behavior. Sutherland used biographical or autobiographical descriptions as data and noted examples of the "diffusion of criminal practices from one situation to another" as evidence that the theory of differential association is useful in explaining white-collar crime.[13]

Other sociologists have pointed out the relevance of differential association, although Marshall B. Clinard has argued that differential association cannot explain all white-collar crime and that personality factors are important as well. Clinard enumerated such individual personality traits as follows: "egocentricity, emotional insecurity or feelings of personal inadequacy, negative attitudes toward other persons in general, the relative importance of status symbols of money as compared with nationalism, and the relative lack of importance of one's personal, family or business reputation."[14]

Other scholars have examined why some organizational executives comply or do not comply with business regulations and found that four theories offer partial explanations, although not one of them alone is sufficient. Of those four theories—opportunity, control, subculture, and differential association (all discussed in previous chapters of this text)—the one that offered the most explanatory power was opportunity theory (see Chapter 5). The authors called for more research and thinking among scholars about the explanations for white-collar crime.[15]

More recent researchers have challenged the early sociological theorists who tended to analyze white-collar crime and white-collar criminals as separate or distinct from other types of crime and other criminals. Travis Hirschi and Michael R. Gottfredson maintain that it is possible to "outline a general theory of crime capable of organizing the facts about white-collar crime at the same time it is capable of organizing the facts about all forms of crime."[16]

Rather than beginning with offenders, as many theorists do, Hirschi and Gottfredson begin with an analysis of criminal events. They look for the characteristics of criminal events that make all crime attractive to potential offenders. According to Hirschi and Gottfredson, the common characteristics are the avoidance of pain and the seeking of pleasure rather than money, success, or peer approval. To get maximum pleasure, the events must occur immediately, be easy to accomplish, and have a certainty of outcome. White-collar crimes, like other crimes, satisfy these characteristics for those in a position to commit them.[17]

Hirschi and Gottfredson conclude that theories that analyze crime by offender typologies, that is, those that compare rapists to burglars to white-collar criminals, should be replaced by their general theory that analyzes the properties of crime. According to them, "The distinction between crime in the street and crime in the suite is an *offense* rather than an *offender* distinction, that offenders in both cases are likely to share similar characteristics."[18] Their theory is based on a combination of control and opportunity theory. Criminals have low self-control, and when presented with an opportunity to engage in criminal activity, they are more likely to do so than persons with a high level of self-control. Thus, self-control and opportunity are the key variables in explaining crime, including white-collar crime.[19]

Some scholars have rejected Gottfredson and Hirschi's approach. Darrell Steffensmeier questions the two researchers' database (they use official *UCR* data on fraud and forgery) as being unrepresentative of actual white-collar crime. He argued that on the basis of gender, age, and race, the offender characteristics of white-collar criminals differ from those of other criminals.[20]

More recently, other scholars have rejected the Gottfredson/Hirschi theory's implication that, in general, white-collar criminals are as versatile and as prone to deviance as common offenders. Insisting that motivation is a factor in white-collar crime and that its omission in Gottfredson and Hirschi's approach is a mistake, these scholars argue that there are "three paths or routes to white-collar crime along which motives, opportunities, and self-control operate differently." The first is that of persons who are impulsive and who pursue their own selfish interests through fraud whenever the opportunity arises. These white-collar criminals fit the Gottfredson/Hirschi theory; they are like criminals who commit non-white-collar crimes. Persons following this path have high offending rates.

The second route is followed by persons with high self-control who calculate their behavior and act aggressively while engaging in crime in pursuit of ego gratification. In between these two routes are persons whose level of self-control is adequate for most situations but who take advantage of criminal opportunities when they have personal problems, such as financial hardships. The Gottfredson/Hirschi theory, critics say, cannot explain these offenders because it does not account for the influence that different circumstances might have on an individual's behavior.[21]

Another explanation of white-collar crime is seen in an analysis that combines motivation and opportunity theory, concluding that white-collar crime is caused by the coincidence of motivation and opportunity, combined with the neutralization of ethical constraints that might inhibit criminal behavior.[22]

Strict liability Holding a person (or a corporation) legally liable for an action of that person or another even though the actor may not have intended to engage in inappropriate or illegal action.

Vicarious liability The placing of legal liability on one person (or corporation) for the action of another. An example would be to hold the owner of a bar responsible for an employee who sold liquor to an intoxicated person who then drove a car and killed another person.

Enterprise liability The process of holding an entire business enterprise legally liable for an event.

Basis of Legal Liability

The general principles underlying the basis of legal liability for criminal behavior have been discussed. Those principles also apply to the crimes presented in this and the following chapter. In these two chapters, however, we are concerned with some acts that may result in criminal liability for the behavior of others. Several legal theories underscore how this is possible.

First, persons may be convicted of a crime under a theory of **strict liability.** For example, a person who serves or sells liquor to an underage customer may be held criminally liable even if he or she did not know that the customer was underage. Second, under a theory of **vicarious liability,** a person may be held criminally liable for the acts of another person. A bar owner may be held liable for the crime of selling to an underage person even if that crime was committed by an employee and without the knowledge of the owner. Preventing the sale of liquor to minors is important enough to society that its laws govern the liability of those in a position to deter this type of behavior. Third, under the theory of **enterprise liability** (also called corporate liability), corporate officers and officials may in some circumstaces be held criminally liable for the acts of their employees.

TYPES OF BUSINESS-RELATED CRIMES: AN OVERVIEW

There are many criminal acts that may be classified as business-related crimes. Some are committed primarily by individuals acting alone, as in the case of embezzlement; others, such as conspiracy, by definition require more than one person; and still others are committed primarily by corporations. This section briefly discusses several crimes. Others are given more attention in following sections or in Chapter 10.

Statutes criminalizing the acts discussed in this chapter may differ from jurisdiction to jurisdiction, but there are common elements. As noted earlier, many of the prosecutions are in federal courts; thus, federal statutes are used primarily to illustrate the crimes discussed.

Avoidance or Evasion of Income Taxes

Income tax fraud is a crime that may be committed individually or in conspiracy with another. Tax evasion is a crime, defined by the federal statute as follows:

> Any person who willfully attempts in any manner to evade or defeat any tax imposed by this title or the payment thereof shall, in addition to other penalties provided by law, be guilty of a felony and, upon conviction thereof, shall be fined not more than $100,000 ($500,000 in the case of a corporation), or imprisoned not more than five years, or both, together with the costs of prosecution.[23]

Pardon An act by a state governor or the president of the United States that exempts an individual from punishment for a crime he or she committed and removes the legal consequences of the conviction. Pardons may be absolute or conditional; may be individual or granted to a group or class of offenders; or may be full or partial, in which case the pardon remits only part of the punishment or removes some of the legal disabilities resulting from conviction.

Some aspects of this statute and its interpretation should be noted. First, the attempt alone completes the crime; eventual success in avoiding or evading taxes adds nothing to the crime. Second, Congress intended that if willfulness, a tax deficiency, *and* an intent to defeat the tax are proved beyond a reasonable doubt, a felony has been committed.[24] Third, the avoidance or evasion of income tax must be *willful,* not just accidental, to be prosecuted under this statute, and "willfulness may not be inferred solely from proof of understated taxes. A specific intent to evade or defeat the tax must be proved by independent evidence of willful affirmative acts."[25] Some high-profile cases of tax fraud are discussed in Exhibit 9.2, which features, among other issues, the presidential **pardon** of Marc Rich.

EXHIBIT 9.2

Business-Related Crimes: High-Profile Cases

The cases of several high-profile business-related crimes came to light in 2001 as President Bill Clinton issued 176 pardons and clemency orders within hours before he left office in January 2001. The most controversial pardon was that of Marc Rich, a 66-year-old Belgian who became a U.S. citizen but who had been a fugitive from justice for approximately 17 years. A billionaire commodities trader, Rich was accused of fraud, income tax evasion, and other business-related crimes; he fled to Switzerland rather than face criminal charges in the United States. Rich and his partner, Pincus Green, promised to donate $1 million a year to a charity that Rich's former wife, Denise Rich, had started in memory of the Riches' daughter, who died of leukemia shortly after the bitter divorce of her parents. Marc Rich had not previously donated to his wife's charity, which involves cancer research, although he had donated millions to cancer research in Israel. Denise Rich had recently donated $1 million to the Clinton library, and some alleged that the Rich pardon was a payback for that contribution, along with the pledges to contribute to Denise Rich's charity.

Another business-related crime is income tax evasion. There are many ways to commit this crime. One case that captured national attention in the 1990s was that of Harry Helmsley, a New York City real estate titan and his wife, Leona, who gained international attention because of their extensive wealth and lavish lifestyles. The Helmsleys and two of their officials were charged with multiple counts of tax evasion, most of which they effected by diverting money from their businesses to buy lavish furnishings and art objects for their personal use. Deducting personal expenditures as business expenses can result in enormous tax savings, but it is a violation of federal tax law. Included were a $500,000 jade art object and a $45,000 silver clock that Leona Helmsley had commissioned for her husband.

Leona Helmsley was convicted and sentenced to four years in prison, fined $7.1 million, and ordered to pay $2 million in restitution for what the judge called naked greed. Because of his health, Harry Helmsley was declared incompetent to stand trial. Leona Helmsley was not imprisoned until after her 1991 appeal (when her conviction was upheld) and the U.S. Supreme Court refusal to review the case. After serving 21 months in prison, Helmsley was released early to a halfway house in 1995, but she was under orders to perform 250 hours of community service, such as stuffing envelopes and wrapping gifts. Her employees reported that they were forced to perform the community services for her. Helmsley was given 150 additional hours of service. She was released from probation in July 1996.

In July 1995 Steffi Graf, the world's top-ranked female tennis player, was accused of tax evasion and was under investigation by German authorities. In July 1996 Graf paid $2 million in taxes to settle her case.

Source: Summarized from media sources.

Bribery Offering money, goods, services, information, or anything else of value for the purpose of influencing public officials to act in a particular way.

Graft Popularly refers to the corruption of public officials to obtain public money or position fraudulently; the federal statute defines graft narrowly as the offering, giving, soliciting, or receiving of anything of value in connection with the procurement of materials under a federal defense program.

Bribery and Extortion

Historically, **bribery** was defined as corruption in the administration of justice. The modern concept of bribery includes the voluntary gift or receipt of anything of value, in corrupt payment for an official act already done or to be done, or with the corrupt intent to influence the action of a public official or any person involved with the administration of public affairs. The federal statute in this area covers bribery and **graft,** which is defined as the offering, giving, soliciting, or receiving of anything of value in connection with the procurement of materials under a federal defense program. The crime does not require proof of an intent to influence the transaction improperly.[26]

State bribery statutes vary but may include the receiving or soliciting, as well as the giving or offering, of a bribe. Bribery statutes are not broad in scope, and generally courts limit bribery to actions within the official capacity of the public servant.

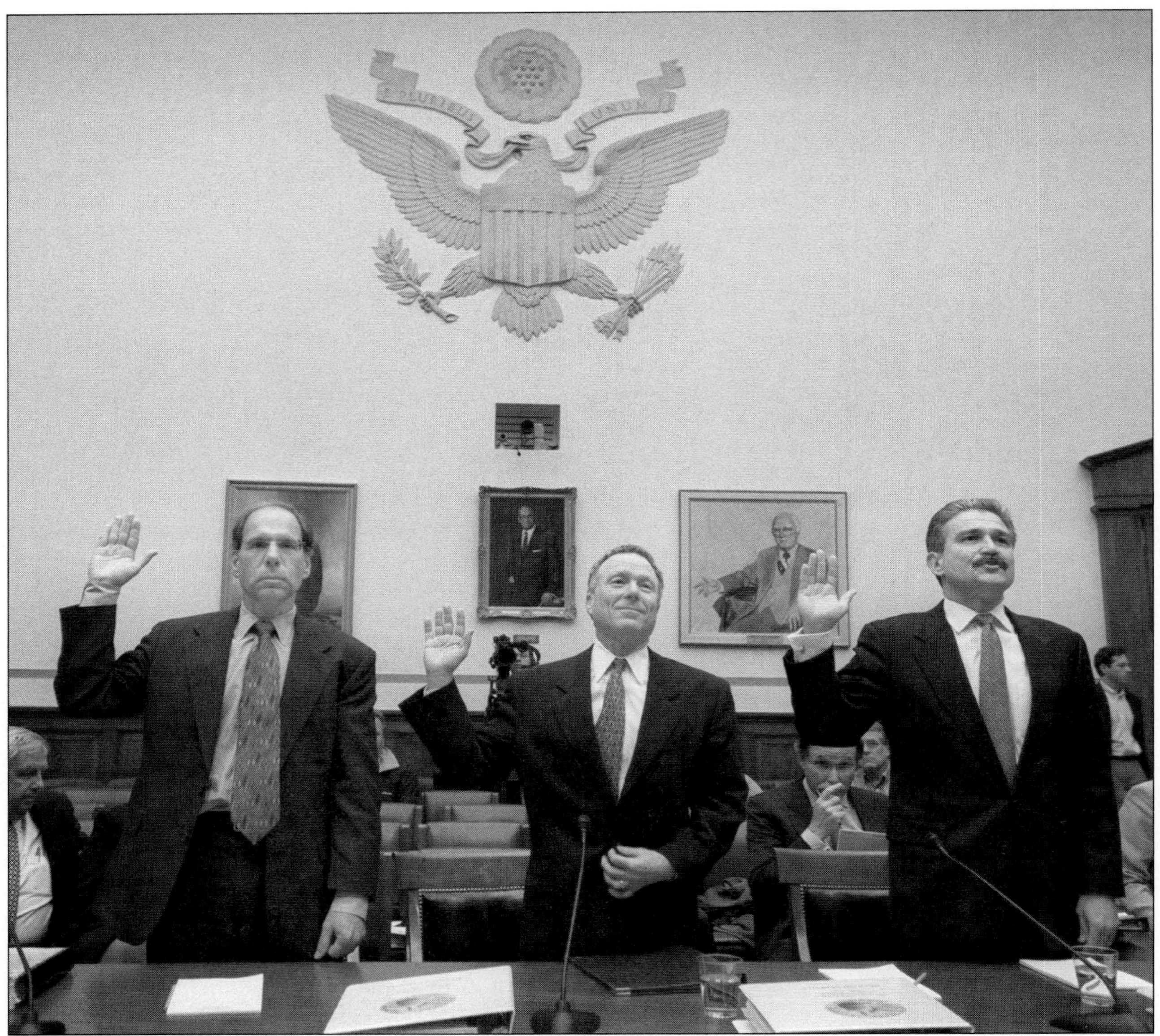

Marc Rich attorney Robert Fink (left), former Marc Rich attorney and current U.S. vice president Richard Cheney's chief-of-staff Lewis Libby (center), and Rich attorney Peter Kadzik (right) are sworn in prior to testifying before the U.S. House of Representatives Committee on Government Reform 10 March 2001 in Washington, D.C. The committee held hearings into allegations of improper activity in the pardons of Marc Rich before President Bill Clinton left office in January 2001. (AFP/Corbis)

Extortion Obtaining property from another by wrongful use of actual or threatened force, fear, or violence, or the corrupt taking of a fee by a public officer, under color of his or her office, when that fee is not due. *See also* **blackmail.**

Although the two crimes are similar, bribery should be distinguished from **extortion,** or **blackmail,** which refers to obtaining property from others by wrongful use of actual or threatened force, fear, or violence, or the corrupt taking of a fee by a public officer, **under color of law,** when that fee is not due.[27]

National attention was focused on extortion in 1997, when Autumn Jackson and two others were convicted of attempting to extort money from entertainer Bill Cosby. Jackson and her mother claimed that Cosby is Jackson's father. Cosby admitted his relationship with her mother but denied he was Jackson's father. He also admitted that he had given Jackson's mother approximately $100,000 over the years to help her with the child and to keep her from revealing her inti-

Blackmail The unlawful demand of money or property by threatening bodily harm or exposure of information that is disgraceful or criminal. *See also* **extortion.**

Under color of law Inappropriate or illegal action taken by government employees (such as law enforcement officers) while acting under the authority of their government positions.

Conspiracy Agreeing with another to join together for the purpose of committing an unlawful act, or agreeing to use unlawful means to commit an act that would otherwise be lawful. The unlawful act does not have to be committed; the crime of conspiracy involves the *agreement* to do the unlawful act.

mate relationship with Cosby, a married man. The jury convicted Jackson (and two others) after hearing the evidence, including an audiotape on which she could be heard asking for $40 million not to tell her story. The tape was made after Cosby's attorney warned Jackson that she was engaging in extortion.

Jackson was sentenced to 17 months in prison. She served about 14 months before a three-judge panel of an appeals court reversed her conviction. The court ruled that the jury should have been given the option of considering whether Jackson believed that she had a rightful claim to the money in light of her belief all of her life that Cosby is her father. The trial judge had ruled that Jackson's belief was not relevant to whether she engaged in extortion. On a rehearing by the entire court, Jackson's conviction was reinstated. The full court ruled that the jury would have convicted Jackson even with the proper instruction.[28] While she was in prison, Jackson gave birth to twins.

Conspiracy

It is assumed that when people act together in criminal acts they may be more dangerous than when they act alone; thus, statutes have been crafted to punish group actions. **Conspiracy** may involve a crime of violence against a person, such as murder, or a property crime, such as distributing counterfeit money. Persons charged with other specific crimes (such as bribery), may also be charged with conspiracy if there is evidence of the additional elements that constitute conspiracy. They may be convicted of the base crime as well as of conspiracy or only of one of the crimes. For example, Terry Nichols was convicted of federal charges of conspiracy and involuntary manslaughter (rather than murder) for his involvement in the Oklahoma City bombings. He was given a life sentence. Timothy McVeigh was convicted of murder as well as conspiracy, sentenced to death, and executed.

Conspiracy is included in this discussion because in many cases it is combined with the crimes committed within the business setting. In addition, conspiracy is frequently an aspect of cases involving organized crime, discussed in Chapter 10.

Under the common law, *conspiracy* was defined as an agreement between two or more persons to commit an unlawful act or to achieve by unlawful means an act not in itself unlawful. The unlawful acts need not be carried out for conspiracy to occur. Although the word *unlawful* might be interpreted to mean *criminal,* early English and American courts interpreted it to include acts that are "corrupt, dishonest, fraudulent, immoral, and in that sense illegal, and it is in the combination to make use of such practices that the dangers of this offense consist."[29] Thus, conspiracy is a useful tool for prosecutors because it is defined broadly.

Today some jurisdictions specify that the act that is the focus of the alleged conspiracy must be a *crime,* whereas others use the term *unlawful,* and still others specify which crimes (or class of crimes) may form the basis of a conspiracy. For example, New York limits *conspiracy in the first degree* to "conduct constituting a class A felony," which includes only the most serious felonies.[30]

Congress has enacted a general conspiracy statute, but federal criminal law includes a number of specialized conspiracy statutes as well.[31]

Embezzlement

The crime of embezzlement, discussed as a property crime in Chapter 8, involves having rightful possession of the property of another and intending to deprive the owner of that property wrongfully. In the upper-class context, normally embezzlement concerns corporate officers or employees and public officers.

The importance of the element of rightful possession is illustrated by a case in which a municipal building inspector threatened to "make it rough" for a contractor unless the contractor paid one-half the usual inspection fee to him personally. The inspector was convicted, but the court of appeals reversed the conviction, stating that the inspector might be guilty of bribery or extortion but he could not be convicted of embezzlement or the related crime of **conversion** (using another person's property without permission) because he did not obtain the money lawfully. This case illustrates the fact that an act might be prosecuted under any of a number of different criminal statutes, depending on their interpretation.[32]

Conversion The process of using the property or goods of another for one's own use and without permission.

A recent high-profile embezzlement case, which resulted in an 11-week trial, ended in an acquittal for Susan McDougal, friend and former business partner of President Bill Clinton and Senator Hillary Rodham Clinton in the failed Whitewater real estate venture. McDougal was accused of forging checks and credit card receipts to embezzle $50,000 from her former employers, conductor Zubin Mehta and his wife.

McDougal is better known for her refusal to testify concerning her association with the Clintons. Her actions earned her a lengthy jail sentence for **contempt** (the violation of a court order). In March 1999 McDougal did testify at her trial on federal charges of criminal contempt and obstruction of justice stemming from her refusal to answer questions before a federal grand jury investigating the Whitewater venture. In January 2001 President Bill Clinton pardoned McDougal for her crimes associated with Whitewater. In the summer of 2001 she settled her civil claim against the Mehtas for slander and malicious prosecution.

Contempt A legal concept imposed on a person who has violated some court order, such as a refusal to abide by a judge's order to behave in court. Contempt may be civil or criminal.

False Advertising

Statutes covering **false advertising** are aimed at protecting two classes of people: the consumer and the competitor. Federal law requires only that the advertising has the capacity to deceive; some state statutes require an intent to mislead. The federal statute seeks to protect members of the buying public from being duped into purchasing items they do not want or intend to buy; therefore, erroneous descriptions of products are illegal, as is *baiting*. The latter involves advertising an especially low price on a product while intending to sell a higher priced, unadvertised product instead.

False advertising The use of untrue statements or other forms of notice to solicit business from the public.

Insider Trading

Since 1986, when several cases of **insider trading** were prosecuted successfully, the U.S. Justice Department has focused on this crime and has won several large cases. Insider trading exists when officers, directors, and stockholders who hold more than 10 percent of the stock of a corporation listed on a national exchange buy and sell corporate shares. **Insider information** is information known to these officers before it is available to the public. Federal law requires that such transactions be reported monthly to the Securities and Exchange Commission (SEC). This requirement is meant to ensure that insiders are not taking undue advantage of the investing public by trading information that enables them to make large profits on their investments at the expense of other investors.

Insider trading Exists when officers, directors, and stockholders who own more than 10 percent of a corporation's stock that is listed on a national exchange buy and sell corporate shares based on insider information known to the officers before it is available to the public. Federal law requires that such transactions be reported monthly to the Securities and Exchange Commission.

Insider information *See* **insider trading.**

Like most areas of criminal law, the laws covering insider trading have changed rapidly and are complicated. Because there are gray areas, some information may be traded without criminal liability. The Justice Department argued successfully in the 1986 cases, however, that the insiders had gone too far. Most of the cases involved selling information about corporate takeovers. Ira B. Sokolow, a 32-year-old investment banker, was convicted and sentenced to one year and a day in prison and three years' probation after he admitted that he sold information about pending takeovers to Dennis B. Levine, the central figure in the largest illegal insider-trading scheme uncovered at that time. Other young Wall Street investors were convicted and faced civil actions as well.

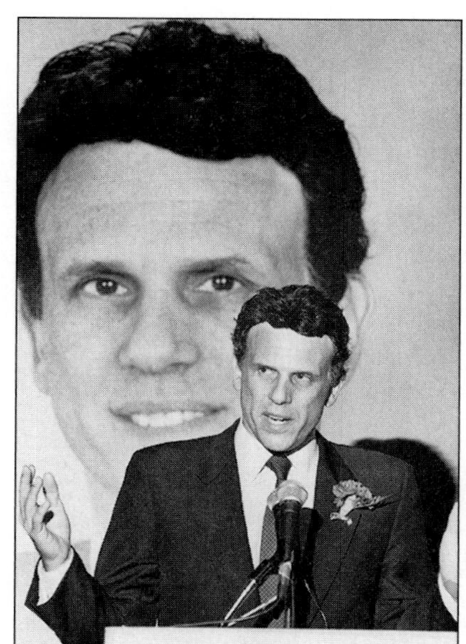

Michael Milken, known for his role in trading junk bonds during the 1980s, stands in front of his own portrait during a speech in 1989 after his conviction on six felony charges stemming from his violation of securities laws. His 10-year sentence was reduced to 2 years, of which he served 22 months before he was released to a halfway house. Milken paid over $1 billion in restitution, fines, penalties, and legal settlements. (UPI/Bettmann/Corbis)

One of the key defendants in the 1986 prosecutions was Ivan F. Boesky, a leading Wall Street stock market speculator who cooperated with federal officials by permitting a secret recording of his conversations with other investors. Boesky agreed to pay a $100 million fine, and to plead guilty to one criminal charge (if others were dropped). Boesky has been barred from the investment business for the rest of his life. He was connected with the insider ring led by Dennis B. Levine, who led the SEC to him. Boesky was released from prison in April 1990. He became a key government witness in cases involving Wall Street scandals.

Michael Milken, the executive who presided over securities firm Drexel Burnham Lambert's junk bond operation, pleaded guilty to six felony counts (none having to do with insider trading; he was indicted on 98 counts) and agreed to pay a $600 million fine. His 10-year prison term was the longest sentence assessed against any defendant in the Wall Street insider trading scandals. Milken entered a federal prison in 1991, but in August 1992 a federal judge reduced his sentence to two years. After serving 22 months in prison, Milken was released to a halfway house in January 1993. Subsequently, he was released on probation, diagnosed with prostate cancer, founded and partially financed the Association for the Cure of Cancer of the Prostate, and appeared to be on the road to rehabilitation as far as criminal activity was concerned. In 1996 his probation was extended while the SEC investigated some of his financial dealings, and in 1997 the government announced that it was focusing on obstruction of justice charges.[33] In March 1998 Milken agreed to pay the SEC $47 million; in exchange, federal prosecutors dropped their investigation into Milken's possible parole violation and terminated his probation.

In the 1970s, junk bonds were not very important in the business world. Most were issued by companies whose previously good credit had deteriorated. The bonds enabled some people to begin or expand businesses, but many companies that went into debt as a result of the junk bonds subsequently failed. Most investors sold off junk bonds, thus driving down the price. Milken bought and sold these bonds, convincing investors that the low prices justified the high risks.

Before President Clinton left office in January 2001, Milken and some of his supporters lobbied for a pardon, noting the significant charitable contributions that Milken had made. Clinton, however, did not grant the request, although he did grant a pardon to Edward Downe Jr., of New York, the former director of a major securities firm who in 1993 pleaded guilty to violating tax and securities laws. Downe was also accused of insider trading that resulted in millions of dollars in profits for his family and friends. Without admitting or denying guilt, Downe agreed to pay the SEC $11 million.[34]

Despite the government's success with prosecutions in the 1980s, many problems arose in the prosecution of insider trading cases. One was that there were no federal statutes aimed specifically at insider trading. Congress attempted to alleviate such problems in 1988 by enacting a statute encompassing insider trading and increasing the penalties that could be assessed for securities violations of this type.[35]

The extent of illegal insider trading is not known, and the government continues to investigate. Repercussions have been felt throughout stock markets in the United States and in Europe. Critics claim that the SEC has gone too far in its interpretations of the law; their opponents argue that these acts are criminal and should be prosecuted vigorously.

Antitrust Violations

Antitrust laws State and federal government statutes designed to protect trade and commerce from unlawful restraints, such as price fixing, price discrimination, and monopolies.

Laws designed to ensure fair competition and free enterprise in the private economic marketplace are known as **antitrust laws.** Historically, the common law attempted to limit restraints on trade and to control monopolies and excessive profits of middlemen. During the second half of the 19th century, Congress expressed concern over abusive practices of large corporations by enacting the Interstate Commerce Act of 1887 and the Sherman Antitrust Act of 1890. The latter has two main provisions:

> Sec. 1: Every contract, combination in the form of trust or otherwise, or conspiracy, in restraint of trade or commerce . . . is declared to be illegal [and is a felony punishable by fine and/or imprisonment]. . .
>
> Sec. 2: Every person who shall monopolize, or attempt to monopolize or combine or conspire with any other person or persons, to monopolize any part of the trade or commerce among the several States, or with foreign nations, shall be deemed guilty of a felony [and is similarly punishable].[36]

The purpose of Section 1 is to prohibit two or more parties from joining together to fix prices. One problem with the court decisions based on this statute, however, is that there is not a clear definition of price fixing. Another difficulty is distinguishing between the legal exchange of information between businesspeople, such as trade associations that disseminate trade news and data, and illegal conduct in the exchange of information that tends to restrain trade unreasonably.

Section 2 of the Sherman Antitrust Act focuses on the control of monopolistic power. Troublesome issues under this section include definitions of the product market, the geographic market, and the market share. The prosecution must prove an illegal purpose and intent along with market structure and power.

The act contains criminal and civil penalties. The U.S. Department of Justice has jurisdiction to prosecute criminal actions, whereas the Federal Trade Commission is limited to administrative and civil jurisdiction. Under the Sherman and Clayton Acts, privately injured parties may sue for treble damages and attorney's fees. Recently, private suits have become increasingly important in antitrust enforcement.

In the fall of 1998 the trial began on antitrust charges filed by the United States against Microsoft concerning allegations that the company founded by Bill Gates "was illegally using its monopoly in operating [computer] system software to gain an unfair advantage in the market for browser software" on the Internet. It was feared, however, that if the government won the suit, the result might be "increased regulation or even a breakup of Microsoft." Microsoft controls approximately 90 percent of the market.[37]

In June 2001 the United States Court of Appeals for the District of Columbia Circuit upheld the district court's "finding of monopoly in its entirety" (specifically, that Miscrosoft violated Section 2 of the Sherman Antitrust Act, reprinted above) but ordered that the district court "must reconsider whether the use of the structural remedy of divestiture is appropriate." The trial court had ordered Microsoft to divide into two companies. The trial judge had made several negative comments about Bill Gates, Microsoft's founder, outside of court. The appellate court chastised the judge for these comments, stating that his ethical violations "were deliberate, repeated, egregious and flagrant," but the court refused to invalidate all of his findings based on these violations. By November 2001, Microsoft and federal prosecutors had reached a settlement agreement, although state prosecutors, who had also filed against the computer giant, were not ready to do likewise.[38]

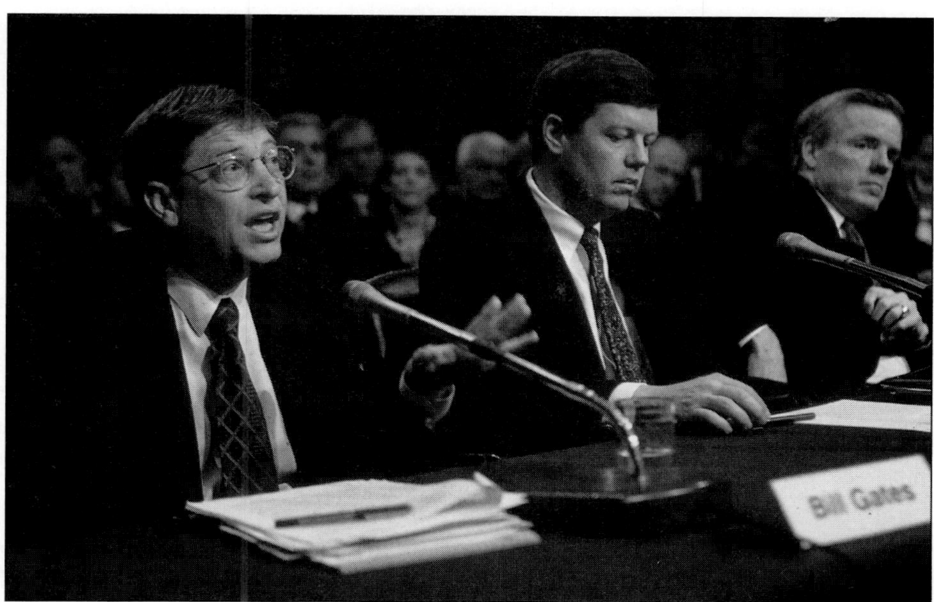

Bill Gates, founder and head of the successful computer company Microsoft, faced antitrust charges in a 1999 trial. In June 2001 a federal court upheld the findings of monoply and ordered the company to divide into two companies. But the court also chastised the trial court judge for some of his inappropriate comments. The federal government and Microsoft reached an agreement by the end of 2001. (Corbis Sygma)

Environmental Crime

For years American industries have been faced with the problem of disposing of hazardous wastes, but in the past two decades the amount of waste has increased dramatically. With that increase has come greater understanding and appreciation of the environmental pollution that results from improper waste disposal. While physical scientists look for better methods of disposal, government agencies wrestle with enforcing the statutes and administrative rules developed to control the problem. Consumer advocates and political activists campaign to alert the public to the hazards of industrial waste and to apply pressure to regulatory agencies charged with the responsibility of enforcing environmental protection laws. Protection of the environment is not without controversy, because regulations to protect the environment may and do conflict with business interests in many cases.

One type of environmental crime involves the improper disposal of toxic waste, which may create hazards for all living creatures and plants. Although medical scientists do not know the extent and nature of the relationship between these hazards and human life and welfare, several health problems such as cancer; genetic mutation, birth defects, and miscarriages; and damage to the lungs, liver, kidneys, or nervous system have been linked to toxic wastes. Contamination of water supplies is one of the greatest hazards of toxic waste.

Most of the attempts to regulate toxic waste disposal involve administrative or civil law. Chapter 1 distinguishes these types of law from criminal law, noting that unless the criminal law is invoked, technically people (and corporations) who violate regulations are not criminals. It may be, as sociologist Edwin H. Sutherland argued, that sociologists should study these violators to develop theories of why people violate regulations and laws, but it is important to distinguish cases brought in the criminal courts from those processed through administrative agencies or civil courts. Unfortunately, this distinction is not always made, which leads people to think that corporations violating administrative regulations or civil laws have violated criminal laws.

There is a question, however, of which type of law—civil, administrative, or criminal—is the most effective regulatory measure. If people suffer property damage and personal injury when regulations and laws are violated, would they be compensated more adequately by filing civil suits against the agency causing the pollution and getting a court order for the agency to discontinue the pollution and pay damages to the victims? Or would society (and individual victims) be compensated more adequately if violators are prosecuted in criminal courts? Or should civil and criminal law be utilized? No one has answered these questions to the satisfaction of most people, but one issue that is critical to an analysis of the question is deterrence. The question of deterrence is relevant to all business crimes, not just corporate crimes.

Congress passed the Comprehensive Environmental Response, Compensation, and Liability Act of 1980 (CERCLA), described as "perhaps the most radical environmental statute in American history." This statute, along with the Resource Conservation and Recovery Act (RCRA), passed in 1976 and subsequently amended, was enacted to provide the Environmental Protection Agency with a mechanism for regulating generation, transportation, disposal, storage, and cleanup of hazardous waste. The RCRA provides civil and criminal penalties for knowing violations.[39]

The existence of statutes providing that environmental pollution is a crime is one issue; enforcing them is another. But the U.S. Department of Justice has increased the number of prosecutions for environmental crimes, and in 1999 a total of 207 years in prison were assessed to defendants convicted of environmental crimes. This was a record number.[40]

Products Liability and Crime

Consumers who are injured by defectively designed, manufactured, or constructed products may sue for damages in civil actions, but the issue for this discussion is whether products liability cases should be prosecuted in criminal courts as well.

On 13 September 1978, Ford Motor Company was indicted by a grand jury in Elkhart, Indiana, for three counts of reckless homicide stemming from the fiery crash of a Ford Pinto that left three teenagers dead. The victims died from burns suffered when the Pinto burst into flames after a low-speed rear-end collision. Although Ford was acquitted on 13 March 1980, this was a pivotal case concerning the criminal liability of corporations for the grossly negligent acts of their employees.

This and other cases illustrate the interrelationship, and often confusion, between civil and criminal law. The families of victims in such cases sued and won large judgments for wrongful deaths, and surviving victims of other such crashes were compensated for their injuries. Some settled out of court; others took their cases to trial. The facts and issues involved are illustrated by the case of Richard Grimshaw, who was 13 when he was a passenger in a Ford Pinto that was rear-ended. The driver of the car was injured and died a few days later. Grimshaw suffered burns over most of his body. He "managed to survive but only through heroic medical measures." He underwent numerous surgeries for skin grafts and was facing another 10 years of surgery at the time his case was appealed. He lost part of several fingers on one hand and portions of his left ear.

Richard Grimshaw brought a civil suit against Ford Motor Company and, after a six-month trial, won a judgment of $12.5 million in compensatory damages and $125 million in punitive damages. Ford's motion for a new trial was denied when Grimshaw accepted a reduction of the punitive award from $125 million to $2.5 million. Ford appealed on a number of legal issues; Grimshaw appealed on other issues. The appellate court upheld the lower court and the judgment stood.

The Pinto represented Ford's attempt in the early 1970s to produce a compact car that would sell for $2,000. The design and production were on a rush schedule. The reasons for considering the design of this car defective are complicated, but at issue was the location of the fuel tank. For design reasons, it was placed behind rather than over the rear axle, as was the custom in other compacts at that time. Because this made the car less crush-resistant, death by fire was more probable in a Pinto than in other compact cars. Evidence revealed that the design defects were known to Ford's corporate executives and that they were warned of the dangers. The cost of adding additional crush space was $15.30 per car, but high-level officials decided to go ahead with the project for cost-saving reasons. The court concluded as follows:[41]

Grimshaw v. Ford Motor Company

Through the results of the crash tests Ford knew that the Pinto's fuel tank and rear structure would expose consumers to serious injury or death in a 20 to 30 mile-per-hour collision. There was evidence that Ford could have corrected the hazardous design defects at minimal cost but decided to defer correction of the shortcomings by engaging in a cost-benefit analysis balancing human lives and limbs against corporate profits. Ford's institutional mentality was shown to be one of callous indifference to public safety. There was substantial evidence that Ford's conduct constituted "conscious disregard" of the probability of injury to members of the consuming public.

The *Grimshaw* case illustrates how gross negligence can be used in a civil suit to award punitive damages to a plaintiff. The fact that Ford was acquitted in the criminal trial does not mean that in a similar case another corporation will not be convicted. Corporations engaging in conduct that is grossly negligent or reckless may find themselves convicted of crimes.

In fact, in December 1999 SabreTech, a corporation dealing with aircraft maintenance, was convicted of charges stemming from the 11 May 1996 fatal crash of a ValuJet Airlines plane. All 110 persons on board the flight from Miami to Atlanta were killed when the plane went down in fire in the Florida Everglades. SabreTech was ordered to pay $11 million in damages to the families of the victims. The company was convicted of improper handling of the hazardous materials that caused the fire in the aircraft.[42]

Defective design and defective manufacture may occur in any product, and the law may provide civil remedies for the injured consumer (or the estate of the deceased). In some cases, if gross negligence or reckless disregard is shown, criminal penalties may be available as well. The same protections extend to other consumer purchases, such as food and drugs. Courts weigh the burden imposed on manufacturers and producers with the need to protect consumers in deciding what type and how much liability to impose.

In a decision involving a company charged with violations of the Federal Food, Drug and Cosmetic Act, the U.S. Supreme Court emphasized the importance of protecting the consumer from adulterated food. In the case before the Court, rats in the company's warehouse contaminated the food. According to the Court, the only defense permitted in these cases is the defendant's evidence that he or she was powerless to correct or prevent the violation.[43]

Workplace Violations

Employers must provide their employees with a safe working environment, but if they do not do this, should they be liable under criminal as well as civil law? The following example illustrates the use of both approaches.

When a fire spread quickly through the chicken-processing plant of the Imperial Food Products, Inc., in Hamlet, North Carolina, in 1991, 25 persons died and 56 were injured. Numerous violations of federal and state requirements were cited, including blocked exits. The owner, Emmett Roe, who was concerned about theft of chicken parts, reportedly ordered the blockage. There were not enough exits for emergencies, and the facility did not have a sprinkler system. Because of these and other violations, Roe was charged with both civil and criminal liability. The insurance company paid $16.1 million in settlements. Roe was convicted of manslaughter and sentenced to 19 years in prison, far less than the maximum of 250 years for 25 counts of manslaughter. The company was fined $808,150 for the violations, which were viewed as willful. Civil lawsuits were filed by survivors against 41 companies whose products within the plant were alleged to have aided the spread of the fire or added toxic products to the smoke.[44] Media reactions to this event are featured in Media Focus 9.1.

In December 1995 the owner of a South Korean mall was sentenced to 10 years in prison after the mall collapsed due to faulty construction and design, killing 501 workers and shoppers and injuring at least 900 others. Victims' families had sought the death penalty. The president of the company (who was also the owner's son) was sentenced to seven years. In addition to their liability for the building, both defendants were found guilty of bribing government officials.[45]

Holding employers and owners criminally liable for the injuries and deaths of their employees (and customers) raises many issues with regard to the lack of security, especially with the increase in violent crimes in the workplace. Workplace violations may also be combined with environmental crimes involving employers, as illustrated by Exhibit 9.3.

This brief overview of some crimes committed within the business world is enhanced by the following section's focus on three areas of fraud and related crimes that have gained attention in recent years.

Media Focus 9.1

The Media and Corporate Crime

In Chapter 9 we discuss Edwin H. Sutherland's contributions to the study of white-collar crime. Sutherland emphasized that most of these crimes are handled by administrative agencies and are not processed through the criminal courts.

More recently, scholars have researched the issue of how the media react to certain crimes of the business world. For example, a scholarly analysis of newspaper coverage of the Imperial Food case discussed in the text illustrates that corporate crime is not always considered *real* crime. Although papers did not attempt to blame the workers or avoid the issue of negligence or the horrors of the injuries and deaths, the articles "showed little consciousness that corporate violence might be seen as a crime." No reports of criminal acts were mentioned until the government took legal action. In other words, the media did not suggest criminal action before such allegations were made. "It was not until the government announced the manslaughter indictments and, in particular, the plea bargain that the criminality of the violence was reported."[1]

1. John P. Wright, Francis T. Cullen, and Michael Blankenship, "The Social Construction of Corporate Violence: Media Coverage of the Imperial Food Products Fire," *Crime and Delinquency* 42 (January 1995): 37–53; quotation is from p. 32.

EXHIBIT 9.3

Workplace Violations and Criminal Law

Employers must provide a safe working environment, but until recently, no criminal action was taken in most cases if they did not do so. In 2000, however, Allan Elias was sentenced to 17 years in prison, the longest term ever assessed to a defendant charged with an environmental crime. Elias was the owner of a chemical-reprocessing facility in a small Idaho town. On 26 August 1996 he ordered 20-year-old Scott Dominguez and other employees, without the benefit of any safety equipment, to clean sludge from the bottom of a 25,000-gallon tank that contained sodium cyanide. Dominguez suffered permanent brain damage as a result of the exposure. In addition to his prison sentence, Elias was ordered to pay Dominguez $5 million in restitution.

Source: "Adding Up Pollution Prosecutions," *National Journal* (21 October 2000), p. 330.

FRAUD AND RELATED CRIMES

The crime of fraud, defined in Chapter 8, refers to the knowing and intentional misrepresentation of circumstances or facts to others with the intention of obtaining money or other items of value, or of inducing another to surrender a legal right. These terms cover a variety of business practices. Fraud-related crimes may be committed by individuals against individuals or by businesses or corporations. We will look at mail and wire fraud, financial institution fraud, and health care fraud.

Mail and Wire Fraud

Most fraud charges are brought in state courts, but the use of mail and wire services has led to the commission of crimes across state lines. Congress therefore enacted the federal fraud statutes to criminalize the use of the postal services or wires to carry out an interstate scheme to defraud people of money or other property rights. The mail fraud statute was passed originally in 1872 and is the oldest of the federal statutes covering crimes traditionally prosecuted in state courts.[46] The wire fraud statute was enacted in 1952.[47]

Because the mail and wire fraud statutes are broad, they are useful to the prosecution in numerous situations, such as the use of the mail or wire to commit bribery, extortion, political corruption, or frauds within business and government settings.

False pretense Representation of some fact or circumstance that is not true and that is meant to mislead the other party.

Federal mail and wire fraud are distinguishable from **false pretense,** which requires a successful effort. Success is not required for a conviction on mail or wire fraud charges.

Financial Institution Fraud

Congress added a federal bank fraud statute in 1984. It was patterned after the mail fraud statute and provides as follows:

> Whoever knowingly executes, or attempts to execute, a scheme or artifice—
> (1) to defraud a financial institution; or
> (2) to obtain any of the moneys, funds, credits, assets, securities, or other property owned by, or under the custody or control of, a financial institution, by means of false or fraudulent pretenses, representations, or promises; shall be fined not more than $1,000,000 or imprisoned not more than thirty years, or both.[48]

This statute includes check kiting (writing checks without sufficient funds), one of the most common forms of bank fraud, as well as crimes associated with the failure of banks and other financial institutions. U.S. attorneys have placed a high priority on prosecuting persons responsible for the failure of savings and loans and other financial institutions. The backlog of cases was so extensive by 1989 that Congress extended the statute of limitations (the time period during which a lawsuit may be filed) for bank fraud and other financial institution offenses from 5 to 10 years.[49]

Government bailouts of the widespread frauds perpetrated on U.S. consumers in the savings and loan industry have cost American taxpayers billions of dollars. Scholars who have analyzed the savings and loan failures note that the environment in which they occurred was ripe for criminal activity. Federal government insurance of the deposits had increased, and little effective oversight was provided by the government for those deposits. Furthermore, there was little risk to the managers, for they were handling other people's money. The situation was ripe for fraud.

Health Care Fraud

Health care fraud, a growing problem in the United States, results in great losses. Federal health care officials estimated in 2001 that health care fraud costs U.S. taxpayers over $25 billion a year and that one-fifth of that total occurs in Miami, Florida. In August 2000 the federal government opened a health care fraud unit in that area. In that month a number of pharmacists, medical equipment firms, and so-called professional patients were indicted for allegedly defrauding Medicare of approximately $3 million through improper billing over a three-year period. The following May six more from Miami were indicted, allegedly involved in the same scheme. Those indicted were charged with a variety of crimes, including false claims, payment or receipt of kickbacks, conspiracy, and money laundering. If convicted, most of the defendants could be sentenced to up to five years in prison, although one may face a 20-year term.[50] Exhibit 9.4 contains other examples of recent cases of health care fraud prosecutions.

Many of the health care frauds occur in Medicare and Medicaid, government health programs. Health care fraud may occur in private health care institutions, but the crime is easier to commit in federal programs due to the size of the programs and the inability of management to respond quickly. It can take months of paperwork to make fast price adjustments in government programs. For example, it took three years for government health programs to reduce payments for home blood glucose monitors from $186 to $59 each, despite the fact that drugstores were selling the products for the lower price. Furthermore, claims processing in government programs can fail to catch these overpayments. It is estimated that *billions* of dollars could be saved if fraud and abuse were curbed in the Medicare and Medicaid programs.

Prosecuting cases of health care fraud is one of the top priorities of U.S. attorneys, who target both civil and criminal fraud committed by both individuals and businesses. In 1999 they issued 371 indictments for health care fraud, a 16 percent increase over those in fiscal year 1998. In 1999 the government recovered over $490 million in health care fraud cases, while Congress appropriated an additional $66 million, which provided 394 new FBI agents plus staff support for this area of prosecution. And in 1998 there were 10 times more suits filed by whistle-blowers than were filed in 1996.[51]

The whistle-blower actions are those brought by informers under a U.S. statute providing that part of the recovered money goes to the person who reports the alleged medical care fraud offenses. In 1999 a $29 million reward was

EXHIBIT 9.4

Health Care Fraud Prosecutions

In recent years U.S. attorneys have focused attention on health care fraud crimes, and they are having increasing success in this area. For example, in the late 1990s a California physician was sentenced to 20 years in prison and ordered to pay $41 million in restitution upon his conviction for fraudulently billing government health care programs as well as private insurance companies. The physician billed for many tests performed on patients whom he diagnosed as gravely ill but who were actually healthy. He billed over $1 billion in fraudulent claims, with over $50 million actually paid.[1]

In the spring of 2001, Dr. Samir S. Najjar, age 53, a Jacksonville, Florida, physician, pleaded guilty to one count of health care fraud and was sentenced to three years in prison and ordered to pay $5 million in restitution. According to a press release from the U.S. attorney's office, Dr. Najjar's "fraudulent schemes included a scheme with local Jacksonville attorneys to fraudulently diagnose over a thousand female patients/clients as suffering from medical problems associated with silicone breast implants in a national class-action lawsuit."[2]

Also in the spring of 2001, Lawrence Friedman, age 53 and the operator of a day care center for the elderly in Brooklyn, New York, pleaded guilty to Medicaid fraud and agreed to pay back $48 million of the money he stole. Among other acts, Friedman billed the government for medical care when he provided social diversions (such as a trip to the movies) to the elderly clients. The judge who sentenced Friedman admonished the state for not auditing Friedman's books, implying that through this negligence the state fostered the fraudulent scheme.[3]

On the corporate front, in the fall of 1998 federal prosecutors filed charges against Columbia/HCA Healthcare (now called HCA—The Healthcare Company), the nation's largest hospital company, alleging that through massive expense-account fraud the corporation had overbilled for programs such as Medicare. In December 2000 the U.S. Department of Justice (DOJ) successfully negotiated its largest settlement in history when Columbia/HCA agreed to pay $745 million in civil damages and penalties and $95 million in criminal fines to settle the government's claims against the national hospital and ancillary health care chain for illegal billing practices and other allegations. In addition, the DOJ negotiated a settlement in its case against the nation's largest hospital management company, Quorum Health Group, which was accused of filing false claims to Medicare. Quorum will pay $85 million to the U.S. government and $2.73 million to the attorney of the whistleblower who brought the allegations to the attention of federal prosecutors.[4]

1. U.S. Department of Justice, *United States Attorney's Annual Statistical Report, Fiscal Year 1996*, p. 29.
2. "U.S. Says Doctor in Breast Implant Scheme Pleads to Health Fraud," *Mealey's Emerging Drugs and Devices* 6, no. 9 (10 May 2001), p. 1.
3. "Man to Pay $48 Million in Medicaid Fraud Scheme," *New York Times* (4 April 2001), p. 12.
4. "Settlement: U.S. *ex rel.* Alderson v. Quorum Health Group," *Health Care Fraud Litigation Reporter* 6 (May 2001), p. 11.

granted to a woman and her lawyer for exposing Medicare fraud at Blue Cross Blue Shield in Illinois.[52]

One U.S. attorney from Massachusetts has proclaimed, "In white-collar crime, this [health care fraud] is certainly the area we have been most active in . . . We have done clinical labs, individual doctors and some national cases . . . There is a fair amount out there to sink your teeth into."[53]

GOVERNMENT-RELATED CRIMES

A variety of crimes may be committed against the government; this section focuses on one: obstruction of justice. Governments may also commit crimes against their citizens. In either case, these crimes may be the same as those discussed in the text thus far, but attention is given here to political crimes, official corruption, and civil rights violations.

Obstruction of justice Interference with the orderly processes of civil and criminal courts, such as refusing to produce evidence, intimidating witnesses, and bribing judges. The crime may be committed by judicial and other officials and might constitute official misconduct in office.

Official misconduct in office Any willful, unlawful behavior by public officials in the course of their official duties. The misconduct may be a failure to act, a wrongful act, or an act that the actor had a right to do but that was performed improperly.

Obstruction of Justice

Some of the crimes discussed previously, such as bribery, may take on additional criminal impact when they are engaged in for the purpose of obstructing justice. Tampering with a jury; intimidating witnesses; bribing or attempting to bribe witnesses, attorneys, judges, or other court personnel; refusing to produce evidence ordered by the court; and refusing to appear when ordered by the court are some of the activities that may constitute **obstruction of justice.** The phrase *obstruction of justice* refers to acts that interfere with the orderly processes of civil and criminal courts. The crime may be committed by judicial and other officials, in which case it might constitute the crime of **official misconduct in office,** which refers to any willful, unlawful behavior by public officials in the course of their official duties. The misconduct may consist of a failure to act or an improperly performed official act. An example of obstruction of justice comes from a case involving two attorneys who tried to convince a convicted drug dealer that on payment of $50,000 they would have his four-year prison sentence reduced to 15 months. The attorneys were convicted and sentenced to five years for each charge, the sentences to be served concurrently. The convictions were upheld on appeal.[54]

Obstruction of justice and other charges were alleged by independent prosecutor Kenneth Starr in the report he delivered to Congress in September 1998 after a four-year investigation of certain alleged activities of President Bill Clinton and others. The report focused on allegations against the president with regard to his "improper relationship" (as Clinton described it) with a White House intern, Monica Lewinsky. The House Judiciary Committee voted for four Articles of Impeachment, which were debated in the full House of Representatives. Clinton was impeached by the House. As noted earlier, he was tried but not convicted by the Senate. The allegations against President Clinton were settled with a plea agreement reached just hours before the president left office. Clinton was investigated, however, for allegations that some of the pardons he issued during his last hours in office may have been improper.

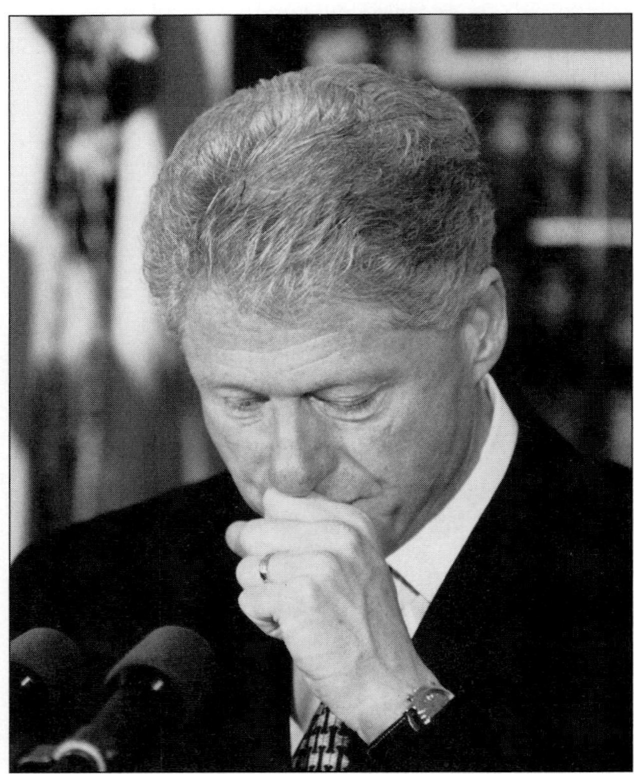

President Bill Clinton was impeached by the U.S. House of Representatives but acquitted by the U.S. Senate on charges of perjury and obstruction of justice stemming from his improper behavior with White House intern Monica Lewinsky and his testimony in the Paula Jones case. Clinton was investigated, but no criminal charges were filed. Clinton was, however, suspended from practicing law in Arkansas and disbarred by the U.S. Supreme Court. (Reuters/Getty Images)

The issue of obstruction of justice arose again in the summer of 2001 after the disappearance of a federal intern, Chandra Levy, in late April. Levy had had an intimate relationship with Gary Condit, the congressman from her hometown in California. Levy was planning to leave Washington to return to California after her internship ended. She canceled her health club membership, cleaned her apartment, and disappeared. There were no signs of foul play or forced entry into her apartment, and it was thought that only her keys were missing. Her purse and identification were found in the apartment. Condit waited about two months before admitting (under pressure) that he had had an intimate relationship with Levy, a single woman.

In the meantime an airline attendant, Anne Marie Smith, who had also allegedly had an affair with Condit, alleged that Condit's office asked her to sign an affidavit stating that she had never had an affair with him. Smith reported this information to the Federal

Bureau of Investigation. It was argued that Condit should be charged with obstructing justice because of his delay in relating the truth about his relationship with Levy as well as his alleged attempts to entice Smith to lie about his relationship with her. As of this writing Levy's case had not been solved. Condit ran for reelection and lost in the primary in February 2002.

Political Crimes and Official Misuse of Power

Watergate A political scandal connected with the Republican White House during the 1972 presidential election campaign. It involved a break-in at the Democratic national headquarters at the Watergate building in Washington, D.C., and eventually led to the resignation of President Richard M. Nixon, the first U.S. president to resign in disgrace. Although Nixon was pardoned by his successor, President Gerald Ford, some of his associates were tried, convicted, and sentenced to prison.

Irangate A term used to refer to the illegal exchange of arms for U.S. hostages in Iran in the 1980s. *See also* **Watergate.**

Until recently, little attention was paid to crimes committed by U.S. government officials against private citizens. This changed after the criminal violations during **Watergate** (the name of the building in which the 1972 break-in at the offices of the Democratic headquarters occurred). The scandal erupted during the administration of President Richard M. Nixon and led to his resignation—he was the first U.S. president to resign in disgrace. Nixon was pardoned by his successor, President Gerald Ford, but some officials in the Nixon administration were indicted, tried, and convicted. Some served prison sentences. The series of events has been described by one writer as follows:

> Watergate revealed that under President Nixon a kind of totalitarianism had already come to America, creeping in . . . in button-down shirts, worn by handsome young advertising and public relations men carrying neat attache cases crammed with $100 bills. Men willing to perjure themselves to stay on the team, to serve their leader. It came in the guise of "national security," a blanket term used to justify the most appalling criminal acts by men determined to preserve their own political power at any cost. It came in the form of the ladder against the bedroom window, miniature transmitters in the ceiling, wiretaps, burglaries, enemies lists, tax audits, and psychiatric profiles.[55]

The Watergate scandal became a symbol of the abuse of power by the government, with part of its name used in subsequent scandals. For example, the Iran-Contra scandal, which began to unfold in 1986, was referred to as **Irangate.** That affair involved numerous allegations concerning the illegal sale of arms to Iran in exchange for the release of U.S. hostages there and the use of some of the profits from those sales to buy arms for the anticommunist Contra rebels in Nicaragua.

Several government officials were convicted of various crimes related to the Iran-Contra scandal. The highest-ranking one, former Central Intelligence Agency (CIA) spy chief Clair E. George, was convicted of lying to Congress. George's first trial ended in a hung jury. Robert G. McFarlane, national security adviser to President Ronald Reagan, and Elliott Abrams, former assistant secretary of state, pleaded guilty to misdemeanor charges of withholding information from Congress. McFarlane was sentenced to two years' probation and 200 hours of community service, along with a $20,000 fine. Abrams was sentenced to two years' probation and 100 hours of community service.

On the same day as Abrams's sentencing, a federal court reversed the five felony convictions against former national security adviser John M. Poindexter. The U.S. Supreme Court refused to hear the case, leaving the appellate court's ruling intact.[56]

A former national security aide, Oliver L. North, also a former Marine Corps lieutenant colonel, captured the nation's attention during his testimony while on trial for numerous counts related to the Iran-Contra affair. North was acquitted of five counts but convicted of aiding and abetting in the obstruction of Congress, falsifying and destroying documents, and accepting an illegal gratuity. He was sentenced to a suspended prison term and a $150,000 fine, placed on probation, and ordered to perform 1,200 hours of community service. A year later one count was reversed by an appeals court that questioned the other counts as well. Subsequently the prosecutor announced that he was dropping all charges against North.[57]

The highest-ranking government official to be indicted in the Iran-Contra affair was Casper W. Weinberger, defense secretary under President Ronald Reagan, who was indicted for lying to Congress. Although one charge against him was dropped, Weinberger was scheduled to go on trial in early January 1993. On 24 December 1992, President George Bush issued pardons for Weinberger, George, McFarlane, Abrams, Alan D. Fiers Jr., and Duane R. Clarridge. Clarridge, a former CIA agent who headed covert CIA operations in Latin America, had been indicted for perjury and making false statements.

Independent counsel Lawrence E. Walsh was furious with President Bush about the pardons, suggesting that the trial of Weinberger would have given prosecutors and the American people the last chance to explore the role that former President Ronald Reagan and then Vice President George Bush may have played in the Iran-Contra scandal. According to Walsh,

> President Bush's pardon of Caspar Weinberger and other Iran-Contra defendants undermines the principle that no man is above the law. It demonstrates that powerful people with powerful allies can commit serious crimes in high office—deliberately abusing the public trust without consequence.[58]

By 1992 the scandal-probing among government officials in Washington, D.C., led one correspondent to state:

> The Justice Department is investigating the FBI. The FBI is investigating the State Department.
>
> The Congress is investigating the White House. And the Central Intelligence Agency, which likes to keep things close to the vest, is investigating itself.[59]

In the summer of 1995 two House subcommittees of Congress investigated the government's 1993 handling of the siege at the Waco, Texas, Branch Davidian compound, and in November 1995 the Senate Judiciary Committee held a two-day hearing to determine what the FBI had done in the intervening years to prevent similar situations. Federal agents from the Bureau of Alcohol, Tobacco and Firearms (ATF) had stormed the 77-acre, heavily fortified cult compound on 28 February 1993. The agents intended to arrest the cult leader, Vernon Howell, also known as David Koresh, on firearms violations. They had arrived in livestock trailers, dressed in black and prepared for a surprise attack. The gunfire from agents and those inside the compound lasted about 45 minutes. Four ATF agents were killed, and many were wounded. Several members of the religious sect within the compound were killed or injured.[60]

FBI agents were called in to assist ATF and local law enforcement agents to lay siege to the compound. On 2 March 1993 Koresh indicated that he and his followers would leave the compound when they received a message from God. Several members, mostly women and children, had been permitted to leave earlier. The week before Easter, Koresh delivered to federal agents a four-page letter he claimed was from God. FBI agents responded that they did not have verification that the message was from God and were trying to get that confirmation. "But if it is the message from God," they said, "then we have to know what the heck the message is." The FBI would not disclose the contents of the communication.[61]

Various other promises were made by Koresh, and in early April he told the FBI that he and his followers would come out after he finished a religious manuscript. Later he asked for word-processing equipment to facilitate his writing.

On 19 April 1993 the 51-day standoff was ended. Federal agents used armored tanks to punch holes in the walls of the compound. Tear gas was injected. According to the FBI, the cult members were told that they should surrender, but they responded instead by firing rounds of gunfire. The compound was set on fire, allegedly at the instruction of Koresh. Only nine members of the cult survived; it was estimated that more than 80 were killed, including 17 children.

Attorney General Janet Reno, in taking responsibility for the attack, stated that the information received by the FBI suggested that the children were in increasing danger from disease and abuse. There was no indication that the cult would commit mass suicide; thus came the decision to move. "Obviously, if I had thought that the chances were great of a mass suicide," Reno said, "I would never have approved the plan."[62]

Not everyone agreed with this government action, however, as the congressional investigations revealed. ATF agents blamed each other, with ATF agent Robert Rodriguez, who had worked undercover at the compound, testifying that he told his bosses that the element of surprise in the February attack was lost and that they lied to the American people about that. Phillip Chojnacki and Chuck Sarabyn, Rodriguez's supervisors, said Rodriguez had not made himself clear and they were not aware that the Davidians knew of their plans. Chojnacki and Sarabyn were fired and then rehired with full benefits and back pay. Director Stephen F. Higgins resigned, but he was not punished, nor did he lose his benefits or pension. He had been with the ATF for 31 years and served as its director since 1983.[63]

At the November 1995 Senate hearings, retired FBI negotiator Clint Van Zandt testified concerning some mistakes admitted by FBI officials. He concluded, "The American people have the right to expect better." The former negotiator told senators that the 1993 Waco siege was "almost beyond repair" when the FBI became involved. He blamed his former colleagues and the ATF for the disaster, stating that the ATF agents "should never have been ordered into such a confrontation."[64]

Also in 1995 Congress held hearings concerning the bloody siege at Ruby Ridge, Idaho, in August 1992, in which government agents shot and killed the 14-year-old son of white separatist Randy Weaver after a fight erupted between the son and officials. FBI agent Lon Horiuchi shot and killed Weaver's wife, who was holding the couple's 10-month-old baby. Another member of the Weaver household was shot and seriously wounded. Horiuchi refused to tesify at the Senate hearings, invoking his Fifth Amendment rights (see Appendix A). At Weaver's trial in Idaho, however, Horiuchi did testify that he fired a shot at Randy Weaver, whom he thought was preparing to shoot at an FBI helicopter (Weaver denied that claim) and that he shot Weaver's wife accidentally. FBI director Louis J. Freeh supported that version of the shooting in his testimony before the congressional hearing. The shooting resulted in the most intensive investigation of the FBI in recent history.[65]

In the Ruby Ridge hearings, U.S. Senator Dianne Feinstein, Democrat from California, asked Freeh whether the FBI had succumbed to a "paramilitary mentality." Freeh said no, but others disagreed. One legal journalist described the Waco and the Ruby Ridge fiascos in these words: "In both . . . the FBI and the ATF dressed up in camouflage and ski-masks and deployed armored vehicles and helicopters to solve problems that, reflection suggests, might well have been solved by making an ordinary arrest."[66]

More recently, FBI officials admitted that the agency had failed to disclose over 4,000 documents to the defense in the Oklahoma City bombing case. The execution of Timothy McVeigh, scheduled for 11 May 2001, was postponed until 11 June 2001 to give the defense time to consider the documents. McVeigh's attorneys argued that the federal government had perpetrated a fraud on the court by not disclosing the documents. Although the matter was being investigated, and the trial judge was critical of the FBI's withholding of evidence, neither that judge nor the appellate court was willing to postpone the execution again. McVeigh decided not to appeal this decision to the U.S. Supreme Court, and he was executed on 11 June. Chapter 12 contains additional discussions of the FBI.

Civil Rights Violations

In recent years attention has been focused on one of the most offensive types of abuse of power by government, the violation of civil rights. After a two-year battle between President George Bush and Congress, a new Civil Rights Act was enacted in November 1991. Among other provisions, the statute reversed or modified some recent Supreme Court decisions that restricted the rights of women and minorities to sue for workplace discrimination.[67] Of relevance here, however, are the violations of civil rights that carry criminal as well as civil penalties.

For years the U.S. Criminal Code has prohibited civil rights violations by government officials. The applicable statute is as follows:

> Whoever, under color of any law, statute, ordinance, regulation, or custom, willfully subjects any inhabitant of any State, Territory, or District to the deprivation of any rights, privileges, or immunities secured or protected by the constitution or laws of the United States, or to different punishments, pains, or penalties, on account of such inhabitant being an alien, or by reason of his color, or race, than are prescribed for the punishment of citizens, shall be fined not more than $1,000 or imprisoned not more than one year, or both; and if death results shall be subject to imprisonment for any term of years or for life.[68]

In a 1968 case involving police brutality, a federal appellate court held that this statute is not limited to cases involving "race, color or alienage." According to the court in *Miller* v. *United States*, "All people regardless of taint or degradation so long as they are inhabitants of a state, territory or district are within the statute's protective embrace. Even suspected criminality or accomplished incarceration furnish no license for the destruction of guaranteed constitutional rights." In *Miller* the defendant police officer had activated his K-9 police dog to attack the suspect for seven or eight minutes.[69]

The four white Los Angeles police officers accused of beating Rodney King during his 1991 arrest were tried for violation of King's federal civil rights after they were acquitted of charges in a state trial. Three of the officers were charged with beating King for 81 seconds, and the fourth, Sergeant Stacey Koon, with failure to restrain the three officers. Two of the officers (Timothy Wind and Ted Briseno) were acquitted. Laurence Powell and Stacey Koon were found guilty and sentenced to 30 months in prison. A federal appeals court upheld the convictions but ordered the trial court to reconsider the sentences, which were shorter than the guideline sentences for their offenses. Koon and Powell appealed to the U.S. Supreme Court, which upheld the principle of judicial discretion under the federal guidelines. The Court agreed with the lower court's decision to lower the sentence because of the victim's misconduct in the incident, the susceptibility the defendants would have to abuse by other inmates, and the burdens they had sustained with successive prosecutions (state and federal). The Court reversed and remanded the case for reconsideration because it abused its discretion "in relying on the other two factors . . . career loss and low recidivism risk." The lower court did not impose longer sentences when it reconsidered the case.[70]

Numerous other examples of police mistreatment of citizens have come to light in recent years. Of particular note are two in New York City. In 1999 Justin

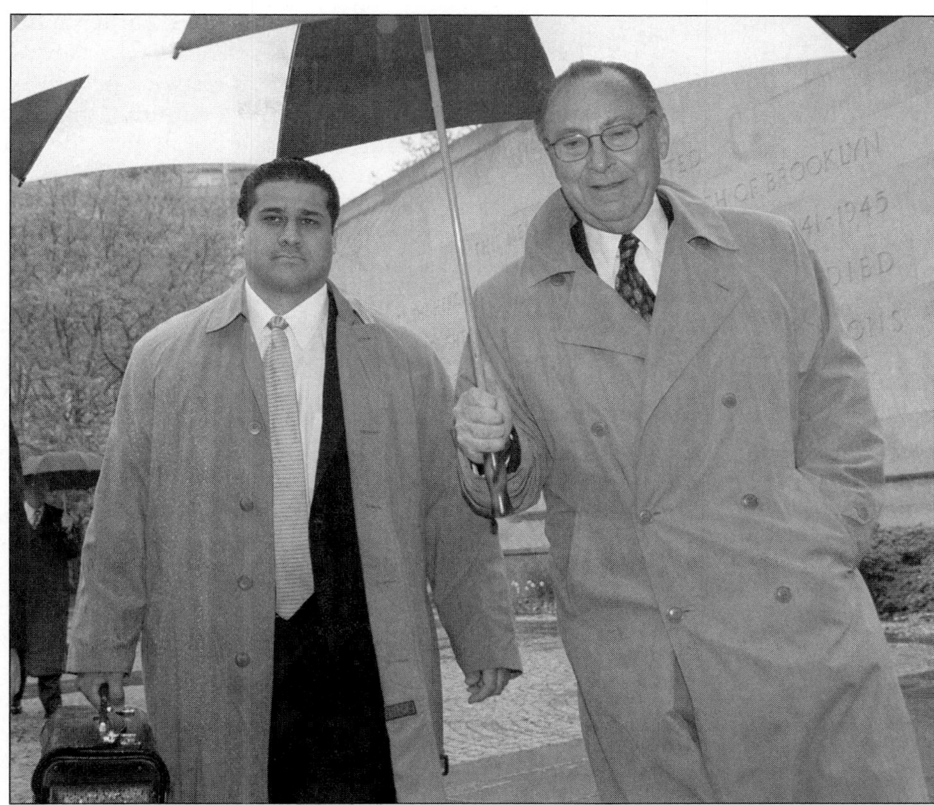

Justin A. Volpe, former New York City police officer, with his attorney before entering a guilty plea for the charge of beating and sodomizing Haitian immigrant Abner Louima. Volpe entered the plea after the trial began and damaging testimony was introduced. Volpe was sentenced to 30 years in prison. (© AFP/Corbis)

A. Volpe pleaded guilty to sodomizing Abner Louima, a Haitian immigrant, and threatening to kill Louima if he reported the incident. Volpe was sentenced to 30 years in prison. In 2001 Louima accepted an $8.7 million settlement of his claims against the city for this brutality.[71]

In 2000 a jury acquitted four white New York City police officers who fired 41 times, killing an unarmed West African immigrant, Amadou Diallo. An anonymous juror reported that the prosecution did not prove its case beyond a reasonable doubt. In 2001 Diallo's mother criticized the police department for permitting the four officers to return to their jobs.[72]

CONTROLLING BUSINESS AND GOVERNMENT-RELATED CRIMES

The sampling of business and government-related crimes in this chapter pertains to those that may be committed by individuals in a business or government setting or by executives acting on behalf of the corporation. One issue in analyzing government or business-related crimes is whether the civil or criminal law should be invoked. Another is whether corporate managers should be held criminally liable for the actions of their employees or whether the civil law is sufficient for these cases.

Chapter 1 distinguishes between criminal and civil law and notes that in some cases corporations (or noncorporate employers) may be held criminally liable for the acts of their employees. Earlier in this chapter we discussed Sutherland's argument that social scientists who study crime should include violators of white-collar crimes in their research even if those violations are handled by administrative agencies or by civil rather than criminal courts.

It is important to keep in mind that the issue is not whether we should attempt to prevent or regulate business and government-related crimes but which is the best method for doing so. Deciding that the civil law is the best response does not mean that the misconduct is considered less serious; it simply means that the civil law is perceived as the best method of control. Criminal charges are hard to prove; negligence is easier. Civil and criminal law are not mutually exclusive, but we must consider the costs in time, attorney fees, and court personnel that are involved in an unsuccessful criminal prosecution. It is important as well to understand that administrative regulation may be more effective than either the civil or the criminal law in controlling corporate conduct.

In the final analysis, business-related crimes are a lot like other crimes:

> Although they differ systematically from common-crime offenses, the white-collar crimes committed by those we studied have a mundane, common, every-day character. Their basic ingredients are lying, cheating and fraud, and for every truly complicated and rarefied offense there are many others that are simple and could be carried out by almost anyone who can read, write, and give an outward appearance of stability.[73]

Regardless of what we think about sentencing those who break the statutes discussed in this chapter, as compared to those who commit traditional property and violent crimes, new sentencing provisions for white-collar criminals went into effect in November 1991 upon recommendation of the U.S. Sentencing Commission, an independent administrative agency within the federal judiciary. (The commission and its purpose are discussed in Chapter 13.) According to the commission, the purpose of these guidelines is to provide just and adequate deterrence, the same purpose that is behind the sentencing guidelines for other crimes. The commission added one new purpose that is not a part of its guidelines for other crimes. The guidelines contain incentives for corporations and other organizations to develop internal mechanisms for "preventing and detecting criminal conduct." The sanctions are severe, but they may be mitigated by corporations that utilize effective compliance programs aimed at prevention and detection. The guidelines emphasize restitution to victims; sanctions that amount to corporate death for corporations that are primarily criminal in nature (this is accomplished by divesting them of their assets); fines (the typical sanction for most offenses) that represent the seriousness of the offense and the ability of the corporation to pay; and supervision of the U.S. Probation Office to assure compliance with imposed sanctions.[74]

In May 2001 the Sentencing Commission recommended even tougher sentencing guidelines for white-collar crimes. The process under the statute that created the commission is that it makes recommendations to Congress in May of each year. If Congress does not react, those recommendations become law in November of that year. Congress could, of course, change the recommendations, but it rarely does so. The new recommendations almost double the penalties for certain insider trading and major fraud crimes, from a maximum term of 37 months to up to 63 months in prison. The current penalty provisions have been described by the manager in one South Florida U.S. attorney's office as "so insignificant . . . that many white-collar criminals consider them merely part of the cost of doing business." The sentencing guidelines have been opposed by many, however, with one South Florida defense attorney referring to those of the U.S. Sentencing Commission as too complex: "You have a better chance understanding a handbook on nuclear devices than you do these sentencing rules."[75]

SUMMARY

This chapter focuses on crimes of the business world as well as those committed by and against the government. Although many of these crimes are economic, personal injury or death may result from crimes such as mislabeling drugs, faulty design or construction of products, or environmental pollution. The erosion of trust and the violations of civil rights that occur when government officials commit crimes destroys the confidence citizens have in the ability of the government to protect them and treat them fairly.

The discussion begins with the problem of defining white-collar crime, looking at the contributions of Sutherland and subsequent sociologists who followed his development of the term. Particular attention is given to the term *corporate crime* and an explanation of how it differs from business-related or white-collar crimes.

The main thrust of the chapter is an examination of several examples of business and government-related crimes. Some, like embezzlement, are committed primarily by individuals in secret; others, like conspiracy, by definition involve more than one person. Crimes committed by government officials in the course of their official responsibilities illustrate the misuse of trust and power that characterizes many of the world's politicians.

The control of white-collar crime is a problem faced directly by the U.S. Sentencing Commission, which has recommended increasing the penalties for many offenses discussed in this chapter. There are some differences, however, between the commission's approach to white-collar and to common-crime offenders. Whether these differences are reasonable is a subject of debate. Whether the criminal penalties are more effective than civil penalties is a subject of debate, too.

The types of crimes and offenders discussed in this chapter cannot always be distinguished from organized crime. Chapter 10 completes the discussion of types of crime and criminals by looking at drug abuse, drug trafficking, and organized crime.

STUDY QUESTIONS

1. Explain and evaluate the use of administrative rather than criminal law to control business-related crimes.
2. Distinguish between *white-collar crime* and *corporate crime.*
3. Discuss the contributions of Edwin H. Sutherland to our understanding of white-collar crime.
4. Enumerate social and political factors that might account for the current emphasis on corporate crime.
5. Discuss the contributions of sociologists since Sutherland to our understanding of white-collar crime.
6. Distinguish strict liability, vicarious liability, and enterprise liability, and relate each to white-collar crime.
7. Why is income tax evasion a serious offense?
8. Define *bribery, extortion, blackmail,* and *graft.*
9. Is conspiracy a civil or a criminal offense? Discuss.
10. Distinguish between *embezzlement* and *employee theft.*
11. Explain *false advertising.*
12. What is insider trading?
13. What is the purpose of antitrust laws? How do you think the Microsoft case will be decided on appeal?
14. How effective do you think we have been in prosecuting environmental crimes?
15. What is the relationship between products liability and crime?
16. Should employers be held criminally liable for workplace violations that lead to injury or death? Explain your answer.
17. What is fraud? Discuss two types.
18. Distinguish between *obstruction of justice* and *official misconduct in office.*
19. Explain what is meant by *civil rights violations* and illustrate your answer.

BRIEF ESSAY ASSIGNMENTS

1. Why has there been little attention paid to the study of corporate crime?
2. What characteristics distinguish white-collar offenders from other offenders? Why do some argue there is no difference between the two groups?

3. Explain why it is difficult to prosecute antitrust violations under the Sherman Antitrust Act of 1890.
4. Discuss why it is easier to commit health care fraud in federal programs than in private institutions.
5. Explain the suggestion that using the civil law (rather than the criminal law) is the best method to address business and government-related crimes.

INTERNET ACTIVITIES

1. Go to the Web and search for recent news and events concerning business and/or government-related crime. What was the offense? Who was involved? What are the short- and long-term impacts of the crimes? Who are the victims? If the offender has been convicted and sentenced, do you think the sentence is fair? In your opinion, should the sentences imposed for business and/or government-related crimes be different from sentences for other types of crime? Why or why not?
2. Check out the National White Collar Crime Center at www.nw3c.org/home.htm. Find and read the white paper on securities fraud. What are the four most prevalent types of securities crime? What is the "pump-and-dump" scam?

NET RESOURCES

www.ncahf.org — The National Council Against Health Care Fraud is a private, nonprofit health agency that provides information and updates on health care fraud. Publications, position papers, task force reports, consumer information statements and links to other health care watchdog sources can be found at the council's website.

www.sec.gov — The U.S. Securities and Exchange Commission's website provides headlines, reports and documentation on activities involving the Securities and Exchange Commission. Site users can access regulatory actions, staff bulletins, litigations, and information on the SEC divisions.

www.consumerlawpage.com/index.html — Maintained by a law firm, the Consumer Law Page offers legal and litigation information and articles on various consumer issues and concerns such as serious injuries, birth defects, toxic chemicals, and defective products.

www.usps.gov/websites/depart/inspect — The U.S. Postal Inspection Service website allows users to access statistics and information on mail fraud and theft, prohibited mail, and other crimes. Publications concerning various crimes and annual postal inspection investigative reports can be found at this site.

www.ftc.gov — One of the Federal Trade Commission's many responsibilities is the enforcement of federal antitrust and consumer protection laws. The FTC's website offers several topic areas, including consumer protection, economic issues, antitrust/competition, and current news releases.

www.epa.gov	The U.S. Environmental Protection Agency's website provides statistics, laws and regulations, environmental resources, and a list of key topics involving environmental protection and enforcement issues.
www.aclu.org	This website provides information on issues and litigation involving the American Civil Liberties Union. Topics include criminal justice, free speech, national security, cyberliberties, and workplace rights.
www.gao.gov/index.html	The U.S. General Accounting Office investigates and reports to Congress on several areas related to this nation's government, such as use of public funds, program review, and evaluation and financial audits. Its website provides numerous publications, reports and articles on various topics investigated by the GAO, plus assistance in using the site to access reports.

ENDNOTES

1. Edwin H. Sutherland, *White Collar Crime* (New York: Holt, Rinehart & Winston, 1959, 1961, paper ed.); originally published in 1949 by the Dryden Press. In 1983 an uncut version of Sutherland's work was published. This version restores the names and case histories and contains an introduction by Gilbert Geis and Colin Goff. It is published by Yale University Press, New Haven, Connecticut.
2. Ibid., p. 9.
3. August Bequai, *White-Collar Crime: A 20th-Century Crisis* (Lexington, MA: D. C. Heath, 1978), p. 2.
4. August Bequai, "Wanted: The White Collar Ring," *Student Lawyer* 5 (May 1977): 45.
5. Justice System Improvement Act of 1979, U.S. Code, Title 42, Section 3701 *et seq.* (1979) [Repealed].
6. Herbert Edelhertz, U.S. Department of Justice, Law Enforcement Assistance Administration, *The Nature, Impact and Prosecution of White-Collar Crime,* (Washington, DC: U.S. Government Printing Office, 1970), pp. 19–20.
7. Marshall B. Clinard, *Illegal Corporate Behavior* (Washington, DC: U.S. Government Printing Office, October, 1979), Abstract.
8. Ibid., p. 18. For a brief but excellent overview of corporate crime, see Nancy K. Frank and Michael J. Lynch, *Corporate Crime, Corporate Violence: A Primer* (New York: Harrow & Heston, 1992).
9. See James W. Messerschmidt, *Capitalism, Patriarchy, and Crime: Toward a Socialist Feminist Criminology* (Totawa, NJ: Rowman & Littlefield, 1986), pp. 99–129.
10. *Statistical Report: United States Attorney General's Office,* Fiscal Year 1996 (Washington DC: U.S. Department of Justice, 1997), pp. 1–4; quotation is from p. 4.
11. John S. R. Shad, quoted in *American Bar Association Journal* 73 (1 June 1987).
12. Donald R. Cressey, *Other People's Money: A Study in the Social Psychology of Embezzlement* (New York: Free Press, 1953), p. 30.
13. Sutherland, *White Collar Crime,* p. 234. See also Edwin H. Sutherland, "Is 'White Collar Crime' Crime?" *American Sociological Review* 10 (April 1945): 132–39.
14. See Marshall B. Clinard and Richard Quinney, eds., *Criminal Behavior Systems: A Typology* (New York: Holt, Rinehart & Winston, 1967), p. 134. The second edition was published in 1986 by Anderson Publishing.
15. Toni Makkai and John Braithwaite, "Criminological Theories and Regulatory Compliance," *Criminology* 29 (May 1991): 191–217.
16. Travis Hirschi and Michael R. Gottfredson, "Causes of White-Collar Crime," *Criminology* 25 (November 1987): 949.
17. Ibid., p. 959.
18. Ibid., pp. 970–71.
19. See Michael R. Gottfredson and Travis Hirschi, *A General Theory of Crime* (Stanford, CA: Stanford University Press, 1990), pp. 23, 180–201.
20. Darrell J. Steffensmeier, "On the Causes of 'White-Collar' Crime: An Assessment of Hirschi and Gottfredson's Claims," *Criminology* 27 (May 1989): 345–58. For a response by Hirschi and Gottfredson, see "The Significance of White-Collar Crime for a General Theory of Crime," *Criminology* 27 (May 1989): 359–71.
21. Michael L. Benson and Elizabeth Moore, "Are White-Collar and Common Offenders the Same? An Empirical and Theoretical Critique of a Recently Proposed General Theory of Crime," *Journal of Research in Crime and Delinquency* 29 (August 1992): 152–272.
22. See James William Coleman, *Criminal Elite: The Sociology of White Collar Crime* (New York: St. Martin's Press, 1985), and Coleman, "Toward an Integrated Theory of White-Collar Crime," *American Journal of Sociology* 93 (September 1987): 406–39.
23. U.S. Code, Title 26, Section 7201 (2001).
24. See United States v. Coppola, 300 F.Supp. 932 (D.C.Conn. 1969), *aff'd.,* 425 F.2d 660 (2d Cir. 1969).
25. United States v. Berger, 325 F.Supp. 1297, 1303 (S.D.N.Y. 1971), *aff'd.,* 456 F.2d 1349 (2d Cir. 1972), *cert. denied,* 409 U.S. 892 (1972).
26. U.S. Code, Title 18, Section 201 et seq. (2001).
27. See U.S. Code, Title 18, Section 1951(b)(2) (2001).
28. Jackson v. United States, 196 F.3d 383 (2d Cir. 1999), *cert. denied,* 530 U.S. 1267 (1999).
29. State v. Burnham, 15 N.H. 396 (1844).
30. New York Penal Code, Section 105.17 (2001).
31. U.S. Code, Title 18, Section 371 (2001).
32. Partian v. State, 225 S.E.2d 736 (Ga.App. 1973).
33. "Milken Leaves Prison for Halfway House Stint," *Orlando Sentinel* (5 January 1993), p. 1D; "Michael Milken," *Dallas Morning News* (29 January 1995), p. 1J; "Now, Obstruction of Justice Is Focus of Milken Inquiry," *New York Times* (14 November 1997), p. 4C.
34. "Dodd Helped Friends Secure Presidential Pardon," *Hartford Courant* (24 February 2001), p. 11.
35. Insider Trading and Securities Fraud Enforcement Act of 1988, U.S. Code, Title 15, Section 78(a) (2001).
36. U.S. Code, Title 15, Section 1 *et seq.* (2001).
37. "Microsoft Winner in Appeal in Keep Software Intact," *New York Times* (24 June 1998), p. 1; "The Microsoft Trial Begins," editorial, *New York Times* (18 October 1998), p. 14; "If Microsoft Loses Case, Remedies Are Thorny," *New York Times* (14 December 1998), p. 1C.
38. For details of the settlement, see "U.S. and Microsoft in Deal, but States Hold Back," *New York Times* (3 November 2001), p. 1.
39. RCRA is codified at U.S. Code, Title 42, Section 9601–9657 (2001), with the 1984 amendments at U.S. Code, Title 42, Section

6901–6991 (2001). CERCLA is codified at U.S. Code, Title 42, Section 9607–9657 (2001).

40. "It's a New World: Polluters Go to Prison," *USA Today* (21 April 2000), p. 3, based on data from the Environmental Protection Agency.
41. Grimshaw v. Ford Motor Company, 174 Cal.Rptr. 348, 384 (4th Dist. 1981).
42. "Service Company Must Pay $11 Million in ValuJet Crash," *New York Times* (15 August 2000), p. 20.
43. United States v. Park, 421 U.S. 658 (1975).
44. "Watch on the Media," *Liability Week* 8 (2 August 1993) (no page number); and "Job Safety: OSHA to Ease Federal Enforcement Role after Upgrades to North Carolina Program," Bureau of National Affairs, Inc., *Daily Report for Executives* (8 March 1995), p. 45.
45. "Owner Sentenced for Mall Collapse," *St. Petersburg Times* (28 December 1995), p. 8.
46. See U.S. Code, Title 18, Section 1341 (2001).
47. U.S. Code, Title 18, Section 1343 (2001).
48. U.S. Code, Title 18, Section 1344 (2001).
49. See U.S. Code, Title 18, Section 3293 (2001).
50. "Feds' Inter-Agency Unit Adds to Medicare Fraud Indictments," *Miami Daily Business Review* (23 May 2001), p. 3.
51. "Out of the Lion's Den Health Care Fraud Enforcement Update," *Nursing Home Litigation Reporter* (20 April 2001), p. 9.
52. "Reward Is $29 Million in Medicare Fraud Case," *New York Times* (30 January 1999), p. 28.
53. "Chasing Health Care Fraud Quietly Becomes Profitable," *New York Times* (23 January 2001), p. 1; quotation is from p. 17.
54. United States v. Machi, 811 F.2d 991 (7th Cir. 1987).
55. David Wise, *The Politics of Lying* (New York: Vintage, 1973), pp. x–xi, as quoted in David R. Simon and D. Stanley Eitzen, *Elite Deviance*, 3d ed. (Boston: Allyn & Bacon, 1990), p. 239.
56. United States v. Poindexter, 951 F.2d 369 (D.C.App. 1991), *cert. denied*, 506 U.S. 1021 (1992).
57. United States v. North, 910 F.2d 843 (D.C. Cir. 1990), *modified, reh'g. denied, in part, en banc*, 920 F.2d 940 (D.C.Cir. 1990), *cert. denied*, 500 U.S. 91 (1991).
58. "Independent Counsel's Statement on the Pardons," *New York Times* (25 December 1992), p. 10.
59. Gary Blounston, "Scandal-Probing Is Flourishing in D.C.," *Miami Herald* (22 November 1992), p. 8.
60. "U.S. Agents Say Fatal Flaws Doomed Raid on Waco Cult," *New York Times* (28 March 1993), p. 1.
61. "Cult Leader Presents F.B.I. with 'Letter from God,'" *New York Times* (11 April 1993), p. 13.
62. "Reno Says Suicides Seemed Unlikely," *New York Times* (20 April 1993), p. 1.
63. "Hearings Show Why Waco Became a Rallying Cry," *Denver Post* (30 July 1995), p. 6D.
64. "Ex-FBI Negotiator Says Agency Faced Hopeless Situation at Waco," *Los Angeles Times* (2 November 1995), p. 14.
65. "Ruby Ridge Probe Now Looking into Possible Cover-Up," *The Recorder* (7 November 1995), p. 1.
66. "Shared Fantasies: We Have Met the Enemy, and They Is [sic] Us," *New Jersey Law Journal* (6 November 1995), p. 26.
67. Civil Rights Act of 1991, P.L. 102–166, 105 Stat. 1071 *et seq.* (21 November 1991).
68. U.S. Code, Title 18, Section 242 (2001). Civil liabilities are provided under U.S. Code, Title 42, Sections 1983 and 1985 (2001).
69. Miller v. United States, 404 F.2d 611 (5th Cir. 1968), *cert. denied*, 394 U.S. 963 (1969).
70. United States v. Koon, 34 F.3d 1416 (9th Cir. 1994), *aff'd. in part, rev'd. in part, remanded*, Koon v. United States, 515 U.S. 1190 (1996).
71. "New York Settles in Brutality Case," *New York Times* (13 July 2001), p. 1.
72. "Mother Responds Angrily to Decision in Diallo Case," *New York Times* (29 April 2001), p. 29.
73. David Weisburd et al., *Crimes of the Middle Classes: White-Collar Offenders in the Federal Courts* (New Haven, CT: Yale University Press, 1991), p. 171.
74. See U.S. Sentencing Commission, *Supplementary Report on Sentencing Guidelines for Organizations* (30 August 1991).
75. "Tougher Federal Sentences Loom for White-Collar Crime," *Broward Daily Business Review* (10 May 2001), p. 12.

CHAPTER

10

▶ John P. Walters speaks to reporters during a 2001 ceremony at the Rose Garden of the White House after President George W. Bush nominated him to be director of the White House Office of National Drug Control Policy. The nomination was confirmed, and Walters became the nation's "drug czar." (© Ron Sachs/Corbis Sygma)

Drug Abuse, Drug Trafficking, and Organized Crime

OUTLINE

Drug Abuse

Data

The Impact of Drug Abuse

- Fetal Abuse
- Economic Cost
- Criminal Activity
- Prison and Jail Overcrowding
- Influence on Criminal Justice System Personnel

The Debate Over Drug Laws

- Federal Laws
- State Laws
- The Legalization Debate
- The Treatment Approach

Illegal Drug Trafficking

Illegal Drug Trafficking Dynamics

Colombian Drug Cartels

- The Medellin Cartel
- The Cali Cartel

The Control of Drug Trafficking

Organized Crime

The Concept of Organized Crime

The History and Organization of Organized Crime

Organized Crime in Other Countries

Organized Crime and Legitimate Business

- Health Care
- The Food Industry
- The Construction Industry
- The Cartage Industry

The Control of Organized Crime

- Statutory Measures
- Prosecutions and Trials

Summary

Study Questions

Brief Essay Assignments

Internet Activities

Net Resources

Endnotes

KEY TERMS

Bootlegging
Drug abuse
Drug trafficking
Extradition
Fetal abuse
Forfeiture
Immunity (criminal)
Loan sharking
Mafia
Money laundering
Organized crime
Prohibition
Racketeering
Syndicate

This chapter focuses on drug abuse, drug trafficking, and organized crime. The activities involved in all of these areas may include some or all of the property and violent crimes that have been discussed previously. All of the three areas on which the chapter focuses are costly to the individuals who are involved and to society as well. Less obvious but nevertheless extensive damage is thrust upon individuals daily by the activities of those associated with organized crime, which has infiltrated legitimate as well as illegitimate businesses throughout the world.

Drug abuse The chronic or periodic misuse of alcohol or other drugs. Drug abuse is considered detrimental to society as well as to the individual abuser. Drug abuse may occur even if the substance has been prescribed by the individual's physician.

Drug trafficking Trading in illegal drugs.

Organized crime The highly structured association of people who bind together to make large profits through illegal and legal means while utilizing graft and corruption in the criminal justice arena to protect their activities from criminal prosecution.

The first two chapters of Part III cover violent and property crimes. Usually violent and property crimes can be distinguished, but, as noted, sometimes it can be difficult to place a crime into only one of these two categories. An act of stealing, such as a purse snatching, may be either theft (a property crime) or robbery (a violent crime) depending on the degree of force used.

The three crime categories covered in this chapter involve both property and violent crimes. **Drug abuse** involves the illegal purchase of drugs, and in some cases other crimes are committed to secure the money for the drugs. Illegal **drug trafficking,** which may or may not be linked with **organized crime,** involves violent as well as property-related crimes. Organized crime results in extensive property losses to businesses and individuals; the hierarchy within organized crime is known for its use of violence to accomplish established goals.

Those who commit the ordinary property and violent crimes discussed in previous chapters are similar in some ways to those who commit the crimes discussed in this chapter. They may do so for personal or business gain or for political reasons. Early sociological analyses noted the interrelationships between business-related crimes and organized crime. Some argue that the relationship is one of mutual benefit, whereas others believe that the structure of legitimate society is necessary for the successful existence of organized crime. But clearly one of the important components of both drug trafficking and organized crime is that many people abuse drugs.

DRUG ABUSE

Chapter 1 discusses the use of the criminal law to control behavior that some people might consider none of the law's business. In that chapter sexual behavior between consenting adults in private is used to illustrate the issues. Drug abuse is another area in which many people believe the criminal law either should not be employed or should be restricted to only some areas.

Some studies show an increase among young teens in the use of marijuana. In this picture a 13-year-old is smoking a joint. (Photo Researchers)

The word *drugs* is used to refer to alcohol, marijuana, cocaine, heroin, and other substances. It is impossible to separate the excessive use of alcohol from abuse of other drugs in terms of effect, as many people who abuse one substance may also abuse others. Nor is it possible to get accurate data on the number of people who abuse drugs, although it is important that we do the best we can in data collection.

Data

A 1997 report stated that in recent years alcoholism had increased among the elderly and teenagers, while another report the same year stated that an increasing number of older high school students used marijuana but that the use of other drugs among this age group had declined.[1] Official government data published that year showed that fewer teenagers were using marijuana and that the use of other drugs had not changed.[2] In 1999, however, the government reported that the use of drugs among persons ages 12 to 17 had dropped significantly since

Media Focus 10.1

A Media View of Marijuana and Violence

Today many people advocate the legalization of marijuana, basing their position on the belief that the drug is not a dangerous one. Unlike crack cocaine, the advocates proclaim, marijuana is not associated with violence. New York City police take a different view, as related in a 2001 *New York Times* article entitled "Violent Crimes Undercut Marijuana's Mellow Image." A person who reads only the title, as many probably did, could reasonably conclude that violence is associated with marijuana use.[1]

A closer reading of the article, however, reveals that police are associating violence with the *sale* of marijuana but not its *use*. For example, one police official states, "The marijuana trade in New York City is controlled and run through the use of violence." Another states that the number of marijuana-related drive-by shootings and other killings has increased in recent years. The cited examples are of persons who made large profits from the sale of the drug. But officials acknowledge that they do not keep data on marijuana-related killings, so these pronouncements may be misleading and even inaccurate. Still, the *Times* headline is impressive; it may have convinced many that smoking marijuana—rather than the profit in selling marijuana—is associated with the violence. Advocates of legalizing the sale of marijuana argue that if the drug were legal, high profits from the sale of the drug would decline—thus lowering the violence. Yet this position, too, is an assumption that may not be accurate.

1. "Violent Crimes Undercut Marijuana's Mellow Image," *New York Times* (19 May 2001), p. 1.

1997 (although the usage was considerably below that of 1977). At the same time, the usage among those 18 to 25 had increased.[3]

High school students are often the subjects of drug use studies. Another major survey that tracks drug use among teens is the Monitoring the Future Study (also known as the High School Senior Study). When this study was initiated in 1975, 30.7 percent of high school seniors reported using an illicit drug in the month prior to the study. This use declined in the years prior to 1992 and then began rising again before another drop between 1997 and 1998. But of particular concern has been the increase in the use of marijuana in this age group. Between 1991 and 1998, the use of marijuana in the month prior to the survey increased from 13.8 percent to 22.8 percent among high school seniors.[4]

The Monitoring the Future Study also asks high school seniors on how many occasions, if any, they used alcohol or other drugs within the 12 previous months and within the past month. The responses in 2000, by type of drug, are reported in Table 10.1. As that table shows, alcohol is the most frequently used drug, with 73.2 percent of high school seniors reporting its use during the past year, while 36.5 percent said they had used marijuana during that time period.

Not all who abuse drugs are arrested; arrest data for drug abuse violations in the year 2000 are given by type of drug in Table 10.2. As that table discloses, most drug abuse arrests are for possession of illegal drugs (81 percent), not for their sale or manufacture. Among possession arrests, by far the greatest percentage, 40.9, is for marijuana.

TABLE 10.1
Reported Drug Use by High School Seniors, 2000

Source: University of Michigan, "Drug Use from the Monitoring the Future Study," press release, December 2000. Reprinted in Bureau of Justice Statistics, *Drugs and Crime Facts* (Washington, DC: U.S. Department of Justice, July 2001), p. 1. On the Internet at www.ojp.usdoj.gov/bjs/dcf/du.htm.

	Used within the Last	
Drugs	**12 Months***	**Month**
Alcohol	73.2%	50.0%
Marijuana	36.5	21.6
Stimulants	10.5	5.0
Hallucinogens	8.1	2.6
Other opiates	7.0	2.9
Sedatives	6.3	3.1
Inhalants	5.9	2.2
Tranquilizers	5.7	2.6
Cocaine	5.0	2.1
Steroids	1.7	0.8
Heroin	1.5	0.7

*Including the last month.

Note: Self-reports of drug use among high school seniors may underrepresent drug use among youth of that age because high school dropouts and truants are not included, and these groups may have more involvement with drugs than those who stay in school.

TABLE 10.2
Arrests for Drug Abuse Violations, 2000

Source: Federal Bureau of Investigation, *Crime in the United States, Uniform Crime Reports 2000* (Washington, DC: U.S. Government Printing Office, 2001), p. 216.

	Sale/Manufacture	Possession
Heroin or cocaine and their derivatives	9.3%	24.2%
Marijuana	5.6	40.9
Synthetic or manufactured drugs	1.1	2.2
Other dangerous nonnarcotic drugs	3.0	13.6
Total	19.0%	81.0%

Cocaine, heroin, and marijuana are not the only substances used by drug abusers. Another drug that is gaining in use—and that has been related to recent acts of violence—is the club drug Ecstasy. Rival gangs have fought over this drug, and dealers have been killed for it; meanwhile, in recent years its use among teenagers has more than doubled. From recreational use by affluent white teenagers, Ecstasy has spread to "virtually every ethnic and class group, and from big cities like New York and Los Angeles to rural Vermont and South Dakota."[5]

The Impact of Drug Abuse

Although some consider the use of controlled substances to be a personal, private issue and not the government's business, there are arguments to the contrary. In addition to the economic, psychological, and physiological problems that may result to the families as well as to the individuals who engage in substance abuse, others may suffer as well. Persons under the influence of controlled substances may (and do) drive and cause injury and death to themselves as well as to others. They may engage in abusive, harassing, or obnoxious behavior. But one area of focus is on the harm that substance abuse may cause to the unborn children of female abusers.

Fetal Abuse

Fetal abuse Abusing a fetus; in some jurisdictions any resulting injury may lead to legal liability; in a few states, killing a fetus may result in murder charges.

A recent area of concern is **fetal abuse,** leading some states to change their homicide statutes to include killing a fetus. For example, California defines murder as "the unlawful killing of a human being, or a fetus, with malice aforethought."[6] This change in the common law view of murder as applying only to persons already born has resulted in convictions for murder for those who kill the fetus of a pregnant woman. The issue here, however, is whether the substance abuse of a pregnant woman, when it causes birth defects or the death of the fetus, should form the basis for a criminal charge against the mother, especially in light of the following evidence. Babies born to mothers who drank alcohol during the last six months of pregnancy are 10 times more likely to develop leukemia during infancy. In addition, mothers who smoke are 50 percent more likely to give birth to babies with mental disabilities than are mothers who do not smoke.[7]

Some jurisdictions have considered prosecuting pregnant women who abuse drugs, but most have not succeeded. A few examples illustrate. In Illinois a grand jury refused to indict a young mother whose infant died shortly after birth and whose death was linked to the mother's use of cocaine. The prosecutor's earlier announcement of his intention to bring charges brought serious criticism on the grounds that such action might deter pregnant drug users from seeking prenatal care. The practice was objected to on the privacy issue as well. One attorney questioned, "If the state can create prenatal patrols for cocaine use, then where would they draw the line?"[8]

The Florida Supreme Court has held that the state's statute prohibiting delivering drugs to minors is not applicable to the case of a woman who ingested illegal drugs while pregnant and gave birth to a drug-addicted baby.[9]

The Connecticut Supreme Court has held that a pregnant woman's cocaine injections shortly before she gave birth did not constitute child neglect in the case of her child, who was born suffering from cocaine withdrawal. The court held that the statute did not cover a pregnant woman's prenatal conduct.[10]

In South Carolina, however, a different result was reached. In 1996 the state supreme court held that in the state's child abuse and endangerment statute the word *child* includes a viable fetus. The case of *Whitmer* v. *State* involved a defendant who "pled guilty to criminal child neglect for causing her baby to be born with cocaine metabolites in its system by reason of Whitmer's ingestion of crack cocaine during the third trimester of her pregnancy." Whitmer was sentenced to eight years in prison. The state supreme court justices stated that they did "not see any rational basis for finding a viable fetus is not a 'person' in the present context." Furthermore, the court found that there was no question that the defendant "endangered the life, health, and comfort of her child."[11]

More recently, in 2001 a South Carolina woman was sentenced to 12 years in prison after she smoked crack cocaine and her fetus died as a result. Regina McKnight, age 24, was convicted of homicide by child abuse. Her stillborn baby was delivered when she was eight and a half months pregnant. McKnight plans to appeal the decision.[12]

The U.S. Supreme Court has ruled that pregnant women suspected of drug abuse may not be tested for drugs without their permission if the purpose of the test is to alert police to their substance abuse. According to the Court, even with the possibility that the substance abuse could endanger the fetus, if the woman does not consent or the officials do not have a warrant, a drug test is an unconstitutional search and seizure.[13]

Another issue regarding drug abuse is the cost to individuals and to society.

Economic Cost

It is estimated that each year between 1989 and 1998 Americans spent $39 to $77 billion on cocaine and $10 to $22 billion on heroin. An estimated $11 billion per year is spent on marijuana, while another $1.5 to $3 billion is spent yearly on other drugs.[14]

In addition to the money spent by individual substance abusers, governments spend large sums on drug control policies. In 2000 the federal government spent nearly $18.5 billion on drug control programs, with the largest percentage of that money being spent in criminal justice systems. A conservative estimate of state spending on drug control is over $81 billion per year, which amounts to over 13.1 percent of the total state spending.[15]

Another cost of drugs is the cost of incarcerating drug offenders, estimated to be over $40 billion annually.[16] As Table 10.3 reports, 59 percent of all federal prison inmates, 21 percent of state prison inmates, and 26 percent of local jail inmates in 1998 were drug offenders.

A third area in which drug abuse creates an impact on individuals, families, and society is in its connection with criminal activity.

TABLE 10.3
Estimated Number of Drug Offenders under Federal, State, and Local Supervision, 1998

Sources: Bureau of Justice Statistics, *Prisoners in 1999* (Washington, DC: U.S. Department of Justice, August 2000); Federal Bureau of Prisons, *Federal Bureau of Prisons Quick Facts* (Washington, DC: U.S. Department of Justice, February 2000); Bureau of Justice Statistics, *Drug Use, Testing, and Treatment in Jails* (Washington, DC: U.S. Department of Justice, May 2000).

	Drug Offenders	Percent of All Inmates
Federal	55,984	59% (95,323)
State	236,800	21 (1,141,700)
Jail	152,000	26 (592,462)

Criminal Activity

One of the stated reasons for criminalizing the use of drugs is that substance abuse has been associated with criminal acts. Table 10.4 contains a summary of the relationship between crime and the use of drugs. Further, government data reveal that adult respondents who use marijuana or cocaine are much more likely to be involved in illegal acts than those who do not use these drugs.[17]

A 2001 government document reports that in 1998 individuals with drug violations constituted 21 percent of state prison populations (up from 6 percent in 1980) and 59 percent of federal prison populations (up from 25 percent in 1980). An estimated 26

TABLE 10.4
Summary of Relationship between Drugs and Crime

Source: Drug-Related Crime, Office of National Drug Control Policy (Washington, DC: U.S. Government Printing Office, March 2000), p. 1.

Drugs/Crime Relationship	Definition	Examples
Drug-defined offenses	Violations of laws prohibiting or regulating the possession, use, distribution, or manufacture of illegal drugs.	Drug possession or use. Marijuana cultivation. Methamphetamine production. Cocaine, heroin, or marijuana sales.
Drug-related offenses	Offenses to which a drug's pharmacologic effects contribute; offenses motivated by the user's need for money to support continued use; and offenses connected to drug distribution itself.	Violent behavior resulting from drug effects. Stealing to get money to buy drugs. Violence against rival drug dealers.
Drug-using lifestyle	A lifestyle in which the likelihood and frequency of involvement in illegal activity are increased because drug users may not participate in the legitimate economy and are exposed to situations that encourage crime.	A life orientation with an emphasis on short-term goals supported by illegal activities. Opportunities to offend resulting from contacts with offenders and illegal markets. Criminal skills learned from other offenders.

percent of all inmates under local supervision were drug offenders. The average cost to incarcerate a person in the United States was $23,542 in the federal system and $20,261 in the state systems. Annual costs to jail one inmate varied from $8,036 to $66,795.[18]

The argument for criminalizing substance abuse is based on an assumption that it causes crime (see, for example, Table 10.5) and thus should be included within the embrace of criminal statutes. Some drug users commit property crimes in order to finance their drug habit. Also, the substance abuser may engage in violent crimes. For example, earlier we mentioned the increase in the use of the drug Ecstasy. According to a recent news article, a pill that can cost less than $1 to manufacture can be sold for $30, and middle- and upper-class students are being recruited to sell the drug to teenagers: "As a result, America's suburbs are being hit with Ecstasy-related drive-by shootings, executions, and assaults as violent international crime groups stake claims to the Ecstasy market." In May 2001 Drug Enforcement Administration (DEA) authorities apprehended a gang that was traveling from state to state, party to party, preying on teens who were high on Ecstasy. The Brooklyn Terror Squad (BTS) "beat up and robbed ravers [participants at raves, all-night dance parties], stole their drugs and then resold them at the same parties," according to federal drug authorities.[19]

TABLE 10.5
Percent of Jail Inmates Who Committed Offense to Get Money for Drugs

Source: Bureau of Justice Statistics, *Profile of Jail Inmates, 1996* (Washington, DC: U.S. Department of Justice, April 1998), p. 1; and Bureau of Justice Statistics, *Drug Use, Testing, and Treatment in Jails* (Washington, DC: U.S. Department of Justice, May 2000), p. 1.

Offense	1996	1999
Total	15.8%	13.3%
Violent	8.8	11.5
Property	25.6	24.4
Drugs	23.5	14.0
Public-order	4.2	3.3

Social scientists have conducted research on the relationship between drugs and crime. In his work published more than 20 years ago, criminologist James A. Inciardi said he found evidence that heroin users were often involved in crimes. After conducting interviews with 356 heroin users who had a long history of drug use, Inciardi concluded, "The data . . . clearly demonstrate not only that most of the heroin users were committing crimes, but also that they were doing so extensively and for the purpose of drug use support." Inciardi's account of the world of drugs was based on his own street research in Miami and New York and on interviews with persons who use, deal, or traffic in heroin and cocaine.[20]

In more recent years Inciardi has studied the relationship between crack cocaine use and crime. In a work published in 2001, Inciardi and a colleague review the findings of these studies. They emphasize that the evidence does not show that drug use *causes* crime—or enslaves drug abusers into crime—for many of the abusers had already engaged in criminal activity before they turned to drugs. But, the authors conclude, "It is clear to us that drugs are driving crime. That is, although drug use does not necessarily initiate criminal careers among users it freezes users into patterns of criminality that are more intense and unremitting than they would have been without drugs."[21]

In 2001 Scott Menard and his colleagues published their analysis of the works of Inciardi and others concerning the relationship between substance abuse and crime. They found support for most of the earlier findings and said, "The most plausible conclusion is that drugs and crime are related by mutual causation: crime affects drug use and drug use affects crime."[22]

Prison and Jail Overcrowding

Every aspect of criminal justice systems is impacted by drug abuse and efforts to control it. Courts are crowded, creating a backlog of cases in the civil division as the courts try to process those in the criminal division. More defense lawyers,

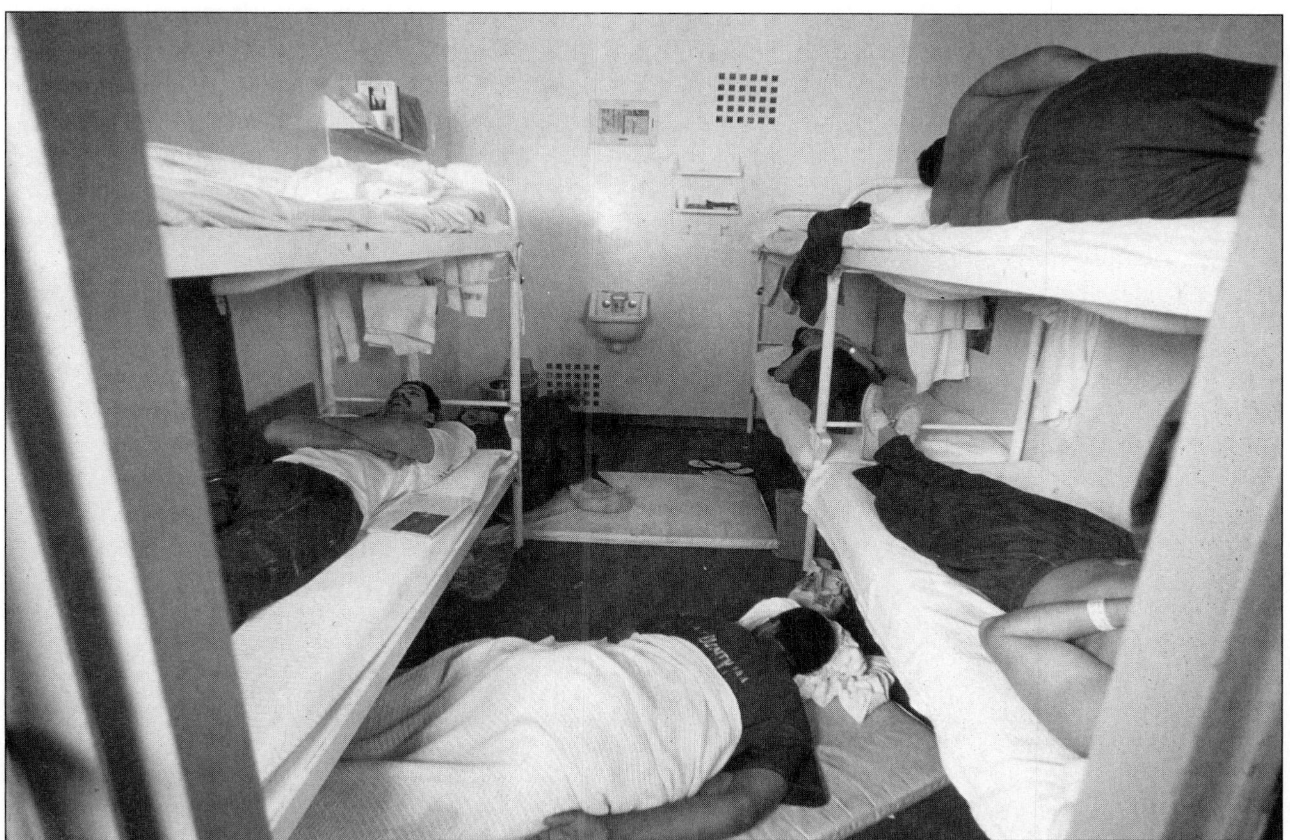

Although every aspect of the U.S. criminal justice systems is impacted by the increase in drug convictions, prison and jail overcrowding is perhaps the most significant result. In this picture, inmates at the Los Angeles County jail are sleeping on the floor because of a lack of beds. (Marc Richards/PhotoEdit)

prosecutors, judges, and all court staff are needed, along with more courtrooms and other facilities. And many jails and prisons are overcrowded in large part because of the number of drug offenders sentenced to serve time or awaiting trial for drug abuse offenses. Consider the following data.

Reports published in November 2000 show that between 1991 and 1997 the percentage of persons held in federal prisons rose from 58 percent to 63 percent, with nearly one-half of those being drug trafficking offenders. In 1997 over one-half of state inmates and approximately one-third of federal inmates were under the influence of alcohol or other drugs at the time they committed their current offense. Between 1991 and 1997 state inmates reported an increased use of drugs, with almost 57 percent reporting drug use within the month prior to the current offense in 1997, compared to 50 percent in 1991. Federal inmates reported an increase from 32 percent in 1991 to 45 percent in 1997.[23]

Drug-related violations also affect prison populations in the return of parolees, accounting for over one-half of parole violators returned to state prisons. Thus, although it is true that prison populations have increased because inmates are serving longer terms, initial and returning drug offenders have contributed significantly to the swelling of prison and jail populations. And although the prison population growth rate is not rising as fast as previously (1999 was the lowest annual growth, 3.4 percent, since 1979), 22 states and the federal system were still operating at or above their capacity, with the federal system operating at 32 percent over capacity.[24]

Influence on Criminal Justice System Personnel

The nation's declared war on drugs (discussed later in this chapter) presents all criminal justice system personnel with some of their most frustrating problems. The escalation of drug trafficking is resulting in corruption, violence, enormous expense, and a crushing blow to all elements of criminal justice systems. Drug offenders have created a "new underworld" within prisons, resulting in the use of drugs to corrupt correctional officers.[25]

Police also face a serious problem—of fighting illegal drugs with inadequate resources while drug offenders tempt them. In 1997 in Chicago, 124 narcotics cases were dismissed because the primary witness for the prosecution in each case was one of the police officers apprehended the previous year for extorting and robbing undercover officers who were posing as drug dealers.[26] The problem of police corruption by drug offenders has led many departments to use random drug testing among officers—and some have called for such testing of all police.[27]

Despite the problems associated with drug abuse, some are calling for changes in drug laws.

The Debate over Drug Laws

Statutes governing the use and sale of controlled substances have emerged over the years. A brief look at these laws and constitutional amendments is important to an understanding of the current situation, for the use of the criminal law to control substance abuse illustrates the successes and problems associated with attempting to control moral behavior by law. We look first at efforts to control alcohol production and consumption and then at the legislation of other drugs.

Prohibition The period in U.S. history (1919–1933) during which it was illegal for anyone to make, sell, or buy alcoholic beverages.

Federal Laws

On 5 December 1983 we marked the 50th anniversary of the repeal of **Prohibition,** the constitutional attempt to control the manufacture, sale, and consumption of alcohol. That year Americans spent $59 billion on alcohol, with an estimated additional $49 billion cost in related work loss, accidents, sickness, and death.[28] Alcohol is also blamed for thousands of deaths each year, constituting the number one cause of death among persons ages 15 to 21. Alcohol is responsible for enormous personal and societal costs caused by illness and absenteeism from work.[29] Thus, the effects of alcohol create more than personal problems; they create problems for society as well. There have been numerous attempts to legislate alcohol abuse.

In 1919 the government enacted the Eighteenth Amendment to the U.S. Constitution, prohibiting the manufacture, sale, and transportation of intoxicating liquors. According to a columnist writing 50 years after that experiment ended,

> It made life both better and worse. With 170,000 saloons closed, alcohol consumption was cut by as much as half, as were arrests for disorderly conduct and drunkenness. The death rate for cirrhosis of the liver was cut two-thirds . . . [but it also] lessened faith in government, made it adventurous and profitable to dare the law, and human to admire those who did it.[30]

Bootlegging The illegal production, use, or sale of alcoholic beverages; the term was used particularly during Prohibition.

The Eighteenth Amendment did not prohibit drinking liquor; it attempted to make liquor more difficult to obtain. But violations of the law were rampant, and **bootlegging** became acceptable to most people. The experiment failed and national Prohibition was repealed in 1933. The result is that we can legally make, sell, and use liquor; but the criminal law is still used to regulate driving under the influence of alcohol and the age at which consumers may legally buy liquor. These uses of the criminal law may be considered appropriate, but they must be distinguished from defining as criminal all manufacture and sales of alcohol (as during Prohibition) or public drunkenness. Many persons arrested for public drunkenness are poor, unemployed, and suffering from acute personal problems. Most are arrested more than once, and many spend so much time in jail that they have been described as serving a life sentence on the installment plan. Such persons are not aided by being placed in jail, and as a result of enforcing criminal laws in this area, the police are diverted from other, more important functions.

The criminal law is used even more extensively to regulate the sale of other drugs. Although in the latter half of the 1800s and in the early part of the 1900s drugs could be purchased in the United States by anyone without penalty, gradually laws were passed to regulate the sale and the possession of drugs.

Although some states had enacted legislation to regulate drugs, the federal government first took action in 1914, when the U.S. Congress restricted the sale and possession of heroin, opium, and cocaine. The Harrison Act of 1914 was originally intended as a tax measure, but it was quickly perceived as restricting the sale, prescription, and use of drugs. Congress added more restrictions to the act over the years, along with enacting other statutes for controlling the use of drugs.

The modern federal war on drugs began with President Richard M. Nixon and developed more extensively during the administration of President Ronald Reagan. Although Reagan's wife, Nancy, urged folks to "just say no" to drug use, legislation under the Reagan administration focused primarily on drug trafficking, especially by those associated with organized crime. In early 1982 the Federal Bureau of Investigation (FBI) was assigned jurisdiction over drug offenses, leading Attorney General William French Smith to declare, "For the first time since its establishment over fifty years ago, the full resources of the FBI will be added to our fight against the most serious crime problem facing our nation—drug trafficking." The FBI's efforts are coordinated with those of the Drug Enforcement Administration (DEA), U.S. attorneys, other agencies in the Department of Justice, and other general agencies.[31]

In June 1982 President Reagan appointed a special group of government agency heads and instructed them to report back to him with suggestions on how to fight drug abuse. Four years later he signed into law the Anti-Drug Abuse Act of 1986, which increased penalties for federal drug-related offenses and provided funding for drug prevention, education, and treatment. Also that year, he issued an executive order authorizing federal agencies to establish programs for drug testing of employees.

As part of the war on drugs, Congress enacted the Anti-Drug Abuse Act of 1988, which directed the president to examine the extent and nature of the drug problem and to propose policies for dealing with it. An Office of National Drug Control Policy (ONDCP) was established in the Executive Office of the President, with the director appointed by the president and confirmed by the Senate.

In September 1989 President George Bush issued his President's National Drug Control Strategy, in which he called for a "larger and more flexible information base in order to help us refine and target our counterdrug efforts." President Bush's drug-control strategy contained provisions for federal grants to state and local agencies for law enforcement purposes, along with numerous provisions for attempts at drug enforcement. It was praised by some and criticized by others, but no significant effects were seen in the fight against drugs, leading some to argue for legalization of drugs. William J. Bennett, the director of ONDCP, and called the *drug czar*, responded that legalization is an idea "seductively simple" and an argument "so dumb only intellectuals would believe" it.[32]

In 1990 Bennett resigned and was succeeded by Robert Martinez, former Florida governor, who was succeeded by President Bill Clinton's appointment, Lee P. Brown, former New York City police commissioner. Brown toned down the war-approach language to illegal drugs. President Clinton kept a rather low profile about drugs despite his frequent references to being tough on crime. When his appointed U.S. surgeon general, Joycelyn Elders, suggested that we study legalizing drugs, a move that she claimed might reduce crime, her comments were not embraced by the White House. In 1994 Elders's son was convicted of drug violations. She subsequently resigned her position for other reasons.

When Brown resigned as drug czar, Clinton appointed Barry R. McCaffrey, a retired four-star army general. McCaffrey alleged that we had become complacent about the war on drugs and that we needed to place greater emphasis on treatment and prevention. In early 1997 President Clinton released his new drug control strategy, which focused on reducing the use of drugs among young people. Critics called the policy a recycled one and emphasized that Clinton had done very little to combat drugs during his first three years in office. Criticism of Clinton's drug policies intensified during the 1996 presidential campaign.

By mid-1998 the Clinton administration had another drug plan for controlling drug trafficking. Among the proposals was the appointment of a federal official to coordinate law enforcement efforts to control the traffic of illegal drugs into the United States at each of the 24 points of entry from Mexico. Drug czar McCaffrey proclaimed, "Only by working together, utilizing the strengths of all of our agencies, can we build a border infrastructure that will defeat the flow of drugs."[33]

In May 2001 President George W. Bush nominated John P. Walters as drug czar. Walters, described as a tough conservative, has long talked about punishing rather than treating drug offenders. He served as the deputy drug director under Bush's father, President George H. Bush. In introducing his nominee, Bush proclaimed that Walters would lead "an all-out effort to reduce illegal drug use. Acceptance of drug use is simply not an option for this administration . . . We emphatically disagree with those who favor drug legalization." Bush said that under legalization "drug use and addiction would soar."[34]

In recent years the U.S. war on drugs has been severely criticized. Critics argue that the war denies to some sick people the drugs needed for treatment, noting that drugs such as marijuana and heroin are helpful in the treatment of cancer pain, nausea due to radiation and chemotherapy, and glaucoma (an eye disease that results in the loss of vision and can cause blindness). The legalization of marijuana for medicinal purposes is discussed below. But with regard to the war on drugs, an internationally acclaimed drug policy expert, Arnold S. Trebach, stated in 1988 that, although they victimize millions, drug policies bring little benefit to anyone. According to Trebach, "We do not now have, and never had, the capability to manage a successful war on any drug."[35]

Social scientists have also been critical of the war on drugs. Three sociologists traced what they described as the failure of the current war on drugs back to the efforts of Harry Anslinger, director of the Federal Bureau of Narcotics (FBN) from 1930 until his retirement (which, they allege, was forced) in 1962. During that period, according to these scholars, Anslinger used measures to discredit, humiliate, and harass Alfred Lindesmith, a sociologist and researcher who argued for approximately four decades that drug addicts should be treated, not punished. One of Anslinger's methods was to discredit a Canadian film, *Drug Addict,* that was developed for training of police and drug counselors. The film embraced the following themes, also supported by Lindesmith:

(1) that addicts and traffickers are recruited from all races and classes;
(2) that high-level drug traffickers are white;
(3) that law enforcement only targets low-level dealers;
(4) that addiction is a sickness;
(5) that addiction to legal and illegal drugs are essentially the same;
(6) that cocaine is not necessarily addictive; and
(7) that law enforcement control of drugs is in the final analysis impossible.[36]

The authors concluded that "in hindsight [the film] appeared to be the last and best chance to create a rational and humane policy on narcotics." Anslinger and his colleagues at the FBN, however, convinced Congress "to stiffen drug penalties and thus set the nation on a course that has led to its current failed policy."[37]

Although not all scholars or politicians would agree with Lindesmith and the other scholars, and certainly many oppose legalizing drugs, it is doubtful that anyone would seriously conclude that we have won the war on drugs or even that we are moving in that direction, especially with our punitive approach of mandatory and long sentences. In fact, a study conducted at the Harvard Medical School emphasized that nearly half of Massachusetts drug offenders who were given long mandatory prison sentences have no record of violence. "Mandatory sentencing laws are wasting prison resources on non-violent offenders and reducing resources available to lock up violent offenders," claimed the chief investigator of the study.[38]

The war on drugs is also very expensive, costing billions of dollars while showing little success. Illegal drugs are still readily available, drug addiction remains a serious problem, and the association between drug abuse and violent and property crimes is high. Further, illegal drug trafficking associated with organized crime in general and drug gangs in particular continues to be a cause of great concern both inside and outside U.S. prisons.[39]

One other issue that should be considered in the war on drugs is whether the government's approach has a differential impact on persons of color and the poor. Three scholars who analyzed National Institute of Justice publications concerning drug control concluded that the war on drugs perpetuates the image of the poor and minorities as a "criminal class." The scholars concluded that "minorities and the poor are affected disproportionately by drug control campaigns, which lead to their overrepresentation in arrests, prosecutions, convictions, and incarcerations." They allege that the studied reports "not only ignore the scholarly literature on race, class, and drugs but also fail to include research by other government agencies . . . that document such biases in drug control." The scholars propose that this is a form of government propaganda—"the distortion of information for the purpose of influencing social action."[40]

Other areas of racial discrimination with regard to the drug war have been suggested. Michael Tonry, a law professor, has alleged that racial disparities in drug sentencing have "steadily gotten worse since 1980." Tonry cites as one example the differential sentences Congress has provided for possession of powder cocaine and crack cocaine. Crack, which is less expensive, is used more by African Americans; power is used more by whites. The differential is 100 to 1. And although the U.S. Sentencing Commission has recommended changing this ratio, it has not been done.[41]

African Americans have argued that they are more often selected for drug prosecutions, but in 1996 in *United States* v. *Armstrong* the U.S. Supreme Court ruled that a defendant who alleges racial bias regarding prosecutorial discretion must show that similarly situated persons of other races are not prosecuted. This case involved crack cocaine and the Court held that the appellants did not show racial bias in the prosecutions of the crime.[42]

One final issue concerning the impact of drug laws on race relates to a 1998 statute providing that for one year after a conviction on drug possession charges and two years after a conviction for selling drugs, college students become ineligible for federal financial aid and loans. Repeat offenders may become ineligible for any future financial aid. The statute had not been enforced, but in 2001, under the Bush administration, some students were notified of their loss of financial aid. It is alleged that the law will impact more heavily on minorities than on whites, as minorities rely more on financial aid and African Americans are more often arrested for drug offenses. According to the executive director of the Drug Reform Coordination Network, "While about 13 percent of the people taking illicit drugs are black, the same as their proportion in the general population, blacks represent 55 percent of the drug convictions. . . . There is every reason to believe there will be some racial disparity in the way this law operates."[43]

State Laws

In addition to the federal government's efforts, states have waged their own wars on drugs. Some state antidrug laws have been upheld; others have been declared unconstitutional. For example, in 1991 the U.S. Supreme Court held that a Michigan statute providing for a life sentence without possibility of parole for possession of more than 650 grams (about 23 ounces) of cocaine did not violate the cruel and unusual punishment clause of the Eighth Amendment to the U.S. Constitution (see Appendix A), but in 1992 the state supreme court held that the statute did violate Michigan's constitutional prohibition against cruel and unusual punishment.[44]

Other severe state laws have been examined. Those of New York, known as the Rockefeller laws, were enacted in 1973 during the administration of New York's governor Nelson Rockefeller. There have been recent calls for revision of those laws, with editorials in the *New York Times* headlined "Drug Laws That Misfired," and "Drug Laws That Destroy Lives." According to the editorials, the harsh penalties have not cut addiction or lowered drug-related crime rates, and the primary result of them has been to overcrowd the state's prisons.[45]

In 2001 attempts were made to ease the Rockefeller laws. New York's governor George E. Pataki, a Republican, supported these attempts, but as of this writing the laws have not been changed significantly. Over the years, however, the sentences of some defendants who had served long terms for drug possession have been commuted; other defendants have been pardoned.

The Legalization Debate

Many agree that some aspects of substance abuse should be included in the criminal law. The production and sale of dangerous narcotics are examples. There is not much agreement, however, on the criminalization of the possession of small amounts of drugs such as marijuana, the use of which is considered by many people to be a private matter. Others say the drug is dangerous. They may cite the evidence from New York City regarding increased violence associated with the drug, which has become rather expensive in that city. According to police, shootings related to marijuana use and sales have gone up in recent years. One area police chief stated, "Some people may think the drug is benign, but the distribution network certainly is not."[46] (See Media Focus 10.1, p. 311.)

Others argue that the prosecution of marijuana possession is not an effective use of the criminal law. In 1995 federal judge Richard Posner, appointed by President Ronald Reagan and considered to be one of the "most brilliant judges in the country," called for legalizing marijuana. According to Judge Posner,

> It is nonsense that we should be devoting so many law enforcement resources to marijuana . . . I am skeptical that a society that is so tolerant of alcohol and cigarettes should come down so hard on marijuana use and send people to prison for life without parole.[47]

In support of Judge Posner's position is the fact that several states—including California—have legalized the use of marijuana for medical purposes. In 2001, however, the U.S. Supreme Court, in a unanimous vote, held that the *federal* statute prohibiting the use of marijuana had been misinterpreted by a lower federal court in California. The lower court had held that a cooperative that supplied marijuana to patients whose doctors prescribed it for medical treatment had an adequate legal defense. The Supreme Court ruling, although involving a technical issue beyond the scope of this discussion, may be viewed as a setback for the trend toward decriminalization of the use of marijuana for medical reasons.[48]

The Treatment Approach

Another approach to drug abuse is to reduce or discontinue punishment and focus on treatment. The treatment approach is seen in the reactions of some jurisdictions, which are moving toward providing treatment and rehabilitation rather than prosecuting substance abuse violations under the criminal law. The following Idaho statute illustrates this trend:

> It is the policy of this state that alcoholics, intoxicated persons or drug addicts may not be subjected to criminal prosecution or incarceration solely because of their consumption of alcoholic beverages or addiction to drugs but rather should be afforded treatment in order that they may lead normal lives as productive members of society.[49]

The statute continues with the declaration that the government should utilize state and federal resources to facilitate research of and treatment for alcoholism and drug addiction.

In the fall of 2000, when California was facing a November vote on Proposition 36, a proposal to focus on treatment rather than punishment of drug offenders, a *New York Times* editorial stated:

> California and the nation have spent the past two decades waging a drug war at an enormous financial and human cost. It is time to try treatment for low-level offenders, as the warehousing approach has so clearly failed.[50]

The California proposition, providing for treatment for first or second minor drug offenses, passed and took effect in 2001. Treatment personnel began preparing for the increase in patients and wondering whether the state would have the resources to deal with the influx. Proposition 36 does not apply to persons who sell or manufacture drugs, but it does apply to minor drug offenders who violate their parole. Funds provided for treatment may not be used for drug testing, and once an offender has completed his or her treatment program, the conviction will be dismissed.[51]

Even more serious than substance abuse, however, is the illegal trafficking in drugs.

ILLEGAL DRUG TRAFFICKING

According to the most recent commission on organized crime, illegal drug trafficking is the most serious problem in organized crime throughout the world. Billions of dollars in profits are generated for the underworld annually through illegal drug sales, and the crime results in "incalculable costs on individuals, families, communities, and governments worldwide." The commission emphasized that, although the influence of organized crime is significant, the individual user of illegal drugs must also be a target of control—without the demand from users, there would be no illegal drug market.[52]

First we will look at illegal drug trafficking and then at organized crime.

Illegal Drug Trafficking Dynamics

Although some illegal drugs are produced in the United States, significant quantities of illegal drugs are smuggled into the country. Illegal drugs are difficult to detect for a number of reasons. They may be hidden in many ways; Exhibit 10.1 describes some of the methods by which cocaine and heroin are smuggled. A careful reading of Exhibit 10.1 makes obvious the difficulties that law enforcement officers encounter in apprehending the smugglers at points of entry. Further problems arise because of the many points of entry into the United States by air, sea, and land and because of the millions of people who cross U.S. borders daily.

Some drugs are smuggled into the United States (or any other country) in small amounts, which are valuable because of the high price they command. Drugs are smuggled in large shipments, too, and divided and sold to dealers. The purity of the drugs may be diluted. There may be several stages in the processes of receiving, distributing, and selling drugs, and the processes may cover a large geographical area, be highly organized, and involve many people.

Violence is common in drug trafficking. It is used to reduce or eliminate competition, expand markets, and intimidate anyone who interferes with the crimes. That includes witnesses, law enforcement, and other personnel. Drug informers and anyone who cheats, steals from, or lies to a drug dealer may be killed.

Another characteristic of illegal drug traffickers is that they may attempt to corrupt public officials. Police are said to be at highest risk because of their arrest power, but corruption occurs at other levels as well. Some examples are

- Selling information about upcoming police raids, agents, and police information.
- Accepting bribes to tamper with evidence or committing perjury in order to protect an illegal drug dealer.
- Stealing drugs from police property rooms or laboratories for personal use or sale.

EXHIBIT 10.1

Methods Used for Smuggling Cocaine and Heroin

BY COURIER

One courier had a half pound of cocaine surgically implanted under the skin of each of his thighs. The cocaine was divided into four one-square-inch packages of one-quarter pound each.

Cocaine was concealed in a stuffed teddy bear. Two teddy bears were found, one was heavier and had a Velcro closure.

Drugs were transported after couriers swallowed latex condoms, balloons, or tips of surgical gloves filled with drugs.

1.7 pounds of heroin were sewn into a compartment of a woman's undergarment.

Cocaine is carried across the border in Arizona on the backs of mules or horses or on foot. Couriers usually travel in groups through canyons or deserts.

Couriers pose as vacationers and pack their luggage with substantial amounts of drugs.

More than a ton of drugs was carried through a concrete-reinforced tunnel (30 feet underground, 5 feet high, and 4 feet wide). Endpoints of the tunnel were a house in Agua Prieta, Mexico, and a warehouse in Douglas, Arizona. The house had hydraulic jacks to raise and lower the floor at the entrance to the tunnel.

IN SHIPPING CONTAINERS

12 tons of cocaine were shipped from Venezuela to Miami inside concrete fencing posts.

Variable amounts of cocaine were containerized and shipped out of Ecuador with such products as shrimp, cacao, and bananas.

150 kilograms of cocaine were flown from Colombia to Honduras, shipped by truck to port, and packaged with crates of plantains, with the fruit on top.

Crack concealed in a box of Cheese Nips was seized in a Greyhound bus station.

225 kilograms of cocaine were packed in false-bottomed metal boxes labeled as toilet seats and bathroom sinks.

Cocaine was found in 17 counterfeit bottles of Pony Malta de Bavaria. The fake bottles were 6.16 ounces, whereas authentic bottles are 6.2 ounces. They were traced to a company called Miami Sweet Import and Export, Inc., and sported an ungrammatical translation of the real company's slogan.

More than a ton of cocaine was found in twelve 55-gallon drums of guava pulp. The cocaine was in plastic packets inside the fruit.

More than 100 of 1,190 cardboard boxes packed with canned fruit were stuffed with cocaine.

Cocaine was wrapped in small plastic packets, wrapped in thick plastic, and buried inside 55-gallon drums of a toxic powdered chemical.

190 pounds of heroin were concealed in a bean-sprout washing machine shipped to Boston from Hong Kong.

2,400 pounds of cocaine were packaged in anchovy cans shipped from Argentina. These cans were weighted and packed to match the surrounding cans, which were packed with anchovies.

800 pounds of heroin were packed into shipments of golf-cart tires.

A shipment containing 25 boxes of live goldfish included dead fish which had been loaded with 3 pounds of heroin.

Peruvian handicrafts and cans marked asparagus were filled with 201 kilograms of cocaine.

Panamanian cocaine smugglers have developed a new technology that combines cocaine with vinyl to produce a material that has been used in making luggage and sneakers. The cocaine is separated from the vinyl after reaching its destination.

SMUGGLING IN AIRCRAFT, BOATS, AND MOTOR VEHICLES

Airdrops of drugs are used so that the pilot of the plane does not have to land. To make the airdrop more precise, some pilots have begun to use high-technology transponders and other homing devices.

3,000 kilograms of cocaine were smuggled in suitcases which were hidden behind interior panels of airplanes. Three former Eastern Airlines baggage handlers smuggled varying amounts in this manner on 13 different flights.

Cocaine was hidden in a secret tank within the fuel tank of a cabin cruiser.

Cocaine was packed in 1-kilogram lots and placed inside plastic pipe which was bolted to the bottom of a banana boat docked in the Bridgeport, Connecticut, Harbor. The pipe was fastened along the center line of the bottom of the ship's hull.

220 pounds of cocaine were found in hidden compartments in a van that could only be opened electronically.

(continued)

EXHIBIT 10.1

Methods Used for Smuggling Cocaine and Heroin, *(continued)*

160 pounds of cocaine were sewn into the interior roof of a family station wagon and transported during a family vacation.

Almost 1,300 pounds of cocaine were concealed in a false compartment in the floor of a motor home.

More than 1,000 kilograms of heroin were found in a truck under eight tons of onions.

Cocaine was packed in cartons and transported in rented moving trucks. Occasionally, large recreational vehicles were used. Both of these methods allow couriers to elude suspicion of out-of-state vehicles and licenses.

Cocaine was enclosed in the gas tank of a car equipped with a baffle which made the left side a separate compartment. The compartment was accessible through a plate attached to the top of the gas tank. The gas gauge worked in a normal manner; however, the car had to be refueled more frequently than other cars.

A front-wheel drive Cadillac had a false drive shaft hump running through the interior of the car to house drugs.

Source: Bureau of Justice Statistics, *Drugs, Crime and the Justice System* (Washington, DC: U.S. Department of Justice, December 1992), pp. 44–45.

- Stealing drugs or money for personal use from sellers and users without arresting them.
- Extorting money or property from drug dealers in exchange for failure to arrest them or seize their drugs.[53]

Another important characteristic of illegal drug trafficking is that, although a few make millions, most drug dealers are not wealthy. Many of the lower-level drug dealers are drug addicts whose habit consumes their profits, and these persons may spend a lot of their time in jail or prison.

Money laundering Hiding the existence, illegal use of, or illegal source of income and making that income appear legal by disguising it.

Finally, **money laundering** plays an important role in illegal drug trafficking. Money laundering is a process of concealing the existence, source, and disposition of money secured from illegal sources. The term is derived from the reference criminals make to "dirty" money that is "laundered clean" so that it can be used openly. For example, large sums of money obtained by selling illegal drugs are channeled through legitimate sources to make it appear that the money has been obtained legally. The transaction might be as simple as sending the cash to another country or as complex as taking over a bank. Large amounts of cash are difficult to handle ($1 million in $20 bills weighs over 100 pounds) and easily stolen. Thus, drug trafficking money may be secured in foreign banks or invested in legitimate stocks, bonds, businesses, or other sources. More complicated money-laundering schemes may involve multiple transactions and financial institutions in several countries.[54] Many money-laundering transactions would be legal if they involved money secured from legal sources or activities.

Colombian Drug Cartels

Two drug cartels in Colombia, South America, are thought to have controlled, at one time, approximately 80 percent of the cocaine traffic in the world. The cartels are named after cities.

The Medellin Cartel

The Medellin Cartel was started in the late 1970s and involved numerous drug lords who found it more feasible to work as a group than individually. They pooled their cocaine and smuggled it into other countries. The cartel became known widely in 1986, when U.S. attorneys drew up an indictment for many of the cartel members and publicized their efforts. According to a news article, "The indictment labeled the cartel the world's biggest drug-smuggling organization and charged it with producing 58 tons of cocaine between 1978 and 1985."[55]

The 1991 surrender in Bogotá, Colombia, of Pablo Escobar, one of the most wanted criminals in the world and a billionaire drug baron, meant that all of the most influential leaders in the Medellin Cartel were either in prison or dead. It was alleged that Escobar ordered the killing of hundreds of Colombians; officials hoped that his surrender would make Colombia a safer place to live. Leaders in the United States speculated that Escobar's incarceration would have little effect on drug trafficking: either he would continue to run his business from prison or others would run it for him. Prior to turning himself in, Escobar declared that he would surrender if his president promised that he would not face **extradition** to the United States, which was holding 10 indictments against him for murder and drug trafficking. Escobar surrendered "hours after an assembly reforming Colombia's constitution decided to scrap extradition, the weapon most feared by Colombia's drug traffickers."[56]

Extradition The process by which an accused is removed from one jurisdiction (usually a state or country) to another for purposes of proceeding with legal actions, such as a trial.

Violence, including the murder of judges, many of whom were bribed, has characterized Colombia's justice system. Officials in the United States speculated that Escobar and his colleagues would make a "mockery of law enforcement

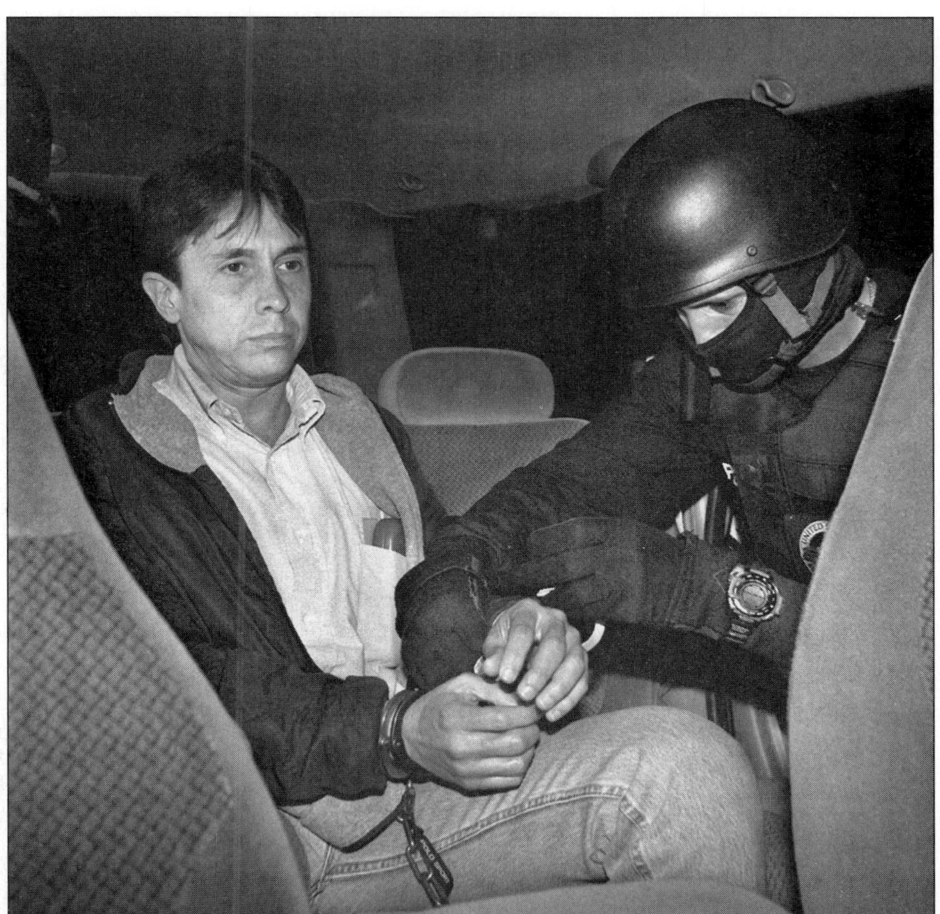

Fabio Ochoa was extradited from Bogotá, Colombia, on 8 September 2001 to face charges on drug trafficking. Here he is assisted from his seat on the airplane by a uniformed officer before being transported to the Miami Federal Detention Center. (Pool Photo Courtesy U.S. Drug Enforcement Administration/Getty Images)

at home and abroad." Perhaps that was correct. Escobar was housed in a private, luxurious, high-security prison located in the hills, with an excellent view. Three of his colleagues who surrendered earlier had comfortable prison quarters that they furnished to their own tastes and where they dined "on their mother's home-cooked meals." It was believed that the traffickers continued to deal in drugs from this "prison."[57]

In July 1992 two government officials were taken hostage when they visited the prison to negotiate the transfer of Escobar and his associates to another prison. After army troops attacked, the officials were freed unharmed, but Escobar and nine of his associates escaped. The inmates were said to be hiding in a tunnel and prepared to fight for their freedom.[58] In 1993, Escobar was killed, essentially ending the power and influence of the Medellin Cartel.

The Cali Cartel

The Cali Cartel (or Cali Mafia) existed alongside the Medellin, and it was suggested that they divided up the lucrative U.S. drug markets. After the decline of the Medellin, the Cali Cartel expanded and gained more power. It was thought to have grossed $7 billion in 1994 in the United States alone and, by 1995, to be in control of 80 percent of the world's cocaine. The head of the U.S. Drug Enforcement Administration (DEA) said of the cartel, "This is probably the biggest organized-crime syndicate there has ever been . . . For their impact, profit and control, they're bigger than the Mafia in the U.S. ever was."[59]

The Cali Cartel has been distinguished from the Medellin by the difference in the way violence was used against public officials. Escobar and his colleagues engaged in the assassinations of high-level public officials. It was claimed that the Cali Cartel members would engage in violence against public officials only if they interfered directly with the cartel's business. Another difference was in the attempt to gain publicity. One drug expert stated that, unlike Medellin members, when Cali Cartel members order a hit, "they don't leave their calling cards."[60]

In June 1995 U.S. officials unsealed a 161-page indictment charging 59 persons allegedly connected to the Cali Cartel with conspiring to smuggle more than 200 tons of cocaine into the United States. By the middle of July 1995, five of the seven Cali Cartel bosses had been arrested in raids that involved 6,000 police and soldiers.

The indictment alleged that from about 1983 the cartel met the Racketeer Influenced and Corrupt Organizations Statute's criterion to be defined as an enterprise. (This statute is discussed later in this chapter.) Specifically, the indictment alleged that the cartel was

> a group of individuals and entities, foreign and domestic, associated in fact for the purposes of importing and distributing cocaine, laundering the proceeds and profits of cocaine trafficking through the use of foreign and domestic corporations and financial institutions, concealing the source and true owners of the finances for the acquisition of these assets and protecting the leaders of the Enterprise from arrest and prosecution.[61]

Subsequent sections of the indictment contained specific charges of racketeering (discussed later in this chapter), conspiracy, money laundering, obstruction of justice, murder, extortion, and other crimes. It was alleged that drugs were smuggled into the United States in frozen broccoli boxes, cement posts, and other such items and shipped to storage and distribution points throughout the country.

Included among the 59 defendants were six U.S. lawyers. Their indictments raised the ire of the criminal defense bar, who claimed they were targeted by U.S. law enforcement officials. Prosecutors argued that the indicted lawyers stepped over the line between acceptable representation of their clients and criminal activity. Four of the six attorneys entered guilty pleas; two,

Michael Abbell and William Moran, went to trial. Their first trial, in 1997, ended with acquittals for the most serious charges (racketeering) and a deadlocked jury on four conspiracy charges. In July 1998 they were convicted of racketeering and money-laundering conspiracy but not of drug-trafficking conspiracy. A warrant was secured for the arrest of Moran, who, upon hearing that a verdict was to be returned shortly by the jury, left the courthouse and never returned.[62] Two months later he was arrested in Mexico City. His bond was revoked pending sentencing. Both Moran and Abbell faced life in prison, but Moran was sentenced to only five years and Abbell was sentenced to more than seven years.

Although some DEA agents claimed to this author in 1995 that the administration had broken the back of the Cali Cartel, in July 2001 Segundo Quinones was sentenced to 30 years in prison. Quinones was the captain of a fishing trawler, the *Layneyd,* that the government seized in connection with a Tampa, Florida–based investigation called Operation Panama Express. Said to be one of the largest drug probes in U.S. history, this operation has targeted Joaquin Mario Valencia-Trujillo, the new leader of the Cali Cartel. At the time of Quinones's sentencing in July 2001, the investigation had seized 80 tons of cocaine worth $1.6 billion. The *Layneyd* was carrying four tons of cocaine when it was seized.[63]

The Control of Drug Trafficking

In recent years, efforts to control drug trafficking in the United States have focused primarily on long prison sentences. Long sentences for drug offenses, however, must be considered in terms of their full impact on criminal justice systems. It is very costly to investigate and prosecute drug cases because of the sophisticated techniques required for intelligence gathering. Trials are long and complicated. Drug traffickers are known to intimidate or even kill witnesses. Danger to witnesses requires the government to protect some through the Witness Program (commonly called the *witness protection program*). This program is sponsored by the U.S. marshals and provides a new identity and a new location for persons who aid the government in dangerous, high-profile prosecutions. This is a very expensive process, and not everyone wishes to have a new identity.

Expensive rewards are used to entice witnesses to give information that will lead to the indictment and arrest of high-level drug traffickers. But even if suspects are convicted and receive long sentences, it is not clear they will serve time in prisons rather than in plush detention facilities, as noted earlier in the case of Escobar. Nevertheless, prison sentencing remains the primary approach in the drug control strategy. In fact, several sections of the Violent Crime Control and Law Enforcement Act of 1994 involved enhanced penalties for drug offenses, including drug trafficking in prisons.[64]

One final weapon of prosecutors in fighting drug trafficking has been to charge defense attorneys who represent persons charged with crimes associated with drug trafficking, as noted in the discussion of the Cali Cartel. In May 2001 Neil Taylor—a Miami, Florida, defense attorney—was tried on charges of money laundering, conspiracy to obstruct justice, and filing false tax returns after he accepted money for legal fees to represent Willie Falcon and Sal Magluta, accused of operating a $2 billion drug trafficking business in Miami. Three other attorneys who represented Falcon and Magluta (who had 40 or more attorneys at various stages) were convicted of drug-related offenses as a result of their representation of these men.

As a result of the government's prosecutions of defense attorneys, some lawyers who had specialized in representing those accused of drug trafficking have ceased doing so. One attorney said in reference to these prosecutions, "This has had a chilling effect on criminal defense lawyers. I and most lawyers will not go near cases where the fees are questionable, because they're absolutely not worth it."[65]

In concluding these sections on drug abuse and trafficking, it is pertinent to note that in March 2001 the government released a report based on a study by 15 economists, criminologists, and psychiatrists assembled by the National Research Council (an arm of the National Academy of Sciences) during the Clinton administration. Although the report took no position on the controversial issue of whether we should focus on punishment or treatment of drug offenders, it did conclude that the data and research available on what works in reducing the demand and supply of drugs are so poor that no reasonable assessments can be made. A spokesman for the Bush White House stated, "We will pay close attention to the report's findings, particularly the need for improved data and research in the area of law enforcement." Among other relevant data in the report is the fact that the $30 billion spent by federal, state, and local governments to combat drugs in 1999 was twice the amount of money the United States spent on the Persian Gulf War of 1991. Finally, the report concluded that "even what might seem the simplest measures of success in the battle against illegal drugs are unreliable."[66]

ORGANIZED CRIME

For a long time the crimes of the underworld have been a source of mystery and excitement and have captured our attention through fictional works such as *The Godfather,* a novel published in 1969 and subsequently made into a movie, both of which have enjoyed immense success.

The ability of underworld criminals to elude law enforcement is well known; in many cases, underworld activities have provided services and commodities that, although labeled illegal by statute, are considered sources of pleasure in our daily lives. In these cases unsuccessful law enforcement may not be viewed as a problem; indeed, attempts to enforce the law may be regarded as a nuisance. Organized crime has infiltrated legitimate businesses in many cases to the extent that the relationship between organized crime and legitimate society is one of cooperation.

The cost of organized crime to society, impossible to determine, goes beyond the loss of property and life and includes the high cost of attempts to control and eradicate organized crime.

The Concept of Organized Crime

The first problem in an analysis of organized crime is to define the concept. There is little agreement on the definition, as noted in Exhibit 10.2, which contains a list and brief discussion of general characteristics of organized crime. In some countries the term *organized crime* is synonymous with *professional crime.* It is true that all professional crime is to some extent organized. Early sociologists used the term *organized crime* to describe professional criminals in contrast to amateur criminals. According to Alfred Lindesmith, organized crime is "usually professional crime . . . involving a system of specifically defined relationships with mutual obligations and privileges." Edwin H. Sutherland and Donald R. Cressey defined organized crime as the "association of a small group of criminals for the execution of a certain type of crime."[67] These definitions include any small group of criminals who organize to engage in their professional work.

Syndicate A group of persons who organize for the purpose of carrying out matters (usually financial) of mutual interest, not illegal by definition, but often associated with illegal activities such as organized crime.

In recent years the term *organized crime* has been used more narrowly. Many people think of organized crime as a national or international **syndicate** that infiltrates businesses at the local and national level. This view is not accepted by

EXHIBIT 10.2

Organized Crime: An Overview

WHAT IS ORGANIZED CRIME?

Although organized crime has been considered a problem throughout the century, no universally accepted definition of the term has been established. The President's Commission on Organized Crime, for example, defines the criminal group involved in organized crime as "a continuing, structured collectivity of persons who utilize criminality, violence, and a willingness to corrupt in order to gain and maintain power and profit."

Some characteristics of organized crime are generally cited:

- **Organizational continuity:** Organized crime groups ensure that they can survive the death or imprisonment of their leaders and can vary the nature of their activities to take advantage of changing criminal opportunities.
- **Hierarchical structure:** All organized crime groups are headed by a single leader and structured into a series of subordinate ranks, although they may vary in the rigidity of their hierarchy. Nationwide organizations may be composed of multiple separate chapters or "families," each unit generally headed by its own leader who is supported by the group's hierarchy of command. Intergroup disputes, joint ventures, and new membership are generally reviewed by a board composed of the leaders of the most powerful individual chapters. For example, La Cosa Nostra currently is estimated to include 24 individual "families" all under the general authority of a "National Commission" comprised of an estimated nine bosses.
- **Restricted membership:** Members must be formally accepted by the group after a demonstration of loyalty and a willingness to commit criminal acts. Membership may be limited by race or common background and generally involves a lifetime commitment to the group, which can be enforced through violent group actions.
- **Criminality/violence/power:** Power and control are key organized crime goals and may be obtained through criminal activity of one type or in multiple activities. Criminal activity may be designed directly to generate "income" or to support the group's power through bribery, violence, and intimidation. Violence is used to maintain group loyalty and to intimidate outsiders and is a threat underlying all group activity. Specific violent criminal acts include, for example, murder, kidnapping, arson, robbery, and bombings.
- **Legitimate business involvement:** Legitimate businesses are used to "launder" illegal funds or stolen merchandise. For example, illegal profits from drug sales can be claimed as legitimate profits of a noncriminal business whose accounting records have been appropriately adjusted. Legitimate business involvement also elevates the social status of organized crime figures.
- **Use of specialists:** Outside specialists, such as pilots, chemists, and arsonists, provide services under contract to organized crime groups on an intermittent or regular basis.

ORGANIZED CRIME GROUPS OFTEN ARE PROTECTED BY CORRUPT OFFICIALS IN THE GOVERNMENT AND PRIVATE SECTOR

Such officials include inspectors who overlook violations, accountants who conceal assets, financial officers who fail to report major cash transactions, law enforcement officers who provide enforcement activity information to drug traffickers, and attorneys who have government witnesses intimidated to change their testimony. The public also supports organized crime by sometimes knowingly or unknowingly purchasing illegal goods and "hot" merchandise.

ORGANIZED CRIME GROUPS ARE INVOLVED IN MANY DIFFERENT ACTIVITIES

In addition to its well-known involvement in illegal drugs, organized crime is also involved in prostitution, gambling, and loan-sharking operations and has been shown to have infiltrated legitimate industries such as construction, waste removal, wholesale and retail distribution of goods, hotel and restaurant operations, liquor sales, motor vehicle repairs, real estate, and banking.

Source: Bureau of Justice Statistics, *Report to the Nation on Crime and Justice: the Data,* 2d ed. (Washington, DC: U.S. Department of Justice, 1988), p. 8.

most social scientists; thus, it is important to distinguish the two major approaches to defining organized crime: (1) the law enforcement perspective and (2) the social and economic perspective.

The most common view of organized crime is the law enforcement perspective. In its 1967 report, the President's Commission on Law Enforcement and Administration of Justice defined organized crime as "a society that seeks to operate outside the control of the American people and their working government." According to that report, organized crime involves thousands of criminals. They operate in a complex organizational structure, and they have rules that are more rigid and more strictly enforced than those of legitimate government. Money and power are their goals. They infiltrate legitimate as well as illegitimate businesses.[68]

A second approach views organized crime as "an integral part of the nation's social, political, and economic life—as one of the major social ills, such as poverty or racism, that grew with urban living in America." Organized crime does involve minority groups, but that involvement is seen by this second perspective as the *process* by which those groups begin to establish themselves and gain power in society. As more acceptable avenues for this process become available, the criminals may move into legitimate enterprises while other groups move into organized crime to begin their process of integration into the society.[69]

Another version of this functional perspective comes from economists who view organized crime as just another economic enterprise. Organized crime supplies goods and services to customers seeking them. Even when the supply is considered illegal by the government at a given time—for example, liquor during Prohibition—the economic process is the same as it would be if the enterprise were not defined as criminal. In organized crime, however, the *proceeds* from these illegal sales are used to engage in other illegal activities, such as corrupting public officials in order to gain protection from prosecution.[70]

These two approaches to the concept of organized crime have some common elements. In both perspectives, the activity is organized and goes on beyond the life of any one particular member. Both perspectives see the need for and the existence of some degree of protection, which is obtained by corrupting public officials. Both perspectives view organized crime as a way of providing illegal goods and services demanded by the public. These similarities have led to the following definition of organized crime as:

> a persisting form of criminal activity that brings together a client-public which demands a range of goods and services defined as illegal. It is a structure or network of individuals who produce or supply those goods and services, use the capital to expand into other legitimate or illegitimate activities, and corrupt public officials with the aim of gaining their protection.[71]

Despite this attempt to articulate a definition of organized crime that is broad enough to include the two perspectives, the view persists of organized crime as roughly synonymous with the national (or international) crime syndicate characterized by Italian membership. This perspective has obvious implications in terms of attempts to eradicate or to control organized crime. It leads to a focus on catching the notorious underworld criminals rather than on making changes in the social system. The lack of a generally accepted definition of organized crime results also in a variety of definitions throughout the states.[72]

The History and Organization of Organized Crime

Many scholars believe that organized crime was not pervasive before the 20th century and that its development as a large-scale operation was a result of Prohibition, discussed earlier in this chapter. They trace the history of organized crime to the Volstead Act, the Eighteenth Amendment, passed in 1919, which made it illegal to sell and distribute alcohol. The "Great Experiment," as some called Prohibition, "provided a catalyst of opportunity that caused organized crime, especially violent forms, to blossom into an important force in American society."[73] Our puritanical approach to the suppression of vice, of which Prohibition is an example, has provided a fertile bed for the growth of organized crime. It can provide the services consumers want but are forbidden by law to obtain.

A study of the history of organized crime must include brief mention of the reports of four major official studies that preceded the most recent government report. The Committee to Investigate Crime in Interstate Commerce (named the Kefauver Committee, after Estes Kefauver, its chair) found widespread involvement of organized crime in gambling and other forms of racketeering.[74] The Select Committee on Improper Activities in the Labor or Management Field (the McClellan Committee) reported numerous incidents of organized criminal activity among labor unions.[75] The 1967 President's Commission on Law Enforcement and Administration of Justice (or, simply, the President's Commission) found that in American cities organized crime is widespread—dominating activities such as gambling, narcotics traffic, and **loan sharking**—and that, in addition, organized criminals have invested some of their money in legitimate businesses in which they have some control indirectly.[76] The National Advisory Committee on Criminal Justice Standards and Goals, which issued its report on organized crime in 1976, concluded that organized crime had infiltrated legitimate as well as illegitimate businesses and was spreading rapidly.[77]

Loan sharking Lending money at very high interest rates and later using extortionate means to force the borrower to repay the loan.

Finally, in July 1983 President Ronald Reagan expressed his concern for the need to combat organized crime in the United States by naming a 20-person organized crime commission. The commission was headed by Judge Irving R. Kaufman of the U.S. Court of Appeals for the Second Circuit. It issued an interim report in 1984 and a final report on labor and management racketeering in 1986. The work of the commission was not without controversy from the outside, but even the members disagreed among themselves on the final report. Nine of them questioned the methods used for reaching conclusions and accused the commission of mismanaging time, staff, and money.[78]

The 1967 President's Commission described organized crime as a highly organized structure with the lords of the underworld at the top. These persons make all the important decisions, and since few are detected, not much is known about their career patterns. At the bottom are those who deal directly with the public and resemble conventional offenders in their career patterns.[79]

Organized crime is directed by a syndicate, a group of persons who organize to carry out their mutual financial interests. There is disagreement about whether there is one or several syndicates in charge of all organized crime in the United States. Some, such as the Kefauver Committee, contend there is one syndicate, the **Mafia,** operating out of New York and Chicago and run by Italians from Sicily.[80] Others deny the existence of the Mafia.[81] The word *mafia* refers to a secret, highly organized hierarchical group involved in racketeering, smuggling, drug trafficking, and other illegal criminal activities. The term is used to encompass other organized crime syndicates, as will be seen below.

Mafia A secret organization with a strict hierarchical structure that is thought to be involved in smuggling, racketeering, drug trafficking, and other illegal activities worldwide. The Mafia infiltrates legal as well as illegal businesses.

According to the President's Commission, organized crime is controlled by 24 groups known as *families.* The size of a family ranges from 20 to 700 members. The families operate as criminal cartels in large American cities; most cities have only one family, although New York City has several. Each family is headed by a *boss,* who has complete authority over the family and can be overruled only by the national advisory commission. Reporting to the boss is the *underboss,* who, like the vice president of a company, acts in the absence of the president and serves as a mediator between the boss and lower-level management. The *consigliere,* or counselor, holds a position analogous to a legal adviser in a corporation. The lieutenants, or *caporegima,* are the middlemen in the management structure. They serve as buffers between the boss or underboss and internal or external conflicts. The lower-level management comprises *soldiers* who "operate the illegal enterprises on a commission basis or own illicit or licit businesses under the protection of the family."[82]

Many social scientists disagree with the use of this bureaucratic analogy, which they say is too rigid to explain the social, economic, and political dynamics of the organized crime family. They describe the family in *kinship* terms, maintaining that organized crime families are called families because many are tied by marriage or blood and because they exhibit some of the complex ties characteristic of families.[83] Others analyze organized crime in terms of an economic system and as an organization of power relationships.[84]

The President's Commission concluded that the organized crime families were in frequent communication and their membership was exclusively Italian. The name of the organization had been changed from the Mafia to La Cosa Nostra (LCN), which means "our thing." The 24 groups controlled other groups that often had members from other ethnic backgrounds. The ultimate authority in the organization was the *commission,* which served primarily as a judicial body. It was made up of 9 to 12 men, not all of equal rank and power. The respect they commanded and the power they wielded appeared to be related to their own wealth, their tenure on the commission, and their positions as heads of large families or groups.[85]

In its 1986 report, a subsequent presidential commission did not define precisely the terms *Mafia* and *La Cosa Nostra* and insisted that although the report was centered on LCN, organized crime was broader than that. LCN, however, was the "group most entrenched in labor and business," infiltrating legitimate business more frequently than any other organized crime group.[86]

Despite the focus on the Mafia and LCN, it is important to emphasize that organized crime is much broader today than ever before, extending to other countries as well.

Organized Crime in Other Countries

The influence of organized crime has been felt around the world. In the early 1990s Italian government officials were making an effort to curb organized crime, which, as the most important private industry in that country, was estimated to gross around $75 billion a year.[87] In 1992, in separate incidents, two of Italy's most senior anti-Mafia crusaders, Judge Giovanni Falcone (along with five of his security guards and his wife, Francesca Morvillo) and Judge Paolo Borsellino (along with five of his guards), were murdered. These were atrocious killings, in which the bodies were literally blown apart by bombs placed underneath the highway on which the officials' motorcade was to pass.

In January 1993 Italian officials captured Salvatore (Toto) Riina, whom they had sought for 23 years. Riina was thought to be the "boss of all bosses" in the organized crime family La Cosa Nostra. He faced several life sentences for convictions obtained in his absence in the 1980s. Riina was accused of taking part in over 100 murders and engaging in extortion, corruption, fraud, and other crimes. Authorities accused him of "masterminding the Sicilian Mafia's growth from a band of island hoods to eminence in the world's billion-dollar cocaine and heroin markets." Riina claimed that he was a worker and knew nothing about LCN. In May 1993 Italian police arrested Benedetto (Nitto) Santapaola, "heir apparent to the leadership of Sicily's Costa Nostra and wanted on many counts of murder."[88]

The trial of 41 mafiosi charged with involvement in the high-tech assassinations of Falcone and Borsellino began in 1995. Salvatore Riina, the chief defendant, and other defendants who attended the trial (held in a windowless courtroom) watched the proceedings from a monitor in a steel cage with bulletproof glass. It was estimated that the trial might take up to two years, with 800 or more people testifying.[89] The trial ended in 1997 with nine acquittals. Life sentences were given to Riina, three of the men suspected of taking over the family after his arrest, and 20 other defendants. Six of the accused who cooperated with the prosecution were given more lenient sentences.[90]

After the 1992 murders of the judges, Italian officials intensified their efforts to eradicate organized crime. They were successful to some extent. By the summer of 1998, new legislation had been enacted, law enforcement had been enhanced and professionalized, 19 of the 30 most wanted organized crime figures had been arrested, and large Mafia assets had been seized. Some argued that the 1992 murders set the stage for massive crackdowns on organized crime, noting that the number of Mafia-type murders fell from 718 in 1991 to only 190 in 1997. Other, more cynical people said that new leaders had emerged, that the chief anti-Mafia prosecutor had resigned because he had not been given the promised resources, and that organized crime retained such a stronghold on industries that small-business owners were committing suicide to escape the power of the Italian Mafia.[91]

One of those arrested and tried for crimes associated with Italian organized crime was Giulio Andreotti, who served seven times as Italy's prime minister. The trial of Andreotti, which began in 1995, featured testimony from over 20 former members of the Mafia. The trial lasted four years and ended in acquittals for Andreotti.

One of those who testified against Andreotti was Tommaso Buscetta, the first major member of the Mafia to break the code of silence and turn against other members. Buscetta became an informer in 1984. After testifying against numerous Mafia figures in the United States, he was given U.S. citizenship and placed under federal witness protection. After a two-year battle with cancer, Buscetta died on 1 April 2000 at age 71. In an interview the previous day, he said that death would be a relief:

> For me, death has been like shade on a sunny day. As a Mafioso I knew I had to get accustomed to its company. It was in the rules. The useless death of others, the unjust death of innocents, convinced me not to remain a Mafioso.[92]

In June 1998 a former influential judge in Rome went on trial for alleged collusion with the Mafia. Two months earlier officials had arrested Vito Vitale, whom they described as "the most dangerous mafioso still at large" and the sole heir to Riina's powerful position in organized crime. Vitale had not been sighted by officials for 30 years, but his influence was well known. Also that year, 24 defendants were convicted for car bombings that damaged important buildings and killed 10 people in 1993. Those crimes were allegedly committed to avenge the arrest of Riina. Of the 24 defendants, 14 were sentenced to the maximum term, life in prison; others were assessed sentences ranging from 12 to 28 years.[93]

By the year 2001 authorities were arguing over whether the Mafia in Sicily was growing stronger or still declining. The Sicilian Mafia was thought to be staging a comeback, led by Bernardo Provenzano, age 68, said to be the current "boss of all bosses" and the most wanted man in Italy. But Provenzano has not been photographed since 1959, so police are not certain of the image of the man they are seeking. Some of Provenzano's associates have been arrested, but thus far not one has turned state's evidence on the boss. One Sicilian judge who has prosecuted numerous Mafia figures claimed in May 2001 that under the leadership of Provenzano the Mafia is "winning again."[94]

One final point on organized crime in Italy is that apparently the unwritten code of honor that once protected women from attacks by the members is dissolving. One member, referring to the death of a woman, noted that she was not killed in error: "She was a target because she knew as much as her husband."[95]

Organized Crime and Legitimate Business

Organized crime infiltrates many illegitimate businesses, such as prostitution, pornography, gambling, and illegal drug trafficking. But organized crime also controls legitimate businesses. In 1972 a federal court in Michigan underscored the involvement of organized crime in legitimate businesses. An excerpt from that case follows.[96]

United States v. Aquino

The Congress finds that (1) organized crime in the United States is a highly sophisticated, diversified, and widespread activity that annually drains billions of dollars from America's economy by unlawful conduct and the illegal use of force, fraud, and corruption; (2) organized crime derives a major portion of its power through money obtained from such illegal endeavors as syndicated gambling, loan-sharking, the theft and fencing of property, the importation and distribution of narcotics and other dangerous drugs, and other forms of social exploitation; (3) this money and power are increasingly used to infiltrate and corrupt legitimate business and labor unions and to subvert and corrupt our democratic processes; (4) organized crime activities in the United States weaken the stability of the Nation's economic system, harm innocent investors, interfere with free competition, seriously burden interstate and foreign commerce, threaten the domestic security, and undermine the general welfare of the Nation and its citizens.

This section overviews the infiltration of organized crime into the health care, meat, construction, and cartage industries.

Health Care

Chapter 9 contains information about fraud in the health care industry. In his testimony before a Senate committee in March 1995, FBI director Louis J. Freeh stated that organized crime had "penetrated virtually every legitimate segment of the health care industry." Freeh alleged that doctors, chiropractors, and attorneys had been corrupted by organized crime and that the list of schemes was extensive.[97]

In 1999 the U.S. General Accounting Office (GAO) issued a report on the infiltration of organized crime into the health care industry, concluding that organized crime is "carving out a role in Medicare, Medicaid, and private insurance health care fraud throughout the country." The GAO identified several fraud schemes, such as using patient brokering, in which "runners" are paid to recruit "patients" to go to health clinics for medical care they do not need. In some cases these "patients" are paid a portion of the "runner's" fee. The results of this and other types of schemes are increased medical costs and increased risks that medical benefits will be exhausted for some individuals whose names are used in the schemes.[98]

Two days before he left office in January 2001, President Bill Clinton issued numerous controversial pardons. One of those pardons was for Glenn Braswell, who was convicted of acts related to health care fraud in Florida. Braswell sold herbal supplements that were advertised as promoting increased bust size, hair growth, and cellulite removal. Braswell was under investigation by the Food and Drug Administration, the Federal Trade Commission, and the Internal Revenue Service at the time the pardon was issued. This pardon was one of several on which the president had not considered the recommendation of the U.S. Department of Justice.[99]

The infiltration of organized crime into the health care fields is not limited to the United States. In 1998 it was announced that the "federal government report on the growing menace of organized crime [in Ottawa, Canada] is chilling. The costs are huge, the consequences extensive—they even reach into areas such as health and the environment."[100]

The Food Industry

The federal government's most recent commission reported that New York is a unique market for organized crime, not only because of the "myriad of goods and services it offers" but also because one-half of the members of La Cosa Nostra are in that state. Organized crime has gained control over a significant portion of the meat industry, a large industry in New York and in the country. Ten percent of consumer spending on beef in this country each year comes from the five New York City boroughs; it is assumed that figures are comparable for the poultry industry. Whereas meat and poultry production and distribution used to be done at local levels, today the industry is vast, complex, and particularly susceptible to infiltration by organized crime, whose members have several advantages over lawfully operated businesses: lower wages, cash from other operations to subsidize their businesses, and a willingness "to use threats or violence to advance their business interests."[101]

Although organized crime continues to maintain a strong hold over the food industry in New York City and continues to use its captive labor unions and reputation for violence to "extort, bribe, cartelize, and otherwise pervert the free market," some progress has been made. In 1995 officials recommended that the city take over the Fulton Fish Market, the largest wholesale seafood distribution center in the country and a company with a history of problems associated with organized crime. Mayor Rudolph Giuliani, who as a prosecutor about to begin a trial of mobsters in 1986 vowed that the "mob will be crushed," achieved some success in his efforts. By the middle of 1996 it was thought that organized crime's control over the Fulton Fish Market had been cut. Giuliani announced regulations that permit the city, which owns at least part of the wholesale meat and produce markets, to conduct background checks on all persons who work in them, take fingerprints, check criminal records, and maintain files on all workers.[102]

By 1997 it was alleged that the mayor's policies had resulted in lowered costs of fish and garbage removal (discussed below) and had "sent a signal that businesses and consumers no longer have to accept the mob as a fact of life."[103]

The Construction Industry

At the time of its study, the latest presidential commission on organized crime estimated that the construction industry did $227 billion in business annually, accounting for approximately 8 percent of the gross national product, and that organized crime added about 20 percent to construction costs. The commission found a substantial infiltration of organized crime in the construction industry in New York City but stated that government responses to the situation "have generally been sporadic and inconsistent. Recent developments had shown more promise," but organized crime has the capability of avoiding and eliminating competition readily.[104]

In 1998 Mayor Giuliani asked the city council to enact licensing regulations on the city's $24 billion construction business. The mayor estimated that most of the high cost of construction (35 percent higher than the national average) resulted from the control of organized crime mobsters engaging in bid-rigging and other illegal practices. At the center of the proposal was a construction commission consisting of five members appointed by the mayor. The commission would have broad powers to regulate and investigate the construction industry. In part, its mission would be to examine the safety records of construction companies, conduct background checks and fingerprint the key officials in the companies, examine tax and financial records, and demand that each company hire independent auditors and monitors "approved by the commission to oversee the company and to guarantee its integrity and fitness to operate in the city." Finally, the commission would be authorized to "deny licenses to companies affiliated with organized-crime figures or who employ subcontracting companies that the commission finds unfit for licenses."[105]

In the spring of 2001 the mayor revised his plan to license contractors, architects, and other industry personnel. The city council's finance committee agreed to consider changes in its plan and to hold hearings on the mayor's proposal. Strong opposition from the construction industry had already been expressed.[106]

In April 2001 five men whom authorities believed were linked to New Jersey's DeCavalcante organized crime family were arrested on charges of extorting money in connection with New Jersey construction projects. One of the five men, Louis A. Luibil, was a member of the planning board.[107]

The Cartage Industry

Under the leadership of Mayor Giuliani, New York City prosecutors charged 23 companies, four trade associations, and 17 individuals with using violence and intimidation to control the city's garbage collection. Garbage carting in that city was controlled almost entirely by these companies, which were in the hands of the Gambino and Genovese crime families. The prosecutor alleged that garbage carting had been controlled by organized crime in New York City for over 50 years. The inflated prices as a result of the infiltration of organized crime were illustrated by the cost for carting at one building: $10,000 under the terms of a contract won by a new group, compared to $100,000 charged by the organized crime–controlled industry.[108] New Yorkers were paying the highest cartage rates in the country, twice those of Chicago and three times those of Los Angeles.[109]

In October 1997 the courts convicted two men alleged to be the most influential Mafia members behind the hold of organized crime over the carting industry. Joseph Francolino Sr. and Alphonse Malangone were found guilty of the most serious charges, those dealing with the state's organized crime control statute. Fourteen of their associates had already pleaded guilty in the five-year investigation. The indictment "estimated that the group had inflated costs for 200,000 customers in the city by as much as $400 million a year." The sentences for these defendants included prison terms up to 30 years and fines totaling $32 million.[110]

In New York City private garbage-hauling is a $1.5-billion-a-year business. In recent years several companies have tried to build a business in New York. In 1992 the nation's second largest waste removal company, Browning-Ferris Industries, began trying to compete for part of the New York City market. The company's sales manager found a dog's head in his yard. A note, "Welcome to New York," was in the dog's mouth. Officials of the company said that although they were concerned about the act, the market is too big to pass up and they would continue in their efforts to work in New York City.[111] Other companies had similar problems, thus demonstrating that it is difficult to operate in that city without a connection to organized crime.

Further evidence of problems arose in 2001 when the private trash haulers in New York City, acting as a unit, told city officials that if the caps were not lifted on their prices, they would leave the city entirely or drop some of their customers. This had been predicted by the Tocci Brothers of Brooklyn, whose operations were closed by the mayor's earlier crackdown on organized crime.[112]

Mayor Giuliani also succeeded in getting the city council to permit the application of background checks (similar to those applied in the food industry) to the carting industry. A federal judge had declined to issue a temporary restraining order against that. The mayor believed that prosecution of organized crime members would not be sufficient to break the hold they had on the city's legitimate industries. "Too often, when top crime figures were indicted or convicted, they were simply replaced by others who kept the corruption going." The city's refusal to grant permits to those who have any connections with organized criminals is thought to have resulted in greater access to competitive bids (in contrast to the monopoly held by organized crime for years), which lowers costs to the industry and eventually to consumers.[113]

The Control of Organized Crime

The above examples, especially that of the cartage industry, illustrate that organized crime is difficult to eliminate or control. Persons involved in organized crime receive significant support from the criminal groups with which they associate. Often the efforts of these specialized groups are focused on gaining a monopoly over a particular kind of criminal activity such as prostitution. They operate through threats, intimidation, bribery, and violence.

Organized crime finds support among outside groups, too. Few top officers are apprehended, and frequently when those at the lower levels are arrested, the higher-ups "fix" the situation and get them released. Organized crime finds protection from those outside, in some cases including the police, attorneys, and judges. For example, in the fall of 1998, Jose Grana Sr. entered a guilty plea in federal court to the charge of conspiring to participate in the affairs of the police department through a pattern of racketeering. He admitted that he bribed West New York police officers to protect his multimillion-dollar gambling business. Several others, including Grana's son, were also charged in a case alleged to involve the police department's acceptance of over $600,000 to protect businesses in prostitution, gambling, and illicit liquor sales. In January 2001 Grana was fined $30,000 and sentenced to 62 months in prison. His son was fined $25,000 and sentenced to 60 months in prison. Alexander V. Oriente, the former police chief of West New York, New Jersey, was sentenced to four years in prison and fined $50,000. The court found that Oriente "had personally presided over a corrupt operation that resulted in $2.5 million to $5 million in bribes and kickbacks from gamblers and pimps."[114]

Immunity (criminal) Exemption from criminal liability for acts that otherwise would be criminal.

In many cases, organized crime members may gain **immunity (criminal)** from prosecution through their political control in a locality. Furthermore, the public is tolerant of the activities of organized crime because of public demand for the goods and services provided. Organized criminals evade the law by infiltrating legitimate businesses, which cannot complain to law enforcement authorities because of their own involvement. Finally, the statutes available for prosecuting organized crime have not always been effective.

Statutory Measures

Legal efforts to control organized crime include several statutes. Robbery; extortion by force, threat, or fear; and extortion under color of law are criminalized by the Hobbs Act, which traces its history to the Anti-Racketeering Act of 1934.[115] The Hobbs Act and other federal statutes were used to prosecute individual crimes, but additional and more powerful tools were needed.

Congress enacted the Organized Crime Control Act of 1970, which has been amended in subsequent years. The stated purpose of this act is "to seek the eradication of organized crime in the United States by strengthening the legal tools in the evidence-gathering process, by establishing new penal prohibitions, and by providing enhanced sanctions and new remedies to deal with unlawful activities of those engaged in organized crime."[116]

Part of the 1970 legislation was the Racketeer Influenced and Corrupt Organizations (RICO) Statute, which has been called the new darling of the prosecutor's tools, replacing conspiracy. This designation refers to the fact that RICO is a very broad statute. Although it was designed to prosecute organized crime, it is broad enough to encompass many white-collar crimes. RICO does not create specific *individual* statutes, such as robbery or extortion, but refers to *patterns* of offenses. Specifically, RICO prohibits the following:

1. the use of income derived from a *pattern of racketeering* to acquire an interest in an enterprise;
2. acquiring or maintaining an interest in an enterprise through a pattern of racketeering activity;
3. conducting or participating in an enterprise's affairs through a pattern of racketeering activity; and
4. conspiring to commit any of these offenses.[117]

Racketeering An organized conspiracy to attempt or to commit extortion or coercion by use of force or threats.

Racketeering refers to the process of engaging in a racket such as extortion or conspiracy for the purpose of obtaining an illegal goal by means of threats. The discussion of the cartage industry in New York earlier in this chapter illustrates the concept: placing persons in fear through threats if they compete in the industry. Those who engage in racketeering may demand money (or something else of value) under threat of violence in return for protection from law enforcement officials, or any other of a number of activities, and so ruin the victim's business by, say, driving up prices.

RICO contains numerous other provisions. For example, since its purpose is to eradicate organized crime in the United States, one section strengthens the legal tools for gathering evidence and adds new remedies, including higher damage awards. To aid the prosecution in gathering information, RICO gives the witness immunity in return for testifying in court or before Congress.

Originally passed to control organized crime, RICO illustrates the difficulty of separating organized crime from white-collar crime, even for purposes of analysis. It is a very broad and flexible statute used for prosecutions against businesspeople; medical, legal, and other professionals; labor union leaders; government officials; and others charged with a variety of white-collar crimes. The statute expands federal law enforcement powers significantly.

RICO is an effective prosecutorial tool because of its breadth of coverage and the fact that it provides both criminal and civil causes of action. In addition, the statute provides stiff penalties, including jail and prison terms as well as treble damages and attorney fees for civil violations. But perhaps its most damaging and controversial element is the provision for **forfeiture** of "any interest . . . acquired or maintained" in violation of the statute. The statute gives the government broad powers "to preserve the availability of the property subject to forfeiture."[118]

Forfeiture The process of taking from an accused items (such as money, a boat, a car) thought to be associated with illegal acts, such as drug trafficking. The property may be taken by the government and held until the case is decided; upon a conviction it may be retained by the government and sold or disposed of in some other way.

The forfeiture provision in particular has raised legal issues. Generally the forfeiture involves civil proceedings, which have a lower burden of proof than criminal proceedings. Under current provisions the government may seize the property of a drug-trafficking suspect even if that person has been acquitted of criminal charges. Prosecutors have done both: brought criminal charges and seized property. Some lower courts held that the dual actions violate the constitutional rights of the accused not to be tried twice for the same offense (see Appendix A, Fifth Amendment, concerning double jeopardy) and that prosecutors must choose civil forfeiture or criminal proceedings, not both. In June 1996 the U.S. Supreme Court held that civil forfeiture proceedings do not constitute punishment and thus do not violate the double jeopardy provision. In *Bennis* v. *Michigan* the Court held that the Fourteenth Amendment's due process clause (see Appendix A) does not prohibit forfeiture proceedings against an innocent owner who was not aware that the property would be used in a crime. *Bennis* involved a petitioner who was co-owner of a car in which her husband forfeited her interest as well as his in a car he used for engaging in illegal acts of prostitution. In January 1996 the American Bar Association asked Congress to revise federal forfeiture laws.[119] Finally, courts have imposed sanctions on attorneys who use RICO improperly—for example, by filing frivolous suits.[120]

In 1998 the U.S. Supreme Court put brakes on the amount that may be forfeited when persons are arrested. In *United States* v. *Bajakajian* a sharply divided Court (voting 5 to 4) held that a forfeiture intended as punishment is unconstitutional if the amount is "grossly disproportional" to the offense. Specifically, the Court held that it was unconstitutional to seize $357,144 in undeclared cash that a Los Angeles man and his family attempted to take in their suitcases on a flight to Cyprus. The only crime the suspect committed was failure to report carrying over $10,000 of currency when leaving the United States for another country.[121]

Statutory measures are available to control money laundering, too. Until 1986 money laundering per se was not a crime. Prior to that time, any illegal activities connected with money laundering were prosecuted under the Bank Secrecy Act of 1970, which required banks to report any domestic transaction of more than $10,000.[122] The Organized Crime Commission concluded that the act was not sufficient for adequate prosecutions because the penalties were too light, and the act did not permit needed government surveillance to detect money-laundering schemes.

The Money Laundering Control Act of 1986 makes money laundering per se illegal and encompasses new offenses related to money laundering and violations of currency transactions.[123] Some provisions of the Anti-Drug Abuse Act of 1986 are useful in prosecutions of money-laundering activities as well.[124]

The Money Laundering Prosecution Improvement Act of 1988 includes provisions that enable financial institutions to require additional information from those who purchase checks, traveler's checks, or money orders in amounts of $3,000 or more. In addition, this legislation authorizes the Treasury secretary to target some types of institutions or geographic areas for further reporting requirements.[125] The Suspicious Activity Reporting Act of 1996 requires banks to report persons who deposit more than $5,000 if the bankers suspect those funds came from an illegal source, but the provisions are sufficiently vague that bankers might overlook illegal transactions and risk being fined or report legal ones and risk losing customers.[126]

Prosecutions and Trials

Some recent examples illustrate the failures and successes in prosecuting organized crime figures.

After considerable expense in one of the longest criminal trials in U.S. history, in August 1988, all 20 defendants in a New Jersey trial were acquitted of 77 counts of credit card fraud, gambling, loan sharking, and illegal drug trafficking. The acquittals were viewed as "a setback in anti-racketeering efforts all over the country."[127]

In 1987 John J. Gotti, whom the government alleged was the leader of the most powerful Mafia family, was acquitted of federal racketeering and conspiracy charges. In 1990 Gotti was acquitted of assault and conspiracy charges. In 1988, Anthony (Fat Tony) Salerno, the alleged boss of the Genovese crime family, along with eight other defendants, was convicted of racketeering. Salerno died in prison in 1992. In 1989 Gene Gotti and John Carneglia were found guilty

John J. Gotti, reputed leader of the Mafia's powerful Gambino family in New York City prior to his incarceration, was acquitted in his 1987 and 1990 trials. But in 1992 he was convicted on numerous counts of loan sharking, gambling, obstruction of justice, tax evasion, murder, and conspiracy to commit murder. He was sentenced to life without parole. Gotti died 10 June 2002. (AP/Wide World Photos)

of drug trafficking, sentenced to 50 years in prison, and fined $75,000 each. Reputedly, both were officers in the Gambino crime family.[128]

In 1992 John J. Gotti was on trial again. The federal prosecutor argued that Gotti had used violence to work his way to the top of organized crime, including arranging the murder of his predecessor, former Gambino boss Paul Castellano. Gotti was indicted on 13 counts, including gangland murders; conspiring to commit murder; gambling; loan sharking; obstruction of justice; and tax evasion. Gotti's trial drew attention from the media and from well-known persons. After his conviction and during his sentencing, Gotti supporters held a vigil outside the courthouse. Some alleged that he did not get a fair trial; others said that they did not know why the government would spend millions of dollars to try Gotti. "All I know is he was very nice to me and my family," said one supporter who asked not to be identified. Gotti and his co-defendant were convicted of all 13 counts and sentenced to life in prison without the possibility of parole. Although Gotti did not speak at his sentencing, his co-defendant did, declaring his innocence of the charges for which he was convicted but admitting that he was "guilty of being a good friend of John Gotti. And if there were more men like John Gotti on this earth, we would have a better country."[129]

Gotti was incarcerated in one of the most secure federal prisons, located in Marion, Illinois, from which it was alleged that he continued to dominate the Gambino crime family through contacts with his son and his brother. Gotti and his attorney were optimistic that Gotti's sentence would be reversed, but in October 1993 the U.S. Court of Appeals for the Second Circuit upheld the verdict, and in May 1994 the U.S. Supreme Court refused to review the case.[130]

Because of his ill health (cancer of the head, neck, and throat) Gotti was moved to the U.S. Medical Center for Federal Prisoners in Springfield, Missouri. In June 2001 his family told the media that although Gotti had not complained, he was not getting adequate medical care. There was speculation regarding how much longer Gotti would live. Gotti died 10 June 2002.

Gotti's son, John A. Gotti, followed in his dad's path and became the reputed leader of the crime family his father had led. But he, too, was apprehended by authorities. In 1998 it was reported that federal officials had offered a plea bargain to the younger Gotti and 10 other mob members who were scheduled for trial in January 1999. Bruce Cutler, Gotti's attorney, said his client was not accepting a plea bargain (reported to involve a 10-year sentence if he would plead guilty to lesser crimes than the major racketeering charges). Gotti was charged with extorting the former owners of a New York City nightclub and profiting from the Gambino family's rackets in "gambling, loan sharking, prepaid telephone card frauds and shakedowns of construction companies in the New York metropolitan area." Gotti was denied bail and jailed from January 1998 until a federal judge ordered his release on bail in August. Cutler had proposed a $10 million bail package, which was financed by 35 "ordinary, common folk of means and good reputation," (in Cutler's words) who put up their homes

John A. "Junior" Gotti, charged with extortion, racketeering, and conspiracy, was released from jail after he agreed to post money to secure a package that included bond of $10 million as well as paying for security to watch him at all times. In the spring of 1999, shortly before his scheduled trial, Gotti asked the judge to return him to jail because of the expense he was incurring. The following week he pleaded guilty in exchange for a maximum sentence of seven years and three months and a $1 million fine. (Rick Maiman/Corbis Sygma)

as collateral. Cutler also proposed that Gotti would pay for the cost of surveillance by a firm hired by the government. His bail package included home confinement as well. By December 1998, however, Cutler was suggesting that Gotti might go back to jail voluntarily because he could not pay all of his bills. Most of his assets were frozen by prosecutors, and he was paying $21,000 a month for the security coverage. Cutler had asked the judge for a rehearing on the bail package. Prosecutors opposed his motion.[131]

In December 1998, allegedly upon the strong advice of his father, Gotti refused the government's plea bargain offer of a six-and-a-half-year prison term and a $1 million fine in exchange for a plea to lesser charges. Gotti faced up to 20 years in prison and forfeiture of approximately $20 million in assets if he was convicted on all of the acts for which he was charged. The government faced a long, expensive, complicated trial with the possibility of acquittals for Gotti and his colleagues because of problems with some of the witnesses. Government prosecutors stated that this was their last plea bargain offer, but shortly before his 1999 trial began, John A. Gotti pleaded guilty in exchange for a maximum sentence of seven years and three months.[132]

In March 1993, despite numerous alleged attempts at jury tampering, Robert Bisaccia was convicted of charges stemming from his position as a captain in the Gambino family. Bisaccia and five other members were convicted of numerous charges (including racketeering, receiving stolen property, and conspiracy) in a 10-month trial that was characterized by frequent outbursts by the defendants as well as alleged jury tampering. Bisaccia was sentenced to 40 years in prison, but his sentence was reversed on appeal. In 1999 he accepted a plea bargain in which he admitted that he committed bribery, conspiracy to commit racketeering, and conspiracy to receive stolen property. Under the plea, Bisaccia was sentenced to 16 years in prison (at least 8 without a chance of parole) and a fine of $20,000 (reduced from the former fine of $100,000).[133]

Other reputed leaders of the Gambino family have been convicted, too. In August 1998 Nicholas (Little Nick) Corozzo was given an 8-year prison sentence, a light sentence considering his "virtual lifetime of racketeering activity" and a plea agreement that he accepted, which would have put him in prison for 10 years. That agreement was dropped when Corozzo failed to pay the $500,000 in restitution to which he and two others had agreed. Although the prosecutor recommended a long sentence, the judge imposed a light one.[134]

Thomas Gambino, a reputed captain in the Gambino family, which was named after his late father, was sentenced to five years in prison but was free on $500,000 bail pending appeal. He lost that appeal in July 1995, but he was permitted to remain free pending an appeal to the U.S. Supreme Court, which refused to hear the case in 1995. Gambino was incarcerated on 3 January 1996. He is not eligible for parole, but if he observes all prison rules, he could be released early.[135]

In January 1993 officials arrested Anthony Salvatore (Gaspipe) Casso, a fugitive from justice who was thought to be one of the most dangerous of today's U.S. Mafia leaders. Casso had disappeared two days before his 1990 trial on federal racketeering charges was to begin. Casso is reputed to be the acting boss of the Lucchese crime family. He was apprehended as he stepped out of his shower and was taken into custody wearing only a towel.[136]

In 1995 Casso began cooperating with federal prosecutors. He informed them that three mobsters plotted to kill 75-year-old Eugene Nickerson, the judge who was scheduled to preside over their racketeering trial. Casso provided information on others of his former "colleagues," leading six of them to plead guilty in exchange for seven-year prison terms, rather than face trials and the probability of much longer prison terms, such as life without parole. In March 1995 Casso pleaded guilty to racketeering charges, which included multiple murders. Under a plea agreement with federal prosecutors, Casso was to be given a lighter sentence than would be normal for one who participated in 15 murders (he claims 37!) as well as other violent crimes. Casso's agreement to testify against other mobsters earned him the desired plea agreement. In 1998, however, the agreement was rescinded on the grounds that while in prison Casso bribed correctional officers to smuggle liquor and food for him and that he lied about some of the persons against whom he testified. In July 1998 Casso was sentenced to 15 life sentences.[137]

In June 2001 Salvatore Gravano, known as Sammy the Bull, pleaded guilty to selling Ecstasy pills in Arizona. Gravano testified against John J. Gotti, his former Gambino crime family boss. Gravano had been in the federal witness protection program but left it to sell Ecstasy with his son and a former business partner. The latter, when confronted with the possibility of prison, gave the government information on Gravano. Gravano faced 15 to 20 years in prison.[138]

These and other successful prosecutions have been due in part to the willingness of mob members to testify against their colleagues. The government rewards them for their cooperation, usually by giving them lesser sentences than they would otherwise receive. In extreme cases, when the informants are threatened by other mob members, they may be placed in the federal witness protection program, discussed earlier in this chapter. A spokesperson for the program has stated that the system has never lost a witness who followed the rules.[139]

Finally, it is important to note that, even with the power of RICO as a prosecutorial tool, not all prosecutions of alleged organized crime figures are successful. After a four-month trial, in July 2001 seven reputed Mafia members were acquitted of multiple murders and other charges. The reputed mob boss Joseph Merlino and six co-defendants faced 36 charges, including racketeering, extortion, drug trafficking, gambling, attempted murder, and murder.[140]

SUMMARY

This chapter completes our analysis of types of crimes and types of criminals by looking at drug abuse, drug trafficking, and organized crime, three areas of criminal behavior that are receiving increasing attention nationally and internationally. The chapter begins with a brief overview of these crimes, their similarities, and their differences.

The discussion of drug abuse includes a look at recent data on the extent and impact of drug abuse. A section on fetal abuse explores the effects that drug abuse may have on the fetuses of pregnant women and considers whether such abuse should be processed within the criminal law. The economic cost of substance abuse is enormous both to individual abusers and their families, to governments, and to society.

The relationship between drug abuse and criminal activity is not fully understood, although we do know that many who abuse drugs are involved in crime as well. And it is a fact that much of the overcrowding of jails and prisons results from drug abuse sentences. Drug abuse also presents criminal justice personnel, such as police and correctional officers, with temptations that may lead to corruption.

A section on the debate over drug laws explores federal and state laws, looking in particular at the federal war on drugs and its critics. The punitive reaction to drug abuse is illustrated by a discussion of the New York Rockefeller laws. Recent reactions to those laws are noted.

A big issue today is whether drug abuse should remain within the criminal law, given its punitive reactions, or should instead be the focus of treatment. We know the drug abuser needs treatment, but we are not sure whether that approach will work. California's passage of a treatment rather than punishment orientation to drug abuse will provide us with some information as the new approach, which took effect in 2001, is put into action.

Although some have called for legalizing the possession of small amounts of marijuana for recreational purposes, such legalization has not become a reality. However, a few states are now permitting the legal use of this drug for medicinal purposes. Challenges in court, led by the U.S. attorney general, are being watched carefully and may negate the purpose of these new statutes.

The discussion of illegal drug trafficking includes a look at the dynamics of this serious area of criminal activity before focusing in particular on two Colombian drug cartels: the Medellin Cartel and the Cali Cartel. The history and nature of each is discussed, along with prosecutions and sentences of those who belonged. The most recent arrests in the Cali case are noted, along with other attempts to control drug trafficking.

The last section of the chapter contains an analysis of organized crime, which is defined and explained in more than one way; the chapter examines the law enforcement perspective and the social and economic perspectives before proceeding with an analysis of the concept of organized crime. The history and structure of organized crime are examined briefly, followed by a comparison between this area of criminal behavior and business-related crimes, discussed in Chapter 9.

Organized crime infiltrates legitimate as well as illegitimate businesses; it provides goods and services that the public wants despite their illegality. Attention is given to the infiltration of organized crime into legitimate businesses: health care, food, construction, and cartage. Such infiltrations provide group support for the activities of organized crime, and thus its control is made more difficult. The discussion of control focuses on statutory efforts and prosecutions, with some of the government's successful trials discussed along with the implications they have had for overall control of organized crime. Organized crime in other countries is discussed as well.

A study of criminal types makes it clear that crime is difficult to analyze by types; categories, even legal ones, are not discrete. There is considerable overlap among the activities involved in crimes of property and of violence and in the characteristics of people who engage in these activities. These four chapters may illustrate that there are more similarities than differences in criminal types. Often the difference lies not in the behavior itself but in the reaction to it. Thus, it is appropriate that attention is given to the official reaction to criminal behavior through an analysis of U.S. criminal justice systems, the focus of Part IV.

STUDY QUESTIONS

1. Summarize the findings of recent studies of data on drug abuse.
2. What is *fetal abuse,* and how should the law relate to this issue?
3. Discuss the economic impact of drug abuse.
4. "Drug abuse causes crime." Discuss the pros and cons of this assertion.
5. To what extent does drug abuse contribute to prison and jail overcrowding?
6. Do you think criminalizing drugs leads to corruption of the police? of correctional officers?
7. Trace the development of federal reactions to drug abuse.
8. Explain what is meant by the *war on drugs,* and evaluate the impact this approach has had on drug use.
9. What are the *Rockefeller laws?* Have they been effective in controlling drug use?
10. Should marijuana possession be legalized? Why or why not?
11. Outline the dynamics of illegal drug trafficking.
12. Distinguish between the Medellin and the Cali Cartels.
13. Define and discuss the importance of money laundering.
14. Define *racketeering,* and discuss the impact of RICO.
15. Analyze the concept of organized crime.
16. Distinguish the two major approaches to the study of organized crime.
17. Explain the hierarchy of an organized crime family.
18. Distinguish between the Mafia and La Cosa Nostra.
19. Discuss organized crime in two foreign countries.
20. State briefly the relationship of organized crime to the following businesses: health care, food, construction, and cartage.
21. How successful has the government been in controlling organized crime? Be specific in your answer.
22. "Organized crime is primarily an issue for the United States." Discuss this statement.

BRIEF ESSAY ASSIGNMENTS

1. Describe the debate surrounding the criminalization of fetal abuse. What has the U.S. Supreme Court ruled concerning this issue?
2. Explain the argument that the war on drugs has had a differential impact on racial and ethnic minorities and the poor.
3. Define and explain *money laundering.* How is it used in illegal drug trafficking?
4. Why is it difficult to define the concept of organized crime?
5. Define and describe the Racketeer Influenced and Corrupt Organizations (RICO) Statute. Why is it an effective tool in the prosecution of organized crime?

INTERNET ACTIVITIES

1. Using your web browser, search for more information about fetal abuse. What are the arguments for and against criminalizing fetal abuse? Which argument do you support? What other social and political issues are intertwined in this complex debate? To get started, go to **www.familypreservation.com** and **www.familywatch.org** and enter "fetal abuse" into these sites' search engines.
2. As indicated in this chapter, the United States is not the only country that experiences organized crime. Go to the Task Force on Organized Crime in the Baltic Sea Region website at **www.balticseataskforce.dk** and look through several reports on trafficking in women, money laundering and foreign gangs.

NET RESOURCES

www.odccp.org/crime_cicp_sitemap.html — The United Nations Office for Drug Control and Crime Prevention website contains news, statistics and reports on drug and criminal justice issues including drug abuse and demand reduction. Also provided on this site is information on terrorism, corruption, organized crime, and trafficking in human beings.

www.ndsn.org — Supported by the Criminal Justice Policy Foundation, the National Drug Strategy Network covers many drug-related topics such as treatment, drug prevention methods, drug policy and reform, and civil liberties and drugs.

www.usdoj.gov/dea — The U.S. Drug Enforcement Administration (DEA) website provides news releases and archives, intelligence reports, and information on major drug operations. A site search engine and links to other drug-related information are also provided.

www.nida.nih.gov — A component of the U.S. Department of Health and Human Services, the National Institute on Drug Abuse maintains a national clearinghouse for drug use resources. The website specializes in the investigation, research, and dissemination of information concerning drug abuse and addiction.

www.drcnet.org — The Drug Reform Coordination Network is an association comprised of activists and citizens nationwide. Its website offers a collection of statistics, publications, and reports all related to drug policy reform. Users can access news and headlines and register to receive free online updates.

www.american.edu/traccc — The Transnational Crime and Corruption Center provides information on sources pertaining to organized crime and corruption in the United States and throughout the international community. In addition to research topics and links, users can access the Organized Crime Watch—NIS, a publication on organized crime and corruption in Russia and the Ukraine.

www.csis.org/goc — As part of the Center for Strategic and International Studies, the Global Organized Crime Project maintains a website of resources and publications on cybercrime, espionage, money laundering, terrorism, and other transnational threats. Information on Asian, Italian, Russian, and global organized crime is also provided.

www.imolin.org — The International Money Laundering Information Network provides reports and analysis, research and information on money laundering and legislation associated with money laundering categorized by country. Links to other related sites such as Interpol, the Financial Action Task Force, and the Asia Pacific Group on Money Laundering can also be accessed.

ENDNOTES

1. Reported in "More People Suffer from Alcoholism," *St. Petersburg Times* (13 March 1997), p. 1; "Survey Suggests Leveling Off in Use of Drugs by Students," *New York Times* (21 December 1997), p. 12.
2. "Fewer Youths Report Smoking Marijuana," *New York Times* (7 August 1997), p. 10.
3. "Use of Illegal Drugs Is Down Among Young, Survey Finds," *New York Times* (1 September 2000), p. 19.
4. Executive Office of the President, Office of National Drug Control Policy, *Drug Use Trends* (Washington, DC: Drug Policy Information Clearinghouse, June 1999), p. 2.
5. "Violence Rises as Club Drug Spreads Out into the Streets," *New York Times* (24 June 2001), p. 1.
6. Cal. Penal Code, Section 187 (a) (b) (2001).
7. "Research Links Alcohol Use and Infant Leukemia," *St. Petersburg Times* (3 January 1995), p. 3, citing the current issue of the *Journal of the National Cancer Institute.*
8. "Here Come the Pregnancy Police," *Time* (22 May 1989), p. 104.
9. Johnson v. State, 602 So.2d 1288 (Fla. 1992).
10. *In re* Valerie D., 613 A.2d 748 (Conn. 1992).
11. Whitmer v. State, 1996 S.C. LEXIS 120 (S.C. 15 July 1996). The statute at issue is codified at S.C. Code Ann., Section 20-7-50 (Supp. 2001).
12. "Woman Is Convicted of Killing Her Fetus by Smoking Cocaine," *New York Times* (18 May 2001), p. 12.
13. "Drug Tests Curbed During Pregnancy," *New York Times* (22 March 2001), p. 1; Ferguson v. Charleston, No. 99-936 (March 2001).
14. Office of National Drug Control Policy, "What America's Users Spent on Illegal Drugs 1988–1998," www.whitehousedrugpolicy.gov/publications/drugfact/american_users_sp.../sectionl.htm.
15. Bureau of Justice Statistics, "Drug Control Budget," www.ojp.usdoj.gov/bjs/dcf/dcb.htm.
16. National Center on Addiction and Substance Abuse, *Behind Bars: Substance Abuse and America's Prison Population* (New York: Columbia University, January 1998), cited in *Drug Treatment in the Criminal Justice System* (Washington, DC: Office of National Drug Control Policy, March 2001), p. 2.
17. *Fact Sheet: Drug-Related Crime* (Rockville, MD: Drug Policy Information Clearing House, National Criminal Justice Reference Service, March 2000), p. 1.
18. *Drug Treatment in the Criminal Justice System* (Washington, DC: Office of National Drug Control Policy, March 2001), pp. 1, 2.
19. "Ecstasy Drug Trade Turns Violent," *USA Today* (16 May 2001), p. 1.
20. James A. Inciardi, "Heroin Use and Street Crime," *Crime and Delinquency* 25 (July 1979): 335–46; Inciardi, *The War on Drugs: Heroin, Cocaine, Crime, and Public Policy* (Palo Alto, CA: Mayfield, 1986).
21. James A. Inciardi and Anne E. Pottieger, "Drug Use and Street Crime in Miami: An (Almost) Twenty-Year Retrospective," in *The American Drug Scene,* 3d ed., eds. James A. Inciardi and Karen McElrath (Los Angeles, CA: Roxbury, 2001), pp. 319–42; quotation is from pp. 337–38.
22. Scott Menard et al., "Drugs and Crime Revisited," *Justice Quarterly* 18 (June 2001): 269–99; quotation is from pp. 269–70.
23. Bureau of Justice Statistics, *Correctional Populations in the United States, 1997* (Washington, DC: U.S. Department of Justice, November 2000), p. 3.
24. Bureau of Justice Statistics, *Prisoners in 1999* (Washington, DC: U.S. Department of Justice, August 2000), pp. 3, 9, 11.
25. "Explosive Drug Use in Prisons Is Creating a New Underworld," *New York Times* (30 December 1989), p. 1.
26. "Drug Cases Are Upended by the Police in Chicago," *New York Times* (27 December 1997), p. 6.
27. See Thomas J. Hickey and Sue Titus Reid, "Testing Police and Correctional Officers for Drug Use after Skinner and Von Raab," *Public Administration Quarterly* 19 (Spring 1995): 26–41.
28. These figures and most of the historical account come from an editorial by John Barbour of the Associated Press, "Fifty Years Ago, America Opened the Bottle Again," reprinted in the *Tulsa World* (4 December 1983), p. 3D.
29. See the report by Joseph A. Califano, former secretary of Health, Education and Welfare, reported in *The 1982 Report on Drug Abuse and Alcholism* (New York: Warner, 1982).
30. Barbour, "Fifty Years Ago."
31. *Justice Assistance News* 3 (March 1982).
32. Quoted in "Drug Czar Criticizes Legalization," *Tallahassee Democrat* (14 December 1989), p. 1.
33. "U.S. Drug Chief Seeks Overhaul of Strategy to Stop Illegal Flow from Mexico," *New York Times* (20 September 1998), p. 17.
34. "Bush Names a Drug Czar and Addresses Criticism," *New York Times* (11 May 2001), p. 16.
35. News release from Macmillan Publishing Company concerning the book by Arnold S. Trebach, *The Great Drug War* (New York: Macmillan, 1988).
36. John F. Galliher, et al., "Lindesmith v. Anslinger: An Early Government Victory in the Failed War on Drugs," *Journal of Criminal Law & Criminology* 88 (Winter 1988): 661–82; quotation is from pp. 670–71.
37. Ibid., p. 681.
38. "Study Casts Doubt on Harsh Drug Sentences," *St. Petersburg Times* (25 November 1997), p. 3.
39. For a discussion of the economics of the drug war, see David W. Rasmussen and Bruce L. Benson, *The Economic Anatomy of a Drug War* (Lanham, MD: Rowman & Littlefield, 1994).
40. Michael Welch at al., "Decontextualizing the War on Drugs: A Content Analysis of NIJ Publications and Their Neglect of Race and Class," *Justice Quarterly* 15 (December 1998): 719–42; quotations are from p. 734.
41. Michael Tonry, "Racial Politics, Racial Disparities, and the War on Crime," *Crime and Delinquency* 40 (October 1994): 475, 483–88. See also Tonry, *Malign Neglect: Race, Crime, and Punishment in America* (New York: Oxford University Press, 1994).
42. United States v. Armstrong, 517 U.S. 456 (1996).
43. "Students Find Drug Law Has Big Price: College Aid," *New York Times* (3 May 2001), p. 12.
44. Harmelin v. Michigan, 501 U.S. 956 (1991).
45. "Drug Laws That Misfired," *New York Times* (5 June 2000), p. 30; "Drug Laws That Destroy Lives," *New York Times* (24 June 2000), p. 28.
46. "Violent Crimes Undercut Marijuana's Mellow Image," *New York Times* (19 May 2001), p. 1.
47. "Legalize Marijuana, Prominent Jurist Says," *USA Today* (14 September 1995), p. 2.
48. U.S. v. Oakland Cannabis Buyers' Cooperative, 121 S.Ct. 1711 (2001).
49. Idaho Code, Section 39–301 (2000).
50. "A Better Approach to Drug Offenders," *New York Times* (26 October 2000), p. 30.
51. "Calif. Rehab Centers Await Influx," *USA Today* (2 July 2001), p 3.
52. President's Commission on Organized Crime, Report to the President and the Attorney General, *America's Habit: Drug Abuse, Drug Trafficking, and Organized Crime* (Washington, DC: U.S. Government Printing Office, 1986), pp. 5–13.
53. Bureau of Justice Statistics, *Drugs, Crime, and the Criminal Justice System* (Washington, DC: U.S. Department of Justice, December 1992), referring to a study by David L. Carter, "Drug-Related Corruption of Police Officers: A Contemporary Typology," *Journal of Criminal Justice* 18 (1990): 88.
54. Ibid., p. 62.
55. "No. 1 Drug Lord Gives Up, Flies to Posh Prison," *St. Petersburg Times* (20 June 1991), p. 1.
56. Ibid.
57. "Drug Baron Gives Up in Colombia as End to Extradition Is Approved," *New York Times* (20 June 1991), p. 1.
58. "Drug Lord, Gang Elude Troops," *Miami Herald* (23 July 1992), p. 1.
59. "Outwitting Cali's Professor Moriarty," *Time* (17 July 1995), p. 30.
60. "Colombia's Weak Courts Hamper Police Efforts to Control Drugs," *Miami Herald* (23 October 1992), p. 1.
61. Grand Jury Indictment, United States District Court, Southern District of Florida, case of United States v. Miguel Rodriguez-Orejuela et al., p. 4. The statute is U.S. Code, Title 18, Section 1961 (2001).
62. "Lawyers Weigh Effects of Conviction of Missing Colleague," *New York Times* (9 August 1998), p. 24.
63. "Drug Boat Captain's Sentence: Thirty Years," *Tampa Tribune* (14 July 2001), p. 3.
64. Violent Crime Control and Law Enforcement Act of 1994, Public Law 103-222 (13 September 1994). See Title IX, Drug Control.
65. "Heat Is on Attorneys in Drug Trafficking Cases; Lawyer Is Accused of Taking 'Dirty Money,'" *Broward Daily Business Review* (25 May 2001), p. 11.
66. "Drug Research Inadequate, White House Panel Finds," *New York Times* (30 March 2001), p. 15.
67. Quoted in Francis A. J. Ianni and Elizabeth Reuss-Ianni, "Organized Crime," in *Encyclopedia of Crime and Justice,* vol. 3, ed. Sanford H. Kadish (New York: Macmillan, 1983), p. 1095.
68. President's Commission on Law Enforcement and Administration of Justice, *The Challenge of Crime in a Free Society* (Washington, DC: U.S. Government Printing Office, 1967), p. 187.

69. Ianni and Reuss-Ianni, "Organized Crime," p. 1095.
70. Ibid., p. 1097.
71. Ibid., p. 1096.
72. Ibid.
73. Howard Abadinsky, *Organized Crime,* 3d ed. (Chicago: Nelson-Hall, 1993), p. 95.
74. Estes Kefauver, *Crime in America* (New York: Doubleday, 1951).
75. Robert F. Kennedy, *The Enemy Within* (New York: Harper & Row, 1960).
76. President's Commission, *Challenge of Crime,* pp. 187–210.
77. National Advisory Committee on Criminal Justice Standards and Goals, *Organized Crime* (Washington, DC: U.S. Government Printing Office, 1973).
78. The President's Commission on Organized Crime was established by Executive Order, No. 12435, July 28, 1983; see U.S. Code, Title 96, Section 1961. The interim report is *The Cash Connection: Organized Crime, Financial Institutions, and Money Laundering* (Washington, DC: U.S. Government Printing Office, 1984). The final report is *The Edge: Organized Crime, Business, and Labor Unions* (Washington, DC: U.S. Government Printing Office, March 1986).
79. The President's Commission on Law Enforcement and Administration of Justice, Task Force Report, *Organized Crime* (Washington, DC: U.S. Government Printing Office, 1967), p. 7.
80. See U.S. Senate Special Committee to Investigate Organized Crime in Interstate Commerce, *Third Interim Report,* Senate Report No. 307, 83d Cong., 1st Sess. (Washington, DC: U.S. Government Printing Office). The report is abridged in Kefauver, *Crime in America.*
81. Giovanni Schiavo, *The Truth about the Mafia* (New York: Vigo Press, 1962).
82. Ianni and Reuss-Ianni, "Organized Crime," p. 1101.
83. See Francis A. J. Ianni and Elizabeth Reuss-Ianni, eds., *A Family Business: Kinship and Social Control in Organized Crime* (New York: Russell Sage, 1972).
84. See Joseph L. Albini, *The American Mafia: Genesis of a Legend,* Reprint (New York: Irvington, 1979).
85. President's Commission, *Challenge of Crime,* pp. 192–93.
86. President's Commission on Organized Crime, p. xviii.
87. "Mafia Wars: Women Now Bloody Targets as Mob Protects Its Own," *Tampa Tribune* (4 February 1990), p. 10.
88. "On Trial as Biggest Boss of Mafia, He's Not So Big," *New York Times* (2 March 1993), p. 5.
89. "Mafia Used Skateboard to Blow Up Investigator," *Reuters, Limited* (13 June 1995), BC cycle; "Anti-Mafia Judge Murder Trial to Be Held September 18," *Agence France Presse* (8 July 1995), International News Section.
90. "Blow to Mafia as Twenty-Four Get Life for Murder," *The Guardian* (London) (27 September 1997), p. 2.
91. "The Long Road Back," *The Herald* (Glasgow, Scotland) (20 July 1998), p. 11.
92. "Tommaso Buscetta: Mafia Insider Turned State's Evidence—and Accused the Former Prime Minister," *The Guardian* (London) (6 April 2000), p. 24.
93. "Mafia Kingpin Held in Sicily," *The Independent* (London) (15 April 1998), p. 9; "World News Briefs; Twenty-Four Guilty in Bombings That Killed Ten in Italy," *New York Times* (7 June 1998), p. 14.
94. "In Sicily, Don Leads Comeback of Mafia," *Boston Globe* (29 May 2001), p. 1.
95. "Mafia Wars: Women Now Bloody Targets."
96. United States v. Aquino, 336 F.Supp. 737, 739 (D.C. Mich. 1972).
97. "Congress Told That Organized Crime Has Penetrated Health Care Industry," *Criminal Law Reporter* 56 (29 March 1995), p. 1595.
98. "Health Fraud Is Fertile Ground for Career Criminals," *Insurance Fraud* 6 (November 1999), no page number given.
99. "Another Dubious Pardon," *U.S. News and World Report* 130 (12 February 2001), p. 26.
100. "We Must Regain the Upper Hand over Organized Crime Groups," *The Financial Post* (29 August 1998), p. 21.
101. President's Commission on Organized Crime, *The Edge,* pp. 213–14.
102. "About Crime: How to Reform a Fishy Business," *Newsday* (3 March 1995), p. 34; "New York Mayor Expands War on Mob," *Dallas Morning News* (7 July 1996), p. 4.
103. "The Mob and the Markets," *New York Times* (12 April 1997), p. 18.
104. President's Commission on Organized Crime, *The Edge,* pp. 217–28.
105. "New Rules Sought for Contractors," *New York Times* (20 June 1998), p. 1.
106. "At Deadline," *Crain's New York Business* (7 May 2001), p. 1.
107. "Five Accused of Bribery," *Ashbury Park Press* (Neptune, NJ) (11 April 2001), p. 1.
108. "Today's News Update," *New York Law Journal* (23 June 1995), p. 1; "Monitors Appointed for Trash Haulers," *New York Times* (23 December 1995), p. 31.
109. "The Garbage Wars: Cracking the Cartel," *New York Times* (30 July 1995), p. 1, Section 3.
110. "Two Convicted as Masterminds of Mob's Hold on Private Garbage Collection," *New York Times* (22 October 1997), p. 19; "Business and Technology: Criminal Justice Defendants in New York City Carting Trial Hit with Prison Terms, Fines," *IAC Newsletter Database* (Business Publishers, Inc., Solid Waste Report) (18 December 1997), Section No. 50, Vol. 28, ISSN: 0038-1128.
111. "To Prosecutors, Breakthrough after Five Years of Scrutiny," *New York Times* (23 June 1995), p. 3B.
112. "Even with Mob Gone, Trash Haulers Have Muscle in New York City," *New York Times* (29 January 2001), p. 21.
113. "Texas Company Agrees to Buy Mafia-Linked Waste Hauler," *New York Times* (23 January 1996), p. 1B; "Progress against Organized Crime," *New York Times* (1 July 1996), p. 12.
114. "Defendant Admits Bribery in Police Corruption Case," *New York Times* (9 September 1998), p. 25; "Ex–New Jersey Police Chief Who Ran a Corrupt Force Is Sentenced and Fined," *New York Times* (6 January 2000), p. 4B.
115. U.S. Code, Title 18, Sections 1951 *et seq.* (2001).
116. Section 1 of Public Law 91-452, 84 Stat. 922 (2001).
117. U.S. Code, Title 18, Section 1962 (2001).
118. U.S. Code, Title 18, Sections 1963(a)(b–h) and 1964(c) (2001).
119. The double jeopardy case is United States v. Ursery, 518 U.S. 267 (1996). See also Bennis v. Michigan, 516 U.S. 442 (1996).
120. See, for example, Fred A. Smith Lumber Co. v. Edidin, 845 F.2d 750 (7th Cir. 1988).
121. United States v. Bajakajian, 524 U.S. 321 (2001).
122. Bank Secrecy Act of 1970, U.S. Code, Title 31, Sections 5311–5326 (2001).
123. U.S. Code, Title 18, Sections 1956 and 1957 (2001).
124. U.S. Code, Title 21, Section 5324 (2001). See also the RICO statute, discussed above, U.S. Code, Title 18, Sections 1961 *et seq.* (2001).
125. U.S. Code, Title 31, Sections 5325–5326 (2001).
126. "Suspicious Activity; Reporting Rules Rely on Bank's Good Judgment," *New York Law Journal* (4 April 1996), p. 5.
127. "Twenty Acquitted in Mob Trial," *New York Times* (27 August 1988), p. 1.
128. "Gotti Brother Sentenced to Fifty Years," *Miami Herald* (8 July 1989), p. 6.
129. "Gotti Sentenced to Life in Prison without the Possibility of Parole," *New York Times* (24 June 1992), p. 1.
130. "After Court Setback, Gotti Faces a Decision," *New York Times* (4 May 1994), p. 16. The case is United States v. Lacascio and Gotti, 6 F.3d 924 (2d Cir. 1993), *cert. denied,* United States v. Gotti, 511 U.S. 1070 (1994).
131. "Gotti's Son and Co-Defendants Are Said to Reject Plea Deals," *New York Times* (11 September 1998), p. 3B; "Gotti Released," *USA Today* (17 September 1998), p. 3; "'Common Folk' Put Up Homes for Mob Suspect," *New York Times* (18 October 1998), p. 30; "Younger Gotti Says Bail Costs and Seizures Impoverish Him," *New York Times* (2 December 1998), p. 27.
132. "Gotti Rejects Deal, Heeding Father's Words, Friends Say," *New York Times* (29 December 1998), p. 15; "Gotti Offered Lighter Term as Setbacks Hamper U.S.," *New York Times* (1 February 1999), p. 3B.
133. "Despite Fears of Jury Tampering, Six Convicted in Mob Trial," *New York Times* (7 March 1993), p. 18; "Mob Suspect Gets Lighter Sentence after Plea Deal," *The Record* (Bergen County, NJ) (10 August 1999), p. 3.
134. "Gotti Pal Gets Eight Years in Prison," *Daily News* (New York) (20 August 1998), p. 8.
135. United States v. Gambino, 818 F.Supp. 536 (E.D.N.Y. 1995), *aff'd.,* 59 F.3d 353 (2d Cir. 1995), *cert. denied,* 517 U.S. 1187 (1996). See also "A Gambino Goes to Jail in 1993 Case," *New York Times* (4 January 1996), p. 6B.
136. "New York Mobster Convicted of Murder," *Miami Herald* (16 June 1992), p. 17; "FBI Arrests Mafia Chieftain in a Hideaway in New Jersey," *New York Times* (20 January 1993), p. 16.
137. "Mafia Chiefs Prefer Jail to Trial Gamble," *The Times* (2 April 1994), Overseas News Section; "Did Mob Aim at Judge?" (2 August 1994), p. 12, Metro; "Plea Deal Rescinded, Informer May Face Life," *New York Times* (1 July 1998), p. 4B; "Rubout King 'Gaspipe' Gets Life Fifteen Times," *New York Post* (9 July 1998), p. 10.
138. "Gravano Pleads Guilty to Selling Drugs," *New York Times* (30 June 2001), p. 12.
139. "Gotti Guns for Mafia Supergrass," *Sunday Times* (4 June 1993), Overseas News Section; "Gotti Tries to Rope Bull," *Daily News (New York)* (4 January 1996), p. 7.
140. "Seven Reputed Mafia Figures Are Acquitted of Murder," *New York Times* (21 July 2001), p. 7.

PART IV

Criminal Justice Systems

Part IV introduces criminal justice systems with three chapters. Chapter 11 focuses on an overview, beginning with a discussion of the basic concepts of U.S. criminal justice systems, followed by a look at the systems effect of changes and an analysis of the exercise of discretion. After a walk through the various stages of the systems from investigation to release, the chapter turns to an analysis of four key constitutional rights of defendants, followed by an overview of victims' rights.

Chapter 12 covers policing in its historical perspective as well as its modern developments. Public and private policing are compared and contrasted. Personnel issues are highlighted, and a section on the nature of policing covers basic police functions as well as police subcultures and the impact of AIDS on policing. Police decision making and discretion in policing are covered as well.

Chapter 13's overview of court systems distinguishes the types of courts; describes the roles of lawyers and judges; and gives accounts of pretrial processes, trials, sentencing, and appeals. The chapter closes with a look at the problem of court congestion.

11

▶ Jeff Pierce, center, holds hands with his aunt Louise Burris, left, and his sister-in-law Esty Pierce during a news conference at the Joseph Harp prison in Lexington, Oklahoma, on 7 May 2001. With the use of DNA evidence, Pierce was released from prison after serving 15 years for a rape that he did not commit. (AP)

U.S. Criminal Justice Systems

OUTLINE

KEY TERMS

Adversary system
Arraignment
Arrest
Booking
Burden of proof
Charge
Criminal justice systems
Defendant
Due process
Equal protection
Grand jury
Habeas corpus
Indictment
Information
Initial appearance
Inquisitory system
Jurisdiction
Jury
Magistrate
Miranda warning
Peremptory challenge
Preliminary hearing
Probable cause
Search warrant
Trial
Venue
Victims' compensation legislation
Voir dire

In this chapter we begin our look into U.S. criminal justice systems by analyzing the philosophy on which they rest. The chapter opens with a discussion of the two major concepts of the adversary system: due process and equal protection. We then examine the effects of changes within criminal justice systems, along with the importance of discretion. Although criminal justice systems, even within the United States, may differ from one jurisdiction to another, all have the same essential stages. Those are examined individually.

The final section of the chapter analyzes four of the basic constitutional rights of defendants: the right to be free from unreasonable searches and seizures, the right not to testify against oneself, the right to counsel, and the right to trial by a jury. These and other constitutional rights are recognized to ensure that the government follows proper procedures in apprehending, charging, and trying people for alleged criminal acts. In some instances, the recognition of defendants' rights may conflict with victims' rights, a subject that is examined as well.

This chapter provides an overview of U.S. criminal justice systems by examining the basic philosophy and concepts on which they rest. The systems are based on the philosophy that the defendant's dignity must be recognized and that he or she is innocent until proven guilty by the government, which must follow proper procedures in presenting its case. Violation of these rules impairs defendants' rights and threatens the foundation of criminal justice systems.

CONCEPTS OF U.S. CRIMINAL JUSTICE

Adversary system One of two primary systems for settling disputes in court. The accused is presumed to be innocent. A defense attorney and a prosecuting attorney attempt to convince a judge or a jury of their respective versions of the case. *See also* **Inquisitory system.**

Inquisitory system A system in which the accused is presumed to be guilty and must prove his or her innocence. *See also* **Adversary system.**

Burden of proof In a legal case, the duty of necessity of proving a disputed fact. For example, in a criminal case the state has the burden of proving the defendant's guilt beyond a reasonable doubt.

Due process A fundamental concept in the U.S. Constitution that a person should not be deprived of life, liberty, or property without reasonable and lawful procedures. The interpretation of what is required by due process rests with the courts.

Criminal justice systems in the United States are based on the **adversary system,** which guarantees numerous rights to persons who are charged with crimes. The adversary system presumes that the best way to get the facts is to have a contest between the two sides—the government and the prosecuting attorney, who together represent society and the victim (in a criminal trial), versus the defense attorney and the defendant. In contrast is the **inquisitory system,** under which the accused is presumed guilty and must prove his or her innocence.

The primary difference between the adversary and the inquisitory systems is the presumption of innocence versus the presumption of guilt, which affects the **burden of proof.** Under the adversary system, the state prosecution has the burden of proving guilt; under the inquisitory system, the defense has the burden of proving innocence. This is a major difference, for in U.S. systems the burden of proof is a critical element. For example, in criminal cases the burden is *beyond a reasonable doubt;* in civil cases it is a *preponderance of the evidence.* Proving that a defendant is guilty beyond a reasonable doubt is a heavy burden, but we impose that stringent standard on the government because of its greater resources and because we believe that it is better to release a guilty person than to convict an innocent one.

An earlier study reported that, up to 1985 in the United States, 345 people were convicted wrongly of capital crimes and that 25 of them were executed.[1] Exhibit 11.1 relates the facts of specific cases of wrongful convictions that have come to light in recent years. Although many people argue that these problems are the result of "inevitable mistakes," several authorities dispute that position. According to one scholar, "A substantially significant number of cases . . . are . . . attributable either to professional dishonesty and deception or to professional incompetence."[2]

The adversary system has aroused considerable criticism, some of which is justified, but it is important to understand its philosophy, which is based on the concepts of *due process* and *equal protection* for all criminal defendants. Both concepts are difficult to define and have been the subjects of numerous court decisions.

A former U.S. Supreme Court justice attempted to explain **due process** in the following frequently quoted statement:

> "Due Process," unlike some legal rules, is not a technical conception with a fixed content unrelated to time, place and circumstances. . . [It] cannot be imprisoned within the treacherous limits of any formula. Representing a profound attitude of fairness between man and man, and more particularly between the individual and government, "due process" is compounded of history, reason, the past course of decisions, and stout confidence in the strength of the democratic faith which we possess. Due process is not a mechanical instrument. It is not a yardstick. It is a process.[3]

The elasticity of the concept of due process does not mean that there are no guidelines; indeed, the U.S. Supreme Court has decided scores of cases concerning

EXHIBIT 11.1

Wrongful Convictions: Innocent Defendants Are Released

U.S. criminal justice systems are based on the philosophy that it is better for ten guilty persons to go free than for one innocent one to be convicted. The adversary system requires that the prosecution must prove guilt beyond a reasonable doubt. But sometimes this does not happen. The concern that innocent people are not only convicted but, in some cases, incarcerated or even executed has led to a national call for a moratorium on capital punishment and a more careful examination of all phases of prosecutions. The following are only a few of the recent examples of persons who have been released from prison after it was discovered that they were wrongfully convicted.

JEFF PIERCE, MAY 2001

Jeff Pierce served 15 years in prison for a rape he did not commit. He was freed in May 2001 because DNA evidence refuted the testimony on which he was convicted. The state judge who vacated Pierce's 65-year sentence said, "The citizens of Oklahoma County have been duped . . . The juries have been lied to for the last 20 years. There are going to be a lot more victims." Pierce was convicted on the basis of evidence from a chemist; all of the cases in which that chemist provided testimony are being investigated. Pierce left prison accompanied by his mother and his brother and was looking forward to seeing his 15-year-old sons, who were infants when he was incarcerated. Pierce and his wife agreed that they would divorce and that she would raise their sons in another state; they were never told that their father was in prison for rape.[1]

PETER LIMONE, FEBRUARY 2001

He served 33 years, two months, and five days before he was released in February 2001. Peter Limone, who was on death row for four years, was released at age 66. His wife, who was convinced of his innocence, visited him regularly and supported their four children during his incarceration. Limone, who was convicted of murder, was "framed by a hit man cooperating with prosecutors and left to languish by Federal Bureau of Investigation agents who apparently knew he was innocent but never spoke out." His lawyer said that what was done to his client "should be chilling to everyone else."[2]

RONALD COTTON, 1995

After serving 11 years for two rapes that he did not commit, Ronald Cotton was released from a North Carolina prison in 1995 and granted a pardon by the state's governor.

How do such wrongful convictions occur? Cotton's attorney, Tom Lambeth, who worked *pro bono* (without pay) on the case, was quick to state that this case was not the result of any malice or malpractice. Referring to our criminal justice system, Lambeth stated:

> It's a human system. I think the jury system is the best system we have, but it's an imperfect system. Eyewitness identification is very imperfect.

Cotton was identified by one of the rape victims as the man who raped her; the second victim did not identify him. The eyewitness identification was crucial in the case, which had sufficient evidence against Cotton to convince two juries to convict him (his first appeal was successful and led to a second trial). Evidence of Cotton's prior conviction (for assault with attempt to rape), for which he served a prison sentence, was admitted because he took the stand to testify in his own behalf. His statements to police were inconsistent, giving the appearance that he was lying and thus was guilty.

Cotton was freed after DNA evidence revealed that he could not have committed either of the two rapes for which he was serving time. The DNA evidence pointed to another man, who confessed and was sentenced for the crimes. DNA, or deoxyribonucleic acid, is contained in all body cells and is measurable. It provides a rather precise way to identify persons if the sample of body fluids containing DNA is large enough for thorough testing.

How do we compensate Ronald Cotton for the 11 years of his life that we took from him? What type of compensation would be sufficient for the suffering he must have endured while incarcerated for a crime he did not commit? The governor's pardon is a first step (after release), for it removes all legal guilt. But the state's provision for a maximum of $5,000 in monetary compensation was not sufficient. After considerable negotiations by his attorney, Cotton was awarded $110,000, and in 1997 North Carolina enacted new legislation, that provides for $500 to $10,000 for each year of wrongful incarceration for a person who is subsequently pardoned by the governor.[3]

(continued)

EXHIBIT 11.1

Wrongful Convictions: Innocent Defendants Are Released, *(continued)*

ED JOHNSON, FEBRUARY 2000

When Ed Johnson's conviction was set aside in February 2000, neither he nor any known relatives were in the courtroom to celebrate—the ruling came almost 100 years after Johnson, a young African American, was convicted of raping a white woman in Chattanooga, Tennessee. In 1906, the U.S. Supreme Court had agreed to review Johnson's case on appeal and had issued a stay of his execution. The next night Johnson was taken from his jail cell by an angry mob that broke into the facility. He was dragged through the city and taken to a bridge, where he was placed in a noose and hoisted above the crowd. He was shot numerous times while his body was swinging. When the rope was severed by a bullet, Johnson's body fell to the bridge, after which one man fired five shots into his head. Before he died, Johnson said, "God bless you all—I am innocent."

Following Johnson's death, the U.S. Supreme Court held its first and only criminal trial, finding Sheriff Joseph Shipp and others guilty of contempt of court for violating the Court's order to keep the appellant safe. Justice Oliver Wendell Holmes rebuked the Chattanooga criminal justice system for its "shameful attempt at justice," and concluded, "In all likelihood this was a case of an innocent man improperly branded a guilty brute and condemned to die from the start."[4]

1. "Man Jailed for Rape Is Freed: Case Led to Chemist Inquiry," *New York Times* (8 May 2001), p. 1.
2. "An Innocent Man Goes Free 33 Years after Conviction," *New York Times* (2 February 2001), p. 12.
3. Summarized from a wire script of *Larry King Live,* Cable News Network, 13 July 1995.
4. "Lynching Victim Is Cleared of Rape, 100 Years Later," *New York Times* (27 February 2000), p. 22.

guidelines. One case is used to illustrate. It is a case that may be familiar to many readers of this text: *In re Gault,*[4] the first case in which the Court heard and decided a juvenile case appealed from a state court.

Until *Gault,* the juvenile court system operated without the due process protections of the criminal court. The juvenile system was based on the philosophy that the child in trouble needed protection and that the juvenile court judge would act as a wise father, making decisions that would be in the best interests of the child. Under this philosophy, the protections of the adult criminal court were not viewed as necessary.

On 8 June 1964 Gerald Gault, age 15, and a friend were taken into police custody in Arizona because of a complaint by a Mrs. Cook. She claimed that the teens had made lewd phone calls to her. Gault's parents were not notified that he was in custody and did not know of this until they returned home that afternoon and asked his brother to look for him.

The day after Gault was, in essence, arrested, a petition was filed, but his parents were not shown that petition. At the initial hearing to detail the evidence against Gault, Mrs. Cook did not testify and no written record was made of the proceedings. At the second hearing, when Mrs. Gault asked for the testimony of Mrs. Cook, she was told that it was not necessary. The judge adjudicated Gerald Gault delinquent even though, when asked, the judge could not recall the section of the state code on which he based that decision. The judge committed Gault to a juvenile institution until he reached the age of majority.

Gerald Gault was not allowed to examine the evidence against him; he was not allowed to present a defense. He was not permitted to cross-examine Mrs. Cook. Yet for an offense that, if committed by an adult, would have resulted in a maximum fine of $50 or a prison term of no more than six months (assessed only after the defendant was granted due process), Gault was committed to a state prison until he reached his majority.

The U.S. Supreme Court reversed the decision in Gault's case. In his opinion, Justice Abe Fortas reviewed the history and purpose of the juvenile court, but he stated that the reality of the court is an unfilled dream. Courts that were designed to act in the best interests of children had become courts of arbitrary and unfair procedures. Justice Fortas explained the importance of due process and of the procedural rules that protect it and concluded, "Under our Constitution, the condition of being a boy does not justify a kangaroo court."[5]

With the *Gault* decision the Court began extending to juveniles some but not all of the elements of due process that are afforded adults who are tried in criminal courts.

Equal protection The constitutional principle that guarantees all people the same treatment in U.S. criminal justice systems regardless of characteristics such as race, ethnicity, religion, or gender.

Like due process, **equal protection** is also a critical concept of U.S. criminal justice systems. Stated simply, equal protection prohibits treating people differently because of their gender, race, ethnicity, and religion. Thus, minorities may not be excluded from juries because they are minorities; nor may persons be excluded because of their gender. But at times it is difficult to prove that what appears to be discrimination is just that—rather than a legitimate use of discretionary power.

An example of this problem is presented in Chapter 10, which looked at the issue of whether prosecutors were targeting African Americans because of their race. When the issue was before the U.S. Supreme Court in the *Armstrong* case (see p. 320), the Court held that although the alleged discrimination would be a violation of equal protection, the defendants did not prove that such discrimination actually occurred.

Because the framers of the Constitution were concerned that the federal government might become too strong, the Bill of Rights was added to protect citizens. The Fourteenth Amendment and other relevant amendments that pertain to some of our most precious rights are reprinted in Appendix A. In early decisions the Supreme Court ruled that the Bill of Rights restricts only the federal government, but gradually the Court has held that most of the provisions apply to the states through the due process clause of the Fourteenth Amendment.

SPECIAL CHARACTERISTICS OF U.S. CRIMINAL JUSTICE SYSTEMS

Two additional characteristics are important to an understanding of all U.S. criminal justice systems. The first is the system effect of all elements and procedures; the second is discretion.

System Effect

Criminal justice systems The agencies responsible for enforcing criminal laws, including legislatures, police, courts, and corrections. Their decisions pertain to the prevention, detection, and investigation of crime; the apprehension, accusation, detention, and trial of suspects; and the conviction, sentencing, incarceration, or official supervision of adjudicated defendants.

U.S. **criminal justice systems** are composed of processes as well as structures. A change in one process or structure has an impact on other elements within the system. Consider a few examples. In September 1992 the chief justice of the U.S. Supreme Court, William H. Rehnquist, warned that the trend toward federalizing crimes was clogging the federal court system. Rehnquist was referring to the congressional practice of enacting new statutes that make federal crimes of acts previously processed only in state courts. He noted that if current practices continued, then by the year 2002 the Ninth Circuit U.S. Court of Appeals would require twice as many federal judges as the entire federal judicial system in 1992. In 1999, Rehnquist issued the warning again, referring to the propensity of Congress to respond to every highly publicized crime.

Another area in which significant changes have occurred in one area of our criminal justice systems as the result of other changes is in the incarceration of more drug offenders, most of whom are serving longer sentences than in the past. State convictions for drug offenses increased as well. These increases at the state and federal levels have had a significant impact on other parts of criminal justice systems. For example, they are the main reason for overcrowded jails and prisons as well as congested courts, and they have required more personnel and more resources in all areas of criminal justice systems. Data on the impact that increases in drug convictions have had on jails and prisons were mentioned in Chapter 10 (see again p. 315).

Another example of the system effect results from the trend in recent years to try juveniles as adults. Many states provide that juvenile cases involving serious offenses (especially violent ones) may be transferred to criminal courts. When the young people in such cases are convicted and sentenced to prison, they are usually sent to adult facilities, most of which are not prepared to deal with the special needs of juvenile offenders. It would appear that little thought was given to this issue when the statutes were enacted, but now, with the increase in juveniles sentenced to prison (rather than to juvenile facilities), authorities are having to face new problems. And although we are often critical of the media for sensationalizing crime, a 25 July 2001 article in the *New York Times* presents the issues in a manner that is objective and informative. The article is summarized in Media Focus 11.1.

These data are not cited to suggest that the arrests, prosecutions, trials, and incarcerations of violent juveniles are not warranted, but rather to show that attempts to handle a situation within one area of a criminal justice system may create problems in other areas. One of the most dramatic examples is the effect that the observing of defendants' rights has on enforcing the law. If we allow police to search and seize without restrictions, and if we torture or trick defendants to the point that they confess, we can have more arrests and more convictions. If we allow neither trials by jury nor many of the other rights in U.S. criminal justice systems, we can speed up the process and decrease court congestion. But these processes would result in crowding more people into prisons, many of which are already overcrowded. More important, such processes would impair the basic philosophy on which U.S. criminal justice systems are based and would deny the rights of defendants (the focus of the last portion of this chapter).

A second special characteristic of criminal justice systems that deserves more attention is the use of discretion.

Discretion

U.S. criminal justice systems permit wide discretion. For example, there are not enough police to enforce all laws. Total enforcement is unwise, as well as impossible, for there may be extenuating circumstances that justify not enforcing some laws. If not all laws are to be enforced, police must make decisions concerning law enforcement. Police officers must decide how to allocate their time, which investigations to conduct, and whether a search is reasonable in a given situation.

Discretion must be exercised by other professionals in criminal justice systems, too, as noted in Exhibit 11.2. Discretion is an inevitable feature of criminal justice systems. Though guidelines, laws, and constitutional amendments may be passed to regulate it, discretion cannot be eliminated. Properly used, it is functional for the system. Many cases should not be prosecuted or tried, and a refusal to arrest may be the best approach in some instances.

One result of discretion is that the number of cases proceeding through the system is considerably smaller than the number coming to the attention of the police. Most felonies that come to the attention of the police will not result in arrests. Some of the accused felons are juveniles and will be transferred to juvenile courts. Some of the remaining adult felony cases will be dismissed without

Media Focus 11.1

Juveniles in Adult Jails: The Ripple Effect

For over a century U.S. criminal justice systems have viewed juvenile offenders as needing the care and protection of a special system. They have been processed through juvenile, not criminal, courts. There have been exceptions, and the incarceration of juveniles in adult jails and prisons has been a concern—one that has increased in recent years. The numbers are significant. Between 1985 and 1998 the number of juveniles incarcerated in adult prisons increased from 3,400 to 7,000.

On 25 July 2001 the *New York Times* printed a lengthy article about the issues that have arisen with the incarceration of juveniles in adult jails and prisons. The article notes that Colorado, Louisiana, Pennsylvania, Texas, Washington, and other states have made special arrangements for their juvenile offenders. In most cases this involves segregating them from adult inmates. These changes were the result of the recommendations made in 1999 by the American Correctional Association (ACA). The ACA suggests limiting the number of juveniles who are transferred to adult criminal courts and subsequently incarcerated in adult jails and prisons; it also suggests that, for those juveniles who are tried and convicted as adults, special provisions should be made.

Juveniles who are incarcerated in adult jails and prisons may be (and often are) physically or sexually assaulted by adult inmates. They may also learn even more about crime from their older colleagues. Furthermore, juveniles in adult facilities are more likely than their counterparts in juvenile institutions to return to crime after their release. They also have a public felony conviction record, in contrast to the private adjudications of the juvenile court.

Perhaps the system impact for which prison and jail officials were not prepared is best summed up in the words of the head of the Louisiana Public Safety and Corrections Department, who said, "The kids were coming to us, and we were jumping up and down like little Johnny in the classroom, waving our hands, saying, 'We need help.'"

It is not just the influence of adult inmates that provides a negative factor when juveniles are housed with them. Juveniles in corrections have different needs. Anyone who has ever fed a growing teen knows that additional food is one of those needs. For example, some juvenile inmates, when asked what the most important motivator in prison was, responded, "Pizza." One official said that this response "shows that [juvenile inmates] are adolescents. They live very much for the minute—which makes them very dangerous inmates. They're not like adult inmates, who will listen to orders of a correctional officer."

Pennsylvania has attempted to meet its problems with juvenile inmates sentenced to prison by building a $71 million facility exclusively for teenage inmates. Pine Grove, a 500-bed institution, was opened in January 2001. Florida enacted a statute requiring that juvenile inmates sentenced to adult prisons must be incarcerated in separate units. And in Texas, juvenile inmates are housed in a separate wing of an adult prison. They spend about one-half of their time in school and the rest in counseling.[1]

But not all states have enough young offenders to warrant building separate facilities for them. If you are in one of those states, though, where do you house a 14-year-old who is convicted of murder? In Florida in 2001 Nathaniel Brazill, who was 13 when he killed his favorite teacher, was sentenced to 28 years without parole. He will be confined in a juvenile center until he is 18, at which time he will be transferred to an adult prison. Another 14-year-old Florida youth, Lionel Tate, was convicted of first-degree murder earlier in 2001. Tate received the mandatory penalty for that crime: life without parole. Both of these and other cases raise the issue of whether we should try juveniles in adult courts and, if so and they are convicted, where we should incarcerate them.[1]

[1]Based on "States Adjust Adult Prisons to Needs of Youth Inmates," *New York Times* (7 July 2001), p. 1.

any charges being filed. Others will be reduced to misdemeanors; some will negotiate pleas, while only a small percentage of those originally charged will actually proceed to trial. Of those found guilty at trial or who plead guilty, most will not be sentenced to prison.[6]

There are many reasons for the decrease in cases through the various stages. In addition to the effect that the exercise of discretion by police or court officials may have, cases may be dismissed because victims or witnesses refuse to testify

EXHIBIT 11.2

Who Exercises Discretion in Criminal Justice Systems?

These Criminal Justice Officials. . .	Must Often Decide Whether or Not or How to—
Police	Enforce specific laws Investigate specific crimes Search people, vicinities, buildings Arrest or detain people
Prosecutors	File charges or petitions Seek indictments Drop cases Reduce charges
Judges or magistrates	Set bail or conditions for release Accept pleas Determine delinquency Dismiss charges Impose sentence Revoke probation
Correctional officials	Assign to type of correctional facility Award privileges Punish for disciplinary infractions
Paroling authority	Determine date and conditions of parole Revoke parole

Source: Bureau of Justice Statistics, *Report to the Nation on Crime and Justice: The Data*, 2d ed. (Washington, DC: U.S. Department of Justice, 1988), p. 59.

and prosecutors do not have enough evidence for convictions without those testimonies. Those involved may agree to testify but fail to appear in court at the appropriate time. Improper or inaccurate statements by attorneys or witnesses, or illegal police behavior during arrest or investigation, may lead the trial judge to exclude evidence that is vital to the case. Without that evidence a conviction is unlikely, so the judge may dismiss the case.

One final point on discretion is important. Juries, police, prosecutors, and judges do not want to release (through acquittal, light sentencing, case dismissals, etc.) people who are dangerous, and they suffer intense criticism when that occurs. This may lead police, court officials, juries, parole boards, and others to exercise discretion conservatively. That is, in an effort to maintain a safe society, they may restrain a person who is not dangerous or even convict a person who is not guilty. Likewise, they may be reluctant to apprehend, convict, and incarcerate persons they believe are not a danger to society. Mistakes may be inevitable and impossible to control, but the system must keep a watchful eye on those who make discretionary decisions for improper reasons, such as to suppress racial minorities or other groups not in current favor with the decision makers.

THE STAGES IN U.S. CRIMINAL JUSTICE SYSTEMS

Criminal justice systems in the United States vary considerably, but they have many common features. They consist of four basic components: police, prosecution, courts, and corrections. The *police,* responsible for entering most people

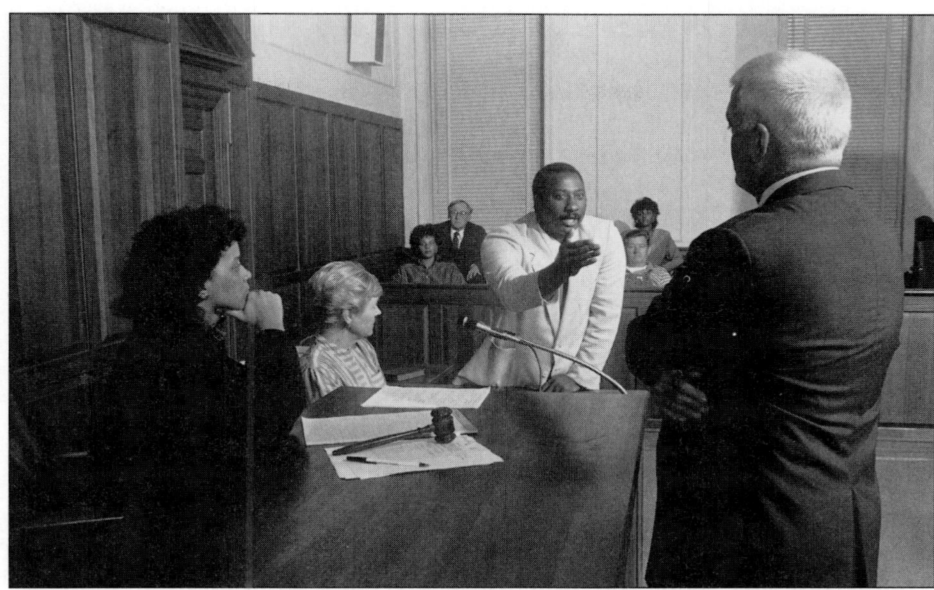

Defense lawyers and prosecutors often disagree, sometimes in front of the jury as well as the judge, but the roles of both are extremely important in adversary systems, such as those in the United States. (Billy Barnes/Stock Boston)

into the system, are also involved in some pretrial procedures. The police are very important, and Chapter 12 focuses on them. The second major component is *prosecution.* The decision to prosecute is a crucial one, involving the discretion of a *prosecuting attorney,* who brings the charges against the accused, and a *defense attorney,* who represents the accused, or the **defendant.**

Defendant In criminal law, the party charged with a crime and against whom a criminal proceeding is pending or has commenced.

Prosecutors and defense attorneys function within criminal court systems. *Courts,* the third major element of criminal justice systems, are presided over by *judges.* The roles of judges, prosecutors, and defense attorneys are discussed in Chapter 13, along with the structure of courts and the concepts of punishment and sentencing. The final component of criminal justice systems is *corrections,* which includes the detainment of some defendants in jail before trial and their confinement in jails, prisons, and other facilities after conviction, discussed in Chapter 14, and the supervision of offenders within the community, the focus of Chapter 15.

Criminal justice systems also feature similar stages, beginning with the investigation of a reported crime. For easy and quick reference, the discussed stages are listed in Exhibit 11.3.

Investigation Prior to Arrest

When police receive a complaint or are observers at a crime scene, they may make an investigation. Police may interview witnesses and obtain information that leads to an arrest. During the investigation, police may detain a suspect briefly and may search for weapons.

Arrest The act of depriving persons of their liberty; taking suspects into custody for the purpose of charging them formally with a crime.

Arrest

Most police encounters do not result in **arrest,** and police have wide discretion at this stage. When a person is arrested, he or she is taken into custody (usually to the police station).

EXHIBIT 11.3

Stages in U.S. Criminal Justice Systems

Investigation prior to arrest
Arrest
Booking
Initial appearance
Preliminary hearing
Information
Grand jury indictment
Arraignment
Reduction of charge
Trial
Sentencing
Appeals and remedies
Incarceration
Release from the system

Booking The process of recording an arrest officially by entering the suspect's name, offense charged, place, time, arresting officer, and reason for arrest; usually done at a police station by the arresting officer.

Initial appearance The defendant's first appearance before a magistrate; this process must take place quickly if the accused has been detained in jail after arrest. At the initial appearance the magistrate decides whether probable cause exists to detain the suspect, and, if so, tells the suspect of the charges and his and her constitutional rights, including the right to an attorney.

Magistrate A lower judicial officer in the state or federal court system.

Charge The formal allegation that a suspect has committed a specific offense; also used to refer to instructions on matters of law given to a jury.

Preliminary hearing A court proceeding before a judge to determine whether there is probable cause to believe that the defendant committed a crime and should be held for trial.

Information The most common formal document used to charge a person with an offense. The prosecutor, acting on evidence from police or citizens, files this document with the court, and it is tested at the preliminary hearing. Unlike the indictment, this procedure does not require participation by the grand jury.

Booking

When the police arrive at the police station with an arrested suspect, the suspect undergoes **booking**—his or her name and the location, time, and purpose of the arrest are entered in the police arrest book, or log. The suspect may be fingerprinted, photographed, and released after booking if it is determined that a crime was not committed or that there is not sufficient evidence to hold the person pending further investigation.

Initial Appearance

Most states have a statutory requirement that, after arrest, the suspect must be taken quickly before a magistrate for an **initial appearance.** The **magistrate,** presumed to be a neutral party, must tell the suspect his or her rights and explain the **charge** (accusation of a crime) against him or her.

Preliminary Hearing

The defendant may waive the **preliminary hearing,** in which the evidence against the accused is considered. If the hearing is not waived, the government's evidence is examined. At this time, the magistrate may either dismiss the charges or bind the suspect over to the grand jury for an indictment, or to the prosecuting attorney for an information. The magistrate may grant bail and set the amount of the bail bond or refuse bail or other forms of release.

Information

If a grand jury is not used, the prosecutor may return an **information,** an accusation based on the evidence available from police officers or private citizens. An information is a formal legal document sufficient to send a suspect to trial.

Grand Jury Indictment

In some jurisdictions, the prosecutor must bring formal charges and have the approval of the **grand jury,** which, after examining the evidence, returns an **indictment,** or a true bill. The indictment serves the same purpose as the information; it requires the suspect to appear before a court that has **jurisdiction** to hear the charges. The grand jury, a specified number of private citizens chosen randomly, meets at periodic intervals to consider whether to indict suspects presented by the prosecution. In addition, the grand jury may conduct investigations on its own.

The Fifth Amendment to the U.S. Constitution (see Appendix A) provides that in federal cases felonies must go through the process of indictment by a grand jury. Some state laws require this process, too. The grand jury may refuse to return an indictment.

Grand jury A group of citizens convened by legal authority to conduct secret investigations of evidence, evaluate accusations against suspects, and issue indictments when appropriate.

Indictment The grand jury's written accusation charging the named suspect with a criminal offense. The grand jury may refuse to return an indictment if jurors do not believe the evidence warrants one.

Jurisdiction The lawful right to exercise official authority, whether executive, judicial, or legislative; the territory of authority within which such power may be exercised. For the police, it refers to the geographical boundaries of power; for the courts, it refers to the power to hear and decide cases.

Arraignment The stage in which the defendant appears before the court, hears the indictment, is given instructions on legal rights, and enters a plea.

Venue Location of a trial; defendants who think they cannot get a fair trial in the jurisdiction in which the alleged crime occurred may petition the court for a change of venue, which is granted at the discretion of the court.

Trial The formal fact-finding process in court in which all evidence in a case is presented and a decision is made by the judge or jury about whether the defendant is guilty, beyond a reasonable doubt, of criminal charges.

Arraignment

After an information or indictment is secured, the suspect must appear before a court for an **arraignment.** After hearing the formal charges and again being informed of his or her rights, the defendant may enter a plea for the first time. If the plea is *not guilty,* a trial date is set. If the defendant has a choice of a trial by a judge or a jury, that decision is made at this stage. Certain pretrial motions may be made, such as a motion to change the **venue** of the trial or to admit or suppress evidence.

Reduction of Charge

For a number of reasons, the charge or charges against the defendant may be reduced. The defendant may agree to plead guilty to lesser charges rather than stand trial on the original charge. At any of the stages in criminal justice systems, the prosecutor may drop charges (although this may require the permission of the judge) or the judge may dismiss charges or entire cases.

Trial

If the case is not dismissed or the defendant does not plead guilty, the case is set for **trial.** Most criminal cases do not go to trial but are resolved prior to that stage. Most trials of minor offenses are brief, lasting perhaps less than an hour or two. In complex cases the trial may continue for weeks or months. Witnesses are questioned by attorneys, victims may testify, and physical evidence such as weapons allegedly used in the crime may be introduced. Rules of evidence are complex and require frequent rulings by the judge.

Judges preside over trials and issue rulings regarding evidence and other issues, but one of their most important roles is to impose sentences on defendants. (Bob Daemmrick/Stock Boston)

Sentencing

After the defendant pleads guilty or is found guilty at a trial, the judge enters a judgment of conviction and sets a date for sentencing. Sentencing in minor cases may occur immediately. In cases involving defendants who have been convicted of several offenses or of one or more serious offenses, normally the judge sets sentencing for a future date to permit time for presentence investigations and recommendations. In some instances the judge determines the sentence; in others the jury may do so. In some jurisdictions the jury recommends a sentence, but the judge does not have to follow its recommendation; in other jurisdictions the judge must follow the jury's recommendation.

Appeals and Remedies

Habeas corpus, writ of A written court order to bring the accused before the court to determine whether the defendant's custody and confinement are lawful under constitutional due process of law.

Defendants may have legal grounds on which to appeal their convictions to an appellate court. They may challenge their confinement through various postconviction remedies such as the writ of ***habeas corpus,*** which is a constitutional challenge to the legality of detention. Through this frequently used procedure, inmates argue that they are being confined illegally because the conditions of confinement violate some federally guaranteed constitutional right.

Incarceration

Convicted persons may be incarcerated in jails, prisons, work camps, boot camps, or other facilities. Others may be permitted to return to the community with or without supervision; many are placed on probation, the most frequently imposed sentence.

Release from the System

Upon completion of a sentence, inmates must be released unless they are confined under special statutes that permit the further detention of persons deemed dangerous to society (such as some sex offenders). Some released inmates are released before the end of their sentences through the parole process. Inmates on parole may be returned to prison to serve the remainder of their terms if they violate parole conditions. Some correctional systems release inmates early to reduce prison overcrowding. Some systems are under federal court order to keep their inmate populations at or below a specified level.

SELECTED CONSTITUTIONAL RIGHTS OF DEFENDANTS

Because the battle would not be evenly matched in a criminal trial if all the powers of the government were thrown against the individual defendant, procedural safeguards have been instituted. The prosecution is required to prove its case beyond a reasonable doubt. Defendants cannot be forced to testify against themselves, and their persons and possessions cannot be searched unreasonably. They are entitled to be notified of the charges against them, to have impartial and public trials by juries of their peers, and to be represented by counsel. If they cannot afford counsel, the state must provide attorneys. Defendants may be tried only once for the same offense, and they are presumed innocent until proven guilty. This section examines some of these constitutional rights. The law regarding these rights is complex, and no attempt is made here to cover every right or every element of the rights that are covered.

Right to Be Free from Unreasonable Search and Seizure

The Fourth Amendment's prohibition against *unreasonable* searches and seizures (see Appendix A) has been tested in numerous cases, many of which have been decided by the U.S. Supreme Court. Unreasonable searches and seizures are prohibited because, according to the Court, the Constitution guarantees citizens a reasonable expectation of privacy. In some cases the invasion of

Search warrant A court-issued writ authorizing an officer to search a person, property, or place.

Probable cause An evidentiary standard; a set of facts and circumstances that justifies a reasonably intelligent and prudent person's belief that an accused person has committed a specific crime or that certain evidence exists in a specific place.

privacy is allowed in order to protect society, but in most instances a search without a valid **search warrant** is a violation of the Fourth Amendment.

The search warrant is to be issued by a neutral magistrate only after a finding of **probable cause,** which means that in light of the facts of the case, a reasonable person would think that the evidence sought exists and that it exists in the place to be searched. The probable cause requirement applies also when an officer is searching without a search warrant.

Despite its preference for warrants, the Supreme Court has allowed some exceptions, explaining, however, that these exceptions are few, specifically established, and well delineated. Some common types of searches are explored next.

Vehicle Stops and Searches

Under some circumstances police may stop and search vehicles that they have reason to believe contain evidence of criminal activity or contraband, such as illegal drugs. For example, if police have a description of a car that was used for leaving the scene of a robbery, they may search the vehicle without a warrant. In other circumstances a warrant is necessary, although in some cases how the police get information that leads to the granting of a warrant has been questioned.

In *Illinois* v. *Gates,* the Supreme Court considered what kinds of facts police must produce to convince a magistrate that they have probable cause to obtain a warrant to search an automobile.[7] In the case, the police department of Bloomingdale, Illinois, received an anonymous letter, which stated that two specified people, a husband and his wife, were engaging in illegal drug sales and that on 3 May the wife would drive their car to Florida. The letter alleged that the husband would fly to Florida to drive the car back to Illinois with the trunk loaded with drugs and that the couple had about $100,000 worth of drugs in the basement of their Illinois home. After receiving this information, a police officer secured the address of the couple and confirmed that the husband had made a 5 May reservation to fly to Florida. Surveillance revealed that the suspect took the flight and spent the night in a motel room registered to his wife. The next morning he left in a car with a woman. The license plate of the car was registered to him. The couple were driving north on an interstate highway used frequently for traveling from Florida to Illinois. Based on these facts, the police secured a search warrant for the couple's house and automobile.

The police, with warrants, were waiting for the couple when they returned to their home in Illinois. Upon searching the house and car, the officer found drugs that the state introduced as evidence at the trial. In upholding the issuance of the search warrant and subsequent admission of the seized evidence, the U.S. Supreme Court established a "totality of circumstances" test for determining whether probable cause to issue a search warrant exists when informants provide information. In *Gates,* independent police verification of the allegations from the anonymous source provided sufficient information on which a magistrate could have probable cause to issue the warrants. Although neither the anonymous letter alone nor the police's conclusions concerning the reliability of the informant were sufficient for probable cause, the extensive corroborating evidence obtained by the police, coupled with the letter and the police's conclusions, provided a reliable basis for issuing the search warrant.

The use of anonymous tips to provide evidence of a crime, giving police the right to stop a vehicle, was tested in 1990 in *Alabama* v. *White.* The Court held that an anonymous tip, furnished by a person who was not known previously to the police, could provide sufficient information and reasonable suspicion to justify an initial stop of a vehicle, when the police had corroborated the informant's data by independent investigatory work. In this case the informant alleged that the suspect, Vanessa White, would leave a specific apartment, get into a brown Plymouth station wagon with a broken right taillight, and drive to a named motel.

She would be carrying illegal drugs. On the basis of this information the police staked out the apartment building, located the described vehicle, and followed that vehicle when White (of whom they had no physical description) entered the car and drove away. The officers stopped the vehicle and told the driver that they suspected that she was carrying illegal drugs. She consented to a search, and illegal drugs were found. She was arrested, tried, and convicted. On appeal she argued that the police did not have reasonable suspicion for the initial stop. The Supreme Court disagreed and emphasized that the police corroborated the information supplied by the anonymous caller.[8]

Although in *White* the suspect gave permission for the automobile to be searched, the Court has ruled that some warrantless searches of automobiles are allowable even without a suspect's permission. In *United States* v. *Ross* the Court held that when police have probable cause to search a lawfully stopped automobile, even without a warrant, they may search any containers inside the car that might be used to conceal the object of the search.[9] Thus, if the car is stopped because police have probable cause to believe that it contains illegal drugs, they may search any container that is capable of concealing drugs. However, it has been held that a warrantless search of a bag in the trunk of a car and thus out of the suspect's immediate reach and control may not be searched incident to a lawful arrest.[10]

Many issues surround the search of containers within an automobile. In 1991 the Court held that, even in the absence of probable cause, the search of a container within the automobile is proper when the suspect consents to a search of the car. In *Florida* v. *Jimeno,* police stopped a car that they believed contained illegal drugs and asked for permission to search the car. The suspect agreed, and the police opened a brown bag that they found on the floor of the car. That bag contained illegal drugs.[11]

In *United States* v. *Johns* the Court ruled that the search of a container within the automobile need not be conducted immediately, and it upheld the warrantless search of containers taken from a truck that police had probable cause to believe contained marijuana. The search of the containers was not conducted for several days.[12]

In *Colorado* v. *Bertine,* the Court upheld the search of a suspect's van after the suspect was arrested for driving while intoxicated. One officer drove the suspect to the police station while another took inventory of his truck, which had not yet been towed. This search, conducted without a search warrant, was upheld because "there was no showing that the police, who were following standardized procedures, acted in bad faith or for the sole purpose of investigation." In addition, police were responsible for the truck since they were having it towed.[13]

In recent years the Court has made some interesting decisions with regard to the investigatory stop as well as searches and seizures. For example, in 2000 all nine justices agreed that a person in suspicious circumstances who flees upon seeing police officers creates reasonable grounds for officers to stop and investigate, but they disagreed on how that principle should apply to a Chicago case. The scene in *Illinois* v. *Wardlow* was an area of the city characterized by heavy trafficking in illegal narcotics. When Wardlow saw police cars, he fled. He was chased down an alley by an officer who discovered that he had a gun. Five members of the Court believed these circumstances gave officers grounds for a stop and search. Chief Justice William H. Rehnquist, writing for that majority, said, "The determination of reasonable suspicion must be based on commonsense judgments and inferences about human behavior"; he then added, "Headlong flight—wherever it occurs—is the consummate act of evasion; it is not necessarily indicative of wrongdoing, but it is certainly suggestive of such." In a dissenting opinion, Justice John Paul Stevens disagreed, stating, "Among some citizens, particularly minorities and those resident in high crime areas, there is also the possibility that the fleeing person is entirely innocent, but, with or without justification, believes that contact with the police can itself be dangerous, apart from any criminal activity associated with the officer's sudden presence."[14]

One issue of significant importance with regard to the investigatory stop is that police have been accused in many cities of engaging in *racial profiling,* that is, stopping people based solely on their race. Generally the complaints are brought by African Americans who allege that police have stereotyped them as law violators. Investigations into these allegations have resulted in settlements. For example, in 1999 the U.S. Department of Justice entered into a consent agreement with New Jersey state troopers. A monitor will oversee whether troopers are following the terms of the agreement. They are not permitted to stop minority motorists unless the race of that person is relevant to the description of a crime suspect for whom they are searching.[15]

Like race, ethnicity is an unacceptable reason for the police stopping a person. In 2000 the Ninth Circuit Court of Appeals ruled that "Hispanic appearance is, in general, of such little probative value that it may not be considered as a relevant factor where particularized or individualized suspicion is required" for a stop. Three Mexicans were stopped about 115 miles east of San Diego, California, by U.S. Border Patrol agents, who gave five reasons for stopping them. One of those reasons was their Hispanic appearance. In *United States* v. *Montero-Camargo,* in holding that ethnicity was not an acceptable reason for the stop, the lower federal court was ruling in opposition to a 25-year-old U.S. Supreme Court case. Apparently the Supreme Court found that decision to be reasonable, for it declined to review the case.[16]

In its 2000–2001 term, the U.S. Supreme Court decided *Indianapolis* v. *Edmond,* holding that when police act on some basis other than individualized suspicion, the reasons why they take such actions should be considered in determining whether they violated a suspect's rights. Several Indianapolis motorists brought this action to get a determination on whether police could use K-9 dogs to circle their cars and search for illegal drugs while other officers were checking driver's licenses and car registrations. The Court did not uphold this practice, in which police admitted that their primary purpose in the stops was to search for illegal drugs. The case did not, however, answer the question of how the Court would rule if searching for drugs was a secondary purpose.[17]

Seizure and Search of the Person

Seizure and search of the person is the most intrusive of all searches and constitutes the greatest invasion of privacy. The Supreme Court has articulated definitions of what constitutes a *search* and a *seizure* and the circumstances under which they are appropriate. First is the issue of what constitutes a seizure of the person.

In a 1980 case the Court held that a seizure occurs when under all the circumstances a reasonable person would not think he or she was free to leave.[18] The "free to leave" test arose in *Florida* v. *Bostick,* in which police boarded a bus bound for Atlanta, Georgia, from Miami, Florida, while it was stopped temporarily in Fort Lauderdale, Florida. Bostick consented to a search of his luggage; illegal drugs were found, and he was arrested.[19]

In *Bostick* the appellant argued that he was not free to leave because the bus on which he was riding was ready to depart when officers boarded to search. He claimed that the officers did not have reasonable suspicion that any of the passengers were carrying illegal drugs or contraband. The Court held that its "free to leave" test has some limitations in cases such as a bus on which one is already a passenger. The test of a reasonable search and seizure under these circumstances is "whether a reasonable person would feel free to decline the officers' requests or otherwise terminate the encounter." The Court sent the case back for trial using that test.

Another case illustrates the Court's development of the law of seizure as it relates to persons. In *California* v. *Hodari D.*, the Court held that when police are chasing a fleeing suspect, that person is not seized until apprehended, and this is true no matter how much force police use. Thus, a "show of authority" by police does not amount to a seizure of the person.[20]

Next are the issues of what constitutes a search, how extensive the search of the person may be, and whether the search requires a warrant. Clearly, police may conduct a warrantless search of the suspect after making a valid arrest. This warrantless search is permitted because of the necessity for arresting officers to protect themselves and others as well as to preserve evidence of a crime. The legality of the search is determined by the legality of the arrest.[21]

Even without an arrest, police may conduct warrantless searches under some circumstances, although those searches are limited. In *Terry* v. *Ohio* the Court acknowledged that officers must be able to protect themselves and others, and so it is reasonable to permit them to pat down a suspect for weapons even though the officers do not have probable cause to arrest. In *Terry* a police officer with 39 years of experience in law enforcement encountered three suspicious men. The officer believed the men were checking out a store for the possibility of a burglary or robbery. After he approached the men and asked their names, the officer conducted a pat-down search for weapons. Two of the men had weapons.[22]

Terry permits officers to conduct a pat-down search for weapons. The Court did not rule concerning discovery of contraband, such as illegal drugs. In 1993, in *Minnesota* v. *Dickerson,* the Court articulated the *plain feel* doctrine (similar to the *plain view* doctrine, discussed below). According to the Court, if during a *Terry* search and before an officer has concluded that the suspect is not armed the officer feels a contraband item "whose contour or mass makes its identity immediately apparent," that item may be seized without a warrant. In *Dickerson* the officer's suspicion was aroused because of the suspect's evasive behavior when he saw officers as he exited a building commonly known to be a crack house. In the course of a proper pat-down search for weapons (none were found), the officer detected a small lump, which felt like it was wrapped in cellophane, in the pocket of the suspect's nylon jacket. Based on his experience, the officer decided the object was crack cocaine. He seized the object and arrested the suspect. Subsequent tests confirmed that it was crack, and the suspect was charged with possessing a controlled substance. In upholding the search, the Supreme Court emphasized that officers may not go beyond the permissible scope of the weapons search to examine the item suspected of being contraband but not a weapon.[23]

In a subsequent case a lower federal court upheld a search and seizure involving a frisk in which an officer used his fingertips to press and probe a suspect's crotch. When the officer felt a hard object that felt to him like crack cocaine, he asked the suspect to drop his pants. During this process the officer used his own body to shield the suspect from the view of others, thus preserving his privacy to a reasonable extent, according to the court.[24]

Some jurisdictions are more restrictive than the Supreme Court in determining proper searches and seizures. For example, a New York court has held that it was not proper for an officer to remove an object from the waistband of a woman while they were frisking her after stopping the vehicle in which she was riding. The stop of the vehicle was lawful. The officer testified that he felt the hard object and asked the woman what it was; she refused to tell him, so he seized what turned out to be crack cocaine. The state argued that the officer feared for his safety when he could not tell the nature of the object and that he should not have to wait for the "glint of steel" before seizing such an object. Under *Terry,* he should be permitted to continue searching until he was sure no weapons were present. The court took the position, however, that a bulge discovered during a frisk cannot be seized unless it looks or feels like a weapon.[25]

Likewise, the Maryland Court of Special Appeals held that an officer's search was intrusive when he pulled up a suspect's shirt. The officer had conducted a pat-down search, during which no weapon was found, and had then seen the suspect put an unknown object in the rear of his waistband. The officer pulled up the suspect's shirt. The court held that the search went beyond that permitted by *Terry;* consequently, the packets of cocaine that fell from the suspect's clothes when the officer tugged on his shirt should have been excluded from the defendant's trial.[26]

Some body searches are even more intrusive and more offensive. In *Rochin* v. *California,* the Supreme Court stated its position on one method of searching a person for evidence of a crime as follows.[27]

Rochin v. California

Having "some information that [petitioner here] was selling narcotics," three deputy sheriffs of the County of Los Angeles, on the morning of July 1, 1949, made for the two-story dwelling house in which Rochin lived with his mother, common-law wife, brothers and sisters. Finding the outside door open, they entered and then forced open the door to Rochin's room on the second floor. Inside they found petitioner sitting partly dressed on the side of the bed, upon which his wife was lying. On a "night stand" beside the bed the deputies spied two capsules. When asked "Whose stuff is this?" Rochin seized the capsules and put them in his mouth. A struggle ensued, in the course of which three officers "jumped upon him" and attempted to extract the capsules. The force they applied proved unavailing against Rochin's resistance. He was handcuffed and taken to a hospital. At the direction of one of the officers a doctor forced an emetic solution through a tube into Rochin's stomach against his will. This "stomach pumping" produced vomiting. In the vomited matter were found two capsules which proved to contain morphine.

Rochin was brought to trial . . . on the charge of possessing "a preparation of morphine" . . . Rochin was convicted and sentenced to sixty days' imprisonment. The chief evidence against him was the two capsules . . .

[W]e are compelled to conclude that the proceedings by which this conviction was obtained do more than offend some fastidious squeamishness or private sentimentalism about combatting crime too energetically. This is conduct that shocks the conscience, illegally breaking into the privacy of the petitioner, the struggle to open his mouth and remove what was there, the forcible extraction of his stomach's contents—this course of proceedings by agents of government to obtain evidence is bound to offend even hardened sensibilities. They are methods too close to the rack and the screw to permit of constitutional differentiation.

The U.S. Supreme Court has upheld some intrusive body searches. It upheld the search of a woman suspected of smuggling drugs at the border. A search of her rectum produced a cocaine-filled balloon. A strip search was conducted only after the authorities, with probable cause to believe the suspect was smuggling drugs, conducted a pat-down search, which revealed that the suspect's abdomen was firm and that she was wearing plastic underpants lined with a paper towel. Using this evidence, authorities secured a warrant to conduct a strip search. Subsequently the suspect excreted 88 balloons containing 80 percent pure cocaine hydrochloride. In upholding the strip search and detention, the Court emphasized that the right to privacy is diminished at the border and frequently must give way to the government's right to enforce laws. The test established by the Court for border strip searches is whether customs officials, "considering all the facts surrounding the traveler and her trip, reasonably suspect that the traveler is smuggling contraband in her alimentary canal."[28]

Strip searches of defendants detained in jail pending trial are permitted under some circumstances. In 1979, in *Bell* v. *Wolfish,* the Supreme Court used a reasonableness test in deciding that the strip searches of inmates after they returned from the visitor's room were necessary for security.[29]

Routine strip searches of persons arrested for violating traffic ordinances are not permissible, even when those persons are booked temporarily at the police station, unless the police have probable cause to believe that the suspects are hiding drugs or weapons. A federal appellate court has held that the civil rights of a woman arrested for two minor traffic offenses were violated when she was strip-searched after her arrest. The court emphasized that the fact that this arrestee would come into contact with other jailed inmates was not a sufficient reason to conduct a strip search under *Bell* v. *Wolfish*. Violence and drugs are not normally associated with the offenses for which she was arrested. Thus, more information is needed to justify a strip search of a person apprehended for traffic violations.[30]

One case of illegal body searches was settled out of court in New York City in 2001. Between 1996 and 1997 officers in Manhattan and Queens jails strip-searched 50,000 or more persons who were arrested for minor offenses, such as loitering, subway violations, or disorderly conduct. In what is reported to be the highest civil rights award against the city, the parties agreed that the city would provide $50 million to be divided among the plaintiffs, with the awards ranging from $250 to $22,500 (or more for plaintiffs who could prove additional emotional damages), depending on the degree of the violation.[31]

Search of the Home

Searches of the home are permissible, although the Supreme Court has restricted the circumstances under which they may be conducted and limited the areas that may be searched. The landmark case on this issue is *Mapp* v. *Ohio*.[32]

Mapp v. Ohio

It appears that Miss Mapp was halfway down the stairs from the upper floor to the front door when the officers, in this highhanded manner, broke into the hall. She demanded to see the search warrant. A paper claimed to be a warrant was held up by one of the officers. She grabbed the "warrant" and placed it in her bosom. A struggle ensued in which the officers recovered the piece of paper and as a result of which they handcuffed appellant because she had been "belligerent" in resisting their official rescue of the "warrant" from her person. Running roughshod over appellant, a policeman "grabbed" her, "twisted [her] hand," and she "yelled [and] pleaded with him" because "it was hurting." Appellant, in handcuffs, was then forcibly taken upstairs to her bedroom where the officers searched a dresser, a chest of drawers, a closet and some suitcases. They also looked into a photo album and through personal papers belonging to the appellant. The search spread into the rest of the second floor including the child's bedroom, the living room, the kitchen and a dinette. The basement of the building and a trunk found therein were also searched. The obscene materials for possession of which she was ultimately convicted were discovered in the course of that widespread search.

At the trial no search warrant was produced by the prosecution, nor was the failure to produce one explained or accounted for. At best, "There is, in the record, considerable doubt as to whether there ever was any warrant for the search of the defendant's home."

The seized evidence was used against Mapp at her trial, and she was convicted. The U.S. Supreme Court reversed.

In 1980 the Supreme Court emphasized the importance of protecting the privacy of the home, noting that "the Fourth Amendment has drawn a firm line at the entrance to the house. Absent exigent circumstances, that threshold may not reasonably be crossed without a warrant."[33] In 1984 the Court held that the Fourth Amendment prohibited the warrantless entry of police into a suspect's home to arrest him for a civil, nonjailable traffic offense.[34] In 1995 the Court reversed a conviction in an Arkansas case in which police, with a search warrant, identified themselves but then entered the unlocked main door of the suspect's home without knocking and seized illegal drugs, a gun, and ammunition.

A unanimous Supreme Court held that in this case it was necessary to "knock and announce." But the Court left open the possibility that under some circumstances (such as those involving officer safety, escaped inmates, destruction of evidence) the knock rule might not be required.[35]

However, if police have a legal right to enter a home (or office or other structure), it is permissible to seize some evidence under the *plain view doctrine* even without a warrant. This privilege was established by the Supreme Court in 1971 in *Coolidge* v. *New Hampshire*.[36] In 1987, in *Arizona* v. *Hicks,* the Court held that probable cause is required to invoke the plain view doctrine, and in 1990 the Court permitted a warrantless "protective sweep," defined as "a quick and limited search of premises, incident to an arrest and conducted to protect the safety of police officers or others. It is confined narrowly to a cursory visual inspection of those places in which a person might be hiding."[37]

In some cases, searches near the home may be conducted as well. The Supreme Court has held that persons have no reasonable expectation of privacy for garbage left outside the curtilage (the enclosed space of buildings and grounds immediately surrounding the home) and thus it may be searched without a warrant.[38] The Court did not answer the question of whether a search would be lawful if the garbage were left within the curtilage. A lower federal appellate court reached that issue in 1991 and ruled that the search would be permissible provided the garbage was left under circumstances making it "readily accessible" to the public. If the garbage appears to be abandoned and exposed to the public, its owner no longer has a reasonable expectation of privacy protecting it from search and seizure.[39]

The Supreme Court has upheld a warrantless aerial surveillance of a defendant's fenced backyard. The search revealed that marijuana plants were being grown there.[40] The Court's holding is based on the assumption that in general a person does not have a reasonable expectation of privacy that would preclude a search of items left in public view or abandoned or obtained by consent.

A case closely related to home searches was decided in 2001, when the Court held that if police believe a suspect will destroy evidence if left alone, they may hold that person outside the home while seeking a search warrant. In the case of *Illinois* v. *McArthur,* police had approached Charles McArthur outside his trailer home in Sullivan, Illinois, telling him that his estranged wife informed the police that McArthur had marijuana hidden under his couch. McArthur refused to let the police in, and for about two hours they held him outside, refusing to let him go inside alone. The Court held that the detention was appropriate.[41]

Finally, in an important case upholding the right of privacy, in 2001 the U.S. Supreme Court held, in a 5-to-4 ruling, that police must first secure a warrant before using a device that detects heat to determine whether an individual was growing marijuana in his home. In *Kyllo* v. *United States* the police secured a search warrant and located over 100 marijuana plants growing in the suspect's home under halide lights. The warrant was secured after a device called Agema Thermovision 210 detected a hot spot in the home. Police had also examined electric bills and analyzed some tips before concluding that the suspect was growing the illegal drug under high-intensity lamps in his home. The heat device located one place in the house that was particularly hot. The issue in the case was whether aiming that device at a private home from a public street constitutes a search. The Court held that it does, with the majority stating that, with regard to searches and seizures, U.S. Supreme Court precedents draw "a firm line at the entrance to the house," and that "That line . . . must be not only firm but bright."[42]

Right Not to Testify against Oneself

The Fifth Amendment (see Appendix A) states that, in a criminal trial, defendants cannot be compelled to testify against themselves. The reason behind the right has been expressed as follows: "We do not make even the most hardened criminal sign his own death warrant, or dig his own grave, or pull the lever that springs the trap on which he stands. We have through the course of history developed a considerable feeling of the dignity and intrinsic importance of the individual man. Even the evil man is a human being."[43]

The prohibitions against physical and mental methods for extracting confessions are illustrated by excerpts from two cases. The first case, *Brown* v. *Mississippi,* gives an example of physical brutality used to elicit confessions from several African American defendants. The only evidence on which the defendants could have been convicted was their involuntary confessions, secured after several whippings. The defendants were convicted and sentenced to death. The Mississippi Supreme Court upheld the convictions. The U.S. Supreme Court reversed. The Court's comments, after describing the beating of the first defendant, were as follows:[44]

Brown v. Mississippi

The other two defendants were also arrested and taken to the same jail. On Sunday night, April 1, 1934, the same deputy, accompanied by a number of white men, one of whom was also an officer, and by the jailer, came to the jail, and the two last named defendants were made to strip and they were laid over chairs and their backs were cut to pieces with a leather strap with buckles on it, and they were likewise made by the said deputy definitely to understand that the whipping would be continued unless and until they confessed, and not only confessed, but confessed in every matter of detail as demanded by those present; and in this manner the defendants confessed the crime, and as the whippings progressed and were repeated, they changed or adjusted their confession in all particulars of detail so as to conform to the demands of their torturers. When the confessions had been obtained in the exact form and contents as desired by the mob, they left with the parting admonition and warning that, if the defendants changed their story at any time in any respect from the last stated, the perpetrators of the outrage would administer the same or equally effective treatment . . .

Because a State may dispense with a jury trial, it does not follow that it may substitute trial by ordeal. The rack and torture chamber may not be substituted for the witness stand.

. . . It would be difficult to conceive of methods more revolting to the sense of justice than those taken to procure the confessions of these petitioners, and the use of the confessions thus obtained as the basis for conviction and sentence was a clear denial of due process . . .

After the prohibition against extracting confessions through physical brutality, some jurisdictions began to concentrate on psychological methods such as interrogation in a police-dominated atmosphere in which the accused is questioned for long periods without rest and without counsel. The interrogator pretended to have evidence of the suspect's guilt and suggested rationalizations for his or her behavior in an attempt to minimize the moral seriousness of the act. Under such pressure, many suspects confessed.

After some of these interrogation techniques were used on Ernesto Miranda, he signed a confession stating that his statement was voluntary. On the basis of that testimony and other evidence, Miranda was convicted of kidnapping and rape and sentenced to 20 to 30 years in prison for each offense, the sentences to run concurrently.

In its 1966 decision in *Miranda,* the Supreme Court emphasized the possibility that under the kinds of psychological pressures used by police on Miranda and other suspects, innocent persons might confess. The Court said that in our system of law, with the tremendous powers of the state in a criminal trial, it is necessary to give defendants procedural safeguards in order to avoid conviction of the innocent as well as coerced confessions from the guilty. The Court interpreted the Fifth Amendment right not to have to testify against oneself as requiring that the police must tell the accused of the specifics of that right. The procedures that the police must follow in the **Miranda warning** are explained by the Court in the following excerpt from the case.[45]

Miranda v. Arizona

As for the procedural safeguards to be employed, unless other fully effective means are devised to inform accused persons of their right of silence and to assure a continuous opportunity to exercise it, the following measures are required. Prior to any questioning, the person must be warned that he has a right to remain silent, that any statement he does make may be used as evidence against him, and that he has a right to the presence of an attorney, either retained or appointed. The defendant may waive effectuation of these rights, provided the waiver is made voluntarily, knowingly and intelligently. If, however, he indicates in any manner and at any stage of the process that he wishes to consult with an attorney before speaking, there can be no questioning. Likewise, if the individual is alone and indicates in any manner that he does not wish to be interrogated, the police may not question him. The mere fact that he may have answered some questions or volunteered some statements on his own does not deprive him of the right to refrain from answering any further inquiries until he has consulted with an attorney and thereafter consents to be questioned.

Miranda warning The rule from *Miranda* v. *Arizona*, which mandates that before persons in custody are interrogated, they must be told of their right to remain silent, that anything they say may be used as evidence against them, and that they have a right to an attorney, who will be appointed if they cannot afford to retain one.

The *Miranda* decision created an immediate controversy. Reactions ranged from the cry that we were licensing people to kill, rape, rob, and steal, to the argument that all the decision did was to extend to all defendants the rights that the Constitution has always guaranteed and that the rich have always enjoyed. In evaluating these criticisms, it is important to understand that the Court is not trying to free guilty people but, rather, to ensure that the rights of the accused are recognized. In many retrials, defendants are convicted again. For example, Miranda was retried without the confession. He was convicted and sentenced to prison. After his release from prison, he was involved in a fight in which he was killed.

The *Miranda* decision has led to extensive litigation. A few decisions illustrate the range of questions considered by the Court in recent years. In *Oregon* v. *Mathiason,* the Court considered whether the *Miranda* warnings would have to be given to a person who went to the police station and confessed after an investigator had left a card at his home. The card invited the suspect, who was on parole, to go to the police station. The police alleged that the suspect went to the station to talk voluntarily, was told that he was under arrest, and then questioned without an attorney. The *Miranda* warning was not given. The police told the defendant that his fingerprints were found at the scene of the crime. That was not true, but when the defendant heard the assertion, he confessed. The Supreme Court held that the confession was not obtained in violation of the suspect's *Miranda* rights: "*Miranda* warnings are required only where there has been such a restriction on a person's freedom as to render him 'in custody.'"[46]

In *Minnesota* v. *Murphy,* the Court considered whether the *Miranda* warnings would have to be given by a probation officer when talking to a client about another crime. When questioned by his probation officer, the probationer admitted that he had raped and murdered a teenage girl. When this confession was used against the probationer at his trial, he was convicted. His attorneys argued that his constitutional rights had been violated because his probation officer had not given him the *Miranda* warning. The Court ruled that the *Miranda* warnings were not required.[47]

If a suspect invokes the right to remain silent until an attorney is present, the police may not interrogate until counsel has been provided, although the Court held in *Edwards* v. *Arizona* that the police may question a suspect who "initiates further communication, exchanges, or conversations with the police."[48] In *Arizona* v. *Roberson,* the Court held that the *Edwards* rule bars police-initiated interrogation following a suspect's request for counsel in the context of a separate investigation. In *Roberson,* the police arrested the suspect at the scene of an alleged burglary and began to question him. They stopped the interrogation when the suspect said that he wanted an attorney. Three days later, while the suspect was still in custody, another officer, who did not know about the previous request for an attorney, advised the suspect of his *Miranda* rights and began to question him about another burglary. The defendant talked, but the Arizona courts suppressed the evidence. The Supreme Court agreed, quoting the Arizona court in an earlier case, that the

> only difference between Edwards and the appellant is that Edwards was questioned about the same offense after a request for counsel while the appellant was reinterrogated about an unrelated offense. We do not believe that this factual distinction holds any legal significance for Fifth Amendment purposes.[49]

The *Miranda* rule does not require that police refrain from questioning a suspect who has requested counsel during a court appearance for a separate crime. In *McNeil* v. *Wisconsin,* the Court ruled that when a suspect requested counsel during his initial appearance in court on an armed robbery charge, that request did not bar police from questioning the suspect on other charges (murder, attempted murder, and burglary) for which he waived his *Miranda* rights and made incriminating statements. He was convicted on the basis of those statements. He appealed, arguing that his invoking the *Miranda* requirements for the robbery charge applied to all questioning even for other charges. The Supreme Court did not agree. The Court held that the *Miranda* rule is *offense-specific.*[50]

A suspect may waive the right to have counsel present prior to police questioning, but that waiver must be made voluntarily, intelligently, and knowingly. An example of an acceptable waiver comes from *Davis* v. *United States,* in which the Court voted 5 to 4 to uphold the conviction of a defendant who was tried for the murder of a fellow serviceman on naval property. After he received the *Miranda* warnings, the suspect signed a waiver of his right to counsel and began talking. Later he stated, "Maybe I should see a lawyer." At that point officers stopped questioning him about the crime and began inquiring whether he wanted counsel. The suspect said he did not wish to speak with an attorney, and interrogation was resumed. The suspect's statements were used against him, and he was convicted. On appeal, the Court upheld the admission of this evidence, stating that the suspect must *request* an attorney.[51] *Davis* is not to be confused with the Court's previous holdings that once a suspect has invoked the right to counsel police must cease interrogation.[52]

Finally, in 2000 the Court ruled that a 1968 congressional attempt to overrule *Miranda* was unconstitutional. In an opinion written by Chief Justice Rehnquist, the Court held that the Miranda rule is a constitutional one and beyond the power of Congress to change. Congress had enacted the statute two years after the Supreme Court decided the *Miranda* case, but it had not been invoked by federal prosecutors, who apparently feared that it might not be held constitutional. According to Rehnquist, writing for the majority of seven justices, "*Miranda* announced a constitutional rule that Congress may not supersede legislatively."[53]

Right to Counsel

The Sixth Amendment (see Appendix A), which provides that in all criminal prosecutions the accused shall have "the Assistance of Counsel for his defense," became a part of the Bill of Rights in 1791. But it was not until 1963 and 1972, as a result of two important cases, that the right to counsel became a reality for most defendants. Our discussion begins with the 1963 decision *Gideon* v. *Wainwright*.[54]

Clarence Earl Gideon's 1961 appeal to the U.S. Supreme Court led to the ruling that indigent defendants are entitled to appointed counsel in all felony cases, not just those involving a possible death sentence. (Bettmann/Corbis)

Clarence Earl Gideon was not a violent man, but he had been in and out of prison for various law violations. At his trial for breaking and entering a poolroom with the intent to commit a misdemeanor, a felony under Florida law, Gideon represented himself but argued that he needed a lawyer. Because he could not afford to retain counsel, he requested the court to appoint an attorney at the state's expense. The judge replied that under Florida law, an indigent was not entitled to a court-appointed attorney except when charged with a crime that could result in the death sentence.

After telling the judge that "the United States Supreme Court says I am entitled to be represented by Counsel," Gideon conducted his own defense, "about as well as could be expected from a layman," according to the Supreme Court. Gideon was convicted and sentenced to five years in prison. On 8 January 1962 the U.S. Supreme Court received a large envelope from Florida prisoner number 003826. Gideon, who had printed his request in pencil, asked the Court to hear his case.

The Court agreed to hear Gideon's case and appointed Abe Fortas, an attorney with a prestigious Washington, D.C., law firm, to represent him. Fortas convinced the Court that it should overrule a previous case in which it had held that the right to counsel appointed at the government's expense if the defendant is indigent applied only to capital cases. The Court, reviewing that earlier decision and other cases, explained the reasons that counsel is important, as the following excerpt from Gideon's case illustrates.

Gideon v. Wainwright

Not only these precedents but also reason and reflection require us to recognize that in our adversary system of criminal justice, any person haled into court, who is too poor to hire a lawyer, cannot be assured a fair trial unless counsel is provided for him . . . The right of one charged with crime to counsel may not be deemed fundamental and essential to fair trials in some countries, but it is in ours. From the very beginning, our state and national constitutions and laws have laid great emphasis on procedure and substantive safeguards designed to assure fair trials before impartial tribunals in which every defendant stands equal before the law. This noble ideal cannot be realized if the poor man charged with crime has to face his accusers without a lawyer to assist him. A defendant's need for a lawyer is nowhere better stated than in the moving words of Mr. Justice Sutherland in *Powell* v. *Alabama:* "The right to be heard would be, in many cases, of little avail if it did not comprehend the right to be heard by counsel. Even the intelligent and educated layman has small and sometimes no skill in the science of law. If charged with crime, he is incapable, generally, of determining for himself whether the indictment is good or bad. He is unfamiliar with the rules of evidence. Left without aid of counsel he may be put on trial without a proper charge, and convicted upon incompetent evidence irrelevant to the issue or otherwise inadmissible. He lacks both the skill and knowledge adequately to prepare his defense, even though he may have a perfect one. He requires the guiding hand of counsel at every step in the proceedings against him. Without it, though he be not guilty, he faces the danger of conviction because he does not know how to establish his innocence."

Since Gideon was convicted of a felony, technically the case applies the right to appointed counsel only to felony cases. In 1972 in *Argersinger* v. *Hamlin,* clarified in 1979 in *Scott* v. *Illinois,* the Supreme Court held that the right to appointed counsel applies to misdemeanors when conviction would result in the *actual* deprivation of a person's liberty.[55]

An important question not answered by *Gideon* is how soon after apprehension a suspect is entitled to appointed counsel. In *Escobedo* v. *Illinois,* the Court ruled that the right to counsel begins before the trial.[56] The Court has decided numerous cases involving the right to counsel during the pretrial and trial processes. In *Brewer* v. *Williams,* the Court emphasized that whatever else the right to counsel may mean, it "means at least that a person is entitled to the help of a lawyer at or after the time that judicial proceedings have been initiated against him."[57] In *Maine* v. *Moulton,* the Court underscored the importance of the right to counsel prior to trial by stating that "to deprive a person of counsel during the period prior to trial may be more damaging than denial of counsel during the trial itself."[58]

The right to counsel is of little value unless the attorney who represents the defendant provides an effective defense. Thus, the right to counsel means the right to effective assistance of counsel, but there is little consensus on the meaning of *effective* assistance.

Lower federal courts have considered this issue, but their answers have varied. A 1984 decision illustrates ineffective counsel. When the defendant's attorney fell asleep during the trial, the court ruled that this was inherently prejudicial. According to the court, an unconscious or sleeping counsel is equivalent to no counsel at all.[59]

In a more recent case a panel of three judges on the Fifth District Court of Appeals returned to the trial court a case involving an alleged sleeping attorney. The panel ruled that there was no evidence concerning when and how long the attorney slept and thus how much information he might not have heard. Therefore, it was not possible to determine whether the inmate (who had been on death row for 16 years when he filed his petition regarding alleged ineffective assistance of counsel) had been prejudiced. Neither the judge nor the prosecutor noticed the defense attorney sleeping, although some jurors and the court clerk testified that he was. The panel sent the case back to the trial court to determine whether more evidence existed. But in August 2001 the full appellate court upheld the lower court's initial decision, stating that the defense attorney repeatedly slept as evidence was introduced and that, "In such circumstances, the Supreme Court's Sixth Amendment jurisprudence compels the presumption that counsel's unconsciousness prejudiced the defendant."[60]

In 1984 the Supreme Court decided two cases on effective assistance of counsel. The first case involved a defendant whose attorney specialized in real estate. He had virtually no experience in criminal law and only 25 days to prepare a defense. The second involved a death row inmate who argued that he did not have effective counsel at the nonjury sentencing stage. In announcing its decision in both cases in *Strickland* v. *Washington,* the Court reinstated the convictions of the defendants, thus overruling the lower federal courts' rulings. According to the Supreme Court's opinion, "The benchmark for judging any claim of ineffectiveness must be whether counsel's conduct so undermined the proper functioning of the adversarial process that the trial cannot be relied on as having produced a just result." To win on the issue of ineffective assistance of counsel, a defendant must be able to prove that his or her attorney's errors "were so serious as to deprive the defendant of a fair trial, a trial whose result is reliable." In *Strickland,* the Court gave some guidelines for determining whether a defendant has had effective counsel; some of those guidelines are reproduced in Exhibit 11.4.[61]

EXHIBIT 11.4
The Supreme Court and Effective Assistance of Counsel

Until recently the Supreme Court had not given much help to lower courts in interpreting what is meant by effective assistance of counsel. In its 1984 decision in *Strickland* v. *Washington* the Court established a two-pronged test: (1) whether the counsel's performance was deficient and (2) whether it prejudiced the defendant. The Court was not very specific, however, on what those two tests mean. Here are some comments from that and other opinions, all cited by the Court in *Strickland.* Can you tell what is meant by effective assistance of counsel by reading these statements?

1. Counsel must be a reasonably competent attorney whose advice is "within the range of competence of attorneys in criminal cases."
2. To show ineffective assistance of counsel, defendants must show that "counsel's representation fell below an objective standard of reasonableness."
3. Counsel owes the client "a duty of loyalty, a duty to avoid conflicts of interest." Counsel must consult with his or her client, advocate that client's cause, and keep the client informed of the important developments in his or her case.
4. Counsel has a duty "to bring to bear such skill and knowledge as will render the trial a reliable adversarial testing process."

Are these statements vague? According to the Court, it is not possible to articulate more specific general standards that could be applied to all cases. Each case must be analyzed individually in light of the particular facts. "More specific guidelines are not appropriate . . . The proper measure of attorney performance remains simply reasonableness under prevailing professional norms."

Source: Summarized from *Strickland* v. *Washington,* 466 U.S. 668 (1984); citations omitted.

Two cases illustrate ineffective assistance of counsel. A Nevada case held that counsel is ineffective when the attorney seeks to advance his own career at the expense of the client's best interests.[62] A Maryland appellate court held that ineffective assistance of counsel is proved when there is a "substantial possibility" that the attorney's errors affected the verdict against the defendant.[63]

In 1993 the Supreme Court held that counsel was not ineffective when the defense attorney failed to object to a decision that was subsequently overruled. Thus, the second requirement of *Strickland,* concerning whether counsel's action prejudiced the defendant, requires more than a mere showing that the outcome would have been different had counsel not made the mistake. It may be that one error would result in ineffective assistance of counsel, but the point is that the totality of counsel's actions must be considered.[64]

Finally, in 2000 the U.S. Supreme Court held that an appellant had ineffective assistance of counsel when the attorney failed to file an appeal within the 60 days permitted for such action. In *Roe* v. *Lucio Flores-Ortega* the defendant gave no instructions to his attorney about filing or not filing an appeal. In such cases, ruled the Court, the question must be asked: Did the attorney consult with the defendant regarding an appeal? "We employ the term 'consult' to convey a specific meaning—advising the defendant about the advantages and disadvantages of taking an appeal, and making a reasonable effort to discover the defendant's wishes." The Court held that there is a constitutional duty to consult "when there is reason to think either (1) that a rational defendant would want to appeal . . . or (2) that this particular defendant reasonably demonstrated to counsel that he was interested in appealing." But the appellant must prove that the ineffective assistance prejudiced him. The case was returned to the lower court to enable the appellant to offer proof that he would have been granted an appeal had his counsel petitioned for one.[65]

Right to Trial by Jury

Jury In a criminal case, sworn persons who hear the evidence at trial, determine certain facts, and render a verdict of guilty or not guilty. In some jurisdictions, juries recommend or determine sentences.

Among other rights, the Sixth Amendment to the U.S. Constitution guarantees the right to a speedy and public trial by an impartial **jury** in the state and county in which the crime occurred (see Appendix A).

The jury system is very important in the United States, which has approximately one-half of all criminal jury trials in the world. In some countries, such as Great Britain, the use of the jury system is declining. Other countries, such as Japan and India, have abolished the jury system, while some countries use professionals to serve as jurors.

The importance of the right to a jury trial was emphasized by the Supreme Court in 1968 in *Duncan* v. *Louisiana:* "Providing an accused with the right to be tried by a jury of his peers gave him an inestimable safeguard against the corrupt or overzealous prosecutor and against the compliant, biased, or eccentric judge." The Court said, however, that this right does not apply to all crimes. It excludes a category of petty crimes or offenses.[66]

In 1989 the Court held that the right to a jury trial does not extend to persons charged with driving under the influence (DUI). In deciding whether a crime is petty and therefore does not qualify for a jury trial, the Court looks primarily at the severity of the penalty that might be imposed if the defendant is incarcerated. In general, a possible sentence of six months or more in prison is considered sufficient to invoke the right to a jury trial.[67] Some states provide greater access to jury trials than required by the Constitution.

The right to a jury trial involves the right to have a jury determine the question of guilt or innocence; it does not mean that a defendant has a right to have the jury make a recommendation or even determine sentencing, although that is permitted in some jurisdictions.

The right to a jury trial is based on the belief that the defendant is entitled to have his or her case decided by those who represent community values. In that regard, the jury may ignore facts, a process that is called *jury nullification.*

The U.S. Constitution provides that a defendant has the right to a trial in the state and county in which the crime is deemed to have occurred (see Appendix A, Sixth Amendment). But the defendant is permitted to ask the court to move the trial elsewhere if it appears that he or she cannot get a fair trial in that jurisdiction. In other words, the defendant may ask for a change of venue.

A defendant is entitled to trial by a jury representative of the community, but that does not mean that he or she is entitled to a jury of any particular composition. Rather, it means that the lists from which jurors are selected must not exclude groups based on criteria such as gender, race, religion, or ethnic background. It addition, it means that actual jury selection may not proceed in a discriminatory manner. But neither must juries be selected in a totally random manner.

Voir dire To speak the truth; the process of questioning prospective jurors to determine their qualifications and desirability for serving on a jury.

Peremptory challenge A challenge by prosecution or defense attorneys to excuse a potential juror from the jury panel. No reason is required. Each side is entitled to a specified number of peremptory challenges.

During the jury selection process, attorneys (or the judge) question those in the jury pool, a process called ***voir dire,*** which means "to speak the truth." The trial judge or the attorneys may excuse potential jurors for *cause,* meaning that they are presumed to be biased in the case. A person may be presumed biased because of prior associations with the defendant or the judge or attorneys or for any number of other reasons, such as the way he or she answers questions.

A second method of excusing potential jurors is through a **peremptory challenge.** When attorneys use this method, they do not need a cause or a reason. The number of peremptory challenges is limited, although the number varies by jurisdiction and by type of case.

In *Batson* v. *Kentucky,* the Supreme Court overturned part of an earlier decision and held that prosecutors may not use the peremptory challenge to exclude African Americans from juries because they believe they will favor their own race. *Batson* is concerned primarily with issues of evidence, but its effect is to make it easier for minority defendants to prove racial discrimination in the composition of the trial jury. Defendants must show that they are members of a defined minority group, that the prosecutor used the peremptory challenge to remove persons of that group from the jury, and that these and other facts "raise an inference that the prosecutor used the practice to exclude the [potential jurors] on account of their race." The prosecution would then have the burden of proving that the exclusion was not based on racial discrimination.[68]

Batson involved an African American defendant challenging the prosecutorial exclusion of African American jurors. In 1991 in *Powers* v. *Ohio,* the Court ruled that a white defendant could challenge a prosecutor's systematic exclusion of African American jurors. The right at stake here is the right of jurors excluded on the basis of their race. The right to a fair trial implies the right of ordinary citizens to participate in the criminal justice system, and their primary way of doing so is through jury duty.[69]

In *Hernandez* v. *New York* the Court upheld a prosecutor's exclusion of two prospective Latino jurors in the trial of a Latino defendant. The Court accepted the prosecutor's argument "that the specific responses and demeanor of the two individuals during *voir dire* caused him to doubt their ability to defer to the official translation of Spanish-language testimony."[70]

On the other hand, in a 1995 case involving the trial of a Hispanic defendant a New York court found unacceptable the prosecutor's reasons for using peremptory challenges to excuse the only three Hispanics in a jury pool. The prosecutor alleged that the computer background of one Hispanic would make him too analytical for the jury. Another, a school security officer, was excused for having had too much contact with young people, which might prejudice him toward the young defendant. A third was excused for various reasons, one of which was that the prosecutor thought he was not intelligent enough. This potential juror had a high school education, and white potential jurors with only high school educations were not dismissed. Two of the three were alleged to have too many contacts with police, a situation normally thought to be favorable to the prosecution. The court concluded that the prosecution used race as a basis for excluding these potential jurors.[71]

In 1992 in *Georgia* v. *McCollum,* the U.S. Supreme Court held that the defense may not use peremptory challenges to discriminate on the basis of race. According to the Court, the trial court erred when it refused to grant the prosecutor's request to prevent the white defendants from using peremptory challenges to eliminate African Americans from the jury. The defendants in this case were accused of committing crimes against African Americans.[72]

In 1994 the Supreme Court applied *Batson* to gender-based peremptories in a *civil* case. In *J. E. B.* v. *T. B.,* a paternity case, the state used its peremptory challenges to exclude nine men from the jury. The case was heard by a jury of 12 women, who decided that the defendant fathered the child in question and should be ordered to make child support payments. The defendant's objection to the use of peremptory challenges to exclude male jurors was rejected by the trial judge and the Alabama Court of Civil Appeals. The Alabama Supreme Court refused to hear the case, but the U.S. Supreme Court held that the exclusion was improper. Justice Harry A. Blackmun stated, "We hold that gender, like race, is an unconstitutional proxy for juror competence and impartiality."[73]

The right to a jury of peers does not include the right of young adults to be tried by a jury composed of other young adults. The absence of young adults on the jury does not necessarily mean that the young defendant's right to be tried by a jury of peers was violated. The defendant must show that the underrepresented group has characteristics that can be defined easily and that the group has common attitudes, experiences, or ideas in addition to a community of interest.[74]

Another issue in selecting an impartial jury concerns the attitudes and beliefs of potential jurors. These attitudes may be so prejudicial that the defendant could not possibly get a fair trial. This issue arises most frequently in the context of capital cases. Should people who are opposed to the death penalty be excluded from juries in capital cases?

Most states base their rules concerning jury selection in capital cases on a footnote of the 1968 Supreme Court opinion. In *Witherspoon* v. *Illinois,* the Court said that potential jurors could be excused for cause if they made it

> unmistakably clear (1) that they would *automatically* vote against the imposition of capital punishment without regard to any evidence that might be developed at the trial of the case before them or (2) that their attitude toward the death penalty would prevent them from making an impartial decision as to the defendant's *guilt.*[75]

In *Wainwright* v. *Witt,* the Supreme Court said that it does not require a ritualistic adherence to the footnote in *Witherspoon;* the proper test for excluding a juror because of views on capital punishment does not require a conclusion that the juror would vote automatically against capital punishment or that the person's bias had to be clear. The test established was whether the person's views on capital punishment would prevent or substantially impair him or her from performing the duties of a juror.[76]

The right to trial by an impartial jury also means that the jurors must not be prejudiced by the media. Defendants cannot have a fair trial if, because of pretrial publicity, the jurors have already made up their minds about the case. Therefore, the Court has issued rulings concerning when pretrial publicity is prejudicial to the defendant. Perhaps the most publicized of these rulings was *Sheppard* v. *Maxwell,* decided in 1966. Dr. Sam Sheppard was convicted of his wife's murder and served 10 years in prison before his conviction was overturned. At his second trial, he was acquitted.[77]

During Sheppard's trial, private telephones were installed to allow the press to transmit their stories as quickly as possible. One station was permitted to set up broadcasting equipment in the room next to the jury deliberation room. With the crowd of media persons and the public, it was impossible for Sheppard to talk privately with his counsel in the courtroom during the trial. Nor was it possible inside the courtroom for counsel to approach the judge out of the jury's hearing. The jurors were exposed to the news media as well.

These and many other facts were considered by the Supreme Court before reversing Sheppard's conviction. Its opinion stressed the importance of the media's First Amendment rights to free speech but also the more important right of the defendant to be tried before an unbiased jury (see Appendix A). In conclusion, it declared, "With his life at stake, it is not requiring too much that petitioner be tried in an atmosphere undisturbed by so huge a wave of public passion . . . The theory of our system is that the conclusions to be reached in a case will be induced only by evidence and argument in open court, and not by any outside influence, whether of private talk or public print."[78] The Court referred to the trial as having a "Roman holiday" atmosphere, complete with murder, mystery, society, and sex.

The influence of publicity on the jury faced the Court again in 1979, when it considered the issue of whether the press could be barred from a pretrial hearing. In *Gannett Co., Inc.* v. *Depasquale,* the Court recognized the importance of openness but refused to recognize a constitutional right of the public to be present at pretrial hearings. The decision reopened the power struggle between the press and the Court, between the rights of the public and the rights of the defendant.[79]

In subsequent decisions, *Gannett* has been eroded. In *Richmond Newspapers, Inc.* v. *Virginia,* the Court ruled that the public and the press have a constitutional right of access to criminal *trials* (*Gannett* dealt with pretrial hearings), but that right is not unlimited. Before trials can be closed, however, the government must explore other alternatives.[80]

Richmond was criticized in the court's later decision in *Globe Newspaper Co.* v. *Superior Court*, which involved a Massachusetts statute that was interpreted by the Massachusetts court to require that the press be excluded during the testimony of a sexual abuse victim who was under the age of 18. The Supreme Court did not agree that blanket exclusion in such cases is appropriate, stating that the facts of each case must be analyzed, and the state must show a compelling reason for excluding the press. Although preserving the psychological welfare of the victim may constitute a compelling state interest, the Supreme Court said that can be done on a case-by-case analysis by looking at the age and maturity of the victim, the victim's wishes, the nature and circumstances of the crime, and other relevant variables.[81]

The Court has held that "the qualified First Amendment right of access to criminal proceedings applies to preliminary hearings" in some circumstances. Those hearings may be closed only if (1) it can be shown that the defendant would not get a fair trial if it were open to the public and press, and (2) a fair trial cannot be provided by less drastic alternatives than closing the trial to the public.[82]

Trial judges have the responsibility of attempting to assess media impact on potential or actual jurors. Judges should take prophylactic measures before the jury is prejudiced and it becomes necessary to declare a mistrial.

VICTIMS' RIGHTS

The discussion thus far has focused on some of the constitutional rights of criminal defendants. The right to be free of unreasonable searches and seizures, the right not to testify against oneself, the right to counsel, and the right to trial by an impartial jury are at the heart of those rights, but they are only a sample of

A decontamination crew dressed in protective suits stands together as an investigator takes photographs outside Ottilie Lundgren's Oxford, Connecticut, home, after the house was declared a crime scene on 30 November 2001. Lundgren, age 94, died of inhalation anthrax on 21 November 2001. (AP)

the provisions of the adversary system to ensure that defendants get a fair trial. Some believe that the pendulum has swung too far, that defendants have too many rights, that society is not protected, and that victims are ignored.

The decade of the 1980s was characterized by a strong movement toward the recognition of victims' rights, evidenced by the implementation of changes directed toward the needs and concerns of crime victims in criminal justice systems. The movement continued into the 1990s and is characterized by two approaches. The first is to increase victims' participation in criminal justice systems; the second is to provide victim compensation.

Throughout most of our history, victims have been ignored by criminal justice systems. In the past decade many jurisdictions have tried to remedy this situation, and they have done so in a variety of ways. For example, the California Penal Code provides that all crime victims and witnesses be treated with "dignity, courtesy, respect, and sensitivity."[83]

Other jurisdictions have made progress since 1982, when the Task Force on Victims of Crime proclaimed that U.S. criminal justice systems were "appallingly out of balance," with defendants obtaining more justice than victims. A recent report concluded that significant improvements had been made in the treatment of victims but that much more needed to be accomplished.[84]

One of the ways victims have been recognized is to permit them to participate in criminal justice systems. Many witnesses and victims need financial and other kinds of assistance before they can participate in criminal proceedings. They may need transportation to court, parking, child care, or other reasonable expenses. They may need medical care and psychological counseling, which are provided in some jurisdictions. Victims have also been permitted to participate in negotiation proceedings with prosecutors and defense attorneys and even with offenders. Many jurisdictions have instituted special training programs to increase the understanding that law enforcement officers, prosecutors, judges and others have of the needs of victims and witnesses. Arrest policies have been revised in many systems. Problems such as domestic violence and child abuse are treated as criminal acts, not domestic problems that should be under the jurisdiction of someone other than criminal justice professionals. Victims may be permitted to express their concerns and opinions on issues such as sentencing or plea bargaining.

The role of victims was limited by the Supreme Court in a 1987 decision, *Booth* v. *Maryland,* in which the Court held that the defendant's constitutional rights are violated when a victim impact statement (VIS) contains certain information, such as the severe emotional impact of the crime on the family, the personal characteristics of the victim, and the family members' opinions and characterizations of the crime and of the offender. When the issue arose in the sentencing phase of a capital case, the Court emphasized the concern that in such serious cases decisions should be based on reason, not emotion. Thus, the jury should not hear this type of information, which "can serve no other purpose than to inflame the jury and divert it from deciding the case on the relevant evidence concerning the crime and the defendant."[85]

In 1991 the Court reversed itself on that ruling as well as another. In *Payne* v. *Tennessee,* the Court ruled that VISs may be used at capital sentencing hearings: "A state may legitimately conclude that evidence about the victim and about the impact of the murder on the victim's family is relevant to the jury's decision as to whether or not the death penalty should be imposed."[86]

A second area of focus in victims' rights is the development of victims' compensation programs. In many cases what victims need most is financial compensation for the property losses they have incurred, medical expenses, or both. This need is recognized by California, where the state constitution's Victim Bill of Rights recognizes a right of restitution of "all persons who suffer losses as a result of criminal activity."[87]

Victims' compensation legislation Legislation that provides financial and other types of assistance to crime victims.

All 50 states have enacted **victims' compensation legislation,** and over 25 states have constitutional provisions for compensation. Enforcement has been a problem, however, and several states have created special agencies to ensure the enforcement of victim compensation provisions. Still, funding for these programs is a problem in many jurisdictions. The federal program is used to illustrate some of the provisions and problems of such a system.

Congress passed the Victim and Witness Protection Act of 1982 (VWPA), which, with subsequent amendments, applies to victims of offenders tried in federal courts. The findings and statement of purpose of the act emphasize the importance of victims' cooperation in criminal justice processes yet note that historically victims have been ignored by the system or "simply used as tools to identify and punish offenders." The legislation recognizes that victims "suffer physical, psychological, or financial hardship first as a result of the criminal act and then as a result of contact with a criminal justice system unresponsive to the real needs of such victims." The act calls for elimination of harassment of victims and witnesses and establishes guidelines for the fair treatment of both. It specifies many other problems faced by witnesses, noting that its purpose is to correct these in the federal system and to provide a model for state victim compensation legislation.[88] The restitution provision of the federal statute has been the subject of litigation. Congress responded to some of the legal issues concerning restitution with language changes in the statute when it enacted the Crime Control Act of 1990.[89]

In 1998, after numerous drafts, the Senate Judiciary Committee passed a proposed constitutional amendment concerning victims' rights. One of the compromises in the proposal was that compensation would be limited to violent crime victims, thus excluding property crime victims. This decision caused a split among some victims' advocate groups.[90]

In 2000 the crime victims' rights constitutional amendment advanced to the Senate but was withdrawn after its sponsors requested that it not be voted on. They apparently knew they did not have the votes to pass the proposal. The Clinton administration had expressed its willingness to support an amendment but had reservations about some of the provisions of this particular proposal. But eventually the administration advised the amendment's sponsors that it would not support the proposal because the concerns of the White House had not been addressed. For example, the White House had insisted on a statement providing that "nothing in [the amendment] shall be construed to deny or diminish the rights of the accused." Proponents of the amendment feared that statement would mean that any time a defendant asserted that his or her rights were being negatively impacted by a victim, the victim's rights would not be recognized.[91]

With regard to the concern about defendant's rights, at its annual meeting in 1997 the American Bar Association considered the implications of the growing victims' rights movement and approved these principles:

- Defendants' rights should not be diminished.
- Victims' rights should not diminish the ability of the trial court to "efficiently and fairly" manage courtroom proceedings.
- Victims' rights should not diminish prosecutorial discretion in charging and plea negotiations.
- Violations of a victim's rights should not give rise to a new cause of action against any public official or public office.
- Government resources for implementing victims' rights should be fully funded.
- The term "victim" should be defined.
- Each jurisdiction should be able to develop its own victims' rights procedures.[92]

In contrast to the Senate's lack of passage of the victim's rights amendment to the U.S. Constitution, in the fall of 2000 it unanimously authorized another five years of life for the Violence against Women Act of 1994. That act contains provision for victims, especially of domestic violence. Additional programs were approved, along with funding for legal counsel for civil cases brought by victims of domestic violence, stalking, and sexual harassment.

New provisions include addressing the abuse of elderly and disabled victims; improving protective orders, especially across state lines; grants for coordinating the work of victims advocates, police, and prosecutors; broadening the definition of cyberstalking to include harassment through e-mail or other electronic means; grants for shelters for battered women and children; and the expansion of some provisions to include crimes such as date rape. When he prepared to sign the bill, President Clinton said the original statute has "made a crucial difference in the lives of hundreds of thousands of women" but that much more needs to be done for female crime victims.[93]

Finally, the National Center for Victims of Crime (NCVC) announced that its priority in the year 2001 would be to secure for victims of property crimes the same type of rights that have been made available to violent crime victims.

Courts may alter evidence rules for witnesses as young as this child. For example, in some cases judges may permit the child to testify without having to view the defendant; in others hearsay evidence rules may be waived. Such decisions must be made on a case-by-case basis, and if the decision violates the defendants' constitutional rights, it will be reversed on appeal. (Gale Zucker/Stock Boston)

DEFENDANTS' RIGHTS VERSUS VICTIMS' RIGHTS

As the above discussion suggests, efforts to compensate victims and to involve them in criminal justice systems may conflict with defendants' rights. One of the most frequently raised issues that create conflicts between victims and defendants is whether or not a sexual abuse victim, particularly a young one, must testify in person in court or whether someone may testify as to what the victim said (hearsay evidence). Normally, hearsay evidence is not allowed because it denies the defendant the opportunity to confront and cross-examine the witness. However, testifying in court can be a very traumatic, even impossible, task for some victims, especially young ones who have been assaulted sexually. This is true particularly when the alleged offender is a victim's relative.

The U.S. Supreme Court considered this issue in 1988 in *Coy* v. *Iowa,* in which the defendant was accused of sexual assault. Note the Court's resolution of the issue of whether it was proper for the alleged victims to testify behind a screen. Had you been on the Court, how would you have decided this issue?[94]

Coy v. Iowa

Appellant was convicted of two counts of lascivious acts with a child after a jury trial in which a screen placed between him and the two complaining witnesses blocked him from their sight. Appellant contends that this procedure, authorized by state statute, violated his Sixth Amendment right to confront the witnesses against him . . .

Appellant . . . argued that, although the device might succeed in its apparent aim of making the complaining witnesses feel less uneasy in giving their testimony, the Confrontation Clause directly addressed this issue by giving criminal defendants a right to face-to-face confrontation. He also argued that his right to due process was violated, since the procedure would make him appear guilty and thus erode the presumption of innocence. The trial court rejected both constitutional claims, though it instructed the jury to draw no inference of guilt from the screen . . .

The Sixth Amendment's guarantee of face-to-face encounter between witness and accused serves ends related both to appearances and to reality . . . The perception that confrontation is essential to fairness has persisted over the centuries because there is much truth to it . . .

The remaining question is whether the right to confrontation was in fact violated in this case. The screen at issue was specifically designed to enable the complaining witnesses to avoid viewing appellant as they gave their testimony, and the record indicates that it was successful in this objective. It is difficult to imagine a more obvious or damaging violation of the defendant's right to a face-to-face encounter . . .

We find it unnecessary to reach appellant's due process claim. Since [the defendant's] constitutional right to face-to-face confrontation was violated, we reverse the judgment of the Iowa Supreme Court and remand the case.

In *Coy* v. *Iowa* the Supreme Court was not saying that in all cases defendants' rights will prevail, but rather that the Court will carefully scrutinize any blanket requirements that infringe on defendants' rights. A question that was not answered by this case was answered in 1990 by the Court. In *Maryland* v. *Craig* a 5-to-4 majority held that a defendant's Sixth Amendment right to confront witnesses at trial (see Appendix A) does not require all confrontations to be face-to-face. In upholding a Maryland statute that permits a child who is the alleged victim of sexual abuse to testify outside the courtroom via television, the Court said that this is permissible provided the reliability of the child's testimony can be determined by other means.[95] Each case must be judged on its individual facts.

SUMMARY

This chapter introduces American criminal justice systems and thus provides the background for the remaining chapters in this section. After distinguishing the adversary from the inquisitory systems, the discussion proceeds to an explanation of the important concepts of due process and equal protection. Two special characteristics of U.S. criminal justice systems—the system effect and the use of discretion—are explored, followed by an overview of the major stages in U.S. criminal justice systems.

The major portion of the chapter focuses on a discussion of four constitutional rights of defendants: the right to be free of unreasonable search and seizure, the right not to testify against oneself, the right to counsel, and the right to a trial by a jury of one's peers. The recognition of victims' rights is discussed, followed by a look at the potential conflicts that arise between the rights of defendants and those of victims.

This chapter shows some of the inevitable tensions and controversies in U.S. criminal justice systems. On the one hand, we believe in individual rights; we do not think the police or any other government officials should be able to interfere in our personal lives without just cause. On the other hand, we want to walk the streets safely, and so we want adequate police protection from crime. When we are victimized, we want our property back and our medical bills paid, and we want the defendants brought to justice. It may be impossible to achieve all of these goals.

It is the tremendous power of the government, a power that can—in the hands of the ruthless—violate our constitutional rights even to the point of conviction for a crime we did not commit, that requires us to provide and maintain some protection for those accused of crime. In protecting their rights, we protect the rights of us all. This need was demonstrated in *A Man for All Seasons,* a play about the life, trial, and execution of the English humanist, author, and statesman Sir Thomas More. More, who lived from 1478 to 1535 (and in 1935 was canonized by the Roman Catholic Church), stated, "Yes, I'd give the Devil benefit of law, for my own safety's sake."[96]

Yet because it is necessary to have the power of law enforcement and the power of prevention, it is essential that we have a professional police force, the focus of Chapter 12.

STUDY QUESTIONS

1. Distinguish the adversary from the inquisitory system, and discuss the role of due process and equal protection in the adversary system.
2. What is meant by the *system effect* of justice systems? Explain how changes in the juvenile court system illustrate this process.
3. Analyze the role of discretion in criminal justice systems.
4. List and define the major steps in U.S. criminal justice systems.
5. Define *probable cause* and analyze its importance with regard to search warrants. Why does the U.S. Supreme Court prefer search warrants to warrantless searches? Discuss search warrants in relation to searches of motor vehicles, homes, and persons.
6. Discuss briefly the legal developments with regard to vehicle searches.
7. State the implications of searches outside but in the vicinity of the home.
8. Should more intrusive body searches be permitted at U.S. borders? Why or why not?
9. Explain the reasons for the *Miranda* warnings.
10. Discuss the legal implications of the *Miranda* rule.
11. Explain the meaning of Clarence Earl Gideon's case and its implications for the right to counsel.
12. What is meant by *effective assistance of counsel?*
13. Define *jury nullification* and discuss its implications.
14. Why is a change of venue permitted?
15. Define *voir dire* and *peremptory challenge* and discuss these concepts in relationship to jury selection based on gender, race, age, and disability.
16. Discuss the implications of a belief in capital punishment to jury selection in a capital case.
17. Explain the role of the media in a defendant's right to a fair trial.
18. To what extent should victims be permitted to participate in the trials and sentencing of their offenders? To what extent should victims be compensated for their suffering?
19. Discuss potential conflicts between recognizing victims' rights and defendants' rights.

BRIEF ESSAY ASSIGNMENTS

1. Define and describe the U.S. Supreme Court's establishment of the "totality of circumstances" in the case of *Illinois* v. *Gates*.
2. Briefly summarize the Supreme Court rulings regarding searches of containers inside vehicles.
3. Explain the "free to leave" test as it relates to the seizure of a person.
4. Discuss the plain view doctrine to seize evidence without a warrant.
5. Briefly describe the case of *Batson* v. *Kentucky* and its impact on jury selection.

INTERNET ACTIVITIES

1. Learn more about trying juveniles in adult court by logging onto the National Association of Sentencing Advocates' website at www.sentencingproject.org and reading the publication entitled "Prosecuting Juveniles in Adult Court: An Assessment of Trends and Consequences." What arguments do the authors make regarding the harm of processing juveniles through the adult system? In your opinion, should juveniles be prosecuted in adult courts? Why or why not?
2. Check out the Northwestern University School of Law Center's site for the Center on Wrongful Convictions at www.law.northwestern.edu/wrongfulconvictions. This center has gained national attention for its investigation and litigation of wrongful convictions. Its work has also influenced the debate on enacting moratoriums on the death penalty.

NET RESOURCES

www.youthlawcenter.com
: The Youth Law Center provides resources to information regarding children's legal rights and protection in the criminal justice system and other social institutions. This site also covers news and legislation regarding juvenile justice and youth rights across the nation.

www.nacdl.org
: The National Association of Criminal Defense Lawyers' website addresses criminal defense topics such as due process, defendant's rights, indigent defense, innocence projects, and fairness issues in the criminal justice system.

www.truthinjustice.org
: The focus of the Truth in Justice website is on persons wrongly convicted in the U.S. criminal justice systems. Recent court cases collected from media sources, police/prosecutor misconduct, and innocence projects are among the topics presented. There are also links to related sites.

www.abanet.org
: The American Bar Association's website provides legal information on a variety of topics through weekly news, briefings, and selected links. Articles and reports from the American Bar Association's online journal can be accessed from this site.

www.neve.org
: The National Center for Victims of Crime's website includes several categories that addresses victims' rights and victimization including public policy, civil litigation and a press center. Users can also access articles and statistics from the site's virtual library.

www.try-nova.org
: A private, nonprofit organization, the National Organization for Victim Assistance offers information and resources on victimization and witness assistance programs on its website. A section on public policy includes information on crime victim and witness rights and a constitutional amendment for crime victims.

ENDNOTES

1. "Twenty-Five Wrongfully Executed in U.S., Study Finds," *New York Times* (14 November 1985), p. 13.
2. C. Ronald Huff, "Wrongful Conviction: Societal Tolerance of Injustice," *Social Problems and Public Policy* 4 (1987): 113.
3. Joint Anti-Fascist Refugee Committee v. McGrath, 341 U.S. 123, 162–163 (1951), Justice Felix Frankfurter concurring.
4. *In re* Gault, 387 U.S. 1 (1967).
5. *In re* Gault, 387 U.S. 1, 19–21, 26–28 (1967).
6. Wayne R. LaFave and Jerold H. Israel, Criminal Procedure (St. Paul, MN: West, 1985), pp. 19–20.
7. Illinois v. Gates, 462 U.S. 213 (1983).
8. Alabama v. White, 496 U.S. 325 (1990).
9. United States v. Ross, 456 U.S. 798 (1982).
10. See United States v. Perea, 986 F.2d 633, 643 (2d Cir. 1993).
11. Florida v. Jimeno, 500 U.S. 248 (1991).
12. United States v. Johns, 469 U.S. 478 (1985).
13. Colorado v. Bertine, 479 U.S. 367 (1987).
14. Illinois v. Wardlow, 528 U.S. 199 (2000).
15. "New Jersey Enters into Consent Decree on Racial Issues in Highway Stops," *Criminal Law Reporter* 66 (5 January 2000): 251.
16. United States v. Montero-Camargo, 208 F.3d 1122 (9th Cir. 2000), *cert. denied,* 531 U.S. 885 (2000).
17. Indianapolis v. Edmond, 531 U.S. 32 (2000).
18. United States v. Mendenhall, 446 U.S. 544 (1980).
19. Florida v. Bostick, 501 U.S. 421 (1991).
20. California v. Hodari D., 499 U.S. 621 (1991).
21. See United States v. Robinson, 414 U.S. 218 (1973).
22. See Terry v. Ohio, 392 U.S. 1 (1968).
23. Minnesota v. Dickerson, 508 U.S. 336 (1993).
24. United States v. Ashley, 37 F.3d 678 (D.C.Cir. 1994).
25. People v. Clark, 625 N.Y.S.2d 306 (App. Div.3d Dept. 1995), *aff'd.,* 86 N.Y.2d 824 (N.Y.App. 1995).
26. Smith v. State, 666 A.2d 883 (Md.App. 1995), *aff'd. and remanded for a new trial,* 693 A.2d 749 (Md. 1997).
27. Rochin v. California, 342 U.S. 165, 166, 172 (1952).

28. United States v. Montoya de Hernandez, 473 U.S. 531 (1985).
29. Bell v. Wolfish, 441 U.S. 520 (1979).
30. Masters v. Crouch, 872 F.2d 1248 (6th Cir. 1989), *cert. denied,* Frey v. Masters, 493 U.S. 977 (1989).
31. "New York to Pay $50 Million over Illegal Strip-Searches," *New York Times* (10 January 2001), p. 1.
32. Mapp v. Ohio, 367 U.S. 643, 644 (1961).
33. Payton v. New York, 445 U.S. 573, 589–590 (1980).
34. Welsh v. Wisconsin, 466 U.S. 740 (1984).
35. Wilson v. Arkansas, 514 U.S. 927 (1995).
36. Coolidge v. New Hampshire, 403 U.S. 443 (1971).
37. Arizona v. Hicks, 480 U.S. 321 (1987).
38. California v. Greenwood, 486 U.S. 35 (1988).
39. United States v. Hedrick, 922 F.2d 396 (7th Cir. 1991), *cert. denied,* 502 U.S. 847 (1991).
40. California v. Ciraola, 476 U.S. 207 (1986). See also Florida v. Riley, 488 U.S. 445 (1989).
41. Illinois v. McArthur, 531 U.S. 326 (2001).
42. Kyllo v. United States, 121 S.Ct. 2038 (2001).
43. Edward Bennett Williams, quoted in Alexander B. Smith and Harriet Pollack, *Crime and Justice in a Mass Society* (Waltham, MA: Xerox, 1972), p. 194.
44. Brown v. Mississippi, 297 U.S. 278 (1936).
45. Miranda v. Arizona, 384 U.S. 436 (1966).
46. Oregon v. Mathiason, 429 U.S. 492 (1977).
47. Minnesota v. Murphy, 465 U.S. 420 (1984).
48. Edwards v. Arizona, 451 U.S. 477, 484–485 (1981).
49. Arizona v. Roberson, 486 U.S. 675 (1988), quoting State v. Routhier, 669 P.2d 68, 75 (1983), *cert. denied,* 464 U.S. 1073 (1984).
50. McNeil v. Wisconsin, 501 U.S. 171 (1991).
51. Davis v. United States, 512 U.S. 452 (1994).
52. See Edwards v. Arizona, 451 U.S. 477 (1981); and Minnick v. Arizona, 498 U.S. 146 (1990).
53. Dickerson v. United States, 530 U.S. 428 (2000).
54. Gideon v. Wainwright, 372 U.S. 335 (1963), which overruled Betts v. Brady, 316 U.S. 455 (1942).
55. Argersinger v. Hamlin, 407 U.S. 25, 37 (1972); Scott v. Illinois, 440 U.S. 367 (1979).
56. Escobedo v. Illinois, 378 U.S. 478 (1964).
57. Brewer v. Williams, 430 U.S. 387, 398 (1977).
58. Maine v. Moulton, 474 U.S. 159 (1985).
59. Javor v. United States, 724 F.2d 831 (9th Cir. 1984).
60. Burdine v. Johnson, 66 F.Supp. 2d 854 (S.D. Tex. 1999), *stay denied, mot. granted, in part, denied, in part,* 87 F.Supp. 2d 711 (S.D.Tex. 2000), *vacated, remanded,* 231 F.3d 950 (5th Cir. 2000), *reh'g. en banc granted,* 234 F.3d 1339 (5th Cir. 2000), *and on reh'g. aff'd.,* 2001 U.S. App. LEXIS 18277 (5th Cir. 2001).
61. Strickland v. Washington, 466 U.S. 668 (1984).
62. See Lawson v. State, 766 P.2d 261 (Nev. 1988).
63. Bowers v. State, 578 A.2d 734 (Md.App. 1990).
64. Lockhart v. Fretwell, 506 U.S. 364 (1993).
65. Roe v. Lucio Flores-Ortega, 528 U.S. 4701 (2000).
66. Duncan v. Louisiana, 391 U.S. 145, 149 (1968).
67. Blanton v. North Las Vegas, 489 U.S. 538 (1989).
68. Batson v. Kentucky, 476 U.S. 79 (1986). The earlier case is Swain v. Alabama, 380 U.S. 202 (1965).
69. Powers v. Ohio, 499 U.S. 400 (1991).
70. Hernandez v. New York, 500 U.S. 352 (1991).
71. People v. Rodriguez, 211 A.D. 2d 275 (N.Y.App.Div. 1st Dept. 1995).
72. Georgia v. McCollum, 505 U.S. 42 (1992).
73. J. E. B. v. Alabama *ex rel.* T. B., 511 U.S. 127 (1994).
74. See Barber v. Ponte, 772 F.2d 982 (1st Cir. 1985) (en banc), *cert. denied,* 475 U.S. 1050 (1988).
75. Witherspoon v. Illinois, 391 U.S. 510, 522 (1968); emphasis in the original.
76. Wainwright v. Witt, 469 U.S. 412 (1985).
77. Sheppard v. Maxwell, 384 U.S. 333 (1966).
78. Sheppard v. Maxwell, 384 U.S. 333, 349 (1966).
79. Gannett Co., Inc. v. Depasquale, 443 U.S. 368 (1979).
80. Richmond Newspapers, Inc. v. Virginia, 448 U.S. 555 (1980).
81. Globe Newspaper Co. v. Superior Court, 457 U.S. 596 (1982).
82. Press-Enterprise Co. v. Superior Court, 478 U.S. 1 (1986).
83. Cal. Penal Code, Section 679 (2001).
84. "States Creating Agencies to Enforce Victims' Rights," *Criminal Justice Newsletter* 29 (1 June 1998), p. 5; "Report Assesses Victims' Progress Since '82 Presidential Task Force," *Criminal Justice Newsletter* 29 (15 June 1998), p. 3.
85. Booth v. Maryland, 482 U.S. 496 (1987), *overruled in part,* Payne v. Tennessee, 501 U.S. 808 (1991).
86. Payne v. Tennessee, 501 U.S. 808. The other case that was overruled is South Carolina v. Gathers, 490 U.S. 805 (1989).
87. Cal. Const. Art. I, Section 28(b) (2001).
88. U.S. Code, Title 18, Section 3663 (2001).
89. U.S. Code, Title 18, Section 3663(a)(3) (2001).
90. "Judiciary Committee Approves Constitutional Amendment," *Criminal Justice Newsletter* 29 (1 June 1998): 5.
91. "Constitutional Amendment Fails to Win Senate Approval," *Criminal Justice Newsletter* 30 (16 May 2000), pp. 1, 2.
92. "ABA Takes Stands on Victims' Rights, Needle Exchange Programs," *Criminal Law Reporter* 61 (20 August 1997): 1458.
93. "Stronger Voice for Victims: Reauthorized Violence against Women Act Expands Scope of Programs," *American Bar Association Journal* 86 (December) 2000), p. 98.
94. Coy v. Iowa, 487 U.S. 1012 (1988), footnotes, citations and case names omitted.
95. Maryland v. Craig, 497 U.S. 836 (1990).
96. Robert Bolt, *A Man for All Seasons* (New York: Vintage Paperbacks, Random House, 1962), pp. 37–38.

12

▶A Connecticut National Guard military police officer stands guard outside Terminal B at Bradley International Airport, representing only one of the newly instituted security measures at all U.S. airports after the terrorist attacks of 11 September 2001. (© Steven E. Frischling/Corbis Sygma)

Police

OUTLINE

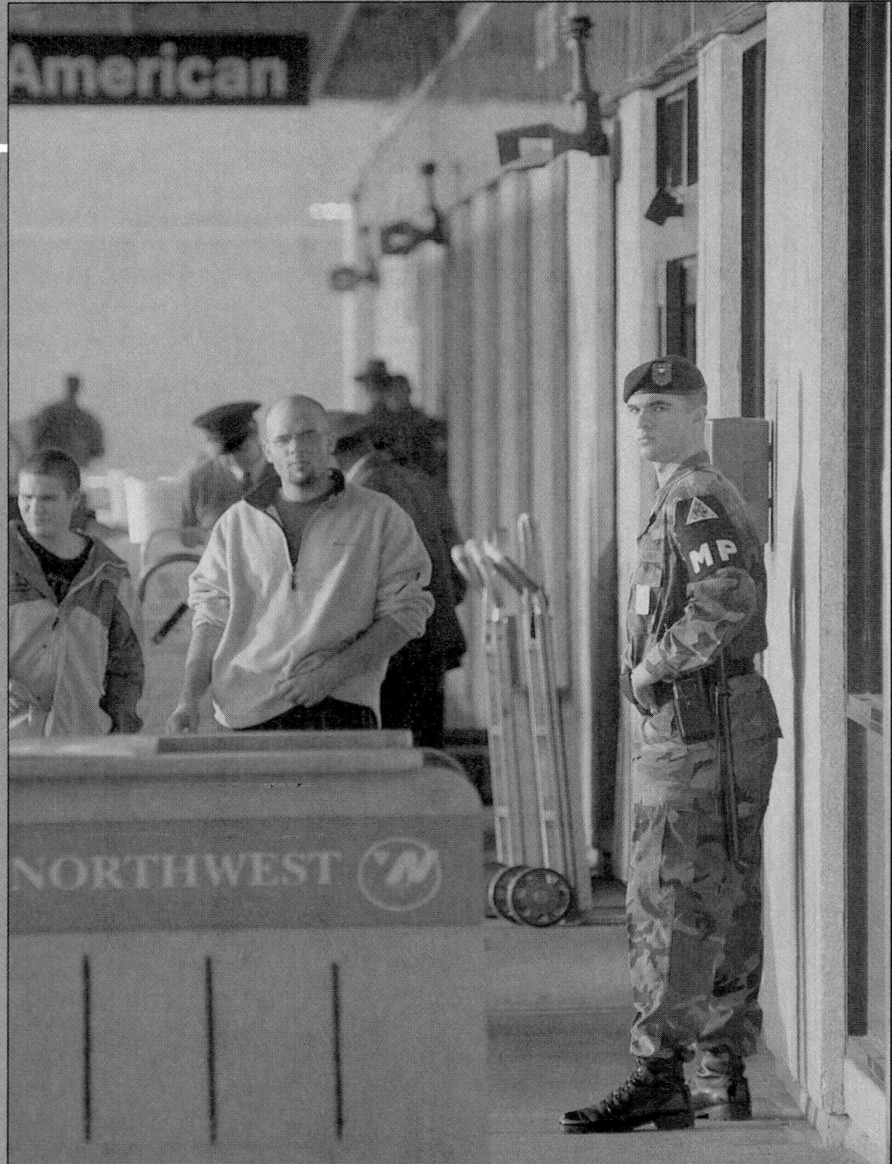

KEY TERMS

Constable
Exclusionary rule
Frankpledge
Good faith exception
Harmful error
Hundred
Inevitable discovery exception
Police
Posse
Proactive
Racial profiling
Reactive
Sheriff
Shires
Tithing
Watch system

This chapter gives a brief history of policing and discusses the levels of public police systems before looking at private security, police personnel, the type of training and education that police officers have had historically, and recent efforts to recruit more women and minorities. A section on the nature of policing focuses on its organization and three functions: law enforcement, order maintenance, and providing community services. We examine the way time is allocated among these three functions and the conflicts and stresses that develop as a result. Police decision making, especially the decision whether to arrest or to use deadly force, and police misconduct are discussed, followed by the control of policing.

Police Local law enforcement officials within the department of government that maintains and enforces law and order throughout a geographical area.

This chapter deals with one of the most important groups of people in American society: the **police,** who are entrusted with the right to protect the citizenry, even when protection requires violence. More is demanded of police than of most other professionals. They are expected to be brave, and not to show fear, shock, surprise, or hurt, even in the face of life's most serious tragedies. Police are told to make decisions quickly and with the calm, cool rationality that most people exhibit only in nontraumatic situations. They are admonished to solve many problems for which society has not found solutions and, in many instances, to perform their jobs in a hostile environment. They are instructed to treat citizens with respect, even when harassed, threatened, and abused verbally and physically.

Police occupy one of the most controversial positions in contemporary society. Although they are hated at times, they are indispensable in a modern complex nation, especially when there is trouble. But many people are not comfortable with police and may react negatively when stopped by them. Police may retaliate with their attitudes, their comments, and in some cases their weapons.

A word of warning is in order for this chapter. Of the many subjects covered in a criminology course, policing may be the most controversial. Policing has moral, religious, philosophical, ethical, and political overtones for many people. Attitudes about who should become police officers and how they should perform their jobs may be based on emotions and politics as well as knowledge, experience, reason, and practicality.

THE EMERGENCE OF FORMAL POLICING

Frankpledge Mutual pledge system in old English law, in which 10 families, constituting a **tithing,** were responsible for the acts of all other members. Ten tithings constituted a **hundred,** which was under the charge of a **constable,** considered to be the first police officer. Hundreds were later combined to form **shires,** similar to counties, over which a **sheriff** had jurisdiction.

Tithing *See* **frankpledge.**

Hundred *See* **frankpledge.**

Constable Term referring to the first police officers who presided over the **hundreds** in the **frankpledge** system. Today the term refers to the municipal court officer whose duties include keeping the peace, executing court papers, transporting prisoners, and maintaining the custody of juries.

Shires *See* **frankpledge.**

Chapter 1 discusses informal social controls that characterize early, primitive societies and that exist to some extent in modern societies. As societies become more complex, formal methods of control become necessary; policing is an important part of that control. As laws emerge, police are needed to enforce them. A brief historical look at policing illustrates the background of modern police systems.

The history of policing begins with *informal policing,* in which all members of a community are responsible for maintaining order. In medieval England, policing was conducted through a system called **frankpledge,** or mutual pledge. Ten families constituted a **tithing;** within a tithing each member was responsible for the acts of all other members.

Later, a **hundred** was developed, made up of ten tithings. The hundred was under the charge of a **constable,** who can be considered the first police officer, responsible for taking care of the weapons of the hundred. Subsequently, hundreds were combined to form **shires,** which were analogous to present-day counties. The shire was under the direction of an officer, appointed by the king, who was called a shire-reeve, a term that came to be pronounced **sheriff.**

With the growth of more complex societies, these informal methods of policing became ineffective. Increased division of labor, a more heterogeneous population, and a lack of social solidarity led to a *transitional type* of policing, for example, the **watch system,** which existed in England and in colonial America. In the watch system, bellmen walked throughout the city, ringing bells and providing police services. Later they were replaced by a permanent watch of citizens and still later by paid constables.

Dissatisfaction with the watch system led to the emergence of the modern type of policing, a movement that began in London. Londoners protested the ineffectiveness of the watch system for dealing with the problems of increased industrialization, rising levels of crime, and a perceived increase and greater severity of public riots. They agitated for a formal police force. Some believed that a police force constantly patrolling the streets would reduce and eventually

Sheriff A county's chief law enforcement officer, usually elected by popular vote, who performs varied functions such as collecting county taxes, supervising some government activities, and serving as the county coroner in some jurisdictions.

Watch system System of policing that existed in early England and colonial America. Bellmen walked throughout the city ringing bells and providing police services. Later they were replaced by a permanent watch of citizens and still later by paid constables.

eliminate crime in the streets. Others feared that the concentration of power that would be necessary for a formal police force would lead to abuses, especially if the force were a national one. Eventually the conflict between these two positions was resolved by the establishment of local police systems.[1]

The first modern police force, the Metropolitan Police of London, was founded in London in 1829 by Sir Robert Peel. The men employed by the force were called *peelers* or *bobbies.* The officers worked full-time; they wore special uniforms, and their primary function was to prevent crime. They were organized by territories and reported to a central government. Candidates had to meet high standards to qualify for a position. Bobbies were respected by Londoners, but recent incidents of corruption, incompetence, and alleged racism have tarnished the image of the once highly esteemed London bobbies.

In time, the rest of England and other countries followed London's example. Some developed a centralized police system, but the United States developed a decentralized one.

PUBLIC POLICING IN THE UNITED STATES

Many of the aspects of the English policing system were brought to the American colonies. Typically, a constable was in charge of towns and the sheriff had jurisdiction over policing counties. Before the American Revolution governors appointed by the English Crown filled these positions, but afterward most constables and sheriffs were selected by popular vote.

Many of the colonies adopted the English watch system. As early as 1631 Boston had a watch system; New Amsterdam (later New York) developed one in 1643. The New York City system was said to be typical of the watch system of policing in this country. Bellmen regularly walked throughout the city, ringing bells and providing police services. They were replaced by a permanent watch of citizens, who were succeeded by paid constables. Professional full-time police were not appointed in New York City until 1845.

Posse A group of private citizens called to assist in law enforcement.

One of the most familiar kinds of policing, which is still in use in a few rural areas, was the **posse.** Under the posse system the sheriff could call citizens over a certain age to assist in law enforcement.

Law enforcement officials were paid by local governments in some of the early American policing systems. Others, however, were paid by private individuals. According to an analysis of police history,

> By the nineteenth century, American law enforcement was a hodgepodge of small jurisdictions staffed by various officials with different power, responsibilities, and legal standing. There was no system, although there were ample precedents for public policing.[2]

Informal policing came under attack early in the United States, as it had in England. It was realized that this system did not provide the expertise and efficiency that was needed to deal with urban riots and the increasing crime and violence that occurred as the country became more industrialized and complex.

Recognition of the need for a formal police system led to the development of a professional police force in Boston in 1837. By the late 1880s, most American cities had established municipal police forces. Today those departments are complex as well as controversial. And unlike the system in England, the U.S. policing system emerged as a decentralized one.

U.S. policing systems operate at the local, state, and federal levels. Rural, county, and municipal police agencies may be found at the local level. Most studies of police focus on municipal policing, although the majority of police agencies are located in small towns, villages, or counties. Rural policing may be the responsibility of only one officer, and these systems must depend on county police agencies for assistance. Officers who work in rural areas may not have had sufficient training. Many work long hours without the prospect of assistance from county officers, and they are paid less than their urban counterparts. Rural policing can be very rewarding for those who enjoy knowing everyone in the community and who like being involved in many activities and maintaining high visibility. Lower crime rates (particularly lower rates of violence), along with less complexity in police and community structures, may be seen as positive elements. Although crime rates have increased in many rural areas, rarely do they involve the violence characteristic of the city.

County policing may cover large geographical areas, creating problems for officers when they need assistance from other areas. Some county (and rural) police agencies may contract with other police agencies for services, a process that is complicated when the county system covers a large territory. Normally, the primary law enforcement officer in the county system is the sheriff, who may have numerous other duties, such as collecting county taxes, supervising some government activities, or even serving as the county coroner.

Municipal police departments are larger and more complex than rural or county departments. They have higher costs and deal with higher crime rates and a more diverse population, but often the officers are better trained, better paid, and more educated. Most of the discussion in this chapter relates to municipal police departments.

Policing at the state level is divided into state police and state patrol. Although their duties may vary from state to state, patrol officers are primarily responsible for traffic control. They are uniformed officers, and they may be permitted to enforce some state laws, but they do not have general powers of state law enforcement. That responsibility lies with the state police. State police officers, in contrast to the state patrol, have enforcement powers over certain regulations such as those concerning fishing and gaming, gambling, horse racing, and the sale of alcoholic beverages.

Most U.S. crimes involve violations of state statutes or local ordinances. Although the United States does not have a national police force, there are congressional statutes that cover federal crimes. These federal statutes are enforced by more than 50 federal agencies, of which the largest and best known is the Federal Bureau of Investigation (FBI) in the Department of Justice. Among its other responsibilities, the FBI is in charge of collecting and disseminating national crime data, published in the *Uniform Crime Reports,* discussed in Chapter 2. The primary function of the FBI is investigative. FBI agents investigate crimes over which federal courts have jurisdiction; but when requested, they may investigate crimes under the jurisdiction of state and local law enforcement agencies.

The history of the FBI is one of controversy. The agency was headed by J. Edgar Hoover from 1924 until his death in 1972, and during much of that time it enjoyed prestige and power. Some scholars allege, however, that under Hoover the FBI was characterized by corruption and other scandals.[3] In recent years the FBI has been faced with lawsuits over hirings and promotions (alleging discrimination against minorities), harassment of agents, and allegations of fraud and other improper behavior on the part of those employed in the FBI lab. The latter allegations were the subject of an intensive investigation by the U.S. Department of Justice (DOJ), which issued a report on the topic in 1997. The DOJ found no evidence of some of the allegations; others were supported. The FBI established a timetable for correcting the problems and agreed to pay Frederic Whitehurst, an FBI chemist who first made the allegations, the sum of $1.1 million. The whistle-blower was reinstated in his job, from which he had been suspended. He reported to work and resigned, as was required by the settlement. The FBI agreed to drop all disciplinary charges against Whitehurst, and the DOJ agreed to pay his legal fees of $258,580.[4]

In July 1993 President Bill Clinton named federal Judge Louis J. Freeh to replace the embattled FBI director William S. Sessions. By August of 1996, Freeh was under fire, with House speaker Newt Gingrich and other influential Republicans calling for his resignation. Freeh remained in office for nearly five more years, but eventually resigned in 2001, at which time the new president, George W. Bush, nominated Robert S. Mueller III, a U.S. prosecutor, to the position. Mueller faced a tough job, as the FBI came under severe criticism in 2001 when the execution of Timothy McVeigh, convicted of the Oklahoma City bombings, was postponed after it was disclosed that the FBI had withheld thousands of documents from the defense. Exhibit 12.1 notes additional and very serious problems that erupted recently and cast the FBI in a negative light.

In addition to the FBI, the DOJ contains other major law enforcement agencies, such as the Drug Enforcement Administration (DEA), the Immigration and Naturalization Service (INS), and the U.S. Customs Service. In late April, after a series of incidents that led them to question the ability of the INS to function efficiently and securely, the U.S. House of Representatives voted 405 to 0 to dismantle the agency, and the Senate is expected to vote likewise. Most federal law enforcement officers are involved in criminal investigation and enforcement. The Bureau of Alcohol, Tobacco and Firearms (ATF) has jurisdiction over laws and licensing requirements regarding the sale of alcohol and other drugs as well as federal gun control laws, and the collection of taxes connected with these areas. The ATF came under criticism when federal agents assaulted the Branch Davidian compound near Waco, Texas (See Chapter 9) in 1993. Four agents were killed, and many cult members and their children perished. Public hearings were held in 1995, and in August of 1996 a House subcommittee accepted a report criticizing Attorney General Janet Reno for her handling of the Branch Davidian siege. Her actions were described as seriously negligent. (See p. 298, Chapter 9, for additional information in this topic.)

EXHIBIT 12.1

Security Problems within the Federal Bureau of Investigation

In July 2001 members of the U.S. Senate expressed outrage at the reports that 449 weapons and 184 laptop computers were missing from the inventory of the Federal Bureau of Investigation (FBI). According to the *New York Times*, "Lawmakers said the latest lapse indicated that the bureau could no longer reliably manage its basic operations." Utah's Republican senator Orrin G. Hatch called the problem "simply inexcusable," and went on to say, "Lax administrative controls over sensitive materials like these cannot be tolerated." Vermont Senator Patrick J. Leahy said, "There are some very, very serious management problems at the F.B.I."[1]

These revelations came shortly after the plea of Robert P. Hanssen, a former FBI agent who was accused of spying for Moscow since 1985. Hanssen pleaded guilty to 15 counts of espionage, attempted espionage, and conspiracy. As the result of his plea, 6 of the 21 counts against him were dismissed and he did not receive the death sentence but rather, life without parole.

Although Hanssen lost his retirement benefits and was required to forfeit the $1.4 million he was paid for spying, his wife is entitled to approximately $38,000 a year in survivor benefits, and was permitted to keep their home and three vehicles. Hanssen was required to undergo debriefings with the FBI, and his sentencing was delayed to give the agency time to assess whether he had been truthful in those sessions.

Before his arrest Hanssen was a respected member of the FBI, a family man, and an openly religious person. Most who knew and worked with him were shocked by his arrest and the revelation that he gave some of the United States' most sensitive security secrets to Russia.

1. "Senators Criticize F.B.I. for Its Security Failures," *New York Times* (19 July 2001), p. 16.

FIGURE 12.1
Highlights of Federal Law Enforcement Officers, 2000
Source: Bureau of Justice Statistics, *Federal Law Enforcement Officers, 2000* (Washington, DC: U.S. Department of Justice, July 2001), p. 1.

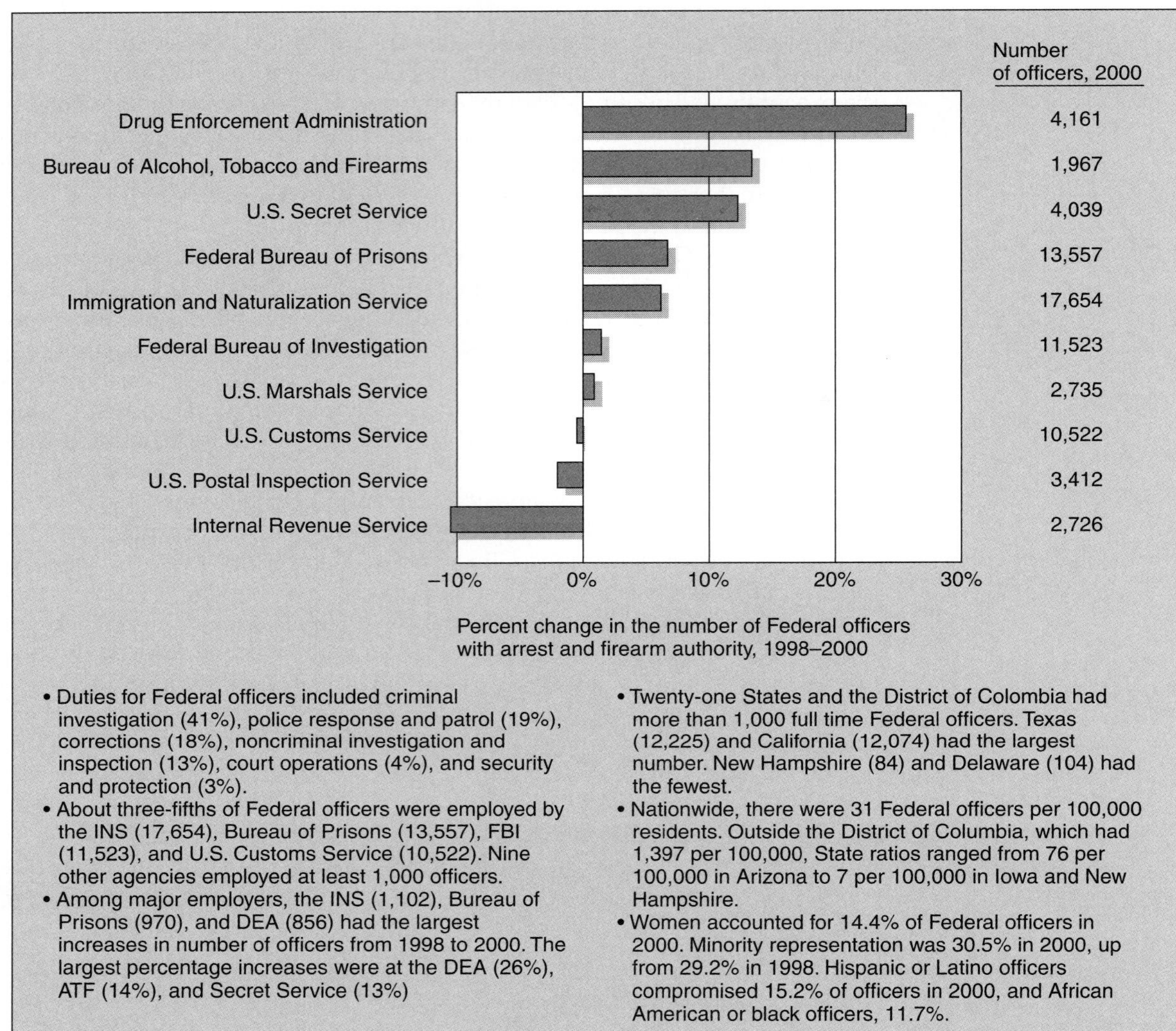

Other federal agencies are involved in law enforcement or licensing. For example, the Food and Drug Administration (FDA) oversees enforcement of laws regulating the sale and distribution of food and drugs, while the Internal Revenue Service (IRS) is charged with enforcing laws regulating federal income tax. Figure 12.1 graphs the numbers and percentages of officers with the major federal agencies.

PRIVATE SECURITY

The problems that arise from decentralized policing, such as understaffed and underfunded public police agencies, accompanied by increased concern with crime, especially violent crime, have led many people to turn to private security firms for protection. Today private (compared to public) security employs more people and is more expensive. Many people see private security as supplemental to public security. Its focus is in specialized areas such as proprietary (in-house) security; guard and patrol services; alarm services; private investigations; armored car services; manufacturers of security equipment; locksmiths; security consultants and engineers; and a miscellaneous category that includes guard dogs, drug testing, forensic analysis, and honesty testing.[5]

The many types of private security services available today may be traced to Allan Pinkerton, who founded Pinkerton's Security Services in 1850. Headquartered in New York City, Pinkerton's is the largest of the private security firms and is responsible for the familiar term *private eye*. Like many other security firms, Pinkerton's contracts to supply private security officers, investigative services, electronic surveillance devices, and private consultants.[6] The agency has been hired abroad as well.

A serious problem with private security has been the lack of standards and quality control. State and federal officials have prepared legislation aimed at controlling private security, but there have been no significant successes in this regard. Efforts must continue, however, for private policing is inevitable, and there is concern that people who are dissatisfied with public policing will focus their attention and money on private security, thus leaving public security without reform pressures and funding. The analogy is made to schools: Many people who can afford to send their children to private schools put little or no effort into reforming public education.

Another type of private security that is growing rapidly is private employment of public police. Although we do not have national data on how many police work off-hours for private security, we do know that the numbers are extensive. Questions of liability and conflict of interests have been raised, but proponents argue that trained police officers are better qualified to perform the tasks of private security than other persons are.[7]

One example of the use of private security is in shopping malls. Most are located on private land and in recent years many of these malls have been the focus of criminal activity. With their sprawling facilities and large parking lots and garages, they are ripe for criminal activity. Although most are safer than city streets, businesspeople are understandably concerned about the safety and welfare of their clients. Private civil lawsuits brought successfully by those who are victimized in malls must also be a factor in the use of private security to minimize crime in malls.

A recent analysis of the relationship between private security and crime incidents at shopping centers led three scholars to conclude as follows:

> In summary, these findings suggest that the level of criminal incidents does not dictate the level of private security. In addition, there is no evidence to suggest that private security measures have a marked preventive effect on the number of criminal incidents that occur in the shopping center. Instead, it seems that private security presence is largely a function of the physical size of the shopping center and the number of shoppers that it draws to the facility.[8]

POLICE PERSONNEL

According to the FBI, as of 31 October 2000, law enforcement agencies in the United States employed 654,601 sworn officers and 271,982 civilians.[9] Media reports can affect the number of people who apply to and remain in police departments, as noted in Media Focus 12.1.

Media Focus 12.1

Policing as Portrayed by the Media

Perhaps it is understandable that a national newspaper such as the *New York Times* would publish a first-page article entitled "City Police Work Losing Its Appeal and Its Veterans." Hopefully, that and similar articles will assist police departments in attracting qualified candidates. But it is a matter of concern that such articles need to be published.

The *New York Times* article went beyond the personnel problems of the New York City Police Department and mentioned similar problems in other large cities. Police departments across the country are having difficulty recruiting young officers while facing an increased number of retirements, some of them early. Further, it is becoming more difficult to entice qualified officers to move up the ranks, especially to that of police chief. Police chiefs are underpaid for the type of work they do, with salaries in large cities ranging from $70,000 to $150,000; these figures are "so low that some officers or sergeants, with overtime, earn more than their bosses."

An assistant police chief in Seattle, who was recruited for the position of chief, said that he absolutely would not consider that position. According to John Diaz, "I work an 11-hour day, but our chief is here before me every day and doesn't leave until I'm gone, and all he gets is attacked in the media all the time. . . . The politics of being police chief has become so insane no one wants the job."

The problem with recruiting for police officers as well as chiefs is coming at a time when crime rates have dropped. And the problems do not stop with the entry-level and top positions. Departments are having difficulty getting officers to take the sergeant's exam and sergeants to take the exam for promotion to lieutenant because lieutenants do not receive overtime pay. The police culture also has an impact on recruiting. As one head of a management and consulting firm stated, "There has been a big change in the culture of policing in the past few years, as lifestyle becomes more important than the sense of public service."

Some argue that the media are partly responsible for the current difficulties in recruiting police and especially chiefs. For example, when the new Seattle police chief was out for a run on his own time, saw a woman who had passed out, administered mouth-to-mouth resuscitation and took her to the hospital, the local media that evening gave only cursory attention to his good deeds. But significant attention was given to a police chase that resulting in injury to a pedestrian, with the police blamed for those injuries.

The article summarized above was published in July 2001. Although the media continue to report negative aspects of policing and police, as perhaps is their duty, the media portrayal of police (and firefighters) since 11 September 2001 has taken a different perspective. Considerable attention has been given to the memorial services for the officers who died in the terrorist acts of that day, their accomplishments during their lives, and their remaining families. And apparently the public has taken a more sympathetic view toward police as well as a greater interest in their jobs. Applications to attend the police academies of some jurisdictions have increased. Most important, there appears to be a greater understanding of the potential for violence for those who work to protect us from the criminal acts of others.

Source: "City Police Work Losing Its Appeal and Its Veterans," *New York Times* (30 July 2001), p. 1.

One of the most important aspects of policing is the recruitment, selection, education, and training of officers. Until recently, most police officers were young white males with a high school education or less. The training they received was at times inadequate for the wide range of duties they performed. Although that picture has changed, there is room for improvement.

Qualifications for Policing

A primary consideration in recruiting potential police officers is, What kind of characteristics should be emphasized? First, an attempt should be made to portray policing to recruits in as realistic a manner as possible. Many of the issues discussed in this chapter are not known to all potential recruits, and they are important. They dispel the myth engendered by movies and television that policing consists of one exciting moment after another. In reality, many police are never involved in a crisis situation; most never fire a gun in the line of duty; and much of their time is consumed by routine, mundane work such as filling out forms and waiting for something to happen.

Second, police departments should focus on the qualities that are important to policing—such as intelligence, good judgment, compassion, tact, courage, objectivity, honesty, emotional stability, and integrity. Third, law enforcement departments should recruit persons who have developed the skills that enable them to use discretion wisely.

Fourth, psychological factors are important, too, for policing is stressful (see the section on police stress later in this chapter). Handling racial tensions in a society in which these tensions appear to be increasing rather than decreasing is not an easy job. Today's law enforcement officers are being accused of misconduct for acts they believe they have conducted appropriately. They may perform their jobs correctly but be suspended pending an investigation, according to the policy in most departments when a suspect is killed by an officer.

Fifth, temperament and personality are important qualifications for policing. Early studies reported that police were emotionally maladjusted, cynical, authoritarian, and impulsive. They were described as being more rigid, punitive, physically aggressive, assertive, and lacking in self-confidence than most other people, and as having a preference for being supervised.[10] It is necessary to analyze the results of these studies carefully. For example, although some studies show that many police officers are cynical, others suggest that they are not cynical toward all aspects of policing. Still others have argued that cynicism is not a trait of police but rather a label from society; police are a heterogeneous, not a homogeneous, group of people who become less, not more, cynical as they grow older and as their length of service on the police force increases. Some reports contend that whatever traits police officers have, such as authoritarianism or punitiveness, were acquired on the force, as recruits do not demonstrate these traits when they begin policing.[11]

In earlier studies of police, the emphasis was on personality, with the assumption that if we could attract different types of people, the quality of policing would improve. But the U.S. Commission on Civil Rights found that the standards used for selecting police recruits do not accurately measure the specific qualities needed for quality job performance. The commission stressed the importance of psychological testing. Analyses of some psychological test results suggest that police applicants are healthier psychologically and more homogeneous than some other applicant groups.[12]

Psychological tests are important, but unless we know how they relate to the specific functions that police must perform, the results will be of little help. We cannot analyze policing without looking at what police do and evaluating the conflicts and stresses they encounter. We need to know their priorities, which are not necessarily related to factors such as background or an authoritarian or nonauthoritarian personality.[13]

The question of the level of education that should be required of police recruits is also a sensitive and controversial issue. Although it might be assumed that experts agree that higher education is important for policing, that is not necessarily the case. Two criticisms of police education must be considered. First, the quality of the earlier educational programs developed specifically for police has been questioned. Many of the curricula focused on technical courses and neglected the broad liberal arts courses that might help officers develop more understanding of the people they encounter. Second, some question whether the goal of a college education for police officers is a reasonable one. Although supporters argue that education increases police officers' sensitivity to issues concerning race and gender and gives additional insights into some of the particular law enforcement and other problems they face on duty, others contend that there is no evidence that higher education has a positive effect on policing.

Another criticism of higher education prerequisites for police applicants is that this might shrink the applicant pool, especially of minority candidates. Additionally, some police unions have expressed opposition to requiring college courses. Finally, there is concern that police education and training have neglected the broader experiences that would enable individuals to tackle many of the professional problems encountered in policing.[14]

It is possible that the routine work of policing is less bearable for a college-educated person. The officer may become bored with the lack of challenge and intolerant of people who have not shared the same kinds of educational experiences. After a review of the literature, two researchers concluded that "intelligence and education do not guarantee success" in policing and that a college degree may "give rise to more dissatisfaction and higher wastage."[15]

Police Recruitment

The establishment of an effective and efficient police force requires careful recruitment and selection, yet the U.S. Commission on Civil Rights found that the standards used in policing were not an accurate measure of the qualities and characteristics that are necessary for performing the job. In addition, the standards discriminated against women as well as racial and ethnic minorities.[16]

The commission underscored the need for police forces to represent the composition of the populations they serve. It noted that a lack of minorities leads to increased tensions and violence in some predominantly minority neighborhoods with high crime rates. Residents of those areas may be reluctant to cooperate with crime prevention efforts if they think they will be discriminated against by police. Women, the most frequent victims of rape and other sexual assaults, may be less willing to report these crimes if there are no women on police forces. Minorities who have been mistreated by white police may not trust them in future interactions. Thus, efforts should be made to recruit female and minority police officers.

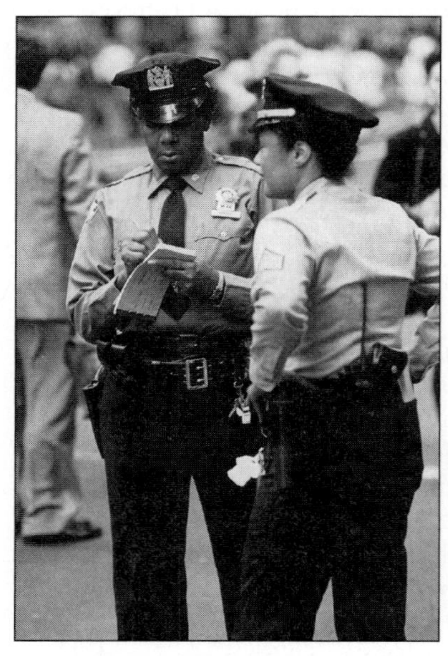

The establishment of an effective and efficient police force requires careful recruitment, selection, and training. In recent years efforts have been made to recruit women and minorities into policing. (Robert Brenner/PhotoEdit)

Female and Minority Officers

Women and minority officers continue to face problems in policing as well as in recruiting. Early studies of minority police officers emphasized their role conflicts. For example, African American offenders expect African American officers to give them a break. If the officers are lenient, this, along with many other actions, results in criticism from white peers.[17]

Some minority officers complain that they are not accepted by white officers, although most say that they believe white officers will come to their aid when they need help. But after hours, many are not accepted as friends. Female officers have made the same complaints and have encountered other problems as well. Many female officers say they experience rejection by some male colleagues and by some members of the public whom they serve. Critics have argued that women cannot handle the physical aspects of policing, but physical differences between men and women do not in themselves mean that women are less capable than men. One female officer, writing about her 13 years of experience, concluded that "the harsh treatment [of female officers] seems to be prevalent throughout law enforcement." She noted that the harassing treatment is more subtle today than earlier, but it still exists: "You can't change attitudes through rules and regulations. Prejudicial feelings run deep and can only change through a slowly evolving process of education and generational levels."[18]

FIGURE 12.2
Female and Minority Local Police Officers

Source: Bureau of Justice Statistics, *Local Police Departments 1997* (Washington, DC: U.S. Department of Justice, February 2000), p. 4.

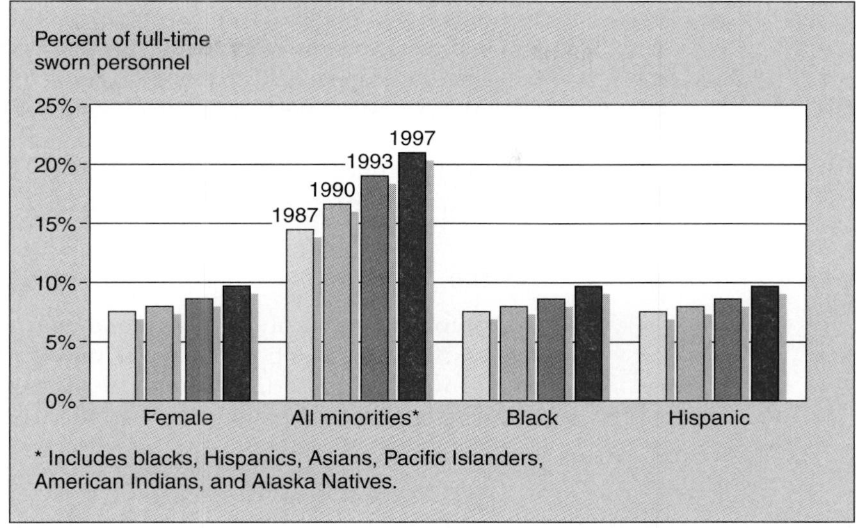

Most of the women and minorities in policing are in beginning positions, such as patrol officers, not in supervisory positions.[19] There are some exceptions, such as the appointment of women as police chiefs, but problems remain. A study by the International Association of Chiefs of Police, published in 1998, reported that nearly 20 percent of the 800 police departments surveyed had no female officers and that overall only 12 percent of officers were women. That figure has not changed significantly in over a decade. In addition, 91 percent of the departments reporting stated that they did not have any women in policymaking positions. Only 123 of the 17,000 police departments in the United States were headed by female chiefs. Gender bias was listed by nearly 10 percent of the reporting departments as the reason why more women had not been promoted. Women who have sued over gender bias have won over one-third of those lawsuits.[20]

A report on women and minorities in policing, published by the Bureau of Justice Statistics in 2000, analyzed data through 1997. The numbers of female and minority police officers from 1987 to 1997 are graphed in Figure 12.2, which demonstrates only small increases in each category.

THE NATURE OF POLICING

Historically, police have had greater responsibility for enforcing the peace than for enforcing criminal laws or traffic ordinances. It was their function to find homes and shelters for women who might be lured away from prostitution; to handle riots and other civil disturbances; to regulate garbage disposal, street sanitation, and explosives; and to inspect bars, liquor stores, and other businesses that require licensing. Numerous social service functions were a part of their jobs as well.

In earlier times, police did not investigate criminal activities—that was the victim's responsibility. Once the victim had identified the suspect, police would assist with apprehension. Victims paid police for helping them regain stolen property. Thus, officers who became experts in finding stolen property could expect greater gain. This action led to specialization in police forces. The practice of getting paid for their services made police give careful attention to those who had the means to pay.

Today most policing differs from the image held by the public and preferred by police—that of the officer chasing and catching dangerous criminals. Considerable time is spent in routine, boring, and nondangerous activities. But the system has developed a structure that gives the greatest rewards for dangerous activities and the fewest for routine functions. This situation creates problems for police, for the department, and for the community. Thus, it is important to look at all police functions. The following discussion focuses on municipal or local policing, but Figure 12.3 details the duties of federal law enforcement officers.

Police Functions

Law enforcement is only one of several police functions, as Exhibit 12.2 demonstrates. Since information gathering may and usually does occur in all three police functions, most discussions categorize the three basic police duties as law enforcement, order maintenance, and service.

FIGURE 12.3
Primary Function of Full-Time Federal Officers with Arrest and Firearm Authority, June 2000

Source: Bureau of Justice Statistics, *Federal Law Enforcement Officers, 2000* (Washington, DC: U.S. Department of Justice, July 2001), p. 2.

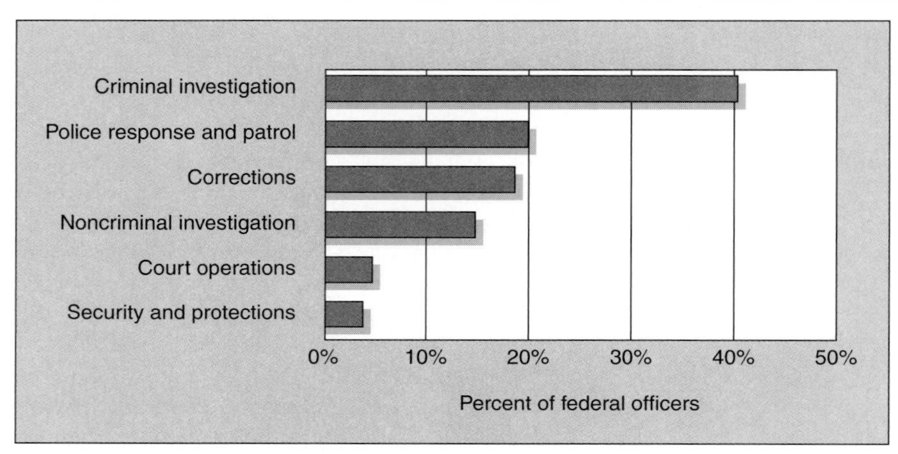

EXHIBIT 12.2
Police Functions

- *Law enforcement:* Applying legal sanctions (usually arrest) to behavior that violates a legal standard.
- *Order maintenance:* Taking steps to control events and circumstances that disturb or threaten to disturb the peace. For example, a police officer may be called on to mediate a family dispute, to disperse an unruly crowd, or to quiet an overly boisterous party.
- *Information gathering:* Asking routine questions at a crime scene, inspecting victimized premises, and filling out forms needed to register criminal complaints.
- *Service:* Conducting a broad range of activities, such as assisting injured persons, controlling animals, or responding to fire calls.

Source: Bureau of Justice Statistics, *Report to the Nation on Crime and Justice: The Data,* 2d ed. (Washington, DC: U.S. Department of Justice, 1988), p. 62.

Law Enforcement

The law enforcement function of policing involves the power to stop, question, detain, and arrest people who violate the law. Law enforcement powers range from stopping traffic violators to apprehending persons suspected of committing serious felonies, which may involve the use of deadly force. As Exhibit 12.2 notes, police gather information and file reports, both important although at times monotonous functions. Securing information may involve investigating crimes, a critical function. The successful prosecution of a case often depends on meticulous, professional, and precise investigative techniques by police. Police must also preserve the evidence they obtain and ensure that its integrity is maintained and that it is available for subsequent criminal trials. Police may be called to testify regarding any or all of these procedures as well as to identify the evidence.

Chapter 11 discussed some of the restrictions that the U.S. Constitution places on police powers, but it is important to understand that those powers to affect the lives of citizens remain wide and significant. Perhaps the enormity of what the police can legitimately do is best illustrated by a 2001 case in which the U.S. Supreme Court held that police may make a full custodial arrest when they see someone breaking the law—even a minor infraction for which a small fine is the maximum penalty. The case involved a Texas mother, Gail Atwater, who, while driving with her children in the car, was stopped by police for failure to wear her seat belt as required by Texas law. Atwater was handcuffed and taken to the police station, where she was held until she posted a $310 bond. The maximum penalty for the violation was $50. In a 5-to-4 decision a bitterly divided Court ruled in *Atwater* v. *City of Lago Vista* that the police had not violated Atwater's constitutional rights when they made the arrest.[21]

It is also important to understand that law enforcement powers do not give police great crime-prevention abilities. In a provocative and often-cited work published in 1968, Herbert L. Packer described what the role of police should be in the area of law enforcement: "Ideally, police should be seen as the people who keep the law of the jungle from taking over."[22]

Finally, in their exercise of discretion police may create problems if they engage in what is referred to as a *zero-tolerance* policy. The approach is perhaps best illustrated by the tenure of William Bratton as the police commissioner in New York City during most of the first term of Mayor Rudolph Giuliani. Bratton made changes in the police department at all levels and focused his zero-tolerance policy on quality-of-life issues, such as removing beggars, prostitutes, petty drug dealers, graffiti scribblers, and other minor offenders from the streets. The approach followed the "broken windows" approach to policing, which was first introduced by James Q. Wilson and George Kelling in 1982. It is based on the belief that if minor offenders who disrupt the quality of life are not removed from the streets, people will be frightened, predatory criminals will be attracted, and crime will escalate.[23]

Bratton and Giuliani credited the zero-tolerance approach and other changes in New York City with the significant decrease in crime in that city during the last part of the 1990s. But one scholar, after examining the city's crime rates and other factors, and comparing them to those in the city of San Diego, which embraced a problem-oriented approach to policing, stated that she found "strong evidence that effective crime control can be achieved while producing fewer negative impacts on urban neighborhoods." Among the negative impacts that Judith A. Greene found in New York City was a significant increase in the filing of citizen complaints before the Civilian Complaint Review Board, along with lawsuits alleging police misconduct and abuse. As noted on p. 420, at least one of the recent lawsuits resulted in a substantial settlement for the plaintiff-victim.[24]

The results of the zero-tolerance policy of New York City's police department also illustrate the system effect we discussed in Chapter 11. If a crackdown on minor offenders who may be viewed as nuisances on the streets results in substantial judgments against the city and the police department when citizens complain of violations of their civil rights, the "cure" may be worse than the "problem."

Order Maintenance

The second function of policing, order maintenance, was defined by James Q. Wilson as the "management of conflict situations to bring about consensual resolution." By *order* Wilson meant the "absence of disorder, and by disorder is meant behavior that either disturbs or threatens to disturb the public peace or that involves face-to-face conflict among two or more persons." An example is domestic disputes. According to Wilson, it is crucial that police, rather than some other professionals, respond to calls involving domestic disputes since such incidents may (and often do) result in violence. Wilson argued that order maintenance is the most important function of police work. Furthermore, police have wide discretion in all areas and often must make decisions in situations characterized by intensive conflicts and hostile participants.[25]

Wilson's position was shared by George L. Kelling, who studied the historical development of policing in the United States. Kelling concluded that as police work becomes more professional, greater emphasis is placed on law enforcement, which is measured more easily than order maintenance. This reduces the emphasis on order maintenance and leads to negative effects without resulting in a decreased crime rate. Kelling, like Wilson, said the evidence pointed out that when police are involved in order maintenance, the relationship between police and community is improved. The result is reduced fear of crime and greater cooperation of citizens with police in crime control.[26]

Carl B. Klockars disagreed with Kelling and Wilson, taking the position that, historically, Americans have considered law enforcement to be the primary

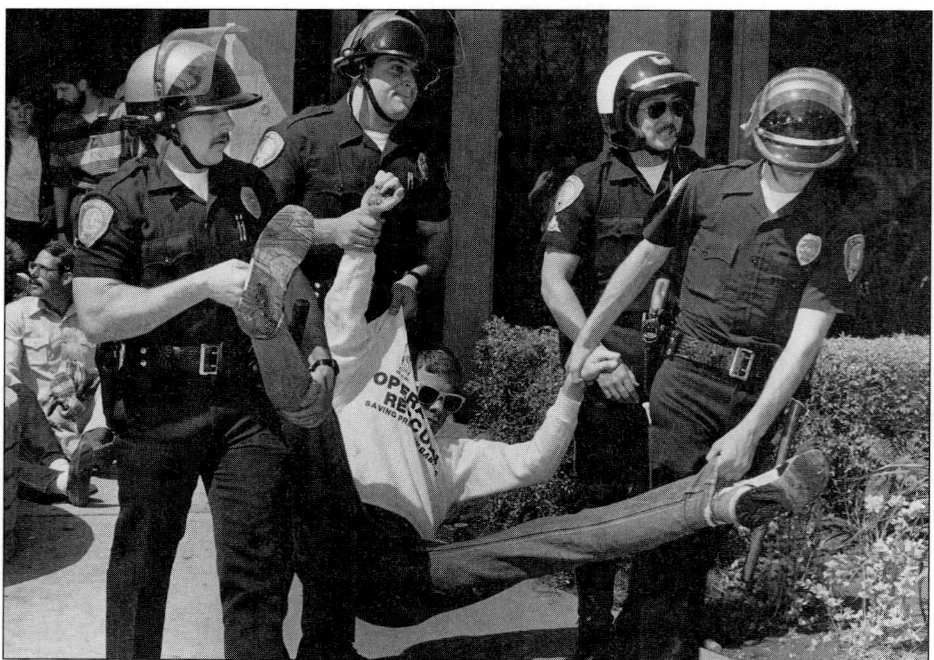

One function of policing is order maintenance. In this photograph, police are arresting a demonstrator during a sit-in at an abortion clinic in Cypress, California. (Spencer Grant/ Stock Boston)

function of policing. To shift that focus, said Klockars, would not reduce the crime rate and would decrease the ability of police to respond to more serious problems and violations. Klockars did not take the position that order maintenance is an unimportant police function but only that greater emphasis should be placed on law enforcement.[27]

Service-Related Duties

The final major function of policing is to engage in a variety of service-related duties. Some people who do not know how to solve a problem (such as killing a snake in the house, getting a cat out of a tree) call the police department for help. Although some service functions are important because of their relationship to crime control and police and community relations, we should not expect police to engage in those that are unrelated to law enforcement.

Policing Models

The structure and manner in which policing occurs may be analyzed by models: the professional model, which is the traditional approach, and the community-oriented model, which involves a community emphasis as well as a problem-solving approach to policing.

The *professional model* of policing is a highly bureaucratic approach characterized by a hierarchical organizational structure in which the police chief is the central authority. All department heads report to the chief. Department heads have subordinates who report directly to them. The chain of command is clear, and the organization has many rules and regulations, with little input from subordinates in regard to making and enforcing them. The police department is organized around specialized functions such as personnel and training, data processing, traffic, patrol, homicide, and sex crimes.[28]

The professional model is efficient; decisions may be made quickly and easily, and the internal control of subordinates is facilitated. The structure may result in high productivity, but its rigidity may cause dissatisfaction among subordinates and result in a department that is too authoritarian and units that are too specialized.

Dissatisfaction with the professional model has led to an approach referred to as *community-oriented policing,* which involves a problem-solving approach by police, along with community involvement. Exhibit 12.3 contains a brief contrast of traditional and community policing.

The *problem-solving approach* to policing is characterized by a less extensive division of labor within the police department, fewer rules and regulations, and fewer authority levels. The emphasis is on gaining the necessary knowledge required for solving problems, and power comes from accomplishing that goal rather than from a title. The approach permits greater participation by subordinates and is based on the assumption that police departments can be more effective if the expertise and creativity of all, including patrol officers, are utilized to solve underlying problems.

A problem-solving approach to policing looks at calls to police not as unique events to be processed individually but as part of a network of events. Problem-solving policing looks for patterns of events and attempts to derive solutions. For example, instead of relying on legal categories such as burglary or robbery, officers are told to group calls into problem categories. What is traditionally called a robbery might be part of a network of prostitution-related robberies committed in specific hotels. By alerting potential customers, hotel owners and managers, and local businesses, and by talking to the prostitutes, police may secure further information. The focus is on underlying *causes* or problems, not on the incident that precipitated an individual call.

EXHIBIT 12.3

Traditional vs. Community Policing: Questions and Answers

Question	Traditional	Community Policing
Who are the police?	A government agency principally responsible for law enforcement.	Police are the public and the public are the police; the police officers are those who are paid to give full-time attention to the duties of every citizen.
What is the relationship of the police force to other public service departments?	Priorities often conflict.	The police are one department among many responsible for improving the quality of life.
What is the role of the police?	Focusing on solving crimes.	A broader problem-solving approach.
How is police efficiency measured?	By detection and arrest rates.	By the absence of crime and disorder.
What are the highest priorities?	Crimes that are high value (for example, bank robberies) and those involving violence.	Whatever problems disturb the community most.
What, specifically, do police deal with?	Incidents.	Citizens' problems and concerns.
What determines the effectiveness of police?	Response times.	Public cooperation.
What view do police take of service calls?	Deal with them only if there is no real police work to do.	Vital function and great opportunity.
What is police professionalism?	Swift, effective response to serious crime.	Keeping close to the community.
What kind of intelligence is most important?	Crime intelligence (study of particular crimes or series of crimes).	Criminal intelligence (information about the activities of individuals or groups).
What is the essential nature of police accountability?	Highly centralized; governed by rules, regulations, and policy directives; accountable to the law.	Emphasis on local accountability to community needs.
What is the role of headquarters?	To provide the necessary rules and policy directives.	To preach organizational values.
What is the role of the press liaison department?	To keep the "heat" off operational officers so they can get on with the job.	To coordinate an essential channel of communication with the community.
How do the police regard prosecutions?	As an important goal.	As one tool among many.

Source: Malcolm K. Sparrow, National Institute of Justice, *Implementing Community Policing,* (Washington, DC: U.S. Department of Justice, November 1988), pp. 8–9.

The Focus on Community-Oriented Policing

Considerable attention has been given to community-oriented policing in recent literature as well as in police departments. George L. Kelling referred to the emphasis on community-oriented policing as follows: "A quiet revolution is reshaping American policing. Police in dozens of communities are returning to foot patrol." Kelling noted that many police were asking citizens what they perceive as their most pressing problems as well as what they thought might be done to solve those problems. Since fear of crime is one of the concerns mentioned most frequently, many police departments are addressing that issue.[29]

Although community policing differs among the various jurisdictions, Herman Goldstein has identified its common characteristics:

- the involvement of the community in getting the police job done;
- the permanent assignment of police officers to a neighborhood in order to cultivate better relationships;
- the setting of police priorities based on the specific needs and desires of the community; and
- the meeting of these needs by the allocation of police resources and personnel otherwise assigned to responding to calls for public assistance.[30]

Community policing may increase police accountability to the community, increase public cooperation with police, reduce fear of crime, and assist police and the community in solving society's most crucial crime problem—drugs.

One of the features of community policing is a return to foot patrol. This practice, reminiscent of earlier days, along with the use of horses or bicycles, makes officers less anonymous and more integrated into their communities. While on foot patrol, police become more visible and more accountable to the public. Police are encouraged to view citizens as partners in crime prevention. Furthermore, more decision making at the patrol level means that those who are best informed of the problems in the community are the ones making important policing decisions.[31]

The recent return to foot patrol began in Flint, Michigan, and has spread to other cities. Experiments of foot patrol in that city and in Newark, New Jersey, produced the following results:

- When foot patrol is added in neighborhoods, levels of fear decrease significantly.
- When foot patrol is withdrawn from neighborhoods, levels of fear increase significantly.
- Citizen satisfaction with police increases when foot patrol is added in neighborhoods.
- Police who patrol on foot have a greater appreciation for the values of neighborhood residents than police who patrol the same areas in automobiles.
- Police who patrol on foot have greater job satisfaction, less fear, and higher morale than officers who patrol in automobiles.[32]

The Flint study revealed a significant (40 percent) reduction in telephone calls for service when police engaged in aggressive foot patrol. A small reduction in crime occurred also. Likewise, officials in Seattle, Washington, reported that community policing has been successful in improving the quality of life for residents and in reducing overall crime.[33]

Wesley G. Skogan, who studied many community-oriented policing programs, commented positively on the results of Chicago's program, calling it one of the most substantial programs he had evaluated. Residents stated that their perceptions of police were more positive and that they saw reductions in crime. The reductions were verified by official data.[34]

A government study of community policing in Indianapolis, Indiana (published in 1998), reported positive results of the approach. Residents perceived that they were safer, "officers with more community policing training were more willing to grant a citizen's request to control another citizen; and the police supervisors interviewed emphasized their support of rather than their control of subordinates."[35]

President Bill Clinton gave strong support to community-oriented policing during his two administrations. In 1994 the Clinton administration announced the down payment on its campaign promise to put 100,000 more police on the street by offering federal grants for hiring police. Later that year Congress enacted a new crime bill that contained a provision for the 100,000 promised officers (see Exhibit 12.4). Under this legislation the federal government provides 75 percent of the costs of employing new officers up to a total of $75,000 during the first three years of a grant, after which the communities are responsible for the full cost unless waivers are granted by the U.S. attorney general. Not all communities are eligible for the grants.[36]

Although community-oriented policing has had its critics, especially among Republicans in Congress, by the fall of 1998 funds had been made available for grants to finance over two-thirds of the promised 100,000 additional police officers.[37] In the year 2000 the U.S. Department of Justice declared the six-year, $9 billion program a partial success although it fell short of putting 100,000 more police on the streets. Criticism remains, however, and it is not yet evident what will happen to the program under the administration of President George W. Bush, although it remains in effect and has received some funding.

Time Allocation

Regardless of the model used, policing involves many problems and issues, one of which is time allocation. As noted earlier, there is disagreement over which of the three functions—law enforcement, order maintenance, and service-related activities—is the most important and how time should be allocated among these functions. In his study, James Q. Wilson reported that 38 percent of police time was spent in service-related duties, followed by 30 percent in order mainte-

EXHIBIT 12.4

The 1994 Crime Act and the Office of Community-Oriented Policing Services (COPS)

The Violent Crime Control and Law Enforcement Act (the Crime Act) was signed into law by President Clinton on September 13, 1994. The expenditures authorized by this legislation included nearly $9 billion for Title I, also known as the Public Safety Partnership and Community Policing Act of 1994. Title I was the basis for the creation of the Department of Justice's Office of Community-Oriented Policing Services (COPS) program. Since 1994, to advance community policing, COPS has provided over $7.5 billion in Federal funds to over 12,000 State and local law enforcement agencies.

The COPS office was charged with changing the practice of policing in the United States by—

- Deploying an additional 100,000 community policing officers
- Facilitating problem-solving efforts and encouraging interactions with communities by officers
- Promoting innovation in policing
- Enhancing existing technologies to assist officers in preventing and responding to crime and its consequences.

To achieve these goals, the COPS program used three primary approaches. The first was to award 3-year grants to agencies for hiring officers. The second was to award grants for acquiring technology and hiring civilians so officers could be redeployed to perform community policing activities. The third was to award grants to agencies for innovative programs with special purposes such as reducing gun violence or domestic violence. All COPS grant programs were designed to supplement local expenditures, not to supplant or replace them. Title I required that COPS funds be distributed equally between jurisdictions above and below a population of 150,000.

The LEMAS data are a rich source of information about community policing; however, they are not intended to be used to determine whether the goals of the COPS program have been met. For more information on the COPS program, see the *National Evaluation of the COPS Program,* National Institute of Justice (NCJ 183643), or visit the COPS website at—www.usdoj.gov/cops.

Source: Bureau of Justice Statistics Special Report, *Community Policing in Local Police Departments, 1997 and 1999* (Washington, DC: U.S. Department of Justice, February 2001), p. 3.

nance, 22 percent in information gathering, and only 10 percent in law enforcement.[38] Those figures differed from a study in Chicago conducted two years earlier by Albert J. Reiss Jr., who found that 58 percent of calls to the police department involved requests about criminal matters and 30 percent were about noncriminal matters.[39]

Later studies, some based on observations of police on patrol rather than on analyses of calls to the police department, show that although police spend more time on law enforcement than on any other activity, less than one-third of police activities involve crimes.[40] One study reported that only 17 percent of calls to police were for nonviolent crimes and 2 percent for violent crimes. Among the other reasons for calls, the largest percentages were for information requests (21 percent), suspicious circumstances (12 percent), public nuisances (11 percent), traffic problems (9 percent), a citizen giving information (8 percent), and interpersonal conflict (7 percent).[41]

Regardless of how activities are categorized, it is agreed that police officers do not spend most of their time in stereotypical police action: catching *serious* criminals. Most policing is **reactive,** not **proactive.** That is, police depend on the cooperation of victims and other citizens for crime reports. Because most crime is not visible to them, police would detect very little crime without these reports.

Reactive The response to criminal behavior in which police rely on notification by alleged victims or others that a crime has been committed instead of taking active measures to detect crimes and identify offenders.

Proactive The response to criminal behavior in which the police detect crimes actively and seek offenders instead of relying on citizens' reports of crimes.

Conflicting Expectations

The variety of police functions and the lack of consensus on how police do or should allocate their time create conflicts over expectations police have for themselves and those of other people, including their colleagues and supervisors. Problem-oriented policing and community policing, or for that matter any other variations in the traditional functions of police, may create conflicting expectations. In addition, police are expected to prevent crime, which they cannot do effectively even with citizens' support, which they do not always get. When they do prevent crime, there is no measure of what they have done. When they engage in order maintenance and service-related functions, they may face hostility in the former and unreasonable demands in the latter; that is, they are asked to solve problems for which they have no solutions.

In addition to expecting the impossible, society is frequently unclear about what police should be expected to do in a given situation. Are they to enforce the law or ignore violations? Because a particular community expects a different type of behavior, police may not always act legally. A study of the reaction of Chicago police to the ambiguity of their role as patrol officers makes the point clearly. Most of them said they preferred not to have patrol duty. Among the many reasons they listed for preferring other duty assignments—more interesting work, higher pay, greater prestige, and greater freedom—the most important was "the officer has a better sense of what is expected of him."[42]

The patrol officer faces other conflicts regarding community expectations. A neighborhood may be composed of persons whose lifestyles include knifings, narcotics, and domestic quarrels. That particular neighborhood may expect the officer to ignore the laws regulating these behaviors. The officer who has worked in areas where such behavior is uncommon may find great resistance when he or she tries to enforce these laws.

Police officers face conflicts over human misery versus evil. When they arrive at the scene of an accident or other tragedy, they must control their emotions. An officer cannot punish the father who is accused of beating his child, nor can he or she get sick at the sight of a mangled body. Police must act with objectivity and perform their jobs as efficiently as possible regardless of the circumstances.

Police face conflict between efficiency and the constitutional rights of citizens, and between honesty and the dishonest activities of some of their colleagues.

Police officers may feel conflict between fear and courage—the desire to be courageous while realizing that they are risking their own health or lives. Order maintenance may take officers into hostile environments. Those who called for help may consider the situation an emergency, but because the officers have been involved in many similar situations, they have learned by experience that the victim's version of the incident may not be reliable. Consequently, they may not be as sympathetic as the complainant desires, and the latter may become upset at this apparent lack of understanding. Furthermore, because only a few calls to police result in arrest, complainants may think that police are not doing their jobs. The problem is that most crimes are property crimes with no clues or witnesses. Even if a suspect is found, officers must fulfill the requirements for making an arrest, and often those cannot be met.

Finally, police experience conflicting expectations with regard to strategies of police administration. This area of strain arises as officers observe administrators wavering between traditional, arrest-oriented policing and problem-solving policing; reactive versus proactive policing; and traditional versus community-oriented policing.

Police Stress

Role conflicts and other problems create stress in policing. Formerly considered a personal problem, stress is viewed now as a corporate problem because of the effect it has on employees. Some businesses retain a professional counselor to assist employees who have difficulty handling stress. Stress causes physical illnesses, resulting in higher medical costs, lower productivity, absenteeism, and premature death, all of which may be costly for businesses as well as for the affected individuals and their families and friends.

Although all people may encounter some stress in their jobs, there is evidence that stress is high among air traffic controllers, lawyers, dentists, physicians, psychiatrists, and law enforcement officers as well as law enforcement administrators. Some argue that law enforcement is the most difficult among all jobs emotionally and psychologically because of the possibility of physical danger. Stress may account for the high divorce rate among police, a rate that according to some studies is higher than in most (or all) other professions.[43]

There is one major difference between policing and most other professions: Police are trained to injure or kill. If the situation requires, they are expected to use force; indeed, they may be sanctioned for not doing so. Officers who kill, however, may be isolated by their colleagues. The routine procedure is to suspend officers pending investigation of a shooting. Even when the investigation shows that the officer was justified in the killing, he or she may continue to experience stress.

Another stressor in policing is the fear by the officers and their families that the officer may be injured or killed in the line of duty. Although most officers are never victimized by the violence of others, the *possibility* of such violence is greater for them than for people in most, if not all, other professions. Fifty-one officers were killed in the line of duty in 2000, an increase of 9 over the previous year. Despite this slight increase, the general trend of violence toward police officers has diminished—a fact that is of little comfort, especially given such acts of violence as that in the Capitol in Washington, D.C., in 1998, which took the lives of two police officers, and the terrorist acts of 11 September 2001.[44]

The stress of policing reaches beyond the individual officer. According to two researchers, "Police work affects, shapes, and at times, scars the individuals and families involved."[45] The effects of stress on police and their families as well as their colleagues has led some departments to initiate stress-reduction programs, a procedure recommended by the Commission on Civil Rights. Some of these programs involve appointing psychologists or other professionals trained in stress reduction to be available to law enforcement officers in the work environment. Others are comprehensive programs that include inpatient treatment facilities and services for law enforcement officers who suffer from job-related stress. Eating and sleep disorders, alcohol and drug addiction, post-traumatic stress, and obsessive-compulsive and anxiety disorders are examples of the problems that may be treated.

The Police Subculture

One of the ways that police officers attempt to cope with stress is to isolate themselves, forming a subculture and associating only with other officers and their families. Social solidarity among police may be the result of the danger that police face, which necessitates the need to help one another. It may be caused by suspiciousness, where police develop a perceptual shorthand to help identify people who might commit an unlawful act. It may be the result of the conflicting demands placed on police. It is difficult for some officers to make friends among nonpolice.

The isolation of police is functional to some extent. It allows them to relate to the public without the undue strain that might result if they were apprehending and arresting their friends. The opposing view is that police isolation is detrimental to police and a disservice to the public. It prevents police from seeing the public's point of view.

Police loyalty is part of an unwritten code of conduct long thought to permeate policing. This traditional loyalty is being diminished in some departments, with more police reporting improper behavior by their colleagues.

In a recent and thorough exploration of the police subculture, John P. Crank illustrates its importance by noting the role the subculture plays when a police officer is killed in the line of duty. The rituals of the services are important and have an impact nationwide, with police from other cities often gathering (frequently on motorcycles) in a huge show of support for policing, respect for their slain colleague, and sympathy for the family. A reviewer of Crank's book states: "Crank notes that police funerals tend to re-awaken the significance of what is meant by being a cop."[46] Certainly that appeared to be the case as thousands mourned the loss of police (and firefighters), along with many others, after the 11 September 2001 terrorist acts.

AIDS and Law Enforcement

A final issue regarding the nature of policing is that the possibility of the transmission of the human immunodeficiency virus (HIV), which causes acquired immune deficiency syndrome (AIDS), by health care professionals to their patients has created some concern among law enforcement personnel. As noted in Chapter 1, AIDS is a deadly disease for which no cure is available. Policing brings officers into close contact with many people, some of whom are suffering injuries that include the loss of blood and other body fluids that carry and can transmit HIV. The converse is citizen attitudes and the concern of other officers about coming into contact with officers who carry HIV.

Although there is no evidence that HIV is transmitted by casual contact, many people are concerned about contacts with persons infected with the virus. Colleagues may react negatively to an officer who has AIDS. Because of this fear, police with AIDS may be afraid to let others know of their condition, fearing that they will be "banished from the wider police fraternity in which most of them came of age, a sort of blue reservoir of strength that they are used to turning to for solace. They cannot imagine telling their colleagues they have a disease that many officers believe is an affliction only of gay men, drug addicts, prostitutes and the homeless." The New York City Police Department provides counseling and referrals for officers with AIDS. These confidential services are provided by a retired officer who is HIV positive.[47]

POLICE DECISION MAKING

Police have considerable decision-making discretion in the performance of their jobs. The decision to interfere with the freedom of another person, even if momentarily, is an extremely serious one. People do not like to be stopped by police; it is a frightening and confusing experience, and some may perceive the police action as discriminatory. Their perceptions may be correct. Police reject this conclusion, saying that they stop people only when they have legal reasons for doing so. The issue is more pronounced when the possibility of an arrest exists. The police officer is not only interfering momentarily with freedom but is setting in motion a process that may result in stigmatization and incarceration.

The decision to stop and question someone or to take a suspect into custody is governed by case and statutory law. This body of law is technical and complicated, but an overview was provided in Chapter 11. The law in this area is related primarily to the *legal seriousness* of the suspected crime, although some studies have found that legal seriousness plays a small part in the decision. Most of the problems that police are called on to resolve are not of a legally serious nature; they are minor problems in which arrests are not usually made. Thus, police may base their decisions to apprehend on criteria other than the legal seriousness of an alleged crime. Radical theory, discussed in Chapter 5, takes the position that policing "reinforces and maintains the class structure of society through its focus on behaviors most likely to be engaged in by the working class and marginal populations."[48]

The Right to Stop and Question

Police must have probable cause to arrest, but probable cause is not required to stop and question in some circumstances. For instance, it is permissible for police officers to stop a person who acts suspicious. They may stop the person and ask for identification, but they may not detain him or her unreasonably, nor may they stop *classes* of people in order to harass them. Some of the legal issues involved in stopping and questioning, as well as frisking and arresting, were discussed in Chapter 11. Here, one case is used to demonstrate the reasons for restricting police in this important area of their work.

On numerous occasions white police officers had stopped a tall, muscular, 36-year-old black man with long hair who jogged frequently in a predominantly white neighborhood. They asked for identification on about 15 occasions over a two-year period. On several occasions, when the jogger refused to identify himself or to answer other questions, he was arrested. He was convicted once and spent several weeks in jail.

According to police, the jogger committed a misdemeanor when he violated a California statute that labeled as disorderly conduct the behavior of a person "who loiters or wanders upon the streets or from place to place without apparent reason or business or who refuses to identify himself and to account for his presence when requested by any peace officer to do so, if the surrounding circumstances are such as to indicate to a reasonable man that the public safety demands such identification."[49]

In deciding that the statute was void because it was vague, the U.S. Supreme Court articulated the importance of individual freedoms. In *Kolender* v. *Lawson* the Court acknowledged that police must be able to exercise some discretion in stop-and-question situations but struck down this statute because, in enacting it, the legislature had not provided sufficient guidelines on that discretion. According to the Court, this statute leaves us free to walk or jog the streets only at the "whim of any police officer."[50]

It is important to understand that the problem with this statute was not that it permitted an initial stop but that there were no standards by which to judge why the police were stopping the jogger. This gives police too much discretion and permits them to stop people for illegal reasons, such as race.

The issue of what type of probable cause is required for the police to stop a person and ask questions arose in *Whren* v. *United States,* decided by the Supreme Court in 1996. This case involved two African American men in an unmarked truck whose vehicle was observed by plainclothes officers in a high drug area in Washington, D.C. The officers noticed that the truck remained for an unusually long time at a stop sign (thus obstructing traffic), after which the driver turned without signaling, and drove away at an unreasonable speed. The truck was stopped, allegedly to warn the driver about traffic violations. As the officers approached the vehicle, they noticed that the passenger was holding plastic bags, which appeared to contain crack cocaine. Both the driver and the passenger were arrested, charged with federal drug violations, tried, and convicted. On appeal they argued that the police did not have probable cause to believe they were violating drug laws but rather stopped them as an excuse to see whether they had illegal drugs. A unanimous Supreme Court upheld the stop, emphasizing that police had a legal right to pull over the vehicle because of a traffic violation. Lack of probable cause to suspect that the driver and his passenger were in possession of illegal drugs was immaterial.

During the same term the Court held in *Ornelas et al.* v. *United States* that when appellate courts consider cases involving investigatory stops and warrantless searches, they must undertake their own independent review of the lower court rulings. In other words, appellate courts may not treat those rulings deferentially, looking only for clear error or abuse of discretion. They must look at all of the facts on which the lower courts based their rulings. According to the Court's opinion, this more detailed and careful review will result in unifying precedent and encourage police to seek warrants when reasonable.[51]

In subsequent cases the Court has held that during routine traffic stops police may order passengers out of cars. Thus, in 1997, in *Maryland* v. *Wilson,* the Court extended the 1997 case of *Pennsylvania* v. *Mimms,* which upheld the right of police to order the driver out of a car after the officer made a legitimate traffic stop.[52]

Also in 1997, in *Richards* v. *Wisconsin,* the Court held that the "knock-and-announce" rule of *Wilson* v. *Arkansas* (decided in 1995) could not be diluted by a blanket waiver for all drug cases. In *Richards* the Court held that if police have a reasonable suspicion that "exigent circumstances" exist, they may enter a home by force without announcing their presence. Such circumstances might be the possible destruction of drugs or other evidence. But the Court said that the issue must be decided on a case-by-case basis, with careful attention given to the particular facts of each case. In *Richards* several officers arrived at a motel where the suspect had allegedly been selling drugs out of his room. One officer was dressed as a maintenance man. Richards opened the door (with the chain on) when the officers knocked, but when he saw an officer in uniform, he slammed the door and locked it. The officers kicked in the door and during their search found cash and cocaine. Richards sought to have the evidence excluded. The Wisconsin Supreme Court recognized a blanket rule for waiving the knock-and-announce rule in felony drug cases. The U.S. Supreme Court rejected that holding but did allow the use of the evidence against Richards on the grounds that exigent circumstances existed.[53]

Wilson and *Richards* did not answer the question of whether property damaged during the entry should factor into the determination of whether a no-knock entry was reasonable. During its 1997–98 term the Court held that a careful reading of those two cases leads to the conclusion that the lawfulness of entering without announcing does not depend on whether property is damaged in the process. In *United States* v. *Ramirez*, the police broke a window in a garage attached to the house. They took this action to prevent the suspect from getting to the weapons thought to be stored there. When the suspect discovered that the breakage was caused by police officers, not burglars, he surrendered. The Court held that breaking the window without announcing their presence was a reasonable action by the police under the circumstances.[54]

The Sociology of Arrest

The Supreme Court has held that "it is not the function of police to arrest. . .at large and to use an interrogating process at police headquarters in order to determine whom they should charge before a committing magistrate on 'probable cause.'"[55]

Police do not stop all people whom they think are violating a law. What explains police decisions to stop and arrest? One variable is the officer's perception of community standards and attitudes and the homogeneity between the police and the community. A study of police activities in relation to community characteristics examined what police do after their initial apprehension of a suspect. The general finding was that police act differently in various settings. Specifically,

1. Police appear to be more active in racially mixed neighborhoods.
2. In racially heterogeneous neighborhoods, police have a greater propensity to offer assistance to residents and to initiate more contacts with suspicious persons and suspected violators . . .
3. In high-crime areas police are less likely to stop suspicious persons, suggesting that the findings evidence a higher level of general police activity in racially mixed neighborhoods . . .
4. Suspects confronted by police have a higher average probability of being arrested in lower-status neighborhoods than in higher-status areas . . .
5. Police are more apt to exert coercive authority in minority and racially mixed communities.[56]

The researcher emphasized that these findings do not mean that police are more prone to arrest African Americans than whites. The *context* of the alleged criminal activity is an important factor in the decision to arrest.

Community expectations may influence police decisions not to investigate or apprehend suspects in some areas. For example, police may not consider places like narrow alleys and abandoned buildings and cars to be areas that the community wishes to be investigated even though they are known to be used for illegal purposes. After they become familiar with an area, the officers know what behaviors to expect, and they may tolerate behavior in one area that would not be considered permissible in another.

Arrests may reflect the preferences of complaining victims, as found in an earlier but extensive and classic study by Donald Black. Black found that arrests were more likely when suspects were disrespectful and when suspects were stopped for serious crimes. He suggested that these factors, not race per se, accounted for higher arrest rates among African Americans than among whites. Others disagree, insisting that police discriminate against African Americans and other minorities in arrests. The solution to this problem is difficult, for as Black's study and many others have shown, police are lenient in their routine arrest practices. Most people who could be arrested are not arrested even when they are apprehended.[57]

In one recent study, however, researchers found some support for the demeanor hypothesis after collecting data in 24 police departments. These researchers considered the display of disrespect but with other variables. For example, in nontraffic contexts, they found that an officer's decision to arrest is not influenced by the suspect's apparent intoxication (from alcohol or other drugs) alone but by that fact combined with the suspect's show of disrespect for the officer. Additionally, they did not find that officers made arrest decisions based on race, gender, ethnicity, or age, but that they expected respect from all suspects.[58]

Racial profiling The reaction by law enforcement officers to potential suspects based solely on their race or ethnicity.

Others would disagree however, as illustrated by the increasing number of incidents of **racial profiling,** in which minorities claim successfully that they are arrested because they are, for example, "driving while black." The increase in complaints has led some police departments to collect data on traffic stops in an effort to determine whether their officers are engaging in racial profiling.

In 2000 it was revealed that as far back as 1996 New Jersey State Police administrators knew that racial profiling was occurring within their ranks, although they denied its existence until 1999. Despite that knowledge, authorities did not take remedial measures.[59] In December 1999 state officials and the U.S. Department of Justice entered into a consent agreement on the issue. Included in that agreement is the provision of an independent monitor to report on whether troopers are following the terms of the consent agreement. Race as a reason for stopping a driver is permitted only if it is relevant to a description of a crime suspect for whom they are looking.[60]

One study in New York City reported that police stop (and often frisk) African Americans and Hispanics at a rate much higher than that for whites. The difference cannot be explained entirely by higher crime rates in the areas of those stops, according to the report issued by the state's attorney general. More than one-half of the stops were of African Americans. The New York City police commissioner criticized the report as "critically flawed in many of its analyses."[61]

Accusations in the police departments in Steubenville, Ohio, and Pittsburgh, Pennsylvania, have resulted in settlements with the DOJ regarding racial profiling.[62]

In April 2000 the Ninth Circuit Court of Appeals held that it is not permissible to use ethnicity as a factor in deciding whether to stop an individual suspected of a crime. The court noted the large number and rapid growth rate of Hispanics in California and concluded that despite a 25-year-old U.S. Supreme Court decision ruling that racial appearance is an appropriate factor for deciding whether a person should be stopped by police, this is not acceptable today: "Hispanic appearance is, in general, of such little probative value that it may not be considered as a relevant factor where particularized or individualized suspicion is required." The case of *United States* v. *Montero-Camargo* involved three Mexicans who were stopped by the U.S. Border Patrol in 1996, about 115 miles east of San Diego. The agents, responding to a tip, gave five factors they considered in their decision to stop the suspects, one of which was their Hispanic appearance. The U.S. Supreme Court refused to review the case.[63]

The Use of Force

Laws regulating the use of force differ, but usually officers may not use deadly force unless they or other persons are threatened with serious bodily harm or death. They may use as much nondeadly force as is reasonably necessary to make an arrest, control a crowd, or engage in any other legitimate police functions.

Generally, a police officer cannot use deadly force to apprehend a misdemeanant (someone who commits a misdemeanor, a less serious offense than a felony), but in some states the act of fleeing is a felony. If a person flees after an arrest, the officer may be permitted to use deadly force, even if the original offense for which the arrest was made was a misdemeanor. Until recently, most jurisdictions permitted officers to fire at a fleeing felon, but these policies have changed. Today federal and many local and state law enforcement agencies prohibit the use of deadly force unless human life is threatened.

Even when a statute permits police to fire a deadly weapon at a fleeing felon, the courts may rule that under some circumstances this action violates the felon's constitutional rights. In 1983 in Tennessee, an officer fired at a 15-year-old who had allegedly broken into an unoccupied residence in a suburban area. The boy was killed by the police officer, who had been taught that it was legal to fire at a fleeing felon.

The boy's father filed a lawsuit against the Memphis police for violating his son's civil rights. The trial court held that the statute and the police officer's actions were constitutional. The court of appeals reversed the decision. The Supreme Court held that the Tennessee statute "is unconstitutional insofar as it authorizes the use of deadly force against . . . an apparently unarmed, nondangerous fleeing suspect." In *Tennessee* v. *Garner* the U.S. Supreme Court stated, "It is not better that all felony suspects die than that they escape. Where the suspect poses no immediate threat to the officer and no threat to others, the harm resulting from failing to apprehend him does not justify the use of deadly force to do so." The Court indicated that the statute might be appropriate in cases in which the officer's firing is based upon probable cause to believe that the suspect poses a threat of serious physical harm or death to the officer or others.[64]

Even with the restrictions on deadly force placed on police by *Tennessee* v. *Garner,* by statutes and by departmental policies, problems with police violence remain. Allegations of police violence and brutality are featured frequently in the media, ranging from physical abuse and harassment to the illegal use of weapons that results in serious injury or death. The issue of excessive force arises most often in civil suits brought against police and police departments, as illustrated by the 1997 beating of Haitian immigrant Abner Louima. Louima alleged that white police officers at a Brooklyn, New York, station house beat him severely and sodomized him with a stick (see Chapter 9). After three weeks of the spring of 1999 trial in this case, resulting in damaging testimony against him, Officer Justin A. Volpe entered a guilty plea and was sentenced to up to 30 years in prison. Other officers were also convicted, but in March 2002, an appellate court overturned on technical grounds the conspiracy to obstruct justice convictions of Charles Schwarz (whose protestations of innocence had captured national attention, including a February 2001 segment of CBS's *60 Minutes*), Thomas Bruder, and Thomas Wiese. These officers may be retried under another federal statute under which the appellate court stated that there may be sufficient evidence to support convictions.[65] In 2001 Louima settled with New York City for $8.7 million.

Vehicle Pursuits

One final area of police discretion that poses potential danger is that of vehicle pursuits in high-speed chases. Because serious injury or death may result for officers, suspects, or bystanders, some departments ban most or all high-speed pursuits. In 1998 the U.S. Supreme Court held that a high-speed police pursuit that ends in a fatality is not a constitutional violation unless the officer acted with "a purpose to cause harm unrelated to the legitimate object of arrest." *Sacramento County, California* v. *Lewis* involved a sheriff's deputy who pursued two boys on a motorcycle after they failed to stop when commanded to do so by another officer. The deputy violated his departmental policy by driving up to 100 miles per hour in a residential area in his pursuit of the suspects. The chase lasted only 75 seconds, but the motorcycle overturned and the deputy's vehicle slammed into the passenger, killing him. The Court held that the deputy did not violate the boy's due process rights during this pursuit since there was no evidence of an intent to harm the suspect or worsen his legal plight.[66]

POLICE MISCONDUCT

Considerable attention has been given to police corruption, especially in large cities such as New York and Los Angeles. According to sociologist Lawrence W. Sherman, "A public official is corrupt if he accepts money or money's worth for doing something that he is under a duty to do anyway, that he is under a duty not to do, or to exercise a legitimate discretion for improper reasons."[67]

In response to an article charging widespread corruption, the mayor of New York City established the Knapp Commission in May 1970. The commission found that police corruption was pervasive within the department and that rookies were subjected to such strong pressures that many succumbed and became corrupt, whereas others became cynical. This attitude was attributed to the departmental belief that corruption should not be exposed and to the code of silence among officers concerning the corrupt activities of their peers.[68]

In the 1980s officials of the New York City Police Department reported that only a small percentage of the city's police officers had been corrupted. The officials claimed that undercover tests of integrity, whereby some officers are assigned to make secret reports on the behavior of other officers, had eliminated organized corruption. Officials noted, however, that the institutionalized, organized corruption found by the Knapp Commission had been replaced by a new type of activity: cheating scams, such as abuse of sick leave, overtime, and military leave. Some officers had been charged with theft and drug violations.

In May 1992 five active New York City police officers and one retired officer were arrested and charged with drug violations in what police call the "most flagrant charge of drug corruption in the city's police force in six years."[69] The following month the FBI began investigating the allegations. In July four officers and two persons retired from the New York City Police Department were arrested for stealing and fencing thousands of counterfeit Chanel handbags.[70] By September even the highest ranking officer in charge of stopping corruption admitted that the task is very difficult: "There has never been a time in this job when we've been presented with more corruption hazards than in the last five years, because of the drug situation."[71]

The Mollen Commission, which conducted a major investigation into alleged corruption in the New York City Police Department, published its final report in 1994. The report compared current corruption patterns to those identified earlier in the Knapp Commission report. Whereas the earlier report found that most officers were "grass-eaters" (those who take bribes routinely) and few were "meat-eaters" (those who look for opportunities to go beyond bribes to more serious crimes), the 1994 report concluded that the current situation was the reverse: "Minor corruption is no longer systemic among the ranks. . . But the 'meat-eaters' are the rule rather than the exception among corrupt cops today."[72]

In 2000 the New York Police Department's commissioner, Howard Safir, resigned to assume a position with a private corporate security firm. He was replaced by Bernard B. Kerik. Although Safir, a longtime friend of Mayor Rudolph Guiliani, was credited, along with the mayor, for the drop in crime in the nation's largest city, he also left behind strained relations with the city's minorities, as we have already noted. Commissioner Kerik did not improve those relations when, in April 2001, he announced that the four police officers who were acquitted in the killing of an unarmed West African immigrant, Amadou Diallo, would keep their jobs. At the announcement Commissioner Kerik expressed his sympathy for Diallo's family, but many minorities are still angered by the killing, the acquittals, and the decision to return the officers to their jobs.

The Los Angeles Police Department (LAPD), still feeling the effects of the 1991 Rodney King beating, which was captured on video by an amateur photographer and shown throughout the world, is facing another crisis. This one, the Rampart scandal (so-called because it took place in the department's Rampart Division), has been described as "the worst corruption scandal in [LAPD] history." The scandal began in 1999 when officer Rafael Perez, who had been caught stealing cocaine from the evidence room, entered into a plea agreement with prosecutors. In the fall of 2000 three officers who were convicted of framing gang members and planting evidence were convicted, but in December 2000 a judge overturned those convictions and ordered a new trial, ruling that prosecutors had not presented sufficient evidence for those convictions and that the jury has misunderstood its instructions. Prosecutors are planning to retry the defendants, and hundreds of cases are being reexamined as a result of the allegations by Perez. Numerous officers have been fired, and an investigation into the department has resulted in a 350-page report on its problems. Perez was sentenced to five years in prison. In November 2000 the city settled for $15 million with Javier Francisco Ovando, a former gang member, now paralyzed after being shot by the police.[73]

As a result of this scandal, the LAPD was placed under the watchful eye of a federal monitor, Michael Cherkasky, who prosecuted notorious Mafia bosses such as John Gotti. Cherkasky is assisted by a team of experts, such as former New York City police commissioner William Bratton. The monitors have five years to reform the LAPD. In April 2002, LAPD police chief Bernard Parks resigned under pressure.

In July 2001 Rafael Perez was released on parole, having served only three of his five years. The judge ruled that Perez had met the terms of his plea agreement and that he had been treated unfairly by being incarcerated in jail rather than prison, which resulted in his obtaining fewer days off his sentence for good behavior.

Why so much corruption among police? Policing is rich in opportunities for corruption, but opportunity is not the only important variable. Variation in police corruption may depend on a police department's type of organization. James Q. Wilson analyzed police departments according to what he termed *styles* of law enforcement: the service style, the legalistic style, and the watchman style. These styles were found to be related to the degree of police corruption, the greatest degree being found among the watchman style.[74]

The *watchman style* emphasizes order maintenance over law enforcement; that is, the law is used to maintain order rather than to regulate conduct. In a department characterized by the watchman style, the police chief tries to limit the discretionary authority of patrol officers. A primary concern is that no one rocks the boat within the department. Police are recruited locally, paid low salaries, given minimum training, not rewarded for higher education, and expected to have other jobs—all factors that may make them more susceptible to corruption.

The *legalistic style* emphasizes specialization, promotional opportunities, and higher education, along with attempts to recruit from the middle class. The law is seen as a means to an end; the police officer tries to be an impersonal agent of the law, uses formal rather than informal sanctions, issues traffic tickets at a high rate, and emphasizes law enforcement over order maintenance or community services.

The *service style* combines law enforcement and order maintenance. Emphasis is on community relations, with police on patrol working out of specialized units (such as narcotics or sexual assault crimes units) and a decentralized command. The pace of work is more leisurely, and more promotional opportunities are stressed. Corruption is not a serious problem, and police are expected to live exemplary private lives.

According to Sherman, police corruption is a problem of both external opportunity and the individual's response. It can be explained only by a close analysis of both variables. Sherman applied theories of community structure and anomie, which state that the degree of anomie depends on the gap between the goals and means to achieve them. Sherman emphasized that anomie can affect the corrupters and the corruptees and that an occupational group might suffer anomie not characteristic of the entire community. Police might have an occupational anomie and therefore be more susceptible to bribes than members of other occupational groups are. In addition, recruits redefine themselves radically in a relatively short period of time, and the process of accepting bribes begins. The key factor is the extent of the corruption in the work group to which the officer is assigned. The process goes by stages, beginning with police perks—free coffee and meals—and moving to a free drink after work, and further to money offered by a motorist. If the officer participates in these stages, he or she may be considered ready by colleagues to be cut in on gambling deals. That offer is hard to turn down, for it represents a chance to participate in the social solidarity of colleagues. Some officers move on to bribes from prostitutes, pimps, or brothel operators and finally into narcotics. Police officers may stop anywhere along the ladder because of their self-concepts, but they are influenced in where they stop by the group definition of how far they can go.[75]

THE CONTROL OF POLICING

The discussions of police stress and corruption are not meant to imply that all or even most officers or administrators are included or that the problems are unique to policing. They may, however, be more obvious in this profession and even more critical because of the power of the police force and the fact that police officers have access to weapons. But because problems do exist, it is important to consider methods for controlling policing. Several approaches are used. We begin with internal controls, which we hope would take care of the problems.

Police Professionalism and Departmental Control

In the final analysis only police can control policing. Discretion is vital in policing, and thus the legislature, the courts, and the community cannot control all police activities. According to Jerome H. Skolnick,

> The needed philosophy of professionalism must rest on a set of values conveying the idea that police are as much an institution dedicated to the achievement of legality in society as they are an official social organization designed to control misconduct through the invocation of punitive sanctions . . . [W]hat must occur is a significant alteration in the ideology of police.[76]

The importance of professionalism was dramatized by a study published in 1970, which reported that the attitudes and behavior of police are not explained by the social variables of class, ethnicity, age, rank, gender, race, and authoritarianism, but by the impact of professionalism.[77] It is important, however, that the public is not misled; police professionalism must be real, not illusory. Thus, in his 1974 work, Peter K. Manning, a scholar of police behavior, contended that police adopt an impossible mandate "that claims to include the efficient, apolitical, and professional enforcement of the law." Because they cannot meet that mandate, they resort to appearances of professionalism that include creating a bureaucracy in police organization (which they see as the best and most efficient way to run the organization), using technology to suggest a scientific perspective of crime, collecting official data and using them to show how efficient they are, and devising styles of patrol that they see as part of bureaucratic efficiency. They develop secrecy, one of their most effective sources of power, because it enables them to act without exposing what they are doing, such as cooperating with organized crime rather than fighting it. Appearances are important, too, because police need convictions for their arrests. For a high rate of convictions, police may cooperate with prosecutors in persuading people to plead guilty to lesser offenses, operating on the assumption that all the people they arrest are guilty and that, if the police apply enough pressure, suspects will confess.[78]

Police departments need to consider revising policies such as those that prohibit lateral entry, which results in promotions only from within the department. Some experts have suggested that police departments develop specialized units, such as a domestic unit, a juvenile unit, and a substance abuse unit with an emphasis on peacekeeping, leaving most of the traditional law enforcement functions to other officers. Still other supporters of professionalism have suggested the creation of crisis intervention units because police receive so many disturbance calls involving family members and friends that might erupt into violence. The aim is to prevent violence. Various methods have been tried, and one that has received considerable attention in recent years is arresting suspects in domestic violence cases even when the alleged victim does not want to press charges.

Community Control

A second method for controlling policing is through the community. In 1981, the U.S. Commission on Civil Rights stated that perhaps "the most valuable asset these officers can possess is credibility with the community they serve."[79] Good police/community relations are particularly important today, since racial and other conflicts between police and the community may escalate into violence. These conflicts reflect larger societal problems, which police cannot solve, but police can work to improve public perceptions of their activities. Actual or perceived negative relationships may lead to violence. Earlier studies reported that people who have positive images of the police are more likely to cooperate with them in crime control. Least likely to cooperate are those who perceive that they are discriminated against—minorities and the poor—and who happen to be the most frequent crime victims.[80]

Community-oriented policing is one way to improve relationships between the police and the community. Another is the involvement of citizens in establishing standards and policies and in enforcing disciplinary action. Civilian review boards were utilized in earlier years, but they were opposed by police; most did not last long and had little power. The U.S. Civil Rights Commission noted the problems with these boards but also suggested that some outside review of alleged police misconduct is appropriate.[81] Historically, community involvement in police policy making and discipline has been a failure.[82] Today, however, some communities are looking again at the possibilities for cooperation in improving the relationship between law enforcement and policing.

Exclusionary rule The Fourth Amendment of the U.S. Constitution provides that "the right of the people to be secure in their persons, houses, papers and effects, against unreasonable searches and seizures shall not be violated and no warrants shall issue, but upon probable cause . . ." Evidence seized in violation of the Fourth Amendment may be excluded from a criminal trial.

Controlling through the Courts

A third method for controlling policing is through the courts. This may take several forms. We have already noted that the Los Angeles Police Department has been put under the control of a federal monitor, who, with his assistants, is in charge of a five-year course to reform that department. Two other court methods of control are the exclusionary rule and the use of criminal and civil lawsuits.

The Exclusionary Rule

The **exclusionary rule** was developed by the U.S. Supreme Court as a method for deterring police from illegal searches and seizures. As early as 1914, the Court held that in federal cases the prohibition against unreasonable searches and seizures would not be effective unless all illegally seized evidence was excluded from trial. In 1961 the Court held that the exclusionary rule applies to cases tried in state courts.[83]

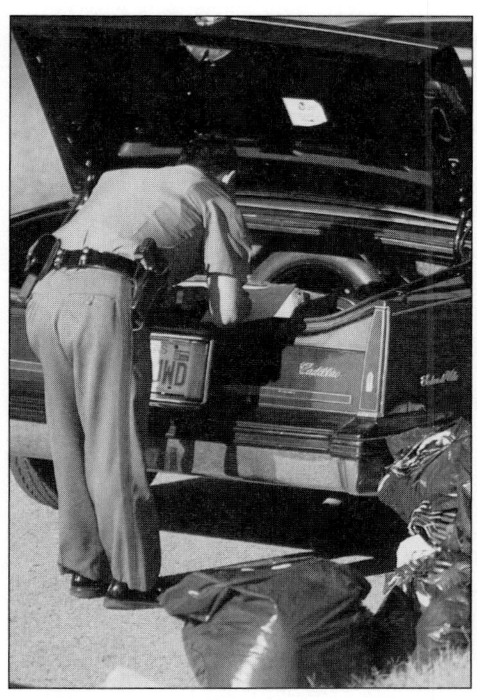

Police search for drugs or other contraband after arresting a motorist. In recent years the U.S. Supreme Court has relaxed the rules on such searches. (Bob Daemmrich/ Stock Boston)

The exclusionary rule serves a symbolic purpose. If police violate suspects' rights in order to obtain evidence to be used in trials, the government is setting a negative example. According to the Supreme Court, when this occurs, the government becomes a lawbreaker: "It breeds contempt for law; it invites . . . anarchy."[84]

The symbolic purpose is important, but the second reason for the exclusionary rule is a practical one. The rule presumably prevents police from engaging in illegal searches and seizures. It is difficult to know whether that is true, because illegal searches may not be reported. The research on the issue is inconclusive. There is evidence, however, that the existence of the rule has led some police departments to increase the quantity and quality of police training, thus educating officers more extensively in what they may and may not do in the area of search and seizure.[85]

In recent years the exclusionary rule has come under attack, with many people calling for its abolition or at least its modification. Generally, the arguments on this side of the issue are the reverse of the arguments in favor of the rule. First is the argument concerning symbolism, which is based on the view that when people see defendants they believe to be guilty going free because of a technicality, respect for the law and for the criminal justice system is undermined. It is the *perception* of letting guilty suspects go free that is crucial. The classic statement on this issue was made by Benjamin Cardozo, then a state court judge and later a justice of the U.S. Supreme Court. Cardozo wrote the 1926 opinion in which the New York Court of Appeals refused to adopt the exclusionary rule for that jurisdiction: "The criminal is to go free because the constable has blundered."[86]

Second, abolitionists contend that the exclusionary rule should be eliminated because it results in the release of guilty people. Third, the possibility of having evidence excluded from a trial because it was not seized properly leads defendants to file numerous motions to suppress evidence, which takes up a lot of court time and contributes to court congestion. In criminal cases, objections to searches or seizures are two of the issues raised most frequently.

Good faith exception An exception to the exclusionary rule in criminal court proceedings. Even if the police seize evidence illegally, the evidence may be used in court if the police had a good faith belief that the evidence was related to the crime and to the suspect who is under investigation.

Several exceptions have been made to the exclusionary rule. Under the **good faith** exception, evidence that is obtained illegally should not be excluded from trial if it can be shown that the officers secured the evidence in good faith, that is, if they reasonably believed that they were acting in accordance with the law. The Supreme Court adopted the good faith exception in *Massachusetts* v. *Sheppard*.[87]

The Court's good faith exception to the exclusionary rule does not require that all states adopt the exception. States may grant defendants greater protection than is required by the Constitution, and some have done so.[88]

Inevitable discovery exception An exception to the exclusionary rule in criminal court proceedings. Illegally seized evidence is admissible if police would have found it later by legal methods.

Another exception to the exclusionary rule adopted by the Supreme Court is the **inevitable discovery exception.** In *Nix* v. *Williams,* the Court held that illegally seized evidence is admissible if police would have found it later by legal methods. In *New York* v. *Quarles,* the Court recognized a *public safety* exception, holding that there are some circumstances in which police are justified in conducting a search or asking questions without first giving the *Miranda* warning. In those instances, illegally obtained evidence is admissible at trial.[89]

In subsequent cases, the Court has decided that evidence seized by officers who had a warrant to search one apartment but, without realizing it, searched a different apartment and found illegal drugs may be used in court because the officers acted in good faith. Excluding that evidence would not deter officers from making such searches since they had acted in the belief that they had the right apartment.[90]

The Court has ruled that defendants' rights are not violated when police, acting in good faith, lose or destroy evidence that could have been used to establish innocence. In *Arizona* v. *Youngblood,* police failed to perform chemical tests on the victim's semen-stained clothes or to refrigerate that evidence for subsequent tests. Test results might have shown that the defendant was not the assailant in that case.[91]

Harmful error An error in legal proceedings that is considered to have resulted in actions so detrimental that some relief, such as a new trial, must be granted. It may also be called a **reversible error** and is in contrast to a **harmless error,** which is a mistake that is not considered serious enough to create the need for remedial action.

In *Arizona* v. *Fulminante,* a sharply divided Court held that the Constitution does not require the automatic exclusion from trial of a coerced confession. According to the Court, a coerced confession is to be evaluated like any other evidence, with the trial judge deciding whether the error was harmless. If so, the confession may be admitted. However, if the confession constituted **harmful error,** meaning that it affected a constitutional right of the defendant and thus is a serious error rather than a simple technical one, the evidence must be excluded.[92]

Criminal and Civil Liability

Another method for attempting to control misconduct by police officers and their supervisors is through criminal and civil liability. Civil litigation against law enforcement officers and their departments and municipalities is extensive, as illustrated by the recent $8.7 million settlement in New York City for the police brutality suffered by Abner Louima, discussed earlier in this chapter. As noted earlier in the chapter, the City of Los Angeles settled for $15 million with one victim, Javier Francisco Ovando, a former gang member who said he was shot in the head and chest and then framed by police. Ovando was paralyzed by the attack. The city council also approved $10.9 million to settle 29 other cases stemming from the Rampart scandal, and over 60 cases were still pending.[93]

There are many legal reasons that may be used in these civil suits. The U.S. Supreme Court has held that inadequacy of training is an acceptable reason, provided the plaintiff can prove that the negligence amounts to deliberate indifference by the police department.[94]

A statute enacted in 1994 provides greater enforcement powers to the Department of Justice (DOJ) to prosecute police who violate the law. It permits investigation and prosecution of patterns or practices of departmentwide misconduct in local police departments, and it authorizes the U.S. attorney general to "acquire data about the use of excessive force by law enforcement officers" and directs him or her to "publish an annual summary of the data."[95]

Finally, federal lawsuits may be brought by those who allege that their federal civil rights have been violated. These suits may be successful even after the officers have been acquitted of state charges. Recall, for example, that the four LAPD officers charged in the Rodney King beating were tried for violating

King's civil rights after they were acquitted of state charges in that incident. Three of the officers were convicted in the federal trial and served time in prison.

At the close of its 2000–2001 term, however, the U.S. Supreme Court did provide additional protection for police officers sued for the use of excessive force. In *Saucier* v. *Katz* the court held that even if an officer's use of force is unreasonable, he or she cannot be held civilly liable if it can be shown that a reasonable officer could make that mistake under the existing circumstances. The case in question involved a brief altercation at the Presidio army base near San Diego, California, in 1994, when Vice President Al Gore was speaking concerning the conversion of the base to a national park. As animal-rights activist, Elliot Katz, age 60, began to unfurl a banner in protest of the conversion, he was dragged by two military police officers and thrown into a van. Katz, who was wearing a leg brace on his fractured foot, fell to the floor of the van but suffered no injuries. He sued the police, alleging that the seizure was unreasonable and thus violated his Fourth Amendment rights (see Appendix A). The Court ruled that the defendant officer was entitled to the immunity defense that is available to officers who make reasonable mistakes in judgment in performing their duties. The Court emphasized that there was a need for heightened security in view of the presence of the vice president and that the complainant was not physically injured.[96]

SUMMARY

After a brief history of policing and overview of U.S. public police systems, this chapter examines the role of private security. Private security has grown significantly, passing public policing in both numbers of employees and total costs. The growth of private security raises many questions, including the fairness issue—is adequate security available only for those who can afford it?—and quality control.

The recruitment, training, and education of police involve many issues. This chapter's overview of qualifications includes a look at the psychology of policing. The chapter also examines the need to increase the numbers of women and minorities in policing. Much of the chapter is devoted to discussing police functions: law enforcement, order maintenance, and community services, along with the controversies that surround them. Models of policing are discussed, with particular attention given to recent developments in community-oriented policing. We examine the attitudes and the hostility police encounter from the public. These and other conflicts and problems have led some police officers to withdraw into themselves, to develop a code of secrecy, and to become isolated from society.

Policing is a stressful job, and some of the causes of stress are discussed, including the problems created by the rapid spread of HIV infection. Police discretion in decision making is examined in the context of the initial stop, questioning, and arrest. The use of force, especially deadly force, is an issue of national concern today. The use of dangerous, high-speed vehicle pursuits is discussed, too.

The widespread traffic in illegal drugs, which produces enormous profits, provides ample opportunity for police corruption. Examples of police who succumb to those opportunities are not difficult to find. Efforts to control corruption have not met with great success in the large cities, such as New York City.

Efforts to control police misconduct are made by the use of police professionalism and departmental control, the community, and the courts. The use of a federal monitor and a group of other experts to reform the Los Angeles Police Department is used to explain one role that courts may play in controlling policing. Courts also employ the exclusionary rule by excluding from trial evidence that has been seized illegally. Criminal and civil liability are other court-related control methods that are being used frequently, with some suits, as noted, resulting in millions of dollars in damages.

Experts have concluded that research on policing has not been adequate because we do not know enough about the police, who occupy one of the most important roles in our criminal justice systems. But we do know the tremendous impact their behavior can have on us as individuals and as a society. We need to understand that the behavior that touches our lives so deeply is significant for police officers as well. Most of them are hardworking and underpaid public servants who are not engaging in corruption or the misuse of police power. They deserve the support of the community in their efforts.

STUDY QUESTIONS

1. Explain briefly the meanings of these words in the context of policing historically: *frankpledge, hundred, shires, constable,* and *watch system.*
2. In what ways, if any, did the watch system influence policing in this country?
3. Distinguish policing levels in U.S. systems.
4. Evaluate policing at the federal level.
5. What current problems face the FBI?
6. Contrast public and private policing.
7. What do you think should be the minimum qualifications for an entry-level police officer? Defend your answer.
8. How have women and minorities been accepted in police departments? What problems do they face? What contributions do they make?
9. Distinguish the three major police functions: law enforcement, order maintenance, service. What should have priority? Why?
10. Define and discuss the implications of zero-tolerance policies in policing.
11. What influence do you think the media have on policing?
12. Describe and evaluate a professional model of policing and contrast it with the problem-solving model.
13. Why has so much emphasis been placed in recent years on community-oriented policing? Evaluate the trend.
14. How should police time be allocated among the three major policing functions?
15. Discuss the major role conflicts officers might encounter in policing.
16. What are the major factors contributing to police stress?
17. Define *police subculture* and evaluate the concept.
18. What unique problems are presented to policing by the rapid spread of AIDS?
19. What is meant by the following statement: "Police must have probable cause to stop"?
20. Explain and evaluate the *no-knock rule* and the *knock-and-announce rule.*
21. What have sociological studies shown us about arrest procedures and policies?
22. Explain the importance of *Tennessee* v. *Garner* to police use of deadly force.
23. What position do you think we should take regarding high-speed police vehicle pursuits?
24. Discuss police corruption historically and indicate the major types of corruption today.
25. What have the New York City and Los Angeles police departments taught us about policing?
26. State the recent problems with police violence.
27. What are the prospects for controlling policing through community action? Through federal courts? Through civil or criminal lawsuits?
28. Define the exclusionary rule, state the reason it exists, and critique the policy. What are the recognized exceptions to the rule?

BRIEF ESSAY ASSIGNMENTS

1. Discuss how policing in rural areas is different from policing in larger municipalities.
2. Describe the debate surrounding police officers and education level. Explain two criticisms of requiring officers to have higher education.
3. Identify and describe common characteristics of community policing.
4. Explain the concept of *racial profiling* and its impact on policing.
5. List and summarize James Q. Wilson's three styles of policing.

INTERNET ACTIVITIES

1. Check out a local law enforcement agency on the Web. How many sworn officers does this agency have? What is the total number of employees? Does the department provide crime statistics for your area? Is there any information on community policing or problem-solving activities and/or programs? Does the department have any specialized investigative units? (e.g., homicide, property, narcotics). Sites such as www.officer.com and www.leolinks.com offer search engines and links to find most law enforcement agencies on the Web.
2. The National Center for Women and Policing website at www.womenandpolicing.org pro-

vides statistics, links, and publications on a variety of issues related to women and law enforcement. Find the article "Equality Denied: The Status of Women in Policing, 2000." According to the article, what is the percent of women in sworn law enforcement positions? How many police agencies have consent decrees? Is a law enforcement agency in your area included in the survey?

NET RESOURCES

www.theiacp.org
Maintained by a nonprofit membership organization, the International Association of Chiefs of Police's website provides information resources consisting of research initiatives, current projects and reports, legislative and policy issues, and links to other related law enforcement sites.

www.ncrle.net
The National Center for Rural Law Enforcement provides news, publications and other information on issues related to rural law enforcement. Users can access model law enforcement policies, associated links, the School Violence Resource Center, and the Criminal Justice Institute.

www.communitypolicing.org
Comprised of five leading police organizations in the United States, the Community Policing Consortium includes on its website various information sources such as publications, community policing, research, and training. A site search engine is also provided.

www.usdoj.gov/cops/home.htm
The U.S. Department of Justice Community Oriented Policing Services website highlights community oriented policing and problem-oriented policing issues. Resource categories include fact sheets, publications, press releases and news on a variety of policing topics. Regional Community Policing Institutes (RCPI) can also be accessed from this site.

www.policeforum.org
A national organization of police executives, the Police Executive Research Forum maintains a website that provides an electronic library, a newsroom, information on legislative issues, current research projects, racial profiling, and links to related sites.

www.aele.org
Americans for Effective Law Enforcement, Inc., is a nonprofit organization whose website features legal publications, professional articles and law reviews, legal and criminal justice links and research sources all related to law enforcement and policing.

www.ins.usdoj.gov
The Immigration and Naturalization Service (INS) website includes information on immigration laws and regulations, access to INS Federal Register publications, administrative decisions, links to other government links, and statistics for various topics related to INS issues and enforcement.

www.policefoundation.org
Police Foundation features resources and publications on current and police foundation research, crime mapping, press releases, and community policing. Links to numerous police and other criminal justice topics and a search engine are also available to site users.

ENDNOTES

1. These methods of policing are discussed in Richard J. Lundman, *Police and Policing: An Introduction* (New York: Holt, Rinehart & Winston, 1980), pp. 15–17.
2. David H. Bayley, "Police: History," in *Encyclopedia of Crime and Justice,* vol. 3, ed. Sanford H. Kadish (New York: Free Press, 1983), p. 1124.
3. Tony Poveda, *Lawlessness and Reform: The FBI in Transition* (Pacific Grove, CA: Brooks/Cole, 1990), p. 1.
4. "F.B.I. to Pay Whistle-Blower $1.1 Million in a Settlement," *New York Times* (27 February 1998), p. 13.
5. William C. Cunningham et al., *Private Security: Patterns and Trends* (Washington, DC: U.S. Department of Justice, August 1991), pp. 1, 2.
6. See William C. Cunningham and Todd H. Taylor, "Ten Years of Growth in Law Enforcement and Private Security Relationships," *The Police Chief* 1 (June 1983): 30, 31.
7. Cunningham et al., *Private Security,* pp. 3, 4.
8. Gang Lee et al., "The Relationship between Crime and Private Security at U.S. Shopping Centers," *American Journal of Criminal Justice* 23 (Spring 99): 156–78; quotation is from p. 173.
9. Federal Bureau of Investigation, *Uniform Crime Reports: Crime in the United States, 2000* (Washington, DC: U.S. Department of Justice, 2001), p. 291.
10. See Arthur Niederhoffer, *Behind the Shield: The Police in Urban Society* (New York: Doubleday, 1969).
11. For an analysis of cynicism among police chiefs see John P. Crank et al., "Cynicism among Police Chiefs," *Justice Quarterly* 3 (September 1986): 343–52.
12. Bruce N. Carpenter and Susan M. Raza, "Personality Characteristics of Police Applicants: Comparisons across Subgroups and with Other Populations," *Journal of Police Science and Administration* 15 (March 1987): 16.
13. Michael K. Brown, *Working the Street: Police Discretion and the Dilemmas of Reform* (New York: Russell Sage, 1981), pp. xii, 7.
14. David L. Carter et al., *The State of Police Education: Policy Direction for the 21st Century* (Washington, DC: Police Executive Research Forum, 1989), p. 15.
15. Elizabeth Burbeck and Adrian Furnham, "Police Officer Selection: A Critical Review of the Literature," *Journal of Police Science and Administration* 13 (March 1985): 62.
16. U.S. Commission on Civil Rights, *Who Is Guarding the Guardians? A Report on Police Practices* (Washington, DC: U.S. Government Printing Office, 1981).
17. Nicholas Alex, *Black in Blue: A Study of the Negro Policeman* (New York: Appleton-Century-Crofts, 1969).
18. Nancy L. Herrington, "Female Cops—1992," in *Critical Issues in Policing: Contemporary Readings,* 3d ed., eds. Roger G. Dunham and Geoffrey P. Alpert (Prospect Heights, IL: Waveland Press, 1997), pp. 385–90; quotations are from p. 388.
19. "Women Being Hired as Officers, but Promotions Found Lagging," *Criminal Justice Newsletter* 20 (19 July 1989): 2.
20. "Female Cops: Nation's Policewomen Are Facing a Bullet-Proof Glass Ceiling," *USA Today* (28 November 1998), p. 1, referring to a soon-to-be published report of the International Association of Chiefs of Police.
21. Atwater v. City of Lago Vista, 2001 U.S. LEXIS 3366 (2001).
22. Herbert L. Packer, *The Limits of the Criminal Sanction* (Stanford, CA: Stanford University Press, 1968), p. 283.
23. See James Q. Wilson and George L. Kelling, "Police and Neighborhood Safety: Broken Windows," *Atlantic Monthly* 249 (March 1982): 28–38.
24. Judith A. Greene, "Zero Tolerance: A Case Study of Police Policies and Practices in New York City," *Crime and Delinquency* 45 (April 1999): 171–87; quotation is from p. 171.
25. James Q. Wilson, *Varieties of Police Behavior: The Management of Law and Order in Eight Communities* (Cambridge, MA: Harvard University Press, 1968), p. 21.
26. See George L. Kelling, "Order Maintenance, the Quality of Urban Life, and Police: A Line of Argument," in *Police Leadership in America: Crisis and Opportunity,* ed. William A. Geller (Chicago: American Bar Foundation, 1985), p. 297.
27. Carl B. Klockars, "Order Maintenance, the Quality of Urban Life, and Police: A Different Line of Argument," in *Police Leadership in America: Crisis and Opportunity,* ed. William A. Geller (Chicago: American Bar Foundation, 1985), p. 316.
28. See the President's Commission on Law Enforcement and the Administration of Justice, *Task Force Report: The Police* (Washington, DC: U.S. Government Printing Office, 1967).
29. George L. Kelling, *Police and Communities: The Quiet Revolution* (Washington, DC: U.S. Department of Justice, June 1988): 1.
30. Herman Goldstein, "Toward Community-Oriented Policing: Potential, Basic Requirements, and Threshold Questions," *Crime & Delinquency* 33 (January 1977): 7.
31. "Community Policing in the 1990s," *National Institute of Justice Journal* 225 (August 1992): 3.
32. George L. Kelling, *Foot Patrol,* National Institute of Justice (Washington, DC: U.S. Department of Justice, 1989), p. 3.
33. National Institute of Justice, *Community Policing in Seattle: A Model Partnership between Citizens and Police* (Washington, DC: U.S. Department of Justice, August 1992).
34. "Community Policing in Chicago Gets High Marks from Evaluators," *Criminal Justice Newsletter* 26 (3 July 1995): 1.
35. National Institute of Justice, Stephen Mastrofski et al., *Community Policing in Action: Lessons from an Observational Study* (Washington, DC: U.S. Department of Justice, June 1998), p. 2
36. Violent Crime Control and Law Enforcement Act of 1994, Public Law 103-322 (13 September 1994). The community policing statute, referred to as "Cops on the Beat," is codified at U.S. Code, Title 42, Section 3796 *et seq.,* (2001).
37. Washington Dateline, PR Newswire (9 September 1998). For recent scholarly analysis of community policing, see Jlihong Zhao and Quint C. Thurman, "Community Policing: Where Are We Now?" *Crime & Delinquency* 43 (July 1997): 345–57; and Brian N. Williams, *Citizen Perspectives on Community Policing: A Case Study in Athens, Georgia* (Albany: State University of New York Press, 1998).
38. See Wilson, *Varieties of Police Behavior,* p. 18.
39. Albert J. Reiss Jr., *The Police and the Public* (New Haven, CT: Yale University, 1971), pp. 63, 64, 71.
40. Richard J. Lundman, "Police Patrol Work: A Comparative Perspective," *Police Behavior: A Sociological Perspective,* ed. Richard J. Lundman (New York: Oxford University Press, 1980), p. 55.
41. Eric J. Scott, *Calls for Service: Citizen Demand and Initial Police Response* (Washington, DC: U.S. Department of Justice, July 1981), p. 26.
42. Wilson, *Varieties of Police Behavior,* p. 53.
43. See Terry Eisenberg, "Job Stress and the Police Officer: Identifying Stress Reduction Techniques," in *Job Stress and the Police Officers: Identifying Stress Reduction Techniques,* ed. William H. Kroes and Joseph J. Hurrell, Proceedings of Symposium, Cincinnati, Ohio, May 8–9, 1975 (Washington, DC: U.S. Government Printing Office).
44. *Uniform Crime Reports 2000,* p. 291.
45. Jerry Dash and Martin Reiser, "Suicide among Police in Urban Law Enforcement Agencies," *Journal of Police Science and Administration* 6 (March 1978): 18.
46. Peter J. Mercier, review of John P. Crank, *Understanding Police Culture* (Cincinnati, OH: Anderson, 1998), in *American Journal of Criminal Justice* 24 (Fall 1999): 153.
47. "A Silent Fraternity: Officers with H.I.V.," *New York Times* (2 August 2000), p. 23.
48. Michael J. Lynch and W. Byron Groves, *A Primer in Radical Criminology,* 2d ed. (New York: Harrow and Heston, 1989), p. 87.
49. Cal. Penal Code, Section 645(e) (1982).
50. Kolender v. Lawson, 461 U.S. 352, 358 (1983).
51. Whren v. United States, 517 U.S. 806 (1996); Ornelas et al. v. United States, 517 U.S. 690 (1996).
52. Maryland v. Wilson, 519 U.S. 408 (1997); Pennsylvania v. Mimms, 434 U.S. 106 (1977).
53. Richards v. Wisconsin, 514 U.S. 927 (1995); Wilson v. Arkansas, 520 U.S. 385 (1997).
54. United States v. Ramirez, 523 U.S. 65 (1998). The federal no-knock statute is codified at U.S. Code, Title 18, Section 3109 (1998).
55. Mallory v. United States, 354 U.S. 449, 456 (1957).
56. Douglas A. Smith, "The Neighborhood Context of Police Behavior," in *Communities and Crime,* ed. Albert J. Reiss Jr. and Michael Tonry (Chicago: University of Chicago Press, 1986), pp. 313–41.
57. Donald Black, "The Social Organization of Arrest," *Stanford Law Review* 23 (June 1971): 1104–09.
58. Robin Shepard Engel et al., "Further Exploration of the Demeanor Hypothesis: The Interaction Effects of Suspects' Characteristics and Demeanor on Police Behavior," *Justice Quarterly* 17 (June 2000): 235–59.
59. "Records Show New Jersey Police Knew of Racial Profiling in '96," *New York Times* (12 October 2000), p. 1.
60. "New Jersey Enters into Consent Decree on Racial Issues in Highway Stops," *Criminal Law Reporter* 66 (5 January 2000), p. 251.
61. "New York Police Stop Minorities Disproportionately, Study Finds," *Criminal Justice Newsletter* 30 (1 July 1999): 1–2.

62. "U.S. Will Monitor New Jersey Police on Race Profiling," *New York Times* (23 December 1999), p. 1.
63. United States v. Montero-Camargo, 208 F.3d 1122 (9th Cir. 2000), *cert. denied,* 121 S.Ct. 211 (2000).
64. Tennessee v. Garner, 471 U.S. 1 (1985).
65. "High Profile Lawyer Team in Louima Brutality Suit Is Raising Questions of Overkill," *New York Times* (9 November 1997), p. 17; "Five Cops Face Fed Trial in Louima Attack," *Daily News* (New York) (19 September 1998), p. 10; "Conviction Voided on Second Officer in Louima Attack," *New York Times* (1 March 2002), p. 1.
66. Sacramento County, California v. Lewis, 118 S.Ct. 1708 (1998). For a recent analysis of vehicle pursuits, see Roger G. Dunham, Geoffrey P. Alpert, Dennis Jay Kenny, and Paul Cromwell, "High-Speed Pursuit: The Offender's Perspective," *Criminal Justice and Behavior* 25 (March 1998): 30–45.
67. Lawrence W. Sherman, ed., *Police Corruption: A Sociological Perspective* (New York: Doubleday, 1974), p. 6.
68. *The Knapp Commission Report on Police Corruption* (New York: Braziller, 1972), p. 260.
69. "New York Officers Charged with Running Drug Ring," *New York Times* (8 May 1992), p. 14.
70. "New York Officers Held in Huge Theft of Handbags," *New York Times* (10 July 1992), p. 16.
71. "Official Says Police Corruption Is Hard to Stop," *New York Times* (20 September 1992), p. 6.
72. "Police Corruption in New York Found Rarer but More Virulent," *Criminal Justice Newsletter* 25 (15 July 1994), p. 1, reporting on the Mollen Commission report released 7 July 1994.
73. "Los Angeles Settles Lawsuit against Police," *New York Times* (22 November 2000), p. 18; "Bad Cops: Rafael Perez's Testimony on Police Misconduct Ignited the Biggest Scandal in the History of the L.A.P.D.: Is It the Real Story?" *The New Yorker* (21 May 2001), p. 60.
74. Wilson, *Varieties of Police Behavior,* pp. 140–226.
75. Sherman, *Police Corruption,* pp. 1–39; 196–201.
76. Jerome H. Skolnick, *Justice without Trial,* 2d ed. (New York: John Wiley, 1975), pp. 238–39.
77. James Leo Walsh, "Professionalism and the Police: The Cop as Medical Student," *American Behavioral Scientist* 13 (May/August 1970): 705–25.
78. Peter K. Manning, "The Police: Mandate, Strategies, and Appearances," in *Crime and Justice in America: A Critical Understanding,* ed. Jack D. Douglas (Boston: Little, Brown, 1974), pp. 171, 186–91.
79. U.S. Commission on Civil Rights, *Who Is Guarding the Guardians?,* p. 2.
80. See Paul S. Benson, "Political Alienation and Pubic Satisfaction with Police Services," *Pacific Sociological Review* 24 (January 1981): 45–64.
81. U.S. Commission on Civil Rights, *Who Is Guarding the Guardians?,* p. 163.
82. See Jack R. Greene, "Police and Community Relations: Where Have We Been and Where Are We Going?" in *Critical Issues in Policing: Contemporary Readings,* 2d ed., eds. Roger G. Dunham and Geoffrey P. Alpert (Prospect Heights, IL: Waveland Press, 1993), pp. 349–368.
83. Weeks v. United States, 232 U.S. 383 (1914); Mapp v. Ohio, 367 U.S. 643 (1961).
84. Olmstead v. United States, 277 U.S. 438, 485 (1928), Justice Brandeis, dissenting.
85. Stephen H. Sachs, "The Exclusionary Rule: A Prosecutor's Defense," *Criminal Justice Ethics* 1 (Summer/Fall 1982): 31, 32. This journal contains a symposium on the pros and cons of the exclusionary rule and is an excellent source on the topic.
86. People v. Defore, 150 N.E. 585, 587 (N.Y.Ct.App. 1926), *cert. denied,* 270 U.S. 657 (1926).
87. Massachusetts v. Sheppard, 468 U.S. 981 (1984). See also United States v. Leon, decided the same day, 468 U.S. 897 (1984).
88. See State v. Novembrino, 491 A.2d 37 (N.J.Sup. 1985).
89. Nix v. Williams, 467 U.S. 431 (1984); New York v. Quarles, 467 U.S. 649 (1984).
90. Maryland v. Garrison, 480 U.S. 79 (1987).
91. Arizona v. Youngblood, 488 U.S. 51 (1988).
92. Arizona v. Fulminante, 499 U.S. 279 (1991).
93. "Los Angeles Settles Lawsuit against Police."
94. Canton v. Harris, 489 U.S. 378 (1989).
95. See U.S. Code, Title 42, Sections 14141–14142 (2001).
96. Saucier v. Katz, 121 S.Ct. 2151 (2001).

CHAPTER

13

▶Young children may be afraid to testify in court, and they lack the experience and knowledge required for some kinds of statements, especially in sexual abuse cases. One way prosecutors have dealt with these problems is to use anatomically correct dolls, which enable children to demonstrate what allegedly happened. (Jim Pickerell/Stock Boston)

Court Systems

OUTLINE

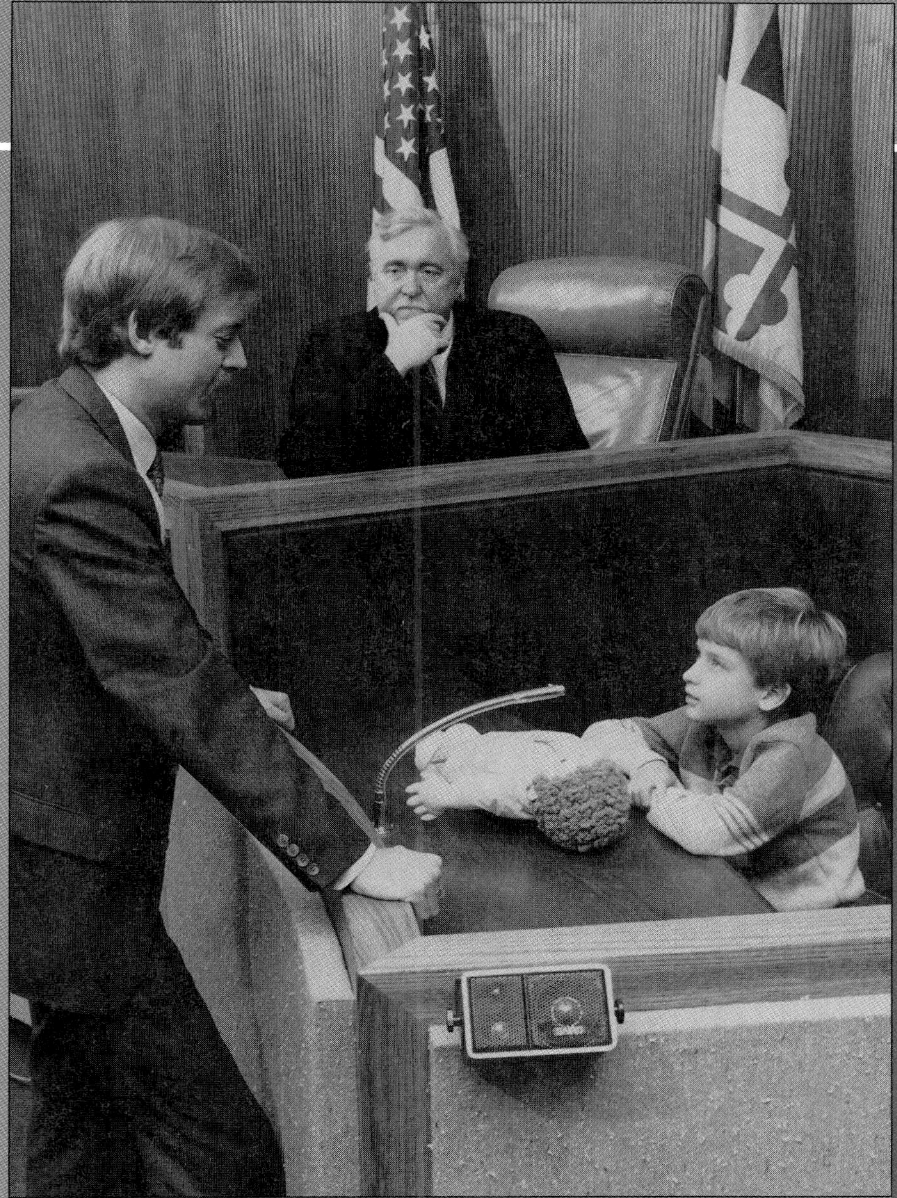

This chapter analyzes criminal court systems. A general overview is followed by more specific discussions of the roles of the prosecution and the defense in criminal cases. The next step, pretrial processes, leads to the topics of bail and plea bargaining. In the section dealing with the trial of a criminal case, the right to a speedy trial and the role of the judge and jury are presented. The analysis of sentencing focuses on current sentencing issues, the sentencing process, and sentence disparity. Attention is given to the appeals process in criminal courts. The chapter closes with an account of court congestion and its solutions.

KEY TERMS

Appeal
Appellant
Appellee
Bail
Bail bond
Capital punishment
Certiorari
Corporal punishment
Defense attorney
Dual court system
Fine
Good-time credit
Judge
Judicial review
Mediation
Plea bargaining
Presumptive sentencing
Preventive detention
Prosecuting attorney
Public defender
Restitution
Sentence
Sentence disparity
Sentencing
Truth in sentencing
Writ

Courts may be considered the crux of criminal justice systems, for it is within them that pretrial, trial, and posttrial motions, petitions, appeals, and other processes such as plea bargaining and sentencing occur. Some of these processes involve not only the legal profession but the public as well.

The importance of courts was emphasized by U.S. Supreme Court chief justice Earl Warren when he declared in the late 1950s, "The delay and the choking congestion in federal courts . . . have created a crucial problem for constitutional government in the United States . . . [I]t is compromising the quantity and quality of justice available to the individual citizen, and, in so doing, it leaves vulnerable throughout the world the reputation of the United States."[1]

Since the 1950s the situation has deteriorated both in state and federal courts, at trial and appellate levels. Court congestion results in delayed trials. Many accused who are not released before trial endure long jail terms in overcrowded facilities. Because their court-appointed attorneys are so busy with trial cases, defendants may not see them during that period. The accused are left with many questions, no answers, and a long wait, often under inhumane conditions. Those who are incarcerated before trial may face more obstacles in preparation for trial and in the reactions of the juries at trial.

The injustices created by an overworked court, in which most cases must be decided quickly and with little individualized attention, are obvious, as is the lack of preparation time available to overworked prosecutors and defense attorneys. The inefficiency and injustice of crowded court dockets and delayed trials project to the public a tainted image of the entire legal system.

COURT SYSTEMS: AN OVERVIEW

The framers of the Constitution established three branches of government—legislative, executive, and judicial. Despite some overlap, these branches are separate and independent, at least in theory. Courts are part of the judicial branch and are empowered to hear and decide civil and criminal cases. Some courts have the power to determine whether acts of legislatures or of Congress fall within constitutional provisions. This power of **judicial review** represents the courts' greatest authority. The highest court of each state determines the constitutionality of that state's laws according to its own constitution, while the U.S. Supreme Court decides whether statutes or court decisions violate the U.S. Constitution or federal statutes.

Judicial review A court's power to determine whether legislative and executive acts and the decisions of lower courts infringe on the rights guaranteed by state constitutions or the U.S. Constitution.

An understanding of some legal terms and concepts is necessary for an analysis of how courts function. One of the most important terms is *jurisdiction,* which refers to the power of the court to hear and decide a case (see Chapter 11). If a court does not have jurisdiction over the subject matter or of the parties who are involved in the action, it may not hear the case. The jurisdiction of some courts is limited by subject matter. For example, some courts may hear only domestic dispute cases, such as divorce, custody, or adoption. Others may hear only civil or criminal cases; those that hear criminal cases may be limited to misdemeanors or felonies.

Jurisdiction may be original, concurrent, exclusive, or appellate. *Original jurisdiction* refers to the court that has the power to hear the case first, that is, the court that may try the facts of the case. If more than one court has jurisdiction, the courts have *concurrent jurisdiction.* When only one court can hear a particular case, that court has *exclusive jurisdiction.* Most decisions of lower courts may be appealed; the courts that have the power to hear and decide those appeals have *appellate jurisdiction.*

Because it is thought that the law needs stability, most courts follow a rule of *stare decisis,* which means to abide by or adhere to cases already decided. The law is flexible, too, and courts may overrule (specifically or by implication) their previous decisions. It is important to distinguish between the rule of the court and the dicta of the judge or justices. At times justices or judges expound on issues that are not part of the court's ruling. Even if these comments represent the opinion of a majority of the court, they must be recognized as *dicta* and not confused with the *holding* or *rule of law* of the case. For this reason, it is necessary to read cases carefully.

Legal reasoning involves a case-by-case analysis. A decided case is read and the facts of a pending case are applied to that one. It is argued that the facts are similar enough that the holding of the decided case should apply or dissimilar enough so that it should not apply. Since the facts differ from case to case, legal reasoning becomes a crucial part of the legal process.

In announcing decisions, usually U.S. appellate courts give written opinions, which may be accompanied by *dissenting opinions* provided by the judges or justices who did not vote with the majority. Judges and justices who concur in the court's opinion may wish to make some additional comments. If so, they write *concurring opinions.* Some opinions are written by justices who concur with part of the court's decision and dissent from the remainder.

In the United States, court decisions are recorded in official reporters. Decisions of the Supreme Court are recorded officially in the *U.S. Reports* and are cited as follows: *Gideon* v. *Wainwright,* 372 U.S. 335 (1963). Prior to being printed in the *U.S. Reports,* Supreme Court cases may be found in other sources, such as *U.S. Law Week* (*USLW*) and the *Supreme Court Reporter* (*S.Ct.*). The cases may be obtained through computer services shortly after the written opinion is released. As soon as a decision is announced, it becomes binding law unless otherwise noted by the court deciding the case. U.S. Supreme Court decisions are binding on all federal courts and on state courts where applicable—that is, where federal statutory or constitutional rights are involved. For more information on how to read a court citation, see Appendix B.

Dual Court Systems

Dual court system The separate judicial structure of various levels of courts within each state in addition to the national structure of federal courts. The origin of the laws violated dictates which court—state or federal—is an appropriate forum for the case. Most state systems consist of lower and higher trial courts, appellate courts, and a state supreme court that governs the interpretation of laws within a state. The federal system includes district trial courts, circuit appellate courts, and the U.S. Supreme Court. Trial courts hear factual evidence, and the issues are decided by a judge or a jury. Appellate court judges review the decisions of lower courts.

The United States has a **dual court system,** consisting of state and federal courts. State crimes are prosecuted in state courts and federal crimes in federal courts. Criminal court systems differ from state to state, but all states have trial courts and appellate courts. In some states, trial courts may hear the serious cases (felonies) as well as the less serious ones (misdemeanors). In other jurisdictions the level is divided, one level of courts hearing felony cases and the other hearing misdemeanors. All states have appellate courts, and some states have an intermediate level of appellate courts. Others have only one court of appeals, usually called the *state supreme court.*

The federal court system has three levels, excluding special courts such as the U.S. Court of Military Appeals. The *district courts* are the trial courts. Cases may be appealed from those courts to the *circuit courts of appeal,* which are called the U.S. courts of appeal. The highest federal court is the *U.S. Supreme Court,* basically an appellate court, although it has original jurisdiction in a few cases. The lower federal courts and the state courts are separate systems; a state court is not bound by the decision of a lower federal court in its district. Cases may be appealed to the U.S. Supreme Court from a state court only if a federal statutory or constitutional right is involved.

Trial and Appellate Courts

Trial and appellate courts should be distinguished. Trial courts hear the factual evidence of a case and decide the issues of fact. These decisions may be made by a jury or by a judge if the case is tried without a jury. When a trial court has ruled

In a case tried before a jury, one responsibility of the jury foreperson is to present the verdict to the court. In some courts, as here, the foreperson reads the verdict aloud in court after the judge has examined the statement. (Jim Pickerell/Stock Boston)

Appeal A step in a judicial proceeding, petitioning a higher court to review a lower court's decision.

Appellant The losing party in a lower court who appeals to a higher court for review of the decision.

Appellee The winning party in a lower court who argues on appeal that the lower court's decision should not be reversed.

against a defendant, he or she may have a right of **appeal** both in the state and in the federal court system, although the defendant does not (except in a few specific types of cases) have the right to appeal to the highest court. Appellate courts hear and decide only a small percentage of the cases appealed.

Appellate courts do not try the facts, such as the defendant's guilt or innocence. In essence, they try the lower courts. The **appellant**—the defendant who was convicted at trial and is appealing that conviction—alleges errors in the trial court proceeding (for example, hearsay evidence admitted, illegal confession admitted, minorities groups excluded from the jury) and asks for a new trial or an acquittal. The **appellee**—the prosecution at trial—argues that either errors did not exist or, if they did, they were not reversible errors, that is, they did not prejudice the court against the appellant and therefore the conviction should stand.

The appellate court may affirm or reverse the lower court's decision. Usually when a decision is reversed, the case is sent back for another trial; that is, the case is *reversed and remanded.* This does not necessarily mean that the defendant is free; in fact, in most criminal cases that are reversed and remanded, the defendant is retried and convicted. A reversal and remand does not violate the Fifth Amendment prohibition against being tried twice for the same offense (see Appendix A). But if the defendant is found not guilty at trial, he or she may not be retried for that offense, although prosecutors might appeal the case on a point of law to get a ruling that may be of benefit in future trials.

THE ROLE OF LAWYERS IN CRIMINAL COURT SYSTEMS

In criminal cases lawyers act as defense or prosecuting attorneys, and each role is very important. They have an ethical obligation to abide by the rules of the courts in which they practice as well as by the rules of the legal profession, state and federal procedures and laws, and constitutional mandates.

Prosecution

Prosecuting attorney A government official whose duty is to initiate and maintain criminal proceedings on behalf of the government against persons accused of committing crimes.

One important role of attorneys in criminal cases is that of the prosecution. The **prosecuting attorney** presents the case for the state or federal government (federal prosecutors are called U.S. attorneys) and is responsible for securing and organizing the evidence against the defendant and for arguing cases that go to trial. Prosecutors have wide discretion. In most cases, they have the power to decide whether or not to prosecute; their decisions are virtually unchecked. Those who decide to proceed with a case over which they have the power to make this decision must return an *information*, an official document that initiates prosecution.

The Fifth Amendment (see Appendix A) requires a grand jury *indictment* in some cases. A grand jury, composed of private citizens, hears evidence presented by the prosecution. If the grand jury believes there is sufficient evidence that the accused committed the crime or crimes in question, it returns an indictment, which begins the official prosecution of the case. In many cases, the prosecutor has considerable control over the grand jury.

Prosecutors have wide discretion in determining which charges to bring or whether to present the case to the grand jury. For example, a person suspected of first-degree murder in a state that has the death penalty could be charged with second-degree murder, which does not carry the death penalty. In some states that defendant could be charged with first-degree murder but not capital murder; or he or she could be charged with first-degree murder, but after conviction and at the sentencing hearing, the prosecutor might not ask for the death penalty. It is also possible that the prosecutor could charge the suspect with manslaughter, depending on the circumstances of the killing.

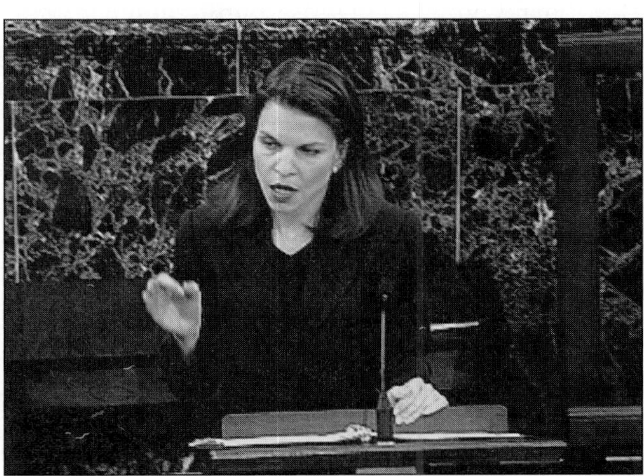

Nicole Seligman, a highly respected Washington, D.C., attorney, was one of President Bill Clinton's attorneys during his trial before the U.S. Senate. (AP Photo/APTN)

Prosecutors may also drop charges after they have been filed. This decision may but does not always require the judge's permission. Once a defendant has been convicted, the prosecutor may be influential in the sentencing process. Prosecutors may differ widely in their decisions.

Prosecutorial discretion is necessary in criminal justice systems. No system can state in advance all cases that should be prosecuted. Decisions must be made in light of the offense, the offender, and the resources of the system. On the one hand, it would be a foolish waste of resources for a prosecutor to insist on taking to trial a case in which the evidence is so weak that there is no chance of a conviction. On the other hand, it would be an abuse of discretion to dismiss the case because the defendant is from a particular race, religion, or gender, or because of other extralegal reasons.

The American Bar Association's *Standards for Criminal Justice* specify that it is the duty of the prosecutor to "seek justice, not merely to convict."[2] Consequently, the prosecutor is not free to use any means available to convict a defendant.

Defense

Defense attorney The attorney who represents the accused in criminal proceedings and whose main function is to protect that individual's constitutional rights.

The Sixth Amendment (see Appendix A) provides that persons accused of committing a crime have a right to counsel. The attorney representing the defendant in a criminal trial is the **defense attorney.** The function of a defense attorney is to protect the legal rights of the accused.[3] The defendant in U.S. criminal justice systems is entitled to a fair trial in which the state must prove guilt beyond a reasonable doubt and in accordance with proper procedures. It is not the function of the defense attorney to prove the defendant's innocence. Attorneys are as bound by the ethics of their profession in the defense of persons they think committed the acts charged as in the defense of those they believe to be innocent. The function of defense attorneys is to give their clients the best advice they can within the law and ethics of the legal profession. Once this function is recognized, the defense of a person who may have committed the criminal act in question is understandable.

This discussion is not meant to suggest that defense attorneys do not abuse the adversary system; some do. Unfortunately, abuses of the system may receive a lot of publicity even though they may be isolated instances that do not reflect on the entire defense bar. But even when abuse occurs, it must be distinguished from the *philosophy* of the system. That philosophy is one of the strongest points of U.S. criminal justice systems—that all persons are presumed innocent until proven guilty and that they may be punished only after the government proves guilt beyond a reasonable doubt. Furthermore, the government must prove its case without violating the accused's constitutional rights.

The right to counsel has been interpreted to include counsel appointed at the expense of the government if the defendant does not have the financial means to retain a private attorney. When counsel is provided at government expense, one of three systems may be used. First, attorneys may be *assigned* to particular indigent defendants. Usually, assignments are made by judges from lists of attorneys who have agreed to serve in this capacity. Second, some jurisdictions use a *contract* system, in which a bar association, private law firm, or individual attorney contracts with the government to provide legal assistance for indigent defendants. Third, many jurisdictions use **public defender** systems, which provide counsel for indigent defendants.

Public defender An attorney whose function is to represent defendants who cannot afford to retain private counsel.

All methods of providing attorneys for indigents have been criticized, although there is some evidence that defense attorneys for indigent defendants perform their services very well. A study conducted by the National Center for State Courts reports that "attorneys who represent indigent defendants perform as well as, and by some measures better than, privately retained defense lawyers."[4] However, a court-appointed attorney with a large caseload, low compensation, low status, and inadequate resources cannot be expected to provide the best legal defense. The burden of improving this situation rests in two places. First, the legal profession should be challenged to discover ways to attract qualified attorneys into criminal defense work; these may include greater prestige and rewards for such work and requiring better law school preparation for criminal cases. Second, society must provide the money and resources necessary to make criminal justice systems work as conceptualized.

PRETRIAL PROCESSES

Chapter 11 briefly covered the main stages that occur from the investigation of a crime through the pretrial, trial, and sentencing phases. The body of law and sociological literature on these processes is extensive. This section focuses on two of the most controversial processes: pretrial release and plea bargaining.

Pretrial Release

One of the most critical periods of criminal justice proceedings is the time between arraignment and trial. The purpose of pretrial release is to enable the defendant to prepare for trial while avoiding the harmful effects of jail deten-

Bail The release of a defendant from custody pending a legal proceeding, such as a trial. *See also* **bail bond.**

Bail bond A legal document stating the terms under which a defendant is granted release from jail prior to a legal proceeding, such as a trial. The bail bond may or may not be secured with money or property pledged by the defendant or others. Technically, if the defendant does not appear at the time and place designated in the document, the court may require the forfeiture of any money or property used to secure the bail bond.

tion. The enormous problems faced by defendants who are incarcerated extend beyond the most obvious one, deprivation of liberty. Pretrial detainees may lose their jobs and acquire the stigma attached to a jail term. They face days of loneliness and idleness, with limited opportunities to talk and visit with family and friends. Often they are confined along with those who have been convicted of crimes and are serving jail terms. These conditions exist even though pretrial detainees are *legally innocent of a crime.*

The Bail System

Courts use several methods for releasing defendants prior to trial, but the most controversial is the bail system. The **bail** system began in England to ensure the presence of defendants at trials, which were held infrequently because judges traveled from one jurisdiction to another. Facilities for detaining defendants before trial were not only terrible but also expensive to maintain. Sheriffs preferred to have someone else take care of defendants who were awaiting trial and so relinquished them to other people, usually friends or relatives. These people served as *sureties.* If the defendants did not appear for trial after they had been placed on bail, the surety was tried. The party furnishing bail was reminded that he or she had the powers of a jailer and was expected to produce the accused for trial. This policy of private sureties was followed in America but was replaced subsequently by a system of posting **bail bond.** There are several types of bail bond, as Exhibit 13.1 notes.

EXHIBIT 13.1
Types of Pretrial Release

Both financial bonds and alternative release options are used today.

FINANCIAL BOND

Fully secured bail The defendant posts the full amount of bail with the court.

Privately secured bail A bondsman signs a promissory note to the court for the bail amount and charges the defendant a fee for the service (usually 10 percent of the bail amount). If the defendant fails to appear, the bondsman must pay the court the full amount. Frequently, the bondsman requires the defendant to post collateral in addition to the fee.

Deposit bail The courts allow the defendant to deposit a percentage (usually 10 percent) of the full bail with the court. The full amount of the bail is required if the defendant fails to appear. The percentage bail is returned after disposition of the case, but the court often retains 1 percent for administrative costs.

Unsecured bail The defendant pays no money to the court but is liable for the full amount of bail should he or she fail to appear.

ALTERNATIVE RELEASE OPTIONS

Release on recognizance (ROR) The court releases the defendant on the promise that he or she will appear in court as required.

Conditional release The court releases the defendant subject to his or her following specific conditions set by the court, such as attendance at drug treatment therapy or staying away from the complaining witness.

Third party custody The defendant is released into the custody of an individual or agency that promises to assure his or her appearance in court. No monetary transactions are involved in this type of release.

Citation release Arrestees are released pending their first court appearance on a written order issued by law enforcement personnel.

Source: Bureau of Justice Statistics, *Report to the Nation on Crime and Justice: The Data,* 2d ed. (Washington, DC: U.S. Department of Justice, 1988), p. 76.

The bail system in the United States is used to ensure the defendant's presence at trial. Early court cases made it clear that bail was not to be used to punish defendants or to protect society. Furthermore, the Supreme Court has ruled that "bail set at a figure higher than the amount reasonably calculated to [ensure that the defendant will stand trial] is 'excessive' under the Eighth Amendment."[5]

According to federal rules and some state statutes, bail may be denied in capital cases and in noncapital cases in which the defendant has a history of fleeing to avoid prosecution. The reason in both cases is consistent with the original purpose of bail—to ensure the presence of the accused at trial. Until recently, this was the *only* legitimate purpose of bail. In 1970, with the passage of the District of Columbia Court Reform and Criminal Procedure Act, **preventive detention** was recognized as a legitimate purpose of bail in that jurisdiction. This statute permits judges to deny bail to defendants charged with dangerous crimes if the government has clear evidence, including consideration of the accused's past and present pattern of behavior, that release would endanger public safety.[6] Some states have similar provisions.

Preventive detention The practice of holding the accused in jail before trial to ensure that he or she does not commit further crimes and is present at trial.

In 1984 Congress passed a comprehensive reform of the federal criminal code, including a provision for preventive detention. Detention is authorized if no conditions of release will reasonably ensure "the appearance of the person as required and the safety of any other person and the community." The act provides that those arrested for drug offenses are presumed dangerous or likely to flee; thus, they may be detained pending trial unless they can prove that it would be reasonably safe for them to be released. The constitutionality of this provision has been challenged in several federal courts, with some upholding its constitutionality and others declaring it unconstitutional. The U.S. Supreme Court ruled in favor of the provision in *United States* v. *Salerno,* decided in 1987.[7]

Like many aspects of criminal justice systems, the use of bail has been connected with extralegal variables. For example, numerous studies note that unemployed persons are more likely than employed persons to be incarcerated after conviction or detained before trial. It is argued that as unemployment increases and the unemployed are perceived as threats by the middle and upper classes, judges will be more punitive, imposing longer sentences or detaining more persons. That argument, however, is not supported by more recent evidence.[8] Further research is needed on the impact that factors such as race, gender, employment status, and ethnicity may have on bail decisions.

An additional problem with bail is that many defendants cannot pay the full amount of bail, thus making it more available to the rich than to the poor. One system designed to remedy this problem is the professional bail bondsman/woman system. In return for a fee, the bail bondsman/woman posts bond for the accused defendant. Theoretically, if the defendant does not appear for trial, the bondsman/woman is required to forfeit the money. In practice, bond forfeitures are rarely enforced. Furthermore, some bondsmen/women do not have the necessary money to produce in cases of forfeiture. To avoid this situation, some jurisdictions require them to prove their ability to pay in case of forfeiture.

The bond system has been criticized, and some states have placed legislative restrictions on the system or eliminated it entirely.

Plea Bargaining

Plea bargaining Negotiations between the prosecution and the defense concerning the nature and number of charges against the defendant, the plea the defendant might enter, punishment that might be recommended, or other issues associated with the trial. The prosecution may agree to some concessions in exchange for a plea or for the defendant's cooperation in providing evidence against other suspects.

Another controversial pretrial process is **plea bargaining,** a negotiation between the prosecution and the defense in which the defense agrees to plead guilty to the current charge(s) or to a lesser charge(s) in exchange for the prosecutor's promise to recommend a light sentence, drop other charges, or make some other concession. The consequences of refusing a plea bargain may be severe and are illustrated by the two juvenile cases discussed in Exhibit 13.2

EXHIBIT 13.2

Plea Bargaining, Adult Courts, and Juveniles

Two 2001 Florida cases involving juveniles illustrate the harshness that can result when plea bargains are rejected. The cases are used here to illustrate that point, but they are also included to demonstrate the current approach toward treating juveniles as adults when they commit murder. The first case also illustrates the trend toward mandatory sentencing.

In January 2001 Lionel Tate, age 14, was sentenced to life in prison without parole after he was found guilty of first-degree murder in the death of a 6-year-old girl with whom he claimed he was play wrestling. Two aspects of Florida law are crucial to this case. First, in cases involving juveniles accused of committing murder, prosecutors have the discretion to try those young persons in adult criminal courts. Second, the law requires a mandatory life-without-parole prison term for defendants convicted of first-degree murder. Thus, once the jury found Tate guilty, the court had to impose life without parole.

The plea bargain in Tate's case is dramatic, for the prosecution had offered Tate a much shorter sentence in exchange for a guilty plea: 3 years of incarceration in a juvenile facility, 1 year of house arrest, and 10 years of probation. Tate's mother, a law enforcement officer, rejected that plea. After he was sentenced, Tate appealed to Governor Jeb Bush for a waiver of the two-year wait to apply for clemency, but the governor denied the request. Famed defense attorney Johnnie Cochran, one of the attorneys who represented O. J. Simpson in his successful defense when he was tried for the murders of his ex-wife Nicole Brown and her friend, Ron Goldman, is heading the appeals case for Tate.

In the second Florida case, 14-year-old Nathaniel Brazill was sentenced to 28 years in prison after he was found guilty of second-degree murder in the shooting death of his favorite teacher. The judge ordered Brazill, who was 13 when he committed the crime, to take an anger management course and to spend two years in house arrest and five years on probation after he finishes his prison term. Brazill, who had been suspended from school earlier on the day of the murder (for throwing water balloons), shot his teacher, Barry Grunow, between the eyes when Grunow refused to let him talk to two girls in the class. Brazill said he intended to scare but not kill his teacher. Brazill's family had rejected a plea bargain of 25 years, the minimum to which he could have been sentenced.

Scholars question the wisdom of trying such young persons in adult criminal courts. Even some who approve of that procedure question permitting prosecutors the discretion to move the cases from juvenile to criminal courts. A recent editorial in the *New York Times* expresses the issue as follows: "Florida, like many other states, has wrongly granted prosecutors too much discretion in making that call." The editorial, in questioning both cases, concludes: "To send 14-year-olds directly to adult prisons for a quarter-century is to give up on them. It may even ensure that they become lifetime criminals."[1]

[1]"Little Adult Criminals," *New York Times* (23 May 2001), p. 26. The remainder of the information was summarized from various media sources.

Not all guilty pleas are the result of plea bargaining. In fact, most convictions are the result of guilty pleas, some of which are based on the defense's decision that pleading guilty is the best choice. Likewise, prosecutorial decisions to reduce or drop charges may be the result of prosecutorial discretion unrelated to a bargain with the defense.

Plea bargaining received the recognition of the Supreme Court in 1971 when it was approved as a means of managing overloaded criminal dockets. The Court declared plea bargaining to be "an essential component" of the criminal process, which "properly administered . . . is to be encouraged."[9] Supporters of plea bargaining argue that the process is necessary because of the tremendous number of criminal cases. Further, plea bargaining saves the state money and time. Not all cases need to go to trial; defendants and society are better served by settling some cases out of court.

Opponents of plea bargaining argue that not all judges and prosecutors honor the deals made between the prosecution and the defense and that innocent defendants are encouraged to plead guilty. Critics express concern that some deals are too good for defendants, that those charged with serious offenses are permitted to plead guilty to less serious offenses, and that some defendants charged with violent offenses get off too lightly.

Another problem with plea bargaining is that defendants may not have access to the probation officer's presentencing report (PSR) prior to entering their plea. For example, in the federal system the PSR may include information that increases the sentencing guideline range (established by legislation and discussed later in this chapter) but that was unknown to the defense or prosecution prior to plea bargaining and the entering of a plea. This additional information may include aggravating or mitigating circumstances, which would permit the imposition of a sentence that deviates from the guideline range and thus might affect plea bargaining. In this way, many federal defendants may be entering pleas without full knowledge of the factors that may be used by judges in determining sentences under the federal guidelines. Approximately 90 percent of all federal defendants enter a plea, and probably most of those involve plea bargaining.

The Supreme Court has placed restrictions on plea bargaining. Specifically, it has recognized the importance of counsel at the plea bargaining stage as well as the need for a public record indicating that the defendant entered the guilty plea knowingly and voluntarily and that the promises made by the prosecuting attorney at the plea bargaining stage were kept. But the Court has upheld the prosecutor's right to threaten to secure a grand jury indictment against the defendant on a more serious charge if the defendant does not plead guilty to the existing charge.

In *Bordenkircher* v. *Hayes*, the defendant was under indictment for passing a hot check for $88.30. The sentence that could have been imposed upon conviction of that offense was 2 to 10 years. The prosecutor told the defendant that he would recommend a five-year sentence if the defendant would plead guilty. If the defendant refused to do so, the prosecutor said he would seek an indictment under the state's Habitual Criminal Act, which provided that upon conviction of a third felony a defendant would receive a mandatory life sentence. The defendant refused to accept the offer, went to trial, and was convicted. In a separate proceeding it was found that he had been convicted of two previous felonies. He was sentenced to life in prison as required by the Habitual Criminal Act. In a 5-to-4 decision, the Court emphasized that although the state may not retaliate against a defendant who chooses to exercise a legal right, "in the 'give-and-take' of plea bargaining, there is no such element of punishment or retaliation so long as the accused is free to accept or reject the prosecution's offer."[10]

To constitute a valid plea bargain, the defendant's plea must be knowledgeable and voluntary. In determining whether a plea is voluntary, the courts consider whether the defendant was represented by counsel; if so, the plea is less likely to be considered involuntary. Furthermore, plea bargains leading to a guilty plea must not be induced by threats or promises to discontinue improper harassment, misrepresentation, unfulfilled promises, or promises that have no relation to proper prosecutorial business, such as a bribe.[11]

An example of an improper plea bargain occurred in an Arizona case. The appellate court held that a guilty plea based on a prosecutor's promise not to oppose the defendant's efforts to obtain conjugal visits with his wife during his incarceration was invalid. Stating that conjugal access is an irrational basis for entering a guilty plea, the court ruled that including this understanding within the plea bargain suggests psychological pressure that invalidates the voluntariness of the defendant's plea.[12]

A 1995 U.S. Supreme Court decision, *United States* v. *Mezzanatto,* might weaken the plea bargaining process. The case involves the federal procedural rule that permits plea bargaining. That rule specifies that statements made by the defendant in the course of a plea bargain may not be used against that defendant at trial if the plea negotiations fail. The rule does not state whether the defendant may waive that provision.[13] In *Mezzanatto* the defendant agreed to the prosecutor's demand that any statement made during plea negotiations could be used against him if the case went to trial. During the negotiations the defendant admitted some involvement in the alleged crime, but his evasiveness led the prosecution to break off negotiations. When the defendant was cross-examined during trial, some of his statements were inconsistent with those he made during plea bargaining. The evidence of those prior inconsistent statements was admitted at trial, and the defendant was convicted. The court of appeals reversed. The Supreme Court agreed to decide the case and settle a split among the federal appeals courts that had ruled on similar cases. The Court reversed, holding that the exclusionary provision of the federal rule could be waived by the defendant.[14]

States are free to abolish plea bargaining, and some have done so, but where plea bargaining is retained its goals must be fairness, less delay, less disparity among sentences, and sentences closer to those that would result from trial. To achieve these goals, the parties to the negotiation must have a reasonable perception of the conviction and sentencing probabilities. The defendant should not be forced to accept a higher bargained conviction or sentence because he or she is in jail, is unable to afford an attorney, has not seen the presentence report, or is represented by a public defender who does not have the time or resources to go to trial. Nor should prosecutors be forced to offer bargains with reduced charges or low sentences because of limited resources.

THE TRIAL OF A CRIMINAL CASE

The trial of a criminal case involves numerous, complicated legal procedures. After a quick overview of the trial process, this section focuses on two major issues in criminal cases: the right to a speedy trial and the roles of the judge and jury.

Although most defendants enter a plea and do not proceed to trail, the trial is a crucial element of criminal justice systems. In recent years the trial has become the focus of television, with some trials televised in their entirety, although some judges do not permit television cameras in the courtroom.

Even when an entire trial is presented to the public, there are proceedings that take place elsewhere, such as in the judge's chambers, that are crucial to the trial proceedings. Judges meet frequently with the prosecution and defense attorneys to work out the details of how the trial will progress. These parties may discuss the need to streamline the presentation of evidence—for example, by reducing the number of witnesses. They may discuss the failure of one party to convey informational documents to the other side, as ordered by the judge in the discovery process. Attorneys may be penalized or the trial may be delayed if these procedures are not followed properly. For example, in 2001 when it was discovered that the FBI had failed to release thousands of documents to the defense in the trial of Timothy McVeigh for the 1995 bombing of the federal building in Oklahoma City, McVeigh's execution was postponed.

Throughout the trial attorneys may file motions with the court, and those motions may affect the remainder of the trial. For example, a successful motion to exclude specific evidence that the opposing side planned to introduce may make it necessary for that side to change its strategy. Also throughout the trial

The top prosecutor in the United States is the U.S. attorney general, who heads the Department of Justice. The current attorney general, John Ashcroft, testifies on 6 December 2001 before the US Senate Judiciary Committee oversight hearing focusing on how to preserve freedoms while defending against terrorism. (©Ron Sachs/Corbis Sygma)

the plea bargaining process may continue and at any time the defendant may, if he or she chooses, be permitted to enter a plea and thus avoid or halt the trial.

At some point, however, the trial will begin. Normally this occurs after all parties are assembled in the courtroom and the bailiff enters to announce that the trial is beginning. All parties will be asked to rise before the judge enters the courtroom. If there are no motions to be heard after the courtroom is called to order for the trial, the judge may proceed with jury selection. In some complicated cases this might take days, weeks, or even months.

Once the jurors are selected and sworn, opening statements may be made, first by the prosecution and then by the defense. During the opening statements the respective sides may give a brief glimpse of what they hope to accomplish during the presentation of evidence. When it is time for that stage, the prosecution presents its evidence first. After each witness finishes testifying, the defense may ask questions in a process called *cross-examination,* after which the prosecution may reexamine its witnesses. After all of the prosecution witnesses are presented and the prosecution rests its case, the defense may present its case.

The defense is not required to present a case. In some cases it will not do so—in effect, the defense rests after the prosecution has presented its case. Why would the defense do this? The defense attorney may feel that the state's evidence is not strong enough to prove the defendant guilty beyond a reasonable doubt and, furthermore, that the defense might weaken its position by putting on its witnesses, especially the defendant. Defendants never have to testify, and many do not. Even an innocent defendant may hurt the defense by testifying.

After all of the evidence is presented, each side may—but is not required to—offer a closing statement. Again, motions might be made. For example, the defense might make a motion for the judge to direct the jury to acquit the defendant, based on the lack of credible evidence to convict. The judge may, but rarely does, grant this motion.

After the closing arguments and processing of any motions, the judge will instruct the jury regarding the law in the case. Usually both the defense and the prosecution will submit information to the judge for that charge; the judge may or may not adopt their language. After the charge is given to the jury, the jurors retire to the jury room and deliberate upon the evidence that has been presented at the trial. They may be sequestered from then until they reach a verdict (in rare cases they may be sequestered as soon as they are sworn in), or they may be permitted to go home at night with instructions not to discuss the case with anyone or to read the paper or watch media information concerning the case.

If the jury cannot reach a verdict after a reasonable time, the judge will declare a mistrial. If the jury does reach a verdict, it will be read in open court after all parties have been notified and given a reasonable time to assemble. After the verdict the jurors may be dismissed—or, in some jurisdictions, they will be told to return at a specified time to hear evidence concerning the sentence if the defendant has been convicted. In other jurisdictions a new jury may be selected for the sentencing hearing or the hearing will be in front of a judge only.

After the defendant is sentenced, he or she may have legal grounds for an appeal. Those who appeal may or may not be released pending the outcome of that appeal. If they are held in custody, they may receive credit for that time served. Those who are sentenced to prison normally will be taken to a facility for classification prior to assignment to a state or federal prison.

Although all of the steps in a criminal trial are important, we have selected two areas of particular significance for further discussion.

The Right to a Speedy Trial

The Sixth Amendment (see Appendix A) provides for the right to a speedy trial. This right does not preclude the defense or the prosecution from asking for and being granted continuances when additional time is needed to prepare. It does mean that the prosecution and defense may not delay unreasonably, but this provision has been challenged many times. Most of the statutes specify some circumstances under which trials may be delayed legitimately, but those provisions are the subject of extensive litigation. An example is the federal provision that delays may occur when they are necessary to "serve the ends of justice."

What constitutes an unreasonable delay must be decided on a case-by-case basis. One decision held that even a 10-year delay between indictment and trial did not deny a defendant her right to a speedy trial. The defendant was charged with conspiracy to import cocaine. To avoid apprehension and prosecution, she fled the jurisdiction prior to the indictment. The government had made diligent efforts to locate her for trial but was unsuccessful for 10 years.[15]

In contrast, in 1992 the U.S. Supreme Court held that a defendant who was indicted in 1980 but not arrested until 1988 had been denied his right to a speedy trial. The defendant in *Doggett* v. *United States* left the country in 1980 and returned in 1982. The government thought he was still out of the country and made little effort to find him. Justice David Souter wrote the opinion for a divided Court, stating that such delays compromise the reliability of a trial in ways that cannot be proved and thus proof is not required. A delay of this magnitude, which was the result of "inexcusable oversights" on the government's part, "far exceeds the threshold needed to state a speedy trial claim."[16]

The trial judge is responsible for monitoring all pretrial procedures and deciding when delays are reasonable and when they are not.

The Trial Decision: Judge or Jury

Although most cases do not go to trial, trials are a crucial part of criminal justice systems, and both judges and juries play a significant role in trials. In a criminal trial the **judge** is the referee. Theoretically, judges are neither for nor against a particular position or issue but are committed to the fair implementation of the rules of evidence and law. Judges must present the case to the jury with a charge, in which they explain the law applicable to the case and give the jury instructions that it must follow in arriving at a verdict. Judges may have significant influence over the jury through their attitudes, their rulings, and their charges. They have an impact on those who testify and on those who are parties to the trial. Trial judges should be considerate and should uphold the highest standards of justice in their courtrooms. The position of the trial judge is a powerful one, for although judges may be overruled, most cases are not appealed.

Judge A judicial officer, elected or appointed to preside over a court of law. Judges are to be the neutral and final arbiters of law and have primary responsibility for all court activities, ranging from monitoring the attorneys and instructing the jury to deciding cases and sentencing those found guilty.

Although some criminal cases are tried before a judge only, most involve juries. Some authorities believe that the jury system is among the great achievements of English and American jurisprudence, whereas others criticize

After a jury convicted British nanny Louise Woodward of second-degree murder, Judge Hiller Zobel overturned that decision, ruling that the evidence supported no more than a manslaughter conviction, which he imposed. Judge Zobel sentenced Woodward to time served and released her from prison. (Getty Images)

it. Sociologists have studied the jury system to gather data on some of the issues, and these studies have become widely recognized in the literature.

Although critics believe that the jury system is an ineffective method for determining facts (the results of empirical research are not clear), there is some support for the system's efficiency and accuracy.[17] The Supreme Court has held that juries understand the evidence presented at trials, but some critics question that conclusion.[18]

A 1995 analysis of the responses of more than 500 jurors in death penalty cases led to the conclusion that "jurors are not playing by the rules." The Capital Jury Project studied how jurors in death penalty cases understand and apply the law, and whether they make arbitrary decisions. The findings disclosed that about half (50.7 percent) of jurors made their determinations about sentencing before they had heard the sentencing evidence. In capital cases in jurisdictions where juries are involved in sentencing as well as in determining the guilt or innocence of the defendant, jurors are supposed to determine the latter first. The court holds a separate sentencing hearing, which can involve evidence that may not be admitted at trial; thus, the defendant does not have the benefit of this evidence if jurors have already made up their minds about sentencing. Considerations of possible punishment should not influence the issue of whether the defendant is guilty.[19]

The assessment of the American jury system is important. Many legal scholars believe it represents the best way to ascertain the truth as well as to administer justice. But one study reports that the public is not so sure. When asked if they thought they could get a fair trial if charged with a crime they did *not* commit, only 51.6 percent of respondents were somewhat confident and only 17.7 percent were very confident that they could.[20]

SENTENCING

Sentencing The postconviction stage in the criminal justice system that includes all those decisions the court makes with regard to the official handling of a person who pleads guilty or is convicted of a crime.

Sentence The decision of the judge or jury, according to statutory law, fixing the punishment for an offender after conviction.

Corporal punishment Infliction of penalties on the physical body.

One of the most important stages in criminal justice systems is **sentencing.** Punishment philosophies, upon which a **sentence** may be based, are discussed in Chapter 3. For offenders, sentencing determines the punishments that are imposed and thus how they will spend the coming months or years. For some, sentencing determines whether they will live or die. For society, the sentencing decision necessitates not only action in particular cases but also recognition of the philosophies that underlie the punishment concept.

Historically, many types of sentences have been imposed, ranging from **corporal punishment** (much of it so painful and brutal that it resulted in death) to probation (the sentence used most frequently in the United States today—see Chapter 15). Offenders may be required to pay a **fine,** or **restitution.** Fines are being assessed more frequently, even in cases of violent crimes. Some offenders are incarcerated in prisons or jails, discussed in Chapter 14.

Current Sentencing Issues

In recent years U.S. criminal justice systems have focused attention on the sentencing of repeat offenders as well as on the increased use of capital punishment.

Fine A type of punishment in which the offender is ordered to pay a sum of money to the state in lieu of or in addition to other forms of punishment.

Restitution A type of punishment in which the offender must reimburse the victim financially or with services. It may be required in lieu of or in addition to a fine or other punishment or as a condition of probation.

Truth in sentencing A concept requiring that actual time served by offenders be closer to the time allocated for the sentence. Many jurisdictions are establishing 80–85 percent as their goal, meaning that offenders may not be released for any reasons until they have served the required percentage of their sentences.

Three Strikes and You're Out

Legislation referred to as *three strikes and you're out* (defined in Chapter 2), available in the federal system as well as in state systems, is illustrated by the California statute, which provides for a mandatory sentence of 25 years to life in prison for conviction of a third felony if prior felonies were for serious or violent crimes. It also provides for tougher sentences for first- and second-time felons and requires an offender to serve 80 percent of a sentence before being released from prison. This mandatory minimum time before release is referred to as **truth in sentencing** and has been adopted in many jurisdictions.[21] Both approaches have been criticized by judges, attorneys, and prison wardens among others, but a 1996 California Supreme Court decision focused on issues surrounding the three-strikes legislation in a dramatic way. Exhibit 13.3 contains details.

Both the truth-in-sentencing and the three-strikes policies illustrate the systems effect that we have spoken about frequently in this text. With inmates serving longer terms under both of these policies, jails and prisons have become overcrowded. For example, according to a 1999 Bureau of Justice Statistics (BJS) report, the average time that violent criminals served in state prisons had increased from 43 to 49 months, with the number of inmates eligible for release falling. In fact, the average number of persons in state prisons increased by 60 percent in the 1990s, although the number of new persons sent to prisons increased by only 19 percent.[22]

Another serious and perhaps unexpected result of the three-strikes legislation is that, apparently because of the seriousness of this approach (long or even life sentences), more defendants are challenging their convictions rather than pleading guilty. In the first few years of the three-strikes legislation in California,

Jerry Dewayne Williams, age 27, shown here in court with his public defender, Arnold Lester, was given a 25-years-to-life sentence after his conviction for stealing pizza from little children. California's three-strikes legislation provides this mandatory sentence upon conviction of a third felony, if the first two were serious. On appeal a judge reduced the first two felonies, thus permitting Williams to be eligible for parole in 2, compared to 23 years. (Tony Barnard/The Los Angeles Times)

EXHIBIT 13.3

Three Strikes and You're Out, But Not If the Judge Disagrees

Three-strikes sentencing legislation took a severe blow from the California Supreme Court in 1996. The court ruled that California judges who believe the imposition of a mandatory sentence of 25 years to life would be too harsh in a particular case are not required to impose that sentence, as discussed later in this exhibit. The California statute provides for the mandatory sentence for persons convicted of a third felony, which may be any felony although the first two must be serious or violent ones. Harsher penalties are mandated for second felony convictions as well.[1]

The California statute has resulted in harsh sentences for offenders convicted of a third felony that is not serious or violent, such as the 25-year sentence for stealing a pizza imposed on Jerry Dewayne Williams, age 27. His prior convictions were for robbery, attempted robbery, drug possession, and unauthorized use of a vehicle. At his three-strikes trial, prosecutors described him as a career criminal who terrorized little kids. "[W]e think our children can sit down in peace in broad daylight, without a 6-foot 4-inch 220-pound ex-con threatening them and taking away food from them."[2]

Williams's sentence and others precipitated protests, but judges who followed the letter of the law had no choice but to impose the harsh penalties. Judges in other cases, however, have challenged the three-strikes mandates. For example, one prosecutor asked for a life sentence for a 43-year-old offender who was found guilty of stealing a $22 Mighty Ducks baseball cap from a shopping mall store. Thomas Kiel Brown was a candidate for the harsh penalty because he had two prior serious felony convictions (for robbery and grand theft). The judge commented, "No judge I know wants to let dangerous criminals loose in the community. But I'm sure the taxpayer doesn't want to spend more than $500,000 to put a petty thief in jail for stealing a cap."[3]

Traditionally, judges have had the power to disregard a prior conviction in making a sentencing decision in a case in which leniency seemed reasonable. Under the California three-strikes law, however, it was presumed that they were not permitted to do so. The California Supreme Court ruled that the state statute did not remove that traditional judicial power, and if it had done so, it would have violated the state constitution. The constitution grants discretion in sentencing to judges, not prosecutors, but the statute provides that only prosecutors have the discretion to disregard a prior conviction. According to a unanimous state supreme court, judges may disregard prior convictions if they believe it is necessary to do so "in the furtherance of justice."

Reaction was immediate and loud. Prosecutors and other supporters of the statute, which was passed in 1994 after the kidnapping and murder of Polly Klaas, criticized the court's decision and lamented the fact that approximately 20,000 offenders might clog the already-crowded courts with sentence appeals. That has not yet occurred (although in February of 1997 a judge reduced some of Jerry Dewayne Williams's prior felonies to misdemeanor convictions, thus making him eligible for release in two rather than 23 years).

Judges praised the California Supreme Court ruling as an appropriate one that restores traditional and necessary judicial discretion, noting that three-fourths of the 18,735 felons sentenced under the

for example, the state experienced a 4 percent increase in trials in nonstrike cases, a 9 percent increase for two-strike cases, and a 41 percent increase in three-strike cases. The increases were not uniform throughout the state, but many judges said that in order to accommodate the increases they had to shift resources from civil to criminal courts.[23]

Three-strikes legislation strains the criminal justice systems and causes disruption for judges, prosecutors, public defenders, and jail officials. It has also been argued that it discriminates against persons because of their race or ethnicity. The author of a study that examined the situation in California three years after the three-strikes legislation took effect said that 43 percent of the defendants sentenced under it were African American although African Americans constituted only 7 percent of the state's population. The author declared, "If one second- and third-strike mandates were sent to prison after convictions for nonviolent felonies.

The California ruling involved a 34-year-old offender, Jesus Romero, whose prior convictions for burglary and attempted burglary were dismissed by the judge faced with imposing a three-strikes sentence following Romero's conviction on cocaine possession. San Diego Superior Court judge William Mudd complained that the legislation "basically castrates a judge" and violates the state constitution by giving all discretion to prosecutors. Rather than sentence Romero to 25 years to life for possession of 13 grams of cocaine, the judge imposed 6 years. Prosecutors appealed and obtained a favorable ruling from the state court of appeal, which held that the judge did not have the power to refuse to impose the mandatory sentence. The state supreme court reversed that ruling.

In 1998 the California Supreme Court attempted to elaborate on the meaning of "in the furtherance of justice" as a means for striking a previous felony to avoid sentencing a defendant under the three-strikes law. It held that a court making the decision must consider

> whether, in light of the nature and circumstances of his present felonies and prior serious and/or violent felony convictions, and the particulars of his background, character, and prospects, the defendant may be deemed outside the scheme's spirit, in whole or in part, and hence should be treated as though he had presently not committed one or more felonies and/or had not previously been convicted of one or more serious and/or violent felonies. If it is striking or vacating an allegation or finding, it must set forth its reasons in an order entered on the minutes, and if it is reviewing the striking or vacating of such allegation or finding, it must pass on the reasons so set forth.[4]

In 1999 the California Supreme Court once again widened the rule regarding three-strikes legislation, expanding the trial judge's power to disregard a defendant's prior felony convictions in sentencing under the statute. The case of *People* v. *Garcia* involved defendant Jerry Garcia, who had five prior serious felonies when he was convicted of two burglaries. The trial judge considered the prior felonies in determining Garcia's sentence for one but not both of the current felonies. He still received a long sentence—31 years—but it would have been even longer had the judge considered the prior felonies in assessing both sentences. The California Supreme Court upheld the judge's decision.[5]

In April 2002 the U.S. Supreme Court agreed to hear two California cases involving the issue of whether a 25-year-to-life sentence upon conviction of a minor property crime under the state's three strike law constitutes cruel and unusual punishment. The decision could result in the reversal of thousands of sentences imposed under the California law and possibly also affect those in other states.[6]

1. See Cal. Penal Code, Title 16, Section 667 (2001).
2. "Theft of Pizza Slice Nets a Twenty-Five-Year Term," *New York Times* (5 March 1995), p. 11.
3. "Judges Hail Change in Their Role," *Los Angeles Times* (21 June 1996), p. 1. The case is People v. Superior Court (Romero), 917 P.2d 628 (Cal. 1996), *review denied sub nom.*, People v. Mosley, 1997 Cal. LEXIS 2873 (Cal. 1997).
4. People v. Williams, 948 P.2d 429 (Ca. 1998), *modified, reh'g. denied*, 17 Cal. 4th 643b (1998).
5. People v. Garcia, 976 P.2d 831 (Ca. 1999).
6. The cases are Lockyer v. Andrade, No. 01-1127 and Ewing v. California, No. 01-6978.

were writing a law to deliberately target blacks, one could scarcely have done it more effectively than 'three strikes.' "[24]

Another problem resulting from three-strikes legislation is the increased shortage of jurors. California already had a shortage, but with the increase in trials due to three-strikes legislation, the problem escalated. Finally, judges and jurors may look for ways to avoid the harsh penalties of the law. Juries can always refuse to convict if they think the mandatory penalty is too severe. Judges have several options, one of which is to reduce the current felony charge to a misdemeanor in some cases.

In conclusion, it could be argued that attempting to deter crime by incarcerating repeat offenders for longer periods of time increases costs and personnel problems in all areas of criminal court systems while offering no evidence

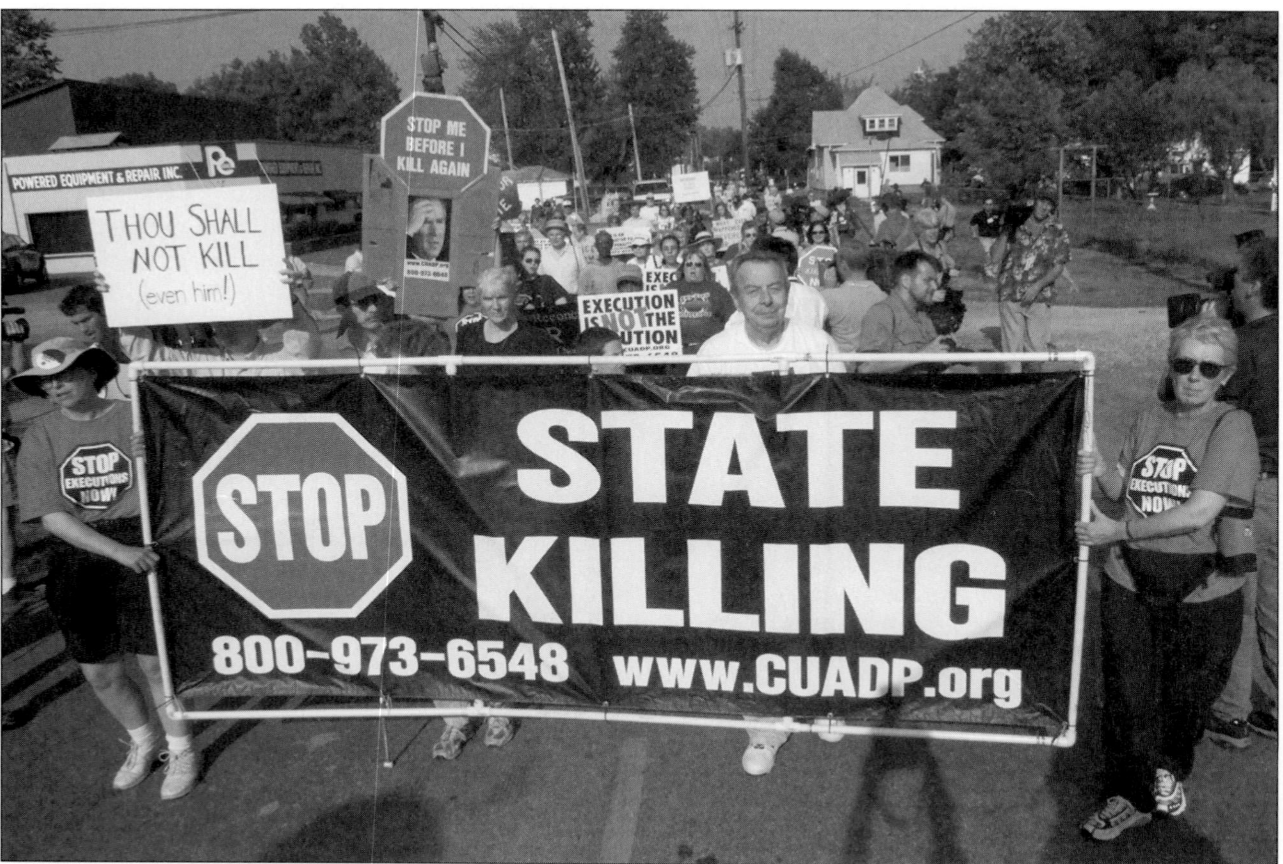

Antideath penalty demonstrators march through the streets of Terre Haute, Indiana 10 June 2001 on their way to the federal penitentiary to protest the execution of Oklahoma City bomber Timothy McVeigh. Supporters of the death penalty also demonstrated. McVeigh was executed on 11 June 2001. (Jim Bourg/Reuters/Getty Images)

that crime is significantly reduced. As some authorities have noted, the new legislation catches the small but not the big fish. "It has resulted in little minnows going to prison while the big fish continue to swim in a sea of crime."[25]

This discussion is not meant to support the position that we should not incarcerate any persons for long periods of time, but rather to illustrate the systems effect that changes in one part of the system may have on other elements of the system. Normally there is little or no planning for these potentially negative side effects of what initially appears to be a great idea for combating crime.

Capital Punishment

Capital punishment The imposition of the death penalty for an offender convicted of a capital offense.

Another major issue in recent years has been the increased use of **capital punishment.** Although capital punishment was used extensively in the past, in 1972 a U.S. Supreme Court decision, *Furman* v. *Georgia,* temporarily halted its use. *Furman* invalidated the Georgia capital punishment statute, ruling that capital punishment cannot be imposed arbitrarily and unfairly; to do so violates the Eighth Amendment's ban on cruel and unusual punishment (see Appendix A).[26] The Court left the door open for states to enact different capital punishment statutes, and many of them have done so. Others have refused to enact the legislation or have failed in their attempts.

In 1977 Gary Mark Gilmore became the first person to be executed since the *Furman* decision. Gilmore, who had given up his right to appeal, was killed by

FIGURE 13.1
Persons Executed, 1930–2001

Source: Bureau of Justice Statistics, *Capital Punishment 1995* (Washington, DC: U.S. Department of Justice, February 1996), p. 2, with updates from news media.

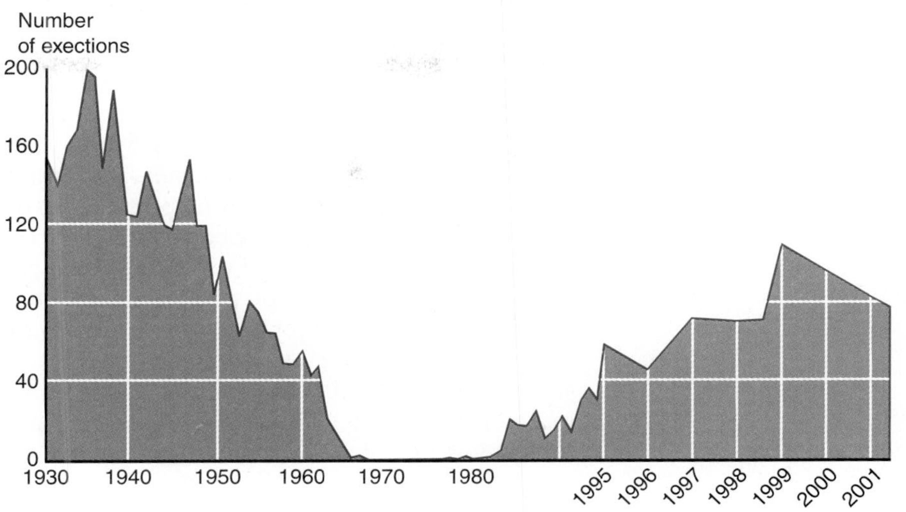

a Utah firing squad. In 1979 John Spenkelink was executed in Florida's electric chair and became the first involuntary execution since *Furman.* As Figure 13.1 shows, only a few executions occurred in the following years, but 56 executions were conducted in the United States in 1995, the highest yearly figure since 1957. That number was surpassed in 1997, when 74 persons were executed, and the 70 executions in 1998 represented only a slight drop. In 1998, Texas, which led the nation in executions, executed its first female in 135 years. Karla Faye Tucker, known as the pick-ax murderer, won the support of people all over the world as she told her story on talk shows and in print, admitting the brutal murders in which she was involved but claiming a new life as a born-again Christian. Despite this support, Tucker was the second woman to be executed in the United States since the reinstatement of the death penalty in 1976.[27] There were 98 executions in 1999, an increase of 28 over the preceding year. In 2000 the number dropped to 85.[28] In 2001 66 persons were executed.

In 1998 a United Nations report called upon the United States to cease executions "until it could ensure that death penalty cases are administered fairly and impartially, in accordance with due process."[29] A moratorium on executions did not gain momentum, however, until Illinois governor George H. Ryan announced in early 2000 that he would impose a moratorium in his state until he could be assured that innocent people were not going to be executed. Some states—such as Texas and Florida—continued to perform executions, but even in those states there were efforts to change the system or to establish a moratorium. And in 2001 the U.S. Supreme Court agreed that during its 2001–2002 term it would hear a case involving the issue of whether it is constitutional to execute a person who was mentally retarded when he committed murder. In June 2002 the U.S. Supreme Court ruled that it is cruel and unusual punishment and thus unconstitutional to execute a mentally retarded person. The case of *Atkins* v. *Virginia* was decided by a 6-3 vote.

Scholars continue to debate the morality of capital punishment and to conduct research on the effects of capital punishment, while most people support the measure and express fascination about its details.

The Sentencing Process

The three basic sentencing models are legislative, judicial, and administrative, and most systems employ one or more of these types. In the *legislative model,* the legislature establishes by statute the length of the sentence for each crime. For example, a burglary conviction carries a sentence of 10 years. Under this model the judge is allowed no discretion at sentencing, nor are prison authorities or parole boards allowed discretion in determining when the inmate is released. This type of sentence is called the *determinate,* or flat-time sentence.

In the *judicial model,* the judge decides the length of the sentence within a range established by the legislature. For example, the legislature determines that for burglary the sentence is from 5 to 10 years, and the judge imposes a sentence within that range. In the *administrative model,* the legislature establishes a wide range of imprisonment for a particular crime. For example, the legislature determines that for armed robbery, the sentence is one day to life, a sentence that is imposed by the judge after the defendant is convicted. The decision to release the inmate is made later by an administrative agency, usually a parole board. The type of sentence imposed in this model is called the *indeterminate* sentence.

There is considerable debate over which of the three sentencing models should be used. Today the trend is away from the administrative model and indeterminate sentencing and toward the legislative model and determinate sentencing. But even this trend illustrates that most sentencing is a combination of the three models. For example, some of the recent legislation permits determinate sentences established by the legislature to be altered judicially if a given case has certain mitigating or aggravating circumstances. This approach is called **presumptive sentencing.**

Presumptive sentencing A method for determining punishment in which the legislature sets a standard sentence in the statute, but the judge may vary that sentence if the case has mitigating or aggravating circumstances.

Presumptive sentencing differs from flat or determinate sentencing in that it does not remove all judicial discretion. It does, however, check the abuse of that discretion by establishing that a deviate sentence is presumed to be improper. Thus, when the sentence is appealed, the sentencing judge has the burden of proving that there are justifiable reasons for deviating from the recommended sentence.

Various combinations of sentence types are used. For example, a defendant may be fined and incarcerated, fined and placed on probation, or fined and ordered to pay restitution. There are combinations of probation and incarceration, too, including

Split sentences—where the court specifies a period of incarceration to be followed by a period of probation

Modification of sentence—where the original sentencing court may reconsider an offender's prison sentence within a limited time and change it to probation

Shock probation—where an offender sentenced to incarceration is released after a period of time in confinement (the shock) and resentenced to probation

Intermittent incarceration—where an offender on probation may spend weekends or nights in jail.[30]

Any of the sentencing models or combinations may be affected by other factors. For example, power may be given to the governor to commute a life sentence to a specified term of years. The state governor (or the president in the federal system) may have the power to pardon an offender (see Chapter 9). It is possible that sentence length may be reduced in accordance with **good-time credit** because of the inmate's good behavior or for time served without an evaluative measure.

Good-time credit Credit resulting in a reduction of prison time; awarded for satisfactory behavior in prison.

Sentence Disparity

Sentence disparity A term used to describe the variations and inequities that result when defendants convicted of the same crime receive varying sentences; may refer also to varying legislative sentences from state to state.

The movement toward determinate sentencing is the result primarily of concern with alleged **sentence disparity,** a concept frequently used but seldom defined. To some, sentence disparity occurs when two people convicted of the same crime are given different sentences by their respective judges. Others claim that disparity exists when legislatures of different states set different penalties for the same offense; thus, robbery with a firearm may result in a 25-year sentence in one state and a 15-year sentence in another. Still others say that sentence disparity exists only when similarly situated offenders receive quite different penalties for the same offense. It is a disparity if a three-time offender in one jurisdiction receives 5 years for armed robbery, whereas a three-time offender in another receives 15 years for the same offense.

The lack of agreement on the meaning of the term makes it difficult if not impossible to interpret the studies of alleged disparity. Nevertheless, numerous attempts—ranging from allegations of racial and gender discrimination to arguments that defendants who receive long sentences are being punished for their unpopular political views—have been made to prove or disprove sentence disparity.

While scholars argue over whether criminal justice systems do or do not discriminate on the basis of extralegal factors (such as age, race, or gender), many people continue to believe that they do. Generally this belief is based on the knowledge that convictions and sentencings (as well as arrests) involve a disproportionate number of African Americans and other minorities. Despite arguments that these differentials are the result of such legal factors as prior criminal records, current offense, and other legally relevant variables, many remain unconvinced.

Law professor Michael H. Tonry, who has studied race and sentencing, concluded that racial disparities have "steadily gotten worse since 1980." Tonry attributed this primarily to the efforts of Republican administrations and legislatures to increase penalties for drug violations. He alleged that they knew these changes would affect minorities negatively while not lowering crime rates. Specifically, he was referring to the 100-to-1 ratio of sentence length for possessing crack cocaine to violating laws regarding powder cocaine. Crack cocaine use is more common among African Americans, while powder cocaine use is more characteristic of whites.[31] Many lower courts that have heard cases on the issues involving statistical differences in sentencing have held that these differences do not prove racial discrimination.[32]

In Chapter 10 we noted that in *United States* v. *Armstrong,* the U.S. Supreme Court held that selective prosecutions in cases involving crack cocaine do not alone support a claim of racial discrimination. The Court ruled that the African American men in Los Angeles who appealed their convictions did not meet the burden of proving unfair racial discrimination.

The debate over whether criminal justice systems discriminate against minorities arises frequently in the context of capital punishment. Several extensive studies have been made in this area, but the U.S. Supreme Court remains unconvinced that the research substantiates unconstitutional discrimination, as demonstrated in the Court's 1987 decision in *McCleskey* v. *Kemp.* McCleskey used an empirical analysis by law professor David Baldus and others to demonstrate that capital punishment is assessed more frequently when the victim is white as compared to African American and, to a lesser extent, when the offender is African American rather than white. The Court would agree only that the study "indicates a discrepancy that appears to correlate with race. Apparent disparities in sentencing are an inevitable part of our criminal justice system." But the Court did not believe the study demonstrates "a constitutionally significant risk of racial bias."[33]

It is also argued that gender discrimination exists in sentencing. Earlier studies reported that women were treated leniently, although some scholars emphasized that any apparent leniency may have been due to differences in the types of crimes committed.[34] Today's critics, however, can point to the increasing success of the battered person syndrome defense of female defendants accused of murdering a spouse or significant other after years of alleged domestic violence. Some of these women have been found not guilty, and others have been found guilty, served prison time, and been released by actions of state governors.

Control of Sentence Disparity

Two approaches are being used to control sentence disparity. In the first, discretion is left with the judge, but efforts are made to control the discretion. In the second, discretion is removed from the judge and placed with the legislature. Judges have wide discretion at the sentencing stage, and various methods have been suggested for controlling it. The threat of removal or being pressured to resign is one approach, which has worked in some cases, particularly when citizens have organized court watches (actually sitting through trials and sentencings to keep an eye on judicial decision making) and publicized controversial sentencing decisions. Recently, however, considerable attention has been given to the establishment of model sentencing guidelines.

Sentence guidelines are seen as a way to control discretion without abolishing it while correcting the disparity that can result from individualized sentencing. A judge who has an offender to sentence may consider the offender's background, the nature of the offense, or other variables without any guidelines. When sentence guidelines are used, the difference is that the relevance of these variables may have been researched, and the judge has a benchmark for reasonable penalties under these circumstances.

There are drawbacks, however, to sentence guidelines. First, some are just guidelines, and there is nothing (except pressure) to prevent judges from ignoring them. In other cases judges must give written reasons for deviating from the guidelines, which may specify general conditions under which the judge may impose a sentence outside the guidelines. Second, empirical evidence suggests that the presence of guidelines has not reduced sentence disparity significantly. Third, there has not been sufficient analysis of the processes used in establishing the guidelines. Finally, even if the sentence guidelines are effective in reducing sentence disparity among judges, the system has no effect on the prosecutor's virtually unchecked discretion in deciding which charges to file; whether to plea bargain; and, if so, how.

Perhaps the most controversial sentence guidelines have been the federal guidelines recommended by the U.S. Sentencing Commission, established as a result of the 1984 revision of the federal criminal code.[35] Those guidelines became law on 1 November 1987 and have been subsequently amended. They were, and they remain, highly controversial, and initially some federal judges refused to enforce them. Others declared them unconstitutional, while still others held that they were constitutional.

In *Mistretta* v. *United States,* the Supreme Court reviewed the history of federal sentencing, including the emphasis on rehabilitation accompanied by indeterminate sentencing, which theoretically gives judges the opportunity to impose a sentence tailored to the rehabilitative needs of an individual offender. After discussing the constitutional issues, the Court held that the federal guidelines do not violate federal constitutional rights.[36]

Reactions to the federal sentencing guidelines continue to vary. The U.S. Sentencing Commission claims that the guidelines have reduced disparities,[37] whereas a study reported by the American Bar Association noted that since the guidelines had been enacted, sentences for young African American men were "significantly higher" than sentences for young white men.[38] University of Chicago law professor Albert W. Alschuler recommends that the federal sentencing guidelines "be relegated to a place near the Edsel in a museum of twentieth-century bad ideas." A federal district judge in Connecticut claims, "We should face the possibility that the basic premise of the guidelines—that the human element should be wiped away from the sentencing process and replaced by the clean, sharp edges of a sentencing slide rule—is itself highly questionable." Numerous federal judges and attorneys have expressed their opposition to the federal sentencing guidelines, and many have called for their abolition.[39]

Determinate Sentences

The most dramatic reaction to alleged sentence disparity has been a return to determinate sentencing. Led by Maine and California (the latter of which used indeterminate sentencing most extensively), most states now have some form of mandatory sentencing. Despite the warnings of advocates of determinate sentencing that a return to this method should not be a piecemeal approach most states did not consider the total impact of their actions when legislating determinate sentences. In many states insufficient attention was given to the consequences of this movement, and the results have been disastrous in some cases. A few problems are considered below.

First, there is the possibility that determinate sentencing leads to greater disparity, although of a different type than before. With discretion removed from judges and with stiff penalties imposed by legislatures, prosecutors might be more reluctant to prosecute, and judges and juries might be more reluctant to find defendants guilty. When either of these possibilities occurs, those defendants receive disparate treatment compared to defendants who committed similar or identical crimes but who are prosecuted and convicted.

Second, determinate sentences may contribute to the increasingly serious problems of jail and prison overcrowding. Just one year after California enacted its broad three-strikes law, it was reported that because of the longer sentences faced by many defendants, judges were setting bail at twice the usual amount for "second-strike" defendants and refusing bail for defendants accused of a third felony. This, along with the refusal of two- and three-strikes defendants to accept plea bargains, increased jail populations. It was estimated in 1995 by Los Angeles County officials that they were housing over 1,000 three-strikes defendants that year; approximately 500 more beds were needed in Orange County to house its increased jail populations.[40]

Third, it is doubtful whether determinate sentencing achieves the goal of decreasing the violent crime rate by deterring crime, and some studies question the effectiveness of three-strikes legislation and other determinate sentences or mandatory minimums. A 1997 report published by the Center on Juvenile and Criminal Justice concluded that crime rates fell more slowly in three-strikes states than in non-three-strikes states. The researchers agreed that

> the data are inconclusive at best. But to tell the public that this legislation works after only two years is inappropriate and misleading. If anything, the initial data demonstrate that three-strikes legislation is not as successful as legislatures had hoped.[41]

A study of 1,175 Massachusetts inmates, published in 1997 by researchers at the Harvard Medical School, concluded that mandatory sentencing laws "are wasting prison resources on nonviolent, low-level offenders and reducing resources available to lock up violent offenders." The researchers noted that the cost of incarceration is between $20,000 and $30,000 a year; thus, it would seem prudent to spend more money on drug abuse treatment and prevention rather than locking up nonviolent, nonserious drug offenders.[42] This study confirmed the findings of a Rand Corporation report published earlier that year. Rand researchers concluded that "providing treatment to hard-core cocaine addicts is eight times as effective in reducing total drug consumption as sentencing dealers to mandatory minimum prison terms." The mandatory minimums might be effective if judges had the discretion to apply them only to high-level dealers, but that is not the case.[43]

Thus, it is not clear that sentencing revisions affect the recidivism rates once the inmates serving those longer terms are released. Furthermore, studies such as one in California reveal that most of the defendants subjected to determinate sentences (70 percent under California's three-strikes law) are nonviolent, nonserious offenders.[44]

A fourth problem is that under determinate sentencing with stiffer penalties, defendants may be less likely to plead guilty and more likely to insist on trials, thus increasing the burden on already-overcrowded court systems. Studies of the earlier stiff drug laws in New York and the mandatory and harsh penalties for carrying guns illegally in Massachusetts reported that many defendants began looking for ways to circumvent the law. Some fled rather than face trial. Judicial decisions showed more favor to defendants, with increased dismissals and not-guilty verdicts. Defendants were more likely to appeal their convictions. In both states, "as the stakes got higher, defendants pursued more dilatory tactics to avoid them."[45] Likewise, just one year after the California three-strikes law was enacted, there was evidence that only 14 percent of second-strike and 6 percent of third-strike cases were plea bargained. That compared to plea bargains in approximately 94 percent of felony cases statewide prior to the enactment of the law.[46]

Fifth, there is evidence that in the California system African Americans have been disproportionately affected by the three-strikes legislation. They have been imprisoned for a third strike "at over 13 times the rate of whites."[47]

In evaluating Florida's return to determinate sentencing, one scholar summed up her conclusions by recommending that other states not follow Florida's example. Pamala L. Griset concluded as follows:

> The power to deprive citizens of their liberty is one of the most awesome responsibilities delegated to government officials. It is difficult to reconcile the proper use of this power with a punishment system that invites geographic disparity, racial discrimination, and unpredictable, unreviewable, and unaccountable sentencing.[48]

These and other issues contribute to the increase in appeals and other challenges to sentences.

APPEALS AND OTHER LEGAL CHALLENGES

Several legal challenges to a criminal conviction, sentence, and subsequent incarceration are available. Defendants who have legal reasons to believe that mistakes were made in their trials may have grounds for an appeal. Immediately after conviction a defendant may have legal grounds for the judge to grant his or her motion for a new trial or for a judgment of acquittal despite the jury verdict. This motion may be successful if the defendant can show that evidence admitted at the trial should have been excluded for some legal reason or that in some other way the defendant's constitutional rights were violated. For example, a defense motion for a judgment of acquittal was granted after a jury convicted Seattle Seahawks wide receiver Brian Blades of manslaughter in the death of his cousin. The defense had argued that the killing was an accident and that the prosecution did not present enough evidence of manslaughter for the judge to send the case to the jury.

If the motion for a new trial or for a judgment of acquittal is not granted (and most are not) the defendant may appeal the conviction on points of law. An appeal of a conviction is made to a court that has appellate jurisdiction over the trial court's decisions, which includes the judge's decisions on evidence and other matters as well as the verdict. In effect, the appellate court looks at the actions of the trial court and decides whether any reversible errors were committed. Most cases are not reversed; most that are reversed are remanded for another trial, and a large percentage of defendants are convicted on retrial.

Writ An order from a court for someone to do something or to give permission to do whatever has been requested.

Defendants may file writs as well. A **writ** is an order from a court for someone to do something or to give permission to do whatever has been requested. It is common for offenders to file a writ of *habeas corpus,* which literally means "you have the body" (see Chapter 11). Frequently this writ is filed by inmates who argue that they are being confined under conditions that violate their constitutional rights. If the writ is granted, the court orders the administrator in charge to produce the person who is claiming that he or she is being confined in violation of his or her rights.

Defendants may also appeal their sentences, but when the legislature has given trial judges wide discretion in determining sentences, appellate courts rarely overturn those decisions. The appellate court shows deference to the judge who has heard and seen the evidence, evidence that is not seen and heard by appellate courts. If, however, the sentence constitutes cruel and unusual punishment, it violates the Eighth Amendment (see Appendix A) and is unconstitutional.

The U.S. Supreme Court

***Certiorari,* writ of** Order issued by an appellate court that has discretion to review a lower court decision and has decided to grant the request to do so. If the appellate court agrees to hear the appeal, it issues a *writ of certiorari,* ordering the lower court to certify the record and send it to the appellate court for review. If the appellate court denies the writ, the decision of the lower court stands.

The highest court of appeals in the United States is the Supreme Court, an institution of great power that elicits considerable controversy. In recent years the Court has received some of the most widespread criticism in its history. Its 1998–99 opening session was marked by demonstrations outside the Supreme Court building, protesting the fact that the justices hire very few minorities as law clerks.

The Supreme Court has almost complete control over which cases it accepts. The Court does this by granting or denying a writ of ***certiorari.*** When the Court agrees to hear a case on appeal, it is said to have granted *certiorari.* Four of the nine justices who sit on the Court must vote in favor of the writ for it to be granted. In an average term, the Court hears fewer than 5 percent of the cases filed. For example, during its 2000–2001 term the Court decided only 85 cases (of which 26 were decided by a margin of only one vote). There are two reasons for this limitation. First, because of time, the Court must limit the number of cases it hears and decides. The problem today is that the number of cases the Court is asked to hear has increased significantly, from approximately 1,000 per year in 1953 to 5,000 or more today.[49]

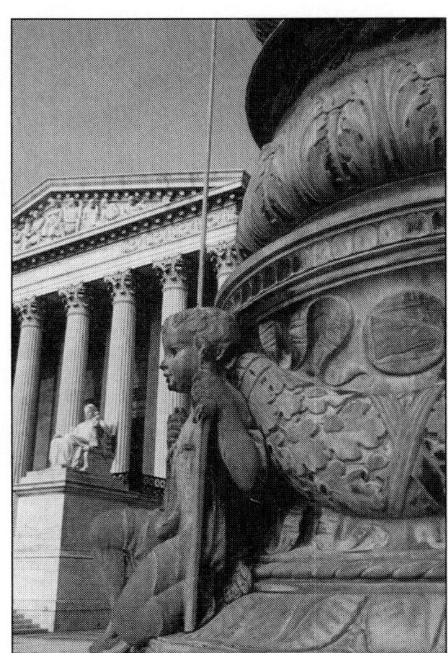

The U.S. Supreme Court building in Washington, D.C., is the symbol of the country's civil and criminal justice systems. (Art Stein/Photo Researchers)

The second reason the Court hears only some of the cases is that the justices view their mission as deciding cases that have an impact beyond the immediate parties. An example is the *Gideon* case, discussed in Chapter 11. The fact that Gideon did not have counsel at his Florida trial was important to Gideon, but the significance of the case went far beyond Gideon and the state.

The Court hears cases when lower court decisions on the issue in question have differed. For example, before the Court decided *Mistretta* v. *United States,* 116 U.S. district court judges had ruled that the federal sentencing guidelines were constitutional, and 158 had ruled they were unconstitutional. Federal appellate courts that had ruled on the issue were divided.[50]

When the Supreme Court rules on an issue that has been in conflict among lower federal courts, its decision becomes the final court resolution of the issue unless or until it is overruled by a subsequent Supreme Court decision. Supreme Court decisions may be nullified by subsequent statutes (provided they are not unconstitutional) or by constitutional amendment.

The principal function of the Supreme Court is to determine whether the litigants' federal constitutional rights have been violated. Controversial court decisions should be considered in the context of constitutional law and a changing society, with its concomitant need for settling conflicts. The law and the Constitution must be flexible enough to deal with different factual situations, which require adjudication as they arise. Additional information on the Court is contained in Media Focus 13.1.

Media Focus 13.1

The Media Focus on the U.S. Supreme Court

At the end of the annual term of the U.S. Supreme Court, various news media, especially the print media, focus on what the Court has (or has not) accomplished during the previous term. As expected, the media puts its own spin on the summary. This focus summarizes *New York Times* reports on the 1999–2000 and 2000–2001 terms of the U.S. Supreme Court. (Both articles were written by the same authors).

In reporting on the 1999–2000 term, the *New York Times* noted that the Court decided fewer cases (73) than in any term since the early 1950s. But, emphasized the article, the Court's decisions covered most of the constitutional range of issues. Under the headline "The Court Rules, American Changes," the article referred to the term as being of "surpassing interest, rich in symbol and substance, a vivid reminder of the Court's power to scramble settled expectations, put old questions to rest and, ultimately, to have the last word."[1]

In summarizing the most important cases, along with who voted for what and with whom, the article noted that 20 cases were decided by a 5-to-4 vote, with the conservative block (Justices William H. Rehnquist, Sandra Day O'Connor, Antonin Scalia, Anthony M. Kennedy, and Clarence Thomas) voting together in 13 of those cases. The other four justices, John Paul Stevens, David H. Souter, Ruth Bader Ginsburg, and Stephen G. Breyer, voted as a block in the majority in only one of the cases decided by one vote.

The *New York Times*'s analysis of the 2000–2001 term was entitled "The Separation of Justice and State." The article noted that although the Court in effect decided the U.S. presidential election, the members of the present Court are far more removed from politics than were those of previous ones. The only current member of the Court who has served in a legislative capacity is Sandra Day O'Connor, a former state legislator. Another interesting fact is that eight of the nine current justices, in contrast to their predecessors (many of whom came from the political branch of government) were judges when they were appointed to the U.S. Supreme Court. Chief Justice Rehnquist was an assistant attorney general in the administration of President Richard M. Nixon. The conclusion, said the writer, is as follows:

> The result has been to transform the Court from an institution that once drew on the collective experience of people who had lived both sides of the vital intersection of law and politics—where the most important cases arise—to one staffed by a smart, highly professional cadre of academic judges who often appear disconnected from the practical implications of the Court's work.[2]

The writer contends that although something has been gained—"a fluidity with legal doctrine in its many nuances"—something has also been lost—"a framework for seeing the world in all its gritty reality from inside the marble cocoon." The suggestion is that if the justices had more practical experience in the real world, they would have known that requiring President Bill Clinton to defend himself against the accusations of Paula Jones (who accused him of sexually harassing her) would have been a time-consuming burden, detracting from the work of the White House.

The writer concludes that with no resignations announced at the end of the term (there had been speculation that such would occur) we might as well step back and analyze the justices with their lack of political backgrounds, realizing that they will continue to decide cases without a feel for the world of political reality.

1. "The Court Rules, America Changes," *New York Times* (2 July 2000), Section 4, p. 1.

2. "The Separation of Justice and States," *New York Times* (1 July 2001), Section 4, p. 1.

COURTS AND CONGESTION

There is no question that most courts, including the Supreme Court as well as the lower appellate courts and trial courts, are overburdened. Recent administrations have taken measures to increase the number of crimes tried in federal courts; Congress has complied with legislation. For example, the Violent Crime Control and Law Enforcement Act of 1994 increased federal jurisdiction over a number of crimes and increased penalties for others, especially those involving illegal drug trafficking.[51] Supreme Court chief justice William H. Rehnquist has warned about the dangers of increasing the number of federal crimes, stating that the trend toward "federalizing" more crimes is clogging the system and poses the danger of "changing the character of the federal judiciary." Rehnquist notes that federalizing crimes has become important politically and that rarely has a Congress met in recent years without making attempts to add more crimes to the federal code. He recommends that Congress address more thoroughly the issues of what should constitute a federal crime and which crimes should be shifted from federal to state courts.[52] State courts are overcrowded, too, with significant increases in caseloads in recent years.

Several methods have been suggested for alleviating court congestion. Former chief justice Warren Burger suggested that frivolous litigation would be discouraged if courts fined lawyers who file such suits. In one case Justice Burger fined an attorney $1,000, stating, "[He] has abused his privilege to practice law by repeatedly filing frivolous papers [and] acting like a small boy who gets a loaded pistol without instruction as to when and how it is to be used."[53] One state judge fined a litigant and his attorneys almost $1 million for a lawsuit he found frivolous.[54] It is important to understand, however, that although fining litigants and their attorneys for filing frivolous civil lawsuits may reduce litigation in civil courts and thus take some pressure off court systems, criminal cases continue to increase in number.

Other suggestions for decreasing court congestion include increasing the numbers of judges and other personnel. The passage of the Omnibus Judgeship Act of 1978 increased the number of federal judges,[55] but (even more than 20 years later) not all of the positions have been filled.

Another suggestion for reducing overcrowding in courts is to create more courts, but that is expensive. In 1982 an additional federal circuit appeals court was added. Reorganization of courts is another suggestion that some state systems have followed. Improving internal management of courts relieves some congestion. For example, shifting judges from one court to another might ease congestion problems during the vacation of a judge in one court. But problems arise when judges are shifted to areas in which they have no experience, for example, from civil to criminal or vice versa, and take on heavy caseloads quickly without time for much learning. Night courts and weekend courts have been used in some cities, particularly large cities with high caseloads, as for example Miami, but such procedures take their toll on participants. Computers have been used to speed up court paperwork.

Mediation The act of attempting to settle claims between parties outside the courtroom; programs for noncourt settlement of disputes were instituted to help reduce the backlog of cases in the court systems.

Alternate dispute resolution is one of the most efficient ways to ease court congestion. In less complicated cases, litigants may use **mediation** rather than court resolution. Mediation has been used successfully in many countries. Mediators may be lay persons with some training in dispute resolution but without the legal training of attorneys. In informal situations, such as within a neighborhood, many disputes may be resolved successfully without the formality and cost of a court trial.

A final suggestion for reducing congestion in our current courts is to add special courts, such as drug courts. The special-court approach was begun in 1989 in Miami, Florida, and is a diversion and treatment approach. The program is an alternative to traditional prosecution in criminal court, and most nonviolent defendants arrested on drug possession charges are funneled into this program. The drug court has been described as follows: "Supervised by a sitting judge, a drug court is an intensive, community-based treatment, rehabilitation, and supervision program for drug defendants."[56] The importance of drug courts as a means for solving court congestion and funneling some offenders through treatment programs rather than prison is reasonable in light of the increase in drug convictions. Since the implementation of the Sentencing

Reform Act of 1984, the proportion of drug offenders sentenced to prison in federal cases increased from 79 to 92 percent. Drug prosecutions in federal courts alone increased from 21 percent of all defendants in 1982 to 36 percent in 1999. Finally, the amount of time a federal drug offender could expect to serve in prison increased from 39.3 months in 1988 to 61.8 months in 1999; and on 30 September 1999, of the 199,185 offenders serving time in federal facilities, 57 percent were there because of drug offenses, compared to only 11 percent for violent crimes, 7 percent for property offenses, 8 percent for an immigration offense, and 9 percent for all others.[57]

Drug courts have been criticized. Evaluators say that, although the recidivism rate is low (about 11 percent), initially the drug courts are more expensive than criminal courts. A participant who completes the program successfully does not go through a criminal court; the charges are dropped. The program includes acupuncture, education courses, vocational services, counseling, fellowship meetings, and strict monitoring through drug testing and court appearances.[58]

In the 1994 criminal code revision Congress included a provision on drug courts. In September 1995 Attorney General Janet Reno announced the award of $6 million in grants to assist 13 communities to improve or build drug court programs, adding to the smaller drug court grants she had announced in August 1995. Congress appropriated $29 million for these grants in 1995 but subsequently reduced that funding to $11.9 million.[59]

By 2001 drug courts were in operation in all states, the District of Columbia, Puerto Rico, Guam, and two federal districts. California led with 142 drug courts, followed by Florida with 65, New York with 63, and Ohio with 49. There was evidence that those who participated in a drug court program had very low use of drugs, with the percentage of clean drug tests ranging from 84 to 98 percent in a survey of 14 drug court programs.[60]

Two other specialized courts have assisted in the court congestion problem. Many jurisdictions have developed special family courts, including some that specialize in domestic violence cases. And in the year 2000 Congress approved legislation that can provide up to $10 million a year in federal money for states to implement mental health courts. These courts are to be designed to target mentally ill persons accused of nonviolent crimes. These defendants are to be diverted from jails and prisons to mental health treatment facilities. According to the Bureau of Justice Statistics, one out of six persons incarcerated in jails and prisons suffers from a mental health problem. As Senator Mike DeWine, who sponsored the bill, said, "Local jails are becoming overwhelmed by the need to care for larger and larger numbers of mentally ill persons. . . It is unacceptable that Los Angeles County and New York jails have essentially become the largest mental health care institutions in our country."[61]

SUMMARY

This chapter presents an overview of courts and their procedures. It begins with a brief explanation of legal terms necessary to understand court functions. It examines the dual court system and the differences between trial and appellate courts. The role of lawyers in criminal court systems is discussed, with a look first at the prosecution and then at the defense. Pretrial processes are discussed, with the focus on the two most controversial processes: granting or denying bail and plea bargaining. The trial of a criminal case is examined, with an emphasis on the right to a speedy trial and the role of the judge and jury in criminal trials.

The sentencing process, one of the most hotly debated topics in criminal justice today, is presented in more detail. After a short discussion of types of sentences, the chapter focuses on the current sentencing issues of three strikes and you're out and capital punishment. An overview of the sentencing process is followed by a discussion of sentence disparity and how it might be controlled. Procedures for appealing convictions and sentences are noted. The Supreme Court, its method of operation, and some of the controversy surrounding it are discussed. The final section focuses on court congestion and suggestions for reducing it, including special courts for cases involving drugs, domestic problems, and mental health.

The importance of the court system cannot be overemphasized, for it is in the courts that the final determination is made of how many criminal justice problems are resolved. Once a person has committed an offense punishable by the state, even if the police's handling of the situation is above question and society has provided all the necessary resources for treatment in whatever setting that may take place, a positive resolution of the problem may be thwarted by the courts. The rights of due process guaranteed by the Constitution may become a farce in the hands of incompetent lawyers and judges. With long delays, trials can become meaningless or unfair. It is incumbent on lawyers, judges, probation officers, and all other functionaries of the courts, as well as society, to make the improvement of courts a primary goal in the war against crime.

Many of the topics discussed in this chapter underscore the importance of discretion in criminal justice systems. Prosecutors have wide discretion in deciding whether to bring charges, which charges to bring, if and when to drop charges, whether to plea bargain, and which sentences to recommend for convicted defendants. Juries exercise discretion in deciding whether defendants are innocent or guilty. Defense attorneys exercise discretion in determining trial strategy and whether to advise their clients to plea bargain. Judges exercise discretion in their supervision of pretrial and trial procedures and in sentencing, for it is obvious that a move toward determinate sentencing does not remove all discretion.

Nor is it wise to attempt to remove all discretion in criminal justice systems. The real questions are where the bounds of that discretion will lie and how discretion may be checked. The control of discretion, not its abolition, should be the issue. The legal profession should recognize and accept the challenge of successful control of judicial and prosecutorial discretion, especially as it relates to sentencing. Some of the problems of criminal justice systems, however, cannot be solved by the legal profession alone. Society must take responsibility for offering adequate legal services for all. The social structure should be appraised in the realization that criminal justice systems do not exist in isolation from the rest of society. Research must be supported, and the tendency to abandon philosophies, such as treatment, before they have been given a real trial should be reexamined. As this author concluded in an earlier publication,

> It is easier to put the offender out of sight than to examine the social structure for cracks. It is easier to punish than to treat. It is easier to abolish the entire system of discretionary sentencing by attacking the abuses than to correct those abuses and provide the resources needed for an adequate implementation of the philosophy of individualized sentencing. It is easier to attack the judges for "leniency" than to examine the need to decriminalize the criminal code or to provide sufficient and well trained probation and parole officers or adequate treatment facilities. It is also easier to lose than to win the war against crime.[62]

STUDY QUESTIONS

1. The chapter begins and ends with a discussion of court congestion. Examine this issue historically and in terms of recent developments.
2. Define *judicial review, jurisdiction (concurrent, appellate,* and *exclusive*), *stare decisis,* and *legal reasoning.*
3. Illustrate the meaning of *dual court system.*
4. Distinguish *appellant* and *appellee* in the context of the appeals process.
5. Define *grand jury* and *indictment.*
6. Define *information* in the context of prosecutorial responsibilities.
7. What is the prosecutor's duty in the criminal justice system?
8. Explain and critique the role of defense attorneys in U.S. criminal justice systems.
9. State the advantages and disadvantages of pretrial release, noting in particular the federal system.
10. Critique the bail system.
11. Evaluate the plea bargaining process.
12. In U.S. criminal justice systems, defendants have a right to a speedy trial. Explain.
13. Contrast the roles of judge and jury in criminal trials.
14. Evaluate U.S. jury systems in criminal cases.
15. Define and evaluate *three-strikes legislation.* Define *truth in sentencing.*
16. Note current issues in capital punishment and evaluate them.
17. Distinguish determinate and indeterminate sentences.
18. Explain presumptive sentences and pardons.

19. What are good-time credits, and should they be retained?
20. Evaluate charges of sentence disparity in U.S. criminal justice systems.
21. Suggest and evaluate ways to control sentence disparity.
22. Define *habeas corpus.*
23. Evaluate the purpose and role of the U.S. Supreme Court.
24. Suggest ways to alleviate court congestion.

BRIEF ESSAY ASSIGNMENTS

1. Explain prosecutorial discretion. Why is it necessary in the criminal justice system?
2. Describe the three systems that may be used when counsel is provided for a defendant at the government's expense.
3. What are the potential problems with the plea bargaining process?
4. Briefly describe the three basic sentencing models.
5. Explain the criticisms of the federal sentencing guidelines.

INTERNET ACTIVITIES

1. Using your Web browser, search for information on sentencing issues and drug policies related to crack cocaine. The Sentencing Project's website at www.sentencingproject.org/brief/brief.htm is a good place to start. What is the sentencing policy? Explain the racial disparity in sentencing for crack/powder cocaine. Do you believe the sentencing differences between crack and powder are justified? Why or why not? What are the overall impacts of this sentencing policy?
2. Choose several criminal justice, social, or court issues and check out www.mediate.com to find information on these topics. What information is provided? For your topic, do you think that mediation can be an effective alternative to the judicial process? Why or why not? What role, if any, do you think mediation will play in the future of the criminal justice process?

NET RESOURCES

www.supremecourtus.gov

At the official website of the U.S. Supreme Court, users can access Supreme Court cases, opinions, rules of the Court, case-handling guidelines and the *Journal of the Supreme Court,* which contains official minutes. Links to related law and judicial websites are also provided.

www.ncsconline.org

The National Center for State Courts is an independent nonprofit organization; its website provides information and links to this country's state and federal courts and international court websites, court statistics, other judicial organizations and the State Justice Institute.

www.ussc.gov

The United States Sentencing Commission's website offers statistics and information on the federal sentencing guidelines, guideline manuals and amendments, reports to Congress, federal register notices, and publications. Links to state sentencing commissions and other related sites are also available.

www.sentencing.org — Comprised of individuals and organizations, the Coalition for Federal Sentencing Reform maintains a website whose topics include a history of the federal sentencing guidelines, a case for reform, fact sheets, links to relevant sites and action alerts.

www.problem-solvingcourts.org — Sponsored by the Center for Court Innovation, the Problem-Solving Courts website offers information and publications on problem-solving courts in areas such as domestic violence, drugs, family treatment, mental health, and guns.

www.ndaa.org — The National District Attorneys Association's website provides a newsroom, district attorney–related links, information on publications covering topics in a variety of areas, special reports, and issues associated with prosecutorial interests.

www.deathpenaltyinfo.org — The Death Penalty Information Center contains resources on numerous topics and issues concerning capital punishment, including women, juveniles, mentally retarded, the U.S. military, race, and the history of the death penalty. Full text reports from the center and a newsroom can also be accessed here.

www.adrr.com — ADR Resources maintained by an individual, has several resources, publications and information on mediation and alternative dispute resolution. In addition to four volumes of mediation essays, free newsletters are available to site users.

ENDNOTES

1. Earl Warren, "Delay and Congestion in the Federal Courts," quoted in *Delay in Court,* ed. Hans Zeisel et al. (Boston: Little, Brown, 1959), p. xxi.
2. American Bar Association, *Standards for Criminal Justice,* Standard 3–1.2(c) (3d ed. 1991).
3. See Ibid., Standard 4–1.2(b) (3d ed. 1991).
4. "Center for State Courts Finds Indigent Defenders Perform Well," *Criminal Justice Newsletter* 23 (15 May 1992): 4.
5. Stack v. Boyle, 342 U.S. 1, 5 (1951).
6. District of Columbia Court Reform and Procedure Act of 1970, D.C. Code Encyl. Section 23-1321 *et seq.* (2001).
7. United States v. Salerno, 481 U.S. 739 (1987). The Bail Reform Act of 1984 is codified at U.S. Code, Title 18, Section 3142(e) (2001).
8. Stewart J. D'Alessio and Lisa Stolzenberg, "Unemployment and Pretrial Incarceration: Does the State Use Imprisonment to Control Labor Surplus?" *American Sociological Review* 60 (June 1995): 350–59.
9. Santobello v. New York, 404 U.S. 257, 260–261 (1971).
10. Bordenkircher v. Hayes, 434 U.S. 357 (1978).
11. Brady v. United States, 397 U.S. 742 (1970).
12. Arizona v. Horning, 761 P.2d 728 (Ariz.App. 1988). For other restrictions on plea bargaining, see New Jersey v. Warren, 558 A.2d 1312 (N.J. 1989).
13. See Federal Rule of Evidence 410 and Federal Rule of Criminal Procedure 11(3)(6) (2001).
14. United States v. Mezzanatto, 513 U.S. 196 (1995).
15. United States v. Blanco, 861 F.2d 773 (2d Cir. 1988), *cert. denied,* 489 U.S. 1019 (1989).
16. Doggett v. United States, 505 U.S. 647 (1992).
17. For an analysis, see Stuart Nagel, "Decision Theory and Juror Decision-Making," in *The Trial Process,* ed. Bruce Dennis Sales (New York: Plenum, 1989), pp. 353–86.
18. Duncan v. Louisiana, 391 U.S. 145 (1968).
19. "Jurors Ignore, Misunderstand Instructions," *American Bar Association Journal* 81 (May 1995): 30–31.
20. "In the Shoes of the Wrongly Accused," *American Bar Association Journal* 81 (June 1995): 32.
21. Cal. Penal Code, Title 16, Section 667 (2001).
22. Bureau of Justice Statistics, *Truth in Sentencing in State Prisons* (Washington, DC: U.S. Department of Justice, 1999), p. 1.
23. "California Court System's Analysis of Three-Strikes Law," *Criminal Justice Newsletter* 20 (15 October 1996), p. 4.
24. "Small-Time Drug Crooks Clog California Prisons" *The Times* (9 March 1996), overseas news
25. "Judges Condemn Set-Minimum Sentences," *USA Today* (10 September 1996), p. 1.
26. Furman v. Georgia, 408 U.S. 238 (1972).
27. "Texas Set to Execute a Female Convict: First in 135 Years," *New York Times* (3 February 1998), p. 1; "Executions, Death Sentences Down in 1998," *USA Today* (21 December 1998), p. 14.
28. Bureau of Justice Statistics, *Capital Punishment 1999* (Washington, DC: U.S. Department of Justice, December 2000), p. 1, updated on the BJS website, www.ojp.usdojgov/bjs/cp.htm (18 January 2002).
29. "United Nations Report Urges Suspension of Death Penalty," *Criminal Justice Newsletter* 29 (17 March 1998), p. 5.
30. Bureau of Justice Statistics, *Probation and Parole 1982* (Washington, DC: U.S. Department of Justice, 1983), p. 2.
31. Michael H. Tonry, "Racial Politics, Racial Disparities, and the War on Crime," *Crime & Delinquency* 40 (October 1994): 475, 483–88. See also Tonry, *Malign Neglect: Race, Crime, and Punishment in America* (New York: Oxford University Press, 1994).
32. See, for example, United States v. Lattimore, 974 F.2d 971 (8th Cir. 1992), *cert. denied,* 507 U.S. 1020 (1993).
33. McCleskey v. Kemp, 481 U.S. 279 (1987).
34. See Darrell Steffensmeier et al., "Gender and Imprisonment Decisions," *Criminology* 31 (August 1993): 411–46; Steffensmeier, "Assessing the Impact of the Women's Movement on Sex-Based Differences in the Handling of Adult Criminal Defendants," *Crime & Delinquency* 26 (July 1980): 344–57; and Kathleen Daly, *Gender, Crime and Punishment* (New Haven, CT: Yale University Press, 1994).

35. See the Sentencing Reform Act of 1984 as amended, U.S. Code, Title 18, Section 3551 *et seq.* and U.S. Code, Title 28, Sections 991–998 (2001).
36. Mistretta v. United States, 488 U.S. 361 (1989).
37. See "Sentencing Guidelines Reduce Disparities, Commission Says," *Criminal Justice Newsletter* 23 (3 February 1992): 3–4.
38. "Mandatory Minimum Sentences Hit," *American Bar Association Journal* 77 (December 1992): 36.
39. "Chorus of Judicial Critics Assail Sentencing Guides," *New York Times* (17 April 1992), p. 2.
40. "Three Strikes Causing Problems in California, Studies Indicate," *Criminal Justice Newsletter* 26 (3 April 1995): 2.
41. "Drop in Crime Said to Be Less in States with Three-Strikes Laws," *Criminal Justice Newsletter* 28 (18 March 1997): 1.
42. "Study Casts Doubt on Harsh Drug Sentences," *New York Times* (reprinted in the *St. Petersburg Times,* 25 November 1997, p. 3).
43. Rand Corporation, *Mandatory Minimum Drug Sentences: Throwing Away the Key or the Taxpayer's Money,* cited in "Mandatory Minimums Ineffective in Cutting Drug Use, Study Finds," *Criminal Justice Newsletter* 28 (15 May 1997): 6.
44. "Three Strikes Causing Problems in California."
45. Kenneth Carlson, *Mandatory Sentencing: The Experience of Two States,* Police Briefs, National Institute of Justice (Washington DC: U.S. Government Printing Office, 1982), pp. 7, 8, 15.
46. "Three Strikes Causing Problems in California."
47. "Drop in Crime Said to Be Less," p. 2.
48. Pamala L. Griset, "Criminal Sentencing in Florida: Determinate Sentencing's Hollow Shell," *Crime & Delinquency* 45 (July 1999): 316–33; quotation is from p. 331.
49. "The Supreme Court Exits," *New York Times* (30 June 2001), p. 24.
50. Mistretta v. United States, 488 U.S. 361 (1989).
51. Violent Crime Control and Law Enforcement Act of 1994, Public Law 193-322 (13 September 1994).
52. "Rehnquist Warns against More 'Federalization' of Crimes," *Criminal Justice Newsletter* 23 (1 September 1992): 6.
53. Clark v. Florida, 475 U.S. 1134 (1986).
54. "Sanctions in Frivolous Suit Come to Nearly $1 Million," *Houston Post* (22 May 1992), p. 1. The case was Metzger v. Casseb, 839 S.W. 2d 160 (Tex.App.1st Dist. 1992).
55. U.S. Code, Title 28, Section 44.133 (2001).
56. Office of National Drug Control Policy, *Drug Treatment in the Criminal Justice System* (Washington, DC: Executive Office of the President, March 2001), p. 4.
57. Bureau of Justice Statistics, *Federal Criminal Case Processing, 1999* (Washington, DC: U.S. Department of Justice, February 2001), p. 1.
58. National Institute of Justice, *Miami's "Drug Court": A Different Approach* (Washington, DC: U.S. Department of Justice, 1993), pp. 1–2.
59. "Attorney General Reno Announces New Drug Court Grants; Successful Program Faces Possible Senate Cut-Off this Week," *U.S. Newswire* (12 September 1995). The enactment statute is found in Sections 50001–50002 of the Violent Crime Control and Law Enforcement Act of 1994, Public Law 103-322 (13 September 1994).
60. *Drug Treatment in the Criminal Justice System,* p. 4.
61. "Congress Approves Grants for Mental Health Courts," *Criminal Justice Newsletter* (24 October 2000), p. 2.
62. Sue Titus Reid, "A Rebuttal to the Attack on the Indeterminate Sentence," *Washington Law Review* 51 (July 1976): 606.

PART V

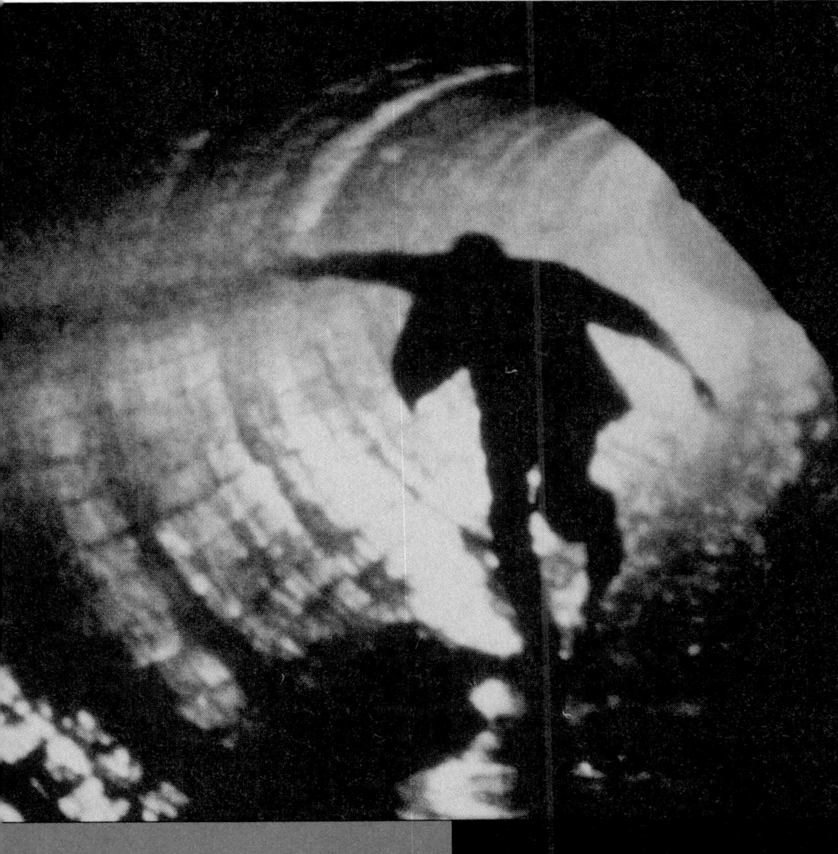

Social Reaction to Crime: Corrections

The final part of this text covers the ways in which society reacts to offenders after they have been processed through court systems. Chapter 14 begins with an overview of the use of jails and prisons for punishment, continues through an examination of early U.S. penal facilities, distinguishes jails and prisons, and addresses their problems of overcrowding. How inmates live in and adjust to prison is discussed, along with prison violence and ways for controlling violence and providing an orderly existence for inmates and officials. Attention is given to inmates' legal rights as well as to the problems inmates and officials face because of the spread of AIDS and tuberculosis.

Prison overcrowding has led to a greater emphasis on alternatives to prison, and recidivism rates have encouraged more thought about preparing incarcerated offenders for reintegration into society. These and other issues are the basis for Chapter 15's analysis of community corrections. The major topics are probation and parole, but attention is also given to the recent and controversial Megan's laws.

CHAPTER 14

▶ Inmates wave sheets asking for peace inside Carandiru Prison in Sao Paulo, Brazil, on 18 February 2001. Rioting inmates in Brazil's largest jail took nearly 8,000 guards and visitors hostage, including hundreds of children, in a revolt that spread to 22 other prisons across the region. This was the largest riot in Brazil's history. (AP)

The Confinement of Offenders

OUTLINE

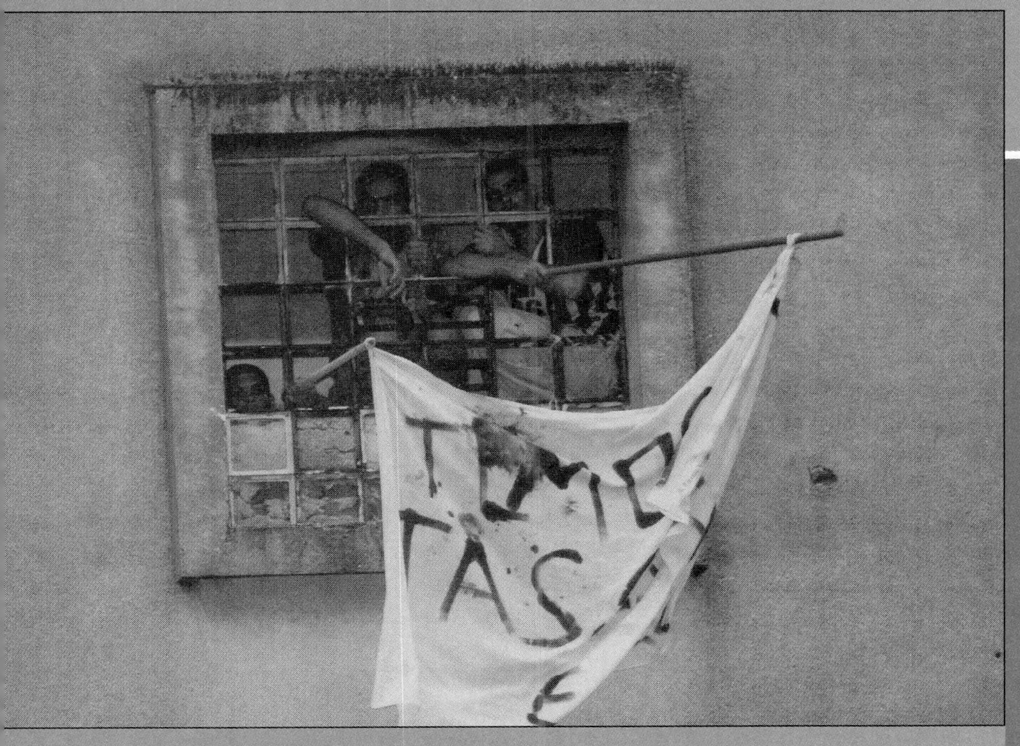

This chapter focuses on the evolution of prisons and jails for the purpose of punishment. It provides a historical background of prisons in Europe and in the United States, distinguishes between prisons and jails, and describes the characteristics of U.S. prisons today. The central problem of overcrowding is examined, and attention is given to privatization of jails and prisons. An analysis of the inmates' social world incorporates discussions of the prison socialization process and a look at the special problems of female, elderly, and mentally ill inmates. The section on prison violence discusses self-inflicted violence as well as violence against others, sexual violence, and prison riots. After briefly noting problems of maintaining control and order within the prison, the chapter overviews inmates' legal rights. It closes with a brief account of prison health issues, especially medical problems such as AIDS and tuberculosis.

KEY TERMS

Deprivation model
Hands-off doctrine
Importation model
Incarceration
Jails
Offenders
Penitentiary
Prison
Prisonization
Reformatory
Transportation

Incarceration Confinement in a jail, a prison, or another penal facility as a form of punishment for a criminal act.

The confinement of offenders as a method of punishment is a relatively recent development. In earlier times offenders were punished using social or psychological methods, often by the victims or their families. Serious (and sometimes not so serious) offenders were subjected to corporal punishments, some of which were so brutal that they caused death. Chapter 3 discussed punishment historically; this chapter focuses on the evolution of **incarceration** as the punishment that follows the determination of guilt.

THE EMERGENCE OF PRISONS FOR PUNISHMENT

Jails Locally administered confinement facilities used to detain persons awaiting a trial or those serving short sentences, usually one year or less.

Transportation The historical practice of deporting criminals to other countries as punishment.

Offenders Persons who commit an offense; used in statutes to describe persons implicated in the commission of a crime.

Prison A state or federal custodial facility for the confinement of offenders serving long terms, usually a year or more.

Penitentiary A state or federal prison or place of punishment used for the confinement of offenders convicted of serious crimes and sentenced for a term of more than one year.

The use of institutions for confining people against their will is ancient. It includes **jails** and other short-term detention facilities, where those awaiting trial or sentencing, execution, **transportation** (deportation to other countries as punishment), whipping, or some other form of corporal punishment were confined. But placing **offenders** in an institution for the purpose of punishment is a relatively modern development.[1]

The transition from corporal punishment to **prison** took place in the 18th century in many European countries. One of the more significant developments was that of hulks (ships used as prisons) in England. The American colonies had rebelled against England's transportation of criminals to the New World; the use of Australia as a penal colony had run into difficulties, too. Crime rates were rising, leading to larger numbers of inmates. Therefore, England legalized the use of hulks, most of which were broken-down war vessels. By 1828 there were 4,000 prison hulks, which were characterized by overcrowding, contagious diseases, lack of work opportunities, unsanitary conditions, lack of ventilation, and corporal punishment. England used prison hulks until the middle of the 19th century, but the use of ships as temporary prisons or jails is a feature of modern incarceration also, a result of the serious overcrowding of most current institutions.

The prison reform movement in Europe provides a lengthy and fascinating area of study that goes beyond the scope of this text. But mention should be made of the great prison reformer John Howard (1726–1790), an Englishman to whom many give credit for the beginnings of the **penitentiary** system. Howard traveled throughout Europe and brought to the attention of the world the sordid conditions under which inmates were confined. In 1777 he published his classic book, *State of Prisons,* which was influential in prison reform in Europe and in the United States.

AMERICAN CONTRIBUTIONS TO THE EMERGENCE OF PRISONS

Despite the existence of prisons in other countries before their emergence in the United States, the new country could claim one unique contribution, at least in theory: the substitution of prison for corporal punishment. Some claim that this idea originated in Europe. Others argue that the prison system began with the Newgate prison in Connecticut and, 20 years later, the Walnut Street Jail in Philadelphia.[2] But credit is usually given to two systems, the Auburn (New York) system and the Pennsylvania system, the latter of which became known throughout the world as the embodiment of the new philosophy.

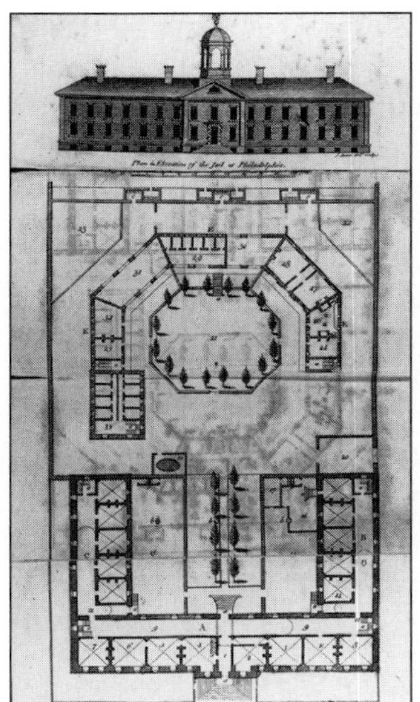

The early Pennsylvania prison known as the Walnut Street Jail was typical of confinement institutions that followed the requirements of a 1790 statute. Inmates spent most of their time in solitary confinement, eating and working in their cells. (Historical Society of Pennsylvania)

The Pennsylvania and Auburn Systems

The Pennsylvania system began in the 19th century, when the Quakers substituted incarceration for corporal punishment. Prison confinement was combined with hard labor rather than with the idleness characteristic of confinement in the English hulks.

The Walnut Street Jail, actually a prison, was typical of the institutions in the Pennsylvania system. It was remodeled to comply with the provisions of a 1790 statute that provided for solitary confinement of offenders. This statute was the beginning of the modern prison system in the United States, for it established the philosophy that was the basis for the Pennsylvania and the Auburn prison systems. Inmates worked an 8- to 10-hour day, in their cells, and they were paid for their work. They received religious instruction. They were allowed to talk to each other only in the common rooms in the evenings. This plan was followed in some other states with variations.

By 1800 some problems in the Pennsylvania system had become obvious. Crowded facilities made work within individual cells impossible; furthermore, there was not enough productive work for the large number of inmates. The Walnut Street Jail failed eventually because of lack of finances, lack of personnel, and overcrowding; but it had gained recognition throughout the world. It has been called the "birthplace of the prison system, in its present meaning, not only in the United States but throughout the world."[3]

The failure of the Walnut Street Jail and other early American prisons led some critics to argue for a return to corporal punishment. But prison reformers were able to get Pennsylvania to enact a statute providing for solitary confinement without labor. The first prison, the Western Penitentiary, was opened in Pittsburgh in 1826, but the lack of work opportunities created problems. Subsequently, the law was changed to permit solitary confinement with inmates working in their cells, setting the stage for Cherry Hill and further developing the Pennsylvania system.

In 1829 Pennsylvania established a prison named for its location in a cherry orchard. This prison represented the first major attempt to implement the Pennsylvania system of solitary confinement of inmates with work provided in their cells. To maintain this system without endangering the health of the inmates or permitting their escape, the architect designed a prison with seven wings, each connected to a central hub by covered passageways. The single cells had individual outdoor exercise yards. Inmates were not permitted to see one another even when taken to chapel. The chaplain spoke from the rotunda, with inmates remaining in their individual cells. The Pennsylvania prison architecture was not popular in the United States but became the model for most of Europe. The system that prevailed in the United States was the New York, or Auburn, plan.

In contrast to the Pennsylvania system, the Auburn plan permitted inmates to congregate but not to communicate. The system was much more economical than the Pennsylvania system. The architecture featured a fortresslike building with a series of tiers set in a hollow frame. Silence was enforced by having inmates eat face-to-back rather than face-to-face. They had to stand with arms folded and eyes down so they could not communicate with their hands; when walking, they had to maintain a lockstep with a downward gaze. They were isolated further by rules limiting contact with the outside world. When they attended religious functions, they sat in boothlike pews that prevented them from seeing anyone other than the speaker.

Auburn's warden, Captain Elam Lynds, believed in strict discipline; he took the position that reformation could not occur until the spirit of the inmate was broken. By 1821 he was placing dangerous inmates in solitary confinement for long periods, a practice that led to mental illness and, in some cases, death. Many inmates pleaded to be permitted to work. A commission appointed to study the prison recommended abolishing solitary confinement and putting all inmates to work.

Both the Auburn and the Pennsylvania prison systems were based on the belief that inmates would corrupt one another if they were permitted to have contact. The Pennsylvania system isolated inmates; the Auburn system permitted congregation but enforced the silent rule. In the Pennsylvania system, the Quaker emphasis on religious training and time for reflection was emphasized; moreover, inmates were expected to read their Bibles and meditate. Corporal punishment was not permitted. The Auburn plan included corporal punishment. The prison systems differed also in architecture. The Auburn plan was less expensive to build, but the Pennsylvania system was more economical to administer. Both systems were severe, although it has been argued that both were improvements over the cruel punishments that existed then in the United States and in Europe.

Prison Expansion

In the late 1800s prison overcrowding became a problem as prison populations increased rapidly. New prisons were built in the early 1900s, including Attica (New York) in 1931 and Stateville (Illinois) in 1925, both still in use today. Most of the prisons built in the early 1900s followed the Auburn plan of architecture. Some programs were available for inmates, and some work was provided, but the work was based on institutional rather than inmate needs. Prison products were sold on the open market, a practice later prohibited by statute because of complaints from private industry. Attempts were made to segregate inmates by classifications such as age, gender, and type of offense. Prison reformers argued that inmates should be treated as individuals and that communication was important. The silent system was abolished, and some attempts were made to increase social activities. But by 1935, for most inmates, "the penitentiary system had again reverted to its original status: punishment and custody."[4]

The 1800s and early 1900s were characterized by an emphasis on probation and parole, discussed in Chapter 15. Of primary concern here is that the prison concept became a total institution for confinement with little, if any, emphasis on reformation. Other scholars have argued that even if prisons were initially intended to be humanitarian, they evolved as institutions for the political and social manipulation of certain classes of people.[5]

The Reformatory Era

Not all early prisons were penitentiaries. In the 1800s some reformers recognized the need to separate children from adults and women from men and to classify offenders by the seriousness of their offenses. A meeting on 12 October 1870, conducted by penologist Enoch C. Wines, led to the emergence of the **reformatory** system, culminating in the establishment of the Elmira (New York) Reformatory in 1876. Elmira became the model for reformatories designed primarily for youthful offenders. Although architecturally Elmira was similar to Auburn, its programs placed a greater emphasis on education and vocational training. Indeterminate sentences with maximum terms, opportunity for parole, and classification of inmates according to conduct and productivity were the greatest achievements of Elmira.

Reformatory Correctional facility that is less secure than a prison or penitentiary and that, at least in theory, has as its primary goal the rehabilitation of offenders.

It was predicted that Elmira would dominate U.S. prison systems. Headed by Zebulon R. Brockway, who was proclaimed by some authorities as the "greatest warden America has ever produced," Elmira "changed the course of corrections by introducing 'scientific reform' and the 'new penology.'" But Elmira was also viewed as an institution that was instrumental in perpetuating sexism and racism and in repressing the lower classes.[6] Thus, although there is disagreement on the place of Elmira in history, it does seem clear that what was designed to be a reformatory was in fact a prison.

Beginning in 1910 the reformatory system declined primarily because of the lack of trained personnel to conduct the education programs and carry on the classification systems adequately. Some of the techniques of management and discipline used at the reformatories were characteristic of prisons. Brockway was accused of using "cruel, brutal, excessive and unusual punishment" to achieve his purpose of reforming inmates. A series of investigations led to recommendations for some changes, such as the improvement of medical care, reduction of overcrowding, and the restriction of whipping, permitting it only on the buttocks. Serious allegations against Brockway were dropped. He continued to rule at Elmira until 1900, "and the Elmira experiment came to an end just as 'prison science' and the 'new penology' were taking hold across the country."[7] Reformatories continued, but many were really prisons, presenting only an illusion of reformation.

The Modern Era of American Prisons: An Overview

In the past few decades significant attempts have been made to change the nature of incarceration. Many of these attempts are related to the use of alternatives to incarceration, discussed in Chapter 15. Changes were made in prisons also. Despite the continued use of many of the fortresslike prisons built in the 1800s and early 1900s, some progressive designs were incorporated into the construction of new prisons. A greater emphasis was placed on rehabilitation combined with improved opportunities for education and vocational training. Treatment programs, at least in theory, were emphasized. Indeterminate sentences were instituted to fulfill the claim that inmates would not be released until they were reformed; reformation would take place through counseling and training.

Despite these alleged changes, many authorities recognize now that most prison reform was illusory; few real changes occurred, and escapes and riots increased. As crime rates climbed, rehabilitation was declared a failure. As sentences were lengthened, inmate populations strained prison capacity. As prison conditions deteriorated, federal courts became active in the inmates' rights movement, which is discussed later in this chapter. Prisons have remained, but the serious conditions of today's institutions have led many to question the so-called reform era.

TYPES OF INSTITUTIONS FOR THE CONFINEMENT OF ADULT OFFENDERS

Most adult offenders are confined in jails, prisons, or community-based facilities. In some jurisdictions adults are detained in *lockups,* which are temporary holding facilities for short-term detention while suspects are awaiting court hearings. Usually lockups are operated by police departments and located at police stations. They may be used to detain juveniles until their parents or other guardians take custody of them from police or they are placed in other facilities. Community-based facilities are discussed in Chapter 15, along with noninstitutional confinement, such as house arrest with electronic monitoring. Jails and prisons are the focus here. Before looking at each individually, inmate populations should be noted.

The jail and prison population of the United States reached 1,725,842 in 1997, representing a 6 percent increase from the previous year. Jail populations, which had been increasing more slowly than prison populations, jumped dramatically, from an average yearly increase since 1990 of 4.9 percent to an increase of 9.4 percent between 1996 and 1997. Approximately 9,100 juveniles were incarcerated in jails, either awaiting trial as adults or serving time after being convicted as adults. By 1998 prison and jail populations had risen to 1.8 million, a record high.[8]

In 1999 the growth of jail and prison populations slowed to 3.4 percent, down significantly from the annual growth rate of 6.5 percent since 1990.[9]

In the year 2000 prison populations began to level off as crime rates fell. In the year ending 30 June 2000, the number of inmates incarcerated in jails rose by 15,206; those in state prisons rose by 27,953, and those in federal prisons rose by 13,501.[10] Exhibit 14.1 contains information about inmates in 2000. Also, during the decade of the 1990s more prisons were built. Both of these facts eased prison overcrowding, although it still exists in many facilities, such as local jails. To some extent jail overcrowding is caused by sentenced offenders being held in jail while awaiting space in prisons that are over the maximum number of inmates allowed by federal court orders. This situation has changed the characteristics of jail inmates, many of whom are serious offenders awaiting transfer to prison. They are housed in jails traditionally used to detain less serious offenders.

Life in prison is symbolized by bars and locks. In many penal institutions inmates spend most of their time in confined areas without meaningful activities or work opportunities. (Sandra Johnson/Index Stock)

For the fourth consecutive year, the percentage increase in female inmates in 1999 surpassed that of males, but the proportion of inmates that were women remained relatively low: 90,688 women compared to 1,276,053 men. Men were 15 times more likely than women to be incarcerated in a state or federal prison. Also in 1999 most states were holding inmates in local jails or other facilities until space was available for them in prisons. Some states were incarcerating their prison inmates in federal facilities for the same reasons. During 2000 the number of women in prisons increased by 1.2 percent, while the number of men increased by 1.3 percent.[11]

The general effect of jail and prison overcrowding magnifies the negative aspects of confinement. Crowded conditions lead to greater contact among inmates, resulting in aggressive and at times violent behavior (including sexual assaults). Overcrowding may also induce stress in inmates *and* staff and lead to physical and mental problems. Another contributor to stress in prison is boredom. Most inmates do not work and have no access to educational or vocational programs. When facilities are overcrowded, the transportation of inmates to and from program sites becomes difficult. Many administrators assign inmates to more time in their cells rather than cope with moving large numbers around the facilities. The educational, recreational, and vocational programs that do exist have long waiting lists. Administrators do not have funds to run enough programs to keep all inmates busy; nor can they hire enough staff to manage large numbers of active inmates. Instead, inmates

EXHIBIT 14.1

Inmates in 2000: Highlights

	Number of Inmates	
December 31	Federal	State
1990	65,526	708,379
1995	100,250	1,025,624
1999	135,246	1,228,455
2000	145,416	1,236,476

- In the last 6 months of 2000, the State prison population declined about 6,200 inmates (down 0.5%)—the first measured decline in the State prison population since 1972 . . .
- At year-end 2000, privately operated facilities housed 87,369 inmates (5.8% of State and 10.7% of Federal inmates); local jails housed 63,140 State and Federal inmates (4.6% of all prisoners).
- On December 31, 2000, State prisons were operating between full capacity and 15% above capacity, while Federal prisons were operating at 31% above capacity.
- Between June 30, 1990, and June 30, 2000, when complete censuses of prison facilities were conducted, the number of State adult correctional facilities increased by 351. At midyear 2000, there were 1,320 State adult facilities, 84 Federal facilities, and 264 privately operated facilities. During the decade, States added more than 528,000 beds (up 81%).
- At year-end 2000, 91,612 women were in State or Federal prisons—6.6% of all prison inmates. Since 1990 the number of male prisoners has grown 77% (reaching 1,290,280 in 2000), while the number of female prisoners has increased 108%.
- Among the more than 1.3 million sentenced inmates at year-end, an estimated 428,300 were black males between the ages of 20 and 39. At year-end 2000, 9.7% of black males age 25 to 29 were in prison, compared to 2.9% of Hispanic males and 1.1% of white males in the same age group.

The total number of prisoners under the jurisdiction of Federal or State adult correctional authorities was 1,381,892 at year-end 2000. During the year the States and the District of Columbia added 8,021 prisoners, and the Federal prison system added 10,170 prisoners. Overall, the nation's prison population grew 1.3%, which was less than the average annual growth of 6.0% since 1990. During 2000 the prison population rose at the lowest rate since 1972 and had the smallest absolute increase since 1980 . . .

Overall, the United States incarcerated 2,071,686 persons at year-end 2000. This total represents persons held in

- Federal and State prisons (1,312,354, which excludes State and Federal prisoners in local jails)
- Territorial prisons (16,130)
- Local jails (621,149)
- Facilities operated by or exclusively for the U.S. Immigration and Naturalization Service (8,894)
- Military facilities (2,420)
- Jails in Indian country (1,775)
- Juvenile facilities (108,965 as of October 1999)

More than 1.9 million [were held] in prisons and local jails.

On December 31, 2000, 1,312,354 inmates were in the custody of State and Federal prison authorities, and 621,149 were in the custody of local jail authorities. Since year-end 1999 the total incarcerated population has increased by 40,388. Including inmates in public and privately operated facilities, the number of inmates in State prisons increased 1.5% during 2000; the number in Federal prisons, 6.6%; and in local jails, 2.5%. During 2000 the total incarcerated population grew 2.1%—less than half the annual average (5.3%) since 1990 . . .

The U.S. prison population rose 1.3% during 2000—the smallest annual growth rate since 1972.

Source: Bureau of Justice Statistics, *Prisoners in 2000* (Washington, DC: U.S. Department of Justice, August 2001), p. 1.

are expected to spend time in their cells or to do menial maintenance work, and many are confined to their cells for more than 10 hours per day.

Numerous solutions to jail and prison overcrowding have been suggested. Several states have enacted statutes granting their governors permission to declare an emergency when prison populations reach a specified level. At that point inmates must be released to provide space for newly convicted offenders. This procedure has led to severe criticism when violent offenders are released, as has occurred in some states. Some jurisdictions have contracted with others to house their surplus inmates, but that is not a viable option in some cases, since many jails and prisons are overcrowded. Others are planning to change or already have changed local ordinances and state statutes to decrease penalties in order to reduce jail and prison populations. Some are seeking funds for renovation and expansion of existing facilities, and others are building new facilities. As noted above, the declining crime rates are also easing overcrowding problems.

Although jails and prisons share some of the same problems, especially with regard to overcrowding, the two types of penal institutions do have some unique features and should be examined independently.

Jails

The Latin root of the word *jail* is *cavea*, meaning "cavity," "cage," or "coop." It has been suggested that jails should be defined as "public cages or coops." As Exhibit 14.2 discloses, jails are used for several purposes.

Ironically, although the jail is the oldest of American penal institutions, less is known about it than about any of the others. Except for an occasional scathing commentary, it has been tolerated but has received little attention. It was not until 1970 that some systematic data on jails became available. At that time the first national jail census was conducted for the Law Enforcement Assistance Administration by the U.S. Bureau of the Census.

Jails can be traced far back into history. They made their debut "in the form of murky dungeons, abysmal pits, unscalable precipices, strong poles or trees, and suspended cages in which hapless inmates were kept."[12] Their main purpose was to detain people awaiting trial, transportation, the death penalty, or

EXHIBIT 14.2

Purposes of Jails

- Receive individuals pending arraignment and hold them awaiting trial, conviction, or sentencing
- Readmit probation, parole, and bail-bond violators and absconders
- Temporarily detain juveniles pending transfer to juvenile authorities
- Hold mentally ill persons pending their movement to appropriate health facilities
- Hold individuals for the military, for protective custody, for contempt, and for the courts as witnesses
- Release convicted inmates to the community upon completion of sentence
- Transfer inmates to Federal, State, or other authorities
- House inmates for Federal, State, or other authorities because of crowding of their facilities
- Relinquish custody of temporary detainees to juvenile and medical authorities
- Sometimes operate community-based programs with electronic monitoring or other types of supervision.

Source: Bureau of Justice Statistics, *Jails and Jail Inmates 1993–94* (Washington, DC: U.S. Department of Justice, April 1995), p. 2.

corporal punishment. The old jails were not escape-proof, and often the persons in charge received additional fees for shackling inmates. Inmates were not separated according to any system of classification. Physical conditions were terrible, food was inadequate, and no treatment or rehabilitation programs existed.

Although allegedly U.S. jails were proposed as a humane replacement for corporal punishment, early jails were not in fact humane places. The conditions in American jails worsened over the years. In 1923 Joseph Fishman, a federal prison inspector, investigator, and consultant, published *Crucible of Crime,* in which he described American jails, basing his descriptions and evaluations on visits to 1,500 jails. He said that some of the convicted would ask for a year in prison in preference to six months in jail because of the horrible jail conditions. Most jails were overcrowded, and inmates did not have adequate food, medical care, or bathing facilities. Separate facilities were not provided for juveniles. Fishman's conclusion might be summarized by his definition of jail as

> an unbelievably filthy institution in which are confined men and women serving sentences for misdemeanors and crimes, and men and women not under sentence who are simply awaiting trial. With few exceptions, having no segregation of the unconvicted from the convicted, the well from the diseased, the youngest and most impressionable from the most degraded and hardened. Usually swarming with bedbugs, roaches, lice, and other vermin; has an odor of disinfectant and filth which is appalling; supports in complete idleness thousands of able-bodied men and women, and generally affords ample time and opportunity to assure inmates a complete course in every kind of viciousness and crime. A melting pot in which the worst elements of the raw material in the criminal world are brought forth blended and turned out in absolute perfection.[13]

In 1931 the American jail was described by the National Commission on Law Observance and Enforcement as the "most notorious correctional institution in the world."[14] By the early 1980s, the American jail was described by noted authorities as "the worst blight in American corrections"[15] and a place where "anyone not a criminal when he goes in, will be when he comes out."[16]

The typical jail in the United States is small and was built between 1880 and 1920. There has been little renovation of its physical facilities. It is located in a small town, often the county seat of a predominantly rural county. These small rural jails constitute the majority of jails but house only a minority of the jail population. Some of them are used infrequently, and usually they are not crowded. Most of the jail population is confined in large urban jails, many of which are targets of court suits on jail conditions.

The fact that the typical jail is financed and administered locally inevitably involves the jail's administration in local politics. Historically, American jails have been under the direction and supervision of the sheriff, usually an elected official. In general, such administrators have shown little interest in jail inspections or improvements. Recently some states have assumed control of their jails, but in most instances the standards remain low, with few if any educational or rehabilitative programs.

Staffing jails is a serious problem. The workers receive low pay and many have little or no training. Jails have low budgets because local governments have less money to spend than state or federal governments; in many communities jails have the lowest priority for local funds. Most jails are understaffed. This absence of adequate supervision gives the inmates little protection from sexual and other violent attacks, and the lack of staff increases the probability that inmates who attempt suicide will be successful. Suicide is the primary cause of death among jail inmates and generally occurs within the first 24 hours of incarceration.

Prisons

Prisons are for the long-term incarceration of offenders. Although frequently the term is used synonymously with *maximum-security* institutions, there are several types of prisons. Historically, maximum-security prisons were the most secure facilities. Most are surrounded by high fences topped with razor wire and are watched by armed correctional officers in observation towers. The architecture of many of these prisons follows the Auburn plan, with large tiers of cell blocks made up of individual cells housing more than one offender each. Theoretically, maximum-security prisons incarcerate only serious offenders or others who might present a security risk. In reality, it is not uncommon to find less serious offenders in these facilities.

Many *medium-security* prisons are surrounded by fences topped with razor or barbed wire; armed correctional officers may or may not be present. Housing architecture, more varied than that of the maximum-security prison, may include individual rooms or dormitories rather than cells. Inmates have greater freedom of movement and theoretically are less serious offenders. Generally *minimum-security* prisons do not have armed correctional officers; many do not have fences or bars. Inmates may be housed in individual rooms or dormitories. They have greater freedom to move about within the institution than in medium- or maximum-security facilities.

In recent years some prisons, or designated wings within a prison, have become *maxi-maxi* institutions, housing the most dangerous inmates. The inmates are confined individually and permitted out of their cells for only short periods,

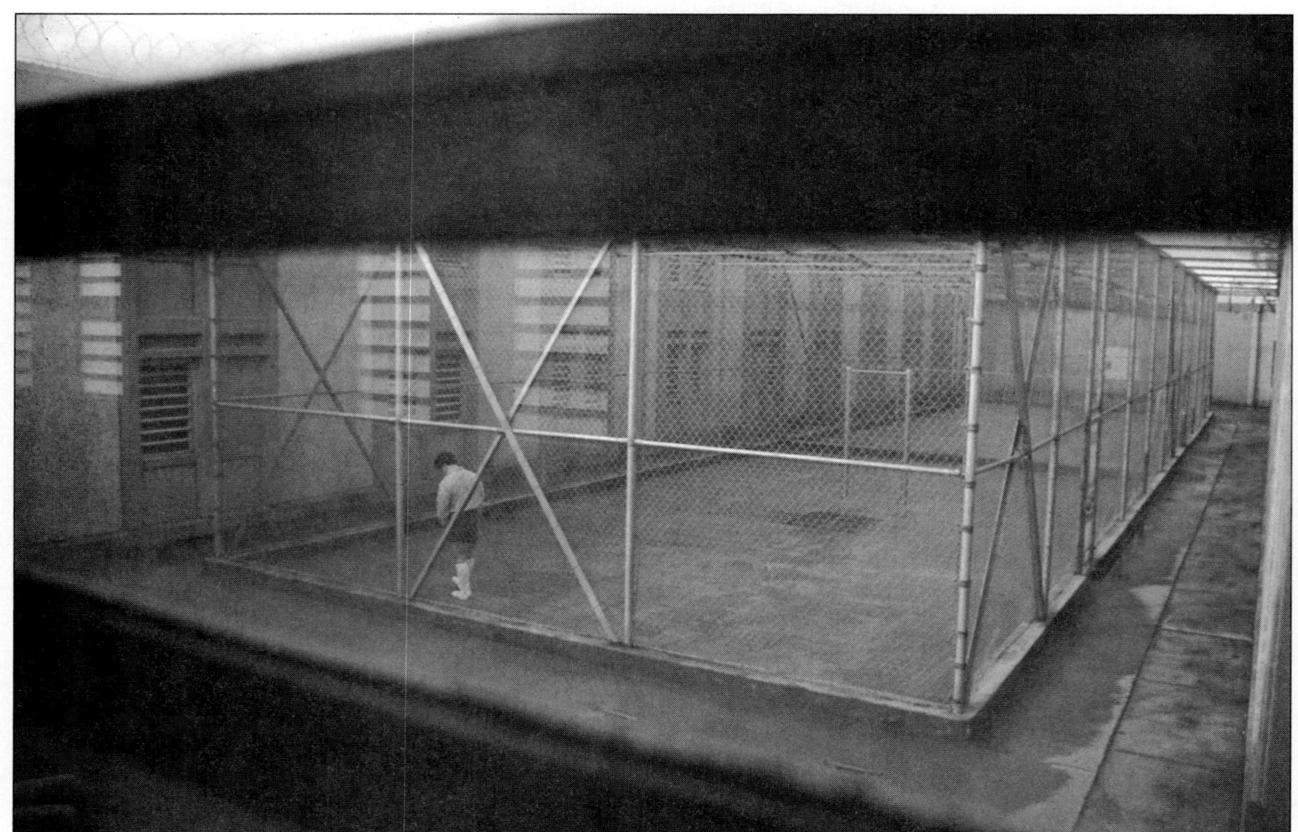

Security is tight in prisons that house the most violent and dangerous inmates. This inmate in the U.S. penitentiary at Marion, Illinois, exercises alone in a secure cage. (Steve Starr/Stock Boston)

for example, one hour a day. In some institutions inmates are shackled when they leave their cells. An example is the federal prison in Marion, Illinois, which houses some of the most dangerous federal inmates, including those thought most likely to attempt escape. Marion has become the model for states that have designated maxi-maxi prisons, giving rise to the epithet "Marionization."

Increased security in the maxi-maxi wings or institutions includes more than perimeter security. After a correctional officer was killed in the Folsom prison in California, all furniture was removed from the Violence Control Unit (which housed the most dangerous offenders). Concrete slabs replaced beds, and epoxy was used to seal electric outlets. The most dangerous inmates were shackled before they were allowed to exercise in the prison yard. In Folsom and other prisons, officials have taken more control over the movement and daily lives of inmates in an effort to decrease prison violence.[17]

There have been problems with maxi-maxi prisons, which have been denounced by human rights groups. The director of the American Civil Liberties Union's Institutionalized Persons Project in Illinois summarized his views of maxi-maxi prisons as follows:

> To build these supermaxes is one thing, but we've gone out of our way to torture these guys and deprive them of human contact in a way that cannot be justified.[18]

Specific maxi-maxi prisons have been attacked, with a report by an organization that monitors human rights worldwide alleging that the two maxi-maxi prisons in Indiana engage in practices that constitute torture under international human rights law. The state's corrections commissioner agreed with some of the report's allegations but argued that this type of institution is necessary to handle inmates who threaten the security of the entire state system.[19]

One year later a report on California prisons noted that from 1988 until 1994, "when whistle-blowers inside Corcoran went to the Federal Bureau of Investigation, the prison's guards shot to death seven inmates and wounded forty-three, more than in all other prisons in the country combined." Although the

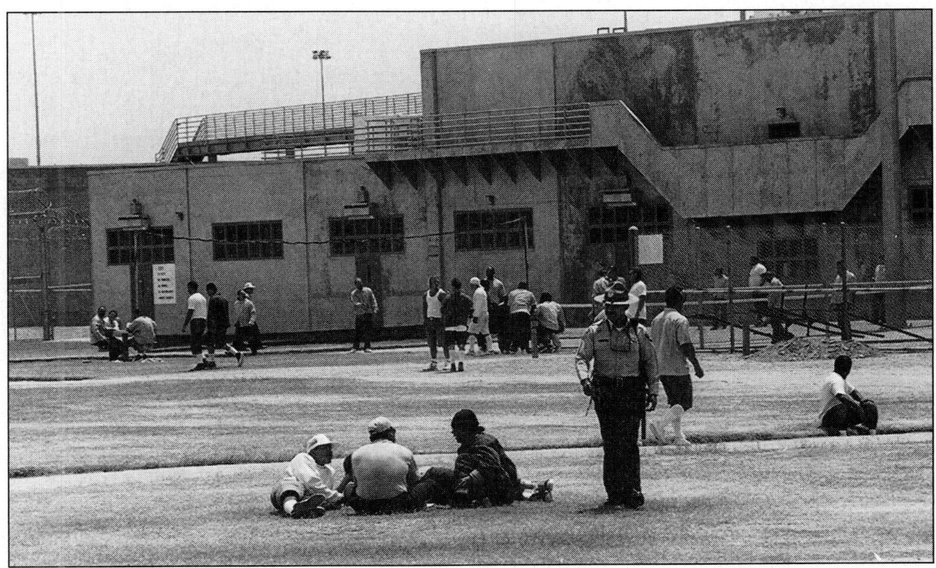

A correctional officer walks through the exercise yard at the Corcoran State Prison in Corcoran, California. This prison houses some of the most violent criminals in California and has been investigated for alleged abuse of inmates by correctional officials. (AP Photo / Scott Anger)

shootings stopped after the complaints were filed, they continued in other California prisons.[20]

Categories other than security levels may differentiate prisons. Some are exclusive by gender; most are for men only. Others house both genders, and although inmates in some co-correctional prisons are permitted limited contact, the rules forbid sexual relations. Problems with housing both genders in the same general facilities have led to their abolition in many systems.[21]

Prisons may also be distinguished as *state* or *federal.* It was not until the 1900s that the federal government established a separate prison system. Before that time, long-term federal inmates were incarcerated in state prisons on a contract basis, and most short-term federal inmates were confined in local jails, also on a contract basis. Today federal prisons are under the jurisdiction of the Federal Bureau of Prisons.

All states have some type of prison system, although the systems vary considerably. Most states have all levels of security, but not all levels are available for female offenders because of their smaller numbers. States differ significantly in the amount of money spent on prisons.

PRIVATE JAILS AND PRISONS

The cost of financing jails and prisons is such a problem today that authorities are looking for innovative ways to finance construction and maintenance of facilities as well as the cost of inmates' care. Some states levy a fee on convicted persons, with the rates usually higher for serious than for minor offenses. In 1992 Congress approved legislation permitting the federal prison system to levy user fees on inmates. It was estimated that approximately 9 percent of new inmates would be able to pay their fees at least for their first year of incarceration and that $48 million might be raised in new revenue through these fees. In a 1995 case the U.S. Court of Appeals for the Second Circuit held that this "cost of imprisonment fine" may be imposed even in cases in which normal fines based on sentencing guidelines are not imposed. Other circuit courts have not agreed on this approach, and the Supreme Court has not decided the issue.[22] One of the disadvantages of the cost of imprisonment approach is that inmates may leave prison without funds and with debts; payment for room and board thus reduces their ability to support their families, pay for educational or other needs, and reintegrate into society when they are released.

A more common plan for financing jails and prisons is privatization. Under privatization a profit-making company, with money from private investors, finances, builds, and owns the jail or prison or contracts to provide some service (such as food or medical care) within the institution. The facility may be leased to the government to operate, leaving the state (or federal government) with no responsibility for upkeep. In some cases, the private company manages the jail or prison. At the end of 1999, 5.5 percent of all state inmates and 2.8 percent of all federal inmates were incarcerated in privately operated prisons. Texas had the largest number, followed by Oklahoma. In five states (New Mexico, Alaska, Oklahoma, Montana, Hawaii), at least 20 percent of the state's inmates were in private facilities.[23]

Privatization of jails and prisons is not a new practice in the United States. Private contracts were rather common in earlier days, but it is the significant increase in prison and jail populations and the cost of maintaining them that has led to the expanded use of privatization in the United States. Similar problems exist in other countries. For example, in 1995 severe overcrowding forced the British Prison Service to announce that a new private jail facility would be built near Nottingham. The news came with an announcement that prison governors described many jails in that country as "scandalous."[24]

Some of the problems with privatization of jails and prisons are illustrated by recent events. In October 1998 four Tennessee inmates escaped from a private prison operated by the Corrections Corporation of America (CCA), which is based in Nashville, Tennessee, but operates prisons in many other states. It took over a month to recapture six inmates (four of whom were murderers) who escaped in July 1998 from a Youngstown, Ohio, prison operated by CCA. Acts of violence occurred in still other prisons operated by the company, leading one Tennessee newspaper to challenge the CCA to "clean up its act, the better to earn public confidence" before any other Tennessee prisons were privatized. The paper alleged that the "disturbing string of incidents at four CCA facilities suggests poor management."[25]

The media have focused on privatization of jails and prisons, emphasizing some of the potential problems: quality control, accountability, security, and cost. The Justice Department has expressed reservations about privatizing federal prisons. The concern is based on a study mandated by a federal statute enacted in 1997, which mandated the closing of the District of Columbia's prison system and placing the inmates under the control of the Federal Bureau of Prisons. The statute also called for privatization of some facilities. The report concluded that although many of the initial legal concerns with privatization may be averted with careful drafting of contracts, there is inconclusive evidence that private prisons are more cost effective and safer than public-run institutions.[26]

One final issue with regard to private prisons is the use of them for juveniles. In 2000 the State of Louisiana agreed to a federal court order effecting major changes in the way that state operates prisons for young men. Among other provisions, the state will no longer send young offenders to Jena, which had been operated by Wackenhut Corrections Corporation, affiliated with the world's largest operator of private prisons, Wackenhut Corporation. Several lawsuits had been filed against Louisiana, alleging that teenage inmates were denied adequate food, clothing, and medical care and were beaten by correctional officers. A second facility, which had been managed by a company operated by friends of the former governor, was also back in the hands of the state department of corrections.[27]

THE INMATE'S SOCIAL WORLD

There are a variety of ways to deal with the stress created by prison life. Some inmates feel they must be active in order to survive the prison experience. Their activities may include watching television or listening to the radio or stereo, obtaining and using drugs, making alcoholic beverages, lifting weights or participating in other physical activities, cleaning cells, scheming, or daydreaming. Some of these activities are becoming impossible, however, as some jurisdictions are cutting back or eliminating cable television and other so-called luxuries of prison life.

Inmates must cope with the physical, social, and psychological problems that result from the worst punishment—the deprivation of liberty. In his classic study of male inmates, Gresham M. Sykes discussed the moral rejection by the community (which is a constant threat to the inmate's self-concept), the deprivation of goods and services in a society that values material possessions, the deprivation of heterosexual relationships and the resulting threat to the inmate's masculinity, and the deprivation of security in an inmate population that threatens his safety and sometimes his health and life.[28]

Everything the inmates do, including the showers they can take and the hours they can sleep, is regulated by the prison staff. Inmates have no autonomy and can show no initiative. They are forced to define themselves as weak, helpless, and dependent, which threatens their self-concept. The prison system rarely, if ever, permits them to function as adults. They face the conflict that

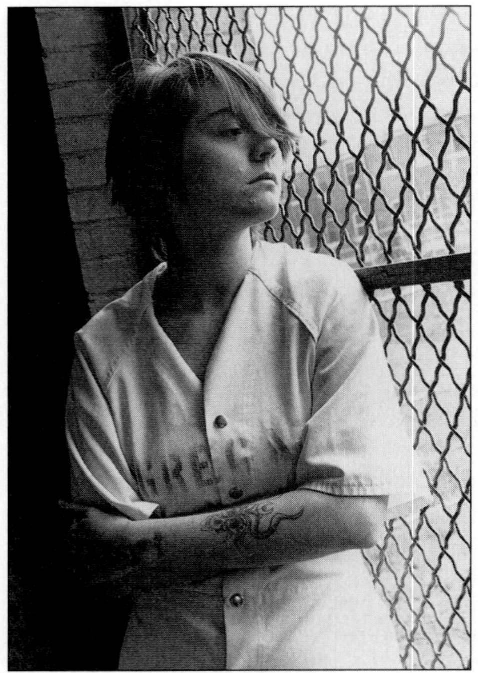

Women who are a threat to themselves or to others may be placed in solitary confinement or administrative segregation, where they are required to wear prison uniforms and lose many of the privileges enjoyed by the general inmate population. (Gale Zucker/Stock Boston)

while the prison's isolated social system stresses adaptation to the inmate subculture, that same system and correctional staff stress preparation for release.

Prisonization

In 1940, a classic study of the prison community was published by Donald Clemmer, who proposed the concept of prisonization to explain the formation of inmate subcultures. He defined **prisonization** as "the taking on, in greater or lesser degree, of the folkways, mores, customs, and general culture of the penitentiary." When a new inmate enters prison, he or she begins the process of prisonization. This process is not the same for all inmates and may be affected by the inmate's personality, environment, and relationships outside prison; whether the inmate joins a primary group in prison; and the degree to which the inmate accepts the codes of prison life. Prisonization may have an effect on the inmate's adjustment after release.[29]

Prisonization The process by which a prison inmate assimilates the customs, norms, values, and culture of prison life.

Clemmer's concept of prisonization was tested empirically by Stanton Wheeler in a study at the Washington State Reformatory. Although Wheeler's findings supported Clemmer's concept, Wheeler also found that the degree of prisonization varied according to the phase of an inmate's institutional career, developing along a U-shaped curve. Inmates tended to be more receptive to the values of the outside world during the first period of incarceration (measured at the end of the first six months) and the last period (last six months before release) and less receptive during the middle, or prison career, period (more than six months remaining). In the last six months of incarceration, when inmates were anticipating their releases back into society, their main reference group shifted from the other inmates within the institution to the society outside. Wheeler concluded that Clemmer's concept of prisonization should be reformulated to include the variable of the career phase.[30]

Subsequent researchers have found some support for Wheeler's U-shaped curve of attitudes.[31] Others, comparing prisonization among male and female inmates, have questioned Wheeler's hypothesis. One study found that although time spent in prison was related significantly to prisonization among female inmates, this was not true among male inmates. For men, variables such as age and attitudes toward law and the judicial system were significant. Among women, attitudes toward race and the police were significant.[32]

More recently, scholars have questioned the methodology of some of the research that shows that prison experiences result in deleterious effects on inmates. They have criticized the research for a lack of attention to psychological factors. One study reports that "psychological functioning was remarkably stable over time in prison." For those who are in prison for a long period, the initial psychological discomfort does not persist over time; nor does the inmate engage in widespread behavioral changes or suffer "general or widespread deteriorative effects." In addition, inmates "did not become social isolates inside of prison, and neither did they lose contact with the outside. Most did not sink into despair or rebellion, but rather their emotional states, health, and conduct in the institutions generally *improved* over time."[33]

Prisonization Models

Sociological analyses of the prisonization process and the emergence of a prison subculture have followed two models: the deprivation model and the importation model.

Deprivation model A model of prisonization based on the belief that the inmate subculture arises from inmates' adaptations to the severe physical and psychological losses imposed by incarceration.

The **deprivation model** is illustrated by Gresham Sykes's position that the inmate subculture is the product of an attempt to adapt to the deprivations imposed by incarceration. Inmates have few alternatives to alleviate their deprivations (including loss of status) and degradation. They cannot escape psychologically or physically; they cannot eliminate the pains of imprisonment. Inmates have a choice of uniting with fellow captives in a spirit of mutual cooperation or withdrawing to seek only the satisfaction of their own needs. In either case, their behavior patterns are adaptations to the deprivations of their environment.

According to the deprivation model, the inmates' social system is functional in that it enables them to minimize the pains of imprisonment through cooperation. For example, the cooperation of inmates in exchanging favors removes the opportunity for some to exploit others and enables them to accept material deprivation more easily. In addition, available goods and services are distributed and shared willingly if the inmates have a cooperative social system. This system helps resolve the problem of personal security, alleviate the fear of further isolation, and restore the inmate's sense of self-respect and independence.[34]

Importation model A model of **prisonization** based on the assumption that the inmate **subculture** arises not only from internal prison experiences but also from external patterns of behavior that inmates bring to the prison.

The **importation model** is illustrated by the work of John Irwin and Donald R. Cressey, who maintained that too much emphasis had been placed on the impact of prison on inmates. They argued that the prison subculture is a combination of several types of subcultures that exist outside the prison and are imported by offenders when they enter.[35]

Scholars have found support for each of these models. Charles W. Thomas emphasized in his research that, like the rest of us, inmates have a past, a present, and a future, and all are related to the prisonization process. New inmates face two social systems in prison: the formal organization (resocialization) and the inmate society (prisonization). Both compete for the inmate's allegiance. The goals of the formal organization are custody and confinement; the goal of inmates is freedom. Because these two social systems conflict, if one succeeds, the other must fail. Since the prison is not a closed system, in explaining the inmate culture we must examine the following factors: preprison experience, both criminal and noncriminal; expectations of staff and fellow inmates; quality of contacts with persons or groups outside the walls; postprison expectations; and immediate adjustment problems. The greater the degree of similarity between preprison activities and prison subculture values and attitudes, the more receptive the inmate is to prisonization. Inmates from the lower social classes are more likely to become highly prisonized. Those who have the highest degree of contact with the outside world have the lowest degree of prisonization. Finally, those with a higher degree of prisonization are among those who have the bleakest postprison expectations.[36]

Leo Carroll criticized the deprivation model in his study of race relations in an eastern prison. The model "diverts attention from interrelationships between the prison and the wider society . . . and hence away from issues such as racial violence." Carroll maintained that the models should not be seen as opposites but as complementary. According to Carroll, the form of inmate subculture that prevails depends on the degree of security and deprivation in the institution. In maximum-security prisons we would expect the deprivation model to prevail, but in prisons with less security and fewer deprivations, the importation model is more likely to dominate. Carroll's research lends support to the importation model, but he concluded that the model was incomplete.[37]

Other researchers have taken the position that the importation and deprivation models should be integrated, that both are important to explaining prisonization. The cross-cultural studies of Ronald L. Akers and his colleagues are examples. The functional or adaptation model was supported only partially by their data from several countries and one U.S. jurisdiction. Their data show that "the inmate culture varies by whatever differences in organization environment there are from one institution to the next."[38]

This integrative approach has been summarized as follows: "The existence of collective solutions in the inmate culture and social structure is based on the common problems of adjustment to the institution, while the content of those solutions and the tendency to become prisonized are imported from the larger society."[39] Thus, it is not sufficient to argue that the importation or deprivation model alone explains the individual adaptations of inmates to prison or the development of an inmate subculture; rather, variables of each are important.

The deprivation model and two other models have been used in recent research to examine prison violence. Some scholars argue that deprivation or *relative* deprivation (changes in deprivation) may lead to violence, while others suggest there is no relationship between deprivation and collective violence. Other scholars take the position that it is not deprivation but *failed prison management*, such as inadequate security and poorly disciplined or poorly trained officers, that is related to inmate problems that may result in collective violence. Another point of view suggests that internal problems are related to prison size. It is much more difficult to maintain order in a megaprison than in a small facility with a lower inmate/officer ratio. Finally, some scholars argue that prisons are not total institutions,[40] and both inmates and prison personnel are influenced by life outside prison. Thus, internal prison order may be influenced by external prison conditions.

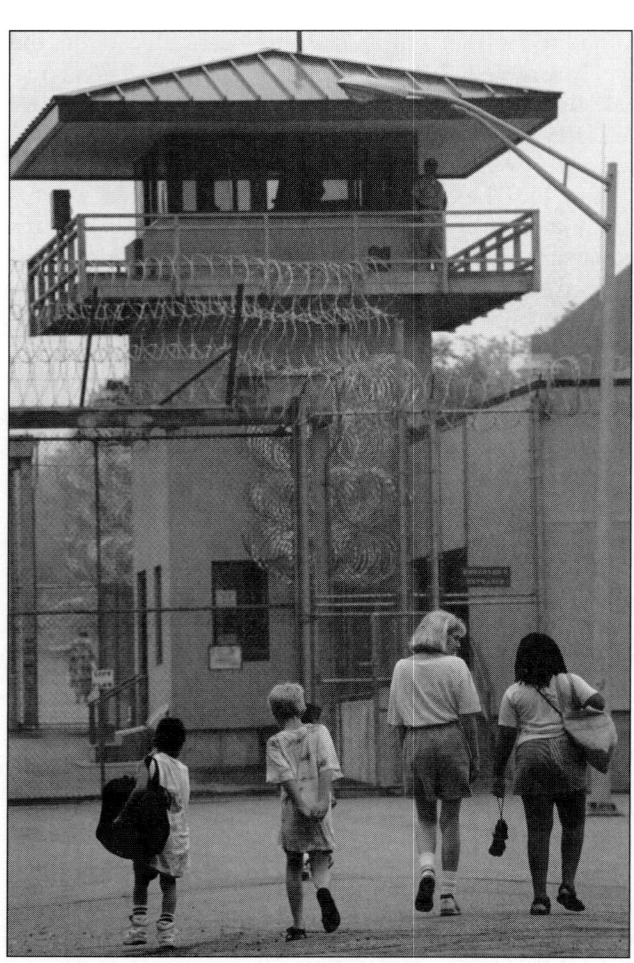

Children of inmates in New York State's maximum-security prison for women at Bedford Hills are escorted to the main gate for a visit with their mothers. Through the summer program at this prison, children are housed overnight or for several days with local families and taken to the prison for daily visits with their mothers. (AP Photo/Kathy Wilens)

An analysis of these various models in the context of data from 371 prisons led the authors to conclude that the deprivation model was least useful in explaining collective violence. There was no evidence that prison order was impacted negatively by prison conditions or that increased security led to disorder, and there was little to suggest the society of captives referred to by Sykes in his earlier studies. Indeed, "there has been little that resembles a 'community' behind the walls for more than two decades." There is no single inmate subculture and no uniform code of behavior among today's inmates. Finally, prison programs—education, vocational, recreational, and so on—are good management tools for keeping control. Poor prison management is a "major structural condition that fails to control, and may promote, individual acts of violence in prison."[41]

These studies on internal prison life serve to reemphasize the need to look at the total social structure, not only of the prison but also of the preprison and postprison experiences in order to understand the effects of imprisonment on the inmate.

Female Inmates

Most of the studies of prisonization were conducted on male inmates, but the few studies of female inmates note some differences in their methods of coping with prison life. Since few inmates are women, it is not surprising that little attention has been given to them. Within recent years, however, the number of female inmates has increased faster than that of males, even though women still constitute only a small percentage of the total prison inmates, as we noted earlier in this chapter.

The increase of women in jails and prisons has created several problems, one of which is discussed here: the problem of how to accommodate female inmates who have young children or who are pregnant (or become pregnant by relationships with correctional officials, either consensual or forced) while they are incarcerated. Some female inmates give birth behind bars, and provisions must be made for the care of their children. Most correctional facilities do not provide accommodations for children. A 2001 report by Amnesty International estimates that incarcerated women in the United States have an estimated 200,000 children under the age of 18.[42] Exhibit 14.3 explains one program for assisting female inmates with their relationships with their children.

EXHIBIT 14.3

Female Inmates and Their Children

Children of prison inmates are the hidden victims of their parents' crimes. Like children of divorced or deceased parents, they often show signs of distress caused by the lack of a stable home life and parental separation, such as depression, aggression, poor school performance, and truancy. Many times they also follow their parents' criminal behavior patterns. To keep mothers and daughters connected and to enhance parenting skills, Girl Scouts Beyond Bars involves mothers in their daughters' lives through a unique partnership between a youth services organization and State and local corrections departments.

Girl Scouts Beyond Bars programs have been implemented in the following States:

- **Maryland.** In 1992 the pilot program began at the Maryland Correctional Institution for Women. More than 30 girls now visit their mothers 2 Saturdays each month. On alternate Saturdays, they attend meetings at a community church, just as girls in other troops would. Before the Girl Scout program started, many of these girls rarely visited their incarcerated mothers.
- **Florida.** Its first program started at the Jefferson Correctional Institution near Tallahassee in early 1994, and a second program soon followed in Fort Lauderdale. The Florida Department of Corrections hopes to expand the program to correctional facilities throughout the State. The program includes formal parenting instruction and transitional services for the mothers and monitoring of the children's school performance, and collaboration with mental health care providers.
- **Ohio.** The Seal of Ohio Girl Scout Council launched the first program in a prerelease center, the Franklin Pre-Release Center in Columbus. When the Girl Scout council expanded the program to the Ohio reformatory for Women in 1994, Ohio became the first to connect the inprison program with the transition to home.
- **Arizona.** Maricopa County (Phoenix) is the first jail site in the country to form a Girl Scouts Beyond Bars partnership. Parents Anonymous and Big Brothers/Big Sisters have also joined the effort.

Girl Scout councils in four other States have also begun Girl Scouts Beyond Bars programs with their corrections partners. While the partnership has demonstrated its ability to increase mother-daughter visitation time, the long-term effect of breaking the cycle of criminal behavior will require a more comprehensive approach on the part of the correctional institution, the Girl Scout council, and the mothers involved.

The program, however, may be used as a model to involve more youth service organizations in crime prevention. Partnerships should include many community service organizations that can provide the range of support services for incarcerated parents and their children to stop negative social behaviors and to break intergenerational cycles of involvement in crime.

Source: National Institute of Justice, *Keeping Imprisoned Mothers and Their Daughters Together: Girl Scouts behind Bars* (Washington, DC: U.S. Department of Justice, October 1995), p. 2.

Some prisons have special facilities in which women can visit with their children in a homelike atmosphere. These facilities may provide a kitchen as well as a play area. The emphasis in some programs is on helping mothers maintain and enhance their relationships with their children and enhance their own self-esteem by being able to care for their children, if only part-time. Other programs help female inmates develop mothering skills as well as vocational skills that will enable them to support their children after their release.

One problem in penal facilities for women that has gained attention in recent years is that of sexual abuse. The 2001 Amnesty International report mentioned earlier, noted sexual abuse of female inmates in all but one state (Minnesota). The executive director of the organization stated that the abuse ranged from consensual sex with prison staff to rape. Some states prohibit sex between correctional officers and inmates but have no prohibitions regarding others who are employed at the prison. Recent sex scandals, however, have led to more extensive legislation of new policies and enforcement of existing rules and statutes, but six states (Alabama, Minnesota, Oregon, Utah, Vermont, and Wisconsin) have no statutes prohibiting sexual relations between inmates and the prison staff.[43]

In April 2001 a study by Human Rights Watch documented that rape is prevalent in U.S. prisons. We have no accurate national data, as one-half of the states do not compile such data. In reporting on this information, a national editorial remarked as follows:

> America's two million prison inmates have been lawfully deprived of their liberty, but they have not been sentenced to physical and psychological abuse. Yet Human Rights Watch found that prison authorities rarely investigate complaints of rape, and prison rapists rarely face criminal charges. Most prisons make little effort to prevent sexual assaults and provide minimal attention for victims.[44]

Elderly, Disabled, and Mentally Ill Inmates

As prison populations have increased in recent years, the institutions have encountered new problems. Today's prison may house older inmates as well as those who are physically disabled or mentally ill. Older inmates can be expected as the normal result of incarcerating more people for longer periods of time. Between 1980 and 1997 the U.S. prison population age 55 or older grew from 9,500 to 30,000. Approximately two-thirds of these inmates had been convicted of violent crimes, and many had received long sentences.[45] Older persons have different needs in areas such as food and medical care. They are more likely to need frequent attention by doctors, which may result in higher medication and surgery costs. In states that have a large retired population, such as Florida, the needs may be particularly acute.

Disabled persons also create a special situation within jails and prisons. And although these individuals were also incarcerated in the past, today we are more cognizant of their needs—we have the Americans with Disabilities Act (ADA) and other statutes for their protection. The ADA and its predecessor, the 1973 federal Rehabilitation Act, have been interpreted as applying to incarcerated persons in some cases.[46]

As a final category of special-needs inmates, the mentally ill should be considered. According to the Bureau of Justice Statistics, in 1997 approximately 16 percent of state inmates and 7.4 percent of federal inmates were identified as mentally ill. Others had some mental problems. Mentally ill inmates were more likely than others to be in prison for a violent offense; nearly 6 in 10 of them reported that they were under the influence of alcohol or other drugs at the time they were arrested for the current offense. Nationally, over a quarter of a million mentally ill persons are incarcerated in jails or prisons.[47] Over three-fourths of them had been sentenced previously for at least one offense prior to the current one; over 78 percent of the women and over 30 percent of the men were sexual abuse victims.[48]

Juveniles in Adult Facilities

Media Focus 11.1 (see p. 357 in Chapter 11), detailed some of the problems that are encountered in adult prisons when juveniles are incarcerated. Today more than 10 percent of incarcerated juveniles are being held in adult facilities, the result of the tougher laws concerning trying juveniles in adult courts when they are accused of committing serious crimes, especially violent crimes. On any given day approximately 14,500 juveniles under the age of 18 are held in adult facilities, 9,100 of those in local jails and 5,400 in adult prisons.[49]

As Media Focus 11.1 noted, one of the problems prison systems face with younger inmates in adult prisons is food. But other issues exist as well. Younger inmates are more impulsive and more difficult to manage. And in states such as Florida (which has the highest number of juveniles tried in criminal rather than juvenile courts), with the reduction in good-time credits that may be earned, juveniles have less incentive to behave. Most of the juveniles incarcerated in adult facilities have records of violence or at least habitual offenses, and they present safety and security issues to the institutions in which they are incarcerated. In short, the incarceration of juveniles in adult prisons and jails "is a burgeoning issue in many correctional systems" and measures should be taken to minimize the impact of this situation. One measure that is essential is the careful classification of each juvenile to "ensure that youths are not improperly housed with adult inmates." Staff who will work with the juveniles should be trained in their particular problems; education and other programs should be adapted to the needs of young persons; and security staff should be adequately prepared to react to violent juveniles in a meaningful manner but without the massive display of force that might be appropriate for adult offenders.[50]

The combined problems of the mentally ill and juveniles should not be handled as some jurisdictions are attempting: by incarcerating mentally ill juveniles in juvenile facilities rather than in mental institutions. Although no official data are available, the Coalition for Juvenile Justice, a federally financed organization in Washington, D.C., which was appointed by the nations' governors, estimated that between 50 and 75 percent of teens in the nation's juvenile justice system suffer from a diagnosable mental disorder, with perhaps 15 to 20 percent of them suffering from a severe disorder. According to one juvenile court judge, "It is a serious national problem . . . In essence, we are criminalizing mental illness among young people who, through no fault of their own, have been abused or neglected by their parents, then bounced around the child dependency system, and finally, because they are untreated, their illness leads them to act out, sometimes violently, so we lock them up in the juvenile justice system."[51]

Finally, review Exhibit 4.4 (see p. 110) concerning the need to provide treatment for drug-addicted inmates.

PRISON VIOLENCE

A common reaction to incarceration is violence, including violence against oneself. Jails and prisons house many violent or potentially violent individuals. It is not unreasonable to expect explosive and bloody behavior from them. Probably the violence among inmates is underreported; many inmates do not report incidents for fear of reprisals from other inmates or the staff. Administrators want to avoid the criticism that comes with the media reports of violence in their prisons, but some prison systems, faced with high rates of violence, have taken extra security precautions such as adding more correctional officers, conducting more searches, or instituting lockdown policies.

The first type of jail and prison violence is inflicted by inmates upon themselves. Some injure themselves to gain attention; others attempt suicide (sometimes successfully). The reasons for self-inflicted violence are varied. They have been linked to overcrowded institutions, extended solitary confinement, and the psychological and physical consequences of being victimized by other inmates. Some inmates who are threatened with homosexual rape or other violence become depressed and desperate about their physical safety. Victims may lack the interpersonal skills and resources that would help fend off would-be aggressors. They may be isolated socially. Another factor contributing to their psychological state is the perception that the only options are fight or flight. Victims know that if they submit to violence they are branded as weak but if they seek help, they are called snitches or rats. Many of those who inflict violence upon themselves are not average inmates. They are young, without histories of drug addiction, past criminal records, or past prison sentences. Frequently prison administrators segregate these inmates, although psychologists recommend human contact and communication as the best method for preventing self-inflicted violence. Many of the problems with sexual aggression first occur when the inmate arrives at the prison or jail.

Newly arrived male inmates may be attacked in dormitories or in cells by two or more established inmates. A study of male sexual aggression in prison found that sexual overtures might involve an actual sexual assault, other physical violence, insulting or threatening language, or propositions.[52] Violence can be precipitated by the aggressor or by the victim. In the first case, the aggressor plans to use violence to coerce his victim before the incident begins. In the second case, the victim reacts violently to sexual innuendo or a proposition perceived as threatening.[53]

The victim may refuse a sexual advance, and the aggressor may react violently to that refusal, interpreting it as an insult or a challenge to fight. Violence may also erupt when gay partners disagree. These arguments, similar to disagreements between heterosexual partners, may pertain to breakups, power, rejection, or pride. Another type of sexual violence in male prisons concerns arguments between two or more rivals over the sexual favors of a third.

Same-gender sexual relationships occur among female inmates as well; but although force may be used, in most cases the relationship is consensual. It develops out of mutual interest, for the purpose of alleviating the depersonalization of the prison, and for gaining status. Women seem to be looking for love, interpersonal support, community, family, and social status.[54] For female inmates the relationship may take the place of the primary groups of their preprison lives. Some female inmates form partnerships not primarily for sexual purposes but to simulate the families they left behind or would like to create. For these women, the relationship with other women may not be sexual, as in the case of male inmates.[55]

Aggression by one inmate against another may be nonsexual, resulting in severe physical injury or even death. The most brutal type of prison violence has occurred during riots, some of which have resulted in extensive property damage, injuries, and even the deaths of inmates or prison officials. Although a few riots occurred early in the history of U.S. prisons, most riots are recent. These differ from earlier ones in that, although they involve the usual complaints about food and conditions, they are more organized. They have been brutal and destructive, too, as Exhibit 14.4 notes. In the 1960s, along with the civil rights and antiwar groups on college campuses and elsewhere, inmates' rights groups developed and expanded. Inmates were viewed as normal persons except that

EXHIBIT 14.4

Selected Incidents of Prison Violence: 1980–2000

LAMESA, TEXAS, APRIL 2000

Thirty-one inmates were injured and one was killed after approximately 300 minority inmates became involved in a riot in a minimum-to-medium-security prison. A dining-hall fight precipitated the disturbance.

CRESCENT CITY, CALIFORNIA, FEBRUARY 2000

Eight inmates were injured, one critically, and one inmate was killed after approximately 200 minority inmates began fighting on the same day on which a federal grand jury indicted two former correctional officers for beating inmates, one of whom died. The Pelican Bay Prison houses the most violent inmates in California and at the time of the riot, the prison held 3,400 inmates in a facility designed to accommodate only 2,280. In a previous riot (1997), six inmates were killed at this institution.

COLUMBIA, SOUTH CAROLINA, 1995

Inmates protesting a new policy requiring them to cut their hair stabbed five officers and took three hostages. The disturbance ended when inmates were permitted to speak with reporters. The rioting inmates claimed to have religious reasons for not wanting their hair cut. The disturbance began with a fight in the dining hall about 8:30 AM and spread with sporadic fires and some fighting breaking out in other places in the prison.

LUCASVILLE, OHIO, 1993

Eight correctional officers were taken hostage when inmates seized a wing of the Southern Ohio Correctional Facility, a state maximum-security prison in Lucasville. Inmates controlled the wing for 11 days. Ten people, including one correctional officer, died.

Among the list of inmate complaints were the religious repression of Muslims and forced integration within cells. Inmates alleged that correctional officers had "blatantly killed innocent people in these jails and called it suicide."[1] In March 1995 the leader of the riot was convicted of aggravated murder (killing another inmate and an officer) and kidnapping.

FORT LEAVENWORTH, KANSAS, 1992

One inmate was killed and three others were injured seriously when approximately 300 inmates participated in a fight, allegedly caused by racial problems, gang violence, and prison overcrowding.

DEER LODGE, MONTANA, 1991

Five inmates were beaten, tortured, and killed by other inmates in a siege that lasted over four hours at the Montana State Prison. Four of the victims were hanged. After seeing an inmate being beaten, prison officials stormed the facility, taking control without resistance from the inmates.

TALLADEGA, ALABAMA, 1991

Cuban detainees, apparently fearing deportation, gained control of a medium-security section of the Talladega Federal Correctional Institution, taking 11 hostages and holding the prison for 10 days before approximately 200 specially trained FBI agents made a predawn raid on the institution. Officials decided to take the facility by force because they feared that one of the remaining hostages would be murdered. The detainees had been among the 125,000 Cubans who came to the United States during the 1980 boatlift. Over 2,000 of them had been declared undesirable by U.S. officials and then were detained in federal prisons pending deportation. In 1987 Cuban detainees staged fiery uprisings at federal prisons in Atlanta, Georgia, and Oakdale, Louisiana.

FOLSOM, CALIFORNIA, 1989

One inmate was killed and 48 were wounded during one of the most violent periods of the Folsom Prison's history. Correctional officers were able to bring the violence, which began in the exercise yard, under control by firing 10 shots into the yard.

ALBANY, NEW YORK, 1988

Five correctional officers were held hostage for 15 hours at the Coxsachie Correctional Facility near Albany, New York. The hostages were taken after an officer and an inmate had an argument in the disciplinary area of the prison, during which one allegedly spat on the other. Inmates in that section are confined to their cells 23 hours a day, with 1 hour a day for exercise, during which the incident began. According to officials, the hostage-taking was not a planned act. Afterward, inmates spent 15 hours trying to decide how to get out of the situation. The correctional officers were assaulted, but none were injured seriously.

(continued)

EXHIBIT 14.4

Selected Incidents of Prison Violence: 1980–2000, *(continued)*

PITTSBURGH, PENNSYLVANIA, 1987

Rioting that led to arson and injuries to three correctional officers, two firefighters, and 24 inmates occurred at the State Correctional Institution of Pittsburgh, a 105-year-old facility that was severely overcrowded at the time. The rioting started after authorities had to evacuate some inmates from their cells to fight a fire apparently caused by faulty wiring. Officers fired warning shots to quell the disturbance.

MOUNDSVILLE, WEST VIRGINIA, 1986

On 1 January 1986, inmates in the West Virginia Penitentiary, wielding homemade weapons, took correctional officers hostage and seized control of the prison. Sixteen hostages were taken. Inmates had control of the prison for 43 hours, during which time they brutalized, tortured, and then killed three inmates who they thought were snitches. One inmate, a convicted child molester and murderer, was dragged up and down the cellblock for other inmates to abuse. Inmates, angered by restrictions on contact visits with family and friends and the cancellation of a Christmas open house, demanded changes in visiting regulations, better meals, control of the temperature in their cells, and improved medical facilities and living conditions. Other demands included a reduction in the inmate population, permission to wear long hair and mustaches or beards, and an opportunity to negotiate with the governor and director of corrections. The inmates demanded that they be treated like human beings, "not like trash and animals." The prison had been placed under court order in 1983 because of unconstitutional living conditions and overcrowding.

SANTA FE, NEW MEXICO, 1980

On 2 February 1980, the worst prison riot in American history occurred at the state prison in Santa Fe, New Mexico. For 36 hours inmates rioted, burning prison facilities and torturing other inmates. At the end of the riot, 33 inmates were dead. The cost of replacing the penitentiary was estimated to be between $60 and $70 million. Survivors reported that inmates were tortured with blowtorches and possibly acetylene torches. Some were decapitated, and others were slashed and beaten.

The New Mexico riot occurred just three weeks after the completion of a special investigation of the prison. The report indicated that the prison was overcrowded, housing 1,200 persons in a facility designed for a maximum of 900. The prison was understaffed. The correctional officers were not trained properly, and their morale was low, partly because of their low salaries. The investigation was prompted by the December 1979 escape of eleven inmates. Management problems were evident in turnover within the administration, for example, five wardens in five years. The state director of corrections had resigned after the December escapes.

Before the New Mexico riot, three inmates had filed suit in federal court alleging that their constitutional rights were being violated in the areas of mail and visiting privileges, food, and treatment (both psychological and medical). They alleged also that overcrowding contributed to the increase in general violence within the prison as well as homosexual rape.

1. "Court OKs TB Tests for Ohio Prison That Had Riots," *Orlando Sentinel* (22 June 1993), p. 6; "Second Hostage Is Freed Unhurt by Ohio Inmates," *New York Times* (17 April 1993), p. 6.

Source: Summarized by the author from media sources.

they suffered from excessive discrimination and reduced opportunities. Thus, these groups focused on equalizing the legal rights and social circumstances of the inmate and the free person.[56]

Riots during this time took a dramatic shift. Although inmates continued to demand improvements in medical care, food services, recreational opportunities, disciplinary proceedings, and educational programs, they began to question the legitimacy of their incarceration. They claimed that they were political victims of an unjust and corrupt system, meaning that they were imprisoned for breaking laws enacted by a political system reflecting an unequal distribution of power. They argued that the sole purpose of criminal justice systems is to protect the entrenched interests of the wealthy and powerful at the expense of the poor and the weak. Today inmates assert that their crimes are justifiable retaliations against a society that has denied them opportunities for social and economic gains. This denial of basic rights in prison, cruel and disproportionate punishment, racial prejudice, and other violations of the system make inmates one of America's deprived minorities. Political protests in prisons began when inmates, like workers and minorities, sought an effective way of expressing their demands and achieving results from the political system.

Organized groups help inmates focus on the expansion of their constitutional rights, better communication between inmates and the outside world, development of meaningful work with fair wages, and restoration of their normal rights and privileges upon release. Inmates want to emphasize the poor prison conditions in the hope that community sympathy and support will lead to reform. It has worked in some instances, but it has not led to substantial prison reform in most cases. For example, the 1971 riot at New York's Attica Correctional Facility resulted in 43 deaths (32 inmates and 11 correctional employees). This riot was described by the investigating commission as "the bloodiest one-day encounter between Americans since the Civil War." After extensive investigation and considerable litigation, reforms were ordered. But in 1985 a federal court judge, hearing another case on Attica, noted that after a peaceful inmate strike about prison conditions, the only thing changed was the flavor of ice cream available for purchase.[57]

Various reasons for prison violence have been cited, but one important factor that must be considered is the presence of gangs within institutions. Gangs have existed in prisons for years, but in the past two decades the violence attributed to gangs has become a more serious problem. A decade ago the director of the Illinois Department of Corrections declared, "Correctional officers today are becoming dangerously outnumbered by gang-affiliated inmates who attempt to exert their special brand of mayhem on all aspects of prison life." The gangs operate on the outside, where they are involved primarily in drugs and violence. Arrests, convictions, and incarcerations of large numbers of these gang members have affected inmate life in Illinois prisons. Within prison, gang members are involved in drug sales, gambling, sexual exploitation, extortion, and murder.[58]

Two years after the Illinois director made the above comments, a gang war erupted in the state prison at Joliet, Illinois. According to prison officials, the inmates who took three correctional officers hostage did so in retaliation for the killing of one of their gang members by a correctional officer. The officer had fired at the inmate after the latter had allegedly stabbed another officer. Three officers were injured.[59]

A final type of prison violence of great concern is that associated with the escape of an inmate, especially from maximum security. In 1988 seven inmates plotted to escape from the nation's largest death row, in Huntsville, Texas. They cut through the fence, moved to a roof, and dropped to the ground outside the prison. All but one surrendered when correctional officers opened fire. Martin E. Gurule escaped, the first inmate to do so from that death row since 1934. His body was found six days later by two off-duty officers who were fishing. The cause of Gurule's death was drowning.[60]

Texas prison officials were not as successful in the case of the Texas Seven, who escaped from the Connally Unit, a maximum-security prison in South Texas, on 13 December 2000. Six were apprehended (the seventh killed himself as law enforcement authorities were closing in) but only after they had spent a month on the run and killed an Irving, Texas, police officer, Aubrey Hawkins, during a Christmas Eve robbery. The admitted leader of the escape, George Rivas, was the first to be tried. His jury of six men and six women were selected and his trial began in August 2001. When asked to enter a plea before the court in a pretrial hearing, Rivas said nothing, and the court entered a not guilty plea for him.[61] Rivas was convicted of first-degree murder.

CONTROL WITHIN PRISONS: THE ROLE OF CORRECTIONAL OFFICERS

In early prisons, wardens and correctional officers controlled inmates and kept prisons secure by separating inmates and by using force. Court interpretations of constitutional rights have changed the methods that may be used for maintaining internal security, but correctional officers continue to play a crucial role in internal control. Although they have the most extensive contact and perhaps the greatest impact on inmates, we know very little about them, because they have seldom been the subject of intensive or systematic analyses.

In the past, correctional officers maintained control within prisons by manipulating inmate social systems. Select inmates were permitted greater freedom within the institution, given power over other inmates, and permitted some infractions of the rules. In exchange, the privileged inmates used their influence in the inmate social-control system to get other inmates to behave. The system worked rather well, but federal judges have prohibited arrangements whereby inmates have control over jobs or privileges or are granted privileges by correctional officers. These restrictions reflect judicial awareness of the corruption that may occur when correctional officers and inmates are too cooperative.

Control of inmates remains a problem, however, and there is evidence that some correctional officers are using force as a control device. Recall, for example, our earlier references in this chapter to the brutality of California correctional officers toward inmates. Another example may be found in New York. For years inmates and correctional officers have battled for control of the special disciplinary unit (referred to by inmates as the "House of Pain") within Rikers Island in New York. In 1998 it was alleged that the officers gave inmates "greeting beatings" when they arrived at the unit. These were to be a preview of more severe disciplinary action.

As the result of the settlement of a lawsuit over the officers' behavior, legal documents supporting inmates' allegations were released. According to the court documents, between the opening of the disciplinary unit in 1988 and the settlement of the lawsuit brought by 15 inmates, correctional officers engaged in over 1,500 instances of force against inmates. Some of these acts resulted in severe injuries, one in death. One provision of the settlement was that two outside consultants would monitor the disciplinary unit for two years.[62]

Even more recently, in Florida in February 2000 four correctional officers were indicted in the 1999 beating death of Frank Valdes, an inmate who had been convicted of the capital crime of killing a correctional officer. The officers denied the charges; the trial began in January 2002 and resulted in the acquittal of all officers. An autopsy revealed that Valdes had swollen testicles, broken ribs, and boot marks on parts of his body.[63]

Also in 2000 two correctional officers at the Nassau County Jail in Uniondale, New York, entered guilty pleas to beating an inmate, Thomas Pizzuto, a former drug addict who was being noisy and demanding drugs. Pizzuto had not engaged in any acts of violence toward the officers, Edward Velaquez and Patrick Regnier, who received 11-year prison sentences. A third officer, Joseph Bergen, was sentenced to five years in prison for altering paperwork in an attempt to cover up the crime.[64]

This brief discussion of correctional officers raises one of the problems of changing one aspect of a system without changing another. The recognition of inmates' rights, long overdue in this country, was done without sufficient preparation of correctional officers and others who work with inmates on a daily basis. There is serious controversy over the resulting problems, and close attention must be given to inmates' rights. Although some people feel that inmates

Media Focus 14.1

The Crisis in Recruiting Correctional Officers

A front-page article in the *New York Times* in 2001 thrust to the national spotlight the problems of staffing prisons. The article, entitled "Desperate for Prison Guards, Some States Even Rob Cradles," focuses on Kansas but contains information about other states as well.

In Kansas the minimum age for correctional officers was recently dropped from 21 to 19 simply because of the difficulty of recruiting candidates for the positions. Several reasons are cited for recruitment problems there and elsewhere: new prisons; low salaries in these positions and higher ones elsewhere; inmates serving longer sentences and thus with fewer incentives to cooperate; more violent inmates; more inmates who are mentally ill or have drug problems. The result is a severe shortage of correctional officers throughout the country. One authority on prisons states that if recruiters were honest, they would advertise like this: "Come to work with us. Have feces thrown at you. Be verbally abused every day."

Some systems lose more officers than they hire in a given year, with an average of 16 percent of officers leaving their jobs in 1999, compared to 9.6 percent in 1991. In some states the departure rate is even higher—for example, 42 percent in Arkansas. Salaries are another factor. Starting salaries for correctional officers are as low as $15,324 in Louisiana and $18,980 in Maine. In Oklahoma one-fifth of correctional officer positions are vacant; the starting salary of $16,742 is below the poverty line for a family of four.

Source: Summarized from, "Desperate for Prison Guards, Some States Even Rob Cradles," *New York Times* (21 April 2001), p. 1.

"get what they deserve," federal courts have ruled that prisons must maintain certain conditions to avoid violation of the Eighth Amendment ban against cruel and unusual punishment (see Appendix A).

It is not easy, however, to recruit qualified persons to serve as correctional officers, especially in the maximum-security prisons. Some of the difficulties and remedies are discussed in Media Focus 14.1.

INMATES' LEGAL RIGHTS: AN OVERVIEW

In 1891 a federal court declared that the convicted felon "has as a consequence of his crime, not only forfeited his liberty, but all his personal rights except those which the law in its humanity accords to him. He is for the time being a slave of the state."[65] Under the rule of that case, prison officials could grant privileges to inmates as they deemed proper. Freedom of speech, freedom to worship in one's religious faith, visits from family and friends, incoming and outgoing mail, and all other important aspects of life inside prison could be regulated by officials.

The past two decades have seen vast changes in inmates' legal rights, as federal courts have abandoned their earlier **hands-off doctrine** toward prisons. In 1974 in *Wolff* v. *McDonnell,* the Supreme Court declared,

Hands-off doctrine A doctrine embraced by federal courts to justify nonintervention in the administration of correctional facilities; has been abandoned recently, but only when federal constitutional rights are at issue.

> But though his rights may be diminished by the needs and exigencies of the institutional environment, a prisoner is not wholly stripped of constitutional protections when he is imprisoned for crime. There is no iron curtain drawn between the Constitution and the prisons of this country.[66]

Prior to this decision, lower federal courts had begun hearing cases in which inmates alleged violations of their constitutional rights. Those and subsequent cases have covered virtually every area of life inside prison. The number of cases is immense. The law changes rapidly in this area, and not all lower federal courts agree on how similar cases should be decided. Thus, in many areas of inmates' rights, there is conflict until the Supreme Court decides an issue. Although the Court has decided relatively few cases in this area, some general points may be made.

It is important to understand that the Supreme Court looks at the total circumstances of a prison environment before deciding whether the alleged conditions violate inmates' rights. That is why the case law on this subject must be read carefully. In addition, some, but certainly not all, of the constitutional rights of defendants discussed in this text in earlier chapters have been applied to inmates.

In general, inmates have been granted the right to practice their religion, to visit with family and friends, to visit with their attorneys and to address the courts, to have a limited due process hearing in discipline cases, and to be free of unreasonable searches and seizures. They must be provided reasonable medical care, be given a sufficient amount of nutritious food, and be fed and housed in sanitary conditions. They may not be abused physically by correctional officers or other prison officials. Theoretically, male and female inmates are entitled to equal protection, although they need not be given identical treatment and facilities. Inmates may not be transferred arbitrarily from one institution to another, but transfers may be made when necessary for security or other recognized penal goals. Inmate rights may be restricted when necessary for internal security.

The Supreme Court has held that the Eighth Amendment (see Appendix A) prohibition against cruel and unusual punishment applies to prisons. This has been interpreted to mean that inmates may not be subjected to corporal punishment such as whippings, but it does not preclude imposing solitary confinement or other deprivations on inmates under appropriate circumstances. Again, the total circumstances must be examined to determine whether the inmate's constitutional rights have been violated. The Court has held that, to be cruel and unusual, conditions "must . . . involve the wanton and unnecessary infliction of pain, [or] be grossly disproportionate to the severity of the crime warranting imprisonment."[67] Further, the Eighth Amendment "must draw its meaning from the evolving standards of decency that mark the progress of a maturing society."[68]

Recent changes in inmates' rights may be illustrated by cases in three areas: physical restraint, smoking, and the Americans with Disabilities Act. The Supreme Court has decided cases in all of these areas. In the first case, the Court interpreted the cruel and unusual clause to mean that inmates may bring suits against prison officials who abuse them physically even if the inmate is not harmed significantly by the abuse. *Hudson* v. *McMillian* involved an inmate, Hudson, who had an argument with a security officer, McMillian. McMillian and Woods, another security officer, handcuffed and shackled Hudson and took him to the administrative lockdown section of the prison. The other pertinent facts and the Court's analysis are contained in the following excerpt.[69]

Hudson v. McMillian

Hudson testified that on the way [to the administrative lockdown area] McMillian punched Hudson in the mouth, eyes, chest, and stomach while Woods held the inmate in place and kicked and punched him from behind. He further testified that Mezo, the supervisor on duty, watched the beating but merely told the officers "not to have too much fun." As a result of this episode, Hudson suffered minor bruises and swelling of his face, mouth, and lip. The blows also loosened Hudson's teeth and cracked his partial dental plate, rendering it unusable for several months. . . .

In *Whitley* v. *Albers*, the principal question before us was what legal standard should govern the Eighth Amendment claim of an inmate shot by a guard during a prison riot. We based our answer on the settled rule that "the unnecessary and wanton infliction of pain . . . constitutes cruel and unusual punishment forbidden by the Eighth Amendment."

What is necessary to establish an "unnecessary and wanton infliction of pain," we said, varies according to the nature of the alleged constitutional violation. For example, the appropriate inquiry when an inmate alleges that prison officials failed to attend to serious medical needs is whether the officials exhibited "deliberate indifference." . . .

By contrast, officials confronted with a prison disturbance must balance the threat unrest poses to inmates, prison workers, administrators, and visitors against the harm inmates may suffer if guards use force. Despite the weight of these competing concerns, corrections officials must make their decisions "in haste, under pressure, and frequently without the luxury of a second chance." We accordingly concluded in *Whitley* that application of the deliberate indifference standard is inappropriate when authorities use force to put down a prison disturbance. Instead, "the question whether the measure taken inflicted unnecessary and wanton pain and suffering ultimately turns on 'whether force was applied in a good-faith effort to maintain or restore discipline or maliciously and sadistically for the very purpose of causing harm' " . . .

[W]e hold that whenever prison officials stand accused of using excessive physical force . . . the core judicial inquiry is that set out in *Whitley:* whether force was applied in a good-faith effort to maintain or restore discipline, or maliciously and sadistically to cause harm . . .

Under the *Whitley* approach, the extent of injury suffered by an inmate is one factor that may suggest "whether the use of force could plausibly have been thought necessary" in a particular situation, "or instead evinced such wantonness with respect to the unjustified infliction of harm as is tantamount to a knowing willingness that it occur" . . .

When prison officials maliciously and sadistically use force to cause harm, contemporary standards of decency always are violated. This is true whether or not significant injury is evident. Otherwise, the Eighth Amendment would permit any physical punishment, no matter how diabolic or inhuman, inflicting less than some arbitrary quantity of injury. Such a result would have been as unacceptable to the drafters of the Eighth Amendment as it is today.

Justice Clarence Thomas wrote a dissent, in which he was joined by Justice Antonin Scalia. They maintained that inmates should have to show serious injuries in their cruel and unusual punishment claims. Thomas argued that the Eighth Amendment "is not, and should not be turned into, a National Code of Prison Regulation."

In the Court's continuing interpretation of the cruel and unusual punishment prohibition, it is clear that although inmates are not entitled to a life of luxury, they are entitled to reasonable accommodations for their health and safety. It is clear also that what constitutes cruel and unusual punishment evolves and changes. So consider the developments regarding smoking that have occurred within the United States in recent years. As a result of medical research findings regarding the harmful effects of secondhand smoke, and the effective lobbying of antismoking groups, many states have enacted statutes regulating where and under what conditions smoking is permitted. Should these regulations extend to prisons?

First, it is important to note that some prison administrations have enacted their own rules regulating smoking, which they may do. The issue is whether inmates have a *constitutional right* to a smoke-free environment. Prior to 1993 lower federal courts differed in their rulings on the issue. In 1993 the Supreme Court decided a case on appeal from a Nevada inmate who alleged that being celled with a five-pack-a-day smoker endangered his health. The lower appellate court held that if tobacco smoke within a prison reaches a level that "poses an unreasonable risk to their [the inmates'] health," it constitutes cruel and unusual punishment and therefore violates the Eighth Amendment (see Appendix A). In *Helling* v. *McKinney* the Supreme Court upheld the federal court and remanded the case, holding that the inmate has a right to prove his case.[70]

The third area of focus involves a 1998 Supreme Court case. In *Pennsylvania Department of Corrections* v. *Yeskey* the Court held that Title II of the Americans with Disabilities Act (ADA) applies to state prisons. That title provides that "no qualified individual with a disability" may be denied the "benefits of the services, programs, or activities of a public entity." Nor may the public entity discriminate against that individual.[71]

Ronald Yeskey was sentenced in 1994 to from 18 to 36 months in a Pennsylvania correctional facility, with a recommendation that he be placed in a motivational boot camp for first-time offenders. He was refused admission, however, because of his medical history of hypertension. He sued, alleging that under the ADA he was being discriminated against. The District Court dismissed the case, holding that the ADA does not apply to inmates in state prisons. The circuit court of appeals reversed, and the U.S. Supreme Court upheld that court, noting that state prisons "fall squarely within the statutory definition of 'public entity,' which includes 'any departmentality of a State or States or local government.'"[72]

In September of 1998 the California Department of Corrections (DOC) settled a lawsuit brought under the ADA by inmates who are developmentally disabled. The DOC has implemented plans to accommodate these and other persons with disabilities in such ways as housing and classification and access to prison programs.[73]

Analysis of Inmates' Legal Rights

What has been the result of recognizing inmates' legal rights? Clearly there have been improvements in living conditions and changes in many prison rules and regulations. Prison systems have been forced into changes that should have occurred without the necessity of legal intervention. Those who complain about judicial intervention and allege that judges are making law might heed the words of Judge William Wayne Justice, speaking about his intervention in a Texas prison case. Admitting that his actions constituted judicial activism ("I was not a potted plant"), Judge Justice emphasized that the requirement to be an impartial judge does not mean a judge must be inactive. The judge's job is to "get the right answer" in the case before him. The judge continued:

> Due process of law does not require that all those who feel aggrieved be able to get what they want from a court. But it does require that when such a person comes to court with a potentially cognizable claim, he be given a chance to say what he wants . . . The right to be heard, whether one's conditions be exalted or lowly, is a right the courts have a duty to vindicate.[74]

Recognition of inmates' rights has been opposed by some correctional officers and other prison officials who claim that it makes their jobs of maintaining security more difficult. Citizens have resented the costs involved. We are left with the basic problem of the conflict that exists between recognizing inmates' constitutional rights while giving prison officials the latitude they need to maintain security within the prison and protect society. The following brief excerpt from *Peterkin* v. *Jeffes* summarizes the problem.[75]

Peterkin v. Jeffes

Based on the factual findings before this Court, we conclude that the totality of the conditions comprising the punishment of prisoners under sentence of death at the State Correctional Institutions at Graterford and Huntingdon does not contravene the Eighth Amendment. We cannot, we believe, emphasize too often that although " 'confinement in a prison . . . is a form of punishment subject to scrutiny under the Eighth Amendment standards,' " courts in assessing these claims "must bear in mind that their inquiries spring from constitutional requirements and that judicial answers to them must reflect that fact rather than a court's idea of how best to operate a detention facility." The primary responsibility for operating prisons belongs to prison administrators, to other state law enforcement officials and to the state legislature. The Eighth Amendment does not authorize a federal court to second guess their decisions nor is it our role to express our agreement or disagreement with their overall policies or theories of prison administration, as long as we find no constitutional violation.

We recognize, as the Supreme Court has documented, that many "courts have learned from repeated investigation and bitter experience that judicial intervention is *indispensable* if constitutional dictates—not to mention considerations of basic humanity—are to be observed in the prisons." Furthermore, we are in agreement with the Court of Appeals for the Second Circuit that "lengthy segregated confinement of the type considered [in this case], after an inordinate lapse of time, may necessitate periodic review to insure that conditions once constitutional have not become cruel and unusual." For the purposes of this case, however, and carefully considering the Supreme Court's teaching that "the Eighth Amendment 'must draw its meaning from the evolving standards of decency that mark the progress of a maturing society,'" we cannot conclude that the totality of the conditions on Pennsylvania's death rows constitute punishment "grossly disproportionate to the severity of the crime[s]."

It is reasonable to expect that prison officials will continue the trend toward decreasing inmate privileges as the public demands stricter punishment and treatment. A 1995 survey revealed that many states had abolished or were phasing out smoking within penal facilities. Several states had banned weightlifting. Maryland suspended its compassionate leave program, which permitted inmates to attend family funerals or visit dying relatives. Rewards for good behavior were abolished in several states; phone calls were being limited more severely; postsecondary education and vocational programs were reduced or eliminated in some states, and many restricted further the amount of personal property permitted in an inmate's cell. According to one legal article, "Prison administrators say reducing inmate privileges is a trend that will not end soon."[76]

Federal legislation enacted in 1996 and a Supreme Court decision make it clear that efforts were being made to curb inmate lawsuits as well as the power of federal courts to order changes in prison conditions.

In 1996 President Bill Clinton signed a budget bill, part of which included the Prison Litigation Reform Act. This act revises portions of the Violent Crime Control and Law Enforcement Act of 1994 and other acts. It limits the power of federal courts to order remedial measures for prison overcrowding. It provides that prospective relief of prison conditions "shall extend no further than necessary to correct the violation of the Federal right of a particular plaintiff or plaintiffs." Even in those cases relief may not be ordered until it is "narrowly drawn, extends no further than necessary to correct the violation of the Federal right, and is the least intrusive means necessary to correct the violation of the Federal right." It specifies that federal courts may not order the construction of new prisons. It limits the power of federal district courts to use discretion in determining whether litigants have exhausted their administrative remedies, by requiring that all other remedies be exhausted before a federal court hears the case. Inmates may not bring civil rights actions for mental or emotional injuries suffered while in custody without "a prior showing of physical injury." It places limitations on awarding attorneys' fees to inmates who file civil suits, and it requires court screening to determine whether cases should be dismissed under any of the provisions of the new act. Damages that are awarded to successful inmates may be used first to satisfy any outstanding restitution orders pending against them. And perhaps one of the most popular provisions with the public

Some prisons and jails have become so overcrowded that temporary facilities have been used for housing inmates. These tents in Phoenix, Arizona, were home to the inmates at the Maricopa County Jail. (Drew Crawford/The Image Works)

is the "no-frills" provision, which precludes the use of funds made available by the act for the following:

(1) in-cell television except for inmates segregated for their own safety
(2) the viewing of R, X, and NC-17 rated movies
(3) any live or broadcasted instruction or training equipment for boxing, wrestling, judo, karate, or other martial art, or any bodybuilding or weightlifting equipment
(4) in-cell coffee pots, hot plates, or heating elements
(5) use or possession of any electric or electronic musical instrument[77]

In 1996 the Supreme Court decided *Lewis* v. *Casey,* which limits the power of federal courts to order extensive changes in inmates' access to courts. In this case the Court limited the interpretations of its 1977 decision, *Bounds* v. *Smith,* which had been read to require states to provide inmates with access to law libraries or to persons with legal training. According to the Court, *Bounds* applies only when inmates attempt to pursue legal claims that have actually been hindered by the lack of legal assistance. According to the Court,

> *Bounds* does not guarantee inmates the wherewithal to transform themselves into litigating engines capable of filing everything from shareholder derivative actions to slip-and-fall claims. The tools it requires to be provided are those that the inmates need in order to attack their sentences, directly or collaterally, and in order to challenge the conditions of their confinement. Impairment of any *other* litigating capacity is simply one of the incidental (and perfectly constitutional) consequences of conviction and incarceration.[78]

The Court did not overturn its previous decision, but it made it more difficult for inmates to get legal assistance. The Arizona case on which it was based included inmates who cannot read, cannot speak English, or cannot use the prison law library because they are confined to their cells. Now, before those inmates and others may obtain legal assistance or meaningful access to the law library, they must show that the lawsuit they wish to file has merit. One might reasonably question how they can do that if they do not have meaningful access to the courts.

Despite the fact that some prison systems have been removed from the jurisdiction of a federal court because they have met the necessary requirements, court supervision remains. In May 2001 Judge William A. Shashy of the Montgomery County Circuit Court ordered the Alabama system to move 1,700 inmates from county jails to state prisons after county sheriffs complained that they could not handle all the inmates awaiting transfer to the prisons to which they were sentenced. When the state had not complied by early July the judge said the state was in contempt of court. Judge Shashy said the court would fine the state for every inmate not removed from a county jail within 45 days. This could cost the state up to $30,000 a day. Only about 250 of the inmates had been moved, and the governor said they could relocate a total of 1,250 inmates by mid-August. The judge was not impressed with the governor's plans.[79]

A judge who toured one jail, in which inmates were sleeping in unsanitary facilities, next to toilets, with as many as 256 inmates in a jail built for 96, wrote a blistering critique of the practice. Judge U. W. Clemon concluded, "The sardine-can appearance of the cell units of [the Morgan County, Alabama Jail] more nearly resemble the holding units of slave ships during the Middle Passage of the 18th century than anything in the 21st century." In Alabama at that time over 11 percent of the state's inmates were housed in county jails rather than prisons, saving the state approximately $70,000 a day. It cost $26 a day to incarcerate an inmate in prison, but the state paid the counties only $1.75 per meal to keep its inmates in jails.[80]

PRISON HEALTH ISSUES

One final area of prison life that should be addressed in light of recent developments is that of the medical health of inmates. First we look at two contagious diseases, tuberculosis (TB) and AIDS, which affect all who live and work within prisons. Both exist in today's prisons and both raise many questions. For example, one solution to prison overcrowding is to incarcerate two or more inmates per cell. That arrangement, however, increases the possibility of the spread of these diseases. Recognition of these problems led officials to close admission to the AIDS unit at the California Medical Facility at Vacaville in 1996 after an outbreak of TB at the prison. Twenty of the prison's AIDS inmates were diagnosed with TB. The weakened immune system of AIDS patients increases their susceptibility to TB.[81]

AIDS is a special problem in jails and prisons because, first, the age group that is at the greatest risk, ages 20 to 39, is that into which most persons in the correctional system fall. Second, this population has a high rate of intravenous drug use, another critical method of transmitting the disease. Thus, many inmates as well as offenders on probation and parole are at high risk for AIDS or have contracted the human immunodeficiency virus (HIV) already.

It is critical that correctional institutions develop policies and practices concerning testing for HIV and AIDS, as well as for protecting the community (and other offenders) from situations in which the virus may be contracted. But policy statements are only a beginning. Continued research on a cure must be

EXHIBIT 14.5

Medical Problems of Inmates, 1997: Highlights

Nearly a third of State Inmates and a quarter of Federal Inmates reported having some physical Impairment or mental condition.

	Percent of Inmates	
	State	Federal
Any condition	31.0%	23.4%
Learning	9.9	5.1
Speech	3.7	2.2
Hearing	5.7	5.6
Vision	8.3	7.6
Mental	10.0	4.8
Physical	11.9	11.1

- 12% of State inmates and nearly 6% of Federal inmates reported having a learning or speech disability.
- Nearly 12% of State inmates and 11% of Federal inmates reported a hearing or vision problem.

More than 1 in 4 State and Federal inmates had been injured after admission to prison.

	Percent of Inmates	
Reported Problem Since Admission	State	Federal
Cold/virus/flu	19.0%	21.9%
Injured	28.2	26.2
Medical problem (exclude injury)	21.4	21.7
Required surgery	7.5	9.6
Other	16.7	15.9

- 21% of State inmates and 22% of Federal inmates said they had a medical problem (excluding injury) after admission; 7% and 10%, respectively, said they had a medical problem that required surgery.

Injuries and other medical problems increase with time in prison.

	Percent of State Inmates	
Time Since Admission	Injured	Medical Problem (Exclude Injury)
Less than 12 mo.	13.2%	15.8%
12–23 mo.	19.8	19.1
24–47 mo.	26.7	20.4
48–71 mo.	36.8	20.3
72 mo. or more	45.9	30.4

- Nearly half of State inmates who had served 6 or more years said they had been injured after admission. Fewer than 20% of those in prison less than 2 years reported an injury.

Medical problems and other conditions more common among older inmates.

	Percent of State Inmates	
	Medical Problems (Exclude Injury)	Physical Impairment or Mental Condition
Gender		
Male	21.0%	30.7%
Female	27.2%	34.4
Age		
24 or younger	12.1%	23.8%
25–34	17.2	26.8
35–44	25.2	34.0
45 or older	39.8	47.6

- 40% of State inmates and 48% of Federal inmates age 45 or older said they had had a medical problem since admission to prison. This problem may have reflected medical conditions existing before admission.
- About a quarter of female inmates and a fifth of male inmates reported a medical problem since admission.

Source: Bureau of Justice Statistics, *Medical Problems of Inmates, 1997* (Washington, DC: U.S. Department of Justice, January 2001), p. 1.

accompanied by intensive education of the general public as well as by the targeted education of high-risk groups and AIDS testing to minimize the spread of the deadly disease.

Finally, inmates have many other health problems. Some enter prison with medical diseases or injuries; others contract them while in prison. The problems are particularly acute for older and female inmates, as noted in Exhibit 14.5, which contains highlights from a 2001 publication of the Bureau of Justice Statistics. Hearing impairments, speech disabilities, mental problems, and physical injuries are only some of the medical problems of inmates. Almost one in six inmates reported some medical problem other than a cold. The findings in Exhibit 14.5 are based on the 1997 Survey of Inmates in State and Federal Correctional Facilities.

SUMMARY

This chapter focuses on prisons and jails as institutions for confining offenders. Both European and American developments contributing to this evolution are discussed, followed by a look at the types of institutions for confining adults. Of particular importance today is the crush of numbers in these facilities. Overcrowding—its extent, its effects, its legal implications, and its potential solutions—is examined. Privatization of prisons and jails is presented and analyzed.

The chapter examines the world of the prison inmate, beginning with the process of socialization in the prison subculture. The issue of whether inmates bring that subculture from the outside or whether it evolves as inmates attempt to adapt to the pains of imprisonment is analyzed.

Problems that have been created primarily by the increase in female inmates are noted. The question of what to do with the children who are abandoned while their mothers are in jails or prisons is raised, too. Along with the unique problems of female inmates, the chapter looks at those of the elderly and the mentally ill before turning to the problems that occur when juveniles are housed in adult prisons.

Prison violence is an aspect of prison life that receives considerable attention when riots occur, but little attention is given to the internal violence of inmates against each other or against themselves. The discussion of sexual attacks notes that this type of violence is common among male inmates. An account of the historical background of riots and the details and causes of more recent riots completes the discussion of violence.

Violence within prisons increases security and control problems. How are inmates controlled? Correctional officers cannot rely on former methods of physical control and the use of inmates who for certain favors would cooperate with officers in maintaining internal control. An overview of inmates' legal rights looks at those rights in general, while recent Supreme Court and congressional efforts to curb inmate lawsuits are summarized. The chapter closes with a look at two major medical issues in prisons: AIDS and tuberculosis.

It is important to recognize that the modern prison is an institution in transition. Prison populations have soared while budgets have been reduced, although some states have added sufficient prison and jail beds to create a surplus. That situation is not expected to remain long, and, in the short run, some of those states (such as Texas) are contracting out space to house inmates from other states.

Prison administrators and correctional officers feel frustrated with their lack of control over prison populations. Other agencies determine how many inmates are sent to prison and when they are released. Many techniques used to accommodate large numbers of inmates are being challenged in the courts, and in some cases, they have been declared unacceptable. Overcrowding is a serious problem for which there are no easy and acceptable solutions.

Society has not yet made the choices that will be necessary to resolve the problems. Do we want prisons only to punish? Or do we want prisons to educate and train offenders to aid their reintegration into society? Are we going to continue to ignore the problems in prisons until riots, with their extensive destruction of property and human life, force us to look at our institutions? Are we willing to acknowledge that, as a society, we must punish criminals but that we must do so in a way that does not wreak havoc on society at the termination of that punishment? Do we want to live in constant fear that our next-door neighbor or the person down the block is an ex-convict and that this offender's treatment in prison was so harsh that his or her cynicism and resentment are worse now than before imprisonment? Are we willing to fund correctional systems that will give us back men and women who are less dangerous and better equipped to manage in the free world? It appears that "we must resign ourselves to spending more money on the people we hate most, or find creative, alternative ways to punish criminals who are not so dangerous that they have to be caged with their heads against toilets."[82]

STUDY QUESTIONS

1. Discuss the relationship between corporal punishment and imprisonment historically and in terms of the development of modern U. S. prison systems.
2. Identify John Howard and note briefly his contributions to the history of prisons.
3. Describe and evaluate the Pennsylvania prison system, noting the place of the Walnut Street Jail and Cherry Hill in that system.
4. Describe and evaluate the Auburn system.
5. Compare early prison expansion with prison overcrowding today.
6. Discuss the evolution of the reformatory system.
7. Evaluate early prison reform.
8. Distinguish lockups, jails, and prisons.
9. Describe jail populations. What accounts for the increase in recent years?
10. Evaluate early jails as a replacement for corporal punishment.
11. Describe briefly the administration and staffing of jails.
12. List and distinguish prison security levels.
13. What are the effects of prison overcrowding?
14. Explain and evaluate privatization of prisons and jails.
15. Define *prisonization* and discuss its impact on inmates' adjustment to prison life.
16. Contrast the deprivation, importation, and integrative models of adaptation to prison life.
17. Describe the problems resulting from the increase of female prison inmates. What are the issues with regard to mentally ill and elderly inmates? Should juveniles in adult facilities be given special attention?
18. Evaluate the causes of inmate deaths.
19. Analyze prison violence.
20. Describe briefly the problems corrections officers face in maintaining control within prisons.
21. Analyze the hands-off doctrine in prison settings.
22. Evaluate recent congressional and Supreme Court efforts regarding prison litigation.
23. Explain the major problems that exist in today's prisons with regard to medical issues.

BRIEF ESSAY ASSIGNMENTS

1. Discuss several effects of jail and prison overcrowding.
2. What are the problems with the privatization of prisons?
3. Explain measures that have been proposed to minimize the negative impact of incarceration upon juveniles.
4. Discuss the reasons and factors contributing to jail and prison violence self-inflicted by inmates.
5. Explain the impact of gangs within correctional institutions.

INTERNET ACTIVITIES

1. Learn more about prison privatization and how it differs from public prisons at www.rppi.org/prison/index.html. What are the most important issues that need to be addressed in the private prison industry? Also go to the Corrections Corporation of America (CCA) website at www.correctionscorp.com/main/media.html. CCA is one of the many private businesses that operate prisons. What are the major differences in how private and public prisons are operated? Do you think prison privatization is a potential solution for jail and prison overcrowding? Why or why not?
2. Check out www.medadvocates.org and click on "Prison Health." This site provides several topics on health-related issues and prisoners such as HIV/AIDS, tuberculosis, hepatitis, elderly prisoners and various health care industry challenges to addressing prison populations.

NET RESOURCES

www.hrw.org

Human Rights Watch's website contains several articles, reports, and news releases on prison conditions, the abuse and treatment of prisoners, and jail detention in both the United States and the international community. Information about other global issues categorized by topic or country, and publications can be accessed here.

www.bop.gov

The Bureau of Prisons is part of the U. S. Department of Justice. Press releases, news events, documents and statistics on incarceration issues and access to the *Federal Prisons Journal* are all provided on the bureau's website. Users can also access the site's search engine, which explores topics within all government agencies.

www.corrections.com

Corrections.com provides headline news and legislation, correctional product and program profiles, and hot topics and issues in corrections. Also included are links and access to organizational websites such as the American Jail Association and the American Correctional Association.

www.correctionalpolicy.com

The Center for Rational Correctional Policy advocates the rethinking of current sentencing practices. The center's website offers statistics on prison populations, state and federal legislative materials, criminal law documents and links, news events, and prisoner resources.

www.correctionalnews.com

Correctional News Online supplies news events, product news, links to correctional industry organizations, features on the correctional institution of the month, and Q&A articles. Free subscriptions to *Correctional News* are also available.

www.nicic.org

The National Institute of Corrections is part of the U.S. Department of Justice. Its website provides information and resources about jails, prisons and community corrections. Publications and reports, news events, Web links, information services, and special topics are offered on this site.

www.prisonactivist.org

Prison Activist is maintained by an organization dedicated to challenging racism and discrimination in the criminal justice system. Topic areas on this site include the prison crisis, alternatives to incarceration, women prisoners, the prison labor industry, prison news, and links to activist/advocacy groups.

www.igc.org/ncia/home.html

The National Center on Institutions and Alternatives' website provides resources and publications on several issues related to incarceration and correctional services. Sentencing advocacy, death penalty mitigation, statistics on racial and ethnic disparity in prison counts, and information about services for various populations can be found here. A site search engine provides links and access to several corrections-related reports and agencies.

ENDNOTES

1. For a history of the development of prisons, see Harry Elmer Barnes, *The Story of Punishment: A Record of Man's Inhumanity to Man,* 2d rev. ed. (Montclair, NJ: Patterson Smith, 1972; originally published 1930).
2. See Alexis M. Durham III, "Newgate of Connecticut: Origins and Early Days of an Early American Prison," *Justice Quarterly* 6 (March 1989): 89–116.
3. Karl Menninger, *The Crime of Punishment* (New York: Viking, 1968), p. 222.
4. Howard Gill, "State Prisons in America, 1787–1937," in *Penology,* ed. George C. Killinger and Paul F. Cromwell (St. Paul, MN: West, 1973), p. 53.
5. See Richard Quinney, *Criminology,* 2d ed. (Boston: Little, Brown, 1979).
6. See the discussion by Alexander W. Pisciotta, "Scientific Reform: The 'New Penology' at Elmira, 1876–1900," *Crime & Delinquency* 29 (October 1983): 613–30; quotation is from page 613. But in *Benevolent Repressing* (New York: New York University Press, 1994), Pisciotta questions the alleged humanitarian reforms of Elmira and other reformatories.
7. Pisciotta, "Scientific Reform," p. 626.
8. Bureau of Justice Statistics, *Prison and Jail Inmates at Midyear 1997* (Washington, DC: U.S. Department of Justice, 1998); Bureau of Justice Statistics News release (14 March 1999).
9. Bureau of Justice Statistics, *Prisoners in 1999* (Washington, DC: U.S. Department of Justice, August 2000), p. 1.
10. Bureau of Justice Statistics, "Prison and Jail Inmates at Midyear 2000," news release, 18 January 2002.
11. *Prisoners in 1999,* p. 7; Bureau of Justice Statistics, "Prison Statistics," news release, 18 January 2002, p. 1.
12. Edith Elisabeth Flynn, "Jails and Criminal Justice," Chapter 2 in *Prisoners in America,* ed. Lloyd E. Ohlin (Englewood Cliffs, NJ: Prentice Hall, 1973), p. 49.
13. Joseph F. Fishman, *Crucible of Crime: The Shocking Story of the American Jail* (New York: Cosmopolis, 1923), pp. 13–14.
14. National Commission on Law Observance and Enforcement, *Report on Penal Institutions, Probation, and Parole,* Report of the Advisory Committee on Penal Institutions, Probation, and Parole (Washington, DC: U.S. Government Printing Office, 1931), p. 273.
15. Daniel Fogel, quoted in "The Scandalous U.S. Jails," *Newsweek* (18 August 1980), p. 74.
16. Norman Carlson, quoted in the *New York Times* (5 January 1982), p. 10B.
17. Quoted in "More Prisons Using Iron Hand to Control Inmates," *New York Times* (1 November 1990), p. 8.
18. "New Prisons Reflect Society," *Orlando Sentinel* (2 August 1998), p. 8.
19. "Rights Group Alleges 'Torture' in Indiana Super-Max Prisons," *Criminal Justice Newsletter* 19 (1 October 1997), p. 1.
20. "California Examines Brutal, Deadly Prisons," *New York Times* (7 November 1988), p. 7.
21. John Ortiz Smykla and Jimmy J. Williams, "Co-Corrections in the United States of America, 1970–1990: Two Decades of Disadvantages for Women Prisoners," *Women and Criminal Justice* 8, no. 1 (1996): 61–76.
22. "Congress OKs Inmate Fees to Offset Costs of Prison," *Criminal Justice Newsletter* 23 (15 October 1992): 6. See United States v. Sellers, 42 F. 3d 116 (2d Cir. 1994), *cert. denied,* 516 U.S. 816 (1995), referring to Section 5E1.2(a) of the federal sentencing guidelines.
23. *Prisoners in 1999,* p. 6.
24. "Pounds 35M Jail Planned as Crisis Grows: Governors Urge Policy Change to End Overcrowding 'Scandal,'" *The Independent* (30 March 1995), p. 10.
25. "Question of Competence," *The Chattanooga Times* (15 October 1998), p. 6.
26. "Justice Department Tells Senate Panel of Doubts on Private Prisons," *Criminal Justice Newsletter* 29 (17 August 1998), p. 6.
27. "Louisiana Settles Suit, Abandoning Private Youth Prisons," *New York Times* (8 September 2000), p. 12.
28. Gresham M. Sykes, *The Society of Captives* (Princeton, NJ: Princeton University Press, 1958), pp. 63–83.
29. Donald Clemmer, *The Prison Community,* 1940 reprint ed. (New York: Holt, Rinehart & Winston, 1958), pp. 298–301.
30. Stanton Wheeler, "Socialization in Correctional Communities," *American Sociological Review* 26 (October 1961): 697–712.
31. See, for example, Peter G. Garabedian, "Social Roles and Processes of Socialization in the Prison Community," *Social Problems* 11 (Fall 1963): 139–52; and Daniel Glaser, *The Effectiveness of a Prison and Parole System,* abridged ed. (Indianapolis: Bobbs-Merrill, 1969).
32. Geoffrey P. Alpert et al., "A Comparative Look at Prisonization: Sex and Prison Culture," *Quarterly Journal of Corrections* 1 (Summer 1977): 29–34.
33. Edward Zamble, "Behavior and Adaptation in Long-Term Prison Inmates: Descriptive Longitudinal Results," *Criminal Justice and Behavior* 19 (December 1992): 409–25; quotations are from pp. 420–21. See also Hans Toch and Kenneth Adams, *Coping: Maladaptation in the Prison* (New Brunswick, NJ: Transaction, 1989).
34. Gresham M. Sykes and Sheldon L. Messinger, "The Inmate Social System," in *Theoretical Studies in Social Organization of the Prison,* ed. Richard A. Cloward et al. (New York: Social Science Research Council, 1960), p. 17.
35. John Irwin and Donald R. Cressey, "Thieves, Convicts and the Inmate Culture," *Social Problems* 19 (Fall 1962): 142–55. For a discussion of the impact that traditional roles of women in our society have on the inmate culture, see Rose Giallombardo, *Society of Women: A Study of a Woman's Prison* (New York: John Wiley, 1966).
36. Charles W. Thomas, "Prisonization or Resocialization: A Study of External Factors Associated with the Impact of Imprisonment," *Journal of Research in Crime and Delinquency* 10 (January 1975): 13–21.
37. Leo Carroll, "Race and Three Forms of Prisoner Power: Confrontation, Censoriousness, and the Corruption of Authority," in *Contemporary Corrections: Social Control and Conflict,* ed. C. Ronald Huff (Beverly Hills, CA: Sage, 1977), p. 40. See also Leo Carroll, *Hacks, Blacks, and Cons: Race Relations in a Maximum-Security Prison* (Lexington, MA: D. C. Heath, 1974).
38. Ronald L. Akers et al., "Prisonization in Five Countries: Type of Prison and Inmate Characteristics," *Criminology* 14 (February 1977): 538.
39. Charles W. Thomas, quoted in ibid., p. 548.
40. See Keith Farrington, "The Modern Prison as Total Institution? Public Perception versus Objective Reality," *Crime & Delinquency* 38 (January 1992): 6–26, rejecting the view that prisons are total institutions, a view developed earlier by Erving Goffman, *Asylums: Essays on the Social Situation of Mental Patients and Other Inmates* (Garden City, NY: Anchor, 1961).
41. Richard C. McCorkle et al., "The Roots of Prison Violence: A Test of the Deprivation, Management, and 'Not-So-Total' Institution Models," *Crime & Delinquency* 41 (July 1995): 317–31; quotations are from pp. 326–29.
42. Cited in "Abuse of Female Inmates Common," *Tallahassee Democrat* (7 March 2001), p. 7.
43. "Study: Sex Abuse Rife in Women's Prisons," *USA Today* (6 March 2001), p. 3.
44. "Rape in Prison," *New York Times* (22 April 2001), p. 16.
45. "America's Aging, Violent Prisoners," *New York Times* (6 July 1997), p. 3E.
46. Bonner v. Lewis, 857 F.2d 559 (9th Cir. 1988), *cert. denied,* 498 U.S. 1074 (1991).
47. Bureau of Justice Statistics, *Mental Health and Treatment of Inmates and Probationers* (Washington, DC: U.S. Department of Justice, July 1999), pp. 1, 3.
48. Ibid., p. 1.
49. *Juveniles in Adult Prisons and Jails: A National Assessment,* a 127-page report, available from the BJA Clearinghouse, Box 6000, Rockville, MD. 20849-6000, as cited in "Juveniles in Adult Prisons 'A Burgeoning Issue,' Study Finds," *Criminal Justice Newsletter* (10 January 2001), p. 6.
50. Ibid.
51. "Concern Rising over Use of Juvenile Prisons to 'Warehouse the Mentally Ill,' " *New York Times* (5 December 2000), p. 14.
52. Daniel Lockwood, *Prison Sexual Violence* (New York: Elsevier, 1980), pp. 16–23.
53. Daniel Lockwood, "Reducing Prison Sexual Violence," Chapter 15 in *The Pains of Imprisonment* (Beverly Hills, CA: Sage, 1982), ed. Robert Johnson and Hans Toch, pp. 257–65.
54. See David A. Ward and Gene G. Kassebaum, "Women in Prison," in *Correctional Institutions,* ed. Robert M. Carter et al. (Philadelphia: Lippincott, 1972), pp. 217–19.
55. See Giallombardo, *Society of Women;* and David A. Ward and Gene G. Kassebaum, "Sexual Tensions in a Women's Prison," in *Crime and Justice: The Criminal in Confinement,* ed. Leon Radzinowicz and Marvin E. Wolfgang (New York: Basic Books, 1971), pp. 146–55.
56. John Irwin, *Prisons in Turmoil* (Boston: Little, Brown, 1980), pp. 94–98.
57. Abdul Wali *v.* Coughlin, 754 F.2d 1015 (2d Cir. 1985).
58. Michael P. Lane, "Inmate Gangs," *Corrections Today* 51 (July 1989): 98, 99. See also David K. v. Lane, 839 F.2d 1265 (7th Cir. 1988).
59. "Inmate Killed and Three Guards Are Hurt in Illinois," *New York Times* (15 July 1991), p. 12.

60. "Death Row Escapee Found Dead," *New York Times* (4 December 1998), p. 16.
61. "Escapee's Trial Seen As Determining Punishment: Lawyers Says Rivas Needs to Testify," *San Antonio Express-News* (1 July 2001), p. 4B.
62. "In Disciplinary Unit, Rikers Island Guards Created a 'House of Pain' for Inmates," *New York Times* (16 August 1998), p. 34.
63. "Guards Indicted in Slaying," *St. Petersburg Times* (3 February 2000), p. 1.
64. "Two Guards Plead Guilty and Describe Fatal Beatings of a Prisoner," *New York Times* (3 January 2000), p. 26.
65. Ruffin v. Commonwealth, 62 Va. 790, 796 (1872).
66. Wolff v. McDonnell, 418 U.S. 539 (1974), *rev'd. in part,* Bell v. Wolfish, 441 U.S. 520 (1979).
67. Rhodes v. Chapman, 452 U.S. 337 (1981).
68. Trop v. Dulles, 356 U.S. 86 (1958).
69. Hudson v. McMillian, 503 U.S. 1 (1992).
70. Helling v. McKinney, 509 U.S. 25 (1993).
71. Pennsylvania Department of Corrections v. Yeskey, 524 U.S. 206 (1998).
72. Pennsylvania Department of Corrections v. Yeskey, 524 U.S. 206 (1998).
73. "California DOC Reaches Settlement in ADA Case," *Corrections Professional* (4 September 1998) (no page number available).
74. William Wayne Justice, "The Origins of *Ruiz* v. *Estelle*," *Stanford Law Review* 43 (November 1990): 6, 12.
75. Peterkin v. Jeffes, 855 F.2d 1021 (3rd Cir. 1988), citations omitted.
76. "States Cut Back on Inmates' Privileges," *National Law Journal* (21 August 1995), p. 22.
77. Prison Litigation Reform Act of 1995, P.L. 104-134 (1998).
78. Lewis v. Casey, 518 U.S. 343 (1996).
79. "Judge to Fine If Alabama Cannot Move Prisoners," *New York Times* (21 July 2001), p. 8.
80. "Alabama's Packed Jails Draw Ire of Courts, Again," *New York Times* (1 May 2001), p. 1.
81. "TB Outbreak at Vacaville Prison," UPI news release (4 January 1996), BC Cycle.
82. Richard Reeves, "High Price of Punishing Criminals," *Tulsa World* (27 June 1982), p. 13.

15

▶ Some inmates are placed in honor farms, which are less secure than prisons. Those who are granted such placement are premitted greater freedon and given more responsibilities than is reasonable in more secure facilities. These inmates are responsible for feeding and milking this cow. (Eastcot/Momatiuk/Woodfin Comp)

Corrections in the Community

OUTLINE

KEY TERMS

boot camps
community-based corrections
community work service
diversion
felony probation
furlough
halfway house
house arrest
intensive probation supervision (IPS)
parole
parole board
parole officers
prerelease program
probation
probation officer
reintegration
shock incarceration
work release

This final chapter examines the practice of handling offenders within the community rather than within institutions. Many offenders are not sentenced to jail or prison; most who are incarcerated return to society, and both they and society should be prepared for that event. If offenders are not prepared – or if we refuse to allow them to succeed upon their return – we can expect many to return to a life of crime. Perhaps some will commit crimes no matter what we do, whereas others might be integrated successfully into the law-abiding society.

This chapter focuses on the methods for handling offenders within the community. After an overview of diversion, the chapter proceeds to a discussion of various types of community corrections before focusing on probation and parole, the major systems under which offenders are supervised within the community. Consideration is given to the problems faced when inmates are released from incarceration, including the recent emphasis on Megan's laws. The chapter closes with a discussion of the future of corrections, including an analysis of the privatization issue, and a look at juvenile justice.

Previous chapters traced the emergence of prisons and the changes in philosophies of punishment and imprisonment. Early reformers thought that offenders should be incarcerated in total institutions. Their segregation from home and society was deemed necessary to remove the evil influences that had led to their criminal behavior. While incarcerated, offenders would have time to think and reflect on their behavior and become involved in religious services and other efforts at reformation.

Before long, prison reformers were declaring that incarceration in total institutions did not reduce the criminal activity of offenders after they were released and that it intensified the problems of those who had served time. In 1777 reformer John Howard referred to prisons as "seats and seminaries of idleness and every vice." In prison, "by the greatest possible degree of misery, you produce the greatest possible degree of wickedness." Jeremy Bentham declared in 1864 that most prisons "include every imaginable means of infecting both body and mind . . . [and that] an ordinary prison is a school in which wickedness is taught . . . All the inmates raise themselves to the level of the worst." In 1890 the English prison system was described as "a manufactory of lunatics and criminals." In 1922 imprisonment was described as "a progressive weakening of the mental powers and of a deterioration of the character in a way which renders the prisoner less fit for useful social life, more predisposed to crime, and in consequence more liable to reconviction." These early declarations have been described as conclusions without evidence;[1] yet as revealed in Chapter 14, empirical research has shown that modern prisons have failed, too.

Probation A judicial determination in which the offender is allowed to remain in the community under conditioned supervision. The term refers also to the component of the criminal justice system that administers all phases of probation.

In 1973 the National Advisory Commission on Criminal Justice Standards and Goals called for an increased emphasis on **probation,** already the most frequently used form of sentencing.[2] During the 1970s the goal of corrections appeared to be the reintegration of the offender into society. In the past two decades, however, we have moved away from a philosophy of rehabilitation and reintegration to one of retribution and just deserts. With that movement, rates of incarceration in total institutions were increased to the point that many states were under court orders to reduce their prison and jail populations.

The need for additional jails and prisons came at a time when construction and operating costs were soaring. As soon as most new, larger facilities were available, they were filled, and many jurisdictions did not have sufficient space to sentence offenders who would otherwise be incarcerated. Some resorted to an early release policy, releasing some inmates to make room for new and more serious offenders. However, in recent years the decreasing crime rates have resulted in extra beds in some jails and prisons. But we have been warned not to become complacent, and we must be cautious in our conclusions about whether these changes represent a long-term trend.

Another solution to overcrowding is to decrease the number of people incarcerated. This is accomplished primarily by diverting the offender from criminal justice systems to other institutions, such as alcohol and drug treatment programs; by imposing fines, restitution, or community work sentences in place of a prison term; or by placing offenders on probation. All of these procedures are controversial, but all have positive features that should be addressed. The use of sentencing alternatives to jail and prison is a sensitive issue, and selling the public on some of these programs is not easy.

There is some encouraging news, however. A 1995 study conducted by the American Correctional Association (ACA) noted that three out of four Americans believe that using a balanced approach toward offenders is better than relying solely on incarceration. The ACA president stated, "The public's mood may not be as punitive as some politicians would have us believe." He emphasized that it is the position of corrections officials that punishment alone will not reduce crime. In the long run, crime will be reduced only through prevention and treatment. The president concluded that we "cannot afford not to pay for literacy programs, vocational training, and drug and alcohol treatment."[3] We will see some evidence of this approach later in this chapter.

Diversion A practice that removes offenders from criminal justice systems and channels them into other agencies, such as social welfare. The term is also used to describe the handling of juveniles in a system separate from adult criminal justice systems and the sentencing of offenders to community-based correctional facilities rather than to prison.

Although more research is needed to determine the extent of acceptance of community-based programs as well as of their effectiveness, we do have data showing that attitudes toward community corrections are more positive among those who are educated about the programs. Court personnel and the general public have similar attitudes about the ranking of community programs by effectiveness: "They rank jail as the least cost effective but the most punitive, severe, safe, and deterring alternative."[4]

There is evidence that recidivism (further violating the law—see Chapter 8) is no higher when community service is imposed instead of incarceration, but the cost savings are significant. These and other community-based approaches are discussed further in this chapter after a brief look at the philosophy of diverting offenders from incarceration facilities.

DIVERSION

One of the solutions to the overcrowding of jails and prisons is to divert some offenders from those facilities into other programs. Technically, **diversion** is meant to funnel the offender away from criminal justice systems and into community programs that might be more beneficial than incarceration. Diversion is used most frequently in juvenile justice systems, where historically offenders have been handled with less formality than is characteristic of adult criminal court systems. Diversion is also used to refer to *pretrial diversion*, the release of the accused pending trial.

In the late 1960s and throughout the 1970s, diversion was a popular concept. Many diversionary programs were developed. Most focused on juveniles, although some provided services for adults. Adult offenders with alcohol and drug problems were typical targets. Some of the evaluations of these programs concluded that instead of diversion, the programs were widening the net, capturing people who would not have been processed through criminal court systems before diversionary programs were begun.

Diversion is used frequently in cases involving substance abuse. Diversion into a treatment program may be a condition of pretrial release. This practice is employed in the federal system.

Table 15.1 illustrates the need for programs offering treatment for drugs. Note that the number of federal inmates in drug treatment programs surpassed the number in any other type of treatment program.

TABLE 15.1
Number of Inmates in Federal Bureau of Prisons Treatment Programs

Source: Federal Bureau of Prisons, *Substance Abuse and Treatment Programs in the Federal Bureau of Prisons: Report to Congress* (Washington, DC: U.S. Department of Justice, January 1999), reprinted in *Drug Treatment in the Criminal Justice System* (Washington, DC: U.S. Department of Justice, March 2001), p. 3.

Program Type	Number of Inmates
Residential	10,006
Transitional	6,951
Nonresidential	5,038
Drug education	12,002

COMMUNITY CORRECTIONS: AN ATTEMPT AT REINTEGRATION

Reintegration A philosophy of punishment that focuses on returning the offender to the community with restored education, employment, and family ties.

The focus on diversion has been accompanied by an emphasis on helping offenders who serve time to reintegrate into the community. **Reintegration** may be defined as "the process of preparing both the community and offender for the latter's return as a productive and accepted citizen . . . The emphasis is on creating the circumstances around him that will enable him to lead a satisfying and law-abiding life."[5]

One method of reducing prison and jail populations and helping offenders reintegrate into the community is to divert them into other programs. These former jail inmates are harvesting spinach for the farmers' market at the Garden Project in San Francisco, a project designed to train former inmates to grow organic produce. (AP Photo/Lacey Atkins)

Community-based corrections An approach to punishment that stresses reintegration of the offender into the community through the use of local facilities. As an alternative to incarceration, the offender may be placed in the community on probation or, in conjunction with imprisonment, in programs such as parole, furlough, work release, foster homes, or halfway houses.

Rehabilitation is the primary legislative goal of **community-based corrections.** Most statutes specify other goals as well: custody/supervision, punishment, restitution, reintegration, employment training, and reduction of prison populations. An example of a statute authorizing community-based corrections is that of California, which reads as follows:

> The Director of Corrections may enter into an agreement consistent with applicable law for a city, county, or city and county to construct and operate community corrections programs, restitution centers, halfway houses, work furlough programs, or other correctional programs authorized by state law.[6]

When we talk about community-based corrections, we must distinguish these facilities and programs from those that may be located in the community but are not, strictly speaking, community based. The degree to which a correctional system is community based can be measured by the frequency, quality, and duration of community relationships, by the number of commitments to large state institutions, by the extent to which other community services are used, and by the degree of involvement by local groups and individuals.

Community correctional centers comprise a wide variety of programs, including residential and nonresidential facilities. Criminal justice systems in the United States and in other countries have experimented with a variety of community-based correctional plans. In some states, such as California and Minnesota, the state assists counties in developing community-based correctional facilities designed to reintegrate or to maintain the offender in the community.[7] Numerous jurisdictions use several methods of community-based corrections; these deserve greater attention.

Community Work Service, Fines, and Restitution

One approach to reintegrating offenders as well as compensating victims is to order offenders to perform community service, pay a fine to the state, or pay restitution to the victim. It is not uncommon to combine two or more of these approaches.

The fine is ordered by the judge and paid by the offender to the state (or county or other entity in which the judge presides). This punishment is used widely in other countries, especially those in Europe; more than three-fourths of English, Swedish, and German cases result in fines. In the United States, fines are often used in combination with other punishments such as probation. Europeans are more likely to use the *day fine,* in which the offender is fined in terms of a day's pay, whereas U.S. systems are more likely to fine according to the crime committed. Some studies, however, suggest that the day fine may be more appropriate in the United States, resulting in increased revenue.[8]

Restitution is a method of reimbursement paid by the offender to the victim. It was approved by the U.S. Supreme Court in 1913 and has received the support of most crime commissions. Restitution is permitted in the federal system by the Victim and Witness Protection Act of 1982, which has been amended subsequently. The Violent Crime Control and Law Enforcement Act of 1994 provides for mandatory restitution for some federal crimes.[9]

Community work service Punishment assigning the offender to community service or work projects. Sometimes it is combined with **restitution** or **probation.**

Restitution and fines are used frequently in conjunction with **community work service** assignments. The assignments may be designed to benefit the victim or the community. Community work service orders are common in European countries. Frequently the assignments involve work in community or government agencies.

All of these approaches sound progressive and advantageous on the surface. They raise revenue, they permit compensation to victims, and they keep offenders working. But there are problems as well. The programs require funding, and with cutbacks in correctional programming some of them have been eliminated or reduced significantly. Victims may overestimate or underestimate their losses. Enforcement problems abound. Because offenders may steal to pay, supervision may be necessary—and that is expensive. The community may react negatively to the presence of offenders working in their midst. The cost of fines and restitution may mean that offenders cannot support their families. Finally, there are legal issues with regard to fines, restitution, and work service. Some of these issues have been resolved by the courts, but others have resulted in contradictory court decisions.

Halfway Houses

Halfway house A prerelease center used to help the inmate in changing from prison life to community life or a facility that focuses on special adjustment problems of offenders, such as a drug or alcohol treatment center. The term is also used to refer to a residential facility used as an alternative to prison for high-risk offenders considered unsuitable for probation.

Sociological theories discussed earlier in the text emphasize the socialization problems characteristic of many offenders. They have not been able to integrate into their environments or bond with significant persons. For many of them the transition from prison to release is difficult, especially if they have been incarcerated for a long time. Some jurisdictions place these offenders in a **halfway house** prior to unconditional release. Programs and supervision within this facility assist offenders to adjust to others and to cope with their own problems. The halfway house may focus on a special problem, such as alcohol or drug treatment, and it may be used in lieu of incarceration rather than as a transition from incarceration to the free world. Halfway houses are used also for some high-risk offenders considered unsuitable for probation.

Halfway houses did not "proliferate and expand their functions to include services for probationers" until the 1960s. There are many studies of halfway houses, but most were conducted during the 1960s and 1970s, when the use of such facilities was extensive. Today in some jurisdictions halfway houses are available for the use of prison administrators who need to solve overcrowding conditions, but many of the facilities are underutilized, perhaps because officials view their use as providing an easy way to do time. Additionally, it is difficult to predict which inmates are most suitable for the programs.

The federal system has provisions for the use of halfway houses, generally during the last 120 to 180 days of an offender's sentence, but most federal inmates are not released from prison until they have completed their sentences. There are several reasons for this: (1) The release criteria are worded vaguely; (2) institutions differ widely in their use of the policy; (3) in many cases plans are not begun soon enough to place the inmates for the recommended time period or at all; and (4) some inmates scheduled for movement to halfway houses do not want to go, perhaps because of the more stringent release requirements, such as securing a job in advance.

Most of the earlier studies of halfway houses examined programs designed for a mixed group of offenders: parolees, probationers, prerelease offenders, and so on. In a more recent analysis of a program designed specifically for probationers, researchers found that only 30 percent of the participants finished the Kalamazoo Probation Enhancement Program successfully. The factors associated with successful discharge from the program were higher age and educational attainment and the absence of a juvenile record.[10]

The use of halfway houses has been criticized by those who view the policy as one of leniency for white-collar criminals. For example, Leona Helmsley, who was convicted of income tax fraud, spent her halfway house time in Le Marquis Hotel in midtown Manhattan after her release from prison. Although the hotel did not provide the elegance of past days, it was an improvement over prison. But the government was quick to note that its provisions, decor, and rules were similar to those of the other 248 federal halfway houses.[11]

Shock Incarceration and Boot Camps

Shock incarceration Process of incarcerating a person for a brief period prior to release on probation or other type of supervision.

One solution to prison overcrowding has been **shock incarceration,** which takes different forms but is designed to incarcerate the offender for a brief period followed by supervision within the community. The term is used synonymously with *shock probation,* which was begun in 1965 in Ohio. Under the Ohio program, the judge could sentence an offender to a brief period of incarceration, followed by probation.

The purpose of the Ohio program was to expose offenders to the shock of prison before placing them on probation but to release them before they were influenced negatively by the prison experience. The program was adopted in some form in other states, although it has been criticized as violating the main purpose of probation, which is to avoid the negative impact of prisons.

Shock probation is different from shock incarceration in that the former involves sending offenders to prison to be exposed to the general prison population and experience. In shock incarceration, however, the offenders are separated from the general prison population. Usually they are placed in special facilities, often called **boot camps.** In the boot camp atmosphere the offender must participate in a strongly regimented daily routine of physical exercise, work, and discipline that resembles military training. Most of the programs include rehabilitative measures such as drug treatment and educational programs. The rationale for boot camps is stated in Exhibit 15.1

Boot camps Correctional facilities designed to detain offenders, primarily juveniles or young adults, for short periods, such as six months; they usually include a regimented daily routine of physical exercise, work, and discipline, resembling military training. Most of the programs include rehabilitative measures such as drug treatment and educational programs.

Since the boot camp programs are relatively new, research on their effectiveness is in its formative stages. Early reports suggest, however, that although those who go through boot camp experiences show greater changes in social attitudes than those who go through regular probation and parole programs, they are just as likely to be returned to prison for committing other offenses during their first year out of the program. Thus, the positive changes the boot camp offenders experience "may not be enough to enable them to overcome the difficulties they face in returning to the home environment." In short, "There is no evidence . . . that shock incarceration will reduce recidivism or improve positive adjustment."[12]

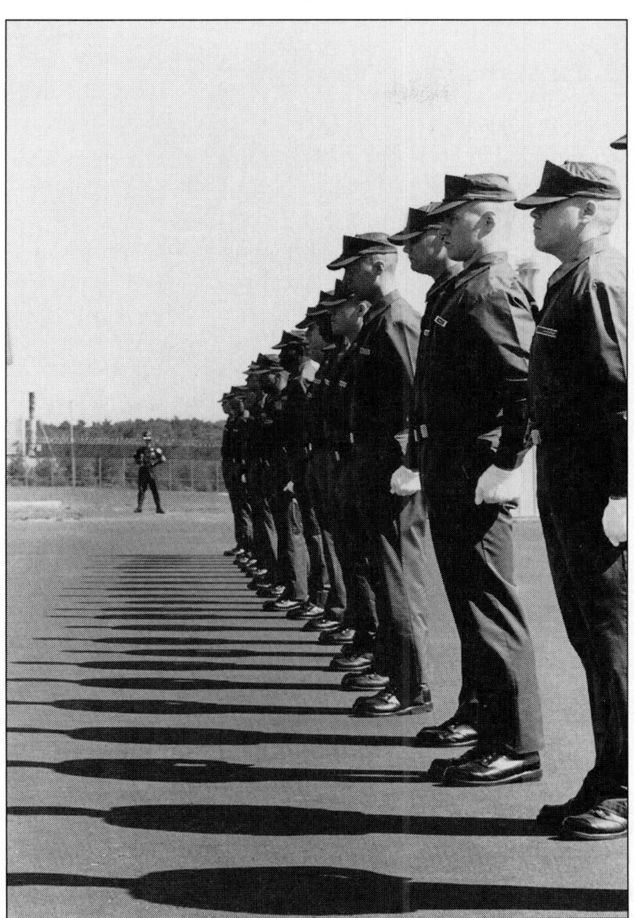

In boot camps offenders must participate in a strongly regimented daily routine of physical exercise, work, and discipline. Boot camps have been carefully scrutinized in recent years, and some have been abolished because of the unreasonable treatment of young inmates. (Susan Pulman / Index Stock)

Some later studies show similar results but are a bit more optimistic. For example, in 1996 the National Institute of Justice published an evaluation of the boot camp programs of three cities, reporting relatively positive results.[13]

Other scholars have criticized the boot camp concept, arguing that the military style does not work even in the military today and that when this style is combined with rehabilitative goals, there are negative consequences. Among those are increased aggression against other offenders and staff, and a "devaluation of women and so-called 'feminine traits' (for example, sensitivity), and other negative effects of an unpredictable, authoritarian atmosphere."[14]

Some jurisdictions have abolished their boot camp programs because of various problems. For example, in August 1997 the California Department of Corrections announced that it was making plans for an immediate phaseout of the only boot camp operated in the adult correctional system, located at San Quentin. The state legislature had approved the program for five years for experimental purposes but failed to renew that commitment in 1997. A study of the state's program found some measures of success, such as the placement of some graduates in jobs paying more than the minimum wage, but there were no significant signs of a reduction of recidivism. Nor was the program a cost-saving one. Although participants spent less time in prison than their non-boot-camp cohorts, their incarceration costs were slightly more than those in prisons because of labor-intensive programs requiring more staff members and other resources.[15] California does, however, maintain boot camp programs in some counties. They are for first-time, nonviolent young offenders.

EXHIBIT 15.1

Rationale for Boot Camps

1. A substantial number of youthful first-time offenders now incarcerated will respond to a short but intensive period of confinement followed by a longer period of intensive community supervision.
2. These youthful offenders will benefit from a military-type atmosphere that instills a sense of self-discipline and physical conditioning that was lacking in their lives.
3. These same youths need exposure to relevant educational, vocational training, drug treatment, and general counseling services to develop more positive and law-abiding values and become better prepared to secure legitimate future employment.
4. The costs involved will be less than a traditional criminal justice sanction that imprisons the offender for a substantially longer period of time.

Source: James Austin et al., *The Growing Use of Jail Boot Camp: The Current State of the Art* (Washington, DC: U.S. Department of Justice, October 1993), p. 1.

Media Focus 15.1

Boot Camps and the Death of an Inmate

Widespread media coverage was given to the story of Tony Haynes, age 14, who died in 2001 while in residence in a boot camp in an Arizona desert. At least 31 young people have died in similar camps since 1980. The Arizona death is under investigation, but the media have reported that, prior to his death, Haynes was beaten by correctional authorities and forced to eat dirt. Two other juveniles also died in boot camps in 2001. Ryan Lewis, also 14, hanged himself in a West Virginia boot camp, and his parents are accusing authorities of failing to recognize his severe depression. And Michael Wiltsie, age 12, died in a Florida boot camp, allegedly after he was restrained on the ground for 30 minutes by a 300-pound counselor.[1]

When Haynes died there were no medical personnel on hand at the camp, and one Arizona paper reported that before his death, the youth vomited dirt. One investigator said they did not know whether the camp had adequate food and water for the youths but that it was 120 degrees the day they visited. Haynes's mother said that her son was in the camp because of behavioral problems (such as shoplifting and slashing his mother's tires) but that he had started to control his anger when he was killed. Some parents were supporting the rigorous approach of the camp, while others were criticizing it.[2]

Investigators were told by some of the other youth at the Arizona camp that they, too, were abused by counselors: They were kicked, punched, forced to swallow mud, and handcuffed if they asked for food or water. The investigation continues.[3]

1. "States Pressed as 3 Boys Die at Boot Camps," *New York Times* (15 July 2001), p. 1.
2. "Desert Boot Camp Shut Down after Suspicious Death of Boy," *New York Times* (4 July 2001), p. 8.
3. "Accounts Put Darker Cloud over Camp," *New York Times* (5 July 2001), p. 13.

After experiencing problems with boot camps, the state of Maryland closed all of them. Georgia began phasing outs its programs after a study by the U.S. Department of Justice gave boot camps a negative evaluation.[16] Media Focus 15.1 contains more recent information on the problems at boot camps.

Day Reporting Centers

A new type of nonresidential supervision program of offenders is spreading rapidly. Day reporting centers (DRCs) are only a few years old; consequently, the research on their success is limited. The concept comes from a British system developed in the early 1970s. Since the early 1980s, the U.S. federal system has utilized a DRC concept through its community treatment centers. Offenders who have completed the program are permitted to report to the centers for treatment while living elsewhere. In 1986 Massachusetts and Connecticut began operating DRCs. Day reporting centers are another low-cost alternative to prisons. They may be combined with electronic monitoring and intensive supervision, housing assistance, education (especially in literacy), job training, and health and personal care. They vary widely in their clientele and in their programming and services.[17]

A recent study notes that DRCs are among the fastest-growing types of correctional supervision. Unlike other community corrections services, which focus on surveillance of offenders, DRCs provide services designed to assist offenders in establishing law-abiding lives in the community. Drug treatment and drug abuse education, assistance on how to locate a job, and training in life skills are examples of the types of services offered. Although reducing jail and prison overcrowding is a goal, the most important aim of these programs is to provide necessary assistance to offenders. Surveillance is important, but it is not a primary mission. The emphasis is on frequent contacts between offenders and the DRC staff.[18]

House Arrest

House arrest A sentence usually combined with probation, that permits the offender to remain at home under supervision. In some cases electronic monitoring of the offender's activities is used in combination with house arrest.

Prison overcrowding in the past two decades has led to another proposed solution—**house arrest,** with or without electronic monitoring. Offenders are placed on probation in their own homes; they must follow specified regulations, including restrictions on when they may leave the premises and for what purposes. House arrest is used extensively in some states to alleviate prison overcrowding and to allow for treatment.

The advantages and disadvantages of house arrest have been summarized by researchers at the Rand Corporation. The advantages include cost effectiveness, social benefits (such as permitting the offender to keep a job and continue interacting with his or her family), flexibility that permits adaptation of the plan to the individual needs of the offender and of the community, and the implementation ease and timeliness. The researchers said:

> Because house arrest sentencing requires no new facilities and can use existing probation personnel, it is one of the easier programs to implement (particularly if no electronic monitoring devices are used). House arrest programs, for the most part, do not require legislative changes and can be set up by administrative decisions. The conditions of house arrest are usually easy to communicate, facilitating implementation.[19]

The disadvantages of house arrest are as follows:

1. House arrest may widen the net of social control.
2. House arrest may narrow the net of social control.
3. House arrest focuses primarily on offender surveillance.
4. House arrest is intrusive and possibly illegal.
5. Race and class bias may enter into participant selection.
6. House arrest compromises public safety.[20]

It is that last disadvantage that is of concern to many. Despite the widespread use and reported success of house arrest, the public reacts to the failures, many of which receive extensive media coverage. In addition, house arrest may be perceived as a luxurious accommodation rather than as punishment. Some research suggests that when house arrest is combined with electronic monitoring, it receives strong public support; but that support is conditional, depending on the type and extent of monitoring and the nature of the crime committed.[21]

Electronic Monitoring

Many participants in house-arrest programs are required to wear electronic devices. These are attached to the offender's ankle or wrist and monitored by a probation officer or a telephone monitoring system. Electronic monitoring was introduced in 1964, but only recently has the practice gained widespread attention and use.

Evaluation of electronic monitoring and house arrest programs must consider the total programs involved. An analysis of three programs in California disclosed, for example, that increasing surveillance did not result in significant decreases in crime, but that when it was combined with counseling, employment, restitution, and community service, the recidivism rates were lower.[22] One study of offenders with drug problems acknowledged the difficulties of success in treating these problems but concluded that the combination of drug treatment programs with electronic monitoring "may offer some help."[23]

Despite these encouragements, it is the failure of electronic monitoring that draws the greatest attention, as illustrated by the following Chicago, Ilinois, case. On 17 August 1992 a burglary suspect, Juan Riviera, was confined to his home

Electronic devices are used to monitor the locations of offenders who have been sentenced to serve time outside of secure facilities. (A. Ramey/Photo Edit)

and wearing an electronic bracelet. That night he managed to free himself of the bracelet, left the house unnoticed by law enforcement authorities, and murdered Holly Staker, an 11-year-old babysitter. Most judges in Staker's district stopped ordering electronic monitoring after her death, stating that they had lost faith in the system.[24] In 1998 Rivera was convicted and sentenced to life without parole.

In April 2001 an Illinois jail was in the news concerning a method of release. The Lake County Jail's day-reporting program had a goal of rehabilitating inmates as well as reducing jail populations. The Lake County Urban League and the Haymarket Center in Chicago shared a contract to operate the program, but after only five months they were losing so much money they had to face terminating the program, which provided counseling and other rehabilitation services for inmates who were released but had to report to the program daily. A maximum of 16 persons had been in the program at any given time, and officials said they needed at least 25 to make a profit; they had hoped for 45. That number was never reached because of strict guidelines for participation and fewer people in the jail. The sheriff did not want to take the risk of releasing some of his inmates. Officials were hoping that the program could be revived, perhaps in another format.[25]

An alternative to electronic monitoring is being used in the state of Florida, where 600 offenders are being watched by a global positioning system (GPS), which uses satellites to track the location of offenders. For example, a GPS can be programmed to inform an official when a sex offender approaches a schoolyard. According to one article on the topic, "The new system costs $9.17 per day, compared to 50 cents a day for a state prison-housed inmate, or $3 per day for conventional electronic monitoring."[26]

PROBATION AND PAROLE: AN OVERVIEW

Probation and parole have been the most frequently used and probably the most controversial alternatives to prison. Probation is a judicial determination that does not involve confinement but does involve conditions imposed by the court.

Probation officers may work with their clients in group therapy sessions in their efforts to assist probationers to adjust to life without crime. (A. Ramey/Photo Edit)

Probation officer The official who is responsible for preparing presentence reports, supervising offenders placed on probation, and helping them integrate into society as lawful citizens.

Parole The continued custody and supervision in the community by federal or state authorities after an offender is released from an institution before expiration of the sentenced term. Parolees who violate parole conditions may be returned to the institution.

In both of these characteristics, it resembles the suspended sentence. The two are distinguished, however, by a third characteristic of probation—supervision, usually by a **probation officer.** The term *probation* refers also to the status of a person placed on probation, to the subsystem of the criminal justice system that handles this disposition of offenders, and to a process that involves the activities of the probation system: preparing reports, supervising probationers, and providing or obtaining services for them.

FIGURE 15.1
Correctional Populations in the United States: 1980–2000

Source: The Bureau of Justice Statistics, correctional surveys as reprinted at http://www.ojp.usdoj.gov/bjs/glance/corr2.htm (19 January 2002), p. 1.

In 2000, almost 6.5 million people were under some form of correctional supervision in the United States. The following diagram shows the trends of correctional populations distributed by how they were confined: probation, prison, parole, jail.

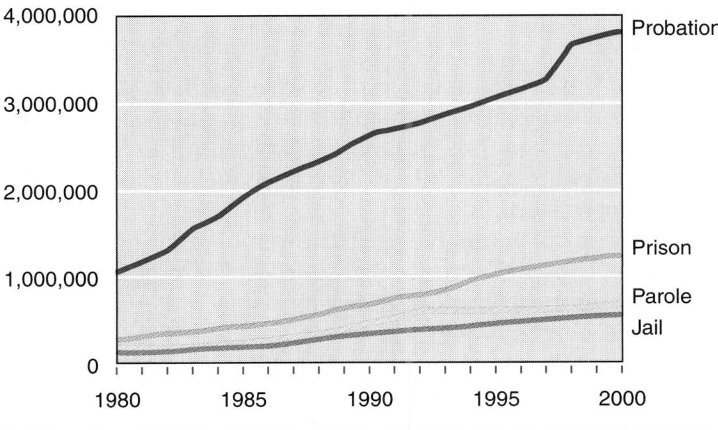

Parole refers to the release of offenders from correctional facilities after they have served part of their sentences. It is distinguished from unconditional release in that usually the parolee is placed under supervision and conditions are imposed on his or her behavior. When offenders are released unconditionally from a correctional facility, the state (or federal government) does not have jurisdiction to supervise their behavior. Unconditional release may occur after the entire sentence or a portion of it has been served and the remainder waived because of good-time credits the inmate has accrued.

The data show that at the end of 2000, nearly 4.6 million adult men and were on probation and parole, which was almost 70,000 more than the previous year. Approximately 3,839,500 adults were on probation and 725,500 were on parole. Of those on probation, 52 percent had been convicted of felonies, while 46 percent were convicted of misdemeanors. Of the probationers, 66 percent were under active supervision. Most of the offenders on parole had been originally sentenced to a term of one year or longer. Women constituted 22 percent of the probationers and 12 percent of parolees. Approximately 64 percent of the probationers were white; 34 percent were black. Among parolees, 55 percent were white, 44 percent were black. Hispanics constituted 16 percent of probationers and 21 percent of parolees.[27]

Figure 15.1 diagrams the data for probation, parole, prison, and jail, showing the trends in the number of persons in the United States under each form of supervision between 1980 and 2000.

FOCUS ON PROBATION

Scholars do not agree on the origin of probation (defined on p. 500), but most trace it, like many other aspects of criminal justice systems, to English common law. Generally U.S. probation is traced to a prosperous shoemaker in Boston, John Augustus, often called the "father of probation." As early as 1841 Augustus introduced into Boston courts the concept of friendly supervision in the community. From his own resources, Augustus paid the fines for many people who were jailed; he worked on rehabilitation as well.[28]

In 1878 Massachusetts became the first state to enact a probation statute officially. By 1900 only five states had probation statutes, but the establishment of the juvenile court in 1899 in Chicago gave impetus to the probation movement. By 1915, 33 states had probation statutes, and by 1957 all states had them. In 1925 a statute authorizing probation in federal courts was enacted.

Probation comes from the Latin word *probare,* which means "to test" or "to prove." Technically, probation, which may be granted only by the court, is a form of sentencing. Often, however, it is considered as a disposition in lieu of sentencing. In some cases the court sentences a defendant to a term of incarceration but suspends that sentence for a specified period of time, during which the offender is on probation. If the terms of probation are not violated, the sentence is not imposed; but if the offender violates probation, he or she may be incarcerated. Because probation is a form of sentencing, which the Supreme Court considers to be a critical stage in criminal justice systems, the defendant is entitled to due process at the probation hearing. Under the U.S. Constitution due process requires that a person may not be deprived of life, liberty, or property without reasonable and lawful procedures (see Appendix A, Amendment Fourteen). This means that the judge may not be unreasonable, arbitrary, or capricious in the decision to grant probation. The defendant is entitled to an attorney at this stage as well as when probation is revoked and the suspended sentence is imposed.[29]

Probation Supervision

Authorities do not agree on important issues in probation, such as whether the size of a probation officer's caseload is related significantly to the success or failure of probationers. But it is clear that traditional probation has problems. Supervision practices and probation conditions vary from jurisdiction to jurisdiction, often with little supervision.

Intensive probation supervision (IPS) Close supervision of probationers by probation officers who have smaller than average case loads.

More recently, the concept of **intensive probation supervision (IPS)** has gained prominence and has focused on another purpose of probation—the diversion of defendants from incarceration. Diversion is seen as one way to attack the problem of prison overcrowding.

In addition to diversion, IPS has other objectives. First, in many jurisdictions, probation caseloads are so high and probation is considered so ineffective, both in helping the offender and in protecting society, that judges may see no alternative to the incarceration of convicted offenders but IPS. Second, despite the increased cost of IPS compared with traditional forms of probation, a difference that results from smaller caseloads, IPS is considerably less costly than incarceration. Third, there is some evidence that IPS has eliminated some of the negative public attitudes toward probation in that it may be viewed as more punitive because of the increased supervision.

There are problems, however. A study of IPS in Texas disclosed the following:

> The IPS program did not alleviate prison crowding and may actually have increased it;
>
> The IPS program costs considerably more than most advocates have realized; [and]
>
> The IPS program was no more effective than routine parole in reducing offender recidivism, as measured by arrests and convictions.[30]

One study of an IPS program designed for drug offenders found that, compared to probationers without IPS, the IPS subjects had more supervision (an average of three hours a month compared to 20 minutes for the non-IPS probationers), but they had more technical violations. There was no significant difference between the two groups in the arrests for new crimes. It was suggested that more intensive supervision coupled with more treatment might produce better results, but it is not known how strict that supervision must be. Furthermore, the costs increase as supervision increases.[31]

Probation Conditions

Regardless of the nature of probation supervision, most judges impose probation conditions. Usually there are restrictions on travel, such as prohibitions against leaving the state or country without permission; prohibitions against the use of alcohol and other drugs; prohibitions concerning associating with questionable people; and requirements of holding a job, attending counseling, or entering substance abuse or other treatment programs. Most probation conditions are upheld, but occasionally appellate courts rule that the trial judge imposed a condition that is not permitted. A few examples illustrate the trend in rulings.

Courts have held that mandatory drug testing is a reasonable probation condition in some cases, such as that of the offender who admitted at sentencing that sometimes he smoked six marijuana cigarettes and drank 14 beers daily, and that he had consumed five beers on the day he committed the burglary for which he was being sentenced. When he tested positive for cocaine, his probation was revoked. He appealed, arguing that mandatory testing was unreasonable. The Hawaii Supreme Court upheld the drug testing, ruling that state law provided for these tests and that they did not represent an unconstitutional invasion of privacy.[32]

A California court ruled that it was unreasonable to require as a probation condition that a female heroin addict not get pregnant. The court noted that the condition was unrelated to the offense in question (child abuse) and that it infringed on reproductive rights, which are fundamental rights. Despite evidence that drug addiction can harm a fetus, the court held that judges have no right to impose their personal views on the offenders they sentence.[33] Critics of such probation conditions warn that the imposition of controls over reproduction discriminate against racial minorities and the poor as well as against women: "Have you ever heard of these punishments being applied to a wealthy woman? Or to a man?"[34]

In contrast, a Pennsylvania court held that it was reasonable to require a female probationer to stay away from her boyfriend for two years. Under Pennsylvania law a probationer may be required to "refrain from frequenting unlawful or disreputable places or consorting with disreputable persons." The probationer was convicted of assisting her boyfriend to avoid apprehension after he entered guilty pleas to numerous burglary counts and absconded before sentencing. The court reasoned that the probationer would have a better chance at rehabilitation if she had no contact with her boyfriend, who subsequently had become her fiancé.[35]

A federal court has held that it was reasonable for a judge to order a probationer to get a paying job rather than become a missionary. The probationer had been ordered to pay restitution and fines after conviction of a series of religious scams.[36] In another case, a federal court ruled that it was unconstitutional to require a convicted drunk driver to attend Alcoholics Anonymous (AA) meetings while on probation. The court acknowledged the spiritual and religious nature of AA meetings and held that requiring one to attend them violated the probationer's First Amendment rights (see Appendix A).[37] In contrast, a California state court held that it is permissible to require a probationer to attend nonspiritual programs aimed at assisting with substance abuse.[38]

RELEASE FROM PRISON

Inmates face many problems upon release from prison. Theoretically, parole release provides assistance in coping with those problems, but in reality not enough assistance is given. Most releasees have limited financial resources or none at all. Many do not have employment, and some do not have residences or families to whom they may return. Most receive indifferent or hostile reactions from the community. Those who have been incarcerated for long periods have the additional problem of catching up on how contemporary society operates. All encounter emotional problems in reacting to the new environment, and many feel depressed, estranged, lonely, and rejected.

Prerelease programs
Institutional programs that assist inmates in adjusting to life after release from incarceration. The programs cover subjects such as money management, job interviewing, and basic social skills.

Some institutions help prepare inmates for release, but the availability of **prerelease programs** is limited. They differ among institutions, ranging from information on etiquette and changing social mores to practical details on how to knot a tie and interview for a job. Some prisons hold prerelease classes, whereas others have prerelease centers or halfway houses.

Some institutions offer training sessions to assist inmates in preparing for release; others offer halfway programs for a gradual reentry into society. Most make some attempt to deal with the two most immediate problems—money and jobs. There are a variety of ways to assist inmates in making the transition. One is to develop prerelease programs. Some of these programs are held within the prison environment, and others take place in prerelease centers. The purpose is to train the offender in the ways of daily living: how to get a job, how to keep a job, how to relate to his or her family, and how to live in a world that may have changed significantly since the offender began the incarceration period. Examples are the shelters in New York that assist female offenders and their children in adjusting to one another.[39]

Prerelease programs may include educational and vocational programs, treatment programs, or life enrichment programs (in which offenders are taught how to control their emotions, plan for the future, and establish goals). They are taught how to manage money, and they may participate in recreational and other leisure activities. Decision making and problem solving are featured as well. They are made aware and given access to databases including state agencies as well as instructed in employment and career issues.

The second major problem of ex-offenders is employment. Several types of programs have been developed to aid ex-offenders in job hunting. For example, in Illinois all inmates within 90 days of release are required to attend two weeks of PreStart, a course that instructs participants in survival skills, goal setting, résumé writing, personal development and self-esteem, job hunting, interviewing skills, stress management, and reintegration into the community. Decision-making skills are discussed as well.[40]

The employment picture is bleak for ex-offenders, however, and many have not had adequate training before or during incarceration. Some jurisdictions are trying to alleviate the problems. For example, Ohio opened its first "work prison" in 1996. Nonviolent, minimum-security inmates live in a community facility while working in the community. They work for nonprofit groups, government agencies, and public schools, earning from $16 to $36 a month at skills that will be useful when they are released.[41]

The importance of work for ex-offenders is illustrated by an analysis of a Texas program for placing parolees in jobs. Re-Integration of Offenders (RIO) provides job placement services for Texas parolees. It was reported that almost 74 percent of offenders who received support services from RIO found employment (with an average hourly wage of $5.15, compared to the then-current minimum wage of $4.25). Researchers concluded that the $8 million per year cost of RIO was worth the expenditure because lower rates of recidivism among participants (23 percent compared to a 38 percent rate for those high-risk offenders who did not participate in the program) reduced incarceration rates significantly.[42]

Furlough and Work-Release Programs

Work-release programs and furloughs are utilized to prepare inmates for release. Although furloughs were introduced in 1918, the extensive use of them or of work release in the United States is recent, stemming from their provision in the federal system by the Prisoner Rehabilitation Act of 1965. Most of the programs in existence today were established by state laws after the 1965 federal law had been enacted.

Furlough An authorized, temporary leave from a prison or other place of incarceration by an inmate for the purpose of attending a funeral, visiting his or her family, or attempting to secure a job.

Work release An authorized absence that allows the inmate to hold a job or attend school but that requires him or her to return to the institution during nonworking hours.

A **furlough** is a brief absence from the institution, usually for a specified purpose other than work or study. Furloughs may be granted to allow inmates to visit sick relatives, attend family funerals, secure employment, obtain a driver's license, meet with future parole officers, arrange for housing, or visit family members. Furloughs may last from several hours to several days. The main advantage of furloughs is that offenders are placed in contact with their families and the outside world. They have a chance to make decisions on their own, away from the closely monitored prison routine, and the community is given time to adjust to them.

In the system known as **work release** the offender is released from incarceration to work or attend school. Inmates may participate in vocational study, take courses at an educational institution, or work at a job in the community. There may be statutory restrictions on eligibility for work release. For example, Minnesota provides that an inmate is eligible for work release if she or he is regularly employed. A state court held that a woman whose husband agreed to pay her $1.50 an hour for housekeeping services would not be eligible. Despite its recognition of the economic value of housekeeping, the court held that housekeeping is not considered employment.[43]

One of the advantages of furlough and work release is that they give offenders an opportunity for close contacts with their families. Close family ties may ease the problems of adjusting to society. In addition, work release enables offenders to provide financial support for their families and helps improve inmates' attitudes toward socially responsible work. Improvements in self-esteem, self-image, and self-respect are additional benefits of work release. Another possible advantage is the lowered cost compared to incarceration.

Inmates on work release may be required to reimburse the state for part of the cost of their incarceration. They pay taxes and may be required to contribute to victim restitution funds.

Offenders who are on work release may have problems in adjusting to the contrast between the community during the day and the institution at night. Indeed, it might be easier to make a complete break with the institution and attempt to readjust to society without having to return to prison. Also, release during the day may eliminate or interrupt participation in some prison programs that are beneficial to the offender. In addition, problems may arise over the use of money earned. Transportation is frequently a problem because many correctional institutions are not located in urban areas where inmates are most likely to find jobs.

A final problem with work release and furlough is the possibility that participants may commit additional crimes or escape from supervision.

FOCUS ON PAROLE

One of the most controversial aspects of criminal justice systems is parole, which involves releasing inmates before they have served their complete sentences. When those releasees commit crimes, especially violent crimes, society is outraged, as illustrated by the case discussed in Exhibit 15.2.

Parole releases have been cause for concern, with the rise in state prison populations due in part to the increasing number of parolees who are returned to prison. During the 1990s there was a 54 percent increase in the number of offenders returned to prison for parole violations. Some of these offenders were released by a parole board decision; others had fulfilled the individual state's legislative requirements for release on parole. Drug offenders were responsible for more than one-half of the parole violators returned to prison.[44] And the most recent analysis from the Bureau of Justice Statistics regarding federal offenders shows that, between 1986 and 1994, 16 percent of them were returned to prison within three years. While 60 percent of those were returned for parole violations, another 30 percent were imprisoned for convictions on new offenses.[45]

Authorities do not agree on the origin of parole. Some trace it to the English system of sending criminals to the American colonies. Criminals were pardoned by the English government after being sold to the highest bidder in America. The buyer became the master of the individual, whose new status was that of indentured servant. The system is similar to parole in that, in order to receive the change in status, an individual agreed to specific conditions similar to the ones imposed by parole boards.[46]

Others claim that the concept of conditioned liberty was introduced first in France around 1830. It was an intermediary step of freedom between prison confinement and complete freedom in the community. Still others trace the history of parole to the reform efforts of Captain Alexander Maconochie, who began the reformatory movement in 1840 in Australia where he was in charge of the worst of England's penal colonies—Norfolk Island. Maconochie eliminated the flat sentence and instituted a system of marks that inmates could earn for good behavior and work. Marks were used to reduce the amount of time served in the prison colony. Maconochie evaluated his term at Norfolk in these words: "I found Norfolk Island a hell, but left it an orderly and well-regulated community." His work was not appreciated by the English, however, and he was recalled. But his reform efforts did have a later effect in England and in America.[47]

Maconochie's system was taken to Ireland by Sir Walter Crofton, who added supervision to the early release program. In 1870 Crofton spoke to the American Prison Association, which adopted a "Declaration of Principles" that

EXHIBIT 15.2

The Failures of Parole: An Officer Is Killed

New York City's mayor Rudolph W. Giuliani proclaimed 14-year veteran police officer Anthony Mosomillo, age 36, not only "an exceptional police officer" but also a hero. Mosomillo was gunned down by a parolee whom he and his fellow officers were attempting to arrest for a parole violation. The suspect, Jose Serrano, managed to get another officer's gun and shoot Mosomillo four times in the neck and body. Before he died, Mosomillo killed Serrano.

As Mosomillo's family and friends mourned, officials tried to ascertain why his killer was out of prison. Serrano was on parole after serving time for a drug conviction, but he was wanted for a parole violation when he was arrested in April 1998 on a minor drug offense. At that time he was released from custody after giving police an alias. He was ordered to return to court on 18 May. Serrano had been fingerprinted, but the prints were not available when he gave police the alias.

When he failed to show up for his 18 May court date, a warrant was issued for his arrest. While Mosomillo and his colleagues were apprehending Serrano, who was hiding under the bed at his girlfriend's house, Serrano's girlfriend, Betsy Ramos, age 34, who was on probation until the year 2005 for her conviction for smuggling heroin, struggled with one of the officers, whose gun was knocked away. Serrano grabbed the gun and began shooting. Mosomillo was taken to the hospital, where he died with his wife and two children, one a toddler, by his side.

The killing of Officer Mosomillo by a parolee led to calls for abolition of New York's parole system. In August 1998 the state enacted a statute that limits access to early release for first-time violent felons. The statute requires that they must serve 85 percent of their maximum sentences before they are covered by mandatory release. Previously these offenders were released after they completed two-thirds of their maximum sentence unless they were involved in disciplinary problems while in prison. The new law, called Jenna's law, is the result of lobbying by the parents of Jenna Grieshaber, who was killed in her Albany apartment by parolee in 1997. The families of Mosomillo and of Grieshaber attended the signing ceremony.

Before the passage of Jenna's law, it was noted that it would not have applied to Serrano, who was convicted of nonviolent drug offenses rather than a violent felony. Ramos was convicted of manslaughter for her role in Mosomillo's death. She was sentenced to 15 years in prison.

Source: Summarized from news media sources.

included parole release. The actual use of formal parole in the United States is traced to 1876 in the Elmira Reformatory in New York State. The plans differed, but all states and the federal government adopted parole eventually. It was used extensively, although in recent years it has been questioned and in some jurisdictions it has been restricted or abolished. By the end of 2000, 15 states had abolished the traditional parole board authority as a form of release from prison, while another 5 states had abolished it for releasing certain violent offenders.[48]

Parole board Normally a panel that decides how much of a sentence offenders serve in the institution and whether they are ready to return to society with continued supervision in the community.

Parole officers The government employees responsible for counseling and supervising inmates released on parole in the community.

The Parole System

The organization of parole is complex. It consists of two main divisions: the **parole board,** responsible for release decisions, and **parole officers,** who supervise parolees. These divisions carry out the four main functions of parole: releasing and placing inmates on parole, supervising parolees, releasing parolees from supervision upon completion of their sentences or proof that they are no longer a risk to the community, and revoking parole when the parolees have violated parole conditions.

The most important stage in the administration of parole is the parole hearing. Until recently the legal requirements at this stage were unclear and the nature of the hearing differed from state to state. Most allowed the inmate to be

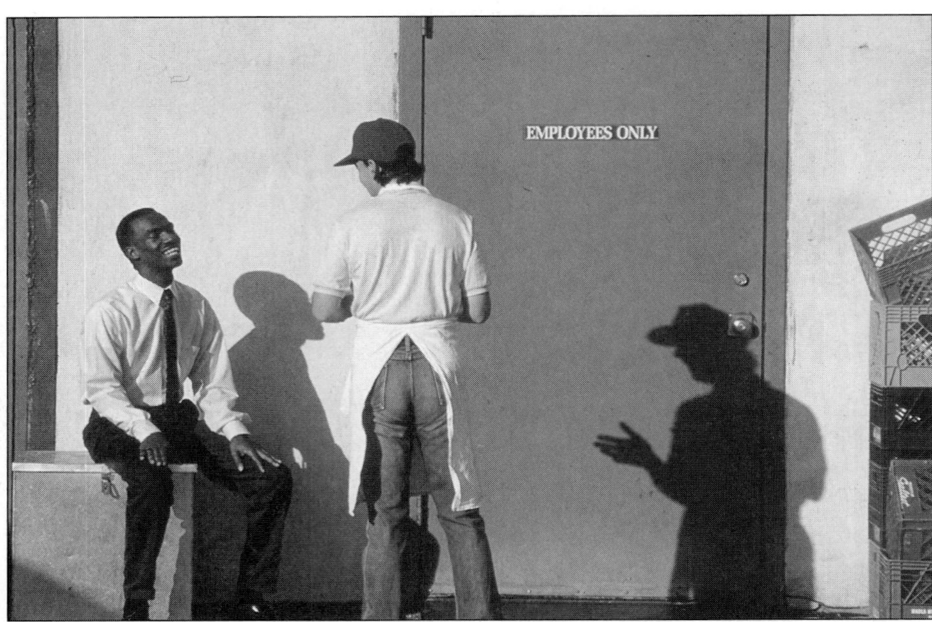

Offenders placed on parole need careful supervision by parole officers. Chris McPhatter, left, is the sentence coordinator for an armed robber on parole in Fayetteville, North Carolina. (Kevin Horan/Stock Boston)

present, but some refused an oral hearing. Some parole boards heard cases with all members present; others divided into panels, with each one hearing and deciding different cases. Usually the hearings were private, attended only by the inmate (where permitted), board members, and a representative of the institution in which the inmate was incarcerated. Reports from family members, psychological or other treatment personnel, or institutional staff members might have been included. Some boards requested information concerning the inmate's plans upon release. Reasons for denial might or might not have been given to the inmates.

Federal courts were divided over the requirements of due process at the parole hearing, but in 1979, in *Greenholtz* v. *Inmates of Nebraska Penal and Correctional Complex,* the Supreme Court held that due process requirements were met by the Nebraska statute that allowed an inmate, at the time of the first parole decision in his or her case, an opportunity to speak on his or her own behalf and, in the case of denial, to receive a statement of the reasons for that denial. The Court held that the Nebraska statute created an expectation of parole that must be protected by due process. Whether that expectation exists in other state statutes would have to be determined by examining each statute. The Court held that due process at the parole hearing does not require the parole board to specify the particular evidence that influenced its denial. The Court did not hold that the U.S. Constitution requires a parole hearing to involve all the elements of due process required at a criminal trial. In a 1995 case the Court criticized the decision but left it standing.[49]

In *Board of Pardons* v. *Allen,* decided in 1987, the Court reaffirmed its decision in *Greenholtz,* holding that Montana's statute created an expectation of parole provided certain conditions are met by the inmate. If the inmate meets those conditions, parole must be granted. Once again, it is the wording of the statute, not the possibility of parole per se, that creates the expectation of liberty that must be protected. The use of *shall* rather than *may* in a statute creates this expectation.[50]

Prior to these court cases, John Irwin emphasized the problems that arbitrary decisions by parole boards could create for inmates. In his classic book, *The Felon,* Irwin said arbitrariness by parole boards created a sense of injustice, which increased the inmate's loss of commitment to conventional society.[51]

Perhaps former Supreme Court justice Hugo Black best summarized the view of many inmates toward the parole board:

> In the course of my reading—by no means confined to law—I have reviewed many of the world's religions. The tenets of many faiths hold the deity to be a trinity. Seemingly, the parole boards, by whatever names designated in the various states, have in too many instances sought to enlarge this to include themselves as members.[52]

The Future of Parole

As the result of highly publicized crimes committed by offenders while on parole as well as the trend toward harsher punishment, some jurisdictions have abolished parole. What happens when parole as a method of release from prison is abolished? Most states with flat-term or determinate sentencing laws allow early release based on good-time credits earned in the institution. The most obvious result of abolishing release by parole boards has been an increase in time served in institutions, but there have been repercussions in other areas. No longer can parole boards reduce acute overcrowding in prisons. Where good-time provisions remain, the control of sentence length has moved from the parole board to prison officials. Individual correctional officers make the basic decisions about inmate conduct and behavior and control their good-time credits. Prosecutors and judges who adjust their charging and sentencing practices have more discretionary power. Thus, abolition of parole may relocate, not remove, discretion.

Earlier chapters note that discretion exists in all areas of criminal justice systems. The exercise of that discretion involves predictions. Police, judges, probation and parole officers, and correctional personnel all make decisions according to such predictions. Our ability to predict accurately is limited, and it may not improve in the near future. But the point is that predictions are made, and discretion is exercised. Nevertheless, the movement to abolish parole has continued.

Others claim that the abolition of parole is a serious mistake. A report by the American Probation and Parole Association and the Association of Paroling Authorities International concluded, "The abolition of parole has been tried and has failed on a spectacular scale. . . The absence of parole means that offenders simply walk out the door of prison at the end of a predetermined period of time, no questions asked."[53] The two organizations began a move toward convincing Americans that parole is not soft on crime, but rather a necessary measure for the release and supervision of releasees. They note that the public thinks parole means shorter sentences but that such is not necessarily the case. Sentences may be determined by the availability of prison space, and releasing inmates because of space shortage and without parole supervision may be dangerous. The report concludes that in all states that have abolished parole "the alternative has resulted in shorter, definite sentences which automatically release offenders at the end of a set sentence."[54]

PROBATION AND PAROLE REVOCATION

Historically, the granting of parole and the revocation of probation or parole were conducted with little, if any, due process. The Supreme Court has ruled that certain due process requirements must be observed at revocation proceedings. In

1967, in *Mempa* v. *Rhay,* the Court ruled that a probationer is entitled to be represented by counsel (state-appointed for indigents) at a combined revocation and sentencing hearing because sentencing is a stage of the actual criminal proceeding "where substantial rights of a criminal accused may be affected."[55]

In 1972 the Court considered parole revocation. In *Morrissey* v. *Brewer,* it held that before parole may be revoked, the parolee is entitled to two hearings. The first is a hearing to determine whether there is probable cause to believe that the individual has violated parole terms. The second and more extensive hearing is to consider the evidence and determine whether parole should be revoked.

In *Morrissey,* the Court stated that (1) the purpose of parole is rehabilitation; (2) until the rules are violated, an individual may remain on parole; (3) full due process rights used in criminal trials do not apply to parole revocation; (4) the termination of liberty by revocation results in "grievous loss," mandating some due process protection; (5) informal parole revocation hearings are proper; (6) parole should not be revoked unless the rules are violated; and (7) the requirements of due process will change with particular cases.[56]

The Supreme Court requires the following elements of due process at the parole revocation proceedings:

1. Written notice of the alleged parole violations.
2. Disclosure to the parolee of the evidence of violation.
3. Opportunity to be heard in person and to present evidence as well as witnesses.
4. Right to confront and cross-examine adverse witnesses unless good cause can be shown for not allowing this confrontation.
5. Right to judgment by a detached and neutral hearing body.
6. Written statement of reasons for revoking parole as well as of the evidence used in arriving at that decision.

The importance of fairness in parole revocation was emphasized by the Supreme Court in the following brief excerpt from the case.[57]

Morrissey v. Brewer

The parolee is not the only one who has a stake in his conditional liberty. Society has a stake in whatever may be the chance of restoring him to a normal and useful life within the law. Society thus has an interest in not having parole revoked because of erroneous information or because of an erroneous evaluation of the need to revoke parole, given the breach of parole conditions. And society has a further interest in treating the parolee with basic fairness: fair treatment in parole revocations will enhance the chance of rehabilitation by avoiding reactions to arbitrariness.

In 1973 in *Gagnon* v. *Scarpelli,* the Court held that *Morrissey's* minimum due process requirements apply to probation revocation hearings but that due process does not require the right to counsel at all revocation hearings. Whether counsel is required by due process should be determined on the basis of the facts of each case. Counsel is required when it is necessary for fundamental fairness. For example, an inmate who has serious communication problems might need counsel at revocation hearings in order for those hearings to be fair.[58]

In *Bearden* v. *Georgia,* the Court held that probation cannot be revoked because an indigent cannot pay a fine and restitution unless there is a determination that the probationer has not made a bona fide effort or that there were no adequate alternative methods of punishment.[59] In *Black* v. *Romano,* the Court held that generally when a court revokes probation and a suspended prison sentence is imposed, the court does not have to indicate that it considered alternatives to prison. This case did not involve the indigency issue regarding failure to pay a fine and restitution as in the *Bearden* case.[60]

Even when following Supreme Court guidelines, it is important to remember that probation or parole revocation is a serious matter. It is possible to grant fair hearings and still revoke probation or parole because of some minor infraction of the rules. For example, in some jurisdictions, any violation of parole conditions results in revocation and the return to prison. In deciding which actions are serious enough to warrant parole revocation, we should keep in mind the potentially harmful effects of incarceration as well as its cost. As budget problems continue to plague corrections systems and many prisons remain overcrowded, we must consider costs when deciding how to punish. Violent offenders are one issue, but violation of a minor parole condition, such as driving a car without the parole officer's permission, is quite another.

A report by the National Institute of Justice disclosed that states are spending large sums of money to incarcerate minor violators of parole and probation conditions. As a result, many jurisdictions have developed revocation guidelines to minimize the problem. Greater use of intermediate sanctions is another alternative adopted by many.

Before turning to an assessment of community corrections, it is important to consider one additional factor: the recent trend toward community notification that sex offenders who have served time in a prison or correctional facility are being released to live in specific areas.

MEGAN'S LAWS

The safety and security of society is a concern anytime an offender is released from incarceration. Various methods are used to try to maintain security. One of the most controversial practices in recent history within U.S. criminal justice systems is the use of *Megan's laws* (see Chapter 2, p. 26). The term derives from the murder of seven-year-old Megan Kanka on 29 July 1994. Megan had been enticed into the home of a neighbor who promised her a puppy. Neither Megan nor her parents nor local law enforcement officials knew that the neighbor, who was on parole, had been convicted of previous sex offenses against young girls and that he lived with two other men, both of whom had been convicted of sex offenses. Knowledge of that information outraged local, state, and national officials and citizens. By 31 October 1994, New Jersey had enacted its Sexual Offender Registration Act, which requires a person who has completed a sentence for conviction of certain designated offenses to register if, at the time of sentencing, his conduct was found to be "characterized by a pattern of repetitive and compulsive behavior." A second requirement involves notifying the community that the sex offender will be living in the neighborhood.[61]

Other jurisdictions followed New Jersey's lead, and by May 1996, 49 states had adopted a version of Megan's law. President Bill Clinton signed a federal version of Megan's law, which mandates the release of information collected through state programs that require the registration of sex offenders if that information is "necessary to protect the public." In June Clinton issued a statement during his weekly radio broadcast in which he endorsed legislation to create a national registry to track sex offenders. He ordered Attorney General Janet Reno to propose guidelines for this process even if a statute were not enacted. As part of its 1994 crime bill, Congress had urged states to establish programs requiring the registration of sexually violent persons, persons convicted of sexually violent offenses, and those convicted of offenses against minors.[62]

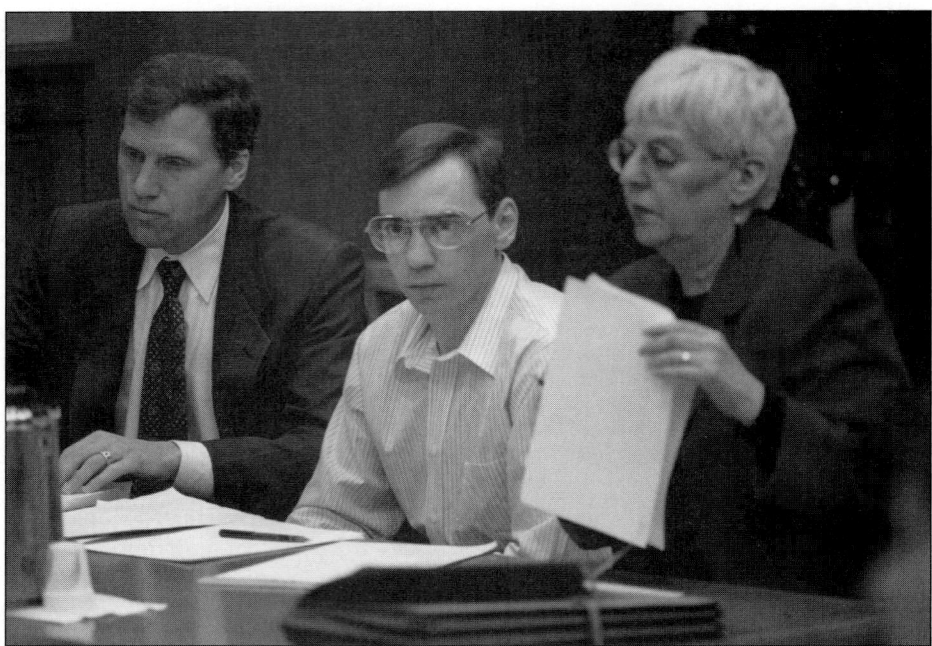

Jesse Timmendequas, center, charged with kidnapping, sexual assault, and felony murder in the death of seven-year-old Megan Kanka, sits between his defense team of Roy Greeman, left, and Barbara Lependorf inside the Hunterdon County Justice Center before the screening of jurors began in Flemington, New Jersey, on 13 January 1997. This crime led to the establishment of Megan's laws throughout the country. These laws require the registration of convicted sex offenders who move into the neighborhoods. Timmendequas, a repeat sex offender, was living across the street from Megan when the crime was committed. He was convicted and sentenced to death. (AP)

In January 2002 New Jersey began posting the names of moderate- to high-risk sex offenders online for the world to access, thus joining 30 states and the District of Columbia in this approach to notifying communities of sex offenders. The state's voters overwhelmingly supported a constitutional amendment in November 2000, and the legislature enacted laws in the spring of 2001. The lawmakers took considerable time in their formulation, hoping to avoid successful challenges to these provisions. The American Civil Liberties Union has announced plans to challenge the postings.[63]

The New Jersey Supreme Court has ruled, however, that the state's Megan's law has limitations with regard to juveniles. Although the original intent of the legislature was that the statute would apply to juveniles, the court decided that this provision would conflict with the state's Code of Juvenile Justice. In July 2001 the court unanimously held that Megan's Law registration requirements "will end at the age of eighteen for offenders who committed a sex crime under the age of fourteen if they can show by clear and convincing evidence that they are not likely to commit another offense." The case on which this ruling was based involved a 17-year-old boy who, when he was 10, sexually molested an 8-year-old girl. The court was struggling to balance the purpose of Megan's law—protection of the public—with that of the Juvenile Code—rehabilitation of the young.[64]

Megan's laws in the various jurisdictions differ both in their registration and notification requirements. With regard to the latter, for example, most statutes require law enforcement officers to provide the notification, but Louisiana offenders are required to notify the public themselves. They must place an advertisement for two days in a local publication, notify school principals, and send postcards to homes located within three blocks (if they live in an urban area) and one mile (if in a rural area). In Oregon probation officers notify the community by going door to door.[65]

Megan's laws have been criticized as inciting violence. In January 1995 a vigilante attack on a paroled sex offender was attributed to New Jersey's version of the law. Two men broke into a home where the parolee was staying. One stated that he was looking "for the child molester." Police were called and arrived before anyone was hurt seriously.[66] In 1998 California's Megan's law was cited as the cause of the death of Michael Allen Patton, who committed suicide five days after law enforcement officials notified community residents that he was living in their area.[67]

Megan's laws have also been challenged in the courts. The challenges are complicated and go beyond the scope of this text. For the most part, however, the requirements have been upheld against arguments that registration and notification constitute punishment by violating the *ex post facto* prohibition, along with that of double jeopardy and due process provisions of the federal constitution. Some courts have required alterations in the specifics of the statutes, but the general provisions have been upheld. In February 2002 the U.S. Supreme Court agreed to hear an appeal from an Alaska petitioner concerning the constitutionality of that state's Megan's law.[68]

In addition to the constitutional issues, however, is the question of whether Megan's laws are effective. Some of the provisions may need to be altered to achieve maximum results. For example, in the summer of 1998 an 11-year-old Connecticut girl was killed after being abducted from her paper route. The man accused of the crime, Jose Torres, age 25, was a resident in the same apartment complex as the victim; she was delivering papers in that area. The Connecticut statute requires that citizens must request information regarding sex offenders living in their areas. The information is filed alphabetically and not by address, so it is difficult to find. In three years only two people checked the register. Citizens vowed to strengthen the state law,[69] but the success of Megan's laws is based on several presumptions.

First, it is presumed that if notification is provided, potential victims will read the notice and act accordingly. This is not always the case, especially in those instances in which the sexual abuser is a family member or friend. Second, it is presumed that law enforcement officials will have accurate data for notification. Third, it is presumed that law enforcement officials will have the resources to perform all their duties associated with community notification of sex offenders. Fourth, it is presumed that community notification will serve as a deterrent to those sex offenders, who will not be inclined to commit a sex crime in their neighborhoods. This presumes that they will not travel to other areas where notification has not occurred. In short, there is reason to question any or all of these presumptions.

Megan's laws are so new that few empirical tests of their effectiveness have been published. One study might be cited, although it utilized a very limited sample. The researchers looked at the cases of 36 sex offenders in Massachusetts who would have been eligible for the community notification registry based on their prior sex crimes. Twelve of those offenders subsequently committed a sex crime against a stranger, while 24 committed crimes against members of their own families, friends, or coworkers. The researchers concluded that if the notification system had no flaws, it could reasonably be assumed that knowledge of 6 of the 12 would have reached potential victims.[70]

THE FUTURE OF CORRECTIONS

In this final section of the book, we will consider some of the issues that our society must face now and in the future. Despite the slight decline in prison populations in some jurisdictions, the reduction of overcrowding in some prison systems, and the decline or leveling off of crime rates, we have in no way solved the crime or incarceration problems. We begin this section with an evaluation of community corrections, focusing on return offenders.

An Evaluation of Community Corrections

Advocates of community corrections argue that, in addition to decreasing the populations of prisons and jails and saving money, the approach benefits in the rehabilitation of offenders. Most evaluations of community corrections, especially probation and parole, involve a study of recidivism, which may include new law violations or violations of the terms of probation or parole or other programs.

Researchers do not agree on the meaning of the term *recidivism* or on how it should be measured. The result is that recidivism data vary. Early studies reported that as many as two-thirds of those released from prison became recidivists. These figures were questioned in the early 1960s in an extensive analysis of federal data by Daniel Glaser, who argued that the best way to study recidivism is to follow a cohort of offenders for a specified period after their release.[71] Earlier studies (especially those of juveniles) did so.[72]

Felony probation Placing on probation an offender convicted of a felony.

More recent studies of recidivism have focused on **felony probation** and parole. Researchers at the Rand Corporation conducted a study of felony probation for the National Institute of Justice. They found that nearly two-thirds of all convicted offenders are placed on probation and that, of those offenders, two-thirds were rearrested, 51 percent were convicted of a new crime, and 34 percent were given a jail or prison sentence. The recidivists committed the crimes of burglary, theft, and robbery. The study pointed out that certain variables were related significantly to recidivism:

Type of conviction crime. Property offenders had the highest rates of recidivism.
Number of prior juvenile and adult convictions. The greater the number, the higher the probability of recidivism.
Income at arrest. Regardless of source or amount, the presence of income was associated with lower recidivism.
Household composition. If the offender were living with spouse and/or children, recidivism was lower.[73]

The Rand researchers acknowledged that felony probation presents great risks. But they warned against premature conclusions based on the reported data: "Rather than castigate probation, critics should realize these findings actually indict the attitudes and policies that placed unrealistic and overwhelming demands on probation agencies."[74] They suggested a more extensive use of intensive probation supervision (IPS).

Other studies of recidivism among felony probationers have been conducted. The largest follow-up study reported that within three years of being placed on probation and while still on probation, 43 percent of felons were rearrested for a felony. One-half of those arrests were for violent crimes (murder, rape, robbery, or aggravated assault) or for drug offenses. Within three years, 46 percent of felony probationers had been sentenced to prison or had absconded (meaning they had failed to report and their whereabouts were not known).[75]

It is important to keep in mind that probation and parole offenders are not equal and that many variables might factor into their success or failure. For example, one study found a lower recidivism rate among offenders who had completed a treatment program as compared to those who had not been involved in treatment.[76] But treatment programs differ, too, and so the nature, type, and extent of the programs must be considered.

Despite recidivism, community corrections must be regarded as a serious alternative to incarceration. Because of financial limitations, high incarceration rates cannot continue, and they are not necessary for security. Yet, some people argue, just as prison is used excessively, so is probation. The problem is that we do not have adequate intermediate sentencing alternatives. In a provocative analysis of the subject, Norval Morris and Michael H. Tonry called for closer scrutiny of sentencing alternatives in between the extremes of incarceration and probation. In particular, they discussed intensive probation, substantial fines, community service, treatment orders, and house arrest and other residential controls. But they insisted that these intermediate punishments must be substantive sentences that are enforced rigorously and are part of a comprehensive sentencing plan.[77]

Others argue that incarceration rates have little effect on crime. If we increase them, we eliminate the possibility of the incarcerated offenders preying on society, but these offenders will be replaced by others. The more people we process through the system the more we release from the system back into society. This argument is referred to as the *rapid replacement hypothesis*.[78] We may be creating a "more experienced criminal 'work force' and ironically a heightened collective potential for crime."[79]

Criminologists Marilyn D. McShane and Frank P. Williams III maintain that the emphasis should not be on alternatives to prison but on prison "as an alternative to other sentences." The evidence suggests that warehousing criminals is not effective and is "prohibitively expensive." McShane and Williams call for greater creativity in correctional policies.[80]

One final problem with community corrections is funding. In recent years many jurisdictions have reduced their prison programs. Some of these reductions have been noted already, but perhaps none is more dramatic than the changes in Harris County (Houston) Texas, which had a probation program described as the "envy of the nation." The program was supported by federally mandated state payments of $34 million a year. It included residential drug treatment centers. Probationers lived at the center at night and left during the day to work in the community's private sector. High-risk offenders participated in a conservation camp, where they worked on public service projects such as cleaning bayous. A super-intensive probation program featured frequent drug tests and required daily check-ins for its participants. The programs lost their funding when the state was no longer required to provide the money to counties to fund alternative programs to incarceration. A large building campaign in Texas has brought relief to the previously overcrowded jails and prisons, and judges must alter the probation terms of the offenders who were in the alternative programs. Some will be incarcerated, some will be freed, and others will report to the remaining reporting system programs, but they will have considerably less supervision. About 500 of the 900 employees of the probation office were terminated.[81]

But something must be done about the high cost of incarceration. Some of the problems were illustrated by the fall 1998 protest by thousands of high school students in California (most of whom were minorities), who argued that the state was spending too much on prisons and too little on education. While the state's budget for higher education decreased by 3 percent, its budget for prisons increased by 60 percent. According to a news article, "The study also found that five black males are in prison for every black male in a state university, while three Hispanic males are added to California's prison population for every one enrolling at a four-year public university."[82]

Criminal justice systems are facing mounting problems and escalating costs. Legislators must consider all of the issues when faced with demands for new legislation. This chapter has shown some of the advantages and disadvantages of processing offenders in some way other than incarceration. But sufficient research is not available to assess the full impact of community corrections. Criminologists should be supported in their efforts to seek funding to find answers to some of society's pressing criminal justice problems.

The Privatization Issue

The high costs of incarceration have led some to suggest that private industry should run correctional facilities. We have already looked at some of the issues surrounding privatization. Here we will focus on an additional one: recidivism. Lonn Lanza-Kaduce and his criminology colleagues at the University of Florida have looked at the issue closely. They began their report by noting that privatization has a long history within correctional systems. In fact, it is rather common for correctional institutions to contract out special services such as education, treatment, medical care, and food. These contracts draw little negative attention. It is the contracting out to the private sector of the total management and supervision of an institution that draws criticism, especially in view of reported abuses in private systems. Lanza-Kaduce refers to some of those abuses; some, especially of juveniles, have been discussed earlier in this text.[83]

Lanza-Kaduce and his colleagues raised some of the ideological issues regarding privatization of correctional facilities, such as the assertion that the private sector is more interested in profit than in effectiveness. They reviewed the cost issue, noting that most studies delving into cost have shown that private facilities can be more cost efficient than public institutions without sacrificing quality. But, the authors note, little attention has been given to distinguishing public and private correctional facilities in terms of recidivism. They studied 198 male releasees from two private facilities in Florida with precision-matched releasees from Florida's public prisons. For the entire sample the investigators measured recidivism over a one-year period. They found lower rates of recidivism among the offenders released from private prisons, and although those from the public and the private institutions were similar in how long it took for them to reoffend and be arrested, those subsequent offenders who had been released from private prisons committed less serious offenses than those released from public prisons. The researchers do not, however, rush to conclude that their study proves that private prisons are more effective than public prisons. The differences could be attributed to several factors, such as programs or other differences in the institutions or the study's methodological limitations. They recommend similar studies on larger samples. But they do believe that their study—described by them as "the first carefully controlled comparative recidivism research" focused on the two types of samples involved—probably does "reflect substantive differences between public and private operations in Florida."[84]

Another assessment of recidivism, although involving less sophisticated methodology, was conducted by the Colorado Department of Corrections, which concluded that its diversion programs are helpful in preventing repeat offenses. Officials claim a 50 percent success rate overall, with juveniles and adults who are placed in diversionary programs rather than sent to prison. Most who did fail the program did so by means of technical violations, such as not reporting on time. Of course, one could always accuse a department of a conflict of interest in reporting its own success, but this report means that the state is going to continue with its diversionary programs, at least for now.[85]

Juvenile Justice

This text focuses primarily on adult criminals, adult courts, and correctional institutions, and space does not permit a thorough analysis of juvenile justice issues, which are normally covered in a separate course. Our discussions throughout the text have noted, however, that the topic of juvenile crime cannot be avoided in the discussion of major crimes in this country. The apparently increasing violence among juveniles has led many jurisdictions to enact legislation providing for transfer of those offenders to criminal courts. Convictions in those courts have led to incarceration in adult facilities, with many resulting problems. The entire concept of the juvenile court and of detention and incarceration for the purpose of rehabilitation has been rethought. A consideration of the future of corrections must embrace an analysis of juvenile justice. Let's consider just a few of the issues raised within the year this text revision is being written.

The special needs of female inmates are addressed in Chapter 14, which notes, among other problems, the issue of child care. But little attention has been given to the needs of female juveniles who are incarcerated. According to a 2001 statement by the American Bar Association, females are the fastest-growing segment of juvenile offenders. Between 1988 and 1997 the number of delinquent acts committed by girls jumped by 83 percent. Girls who are incarcerated are often placed in facilities that do not have adequate programs for their health, education, or vocational training. The care of their children is an additional issue that must be faced.[86]

Another issue regarding female inmates, also discussed in Chapter 14, is that of sexual abuse. The same issue occurs in juvenile facilities. A July 2001 article in a corrections journal related an incident that occurred when 16-year-old Alala Williams entered Alabama's only juvenile lockup for girls. A correctional officer cursed her and called her a "cocky little heifer." Subsequently, other inmates told her about performing oral sex on male workers, and soon she became intimate with one of the officers. She said this activity broke the monotony of prison life and provided her with some of the specialities available, such as sodas. The offender's mother reported the information and sparked an investigation, which has already resulted in recommendations to terminate 15 male officers. Williams and eight other inmates have filed a $171 million federal lawsuit against the agency that runs the institution, the Department of Youth Services. Older female inmates who were once in that section have made similar complaints. The lawsuit alleges rape as well as coerced sexual involvement with correctional officers.[87]

Mental health treatment of juveniles in custody is another issue. In Chapter 14 we noted the needs of adult mentally ill offenders. In July 2001 the Coalition for Juvenile Justice, reporting on a study sponsored by the Juvenile Justice and Delinquency Prevention and the Office of Justice Programs, emphasized the mental health needs of juvenile offenders. Too frequently, these young offenders are not classified appropriately upon intake. This is particularly a problem because, as noted in an article on juvenile mental health, "Intake should be the cornerstone for the intervention process." Staff are not trained to recognize the signs of mental health problems as they develop during incarceration. There is evidence that some mental health programs are effective with juveniles, with a 25 percent lower rate of recidivism than juveniles without such treatment. The treatment should include the following:

Highly structured, intensive programs that focus on changing specific behavior.
Development of basic social and life skills.
Individual counseling that directly addresses behavior, attitudes, and perceptions.

Sensitivity to a youth's race, culture, gender and sexual orientation.
Strong aftercare services . . .
Recognition that youth think and feel differently than adults, especially under stress.[88]

One method of treatment that educators have found to succeed with problem juveniles is art therapy. Prison art programs have been developed and evaluated in three cities: Atlanta, Georgia; Portland, Oregon; and San Antonio, Texas. For example, the YouthARTS project in Atlanta provides literacy education, job training, and art instruction. Intensive training—with one instructor per student—is often used for the first-time offenders between 14 and 16. The sponsors worked closely with personnel in the juvenile court system while planning the program. The evaluation of this program showed that all juveniles who participated improved in "art skills, cooperating with others, participation and communicating effectively with their peers."[89]

Other innovative programs designed for young offenders have shown success. For example, the Special Options Services (SOS) program in Brooklyn, New York, was designed to provide additional services for youths in the federal system. Its founder convinced judges that it would be wise to send some young offenders to this program for counseling, job training, social services, and housing. The program is viewed as an alternative to the harsh federal sentencing guidelines that would apply otherwise. For example, one judge, who was faced with sending to prison a young offender for whom he thought prison would be harmful, was looking for a way to escape the strict federal sentencing guidelines. Potential participants are interviewed by the program's director, who then files a recommendation with the judge. The judge can inform the defendant that he or she will be sent to prison if this program is not completed.[90] It remains to be evaluated but it shows promise for diversion from prison.

Such programs place a greater emphasis on rehabilitation than on warehousing inmates, especially juveniles. This focus characterizes the new movement in Nevada, which proposes to rename the Department of Prisons as the Department of Corrections, a change made years ago in most states, although we still have the Federal Bureau of Prisons. Nevada proposes to create an offender management division and a deputy director of corrections to supervise the state's new programs, which will include job training, education, and development of skills to prepare inmates for release. It will be designed for those who are near release. The program is being proposed because of increasing needs the state faces with the influx of juveniles in adult corrections, the increase in female inmates, and an increase in elderly offenders.[91]

These and similar programs raise the issue of whether we should continue our march toward stricter punishments for juveniles, especially those who commit violent crimes—and whether we should try them in adult criminal courts. Some jurisdictions are rethinking this movement toward the harsh treatment of juveniles, especially when it involves incarcerating juveniles in adult prisons.

In May 2001 the Illinois House of Representatives considered a bill to change that state's laws concerning the transfer of juveniles to adult courts. This effort came as a national report was being issued, alleging racial disparity in the transfers in Cook County (Chicago). Building Blocks for Youth Initiative, a Washington-based coalition, issued a report in April 2001, stating that most of the youths who are automatically sent to adult courts in Cook County are African American or Hispanic. Nine out of 10 of the youth in Cook County who are given prison time are minorities. In Illinois a youth accused of a drug offense within 1,000 feet of a school or public housing automatically goes to adult court for trial. The bill is opposed by many because it does not remove the automatic transfer provision; it retains the provision for those accused of delivering a controlled substance near a school although it does remove automatic transfer for the allegation of intent to deliver.[92]

In August 2001 several Illinois legislators were considering proposing the adoption of a program similar to one used for the past seven years in Ohio. Legislators are becoming concerned about the incarceration of juveniles in adult facilities. Most youth facilities in Illinois are overcrowded, some operating at 175 percent over capacity. Ohio permits local communities to keep the money that the state saves through alternatives to prison for juveniles. Ohio also gives judges more discretion in sentencing juveniles under their Reclaim Ohio program. The Ohio program was begun on an experimental basis in 1994 and extended to the entire state in 1995. Reclaim Ohio has reduced the proportion of juvenile offenders in state custody from 25 to 19 percent, and participating counties, by using the state funds locally, have increased their budgets for alternative programs from $17.1 million to $25.6 million.[93]

One other serious problem with the incarceration of juveniles in adult facilities is that juvenile offenders are more likely to have or contract viral hepatitis. The U.S. Centers for Disease Control and Prevention (CDC) emphasized in 2001 that our 106,000 incarcerated adolescents and young adults are much more likely than nonoffenders of the same ages to use injection drugs and engage in unsafe sex, both behaviors closely related to the contraction of viral hepatitis. The CDC emphasizes that approximately 50 to 75 percent of juveniles who spend time in correctional facilities will also serve time as adults. If they have already contracted this contagious disease, they are likely to infect others in prison; when released, they will infect those outside of prison. Vaccines are available but not entirely effective. Officials are working on a report that will give recommendations for arresting the spread of the disease within prisons.[94]

Other Issues

Numerous other issues discussed within this text must be considered with regard to the future of corrections. Better training of police, along with more personnel; more adequate training of lawyers and judges and more resources in criminal court systems; and revision of sentencing laws are only a few. But most important, as the text has emphasized in numerous places, we must consider the system effect of changes. We cannot make significant changes in one part of the system without expecting changes in another. Thus, if we increase sentences, we will have a shortage of prison space eventually; if we reduce sentences, we may have a surplus of prison beds. The overall picture must be in view as changes are proposed. Most important, we must not become complacent with the recent leveling off of crime.

SUMMARY

This chapter focuses on handling offenders within the community by putting them in community correctional facilities, placing them on probation without a prison term, using boot camps or other forms of shock incarceration, and releasing offenders early from prison on parole. It begins with a brief discussion of the history of corrections before turning to the diversion of offenders from the correctional system. The chapter examines community corrections and the concept of the reintegration of offenders into the community after they have served time in prison. In response to claims that treatment in prison does not work and that incarceration is too expensive, community programs such as work service, fines, restitution, halfway houses, shock incarceration, boot camps, day reporting centers, house arrest, and electronic monitoring are proposed as answers to both problems.

The section on probation and parole begins with an overview and then turns to a more intensive analysis of probation, including a look at probation supervision and probation conditions. An analysis of the problems faced when inmates are released from incarceration involves a look at furlough and work-release programs. Next is a discussion of parole, including its purpose, the nature of the parole system, and the future of parole. Probation and parole revocation have many common features and are discussed together. The legal issues of revocation are noted, with reference applicable to U.S. Supreme Court decisions.

The quickly adopted Megan's laws, which require both registration by sex offenders who return to the community as well as some type of warning system to alert the community to their return, are addressed in terms of their practical and legal significance. The chapter closes with a look at the future of corrections, beginning with an evaluation of community corrections and a discussion of recidivism and how it relates to probation and parole. A second major issue in corrections, privatization of jails and prisons, is analyzed as one solution to overcrowding and high costs. A third important area of concern is that of juvenile justice.

Although they may be necessary for many offenders, prisons have been declared failures. Clearly we cannot continue increasing the incarceration rates without massive expense or the increased use of probation and parole. There are indications that despite their unpopularity, probation and parole will continue to be used for large numbers of offenders. It seems wise, therefore, to study the problems and attempt to improve both systems.

STUDY QUESTIONS

1. Suggest historical changes that may account for the recent increased emphasis on community corrections.
2. Explain and evaluate *diversion.*
3. Define *community-based corrections* and cite examples.
4. Compare *fines* and *restitution.*
5. Explore the concept of community work service.
6. Evaluate the use of halfway houses.
7. Define *shock incarceration* and explain the concept in the context of boot camps.
8. Evaluate the use of boot camps.
9. Discuss day reporting centers.
10. Explain house arrest and electronic monitoring.
11. Distinguish probation and parole and explore the history of each.
12. Explain the process of granting probation.
13. Define and evaluate *intensive probation supervision (IPS).*
14. What are the legal implications of probation conditions?
15. Why are prerelease programs important?
16. Distinguish and evaluate furlough and work-release programs.
17. Explain the functions of parole boards and parole officers.
18. What are the legal issues regarding granting parole?
19. What do you think is the future of parole?
20. What are the legal issues concerning probation and parole revocation?
21. Explain Megan's laws, and evaluate their use.
22. Discuss the pros and cons of community corrections.
23. Evaluate prison privatization.
24. Should juveniles accused of serious crimes be handled in adult criminal courts? Detained or incarcerated in adult jails and prisons? Give reasons for your answers.

BRIEF ESSAY ASSIGNMENTS

1. Discuss several problems inmates face upon release from prison.
2. Explain the challenges for furlough and work-release programs.
3. What are the potential effects of abolishing parole?
4. What are the presumptions of Megan's laws that may adversely affect their success?
5. Describe the difficulty in defining *recidivism* and briefly summarize some of the research findings in this area.

INTERNET ACTIVITIES

1. Using your Web browser, find out more about boot camp programs and services. What types of programs are available? What elements (e.g., physical activity, self-esteem building) are provided in the programs? Start with sites such as www.boot-camps-info.com. Do you think boot camps can prevent and deter juveniles from crime? Why or why not? Do you think boot camps should be abolished?

2. Learn more about national trends in parole by logging onto the National Criminal Justice Reference Service's virtual library at http://virlib.ncjrs.org. Under the subheading "Corrections," find the article entitled "Trends in State Parole, 1990–2000." What are the percent changes in the growth of adults on parole between truth-in-sentencing states and other states? How does time served in your state compare with other states? Describe the major trends in parole.

NET RESOURCES

www.appa-net.org
The American Probation and Parole Association is an international organization comprised of individuals from the U.S. and Canada. Its website offers publications and resources on various aspects of adult and juvenile probation and parole, information on special projects, an information clearinghouse, and a site search engine.

www.cases.org
The Center for Alternative Sentencing and Employment Services provides information on innovative programs and activities designed to address problems in the criminal justice system. Program areas include the Community Service Sentencing Project, the Parole Restoration Project, the Treatment Readiness Project, and a girls' program.

www.communityjustice.org
The Community Justice Exchange is a clearinghouse for community justice issues and information about community justice projects nationwide. The website contains news articles, a "best practices" section on topics such as community courts, and an online library.

www.parentsformeganslaw.com
Parents for Megan's laws is a nonprofit national community and victims right's organization. Its website contains news and special-interest articles, sources on community approaches to sex offenders, information on sexual offender registries, a search engine, and links to nationwide registries.

www.kci.org
The Koch Crime Institute's website provides press releases, a juvenile boot camp directory, white papers, and articles and research links on several topics related to criminal justice, corrections, and juvenile justice.

www.cjcj.org
The Center on Juvenile and Criminal Justice's website offers publications; news stories related to juveniles and criminal justice; information on CJCJ projects; and links to human rights, research, and criminal justice groups. Publications from the Justice Policy Institute, a project of the CJCJ, can also be found on this site.

www.buildingblocksforyouth.org — Building Blocks for Youth focuses on protecting minority youth in the juvenile justice system and advocating for effective policies. This initiative's website includes the latest research summaries, fact sheets and resources on various juvenile justice issues, a newsroom, and a link to state-by-state information on juvenile justice.

ENDNOTES

1. Gordon Hawkins, *The Prison: Policy and Practice* (Chicago: University of Chicago, 1976), pp. 56–59.
2. National Advisory Commission on Criminal Justice Standards and Goals, *A National Strategy to Reduce Crime* (Washington, DC: U.S. Government Printing Office, 1973).
3. "Public Supports Balance in Corrections, ACA Survey Shows," *Criminal Justice Newsletter* 26 (15 June 1995), p. 2.
4. Robert T. Sigler and David Lamb, "Community-Based Alternatives to Prison: How the Public and Court Personnel View Them," *Federal Probation* 59 (June 1995): 3–9; quotation is from p. 6.
5. Robert M. Carter et al., *Program Models: Community Correctional Centers* (Washington, DC: U.S. Government Printing Office, 1980), p. 3.
6. Cal. Penal Code, Section 2910.6 (2001).
7. Minn. Stat. Ann., Section 401.01 *et seq.* (2000).
8. See Laura A. Winterfield and Sally T. Hillsman, *The Staten Island Day-Fine Project* (Washington, DC: National Institute of Justice, January 1993): 1.
9. The federal restitution provisions are codified at U.S. Code, Title 18, Section 3663 (2001). The early Supreme Court case is Bradford v. United States, 228 U.S. 446 (1913). The Violent Crime Control and Law Enforcement Act of 1994, Public Law 103–322 (13 September 1994), amended the victim restitution provisions of U.S. Code, Title 18, Section 3663(a) (2001).
10. For a review of the literature see Kevin I. Minor and David J. Hartman, "An Evaluation of the Kalamazoo Probation Enhancement Program," *Federal Probation* 56 (September 1992): 30–35.
11. "Humbled Helmsley's Halfway Home," *The Plain Dealer* (11 December 1993), p. 2E.
12. Doris Layton MacKenzie et al., "Characteristics Associated with Successful Adjustment in Supervision: A Comparison of Parolees, Probationers, Shock Participants, and Shock Dropouts," *Criminal Justice and Behavior* 19 (December 1992): 437–54; quotations are from pp. 439, 452.
13. Blain B. Bourque et al., National Institute of Justice, *Boot Camps for Juvenile Offenders: An Implementation Evaluation of Three Demonstration Programs* (Washington, DC: U.S. Department of Justice, May 1996), pp. 1–2.
14. Merry Morash and Lila Rucker, "A Critical Look at the Idea of Boot Camp as a Correctional Reform," *Crime & Delinquency* 36 (April 1990): 204–22; quotation is from p. 218.
15. "Poor Evaluation Brings End to California's Boot Camp," *Criminal Justice Newsletter* 28 (1 August 1997): 1.
16. "Maryland Is Latest of States to Rethink Youth Boot Camps," *New York Times* (19 December 1999), p. 1. For a scholarly analysis of boot camps, see Faith E. Lutze and David C. Brody, "Mental Abuse as Cruel and Unusual Punishment: Do Boot Camp Prisons Violate the Eighth Amendment?" *Crime & Delinquency* 45 (April 1999): 242–55.
17. "Day Reporting Centers Growing as a New Intermediate Sanction," *Criminal Justice Newsletter* 22 (15 April 1991): 6.
18. "Day Reporting Centers Spreading as New Intermediate Sanction," *Criminal Justice Newsletter* 26 (2 October 1995): 6–7.
19. Joan Petersilia, National Institute of Justice, *House Arrest* (Washington, DC: U.S. Department of Justice, 1988), p. 2.
20. Ibid., pp. 3–4.
21. See Michael P. Brown and Preston Elrod, "Electronic House Arrest: An Examination of Citizen Attitudes," *Crime & Delinquency* 41 (July 1995): 332–346.
22. For an analysis of the effects of treatment on recidivism, see D. A. Andrews et al., "Does Correctional Treatment Work? A Clinically Relevant and Psychologically Informed Meta-Analysis," *Criminology* 28 (August 1990): 369–404.
23. Annette Jolin and Brian Stipak, "Drug Treatment and Electronically Monitored Home Confinement: An Evaluation of a Community-Based Sentencing Option," *Crime & Delinquency* 38 (April 1992): 158–71; quotation is from p. 168.
24. "Electronic Bracelets Flawed, Suits Claim," *American Bar Association Journal* 81 (April 1995): 30.
25. "Prisoner Counseling Program Could Be Revived," *Chicago Daily Herald* (12 April 2001), p. 4.
26. "Sky Spies Keep Track of Ex-Cons," *Corrections Professional* 6 (27 July 2001): 1.
27. "Probation and Parole Statistics," summary from the Bureau of Justice Statistics, 18 January 2002, www.ojp.usdoj.gov/bjs/pandp.htm.
28. Harry Elmer Barnes and Negley K. Teeters, *New Horizons in Criminology,* 3d ed. (Englewood Cliffs, NJ: Prentice Hall, 1959), p. 554.
29. Mempa v. Rhay, 389 U.S. 128 (1967).
30. Susan Turner and Joan Petersilia, "Focusing on High-Risk Parolees: An Experiment to Reduce Commitments to the Texas Department of Corrections," *Journal of Research in Crime and Delinquency* 29 (February 1992): 34–61; quotation is from p. 57.
31. Susan Turner et al., "Evaluating Intensive Supervision Probation/Parole (ISP) for Drug Offenders," *Crime and Delinquency* 38 (October 1992): 539–56.
32. State v. Morris, 806 P.2d 407 (Hawaii 1991).
33. People v. Zaring, 8 Cal. App. 4th 362 (5th Dist. 1992).
34. Simon Heller, senior staff attorney of the Center for Reproductive Law and Policy in New York, quoted in Stephanie B. Goldberg, "No Baby, No Jail," *American Bar Association Journal* 78 (October 1992): 90.
35. Commonwealth v. Koren, 646 A.2d 1205 (Pa. Super. 1994).
36. United States v. Myers, 864 F. Supp. 794 (N. D. Ill. 1994).
37. Warner v. Orange County Department of Probation, 870 F.Supp. 69 (S.D.N.Y. 1994), *aff'd.,* 1996 U.S. App. LEXIS 23432 (2d Cir. 1996), *vacated, remanded,* 115 F. 3d 1068 (2d Cir. 1997).
38. O'Connor v. California, 855 F.Supp. 303 (C.D.Cal. 1994).
39. "Place to Heal for Mothers Out of Prison," *New York Times* (19 March 1993), p. 11.
40. "Out of Prison, Out of Sight," *Chicago Sun-Times* (25 October 1995), p. 17.
41. "State to Build First 'Work Prison' at Lima," *Columbus Dispatch* (16 February 1996), p. 4B.
42. "Job Placement for Texas Parolees Cuts Recidivism, Study Finds," *Criminal Justice Newsletter* 29 (1 June 1998): 6.
43. State v. Bachmann, 521 N.W.2d 886 (Minn. Ct.App. 1994). The statute is Minn. Stat. 631.425 (2001).
44. Bureau of Justice Statistics, *Prisoners in 1999* (Washington, DC: U.S. Department of Justice, August 2000), p. 11.
45. Bureau of Justice Statistics, *Offenders Returning to Federal Prison, 1986–97* (Washington, DC: U.S. Department of Justice, September 2000), p. 1.
46. Howard Gill, "The Origins of Parole," in *Corrections in the Community: Alternatives to Imprisonment,* ed. George G. Killinger and Paul F. Cromwell Jr. (St. Paul, MN: West, 1974), p. 400.
47. Barnes and Teeters, eds., *New Horizons in Criminology,* 3d ed., pp. 417–22.
48. "Probation and Parole Statistics."
49. Greenholtz v. Inmates of Nebraska Penal and Correctional Complex, 442 U.S. 1 (1979), *criticized in* Sandin v. Conner, 115 S.Ct. 2295 (1995).
50. Board of Pardons v. Allen, 482 U.S. 369 (1987).
51. John Irwin, *The Felon* (Englewood Cliffs, NJ: Prentice Hall, 1970), p. 173.
52. Quoted in Jessica Mitford, *Kind and Usual Punishment: The Prison Business* (New York: Knopf, 1973), p. 216.
53. "Parole Groups Launch Campaign to Curb Abolition Efforts," *Criminal Justice Newsletter* 26 (3 April 1995), p. 5.

54. Ibid.
55. Mempa v. Rhay, 389 U.S. 128 (1967).
56. Morrissey v. Brewer, 408 U.S. 471 (1972).
57. Morrissey v. Brewer, 408 U.S. 471, 484 (1972).
58. Gagnon v. Scarpelli, 411 U.S. 778 (1973).
59. Bearden v. Georgia, 461 U.S. 660 (1983).
60. Black v. Romano, 471 U.S. 606 (1985).
61. The New Jersey Sexual Offender Registration Act is codified at N.J.Stat., Section 2C: 7–1 *et seq.* (2001).
62. The 1996 statute, H.R. 2137, Megan's law, Public Law 104–145 (1996), is codifed at U.S. Code, Title 42, Section 14071(d) (2001).
63. "Sex Offender Registry: Challenge Likely," *New Jersey Lawyer* (30 July 2001), p. 5.
64. *In the Matter of* Registrant J.G., A-18-00 (N.J. 2001).
65. For a discussion of these and other notification requirements, see "Sex Offender Notification Laws Add to Justice System Workloads," *Criminal Justice Newsletter* 28 (15 April 1997): 3.
66. " 'Vigilante' Attack in New Jersey Is Linked to Sex-Offenders Law," *New York Times* (11 January 1995), p. 1.
67. "Death of Sex Offender Is Tied to Megan's Law," *New York Times* (9 July 1998), p. 18.
68. Otto v. John Doe I, No. 01–729.
69. "Killing Shows Connecticut the Limits of Its "Megan's Law," *New York Times* (28 August 1998), p. 19.
70. Anthony J. Petrosino and Carolyn Petrosino, "The Public Safety Potential of Megan's Law in Massachusetts: An Assessment from a Sample of Criminal Sexual Psychopaths," *Crime & Delinquency* 45 (January 1999): 140–58.
71. Daniel Glaser, *The Effectiveness of a Prison and Parole System* (Indianapolis: Bobbs-Merrill, 1964).
72. See, for example, Marvin E. Wolfgang et al., *Delinquency in a Birth Cohort* (Chicago: The University of Chicago, 1972); and Marvin E. Wolfgang et al., *From Boy to Man: From Delinquency to Crime* (Chicago: University of Chicago, 1987).
73. Joan Petersilia, *Probation and Felony Offenders,* Research in Brief, National Institute of Justice (Washington, DC: U.S. Department of Justice, March 1985), p. 4; emphasis deleted.
74. Joan Petersilia, "Rand's Research: A Closer Look," *Corrections Today* 47 (June 1985): 37.
75. Bureau of Justice Statistics, *Recidivism of Felons on Probation, 1986–89* (Washington, DC: U.S. Department of Justice, February 1992), p. 1.
76. Kit R. Van Stelle et al., "Recidivism to the Criminal Justice System of Substance-Abusing," *Crime & Delinquency* 40 (April 1994): 175–96.
77. Norval Morris and Michael H. Tonry, *Between Prison and Probation: Intermediate Punishments in a Rational Sentencing System* (New York: Oxford University Press, 1990).
78. See Sheldon Ekland-Olson et al., *Justice under Pressure: A Comparison of Recidivism Patterns among Four Successive Parolee Cohorts* (New York: Springer-Verlag, 1993).
79. Hee-Jong Joo et al., "Recidivism among Paroled Property Offenders Released during a Period of Prison Reform," *Criminology* 33 (August 1995): 389–410; quotation is from p. 407.
80. Marilyn D. McShane and Frank P. Williams III, "Running on Empty: Creativity and the Correctional Agenda," *Crime & Delinquency* 35 (October 1989): 562–76; quotations are from p. 573.
81. "Judges' Sentencing Options Slashed: Once the Jewel of the Nation, Harris County's Alternative-Sanctions Programs Are Fast Falling under the Budget Cutters' Ax," *Texas Lawyer* (30 October 1995), p. 1.
82. "High School Students in California Protest Spending on Prisons," *New York Times* (2 October 1998), p. 17.
83. Lonn Lanza-Kaduce et al., "A Comparative Recidivism Analysis of Releasees from Private and Public Prisons," *Crime & Delinquency* 45 (January 1999): 28–47.
84. Ibid., p. 42.
85. "Recidivism Report Highlights Colo. Programs' Effectiveness," *Corrections Professional* 6 (4 May 2001), p. 1.
86. "Correctional Educators Must Meet the Needs of the Rising Female Prison Population," *Correctional Educational Bulletin* 4 (30 July 2001), p. 1.
87. "Sex Scandal Breaks at Girls' Prison," *Corrections Professional* 6 (13 July 2001), p. 1.
88. "Teachers Must Handle Mental Health Students with Care," *Correctional Educational Bulletin* 4 (30 July 2001), p. 1.
89. "YouthARTS Project Uses Creativity to Help Juvenile Offenders Avoid Delinquency," *Correctional Educational Bulletin* 4 (02 July 2001), p. 1.
90. "Young Offenders Routed to New Federal Program," *New York Law Journal* (18 June 2001), p. 1.
91. "Nevada Considers Prison System Overhaul to Provide More Training for Inmates," *Correctional Educational Bulletin* 4 (30 May 2001), no page number.
92. "Legislators Consider Easing Law on Adult Trial for Juveniles," *Chicago Daily Law Bulletin* (1 May 2001), p. 1.
93. "House Panel to Study Youth Detention," *Chicago Daily Law Bulletin* (7 August 2001), p. 1.
94. "Imprisoned Youth at High Risk for Viral Hepatitis," *Hepatitis Weekly* (14 May 2001), p. NA; 1086–0223.

APPENDIX A

Selected Amendments of the U.S. Constitution

Amendment I (1791)

Congress shall make no law respecting an establishment of religion, or prohibiting the free exercise thereof; or abridging the freedom of speech, or of the press, or the right of the people peaceably to assemble, and to petition the Government for a redress of grievances.

Amendment IV (1791)

The right of the people to be secure in their persons, houses, papers, and effects, against unreasonable searches and seizures, shall not be violated, and no Warrants shall issue, but upon probable cause, supported by Oath or affirmation, and particularly describing the place to be searched, and the persons or things to be seized.

Amendment V (1791)

No person shall be held to answer for a capital, or otherwise infamous crime, unless on a presentment or indictment of a Grand Jury, except in cases arising in the land or naval forces, or in the Militia, when in actual service in time of War or public danger; nor shall any person be subject for the same offence to be twice put in jeopardy of life or limb; nor shall be compelled in any criminal case to be a witness against himself, nor be deprived of life, liberty, or property, without due process of law; nor shall private property be taken for public use, without just compensation.

Amendment VI (1791)

In all criminal prosecutions, the accused shall enjoy the right to a speedy and public trial, by an impartial jury of the State and district wherein the crime shall have been committed; which district shall have been previously ascertained by law, and to be informed of the nature and cause of the accusation; to be confronted with the witnesses against him; to have compulsory process for obtaining witnesses in his favor, and to have the assistance of counsel for his defence.

Amendment VIII (1791)

Excessive bail shall not be required, nor excessive fines imposed, nor cruel and unusual punishments inflicted.

Amendment X (1791)

The powers not delegated to the United States by the Constitution, nor prohibited by it to the States, are reserved to the States respectively, or to the people.

Amendment XIV (1868)

Section 1. All persons born or naturalized in the United States, and subject to the jurisdiction thereof, are citizens of the United States and of the State wherein they reside. No State shall make or enforce any law which shall abridge the privileges or immunities of citizens of the United States; nor shall any State deprive any person of life, liberty, or property, without due process of law; nor deny to any person within its jurisdiction the equal protection of the laws.

Section 5. The Congress shall have the power to enforce, by appropriate legislation, the provisions of this article.

APPENDIX B

Guide to Legal Citations of Reported Decisions

Pugh v. Locke, 406 F.Supp. 318 (M.D.Ala. 1976), aff'd., remanded sub nom., Newman v. Alabama, 559 F.2d 283 (5th Cir. 1977), *reh'g. denied,* 564 F.2d 97 (5th Cir. 1977), *and rev'd. in part sub nom.,* 438 U.S. 781 (1978), *later proceeding sub nom.,* 466 F.Supp. 628 (M.D.Ala. 1979), *later proceeding,* Newman v. Alabama, 688 F.2d 1312 (11th Cir. 1982), *cert. denied,* 460 U.S. 1083 (1983), *later proceeding sub nom.,* 740 F.2d 1513 (11th Cir. 1984), *dismissed,* 1988 U.S.Dist LEXIS 18634 (M.D.Ala., Dec. 28, 1988).

This case has a number of citations, which is not common among all cases but is common among those involving unconstitutional conditions in prisons and jails. The case is used here because it illustrates so many elements of case citations. There are other citations to *later proceedings* that have been eliminated from the lengthy citation.

Original Citation

[Pugh v. Locke][1] [406][2] [F.Supp.][3] [318][4] [M.D.Ala.][5] [1976].[6]

1. Name of case.
2. Volume number of reporter in which case is published.
3. Name of reporter; see Abbreviations for Commonly Used Reporters, later in this appendix.
4. Page in the reporter where the decision begins.
5. Court deciding the case.
6. Year decided.

Additional Case History

[*aff'd., remanded sub nom.*][7] [Newman v. Alabama][8] [559][9] [F.2d][10] [283][11] [(5th Cir. 1977)][12] [*and rev'd. in part sub nom.*][13] [438][14] [U.S.][15] [781][16] [1978][17] [*later proceeding sub nom.*] or [*later proceeding*][18] [*cert. denied*][19] [*dismissed*][20]

7. Affirmed and remanded (sent back for further proceedings) under a different name. The appellate court told the lower court that it agreed with part of its decision but that some aspect of the decision needed to be reconsidered.
8. The name under which the case was affirmed and remanded.
9. Volume number of the reporter in which case is published.
10. Abbreviated name of reporter (Federal Reporter, second series).
11. Page number on which the opinion begins.
12. The court deciding the case and the date decision was given.
13. Additional history—appeal to U.S. Supreme Court, which reversed the lower court in part, under another name.
14. Volume number of reporter in which Supreme Court decision is published.
15. Abbreviated name of reporter.
16. Page number on which Supreme Court decision begins.

17. Year in which Supreme Court decided the case.
18. The case had a later proceeding under a different name before the Middle District of Alabama court (in 1979) and another before the Eleventh Circuit in 1982.
19. The U.S. Supreme Court refused to grant *certiorari;* thus, the case will not be heard by that Court.
20. The case was dismissed by the Middle District of Alabama court in 1988.

Abbreviations for Commonly Used Reporters for Court Cases

Decisions of the U.S. Supreme Court

S.Ct.: Supreme Court Reporter
U.S.: United States Reports

Decisions from Other Courts: A Selected List

A., A.2d: Atlantic Reporter, Atlantic Reporter Second Series
Cal.Rptr: California Reporter
F.2d: Federal Reporter Second Series
F.3d: Federal Reporter Third Series
F.Supp: Federal Supplement
N.Y.S.2d: New York Supplement Second Series
N.W., N.W.2d: North Western Reporter, North Western Reporter Second Series
N.E., N.E.2d: North Eastern Reporter, North Eastern Reporter Second Series
P., P.2d: Pacific Reporter, Pacific Reporter Second Series
S.E., S.E.2d: South Eastern Reporter, South Eastern Reporter Second Series

Definitions

Aff'd. Affirmed. The appellate court agrees with the decision of the lower court.

Aff'd. sub nom. Affirmed under a different name. The case at the appellate level has a different name from that of the trial court level.

Aff'd. per curium. Affirmed by the courts. The opinion is written by "the court" instead of by one of the judges; a decision is affirmed, but no written opinion is issued.

Cert. denied. Certiorari denied. The Supreme Court, either the state supreme court or the U.S. Supreme Court, refuses to hear and decide the case.

Concurring opinion. An opinion agreeing with the court's decision, but offering different reasons.

Dismissed. The court is dismissing the case from legal proceedings, thus refusing to give further consideration to any of its issues.

Dissenting opinion. An opinion disagreeing with the reasoning and result of the majority opinion.

Later proceeding. Any number of issues could be decided in a subsequent proceeding.

Reh'g. denied. Rehearing denied. The court refuses to rehear the case.

Remanded. The appellate court is sending a case back to the lower court for further action.

Rev'd. Reversed, overthrown, set aside, made void. The appellate court reverses the decision of the lower court.

Rev'd. and remanded. Reversed and remanded. The appellate court reverses the decision and sends the case back for further action.

Vacated. Abandoned, set aside, made void. The appellate court sets aside the decision of the lower court.

GLOSSARY

acquired immune deficiency syndrome (AIDS) A deadly disease discovered in 1979 and spreading throughout the world. The virus that causes AIDS (the human immunodeficiency virus, or HIV) is spread through the exchange of bodily fluids, which occurs most frequently during sexual contact but may occur in other ways such as blood transfusions and the use of contaminated needles. There is no known cure for the disease.

administrative law Rules and regulations made by agencies to which power has been delegated by the state legislature or the U.S. Congress. Administrative agencies investigate and decide cases concerning potential violations of these rules.

adversary system One of two primary systems for settling disputes in court. The accused is presumed to be innocent. A defense attorney and a prosecuting attorney attempt to convince a judge or a jury of their respective versions of a criminal case. *See also* **inquisitory system.**

aggravated assault Technically, an assault is a threat to commit a battery, but often the term is used to refer to a **battery.** In that case, aggravated assault involves an assault or a battery intended to cause serious injury or death and often includes the use of a deadly weapon.

anomie A state of normlessness in society that may be caused by decreased homogeneity and that provides a setting conducive to crimes and other antisocial acts.

antitrust laws State and federal statutes designed to protect trade and commerce from unlawful restraints, such as price fixing, price discrimination, and monopolies.

appeal A step in a judicial proceeding, petitioning a higher court to review a lower court's decision.

appellant The losing party in a lower court who appeals to a higher court for review of the decision.

appellee The winning party in a lower court who argues on appeal that the lower court's decision should not be reversed.

arraignment In criminal practice, the stage in criminal justice systems when the defendant appears before the court, hears the charges, is given instructions on his or her legal rights, and enters a plea.

arrest The act of depriving persons of their liberty; taking suspects into custody for the purpose of charging them formally with a crime.

arson The willful and malicious burning of the property of another with or without the intent to defraud. Burning of one's own property with the intent to defraud is included in some jurisdictions.

assault *See* **aggravated assault.**

attempt crimes Crimes in which the offender engages in some effort to commit a crime but does not carry through with it. Planning is not sufficient; some step must be taken toward committing the criminal act, and a criminal intent must be shown.

bail The release of a defendant from custody pending a legal proceeding, such as a trial. *See also* **bail bond.**

bail bond A legal document stating the terms under which a defendant is granted release from jail prior to a legal proceeding, such as a trial. The bail bond may or may not be secured with money or property pledged by the defendant or others. Technically, if the defendant does not appear at the time and place designated in the document, the court may require the forfeiture of any money or property used to secure the bail bond.

battered person syndrome A syndrome arising from a cycle of abuse by a special person, often a parent or a spouse, that leads the battered person to perceive that violence against the offender is the only way to end the abuse. In some cases the battered person murders the batterer, and in some jurisdictions evidence of the battered person syndrome constitutes a defense to the murder.

battery See **assault.**

behavior theory Theory based on the belief that all behavior is learned and can be unlearned. It is the basis for behavior modification, one approach used for changing behavior in both institutionalized and noninstitutionalized settings.

biocriminology The introduction of biological variables into the study of criminology.

blackmail The unlawful demand for money or property by threatening bodily harm or exposure of information that is disgraceful or criminal. *See also* **extortion.**

booking The process of recording an arrest officially by entering the suspect's name, offense charged, place, time, arresting officer, and reason for arrest; usually done at a police station by the arresting officer.

boot camps Correctional facilities designed to detain offenders, primarily juveniles or young adults, for short periods, such as six months; they usually include a regimented daily routine of physical exercise, work, and discipline, resembling military training. Most of the programs include rehabilitative measures such as drug treatment and educational courses.

bootlegging The illegal production, use, or sale of alcoholic beverages; the term was used particularly during Prohibition.

bribery Offering money, goods, services, information, or anything else of value for the purpose of influencing public officials to act in a particular way.

burden of proof In a legal case, the duty of proving a disputed fact. For example, in a criminal case the state has the burden of proving the defendant's guilt beyond a reasonable doubt.

Bureau of Justice Statistics (BJS) An agency authorized by Congress to furnish an objective, independent, and competent source of crime data to the government. Agency researchers analyze data and issue reports on the amount and characteristics of crime as measured by surveys of the general population who are asked questions about crime victimization.

burglary Breaking and entering any type of enclosed structure without consent and with the intent to commit a felony therein.

capital punishment The imposition of the death penalty for an offender convicted of a capital offense.

career criminals Persons who commit a variety of offenses over an extended period of time or offenders who specialize in particular types of crime, for example, burglary.

carjacking Auto theft by force or threat of force.

case law The aggregate of reported judicial decisions, which are legally binding court interpretations of written statutes and previous court decisions or rules made by courts in the absence of written statutes or other sources of law.

castration Removal of the testes in the male or the ovaries in the female; in earlier times used as a punishment for male rape offenders. In recent times some courts have ordered chemical castration of sex offenders. This process involves using female hormones to alter the male's chemical balance to reduce his sex drive and potency.

causation Causation assumes a relationship between two phenomena in which the occurrence of the former brings about changes in the latter. In the legal sense, causation is the element of a crime that requires the existence of a causal relationship between the offender's conduct and the particular harmful consequences.

***certiorari*, writ of** Order issued by an appellate court that has discretion to review a lower court decision and has decided to grant the request to do so. If the appellate court agrees to hear the appeal, it issues a *writ of certiorari*, ordering the lower court to certify the record and send it to the appellate court for review. If the appellate court denies the writ, the decision of the lower court stands.

charge The formal allegation that a suspect has committed a specific offense; also used to refer to instructions on matters of law given by a judge to the jury.

child abuse Physical and emotional abuse of children, including sexual abuse and child pornography.

civil law That part of the law concerned with the rules and enforcement of private or civil rights as distinguished from criminal law. In a civil suit, an individual who has been harmed seeks personal compensation in court rather than criminal punishment through prosecution.

classical theorists Writers and philosophers who argued that punishment should fit the crime. The popularization of this school of thought led to the abolition of the death penalty and torture in some countries and generally to more humane treatment of criminals.

cognitive development theory Psychological theory of behavior based on the belief that people organize their thoughts into rules and laws and that the way in which those thoughts are organized results in either criminal or noncriminal behavior. This organization of thoughts is called *moral reasoning*, and when applied to law, *legal reasoning*.

cohort The total universe of people defined by an event or events. For example, all students living in Minneapolis in 2002 and enrolled in the eighth grade constitute a cohort. This cohort might be interviewed or given questionnaires to gather data on delinquent behavior. At specified intervals, for example, every five years in the future, the cohort might be tested again to discover the existence of delinquent behavior.

community-based corrections An approach to punishment that stresses reintegration of the offender into the community through the use of local facilities. As an alternative to incarceration, the offender may be placed in the community on probation or, in conjunction with imprisonment, in programs such as parole, furlough, work release, foster homes, or halfway houses.

community work service Punishment assigning the offender to community service or work projects. Sometimes it is combined with **restitution** or **probation.**

computer crime Crime that involves the use of a computer.

concentric circle An ecological theory that divides cities into zones based on environmental and other characteristics and attempts to find a relationship between them and the crime and delinquency rates.

conflict In contrast with the **consensus** approach, the conflict approach views values, norms, and laws as creating dissension and conflict. Conflict thinkers do not agree on the nature or the source of the conflict, nor do they agree on what to call this perspective. The *pluralistic* approach sees conflict emerging from multiple sources, and the *critical* approach assumes that the conflict reflects the political power of the society's elite groups. Also called *Marxist, new conflict approach, new criminology, materialist criminology, critical criminology, radical criminology,* or *socialist criminology.*

consensus An explanation of the evolution of law that considers law to be the formalized views and values of the people, arising from the aggregate of social values and developing through social interaction. Criminal law is viewed as a reflection of societal values broader than the values of special-interest groups and individuals.

conspiracy Agreeing with another to join together for the purpose of committing an unlawful act, or agreeing to use unlawful means to commit an act that would otherwise be lawful. The unlawful act does not have to be committed; the crime of conspiracy involves the *agreement* to do the unlawful act.

constable Term referring to the first police officers who presided over the **hundreds** in the **frankpledge system.** Today, the term refers to a municipal court officer whose duties include keeping the peace, executing court papers, transporting prisoners, and maintaining the custody of juries.

constitutional approach An approach to explaining criminal behavior that assumes that behavior is influenced by the structure or physical characteristics of a person's body.

constructive possession A legal doctrine referring to the condition of having the power to control an item along with the intent to do so.

containment theory An explanation of criminal behavior that focuses on two insulating factors: first, the individual's favorable **self-concept** (definition of self) and commitment to long-range legitimate goals and, second, the pressure of the external social structure against criminal activity.

contempt A legal concept imposed on a person who has violated some court order, such as a refusal to abide by a judge's order to behave in court. Contempt may be civil or criminal.

control group In an experiment with two or more groups, the control group is used as a standard and is not introduced to the experimental variable. The control group is similar to the experimental group in all other relevant factors. Investigators measure the differences between the control and experimental groups before and after the variable that is used with the experimental group.

control theory An explanation of criminal behavior that focuses on the control mechanisms, techniques, and strategies for regulating human behavior, leading to conformity or obedience to society's rules, and that argues that deviance results when social controls are weakened or break down so that individuals are not motivated to conform to them.

conversion The process of using the property or goods of another for one's own use and without permission.

corporal punishment Infliction of penalties on the physical body.

corporate crime An intentional act (or omission of an act when there is a legal duty to act) that violates criminal statutory or case law and that is committed by individuals in a corporate organization for its benefit.

crime An intentional act or omission of an act that violates criminal statutory or case law and for which the state provides punishment.

Crime Classification System (CCS) Collection of crime data based on the severity of crimes and the effect of the crimes on victims.

crime rate In the *Uniform Crime Reports,* the number of offenses recorded per 100,000 population.

crimes known to the police The record of serious offenses for which the police find evidence that the alleged crimes occurred.

criminal justice systems The agencies responsible for enforcing criminal laws, including legislatures, police, courts, and corrections. Their decisions pertain to the prevention, detection, and investigation of crime; the apprehension, accusation, detention, and trial of suspects; and the conviction, sentencing, incarceration, or official supervision of adjudicated defendants.

criminal law The statutes and norms the violation of which may subject the accused person to government prosecution. In general, criminal laws encompass those wrongs considered to be so serious as to threaten the welfare of society.

criminology The scientific study of crime, criminals, criminal behavior, and efforts to regulate crime.

critical criminology *See* **radical criminology.**

cruel and unusual punishment Punishment prohibited by the Eighth Amendment to the U.S. Constitution. The interpretation rests with the courts. Some examples are excessive lengths or conditions in sentences and the death penalty for rape but not murder of an adult woman.

cybercrime Type of computer crime that involves the Internet.

cyberphobia An irrational fear of the Internet or of working with computers.

cyberstalking Stalking someone by use of a computer. *See also* **stalking.**

culture conflict theory An analysis of crime resting on a clash of conduct norms, both of which are accepted partially and lead to contradictory standards and opposing loyalties. *Primary conflict* refers to the clash of conduct norms between two different cultures; *secondary conflict* refers to the clash of conduct norms between groups within a single culture.

defendant In criminal law, the party charged with a crime and against whom a criminal proceeding is pending or has commenced.

defense attorney The attorney who represents the accused in criminal proceedings and whose main function is to protect that individual's constitutional rights.

demonology Belief that persons are possessed by spirits that cause crime and other evil behavior and that this behavior can be eliminated only when the spirits are eliminated.

deprivation model A model of prisonization based on the belief that the inmate subculture arises from inmates' adaptations to the severe physical and psychological losses imposed by incarceration.

determinate sentence A sentence whose length is determined by the legislature, precluding adjustment by the judge, the correctional institution, or the parole board.

determinism A doctrine holding that one's options, decisions, and actions are decided by inherited or environmental factors.

deterrence A justification for punishment based on the prevention or discouragement of crime through fear or danger, as by punishing offenders to serve as examples to potential criminals, or by incarcerating offenders to prevent them from committing further criminal acts.

differential association A person's associations that differ from those of other persons; a theory of crime causation resting on the belief that criminal behavior is learned through associations with criminal behavior and attitudes. A person who engages in criminal behavior can be differentiated by the quality or quantity of his or her learning through associations with those who define criminal activity favorably and the relative isolation from lawful social norms.

differential association-reinforcement A crime-causation theory based on the belief that criminal behavior is learned through associations with criminal behaviors and attitudes combined with a learning theory of operant conditioning. Criminal behavior is learned through associations and is continued or discontinued as a result of the positive or negative reinforcement received.

differential opportunity A theory that attempts to combine the concepts of anomie and differential association by analyzing both the legitimate and the illegitimate opportunity structures available to individuals. Criminal behavior is possible because the environment has models of crime as well as opportunities to interact with those models.

discretion In criminal justice systems, the authority to make decisions and choose among options according to one's own judgment rather than according to specific legal rules and facts. Discretionary decision making may result in positive actions tailored to individual circumstances or in the inconsistent handling of offenders.

diversion A practice that removes offenders from criminal justice systems and channels them into other agencies, such as social welfare. The term is also used to describe the handling of juveniles in a system separate from adult criminal justice systems and the sentencing of offenders to community-based correctional facilities rather than to prison.

domestic violence Violence within the family or other close associations, and including violence against spouses, lovers, housemates, children, and parents.

drug abuse The chronic or periodic misuse of alcohol or other drugs. Drug abuse is considered detrimental to society as well as to the individual abuser. Drug abuse may occur even if the substance has been prescribed by the individual's physician.

drug trafficking Trading in illegal drugs.

dual court system The separate judicial structure of various levels of courts within each state in addition to the national structure of federal courts. The origin of the laws violated dictates which court—state or federal—is an appropriate forum for the case. Most state systems consist of trial courts, appellate courts, and a state supreme court that governs the interpretation of laws within a state. The federal system includes district trial courts, circuit appellate courts, and the U.S. Supreme Court. Trial courts hear factual evidence, and the issues are decided by a judge or a jury. Appellate court judges review the decisions of lower courts.

dualistic fallacy In criminological studies, the assumption that a population has two mutually exclusive subclasses, such as criminals and noncriminals.

due process A fundamental concept in the U.S. Constitution that a person should not be deprived of life, liberty, or property without reasonable and lawful procedures. The interpretation of what is required by due process rests with the courts.

ecological school In criminology, an approach that studies the quantitative relationship between geographic phenomena and crime.

elder abuse The mistreatment of elderly persons, usually the parents of the abuser.

embezzlement Obtaining rightful possession of property with the owner's consent and subsequently wrongfully depriving the owner of that property.

enterprise liability The process of holding an entire business enterprise legally liable for an event.

equal protection The constitutional principle that guarantees all people the same treatment in U.S. criminal justice systems regardless of characteristics such as race, ethnicity, religion, or gender.

exclusionary rule The Fourth Amendment of the U.S. Constitution provides that "the right of the people to be secure in their persons, houses, papers and effects, against unreasonable searches and seizures shall not be violated and no warrants shall issue, but upon probable cause." Evidence seized in violation of the Fourth Amendment may be excluded from a criminal trial.

ex post facto method Referring to a law that provides punishment for an act that was not defined as a crime when the act was committed, or to a law that increases the penalty for a crime committed prior to the enactment of the statute.

extortion Obtaining property from another by wrongful use of actual or threatened force, fear, or violence, or the corrupt taking of a fee by a public officer, under color of his or her office, when that fee is not due. *See also* **blackmail.**

extradition The process by which an accused is removed from one jurisdiction (usually a state or a country) to another for purposes of proceeding with legal actions, such as a trial.

false advertising The use of untrue statements or other forms of notice to solicit business from the public.

false pretense Representation of some fact or circumstance that is not true and that is meant to mislead the other party.

felony A serious type of offense, such as murder, armed robbery, or rape, punishable for a year or longer in prison or a more serious penalty, such as capital punishment.

felony-murder doctrine Doctrine used to hold a defendant liable for murder if a human life is taken during the commission of another felony, such as armed robbery, kidnapping, or arson, even if the defendant did not commit the murder.

felony probation Placing on probation an offender convicted of a felony.

fence A person who disposes of stolen goods.

fetal abuse Abusing a fetus; in some jurisdictions any resulting injury may lead to legal liability; in a few states, killing a fetus may result in murder charges.

fine A type of punishment in which the offender is ordered to pay a sum of money to the state in lieu of or in addition to other forms of punishment.

forcible rape *See* **rape.**

forfeiture The process of taking from an accused items (such as money, a boat, a car) thought to be associated with illegal acts, such as drug trafficking. The property may be taken by the government and held until the case is decided; upon a conviction it may be retained by the government and sold or disposed of in some other way.

forgery Falsely making or altering, with the intent to defraud, a negotiable and legally enforceable instrument, such as a check.

frankpledge Mutual pledge system in old English law, in which ten families, constituting a **tithing,** were responsible for the acts of all other members. Ten tithings constituted a **hundred,** which was under the charge of a **constable,** considered to be the first police officer. Hundreds were later combined to form **shires,** similar to counties, over which a **sheriff** had jurisdiction.

fraud Falsely representing a fact, either by conduct or by words or writing, in order to induce a person to rely on the misrepresentation and surrender something of value.

free will A philosophy advocating punishment severe enough for people to choose to avoid criminal acts. It includes the belief that a particular criminal act warrants a specific punishment without any variation.

furlough An authorized, temporary leave from a prison or other place of incarceration by an inmate for the purpose of attending a funeral, visiting his or her family, or attempting to secure a job.

general deterrence The philosophy of punishment resting on the belief that punishment in an individual case inhibits others from committing the same offense.

good faith exception An exception to the exclusionary rule in criminal court proceedings. Even if the police seize evidence illegally, the evidence may be used in court if the police had a good faith belief that the evidence was related to the crime and to the suspect who is under investigation.

good-time credit Credit resulting in a reduction of prison time; awarded for satisfactory behavior in prison.

graft Popularly refers to the corruption of public officials to obtain public money or position fraudulently; the federal statute defines graft narrowly as the offering, giving, soliciting, or receiving of anything of value in connection with the procurement of materials under a federal defense program.

grand jury A group of citizens convened by legal authority to conduct secret investigations of evidence, evaluate accusations against suspects for trial, or issue indictments when appropriate.

grand larceny A felony involving the theft of property or money over a specified amount or value, in contrast to **petit larceny** (often a misdemeanor), which involves smaller amounts or values. The values for each type of crime may differ among the various jurisdictions.

guilty but mentally ill An alternative to the insanity defense; permits finding that defendants were mentally ill but not insane at the time they committed the crimes charged. They are guilty, and they may be punished, but generally the jurisdictions that have this concept require that these defendants must receive psychiatric treatment while they are confined.

habeas corpus, writ of A written court order to bring the petitioner before the court to determine whether his or her custody and confinement are lawful under constitutional due process of law.

halfway house A prerelease center used to help the inmate in changing from prison life to community life or a facility that focuses on special adjustment problems of offenders, such as a drug or alcohol treatment center. The term is also used to refer to a residential facility used as an alternative to prison for high-risk offenders considered unsuitable for probation.

hands-off doctrine A doctrine embraced by federal courts to justify nonintervention in the administration of correctional facilities; has been abandoned recently, but only when federal constitutional rights are at issue.

harmful error An error in legal proceedings that is considered to have resulted in actions so detrimental that some relief, such as a new trial, must be granted. It may also be called *reversible error* and is in contrast to a *harmless error,* which is a mistake that is not considered serious enough to create the need for remedial action.

hate crimes Defined in the federal criminal code as crimes "that manifest evidence of prejudice based on race, religion, disability, sexual orientation, or ethnicity, including where appropriate the crimes of murder, nonnegligent manslaughter; forcible rape; aggravated assault, simple assault; intimidation; arson; and destruction, damage or vandalism of property."

hedonism The belief that people choose pleasure and avoid pain. In law, its proponents advocate clearly written laws and certainty of punishment without any departure from the prescribed penalties.

homicide A general term including all killings, some of which are deemed to be justifiable or excusable homicides, while others might constitute manslaughter or murder.

house arrest A sentence, usually combined with probation, that permits the offender to remain at home under supervision. In some cases electronic monitoring of the offender's activities is used in combination with house arrest.

hundred *See* **frankpledge.**

identity theft The stealing of an individual's social security number or other important information about his or her identity and using that information to commit crimes, such as removing funds from the victim's bank account.

immunity (criminal) Exemption from criminal liability for acts that would otherwise be criminal.

importation model A model of **prisonization** based on the assumption that the inmate **subculture** arises not only from internal prison experiences but also from external patterns of behavior that inmates bring to the prison.

incapacitation A punishment theory and a sentencing goal, generally implemented by incarcerating an offender to prevent him or her from committing any other crimes. In earlier times incapacitation involved such measures as removing the hands of thieves or castrating rapists.

incarceration Confinement in a jail, a prison, or another penal facility, as a form of punishment for a criminal act.

incest Sexual relations between members of the immediate family who are too close in relationship to marry, such as between siblings, a parent and child, or a grandparent and grandchild.

indeterminate sentence The length of the sentence is determined not by the legislature or the court but by professionals at the institution or by parole boards, which decide when an offender is ready to return to society. The sentence imposed by the judge may range from one day to life.

index offenses Serious crimes as reported by the FBI's *Uniform Crime Reports,* including murder and nonnegligent manslaughter, forcible rape, robbery, aggravated assault, burglary, larceny-theft, motor vehicle theft, and arson.

indictment The grand jury's written accusation charging the named suspect with a criminal offense. The grand jury may refuse to return an indictment if jurors do not believe the evidence warrants one.

individual (or specific) deterrence A punishment philosophy based on the belief that the threat of punishment may prevent an individual from committing any crimes. The use of incarceration is an example.

inevitable discovery exception An exception to the exclusionary rule in criminal court proceedings. Illegally saized evidence is admissible if police would have found it later by legal methods.

information The most common formal document used to charge a person with an offense. The prosecutor, acting on evidence from police or citizens, files this document with the court, and it is tested at the preliminary hearing. Unlike the indictment, this procedure does not require participation by the grand jury.

initial appearance The defendant's first appearance before a magistrate; this process must take place quickly if the accused has been detained in jail after arrest. At the initial appearance the magistrate decides whether probable cause exists to detain the suspect and, if so, tells the suspect of the charges and of his or her constitutional rights, including the right to an attorney.

inquisitory system A system in which the accused is presumed to be guilty and must prove his or her innocence. *See also* **adversary system.**

insanity defense A defense that enables the defendant to be found not guilty because he or she does not have the mental ability required for legal responsibility for criminal behavior.

insider information *See* **insider trading.**

insider trading Exists when officers, directors, and stockholders who own more than 10 percent of a corporation's stock that is listed on a national exchange buy and sell corporate shares based on **insider information** known to the officers (or others) before it is available to the public. Federal law requires that such transactions be reported monthly to the Securities and Exchange Commission.

instrumental Marxism A school of thought in Marxist criminology, which takes the position that the state is the instrument used by those in power to control those they dominate. Instrumental Marxists view the law, the state, and the ruling class as one, which enables the ruling class to take advantage of other classes by determining the nature and enforcement of law.

intensive probation supervision (IPS) Close supervision of probationers by probation officers who have smaller than average case loads.

intent In the legal sense, the design, determination, or purpose with which a person uses a particular means to effect a certain result; it shows the presence of will in the act that consummates a crime.

involuntary manslaughter *See* **manslaughter.**

Irangate A term used to refer to the illegal exchange of arms for U.S. hostages in Iran in the 1980s. *See also* Watergate.

jails Locally administered confinement facilities used to detain persons awaiting a trial or those serving short sentences, usually one year or less.

judge A judicial officer, elected or appointed to preside over a court of law. Judges are to be the neutral and final arbiters of law and have primary responsibility for all court activities, ranging from monitoring the attorneys and instructing the jury to deciding cases and sentencing those found guilty.

judicial review A court's power to determine whether legislative and executive acts and the decisions of lower courts infringe on the rights guaranteed by state constitutions or the U.S. Constitution.

jurisdiction The lawful right to exercise official authority, whether executive, judicial, or legislative; the territory of authority within which such power may be exercised. For the police, it refers to the geographical boundaries of power; for the courts, it refers to the power to hear and decide cases.

jury In a criminal case, sworn persons who hear the evidence at trial, determine certain facts, and render a verdict of guilty or not guilty. In some jurisdictions, juries recommend or determine sentences.

just deserts The philosophy that an individual who commits a crime deserves to suffer for it; also called *retribution.*

justice model A philosophy holding that justice is achieved when offenders receive punishments based on what is deserved by their offenses as written in the law; the crime determines the punishment. In sentencing, this model presumes that prison should be used only as a last resort. Determinate (or flat-time) sentences are set for each offense. Parole is abolished, and early release can be achieved only through good-time credits.

labeling theory An attempt to explain deviance as a social process by which some people who commit deviant acts come to be known as deviants and others do not. Deviance is seen as a consequence of society's decision to apply that term to a person, and deviant behavior is behavior that society labels as deviant.

larceny-theft The taking of personal property without the owner's consent and with the intent to deprive the owner of it permanently. Historically, *petit larceny* involved small amounts, with imprisonment as punishment, and *grand larceny* involved larger amounts and the death penalty. Most modern theft statutes abolish the common law distinctions, and U.S. courts have ruled that the death penalty may not be imposed for larceny-theft.

learning theory Theory based on the assumption that although human aggression may be influenced by physiological characteristics, the activation of those characteristics depends on learning and is subject to the person's control. Social learning determines whether aggressive behavior occurs and, if so, the nature of that behavior.

loan sharking Lending money at very high interest rates and later using extortionate means to force the borrower to repay the loan.

Mafia A secret organization with a strict hierarchical structure that is thought to be involved in smuggling, racketeering, drug trafficking, and other illegal activities worldwide. The Mafia infiltrates legal as well as illegal businesses.

magistrate A lower judicial officer in the state or federal court system.

mala in se Acts morally wrong in themselves, such as rape, murder, or robbery.

mala prohibita Acts that are wrong because they are prohibited by legislation although they may not be recognized by most people as morally wrong.

manslaughter The unlawful killing of a human being by a person who lacks malice in the act; a killing under mitigating circumstances of adequate provocation or diminished capacity, which reduces the offense from murder to manslaughter. Manslaughter may be **involuntary (or nonnegligent),** the result of recklessness while committing an unlawful act such as driving while intoxicated; or **voluntary,** an intentional killing committed in the heat of passion.

marital rape *See* **rape.**

mediation The act of attempting to settle claims between parties outside the courtroom; programs for noncourt settlement of disputes were instituted to help reduce the backlog of cases in the court systems.

Megan's laws Refers to laws requiring the registration of sex offenders when they move to a community. Some jurisdictions require the offenders to notify neighbors; other require only that law enforcement authorities be notified. These laws are named after Megan Kanka, who was raped and murdered by a neighbor who was a released sex offender living with two other such offenders.

mens rea Criminal intent; the guilty or wrongful purpose of the defendant at the time he or she committed a criminal act.

Miranda warning The rule from *Miranda* v. *Arizona,* which mandates that before persons in custody are interrogated, they must be told of their right to remain silent, that anything they say may be used as evidence against them, and that they have a right to an attorney, who will be appointed if they cannot afford to retain one.

misdemeanor An offense less serious than a felony and generally having a penalty of short-term incarceration in a local facility, a fine, or probation.

money laundering Hiding the existence, illegal use of, or illegal source of income and making that income appear legal by disguising it.

murder The unlawful and unjustified killing of another human being (or a fetus in some jurisdictions) with malice aforethought: the intent to kill, the intent to do great bodily harm, an act done in willful disregard of the strong likelihood that death or great injury would result, or a killing committed during the commission of another felony.

National Crime Victimization Survey (NCVS) Victimization data collected and published annually by the Bureau of Justice Statistics (BJS).

National Criminal History Improvement Program (NCHIP) A federal program that provides grants to assist states in improving their crime record systems.

National Incident-Based Reporting System (NIBRS) A method of collecting crime data that views crimes as involving numerous elements. Twenty-two crimes are categorized in this system.

National Youth Survey (NYS) A program for gathering crime data by interviewing adolescents over a five-year period. The program has been structured to overcome many of the criticisms of other self-report studies.

neoclassical school Those who argued that situations or circumstances that made it impossible to exercise free will are reasons to exempt the accused from conviction.

nonnegligent manslaughter *See* **manslaughter.**

obstruction of justice Interference with the orderly processes of civil and criminal courts, such as refusing to produce evidence, intimidating witnesses, and bribing judges. The crime may be committed by judicial and other officials and might constitute official misconduct in office.

offenders Persons who commit an offense; used in statutes to describe persons implicated in the commission of a crime.

official misconduct in office Any willful, unlawful behavior by public officials in the course of their official duties. The misconduct may be a failure to act, a wrongful act, or an act that the actor had a right to do but that was performed improperly.

organized crime The highly structured association of people who bind together to make large profits through illegal and legal means while utilizing graft and corruption in the criminal justice arena to protect their activities from criminal prosecution.

pardon An act by a state governor or the president of the United States, that exempts an individual from punishment for a crime he or she committed and removes the legal consequences of the conviction. Pardons may be absolute or conditional; may be individual or granted to a group or class of offenders; or may be full or partial, in which case the pardon remits only part of the punishment or removes some of the legal disabilities resulting from conviction.

parole The continued custody and supervision in the community by federal or state authorities after an offender is released from an institution before expiration of the sentenced term. Parolees who violate parole conditions may be returned to the institution.

parole board Normally a panel that decides how much of a sentence offenders serve in the institution and whether they are ready to return to society with continued supervision in the community.

parole officers The government employees responsible for counseling and supervising inmates released on parole in the community.

penitentiary A state or federal prison or place of punishment used for the confinement of offenders convicted of serious crimes and sentenced for a term of more than one year.

peremptory challenge A challenge by prosecution or defense attorneys to excuse a potential juror from the jury panel. No reason is required. Each side is entitled to a specified number of peremptory challenges.

petit larceny *See* **grand larceny.**

phrenology Theory of behavior based on the belief that the exterior of the skull corresponds to the interior and to the brain's conformation; thus, phrenologists claim that a propensity toward certain types of behavior may be discovered by examining the bumps on the head.

plea bargaining Negotiations between the prosecution and the defense concerning the nature and number of charges against the defendant, the plea the defendant might enter, punishment that might be recommended, or other issues associated with the trial. The prosecution may agree to some concessions in exchange for a plea or for the defendant's cooperation in providing evidence against other suspects.

police Local law enforcement officials within the department of government that maintain and enforce law and order throughout a geographical area.

positive school Early writers and philosophers who advocated that the study of crime should emphasize the individual, scientific treatment of the criminal, not the postconviction punishment. Adherents believed that the punishment should fit the criminal, not the crime.

posse A group of private citizens called to assist in law enforcement.

preliminary hearing A court proceeding before a judge to determine whether there is probable cause to believe that the defendant committed a crime and should be held for trial.

prerelease programs Institutional programs that assist inmates in adjusting to life after release from incarceration. The programs cover subjects such as money management, job interviewing, and basic social skills.

presumptive sentencing A method for determining punishment in which the legislature sets a standard sentence in the statute, but the judge may vary that sentence if the case has mitigating or aggravating circumstances.

preventive detention The practice of holding the accused in jail before trial to ensure that he or she does not commit further crimes and is present at trial.

prison A state or federal custodial facility for the confinement of offenders serving long terms, usually a year or more.

prisonization The process by which a prison inmate assimilates the customs, norms, values, and culture of prison life.

proactive The response to criminal behavior in which the police detect crimes actively and seek offenders instead of relying on citizen's reports of crimes.

probable cause An evidentiary standard; a set of facts and circumstances that justifies a reasonably intelligent and prudent person's belief that an accused person has committed a specific crime or that evidence sought exists in a specific place.

probation A judicial determination in which the offender is allowed to remain in the community under conditioned supervision. The term refers also to the component of the criminal justice system that administers all phases of probation.

probation officer The official who is responsible for preparing presentence reports, supervising offenders placed on probation, and helping them integrate into society as lawful citizens.

Prohibition The period in U.S. history (1919–1933) during which it was illegal for anyone to make, sell, or buy alcoholic beverages.

Property crimes Those serious crimes not directed toward the person but rather his or her property. The four major property crimes as categorized by the FBI are burglary, larceny-theft, motor vehicle theft, and arson.

prosecuting attorney A government official whose duty is to initiate and maintain criminal proceedings on behalf of the government against persons accused of committing crimes.

psychiatry A field of medicine that specializes in the understanding, diagnosis, treatment, and prevention of mental problems.

psychoanalysis A special branch of psychiatry based on the theories of Sigmund Freud and employing a particular personality theory and method of treatment; the approach concentrates on the individual case study.

public defender An attorney whose function is to represent defendants who cannot afford to retain private counsel.

punishment Any of a series of impositions (such as a fine, probation, work service, incarceration) imposed by the authority of law upon a person who has been determined to be a criminal offender.

racial profiling The reaction by law enforcement officers to potential suspects based solely on their race or ethnicity.

racketeering An organized conspiracy to attempt or to commit extortion or coercion by use of force or threats.

radical criminology Approach to the study of crime and criminals that explores and verifies the connection between economic reality and social phenomena; most radical theorists express a desire to change situations for the betterment of suppressed classes. *See also* **conflict.**

rape Unlawful sexual intercourse (limited to female victims in some jurisdictions); called **forcible rape** if committed against the victim's will by the use of threats or force. **Statutory rape** refers to consensual sexual intercourse with a person who is below the legal age of consent. **Marital rape** occurs when the victim of forced intercourse is the spouse of the alleged offender. *Rape by instrumentation,* a relatively new legal concept, refers to any intrusion by the male penis of any part of a person's body that could be interpreted for the purpose of sexual arousal or gratification or as an act of violence, or the forced intrusion of any object into the genital or anal openings of another person's body.

reactive The response to criminal behavior in which police rely on notification by alleged victims or others that a crime has been committed instead of taking active measures to detect crimes and identify offenders.

recidivism Further violations of the law by released suspects or inmates, or noncriminal violations of conditions by probationers and parolees.

reformatory Correctional facility that is less secure than a prison or penitentiary and that, at least in theory, has as its primary goal the rehabilitation of offenders.

rehabilitation The rationale for the reformation of offenders, based on the premise that human behavior is the result of antecedent causes that may be discovered by objective analysis and that permit the scientific control of human behavior. The focus is on treatment, not punishment, of the offender.

reintegration A philosophy of punishment that focuses on returning the offender to the community with restored education, employment, and family ties.

restitution A type of punishment in which the offender must reimburse the victim financially or with services. It may be required in lieu of or in addition to a fine or other punishment or as a condition of probation.

retribution A punishment theory that contends that an offender should be punished for the crimes committed because he or she deserves it.

revenge A punishment doctrine under which a person who violates the law should be punished in the same way the victim suffered.

robbery Taking personal property from the possession of another against his or her will by the use of force or fear.

routine activity approach An approach explaining crime by means of three elements: (1) likely offenders (people who are motivated to commit crimes), (2) suitable targets (presence of things that are valuable and that can be transported fairly easily), and (3) absence of capable guardians (people who can prevent the criminal activity).

search warrant A court-issued writ authorizing an officer to search a person, property, or place.

selective incapacitation The selection of certain offenders, usually the most serious, for incarceration.

self-concept The image one has of oneself, including an assessment of strengths and weaknesses; a self-image. *See also* **containment theory.**

self-report data (SRD) The method of collecting data by asking people to give information about their prior involvement in crime; based on selected samples of the total population or a subset such as juveniles or incarcerated criminals. Data may be obtained in several ways, such as by anonymous questionnaires or interviews.

sentence The decision of the judge or jury, according to statutory law, fixing the punishment for an offender after conviction.

sentence disparity A term used to describe the variations and inequities that result when defendants convicted of the same crime receive varying sentences; may refer also to varying legislative sentences from state to state.

sentencing The postconviction stage in the criminal justice system that includes all those decisions the court makes with regard to the official handling of a person who pleads guilty or is convicted of a crime.

sheriff A county's chief law enforcement officer, usually elected by popular vote, who performs varied functions such as collecting county taxes, supervising some government activities, and serving as the county coroner in some jurisdictions.

shires *See* **frankpledge.**

shock incarceration Process of incarcerating a person for a brief period prior to release on probation or other type of supervision.

shoplifting The illegal removal of merchandise from stores by customers or persons posing as customers.

socialization The basic lifelong social process by which an individual is integrated into a social group by learning its culture, values, and social roles.

social contract The philosophy that for greater protection, people voluntarily surrender their rights to protect themselves to the government, which must govern by the consent of the people.

sociobiology The application of principles of biology to the study of social behavior.

stalking Defined in the National Violence against Women Survey as "a course of conduct directed at a specific person that involves repeated visual or physical proximity, nonconsensual communication, or verbal, written or implied threats, or a combination thereof, that would cause a reasonable person fear." The term *repeated* means two or more times.

stare decisis Literally, "let the decision stand." The doctrine that courts will abide by or adhere to their previous rulings when deciding cases with substantially the same facts.

status offenses A class of crime that does not consist of proscribed action or inaction, but of the personal condition or characteristic of the accused, for example, being a vagrant. In juvenile law, may refer to a variety of acts that would not be considered criminal if committed by an adult. Examples are being insubordinate or truant, or running away.

statutory law Law created or defined in a written enactment by the legislative body, as opposed to case law.

statutory rape *See* **rape.**

Stockholm syndrome An incongruous feeling of empathy by hostages toward the hostage takers and a displacement of frustration and aggression on the part of the victims against the authorities.

strain theory Refers to the theories of social disorganization, anomie, and subculture that focus on negative social structures and relationships.

strict liability Holding a person (or a corporation) legally liable for an action of that person or another even though the actor may not have intended to engage in inappropriate or illegal action.

structural Marxism Marxist position that although law may be explained by capitalism, it does not always reflect the interests of the ruling class. Structural Marxists look for the underlying forces that shape law, and those forces may create a conflict between capitalism in general and any particular capitalist.

subculture An identifiable segment of society or group having specific patterns of behavior, folkways, and mores that set that group apart from the others within a culture or society.

syndicate A group of persons who organize for the purpose of carrying out matters (usually financial) of mutual interest, not illegal by definition, but often associated with illegal activities such as organized crime.

terrorism Violent acts or the use of the threat of violence to create fear, alarm, dread, or coercion, usually against governments.

tithing *See* **frankpledge.**

theory Part of an explanation, an attempt to relate two or more variables in ways that can be tested. If properly constructed and tested, a theory can be shown to be incorrect or at least questioned. Thus, a theory is more than an assumption. It involves efforts to test the reality of thoughts or explanations about how variables (such as gender) are related to phenomenon (such as criminal behavior).

three strikes and you're out Legislation enacted in most states and in the federal government in recent years and designed to impose long sentences on persons who commit three or more serious crimes or felonies.

transportation The historical practice of deporting criminals to other countries as punishment.

trial The formal fact-finding process in court in which all evidence in a case is presented and a decision is made by the judge or jury about whether the defendant is guilty, beyond a reasonable doubt, of criminal charges.

truth in sentencing A concept requiring that actual time served by offenders be closer to the time allocated for the sentence. Many jurisdictions are establishing 80–85 percent as their goal, meaning that offenders may not be released for any reasons until they have served the required percentage of their sentences.

under color of law Inappropriate or illegal action taken by government employees (such as law enforcement officers) while acting under the authority of their government positions.

Uniform Crime Reports (UCR) The official government source of national crime data; collected, compiled, and published by the Federal Bureau of Investigation.

utilitarianism The philosophy that makes the happiness of the individual or society the main goal and the criterion for determining what is morally good and right. In politics, this means that the greatest happiness of the greatest number is the sole end and criterion of all public action.

venue Location of a trial; defendants who think they cannot get a fair trial in the jurisdiction in which the alleged crime occurred may petition the court for a change of venue, which is granted at the discretion of the court.

vicarious liability The placing of legal liability on one person (or corporation) for the action of another. An example would be to hold the owner of a bar responsible for an employee who sold liquor to an intoxicated person who then drove a car and killed another person.

victims' compensation legislation Legislation that provides financial and other types of assistance to crime victims.

violent crimes Serious crimes against the person (as contrasted to serious crimes against property). The four serious crimes as defined as index offenses by the FBI in its *Uniform Crime Reports* are murder and nonnegligent manslaughter, forcible rape, robbery, and aggravated assault.

voir dire To speak the truth; the process of questioning prospective jurors to determine their qualifications and desirability for serving on a jury.

voluntary manslaughter *See* **manslaughter.**

watch system System of policing that existed in early England and in colonial America. Bellmen walked throughout the city on a regular basis ringing bells and providing police services. Later they were replaced by a permanent watch of citizens and still later by paid constables.

Watergate A political scandal connected with the Republican White House during the 1972 presidential election campaign. It involved a break-in at the Democratic national headquarters at the Watergate building in Washington, D.C., and eventually led to the resignation of President Richard M. Nixon, the first U.S. president to do so in disgrace. Although Nixon was pardoned by his successor, President Gerald Ford, some of his associates were tried, convicted, and sentenced to prison.

white-collar crime The term used to describe violations of the law by persons with higher status; usually the term refers to corporate or individual crimes in connection with businesses or occupations regarded as a legitimate part of society.

work release An authorized absence that allows the inmate to hold a job or attend school but that requires him or her to return to the institution during nonworking hours.

writ An order from a court for someone to do something or to give permission to do whatever has been requested.

XYY chromosome abnormality Presence of an extra Y chromosome in a male. It has been argued that this abnormality is related to criminal behavior, but the evidence of a relationship is not supported strongly. Most courts refuse to admit evidence of this abnormality as a defense to a criminal act.

CASE INDEX

NAME INDEX

GENERAL INDEX